A Flexible Organization for Instructors

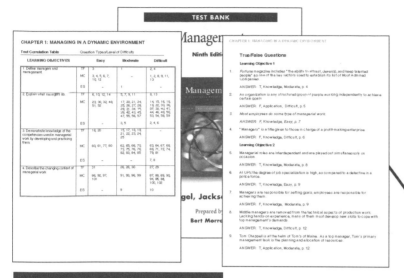

ExamView®

TEST BANK QUESTIONS

are grouped by learning objective, so that you can thoroughly test all objectives—or emphasize the ones you feel are most important. Tables at the beginning of each chapter make it easy to prepare tests that cover the objectives at the level of difficulty appropriate for your students.

MANAGERIAL COMPETENCIES—

communication, planning and administration, teamwork, strategic action, global awareness, and self-management—form the core of a unique framework for assessing and building managerial knowledge, skills, behaviors, and attitudes.

QUESTIONS FOR DISCUSSION AND COMPETENCY DEVELOPMENT

VIDEO CASE

CASE FOR COMPETENCY DEVELOPMENT

ALL LECTURE SUPPORT MATERIALS

come together under their appropriate objectives in the *Instructor's Manual's Annotated Lecture Notes,* for thorough coverage of all objectives. Cues tell you the appropriate times to integrate transparencies, PPT slides, text special features, additional examples, special readings, and Web pages into your lectures—a smorgasbord of teaching aids from which to choose.

Text Special Features
to reinforce Managerial Competencies

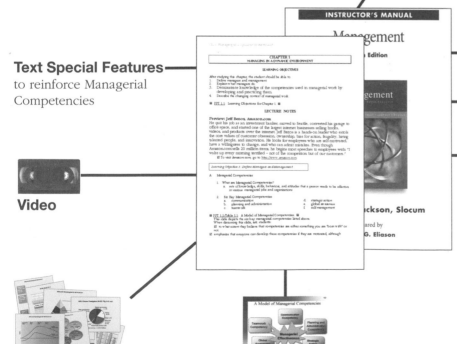

Video

Transparencies

PowerPoint

EDITION 9

Management:
A Competency-Based Approach

DON HELLRIEGEL

Lowry Mays College and Graduate School of Business
Texas A&M University

SUSAN E. JACKSON

School of Management and Labor Relations
Rutgers University

JOHN W. SLOCUM, JR.

Edwin L. Cox School of Business
Southern Methodist University

SOUTH-WESTERN
THOMSON LEARNING

Australia · Canada · Mexico · Singapore · Spain · United Kingdom · United States

Management: A Competency-Based Approach, 9/e, by Don Hellriegel, Susan E. Jackson and John W. Slocum, Jr.

Vice President/Publisher: Jack W. Calhoun
Executive Editor: John Szilagyi
Developmental Editor: Leslie Kauffman, Litten Editing and Production, Inc.
Marketing Manager: Rob Bloom
Production Editor: Margaret M. Bril
Manufacturing Coordinator: Sandee Milewski
Media Technology Editor: Vicky True
Media Developmental Editor: Kristen Meere
Media Production Editor: Mark Sears
Internal Design: Ann Small, a small design studio
Cover Design: Ann Small, a small design studio
Cover Photo: Carlos Alejandro Photography
Photo Researcher: Cary Benbow
Production House: Pre-Press Company, Inc.
Compositor: Pre-Press Company, Inc.
Printer: Transcontinental

Printed in Canada
1 2 3 4 5 04 03 02 01

For more information contact South-Western, 5101 Madison Road, Cincinnati, Ohio 45227 or find us on the Internet at http://www.swcollege.com

For permission to use material from this text or product, contact us by
- **telephone: 1-800-730-2214**
- **fax: 1-800-730-2215**
- **web: http://www.thomsonrights.com**

Library of Congress Cataloging-in-Publication Data

Hellriegel, Don.
     Management/Don Hellriegel, Susan E. Jackson, John W. Slocum.—9th ed.
          p. cm.
     Includes bibliographical references and index.
     ISBN 0-324-05558-7
     1. Management. I. Jackson, Susan E. II. Slocum, John W. III. Title.

     HD31 .H447 2001
     658.4—dc21   00-067936

To Lois (DH)
To Randall (SEJ)
To Ashlyn, Jake, Hunter, and more grandchildren on the way (JWS)

Brief Contents

Part 1   **An Overview of Management**   1

CHAPTER 1   MANAGING IN A DYNAMIC ENVIRONMENT   2
CHAPTER 2   THE EVOLUTION OF MANAGEMENT   40

Part 2   **Managing the Environment**   73

CHAPTER 3   ENVIRONMENTAL FORCES   74
CHAPTER 4   MANAGING GLOBALLY   104
CHAPTER 5   ENTREPRENEURSHIP   132
CHAPTER 6   ETHICS AND CORPORATE SOCIAL RESPONSIBILITY   158

Part 3   **Strategic Decision Making**   189

CHAPTER 7   PLANNING AND STRATEGY   190
CHAPTER 8   FUNDAMENTALS OF DECISION MAKING   218
CHAPTER 9   PLANNING AND DECISION AIDS   242

Part 4   **Organizing**   265

CHAPTER 10   FUNDAMENTALS OF ORGANIZATIONAL DESIGN   266
CHAPTER 11   CONTEMPORARY ORGANIZATION DESIGNS   292
CHAPTER 12   ORGANIZATIONAL CHANGE AND LEARNING   314
CHAPTER 13   MANAGING HUMAN RESOURCES   342

Part 5   **Leading**   373

CHAPTER 14   WORK MOTIVATION   374
CHAPTER 15   DYNAMICS OF LEADERSHIP   402
CHAPTER 16   ORGANIZATIONAL COMMUNICATION   428
CHAPTER 17   MANAGING WORK TEAMS   456
CHAPTER 18   ORGANIZATIONAL CULTURES AND CULTURAL DIVERSITY   484

Part 6   **Controlling and Evaluating**   513

CHAPTER 19   CONTROLLING IN ORGANIZATIONS   514
CHAPTER 20   INFORMATION MANAGEMENT TECHNOLOGY   540

Contents

Preface xvii

Part 1   An Overview of Management 1

Managing in a Dynamic Environment 2

Preview: Jeff Bezos, Amazon.com 4

Managers and Management 4
What Is an Organization? 5 | What Is a Manager? 7 | What Is Management? 7 | Scope of Management 8

What Managers Do 8
General Managerial Functions 8 | Levels of Management 10 | Small-Business Managers 13 | **COMMUNICATION COMPETENCY:** Linda Navarro of Sonnet Supply 13

Managerial Competencies 14
What It Takes To Be a Great Manager 14 | Communication Competency 14 | Planning and Administration Competency 16 | **PLANNING & ADMINISTRATION COMPETENCY:** Homero Resendez of Cemex 17 | Teamwork Competency 18 | **TEAMWORK COMPETENCY:** Honeywell 19 | Strategic Action Competency 20 | Global Awareness Competency 21 | **GLOBAL AWARENESS COMPETENCY:** Coca-Cola 22 | Self-Management Competency 23 | Developing Your Managerial Competencies 25

Management—A Dynamic Process 25
The Restructuring of Organizations 26 | A Changing Workforce 27 | Changing Technology 28 | Globalization 29

Chapter Summary 29
Key Terms 30
Questions for Discussion and Competency Development 30
HJS Management Competencies: Self-Assessment Inventory 32
Video Case: Second Chance Body Armor 39

The Evolution of Management 40

Preview: Toyota's Production System 42

Traditional Viewpoint of Management 42
Bureaucratic Management 45 | **PLANNING & ADMINISTRATION COMPETENCY:** United Parcel Service 48 | Scientific Management 49 | Administrative Management 51 | Assessing the Traditional Viewpoint 52

Behavioral Viewpoint 53
Follett's Contributions 54 | Barnard's Contributions 54 | The Hawthorne Contributions 55 | **TEAMWORK COMPETENCY:** Share It All With Employees, Soup to Nuts 56 | Assessing the Behavioral Viewpoint 57

Systems Viewpoint 57
System Concepts 57 | System Types 58 | **COMMUNICATION COMPETENCY:** Supply-Chain Management at Thomson 58 | Quantitative Techniques 59 | Assessing the Systems Viewpoint 60

Contingency Viewpoint 60

Contingency Variables 60 | Assessing the Contingency Viewpoint 61

Quality Viewpoint 62

The Quality Control Process 62 | The Importance of Quality 65 | **STRATEGIC ACTION COMPETENCY:** Marlow Industries Delivers Quality 66 | Integration of Management Viewpoints and Competencies 66

Chapter Summary 68
Key Terms 68
Questions for Discussion and Competency Development 69
Case for Competency Development: Starbucks 69
Video Case: Sunshine Cleaning, JIAN, and Archway Cookies 70

Part 2   Managing the Environment 73

Environmental Forces 74

Preview: **The Pharmaceutical Industry** 76

The Environment 76

The General Environment 77 | The New Economy 78 | Environmental Stewardship 80 | Demographics 82 | Cultural Forces 84 | **SELF-MANAGEMENT COMPETENCY:** What Are Your Cultural Values? 85

Competitive Forces in an Industry 89

Competitors 89 | New Entrants 90 | Substitute Goods and Services 90 | Customers 91 | Suppliers 91 | **STRATEGIC ACTION COMPETENCY:** Merck 91

Political—Legal Forces 92
COMMUNICATION COMPETENCY: AARP 95

Technological Changes 96
Technology's Role in Strategy 96 | Technology's Role in Manufacturing 97 | Technology's Role in Distribution 97 | **GLOBAL AWARENESS COMPETENCY:** Motorola in China 98

Chapter Summary 99
Key Terms 100
Questions for Discussion and Competency Development 100
Case for Competency Development: The Personal Computer Industry 100
Video Case: Burton Snowboards 102

Managing Globally 104

Preview: **Procter & Gamble** 106

The Global Economy 106

Strategies for International Business 108
Exporting Strategy 109 | Licensing Strategy 110 | Franchising Strategy 110 | Alliance Strategy 110 | Multidomestic Strategy 111 | Global Strategy 112 | **STRATEGIC ACTION COMPETENCY:** Boeing 112

Political—Legal Forces 113
Assessing Political Risk 114 | **PLANNING & ADMINISTRATION COMPETENCY:** Rio Tinto Corporation 116 | Political Mechanisms 117

Global Trade Agreements 119
World Trade Organization 119 | North American Free Trade Agreement 120 | **GLOBAL AWARENESS COMPETENCY:** Mabe 121 | European Union 122

Cultural Forces 123
Views of Social Change 123 | Time Orientation 124 | Language 124 |
TEAMWORK COMPETENCY: Marianne Torrcelli of AT&T 125 | Value Systems 125

Chapter Summary 127
Key Terms 128
Questions for Discussion and Competency Development 128
Case for Competency Development: Grant Gisel of Sierra Systems Consultants 129
Video Case: Enforcement Technology 130

Entrepreneurship 132

Preview: **Yahoo!** 134

Development of Entrepreneurial Activity 134
What Is an Entrepreneur? 134 | How the Environment Encourages Entrepreneurial
Activity 135 | Small-Business Owners 136 | Family Businesses 137

Characteristics of Entrepreneurs 137
Key Personal Attributes 138 | **GLOBAL AWARENESS COMPETENCY:** Masayoshi
Son Builds a Conglomerate from Start-Ups 140 | Technical Proficiency 140 | Managerial
Competencies 141 | **STRATEGIC ACTION COMPETENCY:** Picture This 141 |
COMMUNICATION COMPETENCY: Estée Lauder Built an Image and a Brand 143 |
Assessing Your Entrepreneurial Potential 143 | **SELF-MANAGEMENT**
COMPETENCY: Your Entrepreneurial Quotient 144

Planning and Entrepreneurship 145
Understanding Your Motivations 146 | Deciding Whether to Start or Buy a Business
146 | Assessing the Market 147 | Finding Funds 148 | Going Global? 149 |
Managing a Family Start-Up 150

Entrepreneurship in Large Organizations 152
Intrapreneurs 153 | Fostering Intrapreneurship 153

Chapter Summary 155
Key Terms 155
Questions for Discussion and Competency Development 155
*Case for Competency Development: And Now for Something Completely
Different* 156
Video Case: Yahoo! 157

Ethics and Corporate Social Responsibility 158

Preview: **The Making of a Green Ford** 160

Importance of Ethics and Corporate Social Responsibility 160

Four Forces that Shape Ethical Conduct 161
Societal Norms and Culture 162 | Laws and Regulations 162 | **GLOBAL**
AWARENESS COMPETENCY: Social Accountability 8000 Guidelines Provide Direction
163 | Organizational Practices and Culture 164 | Individual Perspectives 165

Three Approaches to Making Ethical Judgments 165
SELF-MANAGEMENT COMPETENCY: Managerial Values Profile 165 | Utilitarian
Approach 167 | Moral Rights Approach 168 | Justice Approach 170 | Combining
Ethical Approaches 171

Managing Corporate Social Responsibility 172
Stakeholders 172 | Stakeholder Concerns 172 | **STRATEGIC ACTION**
COMPETENCY: Dow Cleans Up Its Act 177 | Evaluating Corporate Social
Performance 179

Encouraging Ethical Conduct 181
PLANNING & ADMINISTRATION COMPETENCY: How Could They Not Know? 181
Organizational Practices 183

Chapter Summary 184
Key Terms 185
Questions for Discussion and Competency Development 185
Case for Competency Development: Passion at Patagonia 186
Video Case: Ben & Jerry's 187

Part 3   Strategic Decision Making 189

Planning and Strategy 190
Preview: **Lucent Technologies** 192
The Planning Function 192

Two Forms of Planning 193
Strategic Planning 193 | **STRATEGIC ACTION COMPETENCY:** Dell's Competitve
Strategies 195 | Tactical Planning 196

Levels of Diversification and Planning 197
Strategic Questions 197 | Types of Business Firms 198 | **COMMUNICATION**
COMPETENCY: GE's Social Architecture 200

Strategic Levels and Planning 200
Corporate-Level Strategy 200 | **PLANNING & ADMINISTRATION COMPETENCY:**
GE's Operating System 203 | Business-Level Strategy 204 | Functional-Level Strategy 204

Phases of Planning 205
Phase 1: Develop Mission and Goals 205 | Phase 2: Diagnose Opportunities and
Threats 206 | Phase 3: Diagnose Strengths and Weaknesses 208 | Phase 4: Develop
Strategies 209 | **STRATEGIC ACTION COMPETENCY:** Dell's New Growth Strategies
210 | Phase 5: Prepare Strategic Plan 211 | Phase 6: Prepare Tactical Plans 211 |
Phase 7: Control and Diagnose Results 211 | Phase 8: Continue Planning 212

Generic Competitive Strategies Model 212
Differentiation Strategy 213 | Cost Leadership Strategy 213 | Focus Strategy 213

Chapter Summary 214
Key Terms 214
Questions for Discussion and Competency Development 214
Case for Competency Development: Gerstner on IBM and the Internet 215
Video Case: Hudson's Somerset Store 217

Fundamentals of Decision Making 218
Preview: **Jim Prevo's Decisions** 220
Role of Decision Making 220

Decision-Making Conditions 221
Certainty 221 | Risk 222 | Uncertainty 223 | **SELF-MANAGEMENT**
COMPETENCY: George Conrades, Akamai Technologies 223

Basic Types of Decisions 224
Problem Types 224 | Solution Types 225 | Routine Decisions 226 | Adaptive
Decisions 226 | Innovative Decisions 227 | **STRATEGIC ACTION COMPETENCY:**
Alliant Foodservice Innovates 228

Models of Decision Making 228
Rational Model 228 | **PLANNING & ADMINISTRATION COMPETENCY:**
Contrasting Controls at American and Southwest Airlines 231 | Bounded Rationality

Model 232 | Political Model 235 | **TEAMWORK COMPETENCY:** Phone.com's
Aversion to Politics 236

Chapter Summary 238
Key Terms 238
Questions for Discussion and Competency Development 238
Case for Competency Development: Jean Simpson's Dilemma 239
Video Case: Next Door Food Store 240

Planning and Decision Aids 242

Preview: **Mike Turillo of KPMG on Knowledge Management** 244

Fostering Knowledge Management 245
Knowledge Management Drivers 245 | Knowledge Management Targets 245 | Enabling
Technology 246 | Enabling Culture 247 | **PLANNING & ADMINISTRATION
COMPETENCY:** Mitre's Introduction of Knowledge Management 247

Fostering Forecasts 248
Delphi Technique 248 | Simulation 250 | Scenarios 251 | **STRATEGIC ACTION
COMPETENCY:** Duke Energy's Scenarios 252

Fostering Creativity 253
The Creative Process 253 | Osborn's Creativity Model 254 | **TEAMWORK
COMPETENCY:** IDEO Brainstorms 256

Fostering Quality 257
Benchmarking 257 | **COMMUNICATION COMPETENCY:** Benchmarking in Site
Services at Cinergy Corporation 259 | The Deming Cycle 259

Chapter Summary 261
Key Terms 261
Questions for Discussion and Competency Development 261
Self-Management Competency Inventory: Personal Creativity 262
Video Case: SP Aviation and Firstbank 263

Part 4   Organizing 265

Fundamentals of Organization Design 266

Preview: **Reorganization of the IRS** 268

Introduction to Organization Design 268
Elements of Organizing 269 | Organizational Structure 271

Basic Types of Departmentalization 272
Functional Departmentalization 272 | Place Departmentalization 275 | **PLANNING
& ADMINISTRATION COMPETENCY:** Starbuck's Organizational Structure 275 |
Product Departmentalization 277 | Customer Departmentalization 278 |
STRATEGIC ACTION COMPETENCY: Novell Reorganizes 279 | Selecting an
Organizational Structure 280

Coordination 280
Unity of Command Principle 281 | Scalar Principle 281 | Span of Control Principle
281 | Coordination and Departmentalization 282 | **TEAMWORK COMPETENCY:**
Cobra's Team Coordination 282

Authority 283
Responsibility 283 | Accountability 284 | Delegation 284 | Centralization and
Decentralization 285 | **SELF-MANAGEMENT COMPETENCY:** Tom Siebel 286 |
Line and Staff Authority 287

Chapter Summary 288
Key Terms 288
Questions for Discussion and Competency Development 289
Case for Competency Development: Peachtree Hospital 289
Video Case: JIAN 290

Contemporary Organization Designs 292

Preview: **Duke Power Reorganizes** 294

Strategic and Environmental Factors 294
Strategic Considerations 294 | Changing Environment 295 | Organic Organization 296

Technology Factors 297
Technological Interdependence 297 | Service Technologies 298

Information Processing Factors 301
Vertical Information Design Strategy 301 | Lateral Information Design Strategy 302 |
PLANNING & ADMINISTRATION COMPETENCY: FastCar Project 303 | Slack
Resources Design Strategy 303 | Self-Contained Design Strategy 304 | **GLOBAL
AWARENESS COMPETENCY:** Yahoo!'s Design 304

Three Contemporary Organization Designs 305
Matrix Organization 305 | Network Organization 306 | **COMMUNICATION
COMPETENCY:** A Three-Firm Alliance Network 307 | Virtual Organization 308 |
TEAMWORK COMPETENCY: AeroTech Builds Virtual Networks 310

Chapter Summary 311
Key Terms 311
Questions for Discussion and Competency Development 312
Case for Competency Development: Ford Motor Company's Transformation 312
Video Case: Bindco, Inc. 313

Organizational Change and Learning 314

Preview: **The Speed of Change at Hewlett-Packard** 316

Types of Organizational Change 316
Degree of Change 317 | Timing of Change 318 | What Is Your Reaction to Change?
319 | **SELF-MANAGEMENT COMPETENCY:** Is Change Your Friend or Foe? 319

Planning for Organizational Change 320
Assess the Environment 320 | Determine the Performance Gap 322 | Diagnose
Organizational Problems 322 | Articulate and Communicate a Vision for the Future 322
| Develop and Implement a Strategic Plan for Change 322 | Anticipate Resistance and
Take Action to Reduce It 324 | **TEAMWORK COMPETENCY:** A Look Inside Outer
Circle 326 | Make Plans to Follow Up 326

Implementing Change 327
Technology-Based Method 327 | Organization Redesign Method 328 | Task-Based
Method 329 | People-Oriented Method 330 | Combining Methods of Change 331

Role of Innovation in Organizational Change 332
Strategic Importance of Innovation 332 | **STRATEGIC ACTION COMPETENCY:**
E-Tailing Charges Up Retailing 332 | Types of Innovation 333 | Architecture for
Innovation 334

Learning Organizations 334
Shared Leadership 335 | Culture of Innovation 336 | **PLANNING &
ADMINISTRATION COMPETENCY:** Learning Audits Improve Organizational Memory
336 | Customer-Focused Strategy 337 | Organic Organization Design 337 |
Intensive Use of Information 338

Chapter Summary 339
Key Terms 339
Questions for Discussion and Competency Development 340
Case for Competency Development: Royal Dutch/Shell 340
Video Case: Central Michigan Community Hospital 341

Managing Human Resources 342

Preview: **Southwest Airlines** 344

Strategic Importance 344
Gaining and Sustaining Competitive Advantage 345 | Consequences for Profitability 346 | Social Value 346

The Legal and Regulatory Environment 347
Equal Employment Opportunity 347 | **GLOBAL AWARENESS COMPETENCY:** Hiring Is No Laughing Matter for Cirque Du Soleil 348 | Health and Safety 349 | Compensation and Benefits 349

Human Resource Planning 350
Forecasts 350 | Competency Inventories 351

The Hiring Process 352
TEAMWORK COMPETENCY: At Dell, Everyone Is on the Recruiting Team 353 | Recruitment 353 | Selection 354

Training and Development 356
Orientation Training 357 | Basic Skills Training 357 | New-Technology Training 357 | Team Training 357 | Career Development 358 | **PLANNING & ADMINISTRATION COMPETENCY:** Developing Leaders at Colgate-Palmolive 358 | Cross-Cultural Training 359

Performance Appraisal and Feedback 360
Strategic Alignment 360 | **COMMUNICATION COMPETENCY:** Making Improvements at Con-Way Transportation Services 361 | Effective Performance Appraisal 362 | Providing Feedback 363

Compensation 364
Attracting and Retaining Employees 366 | Maximizing Productivity 367

Chapter Summary 369
Key Terms 370
Questions for Discussion and Competency Development 370
Case for Competency Development: The Magic of Disney Begins with HRM 371
Video Case: LaBelle Management 372

Part 5   Leading 373

Work Motivation 374

Preview: **Motivation at Medi-Health Outsourcing** 376

Three Approaches to Motivation 376
Managerial Approach 376 | Job and Organization Approach 376 | Individual Differences Approach 377 | Integrating the Approaches 377

Using Goals and Rewards to Improve Performance 377
Setting Goals 377 | **TEAMWORK COMPETENCY:** Goalsharing at Sears 380 | Offering Incentives and Rewards 380 | Self-Management 383 | **SELF-MANAGEMENT COMPETENCY:** Here's Looking at You 384

Effects of Job Content and Organizational Context on Motivation 384

Herzberg's Two-Factor Theory 384 | Job Characteristics 386 | **STRATEGIC ACTION COMPETENCY:** Job Design at Whole Foods Markets 387 | Perceptions of Equity 388 | **GLOBAL AWARNESS COMPETENCY:** The Challenge of International Compensation 389

Individual Differences in Motivation 390

Hierarchy of Needs 390 | Moving Through the Needs Hierarchy 392 | Learned Needs 393

Motivational Forces in Combination 394

Basic Expectancy Theory 394 | The Integrated Expectancy Model 396

Guidelines for Managers 397

Chapter Summary 398
Key Terms 399
Questions for Discussion and Competency Development 400
Case for Competency Development: Motivating High-Tech Workers 400
Video Case: Valassis Communications 401

CHAPTER 15

Dynamics of Leadership 402

Preview: **David Pottruck of Charles Schwab** 404

Leadership and Power 404

Types of Power 405 | Use of Power 406

Traits and Leaders 407

Emotional Intelligence 407 | **SELF-MANAGEMENT COMPETENCY:** Jack Morris's Emotional Intelligence 408 | Ethical Leadership 409

Behaviors and Leaders 409

Theory X and Theory Y 409 | Managerial Grid Model 411 | **COMMUNICATION COMPETENCY:** From No to Yo! 412

Contingencies and Leaders 413

Hersey and Blanchard's Situational Leadership Model 413 | Vroom-Jago Time-Driven Leadership Model 415 | **TEAMWORK COMPETENCY:** Conoco's Empowered Teams 418

Transformational Leaders 419

Visionary 419 | Inspirational 420 | Thoughtful 420 | Considerate 420 | Trustworthy 420 | Confident 420 | **STRATEGIC ACTION COMPETENCY:** Ken Chenault of American Express 421

Leadership Development 422

On-The-Job Learning 422 | Assessment and Training 422 | Coaching and Mentoring 423

Chapter Summary 423
Key Terms 424
Questions for Discussion and Competency Development 424
Case for Competency Development: Your Leadership Style Preference 425
Video Case: Sunshine Cleaning Systems 427

CHAPTER 16

Organizational Communication 428

Preview: **Gordon Bethune at Continental Airlines** 430

The Communication Process 430

Sender (Encoder) 432 | Receiver (Decoder) 432 | Message 433 | **STRATEGIC ACTION COMPETENCY:** Feng Shui At Nortel Telecommunications 436 | Channels 438 | Feedback 441 | **SELF-MANAGEMENT COMPETENCY:** Are You Open To Feedback? 442 | Perception 443

Impact of Information Technology 444
Electronic Mail 444 | The Internet 444 | Teleconferencing 445 | The Downside of Information Technology 445 | **PLANNING & ADMINISTRATION COMPETENCY:** A Hip Workplace 445

Hurdles to Effective Communication 446
Organizational Hurdles 446 | Individual Hurdles 448 | **COMMUNICATION COMPETENCY:** Translation Blunders 449 | Eliminating Hurdles 450

Fostering Effective Communication 451

Chapter Summary 452
Key Terms 452
Questions for Discussion and Competency Development 452
Case for Competency Development: Communication Inventory 453
Video Case: Burke, Inc. 455

Managing Work Teams 456

Preview: **Self-Managed Teams Take Off at General Electric** 458

Importance of Work Teams 458
Work Teams Compared to Other Groups 458 | Why Organizations Use Work Teams 460

Types of Work Teams 461
Problem-Solving Work Teams 461 | Functional Work Teams 462 | Multidisciplinary Work Teams 462 | Self-Managing Work Teams 463 | **COMMUNICATION COMPETENCY:** Quiet, She's Listening 464

A Framework for Team Effectiveness 464
Effectiveness Criteria 465 | Effectiveness Determinants 466

Internal Team Processes 466
TEAMWORK COMPETENCY: Team Assessment Survey 467 | Developmental Stages 468 | Feelings 470 | Behavioral Norms 471 | **PLANNING & ADMINISTRATION COMPETENCY:** These Norms Aren't Normal 471

Diagnosing the Causes of Poor Team Performance 473
Team Design 473 | **GLOBAL AWARENESS COMPETENCY:** NCR's Virtual Teams 474 | Culture 475 | Team Member Selection 476 | Team Training 476 | Reward Systems 479

Chapter Summary 480
Key Terms 480
Questions for Discussion and Competency Development 481
Case for Competency Development: The Utility of Empowered Teams 481
Video Case: Valassis Communications 483

Organizational Cultures and Cultural Diversity 484

Preview: **Architects Build a New Culture** 486

The Elements of a Culture 486
Assumptions 487 | Values and Norms 488 | Socialization 488 | Symbols 488 | Language 488 | Narratives 488 | Practices 489

Basic Types of Organizational Culture 489
Bureaucratic 490 | Clan 490 | **TEAMWORK COMPETENCY:** Mayo Clinic's Patient-Centered Culture 491 | Entrepreneurial 491 | Market 492 | Organizational Implications 493

Organizational Subcultures 494
Subcultures Reflecting National Differences 494 | Subcultures Reflecting Within-Country Differences 494 | Subcultures Reflecting Industry Differences 496 |

Subcultures Reflecting Occupational Differences 497 | Implications of Organizational Subcultures 497

Managing Cultural Diversity 499
Organizational Goals for Managing Cultural Diversity 499 | **PLANNING & ADMINISTRATION COMPETENCY:** More Women Become Partners at Deloitte and Touche 500 | Assessing the Organization 502 | Developing a Plan 503 | **COMMUNICATION COMPETENCY:** GM Executives Listen Up 504 | Implementation 505 | **SELF-MANAGEMENT COMPETENCY:** Diversity Knowledge Quiz 506 | Monitoring and Adjusting 508

Chapter Summary 509
Key Terms 509
Questions for Discussion and Competency Development 510
Case for Competency Development: Cracking Avon's Glass Ceiling 510
Video Case: W. B. Doner, Inc. 512

Part 6   Controlling and Evaluating 513

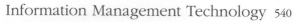

Controlling in Organizations 514

Preview: **FedEx Is on Time** 516

Foundations of Control 516
Preventive and Corrective Controls 517 | Sources of Control 518 | Patterns of Control 519 | **STRATEGIC ACTION COMPETENCY:** Kodak's SUN Plant 519

Creative Effective Controls 520
Cost–Benefit Model 520 | Criteria for Effective Controls 521 | **SELF-MANAGEMENT COMPETENCY:** Tim Koogle, CEO of Yahoo.com 522

Corrective Control Model 523
Define the Subsystem 523 | Identify Key Characteristics 524 | Set Standards 524 | Collect Information 525 | Make Comparisons 525 | Diagnose and Correct Problems 525 | **PLANNING & ADMINISTRATION COMPETENCY:** Computer Monitoriing 526

Primary Methods of Control 526
Mechanistic and Organic Control 527 | Market Control 528 | Financial Control 529 | **COMMUNICATION COMPETENCY:** Hospice of Central Kentucky 534 | Automation-Based Control 535

Chapter Summary 536
Key Terms 537
Questions for Discussion and Competency Development 537
Case for Competency Development: Ethical Behaviors in the Office 538
Video Case: Bindco Corporation 539

Information Management Technology 540

Preview: **Avis Goes Wireless** 542

Role of Information in Organizations 542
Data and Information 543 | Value-Added Resource 543 | **PLANNING & ADMINISTRATION COMPETENCY:** Pillsbury's Data Mining 545

Common Information Technologies 546
Internet 546 | Extranet 547 | Intranet 548 | **STRATEGIC ACTION COMPETENCY:** Countrywide's Internet Challenge 549 | Decision Support System 549 | Expert System 550 | Group Decision Support System 551 | **TEAMWORK COMPETENCY:** MS2 Accelerate 551

Designing Information Systems 552

Information Needs 552 | System Constraints 553 | Goals 553 | Development Stages 553 | Effective Implementation 554

Ethics and Information Technologies 556

Computer Ethics 556 | **SELF-MANAGEMENT COMPETENCY:** Computer Ethics Survey 557 | Privacy Issues 557

Chapter Summary 558
Key Terms 559
Questions for Discussion and Competency Development 559
Case for Competency Development: A B2B Relationship 560
Video Case: Archway Cookies 561

Endnotes E-1

Organization and Internet Index OI-1

Name Index NI-1

Subject Index SI-1

Photo Credits

Chapter 1: p. 1, © Greg Pease/Stone; p. 2, © Walter Hodges/Stone; p. 4, © Time Life Syndication; p. 13 © PhotoDisc; p. 17, © Royalty Free/Corbis; p. 19, © PhotoDisc; p. 22, © AP/Wide World Photos. **Chapter 2:** p. 40, © Walter Hodges/Stone; p. 42, © Mark Richards/PhotoEdit; p. 48, © AP/Wide World Photos; p. 56, © Steven Peters/Stone. **Chapter 3:** p. 73, © PhotoDisc; p. 74, © Michael Newman/PhotoEdit; p. 76, © AP/Wide World Photos; p. 95, © Walter Hodges/Stone; p. 98, © AP/Wide World Photos. **Chapter 4:** p. 104, © Keith Wood/Stone; p. 106, © Bob Krist/Corbis; p. 112, © AP/Wide World Photos; p. 121, © Andy Sacks/Stone. **Chapter 5:** p. 132, © Ed Kashi/Corbis; p. 134, © AP/Wide World Photos; p. 140, © AP/Wide World Photos; p. 141, © AP/Wide World Photos. **Chapter 6:** p. 158, © Jaques Chenet/Woodfin Camp & Associates; p. 160, © AP/Wide World Photos; p. 163, © Social Accountability International; p. 177, © M.K. Denny/PhotoEdit. **Chapter 7:** p. 189, © RF/Corbis; p. 190, © Kaluzny/Thatcher/Stone; p. 192, © Donna Coveney/MIT Department; p. 195, © Reuters NewMedia; p. 203, © AP/Wide World Photos; p. 210, © AP/Wide World Photos. **Chapter 8:** p. 218, © Neil Rabinowitz/Corbis; p. 220, © Dennis Degnan/Corbis; p. 223, © Kuni Takahashi/Akamai; p. 231, © Bud Titlow/Stone; p. 236, © Phone.com. **Chapter 9:** p. 242, © Cindy Charles/PhotoEdit; p. 244, © AP/Wide World Photos; p. 247, © Mitre; p. 252, © Robert Willis/Duke Energy; p. 256, © IDEO. **Chapter 10:** p. 265, © Rob Lewine/Stock Market; p. 268, © AP/Wide World Photos; p. 266, © Chuck Keeler/Stone; p. 275, © AP/Wide World Photos; p. 282, © Andy Sacks/Stone; p. 286, © John Lund/Stock Market. **Chapter 11:** p. 292, © Mark Richards/PhotoEdit; p. 294, © Robert Willis/Duke Energy Archives; p. 303, © Dan McCoy/Rainbow; p. 307, © AP/Wide World Photos. **Chapter 12:** p. 314, © David Oliver/Stone; p. 316, © Corbis; p. 326, © Michael Keller/Stock Market; p. 332, © AP/Wide World Photos. **Chapter 13:** p. 342, © Michael Newman/PhotoEdit; p. 344, © Southwest Airlines; p. 348, © Michael Newman/PhotoEdit; p. 361, © Con-Way. **Chapter 14:** p. 373, © Fisher/Thatcher/Stone; p. 374, © Chromosohm/Joe Sohm/Unicorn Stock Photos; p. 376, © Jean Higgins/Unicorn Stock Photos; p. 380, © AP/Wide World Photos; p. 387, © Julie West/Rainbow. **Chapter 15:** p. 402, © Jose Luis Pelaez Inc./Stock; p. 404, © AP/Wide World Photos; p. 412, © Ariel Skelley/Stock; p. 421, © Todd Gipstein/Corbis. **Chapter 16:** p. 428, © Bruce Ayres/Stone; p. 430, © AP/Wide World Photos, p. 436, © Michael S. Yamashita/Corbis; p. 446, © PHOTOMONDO/FPG. **Chapter 17:** p. 456, © Ryan McVay/PhotoDisc; p. 458, © Stewart Cohen/Stone; p. 464, © Myrleen Ferguson Cate/PhotoEdit; p. 471, © Dan McCoy/Rainbow. **Chapter 18:** p. 484, © Bill Bachmann/PhotoEdit; p. 486, © West Metro Education Program Interdistrict Downtown School/Peter Kerze/Cunningham Group; p. 491, © Jon Feingersh/Stock; p. 504, © Kevin Horan/Stone. **Chapter 19:** p. 513, © Corbis; p. 514, © Chad Slattery/Stone; p. 516, © AP/Wide World Photos; p. 519, © Julie West/Rainbow; p. 526, © Websense; p. 534, © AP/Wide World Photos. **Chapter 20:** p. 540, © Spencer Grant/PhotoEdit; p. 542, © John Coletti/Stock; p. 545, © AP/Wide World Photos; p. 551, © Susie Bodine/MS2.

Preface

OVERVIEW

M anagement is many things. It's leadership, corporate culture, business strategy, organization design, motivation, and ethics—all rolled into one. But, above all, it's supremely challenging and, for that reason, it can also be a great deal of fun. Its focus ranges from understanding entire industries to making and implementing decisions to operating in foreign countries. We expect students who read this book to learn a lot about management—about making a difference, about pulling together, about getting results—and have a good time doing it.

Effective management is the result of hard work and careful planning. The truth is that successfully managing others is an enormously demanding task. As writers with much experience in both academic and professional settings, we demanded a lot from ourselves when we set out to revise the 8th edition of *Management*. In preparing this 9th edition, *Management: A Competency-Based Approach,* we worked hard to deliver a book that is fresh, engaging, and academically solid. We are confident that students and instructors alike will agree that we achieved our goal.

This book offers a lot in terms of content and features. After much research, we developed six managerial competencies—self-management, strategic action, global awareness, teamwork, planning and administration, and communication—and have carefully woven examples of these competencies into every chapter. We chose these competencies after talking with hundreds of managers in all types and sizes of organizations and believe that they are fundamental to managing in a variety of settings.

To make life easier for both students and instructors we offer a wide variety of support materials. Our support package will help instructors teach from the book and fully engage students in learning about management. Details about these materials are presented at the end of this Preface, at the book's home page (http://hellriegel.swcollege. com), and by calling South-Western's Academic Resource Center at 1-800-423-0563.

OUR APPROACH

W e wrote *Management: A Competency-Based Approach* and tailored its support package for use in introductory management classes taught at any level in the university, as well as in junior colleges. Although we recognize that other books and course packages are available for use in introductory management classes, the following are several reasons for using *Management: A Competency-Based Approach*.

STUDENT FOCUS

Students will really like this book. It's current and will grab their interest through a variety of methods, including cases, the Internet, and self-evaluation questionnaires. It has an attractive internal design and sophisticated graphics. Examples used throughout the book will not only make discussions in and out of the classroom lively, but they will also spark independent exploration. Students need to be challenged to go beyond their readings to think actively and interactively about the issues of real-life examples. *Management: A Competency-Based Approach* does that.

We provide an in-depth examination of management fundamentals in informative, concise, and easy-to-read language appropriate for today's managers. We don't beat around the bush, and we're not shy about challenging conventional management practices. Reading this book will be an engaging experience for students, and we believe that it will guide them well as they learn about management and build their management competencies.

Our commitment to student learning is evident throughout the text. The Questions for Discussion and Competency Development section at the end of each chapter will demand students' thoughtful analysis rather than mere regurgitation of material read. The Cases for Competency Development and Video Cases presented at the end of each chapter will help students take more away from the course than just a new and improved vocabulary and a general understanding of various management theories. In our opinion, *active learning* that requires students to approach problems intelligently and to use self-insight to gauge their responses to management issues is a powerful tool. Our text compels students to actively learn and to engage in acquiring managerial competencies.

One of the most important hallmarks of pedagogy that adds value, excites students, and reinforces active learning centers is learning objectives. Every chapter in *Management: A Competency-Based Approach* begins with a statement of Learning Objectives and is organized to allow students to meet each objective. Repetition of each objective in the text where content specific to that objective is covered provides opportunities for self-testing and review. Every chapter ends with a Summary that distills the chapter's main points and is also organized around the chapter's Learning Objectives so that students can easily assess their mastery of the topics presented.

MANAGERIAL COMPETENCIES

We fully expect to set the standard for content that merges the concerns of managers with the managerial competencies that foster excellence. No one can begin to appreciate the role of managers today or in the years ahead without a solid understanding of the competencies needed to manage. What are these managerial competencies? We believe that there are six:

- self-management,
- strategic action,
- global awareness,
- teamwork,
- planning and administration, and
- communication.

These competencies can be learned through feedback and practice, but feedback often comes to students in bits and pieces. In contrast in *Management: A Competency-Based Approach,* we link into a meaningful whole the pieces of information that elsewhere are seldom related to students' performance or to a team's performance. The payoff for students is that we've defined and clarified the competencies necessary for early success in their careers. Throughout the book in a series of specially designed competency boxes, we present students with a variety of ways that they can assess their competencies right now and begin to develop their potential as effective managers. We developed an assessment instrument—provided on CD-ROM as well as at the end of Chapter 1 in the text—for every student to use. After completing this instrument, students can compare their development stages with those of hundreds of other students and practicing managers.

Self-Management Competency. Today's successful manager knows that self-awareness is a crucial vantage point from which to view the operation of an organization and his or her role in that organization. Self-identification of strengths and developmental needs is an important first step in the process of learning to manage others. Our presentation of the self-management competency helps students identify their own strengths and developmental needs in leadership, motivation, ethics, and other areas through a series of experiential exercises and cases. Besides learning about their current strengths (and weaknesses) and developmental needs, students will gain an appreciation for the importance of continual self-assessment throughout their careers.

Strategic Action Competency. Just as artists shape clay to form beautiful sculptures that symbolize important events, managers craft strategies that creatively link the best practices of their organizations to achieve success. Developing broad strategies that can be translated into clear goals and practical action plans is one way that an organization can achieve a competitive advantage. To be sure, risk accompanies all strategic decisions, but the skillful manager acts to devise contingency plans to minimize those risks. Our discussion of the strategic action competency demonstrates how managers of various types of organizations actually develop and apply distinctive strategies to guide their firms.

Global Awareness Competency. Effective managers must stay abreast of important global trends that have significant impacts on their organizations and understand how well their organizations are faring in global markets. Our presentation of the global awareness competency challenges students to recognize the impact of global trends on an organization's plans and growth. The challenges of global expansion and operating in foreign countries demand that students question their own leadership styles, values, and many traditional Western management practices. The main factors for successfully doing business internationally are being sensitive to key cultural differences in countries in which an organization operates and understanding the consequences of cultural differences for the organization.

Teamwork Competency. The ability to cultivate an active network of relationships and to relate well to others is the focus of the teamwork competency. Building solid relationships with others in an organization is crucial because managers must rely on others to help them achieve organizational goals. As organizations rely more and more on teams, managers are forming and staffing teams and monitoring their performance. The right combination of talents is essential for teams to acquire the resources they need to be effective and to achieve their goals. Teamwork requires close collaboration and constant information sharing. Managers can create a healthy environment by forming give-and-take relationships in which they strive to enhance understanding and mutual respect, acknowledge the needs and feelings of others, and productively manage conflict.

Planning and Administration Competency. An organization's design needs to be dynamic. What worked well in the past may no longer serve the needs of an organization or its customers or clients. Effective managers regularly review and adjust the designs of their organizations to meet shifting internal and external needs and the changing competencies of employees. Work gets done when it is well planned, well coordinated, and well monitored. Managers need to push for setting clear and challenging goals, and, when problems arise, they need to step in to help solve them. However, tasks may be neglected when managers spend too much time dealing with trivial problems. Similarly, employees may waste time because of inadequate controls, poor guidance, and slow decision making. Through a series of examples, students will learn how effective managers use the planning and administration competency to create organizations that are increasingly responsive to customer demands with an emphasis on production of quality goods and services.

Communication Competency. The flow of information in an organization is its lifeblood. To maintain and improve the performance of an organization, information must freely flow upward, laterally, and downward. The communication competency strengthens the foundation for successful management. Communication is so fundamental that managers sometimes forget its significance. Communication competency enables managers to lead others—they can't do so without being able to communicate their ideas well. Effective communication includes listening, informing others, fostering open channels, and negotiating with others. Through a series of cases and experiential exercises, students will discover the importance of sharing information with others and of developing a culture in which they and others openly share information. Mastering the communication competency greatly expands a manager's influence and effectiveness.

ENHANCING LEARNING

Every chapter of *Management: A Competency-Based Approach* contains features that make it more teachable, more readable, and more *manageable* than ever before.

Learning Objectives and a Fully Integrated Learning System. The text and all major support materials are organized around Learning Objectives that form the basis of an easy-to-use integrated learning system. Along with the text, the *Study Guide, Test Bank,* and *Instructor's Manual* deliver to instructors and students a fully integrated structure of objectives and content from which to teach and study.

Chapter-Opening Previews. Every chapter opens with a current, real-world story that sets the stage for the topics to be presented in that chapter. These Preview cases, which showcase organizations in the know and in the news, not only reinforce chapter concepts, but also lead into the discussion and whet students' appetites for what is to come. In the Preview for Chapter 1, for example, students read about how Jeff Bezos left his job on Wall Street and borrowed all his parents' retirement money to start Amazon.com. In Chapter 10, students will read about how the IRS has restructured its organization to provide faster and more customer-friendly service.

Graphics. Ask any instructor or student what a management textbook should look like and you will get a consistent response. The graphics must be colorful, must reinforce chapter content, must be easy to read, and must be numerous. If you quickly page through *Management: A Competency-Based Approach,* you will discover that it more than measures up to this standard. Each figure and table is cited in the narrative and tied to the concept under discussion.

Competency Features. Every chapter in *Management: A Competency-Based Approach* contains features set off in boxes that relate the managerial competencies to chapter content. These boxes are not unrelated diversions from the text; rather, they provide information that is fully integrated with the text and can be easily integrated into classroom lectures and discussions. In many instances they challenge students to analyze and evaluate a related Web site. The boxes are for teaching, learning, and reinforcing chapter content. Questions in the *Test Bank* are provided for instructors who want to test material from these boxed features.

Web Insights. This is a **new** feature in the 9th edition. Several Web Insight margin references are placed throughout each chapter, asking students to locate specific information on a company's Web site and to apply this information by answering a related critical-thinking question. The purposes of these Web Insights are to (1) pose some additional questions about an organization discussed in the text and (2) learn how to use the World Wide Web as a research tool.

Key Terms. Key terms appear in boldface in the text, making it easy for students to check their understanding of important terms and concepts. A complete Management dictionary is included on the CD-ROM that accompanies the text and a chapter glossary is included on the Web site.

Internet Sites. In keeping with developing students' managerial competencies, Web sites in each chapter are tied to organizations featured in the text. Questions prompt students to explore, explain, describe, compare, contrast, summarize, and analyze a management practice in a real-world context online. Internet applications may be assigned as individual or team activities. They are also excellent discussion starters. An end-of-book Organizations and Internet index containing URLs cited in the text puts valuable online resources at the instructors' and students' fingertips and allows instructors to develop new Internet-based assignments easily and quickly.

Chapter Summaries. Every chapter ends with a Summary that distills the chapter's main points. Because these summaries are organized around the chapter's Learning Objectives, students can easily assess their mastery of the material presented for those objectives.

Questions for Discussion and Competency Development. Every chapter includes discussion and competency development questions that require students to apply, analyze, discover, and rethink important chapter concepts. Above all, these questions build students' communication competencies because they ask for well-thought-out, well-presented responses.

Case for Competency Development. At the end of most chapters is a brief but substantive case study that enables students to apply chapter concepts to an actual organization's problems—to analyze, evaluate, and make recommendations. These cases cover a wide variety of organizations (Starbucks, IBM, Shell, Disney, Ford, Avon, among others), providing ample opportunities for students to sharpen their problem-solving skills. Internet addresses are provided so that students can update the materials presented in the case and present real-time solutions to the questions posed.

Video Cases. *Prepared by Andre Honoree of Spring Hill College.* The video cases appear at the end of every chapter to reinforce the concepts highlighted in the chapter. The real strength of these cases is their usefulness as benchmarks against which students can measure their understanding of what managers and organizations actually do. The videos feature various organizations, including Yahoo!, Ben & Jerry's, Burton Snowboards, and Archway Cookies. The range of issues addressed in the videos and the accompanying cases provoke interesting and challenging analyses.

SUPPORT MATERIALS

We designed a comprehensive set of support materials to guide instructors and students through not just the basics, but also the subtler issues involved in applying management principles.

STUDENT CD-ROM

The CD-ROM packaged with every copy of the book provides a self-assessment tool for students to use and to reuse as their management competencies mature. Individual ratings can be compared with those of practicing professionals, as well as with those of other students, leading to additional insights and spurring achievement of developmental targets. A Management dictionary, the competency instrument from Chapter 1 of the text, a comprehensive video case, and links to online resources complete this collection of technology-based tools and content.

STUDY GUIDE (ISBN 0-324-05559-5)

Prepared by Andre Honoree of Spring Hill College. Designed from a student's perspective, the value-laden *Study Guide* comes with all the tools necessary to maximize results in class and on exams. Chapter outlines and all exam preparation questions are organized around the text's Learning Objectives so that students can isolate material that is most troublesome to them and focus on it before moving ahead. Answers, along with explicit rationales for the answers, are provided for all self-tests.

INSTRUCTOR'S MANUAL (ISBN 0-324-05560-9)

Prepared by Robert Eliason of James Madison University. Available in print or on CD-ROM, the *Instructor's Manual* emphasizes our integrated learning system. Each chapter includes Learning Objectives, outlines annotated with additional examples and other lecture-enhancing stories and facts, cross-references to text figures (also available as transparencies) and to an expanded set of PowerPoint slides, and complete solutions to all end-of-chapter questions, activities, cases, and video cases.

TEST BANK (ISBN 0-324-05562-5)

Prepared by Bert Morrow of Mississippi State University. Also organized around the text's Learning Objectives, the *Test Bank* is available to instructors in print and on disk. Tables at the beginning of each chapter classify each question according to type, difficulty level, and learning objective so that the instructor can create exams at the appropriate level and with the appropriate mix of question types. Special questions aimed at the content of competency features (boxes) are designated throughout the book. The *Test Bank* contains more than 2,800 true/false, multiple-choice, and essay questions.

A computerized version of the Test Bank is available upon request. ***ExamView Pro* (ISBN 0-324-05563-3),** an easy-to-use test-generating program, enables instructors to quickly create printed tests and online (LAN-based) tests. Instructors can enter their own questions via the word processor provided and can customize the appearance of the tests they create. The QuickTest wizard permits test generators to use an existing bank of questions to create a test in minutes, with a step-by-step selection process.

POWERPOINT PRESENTATION SOFTWARE (ISBN 0-324-05561-7)

Prepared by Justin Neri of James Madison University. More than 200 full-color images supplement course content and extend it through slides drawn from relevant material not available in the text. Commentaries on all slides appear in the Instructor's Manual and provide additional background for lectures.

INSTRUCTOR'S RESOURCE CD-ROM (ISBN 0-324-11282-3)

Key instructor support materials (*Instructor's Manual, Test Bank,* and *PowerPoint Presentation Software*) are provided on CD-ROM, giving instructors the ultimate tool for customizing lectures and presentations.

TRANSPARENCIES (ISBN 0-324-05564-1)

A full set of acetate transparencies is available to adopters of *Management: A Competency-Based Approach* to enhance classroom presentations. All transparencies are tied to lecture outlines presented in the Instructor's Manual.

VIDEOS (ISBNs 0-324-05565-X, 0-324-05566-8, 0-324-05567-6)

Our package includes 20 videos that bring action-based insights right into the classroom. These videos frame management issues in such a way that students must apply some aspect of chapter content to their analyses of the issues.

WEB SITE (HTTP://HELLRIEGEL.SWCOLLEGE.COM)

A rich Web site at http://hellriegel.swcollege.com complements the text, providing many extras for students and instructors. Resources include interactive quizzes; downloadable support materials; supplemental material on operations management; additional cases and Internet exercises; and links to other useful resources.

EXPERIENCING MANAGEMENT (ISBN 0-324-01598-4)

An innovative new product, *Experiencing Management* is a totally online collection of Web-based modules that uses the latest Flash technology in its animated scenarios, graphs, and models. Designed to reinforce key management principles in a dynamic learning environment, *Experiencing Management* maintains high motivation through the use of challenging problems. Try it by visiting http://www.experiencingmanagement.com.

WIZEUP DIGITAL EDITION

The Wizeup Digital Edition of *Management: A Competency-Based Approach* contains the complete South-Western College text, powered by WizeUp software. It features powerful study tools to help students study faster and easier. (Available at http://www.wizeup.com.)

With the digital version students can

- instantly find exactly what they need by using powerful search tools;
- add notes anywhere in their textbooks;
- search, sort, and print their notes to make a custom study guide;
- trade notes digitally with their classmates and professors;
- create custom hyperlinks from their books to the Web or any other digital resource;
- highlight any text and erase highlights if they make a mistake.

All these support materials are available from South-Western College Publishing and from your Thomson Learning representative.

ACKNOWLEDGMENTS

We give special thanks to A. Benton Cocanougher, Dean of the Lowry Mays College and Graduate School of Business, Texas A&M University; to Al Niemi, Dean of the Cox School of Business, Southern Methodist University; and to Barbara A. Lee, Dean of the School of Management and Labor Relations, Rutgers University. They have created an environment that made possible completion of the 9th edition of *Management: A Competency-Based Approach.*

For their outstanding help with many of the essential tasks involved in manuscript preparation and review, we express our deep gratitude to Argie Butler of Texas A&M University and Billie Boyd of Southern Methodist University. Their dedication and ability to laugh when times were bleak made this journey possible.

For the past 18 years, Don and John have known Jerry Moore. He has become almost like an extended member of our families because, not only does he do a superb job of copyediting, but also we have found ourselves arguing over political matters, drug reimbursement policies, and a host of other political/governmental issues. We even argued over electronic editing of manuscripts and how his edits were to be interpreted. We all dreaded to see Jerry's queries because it signaled that we were not communicating clearly and that points were missing or just plain wrong. As Jerry and his wife Mary move into the retirement stage of their careers, we will fondly remember our association with him. He has made a difference in the way we think and write. For this, we are deeply thankful for having worked with him. In our lives, Jerry has made a difference.

Thanks also go to our excellent team of support materials authors. They worked extremely hard to include everything to help the student learn. They are:

Robert Eliason and Justin Neri
James Madison University
Instructor's Manual
PowerPoint Presentation Software

Bert Morrow
Mississippi State University
Test Bank

Andre Honoree
Spring Hill College
Study Guide
Video Cases

Our colleagues and friends at Texas A&M University, Rutgers University, and Southern Methodist University have created an environment that nurtures our professional development. We thank them. We are grateful to our families for their empathy and understanding in letting us devote evenings and weekends to our authors' islands for more than a year. With the completion of this text, we look forward to spending more time with families and friends.

Many reviewers made insightful comments as we prepared the 9th edition. Although there were some differences among them as to what to include, modify, or delete, their comments and suggestions resulted in substantial improvements. We are grateful to the following individuals for sharing their professional insights and suggestions.

Joan Brett
Arizona State University, West

Michael Buckley
University of Oklahoma

John P. Byrne
St. Ambrose University

Elizabeth Cameron
Alma College

Joe Carthey
Northeast Iowa Community College

Gary Christiansen
Northern Iowa Area Community College

Paul Wm. Conco
Campbellsville University

William Cron
Southern Methodist University

Paula Daly
James Madison University

Edwin Gerloff
University of Texas, Arlington

Jennifer George
Rice University

Robert Hanna
California State University Northridge

Charlene Hardy
Walsh University

Warren Imada
Leeward Community College (Hawaii)

Mingfang Li
California State University Northridge

Michael McGill
The Associates First Capital Corporation

Bert Morrow
Mississippi State University

Edward B. Parks
Marymount University

Valentin H. Pashtenko
University of Rhode Island

Joseph Picken
Southern Methodist University

Chester Schriesheim
University of Miami

Charles Snow
Pennsylvania State University

Eric Stark
Washington and Jefferson College

Alex Stajkovic
University of Wisconsin, Madison

Michael Trebesh
Alma College

Don VandeWalle
Southern Methodist University

Jeffrey L. Walls
Indiana Institute of Technology

Cliff Wener
College of Lake County

Angela Zutavern
Booz-Allen & Hamilton

Don Hellriegel
Texas A&M University

Susan E. Jackson
Rutgers University

John W. Slocum
Southern Methodist University

About the Authors

DON HELLRIEGEL

Don Hellriegel is Professor of Management and holds the Bennett Chair in Business in the Lowry Mays College and Graduate School of Business at Texas A&M University. He received his B.S. and M.B.A. from Kent State University and his Ph.D. from the University of Washington. Dr. Hellriegel has been a member of the faculty at Texas A&M since 1975 and has served on the faculties of the Pennsylvania State University and the University of Colorado.

His research interests include corporate entrepreneurship, effect of organizational environments, and organizational innovation and strategic management processes. His research has been published in a number of leading journals.

Professor Hellriegel served as Vice President and Program Chair of the Academy of Management (1986), President Elect (1987), President (1988), and Past President (1989). In September 1999, he was elected to a three-year term as Dean of the Fellows Group of the Academy of Management. He served a term as Editor of the *Academy of Management Review* and served as a member of the Board of Governors of the Academy of Management (1979–1981); (1982–1989). Dr. Hellriegel has occupied many other leadership roles, including President, Eastern Academy of Management; Division Chair, Organization and Management Theory Division; President, Brazos County United Way; Co-Consulting Editor, West Series in Management; Head (1976–1980 and 1989–1994), Department of Management (TAMU); Executive Associate Dean and Interim Dean, Mays College of Business (TAMU); and Interim Executive Vice Chancellor (TAMUS).

He has consulted with a variety of groups and organizations, including—among others—3DI, Sun Ship Building, Penn Mutual Life Insurance, Texas A&M University System, Ministry of Industry and Commerce (Nation of Kuwait), Ministry of Agriculture (Nation of Dominican Republic), American Assembly of Collegiate Schools of Business, and Texas Innovation Group.

SUSAN E. JACKSON

Susan Jackson is Professor of Human Resource Management in the School of Management and Labor Relations at Rutgers University, where she also serves as Graduate Director for the Doctoral Program in Industrial Relations and Human Resources. Prior to joining Rutgers, she taught on the faculties of New York University, the University of Michigan, and the University of Maryland. She received her B.A. in psychology and sociology from the University of Minnesota and her Master's and Ph.D. in organizational psychology from the University of California, Berkeley.

Her primary area of expertise is the strategic management of human resources, and her special interests include managing team effectiveness, workforce diversity, stress and burnout, and the design of human resource management systems to support business imperatives. She has authored or coauthored more than 100 articles on these and related topics. In addition, she has published several books, including *Managing Human Resources: A Partnership Perspective* (with R. S. Schuler); *Strategic Human Resource Management* (with R. S. Schuler); *Diversity in the Workplace: Human Resource Initiatives;* and *Creating Tomorrow's Organizations: A Handbook for Future Research in Organizational Behavior* (with C. L. Cooper). She currently serves as a member of the editorial boards for *Applied Psychology: An International Review; Journal of Applied Psychology; Journal of Occupational and Organizational Psychology; Organizational Dynamics; Journal of Service Research;* and *Human Resource Management Journal.*

Professor Jackson has held numerous positions in professional societies. In the Academy of Management, she currently serves as Representative-at-Large for the Human Resources Division. She also has served as Consulting Editor and Editor of the *Academy of Management Review,* President of the Division of Organizational Behavior, and as a member of the Board of Governors. She is a Fellow in the Society for Industrial and Organizational Psychology, where she has served as Program Chair, and has been a member of the editorial board of the *Frontiers of Industrial & Organizational Psychology,* the Scientific Affairs Committee, Member-at-Large/Long Range Planning Committee, and the Education and Training Committee. She also is a member of the International Association of Applied Psychology, where she has served as Program Co-Chair. In addition, she has served as a consultant to organizations such as General Electric, American Express, Merrill Lynch, Xerox, and the American Assembly of Collegiate Schools of Business.

JOHN W. SLOCUM, JR.

John Slocum is the Chairperson of the Management and Organizations Department and holds the O. Paul Corley Professorship in Organizational Behavior at the Edwin L. Cox School of Business, Southern Methodist University. He has also taught on the faculties of the University of Washington, the Fisher School of Business at the Ohio State University, the Smeal School of Business at the Pennsylvania State University, the International University of Japan, and the Amos Tuck College at Dartmouth. He holds a B.B.A. from Westminster College, an M.B.A. from Kent State University, and a Ph.D. in organizational behavior from the University of Washington.

Professor Slocum has held a number of positions in professional societies. He was elected as a Fellow to the Academy of Management in 1976 for his outstanding contributions to the profession of management and as a Fellow to the Decision Sciences Institute in 1984 for his research in behavioral decision theory. He was awarded the Alumni Citation for Professional Accomplishment by Westminster College, both the Nicolas Salgo and the Rotunda Outstanding Teaching Awards from SMU, and the SMU Alumni Award for Outstanding Service to Alumni. He was the recipient of the inaugural Carl Sewell Distinguished Service Award and a charter member of the *Academy of Management Journal*'s Hall of Fame. He served as President of the Eastern Academy of Management in 1973. From 1975–1986, he served as a member of the Board of Governors, Academy of Management. From 1979–1981, he served as Editor of the *Academy of Management Journal.* In 1983–1984, he served as 39th President of the 8,500-member Academy of Management and Chairman of the Board of Governors of that organization. Currently, he serves as Co-Editor of the *Journal of World Business and Organizational Dynamics.* He is the coauthor of 20 books and has authored or coauthored more than 115 journal articles.

Professor Slocum has served as a consultant to such organizations as OxyChem, ARAMARK, The Associates First Capital Corporation, Fort Worth Museum of Science and History, Pier1, Mack Trucks, Celanese, NASA, Lockheed Martin Corporation, Transnational Trucks, and Key Span Energy.

An Overview of Management

CHAPTER 1
MANAGING IN A DYNAMIC ENVIRONMENT

CHAPTER 2
THE EVOLUTION OF MANAGEMENT

Managing in a Dynamic Environment

1. DEFINE MANAGERS AND MANAGEMENT.

2. EXPLAIN WHAT MANAGERS DO.

3. DEMONSTRATE KNOWLEDGE OF THE COMPETENCIES USED IN MANAGERIAL WORK BY DEVELOPING AND PRACTICING THEM.

4. DESCRIBE THE CHANGING CONTEXT OF MANAGERIAL WORK.

Chapter Outline

PREVIEW: JEFF BEZOS, AMAZON.COM

MANAGERS AND MANAGEMENT

WHAT IS AN ORGANIZATION?
WHAT IS A MANAGER?
WHAT IS MANAGEMENT?
SCOPE OF MANAGEMENT

WHAT MANAGERS DO

GENERAL MANAGERIAL FUNCTIONS
LEVELS OF MANAGEMENT
SMALL-BUSINESS MANAGERS
COMMUNICATION COMPETENCY: Linda Navarro of Sonnet Supply

MANAGERIAL COMPETENCIES

WHAT IT TAKES TO BE A GREAT MANAGER
COMMUNICATION COMPETENCY
PLANNING AND ADMINISTRATION COMPETENCY
PLANNING AND ADMINISTRATION COMPETENCY: Homero Reséndez of CEMEX
TEAMWORK COMPETENCY
TEAMWORK COMPETENCY: Honeywell
STRATEGIC ACTION COMPETENCY
GLOBAL AWARENESS COMPETENCY
GLOBAL AWARENESS COMPETENCY: Coca-Cola
SELF-MANAGEMENT COMPETENCY
DEVELOPING YOUR MANAGERIAL COMPETENCIES

MANAGEMENT—A DYNAMIC PROCESS

THE RESTRUCTURING OF ORGANIZATIONS
A CHANGING WORKFORCE
CHANGING TECHNOLOGY
GLOBALIZATION

CHAPTER SUMMARY

KEY TERMS

QUESTIONS FOR DISCUSSION AND COMPETENCY DEVELOPMENT

HJS MANAGEMENT COMPETENCIES: SELF-ASSESSMENT INVENTORY

VIDEO CASE: SECOND CHANCE BODY ARMOR

JEFF BEZOS, AMAZON.COM

Jeff Bezos, an investment banker, had an idea in the summer of 1994. As he was surfing the Web, he found a site that purported to measure Internet use. It indicated that Internet use was growing by 2,300 percent per year. Bezos believed that people would buy books over the Internet and decided to get in on the rapid Internet growth to sell books online. Many people, including his parents, thought that he was crazy when he quit his job and he and his wife moved from New York City to Seattle. He figured that an average Internet start-up had a one in ten chance of success, but he gave himself a 30 percent chance. He called his parents and said that he wanted to sell books on the Internet. His father said "The Internet? What's that?" Despite their questioning his sanity, Bezos convinced his parents to lend him $300,000, a huge chunk of their retirement savings, to invest in Amazon.

He had decided on books because he wanted to do something that created value for customers. Value would be in a huge selection of books that could be conveniently ordered at a reasonable price. There weren't any mail-order book catalogs that showed thousands, if not millions, of books. A catalog that big would be like a phone book—too expensive to mail. He flew to the American Booksellers Association's annual meeting and discovered that there was no bookseller on the Internet. A few weeks later Bezos formed Amazon, named after the long South American river with limitless branches.

His company was headquartered in his two-bedroom home in Seattle. He and a few friends converted a garage and ran extension cords from every outlet to power three computers. To save money, Bezos went to Home Depot and bought three wooden doors. Using angle brackets and 2×4s, he converted the doors into three desks that cost $60 each. Even today, all the company's employees sit behind a "door desk."

By June 1995, he had created a basic Web site that friends tried to crash. They couldn't because the code was so well written. On July 16, 1995, Amazon.com opened its Web site. During the first 30 days, Amazon sold books in all 50 states and 45 other countries. Bezos knew right then that his idea would grow into something huge. In 1996, the *Wall Street Journal* ran a story about Amazon.com on its front page, which did two things. First, it made a whole new stream of potential customers aware of Amazon.com. Second, it caught Barnes and Noble, Borders, and other booksellers off guard because they didn't have Web sites.

From its start of selling only text-books, Amazon.com now sells a variety of products, including CDs, books, home appliances, software, toys, video games, and other products. Amazon.com sells more than 20 million items from its nine warehouses, which were designed to deliver items efficiently and directly to customers from states with low or no sales tax and are stocked with all its products. The walls of the warehouses are painted white, and the rows of stock shelves shine in fluorescent yellow. Banners float above the aisles listing the company's six core values: customer obsession, ownership, bias for action, frugality, hiring talented people, and innovation. Bezos's obsession with understanding customers' desires and delivering products to them on time have led to a large volume of repeat customer orders, now representing more than 73 percent of Amazon.com orders.

Bezos is a hands-on leader. He believes that hard work and consistency are characteristics that people need to bring to Amazon.com to be successful. He looks for people who have a willingness to change direction and to admit mistakes. People who aren't self-motivated usually don't last long. When he visits a warehouse, he runs through the warehouse to get a feeling of the energy and excitement of the place. He often talks with employees, greeting many of them by name. He begins any speech with: "I wake up every morning terrified—not of the competition but of our customers."[1]

To learn more about Amazon.com, visit the company's home page at

http://www.amazon.com

MANAGERS AND MANAGEMENT

1.

DEFINE MANAGERS AND

MANAGEMENT.

Effective managers such as Jeff Bezos are essential to any organization's overall success, regardless of whether it is a global giant or a small start-up enterprise. Indeed, having talented people is so important to the success of a business that *Fortune* magazine includes "the ability to attract, develop, and keep talented people" as one of the key factors used to establish its list of Most Admired Companies. Since 1995, Jeff Bezos has developed several competencies that have enabled him to perform effectively in his company's top managerial job. A **competency** is a combination of knowledge, skills, behaviors, and attitudes that contribute to personal effectiveness.[2]

Managerial competencies are sets of knowledge, skills, behaviors, and attitudes that a person needs to be effective in a wide range of managerial jobs and various types of organizations. Before reading further, please take time to complete the HJS Management Competencies Self-Assessment Inventory on pages 32–38. We have grouped into categories the scores of hundreds of students and practicing managers against which you can compare your competency scores. Later in this chapter, we describe these competencies in detail.

People use many types of competencies in their everyday lives, including those needed to be effective in leisure activities, in personal relationships, at work, and at school. In this book we focus on managerial competencies. Throughout, we emphasize the competencies that you will need for jobs having managerial responsibility. Specifically, our goal is to help you develop six key managerial competencies:

- communication,
- planning and administration,
- teamwork,
- strategic action,
- global awareness, and
- self-management.[3]

As Figure 1.1 indicates, these six competencies are essential to managerial effectiveness. For now, an overview of what is involved in applying them is sufficient. Table 1.1 identifies several important aspects of each key managerial competency. In practice, knowing where one competency begins and another ends is difficult. You would seldom rely on just one at a time, so drawing sharp distinctions between them is valuable only for purposes of identification and description. Keeping these six managerial competencies firmly in mind will help you think about how the material you are studying can improve your performance in jobs that require you to use them.

WHAT IS AN ORGANIZATION?

Effective managers must pay attention to what goes on both inside and outside their organizations. Regardless of where their attention might be focused at any particular time, managers are part and parcel of organizational settings. Profit-oriented businesses are

Figure 1.1 **A Model of Managerial Competencies**

Table 1.1 | **Six Key Managerial Competencies**

Communication Competency

- Informal communication
- Formal communication
- Negotiation

Planning and Administration Competency

- Information gathering, analysis, and problem solving
- Planning and organizing projects
- Time management
- Budgeting and financial management

Teamwork Competency

- Designing teams
- Creating a supportive environment
- Managing team dynamics

Strategic Action Competency

- Understanding the industry
- Understanding the organization
- Taking strategic actions

Global Awareness Competency

- Cultural knowledge and understanding
- Cultural openness and sensitivity

Self-Management Competency

- Integrity and ethical conduct
- Personal drive and resilience
- Balancing work and life demands
- Self-awareness and development

one type of organizational setting in which managers are found, but they aren't the only one. Undoubtedly, you could write your autobiography as a series of experiences with organizations such as hospitals, schools, museums, sports teams, stores, amusement parks, restaurants, orchestras, community groups and clubs, government agencies, and others. Some of these organizations were small, and others were large. Some were for-profit companies, and others were nonprofit organizations. Some offered products, some offered both products and services, and others offered only services. Some were well managed, and others struggled merely to survive.

We refer to such a group of people as an ***organization*** because each has a structure and strives to achieve goals that individuals acting alone could not reach. All organizations strive to achieve specific goals, but they don't all have the same goals. For example, a goal at FedEx is to offer on-time package delivery service at the lowest prevailing price. A goal at Sony is to create innovative cameras, whereas at Dell Computer a goal is to produce PCs. All these goals, however, are subordinate to the overall goals of increasing profits and market share.

Regardless of an organization's specific goals, the job of managers is to help the organization achieve those goals. In this book, we look at managers in organizations of all types and sizes that have many different goals and many different ways of achieving their goals. Our primary purposes are to help you understand how managers accomplish their goals and to help you develop some of the managerial competencies that you will need to be effective in whatever type of organization you find yourself. Many—indeed, most—of these competencies will be useful to you even if you never have a job with the word *manager* in the title.

WHAT IS A MANAGER?

We've been talking about managers for several pages, so it's time to clarify exactly what the term means. A ***manager*** is a person who plans, organizes, directs, and controls the allocation of human, material, financial, and information resources in pursuit of the organization's goals. The many different types of managers include department managers, product managers, account managers, plant managers, division managers, district managers, and task force managers. What they all have in common is responsibility for the efforts of a group of people who share a goal and access to resources that the group can use in pursuing its goal.

You don't have to be called a manager to be a manager. Some managers have unique and creative titles, such as chief information officer (a person in charge of information systems). People with the job titles of chief executive officer (CEO), president, managing director, supervisor, and coach also are responsible for helping groups of people achieve a common goal, so they too are managers.

Most employees contribute to organizations through their own work, not by directing other employees. Journalists, computer programmers, insurance agents, machine operators, newscasters, graphic designers, sales associates, stockbrokers, accountants, and lawyers are essential to helping organizations achieve their goals, but many people with these job titles aren't managers.

WEB INSIGHT

Access J.C. Penney's Web site at *http://www. jcpenney.com*. Identify the different types of departments and services offered by the company. How does Penney's Web site assist customers in buying certain merchandise?

What sets managers apart, if not their job titles? Simply put, the difference between managers and individual contributors is that managers are evaluated on how well the people they direct do their jobs. Jeff Bezos doesn't fill orders from customers. He hires, trains, and motivates others to manage people who do that job. Vanessa Castagna, executive vice president and chief operating officer (COO) at J.C. Penney, is in charge of revitalizing the company. She announced that J.C. Penney would centralize the buying function and plans to move buying decisions from local store managers to company headquarters in Plano, Texas. She hopes that this policy will enable store managers to spend more time with customers and bring consistency to all J.C. Penney stores. The people who report to Castagna will be responsible for developing a software system that directly feeds sales information from J.C. Penney's 1,150 stores to headquarters and to various suppliers.[4]

WHAT IS MANAGEMENT?

If managers are the people responsible for making sure that an organization achieves its goals, what does the term *management* mean? In everyday usage, people often refer to management as a group of managers in an organization. For example, the CEO and other high-level executives often are referred to as top management. The managers under them may be referred to as middle management, and so on.

The term can also be used to refer to the tasks that managers do. These tasks include planning, organizing, leading, and controlling the work of an organization. Business managers at General Electric (GE) plan, organize, lead, and control activities to ensure that their particular businesses are ranked either first or second against all competitors. CEO Jack Welch has a clear strategy for GE success. Part of this strategy is to improve continuously the quality of GE products and services.

We use the term ***management*** to refer to the tasks and activities involved in directing an organization or one of its units: planning, organizing, leading, and controlling. As you will see, people in many different jobs may be expected to do some management tasks, even if that isn't their main focus. For example, quality control programs such as the one at GE involve employees throughout the entire organization in developing plans for improving quality. When GE Capital Services looks for ways to reduce errors in the bills it sends to credit card customers, managers enlist the help of billing clerks and data processors. They will be empowered to reorganize some of their work and be expected to continue to look for new ways to control quality. In other words, they will be doing some management tasks, but they won't become managers. We reserve the use of *manager* to refer to people in jobs that involve management tasks primarily.

SCOPE OF MANAGEMENT

There are many types of managers and many ways in which managerial jobs differ from each other. One difference is the scope of activities involved. The scope of activities performed by functional managers is relatively narrow, whereas the scope of activities performed by general managers is quite broad.

Functional managers supervise employees having expertise in one area, such as accounting, human resources, sales, finance, marketing, or production. For example, the head of a payroll department is a functional manager. That person doesn't determine employee salaries, as a general manager might, but makes sure that payroll checks are issued on time and in the correct amounts. Usually, functional managers have a great deal of experience and technical expertise in the areas of operation they supervise. Their success as managers is due in part to the detailed knowledge they have about the work being done by the people they supervise, the problems those people are likely to face, and the resources they need to perform effectively.

General managers such as Vanessa Castagna are responsible for the operations of more complex units—for example, a company or a division. Usually they oversee the work of functional managers. General managers must have a broad range of well-developed competencies to do their jobs well. These competencies can be learned through a combination of formal training and various job assignments, or they can be learned simply in the course of trying to adapt and survive in a chosen area. Being adaptable enough to solve whatever problems she ran into has been critical for Ann Livermore, CEO at Hewlett-Packard's Enterprise Computing Solutions Division. She tries to bring freethinkers—the rebels and flakes—into her group to get more diversity in thinking. To increase their effectiveness, she doesn't require them to follow normal operating procedures.

WHAT MANAGERS DO

2.

EXPLAIN WHAT MANAGERS DO.

As we've described the various types of managers, we've given you some idea of what managers do. But these few examples don't show the whole picture by any means. Let's now consider systematically what managers do—the functions they perform and the specific tasks included in these functions.

GENERAL MANAGERIAL FUNCTIONS

The successful manager capably performs four basic managerial functions: planning, organizing, leading, and controlling. However, as you will see, the amount of time a manager spends on each function depends on the level of the particular job. After further describing each of the four general managerial functions, we will highlight the differences among managers at various levels in organizations.

Regardless of their level, most managers perform the four general functions more or less simultaneously—rather than in a rigid, preset order—to achieve organizational goals. Figure 1.2 illustrates this point graphically. In this section we briefly examine the four functions without looking at their interrelationships. However, throughout this book we refer to those interrelationships to help explain exactly how managers do their jobs.

Planning. In general, *planning* involves defining organizational goals and proposing ways to reach them. Managers plan for three reasons: (1) to establish an overall direction for the organization's future, such as increased profit, expanded market share, and

Figure 1.2 **Basic Managerial Functions**

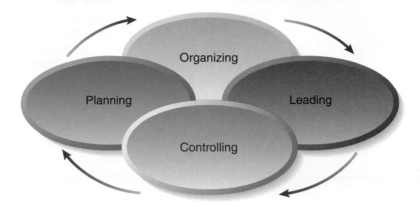

social responsibility; (2) to identify and commit the organization's resources to achieving its goals; and (3) to decide which tasks must be done to reach those goals. Jeff Bezos is a good example of a manager who plans. Through his research, he understood how important the Internet is, which products could be sold over the Internet, what channels of distribution would be needed to deliver products to customers, and how important motivated employees are. In other words, he had a good understanding of what planning involves.

Organizing. After managers have prepared plans, they must translate those relatively abstract ideas into reality. Sound organization is essential to this effort. ***Organizing*** is the process of creating a structure of relationships that will enable employees to carry out management's plans and meet organizational goals. By organizing effectively, managers can better coordinate human, material, and information resources. An organization's success depends largely on management's ability to utilize those resources efficiently and effectively.

Organizing involves creating a structure by setting up departments and job descriptions. For example, the U.S. Postal Service uses a different type of structure than does United Parcel Service (UPS). At the U.S. Postal Service, most employees think of themselves as production workers, and the degree of job specialization is low. Relatively little attention is paid to the marketing function. Most of the decisions are made by top managers, with mail carriers and postal clerks having little to do with decision making. Carriers and clerks are promoted to other jobs as they gain seniority.

In contrast, UPS is organized into two distinct divisions: airline and ground carrier. At UPS, the degree of job specialization is high. Truck drivers don't fly planes, and pilots don't drive trucks. Parcel sorters are located in major hubs around the world and sort parcels for delivery by drivers, who have the most customer contact.

Leading. After management has made plans, created a structure, and hired the right personnel, someone must lead the organization. ***Leading*** involves getting others to perform the tasks necessary to achieve the organization's goals. Leading isn't done only after planning and organizing end; it is a crucial element of those functions. When Lois Dimpfel, vice president of Worldwide Olympic Technology Systems for IBM, was given the assignment to coordinate IBM's technology for the Sydney Olympic Games in 2000, she understood that this task required planning, organizing, and leading simultaneously. With the goal of bringing the games flawlessly to hundreds of millions of people via TV clear in her mind, she organized a team that included hundreds of managers from the United States and Australia. Dimpfel and her team collaboratively planned how to proceed and led in executing those plans.[5]

Controlling. The process by which a person, group, or organization consciously monitors performance and takes corrective action is called ***controlling***. Just as a thermostat sends signals to a heating system that the room temperature is too high or too low, so a management control system sends signals to managers that things aren't working out as planned and that corrective action is needed. Phil Knight is CEO of Nike, the global athletic apparel and shoe company based in Oregon, with annual sales of more than $9 billion.[6] Knight believes that Nike's success is due to its competitive spirit, ability to respond to customers' needs with diverse and genuine products, and its control procedures. In the control process at Nike, Amazon.com, and other organizations, managers

- set standards of performance,

- measure current performance against those standards,

- take action to correct any deviations, and

- adjust the standards if necessary.

WEB INSIGHT

Nike advertises and sells its products and services and furnishes information on sports figures and activities on its Web site at *http://www.nike.com*. In what other ways does Nike use its Web site to stay in touch with changing customer desires?

Nike establishes budgets for each shoe line, such as cross training, aerobic, walking, basketball, and football, and holds its managers responsible for meeting production and financial goals. If a shoe line can't meet its goals, the line is replaced. Knight spends a lot of time traveling globally, visiting retailers. He learns what customers want in terms of product quality, performance, and price. He uses this knowledge when setting performance standards for the firm. At the same time, he reinforces the message that a retailer in Singapore or Shanghai is just as important as one in New York City and that every consumer can count on a consistent commitment to quality.

LEVELS OF MANAGEMENT

Now that we've exposed you to the general functions performed by managers in organizations, let's back up and talk about work settings. So far, we've mostly cited examples of managers in large corporations. But managers and the need for effective management are just as important in small organizations. When Tim Koogle founded Yahoo! in a small basement room in Palo Alto, California, he started with a stack of three flat boxes to which he attached a sign reading: **DO NOT TOUCH**. From this small beginning, Yahoo! now enables millions of customers to view Web pages each month. Yahoo! still doesn't own the servers; it rents them. Koogle knows that, in an intangible world, keeping Yahoo! focused is crucial. At Ford, GM, and other auto manufacturers, making cars requires the use of many different resources. But at Yahoo! the primary resource is brainpower. Employees can start pursuing radically different strategies in the blink of an eye. The company's assets can quickly and utterly become uncoordinated unless Koogle constantly reinforces its strategic focus.[7]

A small organization usually has only one level of management—often the founder or the owner or an executive director. However, large organizations usually have more than one level of management, with varying goals, tasks, responsibilities, and authority. Thus a company's first-line store manager operates very differently than its CEO.[8] Figure 1.3 shows the three basic management levels. We define them with a broad brush here, returning to add detail later in the chapter and throughout the book.

First-Line Managers. In general, *first-line managers* are directly responsible for the production of goods or services. They may be called sales managers, section heads, or production supervisors, depending on the organization. Employees who report to them do the organization's basic production work—whether of goods or of services. For example, a first-line manager at a steel production plant supervises employees who make steel, operate and maintain machines, and write shipping orders. A sales manager at a U.S. automobile dealership supervises salespeople who sell cars to customers in the showroom. An automobile sales manager in Japan works in an office that has computers and telephones similar to a telemarketing center and supervises salespeople who go to people's homes to sell them cars.

This level of management is the link between the operations of each department and the rest of the organization. First-line managers in most companies spend little time

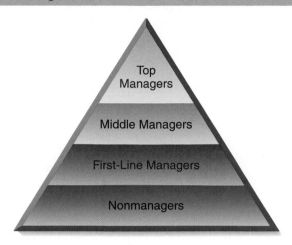

with higher management or with people from other organizations. Most of their time is spent with the people they supervise and with other first-line managers.

First-line managers often lead hectic work lives full of pressure and having little glamour, as Susan Sargent found out.[9] She directs sales representatives who sell home furnishings by phone or e-mail. She expected the sales representatives to feel and act as if they were an extension of the office. But many weren't savvy with their laptops and didn't sell the newest products, mainly because products were introduced to them online. Worse, they took orders for products that were not in stock. There was a real disconnect between the sales representatives and customers. Sargent quickly realized that 80 percent of her day is spent directing the actions of salespeople (leading), making sure that customers' shipments arrive on time, settling disputes among employees, scheduling vacations and overtime, and inspecting products (controlling). She spends relatively little time planning and organizing.

First-line managers usually need strong technical expertise to teach subordinates and supervise their day-to-day tasks. Workers usually develop technical expertise before becoming managers. Sometimes, though, a first-line manager is a recent college graduate who is responsible for the work of both hourly employees and professionals. Such a first-line manager is likely to have little hands-on experience. Lack of experience isn't a problem if the new manager is willing to learn and has the competency to communicate with diverse types of people, to coach and counsel subordinates, and to provide constructive feedback.

Middle Managers. Some managers at larger organizations must focus on coordinating employee activities, determining which products or services to provide, and deciding how to market these products or services to customers. These are the tasks of ***middle managers***, who receive broad, general strategies and policies from top managers and translate them into specific goals and plans for first-line managers to implement. Middle managers typically have titles such as department head, plant manager, and director of finance. They are responsible for directing and coordinating the activities of first-line managers and, at times, such nonmanagerial personnel as clerks, receptionists, and staff assistants. As a middle manager for Lucky Hot Dogs, a company that sells hot dogs from kiosks in New Orleans, every day Jerry Strahan supervises his first-line managers, who in turn manage street vendors. Strahan describes his job as a ringmaster, trying to balance the health department's demands for clean kiosks, vendors' demands for supplies, and first-line managers' demands for recruiting new employees to staff the company's 25 kiosks. He occasionally will scrub carts himself when one of Lucky Dog's maintenance employees doesn't show up for work. He reports daily sales to Lucky Dog's president, Doug Talbot.[10]

Many middle managers began their careers and spent several years as first-line managers. Even so, promotion from the first level of management to middle management is often difficult and sometimes traumatic. The heavier emphases on managing group performance and allocating resources represent the most important differences between first-line and middle managers. The middle manager often is involved in reviewing the work plans of various groups, helping them set priorities, and negotiating and coordinating their activities. Middle managers are involved in establishing target dates for products or services to be completed; developing evaluation criteria for performance; deciding which projects should be given money, personnel, and materials; and translating top management's general goals into specific operational plans, schedules, and procedures.

Middle managers carry out top management's directives primarily by delegating authority and responsibility to their subordinates and by coordinating schedules and resources with other managers. They often spend much of their day talking on the phone, attending committee meetings, and preparing and reviewing reports. Middle managers tend to be removed from the technical aspects of work, so whatever technical expertise they may have is of less direct help to them now. In many organizations today, developing subordinates and helping them move up in the organization is essential to being viewed as a successful manager. When middle managers fail to develop their staffs, low morale and high turnover are likely to follow.

Top Managers. The overall direction of an organization is the responsibility of *top managers*. Michael Dell, CEO of Dell Computer, and Meg Whitman, CEO of eBay, are two such managers who have built hugely successful Internet companies. Typical titles of top managers are chief executive officer, president, chairman, division president, and executive vice president. Top managers develop goals, policies, and strategies for the entire organization. The goals they set are handed down through the hierarchy, eventually reaching each worker.

CEOs and presidents often represent their organizations in community affairs, business deals, and government negotiations. Ray Anderson, CEO of Interface, a billion-dollar-a-year floor-covering company, is a firm believer that a company should try to grow without damaging the earth and manufacture without creating pollution and waste and using excessive amounts of fossil fuels. President Clinton named him to the Council on Sustainable Growth, and he worked with other nations at an environmental summit in Kyoto, Japan, to draft a treaty that committed the 160 industrialized nations of the world to cut their greenhouse-gas emissions by more than 5 percent by 2012. Anderson's main job on the council is to work with a panel of business leaders, environmentalists, and local and federal government officials to deliver policy recommendations on global warming to the White House. He has been instrumental in drafting a bill for Senate consideration that would give early action tax credits to businesses cutting emissions ahead of the schedule set in Kyoto. Royal Dutch/Shell said that it will do so by 2002, General Motors (GM) has pledged to cut energy use by 20 percent by 2002, and recently Toyota has rolled out a hybrid gas/electric car in Japan.[11]

Top managers spend most of their day (over 75 percent) planning and leading. They spend most of their leading time with key people in organizations other than their own. Top managers—like middle managers—spend little time directly controlling the work of others.

Pressures and demands on top managers can be intense. Tightly scheduled workdays, heavy travel requirements, and workweeks of 50 or more hours are common. A true break is a luxury. Coffee is swallowed on the run, and lunch often is eaten during meetings with other managers, business associates, community representatives, or government officials. When there is some free time, eager subordinates vie for a piece of it.

Top managers also face expanding public relations duties. They must be able to respond quickly to crises that may create image problems for their organizations. Imagine that you are Albert Stroucken, president of H. B. Fuller. Headquartered in St. Paul, Minnesota, Fuller manufactures industrial glues, coatings, and paints. Among its products is Resistol, a glue used for making shoes. For many years children in Central America have sniffed Resistol because it provides a temporary euphoria that relieves hunger and hopelessness. The Federal Drug Administration (FDA) has evidence that Resistol's fumes are addictive and can cause brain damage. Fuller has tried to stop Resistol's use as a drug by reducing the toxicity of the glue and restricting its sales in Honduras and Guatemala. It has not added mustard oil, which causes vomiting, to the glue because its sales will decline. Stroucken is faced with the issue of whether Fuller should do more to prevent abuse of its product, including withdrawing it from the market, or continue to make this highly profitable glue.[12]

SMALL-BUSINESS MANAGERS

In small companies, one person—usually the founder or current owner—often carries the whole load. **Small-business managers** are responsible for different types of tasks. Linda Navarro, owner and CEO of Sonnet Supply Company in Hawthorne, California, is a small-business manager. Navarro owns a cutting tool company that caters mostly to the aerospace industry. She began her career with Sonnet in 1977 when she walked into the office and asked for a job.[13] Along the way, Navarro worked in the warehouse, did sales, energized Sonnet's telemarketing program, and subsequently became vice president, then president, and finally CEO and owner. Although she had to overcome a lot of frustrations along the way, Navarro uses her experience to lead her staff of 15 employees. As the firm's CEO, she has learned a great deal about communication, as illustrated in the following Communication Competency feature.

COMMUNICATION COMPETENCY

Linda Navarro of Sonnet Supply

Navarro knows every job at Sonnet and has performed all of them. One of the changes that she has instituted since becoming CEO is an open book management policy. The firm has always been privately owned and financial statements have been private, too. But Navarro insists that employees and customers need to understand what Sonnet's business costs are and how it makes a profit.

Employees are told how to figure costs on each piece of equipment. Rather than an employee knowing one piece of the business, each is trained to operate all equipment and even make sales calls on prospective customers. Navarro wants employees to know that there are bills to be paid and that working efficiently can mean the difference between a big raise and a small raise. If employees know exactly what they need to do as individuals and as a group, they are more apt to strive to reach their

and the company's goals. She frequently refers to her employees as family, and feels a responsibility to help them better their career paths and lifestyles. She selects employees carefully because she wants them to believe in Sonnet and its values. A key value is establishing long-term relationships with customers that are built on trust (e.g., salespeople keeping their word on product delivery schedules) and quality rather than on price.

She also decided to let Sonnet's customers see exactly what its costs are because she grew tired of hearing them complain that Sonnet's prices were too high. She instructs her salespeople to tell customers these costs because she has nothing to hide. She believes that, through developing seminars for customers, Sonnet can add value to its products. For example, since Sonnet's products go into special customer applications, she wants her customers to be

very knowledgeable about Sonnet's product line. The seminars are aimed at helping educate customers, not just to sell them products.

• • •

To learn more about Sonnet Supply, visit the company's home page at

http://www.sonnetsupply.com

As Linda Navarro's activities demonstrate, owners of small businesses don't differentiate among levels of management. As a company grows, however, an owner has to narrow the job's scope and concentrate on certain tasks. For example, an entrepreneur whose strength is in marketing might focus on getting new customers to spur the growth of the business and hire other managers to handle finances and supervise on-site work.

MANAGERIAL COMPETENCIES

3.

DEMONSTRATE
KNOWLEDGE OF THE
COMPETENCIES USED IN
MANAGERIAL WORK BY
DEVELOPING AND
PRACTICING THEM.

We've talked about the various levels of management and what managers do, but you may still be wondering about what it takes to be an effective (or even a great) manager. So, let's look more closely at the competencies that managers need in order to succeed.

WHAT IT TAKES TO BE A GREAT MANAGER

At the beginning of this chapter, we defined *managerial competencies* as sets of knowledge, skills, behaviors, and attitudes that a manager needs in order to be effective in a wide range of managerial jobs and various organizational settings. We identified six specific competencies as being particularly important: communication, planning and administration, teamwork, strategic action, global awareness, and self-management. These competencies are transferable from one organization to the next.[14] Managerial competencies useful to a Farmers Insurance Company sales manager responsible for increasing customer satisfaction throughout a region also would be useful if the manager later took a job at Government Employees Insurance Company (GEICO). They would be useful to the manager of a local coffee shop interested in increasing sales during the breakfast hour and to a project manager in Paris charged with developing a new multimedia game for children. Whether you supervise the work of a small team on the shop floor or serve as CEO of a global company, honing the managerial competencies that we've identified can only enhance your performance.

Regardless of when, where, or how you develop these competencies, you should be able to use them in the future in jobs that you can't yet even imagine holding—or that may not even exist today. One way to enhance your managerial competencies is by studying this book and completing the activities presented at the end of each chapter. By participating in extracurricular activities, you can develop competencies such as communication and teamwork that often can be transferred to a variety of jobs. By taking the appropriate courses and participating in international clubs and associations, you can broaden your knowledge of other countries and build your global awareness competency. By holding an office or taking responsibility for organizing a community event, such as spring cleanup day in the park, you can build your planning and administration competency. Because managerial competencies can be learned through such activities, in addition to on the job, campus recruiters pay a great deal of attention to students' involvement in them, instead of just looking at grade point averages.

COMMUNICATION COMPETENCY

Communication competency is your ability to transfer and exchange effectively information that leads to understanding between yourself and others. Because managing involves getting work done through other people, communication competency is essential to effective managerial performance. It includes

- informal communication,
- formal communication, and
- negotiation.

Communication competency transcends the use of a particular communication medium. That is, good communication may involve having a face-to-face conversation, preparing a formal written document, participating in a global meeting via teleconferencing, giving a speech to an audience of several hundred people, or using e-mail to coordinate a project team whose members work in different regions of the country or the world.

Communication isn't something that you do to other people; it is something that you do with them. It is both informal and formal. Usually, it is a dynamic, give-and-take process that involves both receiving messages from others and sending messages to others. Besides speaking and writing, it involves listening, observing body language, and picking up on the subtle cues that people sometimes use to modify the meaning of their words. Linda Navarro, CEO of Sonnet Supply Company, pays attention to all these communication cues as she visits with employees on the job and with customers. As a member as the Small Business Network Development Forum in Los Angeles, she also applies her communication skills to network with other managers from other lines of business and share best practices.

Of the six managerial competencies that we've identified, communication is perhaps the most fundamental. Unless you can express yourself and understand others in written, oral, and nonverbal (e.g., facial expression and body posture) communication, you can't use the other competencies effectively to accomplish tasks through other people. Nor can you effectively manage the vast network of relationships that link you to other people inside and outside your organization.

The productive employment of workers of all ages, with varying types of work experience and expertise, of both genders and varied cultural and ethnic backgrounds, means that a basic level of communication competency is seldom enough these days. After all, managing effectively means getting all workers to contribute their best ideas and efforts in an intensely competitive global market. At Amazon.com, Jeff Bezos knows that this effort requires plenty of spontaneous, informal communication that is sensitive to the different backgrounds and perspectives of employees and customers alike. Moreover, to be sure that you are understood, you need to become comfortable soliciting and accepting feedback.

Through *informal* communication, managers build a social network of contacts. In China, these connections are known as *guanxi*.[15] In Japan, they're called *kankei,* and in Korea they're called *kwankye.* Whatever language you say it in, maintaining social networks is especially important to managerial work. But in a Confucian society, the web of social contacts maintained through informal communication is central to success. In fact, when business leaders in China were asked to identify the factors most important to long-term business success, *guanxi* was the only factor chosen consistently—ahead of choosing the right business location, selecting the right business strategy, and competitive pricing.[16] Through frequent informal communication, managers in all countries lay the groundwork for collaboration within and outside their organizations.

Being able to communicate in more formal situations also is important to managerial effectiveness. *Formal communication,* such as a newsletter, often is used to inform people of relevant events and activities and to keep people up to date on the status of ongoing projects. Public speeches are another example of formal communication. Whether the audience is company executives, professional peers, shareholders, or members of the community, high-impact public presentations can be used to address stakeholder concerns and enhance the firm's reputation.

Formal communication can also take place at a more personal level, as during conversations with suppliers and clients. Among bankers, for example, formal communication is essential to managing client relationships. Christine Koski, global marketing manager at Celanese Ltd., is in charge of global marketing for the company's chemical group. Her role as a "relationship manager" involves selling the firm's chemicals to many of the world's largest corporations, including Exxon/Mobil, Shell, and DuPont. Although she traveled to more than 25 countries during the past five years and lived in Germany for another five years, she isn't expected to be fluent in the language of every country she visits. But she must be able to communicate, often through an interpreter, in all these cultures. In other words, for Christine Koski, effective communication goes hand in hand with a global perspective. Koski's job also involves *negotiating*—sometimes at great distances. One negotiation with Air Product's plant in Singapore was particularly intense, with down-to-the-wire discussions stretching over days. Working from her hotel room, she needed to build consensus on goals and commitment to achieving them. Good negotiators learn to seek contrary opinions and find ways to respond to the divergent views they uncover. Building consensus and commitment is useful for negotiations with bosses, peers, and subordinates, as well as with clients. Managers also must be able to negotiate to obtain resources for their subordinates and to settle disputes that arise among various stakeholders.[17]

Because managers spend so much of their time communicating, management recruiters look for people who can communicate effectively. In fact, we can't stress enough the importance of good communication. At a time when organizations increasingly expect employees to work with minimal supervision and show more initiative, competent oral, written, and electronic communication is essential. For more details about communication competency, refer to Table 1.2.

Table 1.2	**Dimensions of Communication Competency**

Informal Communication

- Promotes two-way communication by asking for feedback, listening, and creating a give-and-take conversation.
- Has awareness of others' feelings.
- Builds strong interpersonal relationships with people.

Formal Communication

- Informs people of relevant events and activities and keeps them up to date.
- Makes persuasive, high-impact public presentations and handles questions well.
- Writes clearly, concisely, and effectively, using a variety of computer-based resources.

Negotiation

- Negotiates effectively on behalf of a team over roles and resources.
- Is skilled at developing relationships and exercising influence upward with superiors.
- Takes decisive and fair actions when handling problem subordinates.

PLANNING AND ADMINISTRATION COMPETENCY

Planning and administration competency involves deciding what tasks need to be done, determining how they can be done, allocating resources to enable them to be done, and then monitoring progress to ensure that they are done. For many people, planning and administration competency comes to mind first when they think about managers and managing. Included in this competency are

- information gathering, analysis, and problem solving;
- planning and organizing projects;
- time management; and
- budgeting and financial management.

When Jeff Bezos of Amazon.com describes what his workday is like, he puts it this way: "Basically, the whole day comes down to a series of choices." To help him hone his planning and administration competency, Bezos and his staff analyzed his day, and his staff helped him reshape his management approach. Bezos instinctively knew that *information gathering, analysis, and problem solving* are important. He also recognized that customers are a rich source of useful information but that they can easily eat up a whole day. His staff helped him understand that he could delegate the handling of some types of customer phone calls in order to free up 25 percent of his time for meeting directly with customers.

Planning and organizing projects usually means working with employees to clarify broad objectives, discuss resource allocation, and agree to completion dates. Thus Bezos spends 40 percent of his day with employees and customers, 25 percent on the Internet, 10 percent on the telephone, and the rest on paperwork. Because there are more problems and opportunities than he possibly can attend to, Bezos needs to *manage his time* and delegate effectively.

Managers also are accountable for *budgeting and managing financial* resources. Boards of directors and shareholders of public corporations hold CEOs, such as Carly Fiorina at Hewlett-Packard and Michael Brown at EDS, fiscally accountable. In non-profit and government organizations, trustees, various regulatory bodies, and elected officials oversee fiscal management.

One leader who understands the need for effective planning and administration is Homero Reséndez of CEMEX. Based in Monterrey, Mexico, CEMEX was founded in 1906 and last year reported revenues of $4.3 billion.[18] It has operations in 23 countries and is the leading concrete maker in Mexico, Venezuela, and other Latin American countries. The following Planning and Administration Competency feature highlights how Reséndez used his planning and administration competency to manage the firm's growth.

PLANNING & ADMINISTRATION COMPETENCY

Homero Reséndez of CEMEX

Trying to deliver concrete is a tough business anywhere, but doing it in Mexico and other Latin American countries is even more difficult. The weather is unpredictable, labor disruptions are frequent, government inspectors target construction sites for code violations, and traffic jams are common. Meanwhile, a load of concrete must be delivered within 90 minutes or rotation of the cylinder on the back of a truck will ruin the batch.

From the headquarters in Monterrey, Mexico, dispatchers take orders for any of 8,000 grades of concrete and then forward those orders to six regional concrete plants in Mexico, each with its own fleet of trucks. CEMEX tried to train its customers to stick with their orders by imposing financial penalties for changes and demanding longer lead times—but the customers simply ignored the company's demands.

Reséndez knew that CEMEX had to do better than promise delivery within a three-hour window. He turned to FedEx, another operation built entirely around the swift delivery of goods to any and all locations. Reséndez and his team of managers flew to Memphis, Tennessee, and were stunned by FedEx's efficiency and use of information systems to track a customer's order. FedEx's slogan "It's on time, or it's on us" captured the CEMEX team's imagination. The team scheduled another trip to a 911 dispatch center in Houston. Sitting among the

dispatchers, CEMEX managers saw dispatchers field calls reporting heart attacks, fires, and other emergencies with poise and calm. There always seemed to be just enough ambulances and paramedics in just the right parts of town. That's when the idea hit them: Though individually unpredictable, emergencies occurred in sufficient number to allow a pattern to be discerned and planned for.

The team began to question the company's entire planning and administrative setup. Rather than punishing customers with penalties or enforcing long lead times, CEMEX decided to make a last-minute change in the routine. The company launched a project called Sincronizacion Dinamica de Operacions (the dynamic synchronization of operations). CEMEX stopped assigning its delivery trucks to specific zones within a city, setting them free to roam an entire city as one big pool. The company also outfitted its trucks with transmitters and receivers connected to the global-positioning satellite (GPS) system, thereby giving its computer precise, real-time data about the location, direction, and speed of every truck in its fleet. The computer triangulates this information against order destination and mixing plants, all while taking traffic patterns into account. Because many of them have had only six years of formal schooling, CEMEX enrolled its drivers in weekly secondary education classes that lasted two years so that they could

read computer printouts and communicate electronically with dispatchers. Meanwhile, work rules also were changed to help fill orders on time.

The company introduced same-day service at no extra charge, and unlimited order changes became standard operating procedure. If a load fails to arrive within 20 minutes of its scheduled delivery time, the buyer gets back 20 pesos per cubic meter, or about 5 percent of the total bill. With reliability exceeding 98 percent, vehicle efficiency increased by more than 30 percent. Reséndez relied on his information gathering, problem-solving, planning, and organizing skills to increase CEMEX's efficiency.

• • •

To learn more about CEMEX, visit the company's home page at

http://www.cemex.com

In Table 1.3, we highlight the various dimensions that make up planning and administration competency.

Table 1.3	Dimensions of Planning and Administration Competency

Information Gathering, Analysis, and Problem Solving

- Monitors information and uses it to identify symptoms, problems, and alternative solutions.
- Makes timely decisions.
- Takes calculated risks and anticipates the consequences.

Planning and Organizing Projects

- Develops plans and schedules to achieve goals efficiently.
- Assigns priorities to tasks and delegates responsibility.
- Determines, obtains, and organizes necessary resources to accomplish the task.

Time Management

- Handles several issues and projects at one time but doesn't spread self too thin.
- Monitors and keeps to a schedule or changes schedule if needed.
- Works effectively under time pressure.

Budgeting and Financial Management

- Understands budgets, cash flows, financial reports, and annual reports and regularly uses such information to make decisions.
- Keeps accurate and complete financial records.
- Creates budgetary guidelines for others and works within the guidelines given by others.

TEAMWORK COMPETENCY

Accomplishing tasks through small groups of people who are collectively responsible and whose work is interdependent requires **teamwork competency.** Managers in companies that utilize teams can become more effective by

- designing teams properly,
- creating a supportive team environment, and
- managing team dynamics appropriately.

WEB INSIGHT

Teams play a large part in determining the productivity of their members. Access Southwest Airlines' Web site at *http://www. southwest.com* to learn more about the company, including its number-one rating of fewest customer complaints and its inclusion in *Fortune*'s list of the 100 Best Companies to Work for in America. How does Southwest's spirit of teamwork contribute to this recognition?

In a recent study of more than 400 organizations and 80,000 managers, the Gallup Organization, a public opinion poll-taking company, found that the best managed companies used employees in teams.[19] Improving customer service was the main reason given for their use, followed by decreasing absenteeism and improving productivity. At Southwest Airlines, effective teamwork makes it possible for ground crews to turn around a plane at the gate in less than 17 minutes. Regardless of their job titles, all employees work together to get passengers unloaded and loaded. When necessary, pilots, flight attendants, and whoever else is available pitch in to ensure that a flight leaves the boarding gate on schedule.

When people think of teamwork, they often make a distinction between the team members and a team leader. We don't hold this view of teamwork. Instead, we view teamwork as a competency that involves taking the lead at times, supporting others who are taking the lead at other times, and collaborating with others in the organization on projects that don't even have a designated team leader. We hold this view of teamwork competency because most managerial work involves doing all these activities simultaneously.

Designing the team is the first step for any team project and usually is the responsibility of a manager or team leader. But in self-managed teams, the entire team participates in the design. Team design involves formulating goals to be achieved, defining tasks to be done, and identifying the staffing needed to accomplish those tasks. Team members should identify with the team's goals and feel committed to accomplishing them. Members of a well-designed team understand its tasks and how its performance will be measured; they aren't confused about which tasks are theirs and which tasks are some other team's. A well-designed team has just the right number of members. Too many members leave room for free riders; too few create too much stress and leave the team feeling incapable of successfully achieving its goals.

A well-designed team is capable of high performance, but it needs a *supportive environment* to achieve its full potential.[20] All team members should have the competencies needed to create a supportive environment. In a supportive environment, team members are empowered to take actions based on their best judgment, without always seeking approval first from the team leader or project manager. Support also involves eliciting contributions from members whose unique competencies are important for the team and recognizing, praising, and rewarding both minor victories and major successes. A manager having good teamwork competency respects other people and is respected and even liked by them in return. Managers who lack teamwork competency often are viewed as being rude, abrupt, and unsympathetic, making others feel inadequate and resentful. Fundamentally, creating a supportive environment involves coaching, counseling, and mentoring team members to improve their performance in the near term and prepare them for future challenges.

How an organization fosters teamwork is often just as important as teamwork itself. Managers with the greatest likelihood of developing their employees' teamwork competency are those that have input from all levels of the organization, including members of the team, employees that support the team, those who will administer the plan, and even customers. Managers need to pay attention to *managing team dynamics*. If team members remain ignorant about a process, they are more likely to reject it out of hand. People want to be involved. The following Teamwork Competency feature highlights how Honeywell's Commercial Avionics Division develops its employees' teamwork competency.[21]

TEAMWORK COMPETENCY

Honeywell

Honeywell's management charged a team of employees with aligning their pay to the performance of the Commercial Avionics Division. The team's decision was to link workers' pay to division profitability. In its plan, a percentage of each employee's yearly pay is based on the achievement of annual company objectives. This program met with little resistance because it was the employees themselves who decided how the plan would work.

The first step in the plan was for managers in the human resources (HR) department to teach team members, secretaries, engineers, and others in HR some basic concepts of compensation. Armed with this basic knowledge, team members decided to do additional research on their own. Top management provided no guidelines as to how the plan should work; it was up to the team to decide.

The team recommended beginning with a self-funding gainsharing program in which a percentage of each member's pay is at risk, pending achievement of the division's profitability goal. Second, team members also have the opportunity to earn more than their annual salaries when the company has a good year. Third, the team was responsible for all aspects of making the product. Team members took on disciplinary and training issues within the team. The challenge was to learn how to work together and supervise themselves with minimal management direction. Simple things, such as we all need to be at work on time or if you're more than five minutes late, you're docked a day's pay, needed to be addressed by the team. Initially, many team members were frustrated and confused. However, as they learned how to create a supportive envi-

ronment and resolve conflict constructively, the team's productivity soared.

• • •

To learn more about Honeywell, visit the company's home page at

http://www.honeywell.com

Because more and more organizations are relying on teams to improve quality, productivity, and customer service, it becomes increasingly important for you to develop your teamwork competency and become a productive team member. For more detail about teamwork competency, refer to Table 1.4.

<table>
<tr><td>Table 1.4</td><td>Dimensions of Teamwork Competency</td></tr>
</table>

Designing Teams

- Formulates clear objectives that inspire team members to perform.
- Appropriately staffs the team, taking into account the value of diverse ideas and technical skills needed.
- Defines responsibilities for the team as a whole and assigns tasks and responsibilities to individual team members as appropriate.

Creating a Supportive Environment

- Creates an environment in which effective teamwork is expected, recognized, praised, and rewarded.
- Assists the team in identifying and acquiring the resources it needs to accomplish its goals.
- Acts as a coach, counselor, and mentor, being patient with team members as they learn.

Managing Team Dynamics

- Understands the strengths and weaknesses of team members and uses their strengths to accomplish tasks as a team.
- Brings conflict and dissent into the open and uses it to enhance performance.
- Shares credit with others.

STRATEGIC ACTION COMPETENCY

Understanding the overall mission and values of the organization and ensuring that your actions and those of the people you manage are aligned with them involves **strategic action competency**. Strategic action competency includes

- understanding the industry,
- understanding the organization, and
- taking strategic actions.

Today, employees at all levels and in all functional areas are being challenged to think strategically in order to perform their jobs better. They are expected to recognize that shifts in a company's strategic direction are to be expected—even anticipated. Managers and employees who understand the industry can accurately anticipate strategic trends and prepare for the future needs of the organization are less likely to find themselves looking for new jobs when the organization changes direction.

One manager who has proved that he is extremely good at *understanding the industry* in which he operates is Michael Lynton, CEO of the Penguin Group, a company that publishes paperback books and travel guides. The travel-guide industry and its customers are notoriously fickle, yet he has succeeded with *Rouges Guides*. These guides grew out of a simple idea for a series aimed at 30-to-40-year-olds who were interested in roughing it a bit. The company quickly established a brand, and sales are growing at the rate of nearly 20 percent a year. Older established companies, such as Simon and Schuster and John Wiley & Sons, were simply unable to understand that segment of the market. Lynton's success is due in part to his planning and administration competency, which he uses to set up operations that run smoothly even when he isn't there to supervise. But it takes more than a smooth-running operation to be profitable. Early in his career Lynton developed keen strategic insights into the travel industry by working with Michael Eisner at Disney. According to Lynton, "One person, thinking differently, can turn conventional wisdom on its head" seems to be the best advice for any manager who is trying to develop strategic action competency.[22]

This competency also involves *understanding the organization*—not just the particular unit in which a manager works—as a system of interrelated parts. It includes comprehending how departments, functions, and divisions relate to one another and how a change in one can affect others. A manager with well-developed strategic action competency can diagnose and assess different types of management problems and issues that might arise. Such a manager thinks in terms of relative priorities rather than ironclad goals and criteria. All managers, but especially top managers, need strategic action competency. Top managers, such as Michael Lynton, must perceive changes in the organization's environment and be prepared to *take strategic actions*. For more detail about strategic action competency, refer to Table 1.5.

Table 1.5	Dimensions of Strategic Action Competency

Understanding the Industry

- Understands the industry and quickly recognizes when changes in the industry create significant threats and opportunities.
- Stays informed of the actions of competitors and strategic partners.
- Can analyze general trends in the industry and their implications for the future.

Understanding the Organization

- Understands the concerns of stakeholders.
- Understands the strengths and limitations of various business strategies.
- Understands the distinctive competencies of the organization.

Taking Strategic Actions

- Assigns priorities and makes decisions that are consistent with the firm's mission and strategic goals.
- Recognizes the management challenges of alternative strategies and addresses them.
- Establishes tactical and operational goals that facilitate strategy implementation.

GLOBAL AWARENESS COMPETENCY

Carrying out an organization's managerial work by drawing on the human, financial, information, and material resources from multiple countries and serving markets that span multiple cultures requires **global awareness competency**. Not all organizations have global markets for their products and services. Nor do all organizations need to set up operations in other countries to take advantage of tax laws and labor that is cheaper or better trained. Nevertheless, over the course of your career, you probably will work for an organization that has an international component. To be prepared for such opportunities, you should begin to develop your global awareness competency, which is reflected in

- cultural knowledge and understanding, and
- cultural openness and sensitivity.

In the course of growing up and being educated in a particular country or region, people naturally develop cultural knowledge and understanding of forces that shape their lives and the conduct of business.[23] These forces include geography and climate, political processes and orientations, economic systems and trends, history, religion, values, beliefs, and local customs. By the time you become a manager in your home country, your own culture has become second nature to you, so you don't need to devote much time developing further a general knowledge and awareness of it. However, unless you have traveled extensively, or have specifically studied other cultures as part of your education, you probably have much less general knowledge and understanding of other countries, except perhaps those that share a border with your own country. Yet because business is becoming global, many managers are now expected to develop *a knowledge and an understanding* of at least a few other cultures, such as those where suppliers are located or those with newly emerging markets that can help sustain their companies' future growth.

Simply knowing about other cultures isn't sufficient; appropriate attitudes and skills are needed to translate this knowledge into effective performance. An open attitude about cultural differences and a sensitivity to them are especially important for anyone who must operate across cultural boundaries. *Openness and sensitivity* involve, first and foremost, recognizing that culture makes a difference in how people think and act. You can't assume that everyone will think and act as you do, nor that everyone will automatically understand your point of view. Second, openness and sensitivity mean actively considering how another culture might differ from your own and examining how your own culture affects your behavior.

Knowledge about other cultures and an open attitude and sensitivity about cultural differences set the stage for working with people from other backgrounds.[24] In any culture, appropriate language, social etiquette, and negotiation skills help in developing effective work relationships. Depending on your job, you may also need to learn country-specific laws, accounting methods, hiring techniques, and so on. Because there are so many cultures and because predicting which cultures will be most important to you in the future is so difficult, you shouldn't expect to develop global awareness competency relevant to many of the world's cultures. But neither can you put off beginning to build a good foundation.

Because of language and cultural differences, organizations must consider product names when selling in international markets. Inadequate translation can result in a negative image for the product and company. Global markets are complex and often difficult to understand.[25] The following Global Competency feature highlights some problems that Coca-Cola had in its global operations. With a new organizational structure, Coca-Cola hopes to avoid these problems in the future.

GLOBAL AWARENESS COMPETENCY

Coca-Cola

Coca-Cola is the largest soft drink company in the world. In fact, it is massive, employing many thousands of people globally, including 18,000 in Argentina and 6,200 in the company's headquarters in Atlanta, Georgia. Brands such as Fanta, Sprite, and of course, Coca-Cola, have an impact around the world. These names are recognized in many countries, and other brands, also produced by the Coca-Cola Company, are distributed in one or more countries and tailored to specific cultures and tastes of those consumers. Coca-Cola is the market leader in soft drinks in Japan, where it has partnerships with locally owned and managed bottling companies. Japan is one of the most competitive soft drink markets in the world, with 7,000 different brand names and 500 manufacturers.

In January 2000, the Coca-Cola Company underwent a change in its top management. M. Douglas Ivester was replaced as chairman and CEO by Doug Daft, who promptly announced that the company would reduce its workforce worldwide by 21 percent and the Atlanta workforce by 40 percent. Coca-Cola employees in other countries would be affected in several ways by these cutbacks and the changes that would follow. Atlanta is so geographically removed from many of Coca-Cola's overseas operations that top management hasn't been able to oversee and have hands-on input in many overseas facilities and markets. Top management believes that its consumers in 200 nations must be better served and protected.

Changes have come about following two consecutive years of decline in the company's profits and two separate quality issues in Belgium. The Belgian health minister took precautionary measures regarding health-related concerns after bottles filled at the Antwerp bottling facility had an "off taste." It was determined that the carbon dioxide used had affected the taste but presented no actual health problems. The second issue involved an odor on the bottom of some of Coca-Cola's canned products. Independent analysis determined that the cans were safe and that the odor was harmless. Nevertheless, the company, in conjunction with its bottling partner in Belgium, has taken steps to eliminate the odor, which they say was caused by a substance used in the treatment of the cans. They further stated that the offensive odor did not affect product safety.

Daft asserted that "the world in which we operate has changed dramatically, and we must change to succeed. This realignment will better enable the company to serve the changing needs of its customers and consumers at local levels." As a result of the company's new approach to global consumerism, some high-ranking executives will be moved from Atlanta to different countries. What sells and is popular in Atlanta might be a total failure in Argentina or Denmark.

"People have different beverage requirements in different environments," Daft said. "No matter where we operate around the world, we're a local business." Top management at Coca-Cola believes that these changes are necessary if it is to remain the "giant" of the soft drink market, continuing to grow and maintaining its leadership role in a global market.

• • •

To learn more about the Coca-Cola Company, visit the company's home page at

http://www.coca-cola.com

Managers do not share the same cultural knowledge and understanding around the world. Global managers must understand other societies' religions, languages, values, laws, and ethics. Knowing the behaviors fostered by other cultures can help determine which course of action is most appropriate. In the preceding Global Competency feature, obvious mistakes were made that cost Coca-Cola market share and profits. For more detail about global awareness competency, refer to Table 1.6.

T a b l e 1 . 6	*Dimensions of Global Awareness Competency*

Cultural Knowledge and Understanding

- Stays informed of political, social, and economic trends and events around the world.
- Recognizes the impact of global events on the organization.
- Understands, reads, and speaks more than one language fluently.

Cultural Openness and Sensitivity

- Understands the nature of national, ethnic, and cultural differences and is open to examining these differences honestly and objectively.
- Is sensitive to cultural cues and is able to adapt quickly in novel situations.
- Appropriately adjusts own behavior when interacting with people from various national, ethnic, and cultural backgrounds.

SELF-MANAGEMENT COMPETENCY

Taking responsibility for your life at work and beyond involves *self-management competency*. Often, when things don't go well, people tend to blame their difficulties on the situations in which they find themselves or on others. Effective managers don't fall into this trap. Self-management competency includes

- integrity and ethical conduct,
- personal drive and resilience,
- balancing work and life demands, and
- self-awareness and development.

You may be thinking that self-management really doesn't require much time and effort. Dee Hock would disagree. Everyone recognizes a Visa card, but did you know that Dee Hock is the man who built this worldwide powerhouse? Since 1970, when Hock founded Visa, the company has grown from an idea to a service used by half a billion customers. It operates in 200 countries, with an annual volume of roughly $1 trillion. Dee Hock, the man behind this phenomenal success story, isn't a household name, but his success as a manager is unquestioned—which is why he is such a popular speaker at CEO gatherings. When talking to managers about how to succeed, he tells them to "invest at least 40 percent of your time managing yourself—your ethics, character, principles, purpose, motivation, and conduct."[26]

Just as customers expect companies to behave ethically, organizations expect their employees to *show integrity and act ethically*. When recruiting entry-level employees—who don't yet have a long record of employment or much technical expertise—these qualities may be the most important ones that employers look for. According to a recent Gallup Poll, when companies hire young employees, they are far more concerned with the employees' integrity and interest in the job than with their specific technical skills and aptitudes.

Personal drive and resilience are especially important when someone sets out to do something no one else has done and when that person faces setbacks and failures. As its founder, Jeff Bezos needed personal drive and resilience when he decided to start Amazon.com. Because there were no other online companies, banks and venture capital firms were not interested in funding him. It was his parents who originally gave him the $300,000 to start the company.

According to a Catalyst Organization survey of 1,725 women of color managers and *Fortune* magazine's study of 1,735 MBA students, building a family is a top priority for the majority of the respondents. Hoping to have it all, 75 percent gave developing a career a top rating also.[27] Clearly, these future managers won't succeed unless they can find a way to *balance work and life demands*. These demands, which often conflict, and other family concerns led Congress to pass and the president to sign the Family and Medical Leave Act in 1993. In addition, many of the best companies to work for, including Southwest Airlines, Cisco Systems, SAS Institute, and Edward Jones, have other family-friendly policies. However, self-management competency is needed to decide when and how best to take advantage of such policies. New mothers and fathers alike may feel pressure to return to work soon after the arrival of a new family member, rather than take the entire leave allowed them. But having succumbed to work pressures, many experience pangs of guilt or anxiety when they glimpse at the family photo sitting on the corner of the desk. Knowing your own work and life priorities, and finding a way to juggle them all, may be the most difficult management challenge many of you will face.

The dynamic work environment calls for *self-awareness and development* (as well as the ability continually to unlearn and relearn!). That includes both task-related learning and learning about yourself. On the one hand, task-related learning can directly improve your performance in your current job and prepare you to take on new jobs. Learning about yourself, on the other hand, can help you make wiser choices about which types of jobs you are likely to enjoy. With fewer opportunities for promotions and upward advancement, finding work that you enjoy doing is even more important today than in the past. Taking responsibility for your own career development—by understanding the type of work you find satisfying and developing the competencies that you will need—may be the best route to long-term success.

Research shows that people who take advantage of the development and training opportunities that employers offer learn much from them and advance more quickly than those who don't take advantage of them. Derailment awaits managers who fail to develop their competencies. A derailed manager is one who has moved into a position of managerial responsibility but has little chance of future advancement or gaining new responsibilities. The most common reasons for derailment are (1) problems with interpersonal relationships and inability to lead a team (weak in teamwork competency); (2) inability to learn, develop, and adapt (weak in self-management competency); (3) performance problems (weak in planning and administration competency); and (4) having a narrow functional perspective (lacking strong strategic action and global awareness competencies).[28] Table 1.7 provides more detail about self-management competency.

Table 1.7	**Dimensions of Self-Management Competency**

Integrity and Ethical Conduct

- Has clear personal standards that serve as a foundation for maintaining a sense of integrity and ethical conduct.
- Is willing to admit mistakes.
- Accepts responsibility for own actions.

Personal Drive and Resilience

- Seeks responsibility and is ambitious and motivated to achieve objectives.
- Works hard to get things done.
- Shows perseverance in the face of obstacles and bounces back from failure.

Balancing Work and Life Issues

- Strikes a reasonable balance between work and other life activities so that neither aspect of living is neglected.
- Takes good care of self, mentally and physically, and uses constructive outlets to vent frustration and reduce tension.
- Assesses and establishes own life- and work-related goals.

Self-Awareness and Development

- Has clear personal and career goals.
- Uses strengths to advantage while seeking to improve or compensate for weaknesses.
- Analyzes and learns from work and life experiences.

DEVELOPING YOUR MANAGERIAL COMPETENCIES

Throughout this book, both in the text and in the exercises and cases at the end of each chapter, we present material to help you develop the six managerial competencies that we've just described. For example, you've already read about how Linda Navarro uses her communication competency to declare her passion for customer service. You've also seen how Homero Reséndez's planning and administration and self-management competencies helped him develop CEMEX into one of the world's largest concrete makers. And you've learned how employees at a Honeywell division developed teamwork competency to improve their performance. Examples such as these will help you develop an understanding of how all six competencies contribute to performance in jobs that involve managerial work.

MANAGEMENT—A DYNAMIC PROCESS

4.

DESCRIBE THE CHANGING CONTEXT OF MANAGERIAL WORK.

The *process* of obtaining and organizing resources and achieving goals through other people—that is, managing—is dynamic rather than static. Struggling to manage while confronting the new realities of business competition isn't easy. People change, conditions change, technologies change, and the rules change. Managerial thought changes too. It evolves whenever new theories are presented or new practices are tried. If the theories seem to have merit or the practices appear to succeed, their use spreads to more and more organizations until, over a period of time, they become accepted ways of managing. The adoption of Japanese quality control methods by many U.S. firms is an example of the evolution in management thought.[29]

As you launch your career, your challenge will be to succeed in a new era in which change will be the only constant. New forms of organization will emerge. The workforce will be much different, and managers may not even see their employees on a daily basis. Technologies that are just being invented will become commonplace, and global competition will intensify. We describe many of these changes in more detail in Chapters 3–6. Here, we briefly describe and comment on the implications of this dynamic environment for first-line, middle, and top managers.

THE RESTRUCTURING OF ORGANIZATIONS

WEB INSIGHT

Andy Grove, CEO of Intel, writes about organizational changes that companies must make to keep up with the turbulent times coming up in the next decade. Access Intel's Web site at _http://www.intel.com_. What changes does Intel anticipate making in order to keep up with new technologies, new competitors, and customer demands?

In his book, _Only the Paranoid Will Survive_, Andy Grove, CEO of Intel, notes that all industries and companies are going to face turbulent times during the next decade as a result of new technologies, changes in customer demand, and the rise of new competitors.[30] Companies will need to change how they are organized. Although each company will face its unique set of challenges, mergers and acquisitions have been a major source of corporate restructuring, affecting millions of workers and their families. These forms of restructuring often are accompanied by downsizing. **_Downsizing_** is the process of reducing the size of a firm by laying off workers or retiring workers early. The primary objectives of downsizing are similar in U.S. companies and those in other countries:

- cutting costs,
- spurring decentralization and speeding up decision making,
- cutting bureaucracy and eliminating layers of hierarchy, and
- improving customer relations.

Not surprisingly, the ranks of middle managers have been especially hard hit by downsizing. Many companies have fewer middle managers today than they did five years ago. One consequence of this trend is that today's managers supervise larger numbers of subordinates who report directly to them. Because of downsizing, first-line managers have had to assume greater responsibility for the work of their departments. At Nokia's Fort Worth manufacturing plant, first-line managers participate in the production processes and other line activities and coordinate the efforts of specialists as part of their jobs. At the same time, the workers that first-line managers supervise are less willing to put up with authoritarian management. Employees want their jobs to be more creative, challenging, fun, and satisfying and want to participate in decisions affecting their work. Thus self-managed work teams that bring workers and first-line managers together to make joint decisions to improve the way they do their jobs offer a solution to both supervision and employee expectation problems.

Outsourcing means letting other organizations perform a needed service and/or manufacture needed parts or products.[31] Nike outsources the production of its shoes to low-cost plants in South Korea and China and imports the shoes for distribution in North America. These same plants also ship shoes to Europe and other parts of Asia for distribution. Thus today's managers face a new challenge: to plan, organize, lead, and control a company that may have at least some of its operating functions performed by other companies.[32] The most commonly outsourced function is production. By outsourcing production, a company can switch suppliers as necessary to use the supplier best suited to a customer's needs.

As organizations downsize and outsource functions, they become both flatter and smaller. Figure 1.4 illustrates the shifting size and shape of organizations. Unlike the large organizations of the past, the new, smaller firms and often e-commerce firms are less like autonomous fortresses and more like nodes in a network of complex rela-

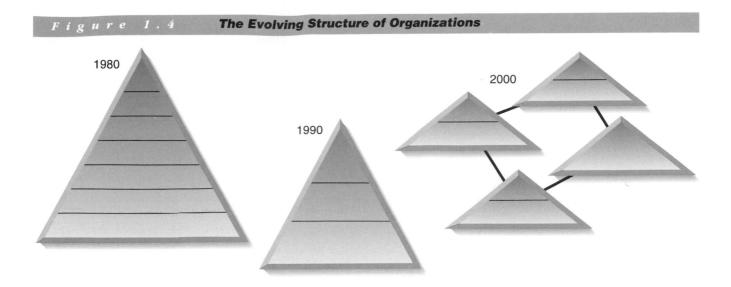

tionships. Network forms of organization are prevalent in high-tech industries, where they gain access to the hot new discoveries being made by scientists in universities and in small, creative organizations. For example, the Internet industry is characterized by networks of relationships among new technology firms dedicated to research and new product development and established firms in industries that can use these new products. John Chambers, CEO of Cisco Systems, readily admits that many of the best ideas and technologies come from outside his firm. Since 1996, Cisco has formed a complex network with small firms that have state-of-the-art software development teams, engage in optical networking and wireless communication, and provide network security.

Being competitive increasingly requires establishing and managing strategic alliances with other firms. In a ***strategic alliance,*** two (or more) firms agree to cooperate in a venture that is expected to benefit both (all).[33] Alliances serve a vital role in extending or creating new resources for a company. For example, American Airlines, Cathay Pacific, Qantas, Canadian Airlines, and British Airways, recently formed the **One**world alliance that is intended to help all five carriers reach parts of the world they were unable to reach before. This alliance gives American Airlines access to Hong Kong, Singapore, and other Asian cities without flying passengers through Tokyo and making them wait hours for connecting flights. It also permits these five airlines to sell seats on each other's flights. In effect **One**world is streamlining and improving the profitability of operations by coordinating different schedules and ticket prices for various markets.

A CHANGING WORKFORCE

At the same time that the size and shape of organizations are changing, the composition of the workforce is changing dramatically. One important change is its age distribution. A large portion of the U.S. workforce now is from the baby-boom generation (77 million people born between 1946 and 1964), but fewer recent college graduates are entering the job market. Between 2000 and 2025, the number of people aged 35 to 47 will decrease by 2 percent, and the number between 60 and 64 will increase by 3 percent. The size of the baby-boom generation created a huge workforce influx. In the late 1970s, for instance, about 3 million people entered the 18-to-24-year-old age group each year. But, in 2000, only 1 million new workers were in this age group, and this number continues to shrink. One implication is that fewer employees now are expected to get more work done. For their organizations to survive, these employees must be highly productive.[34]

Another important change is the increased diversity of the workforce. ***Workforce diversity*** refers to the mix of people from various backgrounds in today's labor force.[35] More and more women are working, for example, resulting in a new gender mix that is nearly balanced instead of being male-dominated. By 2006, women are expected to make up 47.4 percent of the U.S. labor force. Throughout the 1900s, immigration patterns also changed, resulting in more diversity in terms of national heritage. Hispanics, which account for 40 percent of U.S. population growth since 1995, will increase to 50 percent of the growth by 2020. In the 1990s, awareness of increasing workforce diversity grew steadily. A U.S. Department of Labor report, *Workforce 2000*, initially drew attention to this issue by highlighting the changing demographics of the U.S. labor force.

The ***multicultural organization***, with a workforce that includes the full mix of cultures found in the population at large and a commitment to full utilization of its human resources, presents a significant challenge to managers.[36] They will need to come up with creative approaches to managing people with highly diverse backgrounds. At General Mills, the consumer foods company based in Minneapolis, Minnesota, more than half the company's workforce is composed of women and people of color. Beginning in the early 1990s, the company expanded its emphasis on diversity to focus on educating managers and creating a culture that accommodates different work and managerial styles. The business reasons for understanding and embracing diversity include (1) analyzing domestic and global consumer demographics, (2) forging successful alliances with international and minority suppliers, (3) enhancing creativity and growth, (4) increasing productivity, and (5) becoming an employer of choice. CEO Steve Sanger and his senior management staff conduct quarterly reviews of workforce representation and development plans.[37]

CHANGING TECHNOLOGY

In the United States, more than 15 million knowledge workers are employed in high-tech industries—developing, producing, and delivering new electronic and communications-related products. ***Knowledge workers*** are educated people who work with specialized information. They are expected to contribute 33 percent of the growth in the U.S. gross domestic product (GDP) during the next several decades.[38] With information and technology constantly changing, organizations expect them to keep their skills up to date and use them on the job. Rapid changes in technology are transforming all sorts of jobs. Consider the typical sales job at National Gypsum, a company that makes gypsum wallboard used to make walls in buildings. Just a few years ago, a salesperson would visit a construction site and discuss prices, volume, and delivery dates with the architect and construction superintendent. Depending on the size of the territory, a salesperson might call on ten customers a week. Today, with the use of a laptop computer, the same salesperson downloads all the construction plans into the laptop. The volume and price of wallboard can be computed quickly and sent to the architect and construction superintendent via an e-mail attachment. The entire process takes minutes. Salespeople can now call on 80 people per week, and the sales manager can spend time working with the sales force on making effective presentations, rather than resolving minor problems.

New technologies are changing jobs in all types of industries. Already, hundreds of thousands of people are working full or part time at home, connected to an office by means of a computer, modem, and fax machine. Eventually millions of people will work at home instead of commuting to an office.[39] Managers will be responsible for supervising work done by people they may seldom even see. Like managers at FedEx, you may find yourself responding to employees' questions during an in-house TV talk show. Without knowing precisely what the future holds in terms of technology, we can nevertheless be certain that it will be used to reduce simple repetitive tasks, freeing people to spend more time analyzing problems and developing creative solutions.

GLOBALIZATION

During the past 50 years, technological advances in transportation and communications have spurred the growth of international commerce. As a result, many firms evolved from being purely domestic to becoming truly global. The movement of a firm from focusing primarily on a domestic market to one manufacturing and selling products worldwide is known as the **globalization process**. The first step in this evolution is simply to export goods for sale in one or two foreign markets. The next step is to manufacture those goods overseas because that is more efficient than shipping products thousands of miles to markets. Setting up operations close to foreign markets also helps a company better understand its customers. For example, Nokia, a Finnish electronics goods manufacturer and wholesaler, recently opened a large manufacturing plant in Fort Worth, Texas. By doing so, the company hopes to serve the Tandy Corporation, owners of the Radio Shack electronics stores, more efficiently.

What are the implications of globalization for managers? One is that more and more top-level employees will be sent on overseas assignments.[40] These assignments won't be limited to top-level executives, either. When Mercedes-Benz decided to build sport utility vehicles in Alabama, Mercedes sent 160 Alabamans to Germany where they learned their jobs working alongside their German counterparts. In addition, 70 Germans were sent to Alabama to help train the rest of the new U.S. employees. According to a worldwide survey of 351 companies, 43 percent plan to increase the number of employees sent on overseas assignments; only 13 percent plan to reduce overseas assignments in the near future. The most frequent destinations for employees are Asia and Europe, with about 80 percent of companies with expatriates sending their employees to these two regions. Next most popular are North, Central, and South America, which receive expatriates from about 50 percent of the companies.[41]

Middle managers and the professionals they supervise often are the ones being sent on international assignments. Conversely, more and more employees are being hired from other countries. In the United States, domestic labor shortages in certain fields mean that some organizations cannot succeed unless they consider the entire world as their labor market. Similarly, the changing political and economic landscape in Europe means that workers can now more freely move across national borders to find desirable jobs. Thus many middle managers are working with a global workforce without even leaving home.

CHAPTER SUMMARY

In this chapter we introduced several concepts that you need to understand in order to be a successful manager in the years ahead. Because the nature and scope of management are changing so rapidly, no simple prescription can be given for how to manage. Rather, managers today and in the future need to develop six important competencies to enable them to lead dynamic organizations and tackle a variety of emerging organizational issues. You now should be able to do the following.

1. DEFINE MANAGERS AND MANAGEMENT.

Managers establish organizational goals and then direct the work of subordinates, on whom they depend to achieve those goals. Managers acquire and allocate the human and material resources without which organizations couldn't exist. Effective management is essential to the success of an organization.

2. EXPLAIN WHAT MANAGERS DO.

The managerial functions—planning, organizing, leading, and controlling—are what managers do. Managers at different levels in an organization spend their time differently, but they all spend at least some time performing each function. The three basic levels of management are first-line, middle, and top. First-line managers are directly responsible for the production of goods and services. They supervise workers and solve specific problems. Middle managers coordinate the work of several first-line managers or direct the operations of a functional department. They translate top management's goals into specific goals and programs for implementation. Top managers establish overall organizational goals and direct the activities of an entire organization or a major segment of an organization.

Managers at different levels divide their time among the managerial functions quite differently. First-line managers spend most of their time leading and controlling and the rest planning and organizing. Middle managers spend most of their time organizing and leading and the rest planning and controlling. Top managers spend most of their time planning and leading and very little time directly organizing and controlling. Managerial work also varies in scope, broadening at each higher level.

Small-business managers usually perform numerous tasks for their organization. They usually have first–hand knowledge of the production process and also must deal with customers, bankers, and others on a daily basis.

3. **DEMONSTRATE KNOWLEDGE OF THE COMPETENCIES USED IN MANAGERIAL WORK BY DEVELOPING AND PRACTICING THEM.**

To be an effective manager in a dynamic environment requires six managerial competencies: communication, teamwork, planning and administration, strategic action, global awareness, and self-management. You can develop these competencies through study, training, and experience. By doing so, you can prepare yourself for a variety of jobs in various industries and countries. You can continue practicing your managerial competencies by completing the exercises at the end of this chapter.

4. **DESCRIBE THE CHANGING CONTEXT OF MANAGERIAL WORK.**

Four important environmental trends are organizational restructuring, changing workforce, changing technology, and globalization. Through downsizing and outsourcing, organizations are becoming smaller, flatter, and more dependent on strategic alliances with other firms. At the same time, the workforce is getting older and more diverse, which creates many new challenges. They include how to take advantage of the multiple perspectives that employees can bring to bear on issues and problems and how to keep employees satisfied when there is less opportunity for promotion and advancement. New technologies are rapidly changing the nature of work and the workplace. Electronic communications make it possible for people who seldom see each other to work together as a team. New technologies can also free employees from more routine and mundane tasks, giving them more time to spend on problem solving and improving relationships with customers. Globalization requires that managers stay abreast of economic, social, and political trends around the world and understand the implications of these trends for their organizations. It also means that more employees are being sent overseas on temporary assignments.

KEY TERMS

Communication competency, p. 14
Competency, p. 4
Controlling, p. 9
Downsizing, p. 26
First-line managers, p. 10
Functional managers, p. 8
General managers, p. 8
Global awareness competency, p. 21
Globalization process, p. 29
Knowledge workers, p. 28

Leading, p. 9
Management, p. 7
Manager, p. 7
Managerial competencies, p. 5
Middle managers, p. 11
Multicultural organization, p. 28
Organization, p. 6
Organizing, p. 9
Outsourcing, p. 26
Planning, p. 8

Planning and administration competency, p. 16
Self-management competency, p. 23
Small-business managers, p. 13
Strategic action competency, p. 20
Strategic alliance, p. 27
Teamwork competency, p. 18
Top managers, p. 12
Workforce diversity, p. 28

QUESTIONS FOR DISCUSSION AND COMPETENCY DEVELOPMENT

1. What management functions does Jeff Bezos perform at Amazon.com?

2. Identify a small organization. What are the similarities and differences in the jobs of managers in this organization?

3. What challenges does Homero Reséndez of CEMEX face? What competencies are needed to work in this organization?

4. What teamwork competencies are needed in Coca-Cola's new organization?

5. Joe Broadway, a manager for IBM Global Services, says, "The Internet and e-mail are making it easier to communicate with people across cultures." Do you agree or disagree? Why?

6. Think of a team of which you are a member. Using the Teamwork Competency section of the HJS Management Competencies Self-Assessment Inventory on page 36, evaluate the team's effectiveness.

7. Why is it so difficult to become an effective middle manager?

8. **Competency Development: Self-Management.** AT&T Wireless and GTE compete in the cellular telecommunications industry. Identify and investigate the self-management competencies that you would need to develop to get a job at each firm. Visit AT&T's Wireless Service home page at *http://www.attws.com* and GTE's home page at *http://www.gte.com.*

9. **Competency Development: Strategic Action.** In an effort to achieve its potential in sales and revenues, Procter & Gamble recently reorganized itself. During the reorganization, more than 13,000 people were laid off and 30 plants were closed. Visit Procter & Gamble's home page at *http://www.pg.com* to learn how the company is organized and whether Procter & Gamble's market share has increased since the reorganization.

HJS MANAGEMENT COMPETENCIES
Self-Assessment Inventory

Instructions (for self-administration)

Each of the five following statements describes a level of attainment on a dimension of a managerial competency. How well do you think each statement describes you? Following these statements is a list of 95 characteristics that are representative of effective, experienced managers. Next to each characteristic, fill in the number corresponding to the level-of-attainment statement that applies best to you. You may use your textbook CD-ROM to take this inventory and determine your score. Presenting an accurate self-appraisal is important to understanding your current competencies and what you need to do to develop them further.

Level of Attainment

1. I have very little relevant experience. I have not yet begun to develop this characteristic.

2. I think that I am weak in this characteristic. I have had relevant experience, but I have not performed well.

3. I think that I am about average on this characteristic. It will take a good deal of focused effort for me to be consistently effective.

4. I think that I am above average on this characteristic. I need to develop this characteristic further in order to be highly effective.

5. I think that I am outstanding on this characteristic. I need to maintain my strong effectiveness on this characteristic.

Characteristic

_____ 1. Seeks out and listens to others who have contrary opinions.

_____ 2. In speaking with others, is able to make people feel comfortable in different situations.

_____ 3. Varies communication approach when dealing with others from different backgrounds.

_____ 4. Builds strong interpersonal relationships with a diverse range of people.

_____ 5. Shows genuine sensitivity to the feelings of others.

_____ 6. Informs people of events that are relevant to them.

_____ 7. Makes persuasive, high-impact presentations before groups.

_____ 8. When making formal presentations, handles questions from the audience well.

_____ 9. Writes clearly and concisely.

_____ 10. Communicates effectively using electronic media.

_____ 11. Is comfortable using power associated with leadership roles.

_____ 12. Is skilled at influencing superiors.

_____ 13. Is skilled at influencing peers.

_____ 14. When addressing problems, finds solutions that others perceive as fair.

_____ 15. In conflict situations, helps parties move toward win-win situations.

_____ 16. Monitors information that is relevant to ongoing projects and activities.

_____ 17. Obtains and uses relevant information to identify symptoms and underlying problems.

_____ 18. Makes decisions on time.

_____ 19. When taking risks, is able to anticipate negative and positive consequences.

_____ 20. Knows when expert knowledge is needed and seeks it out to solve problems.

_____ 21. Develops plans and schedules to achieve specific goals efficiently.

_____ 22. Prioritizes tasks in order to stay focused on those that are most important.

_____ 23. Can organize people around specific tasks to help them work together toward a common objective.

_____ 24. Is comfortable delegating responsibility for tasks to others.

_____ 25. Anticipates possible problems and develops plans for how to deal with them.

_____ 26. Handles several issues and projects at the same time but doesn't spread self too thin.

_____ 27. Monitors and keeps to a schedule or negotiates changes in the schedule if needed.

_____ 28. Works effectively under time pressure.

_____ 29. Knows when to permit interruptions and when to screen them out.

_____ 30. Knows when to renegotiate established deadlines in order to deliver satisfactory results.

_____ 31. Understands budgets, cash flow, financial reports, and annual reports

_____ 32. Regularly uses budgets and financial reports to make decisions.

_____ 33. Keeps accurate and complete financial records.

_____ 34. Creates budgetary guidelines for others.

_____ 35. Works well within the budgetary guidelines given by others.

_____ 36. Formulates clear goals that inspire team members' commitment.

_____ 37. Appropriately selects team members, taking into account diversity of viewpoints and technical skills.

_____ 38. Provides team members with a clear vision of what is to be accomplished by the team as a whole.

_____ 39. Assigns tasks and responsibilities to individual team members consistent with their competencies and interests.

_____ 40. Creates a process for monitoring team performance.

_____ 41. Creates a team setting in which team members feel that their suggestions make a difference.

_____ 42. Recognizes, praises, and rewards team members for their contributions.

_____ 43. Assists the team in acquiring the resources and support it needs to accomplish its goals.

_____ 44. Acts as a coach, counselor, and mentor for team members.

_____ 45. Is patient with team members as they learn new roles and develop their competencies.

_____ 46. Is aware of team members' feelings.

_____ 47. Understands the strengths and limitations of team members.

48. Brings conflict and dissent within the team into the open and uses them to improve quality of decisions.

_____ 49. Facilitates cooperative behavior among team members.

_____ 50. Keeps the team moving toward its goals.

_____ 51. Understands the history of the industry of which the organization is a part.

52. Stays informed of the actions of competitors and strategic partners in the industry of which the organization is a part.

_____ 53. Is able to analyze general industry trends and understand their implications for the future.

_____ 54. Quickly recognizes when significant changes occur in the industry.

_____ 55. Knows how organizations compete in the industry.

_____ 56. Understands the concerns of all major stakeholders of the organization.

_____ 57. Understands the strengths and limitations of various business strategies.

_____ 58. Knows the distinctive strengths of the organization.

_____ 59. Understands the organizational structure and how work is really accomplished.

_____ 60. Is able to fit into the unique culture of the organization.

_____ 61. Assigns priorities that are consistent with the organization's mission and strategic goals.

62. Recognizes and resists pressures to behave in ways that are not consistent with the organization's mission and strategic goals.

_____ 63. Considers the long-term implications of decisions on the organization.

_____ 64. Establishes tactical and operational goals to implement strategies.

_____ 65. Keeps the unit focused on its goals.

_____ 66. Stays informed of political events around the world.

_____ 67. Stays informed of economic events around the world.

_____ 68. Recognizes the impact of global events on the organization.

_____ 69. Travels to gain first-hand knowledge of other countries.

_____ 70. Understands and speaks more than one language.

_____ 71. Is sensitive to cultural cues and is able to adapt quickly in novel situations.

_____ 72. Recognizes that there is great variation within any culture and avoids stereotyping.

73. Appropriately adjusts behavior when interacting with people from various national, ethnic, and cultural backgrounds.

_____ 74. Understands how own cultural background affects own attitudes and behaviors.

_____ 75. Is able to empathize with those from different cultural backgrounds.

76. Has clear personal standards that serve as a foundation for maintaining a sense of integrity and ethical conduct.

_____ 77. Maintains personal ethical standards under fire.

_____ 78. Is sincere and projects self-assurance; doesn't just tell people what they want to hear.

_____ 79. Recognizes own mistakes and admits to having made them.

_____ 80. Accepts responsibility for own actions.

_____ 81. Seeks responsibility beyond what is required by the job.

_____ 82. Is willing to innovate and take personal risks.

_____ 83. Is ambitious and motivated to achieve goals.

_____ 84. Works hard to get things done.

_____ 85. Shows perseverance in the face of obstacles.

_____ 86. Strikes a reasonable balance between work and other life activities.

_____ 87. Takes good care of self mentally and emotionally.

_____ 88. Uses constructive outlets to vent frustration and reduce tension.

_____ 89. Exercises and eats properly.

_____ 90. Knows how to enjoy leisure time.

_____ 91. Has clear personal and career goals.

_____ 92. Knows own values, feelings, and areas of strengths and limitations.

_____ 93. Accepts responsibility for continuous self-development.

_____ 94. Develops plans and seeks opportunities for personal long-term growth.

_____ 95. Analyzes and learns from work and life experiences.

Scoring and Interpretation

The HJS Management Competencies Self-Assessment Inventory measures characteristics that are representative of the core dimensions of the six basic managerial competencies. These managerial competencies are discussed on pages 14–25.

Transfer the number that you recorded next to each characteristic in the inventory to the corresponding competency dimension in the following list.

COMMUNICATION COMPETENCY

Effective transfer and exchange of information that leads to understanding between yourself and others.

Informal Communication Dimension
1_____; 2_____; 3_____; 4_____; 5_____
Add numbers recorded = _____ / 5 = _____, which equals your average self-assessment on this dimension.

Formal Communication Dimension
6_____; 7_____; 8_____; 9_____; 10_____
Add numbers recorded = _____ / 5 = _____, which equals your average self-assessment on this dimension.

Negotiation Dimension
11_____; 12_____; 13_____; 14_____; 15_____
Add numbers recorded = _____ / 5 = _____, which equals your average self-assessment on this dimension.

Summary: Add the average scores for the three dimensions of this competency = _____ / 3 = _____, which is your overall average self-assessment for communication competency.

PLANNING AND ADMINISTRATION COMPETENCY

Deciding what tasks need to be done, determining how they can be done, allocating resources to enable them to be done, and then monitoring progress to ensure that they are done.

Information Gathering, Analysis, and Problem Solving Dimension
16_____; 17_____; 18_____; 19_____; 20_____
Add numbers recorded = _____ / 5 = _____, which equals your average self-assessment on this dimension.

Planning and Organizing Projects Dimension
21_____; 22_____; 23_____; 24_____; 25_____
Add numbers recorded = _____ / 5 = _____, which equals your average self-assessment on this dimension.

Time Management Dimension

26_____; 27_____; 28_____; 29_____; 30_____

Add numbers recorded = _____ / 5 = _____, which equals your average self-assessment on this dimension.

Budgeting and Financial Management Dimension

31_____; 32_____; 33_____; 34_____; 35_____

Add numbers recorded = _____ / 5 = _____, which equals your average self-assessment on this dimension.

Summary: Add the average scores for the four dimensions of this competency = _____ / 4 = _____, which is your overall average self-assessment for planning and administration competency.

TEAMWORK COMPETENCY

Accomplishing tasks through small groups of people who are collectively responsible and whose work is interdependent.

Designing Teams Dimension

36_____; 37_____; 38_____; 39_____; 40_____

Add numbers recorded = _____ / 5 = _____, which equals your average self-assessment on this dimension.

Creating a Supportive Environment Dimension

41_____; 42_____; 43_____; 44_____; 45_____

Add numbers recorded = _____ / 5 = _____, which equals your average self-assessment on this dimension.

Managing Team Dynamics Dimension

46_____; 47_____; 48_____; 49_____; 50_____

Add numbers recorded = _____ / 5 = _____, which equals your average self-assessment on this dimension.

Summary: Add the average scores for the three dimensions of this competency = _____ / 3 = _____, which is your overall average self-assessment for teamwork competency.

STRATEGIC ACTION COMPETENCY

Understanding the overall mission(s) and values of the organization and ensuring that your actions and those of the people you manage are aligned with them.

Understanding the Industry Dimension

51_____; 52_____; 53_____; 54_____; 55_____

Add numbers recorded = _____ / 5 = _____, which equals your average self-assessment on this dimension.

Understanding the Organization Dimension

56_____; 57_____; 58_____; 59_____; 60_____

Add numbers recorded = _____ / 5 = _____, which equals your average self-assessment on this dimension.

Taking Strategic Actions Dimension

61_____; 62_____; 63_____; 64_____; 65_____

Add numbers recorded = _____ / 5 = _____, which equals your average self-assessment on this dimension.

Summary: Add the average scores for the three dimensions of this competency = _____ / 3 = _____, which is your overall average self-assessment for strategic action competency.

GLOBAL AWARENESS COMPETENCY

Carrying out an organization's managerial work by drawing on the human, financial, information, and material resources from multiple countries and serving markets that span multiple cultures.

Cultural Knowledge and Understanding Dimension

66_____; 67_____; 68_____; 69_____; 70_____

Add numbers recorded = _____ / 5 = _____, which equals your average self-assessment on this dimension.

Cultural Openness and Sensitivity Dimension

71_____; 72_____; 73_____; 74_____; 75_____

Add numbers recorded = _____ / 5 = _____, which equals your average self-assessment on this dimension.

Summary: Add the average scores for the two dimensions of this competency = _____ / 2 = _____, which is your overall average self-assessment for global awareness competency.

SELF-MANAGEMENT COMPETENCY

Taking responsibility for your life at work and beyond.

Integrity and Ethical Conduct Dimension

76_____; 77_____; 78_____; 79_____; 80_____

Add numbers recorded = _____ / 5 = _____, which equals your average self-assessment on this dimension.

Personal Drive and Resilience Dimension

81_____; 82_____; 83_____; 84_____; 85_____

Add numbers recorded = _____ / 5 = _____, which equals your average self-assessment on this dimension.

Balancing Work and Life Demands Dimension

86_____; 87_____; 88_____; 89_____; 90_____

Add numbers recorded = _____ / 5 = _____, which equals your average self-assessment on this dimension.

Self-Awareness and Development Dimension

91_____; 92_____; 93_____; 94_____; 95_____

Add numbers recorded = _____ / 5 = _____, which equals your average self-assessment on this dimension.

Summary: Add the average scores for the four dimensions of this competency = _____ / 4 = _____, which is your overall average self-assessment for self-management competency.

Overall Profile

Instructions. Plot your overall profile of managerial competencies on the following grid, using the *summary average score* for each competency and multiplying the average score for each competency by 20. For example, if your average score on a competency is 3.2, you would multiply it by 20 to obtain a total score of 64 out of 100 possible points on that competency and mark that point on the grid. Then connect the points marked on each vertical line.

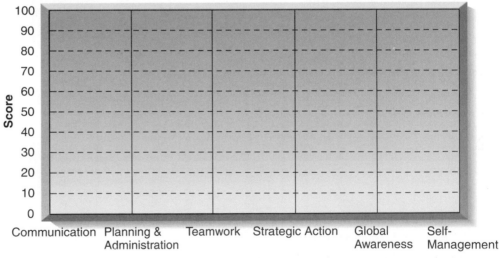

OVERALL INTERPRETATIONS

Score	Meaning
20–39	You have little relevant experience and are quite weak in this competency.
40–59	You are generally weak in this competency but are performing satisfactorily or better on a few characteristics.
60–74	You are generally about average in this competency and above average or better on some characteristics.

Questions

1. What does this profile suggest in relation to needed development in areas of your professional and personal life?

2. Based on the managerial competency in most need of development, identify three possible actions that you might take to reduce the gap between your current and desired level for that competency.

3. Would others who work with you closely or who otherwise know you well agree with your self-assessment profile? On what dimensions might their and your assessments be similar? Different?

4. How do your scores compare to those of hundreds of students and seasoned managers, as shown in the following graph?

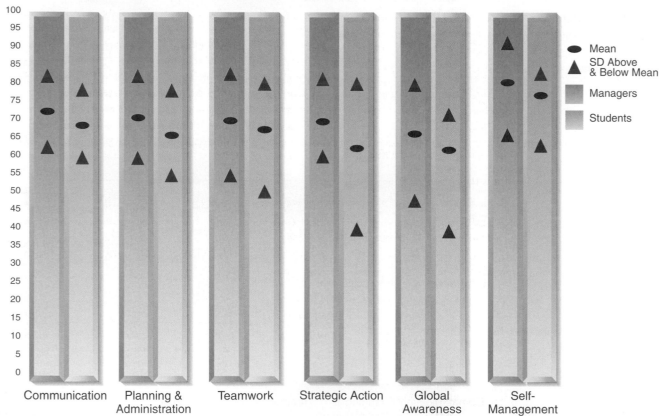

Scores of Managerial Competencies for Managers and Students

Legend: ● Mean ▲ SD Above & Below Mean Managers Students

Competencies: Communication, Planning & Administration, Teamwork, Strategic Action, Global Awareness, Self-Management

Second Chance Body Armor

In 1969, while making a delivery for his pizzeria restaurant in Detroit, Richard Davis was shot and nearly killed by three attackers. During his recovery, Davis was inspired to research and develop a means of personal ballistics protection so that the wearer would have a "second chance" to survive being shot and perhaps even retaliate. Inspired from his near-fatal experience and convinced of the market's need for such a product, Davis founded his own company, Second Chance Body Armor.

Influenced by the military flak jackets worn in the Korean and Vietnamese conflicts, Davis developed a soft, flexible, and concealable panel of ballistic nylon material designed to withstand the firepower of street handguns. He patented his invention as the first comfortable and concealable body armor to cover a person's basic kill zone. Davis quickly realized that the greatest demand and need for his product lay with law enforcement officers.

However, as Davis would soon learn, despite having an innovative and quality product, becoming an entrepreneur requires conquering many challenges. His first challenge was that of financing and resources. Second Chance began as a sole proprietorship with $70 and some antiballistic nylon as assets. Advertising, patents, and development of prototypes therefore would require creative financing. The second challenge was to survive the hectic nature of the first year of the business. As sole proprietor, Davis was responsible for all aspects of the company, including product development, product promotion, bookkeeping, finances, and taxes. Davis admits that, during the first year, he was often behind in his taxes and had to wear many different "hats" in getting the company off the ground.

But perhaps the most important challenge facing Davis was convincing law enforcement officers that his invention worked. Davis accomplished this "missionary work," as he calls it, by performing dramatic live shooting demonstrations on his torso (Davis estimates that he has been shot at least 172 times). These acts convinced law enforcement officers that his body armor was safe and effective and that the company's owner (literally) stood behind his product. Further evidence of the quality and usefulness of the product has since been supplied by the confirmed saving of more than 775 lives of individuals who were wearing the company's body armor.

Davis later incorporated Second Chance, and it has become the world leader in wearable, concealable body armor. But concealable body armor is not all that Davis and his company now produce. They also offer tactical/special-purpose armor jackets, antipuncture corrections vests, and rough stock rodeo protective vests.

Thus, from its humblest of beginnings as a sole proprietorship with little resources or experience, Richard Davis and Second Chance Body Armor have effectively illustrated what an entrepreneur, with innovative ideas and a firm belief in those ideas, can accomplish.

Questions

1. According to Richard Davis, starting your own business is a double-edged sword. What did he mean by that? Would you have added anything else to his statement?

2. What managerial competencies did Davis illustrate when he started his own business?

To learn more about Second Chance Body Armor, visit the company's home page at ***http://www.secondchance.com***.

The Evolution of Management

LEARNING OBJECTIVES

AFTER STUDYING THIS CHAPTER YOU SHOULD BE ABLE TO:

1. DESCRIBE THE THREE BRANCHES OF THE TRADITIONAL VIEWPOINT OF MANAGEMENT: BUREAUCRATIC, SCIENTIFIC, AND ADMINISTRATIVE.

2. EXPLAIN THE BEHAVIORAL VIEWPOINT'S CONTRIBUTION TO MANAGEMENT.

3. DESCRIBE HOW MANAGERS CAN USE SYSTEMS AND QUANTITATIVE TECHNIQUES TO IMPROVE EMPLOYEE PERFORMANCE.

4. STATE THE TWO MAJOR COMPONENTS OF THE CONTINGENCY VIEWPOINT.

5. EXPLAIN THE IMPACT OF THE NEED FOR QUALITY ON MANAGEMENT PRACTICES.

Chapter Outline

PREVIEW: TOYOTA'S PRODUCTION SYSTEM

TRADITIONAL VIEWPOINT OF MANAGEMENT

BUREAUCRATIC MANAGEMENT

PLANNING & ADMINISTRATION COMPETENCY: United Parcel Service

SCIENTIFIC MANAGEMENT

ADMINISTRATIVE MANAGEMENT

ASSESSING THE TRADITIONAL VIEWPOINT

BEHAVIORAL VIEWPOINT

FOLLETT'S CONTRIBUTIONS

BARNARD'S CONTRIBUTIONS

THE HAWTHORNE CONTRIBUTIONS

TEAMWORK COMPETENCY: SHARE IT ALL WITH EMPLOYEES, SOUP TO NUTS

ASSESSING THE BEHAVIORAL VIEWPOINT

SYSTEMS VIEWPOINT

SYSTEM CONCEPTS

SYSTEM TYPES

COMMUNICATION COMPETENCY: Supply-Chain Management at Thomson

QUANTITATIVE TECHNIQUES

ASSESSING THE SYSTEMS VIEWPOINT

CONTINGENCY VIEWPOINT

CONTINGENCY VARIABLES

ASSESSING THE CONTINGENCY VIEWPOINT

QUALITY VIEWPOINT

THE QUALITY CONTROL PROCESS

THE IMPORTANCE OF QUALITY

STRATEGIC ACTION COMPETENCY: Marlow Industries Delivers Quality

INTEGRATION OF MANAGEMENT VIEWPOINTS AND COMPETENCIES

CHAPTER SUMMARY

KEY TERMS

QUESTIONS FOR DISCUSSION AND COMPETENCY DEVELOPMENT

CASE FOR COMPETENCY DEVELOPMENT: STARBUCKS

VIDEO CASE: SUNSHINE CLEANING, JIAN, AND ARCHWAY COOKIES

TOYOTA'S PRODUCTION SYSTEM

The Toyota production system (TPS) is used at its Georgetown, Kentucky, plant and throughout the world. It applies not only to manufacturing, but to almost everything Toyota does from product development to supplier relations and distribution. Toyota sets the industry standards in efficiency, productivity, and quality. How does it maintain these standards?

TPS success depends on highly experienced managers working with a motivated, well-trained workforce. Outside the plant, TPS requires a network of capable suppliers that can match their operations completely with Toyota's. Mike DaPrile, who runs Toyota's Camry assembly facilities, describes it as having three levels: techniques, systems, and philosophy. He comments, "Many plants have put in an *anadon* cord that you pull to stop the assembly line if there

is a problem. A 5-year-old can pull the cord. But it takes a lot of effort to drive the right managerial philosophy down to the plant floor. A lot of people don't want to give the needed authority to the people on the line who deserve it."

In most automobile assembly plants, workers try to overproduce because, once they have filled their quotas, they can take it easy. As a result, work proceeds in starts and stops. At Toyota, overproduction is considered one of the worst forms of waste. Toyota designs the workflow from process to process without peaks or valleys so that the product arrives in just the right quantity for the customer. That results in a smoothly running plant. Because there is no stockpile of parts, suppliers and workers are under tremendous pressure to perform their jobs as scheduled and even to work overtime if they fall behind. A single

breakdown will hamstring the entire operation. Because of recent labor shortages, Toyota has been trying to make jobs easier for workers. It now breaks the assembly line into segments and allows workers to stockpile small inventories of unfinished parts at the end of each segment in case of an interruption.

In a Toyota assembly plant, every movement has a purpose, and there is no slack. The workers experience a smooth flow: retrieving parts, installing them, checking quality, and doing these tasks in comfortable surroundings. Says DaPrile, "We believe in the four S's: sweeping, sorting, sifting, and spick-and-span."[1]

To learn more about Toyota, visit the company's home page at

http://www.toyota.com

TRADITIONAL VIEWPOINT OF MANAGEMENT

1.

DESCRIBE THE THREE BRANCHES OF THE TRADITIONAL VIEWPOINT OF MANAGEMENT: BUREAUCRATIC, SCIENTIFIC, AND ADMINISTRATIVE.

Working for a global company with plants scattered throughout the world is getting to be commonplace. In the past 10 years or so, companies such as Toyota, Procter & Gamble (P&G), Marriott, and Nike, have challenged their managers to manage on a global scale. Managers now lead employees whom they seldom, if ever, see and who may know more about solving a problem than they do. Although new methods of managing employees are needed to keep pace with changes in today's organizations and technology, let's not discard what happened in management before the arrival of the information superhighway. The reason is that management today reflects the evolution of concepts, viewpoints, and experience gained over many decades.

During the 30 years following the Civil War, the United States emerged as a leading industrial nation. The shift from an agrarian to an urban society was abrupt and, for many Americans, meant drastic adjustment. By the end of the century a new corporate capitalism ruled by a prosperous professional class had arisen. Captains of industry freely wielded mergers and acquisitions and engaged in cutthroat competition as they created huge monopolies in the oil, meat, steel, sugar, and tobacco industries. The federal government did nothing to interfere with these monopolies. On the one hand, new technology born of the war effort offered the promise of progress and growth. On the other hand, rapid social change and a growing disparity between rich and poor caused increasing conflict and instability.

In 1886, several important turning points in business and management history occurred. Henry R. Towne (1844–1924), an engineer and cofounder of the Yale Lock Company, presented a paper titled "The Engineer as an Economist" to the American Society of Mechanical Engineers (ASME). In that paper Towne proposed that the ASME create an economic section to act as a clearinghouse and forum for "shop management" and "shop accounting." Shop management would deal with the subjects of organization, responsibility, reports, and the "executive management" of industrial works, mills, and factories. Shop accounting would treat the nuts and bolts of time and wage systems, cost determination and allocation, bookkeeping methods, and manufacturing accounting.

Other events in 1886 influenced the development of modern management thought and practice. During this boom period in U.S. business history, employers generally regarded labor as a commodity to be purchased as cheaply as possible and maintained at minimal expense. Thus it was also a peak period of labor unrest—during 1886 more than 600,000 employees were out of work because of strikes and lockouts. On May 4, 1886, a group of labor leaders led a demonstration in Chicago's Haymarket Square in support of an 8-hour workday. During the demonstration someone threw a bomb, killing seven bystanders. The Haymarket Affair was a setback for organized labor, because many people began to equate unionism with anarchy. In his pioneering study of labor history in 1886, *The Labor Movement in America*, Richard T. Ely advocated a less radical approach to labor–management relations. Ely cautioned labor to work within the existing economic and political system. One union that followed Ely's advice was the American Federation of Labor (AFL), organized in 1886 by Samuel Gompers and Adolph Strasser. A conservative, "bread and butter" union, the AFL avoided politics and industrial unionism and organized skilled workers along craft lines (carpenters, plumbers, bricklayers, and other trades). Like other early unions, the AFL protected its members from unfair management practices. Gompers's goal was to increase labor's bargaining power within the existing capitalistic framework. Under his leadership, the AFL dominated the American labor scene for almost half a century.

Chicago in 1886 also was the birthplace of an aspiring mail-order business called Sears, Roebuck and Company. From its beginning Sears, founded by railroad station agent Richard W. Sears, who sold watches to farmers in his area, characterized the mass distribution system that promoted the country's economic growth. For the first time, affordable fine goods were available to both rural and urban consumers. Also in 1886, the first Coca-Cola was served in Atlanta. This scarcely noticed event launched an enterprise that grew into a gigantic multinational corporation. Other companies that began in 1886 and remain in operation today include Avon Products, *Cosmopolitan* magazine, Johnson & Johnson, Munsingwear, and Westinghouse. Thus 1886 marked the origins of several well-known, large-scale enterprises, modern management thought and practice, and major labor unions.

Why are we recounting such old events in a book that presents modern management concepts? One reason is that many of the concepts and practices established in the early days of management are still used today. Many of the rules and regulations found in organizations today were originally created to protect managers from undue pressures to favor certain groups of people. Today FedEx, American Airlines, and Amazon. com, to name but a few, use rules and regulations for the same reason. A second reason is that the past is a good teacher, identifying practices that have been successful and practices that have failed. Recognizing that employees join organizations for social as well as economic reasons has led many organizations, such as Toyota, Dell, and Lucent Technologies, to use teams to solve problems and base employee pay on team results. A third reason is that history gives a feel for the types of problems for which managers long have struggled to find solutions. Many of these problems, such as low morale, high absenteeism, and poor quality, still exist in many organizations and continue to plague managers.

Looking back also underscores the fact that professional management hasn't been around all that long. In earlier, preindustrial societies, men and women paced their work according to the sun, the seasons, and the demand for what they produced. Small communities encouraged personal, often familial, relationships between employers and employees. The explosive growth of urban industry—and the factory system in particular—changed the face of the workplace forever. Workers in cities were forced to adapt to the factory's formal structure and rules and to labor long hours for employers they never saw. Many were poorly educated and needed considerable oral instruction and hands-on training in unfamiliar tasks.

The emergence of large-scale business enterprises in Canada, the United States, Asia, and Western Europe raised issues and created challenges that previously had applied only to governments. Businesses needed the equivalent of government leaders—managers—to hire and train employees and then to lead and motivate them. Managers also were needed to develop plans and design work units and, while doing so, make a profit, never a requirement for governments! In this chapter we briefly review how management viewpoints have evolved since 1886 to meet those needs.

During the past century, theorists have developed numerous responses to the same basic management question: What is the best way to manage an organization? We continue to study those responses because they still apply to the manager's job. In the following sections we discuss the five most widely accepted viewpoints of management that have evolved since about 1886: traditional (or classical), behavioral, systems, contingency, and quality. These viewpoints are based on different assumptions about the behavior of people in organizations, the key goals of an organization, the types of problems faced, and the methods that should be used to solve those problems. Figure 2.1 shows when each viewpoint emerged and began to gain popularity. As you can see, all five still influence managers' thinking. In fact, one important source of disagreement among today's managers is the emphasis that should be given to each of them. Thus a major purpose of this chapter is to show you not only how each has contributed to the historical evolution of modern management thought, but also how each can be used effectively in different circumstances now and in the future.

Figure 2.1   **History of Management Thought**

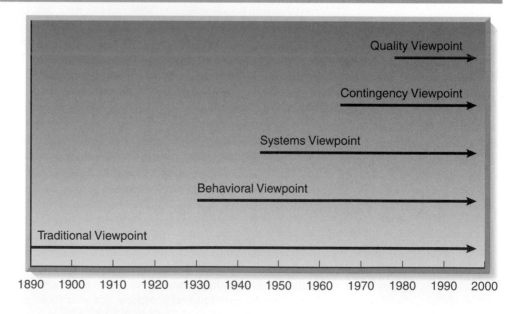

The oldest and perhaps most widely accepted view of management is the *traditional* (or classical) *viewpoint.* It is split into three main branches: bureaucratic management, scientific management, and administrative management. All three emerged during roughly the same time period, the late 1890s through the early 1900s, when engineers were trying to make organizations run like well-oiled machines. The founders of these three branches came from Germany, the United States, and France, respectively.

BUREAUCRATIC MANAGEMENT

Bureaucratic management relies on rules, a set hierarchy, a clear division of labor, and detailed procedures. Max Weber (1864–1920), a German social historian, is most closely associated with bureaucratic management (so named because Weber based his work on studies of Germany's government bureaucracy). Although Weber was one of the first theorists to deal with the problems of organizations, he wasn't widely recognized by managers and scholars in the United States until his work was translated into English in 1947. He was concerned primarily with the broad social and economic issues facing society; his writings on bureaucracy represent only part of his total contribution to social theory.[2]

Bureaucratic management provides a blueprint of how an entire organization should operate. It prescribes seven desirable characteristics: a formal system of rules, impersonality, division of labor, hierarchical structure, a detailed authority structure, lifelong career commitment, and rationality. Together these characteristics represent a formal, somewhat rigid method of managing. Let's take a look at this method, setting aside for the moment all the negative connotations the word *bureaucracy* has today and focusing instead on the system's strengths, consistency, and predictability.

Rules. As formal guidelines for the behavior of employees while they are on the job, *rules* can help provide the discipline an organization needs if it is to reach its goals. Adherence to rules ensures uniformity of procedures and operations and helps maintain organizational stability, regardless of individual managers' or employees' personal desires.

Impersonality. Reliance on rules leads to treating employees impersonally. That is, all employees are evaluated according to rules and objective data, such as sales or units produced. Although the word *impersonality* can also have negative connotations, Weber believed that this approach guaranteed fairness for all employees—an impersonal superior doesn't allow subjective personal or emotional considerations to color evaluations of subordinates.

Division of Labor. The *division of labor* involves dividing duties into simpler, more specialized tasks. It enables the organization to use personnel and job-training resources efficiently. Managers and employees are assigned and perform duties based on specialization and personal expertise. Unskilled employees can be assigned tasks that are relatively easy to learn and do. For example, employee turnover at fast-food restaurants such as McDonald's, Burger King, Hardee's, and Wendy's is over 300 percent a year. Because of the narrow division of labor, most fast-food jobs can be learned quickly and require only unskilled labor. Thus high turnover in this type of business may not create serious service problems.

Hierarchical Structure. Enron, a producer of natural gas and electricity, uses a pyramid-shaped hierarchical structure, as shown in Figure 2.2. A *hierarchical structure* ranks jobs according to the amount of authority (the right to decide) given to each. Typically, authority increases at each higher level to the top of the hierarchy. Those in lower level positions are under the control and direction of those in higher level positions. At Enron, for example, managers at Portland Electric report to the senior vice president of marketing, who in turn reports to the president of energy services. According to Weber, a well-defined hierarchy helps control employee behavior by making clear exactly where each stands in relation to everyone else in the organization.

Authority Structure. A system based on rules, impersonal supervision, division of labor, and a hierarchical structure is tied together by an authority structure. It determines who has the right to make decisions of varying importance at different levels within the organization. Weber identified three types of authority structures: traditional, charismatic, and rational–legal.

- *Traditional authority* is based on custom, ancestry, gender, birth order, and the like. The divine right of kings and the magical influence of tribal witch doctors are examples of traditional authority.

Figure 2.2 **Enron Organizational Chart**

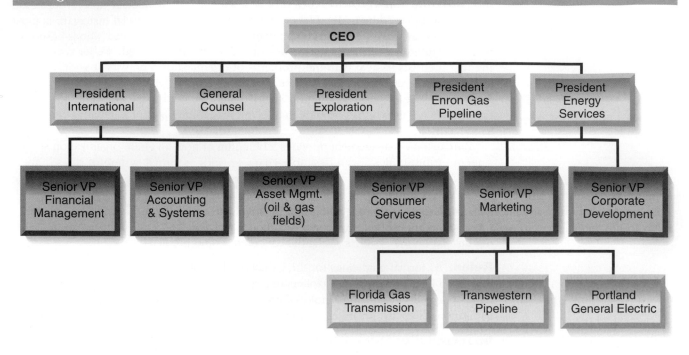

- **Charismatic authority** is evident when subordinates suspend their own judgment and comply voluntarily with a leader because of special personal qualities or abilities they perceive in that individual. Charismatic leaders (e.g., Gandhi, Golda Meir, Martin Luther King, Jr., Jesse Jackson, and Princess Diana) often head social, political, and religious movements. In contrast, business leaders seldom rely solely on charismatic authority, but some, such as Herb Kelleher (CEO of Southwest Airlines), Debbi Fields (founder of Mrs. Fields Cookies), and Cynthia Danaher (vice president of Hewlett-Packard), have used their charisma to motivate and influence subordinates.

- **Rational–legal authority** is based on established laws and rules that are applied uniformly. A superior is obeyed because of the position occupied within the organization's hierarchy. This authority depends on employees' acceptance of the organization's rules.

Lifelong Career Commitment. In a bureaucratic management system, employment is viewed as a *lifelong career commitment;* that is, both the employee and the organization view themselves as being committed to each other over the working life of the employee. Traditionally, Asian organizations, such as NEC, Samsung, Lucky Gold Star, and Toyota, have hired key workers with the expectation—by both parties—that a permanent employment contract was being made. In general, lifelong career commitment means that job security is guaranteed as long as the employee is technically qualified and performs satisfactorily. Entrance requirements, such as level of education and experience, ensure that hiring is based on qualifications rather than connections. The organization uses job security, tenure, step-by-step salary increases, and pensions to ensure that employees satisfactorily perform assigned duties. Promotion is granted when an employee demonstrates the competencies required to handle the demands of the next higher position. Organizational level is assumed to correspond closely with expertise. Managers in bureaucratic organizations, such as the civil service, often rely on the results of written and physical tests, amount of formal education, and previous work experience in making hiring and promotion decisions.

Rationality. The last characteristic of bureaucratic management is *rationality,* which means using the most efficient means available. Managers in a bureaucratic management system operate logically and "scientifically," with all decisions leading directly to achieving the organization's goals. Goal-directed activities then allow the organization to use its financial and human resources efficiently. In addition, rationality allows general organizational goals to be broken into more specific goals for each part of the organization. At Enron, for example, the overall corporate goals are to provide customers with energy, while continuing to achieve superior financial returns to shareholders. A goal of the energy service division is to capture opportunities resulting from the deregulation of electricity and natural gas in the commercial and light industrial markets.[3]

Ranking Organizations by Bureaucratic Orientation. We can use the seven characteristics of bureaucratic management to rank organizations from low to high with respect to bureaucratic orientation. As Figure 2.3 shows, government agencies (e.g., the Internal Revenue Service, or IRS) and some private companies (e.g., McDonald's and Blockbuster Video) rank high. Some creative and innovative companies (e.g., Amazon.com and Cisco Systems) rank low. Such rankings have to be interpreted carefully, however, because differences within organizations make precise measurement difficult. One organization may be highly bureaucratic in its division of labor but only slightly bureaucratic in its use of rules. In another organization these levels may be reversed. Are the organizations equally bureaucratic? No one can say for sure. Moreover, the degree of bureaucracy within an organization may vary considerably among departments and divisions. For example, Sony falls near the middle of the bureaucratic continuum, but its manufacturing plants, which produce standardized household goods (e.g., TVs, radios, clocks, and VCRs), tend to be more bureaucratic than its R&D departments, whose creativity would be stifled by too many rules.

Figure 2.3   **Range of Bureaucracy**

LOW Bureaucratic Structure	MID-RANGE Bureaucratic Structure	HIGH Bureaucratic Structure
• Amazon.com • Cisco Systems • Starbucks	• Pepsi-Cola • Procter & Gamble • Sony	• Internal Revenue Service • Blockbuster Video • McDonald's

---

Benefits of Bureaucracy. The expected benefits of bureaucratic management are efficiency and consistency. A bureaucracy functions best when many routine tasks need to be done. Then lower level employees can handle the bulk of the work by simply following rules and procedures. The fruits of their labor should be of standard (high) quality and produced at the rate necessary to meet organizational goals. At United Parcel Service, the use of rules and regulations for the size and weight of a package enable it to deliver more than 12.4 million packages daily throughout the world.[4] The following Planning and Administration Competency feature provides an excellent example of how bureaucracy can lead to efficiency.

Costs of Bureaucracy. The same aspects of bureaucratic management that can increase one organization's efficiency can lead to great inefficiency in another. Managers at Caterpillar, Ericsson, Siecor, and other organizations report that the orderliness of a bureaucracy often leads to inefficiencies that cannot be tolerated by companies operating in today's changing times. The following are five, often unanticipated, drawbacks of bureaucratic management.[5]

United Parcel Service (UPS) can deliver a small package anywhere in the United States for under $5. It has facilities in more than 200 countries and territories. In 1999, it earned $88 million in profits on revenues of more than $27 billion. How?

The answer is automation and bureaucracy. Mechanized centers sort 51,650 packages per hour. Jobs at UPS centers reflect clearly defined divisions of labor, including sorters, loaders, drivers, and property maintenance personnel. There are eight hierarchical levels from a truck washer to the president. Property maintenance employees are responsible for the washing, fueling, and maintenance of more than 157,000 fleet delivery vehicles and 610 aircraft. Employees who operate sorting machines handle more than 1,100 packages an hour and are allowed no more than one mistake per 2,500 packages. The more than 326,800 employees at UPS handle 12.4 million packages daily exactly the same way because of rules and regulations. Each manager is given several bound policy books spelling out company rules. For example, drivers are

instructed to walk to a customer's door at a brisk pace of 3 feet per second, carrying the package in the right hand and clipboard in the left. They should knock so as not to lose valuable seconds searching for the doorbell.

Technical qualifications are UPS's criteria for hiring and promotion. The company's manual says, "A leader does not have to remind others of authority by use of title. Knowledge, performance, and capacity should be adequate evidence of position and leadership." Special favors are forbidden. Employees set objective performance targets with their bosses. Promotions and salary increases are based on objective performance criteria.

UPS relies on extensive written records and computer systems to store data. Operating costs and production figures are compared to competitors, such as FedEx, DHL, and Airborne. Daily worksheets specifying performance quotas are kept on every employee and department. Employee production records are accumulated weekly and monthly.

UPS pays its drivers $11.50 per hour to start, and within 2 years, drivers should earn $22.00 per hour. With over-

time, many of them expect to earn more than $50,000 per year. In return for this salary, UPS expects maximum performance and closely monitors employees' behavior. For example, a UPS manager watching a driver make deliveries and seeing any wasted seconds will point them out immediately. A mere 30 seconds wasted per delivery can snowball into big delays by day's end.

• • •

To learn more about UPS, visit the company's home page at

http://www.ups.com

1. **Rigid rules and red tape.** Rigid adherence to rules and routines for their own sake is a frequent complaint of employees and customers of many organizations. Such a system leaves little room for individual freedom and creativity. This rigidity may foster low motivation, entrenched "career" employees, high turnover among the best employees, and shoddy work. A significant amount of time and money can be wasted.

2. **Protection of authority.** Managers in a bureaucratic organization may ignore issues of employee productivity while protecting and expanding their own authority. Caterpillar attacked the problem head-on. Management believed that the company couldn't afford to support a maze of corporate buck-passers, so it changed the system by focusing on customer satisfaction. Employees use their PCs to swap essential information and determine exactly what type of engine a customer wants. A computer-controlled monorail system and robots bring employees the engine, parts, and computer-generated information about what to do. This system requires 29 percent fewer people than the old system. Employees work on engines at their own pace and until they are satisfied that the job has been done right.

3. **Slow decision making.** Large, complex organizations depend heavily on timely decisions. In a highly bureaucratic organization, however, adherence to rules and

procedures may take precedence over effective, timely decision making. When that happens, rules take on lives of their own. Formality and ritual delay decisions at every level until all the red tape has been cleared, petty insistence on power and status privileges has been satisfied, and any chance of blame for errors in judgment has been minimized.

4. **Incompatibility with changing technology.** Advancing technology may make bureaucratic management inappropriate. Cindi Fitzgerald, director of wireless Internet for Ericsson, believes that narrowly defined jobs based on rules and regulations generate little trust and sharing of information. There, the technology changes rapidly, and employees must be able to go directly to the person who has the information they need to do their jobs.[6]

5. **Incompatibility with workers' values.** More and more people are being hired by bureaucratic organizations to fill important decision-making positions. These workers' values include performing challenging work, serving clients and customers, and finding innovative solutions to problems. These values often are incompatible with the bureaucratic need for efficiency, order, and consistency. Bureaucratic authority is related to hierarchical position, but most professionals believe that authority stems from personal competence and technical knowledge. Tuy Nguyen, product manager at Siecor Corporation, said, "I have to rely more on the professionalism and commitment of my people than on rules and regulations." Siecor is developing a performance appraisal system that allows team members, peers, and even external customers to evaluate employees' work. The company is having to do so because a manager might not know enough to evaluate a particular person's contributions.

Assessing Bureaucratic Management. Not all bureaucratic organizations are inefficient and unprofitable. In fact, bureaucratic management is still widely and successfully used. This approach is most effective when (1) large amounts of standard information have to be processed and an efficient processing method has been found (as in credit card and insurance companies, the IRS, and traffic courts); (2) the needs of the customer arc known and aren't likely to change (as in the registration of drivers in most states); (3) the technology is routine and stable, so employees can be easily and quickly taught how to operate machines (as at Taco Bell, McDonald's, Burger King, and in toll booths); and (4) the organization has to coordinate the activities of numerous employees in order to deliver a standardized service or product to the customer (as by the IRS, UPS, and the U.S. Postal Service).[7]

SCIENTIFIC MANAGEMENT

As manufacturing firms became larger and more complex in the late 1800s, not all managers could continue to be directly involved with production. Many began to spend more of their time on planning, scheduling, and staffing activities. Also, managers were hard-pressed to keep up with new technologies. As a result, a need was created for operations specialists who could solve the personnel and productivity problems that, if not addressed, could threaten operating efficiency.

Frederick W. Taylor. Thus the stage was set for Frederick Winslow Taylor (1856–1915) to do his pioneering work in scientific management. Whereas bureaucratic management looks at broad organizational structures and work systems, *scientific management* focuses on individuals and their machines or tools. Its philosophy is that management practices should be based on fact and observation, not on hearsay or guesswork.[8] Scientific management is used by Microsoft, Kodak, Mattel, and other manufacturers in their plants, but it is also widely used in service-based organizations, such as FedEx, The Associates First Capital Corporation, and MCI WorldCom.

Taylor, an American mechanical engineer, started out as a foreman at Midvale Steel Company in Philadelphia. He believed that increased productivity ultimately depended on finding ways to make workers more efficient by using objective, scientific techniques. When Taylor worked as a consultant to Bethlehem Steel, for example, he made a science of shoveling. Through observation and experimentation he looked for answers to questions such as the following.

1. Will a first-class worker do more work per day with a shovelful of 5, 10, 15, 20, 30, or 40 pounds?

2. What kinds of shovels work best with which materials?

3. How quickly can a shovel be pushed into a pile of coal and pulled out properly loaded?

4. How long does it take to swing a shovel backward and throw the load a specified horizontal distance at a specified height?

As Taylor accumulated answers to his questions, he developed views on how to increase the total amount shoveled per day. He started a program that matched workers, shovel sizes, materials, and the like for each job. By the end of the third year his program had reduced the number of shovelers needed from 600 to 140 while the average number of tons shoveled per worker per day had risen from 16 to 50. Workers' earnings also increased from $1.15 to $1.88 a day.

Taylor used time-and-motion studies to analyze work flows, supervisory techniques, and worker fatigue. A *time-and-motion study* involves identifying and measuring a worker's physical movements when performing a task and then analyzing the results. Movements that slow production are dropped. One goal of a time-and-motion study is to make a job highly routine and efficient. Eliminating wasted physical effort and specifying an exact sequence of activities reduce the amount of time, money, and effort needed to make a product. Taylor was convinced that having workers perform routine tasks that didn't require them to make decisions could increase efficiency. Performance goals expressed quantitatively (e.g., number of units produced per shift) addressed a problem that had begun to trouble managers—how to judge whether an employee had put in a fair day's work.

Advocates of scientific management stress specialization. They believe that expertise is the only source of authority and that a single foreman couldn't be an expert at all the tasks supervised. Each foreman's particular area of specialization therefore should become an area of authority. This solution is called *functional foremanship,* a division of labor that assigned eight foremen to each work area. Four of the foremen would handle planning, production scheduling, time-and-motion studies, and discipline. The other four would deal with machinery maintenance, machine speed, feeding material into the machine, and production on the shop floor.

What motivates employees to work to their capacity? Taylor believed that money was the answer. He supported the individual piecework system as the basis for pay. If workers met a certain production standard, they were to be paid at a standard wage rate. Workers who produced more than the standard were to be paid at a higher rate for all the pieces they produced, not just for those exceeding the standard. Taylor assumed that workers would be economically rational; that is, they would follow management's orders to produce more in response to financial incentives that allowed them to earn more money. Taylor argued that managers should use financial incentives if they were convinced that increases in productivity would more than offset higher employee earnings.

The Gilbreths. Frank (1868–1924) and Lillian (1878–1972) Gilbreth formed an unusual husband-and-wife engineering team that made significant contributions to scientific management. Frank used a revolutionary new tool—motion pictures—to study workers' motions. For instance, he identified 18 individual motions that a bricklayer uses to lay bricks. By changing the bricklaying process, he reduced the 18 motions to 5, increasing a worker's overall productivity by more than 200 percent. Many of today's industrial engineers have combined Frank Gilbreth's methods with Taylor's to redesign jobs for greater efficiency.[9]

Lillian Gilbreth carried on Frank's work and raised their 12 children after his death. Concerned mainly with the human side of industrial engineering, she championed the idea that workers should have standard days, scheduled rest breaks, and normal lunch periods. Her work influenced the U.S. Congress to establish child-labor laws and develop rules for protecting workers from unsafe working conditions.

Henry Gantt. Taylor's associate, Henry Gantt (1861–1919), focused on "control" systems for production scheduling. His Gantt charts are still widely used to plan project timelines and have been adapted for computer scheduling applications. The ***Gantt chart*** is a visual plan and progress report. It identifies various stages of work that must be carried out to complete a project, sets a deadline for each stage, and documents accomplishments. Gantt also established quota systems and bonuses for workers who exceeded their quotas.[10]

Assessing Scientific Management. Taylor and other early proponents of scientific management would applaud the efforts of KFC, Honda, Canon, Intel, and other organizations that have successfully applied their concepts. Through time-and-motion studies, for example, KFC found that employees took almost 2 minutes to complete a customer's order. To improve performance, KFC instructed employees to acknowledge customers within 3 seconds of arriving at the drive-through window, fill a customer's order within 60 seconds, and arrive at an average service time of 90 seconds. To accomplish these objectives, KFC designed employees' workstations so that employees wouldn't need to take more than two steps to get what they needed, wouldn't lift anything, and from handy shelves could pull down napkins, straws, and other items needed to complete the order. Hundreds of other companies have used Taylor's principles to improve their employee selection and training processes and to seek the one best way to perform each task.

Unfortunately, most proponents of scientific management misread the human side of work. When Frederick Taylor and Frank Gilbreth formulated their principles and methods, they thought that workers were motivated primarily by a desire to earn money to satisfy their economic and physical needs. They failed to recognize that workers also have social needs and that working conditions and job satisfaction often are as important, if not more important, than money. For example, workers have struck to protest working conditions, speedup of an assembly line, or harassment by management, even when a fair financial incentive system was in place. Managers today can't assume that workers are interested only in higher wages. Dividing jobs into their simplest tasks and setting clear rules for accomplishing those tasks won't always lead to a quality product, high morale, and an effective organization. Today's employees often want to participate in decisions that affect their performance, and many want to be independent and hold jobs that give them self-fulfillment.

ADMINISTRATIVE MANAGEMENT

Administrative management focuses on the manager and basic managerial functions. It evolved early in the 1900s and is most closely identified with Henri Fayol (1841–1925), a French industrialist. Fayol credited his success as a manager to the methods he used rather than to his personal qualities. He felt strongly that, to be successful, managers had only to understand the basic managerial functions—planning, organizing, leading, and controlling—and apply certain management principles to them. He was the first person to group managers' functions in this way.[11]

Like the other traditionalists, Fayol emphasized formal structure and processes, believing that they are necessary for the adequate performance of all important tasks. In other words, if people are to work well together, they need a clear definition of what they're trying to accomplish and how their tasks help meet organizational goals.

Fayol developed the following 14 management principles and suggested that managers receive formal training in their application.

1. **Division of labor.** The more people specialize, the more efficiently they can perform their work.

2. **Authority.** Managers have the right and the authority to give orders to get things done.

3. **Discipline.** Members of an organization need to respect the rules and agreements that govern it.

4. **Unity of command.** Each employee must receive instructions about a particular operation from only one person to avoid conflicting expectations and confusion.

5. **Unity of direction.** Managers should coordinate the efforts of employees working on projects, but only one manager should be responsible for an employee's behavior.

6. **Subordination of individual interests to the common good.** The interests of individual employees should not take precedence over the interests of the entire organization.

7. **Remuneration.** Pay for work done should be fair to both the employee and the employer.

8. **Centralization.** Managers should retain final responsibility but should also give their subordinates enough authority to do their jobs properly.

9. **Scalar chain.** A single, uninterrupted line of authority (often represented by the neat boxes and lines of an organization chart) should run rank to rank from top management to the lowest level position in the company.

10. **Order.** Materials and people should be in the right place at the right time. In particular, people should be in the jobs or positions best suited to them.

11. **Equity.** Managers should be both friendly and fair to their subordinates.

12. **Stability and tenure of staff.** A high rate of employee turnover is not efficient.

13. **Initiative.** Subordinates should be given the freedom to formulate and carry out their own plans.

14. **Esprit de corps.** Promoting team spirit gives the organization a sense of unity.

Managers still use many of Fayol's principles of administrative management, but different managers seldom apply them in exactly the same way. Situations vary and so, too, does the application of these principles. At Chapparal Steel the maintenance superintendent receives direction from the plant manager, the chief engineer, and the production manager—violating the unity of command principle. However, the maintenance superintendent has the authority to set priorities for plant maintenance—illustrating the initiative principle.

ASSESSING THE TRADITIONAL VIEWPOINT

Traditional management's three branches—bureaucratic, scientific, and administrative—still have their proponents, are often written about, and continue to be applied effectively. Table 2.1 highlights the points discussed.

Table 2.1	**Characteristics of Traditional Management**	
Bureaucratic Management	**Traditional Management**	**Scientific Management**
Administrative Characteristics		
Rules	Training in routines and rules	Defining of management functions
Impersonality	"One best way"	Division of labor
Division of labor	Financial motivation	Hierarchy
Hierarchy		Authority
Authority structure		Equity
Lifelong career commitment		
Rationality		
Focus		
Whole organization	Employee	Manager
Benefits		
Consistency	Productivity	Clear structure
Efficency	Efficiency	Professionalization of managerial roles
Drawbacks		
Rigidity	Overlooks social needs	Internal focus
Slowness		Overemphasizes rational behavior of managers

Let's summarize what they have in common and what some of their drawbacks are. All three branches of traditional management emphasize the formal aspects of organization. Traditionalists are concerned with the formal relations among an organization's departments, tasks, and processes. Weber, Taylor, the Gilbreths, Gantt, and Fayol replaced seat-of-the-pants management practices with sound theoretical and scientific principles. Managers began to stress the division of labor, hierarchical authority, rules, and decisions that would maximize economic rewards.

The manager's role in a hierarchy is crucial. In organizations, the relationship between expertise and organizational level is strong. Because of their higher position and presumed greater expertise, superiors are to be obeyed by subordinates. Administrative and scientific management's emphasis on logical processes and strict division of labor are based on similar reasoning.

Although they may recognize that people have feelings and are influenced by their friends at work, the overriding focus of traditionalists is on efficient and effective job performance. Taylor considered the human side of work in terms of eliminating bad feelings between workers and management and providing employees with financial incentives to increase productivity. Traditionalists consider job security, career progression, and protection of workers from employers' whims to be important. However, they do not recognize informal or social relationships among employees at work. Taylor and Frank Gilbreth focused on well-defined rules intended to ensure efficient performance, the primary standard against which employees were to be judged.

In assessing the work of the early traditional theorists, you need to keep in mind that they were influenced by the economic and societal conditions facing them at the time. The United States was becoming an industrial nation, unions were forming to protect workers' rights, and laws were being passed to eliminate unsafe working conditions. Even so, most organizations operated in a relatively stable environment with few competitors.

BEHAVIORAL VIEWPOINT

2.

EXPLAIN THE BEHAVIORAL VIEWPOINT'S CONTRIBUTION TO MANAGEMENT.

During the Great Depression, the federal government began to play a more influential role in people's lives. By the time President Franklin D. Roosevelt took office in 1933, the national economy was hovering on the brink of collapse. To provide employment the government undertook temporary public works projects—constructing dams, roads, and public buildings and improving national parks. It also created agencies such as the Social Security Administration to assist the aged, the unemployed, and the disabled.

In one of the era's most dramatic changes, unskilled workers greatly increased their ability to influence management decisions though organization and membership in powerful labor unions. During the 1930s Congress aided unions by enacting legislation that deterred management from restricting union activities, legalized collective bargaining, and required management to bargain with unions. As a result the labor movement grew rapidly, and the Congress of Industrial Organizations (CIO) was formed. In 1937, the autoworkers and steelworkers won their first big contracts. Eventually professionals and skilled workers, as well as unskilled laborers, formed unions to bargain for better pay, increased benefits, and improved working conditions. Following the depression and World War II, a new wave of optimism swept the U.S. economy.

Against this backdrop of change and reform, managers were forced to recognize that people have needs, hold to values, and want respect. Managers were now leading workers who did not appear to exhibit what the early traditional management theorists had thought was rational economic behavior. That is, workers weren't always performing up to their physiological capabilities, as Taylor had predicted rational people would do. Nor were effective managers consistently following Fayol's 14 principles. By exploring these inconsistencies, those who favored a behavioral viewpoint of management gained recognition. The **behavioral** (human relations) **viewpoint** focuses on dealing effectively with the human aspects of organizations. Its proponents look at how managers do what they do, how managers lead subordinates and communicate with them, and why managers need to change their assumptions about people if they want to lead high-performance teams and organizations.

FOLLETT'S CONTRIBUTIONS

Mary Parker Follett (1868–1933) made important contributions to the behavioral viewpoint of management. She believed that management is a flowing, continuous process, not a static one, and that if a problem has been solved, the method used to solve it probably generated new problems. She stressed (1) involvement of workers in solving problems and (2) the dynamics of management, rather than static principles. Both ideas contrasted sharply with the views of Weber, Taylor, and Fayol.[12]

Follett studied how managers did their jobs by observing them at work. Based on these observations, she concluded that coordination is vital to effective management. She developed four principles of coordination for managers to apply.

1. Coordination is best achieved when the people responsible for making a decision are in direct contact.

2. Coordination during the early stages of planning and project implementation is essential.

3. Coordination should address all the factors in a situation.

4. Coordination must be worked at continuously.

Follett believed that the people closest to the action could make the best decisions. For example, she was convinced that first-line managers are in the best position to coordinate production tasks. And by increasing communication among themselves and with workers, these managers can make better decisions regarding such tasks than managers up the hierarchy can. She also believed that first-line managers should not only plan and coordinate workers' activities, but also involve them in the process. Simply because managers told employees to do something a certain way, Follett argued, they shouldn't assume that the employees would do it. She argued further that managers at all levels should maintain good working relationships with their subordinates. One way to do so is to involve subordinates in the decision-making process whenever they will be affected by a decision. Drawing on psychology and sociology, Follett urged managers to recognize that each person is a collection of beliefs, emotions, and feelings.

WEB INSIGHT

What are the core values of Whole Foods Markets? To learn more about the management practices of John Mackey, president of Whole Foods Markets, and how his ideas filter down to each store, visit the company's Web site at *http://www.wholefoodsmarket.com/company*

John Mackey, president of Whole Foods, a supermarket chain that sells only natural foods, believes that Follett's ideas have shaped his management practices. Each Whole Foods Market typically employs between 60 and 140 people and is organized into various teams to develop a sense of cooperation. Each team is responsible for doing its own work and selecting new team members. A candidate must be voted on by the team and receive a two-thirds majority to become a team member. Every 4 weeks, each team meets to discuss problems and make decisions.

Employees also practice self-responsibility. Mackey believes that, by placing responsibility and authority at the store and team level rather than at corporate headquarters, employees are encouraged to make decisions that affect their daily work. Mackey knows that employees will make mistakes because of their inexperience. However, the company is dedicated to learning and growing, and he believes that employees can learn from their mistakes. Recognizing that there are many different approaches to getting things done, Mackey encourages creativity and experimentation at each store and by each employee. He is convinced that only through experimentation can new information be gathered and communication increased among all employees.[13]

BARNARD'S CONTRIBUTIONS

Chester Barnard (1886–1961) studied economics at Harvard but failed to graduate because he didn't finish a laboratory course in science. He was hired by AT&T, and in

1927 he became president of New Jersey Bell. Barnard made two significant contributions to management, which are detailed in his book, *The Functions of the Executive*.[14]

First, Barnard viewed organizations as social systems that require employee cooperation if they are to be effective. In other words, people should continually communicate with one another. According to Barnard, managers' main roles are to communicate with employees and motivate them to work hard to help achieve the organization's goals. In his view, successful management also depends on maintaining good relations with people outside the organization with whom managers deal regularly. He stressed the dependence of the organization on investors, suppliers, customers, and other outside interests. Barnard stressed the idea that managers have to examine the organization's external environment and adjust its internal structure to balance the two.

Second, Barnard proposed the ***acceptance theory of authority***. This theory holds that employees have free wills and thus choose whether to follow management's orders. That is, employees will follow orders if they (1) understand what is required, (2) believe that the orders are consistent with organizational goals, and (3) see positive benefits to themselves in carrying out the orders.

THE HAWTHORNE CONTRIBUTIONS

The strongest support for the behavioral viewpoint emerged from studies carried out between 1924 and 1933 at Western Electric Company's Hawthorne plant in Chicago. The Hawthorne Illumination Tests, begun in November 1924 and conducted in three departments of the plant, initially were developed and directed by Hawthorne's engineers. They divided employees into two groups: a test group, whom they subjected to deliberate changes in lighting, and a control group, for whom lighting remained constant throughout the experiment. When lighting conditions for the test group were improved, the group's productivity increased, as expected. The engineers were mystified, though, by a similar jump in productivity upon reducing the test group's lighting to the point of twilight. To compound the mystery, the control group's output kept rising, even though its lighting condition didn't change. Western Electric called in Harvard professor Elton Mayo to investigate these peculiar and puzzling results.

Mayo and Harvard colleagues Fritz Roethlisberger and William Dickson devised a new experiment. They placed two groups of six women each in separate rooms. They changed various conditions for the test group and left conditions unchanged for the control group. The changes included shortening the test group's coffee breaks, allowing it to choose its own rest periods, and letting it have a say in other suggested changes. Once again, output of both the test group and the control group increased. The researchers decided that they could rule out financial incentives as a factor because they hadn't changed the payment schedule for either group.

The researchers concluded that the increases in productivity weren't caused by a physical event but by a complex emotional chain reaction. Because employees in both groups had been singled out for special attention, they had developed a group pride that motivated them to improve their performance. The sympathetic supervision they received further reinforced that motivation. These experimental results led to Mayo's first important discovery: When employees are given special attention, productivity is likely to change regardless of whether working conditions change. This phenomenon became known as the ***Hawthorne effect***.[15]

However, an important question remained unanswered: Why should a little special attention and the formation of group bonds produce such strong reactions? To find the answer Mayo interviewed employees. These interviews yielded a highly significant discovery: Informal work groups, the social environment of employees, greatly influence productivity. Many Western Electric employees found their lives inside and outside the factory dull and meaningless. Their workplace friends, chosen in part because of mutual antagonism toward "the bosses," gave meaning to their working lives. Thus peer pressure, rather than management demands, had a significant influence on employee productivity.

The writings of Mayo, Roethlisberger, and Dickson that emerged from the Hawthorne studies helped outline the behavioral viewpoint of management. The researchers concluded that behavior on the job is determined by a complex set of factors. They found that the informal work group develops its own set of norms to satisfy the needs of individuals in the work setting and that the social system of such informal groups is maintained through symbols of prestige and power. As a result of their studies, the researchers recommended that managers consider the worker in a personal context (e.g., family situation, friendships, and membership in groups) in order to understand each employee's unique needs and sources of satisfaction. They also suggested that awareness of employee feelings and encouragement of employee participation in decision making can reduce resistance to change.[16]

One manager who has utilized the behavioral viewpoint of management to improve his plant's effectiveness is Ron Ferner of Campbell Soup.[17] To reach the highest level of customer satisfaction in this fiercely competitive industry, he engages employees directly in contributing to the success of the company. He recognizes and rewards employees for their contributions at companywide celebrations and encourages employees to participate in making a wide range of decisions. The following Teamwork Competency feature illustrates how Ferner gets and keeps his employees involved.

TEAMWORK COMPETENCY

Share It All with Employees, Soup to Nuts

When Ron Ferner first joined Campbell Soup in the 1960s, none of the company's executives believed in sharing any kind of information with anybody. Ferner also was skeptical about sharing information because he, along with many others at the time, believed that the principles of scientific management would lead the company to improved profitability. It was a manager's job to stand behind a post and peek out to watch employees work.

By the mid 1980s, Campbell's management had moved to a philosophy of meeting with all employees quarterly. Ferner's plant in Camden, New Jersey, employed more than 1,800 people, requiring 3 days to hold the meetings each quarter. The employees asked questions and managers responded. After many years, the employees got comfortable with asking questions and receiving "real" answers. At first, many managers were reluctant to share information and hesitant to reveal any weakness. According to Ferner, "If you don't talk to employees for 10 years and then show up and say

that today we should start talking, it doesn't work."

At his plant employees were having problems with boxes breaking. Managers started talking to the employees about the problem and quickly realized that the employees had a good handle on what was wrong. The managers encouraged them to call the supplier. The supplier asked some of the employees to visit its plant so that its people could understand the problem. Ferner rented a van and sent some employees to meet with the supplier's employees. Together they solved the problem and Ferner threw a party for the entire plant, congratulating them on their initiative. Their success and the recognition they received boosted the employees' confidence in their ability to identify and solve problems.

The company then decided to provide financial information to all employees, form teams, and ask them about how to improve profitability. The teams came up with a number of suggestions, many of which the company accepted and put into effect. For example, teams

can now be recognized for their contributions. Recognition is self-administered, and anyone can nominate a team. Team members decide which category (i.e., bronze, silver, or gold) of recognition their contribution warrants. The awards range from team gift certificates for dinner to cash payments.

• • •

To learn more about Campbell Soup, visit the company's home page at

http://www.campbellsoup.com

ASSESSING THE BEHAVIORAL VIEWPOINT

The behavioral viewpoint of management goes beyond the traditionalists' mechanical view of work by stressing the importance of group dynamics, complex human motivations, and the manager's leadership style. It emphasizes the employee's social and economic needs and the influence of the organization's social setting on the quality and quantity of work produced. The following are the basic assumptions of the behavioral viewpoint.

- Employees are motivated by social needs and get a sense of identity through their associations with one another.

- Employees are more responsive to the social forces exerted by their peers than to management's financial incentives and rules.

- Employees are most likely to respond to managers who can help them satisfy their needs.

- Managers need to involve subordinates in coordinating work to improve efficiency.

These assumptions don't always hold in practice, of course. Improving working conditions and managers' human relations skills won't always increase productivity. Economic aspects of work are still important to the employee, as Taylor believed. The major union contracts negotiated in recent years, for instance, focus on job security and wage incentives. And, although employees enjoy working with coworkers who are friendly, low salaries tend to lead to absenteeism and turnover. The negative effects of clumsy organizational structure, poor communication, and routine or boring tasks won't be overcome by the presence of pleasant co-workers. The human aspect of the job now is vastly more complex than those advocating the behavioral viewpoint in the 1930s could ever have imagined.[18]

SYSTEMS VIEWPOINT

3.

DESCRIBE HOW MANAGERS CAN USE SYSTEMS AND QUANTITATIVE TECHNIQUES TO IMPROVE EMPLOYEE PERFORMANCE.

During World War II the British assembled a team of mathematicians, physicists, and others to solve various wartime problems. These professionals formed the first operations research (OR) group. Initially, they were responsible for analyzing the makeup, routes, and speeds of convoys and probable locations of German submarines. The team developed ingenious ways to analyze complex problems that couldn't be handled solely by intuition, straightforward mathematics, or experience. The British and Americans further developed this approach (called *systems analysis*) throughout the war and applied it to many problems of war production and military logistics. Later, systems analysis became an accepted tool in the Department of Defense (DoD) and the space program, as well as throughout private industry.[19]

SYSTEM CONCEPTS

A *system* is an association of interrelated and interdependent parts. The human body is a system with organs, muscles, bones, nerves, and a consciousness that links all its parts. In the Preview Case, we described Toyota's production process as a system with employees, teams, and departments that are linked to achieve its goals. An organization also is linked externally to suppliers, customers, shareholders, and regulatory agencies. A competent systems-oriented manager makes decisions only after identifying and analyzing how other managers, departments, customers, or others might be affected by the decisions.

The *systems viewpoint* of management represents an approach to solving problems by diagnosing them within a framework of inputs, transformation processes, outputs, and feedback, as shown in Figure 2.4. The system involved may be an individual, a work group, a department, or an entire organization.

Figure 2.4   **Basic Systems View of Organization**

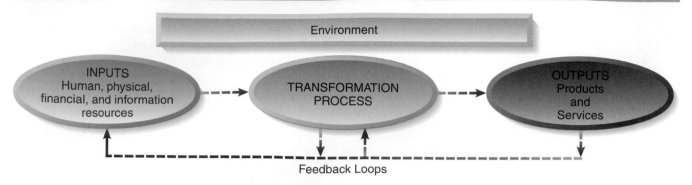

Inputs are the physical, human, material, financial, and information resources that enter a transformation process. At a university, for example, inputs include students, faculty, money, and buildings. *Transformation processes* comprise the technologies used to convert inputs into outputs. Transformation processes at a university include lectures, reading assignments, lab experiments, term papers, and tests. *Outputs* are the original inputs (human, physical, material, information, and financial resources) as changed by a transformation process. Outputs at a university include the graduating students. For a system to operate effectively, it must also provide for feedback. *Feedback* is information about a system's status and performance. One form of feedback at a university is the ability of its graduates to get jobs. In an organization, feedback may take the form of marketing surveys, financial reports, production records, performance appraisals, and the like. A manager's role is to guide transformation processes by planning, organizing, leading, and controlling.

SYSTEM TYPES

There are two types of systems: closed and open. A *closed system* limits its interactions with its environment. At Toyota, the production department operates as a closed system, producing standardized products in an uninterrupted stream. An *open system* interacts with the external environment. Nokia's marketing department constantly tries to identify new products and services to satisfy customers' telecommunications desires. It monitors what competitors are doing and then develops ways to deliver better quality and service at a lower price, constantly receiving feedback from customers as part of this process.

The following Communication Competency feature reveals how Monte Chamberlin, general manager of supply-chain management at Thomson Consumer Electronics in Indianapolis, Indiana, uses a systems viewpoint to manage customer service (key systems concepts are in parantheses). Thomson makes color TV sets (RCA, GE, and ProScan brands). Retail chains such as Circuit City and Best Buy that are among the best customers for Thomson's products had realized inventory cost savings through their dealings with computer and appliance manufacturers, which have their own sophisticated supply-chain programs.[20] Computer makers and retailers, in particular, had long ago discovered the importance of inventory reduction because their products are more valuable than TV sets, yet become obsolete—and lose value—faster.

COMMUNICATION COMPETENCY	*Supply-Chain Management at Thomson*

Monte Chamberlin contacted the people at Dell Computer for assistance (input) in designing a new system. He looked at Dell as an ideal model because of its ability to assemble a large number of different PC models from a small number of components in a short a period of time. After discussing the problem with Dell, he and his team decided that they could reduce by 75 percent the number of assembly steps that weren't common to a wide variety of TV models. Doing so would permit greater manufacturing speed and flexibility (transformation). The team's idea was to bring together a limited number of "generic" sets with few differentiating features to near completion on assembly lines. Then, in a last-minute response to customer orders, routing them through a relatively small number of steps to add features unique to each model would finish the sets (outputs)—a TV maker's version of what PC manufacturers do.

Chamberlin discovered that removing a computer's housing reveals a few unused and unexplained connectors that helped the maker postpone as long as possible the PC's final configuration. The small extra cost of the connectors is more than offset by the flexibility and quick turnaround they permit when customers' orders arrive. This "postponement" strat-egy in the assembly process is one of the systems that Thomson now uses to reduce its response time to market shifts from a few months to just 1 month.

The highest-value component of TV sets is the picture tube. Thomson produces picture tubes in plants in Pennsylvania, Ohio, and Indiana and ships them to plants in Juarez, Mexico, where various suppliers assemble them into finished sets. In the past, trucks northbound from Juarez moved the TVs into distribution centers in El Paso, Los Angeles, and Indianapolis. But now, when a customer places a large order (input) that requires an entire truck, Thomson delivers it directly (transformation process) to the customer (output).

Thomson is also moving to a production planning system based on 1-month sales forecasts from its cus-tomers, which are much more accurate than attempts to predict retail sales several months ahead (input). It has also shifted to receiving orders and shipping TVs weekly (transformation process) instead of monthly, as customers get better at predicting demand and trimming their inventories. It uses a computer software package to keep track of customer delivery dates. The program generates a forecast each week, projecting demand for about 250 different color TV models and can display point-of-sale information from customers as it arrives via the Internet.

• • •

To learn more about Thomson, visit the company's home page at

http://www.thomson-multimedia.com

QUANTITATIVE TECHNIQUES

While some advocates of systems analysis were suggesting that managers look at inputs, transformation processes, and outputs before making a decision, other systems advocates were developing quantitative techniques to aid in managerial decision making. Quantitative techniques have four basic characteristics, as illustrated by the Thomson experience.[21]

1. **The primary focus is on decision making.** Investigation identifies direct actions that managers can take, such as reducing inventory costs.

2. **Alternatives are based on economic criteria.** Alternative actions are presented in terms of measurable criteria, such as shipping costs, sales revenues, and profits.

3. **Mathematical models are used.** Situations are simulated and problems are analyzed by means of mathematical models.

4. **Computers are essential.** Computers are used to solve complex mathematical models, such as statistical process controls, that would be too costly and time-consuming to process manually.

The range of quantitative decision-making tools available to management has expanded greatly during the past two decades. In the past, small businesses such as retail stores, medical offices, mom-and-pop restaurants, and farmers couldn't use systems analysis techniques—but today they can. Owners and managers now have inventory, statistical decision theory, linear programming, and many other aids for solving complex problems. Many of those tools are literally at their fingertips in the form of so ware that can be run on desktop computers. In the emergency room at Presb Hospital in Dallas, a computer on the wall allows the staff to plug in differ modules, which relay the patient's functions to a display screen. Each pulse, blood pressure, and the like—is run by a piece of softwar computer has access to a high-speed local network, so that r monitored remotely. Thus each patient is monitored by components that the staff can change as the medica

In the largest companies, groups of management of business problems by devising their own sophistica on mainframe, networked, and personal computers. Suci such as Caesar's Palace, Bally's, and Harrah's in Atlantic City and Las Vegas increase their profits and improve service. Casinos provide millions of dollars of complimentary services (e.g., food, rooms, and transportation) for high rollers. To reduce the cost of these services and improve the odds that these people will gamble, and therefore lose, in their establishments, casino managers utilize sophisticated information systems that analyze customers' favorite games, betting patterns, accommodation preferences, food and drink choices, and other habits.

ASSESSING THE SYSTEMS VIEWPOINT

Systems analysis and quantitative techniques have been used primarily to manage transformation processes and in the technical planning and decision-making aspects of management. These methods can also be used to improve managers' ability to deal with human resources issues. For example, sophisticated staffing models can be used to map the flow of people into and out of an organization.

Research and development continues to expand the application of information systems in business, which we explore fully in Chapter 20. Moreover, systems analysis is helping computer experts develop hardware, as well as software, with humanlike intelligence. These experts are trying to design computers that are capable of reasoning and processing spoken language. When machines can reason, they, like human beings, will be able to learn from past experience and apply what they have learned to the solution of new problems.

Organizations no doubt will continue to develop more sophisticated systems in order to increase productivity. Such systems will require changes in many aspects of day-to-day operations. These changes will not come without struggle and pain. Yet for organizations to survive managers must use increasingly sophisticated systems in making decisions.[22]

CONTINGENCY VIEWPOINT

4.

STATE THE TWO MAJOR COMPONENTS OF THE CONTINGENCY VIEWPOINT.

The essence of the *contingency viewpoint* (sometimes called the situational approach) is that management practices should be consistent with the requirements of the external environment, the technology used to make a product or provide a service, and capabilities of the people who work for the organization.[23] The relationships among these variables are summarized in Figure 2.5. The contingency viewpoint of management emerged in the mid 1960s in response to the frustration of managers and others who had tried unsuccessfully to apply traditional and systems concepts to actual managerial problems. For example, why did providing workers with a bonus for being on time decrease lateness at one Marriott hotel but have little impact at another? Proponents of the contingency viewpoint contend that different situations require different practices. As one manager put it, the contingency viewpoint really means "it all depends."

Proponents of the contingency viewpoint advocate using the other three management viewpoints independently or in combination, as necessary, to deal with various situations. However, this viewpoint doesn't give managers free rein to indulge their personal biases and whims. Rather, managers are expected to determine which methods are likely to be more effective than others in a given situation.

CONTINGENCY VARIABLES

The relative importance of each contingency variable—external environment, technology, and people—depends on the type of managerial problem being considered. For example, in designing an organization's structure a manager should consider the nature of the company's external environment and the corresponding information processing requirements. Hence the IRS's structure is different from that of Cisco Systems. The IRS has a fairly stable set of customers, most of whom must file their tax returns by April 15

Figure 2.5 **Contingency Viewpoint**

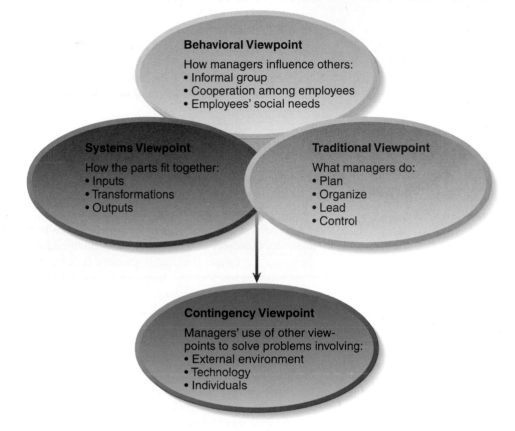

each year. It hires many part-time people during the peak tax season to process returns and answer questions and then lays them off after the peak has passed. In contrast, Cisco Systems has many competitors and a constantly changing set of customers whose demands for switches, routers, and hubs (products that form the "plumbing" of modern communications and networking systems) must be processed immediately. Its continuous information processing requirements call for more reliance on full-time personnel than is necessary at the IRS.

Technology is the method used to transform organizational inputs into outputs. It is more than machinery; it also is the knowledge, tools, techniques, and actions applied to change raw materials into finished goods and services. The technologies that employees use range from the simple to the highly complex. A simple technology involves decision-making rules to help employees do routine jobs. For example, IRS clerks who enter tax information into computers perform routine tasks and work under such rules, requiring few (if any) independent decisions. A complex technology is one that requires employees to make numerous decisions, sometimes with limited information to guide them. A doctor treating an AIDS patient must answer many questions and make many decisions without having much guidance because the technology for treating the disease hasn't yet been perfected.

ASSESSING THE CONTINGENCY VIEWPOINT

The contingency viewpoint of management is useful because of its diagnostic approach, which clearly departs from the one-best-way approach of the traditionalists. The contingency viewpoint encourages managers to analyze and understand situational differences and to choose the solution best suited to the organization, the process, and the people involved in each situation.

Critics argue that the contingency viewpoint really is nothing new. They say that it is merely a meshing of techniques from the other viewpoints of management. The contingency viewpoint does draw heavily from the other approaches. However, it is more flexible than the others, allowing managers to apply the principles and tools from those approaches selectively and where most appropriate. It holds that a manager can use principles from the traditional, behavioral, and systems viewpoints only after properly diagnosing the realities of the situation. Such a diagnosis looks at the nature of a situation and the means by which the manager can influence it.

QUALITY VIEWPOINT

5.

EXPLAIN THE IMPACT OF THE NEED FOR QUALITY ON MANAGEMENT PRACTICES.

Today's organizations are dynamic and, whether large or small, local or global, face formidable new management challenges. Organizations feel pressure from customers and competitors to deliver high-quality products and/or services on time, reward ethical behavior of employees, and develop plans to manage highly diverse workforces effectively. Customer demand for high-quality products and services may be the dominant theme for the foreseeable future. *Quality* is defined as how well a product or service does what it is supposed to do—how closely and reliably it satisfies the specifications to which it is built or provided. Managers in successful organizations are quality conscious and understand the link between high-quality goods and/or services and competitive advantage.

Recall from Chapter 1 that for an organization to be successful it must satisfy customer wants and needs. As Monte Chamberlin at Thomson learned, achieving customer satisfaction through the provision of high-quality goods and services was essential. Thus the focus is the customer, who ultimately defines quality in the marketplace.[24]

Total quality management (TQM) is the continuous process of ensuring that every aspect of production builds quality into the product. Quality must be stressed repeatedly so that it becomes second nature to everyone in an organization and its suppliers. Moreover, training, strategic planning, product design, management information systems, marketing, and other key activities all play a role in meeting quality goals. For example, Toyota requires all employees to undergo hours of training to learn how to use statistical and other measurement tools to ensure quality in its products.

The godfather of the quality movement was W. Edwards Deming (1900–1993).[25] Initially, U.S. managers rejected his ideas, and not until his ideas had helped rebuild Japan's industrial might after World War II were his ideas accepted in the United States. He taught eager Japanese managers how to use statistics to assess and improve quality. In 1951, Japan established the Deming Prize for corporate quality in his honor. Highly esteemed in Japan, this annual prize recognizes the company that has attained the highest level of quality that year.

In 1979, William Conway, president of Nashua Corporation, an office and computer products manufacturer, faced intense competitive pressure from the Japanese. On trips to Japan, he heard competitors praise Deming as a quality guru, and, upon his return, Conway hired Deming. Deming stressed the need for all employees to use statistics to improve quality and productivity, build trust, and work closely with customers. Deming believed that poor quality is 85 percent a management problem and 15 percent a worker problem. After implementing Deming's methods, Nashua's product quality and profits rose markedly.

THE QUALITY CONTROL PROCESS

The quality control process generally focuses on measuring inputs (including customer expectations and requirements), transformation operations, and outputs. The results of these measurements enable managers and employees to make decisions about product or service quality at each stage of the transformation process.

Inputs. Quality control generally begins with inputs, especially the raw materials and parts used in a transformation process. For services, the inputs are based on the information the client provides. Recall that Toyota emphasizes quality control by its suppliers. For almost all parts, Toyota uses only one or two suppliers, which is consistent with one of Deming's prescriptions. On its own, Toyota produces just 30 percent of the parts that go into its cars, compared with about 60 percent at General Motors. Jeffery Dyer, a faculty member at the Wharton School, has studied Toyota's suppliers. He found that Toyota realizes that its cars are only as good as the weakest link in its supply chain. As a result, it developed a set of practices for working with suppliers so that both Toyota and the suppliers learn faster.

WEB INSIGHT

Arvin Industries is 80 years old and has had 3 successive years of increased profits. How does this company stay abreast of current markets and grow to meet changing automotive markets? To learn more about Arvin Industries, visit its Web site at *http://www.Arvin.com*

Arvin Industries is an Indiana-based company that supplies exhaust systems and suspension pieces to Toyota and other automakers. To prepare Arvin to be a supplier, two Toyota engineers spent 7 months in its Indiana plant. They helped improve processes, materials management, and quality in preparation for a Toyota contract—even though the plant was then making parts for a competitor.

One of the best indicators of customer loyalty is the purchase of services. In many businesses, these services are also the sources of greatest profitability. At Lexus, the company has developed a computer system that estimates how much service work the cars that a dealer has sold ought to generate. The computer compares dealers' service billing to its estimates; it also notes which customers have not returned for the first two checkups (1,000 and 5,000 miles) which are free. The computer then generates letters to the customers requesting that they bring their cars in for free service to maintain the cars' warranty.

Transformation Operations. Quality control inspections are made during and between successive transformation stages. Work-in-progress (WIP) inspection can result in the reworking or rejecting of an item before the next operation is performed on it.

The use of statistical process control is one of Deming's key prescriptions. ***Statistical process control*** is the use of quantitative methods and procedures to determine whether transformation operations are being done correctly, to detect any deviations, and, if there are any, to find and eliminate their causes.[26] Statistical process control methods have been available for decades but only in the past 20 years have they been used to any significant extent. They serve primarily as preventive controls.

Sigma is a unit of statistical measurement, which in this context is used to illustrate the quality of a process. The sigma measurement scale (ranging from two to six) describes defects in parts per million. To simplify the concept, let's consider the application of six sigma to writing a text. If defects were measured in misspellings, four sigma would be equivalent to one misspelling per 30 pages of text; five sigma, one misspelling in a set of encyclopedias; and six sigma, only one misspelling in an entire small library, such as a high school library.

Toyota and GE, for example, have adopted the quality goal of ***six sigma,*** which means eliminating defects to the level of 1 per 3.4 million opportunities—or a process that is 99.99966 percent defect free. Five sigma is 233 defects per million, and four sigma is 6,210 defects per million. Most firms operate at the four-sigma level. A key theme in six-sigma programs is the reduction of waste. Toyota trains all employees to seek opportunities to reduce waste in seven areas—called *Toyota's Seven Wastes.* They include

- waste of overproduction (also irregular production such as end-of-month or end-of-quarter surges),
- waste of time on hand (waiting),
- waste in transportation,
- waste of processing itself,
- waste of stock on hand (inventory),
- waste of movement, and
- waste of making defective products.

Outputs. The most traditional and familiar form of quality control is the assessment made after completion of a component or an entire product, or provision of a service. With goods, quality control tests may be made just before the items are shipped to customers. The number of items returned by customers because of shoddy workmanship or other problems is one indicator of the effectiveness of the quality control process. Service providers, such as barbers and hairdressers, usually involve their customers in checking the quality of outputs by asking if everything is okay. However, the satisfactory provision of a service often is more difficult to assess than the satisfactory quality of goods.[27]

Determining the amount or degree of the nine dimensions of quality shown in Table 2.2 is fundamental to quality control. The more accurate the measurement, the easier comparing actual to desired results becomes. Quality dimensions generally are measured by variable or by attribute. ***Measuring by variable*** assesses product characteristics for which there are quantifiable standards (length, diameter, height, weight, or temperature). Consider the quality control process and technology used on the Mercedes-Benz M-class sport utility vehicle at the Mercedes factory in Vance, Alabama.[28] Carmakers have traditionally tracked their body-building accuracy by taking sample vehicles off the assembly line and physically checking a large number of their dimensions with special equipment. Mercedes still does so, running about every 100th body through a measuring machine that checks 1,062 dimensions with sensitive touch probes in a process that takes about 4 hours.

To spot flaws that can develop between those elaborate inspections on every 100th body, Mercedes uses a new vision system. At the end of the body-building line, a body-in-white vehicle—factory language for an unpainted body minus doors, hood, and lift-gate—arrives at the vision station. In a process that takes just 45 seconds, 38 laser cameras mounted on a superstructure check 84 key measurements. Slight dimensional flaws can be identified and corrected before any out-of-tolerance bodies get built. "Before laser gauging, carmakers couldn't do 100 percent inspection. Now we do it," stated Mike Hill, leader of the measurement team.

T a b l e 2 . 2	**The Meaning of Quality**		
		Examples	
Quality Dimension	**Definition**	**Toyota Camry**	**VISA Card**
Performance	Primary good or service characteristics	Miles per galllon, acceleration	Number of merchants who accept the card
Features	Added touches, secondary characteristics	Level of road noise	Credit provisions, interest rates
Conformance	Fulfillment of specifications, documentation, or industry standards	Workmanship, emissions level	Accuracy of monthly account statements
Reliability	Consistency of performance over time	Mean miles to failure of parts	Processing of lost card reports
Durability	Useful life	Miles of useful life (with repair)	Timeliness of automatic card renewals
Serviceability	Resolution of problems and complaints	Ease of repair	Resolution of errors
Responsiveness	Person-to-person contact, including timeliness, courtesy, and professionalism	Courtesy of auto dealer, repairs completed as scheduled	Courtesy of account agents in resolving problems
Aesthetics	Sensory effects, such as sound, feel, and look	Styling, interior finish	Enclosures with monthly statements
Reputation	Past performance and industry/customer regard	*Consumer Reports* ranking, owners' reviews	Advice of friends, *Kiplinger Magazine* ranking

Measuring by attribute evaluates product or service characteristics as acceptable or unacceptable. Measuring by attribute usually is easier than measuring by variable. When Tom Stemberg founded Staples, the office supply superstore, he decided to track customer purchases as a measure of customer loyalty. His solution was to create a membership card good for discounts and special promotions. The company encouraged all its customers to sign up and then entered their membership numbers at the cash register every time they made a purchase. If a customer forgot to bring the card, the cashier could access the account number simply by entering the customer's phone number. The membership application captured basic demographic information; cash-register data gave precise information about preferences, quantities, and frequency of purchase. Together the applications and purchase histories told Staples management which customers and customer segments accounted for most of each store's volume. Staples doesn't need mass mailings to entire geographic markets. Instead, it targets its coupons, mailings, and special promotions to specific customers who have purchased certain products.

THE IMPORTANCE OF QUALITY

Producing high-quality products or services isn't an end in itself. Successfully offering high quality to customers typically results in three important benefits for the organization, as shown in Figure 2.6.[29]

Figure 2.6   **Importance of Quality**

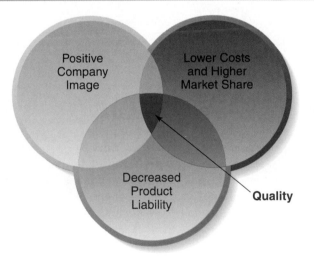

Positive Company Image. A reputation for high-quality products creates a positive image for Maytag, P&G, AT&T, Southwest Airlines, Lexus, and FedEx, among others. A positive image eases recruiting of new employees, increasing sales, and obtaining funds from various lending agencies. For example, Southwest Airlines receives 1,000 applications for each new job it advertises.

Lower Costs and Higher Market Share. In manufacturing plants, higher quality increases productivity and lowers rework time, scrap costs, and warranty costs, leading to increased profits. Improved performance features and product reliability at Toyota enabled the Camry to become the number one selling car in its class in the United States. Many of you have heard Ford's slogan, "Quality Is Job 1," or have seen the advertisement, "The Lonely Maytag Repairman." When Ford refused to introduce its new version of the Thunderbird because it hadn't yet solved some quality problems, it suffered a short-term lag in sales. Ford overcame that lag by increasing its market share after eliminating those problems. In service settings such as State Farm Insurance, Nationwide Insurance, and medical centers, higher quality service can be used to attract and retain new customers. People are willing to pay for excellent service.

Decreased Liability. Product manufacturers and service providers increasingly face costly legal suits over damages caused by faulty, dangerous, and/or misrepresented products and services. Organizations that design and produce faulty products increasingly are being held liable in state courts for damages resulting from the use of such products. The current volume of litigation and possible massive settlements with some 40 states involving cigarette manufacturers—Philip Morris, American Brands, and Liggett and Myers—is the most dramatic example. Successful TQM efforts typically result in improved products and product performance and lower product liability costs.

Decisions about quality should be an integral part of an organization's strategy—that is, how it competes in the marketplace.[30] A core strategy of quality consistently provides the best possible products in their price ranges in the marketplace. Quality therefore must be a basic component of the structure and culture of the organization. Quality isn't simply a program that can be imposed on employees by top management; it is a way of operating that permeates an organization and the thinking of everyone in it. A sign in the visitors' lounge at Marlow Industries reads: "Quality is a strategy, not a program." The following Strategic Action Competency feature indicates how employees at Marlow Industries have integrated quality into the company's operations.[31]

STRATEGIC ACTION COMPETENCY

Marlow Industries Delivers Quality

Raymond Marlow, CEO, thought back to 1987 when the company made thermoelectric coolers and components without much emphasis on quality. Employees would visually inspect the products and ship them to customers. Customers would return products for rework, which caused overtime to skyrocket and shipping costs to increase. The manufacturing cycle time was 15 days, and the order-to-shipment lead time was 16 weeks.

Today, teams of employees are responsible for their operations and satisfying their customers. Employees, not management, control the way products are made and how they are assembled. They created their own statistical control process control flow charts to track quality levels and designed new machinery to increase efficiency. Employees have the authority to fix routine problems (those costing less than $300) without asking for a manager's approval. Employees take the time to do the job right the first time, and management isn't pushing them to ship products just to meet its production goals.

Employees also revamped Marlow's customer relations. Instead of having marketing representatives take calls randomly, customer services are broken down by market segment. Each marketing rep has the authority to resolve problems (over the phone) that will cost as much as $20,000 to fix. Customers are called in advance to let them know when their orders have been shipped. Customers can talk directly to manufacturing employees if they need an answer to a problem.

All these changes have lowered its manufacturing costs by 37 percent, dropped its scheduled overtime costs to almost zero, reduced its order-to-shipment time to 10 weeks, and cut its waste disposal costs by 57 percent.

• • •

To learn more about Marlow, visit the company's home page at

http://www.marlow.com

INTEGRATION OF MANAGEMENT VIEWPOINTS AND COMPETENCIES

In Chapter 1, we identified six management competencies that are essential to your future success as a manager. Each of the five managerial viewpoints stresses at least one of these competencies more than others. Table 2.3 shows the relationships between the management viewpoints and the competencies.

Table 2.3 **Integration of Management Viewpoints and Competencies**

Managerial Competency	Management Viewpoint				
	Traditional	Behavioral	Systems	Contingency	Quality
Communication		X	X	X	X
Planning and administration	X			X	
Strategic action			X		X
Self-management					X
Global awareness			X		X
Teamwork		X		X	X

X = relatively high importance

The traditional viewpoint sought to identify management competencies that efficiently organized the work of employees. Each level of management was assigned specific goals and tasks to accomplish in an allotted time period. The structure of the organization governed relations between manager and employee. It was the manager's job to plan, organize, and lay out the task for the employee; it was the employee's job to follow the manager's instructions. Employees were thought of as "rational" people who were motivated primarily by money.

The behavioral viewpoint focused on developing two competencies: communication and teamwork. It was the manager's job to acknowledge the social and emotional needs of employees and to develop harmonious relationships in the workplace. This viewpoint stressed that employees' behaviors are greatly affected by their interactions with peers. If managers communicated with employees and satisfied their workplace needs, the organization would be effective.

The systems viewpoint stressed that managers should focus on how various inputs, transformation processes, and outputs are related to the organization's goals. The organization was viewed as a "whole," rather than simply the sum of its various departments or divisions. This wholeness requires managers to develop their communication, strategic thinking and action, and global awareness competencies. To develop these competencies, managers use quantitative models to help them understand complex organizational relationships and make appropriate decisions.

The contingency viewpoint draws from each of the other viewpoints and involves a somewhat different set of competencies. Deciding whether to draw on one set of skills in a competency or on several skills across competencies is the job of the manager. How an organization is designed depends on its external environment, the skills of its employees, and the technology used to transform raw materials into finished products. The use of teams, for example, tests the manager's communication and teamwork competencies.

The quality viewpoint stresses meeting customers' expectations in terms of the value (performance and quality) of goods and services. Top management is responsible for putting systems into place to achieve quality. One way for top management to gain the support of employees in such an effort is to design TQM practices that reward employees for meeting quality goals. The TQM philosophy requires a high level of coordination throughout the organization. One way to achieve that coordination is through teamwork. In quality conscious organizations, teamwork means sharing both responsibility and decision making. Managers delegate decision-making authority to employees, permitting them to manage themselves—but only after they have received the necessary training. Deming's philosophy of statistical quality control not only provides a method for analyzing deviations from standards, but it also provides a way to increase communication among employees.

In this chapter we introduced several influential viewpoints and approaches that have shaped managerial thinking during the past 100 years. Ideas from bureaucratic, scientific, and administrative management greatly influenced early managerial practices. Later, new ideas of managing stressed the human or behavioral aspects of managing. During World War II, industry and the armed forces developed sophisticated management systems to coordinate war efforts. Then, as organizations grew and became global, none of the earlier management concepts seemed to apply totally to various situations. The contingency approach stressed that these concepts could be applied under some conditions but not under others. Today's managers are concerned primarily with the quality viewpoint of management as a way to meet consumer demand throughout the world for quality products and services.

1. **DESCRIBE THE THREE BRANCHES OF THE TRADITIONAL VIEWPOINT OF MANAGEMENT: BUREAUCRATIC, SCIENTIFIC, AND ADMINISTRATIVE.**

Max Weber developed a theory of bureaucratic management, which emphasizes the need for a strict hierarchy governed by clearly defined regulations and lines of authority. His theory contains seven principles: a formal system of rules, impersonal management, division of labor, a hierarchical structure, a detailed authority structure, lifelong career commitment, and rationality. Scientific management theorists tried to find ways to make workers more productive. Frederick Taylor thought that management's job was to make individual workers more efficient. That was to be accomplished by improving worker-machine relationships, based on time-and-motion studies. Frank and Lillian Gilbreth also studied how to make workers more efficient. Frank Gilbreth focused on the various physical motions workers used, and Lillian Gilbreth emphasized the welfare of workers. Henry Gantt thought that workers' performance could be charted and thus improved by setting deadlines. Administrative management theorists focused on principles that managers, rather than workers, could use to become more effective. Henry Fayol outlined four functions—planning, organizing, leading, and controlling—that he believed all successful managers use in their work.

2. **EXPLAIN THE BEHAVIORAL VIEWPOINT'S CONTRIBUTION TO MANAGEMENT.**

The behavioral viewpoint emphasizes employees' human and social needs. One of its first proponents, Mary Parker Follett, believed that management should coordinate the efforts of all employees to achieve organizational goals. Chester Barnard's contribution was similar to Follett's. He held, in part, that a manager doesn't have the authority to tell a worker what to do unless the worker accepts that authority. Studies conducted at the Hawthorne plant of the Western Electric Company led to the conclusion that social and human factors can be more important than physical and financial factors in influencing productivity.

3. **DESCRIBE HOW MANAGERS CAN USE SYSTEMS AND QUANTITATIVE TECHNIQUES TO IMPROVE EMPLOYEE PERFORMANCE.**

The systems viewpoint looks at organizations as a series of inputs, transformation processes, and outputs. A system may either be open or closed. Systems analysis advocates that managers use quantitative techniques to solve problems.

4. **STATE THE TWO MAJOR COMPONENTS OF THE CONTINGENCY VIEWPOINT.**

The contingency viewpoint, or situational approach, encourages managers to use the concepts and methods of the traditional, behavioral, and systems viewpoints, depending on the circumstances they face at the time. The three key contingency variables that managers should consider before making a decision are the environment, technology, and people involved.

5. **EXPLAIN THE IMPACT OF THE NEED FOR QUALITY ON MANAGEMENT PRACTICES.**

The quality viewpoint stresses the provision of high-quality products and services at all times. One of the founders of the quality movement was W. Edwards Deming. Long after he had helped Japanese managers make statistical analyses the basis for quality control improvements, his contributions were recognized by U.S. managers. His recommendations included planning for quality, striving for zero defects, using only a few suppliers who have demonstrated that they can deliver quality, and inspecting for quality during the process and not after.

KEY TERMS

Acceptance theory of authority, p. 55
Administrative management, p. 51
Behavioral viewpoint, p. 53
Bureaucratic management, p. 45
Charismatic authority, p. 46
Closed system, p. 58
Contingency viewpoint, p. 60

Division of labor, p. 45
Feedback, p. 58
Functional foremanship, p. 50
Gantt chart, p. 51
Hawthorne effect, p. 55
Hierarchical structure, p. 45
Impersonality, p. 45

Inputs, p. 58
Lifelong career commitment, p. 46
Measuring by attribute, p. 65
Measuring by variable, p. 64
Open system, p. 58
Outputs, p. 58
Quality, p. 62

Rationality, p. 47
Rational–legal authority, p. 46
Rules, p. 45
Scientific management, p. 49
Sigma, p. 63

Six sigma, p. 63
Statistical process control, p. 63
System, p. 57
Systems viewpoint, p. 57
Technology, p. 61

Time-and-motion study, p. 50
Total quality management, p. 62
Traditional authority, p. 45
Traditional viewpoint, p. 44
Transformation processes, p. 58

QUESTIONS FOR DISCUSSION AND COMPETENCY DEVELOPMENT

1. Why should you know about the evolution of management?

2. Visit the *http://www.fedex.com* Web site. What principles of bureaucracy are shown there?

3. What concepts from Mary Parker Follett did Ron Ferner use at Campbell Soup?

4. StrideRite has been named by the editors of *Fortune* magazine as one of the best U.S. companies for which to work. Visit its Web site at *http://www.striderite.com* to discover the principles of management It uses to motivate employees.

5. What challenges face employees who are trying to implement aspects of the behavioral viewpoint in an organization?

6. Using systems concepts, describe the registration process used at your university to enroll students.

7. Visit the *http://www.homedepot.com* Web site. What attributes of quality are illustrated there?

8. **Competency Development: Self-Management.** Merck is a $32.7 billion dollar pharmaceutical company. Visit its home page at *http://www.merck.com* to identify the managerial viewpoints practiced by the company. What managerial competencies would you need to develop if you wanted to work for Merck?

9. **Competency Development: Global Awareness.** How has Burger King been able to maintain its tremendous growth overseas? Visit its home page at *http://www.burgerking.com* to learn how it has used principles of scientific management in its operations around the world.

CASE FOR COMPETENCY DEVELOPMENT

Starbucks

Howard Schultz, chief global strategist of Starbucks, says that his greatest challenge is to attract and manage a worldwide workforce. He believes that Starbucks must provide a motivational system that will cut costs while maintaining high quality. Since going public in 1992, the company's stock has risen by more than 800 percent; its retail sales exceeded $2 billion in 2000; and its profits topped $100 million. Starbucks products can be found in restaurants, hotels, offices, airlines, and in more than 2,600 stores throughout the world.

The Starbucks Support Center is located at Starbucks Coffee Company's headquarters in Seattle. There's energy here—not induced by a caffeine rush—but from associates being involved in a robust blend of teamwork, sense of mission, and challenge. As one of *Fortune* magazine's "100 Best Companies to Work for in America," not to mention one of the world's fastest growing purveyors of indulgence, Starbucks has been giving its employees a daily lift since 1971.

Woven into the company's mission statement is the goal: "Provide a great work environment and treat each other with respect and dignity." It takes more than company declarations to motivate and inspire people. So how does a young, developing company on an aggressive growth track motivate more than 27,000 people and inspire balance and a team spirit?

Starbucks recently agreed to launch a line of Fair Trade–Certified beans. Politically correct coffee is grown on small farm cooperatives rather than large plantations. It sells for $1.26/lb, which goes directly to the farmers rather than to middlemen, who often pay growers less than $0.50/lb. The higher price paid directly to the farmers, who hand-pluck their beans and carry them down the mountain in 100-lb sacks, means that the farmers can afford to send their children to school.

Second is what Starbucks refers to as "a special blend of employee benefits" and a work/life program that focuses on the physical, mental, emotional, and creative aspects of each person. Starbucks developed an innovative work/life program to foster a committed organizational culture—and a long-term partnership. In fact employees at Starbucks are called partners.

Joan Moffat, the Starbucks manager of partner relations and work/life, is responsible for the company's work/life program. It includes on-site fitness services, referral and educational support for child care and elder care, an info line for convenient information, and the Partner Connection—a program that links employees with shared interests and hobbies. Starbucks has comparatively low health-care costs, low absenteeism, and one of the highest retention rates in the industry. "Our turnover rate is 60 percent, which is excellent as compared to the restaurant and retail industry," says Moffat. Moreover, employees reap the benefits of the company's ongoing success.

Starbucks is committed to providing an atmosphere that breeds respect and values the contributions that people make each day, regardless of who or at what level they are in the company. All partners who work a minimum 20 hours a week receive full medical and dental coverage, vacation days, and stock options as part of the Starbucks Bean Stock program. Eligible partners can choose health coverage from two managed care plans or a catastrophic plan. They also can select between two dental plans and a vision plan. Because of the young, healthy workforce, Starbucks has low health-benefit costs. According to Annette King, the HR benefits manager, the company's health-care costs are approximately 20 percent lower than the national average.

The company also provides disability and life insurance, a discounted stock purchase plan, and a retirement savings plan with company matching contributions. These benefits provide a powerful incentive for partners, particularly part-timers, to stay with the company, thus reducing Starbucks' recruiting and training costs. "We have historically had low turnover, most of which can be attributed to the culture and a sense of community," says Moffat.

Three years ago, the HR department began examining how it could become more attuned to employees. For instance, some employees who started with the company when they were in college are now buying homes and dealing with the realities of child care and elder care. Starbucks responded by providing flexible work schedules as part of its work/life program. "Our environment lends itself to meeting multiple life demands. By virtue of our strong sales and accelerated growth, flex schedules have not hurt productivity in the least," says Moffat. "Flexibility is particularly inherent in our stores because of our extended hours of operation and the diversity of our workforce—from students to parents—who need to work alternative hours."

Recent studies have shown that 60 percent of U.S. workers have child-care or elder-care responsibilities. Starbucks recognized—as many other companies have—that partners less encumbered by personal stress and obligations are more innovative and productive. Starbucks implemented several programs that specifically address the life stages and personal needs of its workforce. To help deal with the fast-paced and demanding environment at Starbucks, it also provides referral services for partners and eligible dependents enrolled in the medical plan. It connects them with information that helps make extraordinary life issues more manageable. Moffat herself recently put the program to use when she needed elder-care advice for her grandmother. In another case, a partner needed emergency child care for his ill son. Starbuck's Working Solutions program made prompt arrangements for a certified in-home caretaker, no work was missed, and Starbucks covered half of the cost.[32]

Questions

1. What viewpoint of management is practiced at Starbucks? Explain.

2. Visit a Starbucks coffee shop and, using the quality attributes in Table 2.2, rate Starbucks' product and service quality. How do they stack up against these criteria?

3. What systems concepts are illustrated by Starbucks' employees to fill a customer's order?

4. Why has Starbucks grown to become the largest server of coffee in the world?

For more information on Starbucks, visit the firm's home page at *http://www.starbucks.com.*

VIDEO CASE

Sunshine Cleaning, JIAN, and Archway Cookies

The Evolution of Management Thought video presents three broad characterizations of management thought, reflecting behavioral tendencies, contingency factors, and quality control issues. To illustrate these perspectives of management thought, we present thumbnail sketches of three companies.

Sunshine Cleaning Systems is a janitorial, pressure, and window cleaning business in Florida that puts into practice the behavioral theories of management thought. Its management believes that a good employee must first be a happy employee. Therefore the company not only provides the proper supplies and equipment, but it also has a supportive management style—treating employees with respect and paying relatively good wages. Evidence of its success with this approach is the firm's low employee turnover rate, consistently high customer satisfaction, and profitability.

Headquartered in Silicon Valley, California, JIAN is a software company that illustrates the contingency approach to management. The company applies modern management techniques to the art of building businesses. It does so by providing expert knowledge and effective, timesaving tools that work with the familiar Windows and Macintosh word processing and spreadsheet software. The industry in which JIAN competes is both rapidly changing and unstable, with a fundamental driving principle of constant innovation. The penalty for an inability to adapt is certain failure. To compete in this environment, JIAN looks for individuals who are entrepreneurial and internally motivated and who respond well to change.

Utilizing a virtual organization design, JIAN has strategic alliances with Bindco for manufacturing and distribution of its products and Execustaff for all its human resource functions. This outsourcing allows JIAN to remain small and flexible and to maintain its ability to emphasize teamwork and collaboration in its primary business, software development. Its founder, Burke Franklin, avoids micromanagement. Instead, he uses a questioning technique of management that allows employees to address key questions and solve problems on their own without having to be told what to do.

Archway Cookie Company exemplifies the quality perspective of management thought. Archway is currently the third largest cookie manufacturer in the United States and emphasizes product quality. Its cookies are sold fresh, rather than baked and stored in warehouses to be sold later. The company ensures that its employees are well trained through extensive education and gives them the tools they need to bake quality cookies using only the best ingredients. The lifeblood of the business is the company's relationships with its suppliers. Archway has ongoing relationships with its suppliers. It inspects suppliers' plants and reviews their policies to ensure that they meet the quality standards to which Archway and its customers are accustomed. Finally, quality control (QC) employees inspect all in-coming supplies to the plant with both physical and analytical tests in the company's laboratory. Random samples of finished cookies are also taken, tested, and then kept as references for later comparisons should any problems surface.

Questions

1. Explain why the management of JIAN, Inc., selected the contingency viewpoint of management as its approach.

2. Define total quality management (TQM) and describe which of the three companies is most likely to practice TQM and why.

To learn more about JIAN and Archway Cookies, visit the companies' home pages at *http://www.jianusa.com* and *http://www.archwaycookies.com*.

Managing the Environment

CHAPTER 3
ENVIRONMENTAL FORCES

CHAPTER 4
MANAGING GLOBALLY

CHAPTER 5
ENTREPRENEURSHIP

CHAPTER 6
ETHICS AND CORPORATE SOCIAL RESPONSIBILITY

Environmental Forces

LEARNING OBJECTIVES

AFTER STUDYING THIS CHAPTER YOU SHOULD BE ABLE TO:

1. DESCRIBE HOW ECONOMIC AND CULTURAL FACTORS INFLUENCE ORGANIZATIONS.

2. IDENTIFY THE FIVE COMPETITIVE FORCES THAT AFFECT ORGANIZATIONS IN AN INDUSTRY.

3. DESCRIBE THE PRINCIPAL POLITICAL AND LEGAL STRATEGIES USED BY MANAGERS TO COPE WITH CHANGES IN THE ENVIRONMENT.

4. EXPLAIN HOW TECHNOLOGICAL CHANGES INFLUENCE THE STRUCTURE OF INDUSTRIES.

Chapter Outline

PREVIEW: THE PHARMACEUTICAL INDUSTRY

THE ENVIRONMENT

THE GENERAL ENVIRONMENT
THE NEW ECONOMY
ENVIRONMENTAL STEWARDSHIP
DEMOGRAPHICS
CULTURAL FORCES
SELF-MANAGEMENT COMPETENCY: What Are Your Cultural Values?

COMPETITIVE FORCES IN AN INDUSTRY

COMPETITORS
NEW ENTRANTS
SUBSTITUTE GOODS AND SERVICES
CUSTOMERS
SUPPLIERS
STRATEGIC ACTION COMPETENCY: Merck

POLITICAL–LEGAL FORCES

COMMUNICATION COMPETENCY: AARP

TECHNOLOGICAL CHANGES

TECHNOLOGY'S ROLE IN STRATEGY
TECHNOLOGY'S ROLE IN MANUFACTURING
TECHNOLOGY'S ROLE IN DISTRIBUTION
GLOBAL AWARENESS COMPETENCY: Motorola in China

CHAPTER SUMMARY

KEY TERMS

QUESTIONS FOR DISCUSSION AND COMPETENCY DEVELOPMENT

CASE FOR COMPETENCY DEVELOPMENT: THE PERSONAL COMPUTER INDUSTRY

VIDEO CASE: BURTON SNOWBOARDS

THE PHARMACEUTICAL INDUSTRY

The global pharmaceutical industry is undergoing major changes because of three main factors. The first factor relates to fewer new products entering the market, which is pressuring leading drugmakers to combine in record numbers. In 1999, the value of all mergers and acquisitions in the pharmaceutical and biotechnology industries totaled more than $44 billion, up from $32 billion in 1998. In 2000, Warner-Lambert and Pfizer Corporation merged in the United States. This merger made Pfizer Warner-Lambert the second largest pharmaceutical company in the world, with annual sales of more than $28 billion (about 8 percent of the global market). Its annual R&D budget exceeds $4 billion, and it holds significant market share in all key world markets. In Europe, the combination of Germany's Hoeschst AG and France's Rhone-Polulenc, SA, resulted in a new company, Aventis, which is now the world's largest drug manufacturer. These combined companies represent formidable forces in an increasingly competitive global prescription drug market. These mergers are enabling the merged companies to reduce costs through operating efficiencies by eliminating redundant marketing efforts, manufacturing plants, and R&D efforts. By offering more comprehensive lists of drug products, the merged companies can also provide large blocs of customers with "one-stop shopping" and more competitive prices. In addition, the pooling of individual R&D programs, each with specific strengths, can spur the development of new drugs, such as Viagra, needed to support ongoing sales and earnings growth. Lipitor, a popular cholesterol lowering drug, introduced several years ago by Warner-Lambert, has become the world's largest-selling prescription drug. Annual sales are expected to exceed $10 billion by the time its patent expires in 2010. Pfizer's main objective in its bid for Warner-Lambert was to gain control over the distribution of this popular drug.

The second factor, which is influencing the U.S. pharmaceutical industry primarily, focuses on demographics and third-party payers. On the one hand, the elderly segment of the U.S. population is projected to expand greatly, providing a solid customer base on which drugmakers can grow. Expenditures for prescription drugs are expected to grow at 10.8 percent per year from 2001 through 2004. On the other hand, managed care organizations (HMOs) and government officials are exerting increasing pressures to slow price increases. Currently, the president and Congress are discussing changes in the Medicare law to help those enrolled in the program pay for prescription drugs and to provide a large bloc of consumers for which reductions in overall drug costs can be negotiated with drugmakers.

The third factor, also related primarily to U.S. drugmakers, is the rate of expiration of patents on drugs that generate some $50 billion annually in sales. Some drugmakers may succeed in holding off generic drug competitors through various legal maneuvers, but eventually all patent extensions run out. When a patent expires, generic drugmakers are free to manufacture and market copies of a branded drug at a significantly lower cost. Companies with the most at stake include Eli Lilly and Company, which holds a patent on the popular Prozac antidepressant ($2.3 billion in annual sales); Schering-Plough Corporation, which holds a patent on Claritin antihistamine ($1.9 billion in annual sales); and Merck, which holds patents on Vasotec, Prinivil, Mevacor, and Pepcid (a combined $4 billion in annual sales). Another aspect of the problem is increasing competition from small drug manufacturers that use biotechnology to test new drugs. At the same time, U.S. Food and Drug Administration (USDA) approvals for new drugs is down.[1]

For more information on this industry, visit the FDA's home page at

http://www.fda.gov

THE ENVIRONMENT

1.

DESCRIBE HOW ECONOMIC AND CULTURAL FACTORS INFLUENCE ORGANIZATIONS.

We were selective in choosing the environmental forces to address in this chapter. For example, the international arena is certainly a key part of most managers' environments—today more than ever. However, we mention international forces here only briefly because we devote Chapter 4 to this topic. Also, various groups are pressing for new forms and higher levels of ethical behavior by managers and for increased social responsibility by organizations. We allude to these forces here, but cover them in detail in Chapter 6. Generally, throughout this book, we discuss environmental forces and their management whenever they are relevant to the topic being considered.

We begin this chapter by introducing the basic features of the general environment that organizations operate within: economic and political systems, demographics, and cultural forces. We devote most of the chapter to three types of environmental forces that managers must monitor and diagnose because of their direct or indirect impact on organizations: competitive, political–legal, and technological.

THE GENERAL ENVIRONMENT

The **general environment,** sometimes called the *macroenvironment,* includes the external factors that usually affect all or most organizations.[2] More specifically, as depicted in Figure 3.1, the general environment includes the type of economic system (capitalism, socialism, or communism) and economic conditions (expansionary and recessionary cycles and the general standard of living); type of political system (democracy, dictatorship, or monarchy); condition of the ecosystem (extent of land, water, and air pollution); demographics (age, gender, race, ethnic origin, and education level of the population); and cultural background (values, beliefs, language, and religious influences). All these aspects of the general environment have fundamental implications for managing organizations.

Figure   3 . 1   **The General Environment and Environmental Forces Affecting Organizations**

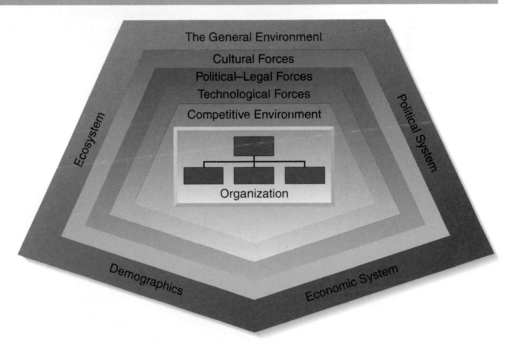

As indicated in the pharmaceutical industry, changes in the general environment are affecting the companies in that industry. For example, to fight off introduction of more generic drugs, pharmaceutical companies holding patents on drugs heavily lobby Congress to introduce bills granting patent extensions on their key (most profitable) products. These companies often argue that they need to recoup the heavy R&D costs incurred to bring products to market. Citizens and powerful lobbying groups, such as the American Association of Retired Persons (AARP), also petition Congress to deny patent extensions, which would increase the availability of generic drugs and to impose restrictions aimed at lowering the costs of drugs. Although the United States remains the world's largest single-country market, people in Latin America, the Far East, and Eastern Europe have increased their use of prescription drugs largely because of government price controls or subsidies and a rising emphasis on self-mediation as the most cost-effective type of care. Finally, pharmaceutical companies are subject to lawsuits alleging adverse side effects from medications. A. H. Robbins, a once-large pharmaceutical company, was driven into bankruptcy several years ago by huge liability judgments stemming from intrauterine contraceptive devices that were later deemed unsafe.

THE NEW ECONOMY

Economics is the discipline that focuses on understanding how people or nations produce, distribute, and consume various goods and services.[3] Important economic issues are the wages paid to labor, inflation, the taxes paid by labor and organizations, the cost of materials used in the production process, and the prices at which goods and services are sold. Free-market competition, private contracts, profit incentives, technological advancement, and organized labor with collective bargaining rights are essential elements of the U.S. economic system and those of a number of other countries. The government (part of the political system) acts as a watchdog over business, providing direction in antitrust, monetary policy, human rights, defense, and environmental matters. Particularly challenging economic and political conditions include the fluctuation of inflation, unemployment, taxes, and interest rates and the environmental and safety regulations covering both the workplace and goods produced. Government ownership of enterprises is the exception, rather than the norm. The economy is not centrally planned, as in North Korea, Cuba, and the People's Republic of China.

Several trends are currently affecting the U.S. and Canadian economies. We briefly review four of these trends, which are shown in Table 3.1.[4]

Table 3.1	**Trends in the New Versus the Old Economy**

New	Old
• Value matters 　　information is key	• Size of organization matters 　　manufacturing is key
• New markets 　　distance vanished	• Defined market segments 　　demographics
• Customers buy activities, not products 　　a click away	• Customers for a lifetime 　　loyalty, repeat business
• Human capital 　　rise of knowledge worker	• Physical and capital assets 　　tangible assets

There is a major emphasis on value. The economies of the past—in the Agrarian Age or the Industrial Age—were characterized by the mass of their outputs, whether crops or steel. Value has shifted from the tangible to the intangible, from steel mills to know-how. Today, manufacturers use more software and less unskilled labor. They are more automated, networked, and integrated than ever before. Thus many manufacturers can reduce their heavy machinery ownership and concentrate on the software that manages production as an important source of value added. Knowledge is embedded in people. Therefore managers are increasingly thinking in terms of the value they are creating by increasing their knowledge. With the economy becoming less about goods and more about the transfer of information and delivery of service, companies in the new economy will focus on ideas and speed. For example, Wal-Mart provides Procter & Gamble (P&G) with daily information on what is selling in which stores. P&G, in return, restocks Wal-Mart's shelves as needed. Wal-Mart achieves greater sales because P&G products are not out of stock when a customer arrives and saves money because P&G carries the inventory. P&G increases its cash flow because it sends supplies only to those stores that need a product, avoiding unnecessary distribution costs.[5]

New Markets. The limitations of geographic borders apply less and less. Firms can increasingly reach customers directly without regard to their or the customers' physical location. In an economy where most everyone is connected, the shortest distance between a customer and the company is one mouse click. The Internet is revolutionary because is has dramatically reduced the cost of communication and coordination in business and personal transactions. Firms such as Travelocity (travel), InsWeb (insurance), Wells Fargo (banking), Charles Schwab (investments), and Amazon.com (book sales) are reaching out directly to customers and in the process are challenging distributors, traditional retailers, and geographic borders. Customers can easily search, evaluate, negotiate, pay for, and take delivery of products at different times and from different providers.

New companies have been formed to provide information and advice to customers so that they can make better decisions. For example, http://www.theknot.com provides advice on wedding planning, including invitations, gift registries, honeymoons, and wedding-related travel. From http://www.garden.com customers can obtain gardening information, garden designs, gardening tips, and the like. More than 70 percent of new car buyers consult with Edmund's or CarPoint on the Internet before purchasing a new car. Edmund's uses Autobytel for dealer searches and negotiations, GEICO for insurance, and Warranty Gold for extended warranties. Customers accessing this Web site can gather and evaluate information, negotiate price and terms, and finance, purchase, and insure a car—all from this single source.[6]

The Key: Customer Convenience. Organizations in the new economy will succeed by creating convenience for its customers. For example, http://www.ebay.com, which calls itself "the world's personal trading community," has sold more than 35 million items. With nearly 1 million items on sale at any time, the company's Web site receives more than 600 million hits per month. What distinguishes eBay from your local flea market is not its sheer scale but the focus on convenience. The system is designed to allow buyers and sellers to search numerous categories and participate in auctions with as little friction as possible. Online tutorials lead customers through a simple four-step process: register, find stuff, bid, and sell. Because eBay does not certify the sellers or the quality of their products, it operates on the principle of caveat emptor—let the buyer beware. By bringing buyers and sellers together, it has created a huge market for resold goods, dramatically cutting the time needed for millions of buyers and sellers to find each other and transact business.

Amazon.com brings readers and publishers together. Ameritrade and E*Trade connect investors and sellers to speed various financial asset transactions. By adding convenience, companies engaged in electronic commerce make their money. They can also expect customers to begin demanding value, including cash payments (digital microcash), for information that they provide as part of electronic transactions. The information that customers give about themselves can, with their permission, be sold to other companies, which customers are learning is another profitable e-business source of income.[7]

Interenterprise Human Capital. In the old economy, the most important assets—capital, plant, and labor—were owned by the organization. To succeed in the new economy, organizations must manage knowledge, not just data or information. That is, knowledge is now an important asset too. ***Knowledge management*** is the creation, protection, development, and sharing of knowledge assets. In the new economy, human capital will have greater power because it is people who create and share knowledge. According to Andy Grove, founder and CEO of Intel, "Our assets leave on the elevator every night." Knowledge workers in many organizations have positioned themselves to be independent entrepreneurs. Grove says that organizations can't own human assets; they can only rent them. Organizations will be forced to develop new ways to compensate employees because knowledge workers increasingly want to share in the wealth they create. Some 88 million N-Geners—the Net Generation (people between the ages of 2 and 22)—will enter the workforces in Canada and the United States between 2000 and 2020. The N-Geners thrive on collaboration and many find the notion of a "boss" somewhat bizarre.[8]

ENVIRONMENTAL STEWARDSHIP

Environmental stewardship is a position that an organization takes to protect or enhance the natural environment as it conducts its business activities.[9] Monsanto is investing billions of dollars to transform itself into a biotech powerhouse capable of helping feed the planet's growing population while, at the same time, being environmentally friendly. An estimated 25 billion tons of the world's topsoil are lost each year, irrigation is increasing the salinity of soil, and arable land is disappearing to development. Air is dirty, water is polluted, and animal species are disappearing. Scientists worry that the planet won't survive the expected doubling of its 5.8 billion population over the next 30 years without instituting strong measures to save it now.[10]

Environmental stewardship at Monsanto requires managers to improve three managerial competencies. First, they need to extend their global awareness competency by creating products for world markets. The company's scientists increasingly will have to focus on state-of-the-art products that have practical value around the world and that are within the economic reach of hundreds of millions of Third World people. Second, Monsanto's managers are allocating resources to stay abreast of rapidly changing technology and push the scientific envelope ever farther. In agriculture, for example, the company's scientists are developing products such as disease-resistant cotton and potatoes. Management is winning government approval of selling genetically engineered seeds in various countries, albeit against some rather vocal opposition in some of them. Finally, Monsanto's management is further developing its strategy to compete against other organizations worldwide.

Monsanto must address the concerns of environmental groups such as Greenpeace, the Sierra Club, and the Union of Concerned Scientists. These groups question whether designer crops can do much to clean up pollution. They also keep a close watch on the manufacture and use of herbicides and other synthetic products. The Audubon Society has broadened its efforts from protection of wildlife to actively monitoring business practices that affect native plants and animals. It was the first organization to propose legal agreements requiring removal of significant amounts of phosphate from water used to refine sugar. The National Resources Defense Council has abandoned some of its earlier views—considered by some to be "fanatic and utopian"—and has displayed a greater understanding of the trade-offs involved in both economic and environmental survival. The organization has begun to move from confrontation to collaboration as a strategy. Nonetheless, some environmental organizations, such as Wise Use, continue to press legislators to adopt stricter laws and regulatory boards that enforce land use and waste disposal regulations to tighten their procedures.

This renewed interest in serving the environment poses numerous challenges to business. With the passage of the U.S. Clean Air Act of 1990 and NAFTA, organizations faced more than a choice—they faced increasingly tough requirements. However, for several years some organizations, such as Shell Oil Company, have supported increased environmental planning and action in response to the radical change in public attitudes. Managers at many organizations are making environmental considerations part of their strategic action competency. They must now think long term, even though profits may suffer in the short term. The following are a few of the actions that organizations should take in heeding the call of renewed environmentalism.[11]

Avoid Confrontation with State and Federal Pollution Control Agencies.

W. R. Grace failed to avoid confrontation over antipollution requirements and currently is involved in expensive restitution for asbestos-related problems and time-consuming and costly asbestos disposal. Browning-Ferris, Waste Management, and Louisiana-Pacific have abused local landfill requirements. In the future, when they bid for city, township, and county refuse collection and disposal contracts, their service plans will be examined particularly closely.

Compensate for Environmentally Risky Endeavors. According to the World Bank, two-thirds of the countries that export tropical forest products are running out of trees. In Central America, the forests have been cleared for cattle ranches. Haiti is almost treeless and once lush El Salvador is a semidesert. Temple-Inland, a manufacturer of corrugated containers, operates mills in both North and South America. Because trees must be cut to make paper and many wildlife species can be endangered because of cutting, the company cuts trees selectively. All cut trees are replaced with seedlings; reforestation takes about 15 years. Recently the company planted 30 million seedlings.

Comply Early with Government Regulations. Because compliance costs increase over time, organizations that act early often have lower costs. Early compliance may also increase their market share, profits, and competitive advantage. In 1997, Toyota unveiled its energy-efficient car, the Prius. It has both an internal combustion engine and an electric motor, which turn on and off independently to provide peak efficiency. Because the Prius gets as much as 66 miles per gallon, owners can save money while they're doing their part to save the environment and comply with U.S. government clean air standards.

WEB INSIGHT

What is "hybrid technology for the real world?" Learn more about saving money while keeping the environment safe. Meet the Toyota Prius on the company's Web site at
http://www.toyota.com

Cut Back on Environmentally Unsafe Operations. In the United States people in the Northeast claim that the sulfur dioxide emitted from coal-fired power plants located primarily in the Midwest are responsible for the acid rain that is killing lakes and trees in the Northeast.

Promote New Manufacturing Technologies. In light of the problems with the earth's ozone layer, Electrolux found that profits from its solar-powered lawn mowers, chain saws lubricated with vegetable oil, and water-conserving washing machines were 3.8 percent higher than profits from the company's conventional products. Similarly, Dixon Ticonderoga, maker of Crayons, introduced a crayon made from soybeans. It is an alternative to crayons made from paraffin wax, which is a by-product of oil refining, and gives the crayons a brighter and richer color.

Recycle Wastes. More than 200 billion cans, bottles, plastic cartons, and paper cups are thrown away each year in developed countries. Many towns and cities have set up recycling programs to reduce the amount of waste to be disposed of and land required for disposal sites. Private companies also are involved in recycling efforts. Sonoco Products Company, one of the world's largest packaging companies, takes its used boxes back from customers so that they don't have to worry about disposing of them. Sonoco benefits because the company uses recycled packaging for more than two-thirds of its raw materials. Other firms with active recycling programs are Safety-Kleen (solvents and motor oil), Wellman (plastics), Jefferson Smurfit (paper), and Nucor (steel). Polyfoam Packers, a Styrofoam manufacturer, has initiated a recycling process that reuses Styrofoam beads.

Management Action Plans. Managers can take the following specific actions to respond to environmental concerns.

- Give a senior-level person well-defined environmental responsibilities. This approach makes environmental concerns a strategic issue.

- Measure everything: waste, energy use, travel in personal vehicles, and the like. Set measurable goals and target dates for environmental improvements. Monitor progress.

- Consider reformulating products in order to use less toxic chemicals in the manufacturing process and cleanup. Try to use materials that won't harm the environment when the consumer eventually discards the product.

- Consider business opportunities for recycling or disposing of products, including having customers return them when the products have reached the end of their useful lives.

- Recognize that environmental regulations are here to stay and that they are likely to become more restrictive. Environmental awareness and behavior (*green behavior*) will have a lot to do with a firm's reputation in the future. Plan for that future by recognizing and acting on this reality today.

Environmental concerns have changed the way producers and consumers alike think about products, the raw materials used to make them, and the by-products of manufacturing processes. In fact, industries have developed a whole new generation of successful products in response to the Clean Air Act and reuse and recycling regulations. For example, Louisiana-Pacific makes various wood products, including particleboard, out of milling scraps.

DEMOGRAPHICS

Demographics are the characteristics of a work group, an organization, a specific market, or various populations, such as individuals between the ages of 18 and 22.[12] Demographics—and in particular, changes in demographics—play an important role in marketing, advertising, and human resource management. Let's consider a few of the broad demographic changes that have occurred in the United States recently and that are expected to continue for the foreseeable future.

Increasing Diversity. The U.S. labor force is becoming more diverse. For example, people with disabilities—aided by passage of the Americans with Disabilities Act several years ago—have been finding more and more ways to become productive employees. Many gays and lesbians no longer try to hide their sexual orientation and want to be dealt with as employees who have rights equal to those of straight people. Older employees now have the right to refuse mandatory retirement and can continue to work as long as they are productive. Obese people are beginning to expect and earn some rights to be treated fairly and equally in the workplace.

By the end of this decade, more than 160 million people will be part of the U.S. labor force, an increase of 21 million from 1998. About 85 percent of new employees will be women and people of color. About 23 million baby-boomers will retire, the majority of whom will be white men. As a result, women and minorities will gradually represent a larger share of the labor force. The overall rate of labor force participation will barely creep upward by 2005, from 66.6 percent to 67.1 percent. The number of Hispanic workers is likely to be some 17.4 million by 2006. This growth will result from continued immigration of young adults, high birth rates, and relatively few retirees. The number of black workers will increase by 15 percent by 2005 and the number of Asian workers by 39 percent. All these trends will make the labor force much more diverse than it is today. In the preceding section, we noted that the U.S. economy has shifted from industrial production to services and information analysis. This shift means that jobs of all kinds are more likely to require some type of specialized skill. One result is that people with little education or training will continue to have a hard time finding meaningful and well-paying work and experience long spells of "labor market inactivity." Currently, home health aides, physical therapists, computer engineers and scientists, special-education teachers, child-care workers, and corrections officers—all of whom must have education and training beyond high school—are among the workers in greatest demand.[13]

Managerial Challenges. Managers are likely to face new pressures from an increasingly diverse workforce.[14] They need to recognize this trend and learn how to manage diversity. Some organizations provide training to help employees at all levels be more tolerant of language, age, race, and ethnic differences; to identify and reject racial and gender preferences in hiring and promotion; and to be responsive to the handicapped. Managers no longer can impose an "Anglo male" organizational culture. Table 3.2[15] highlights some of the factors that managers must address when dealing with a multicultural workforce.

T a b l e 3 . 2	*Multicultural Workforce: What Do People Want?*

Able-Bodied People Want

To develop more ease in dealing with physically disabled people.

To give honest feedback and appropriate support without being patronizing or overprotective.

Disabled People Want

To have greater acknowledgment of and focus on abilities, rather than on disabilities.

To be challenged by colleagues and organizations to be the best.

To be included, not isolated.

Gay Men and Lesbians Want

To be recognized as whole human beings, not just sexual beings.

To have equal employment protection.

To have increased awareness among people regarding the impact of heterosexism in the workplace.

Heterosexuals Want

To become more aware of lesbian and gay issues.

To have a better understanding of the legal consequences of being gay in America.

To increase dialogue about heterosexist issues with lesbians and gay men.

Men Want

To have the same freedom to grow that women have.

To be perceived as allies, not the enemy.

To bridge the gap with women at home and at work.

People of Color Want

To be valued as unique individuals, as members of ethnically diverse groups, as people of different races, and as equal contributors.

To establish more open, honest, working relationships with people of other races and ethnic groups.

To have the active support of white people in fighting racism.

White People Want

To have their ethnicity acknowledged.

To reduce discomfort, confusion, and dishonesty in dealing with people of color.

To build better relationships with people of color based on common goals, concerns, and mutual respect for differences.

Women Want

To be recognized as equal contributors.

To have the active support of male colleagues.

To have work and family issues actively addressed by organizations.

Younger and Older Employees Want

To have more respect for their life experiences.

To be taken seriously.

To be challenged by their organizations, not patronized.

These new employees expect something from their careers, a sense of making a contribution. These better-educated employees want their individual and group needs recognized and met. They desire more control over their destiny, a say in decisions that affect them, and more flexibility in the terms and rewards of employment. They want a fair, open, flexible, and responsive work environment where they can enjoy the workplace, as well as be productive. Many expect to experience the excitement and stimulation of meeting challenging opportunities and problems and the security that comes from being appreciated and supported. People will be less willing to sacrifice personal and family life for career success.

CULTURAL FORCES

Underlying a society and surrounding an organization are various cultural forces, which often are not as visible as other general environmental forces. **Culture** is defined as the shared characteristics (e.g., language, religion, and heritage) and values that distinguish the members of one group of people from those of another.[16] A **value** is a basic belief about a condition that has considerable importance and meaning to individuals and is relatively stable over time. A **value system** comprises multiple beliefs that are compatible and supportive of one another. For example, beliefs in private enterprise and individual rights are mutually supportive. Cultural values aren't genetically transferred. People begin to learn their culture's values from the day they are born, and this learning continues throughout their lives.

Managers need to appreciate the significance of values and value systems, both their own and those of others. Values can greatly affect how a manager

- **views other people and groups, thus influencing interpersonal relationships.** In Japan male managers have traditionally believed that women should defer decision-making responsibilities to men. They belonged at home where they were responsible for raising and educating the children. Until recently, similar views prevailed in many U.S. organizations. But this situation has changed. Many more U.S. managers and government policies/laws view men and women as equals who should be recognized, consulted, and promoted because of their abilities and contributions, not their gender.

- **perceives situations and problems.** Many U.S. managers believe that conflict and competition can be managed and used constructively to solve problems. Many Chinese managers believe that conflict between managers and employees should be avoided.

- **goes about solving problems.** In Korea, managers at Samsung believe that team decision making can be effective. In Germany, managers at Hoechst Chemical believe that individuals should make decisions.

- **determines what is and is not ethical behavior.** One manager might believe that ethics means doing only what is absolutely required by law. Another might view ethics as going well beyond minimum legal requirements to do what is morally right.

- **leads and controls employees.** In the United States, many managers believe in sharing information with employees and relying on mutual trust more than rigid controls. In Mexico, most managers emphasize rules, close supervision, and a rigid chain of command.

By diagnosing a culture's values, managers and employees can understand and predict others' expectations and avoid some cultural pitfalls. Otherwise, they risk inadvertently antagonizing fellow employees, customers, or other groups by breaking a sacred taboo (e.g., showing the bottom of a person's shoe to a Saudi) or ignoring a time-honored custom (e.g., preventing an employee from attending an important religious ceremony in Indonesia).

The framework of work-related values has been used in numerous studies of cultural differences among employees. Geert Hofstede, director of the Institute for Research on Intercultural Cooperation, developed this framework for research on intercultural cooperation in the Netherlands while an organizational researcher at IBM.[17] The findings reported here are based on his surveys of thousands of IBM employees in 50 countries. Hofstede's studies uncovered some intriguing differences among countries in terms of five value dimensions: power distance, uncertainty avoidance, individualism (versus collectivism), masculinity (versus femininity), and Confucian dynamism. Before continuing to read this chapter, please take a few minutes and complete the questionnaire in the following Self-Management Competency feature. Think about the culture in which you now live and study.

SELF-MANAGEMENT COMPETENCY

What Are Your Cultural Values?

INSTRUCTIONS

In the following questionnaire, please indicate the extent to which you agree or disagree with each statement. For example, if you **strongly agree** with a particular statement, you would circle the 5 next to that statement.

1 **Strongly disagree**
2 **Disagree**
3 **Neither agree nor disagree**
4 **Agree**
5 **Strongly agree**

	Strongly Disagree				Strongly Agree

QUESTIONS

1. It is important to have job requirements and instructions spelled out in detail so that employees always know what they are expected to do. — 1 2 3 4 5
2. Managers expect employees to follow instructions and procedures closely. — 1 2 3 4 5
3. Rules and regulations are important because they inform employees what the organization expects of them. — 1 2 3 4 5
4. Standard operating procedures are helpful to employees on the job. — 1 2 3 4 5
5. Instructions for operations are important for employees on the job. — 1 2 3 4 5
6. Group welfare is more important than individual rewards. — 1 2 3 4 5
7. Group success is more important than individual success. — 1 2 3 4 5
8. Being accepted by the members of the workgroup is very important. — 1 2 3 4 5
9. Employees should only pursue their goals after considering the welfare of the group. — 1 2 3 4 5

10. Managers should encourage group loyalty even if individual goals suffer. — 1 2 3 4 5
11. Individuals may be expected to give up their goals in order to benefit group success. — 1 2 3 4 5
12. Managers should make most decisions without consulting subordinates. — 1 2 3 4 5
13. Managers must often use authority and power when dealing with subordinates. — 1 2 3 4 5
14. Managers should seldom ask for the opinions of employees. — 1 2 3 4 5
15. Managers should avoid off-the-job social contacts with employees. — 1 2 3 4 5
16. Employees should not disagree with management decisions. — 1 2 3 4 5
17. Managers should not delegate important tasks to employees. — 1 2 3 4 5
18. Managers should help employees with their family problems. — 1 2 3 4 5
19. Management should see to it that workers are adequately clothed and fed. — 1 2 3 4 5
20. Managers should help employees solve their personal problems. — 1 2 3 4 5
21. Management should see that health care is provided to all employees. — 1 2 3 4 5
22. Management should see that children of employees have an adequate education. — 1 2 3 4 5
23. Management should provide legal assistance for employees who get in trouble with the law. — 1 2 3 4 5
24. Management should take care of employees as they would treat their children. — 1 2 3 4 5
25. Meetings are usually run more effectively when they are chaired by a man. — 1 2 3 4 5

		Strongly Disagree				Strongly Agree
26.	It is more important for men to have professional careers than it is for women to have professional careers.	1	2	3	4	5
27.	Men usually solve problems with logical analysis; women usually solve problems with intuition.	1	2	3	4	5
28.	Solving organizational problems usually requires an active, forcible approach typical of men.	1	2	3	4	5
29.	It is preferable to have a man in a high-level position rather than a woman.	1	2	3	4	5

INTERPRETATION

The questionnaire measures each of the five basic culture dimensions. Your score can range from 5 to 35. The numbers in parentheses are the question numbers. Add the scores for these questions to arrive at your total score for each cultural value. The higher your score, the more you demonstrate the cultural value.

Value 1: Uncertainty Avoidance (1, 2, 3, 4, 5). Your score _____. A high score indicates a culture in which people often try to make the future predictable by closely following rules and regulations. Organizations try to avoid uncertainty by creating rules and rituals that give the illusion of stability.

Value 2: Individualism/collectivism (6, 7, 8, 9, 10, 11). Your score _____. A high score indicates collectivism, or a culture in which people believe that group success is more important than individual achievement. Loyalty to the group comes before all else. Employees are loyal and emotionally dependent on their organization.

Value 3: Power Distance (12, 13, 14, 15, 16, 17). Your score _____. A high score indicates a culture in which people believe in the unequal distribution of power among segments of the culture. Employees fear disagreeing with their bosses and are seldom asked for their opinions by their bosses.

Value 4: Confucianism (18, 19, 20, 21, 22, 23, 24). Your score _____. A high score indicates a culture in which people value respect of and obedience to their elders and conducting business with integrity and dignity. Young employees are expected to follow orders given to them by their elders.

Value 5: Masculinity/femininity (25, 26, 27, 28, 29). Your score _____. A high score indicates masculinity, or a culture in which people value the acquisition of money and other material things. Successful managers are viewed as aggressive, tough, and competitive. Earnings, recognition and advancement are important. Quality of life and cooperation are not as highly prized.

Source: Adapted from P. Dorfman. Culture Values Questionnaire. Las Cruces: New Mexico State University, 2000. Used with permission.

The following discussion focuses primarily on Hofstede's ranking of four regions of the world with respect to each dimension. These rankings are based on the dominant value orientation in each country, with a ranking of 1 for the highest and 50 for the lowest position (relative to all 50 countries in the survey) on each value dimension. Figure 3.2[18] shows the rankings for Canada, Japan, Taiwan, and the United States.

Power Distance. The degree to which influence and control are unequally distributed among individuals and institutions within a particular culture is the measure of its ***power distance***. If most people in a society support an unequal distribution, the nation is ranked high. In societies ranked high (e.g., Mexico, France, Malaysia, and the Philippines), membership in a particular class or caste is crucial to an individual's opportunity for advancement. Societies ranked lower play down inequality. Individuals in the United States, Canada, Sweden, and Austria can achieve prestige, wealth, and social status, regardless of family background.

Managers operating in countries ranked low in power distance are expected to be generally supportive of equal rights and equal opportunity. For example, managers in Canada and the United States typically support participative management. In contrast, managers in Mexico, France, and India do not value the U.S. and Canadian style of participative management. Managers in the United States and Canada try not to set themselves too much apart from subordinates by appearing to be superior or unique. In countries with high power distance, however, a more autocratic management style not only is common but also is expected by employees.

Uncertainty Avoidance. The degree to which members of a society attempt to avoid ambiguity, risk, and the indefiniteness of the future is the measure of its ***uncertainty avoidance***. Individuals in cultures ranked low on this dimension generally are

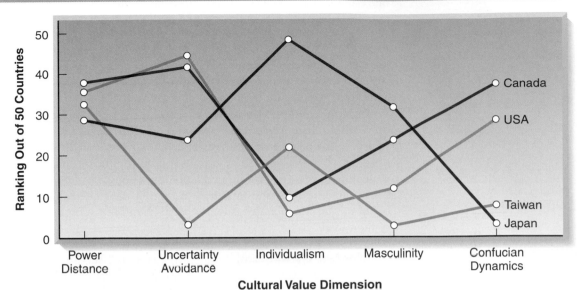

Rank Numbers: 1 = Highest; 50 = Lowest

secure and don't expend a great deal of energy trying to avoid or minimize ambiguous situations. In cultures with high uncertainty avoidance, individuals often try to make the future more predictable by establishing procedures and rules that foster job security. In organizations, high uncertainty avoidance is often associated with built-in career stability (job security), numerous rules governing behavior, intolerance of deviant ideas and behavior, belief in absolute truths, and overreliance on expertise.

In the United States and Canada, employees and managers ranked low on uncertainty avoidance, sharing a relatively high tolerance for uncertainty, compared with workers and managers in Japan and Taiwan. Thus Canadian and U.S. managers are more likely to be receptive to changing rules, open competition, and new ideas than are their counterparts in Japan and Taiwan.

Individualism. A combination of the degree to which society expects people to take care of themselves and their immediate families and the degree to which individuals believe they are masters of their own destinies is its measure of ***individualism***. The opposite of individualism is ***collectivism,*** which refers to a tight social framework in which group (family, clan, organization, and nation) members focus on the common welfare and feel strong loyalty toward one another.

In the United States and Canada, employees ranked high on individualism, a result that agrees with the frequent characterization of these two countries as "I" societies rather than "we" societies. A strong sense of individualism supports and maintains a competitive market-based economic system. High individualism also is consistent with the individual merit and incentive pay systems favored in the United States and Canada. Conversely, group incentives and strong seniority systems are likely to exist in countries with low individualism (high collectivism), such as Taiwan and Japan. Managers and employees in a high-individualism culture move from organization to organization more frequently. They don't believe that their organizations are solely responsible for their welfare, nor do they expect decisions made by groups to be better than decisions made by individuals.

Masculinity. In Hofstede's framework, ***masculinity*** is the degree to which assertiveness and the acquisition of money and material things are valued, as well as the degree of indifference to others' quality of life. The opposite of masculinity is ***femininity***, a more nurturing, people-oriented approach to life. The masculinity dimension also reflects the division of labor among men and women in a society. Canada and the United States probably rank lower today on this dimension than they would have 20 years ago, largely because of the societal changes that have been taking place in role expectations for men and women. In recent years significant social pressures have begun to change stereotyped notions that men should be assertive and women should be nurturing or that gender roles should be clearly differentiated.

In high-masculinity cultures (e.g., Mexico, Japan, Austria, and Italy), women still do not hold many managerial jobs. Men dominate most settings, and an organization's right to influence the private lives of its employees is widely accepted. One researcher observed that Mexico, for example, rigidly defines gender-role expectations: The woman is expected to be supportive of and dependent on men—not to do for herself, but to yield to the wishes of others, caring for their needs before her own. A common belief in Muslim countries is that women should be subordinate to men in all aspects of their lives.

Confucian Dynamism. Confucius was a civil servant in China in about 500 B.C. Known for his wisdom, he developed a pragmatic set of rules for daily life. The following key principles of ***Confucian dynamism*** comprise a pragmatic set of rules for daily life that focus on the treatment of others and personal responsibilities. We illustrate these rules by references to organizational life. First, the stability of society is based on unequal relationships between people. Thus the junior manager owes the senior manager respect and obedience; the senior manager owes the junior manager protection and consideration. Second, the family is the prototype of all social organizations. Thus members of organizations should learn to promote harmony by allowing others to maintain "face," that is, dignity, self-respect, and prestige, particularly in conducting business affairs. Third, people should treat others as they would like to be treated. Thus first-line managers should encourage subordinates to acquire knowledge and skills to enable them to advance, just as these managers would like the middle managers above them to do. Finally, a person's tasks in life consist of acquiring skills and education, working hard, not spending more than necessary, being patient, and preserving the values of the society.

In high-Confucian cultures, such as Japan, Hong Kong, Taiwan, and Korea, management practices such as thrift, gift giving, good manners, and saving face are highly valued. Thrift leads to saving, which provides capital for reinvestment. Welcoming speeches by elder members of the organization and exchanges of small gifts prior to conducting business are important. Seniority is prized and is linked to the size of a person's office, pay, and other perquisites. Such practices emphasize the stability of authority relationships and respect. In the United States, Canada, and the United Kingdom, such management practices are not highly valued or practiced.

Managerial Implications. Understanding culture can make you a better manager even if you never leave your home country. In an increasingly global market, managers in every country must think globally. Even in the United States, most products face tremendous foreign competition. Global competition is a reality, and the number of managers and workers taking assignments in countries other than their own is rapidly increasing.[19] These workers bring aspects of their own cultures into their organizations, neighborhoods, school systems, and homes. Learning how to integrate these workers and their values and ways of doing things into the organization is essential. Although various cultural behaviors may appear similar on the surface, their meanings in different cultures may be quite different. Realizing the importance of these differences helps managers understand their international partners and ultimately to be better managers.

COMPETITIVE FORCES IN AN INDUSTRY

2.

IDENTIFY THE FIVE COMPETITIVE FORCES THAT AFFECT ORGANIZATIONS IN AN INDUSTRY.

Organizations in any industry are directly affected by at least five competitive forces: competitors, new entrants, substitute goods and services, customers, and suppliers.[20] The combined strength of these forces affects long-term profitability, as shown in Figure 3.3. Managers must therefore monitor and diagnose each one, as well as their combined strength, before making decisions about future courses of action. As we noted in discussing the pharmaceutical industry, companies have merged in order to influence character, magnitude, and impact of competitive forces in the industry. In this section, we continue to examine the pharmaceutical industry to illustrate how companies compete.

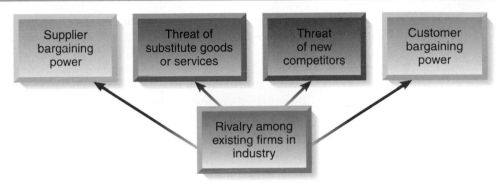

Figure 3.3   Competitive Forces in the Task Environment

COMPETITORS

Aside from customers, competitors are the single most important day-to-day force facing organizations. Bruce D. Henderson, founder and chairman of the Boston Consulting Group, comments: "For virtually all organizations the critical environment constraint is their actions in relation to competitors. Therefore any change in the environment that affects any competitor will have consequences that require some degree of adaptation. This requires continual change and adaptation by all competitors merely to maintain relative position."[21]

WEB INSIGHT

To learn more about international opportunities at Eli Lilly and Company, visit its website at *http://www.lilly.com.* Discover why *Fortune* magazine says it is one of the top 100 companies to work for.

In the Preview Case, we noted that the pharmaceutical industry has become fast-paced and increasingly competitive. Owing to tremendous advances in technology, instead of enjoying a market alone for 3 or 4 years after introduction of a new drug, companies are lucky if the drug is in the market for a few months before a competing medicine is introduced. This situation creates cutthroat product rivalry with leading companies, such as Merck, Abbott Labs, Eli Lilly, and Pfizer Warner-Lambert, attempting to gain market share through massive advertising campaigns. Pharmaceutical companies, which are now allowed by law to advertise their products directly to consumers, spend more than $1 billion per year on advertising. This direct consumer advertising broadens people's understanding of diseases and available treatment and encourages requests for specific branded products.

However, the availability of educational materials on the Internet also has dramatically expanded the public's knowledge of health care and treatment of medical problems. People can now compare the cost of various branded and generic drugs, have their physicians send prescriptions to e-pharmacies, and fill their prescriptions via e-mail.

NEW ENTRANTS

The threat or reality of increased competition in an industry depends on the relative ease with which new firms can compete with established firms. In an industry with low barriers to entry (e.g., the photocopy industry or the fast-food industry) competition will be fierce. The pharmaceutical industry is a particularly interesting case because it has had both high and low barriers to entry during the past 10 years. Economies of scale, product differentiation, capital requirements, and government regulation are four common factors that need to be diagnosed in assessing barriers to entry. Let's see how they have affected the pharmaceutical industry.

Economies of scale are achieved when increased volume lowers the unit cost of a good or service produced by a firm. The potential for economies of scale in the pharmaceutical industry is substantial. The process of bringing a drug to market can take more than a decade and cost more than $500 million. New drugs must achieve enormous sales volumes quickly in order to be profitable.

Product differentiation is uniqueness in quality, price, design, brand image, or customer service that gives one firm's product an edge over another firm's. After 17 years, a prescription drug's patent expires. Generic drugs usually appear immediately, and prices begin to fall. Once this happens, the profitability of the branded drug generally erodes rapidly. Because generic drug companies do not incur the same high costs for R&D, FDA approval, and advertising that the makers of patented drugs do, these savings are passed on to consumers as discounted prices, which are 50 to 90 percent lower than their brand-name competitors' prices. Recently, Glaxo Wellcome's popular Zantac, an antiulcer drug, lost patent protection and generic substitutes now cost 80 percent less than Zantac.

Capital requirements are the dollars needed to finance equipment, supplies, advertising, R&D, and the like. Of 20 drugs entering clinical testing, the FDA estimates that only 1 will ultimately be approved for use. Therefore the costs incurred to bring a new drug onto the market are huge.[22]

Government regulation is a barrier to entry if it bars or severely restricts potential new entrants to an industry. Once the FDA approves a drug, the FDA continues to monitor the drug, often requesting additional testing. The FDA determines label content, which must include a detailed description of the drug, its chemical composition, indications, contraindications, and side effects. If the safety of the drug is questioned because of defective packaging, misleading labeling, failure to meet content uniformity, or lack of effectiveness, the costs can be staggering. When American Home Products had to recall its Redux and Pondimin diet drugs because testing linked the drug with heart valve problems, the company lost $3.75 billion.

SUBSTITUTE GOODS AND SERVICES

In a general sense, all competitors produce substitute goods or services, or goods or services that can easily replace another's goods or services. For example, the introduction of desktop publishing systems by IBM, Apple, and Dell enabled graphic design companies to use personal computers (PCs) to design and typeset brochures, catalogs, flyers, and even books. Desktop publishing or typesetting software thus substitutes for the services of typesetting firms at a fraction of their cost. Many organizations (e.g., Amoco, The Associates First Capital Company, and Lockheed Martin) commonly use fax, e-mail, and/or overnight delivery services as a substitute for long-distance telephone calls and the U.S. Postal Service. Substitutes are a powerful force in the pharmaceutical industry. The threat of substitution is largely based on the formula in the patent.

In 2000, Merck lost patent protection on four drugs that accounted for more than 25 percent of its sales and more than 50 percent of its profitability. Thus Merck will face competition from generic substitutes and stands to lose 80 percent of its market share.[23]

CUSTOMERS

Customers for goods or services naturally try to force down prices, obtain more or higher quality products (while holding price constant), and increase competition among sellers by playing one against the other. Customer bargaining power is likely to be relatively great under the following circumstances.

- **The customer purchases a large volume relative to the supplier's total sales.** Health maintenance organizations (HMOs) and other managed care organizations list drugs approved for reimbursement. Managed care's share of the pharmaceutical market exceeds 75 percent.

- **The product or service represents a significant expenditure by the customer.** Customers generally are motivated to cut costs that constitute large portions of their total costs. Third-party payers encourage patients to use generic drugs over branded drugs to save money.

- **Large customers pose a threat of backward integration.** Backward integration is the purchase of one or more of its suppliers by a larger organization as a cost-cutting or quality-enhancing strategy. No HMO has purchased a pharmaceutical drug manufacturer nor has the government, through its Medicare and Medicaid programs, done so. However, the government, organizations such as AARP, and Medigap insurers have tried to hold the cost of drugs down for many patients.

- **Customers have readily available alternatives for the same services or products.** A consumer may not have a strong preference between a generic and a branded drug. In terms of dollars, the retail market for generic pharmaceuticals is expected to reach $20 billion by 2005, up from $14 billion in 1999. The force behind this increase is the desire by consumers to save money.

SUPPLIERS

The bargaining power of suppliers often controls how much they can raise prices above their costs or reduce the quality of goods and services they provide before losing customers. Copyrights and patents generally increase supplier strength for defined periods of time. This protection prevents suppliers from copying branded drugs and distributing generic drugs. In general, high supplier strength in the pharmaceutical market tends to be relatively short-lived.

The following Strategic Action Competency feature describes how Merck competes in the volatile pharmaceutical industry.[24] Merck is the largest drug manufacturer in the United States and ranks number two in the world behind Aventis. With sales of more than $32 billion and employing more than 62,000 people, more than one-third of the company's sales are in drugs that focus on people's cardiovascular health. The Merck-Medco Managed Care Division manages pharmacy benefits for more than 52 million people.

STRATEGIC ACTION COMPETENCY   *Merck*

Merck manufactures drugs in 20 different therapeutic categories approved by the FDA. In a recent year, it invested $2.4 billion in research and development. Its R&D effort was instrumental in manufacturing and marketing VIOXX, a drug for osteoarthritis and acute pain. VIOXX has become the fastest growing prescription arthritis medicine in the United States, commanding a market share of 48 percent in its class of medication.

To maximize and expand product offerings, Merck recently signed a licensing agreement with Kyorin Pharmaceutical Co., Ltd., to develop and market a new drug for the treatment of diabetes. It acquired SIBIA Neurosciences to expand its research and marketing capabilities in diseases related to the central nervous system. Merck has also entered into a number of collaborative agreements with specialized high-tech companies. For example, its collaboration with Vical to help develop vaccines, using the latest genetic technology, and with Aurora Biosciences on genomics technology, are two such examples. According to Merck's president, Raymond Gilmartin, the only sustainable advantage a company can have is the ability to innovate. Collaborating with other organizations helps control the massive R&D outlays required in the industry.

To reduce costs of distribution, Merck-Medco built a state-of-the-art automated pharmacy in Las Vegas, Nevada, using robotics and other technologically advanced logistical processes to increase efficiency and safety. The average large retail drug store generally dispenses about 500 prescriptions a day. The Las Vegas

pharmacy dispenses 5,000 prescriptions per hour, or 18 million prescriptions a year. It recently established an Internet Web site, http://www.merckmedco.com, that is capable of dispensing more than 250,000 online prescriptions per month. In 1999, it entered into an agreement with CVS/pharmacy, the number one online drugstore in the United States, to enhance further the services provided on its Web site. Merck-Medco also offers doctors the convenience of ordering vaccines and getting relevant information online from http://www.vaccinesbynet.com. Anyone can also receive the latest health-related information free by browsing Merck's Web site http://www.merckhomeedition.com.

Merck is constantly monitoring changes in legislation proposed by Congress and the administration. Merck is actively supporting legislation that would guarantee prescription drug coverage in any new Medicare legislation. Such coverage is especially important to Merck, which is losing patent protection for four drugs that had sales in excess $3.8 billion in 2000.

• • •

To learn more about Merck and the pharmaceutical industry, visit the company's home page at

http://www.merck.com and
http://www.hoovers.com

POLITICAL–LEGAL FORCES

3.

DESCRIBE THE PRINCIPAL POLITICAL AND LEGAL STRATEGIES USED BY MANAGERS TO COPE WITH CHANGES IN THE ENVIRONMENT.

Societies try to resolve conflicts over values and beliefs through their political and legal systems. For instance, in the United States and Canada the concepts of individual freedom, freedom of the press, property rights, and private enterprise are widely accepted. But legislative bodies, regulatory agencies, interest groups, and courts—often in conflict with one another—define the meaning and influence the actual interpretation of these concepts.

Many political and legal forces directly affect the way organizations operate. For the pharmaceutical industry in particular, changes in political forces have been especially significant during the past 25 years and will continue to be in the future. To achieve organizational goals, managers must accurately diagnose these forces and find useful ways to anticipate, respond to, or avoid the disturbances they cause.

For many industries (e.g., financial services, including banking), government regulation is a central aspect of their environments. Consider, for example, how two federal credit laws affect lenders and borrowers in the United States.

- The *Equal Credit Opportunity Act* entitles the customer to be considered for credit without regard to race, color, age, gender, or marital status. Although the act doesn't guarantee that the customer will get credit, it does ensure that the credit grantor applies tests of credit-worthiness fairly and impartially.

- The *Truth in Lending Act* says that credit grantors must reveal the "true" cost of using credit—for instance, the annual interest rate the customer will be paying. In the case of a revolving charge account, the customer must also be told the monthly interest rate and the minimum monthly payment required.

As shown in Figure 3.4, managers can use five basic political strategies to cope with turbulence in their environments: negotiation, lobbying, alliance, representation, and socialization. These strategies aren't mutually exclusive, are usually used in some combination, and each often contains elements of the others. Negotiation probably is the most important political strategy because each of the other four strategies involves to some degree the use of negotiation.

Negotiation is the process by which two or more individuals or groups, having both common and conflicting goals, present and discuss proposals in an attempt to reach an agreement.[25] Negotiation can take place only when the two parties believe that some form of agreement is possible and mutually beneficial. Recall the strike several

Figure 3.4 **Managerial Political Strategies**

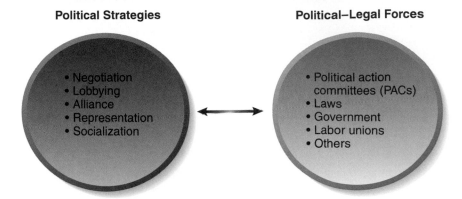

Political Strategies

- Negotiation
- Lobbying
- Alliance
- Representation
- Socialization

Political–Legal Forces

- Political action committees (PACs)
- Laws
- Government
- Labor unions
- Others

years ago by the International Association of Machinists and Aerospace Workers against Lockheed Martin for higher wages and increased job security. Negotiators representing the company and the union presented various proposals in an attempt to reach an agreement. Not until both parties realized that some agreement was necessary, did they agree on and ratify a new contract.

Lobbying is an attempt to influence government decisions by providing officials with information on the anticipated effects of legislation or regulatory rulings.[26] Congress and regulatory agencies, such as the Securities and Exchange Commission (SEC), the Federal Communications Commission (FCC), and the Food and Drug Administration (FDA), are the targets of continual lobbying efforts by organizations affected by their decisions. Organizations whose stability, growth, and survival are directly affected by government decisions typically use their top managers to lobby for them. Motorola, Microsoft, Coca-Cola, and Atlantic Richfield, among others, lobbied Congress to pass the favored nation trade status for China after defiant student demonstrators were killed on Beijing's Tiananmen Square. These organizations agree that human rights violations have occurred in China but that its market is too attractive to be ignored.

Only the largest organizations (e.g., NBC, AT&T, and Exxon) can afford to lobby for themselves. The most common form of lobbying is by associations representing the interests of groups of individuals or organizations. Approximately 4,000 national lobbying organizations maintain staffs in Washington, D.C. An additional 75,000 state and local associations and organizations occasionally lobby Washington's decision makers. Two of the largest associations representing business interests are the National Chamber of Commerce, with about 36,000 business and other organizational members, and the National Association of Manufacturers (NAM), with about 12,500 member corporations. The American Association of Retired Persons (AARP), with more than 30 million members, is the largest U.S. association representing individual interests. The AARP lobbies on behalf of U.S. citizens aged 50 and older and has a paid staff of 1,600, with headquarters in the heart of the nation's capital.

WEB INSIGHT

What legislation is the National Association of Manufacturers (NAM) currently watching and attempting to influence? To answer this question, visit NAM's Web site at *http://www.nam.org*

An ***alliance*** is a unified effort involving two or more organizations, groups, or individuals to achieve common goals with respect to a particular issue.[27] Alliances, especially those created to influence government actions, typically form around issues of economic self-interest, such as reducing R&D costs in the pharmaceutical industry. Other issues include government policy (e.g., the control of raw materials or taxes), foreign relations (e.g., the control of foreign sales or investment in overseas plants), and labor relations (e.g., the control of industrywide salaries and benefits, as within the construction industry or the National Football League). Alliances often are used for the following purposes.

- Oppose or support legislation, nomination of heads of regulatory agencies, and regulations issued by such agencies. Boeing, Gruman Aircraft, and Lockheed Martin have all supported the Federal Aviation Administration's (FAA's) crackdown on substandard counterfeit airline parts that have come into the United States from South Korea, Vietnam, and Russia.

- Improve competitiveness of two or more organizations through collaboration. Corning Glass Works uses multiple joint ventures with foreign partners such as Siemens (Germany), Samsung (Korea), Asahi Chemical (Japan), and Vitro (Mexico) to penetrate and thrive in a growing number of glass markets.

- Promote particular products or services, such as oranges, computers, and electricity. For example, the Edison Electric Institute promotes both the use and conservation of electrical energy.

- Construct facilities beyond the resources of any one organization, such as new plants. GM and Delphi have built a $1 billion automobile plant in Shanghai, China.

- Represent the interests of specific groups, such as women, the elderly, minorities, and particular industries. The NAM lobbies Congress to pass legislation favorable to its members, including restricting imports of foreign goods such as shoes and automobiles, and trying to open new markets in foreign countries such as the sale of rice in Japan.

An alliance both broadens and limits managerial power. When an alliance makes possible the attainment of goals that a single individual or organization would be unable to attain, it broadens managerial power. When an alliance requires a commitment to making certain decisions jointly in the future, it limits managerial power. Members of OPEC periodically negotiate production levels and the price they will charge for oil. These agreements are intended to broaden OPEC's power by generating more revenue for its members. However, to be successful in this endeavor, OPEC members must abide by the agreed production limits.

A *joint venture,* which typically involves two or more firms becoming partners to form a separate entity, is a common form of an alliance. Each partner benefits from the others' competence, which allows them to achieve their goals more quickly and efficiently. For example, Wal-Mart formed a joint venture with America Online to set up a large e-commerce presence on the Internet.[28] Wal-Mart realized that the longer it waited to get into the e-commerce market, the more serious would become growing e-commerce competition. America Online became a suitable joint venture partner because of its more than 32 million members. Wal-Mart is now learning the details of managing e-commerce and selling digital services in a retailing environment. Other retail giants, such as Sears and J.C. Penney, have little presence on the Internet and no comparable portal and will have to scramble to compete in e-commerce in the future.

Representation involves membership in an outside organization that serves the interests of the member's organization or group. Representation strategy often is subtle and indirect. School administrators often receive paid time off and the use of school resources to participate in voluntary community associations that might support the school system, such as the PTA, Chamber of Commerce, Elks, Kiwanis, Moose, Rotary, and United Way. A more direct form of representation, often based on some legal requirement, occurs when a specific group selects representatives to give it a voice in an organization's decisions. For example, union members elect officers to represent them in dealing with management.

Corporate boards of directors, the top-level policy-making groups in firms, are elected by and legally required to represent shareholders' interests. The National Association of Corporate Directors, however, suggests a much broader role for board members: They should ensure that long-term strategic goals and plans are established; that a proper management structure (organization, systems, and people) is in place to achieve these goals; and that the organization acts to maintain its integrity, reputation, and responsibility to its various constituencies. The board's responsibility to monitor and control the actions of the chief executive officer and others in top management is essential to its representing the interests of the shareholders.

Socialization is the process by which people learn the values held by an organization and the broader society. The assumption is that people who accept and act in accordance with these basic values are less likely to sympathize with positions that threaten the organization or the society. The so-called American business creed stresses the idea that a decentralized, privately owned, and competitive system in which price is the major regulator, should be continued and that citizens should oppose government actions that interfere with or threaten this system. Most U.S. and Canadian businesspeople subscribe to these beliefs and act on them.

Socialization includes formal and informal attempts by organizations to mold new employees to accept certain desired attitudes and ways of dealing with others and their jobs.[29] At its headquarters in Crotonville, New York, GE introduces thousands of its managers to the company's values and philosophy. These values include identifying and eliminating unproductive work in order to energize employees and encourage creativity and feelings of ownership at all levels. Conoco uses its virtual university to train managers. Employees can download courses from its Web site and/or attend courses at its Woodlands, Texas, location. Of course, top management's attempts may be offset or reinforced by the expectations of and pressures exerted by workers or other groups within the organization.

The use of socialization strategies by organizations is subject to broader cultural forces. In the United States and Canada the importance of individualism limits the extent to which organizations can use socialization strategies. Too much of what may be perceived as the "wrong kind" of socialization is likely to be met with resistance and charges of invasion of privacy or violation of individual rights.

The AARP uses many of these political strategies to gain support for its programs. Founded in 1958 by Dr. Ethel Percy, it now has more than 30 million members. Its goal is to educate older Americans (50 years old or older) on issues that face them, ask political candidates for clarification of their positions on issues that affect senior citizens, and increase voter participation. AARP does not endorse political candidates or contribute money to their campaigns. However, it does organize forums at which candidates can discuss particular issues for older Americans. Working with and through various other organizations, AARP advises members about health, auto, and home insurance, investment opportunities, mail-order pharmacy services, travel, and legal services, among others, and provides discounts for its members for some of these services.

As the leading advocate for older Americans, AARP engages in legislative and consumer advocacy on many subjects.[30] The following Communication Competency feature describes how AARP uses various political strategies to communicate its goals in three areas: Social Security, Medicare, and long-term care. The political strategies are indicated in parentheses.

COMMUNICATION COMPETENCY

AARP

Few currently retired people or those who will retire by 2005 will outlive their Social Security benefits under the program as it is now constituted. However, by 2034, the burden on Social Security will be greater than the payments going into the trust fund. Approximately 28 percent of the people receiving benefits today are under 65, including more than 4 million children with a deceased or disabled parent. Although Social Security was never intended to be a person's sole retirement income, 16 percent of its beneficiaries have no other income and more than 50 percent of older people rely heavily on Social Security income. To ensure that the system is properly funded, AARP has pressured Congress (lobbying strategy) to make adjustments in contribution rates, in annual cost of living adjustments, and investment of the trust fund. The organization has presented arguments against investing in the stock market, even though it routinely outperforms other investments, such as U.S. Treasury Bills. The argument presented is that most Americans with modest savings have little experience managing stock market investments and lack the skills needed to do so.

AARP was a driving force (representation strategy) for the 1997 Balanced Budget Act, which ensures that Medicare will be solvent through 2007. Under this act, Medicare makes regular monthly payments to certain health-care organizations (HMOs) that older people can use. It also supported the enactment of a Medical Savings Account, which combines purchasing a catastrophic health insurance policy with an individual medical plan, something like an IRA.

AARP is also concerned about long-term care. More than 6 million elderly people need some help in caring for themselves. As people grow old, they grow more frail and often suffer from chronic and debilitating illnesses. Maintaining a person in a nursing home costs $35,000 to $50,000 per year, and each home visit by a nurse or physical therapist costs as much as $100. Medicare pays for such services only for a limited period of time after a person is released from a primary care facility (e.g., a hospital), and the remainder must come from a person's savings or from the person's family. Older people who go into a nursing home can be covered by Medicaid but only after they spend down their assets (e.g., sell their homes, stocks, and deplete almost all their savings). AARP is trying to educate (socialization strategy) older people about different financing choices. But any financing program would require strong consumer protections and be easy for older people to understand and use. The organization is lobbying Congress to establish national standards to measure, assess, and ensure the quality of long-term care.

• • •

To learn about AARP, visit the organization's home page at

http://www.aarp.org

TECHNOLOGICAL CHANGES

4.

EXPLAIN HOW TECHNOLOGICAL CHANGES INFLUENCE THE STRUCTURE OF INDUSTRIES.

In Chapter 2 we defined *technology* as a transformation process that changes organizational inputs into outputs. Thus technology is the knowledge, tools, techniques, and actions used to transform ideas, information, and materials into finished goods and services. A technology may be as simple as making coffee at a restaurant or as complicated as driving the Pathfinder on Mars.

Technological change plays an increasingly pivotal role in an organization's environment, building on the present and helping create the future. Many new technologies are radical enough to force organizations, especially in high-tech industries, to reconsider their purposes and methods of operation or face extinction. The United States and several other industrial societies have become information societies. This shift was made possible by the explosion of computer-based and telecommunications technologies. One example is the PC and its integration with mainframe computers and telecommunications systems to form supernets. Through them, organizations can collect, process, and transmit vast amounts of data quickly and economically. For instance, Kodak now supplies photographic dealers with a microcomputer and software system that enables them to order Kodak products directly rather than through wholesalers. The management of information technology is woven into various chapters of this book, but here we briefly examine technology's role in three areas: strategy, manufacturing, and distribution channels.

TECHNOLOGY'S ROLE IN STRATEGY

Computer-based information technologies are now essential in most organizations, which is one reason for our including technological change in this chapter. In the 1970s, one of every two watches sold in the United States was a Timex product. Yet by the mid 1990s, the company's market share was less than 5 percent. Seiko, Citizen, Pulsar, Accutron, and Swatch now dominate this market. Why? As the watch industry moved from mechanical to electronic, Timex didn't change its strategy and continued to build watches that relied on older technology. Innovations in quartz crystal chemistry and light-emitting diode (LED) semiconductors made Timex's technology obsolete. Electronic watches overwhelmed the marketplace and brought prices down, causing Timex to lose most of its market share. Similarly, in today's automobile industry, ceramic-based engines and sophisticated battery-powered systems hold the promise of greater efficiency and performance than internal combustion engines can provide.

Information technology creates options, including the following, that simply weren't feasible with older technologies.[31]

- Computer-aided design linked to versatile, computer-controlled machines permits short production runs of custom designs with economies of scale approaching those of traditional large-scale manufacturing facilities.

- Consumers can shop via home pages on the Internet and "electronic shopping malls" more easily than using the Yellow Pages and telephones and going to shopping centers or individual outlets.

- With online, real-time financial management systems, managers can determine profit and loss positions daily, which was impossible with manual methods and earlier stages of computer technology.

- Retail banking customers can perform numerous banking functions from remote locations, including shopping centers, apartment building lobbies, corporate offices, out-of-state banks, and even their homes with PCs.

TECHNOLOGY'S ROLE IN MANUFACTURING

Advances in design and manufacturing technology have made it possible to reduce substantially the amount of time required to introduce a new product into the market. The use of computers and statistical analyses in manufacturing have also boosted quality, with machines and processes integrated by means of common databases and routines that simplify procedures and reduce the potential for human error. Perhaps the most significant contribution of advanced manufacturing technologies is that of mass customization—that is, the ability to produce a wide variety of a product by using the same basic design and production equipment but making certain modifications to meet the demands of a broader market. For example, Levi Strauss has successfully used computer-assisted design (CAD) systems to help design customized leather outfits and jeans for customers. Using an engineering workstation and advanced software, Levi Strauss can measure a customer's specific contours, body shape, weight, and preferences to create a customized pattern that becomes the basis for a perfectly fitting suit, pair of jeans, or dress in a short time. A customer's color and style preferences, as well as body measurements, are then directly fed into a computer that is electronically linked to a highly flexible stitching and finishing operation. Currently, most Levi Strauss outlets carry somewhere between 80 and 100 different varieties of jeans and outfits. With the use of new manufacturing and customization capabilities, company management believes that it will have between 400 and 500 variations on the shelves in the near future.[32]

TECHNOLOGY'S ROLE IN DISTRIBUTION

In the late 1990s, perhaps the single greatest change in distribution was the strong presence of the Internet and the World Wide Web, which provided online ordering, distribution, and sales. When Jeff Bezos created Amazon.com (see Chapter 1), suddenly the Internet threatened established retail booksellers, such as Barnes and Noble and Borders. Internet brokerage houses, Ameritrade, and E*Trade allow customers to access their accounts directly to buy and sell stocks. These services bypass those offered by traditional firms. Internet shopping also has replaced the department store for many customers. Combining Internet access and traditional catalog sales has enabled Lands' End, Early Winters, Touch of Class, and L. L. Bean to reach customers whose specialized needs are not effectively satisfied by existing "brick-and-mortar" department stores and discount chains.

Pitney Bowes, a company best known for making postage machines, is now facing a similar type of challenge from the rise of the Internet. Since 1920, Pitney Bowes has provided organizations with machines that allow them to affix the right amount of postage to letters and packages. In late 1998, companies such as E-Stamp, Stamp Master, and many others started designing Web sites that enable customers to pay for postage over the Internet, download customer-specific sets of coded data into their computers, and print out their own mailing labels and envelopes. In effect, the Internet, with permission of the U.S. Postal Service, now allows customers to print their own stamps. In response, Pitney Bowes has introduced its own version of user-friendly, Internet-based software to help customers order prepaid postage with greater ease.[33]

Building an international information highway now extends far beyond simple message systems and bulletin boards. Satellites, cellular towers, and fiber-optic telephone cables allow individuals and companies to exchange voice, data, and graphic messages in real time. Futurists speculate that within 5 to 10 years everyone will have personal numbers for all the telecommunications devices they use; that wireless technology will replace twisted pair, coaxial, and fiber-optic cable; and that telephone, fax, and computing will be integrated in handheld devices. Already, in many countries, including the United States, Sweden, Japan, and the United Kingdom, telephone customers have personal cards that they can slip into such a device and receive calls anywhere in their calling areas. Malaysia, China, and other developing countries are bypassing wired systems in favor of cellular technologies. And personal communicators made by Toshiba, Sony, and others permit phone, fax, and computing with a pen input screen. As a result, organizations have changed their business strategies to compete in the high-tech world.

While Congress debates U.S.–Chinese relations and China's human rights record, China is proving irresistibly attractive to the world's most advanced technology companies. Northern Telecom, Intel, and Philips now manufacture semiconductors in Shanghai. Sweden's Ericsson makes telephone switches in Nanjing, and IBM assembles PCs in Shenzhen. The following Global Awareness Competency feature highlights Motorola's business strategy in China.[34] The company is currently completing a $560 million chip plant in Tianjin, a northern port city. By 2005, it expects to employ more than 10,000 people and invest an additional $1.9 billion in a world-class chip manufacturing plant there.

GLOBAL AWARENESS COMPETENCY

Motorola in China

Motorola's operation in China rests on two key beliefs that guide all its actions worldwide—respect for the dignity of the individual and uncompromising integrity. These beliefs help Motorola maintain its competitive advantage in a highly competitive industry.

Since Motorola first entered China in 1993, the production of cellular phones has increased by more than 400 percent, with sales exceeding $3.4 billion annually. Cellular phones will become the dominant method of communication because of the extremely large costs of the alternative: laying and installing telephone cables and lines throughout the country. Moreover, China has more than 600,000 miles of roads,

but less than 40,000 miles of it are paved modern highways, so drivers can rarely cover more than 300 miles a day. Similarly, it takes about 17 days to go by train from Shanghai to Guangzhou (1,125 miles), a city outside Hong Kong. Cellular phones require state-of-the-art manufacturing facilities, so a high-tech company from outside China had to be involved. However, politically the company—in this case Motorola—had to set up cooperative relationships between itself and host country companies. For example, it recently established a joint venture with Beijing Mobile Communication Corporation to manufacture wireless phones. It also worked with that com-

pany to devise a high-speed data transport service. Such a system allows sub-scribers to send and receive information via a mobile terminal on radio channels or the Internet. This system will open the mobile market to a wealth of data applications, including e-commerce and data transfer. This new technology combines voice, data, and multimedia in one network.

Motorola also created joint ventures with Leshan Radio Factory for the manufacture of semiconductors and Nanjing Panda Electronics to establish centers for continual education. Chip production requires advanced hi-tech and complex technical competencies,

so Motorola must train production employees and managers. This training involves the use of Deming's quality control principles (see Chapter 2) and adherence to Motorola's six-sigma rule—fewer than four defective parts per million. Employees are also taught principles of human relations, motivation, organizational change, and other subjects. Motorola founded Project Hope, a nonprofit program to help raise the literacy rate in poverty stricken areas. More than 300 million Chinese (about 25 percent of China's population) are illiterate, and primary educa-

tion for children is too much of a financial burden for many families, who have an average income of less than RMB 480 yuan (about US $50). Through Project Hope, Motorola has built schools, provided teachers, and provided financial assistance to families.

• • •

To learn more about Motorola's China operation, visit the company's home page at

http://www.motorola.com

The information superhighway via the Internet represents a significant change in technology for all companies. Like the computer-driven engineering technologies that revitalized manufacturing, the information superhighway has the ability to change the basic ways in which people communicate at work and home. Consider the International Cargo Management System. With this information system, Seal and other cargo carriers can send an electronic guard with cargo that will let the shipper visually inspect the product's location and condition. When the container is on land, the signal is sent via cellular carrier. When the cargo is at sea, the signal is sent via ship-to-shore radio or phone or global communication satellites. It is more than a cute gadget because theft is a major cost for shippers; more than $5 billion in losses are reported annually in the United States alone.

The information superhighway will affect every organization in the years ahead. Because it represents new technology, this component of the environment undoubtedly will bring change to the political–legal arena, as customers and managers struggle with the problems of having confidential information travel around the world and with equipment and operator safety.

CHAPTER SUMMARY

The purpose of this chapter was to help you develop your planning and administrative, strategic thinking and action, global awareness, and communication competencies with respect to an organ-ization's environment. We discussed and presented examples of various practices that organizations can use in coping with their environments. We indicated that an organization's environment can be broken into four segments: economy and culture, competition, politics, and technology. Various competitive forces have impacts on these segments, creating both opportunities and threats that will challenge you to use all the competencies you acquire.

1. **DESCRIBE HOW ECONOMIC AND CULTURAL FACTORS INFLUENCE ORGANIZATIONS.**
The environment includes the external factors that usually af-

fect organizations, either directly or indirectly. It encompasses the economic system and current economic conditions, political system, natural resources, and the demographics of the population within which organizations operate. Cultural forces, primarily working through value systems, shape the viewpoints and decision-making processes of managers and employees alike. Hofstede's work-related value framework has five dimensions: power distance, uncertainty avoidance, individualism, masculinity, and Confucian dynamism.

2. **IDENTIFY THE FIVE COMPETITIVE FORCES THAT AFFECT ORGANIZATIONS IN AN INDUSTRY.**
Managers must assess and respond to five competitive forces in the environment: competitors, new entrants, substitute goods and services, customers, and suppliers.

3. DESCRIBE THE PRINCIPAL POLITICAL AND LEGAL STRATEGIES USED BY MANAGERS TO COPE WITH CHANGES IN THE ENVIRONMENT.

Political–legal issues, which used to be in the background, now often directly influence the way organizations operate. Five political strategies that managers use in coping with political–legal forces in the environment are negotiation, lobbying, alliances, representation, and socialization.

4. EXPLAIN HOW TECHNOLOGICAL CHANGES INFLUENCE THE STRUCTURE OF INDUSTRIES.

Technological forces in the environment are rapidly changing the specific knowledge, tools, and techniques used to transform materials, information, and other inputs into particular goods or services. We examined how technological changes affect three areas of an organization: strategy, manufacturing, and distribution.

KEY TERMS

Alliance, p. 93
Capital requirements, p. 90
Collectivism, p. 87
Confucian dynamism, p. 88
Culture, p. 84
Demographics, p. 82
Economics, p. 78
Economies of scale, p. 90
Environmental stewardship, p. 80

Femininity, p. 88
General environment, p. 77
Government regulation, p. 90
Individualism, p. 87
Joint venture, p. 94
Lobbying, p. 93
Masculinity, p. 87
Negotiation, p. 92
Power distance, p. 86

Product differentiation, p. 90
Representation, p. 94
Socialization, p. 94
Uncertainty avoidance, p. 86
Value, p. 84
Value system, p. 84

QUESTIONS FOR DISCUSSION AND COMPETENCY DEVELOPMENT

1. How might the four trends in the new economy affect your college or university?

2. Why is environmental stewardship becoming a concern for many businesses?

3. Visit the Web site *http://www.greenpeace.org*. What political strategies affecting international organizations are being used by Greenpeace?

4. What implications do the changing demographic patterns in the United States have on diversity for organizations such as Texas Instruments and McDonald's for staffing and promotional opportunities?

5. What are the five dimensions of culture in a society? Assuming that you took a job with Wal-Mart in Mexico, what are some values that you would need to be aware in order to be a productive employee? What competencies might you need to develop?

6. Visit the Web site *http://www.hoovers.com*. Click on the telecommunications industry. Using the five-force industry model, describe the key competitive issues in that industry.

7. How has Amazon.com (*http://www.amazon.com*) used the Internet to change the technologies used in the retail book

industry? How did these changes affect the strategies and distribution systems of its competitors, such as Barnes and Noble and Borders?

8. What political strategies have the U.S. tobacco companies used in their attempts to control the lawsuits against their industry? Have these strategies been successful?

9. **Competency Development: Planning and Administration.** In 1963, Gary Comer founded Lands' End. Today, the company employs more than 8,000 people and has a catalog business with customers from the United States, Germany, France, and Japan. These catalogs offer more than 2,500 different products. Visit the company's home page at *http://www.landsend.com* and find three examples of how managers' planning and administration competencies are applied at Lands' End.

10. **Competency Development: Teamwork.** Rubbermaid makes extensive use of teams to come up with ideas for new products. A highly innovative company, Rubbermaid introduces about 350 new products a year. It typically spends 14 percent of its profits on R&D. To learn more about how Rubbermaid uses teams to achieve its competitive advantage, visit the company's home page at *http://www.rubbermaid.com*.

The Personal Computer Industry

Ever since its mass production and distribution began in the early 1980s, the personal computer (PC) has become a mainstay in the office, laboratory, factory, home, briefcase, and now, even in the car. Personal computers are available for sale in almost every mass merchandising outlet, not only in such electronics retailing outlets as Best Buy, Circuit City, and Radio Shack. They also are available from manufacturers and distributors over the telephone and online over the Internet, a phenomenon that itself can be traced directly to the massive growth and proliferation of PCs.

Makers of PCs include such well-known names as Apple Computer, Compaq Computer, Hewlett-Packard, IBM, Dell Computer, Gateway, Packard Bell, and many new start-ups. In fact, there are so many PC manufacturers today that new entrants can easily enter the industry—and disappear just as quickly, as in the case of AST Research and other once-thriving companies. Toward the end of 1998, the top five PC makers—Compaq, IBM, Dell, Hewlett-Packard, and Gateway—commanded 41 percent of the U.S. market. If there is one word that describes competition in the PC industry, it is unrelenting.

The dominant operating system standard in the industry is Microsoft's Windows. It features a set of efficiently organized software instructions, meaningful icons, and easy point and click operation via a mouse. In many ways, the tremendous growth of the PC industry throughout the 1990s can be traced to the several versions of the Windows operating system that have greatly eased the way for users to operate their machines. Windows makes it possible for users to load a variety of different programs into their PCs quickly and conveniently. Because of the tremendous popularity of this operating system, literally thousands of different broad-based software applications (e.g., word processing, spreadsheet, Internet access, etc.) have been designed to use its format to make the computer more versatile. However, with the government's court-approved plan to break up Microsoft, which is being appealed, it remains to be seen whether the company can retain its dominant share of the software market.

Personal computers are easy to manufacture, although the highest quality machines often use many customized parts. For example, the "average" PC requires only an Intel microprocessor (or equivalent chip) as its central processing unit (CPU), a hard disk drive (which provides long-term storage of programs and data), a CD-ROM drive (for audio play and downloads of extremely memory-intensive software programs), a few printed circuit boards, a keyboard, and a monitor. Each new firm that enters the industry hopes to undercut an established firm through lower prices. The average price of PCs has dropped by about 15 to 20 percent every year for the past 3 years. Since 1997, the biggest growth of PCs has occurred in models selling for less than $1,000, which now pack as much power and speed as models that sold for more than $3,500 just a few years ago.

Economies of scale in PC production are moderate, but the availability of manufacturing capacity and standardized, off-the-shelf technology makes assembly easy and inexpensive. Aside from the microchips and the software operating systems (both of which can be readily purchased or licensed), few proprietary technologies or techniques are involved in PC manufacture and distribution. Manufacturers can even custom-manufacture machines for individual customers according to their specific needs for speed, power, number of different peripherals (e.g., scanners, printers, CD-ROM and DVD drives, and sound and video cards), and price.

The PC industry serves millions of knowledgeable and powerful buyers. With hundreds of suppliers to choose from, customers are ruthless in their search for higher value (better quality and lower cost). Until about 1990, the majority of PC buyers were large and small businesses that used the machines to increase their productivity. Then the market for individual buyers exploded. Regardless of who uses a PC or what it is used for, the consumer is demanding and savvy. The PC market has already become similar to those for color television sets during the 1970s and VCRs during the 1980s, with most customers fully aware of the options they need and how much those features should cost. Most PCs have a minimum standard of quality, power, speed, and memory, so competition turns largely on price. For example, the price of the latest streamlined PC models from Compaq and Gateway (based on later Intel-class chips, but with few peripherals) dropped from $1,000 in 1997 to $599 in 1999.

Knowledgeable buyers also mean that some customers will not base their purchase decisions solely on price. This situation is particularly true for business and corporate buyers, who often want superior maintenance, software upgrades, and repair services. In most cases, businesses will either purchase directly from large PC manufacturers or from value-added resellers who will perform much of the maintenance, warranty work, and system upgrades when new technologies or software applications enter the market. Thus some PC makers have opportunities to stake out important market niches with customers who seek additional security and fast service for their machines.

Some of the most important suppliers to the PC industry are the manufacturers of microprocessors, memory and graphics chips, and printed circuit boards, which represent the guts of the machine. Large chip makers with the capability and manufacturing prowess to make both PC components and the PC itself include Intel, AMD, National Semiconductor (Cyrix unit), IBM, Motorola, Toshiba of Japan, Acer of Taiwan, and a host of smaller semiconductor manufacturers. Important disk drive suppliers to the PC industry include companies such as Seagate, Quantum, Western Digital, Applied Magnetics, and Read-Rite. These companies themselves compete fiercely in designing new generations of ever smaller and more powerful disk drives. Major manufacturers of printers include Hewlett-Packard, Canon, Seiko-Epson, and Lexmark, all of which are technological leaders in peripherals businesses. The traditional names in consumer electronics—Sony, Philips, Matsushita, and others—are key players that make many of the CD-ROM and DVD components.

Although few direct substitutes currently exist for low-priced standard PCs, the potential clearly exists for new products and technologies to redefine and reshape the way PCs are designed, made, sold, and used. Even smaller PCs have already made significant inroads into this market, as with the explosion of laptop, notebook-sized computers. Laptop models are more stylish and replace the bulky monitors and keyboards associ-ated with conventional PCs. However, the real growth in substi-tute products will likely occur with the growing availability of hand-held, palm-top computers that can perform many PC func-tions without a keyboard. These hand-held machines may very well signify the rise of new wireless network appliances that also serve as communication devices and may eventually replace other devices such as the cellular phone, the pager, and even the laptop itself over time.[35]

Questions

1. Using the competitive forces in the environment shown in Figure 3.3, analyze the PC industry. How competitive is it?

2. How might changes in the economy affect the PC industry by 2005?

3. How might the rapid changes in computer technology affect firms competing in the PC industry?

Burton Snowboards

In the mid 1960s, Jake Burton was one of the thousands of young people who enjoyed surfing on snow with Sherman Poppen's Snurfers. In 1977, Burton was surprised to discover that, in the intervening years, the industry had not developed, expanded, or innovated much. Noting this lack of development in snowboards, Burton quit the Manhattan business world, moved to Londonderry, Vermont, and started designing and testing his own snowboards. From his recognition of a product need, the possibility of a profitable market niche, and commitment to a quality product came the world's first snowboard factory—Burton Snowboards.

Like most new small businesses, the early years were filled with change and hard work. In just its second year, Burton moved the company into a farmhouse in Manchester, Vermont. Working out of his home, a group of four to five workers produced, sold, and repaired all the Burton snowboard models. The company's toll-free customer service line rang in Burton's bedroom throughout the night. He would often load his car and visit as many as 10 shops a day, pitching the company's boards to shopowners whenever orders were low.

In the 1980s, Jake realized that, for the sport to grow in popularity, it had to become more than just a cult sport in which snowboarders used sledding hills or snow-covered golf courses. Burton lobbied eastern U.S. ski resorts to open their lifts to snowboarders, and one by one they did. As more resorts opened to snowboarders, the demand for the company's snowboards and innovations in them increased rapidly.

For example, edgeless wooden boards that were best suited for powder weren't optimal for the icy conditions of eastern ski resorts. These conditions still drive innovation at Burton Snowboards. The company's basic policy is that, if a board doesn't work in Vermont, it doesn't get made. As the company continued to grow, Burton moved the company to a modern day facility in Burlington, Vermont.

To remain the world's leader in snowboarding and snowboarding accessories, Burton must constantly monitor the company's external environment. He realizes that the environment's most influential factors are snowboarding's social trends. Participants in snowboarding have their own slang, dress, and activities that dominate the industry's culture. It is Burton's responsibility to ensure that the company's products match the changing tastes and preferences of this dynamic group. Although the company produces a product for all ages, its primary target age group is 12 to 35. However, the preferences of this group aren't homogenous, so the company develops different boards for various segments of it.

The company has a strong commitment to technological innovation, annually redesigning and updating its core products. It takes advantage of the latest computer innovations, allowing it to simulate the hills and mountains that its boards will "surf" and improve product design before actually making a prototype.

Burton Snowboards has led the industry by being the innovator and has attracted many competitors who often copy or imitate its earlier designs. The industry also is steadily consolidating small competitors into larger corporations. However, Burton believes that the company's future is secure so long as it remains focused on serving its core consumers. To do so, Burton Snowboards needs to remain committed to producing the highest quality (even if that means higher costs) and most innovative snowboards on the market.

Questions

1. Describe the environmental factors affecting Burton Snowboards.

2. Identify which of the five competitive forces in the industry have the greatest impact on Burton Snowboarding.

3. Is socialization a major factor at Burton Snowboards? Explain your answer.

To learn more about Burton Snowboards, visit the company's home page at *http://www.burton.com*.

Managing Globally

AFTER STUDYING THIS CHAPTER YOU SHOULD BE ABLE TO:

1. STATE SEVERAL CHARACTERISTICS OF THE GLOBAL ECONOMY.

2. DESCRIBE SIX STRATEGIES USED BY ORGANIZATIONS IN INTERNATIONAL BUSINESS.

3. EXPLAIN THE IMPACT OF POLITICAL–LEGAL FORCES ON INTERNATIONAL BUSINESS.

4. DISCUSS HOW THREE MAJOR TRADE AGREEMENTS AFFECT GLOBAL COMPETITION.

5. DESCRIBE HOW A COUNTRY'S CULTURE CAN AFFECT AN ORGANIZATION'S BUSINESS PRACTICES.

Chapter Outline

PREVIEW: PROCTER & GAMBLE

THE GLOBAL ECONOMY

STRATEGIES FOR INTERNATIONAL BUSINESS
EXPORTING STRATEGY
LICENSING STRATEGY
FRANCHISING STRATEGY
ALLIANCE STRATEGY
MULTIDOMESTIC STRATEGY
GLOBAL STRATEGY
STRATEGIC ACTION COMPETENCY: Boeing

POLITICAL–LEGAL FORCES
ASSESSING POLITICAL RISK
PLANNING AND ADMINISTRATION COMPETENCY: Rio Tinto Corporation
POLITICAL MECHANISMS

GLOBAL TRADE AGREEMENTS
WORLD TRADE ORGANIZATION
NORTH AMERICAN FREE TRADE AGREEMENT
GLOBAL AWARENESS COMPETENCY: Mabe
EUROPEAN UNION

CULTURAL FORCES
VIEWS OF SOCIAL CHANGE
TIME ORIENTATION
LANGUAGE
TEAMWORK COMPETENCY: Marianne Torrcelli of AT&T
VALUE SYSTEMS

CHAPTER SUMMARY

KEY TERMS

QUESTIONS FOR DISCUSSION AND COMPETENCY DEVELOPMENT

CASE FOR COMPETENCY DEVELOPMENT: GRANT GISEL OF SIERRA SYSTEMS CONSULTANTS

VIDEO CASE: ENFORCEMENT TECHNOLOGY

PROCTER & GAMBLE

When Durk Jager took over as CEO of Procter & Gamble (P&G) in 1999, his charge was to restructure P&G so that it could achieve its full growth potential in sales and revenues. The sales goal for P&G in 2005 was $70 billion, or almost double that of 2000. P&G, which sells more than 300 brands to 5 billion consumers in 140 countries, needed to change its structure to achieve those goals. Jager restructured P&G into seven product groups—baby care, beauty care, fabric and home care, feminine protection, food and beverage, health care and corporate new ventures, and tissues and towels—instead of four geographic units (North America, Europe, Asia, and Latin America). Under the old geographic structure, a laundry product in Europe might compete for marketing funds against P&G diaper or tissue products in Asia. These seven global product managers have responsibility for profitability of existing and new brands and have the resources to respond quickly to competitors and customers. P&G also established a single global business service organization whose mission is to provide essential business services such as accounting, employee benefits and payroll, purchasing, information, and technology to the entire company. By establishing this new structure, Jager hoped to achieve significant economies of scale while improving overall quality and speed of services. He chose this design because of P&G's previous inability to establish brands around the world.

In mid 2000, Jager resigned and was replaced by A. G. Lafley. Although there were many reasons for Jager's quick departure, including disappointing sales and revenues and the introduction of too many new products, P&G's global arena had significantly changed. For example, with China's entrance into the World Trade Organization, numerous local Chinese competitors now compete with P&G in world markets. In Zhongshan, China, Disposal Soft Goods, a manufacturer of throw-away diapers, an unattainable luxury for millions of Chinese a few years ago, is a major competitor of P&G's. With the ability to manufacture more than 300 million diapers a year and 19 million Chinese babies born each year, the Chinese company has the ability to sell its diapers in markets that have been traditionally held by P&G, especially in China, Malaysia, and New Zealand. In addition to facing new competitors, P&G's profits were lower because of the euro's (Europe's common currency) slump against the U.S. dollar. For P&G the higher exchange rate means that its products aren't as competitive as they used to be on price with goods manufactured by European competitors, such as Unilever and Nestlé.

The challenges facing Lafley are to focus P&G on food and pharmaceuticals. Food and beverages—mainly Pringles potato chips, Folgers coffee, Crisco shortening, and Jif peanut butter—contribute 11 percent of P&G total sales. That's small when compared to laundry and cleaning products (30 percent), paper goods (29 percent), and beauty care (21 percent). Food and beverages face strong international competition because customers' preferences are determined by local customs more than global brand awareness. Pharmaceuticals, which contributed less than 2 percent of P&G's revenue, are even more marginal. Pharmaceuticals are financially attractive because they bring higher profit margins, but global competition is fierce.[1]

To learn more about Procter & Gamble, visit the company's home page at

http://www.pg.com

THE GLOBAL ECONOMY

1.

STATE SEVERAL CHARACTERISTICS OF THE GLOBAL ECONOMY.

Procter & Gamble's situation illustrates the effect of several global forces that an increasing number of companies face—intense rivalry among competitors, pressures on prices, need for cost cutting, diversification into related lines of business, and the impact of changes in the financial arena on profitability. Table 4.1 highlights some of the more important trends in the global economy.

In a global economy, products are shipped anywhere in the world in a matter of days, communication is instant, and new product introductions and their life cycles are shorter—with 6 months the norm in some high-tech industries. For example, more than two-thirds of Xerox's revenue is generated from sales outside the United States. Therefore what happens in the financial markets in Asia, Europe, Latin America, and Africa is of vital interest to Xerox. The fall of the euro against the U.S. dollar has been blamed for lower profits for Xerox, P&G, McDonald's, and Office Depot, among others.

Table   4.1   **Global Economic Trends**

- Increased competition
- Shortened product life-cycles
- Importance of exports and imports
- Worldwide communication
- New countries emerge
- Borderless organizations
- Worldwide labor pool

Exports and imports of goods and services represent about 30 percent of the U.S. gross domestic product, up from less than 21 percent in 1992. Trade is now so important to the U.S. economy that one job in six depends on it. Yet a recent poll revealed that 55 percent of the population thought that expanded trade leads to a loss of U.S. jobs. When asked to identify the biggest threat to U.S. jobs, 52 percent said that it was cheap foreign labor. This attitude reflects the fact that trade is often portrayed in the media as a war between nations in which countries that export more than they import win, whereas countries that import more than they export lose. Since 1995, U.S. exports of goods and services have soared 40 percent, accounting for much of the overall growth in the economy. However, imports have been growing more than exports, in part because the economy has expanded, which gave U.S. consumers more money to spend.[2]

The nature of trade is changing dramatically. Increasingly, trade takes place between different parts of the same corporation or through alliances (joint ventures). Asking whether a product—computer, car, or shirt—has been "Made in the USA" or "Made in Canada" has become almost meaningless. Grand Union is 100 percent owned by Generale Occidentale of France, and A&P is 55 percent owned by the Tengelmann Group in Germany. Miles Laboratories, a major pharmaceutical company, is 100 percent owned by Bayer AG of Germany, and Alcon Laboratories is 100 percent owned by Nestlé, S.A., of Switzerland. Although many executives tend to think in terms of managing a U.S. company overseas, they may well find themselves employed by a non-U.S. organization as a local manager to run its U.S. affiliate. The production of components for cars, vacuum cleaners, PCs, and many products is increasingly scattered around the world.[3]

Another driving force is the information revolution that now permits instantaneous worldwide communication.[4] The globalization of business has placed a premium on information. "Information technologies are the most powerful forces ever generated to make things cost-effective," says John S. Mayo, president of Lucent Technologies. Entrepreneurs in the industrial nations, especially the United States, are spearheading the Internet boom, building fiber-optic networks, and offering myriad new products and services on the World Wide Web. Sun Microsystems offers 24-hour technical assistance throughout the world with a single phone number drawing on employee teams in California, London, and Sydney. The teams coordinate their efforts electronically through a sophisticated information system. Within the next 15 years, the number of computers and communications satellites is projected to double. The number of wireless communications networks will rise from 34 million to more than 1.3 billion. The number of Internet users will grow from 70 million in 1997 to more than 1.2 billion by 2002. These figures are astounding when you realize that one-half the world's population has never even used a phone!

The drive for increased openness—both economically and politically—is happening. The collapse of Communism in 1989 created a new group of rapid-growth countries in Central and Eastern Europe. The development of market institutions (e.g., banks and stock markets) that provide for effective corporate governance in many of these

WEB INSIGHT

To learn more about Sun Microsystems' worldwide operations, visit the company's Web site at _http://www.sun.com_. You'll be able to access new and existing product information from almost any country 24 hours a day.

countries (e.g., Slovakia, Croatia, and Kazakhstan) have been developing slowly. The lack of strong legal frameworks has allowed increases in bribery and corruption. The lack of well-defined property rights that convey ownership and transferability has also led to problems. However, the rapid and widespread adoption of market-based policies in these emerging economies has been significant.[5]

Privatization permits organizations to adapt their strategies to meet the demands of the market and places the burden on top managers of managing their organizations effectively and efficiently. Privatization also means an increasing number of joint ventures with foreign firms and usually the adoption of more modern management practices. When GE created a joint venture with a manufacturer of light bulbs in Hungary, GE managers with global experience were called in to help the Hungarian company improve its production to world-class standards.

As domestic policies are becoming more market-oriented, governments are opening their countries to multinational trade and joining regional trade associations. New strategic partnerships of foreign and domestic organizations are emerging. Governments everywhere are pursuing market-based economic policies. Multinational corporations are accelerating the exchange of innovations across open borders. Global investors are pressuring companies to open their books. People are demanding stronger political and economic rights, as shown by Vicente Fox's election as president of Mexico. Mr. Fox's party, the National Action Party, won the election on the basis of improving educational opportunities for all Mexicans. The party hopes that, through education, more than 1.3 million unemployed Mexicans will be able to enter the labor force and make valuable contributions to society.

One of the most important factors that has fueled the growth of the global economy is the prevalence of labor and resources in different parts of the world.[6] Many textile, housewares, and toy manufacturers have opened overseas operations because of low labor costs. Toy companies, such as Mattel and Hasbro, have significant production operations in China where the average worker earns U.S. $120 per month. Such low labor costs enable these companies to offer high-quality toys at low cost. The presence of these companies has also helped stimulate the development of local economies. Many U.S. firms are locating some of their most sophisticated operations in regions having abundant sources of highly skilled, technical personnel. Texas Instruments has established a state-of-the-art software development site in Bangalore, India, to work with highly skilled computer technicians.

We discuss these and other forces that are driving and restraining the global economy throughout this chapter. Although any type of organization may act globally, most that do are for-profit businesses. Therefore the material covered in this chapter applies primarily to them.

STRATEGIES FOR INTERNATIONAL BUSINESS

2.

DESCRIBE SIX STRATEGIES USED BY ORGANIZATIONS IN INTERNATIONAL BUSINESS.

Organizations typically choose among six strategies for conducting international business. They range from low to high in complexity and in resource commitment, as shown in Figure 4.1. *Complexity* refers to the structure of the organization (e.g., number of hierarchical levels, number of staff people, and number of departments) and the amount of coordination required to deliver a product or service to customers. *Resource commitment* refers to the amount of tangible financial assets and information support systems that the organization dedicates to its global strategy.

Organizations can change their strategies over time as they learn from their experiences. Celanese Chemical Corporation used an export strategy to sell its chemicals in Thailand, China, Vietnam, and other Southeast Asian countries in the early 1990s. One person covered this territory and needed little support from the organization headquartered in Dallas, Texas. As its chemical business grew during the 1990s, Celanese

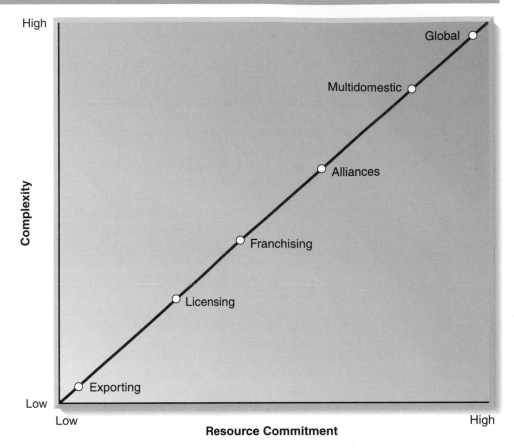

High

Complexity

Low

Low   Resource Commitment   High

Global
Multidomestic
Alliances
Franchising
Licensing
Exporting

changed its international strategy to become a global chemical company. As Celanese changed its strategy, its organizational structure became more complex and it committed larger amounts of resources to its far-flung operations. It built a $300 million dollar plant in Singapore and hired 100 local employees to staff that operation. The Singapore operation's output is coordinated with its other plants in Texas, Canada, and California to provide chemical products worldwide.[7]

EXPORTING STRATEGY

The **exporting strategy** involves maintaining facilities within a home country and shipping goods and services abroad for sale in foreign markets. When a domestic firm decides that it wants to move toward global operations, its first priority should be to build a global customer base. All that is necessary is a Web page and some promotion to direct potential customers to its location. Exporting is a practical means for small or medium-sized organizations with little financial resources to invest but who are facing increased competition in their domestic markets. For many such firms, exporting is the primary strategy of international operations. Tim Luberski, CEO of California Sunshine, uses this approach. California Sunshine is a leading exporter of U.S. dairy products, including milk, eggs, yogurt, and sour cream. Extended product dating and rapid delivery allow them to be sold virtually around the world. California Sunshine customers can order products directly on the Internet at http://www.hiddenvilla.com. With three large warehouses located next to international airports, California Sunshine guarantees product delivery within 72 hours.[8]

A variation on exporting (or importing) is **countertrade,** an agreement that requires companies from the exporting nation to purchase products of equivalent value from the importing nation. Countertrade affects up to 30 percent of all world trade. When a nation's banking system is poor, as is the case in many developing African and Eastern European nations, countertrade may be the best form of pricing. An estimated 90 percent of Russian transactions for imports involve some form of countertrade. For years, PepsiCo exported syrup and related soft drinks items to Russia in exchange for vodka. In a bizarre deal, Polish coal was exchanged for concerts given by the Swedish rock band Abba in Poland.

LICENSING STRATEGY

A *licensing strategy* involves a firm (the licensor) in one country giving other domestic or foreign firms (licensees) the right to use a patent, trademark, technology, production process, or product in return for the payment of a royalty or fee.[9] This contractual arrangement also may involve the licensor in providing manufacturing, technical, or marketing expertise to the licensee. A simple licensing arrangement involves U.S. and Canadian book publishers giving foreign publishers the right to translate a book into another language and then publish, market, and distribute the translated book. The licensor doesn't have to worry about making large capital investments abroad or becoming involved in the details of daily production, marketing, or management. PepsiCo and Coca-Cola have licensing agreements with bottlers/distributors in most countries of the world.

Technological and market forces are combining to stimulate use of the licensing strategy. The reason is that licenses can be used to disseminate new technologies rapidly to new markets. Image Entertainment, Inc., a leading licensee and distributor of DVD programming in the United States recently announced a licensing agreement with Nippon Columbia of Japan. It will enable customers to view programs such as the Eagles' "Hell Freezes Over" or Peter Frampton's, "Live in Detroit," distributed by Image Entertainment throughout Australia and New Zealand. Martin Greenwald, Image's president, believes that the licensing agreement is a means to become a global force in video distribution. Image is also in the process of finalizing additional licensing agreements for other parts of the world.[10]

FRANCHISING STRATEGY

A *franchising strategy* involves a parent organization (the franchiser) granting other companies or individuals (franchisees) the right to use its trademarked name and to produce and sell its goods or services. It is a special type of licensing agreement whereby the franchiser not only provides the product, technology, process, and/or trademark, but also most of the marketing program. In nearly any major city around the world, you are likely to find McDonald's, Burger King, Kentucky Fried Chicken (KFC), Marriott, or Holiday Inn, among others. They are there because local entrepreneurs have bought franchises. Franchising permits companies to maintain marketing control while passing along many of the costs, risks, and responsibilities to the licensees. The franchiser provides franchisees with a complete assortment of materials and services for a fee. Franchisees often function somewhat independently from the parent company but benefit from being part of a larger organization. However, the franchiser usually is actively involved in training, monitoring, and controlling certain actions of the franchisee to ensure that it conforms to the franchise agreement.

ALLIANCE STRATEGY

An *alliance strategy* involves agreeing with other organizations to pool physical, financial, and human resources to achieve common goals. *Global strategic alliances* are joint ventures that involve actions taken internationally by two or more companies contributing an agreed upon amount of resources.[11] This approach may be preferred when competition is tough or technology and capital requirements are relatively large for one partner. General Motors has global alliances with Suzuki, Isuzu, and Toyota. Ford has allied with Nissan and Mazda. General Mills created a global strategic alliance with Nestlé in Europe, called Cereal Partners Worldwide, to compete against the growing global market share of Kellogg's. General Mills and Nestlé agreed to pool part of their product lines and distribution systems.

The following factors have stimulated the formation of alliances, especially joint ventures.[12]

- The need to share and lower the costs of high-risk, technologically intensive development projects, such as computer-based information systems. Toshiba, for example, is allied with several U.S. firms (United Technologies, Apple Computer, Sun Microsystems, and Motorola) and European firms (Olivetti, Siemens, Rhore-Poulenc Ericsson, and SGS-Thompson). The partners are simultaneously owners investing capital, customers routing calls via satellites, and suppliers of technology to the venture.

- The desire to lower costs by sharing the large fixed-cost investments for manufacturing plants in some locations and in industries such as autos, steel, and appliances. To reduce manufacturing costs, Ford and Volkswagen formed a joint venture to make four-wheel-drive vehicles in Portugal.

- The desire to learn another firm's technology and special processes or to gain access to customers and distribution channels. Samsung entered into a joint venture with GE to produce microwave ovens and later became a competitor of GE's in the full line of household appliances.

- The desire to participate in the evolution of competitive activity in growing global industries. Royal Crown Cola Company signed a joint venture agreement with Mexico's Consorcio Aga to help RC Cola boost its sales there. In addition to licensing its brands, RC Cola provides advertising, promotional, and technical support to Consorcio Aga.

Alliances provide entry into markets that are risky because of strict political requirements or great economic uncertainty. For example, China usually doesn't permit foreign corporations to establish wholly owned subsidiaries there—they must form some sort of alliance with Chinese participants. Finally, domestic partners are likely to have a deeper understanding of how to deal with great political and economic uncertainty in countries such as China and Russia.

MULTIDOMESTIC STRATEGY

A *multidomestic strategy* involves adjusting products, services, and practices to individual countries or regions (e.g., Pacific Rim versus Western Europe versus North America).[13] Procter & Gamble, General Mills, Philip Morris, and PepsiCo all practice multidomestic strategies. Pressures for local customizing to respond to differences in customer demand, distribution channels, host government demands, and/or employee needs drive this strategy. It is based on the assumption that the benefits of local response will outweigh the extra costs of customizing. These companies view the world as a whole of unique parts and deal with each part individually. Thus a multidomestic company treats each market separately because of differences in tastes and competitive conditions.

Under a multidomestic strategy, each major overseas subsidiary usually is somewhat independent. Often each is a profit center and contributes earnings and growth according to its market opportunity. A *profit center* is an organizational unit that is accountable for both the revenues generated by its activities and the costs of those activities. Its managers are responsible for generating revenues and minimizing costs to achieve the unit's profit goals. Coca-Cola is well known in the United States for its Coca-Cola, Diet Coke, Sprite, Diet Sprite, and Mello Yellow brands. In Australia, it sells carbonated beverages under the brand names of Skysurfer and Life. The sweetness levels are vastly different from those in the United States. The company's world headquarters in Atlanta, Georgia, maintains overall financial control and coordinates broad marketing (including product line) policies worldwide. A multidomestic strategy also means that some R&D—and even production—may be handled in the home country. But specific marketing and transportation operations usually are delegated to managers in each nation or region.

Frito-Lay uses a multidomestic strategy in tailoring its snack foods to taste preferences around the world. For example, Janjaree Thanma directs marketing research for Frito-Lay in Thailand. Interestingly, after testing 500 flavors for its chips with Thai consumers, the results showed that their preference was for U.S. flavors, such as barbecue.

GLOBAL STRATEGY

A **global strategy** stresses worldwide consistency, standardization, and relatively low cost.[14] Subsidiaries in various countries are highly interdependent in terms of goals, practices, and operations. As much as possible, top managers focus on coordination and mutual support of the firm's worldwide activities. For example, a Black & Decker subsidiary in one country might manufacture certain parts for families of products; subsidiaries in other countries do the same with regard to other parts. The subsidiaries then exchange components to complete assembly of their particular products. Profit targets vary for each subsidiary, reflecting its importance to the company's total system.

The customers of global firms have needs that are basically similar in many countries. Thus primary marketing strategies are highly transferable across national boundaries. For example, the marketing of Intel's Pentium chips to computer manufacturers in various countries has many similarities. Customers' technical standards are relatively compatible, and, for the most part, governments don't regulate computer chip production and sales practices. American Express Company also realizes the benefits of a global strategy by emphasizing the ideas of quality, security, and safety. One of American Express's goals is to create the world's most respected brand name. Travelers around the world recognize the reliability and quality symbolized by the American Express logo. Travelers who encounter trouble can go to any American Express office for emergency replacement of traveler's checks or lost or stolen credit cards. In addition, all offices are equipped to send emergency telegrams and messages to families, consulates, and other contacts for people in need of such services.

An increasing number of multinational corporations are using global strategies. They include Caterpillar and Komatsu (heavy construction equipment); Kodak and Fuji (film); and Texas Instruments, Intel, and Hitachi (semiconductors). As demonstrated in the following Strategic Action Competency feature, Boeing, the world's largest commercial aircraft manufacturer, uses this strategy. In 1999, its $57,993 billion in sales earned Boeing a profit of $2,309 billion dollars.[15]

STRATEGIC ACTION COMPETENCY

Boeing

Since its beginnings in 1916, Boeing has consistently been known for its line of aircraft, such as its World War II and Cold War bombers and its commercial 727, 737, 747, 757, 767, and 777 jets. Its planes are used by most nations' commercial airlines. It has remained America's number one exporter for the past 5 years, deriving more than half of its sales from customers outside the United States. Since the late 1980s, Boeing has faced a growing challenge from Airbus. With the ongoing financial assistance of several European countries, Airbus has steadily increased its market share at Boeing's expense. Boeing acquired its

U.S. rival, McDonnell-Douglas, to boost sales in the medium-range aircraft market (less than 2,000 miles). Still with the steady rise of Airbus and potentially new companies in Japan, China, and elsewhere, Boeing faces fierce competition. To maintain its share of the market, Boeing has identified four pillars of its global strategy: R&D investment, economies of scale, focused global marketing, and product enhancement.

The cost of designing and developing a new plane, such as the 777, exceeds $4 billion. This huge development cost serves as a great barrier to entry and keeps many other manufacturers,

such as Lockheed Martin, from entering the commercial airplane industry. Boeing's commitment to learning and using state-of-the-art computer-aided design (CAD), metallurgy, electronics, and low-cost assembly techniques are invaluable in reinforcing Boeing's ability to tackle complex engineering problems.

Manufacturing and assembly of key aircraft components are highly capital-intensive operations whose costs need to be spread over many aircraft. To ensure both high quality and low assembly cost, Boeing has concentrated most of its key component, assembly, and systems integration operations near its main plant in Seattle, Washington. All assembly operations take place in Boeing's Everett, Washington, plant, which covers more than 40 acres. This one plant can assemble more than 400 planes a year. Using the latest in computer-aided manufacturing (CAM) techniques, Boeing can now build wings for its 777 airframe in 10 days, as opposed to 80 days in the past. It also uses composite materials that are stronger and lighter than metal beams in constructing the aircraft's frame.

Boeing prides itself on having developed aggressive global marketing teams. These teams are able to match customers' needs with Boeing's aircraft and provide generous financing and pricing terms to the customer. Effective global marketing requires a highly sophisticated, knowledgeable, and well-trained sales force to keep Airbus and other rivals (e.g., Embraer and Bombardier) from reaching new customers. It maintains parts at various locations throughout the world to avoid maintenance failures and minimize downtime. It has even set up satellite offices at British Airways, Lufthansa, and Japan Airlines, to ensure that these customers receive the latest technical developments and immediate servicing of their aircraft.

Finally, Boeing continuously seeks ways to improve its planes. For example, it has several variations of its popular 737 line to meet the special needs of Southwest Airlines and other low-cost carriers. Each plane features some variations, but they are made without sacrificing the common design, which makes for easy service and parts replacement.

• • •

To learn more about Boeing, visit the company's home page at

http://www.boeing.com

Various needs must be addressed for a multinational's global strategy to be successful.[16] The following are six such needs.

1. The firm needs to be a significant competitor in the world's most important regional markets—North America, Europe, and Asia.

2. Most new goods and services need to be developed for the whole world—such as American Express Company's financial services and Kodak's film and related products.

3. Profit targets need to be based on product lines—such as Boeing's line of jet aircraft—rather than countries or regions of the world.

4. Decisions about products, capital investment, R&D, and production need to be based on global considerations—such as Kodak's and Fuji's strategic location of plants for producing film and related products in various regions of the world.

5. Narrow-minded attitudes—such as "this isn't how we operate here"—need to be overcome. Some ways to shape work-related attitudes and values include training employees to think globally, sending them to various countries for first-hand exposure, and giving them the latest information technology. Merrill Lynch recently spent more than $800 million on 25,000 state-of-the-art workstations. The upgraded technology will further enhance the ability of employees to communicate with each other and the firm's customers, almost on a real-time basis throughout the world.

6. Foreign managers need to be promoted into senior ranks at corporate headquarters.

POLITICAL–LEGAL FORCES

3.

EXPLAIN THE IMPACT OF POLITICAL–LEGAL FORCES ON INTERNATIONAL BUSINESS.

Organizations that engage in international business must cope with a web of political and legal issues. Therefore management must diagnose these issues accurately in order to understand the risks and uncertainties involved in international business. Recall from Chapter 3 that managers may use one or more of five political strategies—negotiation, lobbying, alliance, representation, and socialization—to reduce political risk.

Political risk is the probability that political decisions or events in a country will negatively affect the long-term profitability of an investment. Of concern to all international and global corporations is the political risk associated with resource commitments in foreign countries.[17]

ASSESSING POLITICAL RISK

Political risk factors may be grouped into five principal categories: domestic instability, foreign conflict, political climate, economic climate, and corruption. As Figure 4.2 shows, managers may estimate the seriousness of the political risk associated with conducting business in a country by assessing various factors in each category.

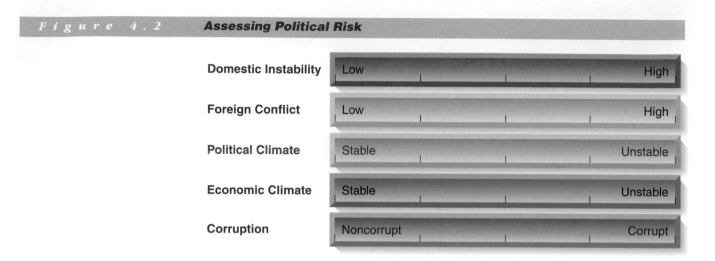

Figure 4.2 **Assessing Political Risk**

Domestic instability is the amount of subversion, revolution, assassinations, guerrilla warfare, and government crisis in a country. Haiti and Fiji have histories of domestic instability that have generally discouraged foreign investment.

Foreign conflict is the degree of hostility that one nation expresses to others. Such hostility can range from the expulsion of diplomats to outright war. The invasion of Kuwait by Iraq is one of the more dramatic recent examples. In August 1990, then President George Bush determined that the actions of the government of Iraq were an unusual and extraordinary threat to the national security and foreign policy of the United States. Under authority granted by the U.S. Export Administration Act of 1979, the government imposed a ban on trade with Iraq, which directly affected many firms. This ban and the tensions with Iraq continue. The political risk for Iraq is very high.

Political climate is the likelihood that a government will swing to the far left or far right politically. Managers may evaluate variables such as the number and size of political parties, number of factions in the legislature, role of the military in the political process, amount of corruption in government, effectiveness of political leadership, influence of organized religion in politics, extent of racial and nationality tensions, and quality of the governmental bureaucracy. Currently, Russia is considered to have a risky political climate because of the instability of its government, opposing political forces, and widespread corruption.

The **economic climate** reflects the extent of government control of markets and financial investments, as well as government support services and capabilities. These factors include government regulatory and economic control policies (wages, prices, imports, and exports); government ability to manage its own economic affairs (inflation, budget surpluses or deficits, and amount of debt); government provision of support services and facilities (roads, airports, electricity, water, and refuse and sewage disposal), often referred to as *infrastructure;* and government capabilities in general.

Corruption relates to the degree to which institutions, including the government, are perceived to be untrustworthy, are open to bribes, and conduct fraudulent business practices.[18] Corruption in the United States, Canada, and other Western countries is viewed as wrong. Recently the corruption of key Japanese and Korean government officials led to their leaving their government posts. However, former Indonesian President Suharto and his family are worth more than $15 billion, despite his annual salary of $36,000. Many people believe that the family wealth was acquired from corrupt business practices, such as Baligate.

Transparency International has compiled a Corruption Perception Index from research on 99 countries.[19] Although this list is based on perceptions rather than actual corruption, it is a good proxy for corruption in a country. This index is widely used by organizations and the U.S. government in making judgments about business practices in countries. As shown in Table 4.2, both Denmark and Finland are perceived as less corrupt than the United States and that Nigeria and Cameroon are among the most corrupt nations.

Table 4.2	Corruption Perceptions
Country Rank*	**Country**
1	Denmark
2	Finland
5	Canada
18	United States
25	Japan
36	Greece
45	Brazil
58	Mexico and China
72	India
82	Russia
98	Nigeria
99	Cameroon

*Ranked from least corrupt (1) to most corrupt (99).

The U.S. government has had a greater tendency than most other governments to impose export controls unilaterally as a way to advance its foreign policy. Opponents claim that unilateral export controls cost U.S. businesses billions of dollars per year in sales. Pressure groups continually lobby the U.S. government to impose sanctions on various countries, which generally means limiting the ability of U.S.-headquartered companies to do business with or in those countries. The Teamsters, International Ladies Garment Workers Union, and International Longshoremen's Association, among other unions, want trade sanctions invoked against countries that don't follow U.S. labor standards. Environmental groups want sanctions applied to countries that violate environmental standards. Human rights groups want sanctions imposed to combat political oppression. Many of these groups aren't content for the sanctions to restrict the activities of U.S. companies only. They also want to target every company in every foreign country that trades with the nation whose actions offend their sensibilities. For example, consider some of the political challenges that Nike has faced.

WEB INSIGHT

Is your college or university a member of the Worker Rights Consortium? You can find out by visiting the organization's Web site at *http://www.workersrights.org*. Learn more about the codes of conduct that have been developed by students like yourself to ensure that goods are produced under conditions that respect the basic rights of workers.

- The company has raised wages and barred children from working at its overseas plants, but students at the University of Oregon and Michigan endorse a Worker Rights Consortium. Backed by organized labor, this group makes surprise visits to Third World factories and demands "fair living wages." Students protested its athletes wearing the Nike swoosh and demanded that their universities cancel contracts with Nike.

- Nike found itself in an international firestorm over human rights issues in Indonesia and agreed to open schools and pay for the education of children from poor families working in its plants.

In Algeria, where foreigners—and journalists—are favorite assassination targets, expatriate workers sign on for a soldier's life. Bechtel employees, working on a major international pipeline project, lived in compounds protected by trenches, barbed wire fences, and guard towers. No women, children, or visits to neighboring towns were allowed.

Shell, the largest foreign operator in Nigeria, came under fire from human rights groups that called—in vain—for the giant oil company to withdraw from the country. If Shell had agreed, withdrawal would have been very difficult because it has been working in Nigeria, Africa's most populous nation, for 60 years. Shell and its partners employ 5,000 workers and produce half the oil produced in Nigeria, which is a member of OPEC.

The federal Overseas Private Investment Corporation (OPIC) sells risk insurance and lends money to U.S. companies venturing into politically risky countries. According to Ruth Harkin, president of OPIC, since 1992, the agency has sold $1.6 billion worth of political-risk insurance for 40 different overseas oil and gas projects. "We will go up to $200 million per project," Harkin said. "And we'll charge you plenty for it too, but nonetheless, it's worth it. I can assure you."

The following Planning and Administration competency feature highlights the political risk facing Robert Wilson, CEO of the Rio Tinto Corporation, a mining company headquartered in London.[20] It has operations in 40 countries around the world and employs more than 34,000 people. Its annual sales and profits exceed $9.3 billion and $1.2 billion, respectively. Wilson believes that, during the past 30 years, the nature of political risk has changed for corporations. In the 1970s and 1980s, the main political risk for global firms was the possibility that foreign government would impose unilateral profit restrictions on firms operating on their soil. In the 1990s, the greatest political risks involved were the challenge of creating good relationships with key elected government officials and forecasting public opinion. The countries posing the greatest political risk for Rio Tinto are Australia and the United States.

PLANNING & ADMINISTRATION COMPETENCY

Rio Tinto Corporation

Why the United States? Environmentalism. It took more than 20 years to get a copper-mining project approved in Wisconsin. During that time, Rio Tinto went through four public hearings and interminable reviews. The public's support for the project went from strong to very weak. In the end, Wilson and his staff faced people who opposed development at any cost. The environmentalists were concerned about water use, pollution, and other factors that might harm the environment. Some of them were elected to local government offices and the state legislature by Wisconsin voters during this time and became a driving force that Rio Tinto has to contend with in their attempts to pass stringent anti-pollution legislation.

How does Rio Tinto manage its political risks? First, it does not make po-

litical donations to any political party because there is the risk that the government will change. When Rio Tinto started its Escondida project in Chile, the military junta controlled the country. When Chile returned to democratically elected government in the late 1980s the government was unstable. To avoid making donations to any of the political parties, Rio Tinto's managers set up financing arrangements that took sales revenues offshore. They also brought in firms from three different countries to broaden the range of firms and countries involved with the project.

Second, Rio Tinto tries to gain support of people in local communities, especially doctors and educators. In other words Rio Tinto establishes open communication so that people in the community can see it as a productive force. Local managers are given the authority

to solve problems locally without bringing everything back to headquarters. For example, when there was a movement to unionize the workforce at the Gordonstone coal mine in Queensland, Australia, the local mining managers met with workers in an attempt to maintain production at the mine during organizing and negotiating efforts.

Third, investments are always made in U.S. dollars, rather than pounds sterling because sterling prices fluctuate and have been devalued against the dollar. For the investor, this approach takes some of the economic risk out of their investment decisions.

• • •

To learn more about Rio Tinto, visit the company's home page at

http://www.riotinto.com

POLITICAL MECHANISMS

Governments and businesses utilize a variety of political strategies, as we discussed in Chapter 3, to cope with political and legal forces. In this section, we go beyond those strategies to explain two significant types of international political mechanisms: (1) protectionism and (2) bribery and extortion. We support neither but want you to be aware of actual practices that you are bound to encounter someday in international business.

Protectionism. *Protectionism* refers to the many mechanisms designed to help a home-based industry or firms avoid (or reduce) potential (or actual) competitive or political threats from abroad. Tariffs, quotas, subsidies, and cartels are among the most widely used political mechanisms. Protectionism has both strong advocates and opponents. Generally, it works against consumers' interests by raising prices. Advocates claim that it protects home-country industries and jobs against unfair competition from countries with subsistence wages and special subsidies. Therefore whether companies, business associations, and employee groups favor or oppose a particular protectionist measure depends on how it may affect their particular interests.

A *tariff* is a government tax on goods or services entering the country. Its primary purpose is to raise the price of imported goods or services. As a result, domestic goods and services gain a relative price advantage. The sugar lobby in the United States is very powerful. Sugar growers seek to protect their market by pouring millions of dollars into political campaigns and being rewarded with special tariffs and import quotas to protect their industry. The intent of these protective measures, which have existed for more than 50 years, is to preserve about half the domestic market for U.S. sugar producers. As a result, U.S. consumers pay about three times the world price for sugar.

Heartland-By-Products, a Michigan producer of molasses, imports a sugar-molasses mixture from Canada. An agreement with the U.S. Customs Service in 1995 stipulated that this mixture was not covered by sugar restrictions, and Customs approved its importation without levying the sugar tariff. Recently, the Customs Service, under pressure from sugar lobbyists and Senator John Breaux of Louisiana, reversed its decision and indicated that Heartland would have to pay a tariff on its imported mixture, claiming that the company was "smuggling sugar into the country in the form of molasses." The price Heartland now pays for sugar imported from Canada rose 7,000 percent. Heartland is now in the courts trying to overturn this decision.[21]

A *quota* is a restriction on the quantity of a country's imports (or sometimes, on its exports). Import quotas generally are intended to guarantee home-country manufacturers access to a certain percentage of the domestic market. Most experts agree that, if protectionism is politically unavoidable, tariffs are preferable to quotas. The reason is that quotas fix the levels of imports entering a country and thus freeze markets. Labor unions and members of Congress have argued against further opening of U.S. markets at a time of trade deficits, arguing that quotas protect U.S. industries from low-cost manufacturing abroad. However, if quotas were lifted, domestic producers would then have to become more productive and efficient to maintain market share. Quotas are a hidden tax on consumers, whereas tariffs are a more obvious tax.

A *subsidy* is a direct or indirect payment by a government to domestic firms to make selling or investing abroad cheaper for them—and thus more profitable. Indirect payments are illustrated by some of OPIC's activities. This self-sustaining U.S. government agency helps qualified U.S. investors establish commercial projects in developing countries by offering reinvestment assistance and financing. Its political-risk insurance program provides coverage for eligible projects against losses from government seizure of assets; nonconvertibility of local currency into U.S. dollars; and damage caused by war, revolution, insurrection, or strife.

Many countries provide subsidies to farmers whose products are then able to compete on price in global markets. Consider the worldwide average subsidies given to farmers for six products: wheat, 48 percent; rice, 86 percent; sugar (refined white), 48 percent; beef, 35 percent; and pork, 22 percent.

A **cartel** is an alliance of producers engaged in the same type of business, which is formed to limit or eliminate competition and control production and prices.[22] Governments impose tariffs and quotas and grant subsidies. In contrast, cartels operate under agreements negotiated between firms or governments, as in the case of OPEC. A primary goal of any cartel is to protect its members' revenues and profits by controlling output and therefore prices. International cartels currently exist in oil, copper, aluminum, natural rubber, and other raw materials. The best-known cartel is OPEC, which was formed in 1960. The recent history of the oil industry and OPEC clearly demonstrates that cartels often face uncertainty and have to cope with rebellion among their members. In recent years, OPEC hasn't been very effective in controlling oil production by member countries. Some members, especially Nigeria and Venezuela, often can't agree on prices or quantities to be produced. Law forbids U.S. firms to form or participate directly in cartels because their purpose is at odds with preserving competitive markets and individual rights based on private property.

Bribery and Extortion. A **bribe** is an improper payment made to induce the recipient to do something for the payer. Bribes are illegal in Canada and the United States but not in some countries. By offering a bribe, the payer hopes to obtain a special favor in exchange for something of value (e.g., money, a trip, or a car). In recent years, the growing moral revulsion against bribery and other forms of corruption has swept politicians from office in Brazil, Italy, and Japan. In Italy, state prosecutors exposed an elaborate web of relationships among the Mafia, politicians, and business executives. Bids for highways, sewers, and other public projects now come in as much as 40 percent below past bids for comparable projects. However, this example is not to suggest that Italy—or any country for that matter—is free from political and business corruption.

Extortion is a payment made to ensure that the recipient doesn't harm the payer in some way. The purpose of extortion is to obtain something of value by threatening harm to the payer. When Coca-Cola entered the Russian market, it refused to respond to extortion efforts by the Russian Mafia. In retaliation, the Russian Mafia launched a bazooka attack on the bottling plant that Coca-Cola was building in Moscow. In addition, the Mafia attempted to intimidate many of the company's Russian distributors.

Bribery and extortion are practiced throughout the world. These practices occur most frequently in Indonesia, Azerbaijan, Honduras, Tanzania, Yugoslavia, and several other countries. In fact, some countries culturally define certain forms of bribery and extortion as an acceptable, appropriate, and expected form of gift giving. Belgium, France, Sweden, Greece, and Germany allow or tolerate the tax deductibility of foreign bribes. The United Nations and the World Bank are attempting to get members to criminalize bribery and extortion—as has the U.S. government.

The U.S. Foreign Corrupt Practices Act of 1977 makes it a crime for U.S. corporations or individuals to offer or make payments to officials of foreign governments or companies for the purpose of obtaining or retaining business.[23] The act established specific record-keeping requirements for publicly held corporations, making difficult the concealment of political payments prohibited by the act. Violators—both corporations and individuals—face stiff penalties. A company may be fined as much as $1 million, and a manager who directly participates in or has knowledge of any violations of the act faces up to 5 years in prison and/or $100,000 in fines. Furthermore, the act prohibits corporations from paying any fines imposed on their directors, managers, employees, or agents.

The act doesn't prohibit grease payments to employees of foreign governments whose duties are primarily procedural or clerical. **Grease payments** are small payments—almost gratuities—used to get lower level government employees to speed up required paperwork. Such payments may be required to persuade employees to perform their normal duties. Prohibiting grease payments would put U.S. firms at an extreme competitive disadvantage when conducting business abroad. Such a prohibition also would be very difficult to enforce. For example, Paul Gimona of Rome, Italy, is a manufacturer's representative and sole distributor of a high-tech Swedish oil flow detector. His territory includes the United Arab Emirates, Egypt, and other Mideast oil-producing countries. To get his company's device installed in pipelines as they are built, he must pay an unofficial fee to local officials who then approve the projects.

GLOBAL TRADE AGREEMENTS

4.

DISCUSS HOW THREE MAJOR TRADE AGREEMENTS AFFECT GLOBAL COMPETITION.

We discussed five competitive forces in Chapter 3: competitors, new entrants, substitute goods and services, customers, and suppliers. These forces apply whether a firm competes locally (say, in the Denver, Colorado, area), nationally (say, in Mexico), regionally (say, in Europe), or worldwide. In this section we briefly review three significant agreements that directly affect one or more of the five competitive forces. These agreements heighten the market-based competitive pressures on firms.

WORLD TRADE ORGANIZATION

The ***World Trade Organization*** (WTO) was established in 1995 as an outgrowth of the General Agreement on Tariffs and Trade (GATT).[24] This agreement represented a series of negotiated understandings regarding trade and related issues among the participating countries. Twenty-three countries signed the first GATT in 1947. By 2005, world trade in merchandise and commercial services is forecasted to exceed $8 trillion (1 trillion is 1,000 billion), or $2 trillion more than in 2000.

The WTO has 136 member countries, which account for about 95 percent of world trade. The key functions of the WTO include

- administering WTO trade agreements,
- providing a forum for trade negotiations,
- handling trade disputes between nations,
- monitoring national trade policies,
- providing technical assistance and training for people in developing countries, and
- cooperating with other international organizations, such as the European Union (EU), the Association of South East Asian Nations (ASEAN), and the association formed as a result of the North American Free Trade Agreement (NAFTA).

Three principles are fundamental to WTO operations. The *most favored nation principle* means that when country A grants a tariff concession to country B, the same concession automatically applies to all other countries that are members of WTO. The *reciprocity principle* means that each member country will not be forced to reduce tariffs unilaterally. A tariff concession is made only in return for comparable concessions from the other countries. The *transparency principle* means that tariffs are to be readily visible to all countries. Presumably, tariffs are the only permitted form of restriction. WTO doesn't allow internal taxes and regulations to be applied to imported goods if they aren't equally applied to domestic goods. However, there are exceptions to these principles. For example, the escape clause provides that, if a product is being imported into a country in such increased quantities that it causes or threatens to cause serious injury to domestic producers of that product, the importing country may temporarily increase the tariff on that product.

Under WTO provisions, trade negotiations also may take place directly between two or more countries. One significant trade dispute between the United States and China relates to the lack of enforcement of intellectual property rights.[25] Global losses caused by software piracy (mostly through direct copying of software products) were estimated at $16 billion in 2000. The economic incentives for pirates are huge. AutoCAD R12, for example, is a program that enables architects to design in three-dimensions. It would cost $4,000 if brought legally, but at the Golden Arcade in Hong Kong, it costs $100. If you have ever been to Hong Kong, the temptation to buy counterfeit CDs and other electronic gadgets is almost irresistible. In China, Russia, the Philippines, and 19 other countries, about 90 percent of the software sold in 2000 was illegally produced (pirated).

After intense negotiations that were filled with threats, China signed an accord in late 1995 to police and enforce U.S. intellectual property rights. As part of the agreement, China agreed to (1) establish at least 22 task forces to oversee an antipiracy campaign and (2) to consult with the United States regularly over a 3- to 5-year period. Specifically, China agreed to

- launch raids against retail outlets and inspect factories alleged to be engaging in piracy;

- strengthen penalties against enterprises found to be producing pirated products and increase the power of enforcers to crack down on violators;

- end quotas and licensing requirements on audiovisual and software imports; and

- allow audiovisual and computer software companies to form joint ventures in China.

Although progress has been made, critics claim that China hasn't vigorously enforced the provisions of the agreement. Trade controversies continue with China.

NORTH AMERICAN FREE TRADE AGREEMENT

The **North American Free Trade Agreement** (NAFTA) went into effect in 1994 to increase free trade among the United States, Canada, and Mexico. NAFTA essentially created a giant free-trade zone stretching from the Yukon to the Yucatan by removing barriers to trade, such as tariffs, quotas, and licenses among the United States, Canada, and Mexico. This free-trade zone covers more than 8.2 million square miles, 400 million consumers, and $600 billion in annual economic activity. NAFTA represents an extension of the Canada–United States Free Trade Agreement, which went into effect in 1989.[26]

Over a 15-year period, NAFTA is to reduce and eliminate numerous tariffs and most nontariff barriers among the three countries. Although full elimination of certain tariffs will not take place until 2009, over 70 percent of the goods imported from Mexico may now enter the United States without tariffs. At the same time, over 50 percent of U.S. exports to Mexico are now tariff-free. The agreement also realizes long-held goals of fostering trade in services and liberalizing foreign investment rules. NAFTA tightens the protection of intellectual property (copyrights, trademarks, and patents, in particular). Eighty-eight percent of Mexico's exports are now to the United States and Canada. The benefits to the United States and Canada are the ability of manufacturers to produce goods more cheaply, especially in maquiladora plants, and the ability to move raw materials easily among the three countries. **Maquiladora plants** are foreign-owned industrial plants located in Mexico that border the U.S. states of Texas, New Mexico, Arizona, and California. These plants employ more than 1.4 million people, house roughly 40 percent of Mexico's manufacturing, and pay more than five times Mexico's minimum wage.[27]

Although NAFTA further opened Canadian and U.S. markets, the most significant liberalization applies to Mexico. NAFTA expands Canadian and U.S. companies' ability to establish or purchase businesses in Mexico and increases their ability to sell if they want to leave. NAFTA loosens previous restrictions on expanding operations in Mexico and removes restrictions on transferring profits to other countries.

Despite much liberalization, NAFTA retains certain protectionist provisions, some of which may persist with no time limit. NAFTA temporarily protects sensitive industries (e.g., agriculture, minerals, banking, textiles, and apparel) by stretching out the phase-in time for lifting restrictions that apply to them. NAFTA also contains other types of protection that are permanent and appear to raise trade barriers above pre-NAFTA levels. In some industries—notably automobiles, textiles, and apparel—NAFTA imposes higher North American content rules. Under the previous Canada–United States Free Trade Agreement, for example, automobiles could be imported duty-free if they contained at least 50 percent Canadian and U.S. inputs. For auto imports to receive NAFTA benefits, the North American rule is now 62.5 percent. For textiles or apparel to qualify for "free" trade under NAFTA, all components—beginning with the yarn or fiber—must be produced in North America.

The service industries that received the most attention during NAFTA negotiations were finance, insurance, transportation, and telecommunications. NAFTA doesn't change requirements for foreign banks' entry into the United States and Canada. But the opening of the Mexican financial system is among the agreement's most significant achievements. Requirements for entry into brokerage, bonding, insurance, leasing, and warehousing were liberalized even more than they were for banking.

NAFTA and WTO certainly don't eliminate all trade problems among the member countries. But they do provide frameworks through which such problems can be resolved. By increasing the competitive forces that act on firms, the ultimate goals of WTO and NAFTA are to achieve greater efficiency and consumer satisfaction. However, as legal documents that were politically negotiated, they contain provisions, loopholes, and exceptions that will be tested over the decades to come. The provisions of these agreements no doubt will be welcomed or resisted, depending on their effect on a particular country, industry, labor organization, or firm.

The following Global Awareness Competency feature describes how Luis Avalos, CEO of Mabe, a $1 billion a year manufacturer of appliances in Mexico that employs more than 15,000 people, has been able to grow at annual rates of 15 to 20 percent since the passage of NAFTA.[28] Mabe exports refrigerators, ranges, heating elements, compressors, and washers to the United States, Canada, and Central and South American countries. Mabe manufactures these products for a variety of companies, including GE and IEM. It has been able to develop world-class manufacturing capabilities and innovative management practices under Avalos's leadership. This feature also highlights why Avalos chose to locate Mabe in Mexico instead of other Latin American countries.

GLOBAL AWARENESS COMPETENCY

Mabe

With the passage of NAFTA, Mexico has become a very competitive nation because of the low cost of labor, good relationships with unions, and well-trained engineers. To remain competitive, Mabe had to locate plants in areas of a country where there was an educated workforce. For example, Mabe had to have employees who could make products that met GE's demands for six-sigma quality. In Mexico, it is easy to find workers with at

least a high school education. A high school education provides them with a basis of general knowledge and level of mathematics that allows them to be trained. The engineering programs at Mexican universities are first rate, many comparable to those in the United States.

To ensure a high-quality workforce, Mabe invests heavily in training. At least 6 percent of an employee's working hours are spent in training. This emphasis on

training allows employees to become more specialized in their areas of expertise or to develop managerial competencies. The average Mexican employee at Mabe works a 45-hour week. Therefore, in 1 year, that employee receives about 3 weeks of training. At the new $250 million Mabe factory designed to build side-by-side-door refrigerators for export to the United States, employees are assigned to self-managed teams. Employees are trained in setting objectives, learning how to measure defects, assume responsibility for six-sigma-level quality, the amount of scrap, and equipment maintenance. Management clearly communicates Mabe's objectives, and team members become real doers.

Mexico does not have labor unions whose goals are based on antimanagement ideologies, such as those found in some other Latin American countries. Presently, labor unions are focusing on promoting job stability for their members. The benefits for Mabe are that

unions work with their members to help them arrive at work on time, be honest, and provide workplace stability. There is a sense of cooperation and consensus between management and unions. Mabe has also introduced scholarships for the unemployed in an area to help them develop the skills needed to enter or reenter the workforce.

• • •

To learn more about Mabe, visit the company's home page at

http://www.mabe.com.mx

EUROPEAN UNION

The ***European Union*** (EU), called the European Community (EC) until 1994, has 15 members: Austria, Belgium, Denmark, Finland, France, Germany, Greece, Ireland, Italy, Luxembourg, the Netherlands, Portugal, Spain, Sweden, and the United Kingdom. These countries are home to some 400 million consumers.[29] Additional countries that may soon join the EU are Hungary, Iceland, Poland, and the Czech Republic. The potential membership of other countries (Turkey, Slovakia, Estonia, Latvia, Lithuania, and other newly independent countries from the former Soviet Union) remains to be determined.

The goals of the European Union include creating a single market among member countries through the removal of trade barriers (e.g., tariffs) and establishing the free movement of goods, people, services, and capital. Implementation of activities to achieve these and other goals officially began at the end of 1992. In addition, the changes go beyond economic interests to include social changes as well. Educational degrees have already been affected. The EU Council of Ministers issued a directive that recognizes diplomas of higher education across national boundaries. This action makes it easier for professionals to work in different countries. Most member countries have developed master's degree programs in business administration that are compatible with the others' and those in the United States.

The EU clearly is more than an economic union: It is a state of mind and a political force. Eventually, it should lead to less government interference in economic activities. Meeting uniform quality standards and worker safety and environmental controls will be expected of all companies who trade in the EU. The ***International Organization for Standardization*** (ISO) issues certification standards for excellence in quality that serve a purpose similar to that of the Deming Prize in Japan and the Baldrige Award in the United States.

An essential stage of the EU program is to complete formation of a common internal market. That involves eliminating

1. physical barriers at each country's borders, which prevent the free flow of goods and people;

2. technical barriers, which prevent goods and services produced or traded in one member nation from being sold in others;

3. fiscal barriers, such as red tape and the different national tax systems, which hinder cross-border trade; and

4. financial barriers, which prevent the free movement of investment capital.[30]

The EU has introduced a common currency, the euro. Its valuation against the U.S. dollar is monitored by an independent central bank in Frankfurt, Germany. The value of the euro has been falling against the dollar, but merchants and others cannot accept the euro as payment for goods and service until 2002. Until then, each of the 15 member nations will continue to use its own currency in financial transactions.

The European Commission is the EU's executive body and sole initiator of legislation. The commission claims that 95 percent of the legislative measures set out in the 1992 program have been adopted. However, the toughest issues weren't addressed in the 1992 program, including agreement on a common immigration policy. Some member nations are concerned that they'll be flooded with immigrants as the result of an open door policy. As unemployment has risen in Eastern Europe, the frontiers of the EU have been tightened. It is now virtually impossible to enter the member nations legally as an economic migrant. An applicant rejected by one member nation can no longer apply to any other member nation.

The EU has already increased market opportunities, fostered competition, and encouraged competition from the outside. The removal of transnational trade restrictions and the relaxation of border controls based on economic restraints have had a considerable impact on U.S. and Canadian companies. For example, NBC, with no previous global experience, acquired controlling interest in Europe's Super Channel. It is now beaming its programs to about 65 million homes and hotels throughout Europe.

Many non-Europeans continue to be concerned that the supposedly free market of Europe will be anything but free to outsiders.[31] The EU Commission has pressured U.S. and Japanese firms to conduct more R&D and production in Europe or face the risk of increased tariffs and other barriers. Restrictions still apply to non-EU banks and security firms unless foreign countries (e.g., the United States, Canada, and Japan) grant reciprocal rights. These restrictions range from limiting the right to acquire banks in EU countries to special taxes on foreign banks operating there.

Various alternative strategies are available to U.S. and Canadian enterprises. One strategy is to export goods and services to the EU. In general, though, North American firms have had only limited success in doing so. The most successful strategy has been to set up subsidiaries or branches in one or more of the EU countries. The advantages of subsidiaries have been demonstrated by well-established companies such as Opel (a subsidiary of GM in Germany), Ford, and IBM. Some companies have consolidated their previous positions in Europe. For example, UPS purchased eleven companies in EU nations to strengthen its market position.

CULTURAL FORCES

5.

DESCRIBE HOW A COUNTRY'S CULTURE CAN AFFECT AN ORGANIZATION'S BUSINESS PRACTICES.

The cultural forces that we discussed in Chapter 3 underlie the day-to-day competitive and political forces operating within and among nations. Four aspects of a culture that have direct implications for international management are views of social change, time orientation, language, and value systems.

VIEWS OF SOCIAL CHANGE

Different views of the need for social change and its pace can have a significant impact on an organization's plans for international operations.[32] The people of many non-Western cultures, such as those of India, Saudi Arabia, and China, view change as a slow, natural progression. For them change is part of the evolution of human beings and the universe, guided by a Supreme Being, and the attitude toward it tends to be passive (or even reactive). In contrast, the people of Western cultures tend to view change differently. For them change can be shaped and controlled to achieve their own goals and aspirations, and the attitude toward it tends to be active. Therefore Western managers assigned to non-Western countries often run into difficulty when trying to introduce innovations too rapidly. In cultures that hold a passive/reactive view of change, new ways of doing things often must go hand in hand with a painstaking concern for their effect on interpersonal relationships. Moreover, people in nations such as India, Italy, and Turkey that are characterized by high uncertainty avoidance also are likely to resist or react cautiously to social change. Managers plunged into these cultures have to recognize this viewpoint, plan for it, and manage change accordingly.

TIME ORIENTATION

Many people in the United States and Canada think of time as an extremely scarce commodity. They often say that "time is money," or that "there is too little time." Several popular books on time management show an almost frenetic concern with how managers should plan their days. The need to set and stick to tight deadlines for accomplishing tasks is a basic tenet of this style of management.

In some cultures, however, time is viewed more as an unlimited and unending resource. For example, Hindus believe that time does not begin at birth or end at death. The Hindu belief in reincarnation gives life a nontemporal, everlasting dimension. Because of such attitudes, employees, customers, and suppliers in some cultures are quite casual about keeping appointments and meeting deadlines—an indifference that can be highly frustrating to Canadian and U.S. managers who have to deal with them.

Traditionally, the Mexican attitude toward time can best be summed up in the word mañana, meaning "not today"—but not necessarily tomorrow either! A manager in Mexico might say, Yes, your shipment will be ready on Tuesday. You arrive on Tuesday to pick it up but find that it isn't ready. No one is upset or embarrassed; they say politely that the paperwork hasn't been processed yet or offer some other explanation. Time commitments are considered desirable but not binding promises. However, this attitude toward time is changing among Mexican businesspeople and professionals. As lifestyles become more complex and pressures for greater productivity increase, many more people in Mexico are paying attention to punctuality and meeting time commitments.

LANGUAGE

Language serves to bind as well as to separate cultures.[33] Fluency in another language can give an international manager a competitive edge in understanding and gaining the acceptance of people from another culture. However, the ability to speak a language correctly isn't enough: A manager must also be able to recognize and interpret the nuances of phrases, sayings, and nonverbal gestures.

The story is told of several U.S. executives who were trying to negotiate with their Japanese counterparts. The American head negotiator made a proposal. The Japanese head negotiator was silent. His silence meant that he was considering the offer. The American, however, took his silence to mean that the offer wasn't good enough. So the American raised the offer! Again the Japanese considered in silence, and again the silence prompted the American to raise the offer. Finally, the American reached his limit, and an agreement was struck. The Japanese head negotiator had obtained several concessions simply because the American negotiator had misread his silence.

The following Teamwork Competency feature provides additional perspective on the need to be sensitive to unique patterns of language and communication with those from other cultures.[34] As you will read, Marianne Torrcelli at AT&T experienced some difficulties in managing global teams. Because top management wants to groom global managers, managers must understand the behaviors of people in various parts of the world and learn how to lead these people effectively. To be successful, a manager in the global economy must understand the effect of diverse cultures on organizational behavior—not always an easy task.

TEAMWORK COMPETENCY

Marianne Torrcelli of AT&T

"The U.S. team members are driven by the exact dates on the schedule," explained Marianne Torrcelli, leader of a U.S. AT&T team working in Mexico and the United Kingdom. "The team members are disappointed and feel a sense of urgency when the schedule is not met. We believe that 'Time is Money,' and that missed dates equate to potential jeopardy in project completion, which results in lost revenue. To prevent that, the U.S. AT&T team responds quickly to emergency situations, focuses on critical issues, engages additional resources, and works overtime. The job takes priority over family."

"But in Mexico," Torrcelli observed, "as long as work items are being addressed—even if they are not on schedule—the U.S. team members feel comfortable that they will be completed at some point. The 'schedule' is not in jeopardy. We understand that in Mexico there isn't a sense of urgency the U.S. AT&T team members feel when critical task delivery times are missed. The 'mañana syndrome' is real. The Mexican team members have an outstanding commitment and dedication to the project, but they place their family before work. The work can be done 'mañana.'"

"It's different in the UK. Their employees understand the concept of 'schedule' the way Americans do. They also understand the need to complete tasks on time and that when an emergency situation arises, the team members need to respond quickly. But the British team members maintain a balance between work and their personal lives. For example, they never work extensive overtime to resolve a critical issue."

• • •

To learn more about AT&T, visit the company's home page at

http://www.att.com

VALUE SYSTEMS

In Chapter 3, we discussed the importance of value systems and described five value dimensions: power distance, uncertainty avoidance, individualism (versus collectivism), masculinity (versus femininity), and Confucian dynamism. Obviously, differences in cultural values affect how managers and professionals function in international business.

Because of continuing interest in the competitive challenge of Japanese firms, let's look at some of the differences in Japanese and U.S. values and a few of the management implications of these differences. Although the Japanese economy has been in a recession and the halo of the superiority of Japanese management has been tarnished, Japan is still a major trading partner of many industrialized nations around the world.

U.S. and Japanese Societies. *Collectivism* means that people identify strongly with the groups to which they belong—from the family unit to the society as a whole. It emphasizes group goals and interdependence with others. Groups aren't thought of as collections of individuals. Rather, groups exist first and absorb individuals into them. Consequently, the individual is governed by the norms (rules) of each group. The Japanese form of collectivism leads to greater group cohesion than is usually found in the United States. The short-term sacrifice of the individual's wants for the benefit of the group is commonly accepted. As a result, Japanese achievements tend to be group-oriented. Furthermore, because the Japanese value system is less diverse than that in the United States, severe conflicts caused by underlying differences in values occur less frequently.

There is now a profound shift in the mood of Japanese.[35] The economic slide of the 1990s was rooted in Confucian values in which deference to authority and Japan's dedication to growth were the bases of many business decisions. Top managers at banks and telecommunications (especially NTT), long the most protected of all industries, fear that their fail-safe guarantees are gone. Banks and other institutions are restructuring themselves to survive, which has allowed "outsiders" to begin to influence Japan's cultural values. A top running Japanese television show, *Money Angels*, focuses on financial advice. The show's sponsors, the U.S. investment bank Goldman, Sachs, and Company, is selling millions of dollars in mutual funds and raising money for Japanese companies needing cash. In 2000, foreign investment in Japan was running at a rate some three times faster than in 1999. The presence of more foreign corporations is also casting traditional Japanese banks in an unfavorable light because Japanese investors are earning three times more on their investments than in their own banks.

Japan's silent majority is using the Internet to voice opinions directly to the media instead of following Confucian values dictating that people obey their elders and not question their orders.[36] For example, Toshiba Corporation recently issued a public apology to an irate customer who assailed the electronics giant on the Internet because of shoddy workmanship on a videocassette recorder. In Kobe, the local government ignored a citizens' group opposed to a new airport until it went on the Internet. In Japan as in other societies, information now equals power.

U.S. and Japanese Organizations. The fundamental societal differences that we've been discussing are reflected in some very basic differences between U.S. and Japanese organizations. Do these differences mean that U.S. or Japanese managers can't transfer to their organizations any of the ideas that have worked so well in each other's countries? Not at all.[37] Several Japanese management practices—such as the widespread use of team management and quality control—have been successfully adapted to U.S. operations. Over the years, U.S. organizations have created their versions of team management that reflect the need for timely decision making. Some Japanese organizations are now adopting some of these modifications.

In identifying differences between the two nations' organizations and management practices, we are painting with a broad brush. Table 4.3 broadly characterizes and compares U.S. and Japanese organizations based on six dimensions that are strongly influenced by the contrasting values of the two nations. The themes of individualism in the

Table 4.3	Tendencies of Many U.S. and Japanese Organizations	
Dimensions	**Many (Not All) Major U.S. Organizations**	**Many (Not All) Major Japanese Organizations**
Employment	Short term on average, but varies widely; unstable and insecure	Long term for males (recent decline in lifetime employment); moderately secure and stable
Salary and promotion	Merit pay based on individual contribution; rapid promotion in career	Seniority-based early in career; more merit pay later
Attitude toward work	Individual responsibilities	Collective responsibilities; group loyalty, duty-oriented
Decision making	Individual-oriented; relative top-down emphasis	Consultation oriented; bottom-up emphasis
Relationship with employees	Depersonalized; emphasis on formal contacts	Personalized; employee treated more as family member; paternalism
Competition	Relatively free and open among individuals	Low among individuals within groups; high among groups

United States and collectivism in Japan are readily apparent. The word "lifetime" employment is misleading because employment doesn't last for a lifetime; most workers in Japan must leave their job between the ages of 55 and 60 according to law. Guaranteeing employment was no problem when the economy was growing at an annual rate of 10 percent.

Job security (e.g., "lifetime" employment) is possible for three reasons: First, Japanese corporations pay their employees a bonus, typically twice a year. Corporations are allowed to pay a small bonus in a bad year or even defer the payment of a bonus to the second year. Therefore full-time employees tend to stay even when times are tough. Second, firms use temporary workers, mostly women, who are immediately laid off when business slows. Third, large Japanese firms, such as Mitsubishi, Mitsui, Toyota, Nissan, Hitachi, Matsushita, and Toshiba are core members of *keiretsu* systems (industrial groupings), and they act as a parent to other members of the group. A parent company guarantees purchases and financial, managerial, and technological assistance in exchange for shares of stock and other financial arrangements. These core members often use member firms as buffers and assign workers to them. Therefore, when the automobile slump hit Japanese companies in 1998, the major companies controlled their payrolls by slashing overtime, eliminating wage increases, freezing new hires, and encouraging early retirement.[38]

Changing Patterns. Exceptions to the traditional patterns in Japanese organizations are becoming more numerous. One of the consequences of so-called lifetime employment is that Japanese companies kept mediocre employees. In Japan, the primary objective of a firm was not to increase shareholders' wealth, but to protect employee welfare. However, the shares of a large number of corporations are now traded on the Tokyo Stock Exchange, and their shareholders want a decent return on their money. Thus shareholders are no longer tolerating a no-layoff policy that restricts the reallocation of assets and weakens the company's financial base.

Highly capable and assertive individuals do leave their organizations and start businesses of their own or join smaller organizations. In the past, firms started by individualistic entrepreneurs included Honda, Sony, and Matsushita. Small Japanese enterprises (300 or fewer employees) can't afford to offer extensive fringe benefits, as do the giant corporations. Small firms also are able to offer less job security because they are less secure in their markets. Owing to the recent recession in Japan, even large corporations such as Toyota have had to create a new category of temporary (contract) professional workers and have had to (painfully) lay off regular employees.

Some young Japanese workers aren't as devoted as the preceding generation is to long hours of hard work. Many young Japanese realize that some aspects of Western lifestyles are preferable to their own. Some accept the concept of flexible individualism—not the rugged U.S. variety but a simple desire for self-expression in their work, lifestyles, and possessions. Husband and wife now sometimes share child rearing and other household duties, once relegated completely to women. Materialism is leading some families to have two wage earners. These trends in Japan appear to be a result of its increasingly global economic participation, which is modifying its once homogeneous culture.

CHAPTER SUMMARY

In this chapter, we focused on various global considerations for those engaging in international business. Organizations and individuals—both as employees and consumers—are increasingly touched by global forces and issues.

1. STATE SEVERAL CHARACTERISTICS OF THE GLOBAL ECONOMY.

Organizations are becoming more global in their operations, and globalization of commerce will continue to accelerate. Societies also are becoming more global. During this next decade, these shifts will affect organizations in several important ways. First, communication is instant, placing a premium on information; second, organizations are becoming boundaryless, with operations spanning the globe; third, governments are becoming more democratic; and fourth, there is highly skilled labor in many different parts of the world.

2. DESCRIBE SIX STRATEGIES USED BY ORGANIZATIONS IN INTERNATIONAL BUSINESS.

The strategies used by many international businesses include exporting, licensing, franchising, alliance, multidomestic, and global. These strategies vary in terms of their relative complexity (reflected in organization design) and resource commitments required to effectively implement the strategy. Organizations use different strategies over time as they learn how to adjust their operations to the demands of their global marketplaces.

3. EXPLAIN THE IMPACT OF POLITICAL–LEGAL FORCES ON INTERNATIONAL BUSINESS.

International business operations create new complexities, risks, and uncertainties. Broad political–legal issues include domestic instability, foreign conflict, political climate, economic climate, and corruption. Political mechanisms utilized in international business include tariffs, quotas, subsidies, cartels, bribes, and extortion.

4. DISCUSS HOW THREE MAJOR TRADE AGREEMENTS AFFECT GLOBAL COMPETITION.

The World Trade Organization (WTO) helps open markets and reduce barriers (e.g., tariffs) among its 136 member nations. The North American Free Trade Agreement (NAFTA) further reduces barriers, encourages investment, and stimulates trade among Canada, Mexico, and the United States. The European Union (EU) is an organization of 15 countries. Its primary goals are to create a single market and allow the free movement of goods, services, people, and capital among its members. The ultimate goal is to improve the standard of living and quality of life for the citizens of the member countries.

5. DESCRIBE HOW A COUNTRY'S CULTURE CAN AFFECT AN ORGANIZATION'S BUSINESS PRACTICES.

The primary cultural factors that can influence how an organization is managed include views of social change (passive or active), time (scarce or unlimited), language (verbal and nonverbal differences), and value systems (individualism versus collectivism). Special attention was given to understanding how cultural issues have led to differences in the management system in Japan and the United States.

KEY TERMS

Alliance strategy, p. 110

Bribe, p. 118

Cartel, p. 118

Corruption, p. 114

Countertrade, p. 109

Domestic instability, p. 114

Economic climate, p. 114

European Union, p. 122

Exporting strategy, p. 109

Extortion, p. 118

Foreign conflict, p. 114

Franchising strategy, p. 110

Global strategic alliances, p. 110

Global strategy, p. 112

Grease payments, p. 118

International Organization for Standardization, p. 122

Licensing strategy, p. 110

Maquiladora plants, p. 120

Multidomestic strategy, p. 111

North American Free Trade Agreement, p. 120

Political climate, p. 114

Political risk, p. 113

Profit center, p. 111

Protectionism, p. 117

Quota, p. 117

Subsidy, p. 117

Tariff, p. 117

World Trade Organization, p. 119

1. Identify at least three challenges facing Procter & Gamble.

2. What are some of the competencies you need to develop to become an effective global manager? How can your course work in school help you do so?

3. What are some of the problems facing the people of Japan?

4. What role do culture and society play in creating ethics for people in global organizations?

5. Suppose that Mabe wanted to open four new plants overseas. Name four countries that might represent a high degree of risk for such operations (go to *http://www.countrydata.com*). Would Mabe be better off exporting to those countries? Explain.

6. Has NAFTA been good or bad for U.S. manufacturing companies? What are two of the current problems for transportation companies under the NAFTA trade agreement?

7. Has the EU stimulated trade in Europe? How has it affected nations that are not members of the EU?

8. **Competency Development: Communication:** Imagine that you have just become an export manager of a firm and need to become fluent in Japanese during the next 6 months before beginning an assignment in Kyoto. Visit the Boston Language Institute at *http://www.boslang.com* and learn how you can become fluent in Japanese.

9. **Competency Development: Self-Management:** Overseas business etiquette and cross-cultural awareness can make or break a deal. The simple handshake in the United States needs to be replaced by a bow in Asia. Many Americans rush to eat lunch and do business. In Mexico managers view lunch as a time to relax and enjoy getting to know their colleagues. Lunch usually lasts several hours. How important is punctuality? What nonverbal gestures are appropriate? To determine the business etiquette in various countries, go to *http://www.globalprotocol.com*.

CASE FOR COMPETENCY DEVELOPMENT

Grant Gisel of Sierra Systems Consultants[39]

Grant Gisel has been president of Sierra Systems Consultants since 1973. Recently Sierra Systems ranked in the top 10 of Canada's 100 information technology service companies, according to a survey in the *Financial Post*. The firm provides information consulting services and has partnerships with PeopleSoft, SAP, Oracle, Microsoft, IBM, Netscape, and Sun Microsystems. Following are excerpts from a recent interview with Gisel.

What is the extent of your involvement in strategic alliances?
Strategic alliances are very important to Sierra. Before 1980, we really didn't have any alliances and were proud of this fact. However, during the last 8 or 9 years, our business strategy has evolved to the point where more than 50 percent of our revenue is related in some way to strategic alliances that we have created.

What was the motivation for forming alliances?
There are three primary reasons for Sierra's involvement. First is to provide better service to our customers. We look at relationships with IBM, SAP, and others as a way of bringing a more complete solution to their problem than Sierra could provide alone. Second, the alliances allowed us to take on bigger projects than we would have been able to undertake on our own. By partnering with others, we've been able to build a team that could take on much larger assignments than we would have

been able to do, or that was financially feasible. Third, alliances have allowed better professional opportunities for our staff to develop their managerial competencies.

Which alliances have been most difficult?
The most difficult parts of an alliance by and large revolve around projects where there has been money lost, and the remains must be divided between the alliance partners. There are sometimes difficulties and misunderstandings that surface as a result. But you should be working on trying, from a communications point of view, to make sure that those things don't happen. Often times we have done business with a partner before and think that we have an understanding of the project. Each new project needs to be carefully thought out.

What do you do to achieve success?
Sierra needs to know why we're doing this. That is, we need to undertake our motivation for forming an alliance and specifically state what Sierra can contribute. We must be realistic not to oversell. In the long term, trust and credibility will be a risk if this occurs. We try not to form too many alliances at once; we focus on quality relationships, not quantity. Forming an alliance with others who have a good track record in previous alliances is critical. We consider whether the partner has complementary capabilities, cultural compatibility, and good chemistry among members of senior management. We assess our strengths and weaknesses as well as those of our partner. We map out a

negotiating strategy in advance and determine which issues are nonnegotiable and which are flexible. We consider what is important to protect and outline key issues, such as management's role, ownership of intellectual property, fees of licensing and technology, marketing plans, and exit terms. Ensuring that Sierra and its partner have clearly defined responsibilities and agreed upon due dates for parts of the project to be completed is critical.

Often times, a client will try to play one partner off against another. If the partnership allows that to happen, it becomes very difficult to be successful. Whether we like it or not, as our industry gets involved in larger and larger projects, we're going to be involved in partnerships.

Finally, we develop a culture that suits the alliance, rather than borrowing the culture from the partners. That means spelling out the forms of communications (e-mail, fax, face-to-face meetings) to be used and means for resolving conflicts. Both parties need to staff the alliance with their best people. When we cross international boundaries, we always staff with people who have had international experience, multiple language skills, and if possible, who have lived in the country. We provide them with training and rewards for achieving the alliance's goals. Both partners need to support activities that will enable the alliance to grow and its people to learn.

Questions

1. Can the reasons for Sierra Systems Consultants entering into strategic alliances be applied to other firms? Go to *http://www.alexisgill.com* to learn how successful firms develop their employees' competencies to manage alliances effectively.

2. What political–legal issues might affect a partnership?

3. How has NAFTA helped Sierra grow?

Enforcement Technology

Enforcement Technology, Inc. (ETEC), provides online automated parking and traffic citation management systems and services for cities, counties, states, provinces, countries, colleges, and universities in both the United States and abroad. Since its incorporation in 1986, ETEC has expanded to serve more than 450 agencies in 50 states and eight countries. Today it is the worldwide leader in hand-held parking and traffic enforcement technology, manufacturing and servicing its own hardware and software.

The ETEC products are known worldwide as Automated Citation Management Systems (AutoCITE) and consist of two major systems. One is the Automated Citation Issuance System (AutoISSUE), the enforcement system used to issue parking and traffic citations in the field. These citations are then downloaded and compiled on a PC at a company office. The second system is the Automated Citation Processing and Collection System (AutoPROCESS), which provides all the processing and collection functions for the company's clients.

The ETEC parking enforcement service centers currently process more than 4 million parking citations a year. As part of their basic processing and collection contracts, they also provide follow-up on delinquent citations and citations issued to out-of-state vehicles. The company has been very successful in improving the collection rates (fines paid) for its clients throughout the world.

In the United States, ETEC provides all the services that a client might want because the firm has a good grasp of the U.S. market and its clients' needs. However, management knows that ETEC's continued growth and success internationally must be based on successfully serving unique markets throughout the rest of the world. This realization is reflected in its global strategies.

ETEC routinely engages in strategic alliances or partnerships when entering foreign markets. It applies a "when in Rome do as the Romans do" philosophy to its international ventures, believing that it must understand the market rather than try to change it to be more like the U.S. market. By having a local partner, ETEC gains immediate insights into the host nation's culture, laws, customs, and currency issues—all of which can have an impact on its products and how they are delivered.

ETEC practices a relatively simple global pricing strategy, whereby all prices are pegged to the U.S. dollar and all exchange rate risks are passed on to its customers. Finally, when deciding on which global markets to enter, ETEC enjoys the luxury of having potential clients approach the company. ETEC then decides which ventures best fit its overall global strategy.

Questions

1. Explain why ETEC chooses local partners for its operations in other countries.

2. Explain the international business strategy options from which ETEC must choose to compete internationally. Which method(s) does it utilize most often?

To learn more about Enforcement Technology, Inc., visit the company's home page at ***http://www.autocite.com***.

Entrepreneurship

LEARNING OBJECTIVES

AFTER STUDYING THIS CHAPTER YOU SHOULD BE ABLE TO:

1. EXPLAIN WHAT ENTREPRENEURS DO AND DESCRIBE HOW THE ENVIRONMENT SUPPORTS THEIR ACTIVITIES.

2. DESCRIBE THE PERSONAL CHARACTERISTICS THAT CONTRIBUTE TO ENTREPRENEURS' SUCCESS.

3. DESCRIBE THE PLANNING REQUIREMENTS ASSOCIATED WITH BECOMING A SUCCESSFUL ENTREPRENEUR.

4. RECOGNIZE INTRAPRENEURS AND THE ORGANIZATIONAL CHARACTERISTICS THAT ENCOURAGE INTRAPRENEURSHIP.

Chapter Outline

PREVIEW: YAHOO!

DEVELOPMENT OF ENTREPRENEURIAL ACTIVITY
WHAT IS AN ENTREPRENEUR?
HOW THE ENVIRONMENT ENCOURAGES ENTREPRENEURIAL ACTIVITY
SMALL-BUSINESS OWNERS
FAMILY BUSINESSES

CHARACTERISTICS OF ENTREPRENEURS
KEY PERSONAL ATTRIBUTES
GLOBAL AWARENESS COMPETENCY: Masayoshi Son Builds a Conglomerate from Start-Ups
TECHNICAL PROFICIENCY
MANAGERIAL COMPETENCIES
STRATEGIC ACTION COMPETENCY: Picture This
COMMUNICATION COMPETENCY: Estée Lauder Built an Image and a Brand
ASSESSING YOUR ENTREPRENEURIAL POTENTIAL
SELF-MANAGEMENT COMPETENCY: Your Entrepreneurial Quotient

PLANNING AND ENTREPRENEURSHIP
UNDERSTANDING YOUR MOTIVATIONS
DECIDING WHETHER TO START OR BUY A BUSINESS
ASSESSING THE MARKET
FINDING FUNDS
GOING GLOBAL?
MANAGING A FAMILY START-UP

ENTREPRENEURSHIP IN LARGE ORGANIZATIONS
INTRAPRENEURS
FOSTERING INTRAPRENEURSHIP

CHAPTER SUMMARY

KEY TERMS

QUESTIONS FOR DISCUSSION AND COMPETENCY DEVELOPMENT

CASE FOR COMPETENCY DEVELOPMENT: "AND NOW FOR SOMETHING COMPLETELY DIFFERENT"

VIDEO CASE: YAHOO!

YAHOO!

As graduate students at Stanford University, David Filo and Jerry Yang didn't have search engines to keep track of all the Web sites they found. As their list of interesting sites grew, they needed a way to sort and keep track of them. Out of necessity grew their invention—a search engine that locates material and software that classifies and organizes it all. When they first posted it for the public, visitors loved the site so much that the university's computer system couldn't support all the traffic! Pressured by university officials to find a company that was willing to host their service, Filo and Yang dropped out of their Ph.D. program and went into business. Their service went public under the name Yahoo!, meaning "Yet Another Hierarchical Officious Oracle," and was an instant success.

Yahoo!'s founders didn't progress from a student electronic filing system to a global portal whose pages are viewed by some 100 million people per month by accident. According to the venture capitalist who funded the Yahoo! start-up, "Jerry . . . wanted to build a business that is really lasting." Yang and Filo—the "Chief Yahoos"—were a team from the start, and they soon added others to it. They hired their CEO, Tim Koogle, the first year. Soon after, they hired COO Jeffrey Mallett. In the second year, the team began executing an advertising strategy. By the third year, they could focus on increasing revenue to fund further expansion.

Planning in the early years was difficult because they were creating a new market, so taking calculated risks was a part of everyday life. For example, they expected seasonal fluctuations in advertising costs, but they couldn't predict the pattern with any confidence. Cancellation of a few major advertising contracts could have had severe consequences, yet they couldn't let this risk deter them from investing heavily to pursue new opportunities.

The daily handling of such business issues falls mostly on the shoulders of Koogle and Mallett. Filo has the strongest technical skills, and he guides the team as it makes big strategic decisions about the content and structure of Yahoo!: "He's one of the best strategic thinkers we have and has great business instincts. We always listen to him because he has a great feel for how the products and technology can or can't scale up," explains Yang.

Global awareness also benefits Yahoo!. Yang was born in Taiwan and moved to the United States as a teenager. Both his language skills and knowledge of Asian cultures have proved useful. When he visited Beijing University to promote the company, he schmoozed with students, talking in Mandarin. By the time he returned home, he had negotiated a new partnership with Founder, a state-owned Chinese software maker.

In many ways, Yang is the "big picture guy," who dreams up visions of what the company can be and do. Yang says the biggest limitation they face is how fast they can come up with new ideas: "We're constrained by how fast our brains can work, more than anything else." Despite this constraint, investors seem confident that Yahoo! has successfully made the shift from a small start-up to a major player in a new industry.[1]

For additional information, visit the company's home page at

http://www.yahoo.com/info/investor/

DEVELOPMENT OF ENTREPRENEURIAL ACTIVITY

1.

EXPLAIN WHAT ENTREPRENEURS DO AND DESCRIBE HOW THE ENVIRONMENT SUPPORTS THEIR ACTIVITIES.

Entrepreneurial activity has long been a hallmark of the business scene in the United States. Although big business often gets more attention in the media, small start-ups have fueled the rapid economic growth of recent years.

WHAT IS AN ENTREPRENEUR?

Entrepreneurs are people who create new business activity in the economy. Often they do so by starting new companies. But they can also create new business activity by introducing a new product or creating a new market. Thus managers in large corporations engage in entrepreneurial activity when they develop new product lines or establish new divisions to enter markets they hadn't penetrated before. In the broadest sense, then, entrepreneurs manage resources in order to create something new—a new business, a new product or service, or even a new market.

Highly successful entrepreneurs often are differentiated from less successful entrepreneurs by how quickly they increase their new business activities. The most successful are those whose businesses grow most rapidly. They find market opportunities that others may have overlooked and form a vision of how to exploit these opportunities. They position themselves well in markets that are shifting or are untapped. In this sense, they are innovative and creative. They accurately predict the direction markets are moving and then prepare to serve those markets before others are ready to do so.

People often think that entrepreneurs succeed primarily because they invent new products or services, such as the Yahoo! search engine, but that isn't the case. Most successful entrepreneurs begin by offering a higher quality product or service, rather than by introducing something completely new. They make small modifications to what others are already doing. After they get started, they listen to customers and come up with still other modifications. Then they quickly adapt what they're doing—and they repeat this process over and over.[2] Offering exceptional quality led to success for Ben Cohen and Jerry Greenfield. They started Ben & Jerry's Ice Cream in 1963 after enrolling in a $5 correspondence course on ice cream making from Penn State University. They started making super premium ice cream with chunks of fruit, which appealed to customers who didn't like regular ice cream. At that time, the big ice cream manufacturers (e.g., Kraft, Pillsbury, Sealtest, and Borden's) weren't in the super premium market.[3]

Jake Burton is another entrepreneur who got his start in Vermont. He succeeded by improving on the design of a product that he first got to know as a 14-year-old. Shortly after college, he relocated from New York City and founded Burton Snowboards. "A lot of people think I invented snowboarding," he says. "But that's not true." The basic design for a snowboard had already been developed by Brunswick, the company that developed bowling alleys. But Brunswick never made the product a success. The philosophy of Burton Snowboards is to improve on what's available, based on an understanding of what customers really want. Burton had learned that "if the original product is a hassle for people, they'll fork over money for something that's better."[4]

HOW THE ENVIRONMENT ENCOURAGES ENTREPRENEURIAL ACTIVITY

During the past 10 years, entrepreneurs have created several million new businesses throughout the world. One of every six business students says that owning a company is a personal goal, and forecasters predict a large number of organizational births well into the future. In particular, an explosion in venture creation by women, immigrants, and members of minority groups is anticipated. The proportion of new business start-ups involving female entrepreneurs rose from 24 percent in 1975 to 40 percent in 2000.[5]

Does this explosion reflect a boom in "born entrepreneurs" a generation ago? No. Rates of entrepreneurship ebb and flow with environmental conditions.[6] In the United States, entrepreneurship rates rose dramatically during the 1920s and then declined during the 1930s. They rose again after World War II but then declined from the 1950s until the late 1980s. The past decade has been another period of rising entrepreneurship, initiated by innovations in microelectronics, computers, telecommunications, and information technologies. Low interest rates and higher rates of immigration also seem to contribute to higher rates of entrepreneurial activity. As more and more people become successful entrepreneurs, creation of a more favorable social climate spurs others to take the entrepreneurial plunge.[7] Political and economic factors also play a role. To stimulate entrepreneurship, many governments throughout Asia and Europe have begun loosening regulatory constraints and changing their tax laws. Their objective is to ensure that their countries participate fully in the entrepreneurial boom that new technologies are making possible.[8]

Local conditions can also stimulate entrepreneurship. Economists often argue that costs (i.e., tax rates) are an important factor, but CEOs suggest that other factors are more important. For some industries, such as entertainment, easy networking is crucial. Positioned between Hollywood and the video production centers of Venice and Santa Monica, California, Culver City is the kind of place where entrepreneurs can easily meet with other CEOs or potential clients for informal discussions at local coffee shops. Silicon Swamp, the term used to describe several counties near Washington, D.C., also is good for networking. MCI Communications located there for easy lobbying access to regulators. Then a virtual cycle of entrepreneurship began. MCI executives with new ideas gradually headed off to start their own companies. "Just as there are six degrees of separation between any two people on the globe, almost all of the telecom firms here can trace their roots back to MCI," explained one venture capitalist. The new start-ups, in turn, attracted other new talent, as well as new venture capital.[9] North Carolina's Research Triangle, near Raleigh, Durham, and Chapel Hill, has a different type of special appeal. It attracts engineers and software people and has become a mecca for science-based start-ups. A big advantage is its close proximity to the three major universities in those cities (North Carolina State, Duke, and the University of North Carolina).[10] The region also is home to many new-venture incubators.

The term ***incubator organization*** applies to organizations that support entrepreneurs. They rent space to new businesses or to people wanting to start businesses. They often are located in recycled buildings, such as warehouses or schools. They serve fledgling businesses by offering administrative services, providing management advice, and offering assistance with financing.

An incubator tenant can be fully operational the day after moving in, without having to buy phones, rent a copier, or hire office employees. Nonprofit incubators may offer these services free, but entrepreneurs often share some of their profits with for-profit incubators. In New York City, venture capital companies provide incubator space to dot-com startups as a way to nurture their investments. Some venture capitalists also view incubators as an easy and risk-free way to watch how a start-up is developing and then make better decisions about which ones to invest in most aggressively. For investment companies located in New York, for example, it's much easier to support and evaluate a start-up located in nearby warehouse space than one headquartered in a Silicon Valley garage.[11]

SMALL-BUSINESS OWNERS

Some people use the term *entrepreneur* incorrectly to mean *small-business owner*. The U.S. government defines a small business as a company employing fewer than 500 people. So, the term ***small-business owner*** simply refers to anyone who owns a major equity stake in a company with fewer than 500 employees. The Small Business Administration (SBA) is the agency of the federal government responsible for supporting the development of small-business activity, and it offers many useful resources to help people establish and effectively manage such businesses. According to SBA statistics, in 2000 there were 24 million small businesses in the United States, representing 40 percent of U.S. companies and creating three-fourths of all new jobs. So understanding this type of company and the type of people who might run them is important.

Many entrepreneurs are small-business owners for awhile, but not all small-business owners become entrepreneurs. That is, not all small-business owners introduce new business activity. People can become owners of small businesses by purchasing companies, inheriting them, buying franchises, and other means. Furthermore, many such owners are content to keep their businesses small and don't expand their businesses like successful entrepreneurs do.

It's easy to imagine that working for yourself might be better than working for someone else. But even if you aren't the business owner, working in a small company is different from working for a large company. Satisfaction is one big difference. According to a recent Gallup poll, companies with fewer than 50 employees have the most satisfied workforces. The breakdown of "extremely satisfied" employees is shown in Figure 5.1.[12]

Small companies definitely have some drawbacks, often including lower pay and few, if any, medical and other insurance benefits. But for most people, the drawbacks are offset by a more favorable work climate. In a small business, employees are expected to use many skills and wear many hats. They can more easily see how their work relates to the company's mission and how their performance affects the company's profitability.[13]

Figure 5.1 **How Company Size Relates to Employee Satisfaction**

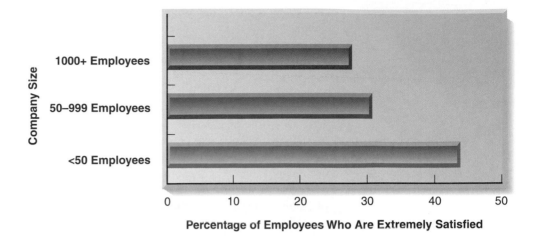

FAMILY BUSINESSES

WEB INSIGHT

What types of special issues do family-business owners face and how can they deal with these issues? Visit *http://www.fambiz.com* for some initial ideas.

When people think of small businesses, they often think of family businesses. Actually, a family business may be either large or small. It may be growing rapidly—that is, an entrepreneurial enterprise—or it may be growing slowly. There is no government definition of *family business,* but most often the term is used to describe a business owned and managed mostly by people who are related by blood and/or marriage. Often these businesses are passed down from one generation to the next. Kohler Company, which is known for its plumbing fixtures, is an example. Kohler was founded 125 years ago by the inventor of the modern bathtub. Since then, this private company has diversified into furniture, small engines, and golf resorts—yet, it is still controlled by the original family and it still employs many family members.

As we explain later in this chapter, pressures to expand a business can create a great deal of stress for entrepreneurs and the people who work with and for them. When those people also are family members, especially knotty problems can arise. Some families handle these pressures by turning over management of their start-ups to professionals. Other families find ways to keep their businesses growing while maintaining management and ownership control. Seph Barnard, CEO of Tape Resources, almost sold his company because trying to run the 10-year-old business as though it were still a start-up had exhausted him. As Barnard's company grew, he continued to monitor everything closely, refusing to delegate to others. Eventually he nearly ruined his health and lost his family. When someone offered to buy his firm, he just couldn't give it up. He knew that he would have to change his management style, however, and finally began letting others share the managerial workload.[14]

CHARACTERISTICS OF ENTREPRENEURS

2.

DESCRIBE THE PERSONAL CHARACTERISTICS THAT CONTRIBUTE TO ENTREPRENEURS' SUCCESS.

Each year, *Inc.* magazine identifies the 500 most rapidly growing private companies in the United States. To qualify for this list, a company must be at least 5 years old. About 80 percent are between 5 and 10 years old. Who are the CEOs of these companies? These highly successful entrepreneurs are well educated, with 85 percent having a college degree and 40 percent having some type of graduate degree. Only 15 percent hold an MBA, however. When they first started, most hoped that their businesses would merely survive or expected that they would grow slowly.[15]

If so few highly successful entrepreneurs started out with the goal of heading a rapidly growing company, how did they get started? When successful entrepreneurs were asked to explain why they started their own companies, the most frequent reason they gave was to work for themselves and control their lives (41 percent). Other reasons included creating something new (12 percent), proving that they could do it (9 percent), not feeling rewarded in their old jobs (8 percent), being laid off (5 percent), and a variety of miscellaneous reasons (11 percent). The desire to be their own bosses often becomes strong when people discover that they can't accomplish their career goals in a large organization.[16]

The many studies of entrepreneurs that have been conducted over the years indicate that those who succeed have several characteristics in common. These characteristics include some key personal attributes and strong technical and/or managerial skills. As shown in Figure 5.2, the combination of all of these characteristics increases the probability of entrepreneurial success.

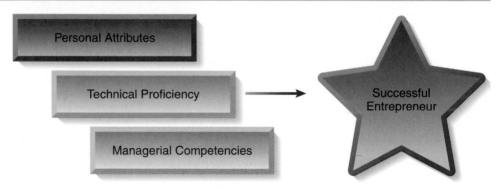

Figure 5.2 **Characteristics of Entrepreneurs**

KEY PERSONAL ATTRIBUTES

Because entrepreneurial activity is so important to economic growth, researchers have sought to understand what contributes to successful entrepreneurship. Obviously, business conditions are one important factor. But even with the best of business conditions, not everyone becomes an entrepreneur nor do all entrepreneurs become successful. A study of inventors who worked for three of the country's largest national research laboratories documented this point. The researchers were interested in explaining the differences between inventors who eventually left the labs to start their own companies and those who didn't. Was it something about the environment within a lab that caused some inventors to leave and become entrepreneurs? Or was it the personal attributes of the inventors? The study showed that both were important but that differences in personal attributes were more important than differences among the labs.[17] The personal attributes that most entrepreneurs share are a strong need for achievement, a desire to be independent, self-confidence, and the willingness to make sacrifices for the sake of the business.[18]

Need for Achievement. The need for achievement—a person's desire either for excellence or to succeed in competitive situations—is a key personal attribute of successful entrepreneurs. High achievers take responsibility for attaining their goals, set moderately difficult goals, and want immediate feedback on how well they have performed. David McClelland and others have conducted extensive research into the human need for achievement. Their findings indicate that perhaps only 5 percent of the U.S. population is characterized by a predominant need to achieve.[19] For most people, power needs and the need for affiliation are more important than the need for achievement. A strong drive to achieve is something that sets successful entrepreneurs apart from everyone else. Entrepreneurs learn to set challenging but achievable goals for themselves and for their businesses and, when they achieve them, to set new goals.

Desire for Independence. Entrepreneurs often seek independence from others. As a result, they generally aren't motivated to perform well in large, bureaucratic organizations. They have internal drive, are confident of their own abilities, and possess a great deal of self-respect.

Many of these feelings were familiar to Catherine Hughes. As CEO of Radio One, she became the first African-American woman in the United States to head a publicly traded company. Hughes got started in business more than 20 years ago. That's when she took on the challenge of running Howard University's ailing radio station. Within a few years, she had bought her own station, WOL-AM, with the help of a $600,000 loan. The cost of servicing the loan was so steep that she had to live at the radio station. Hiring adequate staff was also a problem, so she filled in as a DJ and talk show host. Despite these hardships, Hughes was happy, saying, "I was thinking of programming ideas, recruiting people, putting together sales packages. It was finally my show." Today, the show that Hughes runs is a $50 million business with about 30 stations around the country.[20]

Self-Confidence. A successful track record does much to improve an entrepreneur's self-confidence and self-esteem. It enables that person to be optimistic in representing the firm to employees and customers alike. Expecting, obtaining, and rewarding high performance from employees is personally reinforcing, and it also provides a role model for others. Most people want an optimistic and enthusiastic leader—someone they can look up to. Because of the risks involved in running an entrepreneurial organization, having an "upbeat" attitude is essential.

Self-Sacrifice. Finally, successful entrepreneurs have to be self-sacrificing. They recognize that nothing worth having is free. That means giving up the 2-week vacation, the golf game every Saturday, or the occasional trip to the mountains. Success has a high price, and they are willing to pay it. For Catherine Hughes, living out of a sleeping bag at her radio station was a sacrifice. Having her car repossessed because she couldn't afford the payments on both her car and her station was a sacrifice. But perhaps her biggest sacrifice was selling a rare gold pocket watch because she needed the $50,000 it brought in. Made by slaves, the watch had belonged to her great-grandmother. Such sacrifices can be a tough reality for entrepreneurs.

Entrepreneurs: Made, Not Born. Although entrepreneurs are different from most people, they probably weren't born that way. They develop personal attributes over the years, but they acquire many of their key attributes early in life, with the family environment playing an important role. For example, women who were born first into a family tend to be more entrepreneurial than women born later into a family, perhaps because the first child receives special attention and thereby develops more self-confidence. Entrepreneurs also tend to have self-employed parents. The independent nature and flexibility shown by the self-employed mother or father is learned at an early age. Such parents are supportive and encourage independence, achievement, and responsibility.[21]

Changing personal attributes isn't easy, especially by the time people reach adulthood. Nevertheless, doing so may well be worth the effort. The best way is to engage in entrepreneurial behavior. Successful entrepreneurial experiences can lead to development of new ways of thinking and spur motivation.

The idea that entrepreneurial success breeds more entrepreneurial activity may explain why many entrepreneurs start multiple companies during their lifetimes. When the successful founder of the retail catalog *Gardeners Eden* sold her business to Williams-Sonoma, she didn't stop being an entrepreneur. She launched another new business—the mail-order flower company Calyx & Corolla. For some people entrepreneurship itself becomes a career. Rather than managing a business solely for income or growth, these individuals use their companies as springboards to start or acquire other ventures and then repeat the process, which is known as the ***corridor principle***.[22] That is, opening a business is analogous to entering a passageway. As you walk along it, you notice new corridors to explore. If you get hooked on exploring the corridors, you become a ***serial entrepreneur***. As the term suggests, a serial entrepreneur is a person who founds and operates multiple companies during a career. Martha Stewart is a serial entrepreneur. Her array of businesses includes television and radio shows, products sold through big retailers such as Kmart and Sears, the Martha by Mail catalog, and an e-business called marthastore.

In Japan and other countries, a new type of super-serial entrepreneur is emerging. Some people call them Net builders, referring to the web of interconnected businesses they develop and support. As described in the following Global Awareness Competency feature, these entrepreneurs aren't satisfied to nurture just one start-up at a time—they run several related companies at the same time.[23]

Masayoshi Son Builds a Conglomerate from Start-Ups

Perhaps it is natural for new start-up companies to keep close links to other start-up companies. But Masayoshi Son has taken this idea to the extreme. By the age of 42, he has already built a Net empire that includes 300 Internet companies scattered throughout the United States, Europe, Japan, and other parts of Asia. Son's entrepreneurial energy has always paid off. At the age of 16, he moved from Japan to attend the University of California at Berkeley. There he earned his first million dollars by importing Japanese arcade games and installing them around the campus. At the same time, he was developing computer games and applying for a patent on a pocket-sized electronic translator.

As founder and CEO of Softbank, Son oversees about $4 billion in venture capital investments for his many companies. Within 5 years, he hopes to expand his reach to include 800 Internet ventures. To achieve this goal, he plans

to import Web-based companies that have been successful in other countries, set them up in Japan, Korea, or elsewhere in Asia, and then take them public. Years ago, a similar model was used to expand Japan's *zaibatsu,* which started out as small retailers and grew into global conglomerates with controlling interests in interlocked trade, insurance, and shipping companies. In today's electronics-dominated markets, *net-batsu* is the new term used to describe such corporate groups.

Like the dot-com companies listed on U.S. stock exchanges, the market capitalization of *net-batsus* has soared. Softbank's share price rose from $72 to $1,500 in a year, surpassing Sony Corporation in total market value. Some observers hope that Son's success will stimulate other Japanese entrepreneurs to take the big risks needed for success in the new economy. "We're going to need lots and lots of entrepreneurs to

rebuild Japan," observed Joichi Ito, the 33-year-old chairman of Infoseek Japan.

• • •

To learn more about Softbank, visit the company's home page at

http://www.sbholdings.com

TECHNICAL PROFICIENCY

Entrepreneurs often demonstrate strong technical skills, typically bringing some related experience to their business ventures. Successful automobile dealers usually have acquired a fair amount of technical knowledge about selling and servicing automobiles before opening their dealerships. Nike's cofounder Bill Bowerman used his technical knowledge to design revolutionary footwear. As a track coach, he supported the careers of 19 Olympians. As a businessman, he developed the waffle outer sole and found myriad ways to keep making running shoes lighter and lighter. Technical proficiency is especially important in the computer industry, which is home to about 30 percent of the fastest growing U.S. firms. Both David Filo and Jerry Yang were Ph.D. candidates in electrical engineering at Stanford University when they first began developing the software and databases that eventually became Yahoo!. Like many entrepreneurs, they used their technical skills to create something they found useful.

MANAGERIAL COMPETENCIES

Managing a rapidly growing entrepreneurial company can be immensely challenging. To succeed requires drawing on the various managerial competencies described throughout this book.

Strategic Action Competency. Entrepreneurial success is often attributed to opportunistic behavior and being in the right place at the right time. Opportunity and luck may play some role in success, but sound strategic decisions also are important. A study of 906 CEOs who were winners of awards in the Ernst & Young LLP Entrepreneur of the Year Program revealed several leading strategic practices they had used to sustain rapid growth for their companies. Some of the most common strategic practices identified were

- delivering products and services that were perceived as the highest quality to expanding market segments;
- cultivating pace-setting new products and services that are first to market;
- delivering products and services that demand average or higher pricing;
- using new products and services to expand revenue by about 20 percent annually;
- generating new customers that expand revenue by about 30 percent annually;
- focusing marketing expenditures on a high-quality sales force that can rapidly expand the company's geographic presence;
- maintaining financial control of the firm; and
- linking the entrepreneur's long-term objectives to a defined exit strategy.

WEB INSIGHT

Starting a new business and succeeding is easier if you have someone to ask for advice when making important strategic decisions. The Service Core of Retired Executives (SCORE) is one place to find such advice. But are there any retired executives who know about doing business on the Internet? Visit *http://www.score.org* to find out. For what types of business would it be easiest to find help?

Although the study identified these common strategic practices, the entrepreneurs hadn't necessarily formulated them as goals early in the lives of their firms. For many, these practices emerged through their daily actions. Making decisions that support growth is an ongoing activity that occurs day in and day out. Thus a good approach is to treat a new venture like an experiment. It should be guided by a clear strategic plan focused on satisfying customers, but decisions about how to achieve the goals should be based on trying various approaches and learning by observing what happens.[24]

Serial entrepreneur Steve Jobs has honed his strategic action competency through years of experience, first at Apple and later at Pixar. The following Strategic Action Competency feature illustrates how Jobs's strategic action competency helped him resuscitate Pixar, win an Academy Award, and build a small business into a major movie studio.[25]

STRATEGIC ACTION COMPETENCY

Picture This

Today, the Pixar company name is as familiar to most people as its first two hit movies: *Toy Story* and *A Bug's Life*. Not so back in 1986, when Steve Jobs paid George Lucas $10 million for a small special effects company. Jobs had just left the first company he founded, Apple Computer, and was looking for a new

challenge. At the time, Pixar was little more than a band of special effects techies who did whatever was needed to spice up the movies that George Lucas produced.

At first, Jobs's vision was simply to turn the ailing company into a successful supplier of animation. But within a

few years he wanted to do more. Rather than doing a few special effects here and there as needed, he imagined producing full-length, fully animated movies. To do so required a strategic partner. Jobs and his Pixar team had a deep understanding of their own organization and a good grasp of the movie industry. But they knew that success in this industry required more than making a great movie. Marketing muscle and access to distribution channels for the movie and its associated products were essential, too.

Jobs chose to partner with the Walt Disney Company. First he cut a three-movie deal that gave Pixar the rights to 10 percent of the profits. Pixar would produce the movies; Disney would market and distribute them and retain 90 percent of the profits. One of those movies, *Toy Story,* was a huge success. Buoyed by its success, Jobs developed a new vision: Rather than work for Disney, he sees a future in which Pixar is the next Disney. "In Hollywood, there are very few brands—really just two—Disney and Spielberg. We want to be one, too," says Jobs.

To raise funds and gain some bargaining power, Jobs took Pixar public in 1995. The initial public offering (IPO) was the biggest of the year. Then he struck a new deal with Disney. This time, Pixar and Disney would be equal partners for five films, sharing the profits 50–50. The first movie produced under the new deal was *A Bug's Life*—another hit! *Toy Story 2* and *Monsters, Inc.,* soon followed.

Although the partnership with Disney seems to be working well, some observers predict that Pixar will lose out in the end. Pixar is completely dependent on Disney, they say. Steve Jobs's fans aren't worried, however. As part of his deal with Disney, he negotiated the rights to start talks with other studios after finishing the third of the five movies. As one former Pixar executive explained,

Jobs has the "brains, energy and chutzpah to protect Pixar's interests."

• • •

To learn more about Pixar Animation Studios, visit the company's home page at

http://www.pixar.com

Planning and Administration Competency. Though plans may have to be changed along the way, planning is nevertheless important for entrepreneurial companies, and nearly 80 percent of successful entrepreneurs put their plans in writing. As you might expect, the planning horizon is relatively short. Half the time it covers less than 3 years. Written monthly plans that cover periods of 12 to 24 months are common. As the time frame grows longer, the plans tend to become more general. For example, some may state only annual goals.

Administering the plan is important, too. Here staffing activities can be key.[26] In the start-up phase, when funds are scarce and the company has no track record, attracting top-notch employees is difficult. Founders often do most of the crucial work themselves. But to grow, they soon must hire new talent. Once the talent has been brought on board, successful entrepreneurs tie management compensation to performance against the plan, on a monthly or quarterly basis. They also use the plan to work with employees to set job performance standards jointly.[27]

Compared to more established companies, Yahoo! and other start-ups must base plans and make administrative decisions on very little hard data. Founders can't avoid uncertainty, but they can't allow it to paralyze them either.[28]

Teamwork Competency. Successful entrepreneurs are extremely hard working and task oriented, but they aren't lone wolves—one person can do only so much alone. Unless they can build effective teams, their organizations' growth will eventually reach a limit. Successful entrepreneurs are self-starters who usually support subordinates and their programs enthusiastically. Entrepreneurs also maintain good relationships with their venture partners.[29]

The study of 906 entrepreneurs previously described found that the majority of successful companies had a particularly effective top-management team. Only 3 percent of these CEOs acted alone in the top-management role. Such teams tended to be small, with 67 percent ranging in size from three to six managers, and diverse in terms of functional background. Team balance and innovation were achieved by mixing people who had previously worked closely together with people who hadn't. These management teams all used a collaborative decision-making style.

Communication Competency. For a budding entrepreneur with an idea and ambition, but little else to work with, being able to communicate effectively is essential to gaining the cooperation and support needed to turn a vision into reality.[30]

As described in the following Communication Competency feature, Estée Lauder used her communication skills to build a cosmetics empire that is worth more than $6 billion and operates in more than 100 countries.[31] Like most family businesses, the company started out as a "nice little business," with Mrs. Lauder selling skin creams developed by her uncle, who was a chemist. Its growth was due to Mrs. Lauder's ability to convince both customers and the CEOs of department stores that her brand was better than all the others.

COMMUNICATION COMPETENCY

Estée Lauder Built an Image and a Brand

Beauty products were already saturating the market when Estée Lauder started out as a 40-something entrepreneur. Nevertheless, Estée Lauder (originally named Josephine Esther Mentzer by her immigrant parents) convinced the world that her products were better than any others. She used her powers of persuasion to get in to see the right people and to make her case. More than 50 years later, Stanley Marcus, then the president of Neiman Marcus, still can remember his encounter with her. She delayed him from leaving work at the end of a day as she explained: "I have the most wonderful beauty products and they must be in your store." When Marcus tried to put her off, telling her to go see the marketing manager, she persisted. "I've done that, and he said I should come back another day.

But you see, Mr. Marcus, I don't have time for that because my products must be in your store right away." When asked how much space she needed, she replied that space wasn't important. Just 4 or 5 feet were all she wanted. Then he asked when she could deliver the merchandise. It turned out that she had brought it with her. The next day, she set herself up near the store entrance and greeted every customer with "Try this. I'm Estée Lauder and these are the most wonderful beauty products in the world." Marcus described her sales style as gracious and very determined. "It was easier to say yes to Estée than to say no." Her son, Leonard Lauder, was equally effective when he took over as CEO upon his mother's retirement. A Rite Aid executive was so impressed by a handwritten note he sent af-

ter visiting her store that she saved it for several years. "That seems silly, right? I mean, I get vendors' letters every day, but this one was different," she explained.

In this business, the key to success is persuading people to buy very simple products that they probably don't really need—and make them feel good for having spent their money. As was true in the company's start-up days, one-to-one communication still plays a big role in selling cosmetics. Today, the Estée Lauder company controls over 45 percent of the global cosmetics market, with volume three times that of its nearest competitor.

• • •

To learn more about the Estée Lauder Companies, visit their home page at

http://www.elcompanies.com

Much of the communication that occurs in larger companies takes the form of speeches, written reports, formal proposals, and scheduled reviews. In small companies, most communication is direct and less formal. When Paul Ralston moved from his marketing job at Body Shop International PLC to Autumn Harp, where he later became president, he noticed the difference immediately. Communication often got bogged down at Body Shop in a proliferation of memos and e-mail. According to Ralston, "You would get a lot of stuff to read, and you didn't know where it fit in." At Autumn Harp, communication was mostly face to face, according to Ralston: "If you needed to talk to someone, you put your head around a wall."[32] For global entrepreneurial firms, communicating effectively can be more challenging. A maker of premium pet foods, IAMS, meets this challenge by sending its handful of expatriate employees home-country magazines and newsletters and keeping in touch through frequent phone calls.

ASSESSING YOUR ENTREPRENEURIAL POTENTIAL

By now, you may be wondering whether you have what it takes to be a successful entrepreneur. Although no one can predict your success, the characteristics that many entrepreneurs have in common—including family background, motivation, and personality traits—can give you a rough idea of your potential. To learn more, complete the questionnaire presented in the following Self-Management Competency feature. Northwestern Mutual Life Insurance Company in Milwaukee prepared this quiz to help you and others like you to get an idea of whether you might have a head start or a handicap if you go into business for yourself.[33]

Begin with the score of zero. Add or subtract from your score as you respond to each item.

1. Significantly high numbers of entrepreneurs are children of first-generation U.S. citizens. If your parents were immigrants, add 1. If not, subtract 1. _____

2. Successful entrepreneurs were not, as a rule, top achievers in school. If you were a top student, subtract 4. If not, add 4. _____

3. Entrepreneurs were not especially enthusiastic about participating in group activities in school. If you enjoyed group activities—clubs, team sports, and so on—subtract 1. If not, add 1. _____

4. Studies of entrepreneurs show that, as youngsters, they often preferred to be alone. Did you prefer to be alone as a youngster? If yes, add 1. If no, subtract 1. _____

5. If you started an enterprise during childhood—lemonade stands, family newspapers, greeting card sales—or ran for elected office at school, add 2 because enterprise usually appeared at an early age. If you didn't initiate enterprises, subtract 2. _____

6. Stubbornness as a child seems to translate into determination to do things your own way—certainly a hallmark of proven entrepreneurs. So, if you were a stubborn child, add 1. If not, subtract 1. _____

7. Caution may involve an unwillingness to take risks, a handicap for those embarking into previously uncharted territory. Were you cautious as a youngster? If yes, subtract 4. If no, add 4. _____

8. If you were daring, add 4. _____

9. Entrepreneurs often speak of pursuing different paths—despite the opinions of others. If the opinions of others matter to you, subtract 1. If not, add 1. _____

10. Being bored with a daily routine is often a precipitating factor in an entrepreneur's decision to start an enterprise. If an important motivation for starting your own enterprise would be changing your daily routine, add 2. If not, subtract 2. _____

11. If you really enjoy work, are you willing to work long nights? If yes, add 2. If no, subtract 6. _____

12. If you would be willing to work "as long as it takes" with little or no sleep to finish a job, add 4. _____

13. Entrepreneurs generally enjoy their activity so much that they move from one project to another—nonstop. When you complete a project successfully, do you immediately start another? If yes, add 2. If no, subtract 2. _____

14. Successful entrepreneurs are willing to use their savings to start a project. If you would be willing to spend your savings to start a business, add 2. If not, subtract 2. _____

15. If you would be willing to borrow from others, too, add 2. If not, subtract 2. _____

16. If your business failed, would you immediately work to start another? If yes, add 4. If no, subtract 4. _____

17. If you would immediately start looking for a good paying job, subtract 1. _____

18. Do you believe entrepreneurship is "risky"? If yes, subtract 2. If no, add 2. _____

19. Many entrepreneurs put long-term and short-term goals in writing. If you do, add 1. If you don't, subtract 1. _____

20. Handling cash flow can be crucial to entrepreneurial success. If you believe that you have more knowledge and experience with cash flow than most people, add 2. If not, subtract 2. _____

21. Entrepreneurial personalities seem to be easily bored. If you are easily bored, add 2. If not, subtract 2. _____

22. Optimism can fuel the drive to press for success. If you're an optimist, add 2. If you're a pessimist subtract 2. _____

A score of 35 or more: You have everything going for you. If you decide to become an entrepreneur, you ought to
achieve spectacular success (barring
acts of God or other variables beyond
your control).

A score of 15 to 34: Your background,
skills, and talents give you an excellent
chance for success in starting your
own business. You should go far.

A score of 0 to 14: You have a head start
on the ability and/or experience in running
a business and ought to be successful in
opening an enterprise of your own if you
apply yourself and develop the necessary
competencies to make it happen.

A score of minus 15 to minus 1: You
might be able to make a go of it if you
ventured out on your own, but you
would have to work extra hard to compensate for a lack of advantages that
give others a "leg up" in beginning their
own businesses.

A score of minus 43 to minus 16: Your
talents probably lie elsewhere. You
ought to consider whether building your
own business is what you really want to
do because you may find yourself working against your true preference. Another work arrangement—such as working for someone else or developing a
career in a profession or an area of
technical expertise—may be far more
attractive to you and therefore allow you
to enjoy a lifestyle appropriate to your
abilities and interests.

PLANNING AND ENTREPRENEURSHIP

3.

DESCRIBE THE PLANNING
REQUIREMENTS
ASSOCIATED WITH
BECOMING A SUCCESSFUL
ENTREPRENEUR.

Research has shown that, before going into business, entrepreneurs who are successful typically plan more carefully than those who fail.[34] One tool that helps
them do so is the business plan.[35] A *business plan* describes the basic idea that is the
foundation for the start-up and outlines a step-by-step process showing how that idea
can be turned into reality. Table 5.1 shows the major components of a business plan.[36]

Table 5.1	Components of a Business Plan	
	Introduction and Overview	**Executive summary:** One to three pages that summarize the key points in the business plan and generate excitement in the person reading it.
		Vision and mission: State the business philosophy and the basic business strategy. A code of ethics also should be included.
		Product or service: Explain what it is and how it is unique. Why will people want to buy it? What is the source of competitive advantage?
		Current status of the venture: If an existing company is involved, describe it. If this is a start-up, explain the degree to which the idea has begun to be implemented.
	Details of Major Business Components	**People:** Identify the key players—the management team, active investors, and directors—and explain how employees will be recruited and retained.
		Marketing: Identify the market and target customers; explain how they will be attracted; describe marketing and pricing practices.
		Operations: Describe the business facilities (location, equipment), quality, and inventory control procedures, sources for supplies and purchasing practices.
		Financial Plan: State financial needs and planned sources of capital, debt, and personal equity positions. Provide historical data; describe expectations for 3 to 5 years out by including a projected income statement, a projected cash flow statement, a projected balance sheet, and a break-even analysis of profits and cash flow.
	Supplements	Include any additional details relevant to the plan. Often included are
		• personal data sheets on owners, lead entrepreneurs, and key skilled managers;
		• supporting information on materials purchasing, vendors, quotes, and prices;
		• facility plans, layouts, manufacturing requirements, and equipment needs; and
		• credit reports, bids, contracts, and other appendices that would be helpful to investors.

Entrepreneurs must answer the following types of questions in their business plans.

WEB INSIGHT

There's plenty of help available for people who are putting together a business plan. If you were putting together a plan, how would you get started? Visit *http://www.bplans.com* and *http://www.toolkit.cch.com* for some ideas.

1. What are my motivations for owning a business?
2. Should I start or buy a business?
3. What and where is the market for my product or service?
4. How much will it cost to own the business, and where will I get the money?
5. Should my company be a domestic or global company?
6. How will growth be managed?

UNDERSTANDING YOUR MOTIVATIONS

People become business owners for various reasons. Some want to make a hobby or craft pay off. Others enter businesses owned by family members. Still others choose an industry on the basis of their assessments of the growth and profit potential in that industry. One way to think about business opportunities is to classify them as lifestyle, small but profitable, and high-growth ventures. Your motivation for owning a business may fit better with some types of business opportunities than others.

You've already read about several high-growth ventures in this chapter. These organizations have created substantial wealth for their founders, as well as others who hold a financial stake in them. Such businesses help the owners satisfy a strong need for achievement. By comparison, a *lifestyle venture* is designed to meet the founder's desire for independence, autonomy, and control. Such ventures often remain small and may even be limited to a sole proprietor. Michael Bryant's business fits this description. Bryant is the sole employee of Career Transition, located in Baltimore on the second floor of his home. A consultant, Bryant helps people decide what to do with their lives. Many of his clients are sent by organizations that hope he will be able to help the employees they are laying off find new jobs, but some come to him on their own. Bryant also helps downsizing organizations with their strategic planning and offers seminars on time management and communication. He has few expenses, works a 4-day week and brings in about $100,000 in a good year.

He describes himself as being as happy as "a pig in slop!" His satisfaction comes from practicing his craft, running his own business, and enjoying a lifestyle that permits him to be around when his kids come home from school and when the sun sets on his property. Bryant believes that his small business is nearly ideal. "My meetings are great," he says. They are held where he wants them, with only the people he wants to attend, and they end when he says. "My personnel problems are under control. . . . There are no disturbances. And the employees are really mature about what the boss needs to get done." And he distributes all his profits to himself.[37]

Bryant clearly is satisfied with his small-business operation, and in this regard he isn't unique. In general, entrepreneurs who emphasize noneconomic goals, such as "to do the kind of work I want to do," are more satisfied than those whose motivation is primarily economic gain.[38] Of the millions of small-business owners like Bryant in the United States, many find that staying in touch with other CEOs who run similar businesses is useful and rewarding. Networking among these small-business owners is facilitated by the Small Business Advancement National Center and several affiliated regional Small Business Development Centers, which enable owners to learn about resources that are available locally.

DECIDING WHETHER TO START OR BUY A BUSINESS

Prospective entrepreneurs who have the option to "start or buy" begin by weighing the advantages and disadvantages of each strategy. Sometimes, of course, the decision to start a business is made for them. If they don't have the financial resources necessary to purchase an existing company, they have no choice but to start their own. Even if they have the resources, though, suitable businesses may not be available. This situation is likely to be the case if an entrepreneur has a truly new idea. However, if they have the resources, entrepreneurs often find that buying an existing company—perhaps one that the current owner is having difficulty managing—is a good idea. Leonard Riggio used this approach when he started Barnes and Noble back in 1971. He secured a $1.2 million loan to purchase a failing 100-year-old bookstore on Fifth Avenue in New York City. Today, Barnes and Noble has about 15 percent of the U.S. market, with more than $3 billion in annual revenues.[39]

A middle ground between starting a business and buying an existing business is to invest in and run a franchise. A *franchise* is a business operated by someone (the franchisee) to whom a franchiser grants the right to market a good or service. The franchisee pays a franchise fee and a percentage of the sales to the franchiser. In return the franchisee often receives financial help, training, guaranteed supplies, a protected market, and technical assistance in site selection, accounting, and operations management. McDonald's, Domino's Pizza, Jiffy Lube, AAMCO Transmissions, and Jenny Craig Diet Centers, to name but a few, all use franchises to market their products. Whoever enters a franchise agreement obtains a brand name that enjoys recognition among potential customers. However, franchisees are their own bosses only to a degree. They can't run their businesses exactly as they please. They usually have to conform to standards set by a franchiser, and sometimes they must buy the franchiser's goods and services. But many people want to operate a franchise in the first place for these very reasons.

Buying an existing firm can be complex and may involve considerable risk. The seller may not reveal some hidden problems—and may not even be aware of others. Also, many a new owner has thought that he or she was buying goodwill, only to have the previous owner open a competing firm and lure away the established clientele. A prospective buyer is wise to specify, in the purchase agreement, restrictions limiting the previous owner's ability or right to compete with the new owner. Such restrictions may limit the types of businesses that the previous owner can operate in a certain area and/or for a stipulated period of time.

As we have previously noted, new ventures frequently spring from an incubator organization, where entrepreneurs may develop the skills and knowledge needed for starting their own businesses. When deciding what type of business to own, people should begin by examining their competencies and the contacts they can bring to their future companies. Prospective entrepreneurs should carefully examine factors such as expected revenue, initial investment required, and intensity of competition. Such an analysis often turns up existing businesses that may be purchased. In addition to exploring the Internet, business magazines such as *Inc., Entrepreneur,* and *Venturing* can be good sources of ideas for new ventures.

Learning about businesses available for purchase and negotiating the purchase agreement often require the assistance of experts. Bankers, accountants, attorneys, and other professionals may be aware of an opportunity to buy a business before it is publicly announced. A business broker may help the prospective owner find a firm and act as intermediary for the sale. Usually, an attorney prepares or reviews the sale documents.

Other questions the prospective owner should consider include the following.

- Is there a way that I can begin the enterprise in stages or with a limited investment?

- Can I run the company at first as a home-based business?

- Can I continue working for someone else and put in time on my own business after hours?

- To what extent can I draw on relatives to help me, perhaps simply by answering the phone while I work at my regular job?

ASSESSING THE MARKET

The market assessment and forecasting techniques described in Chapter 9 often are overlooked in planning for business ownership. Entrepreneurs frequently are so excited about their business ideas that they assume others will feel the same way. Their market research may consist of asking the opinions of a few friends or relatives about the salability of a product. Such discussions convinced CEO Nancy Deyo, founder of Purple Moon, that money was to be made by selling entertainment software for girls. She was right. The emerging market for software entertainment for girls aged 7 to 12 saw CD-ROMs and online products for girls increase tenfold within a year.[40] However, many aren't so fortunate.

More systematic information that can be used in targeting and analyzing markets is available from the federal government, which compiles an enormous amount of data on products, industries, consumers, and other market-related categories. Pubic opinion and market polls also provide information.

How should a business plan identify the target market? Typical questions derived from a business plan (see Table 5.1) are listed in Table 5.2.[41] These questions focus on the attractiveness of the market and on the firm's ability to capture a share of that market.

Table 5.2	*Market Issues Facing the Entrepreneur*

- Who exactly constitutes your market? Describe the characteristics (age, gender, profession, income, and so on) of various market segments.
- What is the present size of the market?
- What strategy will you use to attract, expand, and keep this market?
- How are you going to price your products or services to make a fair profit and, at the same time, be competitive? Will you have different pricing for different market segments?
- What percentage of your annual revenue will you try to generate from new products and services?
- What percentage of annual revenue will you invest in developing new products and services?
- How will you market your products and services?

John Doerr, one of the most successful venture capitalists of all time, says that the best business plans are short. He likes to learn the details by talking with the people who will implement the plan. When he meets people to talk about their business plans, he asks himself, "Are these the people I want to be in trouble with for the next 5, 10, 15 years of my life?" Knowing that any start-up will experience unforeseeable problems, he says that for him the investment decision comes down to the management team. "I always turn to the biographies of the team first. For me, it's team, team, team." Among those he has backed are Sun Microsystems, Genentech, Healtheon, Netscape, Excite, and Amazon.com. Obviously, he is an excellent judge of whether a start-up team has what it will need to be a success.[42]

FINDING FUNDS

Entrepreneurs are likely to overestimate their income and tend to underestimate their costs. The new-venture plan should identify anticipated costs of opening the business (e.g., deposits, fixtures, and incorporation fees). It should also include a month by month projection of the cost of goods or services sold and the firm's operating expenses for the first 1 to 3 years.

The entrepreneur must plan for obtaining funds to handle expenses associated with the start-up phase that revenues can't initially cover. Getting financial support is one of the most important activities that differentiates people who just think about having their own business from those who actually start one.[43] Furthermore, the larger the amount of resources obtained, the better the odds are of being able to continue in business for the long term.[44]

Common sources of funds include the entrepreneur and other members of the venture team, family and friends, financial institutions such as banks and venture capital firms, and angels. *Venture capitalists* are like bankers. They are organized as formal businesses, but because they aren't subject to the same state and federal regulations as banks, they can take greater risks in making investments. Generally, venture capitalists expect their investments to reap return 25 to 35 percent annually. To make sure that happens, they get much more actively involved in the ventures they fund than bankers do. Indeed, according to one recent study, they spend 40 percent of their time monitoring businesses they have funded and serving as consultants or directors.[45] To get information about venture capitalists, entrepreneurs can contact investment research firms, venture capital clubs, or the Entrepreneurial Development Institute. But for really quick responses, they can post their business plans on the Internet. Numerous Internet sites now serve as matchmakers for entrepreneurs and venture capitalists. Experts predict that within 5 years or less, most venture financing will occur online.[46]

An *angel* is a private individual who invests directly in firms and receives an equity stake in return. Often such a person also acts as a business advisor to the founder. Angels seem to have some altruistic motives and often make less stringent demands than do venture capitalists. Like serial entrepreneurs, angels truly enjoy seeing a business grow and watching a start-up venture mature into a viable business. Angel Norm Brodsky has had this experience many times as an entrepreneur himself and now enjoys supporting others. "Yes, making money is important," he says. "I wouldn't go into deals unless I thought I could get my capital back and make a good return. But I really don't do this type of investing for the money anymore. I'm more interested in helping people get started in business."[47]

A sound business plan is essential to demonstrate to potential lenders and investors the viability of the proposed enterprise. Once funding has been obtained, entrepreneurs should provide their financial backers with timely information and establish a trust relationship with them. This approach tends to reduce the extent to which investors feel the need to intrude into the business, and it enhances the likelihood of their reinvesting in the future.[48]

GOING GLOBAL?

Most new-venture entrepreneurs begin with a domestic focus, but a growing number establish their firms as global start-ups. Of the fastest growing start-ups in recent years, 38 percent have some international sales.[49] Logitech—which manufactures a widely used computer mouse—is a well-known global start-up. Founded in 1982 by a Swiss and two Italians, this firm was headquartered in California and Switzerland and then expanded in Ireland and Taiwan. Within 7 years, it had captured 30 percent of the computer mouse market. A more recent global start-up is iMediation, a provider of e-commerce services. The company was launched simultaneously in Germany, France, and the United States by managers of eight different nationalities. According to iMediation's CEO, Didier Benchimol, the challenge for a global start-up is to achieve a global reach through superb strategic execution in each location.[50]

Because global start-ups pose some special challenges to management, the decision to found a global firm should be made only after careful analysis. Figure 5.3 depicts the key factors affecting the decision about whether to found a domestic or global start-up. Specific considerations include the following.[51]

1. Are the best human resources dispersed among various countries? If yes, it may be easier to operate as an international company than to convince potential employees to move to your hometown.

2. Would foreign financing be easier or more suitable? If yes, consider whether the advantages of foreign financing are sufficient to offset the advantages of relying on domestic sources to meet other resource needs.

3. Do target customers require a venture to be international? If yes, a global approach may be necessary to acquire a reasonable share of the market.

4. Will worldwide communication lead to quick responses from competitors in other countries? If yes, the best domestic defense may be an international offense.

5. Will worldwide sales be required to support the venture? If initial expenses (e.g., R&D) will be high, worldwide sales may be necessary to generate sufficient revenue to support the venture.

6. Will domestic inertia be crippling if internationalization is postponed? Changing the ethnocentric policies, procedures, product designs, and advertising strategies of your established domestic company may be more difficult than building a globally effective firm from the beginning.

MANAGING A FAMILY START-UP

Family-owned businesses are an integral part of the U.S. economy. Unfortunately, however, a family business often begets a family feud, which can destroy both the family and the business. For the employees of such a firm, getting caught in the cross fire is an occupational hazard, which no one really knows how to prevent. Family feuding often leaves employees wondering whether to look for new employment. Karen Langley (not her real name) explains why she eventually left the small family-owned company that she once worked for. The father, his sons, and their cousins fought constantly over the business, engaging in behavior that could best be described as back-stabbing. "It was very uncomfortable," she says. Distrust within the family was high, and it eventually spread beyond the family. One family member began accusing employees of stealing and began lurking around trying to watch everyone. "It really became impossible for me to stay there," she explained.[52]

Not every family business has these problems, of course. Janice Bryant Howroyd started her family business, ACT*1 Personnel Services, in part to serve her family. She employs seven brothers, sisters, nieces, and nephews who handle everything from marketing and accounting to technology. Her two teenage children own 49 percent of the $67 million business (mom owns the other 51 percent).[53] To increase their probability of success, families should take actions to ensure that the conditions shown in Figure 5.4 are in place. The following are some specific steps to take.

1. Decide who is responsible for what. Jobs in companies just starting up shouldn't be too narrowly defined. Families should recognize each other's areas of expertise to determine who is best able to make each decision.

2. Draw up a legal agreement specifying how to dispose of, or reallocate the equity in, the business when the current head of the business steps down or dies. This task may include developing a specific plan for deciding succession issues. In-

vestors and other outsiders have an interest in family member accord on how to handle management transitions.

3. Agree on how a decision will be made about whether and when to sell the business.

4. If the business will employ other family members, agree on the hiring criteria to be used before considering any particular family member.

5. Settle fights as they come up. If a family member does something on the job that makes another angry, correcting the problem requires that it be brought into the open.

6. Establish a board of advisers. Sometimes outsiders are needed to mediate a conflict or at least to provide a fresh perspective.

Figure 5.4   **Successful Family Businesses**

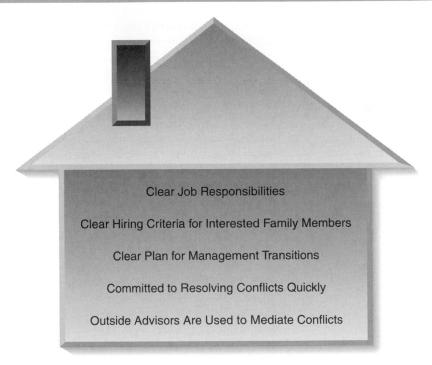

Clear Job Responsibilities

Clear Hiring Criteria for Interested Family Members

Clear Plan for Management Transitions

Committed to Resolving Conflicts Quickly

Outside Advisors Are Used to Mediate Conflicts

Similar to other types of businesses, family businesses have to address survival and operational issues. Survival issues may arise only once in the lifetime of the owners and the enterprise, but the way they are resolved may determine whether the firm will continue to exist. More than two-thirds of family-business owners want family ownership to continue into the next generation, but few have tackled the issues that need to be addressed to make that happen, which include

1. ensuring equitable estate treatment,

2. preparing for ownership transfer,

3. minimizing estate taxes,

4. ensuring the financial security of the senior generation, and

5. selecting and developing a successor.

Operational issues arise almost daily. Left unattended, they may become crises or even survival issues. Many operational issues that cause problems in family businesses are similar to those that might cause conflict in other types of businesses. However, because family members often are affected, emotional reactions can be more unpredictable. Particularly problematic is how to balance the need to make decisions that acknowledge both economic and "rational" criteria and personal relationship and family obligation criteria. Various family members may feel differently about the importance of these two sets of criteria, making disagreements difficult to resolve through consensus. In addition, whereas severing a relationship completely is a reasonable path to take when normal business relationships become frayed, severing relationships is an extreme and sometimes devastating way to react to frayed relationships in a family business.

If operational and relationship issues aren't resolved, the family itself may not survive. The experiences of Mary and Phil Baechler, unfortunately, aren't uncommon. Six months after Mary and Phil had their first child, Travis, Phil invented a jogger's stroller. When Phil and Mary took turns jogging, with Travis in the stroller, people would ask where they could purchase one. Mary's father finally convinced them to start a business. So with $8,000, they founded Racing Strollers in 1984.

After the Baechlers placed a small ad in *Runner's World,* customers started calling at all times of the day and night, assuming that operators were standing by to take orders. Mary couldn't stand putting a customer on the answering machine and spent countless hours taking orders. Phil just let customers put their orders on the answering machine. Mary had the ambition to make it big, always going that extra mile for a customer. Phil wasn't as driven and didn't go that extra mile. He enjoyed being an artist and designer, wanting only a sense of fulfillment and reasonable financial security. Mary viewed the business as a religion and got hooked on making money. Phil wanted a life away from work once they got home. He didn't want to hear about problems at Racing Strollers. Mary took all the problems home and wanted to discuss them.

After several years of nearly going broke, the business became profitable. While the business was doubling at least once a year, the marriage paid the price. When the stress, urgency to move the business forward, and neglect of the family clearly put too much strain on their marriage, the Baechlers had to make a choice. Mary finally chose business over marriage, and the couple started divorce proceedings. Mary became CEO of the company, under a new name, The Baby Jogger Company. The new company continues to sell the original stroller as well as several other models developed since then. Mary still owns the business, but a new CEO has taken over day-to-day operations. CEO Colette Berkheimer started with the company in 1988, as a secretary and grew with it. "We were really small back then, so you didn't just do the job you were hired for. You got to do a little bit of everything! I committed myself to learning everything about every aspect of this business."[54]

Anyone employed in a family firm—whether a family member or an outsider—is affected by how the family gets along. Their relationships and interactions influence the company's competitive position and survival prospects, career advancement opportunities, employee motivation and morale, and employee quality of life at work as well as at home.

ENTREPRENEURSHIP IN LARGE ORGANIZATIONS

4.

RECOGNIZE INTRAPRENEURS AND THE ORGANIZATIONAL CHARACTERISTICS THAT ENCOURAGE INTRAPRENEURSHIP.

Leaders recognize that entrepreneurial behavior within their companies can produce growth and profits. In fact, such behavior is essential for long-term survival. Thus corporate entrepreneurship, once considered a contradiction in terms, has become widely accepted in successful companies. [55]

Consider for a moment why an organization exists. It has a mission and some goals to be accomplished, which require the efforts of more than one person. At the very least, a business has a long-term goal of satisfying customers so that it can become and remain profitable.

Fundamental to organizing is dividing up the work. Managers may think that they have organized successfully when they have brought different interests together, minimized conflict, increased stability, and reduced uncertainty. But they often overlook the effects of those organizing efforts on entrepreneurial tendencies. Is the new climate conducive to change? Will disruption be tolerated? Is redirection possible?

Large organizations usually are formally structured for efficiency. Their managers run operations in such a way that the same activities will continue indefinitely into the future. Obviously, this approach often is at odds with innovation and change. Employees come to take the working environment for granted, and individual efforts to foster change may be met with resistance. What then can be done to encourage entrepreneurship when a company needs to be revitalized? The answer lies in changing—perhaps even inciting a revolution in—an organization's practices. One way to do so is for the company to support intrapreneurs.

INTRAPRENEURS

The term *intrapreneur* was coined to describe someone in an organization who turns ideas into profitable realities.[56] Introduction of the IBM personal computer represents an intrapreneurial activity. The company assigned development of the PC to Philip Estridge. He and his group proceeded to violate many time-honored IBM traditions. They used outside suppliers to speed up development and hold down costs, rather than depending solely on other IBM divisions. And they marketed PCs directly through retailers, rather than relying on IBM's sales organization. Estridge was able to accomplish his vision because initially he had the support of top management. Owing to differences that eventually arose between Estridge and corporate management, he left IBM in 1994, however. At 3M, Art Fry was one of the company's many successful intrapreneurs. Fry invented Post-it Notes and convinced 3M of their usefulness about 20 years ago. "When I first started telling people about my idea for Post-it Notes, no one understood what I was talking about. People had never heard of a 'repositionable note,' and they couldn't conceive of such a phenomenon. I had to launch my own campaign to get the project off the ground," he recalls.[57]

A more recent example of intrapreneurship was the creation of CNNFN, which is CNN's financial news station. In that case, Lou Dobbs took the lead. He not only got the station up and running, he also served as the news anchor for the channel's daily financial news program, which was then called *Moneyline News Hour with Lou Dobbs*. Like Estridge, Dobbs eventually left CNN owing to differences that arose between him and corporate management. Within a few months, he had founded a new venture called iSpace.com.

Not every employee can become a successful intrapreneur. It requires unusually well-developed strategic action, teamwork, and communication competencies. The person who is going to establish a new intrapreneurial venture must have a dream. Yet this dream, almost of necessity, is going to be at odds with what the rest of the organization is doing. So, to establish the new venture, the individual will have to sell that dream to others while simultaneously challenging the organization's beliefs and assumptions. Having successfully communicated a dream that others buy into, developing the venture requires that the intrapreneur build a team to work on the venture, crossing departmental lines, structures, and reporting systems. Intrapreneurial activities can cause some disruption, particularly in large organizations where each manager's "turf" has been staked out carefully over the years, so being diplomatic and avoiding win-lose conflicts is essential. Even organizational diplomats aren't immune to the frustrations that occur throughout the establishment of any new intrapreneurial venture, so a strong support team is needed to carry the intrapreneur through endless trials and tribulations.

FOSTERING INTRAPRENEURSHIP

Top management can foster an intrapreneurial culture by eliminating obstacles and providing incentives for intrapreneurship.[58] Organizations that redirect themselves through innovation have the following characteristics.

- **Commitment from senior management.** Such commitment must include a willingness to tolerate failure. Top managers must regularly communicate their commitment to intrapreneurial activities—and back their words with actions.

- **Flexible organization design.** Intrapreneurial organizations are designed for fast action. Management gives information—and the authority to make decisions—to those best positioned to react to changing market conditions. These people often are first-line managers.

- **Autonomy of the venture team.** Closely aligned with flexibility is maintaining a hands-off policy in day-to-day management of the team charged with implementing an innovation. Successful intrapreneurs usually are allowed considerable leeway in their actions.

- **Competent and talented people who exhibit entrepreneurial behaviors and attitudes.** A willingness to volunteer isn't sufficient reason to assign someone to a venture team—that person also must be competent in that or a related area. Competent volunteers usually have experience in, or have received training for, new-venture creation. Some companies conduct formal training programs; others establish mentor or coaching relationships. Even so, most intrapreneurs have experienced at least one failure before achieving successes that more than offset early losses.

- **Incentives and rewards for risk taking.** Intrapreneurs may not be willing to risk their careers and undergo the frustration of forcing change only for the satisfaction of giving life to their ventures. The developers of successful ventures should be generously compensated. Intrapreneurship should not be a dead-end activity; rather, it should be linked to an identifiable career path of advancement.

- **An appropriately designed control system.** Nothing is more stifling to an intrapreneurial activity than bureaucratic controls. Nevertheless, despite the potential contradiction between strong controls and the intrapreneurial spirit, senior management can't give up its accountability for new-venture projects. Controlling internal innovations means collecting and analyzing data that enable management to predict, to a reasonable degree, where the new-venture team is headed. It also involves ensuring that the team understands the difference between intrapreneurial behavior and irresponsible risk taking.

Islands of intrapreneurial activity have been called **_skunkworks_**. The subculture within a skunkworks is similar to those in many incubator organizations. Formal rules and procedures are ignored in favor of experimentation and innovation. Violations of reporting policies and review procedures are tolerated by top management, however, only as long as the team stays focused on helping the company bring new products and services to market ahead of competitors.[59] As is true for stand-alone new ventures, tying performance to rewards can keep a skunkworks team focused on its goal. Incentives should reward its cooperation with other parts of the organization and those in units that cooperate with and support the intrapreneurial project. Finally, in order for intrapreneurial activities to occur, top management must provide appropriate leadership. People generally are recruited to intrapreneurial activities by charismatic leaders, who support norms and values that foster innovative activity.

Of course, a large organization isn't likely to support a particular skunkworks operation forever. If the effort succeeds, operations will be formalized, and the team might become the nucleus around which a new divison is formed. If the effort fails to meet expectations, it might be closed down. A third possibility is to spin off the skunkworks and allow it to operate as a separate subsidiary. This approach allows the parent organization to obtain a return on its investment while keeping the entrepreneurial spirit alive.

CHAPTER SUMMARY

Entrepreneurial activity fluctuates over time, but currently is on the rise in the United States. Many people think of entrepreneurs and small-business owners as being the same, but that isn't necessarily the case.

1. EXPLAIN WHAT ENTREPRENEURS DO AND DESCRIBE HOW THE ENVIRONMENT SUPPORTS THEIR ACTIVITIES.

Entrepreneurs are people who create new business activity in the economy. If they do so by starting a new company, entrepreneurs are also small-business owners. Other entrepreneurs create new business activity within large organizations. Often the reasons that entrepreneurs give for starting their own companies are to be their own bosses and have more control over their lives. When they start their companies, the goal of many entrepreneurs is for the business to grow slowly. When their companies grow rapidly for a sustained period of time, however, they are considered to be more successful. Rapid technological change, low interest rates, and high immigration rates all stimulate entrepreneurial activity. Local conditions that meet the needs of entrepreneurs—such as a good labor force and easy networking—also can stimulate entrepreneurial activity.

2. DESCRIBE THE PERSONAL CHARACTERISTICS THAT CONTRIBUTE TO ENTREPRENEURS' SUCCESS.

Personal characteristics of entrepreneurs include the need for achievement, desire for independence, self-confidence, and willingness to make personal sacrifices. These characteristics often are developed early in life and seem to be shaped greatly by the family environment. Having a parent who was an entrepreneur and being involved in entrepreneurial activities increase the likelihood that a child will become an entrepreneur. Entrepreneurs usually are technically proficient in areas related to their busi-

nesses. Managerial competencies are as important for entrepreneurs as they are for other managers. Strategic action, planning and administration, teamwork, and communication competencies seem to be especially important for entrepreneurs.

3. DESCRIBE THE PLANNING REQUIREMENTS ASSOCIATED WITH BECOMING A SUCCESSFUL ENTREPRENEUR.

Entrepreneurs can improve their chances for success by creating a business plan and following it. A prospective entrepreneur must consider questions such as: (1) What are my motivations for owning a business? (2) Should I start a business or buy one? (3) Is there an adequate market for my product or service? (4) How much will it cost, and where will I obtain the start-up funds? (5) Should I start a domestic or global organization? (6) How will I manage growth? and (7) What is involved in running a successful family business? Operating a family business leads to some unique opportunities and some special problems. Failure to manage them can spell doom for the company as well as the family.

4. RECOGNIZE INTRAPRENEURS AND THE ORGANIZATIONAL CHARACTERISTICS THAT ENCOURAGE INTRAPRENEURSHIP.

Within an organization, intrapreneurship involves turning ideas into marketable products and services. Fostering intrapreneurship and successfully marketing new ventures require a commitment by management, flexible organizational structures, autonomy of the venture team competent and talented intrapreneurs, incentives and rewards for risk taking, and appropriate control systems. To encourage innovation and prevent formal rules and procedures from interfering with the development of new ideas, large organizations often set up skunkworks. Their activities are less formalized, and they usually have unique subcultures.

KEY TERMS

Angel, p. 149
Business plan, p. 145
Corridor principle, p. 140
Entrepreneur, p. 134
Family business, p. 137

Franchise, p. 147
Incubator organization, p. 136
Intrapreneur, p. 153
Lifestyle venture, p. 146
Serial entrepreneur, p. 140

Skunkworks, p. 154
Small-business owner, p. 136
Venture capitalists, p. 148

QUESTIONS FOR DISCUSSION AND COMPETENCY DEVELOPMENT

1. What does it take to start an entrepreneurial business?

2. Why have more women and members of minority groups become actively involved in entrepreneurial activities recently?

3. What is the most common strategy of fast-growing companies, and why is this strategy so effective?

4. Why would an entrepreneur prefer to launch an entirely new venture rather than buy an existing firm?

5. Why are governments around the world eager to create conditions that support entrepreneurial activity?

6. **Planning and administration competency.** Obtaining funding for a new venture is one of the key steps that can lead to success. Investigate what you should do to increase your chances of developing a business plan that appeals to venture capitalists and angels and identify some specific possible sources of funds. Begin your research by visiting sources such as ***http://www.universityangels.com***.

7. **Teamwork competency.** Teamwork is important to any small business, including a family business. What are some of the special problems that family businesses seem to experience when it comes to working together as a team? Develop a short list of recommendations for families that want to maintain a positive team atmosphere. Begin your research by visiting ***http://www.fambiz.com***.

CASE FOR COMPETENCY DEVELOPMENT

"And Now for Something Completely Different"[60]

Jirka Rysavy built Corporate Express into the world's largest direct-to-business office supply company. When he started, the business was a money-losing stationery store in Boulder, Colorado. He bought it by paying $100 and agreeing to assume the store's $15,000 debt. During the first year, he closed the stationery storefront, dropped the company's small accounts, and focused on corporate clients. Rysavy's vision was to become "the IBM of office supply companies." When sales grew by 800 percent that year, the vision began to seem feasible.

Corporate Express wasn't Rysavy's first start-up attempt. By the time he bought the stationery store, he already had opened another company to distribute environmental products. He was also a founding partner of Traders of the Lost Arts, a shop that sold Third World crafts. His success with these other small businesses may have helped him convince First Interstate Bank to finance a $7.8 million purchase of the poorly performing stationery division of Denver's NBI. Through this and similar acquisitions, Corporate Express grew from 11 employees to 23,000 employees, and from $2 million in annual revenues to $3.2 billion. Companies such as Hewlett-Packard, Sun Microsystems, and Exxon saved millions of dollars annually by outsourcing their stockrooms to Corporate Express.

How did this Czechoslovakian émigré who was flat broke in 1984 make his assets grow to nearly $50 million in about a decade? His ability to stay focused is surely part of the story. For many of those years, he chose to live alone in a small mountain cabin with no TV or running water—he continued to live like that even after becoming quite wealthy. Being comfortable with risk also helped. Even when Corporate Express's stock price fell by 41 percent in 1 day, he just went home at the end of the day and followed his usual routine—a vegetarian dinner, a few hours of meditation, and a good night's sleep. "To panic in a crisis is the worst thing you can do," he explained. Instead of panicking, Rysavy had his mind on expansion and growth.

In 1997, Rysavy shifted responsibility for the company's daily operations to a boyhood pal in order to focus his own energy on leading the company's diversification into software distribution services and overseas growth. Two years later, Internet-based business-to-business activity exploded. Corporate Express was well positioned to ride this new wave, but Rysavy chose not to take the ride himself. Instead, he sold Corporate Express to Buhrman, an office products firm headquartered in Amsterdam. Rysavy took a seat on the board of directors for the merged companies, but now most of his energy is refocused on the firm he had created in 1988—Gaiam, Inc.

Gaiam is an environmentally friendly company that designs and sells "green" products and services. The company's mission is to "become the source for individuals and businesses interested in natural health, ecological lifestyles, personal growth, and sustainable commerce." Besides individual consumers, Gaiam's customers include such giants as Kmart, Target, and Amazon.com. The company prides itself on involvement in activities that give back to the community and the environment. For example, it works with the Arbor Day Foundation and the Rain Forest Rescue organization to plant new trees and preserve existing trees throughout the world. Closer to home, it works with Habitat for Humanity and Community Food Share, as well as various other community service organizations.

Questions

1. Compared to Corporate Express, Gaiam seems more like a lifestyle venture that reflects Rysavy's personal values as an approach to living. Can a lifestyle venture with such a specialized focus grow and thrive in the hands of a serial entrepreneur?

2. If the company grows, will it be able to maintain its core value of being environmentally friendly? What should Gaiam do to help ensure that this happens?

3. How long do you think Rysavy will stay as CEO of Gaiam before deciding to build yet another company? Explain.

To learn more about how Jirka Rysavy's second entrepreneurial venture is doing, visit the company's home page at ***http://www.gaiam.com***.

Yahoo!

Started by two Stanford electrical engineering Ph.D. candidates as a way simply to keep track of their personal interests on the Web, Yahoo!, Inc., has since become one of the most recognized brands associated with the Internet. In 1994, the company's founders, David Filo and Jerry Yang, realized that their personal lists of Web sites were becoming too cumbersome and decided to develop a customized database to simplify such information. They also realized that such a system would benefit greatly the many thousands of people and organizations that were beginning to use the Internet. As a result, Filo and Yang developed customized software to help users locate, identify, and edit material stored on the Internet, and Yahoo! emerged. Then, in 1995, Marc Andreessen (cofounder of Netscape Communications) invited Filo and Yang to move their files to Netscape's larger computers.

As Yahoo! evolved from a hobby to a business, Filo and Yang made several wise management planning and control function decisions. First, because of the highly competitive nature of the industry, Yahoo!'s three-part corporate strategy emphasizes the need for continuous product innovation. Second, the founders selected an organization design that reflects the rapidly changing Internet environment. Finally, the firm's cultural values stress continuous improvement, customer satisfaction, and product integrity. Filo and Yang's understanding of the importance of the planning and controlling managerial functions has greatly contributed to Yahoo!'s success.

As the first online navigational guide to the Web, Yahoo!, Inc., has become a global Internet communications, commerce, and media company serving more than 150 million people worldwide. It is currently the industry leader in terms of traffic, advertising, household, and business user reach. Also, to enhance its Web presence, the company has diversified by offering a variety of online business services, including audio and video streaming, store hosting and management, and Web site tools and services. Headquartered in Santa Clara, California, the company's global Web network includes 23 properties outside the United States, with offices in Europe, Latin America, Canada, and the Pacific Rim.

Questions

1. Explain how Yahoo! emphasizes product innovation in its corporate strategy.

2. Discuss how Yahoo!'s organization design accurately reflects and addresses the rapidly changing Internet environment.

3. Yahoo! is successful because of the teamwork competency of its managers. Define *teamwork competency* and what is needed to achieve it.

To learn more about Yahoo!, visit the company's home page at ***http://www.yahoo.com***.

Ethics and Corporate Social Responsibility

AFTER STUDYING THIS CHAPTER YOU SHOULD BE ABLE TO:

1. STATE THE IMPORTANCE OF ETHICS FOR INDIVIDUAL EMPLOYEES AND ORGANIZATIONS.

2. DESCRIBE FOUR FORCES THAT INFLUENCE THE ETHICAL BEHAVIOR OF INDIVIDUALS AND CORPORATE SOCIAL RESPONSIBILITY.

3. DESCRIBE THREE APPROACHES THAT PEOPLE USE WHEN MAKING ETHICAL JUDGMENTS.

4. EXPLAIN HOW THE CONCERNS OF STAKEHOLDERS INFLUENCE MANAGERS' ETHICAL DECISIONS.

5. DESCRIBE HOW INDIVIDUALS AND ORGANIZATIONS CAN CONTRIBUTE TO IMPROVING ETHICAL CONDUCT IN THE WORK SETTING.

Chapter Outline

PREVIEW: THE MAKING OF A GREEN FORD

IMPORTANCE OF ETHICS AND CORPORATE SOCIAL RESPONSIBILITY

FOUR FORCES THAT SHAPE ETHICAL CONDUCT

SOCIETAL NORMS AND CULTURE

LAWS AND REGULATIONS

GLOBAL AWARENESS COMPETENCY: Social Accountability 8000 Guidelines Provide Direction

ORGANIZATIONAL PRACTICES AND CULTURE

INDIVIDUAL PERSPECTIVES

THREE APPROACHES TO MAKING ETHICAL JUDGMENTS

SELF-MANAGEMENT COMPETENCY: Managerial Values Profile

UTILITARIAN APPROACH

MORAL RIGHTS APPROACH

JUSTICE APPROACH

COMBINING ETHICAL APPROACHES

MANAGING CORPORATE SOCIAL RESPONSIBILITY

STAKEHOLDERS

STAKEHOLDER CONCERNS

STRATEGIC ACTION COMPETENCY: Dow Cleans Up Its Act

EVALUATING CORPORATE SOCIAL PERFORMANCE

ENCOURAGING ETHICAL CONDUCT

PLANNING & ADMINISTRATION COMPETENCY: How Could They Not Know?

ORGANIZATIONAL PRACTICES

CHAPTER SUMMARY

KEY TERMS

QUESTIONS FOR DISCUSSION AND COMPETENCY DEVELOPMENT

CASE FOR COMPETENCY DEVELOPMENT: PASSION AT PATAGONIA

VIDEO CASE: BEN & JERRY'S

THE MAKING OF A GREEN FORD

In his day, Henry Ford made history by adopting an employee-friendly policy—paying his employees $5 for a day's work. A century and three generations later, Bill Ford, Jr., Henry's great-grandson hopes to make history by showing that big auto manufacturers don't have to sacrifice profits in order to help save the environment. Not everyone at the company thinks he's on the right track. One of Bill Ford's first attempts to put environmental issues on the company's agenda occurred 10 years ago, after he had just been promoted to director of business strategy. Soon after sending out a memo announcing that he would hold a meeting to discuss environmental issues, the company's lawyer visited him. His message? That Bill couldn't hold the meeting and that he intended to tell people not to go. The meeting was held anyway, but not many people attended—other than the lawyers! Even as the director of business strategy, Bill Ford had too little influence

to create much momentum for his environmental mission.

As chairman, Bill Ford may finally be in a position to make a real difference. His mission is nothing less than to change the face of industry. He recently pulled Ford out of the Global Climate Coalition—a group that combats the spread of theories about global warming. Within 3 months, DaimlerChrysler, GM, and Texaco had followed his lead. When a disastrous explosion destroyed much of the old Ford Rouge plant, he hired an architect known for his environmentally friendly designs to direct its rebuilding. Contrary to the image many people have of industrial corporate leaders, Bill Ford believes that his company does best for its shareholders by doing good in the community, taking care of employees, and safeguarding the environment. Even union leaders, such as the president of UAW Local 600, acknowledge that Bill Ford is different: "His concern for people,

for the community, for the environment—those are things you just don't see in industrialists." Activist Robert Massie agrees. "I think Bill Ford has the potential for being a really thrilling corporate leader. It's funny for me to talk like this. Ralph Nader would say to me, 'What did he [Bill Ford] put in your coffee?'"

Of course, not everyone is so supportive. Explains Ford, "There are people who think I'm a Bolshevik, and that this is all a major distraction at best and heresy at worst. But I really don't care. I'm in this for my children and my grandchildren. I want them to inherit a legacy they're proud of. I don't want anybody. . . to have to apologize for working for Ford Motor Company. I want them to look and say, 'What a difference we made!'"[1]

To learn more about Bill Ford, Jr., and the Ford Motor Company, visit the company's home page at

http://www.ford.com

IMPORTANCE OF ETHICS AND CORPORATE SOCIAL RESPONSIBILITY

1.

STATE THE IMPORTANCE OF ETHICS FOR INDIVIDUAL EMPLOYEES AND ORGANIZATIONS.

Bill Ford, Jr., is working to make his company a leader by adopting a proactive approach to corporate social responsibility. Driven by his personal ethical values, he wants to see Ford Motor Company make a positive difference by going beyond the minimum standards imposed by laws and government regulations. His ethical approach is based on the assumption that managers and employees should be guided by more than narrow economic interests; that personal and societal values should also guide a company's actions. Is he alone in these beliefs? Apparently not. A survey of students at 50 business schools found that half the respondents would accept lower pay to work for a company they believed was "very socially responsible." Forty-three percent said that they wouldn't take a job at a company that wasn't socially responsible.[2] So Ford's commitment to socially responsible practices may make it more attractive to many students seeking employment.

Interestingly, men and women seem to differ when it comes to judging ethical behavior in business situations. When researchers analyzed data from more than 20,000 people, they found that women were more likely to view specific business practices as unethical. Compared to men, women seem to be especially critical of rule breaking and insider trading. Men tend to accept such practices unless it is clear that someone suffered monetary consequences. These gender gaps are especially large among students. Are the differences a matter of biology? Probably not. Gender differences in judgments about ethical behavior seem to decline as people gain work experience, although they don't disappear.[3] These and other research results suggest that personal ethics reflect the experiences that people have over time.

Ethical issues facing managers and employees have grown in significance in recent years. By some estimates, fraudulent activities cause 30 percent of U.S. business failures.[4] No industry seems to be immune. Business scams have brought down financial institutions such as Cendant, discount retailers such as Phar-Mor, and even businesses based on religion, such as Jim Bakker's PTL ministry. These and numerous other high-profile scandals have drawn stakeholders' attention to the effects of unethical business practices and fueled demands for reform.[5]

In this chapter, we briefly describe four forces that influence and define ethical and unethical decisions and behavior—societal norms and values, laws and regulations, organizational practices and culture, and individual perspectives. Then we ask you to consider your own approach to ethical problems. You will discover how much your personal judgments are influenced by utilitarian thinking, a concern for moral rights, and a belief in maintaining a sense of justice. We then describe the stakeholder approach to considering issues of ethics. An analysis of stakeholders' interests can help decision makers recognize the unavoidable conflicts among them and aid in the search for solutions that balance and respect those interests. Finally, we discuss the issue of how you should behave if you witness unethical or illegal business practices.

FOUR FORCES THAT SHAPE ETHICAL CONDUCT

2.

DESCRIBE FOUR FORCES THAT INFLUENCE THE ETHICAL BEHAVIOR OF INDIVIDUALS AND CORPORATE SOCIAL RESPONSIBILITY.

In the most elementary sense, *ethics* is a set of values and rules that define right and wrong conduct. These values and rules indicate when behavior is acceptable and when it is unacceptable. What is considered ethical may depend on the perspective from which ethical issues are considered. Figure 6.1 identifies the four basic forces that influence the ethical conduct of individuals and organizations. Rarely can the ethical implications of decisions or behaviors be understood by considering only one of these forces.

| Figure 6.1 | **Forces That Shape Ethical Conduct** |

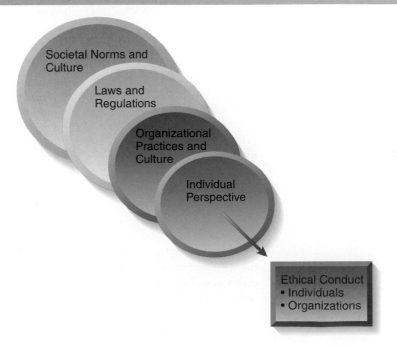

SOCIETAL NORMS AND CULTURE

A large part of any view of what is ethical comes from the society in which the behavior occurs. The media expose and report on decisions and behaviors, which then are judged publicly by many different critics and interest groups. In 1966, public interest groups acting through the U.S. Surgeon General forced tobacco companies to put warning labels on cigarette packaging. In 1971, pressure from these same groups forced tobacco companies to agree to ban tobacco ads on TV and radio. More recently, continued pressure from groups working on behalf of the public interest has resulted in even more severe restrictions on this industry. And the public protests continue. For the past 3 years, students at schools such as Yale and Cornell have been trying to persuade university officials to disinvest their tobacco company stocks.[6]

Dozens of studies have shown that smoking and chewing tobacco have negative health consequences, including an estimated 400,000 deaths annually in the United States alone. Tobacco companies have come under attack because many citizens believe that the companies behaved unethically. Covering up or ignoring the health risks associated with their products, designing addictive products, and youth-targeted advertising are some of the practices that many people consider to be unethical, regardless of whether they were actually illegal. When the Attorneys General of 40 states decided that the tobacco companies should be held legally liable for the health-related costs of smoking, the potential financial implications were so great that the tobacco companies agreed to a settlement that is costing them many billions of dollars. As part of the deal, they agreed not to oppose a new tax on cigarettes, to take actions to attempt to reduce teen smoking, and to withdraw advertising believed to be especially appealing to youth.[7]

LAWS AND REGULATIONS

What a society interprets as ethical or unethical frequently ends up being expressed in laws, government regulations, and court decisions. ***Laws*** are simply society's values and standards that are enforceable in the courts. The legality of actions and decisions doesn't necessarily make them ethical, however. At one time, for example, U.S. organizations could legally discriminate against women and minorities in hiring and promotions. As a consensus developed that such discriminatory practices were unethical, laws such as the Civil Rights Act of 1964 were passed to stop the practices and ensure equal employment opportunities for all citizens. The legal concept of employment-at-will provides another example of the interplay between changing societal views and changes in the law. ***Employment-at-will*** is a traditional common-law concept holding that employers are free to discharge employees for any reason at any time and that employees are free to quit their jobs for any reason at any time. Historically, employers often dismissed employees without explanation (at will). During the past 25 years, though, courts have modified the freewheeling notion that employees can be fired for any reason. Table 6.1[8] lists lawful and unlawful reasons for dismissing employees.

Research on corporate illegal behavior shows that it is bad for a company's reputation and profitability. After a corporation or one or more of its top executives has been convicted of illegal behavior, profits decline and sales slow for as long as 5 years. If a firm is convicted of multiple wrongdoings, the public is especially harsh in its views of the firm. Surprisingly, however, neither the public's reaction nor the negative impact on profits seems to be sufficient to convince wayward firms to change their ways. Even though performance declines after a conviction, a firm that engaged in illegalities in the past is likely to be convicted again in the future.[9]

When behavior is clearly unethical *and* illegal, taking a stand that satisfies both the courts and the public is relatively easy. In that case individual employees also have clear knowledge of what's right and what's wrong. But in many areas of business practices, judgments about right and wrong fall within a gray area of ambiguity. How should employees behave when the laws are unclear or conflicting or when societal opinions have shifted and old laws are being questioned as unethical? Under these circumstances, employees must look to the standards, policies, and practices of their organization and to their personal values and beliefs.

Table 6.1   **Lawful and Unlawful Reasons for Dismissing Employees**

Permissible Reasons

- Incompetence in performance that does not respond to training or to accommodation
- Gross or repeated insubordination
- Civil rights violations such as engaging in harassment
- Too many unexcused absences
- Illegal behavior such as theft
- Repeated lateness
- Drug activity on the job
- Verbal abuse
- Physical violence
- Falsification of records
- Drunkenness on the job

Unacceptable Reasons

- Blowing the whistle about illegal conduct by their employers (for example, opposing and publicizing employer policies or practices that violate laws such as the antitrust, consumer protection, or environmental protection laws)
- Cooperating in the investigation of a charge against the company
- Reporting Occupational Safety and Health Administration violations
- Filing discrimination charges with the Equal Employment Opportunity Commission or a state or municipal fair employment agency
- Filing unfair labor practice charges with the National Labor Relations Board (NLRB) or a state agency
- Filing a workers' compensation claim
- Engaging in concerted activity to protest wages, working conditions, or safety hazards
- Engaging in union activities, provided there is no violence or unlawful behavior
- Complaining or testifying about violations of equal pay, wage, or hour law
- Complaining or testifying about safety hazards or refusing an assignment because of the belief that it is dangerous

If a company operates in many different countries, local standards for ethical conduct may differ greatly from one location to the next. Hence developing ethical guidelines that make sense in various settings can be a complex task.[10] Some companies apply U.S. standards for ethical conduct universally in the belief that this approach won't violate ethical principles elsewhere. Other companies adapt to local practices, arguing that ethical standards make sense only when considered within a particular societal context.

A third alternative is to use the ***Social Accountability 8000 certification guidelines*** as standards for global business practices. As described in the following Global Awareness competency feature, these standards are intended to reflect expectations for good corporate citizenship in any culture.[11]

GLOBAL AWARENESS COMPETENCY

Social Accountability 8000 Guidelines Provide Direction

Being a good corporate citizen is important no matter where an organization does business. But how do managers know what good citizenship is, especially when they do business in dozens of different countries? It may be possible simply to learn and conform to the minimum requirements set by local laws and customs, but this approach complicates running a global business. It may be easier for companies to follow a single set of guidelines that ensure good citizenship in any country. Providing such guidelines is the objective of the Social Accountability 8000 (SA 8000) certification process. Created by the Council on Economic Priorities Accreditation Agency, which is now called Social

Accountablity International, the SA 8000 standards address business practices in the following areas: child labor, forced labor, health and safety, collective bargaining, discrimination, disciplinary action, working hours, and compensation.

The procedures for obtaining SA 8000 certification are similar to those used for ISO 9000 quality certification. Companies voluntarily participate in an intensive audit and agree to additional scheduled and unannounced inspections. Qualified companies receive the right to publicize their SA 8000 status. Supporters of SA 8000 certification argue that global standards such as these can be especially helpful to global companies that rely on suppliers located all over the world.

By requiring their suppliers to obtain SA 8000 certification, global companies such as Toys R Us and Avon can feel more confident that their goods and services will not be subject to protests over unethical business practices.

• • •

To learn more about SA 8000 certification, visit the home page of Social Accountability International at

http://www.cepaa.org

ORGANIZATIONAL PRACTICES AND CULTURE

Organizations influence employee actions both formally and informally. To provide formal guidance for employees, an organization can state clear policies that define ethical and unethical conduct. A ***code of ethics*** states the principles that employees are expected to follow when acting on behalf of the organization. Codes of ethics help employees understand the organization's norms and values, and provide basic rules for deciding what behavior is acceptable. Additional formal guidance may be offered through training programs that describe difficult ethical situations that employees may face and offer advice about how to deal with them.

The basic informal source of guidance is top management's behavior, which demonstrates the ethical principles that are important to the organization.[12] Unless top managers are very clear in the signals they send, however, employees can easily misinterpret what the organization values most. Consider what happened at Columbia Hospital Corporation of America. Managers at headquarters set quotas for doctors. The quotas were reasonable and most doctors achieved them. Management then decided to set more difficult "stretch" goals. These goals were challenging, but most doctors worked hard enough to achieve them. Managers set the next round of goals even higher. Some doctors fell short of the goals and began to fear the consequences. Out of fear, they figured out ways to "game" the system and appeared to be meeting their goals. Managers again increased quotas so that even the most hard-working doctors couldn't reach them. They, too, began to game the system. The process continued until eventually no one could achieve the goals honestly. By then, almost all the organization's employees had learned how to play the "game," and everyone felt entitled to cheat to protect their jobs.

Situations like the one just described are all too common. One survey of more than 4,000 employees found that 29 percent felt pressure to engage in conduct that violates their companies' business standards in order to meet organizational goals. About 25 percent reported that their managers looked the other way and ignored unethical conduct in order to achieve their goals.[13] Ignoring such conduct is apparently what happened at PriceWaterhouseCoopers (PWC), where at least half the 2,700 U.S. partners owned stock in companies that the firm audited. The practice is explicitly prohibited. The company tried to defend the fact that 1 of every 20 employees committed violations by describing the violations as "technical" in nature and unintentional. The Securities and Exchange Commission (SEC) rendered a harsher judgment. It concluded that PWC "made little or no effort to comply with" the most basic rules of auditor independence. Worried that the entire industry may be ignoring the rules, the SEC quickly began investigating all the other major public accounting firms.[14]

INDIVIDUAL PERSPECTIVES

Individuals have their own values and a sense of what is right or wrong. Sometimes an individual's view of what is ethical converges with the views of their organization and the larger society, but not always.

Psychological studies of ethical behavior suggest that people develop morally, much as they do physically, from early childhood to adulthood. As they develop, their ethical criteria and patterns of moral reasoning change. For children, the meaning of right and wrong is determined mostly by behaviors that are punished and behaviors that are rewarded. That is, only the immediate consequences of an action determine whether it's good or bad.[15] An employee who thinks like this would believe that the only reason not to steal money from an employer is the certainty of getting caught and then fired or even arrested. Most organizations don't want employees who use such simple reasoning to guide their behaviors when faced with ethical dilemmas.

Adults usually have more complex rules for judging what is right and wrong. They may take into account what pleases or helps friends or family and strive to be seen as a "good person" who is not motivated simply by self-interest. Doing one's duty, showing respect for authority, and maintaining the social order for its own sake may also be considered important when a person is deciding how to behave. Suppose, for example, that you work in an organization where employees commonly take paid sick days even when they aren't sick. Employees view these leave days as something the company owes them. However, the company policy states that sick days are allowed only for legitimate illnesses. If you worked in this organization, you would have to rely on your own individual perspective to decide how to behave. Would you abide by the organization's formal rules and take time off only when you were really sick? Would you inform the company that you knew that others were abusing the sick leave policy? Or would you be more interested in getting along with your peers and helping everyone get as much time off as possible? Or would you actively work to modify the rule in a way that does no harm to either your colleagues or the company as a whole? For example, you could encourage your employer to specify an allowable number of days off per year and allow employees to take these days for whatever reasons they choose. How you would approach the hypothetical example involving sick leave reflects your individual values and may reflect your general approach to resolving ethical dilemmas.

THREE APPROACHES TO MAKING ETHICAL JUDGMENTS

3.

DESCRIBE THREE APPROACHES THAT PEOPLE USE WHEN MAKING ETHICAL JUDGMENTS.

We have shown that an individual's ethical judgments can be shaped by many factors—the norms of society, laws, an organization's culture, and even the person's gender. How do you approach ethical questions? The following Self-Management Competency feature will give you insights into your general approach to ethical behavior. Before continuing to study this chapter, please take a few moments to fill out the Managerial Values Profile questionnaire.[16] Then calculate your three scores.

SELF-MANAGEMENT COMPETENCY

Managerial Values Profile

The Managerial Values Profile is designed to help managers identify the value premises that guide their managerial actions. The results can be useful for people who want to understand better the determinants of their own actions, as well as those who want to broaden their perspectives on managerial ethics.

INSTRUCTIONS

Twelve pairs of statements or phrases follow. Read each pair and check the one that you most agree with. You may, of course, agree with neither statement; in that case, you should check off the statement that you least disagree with, the "lesser of the two evils." It is essential that you select one and only one statement or phrase in each pair; your Managerial Values Profile cannot be scored unless you do so.

_____ 1. The greatest good for the greatest number	_____ 2. The individual's right to private property
_____ 3. Adhering to rules designed to maximize benefits to all	_____ 4. Individuals' rights to complete liberty in action, as long as others' rights are similarly respected
_____ 5. The right of an individual to speak freely without fear of being fired	_____ 6. Engaging in technically illegal behavior in order to attain substantial benefits for all
_____ 7. Individuals' rights to personal privacy	_____ 8. The obligation to gather personal information to insure that individuals are treated equitably
_____ 9. Helping those in danger when doing so would not unduly endanger oneself	_____ 10. The right of employees to know about any danger in the job setting
_____ 11. Minimizing inequities among employees in the job setting	_____ 12. Maintaining significant inequities among employees when the ultimate result is to benefit all
_____ 13. Organizations must not require employees to take actions that would restrict the freedom of others or cause other harm	_____ 14. Organizations must tell employees the full truth about work hazards
_____ 15. What is good is what helps the company attain ends that benefit everyone	_____ 16. What is good is equitable treatment for all employees of the company
_____ 17. Organizations must stay out of employees' private lives	_____ 18. Employees should act to achieve organizational goals that result in benefits to all
_____ 19. Questionable means are acceptable if they achieve good ends	_____ 20. Individuals must follow their own consciences, even if it hurts the organization
_____ 21. Safety of individual employees above all else	_____ 22. Obligation to aid those in great need
_____ 23. Employees should follow rules that preserve individuals' freedom of action while reducing inequities	_____ 24. Employees must do their best to follow rules designed to enhance organizational goal attainment

SCORING YOUR MANAGERIAL VALUES PROFILES

Below, circle the numbers of the statements or phrases that you checked off. When you have circled the numbers of all of your choices, add up the *number of circled items* in each column. Put this number in the row marked "Total." The total for any column can range from zero to eight. The higher your score, the more these values are important to you.

Utilitarian	Moral Rights	Justice
1	2	4
3	5	8
6	7	9
12	10	11
15	14	13
18	17	16
19	20	22
24	21	23
Total: _____	_____	_____

UTILITARIAN APPROACH

If your approach to ethical dilemmas is to weigh all the potentially positive outcomes of your action and compare them to all the possible negative outcomes, you probably had a high utilitarian score. People guided by the **utilitarian approach** focus on behaviors and their results, not on the motives for such actions.[17] A manager or employee guided by this approach considers the potential effects of alternative actions from the perspective of the accepted social contract. The alternative chosen is supposed to benefit the greatest number of people, although such benefit may come at the expense of the few or those with little power. In other words, a good alternative may harm some people, but even more people will be helped in some way.

According to classic capitalist theory, the primary managerial obligation is to maximize shareholders' profits and their long-term interests. Nobel Prize–winning economist Milton Friedman is probably the best-known advocate of this approach.[18] Friedman argues that using resources in ways that do not clearly maximize shareholder interests amounts to spending the owners' money without their consent—and is equivalent to stealing. According to Friedman, a manager can judge whether a decision is right or wrong by considering its consequences for the company's economic needs. The utilitarian approach prescribes ethical standards for managers and employees in the areas of organizational goals, efficiency, and conflicts of interest.[19]

Achieving Organizational Goals. The utilitarian approach asserts that businesses operating in a competitive market system can achieve the greatest good for the greatest number by maximizing profits. According to this logic, a company that achieves high profits can offer the highest quality products at the lowest prices for consumers. Profits are seen as the reward for satisfying consumers. If profits get too high, new competitors will enter the market, thereby increasing the supply of high-quality goods and pushing prices down.

According to Friedman, no firm *unilaterally* should go beyond what the law requires—to help preserve the environment, for example. Doing so would only reduce that firm's profits and would do nothing to eliminate the pollution caused by its competitors. Bill Ford, Jr., must successfully argue against this logic as he strives to adopt environmentally friendly practices at Ford Motor Company. Friedman contends that the government is responsible for protecting the environment and should pass environmental laws and regulations that apply to *all* companies. Companies that voluntarily go beyond what is required by law may lose out in the long run because their competitors will have lower costs and thus lower prices.

The utilitarian focus on company profits drives some companies to assess how all activities—even so-called "charitable" contributions—are related to business performance. A survey of contributions managers illustrates how prevalent this approach is. The survey found that two-thirds of the contributions managers were struggling to show how their company's donations and community service programs contributed to corporate goals.[20]

Efficiency. Managers and employees alike should try to attain organizational goals as efficiently as possible. Efficiency is achieved by minimizing inputs (e.g., labor, land, and capital) and maximizing outputs. If technologies are available that allow an organization to produce goods or deliver services at a lower cost, it should use them. It should do so regardless of the consequences in terms of layoffs, retraining costs, or moving production overseas to obtain lower wages and be subject to fewer restrictive regulations. According to the utilitarian approach, should a company be concerned with whether an overseas production facility that it relies on meets SA 8000 certification standards? If you said *no,* you answered correctly.

Conflicts of Interest. Managers and employees alike should not have personal interests that conflict with the organization's achievement of its goals. A purchasing agent having a significant financial interest in one of the firm's major suppliers faces a potential conflict of interest. Again, the reason for this proscription relates to profitability. In this case, the purchasing agent might be motivated to purchase from that supplier, even when the price or quality isn't the best available. In the case of accounting firms such as PWC, owning stock in a company they audit may lead to a desire to give a more favorable audit result in order to maintain the value of their shares of stock.

Nonprofit organizations too must be careful to avoid conflicts of interest as they struggle to support their activities. In the arts, for example, critics are quick to raise concerns when commercial considerations threaten to reduce the support that artistic institutions provide for independent artists. When the Solomon R. Guggenheim Museum announced that it would honor Italian designer Giorgio Armani by having an exhibit of his work, it was criticized for being influenced by a $15 million gift that Armani had given the museum several months earlier. This potential conflict of interest followed soon after the Guggenheim held an exhibit titled "Art of the Motorcycle," which was sponsored by BMW. Museum directors usually make decisions involving potential conflicts of interest on a case by case basis. In reaction to decisions such as those made by the Guggenheim—which are increasingly common at major museums—pressure to take a more systematic approach is growing. Recently, for example, the Association of Art Museum Directors created a committee to review its professional practice guidelines on finances.[21] In the absence of clear guidelines, managers of nonprofit organizations are left in the uncomfortable position of balancing the nonfinancial, value-based goals of their organizations with the ever-present need to generate revenue to pursue those goals.

Conflicts of interest can sometimes be difficult to judge. At PWC, for example, many of the people involved felt that the rules barring employees from owning stock in companies that the firm audits are outdated and largely irrelevant today because stock ownership is so widespread. Identifying conflicts of interest can be even trickier when cultural differences are added to the mix, as one U.S. businessman discovered when on assignment in Russia. He was working with a senior Russian partner, who also happened to own some other businesses. When the Russian began to "borrow" company materials and equipment, the U.S. partner viewed his behavior as unethical. The Russian saw no conflict of interest; using the equipment in two companies of which he was an owner seemed both reasonable and efficient.[22]

The utilitarian approach is consistent with strong values of individualism, acceptance of uncertainty, and masculinity, as defined in Chapter 3. These values support profit maximization, self-interest, rewards based on abilities and achievements, sacrifice and hard work, and competition.[23] Many economists espouse the utilitarian approach, but it receives less support from the general public. During the past 25 years, utilitarian ethics have been increasingly challenged and tempered by the moral rights and justice approaches.

MORAL RIGHTS APPROACH

The **moral rights approach** holds that decisions should be consistent with fundamental rights and privileges (e.g., life, freedom, health, and privacy), as set forth in documents such as the first 10 amendments to the U.S. Constitution (the Bill of Rights) and the United Nations' Declaration of Human Rights.[24] Several U.S. laws require managers and other employees to consider these rights as guides for decision making and behaviors.

Life and Safety. In the United States, many laws require businesses to comply with society's view of appropriate standards for quality of life and safety. Employees, customers, and the general public have the right *not* to have their lives and safety unknowingly and unnecessarily endangered. For example, this moral right in large part justifies the U.S. Occupational Safety and Health Act (OSHA) of 1970, which contains many requirements designed to increase the safety and healthfulness of work environments. Among other things, OSHA and its implementing regulations restrict the use of asbestos, lead-based paint, and various toxic chemicals in the workplace. Businesses operating in other countries often find that laws are less restrictive there, so they must choose whether to meet only the standards of the host country or exceed those legal requirements. General Motors chose to use a higher standard than required for its operations in Mexico. Although it wasn't legally required to do so, the company spent more than $10 million to install small stand-alone sewage treatment systems in towns throughout Mexico. According to Lee Crawford, a managing director working there, "It was just something we felt was the right thing to do. . . . Water is one of the biggest single problems in Mexico." As an indication of how important these projects were to that country, the Mexican government honored GM with its Aguila Azteca award for humanitarian service.[25]

Like the quality of water, the quality of housing that people can afford affects their overall quality of life. Wages and housing costs, in turn, limit what people can afford. In California's Silicon Valley, many people highly skilled in computer and electronics technology have become millionaires by the age of 30. Their wealth has helped drive up housing costs by 65 percent in 5 years. At the same time, increased reliance on outsourcing and subcontracting has driven down wages of less-skilled, nontechnical employees—they make 10 percent less today than they did a decade ago.[26] A utilitarian approach would view this growing gap between the economic haves and have-nots as contributing to efficiency and profitability. A moral rights perspective would suggest that thriving corporations should distribute their wealth more evenly to ensure that all employees involved in their business can afford decent housing.

Truthfulness. Employees, customers, shareholders, and the general public have the right *not* to be intentionally deceived on matters about which they should be informed. The classic legal concept of *caveat emptor*—"let the buyer beware"—used to be the defense for a variety of shady business practices. During the 1950s and 1960s, an increasingly aware public began to challenge the ethics of such a position. Shifting societal attitudes and values concerning *appropriate* behavior by businesses led to a flood of U.S. consumer legislation during the late 1960s and early 1970s, which substantially diminished the influence of that concept. Today, quality improvement practices and customer-oriented practices make such an approach to customer relations risky. Nevertheless, the rapid speed of change inevitably means that there will always be opportunities legally to withhold information—and thereby deceive customers, shareholders, employees, and the general public.

Privacy. The moral right of citizens to control access to personal information about themselves and its use by government agencies, employers, and others was the basis for the U.S. Privacy Act of 1974. The act restricts the use of certain types of information by the federal government and limits those to whom this information can be released. The 1988 Video Privacy Protection Act is an example of a more specific law designed to ensure that privacy rights are respected. This act forbids retailers from disclosing video rental records without the customer's consent or a court order. For example, a customer who rents exercise videos need not worry about getting on mailing lists for exercise equipment catalogs, fitness magazines, and the like.

With the availability of an array of new information technologies (especially computers and videos), enormous concern has been expressed about invasions of privacy.[27] A few of these privacy issues include drug testing, honesty testing, confidentiality of medical and psychological counseling records, managerial monitoring of e-mail and work performed on computers, access to credit records, and the gathering and sale of personal information gleaned from the Internet.

Video monitoring is an example of the use of one technology that has become widespread, despite the negative reaction many people have to the idea of having everything they do recorded on tape. For example, at hundreds of Dunkin' Donuts shops, the walls have ears that can hear conversations between customers as they wait in line to be served, as well as monitor conversations among employees. Franchise owners believe that this form of intrusion is necessary to increase security and keep employees on their toes. But some employees and customers have expressed concerns. They feel like they are being spied on. People react in a similar way when they hear about software programs designed to keep track of their accessing of Web sites via the Internet.

Freedom of Conscience and Speech. Often speech is a vehicle for expressing matters of conscience. So freedom of speech is closely related to freedom of conscience. Thus individual employees have the right to refrain from carrying out orders that violate their moral or religious beliefs. They also have the right to criticize the ethics or legality of their employers' actions, so long as the criticisms are conscientious and truthful and do not violate the rights of others within or outside the organization.

The freedoms of speech and conscience have often been at the center of ethical debates associated with new media, such as the Internet. Should executives at Yahoo! accept advertisements from companies engaged in pornographic activity? Advertisements for pornographic products and services have long been banished from broadcasts of the major television networks. But the culture of the Internet supports aggressive adherence to principles of free speech. Permitting such advertising may be consistent with the principle of free speech for advertisers. However, parents whose children are exposed to pornography on the Web often express other concerns. Knowing of these concerns, a manufacturer of snacks that knows its logo might appear next to a pornography ad needs to think carefully about whether to advertise on that Internet site.[28]

As a guide to ethical decision making in organizations, the moral rights approach serves as an effective counterweight that protects the nonbusiness sectors of society from overenthusiastic capitalists strictly following the utilitarian approach. However, as a guide to ethical behavior in organizations, the moral rights approach says more about what organizations should *avoid* doing—that is, violating the moral rights of employees, customers, and members of society—than it does about what *to* do. The justice approach provides more guidance in this regard.

JUSTICE APPROACH

The *justice approach* involves evaluating decisions and behavior with regard to how equitably they distribute benefits and costs among individuals and groups.[29] To ensure just decisions and behavior, the proponents of this approach argue that three principles should be followed when designing management systems and making organizational decisions: the distributive justice principle, the procedural fairness principle, and the natural duty principle.

Distributive Justice Principle. The *distributive justice principle* morally requires that individuals not be treated differently on the basis of arbitrarily defined characteristics. It holds that (1) individuals who are similar in relevant respects should be treated similarly, and (2) individuals who differ in relevant respects should be treated differently in proportion to the differences between them. A legal regulation that supports the distributive justice principle is the U.S. Equal Pay Act of 1963. It made illegal the payment of different wages to women and men when their jobs require equal skill, effort, and responsibility and are performed under similar working conditions. Prior to the passage of this act, it was common for women to be paid at two-thirds the rate of men doing the same work. The practice of unequal pay for men and women doing equal work was a holdover from practices adopted during World War II, when many women entered the workforce to replace men who left the factories to go into the armed services.[30]

Perceptions about what constitutes distributive justice also are behind recent concerns over the growing disparity between the compensation packages that CEOs receive and the pay levels of everyone else. Should the average daily compensation for CEOs be more than most workers make in an entire year? Is it fair for the average CEO's pay be rising at a rate that is six or seven times the rate of increase for other workers? According to the distributive justice principle, these pay levels rates of increase are ethical if the contributions of a CEO are proportionately greater and if the value of the contributions has been increasing at a much faster rate than those of the average worker.[31]

Fairness Principle. The *fairness principle* morally requires employees to support the rules of the organization so long as the organization is just (or fair) and employees have voluntarily accepted some benefits or opportunities in order to further their own interests. Employees are then expected to follow the organization's rules, even though those rules might restrict their individual choices. For example, if an applicant was informed that accepting a job offer would later involve being subjected to random drug testing and continuous video monitoring, the organization could expect the employee also to accept these conditions of employment. Under the fairness principle, both the organization and its employees have obligations and both should accept their responsibilities. Their mutual obligations can be considered fair so long as they were voluntarily agreed to, they were spelled out clearly, and they are consistent with a common interest in the survival of the organization.[32]

Perceptions of fairness often reflect people's reactions to the procedures used to resolve problems. Acceptable processes lead to perceived *procedural justice*. For example, a company's management practices are more likely to be perceived as fair when a formal process is in place for investigating employees' grievances and taking remedial actions, when needed.[33] Similarly, top managers working in foreign subsidiaries are sensitive to issues of procedural justice. Believing that their multinational employers use fair procedures in making resource allocations inspires them to go beyond the call of duty in their work and leads to more cooperative and creative behavior.[34]

Natural Duty Principle. In exchange for certain moral rights, people must accept certain responsibilities and duties. The ***natural duty principle*** morally requires that decisions and behavior be based on universal principles associated with being a responsible member of society. Four universal duties are

- to help others who are in need or in jeopardy, provided that the help can be given without excessive personal risk or loss;

- not to harm or injure another;

- not to cause unnecessary suffering; and

- to support and comply with just institutions.

In exchange for accepting these duties or responsibilities, a person is entitled to certain rights. The natural duty principle complements the moral rights approach. For example, if a manager has the right to safety at work, as suggested by the moral rights approach, this right can best be ensured if employees also agree that they have a duty not to harm others. If everyone acted according to this principle, problems such as workplace violence would not occur. In addition, a manager's right to privacy should be complemented by a willingness to comply with privacy laws and regulations, as well as cultural norms regarding what constitutes invasions of privacy, in dealing with employees.

COMBINING ETHICAL APPROACHES

No approach to ethical decisions can be said to be the "best" approach. Each one has strengths and weaknesses.[35] Managers in many U.S. organizations regularly use the utilitarian approach when solving business problems. Consistent with this approach, which values the goals of efficiency, productivity, and profit maximization above all others, they consider issues of moral rights and justice only to the degree required by law. In many European countries, however, managers appear to be more likely to develop solutions that are relatively more consistent with the moral rights and justice approaches. These approaches give greater weight to long-term employee welfare than to short-term organizational efficiency and profits. Although differences in cultural norms and values help explain some differences in how managers approach ethical decisions, there may be great variation among managers within any organization. Organizational cultures and differences in managers' personal perspectives help account for such differences.

Using all three approaches to ethical decision making increases the probability that decisions and behaviors will be judged as ethical by others holding a wide range of values and beliefs. Many organizational practices in the United States reflect solutions that were developed by managers who gave the most weight to the utilitarian approach but also believed that doing what was right was one way for the company to do well. The adoption of pollution prevention technologies that exceed government requirements illustrates this approach. To achieve the goals of being both a clean manufacturer and remaining profitable, many U.S. and Japanese plants have used employee involvement in continuous improvement activities. This approach helped Toyota and Honda beat other auto companies in bringing to market fuel-efficient cars. Toyota's Prius is powered by a combination of gasoline and electricity. It gets 66 miles per gallon and has a range of 870 miles. It's an example of the type of product that Bill Ford, Jr., would like to see the Ford Motor Company produce. In fact, shortly after Honda and Toyota introduced their combination cars, Ford announced that it would introduce a combination sport utility vehicle in 2003. Apparently, the utilitarian emphasis on short-term profits had slowed progress on "green" cars by Ford and other U.S. automakers.[36]

MANAGING CORPORATE SOCIAL RESPONSIBILITY

4.

EXPLAIN HOW THE CONCERNS OF STAKEHOLDERS INFLUENCE MANAGERS' ETHICAL DECISIONS.

Despite the prevalence of the utilitarian approach among U.S. managers, most know that they have many responsibilities, which engage them in a wide range of activities. Even if they believe that financial considerations must always be given highest priority, they recognize that long-term success requires attending to the concerns of different groups of people. A manager's job can be thought of as a series of attempts to address the concerns of these groups, or stakeholders.[37]

STAKEHOLDERS

Individuals or groups that have interests, rights, or ownership in an organization and its activities are known as **stakeholders**. Those who have similar interests and rights are said to belong to the same stakeholder group. Customers, suppliers, employees, and strategic partners are examples of stakeholder groups. Each has an interest in how an organization performs and interacts with them. These stakeholder groups can benefit from a company's successes and can be harmed by its mistakes. Similarly, an organization has an interest in maintaining the general well-being and effectiveness of stakeholder groups. If one or more stakeholder groups were to break their relationships with the organization, the organization would suffer.

For any particular organization, some stakeholder groups may be relatively more important than others. The most important groups—the primary stakeholders—are those whose concerns the organization must address to ensure its own survival. Secondary stakeholders are also important because they can take actions that can damage—but not destroy—the organization. Public opinion leaders, political action groups, and the media are secondary stakeholders for many organizations.[38]

Figure 6.2 identifies the many stakeholders that may have an interest in a particular corporation. Note that no distinction is made between primary and secondary stakeholders. The reason is that the importance of each stakeholder group varies from one firm to the next. In general, customers, employees, government regulators, society, and shareholders are primary stakeholders for most U.S. companies.

STAKEHOLDER CONCERNS

Each group of stakeholders has somewhat different concerns. That is, each cares more about some aspects of an organization's activities and less about others.

Customers. Many organizations say that they put the concerns of their customers or clients first. For U.S. companies, that often means improving the quality of products and services while keeping costs in check. Managers have introduced TQM programs for both external customers and suppliers and internal customers in other departments who purchase or supply products or services.

Before Christopher Galvin became CEO of Motorola, he made his mark by transforming that company's culture from "a loose confederation of warring camps" to a team-based, customer-focused organization. In 1987, the Paging Division was producing large numbers of defective products. Galvin's quality target was to lower the defect level to six sigma (about 1 defect in 14 million pagers). Using robotic technologies, teamwork, and quality improvement techniques, the plant substantially reduced both defects and the time required to manufacture pagers. Since becoming CEO, Galvin has turned the entire company around. His customer-oriented changes didn't yield immediate results, however. During the change process, Galvin was skewered by the business media as the company's share price fell. In the long run, his willingness to put customers' long-term needs ahead of shareholders' short-term concerns benefited both groups.[39]

Pressures to improve profits and be responsive to shareholders sometimes mean that customers' concerns are temporarily forgotten. Sears discovered just how powerful its customers were when the company set up an incentive system that had severe unintended consequences. Faced with declining revenues and reduced market share, management adopted new goals and incentive programs. It wanted to improve the profitability of the auto repair and service business. Goals called for larger numbers of parts and services such as springs, shocks, alignments, and brake jobs to be sold each shift. Pressure from top management on service managers and mechanics combined with rewards for meeting the new goals pushed some sales employees to use unethical sales tactics. In the rush to meet their goals, the quality of repair service slipped. Consumers filed hundreds of complaints accusing the company of selling unnecessary parts and services in more than 40 states.[40] Cheating and not satisfying customers obviously tarnished Sears's reputation. Solving those problems was costly, time-consuming, and embarrassing to the company and its employees.

Some consumers make a special point of purchasing products and services only from companies with outstanding reputations for ethical conduct and social responsibility. This is one way to express their personal ethical perspectives. Others go public when they have concerns about unethical practices. Consumers concerned about human rights have protested conditions in offshore apparel manufacturing, affecting a large number of companies. Conditions in several shoe manufacturing plants in China illustrate the problem. Some 50,000 employees, many of them younger than the Chinese minimum age of 16 for working in factories, make products for Nike, Adidas, Reebok, LA Gear, Puma, and New Balance. For many years, these workers weren't even paid the Chinese minimum wage of $1.90 per day, with no benefits. Mandatory overtime hours typically amounted to 80 hours per month, or double the amount allowed by Chinese law. Some employers attempted to reduce employee turnover by requiring employees to pay a "deposit" equivalent to 2 weeks of pay. Employees forfeited the deposit if they left before their employment contracts expired. Other employers confiscated migrant workers' identification papers so that they couldn't job hop or even remain in the city.[41]

For awhile, CEOs like Nike's Phil Knight shrugged off the protests. But college students made it clear that they didn't want their university sports teams to wear apparel made in sweatshops. They demanded that these companies disclose the names and addresses of their factories. Knight finally agreed to these demands, and other CEOs then followed. Eventually, several of the companies affected began working toward a longer term solution, which involves independent monitoring and reporting of factory conditions.[42]

Employees. Many of the concerns that employees have today reflect changes in the structure of organizations and the fact that work is a major activity in their lives. How a company should treat employees during times of change is a key issue raised by this group of stakeholders. When IBM restructured its organization in the early 1990s, it terminated more than 100,000 employees, many at the middle-management level. Just as the economy was absorbing the shock of layoffs at IBM, AT&T announced that it expected to lay off 40,000 employees. Both IBM and AT&T had been known as companies that provided job security. Employees felt betrayed, and the media vilified AT&T's CEO Bob Allen. In the end AT&T made fewer layoffs than he had originally announced. Many people believe that the company decided against laying off so many people because of the public's adverse reaction. It sent a clear message that laying off so many people was ethically untenable.

Pay and benefits are another area of concern to employees. Of nearly equal importance to employees are fair pay, secure and affordable health insurance, paid sick leave, and assured pension and retirement benefits.[43] A decade after it made headlines with its layoffs, IBM was again being criticized for treating employees unfairly. This time it was because the company announced a new benefits plan, called a *cash balance plan*. Cash balance plans are a relatively new approach to helping employees prepare financially for retirement. Such plans tend to be good for younger employees because they allow employees to take their retirement savings with them when they leave a company. But for older employees who have been at a company a long time—which was true for many at IBM—these new plans can reduce retirees' annual retirement incomes by several thousand dollars.[44] What employees lose, the company saves. Employees were outraged, and everyone in the country heard about it. Soon IBM executives worked out a solution that minimized the negative impact of the new plan on the company's most senior employees. However they go about it, progressive companies understand that satisfying employees' concerns and views about fair treatment must be part of any financial or benefits plan.

Society. When discussing stakeholders in the broader society, we are referring to all the communities affected by an organization, including those at the local, national, and international levels. Socially responsible organizations stay attuned to public opinion and use it as one source of information that may shape their own management practices. With heightened public interest in corporate social responsibility, many companies are discovering that they can't avoid having people evaluate how well they perform in this respect.[45]

Charitable contributions are one way that corporations can respond to this concern. For example, the Post Division of General Foods donates cereals to a national school-breakfast program. Ann Fudge, president of the division, says, "Lots of kids go hungry, which does not put them in a position to learn. Working with public school systems, we donated cereal to help these kids get the nutrition they need. Every company can find a way to improve the lives of kids in their community."[46]

Being able to give back to the community is one of the few reasons to bother making a profit, according to the cofounder Ben Cohen of Ben & Jerry's. Each year, 7.5 percent of Ben & Jerry's pretax profits go to social causes.[47] A commitment to community concerns often involves more than simply donating money. For Ben & Jerry's, it also involves seeking out nonprofit groups to run some of its shops, with shop revenues then being used to help support the nonprofit groups.[48] Having employees giving time and assistance is another way to contribute. Often, voluntary labor is a community's biggest need. One of the most ambitious volunteer programs—one that often serves as a benchmark for other companies—is the We Are Volunteer Employees (WAVE) program, supported by the Fannie Mae and Freddie Mac Foundation. Key components of this program are described in Figure 6.3.[49]

| Figure 6.3 | **The WAVE Program** |

Key Components of the
We Are Volunteer Employees (WAVE) Program
- Volunteer matching service that helps employees connect with volunteer opportunities
- Group projects that are coordinated by "issues" committees (e.g., AIDS/HIV, homelessness)
- Corporatewide and regional recognition programs
- "Dollars for Doers" grants that match the hours employees work with donations for the agencies they serve
- Team building for executives based on volunteer service
- 10 hours paid leave time per month for volunteer activities

To learn more about Fannie Mae, visit
www.fanniemae.com

To learn more about Freddie Mac, visit
www.freddiemac.com

WEB INSIGHT

Which companies have recently received the Ron L. Brown Award for Corporate Leadership? To find out, visit *http://www.ron-brown-award.org*. Consider the socially responsible activities these companies are involved in. Are their top managers most motivated by the utilitarian, moral rights, or justice approach?

To encourage companies to become involved in their communities, in 1997 the federal government established the ***Ron Brown Award for Corporate Leadership,*** which rewards leadership in employee and community relations. Named after the late secretary of commerce, who died in an airplane accident while on government business in Bosnia, the award complements the Malcolm Baldrige National Quality Award. The Ron Brown Award encourages business leaders to move away from the traditional, utilitarian model of business and become more active in contributing to society. Rather than deny their social responsibility, or resist it by doing the least possible amount, many companies are choosing to do everything that is legally required and to look for areas in which they can do even more. IBM, Anheuser Busch, and BankBoston are examples of companies that have successfully competed for the distinction of winning this award. For more details about the Ron Brown Award, see Figure 6.4.[50]

Within a community, members of employees' families represent an important constituency for employers. Attending to the needs of employees' families builds an organization's reputation and goodwill in the community. Heineken, the Dutch brewery, has a global workforce of 36,000 employees. Nearly half live and work at one of 25 facilities in Africa. These employees and their families—more than 60,000 people—enjoy access to the company's staff of doctors and nurses, a medical training facility, and a pharmacy. As Heineken continues to expand in Africa, it plans to upgrade the local medical facilities in each community it enters to ensure that they meet the company's standards.[51]

The Natural Environment. In addition to being concerned about the people in its community, societies also are becoming increasingly concerned about the natural environment.[52] Conducting business in a way that protects the natural environment while making economic progress, thus meeting the needs of the present generation without compromising the ability of future generations to meet their own needs, is referred to as ***sustainable development***.[53] In 1987, the Brundtland Commission of the United Nations introduced the concept of sustainable development. The idea behind it is that

Figure 6.4   **The Ron Brown Award for Corporate Leadership**

The Ron Brown Award

Principles of Excellence

- Top management must demonstrate commitment to corporate citizenship.
- Corporate citizenship must be a shared value of the company that is visible at all levels.
- Corporate citizenship must be integrated into a successful business strategy.

Characteristics of Programs and Practices that Demonstrate Excellence

- Distinctive, innovative, and effective; they represent "best practices" when compared to competitors.
- Impact on the people they were designed to serve is significant and measurable.
- There is broad potential for social and economic benefits for U.S. society.
- Sustainable and feasible within a business environment and mission.

financial performance, environmental integrity, and social equity are goals that organizations can and should pursue in unison.

At Interface, a carpet maker based in Atlanta, sustainable development drives decisions at all points in the business process—from the R&D lab to the factory floor to distribution and installation. The company's basic business is turning petrochemicals into textiles, traditionally a high-pollution industry. Founder and CEO Ray Anderson wants to change that. He is striving to be "the first fully sustainable industrial enterprise, anywhere. I want to pioneer the next industrial revolution," he says. For Interface, this requires eliminating all toxic emissions, finding ways to consume and reuse all "waste," making all transportation as efficient as possible, and educating employees, customers, and suppliers about the meaning of the company's commitment to sustainability.[54]

Local laws and regulations govern business actions related to pollution and the use of natural resources. International standards for environmental management have been developed, also. The European Union's Eco-Management and Audit Scheme (EMAS) and the International Organization for Standardization's 14000 (ISO 14000) standards are examples of environmental policy statements designed to provide guidance to multinational businesses. By meeting the ISO 14000 standards, companies such as the Lear Corporation and Volvo of North America can certify that they have developed responsible environmental policies. Such certification may, in turn, be used by local community decision makers when deciding whether to permit a business to operate in the area.[55]

For many industries, being profitable while addressing society's need for a healthy environment has been a difficult challenge. Figure 6.5[56] illustrates the many forces that must be balanced by organizations that seek to address environmental issues. For those that depend on the environment to sustain their businesses, meeting this challenge is a strategic imperative.

Figure 6.5   *Forces that Drive Corporate Responses to Environmental Issues*

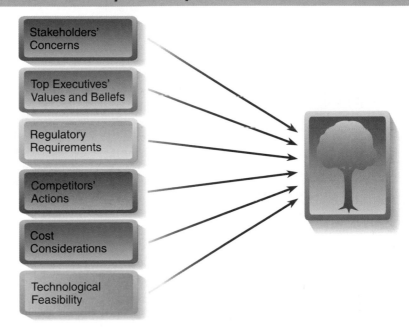

Research shows that companies that actively address environmental issues benefit in a variety of ways. Most obviously, they build reputations of being socially responsible. But they also develop new and valuable organizational capabilities. They learn to integrate the concerns of multiple stakeholders when making key decisions, and they also further develop abilities to innovate and learn.[57] One approach to meeting this challenge is described in the following Strategic Action Competency feature.[58]

Dow Cleans Up Its Act

"Dow's negligence has endangered our community" read the headlines in the *Detroit Free Press*. The story that followed described how a Dow contractor had repeatedly spilled toxic dust in the Midland, Michigan, area, which serves as company headquarters. Publicly, environmentalists and the company battled for favorable coverage in the press. Privately, however, the company

and local activists continued working together on a project they had started months earlier. The goal of everyone involved was to reduce toxic chemical emissions coming from Dow's huge facility by 35 percent while also improving the company's profitability. In other words, neither the environment nor profitability would gain at the expense of the other. Both should come out winners.

To achieve its goal, Dow invited five local activists who had been vocal critics of Dow to work with company managers. They began by making a list of 26 chemicals of most concern to them. Dow also hired several experts and a mediator to work with the team of managers and critics as they searched for "low-hanging fruit." The idea was to find ways to make *big* reductions. Dow management thought that doing so would be difficult because it had been working for 20 years on pollution control. The environmentalists also thought that it would be difficult. After all, if there were easy ways to improve profitability, wouldn't the company have already exploited them?

These concerns turned out to be unwarranted. Many opportunities for improvement were discovered. By the end of the project, called the Michigan Source Reduction Initiative, Dow's emissions were down by even more than its original goal. Its investment of $3.1 million would yield expected savings of $5.4 million per year. In addition, for some of

the company's businesses, product quality improved. For other of its businesses, production capacity increased. Carol Browner, administrator of the U.S. Environmental Protection Agency (EPA) was as pleased with the results as Dow was. According to Browner, "This partnership will almost certainly become a model nationally among companies looking to improve the environment and improve their bottom line."

• • •

To learn more about Dow Chemical, visit the company's home page at

http://www.dow.com

Owners and Shareholders. For many nonprofit and government agencies who are supported primarily through taxes, the concerns of owners and shareholders are essentially those of society at large. But for privately owned companies and those whose shares are publicly traded, the concerns of owners—that is, shareholders—may be quite different from those of society in general.

Most shareholders invest their money in companies for financial reasons. At a minimum, they want to preserve their capital for later use. During the past decade, the majority of publicly traded shares have moved from the hands of individual investors to institutional investors, who trade on behalf of individuals. The job of institutional investors, such as the California Public Employees Retirement System (CALPERS) and the Teachers Insurance and Annuity Association (TIAA), is to make money by choosing which companies to invest in. Their perspective on corporate issues is to make profit generation the firm's top priority. As professional investors, these shareholders have considerable power to influence management's decisions.

Finding Win–Win Solutions. Clearly, the primary concerns of various stakeholder groups differ, as do their views about the appropriate role of business in society. Some managers would agree with Chrysler Chairman Robert Eaton, who said, "The idea of corporations taking on social responsibility is ridiculous. You'll simply burden industry to a point where it is no longer competitive." Other managers would agree with the view of most people, who reject the idea that making money is the only role of business. In fact, socially responsible corporations are the more attractive alternative for prospective employees.[59] Such differences in perspective make managing effectively a challenge.[60] As the example of Dow Chemical shows, developing strategic alliances with relevant stakeholder groups—even those who are critical of the organization—can be an effective response to this challenge.[61] Through their alliance with community activists and critics, Dow found integrative solutions that address the concerns of *both* shareholders and environmentalists. Dow's approach results in win–win outcomes—they did not simply negotiate a compromise that required each side to lower its goals.

Conflict among stakeholders is common, but so are shared interests. For Robert "Joe" Murphy, president of Community Grocers, Inc., in Mount Ayr, Iowa, satisfying customers goes hand in hand with satisfying shareholders and being a socially responsible business. When the town's only surviving grocery store moved to the outskirts, Murphy sought financing to support a local grocery store from members of the community. In a town of only 1,700 people, Murphy persuaded 322 to invest in his venture. The townspeople-turned-investors were also Murphy's customers. They wanted great service, fresh produce, and of course, healthy returns. Murphy found that he could satisfy all their expectations. "Keeping a shareholder happy is no more than keeping the general public happy," he observed.[62]

The successes of other customer-driven companies support this view. Michael Treacy and Fred Wiersema studied the performance of 13 well-known customer-oriented firms, such as FedEx, Wal-Mart, and Intel. They compared the performance of these firms to others in the same industries. Over a period of 5 years, the revenues of these 13 companies grew 3.2 times faster than their competitors. Profits were 2.1 times as great as their competitors'.[63]

Would you be surprised to learn that some investors want to know that a company treats its employees well? CALPERS is one investor that bases stock purchase decisions partly on how companies treat their employees. Perhaps these investors know that having satisfied employees goes along with having satisfied customers, especially in the services sector. Managers and employees who hate their jobs can't give the best possible service to customers. Conversely, when customers are happy, employees feel a sense of pride and satisfaction at being part of the company.[64]

Employee-friendly companies also have a competitive advantage in attracting the highly skilled workers they need. After being on the job for awhile, employees who are more satisfied with how they are treated are more willing to do a little extra for the organization. Managing employees well can also benefit shareholders in other ways. For example, companies that have good records of equal employment opportunity and nondiscrimination perform better in the financial markets and have higher annualized returns than those with poor records. Other research suggests that good economic performance goes hand in hand with being environmentally responsible. Studies such as these support the idea that economic concerns need not be divorced from ethical concerns. Behaving ethically can be profitable.[65]

EVALUATING CORPORATE SOCIAL PERFORMANCE

With heightened public interest in corporate social responsibility, many companies are discovering that they can't avoid having people evaluate how well they perform in this respect. Business publications such as *Fortune* magazine rank various aspects of organizational performance annually. And, as already noted, the Ron Brown Award encourages business leaders to move away from the traditional, utilitarian approach of business and actively contribute to society. One approach to evaluating an organization's social and ethical performance is to consider whether it merely reacts to ethical concerns as they arise or anticipates and addresses ethical concerns affirmatively. Another approach is to look at the results of a formal social audit.

Affirmative Social Responsibility. An affirmative approach to social responsibility is the most difficult, complex, and expensive concept for organizations to address. *Affirmative social responsibility* involves accepting five categories of obligations.[66]

- **Broad performance criteria.** Managers and employees must consider and accept broader criteria for measuring the organization's performance and social role than those required by law and the marketplace.

- **Ethical norms.** Managers and employees must take definite stands on issues of public concern. They must advocate ethical norms for the organization, the industry, and business in general. These ethical norms are to be advocated even when they seem detrimental to the immediate profits of the organization or are contrary to prevailing industry practices.

- **Operating strategy.** Managers and employees should maintain or improve current standards of the physical and social environment. Organizations must compensate victims of pollution and other hazards created, even in the absence of clearly established legal grounds. Managers and employees need to evaluate possible negative effects of the organization's plans on other stakeholders and then attempt to eliminate or substantially reduce such negative effects before implementing the plans.

- **Response to social pressures.** Managers and employees should accept responsibility for solving current problems. They need to be willing to discuss activities with outside groups and make information freely available to them. They also need to be receptive to formal and informal inputs from outside stakeholders in decision making.

- **Legislative and political activities.** Managers must show a willingness to work with outside stakeholders for enactment, for example, of environmental protection laws. They must promote honesty and openness in government and in their own organization's lobbying activities.

Social Audits. Managers measure what matters to them. Those who are concerned about their company's social performance should conduct a social audit. A *social audit* identifies, monitors, and evaluates the effects that the organization is having on its stakeholders and society as a whole. In contrast to a financial audit, a social audit focuses on social actions rather than fiscal accountability and measures achievement under the affirmative social responsibility concept. Many firms conduct such audits, including Shell, Levi Strauss & Company, AT&T, McDonald's, and Johnson & Johnson. Table 6.2[67] illustrates the concerns of important stakeholders that often are represented in a social audit. Such audits are necessary because even the most conscientious companies can have some employees who fail to meet ethical standards of conduct.

T a b l e 6 . 2	*Stakeholders' Concerns When Evaluating Organizational Performance*
Stakeholder Group	**Examples of Concerns**
Owners, investors, or other financial supporters	Financial soundness
	Consistency in meeting shareholder expectation
	Sustained profitability
	Average return on assets over 5-year period
	Timely and accurate disclosure of financial information
Customers, clients, or patrons	Product/service quality, innovativeness, and availability
	Responsible management of defective or harmful products/services
	Safety records for products/services
	Pricing policies and practices
	Honest, accurate, and responsible advertising
	Respect for customers' privacy concerns
Employees	Nondiscriminatory, merit-based hiring and promotion
	Diversity of the workforce and quality of work life
	Wage and salary levels and equitable distribution
	Availability of training and development
	Workplace safety and privacy
Community	Environmental issues
	Environmental sensitivity in packaging and product design
	Recycling efforts and use of recycled materials
	Pollution prevention
	Global application of environmental standards
	Community involvement
	Monetary charitable contributions
	Innovation and creativity in philanthropic efforts
	Product donations
	Availability of facilities and other assets for community use
	Support for employee volunteer efforts

5.

DESCRIBE HOW
INDIVIDUALS AND
ORGANIZATIONS CAN
CONTRIBUTE TO
IMPROVING ETHICAL
CONDUCT IN THE WORK
SETTING.

Unethical conduct will never be eliminated, but there are ways to reduce it. At the personal level, employees who find themselves in a position of knowing about unethical behavior must decide what to do about it. At the organizational level, managers can implement a variety of organizational practices to support ethical conduct.

Whistle-Blowing. Employees who report unethical or illegal actions of their employers to other people or organizations that are capable of taking corrective action are referred to as **whistle-blowers.** If you knew that a coworker was behaving illegally or unethically, would you report it to someone? If so, who would you tell—someone inside the company or someone on the outside?

WEB INSIGHT

What is the National Whistle-Blower Center? What information does it provide that may be useful to people who may be considering blowing the whistle about an unethical activity? Find out by visiting this nonprofit organization's home page at ***http://www. whistleblowers.org***.

Researchers have studied whistle-blowing for several years. These studies indicate that whistle-blowers aren't very different from other employees. They don't seem to be at a higher stage of moral development, nor are they either more or less loyal to the company than their fellow workers. Instead, they tend to be people who happen to know about the wrongdoing and believe that by acting they can do something to stop it.[68] That's a good description of the two whistle-blowers at Cendant Corporation described in the following Planning and Administration Competency feature, who revealed how poorly that company's managers had exercised their authority and responsibilities.[69]

PLANNING & ADMINISTRATION COMPETENCY

How Could They Not Know?

When the news hits that a company has "cooked the books," the story is likely to include statements from top-level executives claiming that they had no knowledge of the scandal. But the response from the public often is, "How could they not know!?" That's how many people reacted when the CEO of CUC International, Walter Forbest, insisted that he had no knowledge of a scheme that extended over at least 5 years and created at least $500 million in fake profits. Is it possible that a CEO could be so oblivious? Two whistle-blowing accountants at Cendant Corporation were effective in exposing the scandal partly because they had so much information about wrongdoing that they simply could not be ignored. They chose to blow the whistle to the company's board of directors.

Cendant was created by a merger between CUC International and HSF.

At the time of the merger, HSF was considered to be a great success story. The share price of this real estate brokerage franchiser had tripled in just 2 years. It controlled well-known subsidiaries such as Century 21, Howard Johnson, and Avis. CUC's share value had increased steadily for several years and did especially well during the merger talks. Its business was a discount shopping club. In terms of its administrative and accounting systems, HSF was a tightly run organization. In contrast, CUC had primitive systems and no long-term planning, and individual divisions were left to do much as they pleased. One HSF executive described CUC managers as being "like children playing at business."

During the due diligence phase before the merger, HSF management found it difficult to get accounting infor-

mation from CUC, but CUC's independent auditors' report assured HSF that CUC and its books were clean. Shortly after the merger was finalized, however, a different reality was revealed. At a "routine" budget meeting, two CUC accounting executives told Cendant executives about widespread fraud at CUC. In the following weeks, investigations identified 20 CUC controllers who were involved in fraudulent practices. Records had been backdated and falsified, information had been withheld from outside auditors, and accounting data had been simply manufactured as needed.

• • •

To learn more about Cendant, visit the company's home page at

http://www.cendant.com

When you see wrongdoing occur, your goal should be to find a way to stop it. Simply confronting the person involved may be all that you need to do. However, blowing the whistle yourself or encouraging others to blow the whistle doesn't always make sense. It is a step that you should take only after making other less drastic efforts to change the situation. That is, blow the whistle only as a last resort and when you're likely to achieve a useful outcome—and in full recognition of the possible consequences to yourself. Table 6.3[70] lists some of the questions that you need to ask yourself if you're considering blowing the whistle.

Table 6.3	Questions to Ask Yourself If You're Thinking About Blowing the Whistle*
Do the characteristics at the right describe you, the whistle-blower?	Do you have credibility with middle and upper managers in the organization?
	Do you have power in the organization (professional status, long tenure, or control over resources)?
	Are you willing to identify yourself?
	Are you prepared to leave the organization if that becomes necessary?
Do the characteristics at the right describe the person to whom you plan to report the wrongdoing?	Does the person have credibility?
	Is the person powerful?
	Is the person supportive of you?
Do the characteristics at the right describe the person being accused of wrongdoing?	Is the person's credibility questionable?
	Does the person have relatively low power and status?
Do the characteristics at the right describe the wrongdoing you intend to report?	Does the organization depend on the wrongdoing to achieve its goals? (If yes, then you will be more effective if you report the wrongdoing to an external source instead of an internal source.)
Do the characteristics at the right describe the evidence you have?	Do you have written documents?
	Does your evidence come from more than one source?
	Is the evidence unambiguous?
	Do you have evidence of illegal behavior?
Do the characteristics at the right describe the organizational context?	Is reporting the wrongdoing related to doing a normal part of your job?
	Does the organization have a strong ethical culture and clear rules for how wrongdoing will be treated?
	Do you feel you can trust your superiors to not retaliate against you?

*The more times your answer is "Yes," the more likely your whistle-blowing efforts will be effective.

If your answers to these questions indicate that your whistle-blowing isn't likely to stop the wrongdoing, you should consider other courses of action. For example, you might try to persuade other employees to act with you; ignoring or firing a group of employees who report wrongdoing is more difficult than taking action against one person. Another alternative is to consider leaving the company. This action may not stop the wrongdoing, but at least it will ensure that you don't get caught up in the situation and possibly end up being drawn into the wrongdoing yourself. If the wrongful activity is causing serious harm to people, however, walking away from the situation may only result in feelings of guilt.

In addition to considering whether they will be effective whistle-blowers, employees should consider whether they are likely to experience retaliation for blowing the whistle.[71] Employees who work for federal contractors are protected from retaliation by the False Claims Act. Its goal is to encourage employees to blow the whistle on unethical employers who have been awarded federal contracts. Many state laws also protect whistle-blowers from retaliation by employers. Some states protect only those whistle-blowers who go outside the company (e.g., telling a newspaper reporter) to report wrongdoing. Other states protect only those whistle-blowers who report wrongdoing to someone inside the company (e.g., writing a letter to the CEO). Regardless of such laws, fear of retaliation is a reasonable concern. In particular, retaliation against whistle-blowers is likely to occur under the following circumstances:

- The allegation of wrongdoing has little merit.
- The accusations are made to someone outside the company.
- The whistle-blower has little support from top management or middle management.

ORGANIZATIONAL PRACTICES

WEB INSIGHT

Organizations are using many creative ways to improve ethical conduct. Visit the Ethics Resource Center at *http://www.ethics.org* and the International Business Ethics Institute at *http://www.business-ethics.org* to learn more about these activities. What are the three most important actions that managers can take to encourage ethical conduct among employees?

Giving whistle-blowers legal protection isn't enough to encourage whistle-blowing.[72] The corporate culture must also encourage whistle-blowing. As shown in Table 6.4, an organization can do much to minimize wrongdoing and support ethical behavior. Most companies have written standards describing their codes of ethics, which are explained during the orientation of new employees. But the majority do not provide additional ethics training or refresher courses for more experienced employees. Having a code of ethics but doing little to enforce it may be worse than doing nothing at all, according to the results of one study. If employees believe that a code of ethics has been adopted merely as window dressing to protect top managers in the event of a scandal, they can become cynical and less committed to the company.

Table 6.4	*Organizational Practices for Minimizing Wrongdoing*

- Document the organization's ethical rules through a written code of ethics.
- Have someone designated as an ethics officer, who is responsible for monitoring the organization's adherence to its stated standards.
- Appoint an ethics committee to oversee the organization's ethics initiatives and supervise the ethics officer.
- Emphasize the importance of ethical conduct in training and development programs to ensure that employees understand what behaviors are considered unethical by the organization.
- Evaluate employees' adherence to ethical guidelines and use these evaluations when making decisions about pay and promotions.
- Provide ways for employees to report the questionable actions of peers and superiors, such as by providing an ethics hot line.
- Develop enforcement procedures that contain stiff disciplinary and dismissal procedures and follow through by using these procedures when appropriate.
- Constantly communicate the organization's ethical standards and principles, using all channels of communication possible. Recognize that the actions of top managers are especially important in communicating ethical standards.
- Treat allegations of wrongdoing seriously, while at the same time ensuring that both the whistle-blower and the person accused of wrongdoing are treated fairly.

Levi Strauss & Company's approach to ethical management is as familiar to business leaders as its jeans are to teenagers. Its mission statement begins, "The mission of Levi Strauss & Co. is to sustain responsible commercial success as a global marketing company of branded apparel." Its aspiration statement goes on to say, "We all want a company people can be proud of, . . ." which includes "leadership that epitomizes the stated standards of ethical behavior." At Levi Strauss, ethical leadership extends well beyond company walls to its dealings with some 500 cutting, sewing, and finishing contractors in more than 50 countries. Despite cultural differences in what are viewed as ethical or as common business practices, the company seeks business partners "who aspire as individuals and in the conduct of all their businesses" to ethical standards compatible with those of Levi Strauss. The company actively promotes ethical business practices through activities such as membership in Business for Social Responsibility—an alliance of companies that share their successful strategies and practices through educational programs and materials.[73]

Incorporating social responsibility into an organization's mission statement and major corporate policies is one way to communicate that top management is serious about ethical conduct. Another way is to invest in training for all employees. Lockheed Martin Corporation invested both time and money to develop a company game called The Ethics Challenge. By playing this interactive multimedia game, employees can improve their knowledge of ethics and problem-solving skills. The game presents employees with scenarios of actual ethical incidents within the company and requires them to solve the problems. Examples from the game are then discussed during training workshops conducted by company managers. "It was a pretty big gamble to take something as serious as ethics training and turn it into a game," said the company's director of ethics communication and training. "We wanted to do something unusual that stood out from all the other training that our employees get. Our sense is that it is an effective tool to increase ethics awareness." To keep ethical issues salient, the company also issues an ethics calendar and a screen saver that shows the company's key values.[74]

CHAPTER SUMMARY

In this chapter we examined the importance of ethical and socially responsible business decisions. What is viewed as ethical is likely to vary among an organization's many stakeholders, as well as among different cultures. These differences mean that, ultimately, individuals must accept responsibility for their own conduct.

1. STATE THE IMPORTANCE OF ETHICS FOR INDIVIDUAL EMPLOYEES AND ORGANIZATIONS.

Concerns about ethics in business are increasing. Many business students say that they would prefer to work for organizations with good reputations for being ethical and socially responsible. At the same time, scandalous business practices are continually being revealed in the business media. Managers and other employees can learn to recognize ethical issues and deal with them effectively by understanding the forces that affect ethical conduct and the different perspectives that can be used to make ethical judgments.

2. DESCRIBE FOUR FORCES THAT INFLUENCE THE ETHICAL BEHAVIOR OF INDIVIDUALS AND CORPORATE SOCIAL RESPONSIBILITY.

The four forces that influence a person's ethical conduct are societal norms and culture, laws and regulations, organizational practices and culture, and the individual's own perspective. All four forces act together to influence ethical conduct. Societal norms and culture comprise shared values that underlie standards for acceptable behavior. Laws and regulations reflect societal standards that are enforceable in the courts. Organizational practices and culture include both formal policies, such as a code of ethics, and informal norms, such as how managers

define acceptable employee performance. Finally, an individual's own perspective on what is right and wrong can influence how that person responds to the other three forces.

3. DESCRIBE THREE APPROACHES THAT PEOPLE USE WHEN MAKING ETHICAL JUDGMENTS.

Managers and employees commonly rely on one or some combination of three ethical approaches to guide decision making and behavior. The utilitarian approach focuses on decisions or behavior that are likely to affect an organization's profitability. For businesses, profits indicate financial and economic performance. The moral rights approach upholds a member of society's fundamental rights to life and safety, truthfulness, privacy, freedom of conscience, free speech, and private property. The justice approach advocates impartial, equitable distribution of benefits and costs among individuals and groups, according to three principles: distributive justice, fairness, and natural duty.

4. EXPLAIN HOW THE CONCERNS OF STAKEHOLDERS INFLUENCE MANAGERS' ETHICAL DECISIONS.

The diverse values and ethical approaches prevalent in advanced economies introduce a great deal of complexity for organizations that attempt to act in socially responsible ways. One approach that an organization can use to ensure socially responsible actions is to consider how its actions affect important stakeholders. Each group of stakeholders has different concerns. Sometimes these concerns conflict; at other times they mesh. Thus finding solutions that address the concerns of multiple stakeholders becomes an important strategic task.

5. **DESCRIBE HOW INDIVIDUALS AND ORGANIZATIONS CAN CONTRIBUTE TO IMPROVING ETHICAL CONDUCT IN THE WORK SETTING.**

The goal of whistle-blowing is to stop illegal or unethical wrongdoing. A whistle-blower is more likely to be effective (1) when he or she has credibility, power, and support within the organization; (2) when written evidence of the wrongdoing is available; (3) when the business doesn't depend on the wrongdoing to achieve its goals; and (4) when the person being accused of wrongdoing has relatively low credibility and power. Organizations that seek to minimize wrongdoing should have procedures in place to encourage whistle-blowers to take action and assure them that such action won't result in retaliation against them. Other appropriate management practices include having a written code of ethics, designating an ethics officer and offering an ethics hotline, providing ethics training, and including adherence to ethical standards as criteria for making pay and promotion decisions.

KEY TERMS

Affirmative social responsibility, p. 179
Code of ethics, p. 164
Distributive justice principle, p. 170
Employment-at-will, p. 162
Ethics, p. 161
Fairness principle, p. 171
Justice approach, p. 170

Laws, p. 162
Moral rights approach, p. 168
Natural duty principle, p. 171
Ron Brown Award for Corporate
Leadership, p. 175
Social Accountability 8000 certification
guidelines, p. 163

Social audit, p. 180
Stakeholders, p. 172
Sustainable development, p. 175
Utilitarian approach, p. 167
Whistle-blowers, p. 181

QUESTIONS FOR DISCUSSION AND COMPETENCY DEVELOPMENT

1. Think about your experiences during the past few weeks and identify a situation that required you to make a difficult ethical decision. How did you think through the problem you faced? Did you use the utilitarian, moral rights, or justice approach? Explain how the approach you used influenced your decision and behavior.

2. One way to simplify your approach to ethical decision making is to consider whether an action is legal or illegal. Is this a good approach to ethical conduct? Explain.

3. Managers are important in setting the ethical tone for employees. If you work for an unethical manager, chances are you may eventually feel some pressure to act in ways that you consider unethical. Suppose that you suspect that your boss is not completely honest when reporting the sales figures for your unit. What should you do?

4. As the boundaries of the workplace have become more fuzzy and flexible, so have the boundaries of private life. Many people take work home with them and stay in almost constant touch with their colleagues or customers via e-mail or voice mail. Similarly, they may conduct some of their private business from their office at work. What types of personal activities are fairly conducted while you're at work, if any? Is it fair for employers to expect employees to be constantly "connected" to their workplace but not allow them to make personal telephone calls or shop on the Internet while at work? Explain.

5. Are some occupations or some industries more likely to have employees who break the law or behave unethically? Conversely, are some occupations or some industries less likely to have employees who break the law or behave unethically? If you answer *yes*, explain how the four forces described at the beginning of this chapter could account for these differences.

6. **Communication Competency.** Organizations communicate their ethical principles in a variety of ways: through the behavior of leaders, in writing, by offering training programs, through performance assessment methods, and so on. Visit the home page of the Ford Motor Company at **http://www.ford.com**. Describe the ethical principles that Ford communicates to people who visit this site. Be sure to consider the perspective of potential customers, employees, and shareholders.

7. **Teamwork Competency.** As a student, you are almost certain to work in a team with other students on some class assignments—for this course or other courses. What can you and the members of your team do to manage the ethical conduct of your team? Would it be useful to develop a code of conduct for your team? Explain your answer.

Passion at Patagonia

A recent visit to Patagonia's home page revealed that the company wanted to fill two positions: director of supply-chain integration and Internet program manager. Hundreds of potential job applicants could have the technical skills and managerial competencies needed for these jobs, but how many would fit this description: "Demonstrated Environmental Activism is a requirement"?

At Patagonia, a company that designs and manufactures specialty sportswear, social responsibility and activism seem to be more important than financial success. And as long as founder and entrepreneur Yvon Chouinard is still around, that's not likely to change at this privately held company. Chouinard spends most of his time far away from the company, leaving day-to-day management tasks to professional managers. But even those managers who are directly responsible for watching the company's financial health have been carefully screened to ensure that their values are in line with those of the activist founder. A chief financial officer (CFO) who thinks that profitability is all she needs to worry about might find it difficult to adjust to working in a company that is used as a tool for social change.

In the past, Chouinard openly expressed his disrespect for traditional business values—he referred to most businesspeople as "greaseballs." Nevertheless, a company the size of Patagonia, which faces strong competition from companies such as L.L. Bean, REI, and Lands' End, can't thrive if it ignores the advice of its accountants and financial experts. But can CFOs who care as much about the environment as they do about profits really be counted on to keep the company financially sound?

For years, Patagonia did extremely well, growing steadily to reach $24 million in annual sales by the mid 1980s. Then it quickly tripled in size. Chouinard had set a goal of $250 million in annual sales because he wanted more funds in order to pursue his social causes. To encourage growth, he seemed to hire everyone he met whose values fit the company's goal, despite warnings from his professional management team. Eventually, financial problems mounted to a point where they could no longer be ignored. In 1991, Patagonia was forced to lay off 20 percent of its workforce and Chouinard was forced to rethink his approach to business. Can a company that wants to make the best quality outdoor clothing in the world become the size of Nike? Was the idea of improving the environment incompatible with manufacturing clothing—when the process of producing such goods is itself a process that pollutes the environment? Which is the more socially responsible course of action: trying to use a business to lead the process of change or getting out of business altogether?

Chouinard spent several months thinking long and hard about such questions. In the end, he decided to stay in business and continue to use Patagonia as a tool for creating change. The company mission statement asserts that "Patagonia exists to use business to inspire and implement solutions to the environmental crisis." He also committed his company to a course of action that was intended to ensure the company's survival for another 100 years. It dropped 30 percent of its clothing lines, reduced its advertising, and began making major changes in its manufacturing processes, based on the results of its environmental audit results. Because Chouinard owns Patagonia, he can run the company in a way that is consistent with his values and passion for the environment.

At Patagonia, employees are treated as well as the environment. It ranks among *Fortune* magazine's 100 Best Companies to Work For, in part because it does so well in balancing work and life. Many of the company's practices support employees' passions for life outside work. Among the training programs it offers are surfing, introduction to French culture, and sewing. Employees also can take internships with community groups that the company supports, such as the Great Basin Bird Conservancy in Nevada. A generous vacation policy also gives employees time to pursue outside interests. Because the company hires employees with interests that are compatible with an outdoors orientation, their free time often is spent in activities that are similar to those engaged in by customers. When they return to work, chances are they'll bring back one or two new ideas that can be translated into improved products or services.

Despite Patagonia's success, some people wonder whether the company can continue to stay in business as a clothes manufacturer and, at the same time, have a net positive impact on the environment. Others wonder whether its employee-friendly policies can succeed as it expands internationally. A case in point arose with the company's only female manager in Japan. Consistent with company policy and the U.S.-based company's culture, this manager began to bring her child to work occasionally. The other managers were critical of her for doing so and began speaking unkindly about her. When confronted with this issue, the director of human resources had to find a solution that she considered ethical in the context of both the company's culture and Japanese culture.[75]

Questions

1. Based on what you know about Patagonia, what approach to ethical decision making do you think is used by most managers in the company?

2. Should the Japanese manager be allowed to continue to bring her child to work in accordance with the company's policies and practices? Explain.

3. If a company commits to being environmentally friendly, how can its managers use their communication competencies to support the organization's pro-environment values?

4. At Patagonia, social responsibility is as important as financial success. Unless the company succeeds financially and survives, however, its concerns about social responsibility will be irrelevant. Explain how Patagonia managers can use their planning and administration competencies to help this company integrate and achieve these two important goals.

To learn more about Patagonia, visit the company's home page at *http://www.patagonia.com.*

Ben & Jerry's

Ben & Jerry's Homemade, Inc., was purchased by the consumer giant Unilever in the summer of 2000. Despite this acquisition, Ben & Jerry's remains a major competitor in the ice cream and frozen yogurt industries by not straying far from its humble beginnings and dedication to social responsibility.

The company's founders are childhood friends Ben Cohen and Jerry Greenfield. Armed with only $12,000 ($4,000 of which was borrowed), a $5 correspondence course on ice cream making, and an old-fashioned rock salt ice cream maker, the two opened their company in 1978 in a renovated gas station in Burlington, Vermont. Their business soon began to prosper, and they became known for their innovative flavors made from fresh Vermont milk and cream. The company grew and diversified until today it makes and distributes ice cream, low-fat ice cream, frozen yogurt, sorbet, and novelty products nationwide and in selected foreign countries. Retailers that handle its products include supermarkets, grocery stores, convenience stores, franchised Ben & Jerry scoop shops, and restaurants.

For the first 10 years the company operated as a village culture whereby the values of the company were passed on orally rather than as a formal written document. However, in 1988, as the company began to grow rapidly, the founders and employees decided to write a formal mission statement for the company. This statement explains what the company stands for and has three interrelated parts, addressing product, economic, and social concerns. Ben & Jerry's is committed to making quality products, achieving economic rewards for its shareholders, and meeting its social mission by having a commitment to its community. All three parts are viewed as working in harmony to achieve the company's goals.

One example of how Ben & Jerry's attempts to achieve the social aspect of the company's mission is through its philanthropic efforts. It annually gives 7.5 percent of its pretax earnings to three beneficiaries: the Ben & Jerry's Foundation, employee community action teams at five Vermont locations, and projects supported by corporate grants made by its director of social mission development. These support projects are models for social change and exhibit creative problem solving and give hope to many people. The foundation, for example, is managed by nine employees who consider proposals relating to children and families, disadvantaged groups, and the environment.

Cohen and Greenfield believe that the company enjoys its current position in the marketplace by "brand equity" generated by its foundation work and other socially responsible actions. Brand equity is manifested by consumers who choose Ben & Jerry's, are brand loyal in their continuing purchases, and buy shares of stock in the company. Being socially responsible is viewed by everyone at Ben & Jerry's as fulfilling its mission, not as a drain on its resources.

Questions

1. Describe and give examples of how Ben & Jerry's actions reflect the company's mission.

2. Is Ben & Jerry's argument that "brand equity" is responsible for the company's continued success valid? Explain.

3. Does Ben & Jerry's meet the five obligations of affirmative social responsibility?

To learn more about Ben & Jerry's, visit the company's home page at *http://www.benjerry.com*.

PART

3

Strategic Decision Making

CHAPTER 7

PLANNING AND STRATEGY

CHAPTER 8

FUNDAMENTALS OF DECISION MAKING

CHAPTER 9

PLANNING AND DECISION AIDS

Planning and Strategy

1. EXPLAIN THE ROLE OF THE PLANNING FUNCTION.

2. DESCRIBE THE COMPONENTS OF TWO BASIC FORMS OF PLANNING.

3. DISCUSS THE EFFECTS OF LEVEL OF DIVERSIFICATION ON THE COMPLEXITY OF PLANNING.

4. DESCRIBE THE THREE BASIC LEVELS OF STRATEGY AND PLANNING.

5. STATE THE EIGHT PRIMARY PHASES OF THE PLANNING PROCESS.

6. EXPLAIN THE GENERIC COMPETITIVE STRATEGIES MODEL.

Chapter Outline

PREVIEW: **LUCENT TECHNOLOGIES**

THE PLANNING FUNCTION

TWO FORMS OF PLANNING

STRATEGIC PLANNING
STRATEGIC ACTION COMPETENCY: Dell's Competitive Strategies
TACTICAL PLANNING

LEVELS OF DIVERSIFICATION AND PLANNING

STRATEGIC QUESTIONS
TYPES OF BUSINESS FIRMS
COMMUNICATION COMPETENCY: GE's Social Architecture

STRATEGIC LEVELS AND PLANNING

CORPORATE-LEVEL STRATEGY
PLANNING AND ADMINISTRATION COMPETENCY: GE's Operating System
BUSINESS-LEVEL STRATEGY
FUNCTIONAL-LEVEL STRATEGY

PHASES OF PLANNING

PHASE 1: DEVELOP MISSION AND GOALS
PHASE 2: DIAGNOSE OPPORTUNITIES AND THREATS
PHASE 3: DIAGNOSE STRENGTHS AND WEAKNESSES
PHASE 4: DEVELOP STRATEGIES
STRATEGIC ACTION COMPETENCY: Dell's New Growth Strategies
PHASE 5: PREPARE STRATEGIC PLAN
PHASE 6: PREPARE TACTICAL PLANS
PHASE 7: CONTROL AND DIAGNOSE RESULTS
PHASE 8: CONTINUE PLANNING

GENERIC COMPETITIVE STRATEGIES MODEL

DIFFERENTIATION STRATEGY
COST LEADERSHIP STRATEGY
FOCUS STRATEGY

CHAPTER SUMMARY

KEY TERMS

QUESTIONS FOR DISCUSSION AND COMPETENCY DEVELOPMENT

CASE FOR COMPETENCY DEVELOPMENT: GERSTNER ON IBM AND THE INTERNET

VIDEO CASE: HUDSON'S SOMERSET STORE

LUCENT TECHNOLOGIES

Lucent Technologies is a major corporation in the network communications industry with more than 150,000 employees and $38 billion in sales. It is a major provider of telecom equipment, integrated circuits, broadband networking services, and related software. Richard McGinn is chairman and CEO of Lucent Technologies. The following are some of his perspectives on the strategic planning issues and perspectives facing this firm.

At Lucent Technologies, we like to say that we are at the center of the communication revolution—and we are. It is a revolution that requires and demands a constantly changing inventory of talent and technology to gain ground and to hold ground. It is a revolution that requires us to change rapidly and responsibly. Today, our industry is expanding and evolving, fueled by

e-commerce—e-everything—and a tremendous expansion of technology. The communication revolution demands a deep understanding of technology as a fundamental.

How does a company, through its strategy and through the execution of that strategy, extract value and meaningful growth from one of the fastest-growing industries in the world? How do we transform knowledge to create the networks and services and applications that companies and individuals want today? How do we manage technology into an advantage that translates into climbing numbers on our bottom line?

To a great extent, Lucent's growth is a function of strategy and execution. However, it is also the result of an unrelenting drive to be first to market, to address opportunities that emerge, and to really

drive ourselves and our teams to achieve. The surge in our bottom line demonstrates that we are learning how to be a business that extracts value from the industry and from the work that we do.

Are we comforted or satisfied or proud? What we know is that no matter what area we are working in there is at least one very good competitor out there whose job is to take away our children's bread money. In all areas, there are competitors attracting attention, attracting investment, and attracting customers. In semiconductors, Texas Instruments is a huge competitor. In wireless, it's Ericsson of Sweden. In data networking, it's Cisco. In optical, it's Nortel.[1]

To learn more about Lucent Technologies, visit the company's home page at

http://www.lucent.com

THE PLANNING FUNCTION

1.

EXPLAIN THE ROLE OF THE PLANNING FUNCTION.

Lucent Technologies has developed new strategies and lines of business since it was spun off from AT&T in 1994. At that time, telecommunications equipment was its only business. Through effective planning, leadership, and overall management, Lucent Technologies was identified in the top 10 of "America's most admired companies" in 2000.[2] In this chapter we describe some of the fundamentals of planning and development of strategic options that Lucent Technologies and other organizations apply.

In Chapter 1, we defined *planning* as identifying organizational goals and developing ways to reach them. We consider planning a basic general managerial function because it sets the framework and direction for the organizing, leading, and controlling functions.[3] In addition, the ability to plan by an individual, team, or organization is embedded in each of the six managerial competencies that we develop throughout this book.

The role of planning and strategic thinking at Lucent Technologies is suggested in the following remarks by Richard McGinn:

> *Today, our vision of communications networking is proving true. You can look at the technology decisions we have made. More importantly, you can look at the networks our customers are building and the moves our competitors are making to keep up. Over the last three years, the world has indeed evolved into a network of networks—just as we predicted and planned for. Some of those networks are wireline, some wireless. They rely on a variety of switching technologies—ATM, IP, and circuit. These networks overlap and connect. People talk, send data, and surf the Internet over a variety of networks and access points. It doesn't matter to them what the network is, so long as the service is available, fast, and reliable.[4]*

Why plan? When used by competent leaders and managers, planning should assist them in (1) discovering new opportunities, (2) anticipating and avoiding future problems, (3) developing effective courses of action (strategies and tactics), and (4) comprehending the uncertainties and risks with various options. Planning should also improve the odds of achieving an organization's goals by adapting and innovating to create desirable change, improving productivity, and maintaining organizational stability. Realization of such goals enables the organization to achieve long-term growth, maintain profitability, and survive. If done properly, planning fosters organizationwide learning, including the discovery of key problems, opportunities, and new strategies. A key goal of this chapter is to help you develop the ability to plan effectively.[5]

TWO FORMS OF PLANNING

2.

DESCRIBE THE COMPONENTS OF TWO BASIC FORMS OF PLANNING.

In this section we identify and describe the components of two basic forms of planning: strategic planning and tactical planning.[6]

STRATEGIC PLANNING

Strategic planning is the process of (1) diagnosing the organization's external and internal environments, (2) deciding on a vision and mission, (3) developing overall goals, (4) creating and selecting general strategies to be pursued, and (5) allocating resources to achieve the organization's goals. Managers and others must take an organizationwide or divisionwide approach in the process of strategic planning. The focus is on developing strategies that deal effectively with environmental opportunities and threats in relation to the organization's strengths and weaknesses.

In more sophisticated organizations, strategic planning includes ***contingency planning***—preparation for unexpected, major, and quick changes (positive or negative) in the environment that will have a significant impact on the organization and require immediate responses. This process begins with managers developing scenarios of major environmental events that could occur. A contingency plan for a dramatic negative event could be developed for responding to a disaster (e.g., an earthquake, flood, or fire destroying a company's manufacturing plant) or for managing a crisis (e.g., the viruses—such as the "Love Bug" virus in 2000—transmitted over the Internet that are increasingly invading companies' computer files and software). Similarly, a contingency plan for a dramatic positive event could be developed for responding to customer demand for products (goods and/or services) that overwhelms the firm's current capacity. Alteon WebSystems, founded in 1996 and based in San Jose, California, was overwhelmed by the surge in demand (over 140 percent in one quarter) in 1999 for its products—Web switches and server adapters. Joe Booker, Alteon's chief operating officer recalls that "we cried, begged, pleaded, and threatened suppliers. We even offered expediting fees and Alteon stock to some of them."[7] Why the crisis? If Alteon couldn't deliver the switches on time, it would lose both current and potential customers and threaten the planned initial public offering (IPO) of its stock.

Generally, three to five potentially critical and unanticipated events should be planned for. The attempt to consider more such events is likely to make the contingency planning process too time consuming and unmanageable. Contingency planning forces managers to be aware of possibilities and outline strategies to respond to them. It supports orderly and speedy adaptation, in contrast to panic–like reactions, to external events beyond the organization's direct control.

In Chapters 3 and 4 we discussed many forces—both domestic and global—in the environment that managers and others must scan and diagnose in strategic planning and the daily management of their organizations. We now review the four main aspects of strategic planning that managers can directly influence: vision and mission, goals, strategies, and resource allocation.

Vision and Mission. A *vision* expresses an organization's fundamental aspirations and purpose, usually by appealing to its members' hearts and minds. A vision statement adds soul to a mission statement if it lacks one. Over time, traditional statements of mission (e.g., stating the business the organization is in) may change, but the organization's vision may endure for generations.[8] The following statements represent the visions of three organizations.[9]

- **Lucent Technologies:** Building the next generation of communications networks now.

- **Cisco Systems:** Leading the Internet economy and helping change the way we work, live, play, and learn.

- **Dell Computer:** There is a difference at Dell. It's the way we do business. It's the way we interact with the community. It's the way we interpret the world around us—our customers' needs, the future of technology, and the global business climate. Whatever changes the future may bring, our vision—Dell Vision—will be our guiding force.

Cisco systems is a major competitor of Lucent Technologies and Dell Computer is a major customer of Lucent Technologies and Cisco Systems. Dell also relies on their networking products and systems, which enable Dell's personal computers and servers to communicate over the Internet, telephone lines, satellites, and other networks.

Most organizations don't have a vision statement. More often an organization will have a mission statement only. Its **mission** is the organization's purpose or reason for existing. A mission statement often answers basic questions such as (1) What business are we in? (2) Who are we? and (3) What are we about? It may describe the organization in terms of the customer needs it aims to satisfy, the goods or services it supplies, or the markets it is currently serving or intends to serve in the future. Some mission statements are lengthy, but others are quite brief. The following statements illustrate how three organizations express their missions.

- **Lucent Technologies:** To provide customers with the world's best and most innovative communications systems, products, technologies and customer support, and to deliver superior, sustained shareowner value.

- **Cisco Systems:** To shape the future of the Internet by creating unprecedented value and opportunity for our customers, employees, investors, and ecosystem partners.

- **Dell Computer:** To be the most successful computer company in the world at delivering the best customer experience in markets we serve. In doing so, Dell will meet customer expectations of: high quality, leading technology, competitive pricing, individual and company accountability, best-in-class service and support, flexible customization capability, superior corporate citizenship, and financial stability.

A mission statement is meaningful only if it acts as a unifying force for guiding strategic decisions and achieving an organization's long-term goals. The mission statement should encourage the organization's members to think and act strategically—not just once a year but every day.

Goals. *Organizational goals* are the results that the managers and others have selected and are committed to achieving for the long-term survival and growth of the firm. These goals may be expressed both qualitatively and quantitatively (what is to be achieved, how much is to be achieved, and by when it is to be achieved).

Richard McGinn notes that, when Lucent Technologies left the AT&T fold, its top management set six key organizational goals for it to meet within 3 years.

- Achieve double-digit (10 percent or more) revenue growth per year—it had been growing 5 to 6 percent per year as part of AT&T (quantitative goal).

- Maintain best-in-class quality (qualitative goal).

- Improve (reduce) sales, general, and administrative expenses and the cost structure of the business (qualitative goal).

- Invest in research and development at a higher level—up to 11 percent of sales (quantitative goal).

- Reduce tax rates (qualitative goal).

- Increase return on assets from about 5 percent to 10 percent (quantitative goal).

Lucent Technologies achieved all these organizational goals by the target date.[10]

Strategies. *Strategies* are the major courses of action selected and implemented to achieve one or more goals.[11] In Chapters 3 and 4 we reviewed several competitive strategies that managers use to deal with threats and take advantage of opportunities. They include the alliance strategy, exporting strategy, licensing strategy, multidomestic strategy, and global strategy. In this chapter, we discuss additional general and firm-specific strategies.

A key challenge is to develop strategies that are at least partially unique relative to competitors or to pursue strategies similar to those of competitors but in different ways. Strategies will have the greatest impact when they position an organization to be different in one or more aspects from its competitors. Michael Porter, a professor at the Harvard Business School and widely regarded as one of the foremost thinkers on strategic management, comments: "Operational effectiveness means you're running the same race as your competitors, only faster. But strategy is choosing to run a different race because it is the one you've chosen to win. . . . Strategy is not accidental. It is a purposeful process."[12]

The following Strategic Action Competency feature provides a glimpse of the competitive strategies employed by Dell Computer.[13] Dell Computer and most other successful organizations use multiple strategies that serve to complement and support each other. This approach is consistent with the systems view of organizations.

STRATEGIC ACTION COMPETENCY

Dell's Competitive Strategies

Dell Computer developed four inter-related competitive strategies. In brief, they are speed to market; superior customer service; a fierce commitment to producing consistently high quality; custom-made computer systems that provide the highest performance and the latest relevant technology to customers; and early exploitation of the Internet.

In a recent speech, Michael Dell, chairman and CEO of Dell Computer, discussed some of these strategies. His remarks comprise the remainder of this feature.

Dell's key competitive advantages are grounded in our unique, direct business model. We entered the business with no channel conflicts; we were

and still are the entire channel, from procurement through service. As a result, Dell has one integrated process for managing the entire value chain, from component supplier to end customer—and we control all the aspects in-between.

This integrated process provides inherently lower cost by eliminating middlemen margins, as well as from the cost efficiencies of higher quality that result from greater control and "fewer touches" of both product and process. In fact, our customer-centric business, and ability to view the entire spectrum of a customer's experiences with Dell, enables us to efficiently organize our company around well-defined customer segments. Each of our customer-oriented business seg-

ments controls its own product, manufacturing, sales, and support operations. Dell's ability to segment the market to provide closer understanding of distinct customer needs, and to tailor products and services accordingly, is the key to having the lowest cost and most effective service for each segment.

Any business is ultimately a series of transactions and interactions; the Internet is profoundly affecting the cost of transactions and the efficiency with which these interactions occur. Let me provide two examples. Each online purchase produces an average of 40 per-cent fewer order status calls for Dell, and 15 percent fewer technical support calls, which is a savings of $3 to $8 per call.

The Internet also is contributing to the cost savings that result from im-proved quality, as well as enhanced customer service. We have created web-based links with our suppliers and customers to improve the speed of infor-mation flow throughout the value chain and literally bring suppliers and cus-tomers inside our business. On the sup-ply side, these Web-based links have greatly accelerated the speed of cus-tomer feedback on quality, as well as allowing suppliers to more rapidly adjust their product mix to customer demand, which improves their inventory and cost efficiency.

• • •

For more information about Dell Com-puter, visit the company's home page at

http://www.dell.com

Resource Allocation. *Resource allocation* involves dividing money, people, facilities and equipment, land, and other resources among various current and new business opportunities, functions, projects, and tasks. As part of the strategic planning process, resource allocation generally boils down to earmarking money, through bud-gets, for various purposes.

Cisco Systems, headquartered in San Jose, California, is a major provider of prod-ucts that link networks and power the Internet, including routers and switches. A *router* is the part of a communications network that receives transmissions (e.g., e-mail messages) and forwards them to their destinations. *Switches* are circuitry components that govern signal flow over the Internet and other electronic networks. Major strate-gic resource allocation decisions made recently by Cisco's top management include the purchase of 40 companies between 1993 and 2000 and budgeting $10 billion to acquire additional companies that service and provide products for the Internet and other electronic networks. In addition, management must make other types of strategic decisions each year. Resources must be allocated to each line of business (e.g., routers and switches), R&D efforts, employee merit pay and incentive systems, corporate contributions to charity and public service initiatives, construction of new manufacturing facilities, marketing and sales activities, general and administrative functions, and so on. One of the strategic resource allocation guidelines at Cisco Sys-tems is to keep general and administrative costs relatively constant as a percentage of net sales, specifically at about 3.1 to 3.4 percent. Another allocation guideline at Cisco for the near future is to increase R&D expenditures at a rate similar to or slightly greater than sales growth rate. These expenditures currently are about 13 percent of net sales at Cisco.[14]

TACTICAL PLANNING

Tactical planning involves making concrete decisions regarding what to do, who will do it, and how to do it—with a normal time horizon of a year or less. Middle and first-line managers and teams often are heavily involved in tactical planning. It normally in-cludes developing quantitative and qualitative goals that support the organization's strategic plan, identifying courses of action for implementing new initiatives or improv-ing current operations, and formatting budgets for each department, division, and proj-ect within the guidelines set by higher level management.

Departmental managers and employee teams develop tactical plans to anticipate or cope with the actions of competitors, to coordinate with other departments, customers, and suppliers, and to implement strategic plans. The information presented in Table 7.1 demonstrates that tactical planning differs from strategic planning primarily in terms of shorter time frames, size of resource allocations, and level of detail. However, the two forms of planning are closely linked in a well-designed planning process.

Dimension	Strategic Planning	Tactical Planning
Intended purpose	Ensure long-term effectiveness and growth	Means of implementing strategic plans
Nature of issues addressed	How to survive and compete	How to accomplish specific goals
Time horizon	Long term (usually two years or more)	Short term (usually one year or less)
How often done	Every one to three years	Every six months to one year
Condition under which decision making occurs	Uncertainty and risk	Low to moderate risk
Where plans are primarily developed	Middle to top management	Employees, up to middle management
Level of detail	Low to moderate	High

LEVELS OF DIVERSIFICATION AND PLANNING

3.

DISCUSS THE EFFECTS OF LEVEL OF DIVERSIFICATION ON THE COMPLEXITY OF PLANNING.

In this section we review strategic considerations involved in making diversification decisions. Such decisions serve to define different types of firms and the complexity of planning associated with each type.

STRATEGIC QUESTIONS

Diversification refers to the variety of goods and/or services produced by an organization and the number of different markets it serves. The amount of diversification directly affects the complexity of an organization's strategic planning. Strategic changes in the amount of diversification should be guided by answers to questions that help top managers identify the potential risks—and opportunities—that diversification presents. The following are four such strategic questions.

- What can we do better than other firms if we enter a new market? Managers may base diversification or new start-ups on vague definitions of their businesses rather than on a systematic analysis of what sets them apart from current or potential competitors. Based on extensive study, the top management at Lucent Technologies concluded that the firm should become a force in the broadband (voice, video, and data) networking market by purchasing a variety of firms specializing in this area.

- What strategic resources—human, financial, and others—do we need to succeed in the new market? Excelling in one market doesn't guarantee success in a new one. The competencies required to be competitive in one type of business may not transfer to another type of business. Several years ago, PepsiCo spun off the Pizza Hut, Taco Bell, and KFC fast-food restaurant chains into a new stand-alone company. PepsiCo's top management concluded that the company's previous diversification into the restaurant business was diverting the focus of top management from its core drink business.[15]

- Will we simply be a player in the new market or will we emerge a winner? Diversifying or new start-up companies may be outmaneuvered by current competitors in the line of business the firm is entering. The reason is that managers may have failed to consider whether their organizations' strategic resources can be easily imitated, purchased on the open market, or replaced by other competitors. Also, entry by the firm may stimulate the current competitors to become much more effective and efficient. For example, Toys "Я" Us, with more than 1,600 stores, responded aggressively when several Internet-based toy retailers entered the market. The firm established its own Internet-based retailing arm and allowed customers to return items ordered over the Internet, if there were problems with the order, to one of its "bricks-and-mortar" stores. This approach eliminated the need for customers to return items through the mail. With its buying power, Toys "Я" Us was able to meet the price competition of the new competitors head on. Most have now gone out of business. Although Toys "Я" Us initially had a variety of problems with its online sales and service, they have been resolved.[16]

- What can we learn by diversifying, and are we sufficiently organized to learn it? Astute managers know how to make diversification a learning experience. They anticipate how new businesses can help improve existing businesses, act as stepping-stones to markets previously out of reach, or improve organizational efficiency. Dell's diversification from being a provider of just PCs to a provider of servers as well is such a stepping-stone extension.

TYPES OF BUSINESS FIRMS

An organization may be a single business (even a dominant business) in a market or diversified into related businesses or unrelated businesses. Figure 7.1 indicates that the level of diversification and the complexity of strategic planning are directly related. A firm that produces varied goods or services for unrelated markets often must have a complex planning process. In contrast, a firm involved in a single product line or service needs a less elaborate planning process.

Figure 7.1 **Level of Diversification and Planning**

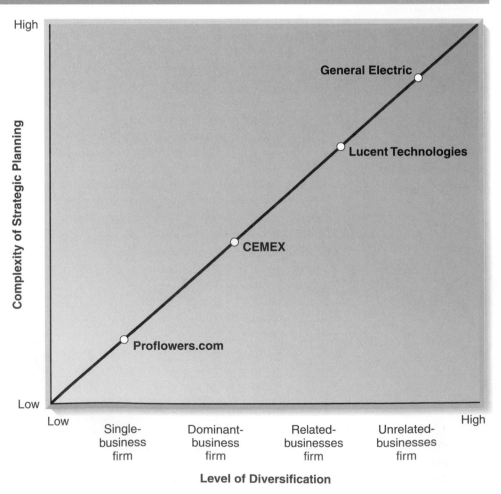

WEB INSIGHT

What types of flowers and services are available through the Web site at *http://www.proflowers.com*? Would you be willing to place an online order with this firm? Why or why not?

A **single-business firm** provides a limited number of goods or services to one segment of a particular market. Proflowers.com is an on-line florist with headquarters in La Jolla (near San Diego), California, that started in 1998. The company's growers fill online orders at the farm and ship the flowers to customers via FedEx; they arrive a day or two after being cut. Proflowers's strategy is to sell fresher flowers at a lower cost. Bill Strauss, C.E.O. of Proflowers.com, comments: "The U.S. per capita consumption of flowers is one-fourth the European average because flowers have traditionally moved from growers to distributors to retailers, adding cost and reducing vase life with every transaction. With FedEx, we leverage the Internet to deliver direct from the grower to the consumer."[17] Proflowers.com is a single-business Internet firm that sells flowers, not a flower company that wants to sell online.

A **dominant-business firm** serves various segments of a particular market. The term *market* refers collectively to the various users of a particular product line. As noted in Chapter 1, CEMEX, headquartered in Monterey, Mexico, is one of the three largest cement manufacturers and ready-mix producers in the world. With approximately 60 million metric tons of capacity, it has operations in 23 countries and trade relations with 60 others. CEMEX's business strategy is to

- build on its core cement and ready-mix concrete capabilities;
- concentrate on high-growth developing markets; and
- maintain high growth by channeling available cash to selective investments that will further its geographic diversification.[18]

A **related-business firm** provides a variety of similar goods and/or services. Its divisions generally operate in the same or similar markets, use similar technologies, share common distribution channels, and/or benefit from common strategic assets. Lucent Technologies approximates a related-business firm with its four primary business segments.

- *Service provider networks:* Products include switching and transmission systems for voice and data, data networking routing switches and servers, and wireless network infrastructure.
- *NetCare professional services:* Services include network planning, design, implementation, maintenance, and software.
- *Microelectronics and communications technologies:* Products include integrated circuits for wireless and communications, computer modems and networks, and optical fiber.
- *Bell Labs:* Provides basic research and development for other Lucent units.

An **unrelated-business firm** provides diverse products (goods and/or services) to many different markets. Often referred to as a conglomerate, such a firm usually consists of distinct companies that have little or no relation to each other in terms of goods, services, or customers served. Many North American firms have backed away from such diversification by selling off unrelated businesses. For the most part, the volume and diversity of information needed to plan for and manage such firms was overwhelming. As a result, their top managers often reverted to planning and controls through financial data that focused on the past and near-term for making strategic decisions. Many other types of problems also arose, such as too little investment in long-term R&D.[19]

WEB INSIGHT

General Electric has many lines of business. Go to GE's listing of them at *http://www.ge.com/businesses.htm*. Select one of these businesses and click to its Web site. What mission and key services/goods are described in this business?

General Electric (GE), ranked by *Fortune* magazine as the most admired company in 1998, 1999, and 2000, is one of the few successful unrelated-business firms.[20] GE is a diversified services, technology, and manufacturing company with approximately 340,000 employees worldwide and more than $112 billion in annual sales. GE has 36 lines of business, including aircraft engines, appliances, capital services, financing, lighting, medical systems, NBC, plastics, and power systems, among others.[21]

In the following Communication Competency feature, Jack Welch, CEO of GE, suggests that the firm's unique communication system and culture—what he calls *social architecture*—provides one of the anchors to its success.[22] Note his emphasis on (1) promoting two-way communication by asking for feedback, listening, and creating a give-and-take conversation between organization levels and across business lines; and (2) informing employees of relevant events, and activities and keeping them up to date. Later in the chapter, we present Welch's perspective on the other anchor to GE's success—its *operating system*.

COMMUNICATION COMPETENCY

GE's Social Architecture

GE's current social architecture began to form in the early '80s when we became convinced that the only way a company like ours could move quickly and successfully through times of radical change was to use every mind in the Company and to involve everyone in the game—to leave no one, and no good idea, out. To achieve this radical cultural transformation, we developed something we called "Work-Out," which is based on the simple premise that those closest to the work know it best. Over the years, there have been literally hundreds of thousands of Work-Out "town meetings," where the views and ideas of every employee, from every function, in every business, were solicited and turned into action—usually on the spot. People saw

the value we attached to their intellect and their ideas—and as a result, their ideas began to flow in torrents.

The second facet of the social architecture involved the cultivation of what we call "boundaryless" behavior by the removal of every organizational and functional obstacle to the free and unimpeded flow of ideas—inside the Company across every operation, and outside the Company from the best thinking in world business. We measured this boundaryless behavior in our leadership—and rewarded or removed people based on it. We anonymously survey thousands of employees every year to measure our progress and see if our rhetoric matches their reality. When it does not, we take action.

The combination of involving everyone in the game and of responding to this flow of ideas and information turned GE into what we are today—a learning company. By becoming a learning company, we have taken market and geographic diversity, the traditional handicap of multibusiness companies, and turned them into a decisive advantage—unlimited access to the most enormous supply of best ideas, information, and intellectual capital the business world has to offer.

• • •

For more information about General Electric, visit the company's home page at

http://www.ge.com

STRATEGIC LEVELS AND PLANNING

4.

DESCRIBE THE THREE BASIC LEVELS OF STRATEGY AND PLANNING.

Plans and the strategies embedded in them are normally developed at three primary levels at dominant-business (e.g., CEMEX), related-business (e.g., Lucent Technologies), and unrelated-business (e.g., General Electric) firms. Figure 7.2 shows some of the executives involved in planning at these levels for GE. For single-business firms, plans and strategies are developed at two primary levels—the business level and the functional level.

CORPORATE-LEVEL STRATEGY

Core-Focus. Corporate-level planning and strategy guides the overall direction of firms having more than one line of business. The amount of diversification determines the complexity and scope of planning and strategy formulation required. **Corporate-level strategy** focuses on the types of businesses the firm wants to be in, ways to acquire or divest businesses, allocation of resources among the businesses, and ways to develop learning and synergy among those businesses. Top corporate managers then determine the role of each separate business within the organization.[23]

Figure 7.2 **General Electric's Strategy and Planning Levels**

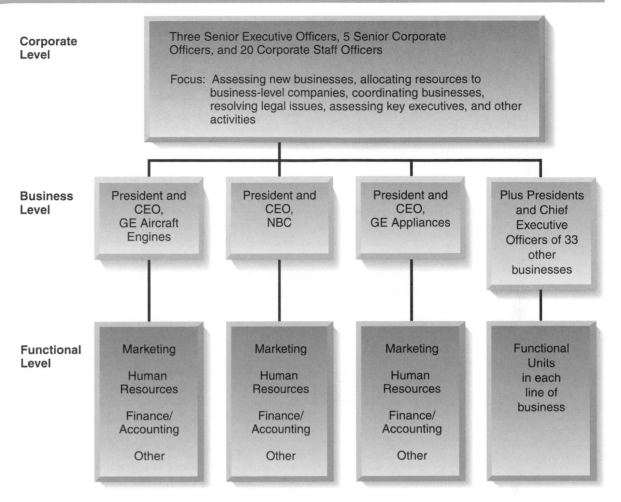

Corporate Level

Three Senior Executive Officers, 5 Senior Corporate Officers, and 20 Corporate Staff Officers

Focus: Assessing new businesses, allocating resources to business-level companies, coordinating businesses, resolving legal issues, assessing key executives, and other activities

Business Level

President and CEO, GE Aircraft Engines

President and CEO, NBC

President and CEO, GE Appliances

Plus Presidents and Chief Executive Officers of 33 other businesses

Functional Level

Marketing

Human Resources

Finance/ Accounting

Other

Marketing

Human Resources

Finance/ Accounting

Other

Marketing

Human Resources

Finance/ Accounting

Other

Functional Units in each line of business

One of GE's corporate-level strategies is to operate as a *learning company* that takes advantage of the diversity of markets and geographic areas served. As indicated in Figure 7.2, the corporate level at GE includes 3 senior executive officers (chairman of the board and CEO and 2 vice chairmen of the board and executive officers), 5 senior corporate officers (senior vice presidents of human resources, R&D, general counsel/legal, information systems, and finance) and 20 corporate staff officers (vice presidents of auditing, mergers and acquisitions, corporate communications, leadership, financial planning, environmental programs, governmental relations, and 13 other areas). With a total of 28 officers and additional support staff involved, the planning and strategy formulation process at GE's corporate level is complex and broad in scope.

One of the functions of corporate-level management is to guide and review the performance of strategic business units. A ***strategic business unit*** (SBU) is a division or subsidiary of a firm that provides a distinct product or service and often has its own mission and goals. An SBU may have a well-defined set of customers and/or cover a specific geographic area. An SBU is usually evaluated on the basis of its own income statement and balance sheet. The top managers of each SBU are responsible for developing plans and strategies for their units. These proposals normally are submitted to corporate headquarters for review. Top corporate management, as at GE, is involved in determining which SBUs to start, acquire, or divest. Corporate-level management also decides whether to allocate the same, less, or more financial and human resources to the various SBUs. Figure 7.2 shows specifically 3 of the 36 strategic business units at GE. Among these other SBUs are GE Capital, GE Capital Commercial Finance, GE Lighting, GE Medical Systems, GE Plastics, and GE Power Systems.

Growth Strategies. There are a variety of corporate-level growth strategies.[24] Five of the more common strategies are forward integration, backward integration, horizontal integration, concentric diversification, and conglomerate diversification.

In pursuing a *forward integration strategy* a company enters the business of its customers, moving it closer to the ultimate consumer. This approach is sometimes called a *downstream strategy*. For example, Lucent Technologies acquired International Network Services in 1999, a global provider of network consulting, design, and software solutions. This acquisition moved Lucent closer to many of its ultimate customers by providing the expertise needed to help them to define and meet their network needs. Lucent now has more than 5,500 consultants, technicians, and engineers in communications networking.[25] Prior to this acquisition, Lucent often worked with and through International Network Services, among other such firms, in solving networking problems of its ultimate customers.

When a company pursues a *backward integration strategy*, it enters the businesses of its suppliers, usually to control component quality, ensure on-time delivery, or stabilize prices. This approach is sometimes called an *upstream strategy*. It is implemented by acquiring suppliers or by creating new businesses that provide the same goods or services as the organization's suppliers. For example, Amazon.com recently acquired Junglee Corporation, an Internet company that started in 1996 and grew to 50 employees in 2000. It had introduced a virtual-database technology that extracts product information and prices from sites strewn across the Internet and integrates the information into a single database. This database enables users to comparison shop for a wide range of products. Amazon.com recognized that, as the popularity of e-commerce grows, the ability to give consumers more and better organized information than they could obtain through hyperlinks would become a vital technology.[26] Rather than developing a technology to compete with Junglee, Amazon.com's management decided to purchase this supplier of online comparison shopping software.

A company implementing a *horizontal integration strategy* acquires one or more competitors to consolidate and extend its market share. For example, in 2000, United Airlines (UAL Corporation) and US Airways announced a merger agreement, which is subject to the approval of the U.S. Justice Department. United claims that four aspects of the merger, in particular, will make the new company more competitive than the two companies were as separate entities.

- US Airways customers will gain the benefits of United's global route system.
- The combination brings together United's extensive east–west system with US Airways' comprehensive north–south routes, creating an efficient nationwide network.
- US Airways' hubs in Charlotte, Philadelphia, and Pittsburgh will increase the number and frequency of U.S. and international flights, providing better service for customers.
- The frequent-flyer programs will be consolidated, offering passengers more destinations than other airline programs.[27]

A growing alternative to traditional forms of backward, forward, and horizontal integration is the *alliance strategy*. As suggested in Chapter 4, this strategy involves two or more organizations pooling physical, financial, human, technological, and/or other resources to achieve specific goals. For example, in 2000, GE Industrial Systems and Cisco Systems formed a new company, GE Cisco Industrial Networks, headquartered in Charlottesville, Virginia. The goal of GE Cisco is to increase customers' productivity by creating an Ethernet-based network infrastructure to deliver the benefits of enterprisewide communication. The alliance's capabilities are based on GE's experience with control technology, factory automation, and manufacturing, and Cisco Systems' expertise in network infrastructures.[28]

When utilizing a *concentric diversification strategy*, sometimes called *related diversification,* a firm acquires or starts a business related to the organization's existing business in terms of technology, markets, or products. Frequently, a related-business enterprise acquires another company or starts a new venture. Some common thread must link the two firms, such as the same general set of customers and markets, similar technology, overlapping distribution channels, compatible managerial competencies, or similar goods or services. For example, top management at America Online (AOL) and Time Warner viewed their merger in 2000 as a form of concentric diversification. AOL's business lines include interactive services, America Online, CompuServe, and the Netscape Navigator and Communicator browsers (applications that allow users to download Web pages and view them on their own computers). Time Warner business lines include 33 magazines (e.g., *Time, People,* and *Sports Illustrated*), book publishing, Warner Brothers Studios, CNN, TNT, and HBO. Management contends that the merger will capitalize on the convergence of entertainment, information, communications, and online services—all driven by the technologies of the Internet and the digital market-place. One immediate benefit to AOL is that it gains access to Time Warner's cable de-livery and broad content. In turn, Time Warner gains access to 23 million AOL sub-scribers and a well-established vehicle for expanded e-commerce.[29]

In pursuing a ***conglomerate diversification strategy,*** a firm adds what appears to be unrelated goods or services to its line of businesses. A firm may acquire another company or start a venture in a totally new field. Diversified enterprises operating unre-lated businesses most often purchase established companies. As mentioned previously, this corporate-level strategy is usually viewed with skepticism but GE is an exception. The following Planning and Administration Competency feature presents excerpts of GE's CEO and Chairman of the Board Jack Welch's views on the other main anchor to his firm's success—GE's *operating system.*[30] We reviewed the *social architecture* anchor at GE previously.

PLANNING & ADMINISTRATION COMPETENCY

GE's Operating System

The operating system of GE was devised to channel and focus ideas and informa-tion (such as from Work-Out sessions) and put it to use through the medium of Companywide "initiatives." This system tracks, measures, and can be expanded as initiatives take hold and flourish. This operating system is based on an informal but intense regular schedule of reviews designed to create momentum for the ini-tiative. It progresses with a drumbeat regularity throughout our business year—year after year.

A typical initiative—Product Serv-ices, say, or Six Sigma Quality—was launched at the meeting of our 600 global leaders in January. A commit-ment to the initiative is made. Every subsequent event in the Company is developed around implementing and expanding the initiative: resources are allocated; high-visibility jobs are created; intense communications start throughout the businesses; and work begins.

Each quarter throughout the year, the leaders of our businesses meet to share what each of them has done to drive the initiative. At these meetings, leaders rang-ing from the Reinsurance CEO, to the NBC executive, to the head of the Indus-trial Systems business describe how they are implementing the particular initiative in their own operations. The incredible amount of learning that comes from this shared experience expands the initiative and energizes their efforts.

This takes us full circle to January, when the 600 global leaders of our Company meet and focus, once again, on the initiatives. The initiative from the prior January usually occupies the entire first day, and the role models present their stories and share their learning. On Day 2, new ideas around other ongoing initiatives—some several years old—are shared. This year, for example, the first full day was on e-business. Day 2 cov-ered new thinking in Globalization, Six Sigma, and Product Services. This oper-

ating system propels what has become a "learning engine" and embeds these initiatives in the DNA of the Company.

• • •

For more information about General Electric, visit the company's home page at

http://www.ge.com

BUSINESS-LEVEL STRATEGY

Business-level strategy refers to the resources allocated and actions taken to achieve desired goals in serving a specific market with a highly interrelated set of goods and/or services. The focus is on ensuring competitiveness by using the firm's present and continuously developing core organizational competencies in specific markets.[31] At GE, business-level strategies are developed for GE Medical Systems, GE Lighting, and the company's 34 other lines of business. At AOL Time Warner, business-level strategies are developed for America Online, Warner Brothers Studios, HBO, and its various other lines of business. As previously noted, for a single-business firm no distinction is made between business-level and corporate-level strategies. For example, the top managers at Proflowers.com focus primarily on what we normally think of as business-level strategies and planning.

Top managers of a firm or SBU focus on planning and formulating strategies for (1) maintaining or gaining a competitive edge in serving its customers, (2) determining how each functional area (e.g., production, human resources, marketing, and finance) can best contribute to its overall effectiveness, and (3) allocating resources among its functions.

A focus on customers is the foundation of successful business-level plans and strategies. This focus requires attention to three basic questions.

- Who will be served? Customer needs and demand may vary according to demographic characteristics (e.g., age, gender, income, occupation, education, race, nationality, and social class); geographic location; lifestyle choices (e.g., single or married, with or without children); type of customer (e.g., manufacturers, wholesalers, retailers, or end customers); and so on. Proflowers.com serves consumers of flowers and related products.

- What customer needs will be satisfied? Proflowers.com serves the needs of consumers who want to show their appreciation of or love for others and consumers who purchase flowers for aesthetic satisfaction and beautification.

- How will customers' needs be satisfied? Proflowers.com uses its capabilities in information technologies, including the Internet, to create relationships with customers and growers and to provide speedy distribution and tracing through FedEx.

FUNCTIONAL-LEVEL STRATEGY

Functional-level strategy refers to the interrelated actions and resource commitments established for operations, marketing, human resources, finance, legal services, accounting, and the organization's other functional areas. Functional-level plans and strategies should support business-level strategies and plans. At the functional level, these tasks often involve a combination of strategic and tactical planning. Table 7.2 provides examples of the issues that management in various types of firms usually address in developing functional-level plans and strategies.

Operations strategies specify how the firm will develop and utilize its production capabilities to support the firm's business-level strategies. ***Marketing strategies*** address how the firm will distribute and sell its goods and services. ***Finance strategies*** identify how best to obtain and allocate the firm's financial resources.

In Chapter 13 we discuss a number of issues central to developing a functional plan and strategy in human resource management. These issues include the legal and regulatory environment, staffing, training and development, performance appraisals, and compensation.[32] For example, Home Depot recently implemented a new staffing initiative. The company's automated Job Preference Program provides managers with the names of prescreened candidates, suggests interview questions for the positions to be filled, and presents answers they should listen for in response to the suggested questions. This computerized staffing aid has helped to broaden the pool of qualified applicants. Job applicants apply at kiosks in stores or by calling an 800 number. They are given a 40- to 90-minute basic skills test that helps screen out unqualified candidates prior to person-to-person interviews. The promotion part of the system requires current employees to register online for jobs that they may want in the future. Employees are

Sample Functions	Sample Key Issues
Human resources	• What type of reward system is needed?
	• How should the performance of employees be reviewed?
	• What approach should be used to recruit qualified personnel?
	• How is affirmative and fair treatment ensured for women, minorities, and the disabled?
Finance	• What is the desired mixture of borrowed funds and equity funds?
	• What portion of profits should be reinvested and what portion paid out as dividends?
	• What criteria should be used in allocating financial and human resources to projects?
	• What should be the criteria for issuing credit to customers?
Marketing	• What goods or services should be emphasized?
	• How should products be distributed (e.g., direct selling, wholesalers, retailers, etc.)?
	• Should competition be primarily on price or on other factors?
	• What corporate image and product features should be emphasized to customers?
Operations (manufacturing)	• What should be the level of commitment to total quality?
	• How should suppliers be selected?
	• Should the focus be on production runs for inventory or producing primarily in response to customer orders?
	• What production operations should be changed (e.g., automated or laid out differently) to improve productivity?

encouraged to update their profiles regularly at kiosks in employee break rooms. The system is networked so that if someone applies, say, at a Home Depot store in a suburb of Atlanta, the application goes to any store within commuting distance in the Atlanta area. Managers may interview and promote only employees who have expressed an interest in the position, and they must interview at least three people.[33]

PHASES OF PLANNING

5.

STATE THE EIGHT PRIMARY PHASES OF THE PLANNING PROCESS.

In this section, we expand on some of the concepts and issues discussed to this point and present them as phases of business-level planning. We give more attention to functional-level planning and strategies in Chapters 9, 10, 13, and 19.

The planning process that we present applies primarily to single-business firms (or SBUs) and highly related–business firms. It comprises a sequence of eight primary phases, which are summarized in Figure 7.3. However, these phases do not necessarily have to be undertaken in strict sequence for the planning effort to be successful. In practice, managers and teams, such as at Proflowers.com, involved in business-level planning often jump back and forth between phases, or even skip phases, as they develop their plans.

PHASE 1: DEVELOP MISSION AND GOALS

We noted previously that an organization's mission(s) and goals are guided by considering questions such as What business are we in? What are we committed to? and What results do we want to achieve? General goals provide a sense of direction for decision

Figure 7.3 **The Planning Process**

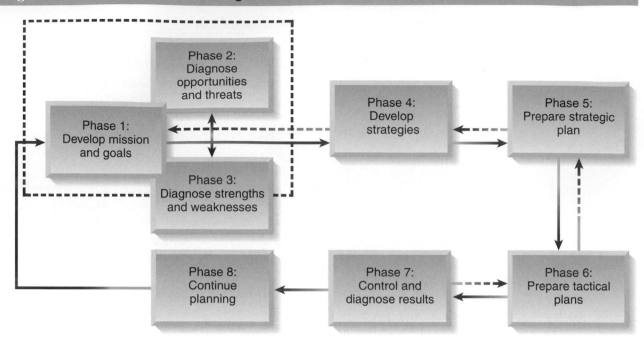

making and may not change from year to year. The mission(s) and goals are not developed in isolation, as indicated by the two-way arrows in Figure 7.3. They are affected by an assessment of environmental threats and opportunities (phase 2) and strengths and weaknesses (phase 3).

For example, the vision of Home Depot is broad and general: *responding and changing to meet customer needs.* Its mission is more targeted: *to become a total solutions provider to all home improvement customers.* In a recent fiscal year, Home Depot developed three general goals, which were made more concrete through a number of narrower goals. The general goals were

- to continue a pattern of strong and consistent sales and earnings growth,
- to increase our ability to be a total solutions provider to do-it-yourself and professional home improvement customers, and
- to lead the marketplace to a better world.[34]

PHASE 2: DIAGNOSE OPPORTUNITIES AND THREATS

In Chapters 3 and 4, we discussed environmental forces—internal and external, domestic and global—that can affect an organization. These forces represent both opportunities and threats for an organization. Strategic planning helps managers identify these opportunities and threats and take them into account in developing an organization's mission, goals, plans, and strategies. Political forces and stakeholders within and outside the organization play a key role in determining its mission and goals, as well as exerting pressures for changing them. Top managers negotiate with powerful stakeholders (boards of directors, banks, governments, major customers, and suppliers) in an attempt to influence those forces.

In Chapter 3, we reviewed the framework suggested by Michael Porter for diagnosing the competitive forces in an industry that a firm faces at any particular time. This framework (see Figure 3.3 and related discussion) includes five competitive forces: competitors, customers, suppliers, new entrants, and substitute goods and services. The combined strength of these forces affects the long-run profit potential in an industry. That, in turn, affects each individual firm's (or SBU's) overall profit potential, growth prospects, and even likelihood of survival. Strategic planning must include an assessment of these forces. Numerous specific variables affect the strength of each force, but a review of all the variables is beyond the scope of this book. Here, we simply review each force and highlight its potential impact on a firm's strategic planning.

Competitors. The rivalry among existing competitors in an industry varies with top management's view of threats or opportunities, the strategies a firm pursues, and competitor's reactions to those strategies. These reactions and strategies include price increases or decreases, advertising campaigns, introduction of improved or new goods, changes in customer service, and so on. Three of the variables affecting the strength of rivalry among competitors within an industry are the number of firms, the rate of industry growth, and level of fixed costs.

The many manufacturers (mostly assemblers) of personal computers, high rate of growth in demand for PCs, and ever improving computer-based capabilities have combined—along with other factors—to create intense rivalry among firms in the industry. Through endless combinations of price cuts, improved features, and service enhancements, global and local suppliers of PCs have attempted to gain a competitive edge over their competitors. Global PC firms include—among others—Dell, Compaq, Gateway, Hewlett-Packard, IBM, Micron, and AST.

New Entrants. The entry of new competitors often is a response to high profits earned by established firms and/or rapid growth in an industry. The difficulties that new competitors experience are significantly influenced by the barriers to entry and the reactions of established competitors. Barriers to entry are factors that make entering an industry relatively easy or relatively difficult. Two important barriers are economies of scale (lower costs as volumes increase) and capital requirements to become a competitor.

The Internet has created a revolution of new firms entering the market of traditional firms. For example, many brick and mortar travel agencies have closed, merged, downsized, or changed their strategies as a result of online travel services—such as Expedia.com, Travelocity.com, Travelzoo.com, and Trip.com—and the development of online passenger reservation systems by airlines.

Customers. The bargaining power of customers depends on their relative ability to play one firm off against another in order to force down prices, obtain higher quality, or buy more goods or services for the same price. As a result of deregulation, new computer-based technologies, digital convergence, and new competitors, the power of customers in purchasing telecommunications services has increased substantially over the past dozen years.

The bargaining power of customers is likely to be great in the following situations.

- A small number of customers purchase relatively large volumes from the seller. Major automobile manufacturing firms buy tires from a few makers.

- Customers purchase standard and undifferentiated goods or services. Customers perceive little difference between many telecommunications services, such as long distance or wireless service.

- Customers can easily switch from one seller to another. Long distance telephone service providers, such as MCI, Sprint, and AT&T, make switching easy.

Suppliers. The bargaining power of suppliers increases when they can increase or protect market share, raise prices, or eliminate certain features of their goods or services with little fear of losing customers. The situations that tend to make suppliers more powerful are similar to those that make customers more powerful. The bargaining power of suppliers is likely to be great in the following situations.

- A small number of suppliers sell to a large number of customers in an industry. Microsoft was found guilty by a federal court of abusing its supplier power.

- Suppliers don't have to worry about substitute goods or services that their customers can readily buy. Microsoft was found guilty by a federal court of making its customers purchase its browser with its Windows products.

- Supplier's goods or services are differentiated. Intel attempts to differentiate its microprocessors (computer chips) through mass advertising to PC purchasers.

Substitute Goods or Services. The threat of substitute goods or services depends on the ability and willingness of customers to change their buying habits. Substitutes limit the price that firms in a particular industry can charge for their products without risking a loss in sales. Cable television operators are being challenged by providers of digital satellite television transmission. Brinks and other armored car and guard operators are being threatened by the increase in the number of electronic surveillance firms.

PHASE 3: DIAGNOSE STRENGTHS AND WEAKNESSES

The diagnosis of strengths and weaknesses enables managers to identify an organization's core competencies and to determine which need to be improved. This diagnosis includes the organization's relative competitive position, ability to adapt and innovate, human resource skills, technological capabilities, financial resources, managerial depth, and the values and background of its key employees. **Core competencies** are the strengths that make an organization distinctive and more competitive by providing goods or services that have unique value to its customers. From a business-level perspective, core competencies fall into three broad groups: superior technological know-how, reliable processes, and close relationships with external stakeholders. A *reliable process* involves delivering an expected result quickly, consistently, and efficiently with the least inconvenience to customers.[35]

Citigroup has sophisticated financial and market trading know-how (technological core competency). It uses local customer contacts in various countries and its global network of affiliates to develop international business (close external relationships core competency). As a result, Citigroup now provides numerous financial services through its global network to more than 100 million customers worldwide. Its mission is to provide its customers "any banking service, anywhere, anytime, in any currency in any way they choose" without losing transactions and without bureaucratic delay (reliable processes core competency). Citigroup has developed a solid reputation with customers for executing cross-border transactions by assigning each customer a single contact person to build customer confidence in the handling of such transactions.[36] Ideally, a firm's core competencies make simple imitation of that firm difficult. For example, Citigroup's competitors do not have its ability or reputation for delivering easy foreign exchange trading to consumers. Their reliability is less because they have a more limited network of affiliate banks around the world and must rely more on correspondent banks, which also increases their costs.

Core organizational competencies represent strengths, as do an individual's managerial competencies. Most individuals find that assessing their strengths is easier than assessing their weaknesses. The same is true of organizations when assessing their strengths and weaknesses. Weaknesses often are blamed on specific managers and employees. As a result, statements of organizational weaknesses may be perceived as personal threats to their positions, influence, and self-esteem. But weaknesses are not self-correcting and are likely to become worse if not openly dealt with in the strategic planning process.

Recall from Chapter 1 that *outsourcing* means letting other organizations perform a needed service and/or manufacture needed parts or products. An increasing number of firms are outsourcing part or all the tasks and functions that are not a core competency or represent a current or potential weakness. Partial outsourcing of information technology tasks to firms such as EDS, IBM, Andersen Consulting (which has changed its name to Accenture), and Computer Sciences Corporation (CSC) has become increasingly common.[37] For example, DuPont, the huge chemical firm, outsources 75 percent of its information technology tasks to CSC and Accenture.[38]

Table 7.3 provides a basic framework for beginning the assessment of some business-level and functional-level strengths and weaknesses. The framework is in-

Table 7.3 **Sample Factors in Diagnosing Strengths and Weaknesses**

Instructions: Evaluate each issue on the basis of the following scale.

A = Superior to most competitors (top 10%).

B = Better than average. Good performance. No immediate problems.

C = Average. Equal to most competitors.

D = Problems here. Not as good as it should be. Deteriorating. Must be improved.

F = Major cause for concern. Crisis. Take immediate action to improve.

Category	Issue	Scale				
		A	B	C	D	F
Information technologies	Networking capabilities	—	—	—	—	—
	Speed of introduction	—	—	—	—	—
	Enhance service to customers	—	—	—	—	—
	Enhance product features	—	—	—	—	—
Human resources	Employee competencies	—	—	—	—	—
	Reward systems	—	—	—	—	—
	Commitment to learning	—	—	—	—	—
	Team orientation	—	—	—	—	—
	Other	—	—	—	—	—
Marketing	Share of market	—	—	—	—	—
	Channels of distribution	—	—	—	—	—
	Advertising effectiveness	—	—	—	—	—
	Customer satisfaction	—	—	—	—	—
	Other	—	—	—	—	—
Finance	Ability to obtain loans	—	—	—	—	—
	Debt-equity relationship	—	—	—	—	—
	Inventory turnover	—	—	—	—	—
	Usefulness of financial reports	—	—	—	—	—
	Other	—	—	—	—	—
Manufacturing	Per unit cost	—	—	—	—	—
	Inventory control	—	—	—	—	—
	Flexibility	—	—	—	—	—
	Quality process	—	—	—	—	—
	Other	—	—	—	—	—

tended for a single-business firm or an SBU. In some firms, top, middle, and first-level managers develop statements of opportunities, threats, strengths, and weaknesses for their areas of responsibility. Issues assessed by mid-level plant managers usually are quite different from those considered by top managers. Plant managers are likely to focus on manufacturing opportunities, threats, strengths, and weaknesses, whereas top managers are likely to focus on current and potential competitors, legislation and government regulations, societal trends, and the like. The key issues, regardless of their source, need to be addressed in the organization's strategic plan.

PHASE 4: DEVELOP STRATEGIES

The development of strategies must be evaluated in terms of (1) external opportunities and threats, (2) internal strengths and weaknesses, and (3) the likelihood that the strategies will help the organization achieve its mission and goals. Firms such as GE and AOL Time Warner have many SBUs. Thus the development of corporate-level and business-level strategies for such organizations is very complex.

Three basic growth strategies are common to business-level planning and strategy. A *market penetration strategy* involves seeking growth in current markets with current products. A firm might increase market penetration by (1) encouraging greater use of the product (e.g., getting current AT&T customers to use its long-distance service more often); (2) attracting competitors' customers (e.g., getting Dell customers to purchase Compaq PCs); and (3) buying a competitor (e.g., American Airlines buying US Airways). Market penetration also may be achieved by increasing the total size of the market by converting nonusers into current users (e.g., getting more consumers to use America Online).

A *market development strategy* requires seeking new markets for current products. Three principal ways of doing so are (1) entering new geographic markets (e.g., Dell's expansion from North American operations to global manufacturing and sales); (2) entering target markets (e.g., Meredith Corporation's introduction of an online magazine—*Successful Farming*—for farmers because many of them have PCs connected to an Internet service); and (3) expanding uses for current products and facilities (e.g., Warner Cable's use of its cable lines to carry new multimedia products and services through the Internet, rather than just television signals).

A *product development strategy* involves developing new or improved goods or services for current markets. Approaches that can be used to develop enhanced products include (1) improving features (e.g., increased leg room in the interior of the Honda Accord); (2) increasing quality in terms of reliability, speed, efficiency, or durability (e.g., Dell Computer's steady introduction of new lines of PCs); (3) enhancing aesthetic appeal (e.g., introduction by several manufacturers of more stylish PCs, triggered by the colorful line of Macs); and (4) introducing new models (e.g., Maytag's new line of washing machines with electronic sensors to get clothes cleaner).

As suggested in the following Strategic Action Competency feature and throughout this book, the array and diversity of business-level and corporate-level strategies are much greater than suggested in this chapter. It reports on some of the new strategies being implemented at Dell Computer as a result of the explosive growth of Internet use and changes in the marketplace for PCs.[39]

STRATEGIC ACTION COMPETENCY

Dell's New Growth Strategies

Michael Dell, CEO and chairman of the board of Dell Computer, comments: "People associate us with the PC and Windows. That's an easy association to make, but it's not really an accurate description of the company anymore." Fred Hickey, editor of *High-Tech Strategist,* adds: "The party's over. PCs have become a commodity just like televisions. Dell's the leader in a dying market." Michael Dell insists he can sidestep PC market changes by moving into other product areas, such as high-end servers and services. "Change is not something we've ever shied away from," he says.

The Internet, Michael Dell suggests, is pulling companies like Dell in two directions—toward the "core," where servers and huge storage systems re-

side, and the "edge," comprising PCs, cell phones, and hand-held devices. On the one hand, Dell is moving upstream, providing servers and storage systems that compete with those of Sun Microsystems. On the other hand, Dell is moving downstream, selling low-cost PCs and reselling hand-held devices that other companies make. Moreover, Dell is moving sideways into services—Web hosting and storage to drive new revenue streams. Dell states: "The real Holy Grail is the servers and storage systems that will sit at the center of that network." He predicts the server industry's sales will grow twentyfold in 5 years.

As Dell pushes beyond the PC market, another growth strategy is Dell Ventures, an investment arm formed in 1999. It has put more than $100 million

into 90 companies, figuring not only to make money as these firms grow but also to use these partners to support Dell's growth. Interliant, a Web hosting company in Purchase, N.Y., sold a stake to Dell in 2000. The company immediately entered the Web hosting business by reselling Interliant's service. Dell hopes to benefit three ways. First, the company steers customers to Interliant and takes a percentage of sales. Second, Dell sells its servers to Interliant to support those new customers. Finally, its support increases Interliant's sales, which should drive up the value of Dell's stake in Interliant. "They buy our infrastructure, we put them in front of our customers," Dell says.

Dell is taking on Sun Microsystems, the market leader in servers, with the same strategies it used against Compaq and IBM in the PC market: sell direct, win on price, and keep customer loyalty with quality. For example, Dell recently sold two storage subsystems to Mirage Resorts, for the Bellagio Casino in Las Vegas. Says Glenn Bonner, Mirage's chief information officer, "You can put in a $50,000 Dell server, and it competes with an IBM midrange computer that costs $375,000. Now that's something I'm going to look at."

• • •

For more information about Dell Computer, visit the company's home page at

http://www.dell.com

PHASE 5: PREPARE STRATEGIC PLAN

After developing alternative strategies and selecting among them, management is ready to prepare the written strategic plan. As suggested by the discussion in this and previous chapters, the written plan should contain sections that address

- organizational mission and goals;
- goods and/or services offered, including what makes them unique;
- market analysis and strategies, including opportunities and threats and contingency plans if things don't go as expected;
- strategies for obtaining and utilizing the necessary technological, manufacturing, marketing, financial, and human resources to achieve the stated goals, including capitalizing on strengths and overcoming weaknesses, as well as contingency plans in these areas;
- strategies for developing and utilizing organizational and employee competencies; and
- financial statements, including profit-and-loss, cash-flow, and break-even projections.

PHASE 6: PREPARE TACTICAL PLANS

Tactical plans are intended to help implement strategic plans. As indicated in Figure 7.3, middle and first-line managers and employee teams normally base tactical plans on the organization's strategic plan. (See Table 7.1 for a summary of the features of tactical planning.) Cameraworld.com, headquartered in Portland, Oregon, sells quality camera and related products online and via telephone. The firm recently implemented a tactical plan for improving its order fulfillment and shipping system. Specifically, the warehouse was relocated and reorganized and its equipment enhanced to speed up shipping. Frequently ordered items were moved closest to the packing and shipping stations, and rarely ordered items were moved to the back of the warehouse. The company increased the number of packing stations from one to four and increased the number of PCs in the warehouse from one to five.[40]

PHASE 7: CONTROL AND DIAGNOSE RESULTS

Controls are needed to ensure implementation of plans as intended and to evaluate the results achieved through those plans. If the plans haven't produced the desired results, managers and teams may need to change the mission and goals, revise the strategies, develop new tactical plans, or change the controls utilized. A thorough assessment of results will reveal specific changes that need to be incorporated in the next planning cycle. In Chapter 19, we discuss the controlling function in organizations. Controls help to reduce deviations from plans and provide useful information to the ongoing planning process.

PHASE 8: CONTINUE PLANNING

Planning is a continuing and ongoing process. The external (e.g., new competitors) and internal (e.g., expectations of new employees) environments are constantly changing. Sometimes these changes are gradual and foreseeable. At other times, they are abrupt and unpredictable. Rapid development of the Internet is being experienced by many organizations, such as Toys "Я" Us, as one of those abrupt and unpredictable forces.[41]

GENERIC COMPETITIVE STRATEGIES MODEL

6.

EXPLAIN THE GENERIC COMPETITIVE STRATEGIES MODEL.

The **generic competitive strategies model** provides a framework of three basic business-level strategies for a variety of organizations in diverse industries.[42] This model is called *generic* because all types of organizations can use it, whether they are involved in manufacturing, distribution, or services. Figure 7.4 shows the basic parts of this model. The strategic target dimension (vertical axis) indicates how widely the good or service is intended to compete—throughout the industry or within a particular segment of the industry. The source of advantage dimension (horizontal axis) indicates the basis on which the good or service is intended to compete—uniqueness as perceived by the customer or low cost (price) to the customer. The various combinations of these two variables, strategic target and source of advantage, suggest three different generic competitive strategies: differentiation strategy, cost leadership strategy, and focus strategy. The three basic growth strategies—market penetration, market development, and product development—may be used in combination with each of these competitive strategies.

| *Figure 7.4* | **Generic Competitive Strategies Model** |

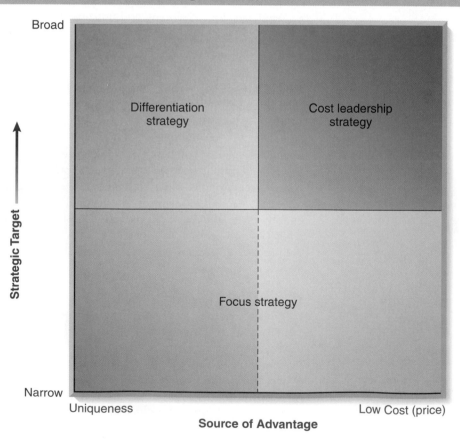

DIFFERENTIATION STRATEGY

The ***differentiation strategy*** involves competing with all other firms in the industry by offering a product that customers perceive to be unique. This strategy is dominant in much of the auto industry. Most automakers attempt to create unique value (benefits) by influencing customer perceptions and/or providing real differences for each automobile make and model. They use various strategies, including, among others, innovative product design (BMW), high quality (Toyota), unique brand image (Mercedes-Benz), technological leadership (Honda's four-wheel steering), customer service leadership (Lexus), an extensive dealer network (Ford and GM), and product warranty (Mazda's introduction of the bumper-to-bumper warranty). The long-term effectiveness of the differentiation strategy depends on how easily competitors can imitate the unique benefits provided by the firm. As soon as most or all competitors imitate the offering (such as a bumper-to-bumper car warranty), it no longer is an effective means of differentiation.

COST LEADERSHIP STRATEGY

The ***cost leadership strategy*** means competing in the industry by providing a product at a price as low as or lower than competitors' prices. This strategy requires a constant concern with efficiency (e.g., reduction in per unit costs). Several essential actions are associated with a cost leadership strategy: (1) utilizing facilities or equipment that yield high economies of scale; (2) constantly striving to reduce per unit overhead, manufacturing, marketing, labor and follow-up service costs; (3) minimizing labor-intensive personal services and sales forces; and (4) avoiding customers whose demands would result in high personal selling or service costs. High volume and/or rapid growth often are needed for profitability with the cost leadership strategy.

Online personal investing and financial services firms through the Internet, such as E*Trade, use the cost leadership strategy.[43] E*Trade emphasizes its low commission and margin rates on its Web site by statements such as: "You simply get more for less at E*Trade. Compare us to the competition. . . . Our combination of low costs and value-added resources is hard to beat."[44] Listed stocks may be traded as low as $14.95 for as many as 5,000 shares in a single trade.

FOCUS STRATEGY

The ***focus strategy*** involves competing in a specific industry niche by serving the unique needs of certain customers or a specific geographic market. A *niche* is a specialized group of customers (e.g., teenagers, physicians, or retirees) or a narrowly defined market segment that competitors may overlook, ignore, or have difficulty serving (e.g., an inner-city area being redeveloped or rehabilitated). Organizations attempt to create a unique image for their products by catering to the specific demands of the selected niche and ignoring other potential customers. Strategic actions associated with the focus strategy are adaptations of those associated with differentiation and cost leadership strategies but are applied to a specific market niche.

Jollibee Foods, a family-owned fast–food company in the Philippines, successfully uses the focus strategy. The company first overcame intense competition from McDonald's in its home market, partly by upgrading service and delivery standards but also by developing rival menus customized to local tastes. Along with noodle and rice meals made with fish, Jollibee created a hamburger seasoned with garlic and soy sauce—allowing it to capture 75 percent of the burger market and 56 percent of the fast-food business in the Philippines. Having learned what it takes to compete with multinationals, Jollibee management had the confidence to expand abroad, applying its focus strategy. Using its tested recipes, the company has established dozens of restaurants near large Filipino expatriate populations in Hong Kong, the Middle East, and California.[45]

We do not want to leave you with the impression that any one strategy ensures success. A successful firm tends to develop and utilize a *set* of strategies that integrate functions, resources, and competencies to meet market demands, as a symphony orchestra requires a score and conductor to integrate its many components to play in harmony.[46]

CHAPTER SUMMARY

In this chapter, we focused on the development of your planning and administration and strategic action competencies. We emphasized the features of strategy formulation and planning at the corporate and business levels.

1. EXPLAIN THE ROLE OF THE PLANNING FUNCTION.

Planning is the most basic managerial function. It helps an organization adapt to change by (1) identifying opportunities, (2) anticipating problems, and (3) developing appropriate strategies and tactics. If done properly, planning identifies risks and opportunities, facilitates entrepreneurship, and fosters learning.

2. DESCRIBE THE COMPONENTS OF TWO BASIC FORMS OF PLANNING.

Strategic planning emphasizes the development of an organization's mission and vision, goals, general strategies, and major resource allocations. Tactical planning emphasizes the shorter term detailed decisions regarding what to do, who will do it, and how to do it. Tactical planning provides the specific actions for implementing strategic plans.

3. DISCUSS THE EFFECTS OF LEVEL OF DIVERSIFICATION ON THE COMPLEXITY OF PLANNING.

The primary levels of diversification include (1) single-business firm, (2) dominant-business firm, (3) related-business firm, and (4) unrelated-business firm. The complexity of strategic planning increases as an organization becomes more diverse in terms of the range of goods and services it provides and the markets it serves.

4. DESCRIBE THE THREE BASIC LEVELS OF STRATEGY AND PLANNING.

Corporate-level strategy focuses on the activities of various businesses (or product lines) within a parent organization. Corporate-level growth strategies include forward integration, backward integration, horizontal integration, concentric diversification, and conglomerate diversification. Business-level strategy focuses on the operations and performance of a single-business firm or strategic business unit (SBU). Functional-level strategy focuses on the actions for managing each functional area. It specifies how each function will contribute to the organization's business-level strategies and goals.

5. STATE THE EIGHT PRIMARY PHASES OF THE PLANNING PROCESS.

The planning process includes eight interrelated phases: (1) develop the organization's mission and goals, (2) diagnose opportunities and threats, (3) diagnose strengths and weaknesses, (4) develop strategies (e.g., growth strategies of market penetration, market development, or product development), (5) prepare a strategic plan, (6) prepare tactical plans, (7) control and assess the results of both strategic and tactical plans, and (8) continue the planning process.

6. EXPLAIN THE GENERIC COMPETITIVE STRATEGIES MODEL.

The generic competitive strategies model provides a framework of three basic business-level strategies (differentiation, cost leadership, and focus) that are applicable to various sizes and types of organizations in diverse industries.

KEY TERMS

Backward integration strategy, p. 202
Business-level strategy, p. 204
Concentric diversification strategy, p. 202
Conglomerate diversification strategy, p. 203
Contingency planning, p. 193
Core competencies, p. 208
Corporate-level strategy, p. 200
Cost leadership strategy, p. 213
Differentiation strategy, p. 213
Diversification, p. 197
Dominant-business firm, p. 199

Finance strategies, p. 204
Focus strategy, p. 213
Forward integration strategy, p. 202
Functional-level strategy, p. 204
Generic Competitive strategies model, p. 212
Horizontal integration strategy, p. 202
Market development strategy, p. 210
Market penetration strategy, p. 210
Marketing strategies, p. 204
Mission, p. 194
Operations strategies, p. 204

Organizational goals, p. 194
Product development strategy, p. 210
Related-business firm, p. 199
Resource allocation, p. 196
Single-business firm, p. 199
Strategic business unit "(SBU)", p. 201
Strategic planning, p. 193
Strategies, p. 195
Tactical planning, p. 196
Unrelated-business firm, p. 199
Vision, p. 194

QUESTIONS FOR DISCUSSION AND COMPETENCY DEVELOPMENT

1. Review Richard McGinn's comments in the Preview Case regarding Lucent Technologies. What managerial competencies, and specific elements of those competencies, does McGinn reflect in his comments? You may find it helpful to review the section on *Managerial Competencies* in Chapter 1 before responding to this question.

2. If you were to develop a contingency plan for yourself, what three "environmental" factors would you include in it? Assume a 3-year time period for yourself.

3. Review the Strategic Action Competency on Dell's competitive strategies. Based on the generic strategies model, what is the dominant generic strategy at Dell? Why? Does this competency feature suggest any other aspects of a generic strategy?

4. Lucent Technologies and Cisco Systems are direct competitors in several lines of business. Search their Web sites and identify five specific products or services for which they are direct competitors. Their home pages are ***http://www.lucent.com*** and ***http://www.cisco.com***, respectively.

5. From your findings in answering Question 4, select one of the goods or services identified. Compare at least four of the features (or attributes) of this good or service as presented on the Web sites of Lucent Technologies and Cisco. Based on your assessment, which good or service do you prefer? Why?

6. General Electric is a highly successful unrelated-business firm. What are GE's stated values? Are the descriptions of its *social architecture* and *operating system* consistent with these values? Explain. The statement of values may be found on its Web site as follows: (1) go to ***http://www.ge.com/investor/annuals.htm***; and then (2) find *Corporate Info* on the directory shown and click the entry *GE Values*.

7. **Competency Development: Strategic Action Competency.** Granite Rock, headquartered in Watsonville, California, sells crushed gravel, concrete, sand, and asphalt. The family-owned business has some 600 employees and is led by Bruce and Steve Woolpert (brothers) who serve as co-presidents. Several years ago, they set a company goal of providing total customer satisfaction and achieving a reputation for service that met or exceeded that of Nordstrom, the upscale department store that is well known for delighting its customers. As one means of achieving this goal, they adopted a radical policy called "short pay." At the bottom of every Granite Rock invoice is the statement: "If you are not satisfied for any reason, don't pay us for it. Simply scratch out the line item, write a brief note about the problem, and return a copy of this invoice along with your check for the balance." It isn't a refund policy, so customers don't need to return the product or even need to call and complain. They have complete discretionary power to decide whether and how much to pay based on their satisfaction level.[47] Identify at least three implications for planning related to the stated goal and "short pay" policy at Granite Rock. What business-level strategy is Granite Rock following? Based on Granite Rock's goal and policy, what are the three management competencies, and the elements of each, that are most likely to be crucial in ensuring that its policy does not bankrupt the firm?

8. **Competency Development: Global Awareness Competency.** As domestic markets mature, many companies look overseas for expansion. One of the catchphrases in retailing is globalization. Many retailers are learning the substantive differences and subtleties involved in conducting business in new international markets. In the case of U.S. retailers, the fact that 95 percent of the world's population lives elsewhere serves as a strong incentive for international trade. Select one major retailer—such as Pier 1, Sears, Wal-Mart—and investigate its Web site. What in-store concepts and practices have been transferred intact and what, if any, have been modified—either globally or in a particular country? Have any changes in the size of its stores been necessary? If yes, why? Are there any differences in the level of services provided in this retailer's international markets?

9. **Competency Development: Teamwork Competency.** AES Corporation, a global electricity company based in Arlington, Virginia, uses empowered teams in facilities located throughout the world. Chairman Roger Sant explains, "[The employees] have total responsibility for decisions. They are accountable for results. What they do every day matters to the company . . . every AES person is a mini-CEO."[48] Identify at least three of the implications for how business-level and functional-level planning should be undertaken with a commitment by top management to the use of empowered teams at all organizational levels. For more information on the AES Corporation, visit this company's home page at ***http://www.aesc.com***.

CASE FOR COMPETENCY DEVELOPMENT

Gerstner on IBM and the Internet

The mission statement of IBM declares:

At IBM, we strive to lead in the creation, development, and manufacture of the industry's most advanced information technologies, including computer systems, software, networking systems, storage devices, and microelectronics. We translate these advanced technologies into value for our customers through our professional solutions and services businesses worldwide.

Louis Gerstner, Jr., serves as Chairman and CEO of IBM. The following are excerpts from his Letter to Shareholders in IBM's *1999 Annual Report*.

The fact is, 1999 was the year e-business and the global Internet economy came of age. It was a tidal wave, sweeping everything before it, driving new levels of megamerger activity, carrying thousands of entirely new businesses to unprecedented levels of wealth (much of it probably unsustainable), submerging almost as many others, and rearranging the landscape of commerce.

One conservative estimate is that the e-business opportunity will approach $600 billion by 2003, and it could well be even larger than that. While the overall information technology (I/T) industry grows at around 11 percent, the e-business portion is growing much faster—around 22 percent.

We know how open the field is and how huge the stakes are. It's tough to be fast, focused and feel a sense of discomfort in a period of explosive change. But that's what we have to do. As the race begins, these are our top three goals:

(1) *Accelerate our growth.* A hyperdynamic marketplace such as we see today values *trajectory*—that is, the potential for growth—more than current market position. That's good for IBM, because we're entering a period of explosive demand for everything we have—hardware, software, services, component technology, expertise—the whole portfolio. There's no question the opportunity is there, but thus far we haven't captured our rightful share across all segments.

We will continue to shift our portfolio toward the highest-growth e-business opportunities. In this regard, we passed an important milestone last year. Our three major growth engines—services, software, and component (OEM) technology—now provide more than half (in fact, nearly 60 percent) of IBM's revenue. Conversely, we are exiting businesses where we can't achieve our growth objectives, or where partnership is the preferred strategy. That's why we formed a networking solutions alliance with Cisco Systems last year. And it's why we scaled back our enterprise application software efforts in 1999, instead partnering with leading software developers like Siebel Systems, i2 Technologies, SAP, and Telcordia Technologies.

(2) *In all things, innovate.* By innovation I don't just mean technology—though of course I mean that, too. With our seventh straight year of patent leadership and another record total (2,756 U.S. patents in 1999), IBM's position as the world's premier commercial center of technology innovation is unchallenged. We will continue to invest in that. We will also continue to speed those innovations—such as copper chips and record-setting hard disk drives—into products (our own, and those of our customers). And we'll continue taking on "grand challenges" that bring technology breakthroughs to bear on previously intractable problems. For example, in December 1999, IBM Research announced a $100 million push to build a supercomputer named "Blue Gene"—500 times more powerful than today's fastest computers—that initially will be used to model the mysterious folding of human proteins.

But innovation at IBM has never been about technology alone, or for its own sake. Especially now, when the competitive environment demands that we create radically new ways in which we go to market, attract new employees, and structure relationships with customers and partners. For instance,

we have stepped up our efforts to reach out to Internet start-ups—through novel incubator programs and more than $700 million in planned start-up financing and venture capital investments. We form relationships with dotcoms while they're still in the incubator, so we can help them make technology decisions before they launch. Just as important, we get to see beyond the current technology horizon, understand the trends, and deploy that learning directly in IBM. (And, by the way, we've already seen a tidy return on our investments.)

(3) *Shape the new face of IBM.* What will "IBM" mean to customers, potential customers and employees, and the public at large in the years ahead? Our brand used to be touched and our company experienced primarily through our products. But going forward, a smaller percentage of our customers will buy an item with "IBM" stamped on it. Instead, when they experience the benefits of our innovative technology, much of it will be inside other companies' branded products, or at work behind the scenes in the computing infrastructure of the Net.

Even more important, they'll experience IBM in the person of another human being. Sometimes within the next five years, more than half of our revenues and workforce will come from services. This will mean that, very soon, revered IBM brand attributes like quality, reliability, and innovation will primarily be descriptions of IBM people—their knowledge, ideas, and behavior—just as today they describe IBM ThinkPads, servers, and software.[49]

Questions

1. What strengths, weaknesses, opportunities, and threats are suggested in Louis Gerstner's comments?

2. What corporate-level strategies are illustrated in his statements?

3. Are the stated goals of IBM consistent with its stated mission? Explain.

4. In his Letter to Shareholders, Gerstner also states: "This year I'd like to mention three other important developments (actually, they are more like new realities) that are now taking hold." What are these developments? To answer this question, read pages 5–7 of IBM's *1999 Annual Report,* which may be found at ***http://www.ibm.com/annualreport/1999/.***

5. What are the key differences between the Letter to Shareholders in *IBM's 1999 Annual Report* and the annual report for the most recent year? IBM's most recent annual report and the annual reports for the previous 5 years are listed at ***http://www.ibm.com/annualreport/.***

To learn more about IBM, visit the company's home page at ***http://www.ibm.com.***

Hudson's Somerset Store

Hudson's Department Stores are part of the fourth largest retailing chain in the United States—the Target Corporation (formerly, Dayton Hudson, Inc.). The retail giant has three major lines of retailing: Mervyn's, Target, and a group of department stores (including Dayton's, Hudson's, and Marshall Field's). The Minnesota-based company decided to develop new upscale stores and first opened one such store—a Hudson's store—in Somerset, Michigan, a wealthy Detroit suburb.

The design of Hudson's Somerset store was heavily influenced by a Marshall Field's store in Northbrook, Illinois (a Chicago suburb), a trendsetter in merchandising and layout design. Both facilities were created by Andrew Markopoulos (Hudson's senior vice president of visual merchandising and design), whose intent was to combine classic department store traditions (e.g., luxurious wood and marble materials) with contemporary layouts to ensure easy and convenient shopping.

The Somerset location features wide aisles that form a simple X shape and branch off a circular atrium like the spokes of a wheel. The store has minimal interior walls, allowing the atrium to be visible from each floor. Each department is wedge shaped and has contrasting décor to make it easy for customers to tell one department from another.

Despite having the Marshall Field's store as a model, a planning committee of Hudson's employees was involved in making many planning and design decisions for the new store. Committee membership deliberately included employees from various departments and levels of administration. The intent was to keep everyone involved and informed during design and construction so that when overlapping issues arose, they could be attacked head on and resolved quickly.

The committee's role and tasks changed over time. Initially, its members set deadlines and general goals as they discussed all aspects of the new store. However, as work on the store progressed, they began to concentrate on area-specific issues.

The planning process was successful, as evidenced by the store coming in under budget and now being considered the company's benchmark store. The committee kept detailed records and provided timely feedback to headquarters about the process and what the committee members learned from being involved in it. Hudson's management now uses this information in developing other new upscale stores.

Questions

1. What type of planning process did the Hudson's committee utilize at the beginning of the Somerset store's development? Explain.

2. What are some of the recommendations that Hudson's employees offered for future planning projects?

3. The decision by Target's management to develop more upscale department stores is emblematic of which of the following basic growth strategies: market penetration, market development, or product development?

To learn more about the Target Corporation, visit the company's home page at ***http://www.targetcorp.com***.

Fundamentals of Decision Making

LEARNING OBJECTIVES

AFTER STUDYING THIS CHAPTER YOU SHOULD BE ABLE TO:

1. EXPLAIN THE ROLE OF DECISION MAKING FOR MANAGERS AND EMPLOYEES.

2. STATE THE CONDITIONS UNDER WHICH INDIVIDUALS MAKE DECISIONS.

3. DESCRIBE THE CHARACTERISTICS OF ROUTINE, ADAPTIVE, AND INNOVATIVE DECISIONS.

4. EXPLAIN THE FEATURES OF THREE BASIC MODELS OF DECISION MAKING.

Chapter Outline

PREVIEW: JIM PREVO'S DECISIONS

ROLE OF DECISION MAKING

DECISION-MAKING CONDITIONS

    CERTAINTY

    RISK

    UNCERTAINTY

    SELF-MANAGEMENT COMPETENCY: George Conrades, Akamai Technologies

BASIC TYPES OF DECISIONS

    PROBLEM TYPES

    SOLUTION TYPES

    ROUTINE DECISIONS

    ADAPTIVE DECISIONS

    INNOVATIVE DECISIONS

    STRATEGIC ACTION COMPETENCY: Alliant Foodservice Innovates

MODELS OF DECISION MAKING

    RATIONAL MODEL

    PLANNING AND ADMINISTRATION COMPETENCY: Contrasting Controls at American and Southwest Airlines

    BOUNDED RATIONALITY MODEL

    POLITICAL MODEL

    TEAMWORK COMPETENCY: Phone.com's Aversion to Politics

CHAPTER SUMMARY

KEY TERMS

QUESTIONS FOR DISCUSSION AND COMPETENCY DEVELOPMENT

CASE FOR COMPETENCY DEVELOPMENT: JEAN SIMPSON'S DILEMMA

VIDEO CASE: NEXT DOOR FOOD STORE

JIM PREVO'S DECISIONS

To install an enterprise resource planning (ERP) system at Green Mountain Coffee, Inc., of Waterbury, Connecticut, Jim Prevo had to take his team—and his company—on a risky, 3-year journey. "An ERP implementation is like the corporate equivalent of a brain transplant," says Prevo, vice president and chief information officer (CIO) at the wholesaler and retailer of specialty coffees. "We pulled the plug on every company application and moved to PeopleSoft (software). The risk was certainly disruption of business, because if you do not do ERP properly, you can kill your company, guaranteed."

Green Mountain had operated on homegrown computer software applications that had become inadequate as the company increased revenue by 30 percent annually, beginning in 1993. By 1996, the firm was unable to manage its inventories electronically. That meant keeping extra inventories to ensure that

orders could be filled—and even then, they sometimes couldn't. "What was at stake was our long-term ability to grow," Prevo says.

But ERP wasn't the project that the top executives had asked Prevo's department to undertake. The initial plan was for a 5- to 12-month in-house revamping of the company's software. Believing that that approach wouldn't solve Green Mountain's problems, Prevo sold the executive leadership on a 3-year ERP project instead. He managed to do so even though Prevo had to explain that installing an ERP system was a bet-the-company strategy: If it didn't work, the company could be out of business. "A CIO or IT (information technology) leader must make the judgment of when the risk is low enough to make the jump," Prevo says.

To make the project work, Prevo had to be a leader without being the line manager of everyone on the cross-

functional team. Luckily, he had the background. "I used to be a software engineer at Digital Equipment . . . so I had a great deal of experience managing teams where I had influence but not authority," Prevo says. Once the People-Soft project began, Prevo found himself trying to keep the implementation team's spirits up in the face of glitches that always come with an ERP installation. For Green Mountain, they included on-line sales functions that didn't work properly and servers that were swamped by the new workloads.

"Jim was in a leadership role in this project, and he added a tremendous degree of insight and support," says Robert Stiller, CEO of Green Mountain Coffee.[1]

To learn more about Green Mountain Coffee, visit the company's home page at

http://www.greenmountaincoffee.com

ROLE OF DECISION MAKING

1.

EXPLAIN THE ROLE OF DECISION MAKING FOR MANAGERS AND EMPLOYEES.

Under less risky circumstances, managers and employees make decisions every day, as Jim Prevo did, using a process that contains the same basic elements. He defined the problem (e.g., totally inadequate software applications for growth), gathered information (e.g., getting information on new enterprise resource planning systems), identified and assessed alternatives (e.g., improve current application or go with a new ERP system), and then decided and recommended what to do. Fortunately, when most managers make recommendations or decisions, relatively few face the potential adverse consequences that Prevo did if the ERP project had failed. All, however, encounter a wide range of decision-making situations.

In this chapter, we present the basics of ***decision making***, which include defining problems, gathering information, generating alternatives, and choosing a course of action. We discuss how managers and employees can base various types of decisions on the nature of the problem to be solved, the possible solutions available, and the degree of risk involved.

Effective managers rely on several managerial competencies to make and implement decisions. In turn, decision making underlies most managerial competencies. For example, Prevo's decision and recommendation to implement the ERP planning project demonstrated his strategic action competency. He used his communication competency to explain what would be involved and to convince other managers in the company of the wisdom of this risky strategy. Prevo relied on his planning and administration competency and teamwork competencies to make the project work.

DECISION-MAKING CONDITIONS

2.

STATE THE CONDITIONS
UNDER WHICH
INDIVIDUALS MAKE
DECISIONS.

The conditions under which individuals make decisions are influenced by developments and events that they can't control but that may in the future influence the results of their decisions.[2] In our discussions of general and global environmental forces in Chapters 3 and 4, we identified and discussed forces that managers and employees often must deal with. In Chapter 6, we noted the impact that key stakeholders can have on decisions involving ethical and social responsibility issues. Thus decisions are affected by forces that can range from new technologies or the entrance of new competitors into a market to new laws or political turmoil. In addition to identifying and measuring the strength of these forces, managers must estimate their potential impact. Green Mountain Coffee faced the prospect of potentially huge benefits or potential disaster when its management decided to implement the ERP project. The impact of such actions always is felt in the future, either sooner or later. Managers and others involved in forecasting and planning may be hard-pressed to identify the implications of decisions, especially when they may not occur until years later. Recall that the ERP project at Green Mountain Coffee involved a 3-year time horizon for full implementation—and the full impact of the changes probably wouldn't be felt until even later. This period contrasts with the 5- to 12-month horizon for revamping the company's current software. Decision makers such as Jim Prevo have to base their decisions and recommendations on available information. Hence the amount and accuracy of information and the depth of individual's managerial competencies (see Chapter 1) are crucial to sound decision making.

The conditions under which decisions are made can be classified as certainty, risk, and uncertainty.[3] These conditions are shown as a continuum in Figure 8.1. When individuals can identify developments and events and their potential impact with total predictability, they make decisions under the condition of certainty. As information dwindles and becomes ambiguous, the condition of risk enters into decision making. Individuals begin to base their decisions on either objective (clear) or subjective (intuition and judgment) probabilities. The decision to proceed with the ERP project at Green Mountain Coffee was made under a condition of risk that involved subjective probabilities. The condition of uncertainty means that individuals have little or no information about developments and forces on which to base a decision. Because of that uncertainty, decision makers may be able to make only a reasonable guess as to possible outcomes from the decision.

Figure 8.1 **Conditions Under Which Decisions Are Made**

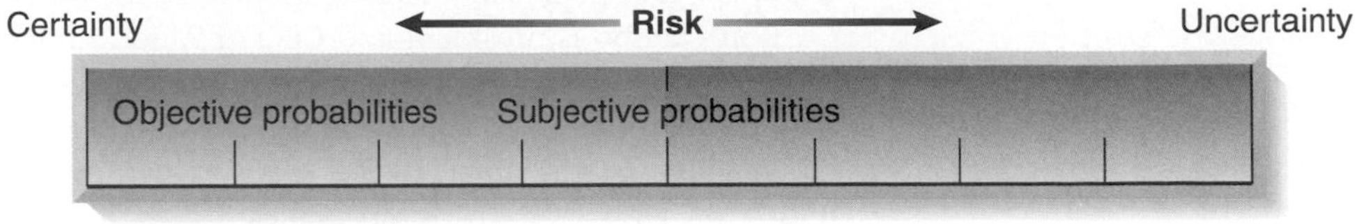

CERTAINTY

Certainty is the condition under which individuals are fully informed about a problem, alternative solutions are known, and the results of each solution are totally predictable. The condition of certainty at least allows exact anticipation (if not control) of events and their consequences. This condition means that both the problem and alternative solutions are totally known and well defined. Once an individual has identified alternative solutions and their expected results, making the decision is relatively easy. The decision maker simply chooses the solution with the best anticipated result.

Decision making under the condition of certainty is the exception for most managers and professionals. However, first-line managers make some day-to-day decisions under conditions of certainty or near certainty. For example, a surge in packages around a holiday period may cause a first-line manager at the FedEx center in Memphis, Tennessee, to ask 10 employees to work 2 hours of overtime. The manager can determine the cost of the overtime with certainty. The manager also can anticipate with near certainty the number of additional packages that will be processed. Thus the actual labor costs for handling the packages can be calculated with near certainty before the overtime is scheduled.

RISK

Risk refers to the condition under which individuals can define a problem, specify the probability of certain events, identify alternative solutions, and state the probability of each solution leading to the desired result.[4] Risk generally means that the problem and alternative solutions fall somewhere between the extremes of being certain and being unusual and ambiguous.

Probability is the percentage of times that a specific result would occur if an individual were to make a specific decision a large number of times. The most commonly used example of probability is that of tossing a coin: With enough tosses of the coin, heads will show up 50 percent of the time and tails the other 50 percent. Insurance companies make intensive use of the probability concept in setting all kinds of premium rates.

The quality of information available to an individual about the relevant decision-making condition can vary widely—as can the individual's estimates of risk. The type, amount, and reliability of information influence the level of risk and whether the decision maker can use objective or subjective probability in estimating the result (see Figure 8.1).

Objective Probability. *Objective probability* is the likelihood that a specific result will occur, based on hard facts and numbers. Sometimes an individual can determine the likely result of a decision by examining past records. For example, although Allstate, Farmer's, and other life insurance companies can't determine the year in which each policyholder will die, they can calculate objective probabilities that specific numbers of policyholders, in various age categories, will die in a particular year. These objective probabilities are based on the expectation that past death rates will be repeated in the future.

Subjective Probability. *Subjective probability* is the likelihood that a specific result will occur, based on personal judgment and beliefs. Such judgments vary among individuals, depending on their intuition, previous experience with similar situations, expertise, and personality traits (e.g., preference for risk taking or risk avoidance).

Ron Dembo is president and CEO of Algorithmics, Inc., and a leading authority on risks in business. His firm sells software—applications with names such as Risk Watch and Risk Mapper—to banks, insurers, and other firms that need assistance in measuring and managing their financial risks. His comments are directly relevant to decisions made under risk with subjective probabilities:

> The world is much riskier today because everything is much more interconnected.... If you're not managing risk, you can't claim to be managing your business.... Managing risk means thinking about the future, not about the past. Some of the best minds in business misunderstand this point. We all get comfortable basing our strategies for the future on the past. That's why risks that we didn't anticipate can take us by surprise—and why it's so hard to reckon with events for which there is no precedent.[5]

WEB INSIGHT

See the current Form 10-K for E*Trade. Review the section on risk factors. What differences and similarities are there in stated risks for the current year with those listed here for 2000? Go to **http://www.hoovers.com**, keystroke "E*Trade," and click "GO." Find and click "Real-time SEC filings" in the index for E*Trade.

E*Trade, the online personal financial services firm, has customers in all 50 states and 119 countries from Aruba to Zambia. It is one of the leaders in providing "anytime, anywhere, any device" access to financial information and transaction capabilities.[6] The management of E*Trade recognizes many risks—and uncertainties—in its business. In the filing of its annual 10-K form with the Securities and Exchange Commission, E*Trade management annually identifies "Risk Factors," which actually include uncertainties as well, for review by all interested parties. This form is a public document and must be submitted for all firms traded on major U.S. stock exchanges. A few of the risk factors—including uncertainties—that E*Trade management set forth in its submission of the 10-K form in 2000 include the following.

- We could suffer substantial losses and be subject to customer litigation if our systems fail or our transaction processing is slow.

- Our security could be breached, which could damage our reputation and prevent customers from using our services.

- There can be no assurance that we will be able to compete effectively with current or future competitors or that such competition will not have material adverse effect on our business, financial condition, and operating results.

- Our future success depends, in part, on our ability to develop and implement our services and products. There are significant technical risks in the development of new services and products or enhanced versions of existing services and products.[7]

UNCERTAINTY

Uncertainty is the condition under which an individual doesn't have the necessary information to assign probabilities to the outcomes of alternative solutions. In fact, the individual may not even be able to define the problem, much less identify alternative solutions and possible outcomes. Uncertainty often suggests that the problem and the alternative solutions are both ambiguous and highly unusual.[8]

Dealing with uncertainty is an important facet of the jobs of many managers and various professionals, such as R&D engineers, market researchers, and strategic planners. Managers, teams, and other professionals often need to *absorb uncertainty* by using their intuition, creativity, and all available information to make a judgment regarding the course of action (decision) to take. The following Self-Management Competency feature presents the views of George Conrades, chairman and CEO of Akamai Technologies.[9] Headquartered in Cambridge, Massachusetts, this firm provides software products to enhance the way the Internet works. Akamai's software enables companies, especially Web site operators, to store their content closer to the customer and deliver it over the least congested route at any given moment. Conrades's comments suggest a keen self-awareness along with personal drive and resilience in the role he plays as CEO in absorbing uncertainty to keep Akamai moving forward.

SELF-MANAGEMENT COMPETENCY

George Conrades, Akamai Technologies

I play three roles, all of which support the execution of our business model. First is to ensure that we stay focused on our business, that we not get distracted. Second is coordination— making sure our management and organization stay as flat as possible and that everybody keeps communicating. And the third role is to absorb uncertainty—to be the guy who, after thorough, wide-open discussions, drives the group to a decision.

We operate in an environment—the Internet—where there's an enormous amount of uncertainty. You can't be sure what's going to happen tomorrow, never mind next year. The danger is that the uncertainty can lead to paralysis. I'm the guy in the organization who absorbs the uncertainty. I'm the one who says, "Okay, we've talked through this enough. Let's do it and see what happens." By taking on the risk, I free the organization to act.

Now, absorbing uncertainty doesn't mean resolving uncertainty. The uncertainty is always there, and it always will be. We understand that—in fact, it's built into the way we manage the business. Every Monday the entire management team gathers together, and we argue about the key challenges we face. One person throws out an idea, and the rest of us tear into it: What are the assumptions underlying that idea? What's the logic? What are the implications? We're intellectually ruthless, and we all cherish that ruthlessness. It's the cornerstone of our culture, really. We never let it get personal. It's always constructive—aimed at ripping a question apart so we can be as sure as possible that we come to the best decision.

My role is to be the referee in those discussions. I'm an active participant in them, but I'm also the guy who steps back from the fray, synthesizes everything that's been said, and makes sure the argument's moving forward rather than in a circle. I might jump up to the white board, for instance, to capture the key ideas and force people to focus on them. I'm also the guy who says, "Enough." When it's clear we've gone as deep as we're going to go, I stop the debate, and we finalize the decision. I'm careful to never play that role in an authoritarian, top-down way.

• • •

To learn more about Akamai Technologies, visit the company's home page at

http://www.akamai.com

BASIC TYPES OF DECISIONS

3.

DESCRIBE THE CHARACTERISTICS OF ROUTINE, ADAPTIVE, AND INNOVATIVE DECISIONS.

No single decision-making method can be used in the various situations encountered by managers and employees. As a start, the decision maker needs to define accurately the problem at hand, move on to generating and evaluating alternative solutions, and finally make a decision. Doing so, however, is not this simple in reality.

The considerations of certainty, risk, and uncertainty provide an underpinning to the basic types of decisions—routine, adaptive, and innovative. They reflect the types of problems encountered and the types of solutions considered. Figure 8.2 presents the different combinations of problem types (vertical axis) and solution types (horizontal axis) that result in the three types of decisions. The diagonal line from lower left to upper right shows the related conditions of certainty, risk, and uncertainty.

PROBLEM TYPES

The types of problems that managers and others deal with range from the relatively common and well defined to the unusual and ambiguous. The bank teller with an out-of-balance cash drawer at the end of the day faces a common and well-defined problem. In contrast, managers and other professionals must deal with unusual and ambiguous problems. When the number of such problems escalates with short time frames for resolution, a pattern of *fire fighting* may occur with linked elements, such as the following, creating unsatisfactory results.

- *Solutions are incomplete.* Too many problems are patched, not solved. That is, superficial effects are dealt with, but the underlying causes are not fixed.

- *Problems recur and cascade.* Incomplete solutions cause old problems to reemerge or actually create new problems, sometimes elsewhere in the organization.

- *Urgency supersedes importance.* Ongoing problem-solving efforts and long-range activities, such as developing new processes, are repeatedly interrupted or deferred because fires must be extinguished.

- *Some problems become crises.* Problems smolder until they flare up, often just before a deadline.[10]

Figure 8.2   **Framework for Decision Making**

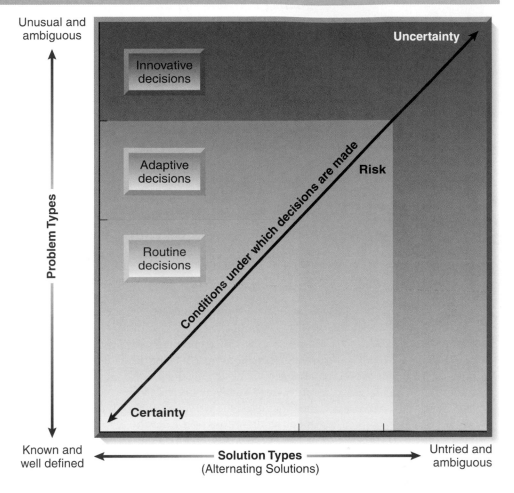

SOLUTION TYPES

The types of solutions available also range from the known and well defined to the untried and ambiguous. What happens when Shirley Coyle, a bank teller at a Bank of America branch, has an out-of-balance cash drawer? In brief, she follows a specific, well-defined procedure—check all deposit slips against deposit receipts and cash tickets and recount all the cash. In contrast, managers and other professionals often must develop solutions that are untried and ambiguous. *Management Review* magazine asked experts to nominate the 75 greatest management decisions (solutions) ever made. The only link between them was that they were successful and had a major impact. At the time the nominated decisions were made, all were untried and most involved ambiguous solutions. Three of the nominees of special interest were the following.

- In desolate post–World War II Japan, Toyota listened to an obscure American statistician, W. Edwards Deming, who arrived unheralded in 1947. Deming introduced Toyota to quality techniques, and it changed the world of manufacturing.

- Ignoring market research, Ted Turner launched the Cable News Network in 1980. No one thought a 24-hour news network would work. It did.

- When the Wilson family of Memphis went on a motoring vacation, they discovered it was not much fun to stay in motels that were either too expensive or too slovenly. So Kemmons Wilson built his own. The first Holiday Inn opened in Memphis in 1952.[11]

ROUTINE DECISIONS

Routine decisions are the standard choices made in response to relatively well-defined and common problems and alternative solutions. How to make various routine decisions is often covered by established rules or standard operating procedures or, increasingly, in computer software, such as computerized airline reservation systems. Placing orders online, cleaning buildings, processing payroll vouchers, packing and shipping customers' orders, and making travel arrangements are but a few examples of tasks requiring routine decisions. Managers and employees need to guard against the tendency to make routine decisions when a problem actually calls for an adaptive or innovative decision.[12] Doing so results in ***active inertia***—the rigid devotion to the status quo by attempting to do more of the same old thing better. At times, even leading companies, such as GM and J.C. Penney, become stuck in the routine ways of thinking and working that brought them initial success. When their environments change significantly, their once winning formulas bring stagnation, declining profits and value, or even failure.

McDonald's is a company whose routines hindered its response to changing market conditions. In the early 1990s, McDonald's operations manual comprised 750 pages detailing every aspect of a restaurant's business. For years, the company's focus on standardized processes, all dictated by headquarters, had allowed it to introduce its standard formula rapidly in market after market. This approach ensured the consistency and efficiency that attracted customers and dismayed rivals.

However, McDonald's also displayed active inertia. Consumers were looking for different foods, and competitors such as Burger King and Taco Bell were capitalizing on the shifts in taste by launching new menu items. McDonald's was slow to respond to the changes. Its historical strength—a single-minded focus on refining its mass-production processes—suddenly became a weakness. By requiring menu decisions to pass through headquarters, the company stifled innovation and delayed action. Its central development kitchen, removed from the actual restaurants and their customers, developed a series of products—such as the McPizza, McLean, and Arch Deluxe—but all failed to entice diners.[13] Starting in 1997, McDonald's began to implement a series of adaptive decisions to overcome its active inertia.

The key to the continuing usefulness of routine decisions is to review constantly the need to retain or change them through meaningful strategic and tactical planning. Consider the following effective application of complex and sophisticated routine decisions that are supported by computer software and databases. Capital One Financial Corporation is one of the 10 largest issuers of credit cards with about 20 million customers and 11,000 employees. The customer-service telephones at Capital One ring more than 1 million times a week. People call to ask about their MasterCard balances, whether a recent payment was received, or why the interest rate has jumped. Here's what happens before a caller hears the first ring.

The instant the last digit is punched, high-speed computers are activated. They are loaded with background information on one in seven U.S. households and with exhaustive data about how the company's millions of customers behave. The computers identify who is calling and predict the reason for the call. After reviewing 50 options, the computers pick the best option for each situation. The computers also pull and pass along about two dozen pieces of information about the person who is calling. They even predict what the caller might want to buy—*even though he or she isn't calling to buy anything*—and then the computers prepare the customer-service rep to sell that item, once the original reason for the call has been addressed. All these steps—the incoming call, the data review, the analysis, the routing, and the recommending—happen in just one-tenth of a second.[14]

ADAPTIVE DECISIONS

Adaptive decisions refer to choices made in response to a combination of moderately unusual problems and alternative solutions. Adaptive decisions typically involve modifying and improving on past routine decisions and practices. Adaptive decisions often reflect the concept of **convergence**—a business shift in which two connections with the customer that were previously viewed as competing (e.g., bricks-and-mortar bookstores and Internet bookstores) come to be seen as complementary. Those customer connections can include previously competing sales channels, product categories, or distribution channels.

WEB INSIGHT

Go to the Web site for Lands' End at *http://www.landsend.com*. Evaluate its ease of use for consumers in making purchase decisions.

A case in point of adaptive decisions and convergence is Lands' End—a direct merchant of traditionally styled clothing for men, women, and children. The headquarters and main distribution center are located in Dodgeville, Wisconsin.[15] Lands' End no longer sees its Internet and toll-free phone sales as competing. Instead, an Internet customer can click on a Web site button and within 20 seconds talk to a customer service representative who can feed personalized images to the customer's Web browser.[16]

Adaptive decisions also reflect the concept of **continuous improvement**—which refers to a management philosophy that approaches the challenge of product and process enhancements as an ongoing effort to increase the levels of quality and excellence.[17] It involves streams of adaptive organizational decisions made over time that result in a large number of small, incremental improvements year after year. Continuous improvement requires a commitment to constant diagnosis of technical, organizational, and managerial processes in search of improvements. In part, the process resembles the wheel in a hamster cage—a ladder wrapped onto a cylinder, with no beginning and no end. Each "turn of the wheel" improves an existing product and/or process. Year after year the organization's products and processes keep getting better, more reliable, and less expensive. Continuous improvement is driven by the goals of providing better quality, improving efficiency, and being responsive to customers.[18]

Larry Carter is the chief financial officer of Cisco Systems. Recall from Chapter 7 that Cisco is a major provider of products and services that enable firms to use the Internet effectively. Several years ago, Carter implemented an improvement project to serve the company's sales personnel better. They were upset because they spent too much time filling out expense reports and had to wait weeks to get reimbursed. So Cisco moved expense reporting to the Web and made it virtually instantaneous for all employees. Carter then worked to automate paying commissions—a major step toward real time because it meant calculating revenues and commissions as orders were entered. He next improved accounting, setting all cutoffs for the same time (Saturday midnight, Pacific Time) and converting 50 different ledgers into one global chart of accounts. Then, using total quality tools to measure everything—from invoice holds by reason to time-sheet errors by cause—Carter steadily improved the integrity of Cisco's data. It took 4 years, but Cisco now has real-time management accounting.[19]

INNOVATIVE DECISIONS

Innovative decisions are choices based on the discovery, identification, and diagnosis of unusual and ambiguous problems and/or the development of unique or creative alternative solutions. Again, the solutions frequently involve a series of small, interrelated decisions made over a period of months or even years. In particular, leading-edge innovations may take years to develop and involve numerous professional specialists and teams. Because innovative decisions usually represent a sharp break with the past, they normally don't happen in a logical, orderly sequence. Such decisions are typically based on incomplete and rapidly changing information. Moreover, they may be made before problems are fully defined and understood. To be effective, decision makers therefore must be especially careful to define the right problem and recognize that earlier actions can significantly affect later decisions.[20]

Alliant Foodservice, Inc., is one of the nation's largest broadline food-service distributors, operating a coast-to-coast network of 44 distribution centers and food processing facilities. Headquartered in Deerfield, Illinois, Alliant has about 11,000 employees and serves some 100,000 customers, including independent and multiunit restaurant operations, hotels, contract food-service operations, and health-care facilities. The following Strategic Action Competency feature describes the innovative decisions being made to transform the company's distribution system.[21]

STRATEGIC ACTION COMPETENCY

Alliant Foodservice Innovates

Several years ago, James Roger, chairman of Alliant Foodservice, realized that if Alliant didn't act fast, it would get squeezed out by online rivals able to connect buyers and sellers directly, without interference by middleman distributors—such as his own $6 billion, privately held firm. To lead the transformation in the company's distribution system, he hired Earl Mason, who had previously served as an executive at Compaq, as CEO.

At the center of Mason's plan is AlliantLink.com, a Web site that lets restaurants, hospitals, and hotels, among others, order goods without catalogs, faxes, and phones. Traditionally, food orders are placed by buyers sifting through pages of catalogs listing everything from lettuce to beef cuts and then choosing the products that fit the week's menu. The lists are gener-

ally faxed a few times a week between restaurants and food distributors such as Alliant and Sysco Corporation, the leading distributor with annual sales of $16 billion.

Alliant's Web site is connected to a database that keeps tabs on what's in stock—and what isn't—in 44 Alliant warehouses throughout the United States—all in real time. These warehouses are the "bricks and mortar" part of Alliant's business, the distribution arm of the company that delivers 1 million cases of food and supplies every day. By connecting the food service to the Web site, Mason created what he calls Alliant Exchange, Inc., a holding company for the two-pronged (bricks and mortar and Web-based) operation.

Historically, the distribution process generated costly errors. Already, the

new system with its improved technology has reduced errors by more than 60 percent. For example, returns have been cut dramatically. Formerly, catalogs limited descriptions of food to 19 characters, making it difficult for customers to know which foods best fit their needs. On average, there were 14 returns per 1,000 cases delivered. By using AlliantLink.com, customers get vivid pictures and details of each product. Returns now are only 3 returns per 1,000 cases shipped; the goal is 0.3 returns per 1,000 cases.

• • •

For more information about Alliant Foodservice, visit the company's home page at

http://www.alliantfs.com

MODELS OF DECISION MAKING

4.

EXPLAIN THE FEATURES OF THREE BASIC MODELS OF DECISION MAKING.

The material presented to this point provides the foundation for discussing three models of decision making: rational, bounded rationality, and political. These models have been developed to represent different decision-making processes, and each provides valuable insights into those processes.

WEB INSIGHT

Go to the Web site at *http://www. HelpMakingDecisions.com*. How does this service attempt to guide you in making rational decisions? Describe one of the testimonials given about using this model.

RATIONAL MODEL

The *rational model* prescribes a set of phases that individuals or teams should follow to increase the likelihood that their decisions will be logical and optimal. A *rational decision* results in the maximum achievement of a goal within the limitations of the situation. The rational model usually focuses on means—how best to achieve one or more goals. Moreover, this process may be used to assist in identifying, evaluating, and selecting the goals to be pursued.

Figure 8.3 shows the rational model of decision making as a seven-phase process. It starts with defining and diagnosing the problem and moves through successive phases

Figure 8.3   **Phases of Rational Model of Decision Making**

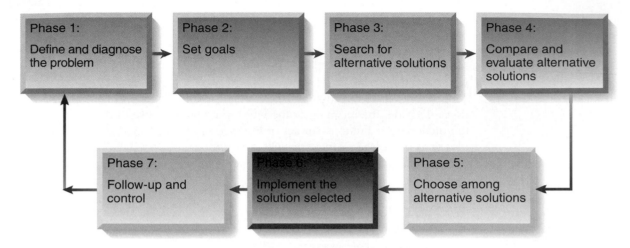

Influence of external and internal environmental factors and stakeholders

to following up and controlling. When making routine decisions, individuals can follow these phases easily. In addition, people are more likely to utilize this process in situations involving conditions of near certainty or low risk, that is, when they can assign objective probabilities to outcomes. Routine decisions under conditions that approximate certainty obviously don't require using all the phases in the model. For example, if a particular problem tends to recur, decisions (solutions) may be written as standard operating procedures or rules. Moreover, individuals or teams rarely follow these seven phases in sequence when making adaptive or innovative decisions.[22]

Phase 1: Define and Diagnose the Problem. The rational model is based on the assumption that effective decisions (solutions) are not likely if managers, teams, or individual employees haven't identified the real problems and their possible causes. Problem definition and diagnosis involves three skills that are part of a manager's planning and administration competency: noticing, interpreting, and incorporating. *Noticing* involves identifying and monitoring numerous external and internal environmental factors and deciding which ones are contributing to the problem(s). *Interpreting* requires assessing the factors noticed and determining which are causes, not merely symptoms, of the real problem(s). Finally, *incorporating* calls for relating those interpretations to the current or desired goals (phase 2) of an individual department or the organization as a whole. If noticing, interpreting, and incorporating are done haphazardly or incorrectly, the individual or team responsible for making the decision ultimately is likely to select a poor solution.

Let's consider an example of the need for sound problem definition and diagnosis. Several years ago, a new management team took over at Greyhound Lines and quickly made an incorrect diagnosis of the key problems facing the firm. The team concluded that Greyhound's problem was that it did not operate like an airline business but that it should. A whole series of inferences logically flowed from acceptance of that definition of the problem: (1) the airline business model would work in the bus industry; (2) the major difference between the airlines and Greyhound was in marketing; (3) a computerized reservations system was the key to improved marketing and the more efficient management of bus operations; (4) a reservation system based on the airline model would be simple and inexpensive to develop; and (5) even though revenues were declining, costs could be cut even faster, buying time to implement the new marketing strategy.

Unfortunately, this definition of Greyhound's problem and the related inferences were incorrect. The differences between the airline and bus industries were much greater than the superficial diagnosis suggested. As a consequence of the disastrous results, Craig Lentzsch, a bus industry veteran, was hired as the new CEO. He and fellow executives rediagnosed and redefined the fundamental problems facing Greyhound. As a result, they discarded the airline business model; scrapped the reservation system; established an everyday low-price structure; increased frequency of service on popular routes; and implemented flexible scheduling of its equipment, drivers, and other resources to meet peak travel demand.[23]

A basic part of effective problem definition and diagnosis is asking probing questions. Consider the meaning of the word *question*. Our use of the word goes beyond the dictionary definition—an act or instance of asking—and is closer to the multiple meanings expressed by two creativity experts.

- A question is an invitation to creativity.
- A question is an unsettled and unsettling issue.
- A question is a beginning of adventure.
- A question is a disguised answer.
- A question pokes and prods that which has not yet been poked and prodded.
- A question is a point of departure.
- A question has no end and no beginning.[24]

Phase 2: Set Goals. *Goals* are results to be attained and thus indicate the direction toward which decisions and actions should be aimed. *General goals* provide broad direction for decision making in qualitative terms. For example, one of the general goals of the Smithsonian Institute in Washington, D.C., is to serve as an educational resource for the people of the United States and the rest of the world. *Operational goals* state what is to be achieved in quantitative terms, for whom, and within what time period. For example, Craig Lentzsch, CEO of Greyhound Lines, stated the following goal to the firm's employees in a 1999 company newsletter: "In the year 2003, only four years in the future, we will be a $2 billion company. That's our goal and I'm confident we will get there."[25] Annual revenues were about $850 million when he stated this goal. It specified what in quantitative terms ($2 billion in revenues), for whom (Greyhound Lines), and a measurable time period (4 years).

Goals aren't set in a vacuum. As mentioned in earlier chapters, various stakeholders (e.g., customers, shareholders, suppliers, and government agencies) have an impact on an organization and its employees. This impact is felt in the goal-setting revision process. As suggested previously in Figure 8.3, stakeholders play a crucial role in shaping the problems identified, goals selected, alternatives considered, and choices made by managers and employees. The relative range of choices that organizations have in setting goals varies greatly, depending on the magnitude of stakeholder power.[26] Organizations can have many choices in setting goals when external stakeholder power is relatively low—as, for example, at GE and Dell Computer. They are market leaders in their industries and have sufficient human, technological, and financial resources to shape and satisfy stakeholders.

Phase 3: Search for Alternative Solutions. Individuals or teams must look for alternative ways to achieve a goal. This step might involve seeking additional information, thinking creatively, consulting experts, undertaking research, and taking similar actions. Recall the initial alternatives generated by Jim Prevo of Green Mountain Coffee in the Preview feature: (1) do nothing, (2) revamp and improve the company's home-grown software applications, or (3) install a totally new enterprise resource planning (ERP) system. Each of these alternatives had risks.

Phase 4: Compare and Evaluate Alternative Solutions. After individuals or teams have identified alternative solutions, they must compare and evaluate these alternatives. This step emphasizes expected results and determining the relative cost of each alternative. Recall that the ERP alternative at Green Mountain Coffee had potentially much greater positive results, but significantly higher short-term costs, than the other alternatives. In addition, the ultimate potential adverse cost—disruption of operations—could be crucial. As Jim Prevo commented: "An ERP implementation is like the corporate equivalent of a brain transplant. We pulled the plug on every company application and moved to PeopleSoft (software). The risk was certainly disruption of business, because if you do not do ERP properly, you can kill your company, guaranteed."

Phase 5: Choose among Alternative Solutions. Decision making is sometimes viewed as having made a final choice. Selecting a solution, as suggested here, is only one step in the rational decision-making process. Many managers complain that when recent college graduates receive a project assignment, they tend to present and propose only one solution. Instead of identifying and evaluating several feasible alternatives, the new graduate presents the manager with the option only of accepting or rejecting the alternative presented. Although choosing among alternative solutions might appear to be straightforward, it may prove to be difficult when the problem is complex and ambiguous and involves high degrees of risk or uncertainty, as experienced by Jim Prevo. Each of the alternatives he considered had risks and consequences. In the final analysis, Prevo concluded that the only alternative with major positive consequences was to install the new ERP system.

Phase 6. Implement the Solution Selected. A well-chosen solution isn't always successful. A technically correct decision has to be accepted and supported by those responsible for implementing it if the decision is to be acted on effectively. If the selected solution can't be implemented for some reason, another one should be considered. We explore the importance of participation in making a decision by those charged with implementing it in Chapters 15 and 17.

Phase 7: Follow-Up and Control. Implementing the preferred solution won't automatically achieve the desired goal. Individuals or teams must control implementation activities and follow up by evaluating results. If implementation isn't producing satisfactory results, corrective action will be needed. Because environmental forces affecting decisions change continually, follow-up and control may indicate a need to redefine the problem or review the original goal. Feedback from this step could even suggest the need to start over and repeat the entire decision-making process. The following Planning and Administration Competency feature reveals significant differences in how two airlines—American and Southwest—used different control practices with different results in pursuit of the same goal: improved on-time performance.[27] American Airlines has since modified this aspect of its control practices.

PLANNING & ADMINISTRATION COMPETENCY

Contrasting Controls at American and Southwest Airlines

Each time a non-weather–related flight delay occurred at American Airlines, managers on duty were responsible for figuring out what caused it. Immediate penalties—in the form of having to explain what happened, threats of punitive consequences, and more—accompanied delays.

This approach had the unintended effect of encouraging employees to look out for themselves and avoid being singled out by management. As a result, they focused less on shared goals of on-time performance, accurate baggage handling, and satisfied customers and more on CYA. "If you ask anyone here, what's the last thing you think of when there's a problem," said a ramp supervisor, "I bet your bottom dollar it's the customer. And these are guys who bust their

butts everyday. But they're thinking how do I keep my ___ out of the sling."

American's control practices also resulted in a great deal of time spent trying to sort out the cause of delays. "There is so much internal debate and reports and meetings," said one field manager. "This is time that we could be focusing on the passengers." Another result appeared to be frequent misidentification of the problem. "We have delay codes for when the Pope visits, or if there are beetles in the cockpit," said another field manager only half in jest, "but sometimes a problem occurs routinely and we have no code for it. What usually happens is a communication breakdown, but we have no code for that. So we tag it on the last group off the plane."

Determining the cause of delays had been a conflict-ridden process at Southwest, as it was at American, and it often deteriorated from problem solving to finger pointing and blame avoidance. Southwest countered this tendency in the early 1990s by instituting a "team delay" approach that allowed less precise reporting of the cause of delays. The goal was to encourage learning, not pinpoint individual blame. According to Jim Wimberly, executive vice president of operations, "We had too many angry disagreements between flight attendants and gate agents about whose delay it was. It

was too hard to determine whose fault it was." One of Southwest's chief pilots explained, "The team delay is used to point out problems between two or three different employee groups in working together. We used to do it [in the following way]: If people were still in the jetway at departure time, it was a station delay. If people were on board at departure time, it was a flight crew delay. But now if you see everybody working as a team, and it's a team problem, you call it a team delay. It's been a very positive thing."

The reduced precision of performance measurement did not appear to concern Southwest leaders. "We could have more delay categories," said Wimberly. "But we'd only end up chasing our tail." At Southwest, the role of headquarters appeared to be supportive rather than punitive. The relationship between field and headquarters was characterized by a two-way flow of information and a focus on learning.

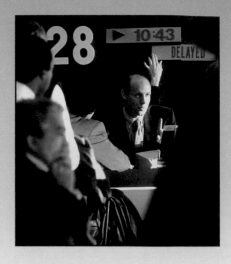

• • •

To learn more about American Airlines and Southwest Airlines, visit their home pages at

http://www.americanairlines.com and *http://www.iflyswa.com*

The rational model might be thought of as an ideal, nudging individuals or teams closer to rationality in making decisions. At best, though, human decision making rarely approximates this ideal, especially under conditions of risk with subjective probabilities and uncertainty. When dealing with some types of problems, people don't even attempt to follow the rational model's seven phases.[28] Instead, they apply the bounded rationality or political models. Observations of actual decision-making processes in organizations suggest that individuals often modify or even ignore the rational model, especially when faced with making certain types of adaptive and innovative decisions.

BOUNDED RATIONALITY MODEL

The **bounded rationality model** represents people's tendencies (1) to select less than the best goal or alternative solution (i.e., to satisfice), (2) to engage in a limited search for alternative solutions, and (3) to have inadequate information and control over external and internal environmental forces influencing the outcomes of decisions.[29] Herbert Simon, a management scholar, introduced this model in the mid 1950s. It contributed significantly to the Swedish Academy of Sciences' decision to award him the 1978 Nobel Prize in economics for his "pioneering research into the decision-making process within economic organizations." This model emphasizes the limitations of rationality and thus provides a better picture of the day-to-day decision-making processes used by most people. It partially explains why different individuals make different decisions when they have exactly the same information.

Satisficing. *Satisficing* is the practice of selecting an *acceptable* goal or alternative solution rather than searching extensively for the best goal or solution. An acceptable goal might be easier to identify and achieve, less controversial, or otherwise safer than the best available goal. As shown in Figure 8.4, the factors that result in a satisficing decision often are limited search, inadequate information, and information processing

Figure 8.4 **Factors Influencing a Satisficing Decision**

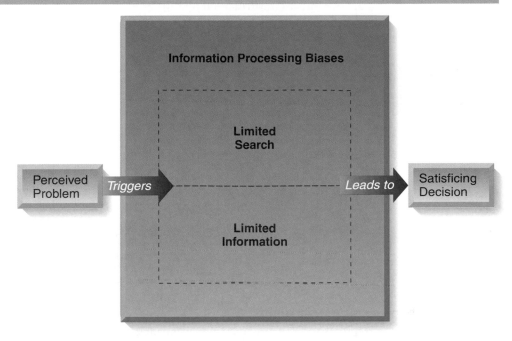

bias. However, the achievement of quality improvement goals often is a result of a series of satisficing decisions. Recall from Chapter 2 that W. Edwards Deming taught management that the greatest cause of defective products was poorly designed processes. Many successful organizations map, measure, and continuously improve their processes incrementally to reach higher levels of quality.

In an interview on the bounded rationality model, Herbert Simon explained satisficing this way:

> *Satisficing is intended to be used in contrast to the classical economist's idea that in making decisions in business or anywhere in real life, you somehow pick, or somebody gives you, a set of alternatives from which you select the best one—maximize. The satisficing idea is that first of all, you don't have the alternatives, you've got to go out and scratch for them—and that you have mighty shaky ways of evaluating them when you do find them. So you look for alternatives until you get one from which, in terms of your experience and in terms of what you have reason to expect, you will get a reasonable result.*

But satisficing doesn't necessarily mean that managers have to be satisfied with whatever alternative pops up first in their minds or in their computers and let it go at that. The level of satisficing can be raised—by personal determination, by setting higher individual or organizational standards (goals), and by use of an increasing range of sophisticated management science and computer-based decision-making and problem-solving techniques.[30]

Limited Search. Individuals usually do not make an exhaustive search for possible goals or alternative solutions to a problem. They tend to consider options until they find one that seems adequate. For example, when trying to choose the "best" job, college seniors can't evaluate every available job in their fields. If they tried to, they probably would reach retirement age before obtaining all the information available. In applying the bounded rationality model, students would stop searching for alternatives as soon as they hit on an acceptable one.

Some research suggests that adding information does not yield better decisions than the smaller amount of information originally available. This result can be caused by several factors: information overload; the tendency to focus on issues that may only represent symptoms, for which information is readily available; or the improper processing of information, which leads to a false sense of certainty (security).[31] Also, consider the following perspective on limited search by entrepreneurs:

> *Entrepreneurs do not approach the starting of a new venture from a sequential and methodological perspective. If they approached the start-up process in a more comprehensive manner, the venture would probably never be started due to the lack of information, or, where sufficient information was available, the probabilities of success would be so low that the venture would rarely be pursued. However, with entrepreneurs, their biases and heuristics (personal decision rules) indicate that there is a major opportunity to be capitalized on and/or that problems with fulfilling their expectations for the venture do not exist or will be addressed later.[32]*

Limited Information. Bounded rationality also suggests that people frequently have inadequate information about the (1) precise nature of the problems facing them, (2) range of feasible alternatives, and (3) consequences of each alternative. These conditions create a condition of ***ignorance***—the lack of relevant information or the incorrect interpretation of the information that is available.

WEB INSIGHT

S.C. Johnson Wax is a family-owned company. What is its stated guiding corporate philosophy regarding decision making? To answer this question, visit S.C. Johnson's Web site at *http://www.scjohnson.com/family/*.

S.C. Johnson Wax took advantage of the ignorance of its competitors when estimating sales potential in Central and Eastern Europe. Its competitors used official government data, which showed that Russia and Poland rank below Spain on per capita gross domestic product. However, the actual purchasing power in most East European countries is much higher than reported in government figures. The official data do not take into account the "black" economy in that region, which is estimated to generate between 25 and 50 percent of all income. S.C. Johnson Wax capitalized on the ignorance of this fact by its competitors. After just 5 years, its sales volume in Poland is already 50 percent of that in Spain where it has operated for more than 30 years.[33]

Information Processing Biases. People often fall prey to information processing biases when they engage in decision making. These biases include the following.[34]

- The ***availability bias*** refers to easy recall of specific instances of an event that may lead individuals to overestimate how frequently the event occurs. People who have recently seen a serious automobile accident often overestimate the frequency of such accidents.

- The ***selective perception bias*** refers to the concept that people often expect to see what they do see. People tend to seek information consistent with their own views and downplay conflicting information. Some people eagerly leap from a tower 100 feet above the ground with only a bungee cord between them and certain death. Yet these same people may not be willing to live near a closed plant that has been declared a superfund cleanup site.

- The ***concrete information bias*** refers to recollection of a vivid, direct experience usually prevailing over abstract information. A single personal experience may outweigh statistical evidence. An initial bad experience on the job may lead an employee to conclude that most managers can't be trusted and are simply out to exploit their subordinates.

- The ***law of small numbers bias*** refers to the tendency to view a few incidents or cases as representative of a larger population (i.e., a few cases "prove the rule") even when they aren't. Widely publicized, but infrequent, events of excessive use of force by a few police officers often instantly trigger characterizations of most police officers as people who regularly engage in extreme use of force and aggression.

- The **gambler's fallacy bias** refers to people seeing an unexpected number of similar events that lead them to the conviction that an event not seen will occur. For example, after observing nine successive reds turn up on a roulette wheel, a player might incorrectly think that chances for a black on the next spin are greater than 50/50. They aren't!

Competent and experienced decision makers tend to minimize these biases and the quick acceptance of satisficing. Their many experiences enable them quickly to gain an accurate sense of what's going on in the situation. They recognize typical and effective ways of reacting to problems. Their deep sets of experiences enable them to see patterns and anomalies that serve as warning signs. Competent individuals do not settle on the first thought—definition of the problem or solution—that comes to mind. They have typically encountered the adverse consequences of this approach in the past and have thus learned from experience.[35]

POLITICAL MODEL

The **political model** represents the decision-making process in terms of the self-interests and goals of powerful external and internal stakeholders. Before considering this model, however, we need to define power. **Power** is the ability to influence or control individual, team, departmental, or organizational decisions and goals. To have power is to be able to influence or control the (1) definition of the problem, (2) choice of goals, (3) consideration of alternative solutions, (4) selection of the alternative to be implemented, and ultimately (5) actions and success of the organization. Political processes are most likely to be used when decisions involve powerful stakeholders, decision makers disagree over choice of goals, and analysts fail to search for alternative solutions.[36] These factors are highly interrelated, as shown in Figure 8.5.

| Figure 8.5 | **Political Model of Decision Making** |

Divergence in Problem Definition. In the political model, external and internal stakeholders attempt to define problems to their own advantage. Conflicts occur when various stakeholders have different perceptions about the nature and sources of problems.

When things go wrong within politically based or oriented organizations, one or more individuals may be singled out as the cause of the problem. **Scapegoating** is the casting of blame for problems or shortcomings on an innocent or only partially responsible individual, team, or department. By implication, the other people who might be responsible for the problem are considered to be free from blame. Individuals or organizational units may use scapegoating to preserve a position of power or maintain a positive image.

Top management at Flour Corporation used this tactic several years ago. When the company was charged with financial fraud during cleanup work at a closed nuclear-weapons fuel factory near Cincinnati, Ohio, it scapegoated one of its engineers for causing its problems. The General Accounting Office (GAO)—the investigative arm of Congress—cited Flour for cost overruns, missing inspection records, leaking containers of hazardous waste, and substance abuse problems. Flour originally denied the allegations, noting that they were overstated and highly prejudicial. It also alleged that the U.S. Department of Energy impeded the company's own internal investigation. Flour eventually settled the lawsuit brought by the U.S. Justice Department to preserve the continuity of its operations.[37]

In contrast to the scapegoating and narrowly self-serving problem definition that occurred at the Flour Corporation, the following Teamwork Competency feature describes top management's efforts at Phone.com to minimize such political behaviors.[38] Phone.com's mission is to develop, market, and support infrastructure software and applications that enable the convergence of the Internet and mobile telephony. The firm is headquartered in Redwood City, California, and has offices in London and Tokyo. The firm focuses on (1) creating an environment in which effective teamwork is expected, recognized, praised, and rewarded; and (2) bringing conflict and dissent into the open and using it to enhance performance.

TEAMWORK COMPETENCY

Phone.com's Aversion to Politics

Bob Linder, vice president of marketing for Phone.com, comments on politics and the company's culture. "When you grow by acquisition, there is a danger in preserving the company's culture and values. To preserve the company culture, we instituted a very methodical orientation and training about the company's values, something smaller companies often forget about. One value is, we do not allow politics. A political act is grounds for an employee's termination. 'Politics' means any act that is in your own self-interest but that is not in the interest of the company, or harms another person in the company.

"An example is scheming to make somebody look bad or trying to blame someone else for your mistake—the kind of classic political backstabbing you get in large companies when everyone is out for their own glory as opposed to the good of the company. The negative way is to say no politics, or you get fired. The positive way is to say everyone must have the company's interest at heart.

"Within our management team, we follow that religiously. So whenever I hear someone in my group saying that another group is useless or incompetent, or a particular person is incompetent, I just say, 'Look, don't tell it to me. Go tell it to them. It doesn't do any good to tell me and moan about it. Go face it.' It's a very straightforward culture. So we enumerated all our core values and put them on a Web site. This is what everyone lives by in this company."

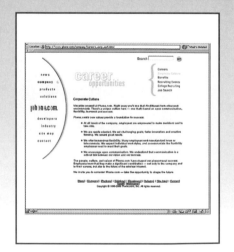

Alain Rossman, the chairman and CEO, also comments. "We have a set of values we stick to that are pretty simple. We are results-oriented. So we say, 'Folks, the biggest thing you've got to do is forget your ego, forget politics, think about results.' We've achieved a flexible culture where people understand that nothing matters but surviving the hypergrowth, the tornado. You have to shed the personal side and think, 'If I'm not the right person, who is the right person?' It helps that everybody is a shareholder, and there are tremendous rewards for succeeding. That lines up the whole thing."

• • •

To learn more about Phone.com [which merged with software.com], visit the merged company's home page at

http://www.openware.com

Divergence in Goals. The political model recognizes the likelihood of conflicting goals among stakeholders and that the choice of goals will be influenced strongly by the relative power of stakeholders. Often no clear "winner" will emerge, but if power is concentrated in one stakeholder, the organization's primary goals will likely reflect that stakeholder's goals. Phone.com's Alain Rossman stated: "It helps that everybody is a shareholder, and there are tremendous rewards for succeeding. That lines up the whole thing." Clearly, this policy helps align the goals of the employees with those of the organization and top management. As Phone.com prospers, so do the employees.

A balance of power among several stakeholders may lead to negotiation and compromise in the decision-making process. Although a balance of power may lead to compromise, as in most union–management negotiations, it also may lead to stalemate. In the UPS strike several years ago, both union and management had to compromise their original positions to break the stalemate and settle the strike.[39] Recall that a common political strategy is to form a coalition (alliance) when no one person, group, or organization has sufficient power to select or implement its preferred goal. Many health-related organizations and associations—such as the American Cancer Society, American Heart Association, and American Medical Association—have formed an informal coalition with Congress to fight smoking and the tobacco interests.

Divergence in Solutions. Some goals or the means used to achieve them may be perceived as win–lose situations; that is, my gain is your loss, and your gain is my loss. In such a situation, stakeholders often distort and selectively withhold information to further their own interests, as both management and union officials did in the Teamsters strike against UPS. Such actions can severely limit the ability to make adaptive and innovative decisions, which, by definition, require utilizing all relevant information, as well as exploring a full range of alternative solutions.

Stakeholders within the organization often view information as a major source of power and use it accordingly. The rational decision-making model calls for all employees to present all relevant information openly. However, managers and employees operating under the political model would view free disclosure as naïve, making achievement of their personal, team, or departmental goals more difficult.[40] To complicate the picture, information often is (1) piecemeal and based on informal communication (Did you know that . . . ?); (2) subjective rather than based on hard facts (Those computer printouts don't really matter around here.); and (3) defined by what powerful stakeholders consider to be important (What does the boss think? or How will the board respond?).

Co-optation is one of the common political strategies used by stakeholders to achieve their goals. *Co-optation* refers to bringing new stakeholder representatives into the strategic decision-making process as a way to avert threats to an organization's stability or existence.[41] An example is placing a banker on a firm's board of directors when the firm needs to borrow money. Also, some organizations have created junior executive committees as a way to involve middle managers in selected strategic issues and gain their support in implementing a chosen course of action.

Despite the common view, the political model is not necessarily bad. As with the other two models—rational and bounded rationality—it can be useful and appropriate, especially for resolving conflicts among stakeholders with divergent goals and/or divergent preferences for actions to be taken. If the political model is implemented with an underpinning of basic ethical principles as discussed in Chapter 6, it is likely to lead to constructive decisions and outcomes.

CHAPTER SUMMARY

This chapter introduced you to the basics of decision making. We discussed basic decision-making concepts and models that are used by managers and other professionals in organizations. Chapter 9 presents several planning and decision aids that improve the chances of making effective decisions.

1. EXPLAIN THE ROLE OF DECISION MAKING FOR MANAGERS AND EMPLOYEES.

Decision making involves identifying problems, gathering information, considering alternatives, and choosing a course of action from the alternatives generated. Decision making abilities are needed to develop and implement all six managerial competencies—communication, teamwork, planning and administration, strategic action, global awareness, and self-management. Managers and employees are required to make various types of decisions in a variety of situations daily.

2. STATE THE CONDITIONS UNDER WHICH INDIVIDUALS MAKE DECISIONS.

Individuals make decisions under circumstances that represent the probability of events occurring over which they have no control but that may affect the outcomes of those decisions. Such conditions may be viewed as a continuum from certainty to risk to uncertainty. Decision making becomes more challenging with increasing levels of risk and uncertainty.

3. DESCRIBE THE CHARACTERISTICS OF ROUTINE, ADAPTIVE, AND INNOVATIVE DECISIONS.

Routine decisions are relatively well defined and address common problems and solutions. Adaptive decisions address somewhat unusual problems and/or solutions of low to moderate risk. Innovative decisions address very unusual and ambiguous problems and/or solutions of high risk or uncertainty. In general, managers and professionals become more highly valued as they increase their ability to make effective adaptive and innovative decisions.

4. EXPLAIN THE FEATURES OF THREE BASIC MODELS OF DECISION MAKING.

The rational model prescribes a sequence of seven phases for making decisions: (1) define and diagnose the problem, (2) set goals, (3) search for alternative solutions, (4) compare and evaluate alternative solutions, (5) choose among alternative solutions, (6) implement the solution selected, and (7) follow up and control the results. In contrast, the bounded rationality model describes a pattern that tends to be more descriptive of how managers and others often make decisions. It represents tendencies to satisfice, engage in a limited search for alternative solutions, have limited information, and use various biases to obtain and process information. This model recognizes the practical limitations on individuals when they make decisions. The political model emphasizes the impact of multiple stakeholders with power on decision making. Political decision making is triggered when stakeholders hold divergent views about problem definitions, desired goals, and/or preferred solutions. Various political strategies, including co-optation and scapegoating, come into play under such circumstances.

KEY TERMS

Active inertia, p. 226
Adaptive decisions, p. 226
Availability bias, p. 234
Bounded rationality model, p. 232
Certainty, p. 221
Concrete information bias, p. 234
Continuous improvement, p. 227
Convergence, p. 227
Co-optation, p. 237
Decision making, p. 220

Gambler's fallacy bias, p. 235
General goals, p. 230
Goals, p. 230
Ignorance, p. 234
Innovative decisions, p. 227
Law of small numbers bias, p. 234
Objective probability, p. 222
Operational goals, p. 230
Political model, p. 235
Power, p. 235

Probability, p. 222
Rational decision, p. 228
Rational model, p. 228
Risk, p. 222
Routine decisions, p. 226
Satisficing, p. 232
Scapegoating, p. 236
Selective perception bias, p. 234
Subjective probability, p. 222
Uncertainty, p. 223

QUESTIONS FOR DISCUSSION AND COMPETENCY DEVELOPMENT

1. Review the Preview feature regarding Jim Prevo's decision. Identify at least two risks and two uncertainties involved with the two key alternatives for Green Mountain Coffee—adopt the enterprise resource planning (ERP) system or revamp the company's current software.

2. Did your decision to enroll in this course involve bounded rationality? Explain your answer.

3. Identify two adaptive or innovative decisions that you have made during the past year or so. Describe how you made them.

4. Review the Self-Management Competency feature on George Conrades of Akamai Technologies. He discusses one of his roles as "absorbing uncertainty." Have you ever absorbed uncertainty for others? Explain. In what ways has your instructor in this course absorbed uncertainty for you?

5. Think of an important decision that you have made during the past year or so. In what ways did your process of making this decision match or vary from each of the phases of the rational model?

6. For the decision identified in Question 5, in what ways did your process of making it match or vary from each component in the political model?

7. **Competency Development: Communication.** Owens Corning left its 28-story headquarters building in Toledo, Ohio, for a new 3-story structure a few blocks away. Glen Hiner, CEO and chairman of the board, comments: "People referred to management as the 28th floor. It had a stigma to it. It was restrictive. In the new building the leadership is in the middle of the second floor—the middle of the middle—accessible by all."[42] Review the dimensions of the communication competency in Table 1.2. Which of these dimensions does Hiner hope to improve by changing the physical location of top management? Will that change be sufficient to improve the communication competencies of top managers? Explain. In what ways may increasing communication competencies improve decision making at Owens Corning? This firm is one of the world's top makers of fiberglass and composite materials with more than 20,000 employees. To learn more about Owens Corning, visit the company's home page at **http://www.owenscorning.com**.

8. **Competency Development: Planning and Administration.** Scott McNealy is the chairman and CEO of Sun Microsystems, headquartered in Palo Alto, California. Sun's vision is to enable "computers to talk to each other no matter who built them." McNealy was asked recently "what metrics matter most to him." That is, what indicators does he track to determine whether Sun Microsystems measures up? Consider his reply: "There are few metrics that I pay closer attention than 'system uptime'—how often Sun systems are up and running at customer sites. The most important commitment that we can make as a company is to share our customers' risk. Most of our customers face the same risk: computer systems that go down when people need them.

   "That's why we assemble real-time data on system availability at customer sites. We use that data to determine the causes of downtime. We also use that information to educate people, to improve processes, to implement enhancements: whatever it takes to help our customers maximize uptime—which, in turn, maximizes their ability to serve their customers."[43]

   What phases of the rational model of decision making are illustrated in McNealy's comments? Explain. To learn more about Sun Microsystems, visit the company's home page at **http://www.sun.com**.

CASE FOR COMPETENCY DEVELOPMENT

Jean Simpson's Dilemma[44]

After work, Jean Simpson sat with a friend, sipping Chardonnay in a quiet corner at Charlie's Grill. "You won't believe the conversation I just had," she said. With uncharacteristic anger, she went on to describe what had happened.

Simpson works in sales for Salient, Inc., a medium-sized manufacturing company in Milwaukee, Wisconsin, that produces a specialized line of hi-tech peripherals sold to computer hardware companies. Until recently, nearly all its sales were in the United States. But that changed a year ago when Salient decided to market worldwide. In the process, it hired Simpson and a few others to put together a fast-track sales program, offering substantial bonuses for reaching stretch goals.

Fluent in French, Simpson was assigned to sales in Quebec, Canada. She saw this as a professional challenge to demonstrate what she could achieve. Two weeks ago she had marked her first year anniversary, and her sales were well over the top of annual goals.

This morning she had met with the head of human resources for a performance review. "That's when the wheels fell off the wagon," she muttered between bites of smoked salmon. Wide-eyed, her friend Sara Cummings just listened. "Instead of congratulating me and handing me a bonus check, the guy told me that I should be happy that I was still working, since the company's financial picture was rocky." When I reminded him that I had a signed contract about the bonus, he repeated that under the difficult company circumstances, I could keep my job.

Although the job market for someone like herself was fairly good, Simpson thought that she would likely be denied a good recommendation. Putting down her wine glass, she sighed, "God, this is so unfair. What should I do?"

Questions

1. Analyze this situation by using the phases of the rational model of decision making. Make any assumptions that you consider necessary. If you were Jean Simpson, what would you do, based on this model?

2. Analyze this situation by using the political model of decision making. Make any assumptions that you consider necessary. If you were Jean Simpson, what would you do, based on this model?

3. What are the similarities and differences in your analyses and chosen courses of action as a result of applying these two different models?

Next Door Food Store

The Next Door Food Store convenience chain is headquartered in Mt. Pleasant, Michigan, and has more than 30 locations throughout the state. The company's stores have evolved since their creation in 1920 into "a whole lot more than the corner gas station," according to company President David C. Johnson. The company's management has a strong commitment to innovation and has never been afraid of change or making difficult decisions. This willingness to change is illustrated by the company's decision to create the first combination gas station and convenience store in northern Michigan (in Charlevoix) in 1978. The remodeled gas station was so successful that management quickly converted all its locations to the new layout, a decision that led to a doubling of the company's size by 1989. In 1994, the chain decided to add Subway sandwich shops to its stores, which in turn attracted other food service franchises to Next Door store locations.

Early on, executives at Next Door realized that consumers' wishes and concerns should serve as guides to their decision making. To satisfy consumers, yet make rational decisions in the interests of the chain, management had to determine which items each store should carry and how to distribute these items to the stores. To address these fundamental product and distribution issues, management first considered the goals of the company and the constraints facing it. The goals of Next Door Food Store cover four main areas: (1) to maintain a variety of products that meet customer demands; (2) to keep distribution costs as low as possible; (3) to minimize inventory levels; and (4) to utilize just-in-time (JIT) inventory systems in cooperation with suppliers.

Decisions regarding product and distribution issues were also influenced by several constraints. First, the sales volume of each small store was quite low relative to that of large supermarkets. Second, each location has relatively small shelf and storage space. Third, the limited number of convenience stores meant that the company would not enjoy economies of scale in purchasing. Fourth, the company's more than 30 stores were scattered throughout the state. Finally, the company did not have its own trucks for shipping goods to its stores.

Based on these goals and constraints, Next Door's management considered two options: (1) build and operate its own warehouse and distribution network or (2) rely on other wholesalers and distributors to supply its stores.

Next Door's management realized that the first option would be a tremendous drain on the firm's financial and human capital. The company would have to build and operate a facility and then hire and train a large number of additional employees. The second option would not impose such a large financial burden on the firm and would place these responsibilities on existing wholesalers and distributors that had the experience, modes of transportation, and warehousing capabilities needed to serve the needs of all the company's stores. Considering all the factors involved, management determined that option two was the best approach for the firm to take.

Questions

1. In what ways does Next Door Food Store rely on its wholesalers and distributors?

2. What fundamental mistake did Next Door Food Store commit when it decided to enter into an exclusive agreement with Coca-Cola?

To learn more about Next Door Food Store, visit the company's home page at *http://www.nextdoor1.com*.

Planning and Decision Aids

AFTER STUDYING THIS CHAPTER YOU SHOULD BE ABLE TO:

1. EXPLAIN KNOWLEDGE MANAGEMENT AS A MEANS OF CREATING AND UTILIZING AN INFORMATION BASE AND BUILDING ON AN ORGANIZATION'S INTELLECTUAL ASSETS.

2. DESCRIBE THE BASIC FEATURES OF THE DELPHI TECHNIQUE, SIMULATION, AND SCENARIO FORECASTING AIDS.

3. USE OSBORN'S CREATIVITY MODEL TO STIMULATE ADAPTIVE AND INNOVATIVE DECISIONS.

4. APPLY TWO QUALITY MANAGEMENT DECISION AIDS—BENCHMARKING AND THE DEMING CYCLE.

Chapter Outline

PREVIEW: MIKE TURILLO OF KPMG ON KNOWLEDGE MANAGEMENT

FOSTERING KNOWLEDGE MANAGEMENT
KNOWLEDGE MANAGEMENT DRIVERS
KNOWLEDGE MANAGEMENT TARGETS
ENABLING TECHNOLOGY
ENABLING CULTURE
PLANNING AND ADMINISTRATION COMPETENCY: Mitre's Introduction of
Knowledge Management

FOSTERING FORECASTS
DELPHI TECHNIQUE
SIMULATION
SCENARIOS
STRATEGIC ACTION COMPETENCY: Duke Energy's Scenarios

FOSTERING CREATIVITY
THE CREATIVE PROCESS
OSBORN'S CREATIVITY MODEL
TEAMWORK COMPETENCY: IDEO Brainstorms

FOSTERING QUALITY
BENCHMARKING
COMMUNICATION COMPETENCY: Benchmarking in Site Services at Cinergy Corporation
THE DEMING CYCLE

CHAPTER SUMMARY

KEY TERMS

QUESTIONS FOR DISCUSSION AND COMPETENCY DEVELOPMENT

SELF-MANAGEMENT COMPETENCY INVENTORY: PERSONAL CREATIVITY

VIDEO CASE: SP AVIATION AND FIRSTBANK

MIKE TURILLO OF KPMG ON KNOWLEDGE MANAGEMENT

The mission statement of KPMG asserts that "KPMG is a global network of professional advisory firms whose aim is to turn knowledge into value for the benefit of its clients, its people, and communities." Mike Turillo is the International Chief Knowledge Officer of KPMG. The following are some of his perspectives on knowledge management.

The state of knowledge management today is like the advent of the crystal radio early in the last century. Back then you had someone who had a need to broadcast, and someone who had a need to receive. The crystal was a phenomenal breakthrough. It allowed us to do things in communicating with one another that we had never been able to do before. We had gone about as far as we could in communicating and collaborating not just as businesses, but as a society.

In the past three or four years, technology has created another crystal radio for us. It allows us to take vast amounts of data, assimilate and filter them, put them into our context, and begin to be serious about collaborating in a real-time method. To my colleagues who think this is phenomenal, I remind them that this is just the crystal radio, or the transition from silent films to talkies. I tell them, "You ain't seen nothing yet."

There were significant impediments in creating the shift from a knowledge-hoarding culture to one of knowledge sharing. It takes time to convince people that they will be penalized if they continue previous behavior, and rewarded as they embrace the new one. The senior members of the firm age 50 and over are at the point where they have gone about as far as they can go. With their egos kind of in check, they are all for "whatever I can do to make the company work better." For those under 30, it's been, "Anything I can do to succeed, any tool that you can give me," plus a healthy attitude they bring with them about collaboration and working together, "we're absolutely for it." The age group of 30 to 50 are the ones we really had to work with. Can't blame them. They have already developed habits and patterns. They came into the business with some understanding of what the rules were, and now somebody is changing them. They say: "OK, I get it, but please, you've got to help me understand how I am going to master it."[1]

To learn more about KPMG, visit the company's home page at

http://www.kpmg.com

As suggested by Mike Turillo's remarks, knowledge management is both a philosophy about information sharing and an aid to planning and decision making. ***Knowledge management*** (KM) is the art and science of creating, measuring, distributing, enhancing, evaluating, and integrating the information base of an organization and building on its intellectual assets. In this chapter, we highlight and describe the features of KM. We also present seven planning and decision aids that can be used (1) at various organizational levels, (2) in virtually all functional areas (e.g., marketing, finance, human resources, and auditing), and (3) for aiding in the analysis essential to planning and decision making associated with many types of organizational issues and problems. However, we do not discuss general planning and decision aids (e.g., break-even analysis and payoff matrix) in this book. They are commonly presented and discussed in depth in other business courses (e.g., accounting, finance, and marketing). We begin by discussing the fundamentals of knowledge management, which increases the likelihood of the effective use of the other aids. Next we review the basics and limitations of forecasting and the essentials of three commonly used forecasting techniques: the Delphi technique, simulation, and scenarios. Then we address the need for creativity in many situations by reviewing—from among dozens of aids—Osborn's creativity model. We conclude the chapter with two aids that are designed specifically to improve quality—benchmarking and the Deming cycle.

FOSTERING KNOWLEDGE MANAGEMENT

1.

EXPLAIN KNOWLEDGE MANAGEMENT AS A MEANS OF CREATING AND UTILIZING AN INFORMATION BASE AND BUILDING ON AN ORGANIZATION'S INTELLECTUAL ASSETS.

Knowledge Management is generally viewed as consisting of three main components.

- *Explicit knowledge:* published and internally generated reports and manuals, books, magazines and journals, government data and reports, online services, newsfeeds, and the like.

- *Tacit knowledge:* the information, competencies, and experience possessed by employees, including professional contacts and cultural and interpersonal dimensions—openness, the lessons to be gleaned from successes or failures, anecdotal fables, and information sharing. This knowledge may be unconsciously understood and applied, difficult to express, often developed from direct experiences and action, and typically shared through conversations involving storytelling and shared experiences.

- *Enabling technologies:* intranets, Internet, search engines, and work-flow software.[2]

WEB INSIGHT

Knowledge Inc. is a monthly online executive newsletter that covers trends in knowledge and intellectual capital management. Go to its Web site at *http://www.knowledgeinc.com*. Click *The Smart Enterprise* and then click one of the case studies listed. What did you learn by reading the case study?

KNOWLEDGE MANAGEMENT DRIVERS

The Information Age has replaced the Industrial Age. The balance sheet, which typically measures physical assets (e.g., land, factories, equipment, and cash), is increasingly measuring a new asset—knowledge. Knowledge is becoming more valuable than physical or financial assets, or even natural resources. Information and knowledge (e.g., experience, advice, best practices, and communication) are the new competitive weapons.

The serious risks of not taking steps to manage knowledge assets and processes are driving organizations to reevaluate their knowledge strategies. In doing so, they are finding some rather severe shortcomings in their systems, including the following.

- *Productivity and opportunity loss*—a lack of knowledge where and when it is needed; a knowledge base that is not usable.

- *Information overload*—too much unsorted and nontargeted information.

- *Knowledge attrition*—according to some estimates, the average organization loses half its knowledge base every 5 to 10 years through obsolescence and employee and customer turnover.

- *Reinventing the wheel*—lack of standards and infrastructure for creating, capturing, sharing, and applying best practices or lessons learned.

Strategic importance must be placed on overcoming these and other such shortcomings to ensure that the right knowledge is available to the right person at the right time.[3]

KNOWLEDGE MANAGEMENT TARGETS

The application of KM has three natural targets: an organization's teams, customers, and workforce.[4]

Teams. Collaboration is often crucial to ensuring that goods and services are designed to meet customer needs. By obtaining input from sales, marketing, engineering, design, and other groups, KM provides both a method of sharing ideas and identifying best practices in design and development. By bringing together the ideas and information of each group, a project team can move ahead more quickly and efficiently. It becomes aware of work being done elsewhere in the organization, thereby reducing duplication and enhancing intergroup problem solving. Procter & Gamble (P&G)—manufacturer of numerous consumer products such as soap, toothpaste, and cosmetics—has researchers in 22 technical centers on four continents. One component of P&G's KM system is the *Innovation Net,* an intranet developed to provide them with specialized databases and knowledge. It also contains information on research being conducted throughout P&G, enabling researchers to identify others who are working on similar problems. Innovation Net also supports the creation of *communities* of researchers at P&G who are linked by their own broad professional interests, not just specific business needs or problems. Sixteen such communities operate through Innovation Net (e.g., life sciences and biotechnology, microbiology, and computer-aided design). Innovation Net supports and enhances face-to-face communication among these researchers; it isn't a substitute for them.[5]

Customers. Satisfied customers are the foundation of a company's continuing success. Tracking ongoing contacts with customers—their issues, buying patterns, and expectations—is essential in developing and improving those relationships. Knowledge management can facilitate this process. In environments where change is a constant, organizations are challenged constantly to revise strategies affecting every area, from the supply room to the executive suite. Don Holthouse is the director of corporate strategy and knowledge initiatives at Xerox. He managed the firm's development of a KM system, named Eureka, for its 25,000 service representatives around the world. Eureka is an enormous computer-aided knowledge source to help service reps solve particularly difficult problems. Holthouse comments: "Once in about a thousand service calls, there is a problem nobody has seen before. The service rep is out there trying to fix it at the customer site. That takes a long time and costs a lot. So the question then becomes: How to capture that solution from the service rep who is the only one who knows?" The answer was to have the service reps input their experiences into Eureka, relating how they successfully dealt with unusual and difficult service problems. Eureka now contains some 25,000 such "reports," organized by means of an easy-to-use classification system. These reports include communications such as a note from a rep in Brazil thanking a Canadian counterpart for a suggestion that a $0.90 connector could save Xerox from having to replace a $40,000 machine. The knowledge being captured, distributed, enhanced, created, and integrated through Eureka is now being fed to other Xerox units, not just to the service representatives.[6]

Workforce. An organization's single most valuable asset is its workforce. Knowledge management can track employees' skills and abilities, facilitate performance reviews, deliver training, provide up-to-date company information, manage benefits, and improve employee knowledge and morale. Rapidly changing market conditions can catch a company short in terms of needed valuable employee skills. Knowledge management systems should be able to anticipate and identify skill gaps and provide mechanisms for training employees in new skills.

ENABLING TECHNOLOGY

Technology is the KM enabler. It provides the foundation for solutions that automate and centralize the sharing of knowledge and fostering innovation. Recall the Preview feature and Mike Turillo's comment on the role of technology in KM at KPMG: "In the past three or four years, technology has created [the equivalent of] another crystal radio for us. It allows us to take vast amounts of data, assimilate and filter them, put them into our context, and begin to be serious about collaborating in a real-time method." Choosing a set of technologies on which to build KM involves addressing at least two critical issues.[7]

First, the technologies should deliver only the relevant business information to users but quickly and from every feasible source. A by-product of the speed at which technologies change is the creation and storage of knowledge in many different places. The technology used should support exploration of new ideas and solutions to problems and make existing knowledge easily available to both developers and users. Xerox's Eureka is an example of such technology.

Second, because of the increasing mobility of knowledge workers, technologies used need to comprise a variety of devices—from telephones to laptop computers. The ability to obtain and deliver information is useless if it cannot be transmitted to where a decision needs to be made. In Chapter 20, we discuss some of the technologies utilized in KM.

ENABLING CULTURE

Organizations consistently identify cultural issues as the greatest barriers to the successful implementation of KM.[8] Recall the Preview feature and Mike Turillo's views of the cultural issues associated with implementing KM at KPMG: "There were significant impediments in creating the shift from a knowledge-hoarding culture to one of knowledge sharing. It takes time to convince people that they will be penalized if they continue previous behavior, and rewarded as they embrace the new one." Overcoming these cultural barriers requires that an organization create an atmosphere where sharing knowledge and innovating is valued and rewarded, both implicitly and explicitly. If people feel alone or unrewarded in changing their behaviors, they will not respond positively to the application of knowledge management.

The Mitre Corporation is a nonprofit organization, is headquartered in Bedford, Massachusetts, and works with government clients to address issues of national importance through the combined use of systems engineering and information technology. Its major clients include the U.S. Department of Defense, the U.S. intelligence community, the Federal Aviation Administration, and the Internal Revenue Service.[9] The following Planning and Administration Competency feature describes Mitre's introduction of KM and its relation to creating major cultural change in the organization.[10]

PLANNING & ADMINISTRATION COMPETENCY

Mitre's Introduction of Knowledge Management

Mitre's KM infrastructure has helped transform the organization through the sharing of information, which is expected and rewarded. Mitre has invested $7.2 million in KM, netting a return on investment of an estimated $62 million in reduced operating costs and improved productivity.

When President Victor A. De-Marines took office in early 1996, he concluded that Mitre was not utilizing its expertise as well as it could. "We had a culture where fiefdoms had developed their own pockets of knowledge," De-Marines says. Worse, these fiefdoms acted like rivals and, faced with increasing budget scrutiny from the government, DeMarines believed that this internal rivalry compromised Mitre's ability to deliver the level and quality of services warranted by the government's investment in them. Says DeMarines, "We had to develop a culture for sharing."

But to achieve and sustain such a culture shift, Mitre needed an information architecture that would not just enable but encourage sharing. DeMarines brought this problem to Andrea Weiss, a

20-year Mitre veteran promoted to be the company's first-ever CIO. Weiss knew how Mitre worked. "If you wanted an answer to a question, you had to have a 'people network,' Weiss says. "You needed to know someone who knew someone who knew who was expert in that." DeMarines challenged Weiss to help change this culture—to build a KM system that would allow Mitre executives to, as Weiss says, "know what we know, use what we know, and bring it all to bear on all of our customers' jobs."

To achieve DeMarines's goal, Weiss had to enrich its basic network with information deemed essential to employees' everyday lives. Weiss and her team met with senior managers and rank-and-file employees and emerged with a set of business requirements that resulted in the following KM features.

- *Corporate Directory:* Not just names, phone numbers, and e-mail addresses, this application includes personal profiles and résumés of all Mitre employees, as well as any material they may have published in their areas of expertise.

- *Lessons Learned Library:* The Systems Engineering Process Library (SEPL) captures best practices of key software systems deployed throughout Mitre. The Risk Assessment and Management Program (RAMP) collects and stores 10 years' worth of lessons learned from all Mitre projects.
- *Improved Efficiency Reports:* All the necessary HR documents—time sheets, service requests, and so

on—can be filled out online, as can property inventory and tracking forms (key documents in a government-funded organization). A facility-scheduling application lets users locate, schedule, and equip meeting space at Mitre's various locations.

Mitre's more than 4,000 employees interact with the system daily. The KM system's primary Web servers record as many as 10 million transactions per month. Internally, each of Mitre's business units is developing programs to extend KM companywide. Outside the system's firewall, a new KM extranet lets

select customers benefit from Mitre's project information and technical expertise.

• • •

To learn more about Mitre, visit the organization's home page at

http://www.mitre.org

FOSTERING FORECASTS

2.

DESCRIBE THE BASIC FEATURES OF THE DELPHI TECHNIQUE, SIMULATION, AND SCENARIO FORECASTING AIDS.

WEB INSIGHT

Go to the web site at *http://www.e-forecasting. com/index.html*. What types of forecasts are available through this online service?

Forecasting involves projecting or estimating future events or conditions in an organization's environment. Forecasting is concerned primarily with external events or conditions beyond the organization's control that are important to its survival and growth. An example is e-Forecasting.com's forecast that annual demand for PCs worldwide will reach 304 million units in 2005, up from the estimated demand of 182 million units in 2000.[11] Much forecasting is based on extrapolation. **Extrapolation** is the projection of some trend or tendency from the past or present into the future. The simplest, and at times most misleading, form of extrapolation is a linear, or straight-line, projection of a past trend into the future.[12] For example, many investors were shocked and dismayed in 2000 when the forecasts of most market analysts in 1999 for continuing double digit percentage stock market gains were not realized.

Cheryl Russell, a well-respected demographer and forecaster, warns of four forecasting pitfalls.

- *Listening to the media.* Tracking trends through headlines is asking for trouble. The media often distort trends, blow fads up into trends, or completely miss trends.

- *Assuming that things are going to return to the way they used to be.* The belief that trends are like a swinging pendulum—going one way, then the other—is a nice concept, but things really don't work that way.

- *Hearsay.* The neighbors are doing it, or everyone says that they know someone doing it, so therefore a trend must exist.

- *Tunnel vision.* The business media provide only a narrow view of what's going on in the world. Reading or obtaining material in other ways about other aspects of life provide an expanded view of the world.[13]

Even though forecasting is risky, it's still necessary. Managers and teams at all levels have to use whatever is available to them in anticipating future events and conditions. Three forecasting aids—the Delphi technique, simulation, and scenarios—are often used in planning and decision making. Because all of them focus on understanding possible futures, they aren't mutually exclusive and may well be used with one another.

DELPHI TECHNIQUE

The **Delphi technique** is a forecasting aid based on a consensus of a panel of experts. The experts refine their opinions, phase by phase, until they reach a consensus. Because the technique relies on opinions, it obviously isn't foolproof. But the consensus arrived at tends to be much more accurate than a single expert's opinion. The Delphi process replaces face-to-face communication and debate with a carefully planned, orderly program of sequential impersonal exchanges. The first decision that has to be made involves the selection of a group of experts.[14]

Delphi Questionnaires. The heart of the Delphi technique is a series of questionnaires. The first questionnaire may include generally worded questions. In each later phase, the questions become more specific because they are built on responses to the previous questionnaire.[15]

Table 9.1 shows a Delphi technique questionnaire developed for your use. It is concerned with possible developments in e-commerce as applied to automobile dealerships. You might want to take a few minutes now to respond to these questions.

Table 9.1   **Delphi Questionnaire: Automobile Dealers and E-Commerce**

Introduction: The eight questions here are concerned with future possible developments for automobile dealerships as a result of electronic commerce (EC). In addition to giving your answers to each question, you are asked to rank the questions from 1 to 8. The ranking 1 means you think that you have the highest probability of making an accurate projection for this question relative to the others. The ranking 8 means you regard your answer as least probable relative to other years identified. Please rank all questions, using every number from 1 to 8 only once. "Never" is also an acceptable answer.

Rank (1–8)	Questions	Year
_____	1. By what year will 60 percent of new automobile sales take place through EC, either through a dealer or direct with a manufacturer?	_____
_____	2. By what year will 35 percent of used car sales take place through EC?	_____
_____	3. By what year will 40 percent or more of automobile loans be obtained through EC?	_____
_____	4. By what year will the number of new car dealerships be reduced by one-third as compared to 2001?	_____
_____	5. By what year will 50 percent or more of appointments for new car warranty work be scheduled through EC?	_____
_____	6. By what year will 50 percent or more of new car sales occur directly between the manufacturer and consumer through EC?	_____
_____	7. By what year will 50 percent or more of new car sales be custom ordered for a manufacture through EC rather than purchased from inventory (e.g., a dealer's lot)?	_____
_____	8. By what year will 65 percent of consumers use the Internet to compare and evaluate the features and prices of automobiles?	_____

Phases. The Delphi technique involves three phases.

1. *A questionnaire is sent to a group of experts.* These experts remain unknown to one another. The questionnaire requests numerical estimates of specific technological or market possibilities. It asks for expected dates (years) and an assignment of probabilities to each of these possibilities. Respondents are asked to provide reasons for their expressed opinions. This process may be conducted via e-mail, fax, or regular mail.

2. *A summary of the first phase is prepared.* This report may show the median and quartile ranges of the responses. The report, along with a revised questionnaire, is sent to those who completed the first questionnaire. They are asked to revise their earlier estimates, if appropriate, or to justify their original opinions. The reasons for the possibilities presented in the first phase by the experts are critiqued by fellow respondents in writing. The technique emphasizes informed judgment. It attempts to improve on the panel or committee approach by subjecting the views of individual experts to others' reactions in ways that avoid face-to-face confrontation and provide anonymity of opinion and of arguments advanced in defense of those opinions.

3. *A summary of the second phase is prepared.* This report usually shows that a consensus is developing. The experts are then asked in a third questionnaire to indicate whether they support this emerging consensus and the explanations that accompany it. To avoid blind agreement, they are encouraged to find reasons for *not* joining the consensus.

Three phases generally are recommended. Although more phases could be used, the experts often begin dropping out after the third phase because of other time commitments. The number of participating experts may range from only a few to more than 100, depending on the scope of the issue. A range of 15 to 20 is recommended for a very focused issue. As the sample size (number of experts) increases, the amount of coordination required also increases, as do costs.

SIMULATION

A *simulation* is a representation of a real system. A simulation model usually describes the behavior of the real system (or some aspect of it) in quantitative and/or qualitative terms. Simulation often is used to forecast the effects of environmental changes and internal management decisions on an organization, department, or SBU. The goal of simulation is to reproduce or test reality without actually experiencing it. Most simulations are intended to let management ask numerous "what if" questions. For example, What profits can we anticipate next year if inflation is 8 percent and we continue current pricing policies? or What profits can we expect next year if inflation is 2 percent and we open two new plants? To answer such questions, analysts often develop complex equations and use computers to perform many of the step-by-step computations required. Such models can be used to simulate virtually any issue of interest (e.g., profits, sales, and earnings per share) for which a forecast is needed.

Tango! Simulation. Tango! is a business simulation offered by Celemi, a Swedish training and consulting firm. Tango! dramatizes the challenges of managing knowledge-intensive organizations. Teams ("companies") of four or five members use this simulation to compete with similar teams representing other companies to build the highest market value. The game runs 4 or 5 "years," each of which takes a couple of hours to play. Each company starts with a small staff and a few customers, for which they do projects—some easy, some challenging—every year. At the start of a new year, the companies can hire new recruits who enter the labor market, represented by cards; each year they can go after new customers represented by another stack of cards. In later stages of the game, companies can headhunt from one another or try to steal customers.

The companies get paid for completing projects. Success depends on matching the customer with the right talent—staffers whose skill and "chemistry" meet the customer's needs. The money—a generic currency called M—eventually turns into equity. But the companies also build intangible assets. In Tango!, the intangibles are image—reputation earned by completing challenging projects—and know-how. Companies build know-how by increasing the skills and abilities of individual employees (through demanding projects or training) or by building shared knowledge through R&D—to which values of M are also assigned. In real life, the value of knowledge-intensive companies is based at least as much on talent as on tangibles. Similarly, market value in Tango! is defined as the sum of financial and intellectual assets.[16]

Table 9.2 lists the common types of business simulation models. It is based on the types of simulation models that Marc Stanley & Co. can help a firm develop. Headquartered in Wilton, Connecticut, Marc Stanley is but one of many consulting firms that provide such assistance.

Virtual Reality. *Virtual reality* (VR) is a surrogate environment created by communications and computer systems.[17] The term denotes a simulated environment into which a user "enters," moves around, and interacts with objects. Virtual reality fulfills the sensory requirements of human beings for sight, sound, and movement. One of the earliest practical uses of VR was the training of pilots in flight simulators. Entertainment manufacturers are increasingly using it in their video games.

The advantage of VR as a planning aid is the freedom it allows for experimentation. The pace of action may be slowed down or speeded up. Processes that occur rapidly can be slowed down for more careful study. Processes that extend over long periods of time can be speeded up to reveal more clearly the consequences of particular actions. Actions that can't be replayed in the real world can be redone countless times. Complexity can be simplified by uncoupling variables that are interlocked in reality.

Virtual reality can be as simple as a computer-based representation of an architect's sketchpad. The architect can draw and talk through moves in a spatial-action language,

Budget Models

- All levels of organization

Treasury and Financial Models

- Cash management
- Income statements
- Cash flow projections
- Foreign exchange management
- Stock and commodity prices

Marketing Models

- Sales budgets
- Pricing
- Market share projections
- Advertising and marketing plans
- Effects of competitor's actions

Operations Models

- Inventory costs
- Materials costs
- Production costs
- Purchasing
- Facility utilization

Human Resources Models

- Compensation
- Optimum staffing levels
- Measurements of productivity

Strategic Planning Models

- Scenario planning
- Political/economic forecasts
- Business war-gaming

leaving traces that represent the forms of building on a site. Because the drawing can reveal qualities and relations unimagined beforehand, moves can function as experiments—for example, discovering that certain building shapes don't fit the slope of the land or that classrooms are too small.

To better arm professionals responsible for fire investigations, an innovative CD-ROM based training tool called *interFIRE VR* has been developed. It utilizes VR technology to improve fire investigation skills, increase successful arson prosecutions, and reduce the estimated $2 billion that insurers and policyholders pay each year for unresolved cases. Information on the CD-ROM is available at http://www.interfire.com.[18]

SCENARIOS

Scenarios are stories that help people recognize and adapt to changing features of their environments. Scenarios provide a way to identify alternative paths that may exist for an organization in the future and the actions that likely are involved in going down each of those paths.[19]

Scenarios are analogous to answering "what if" questions. For example, considering the most pressing external forces our industry or organization is likely to face, how can we spin them all together in a narrative story, or how can we weave in the certainties and uncertainties of a future world to create new perspectives? Some of the most creative, convention-breaking thinking occurs during mapping out extreme scenarios—for instance, a fundamentally different but better world. However, the number of scenarios under consideration should be limited to prevent decision making from becoming unwieldy. The three most common categories of scenarios used in organizational planning are (1) the company's worst nightmare, (2) a fundamentally different but better world, and (3) more of the same (equivalent to the status quo) but better.[20]

Planners at Ford, Wal-Mart, and other firms might use scenarios to address questions such as: What future opportunities might exist for e-commerce? How could developments in e-commerce dramatically change traditional retailing distributions? or What types of strategies might be useful in preventing, diverting, encouraging, or dealing with the possible future of e-commerce?[21]

Scenarios are quite useful in forcing those involved in planning to evaluate preliminary plans against future possibilities. The following Strategic Action Competency feature reports on Duke Energy's use of scenarios in its strategic planning process.[22] Duke Energy is a global energy company with headquarters in Charlotte, North Carolina. The scenarios presented were designed to help top management (1) understand the industry and quickly recognize when changes in the industry create significant threats and opportunities; (2) analyze general trends in the industry and their implications for the future; and (3) understand the strengths and limitations of various business strategies.

STRATEGIC ACTION COMPETENCY

Duke Energy's Scenarios

At Duke Energy Corporation, executives are at work on what they call a "wind tunnel for testing strategy." They have tried to test the company's ambitious growth plans against various economic winds that might blow either in their favor or against them.

As senior executives gathered for a 2-day strategy meeting in 2000, they confronted three scenarios for the next few years that were developed by Duke's strategy group. One scenario is called the *Economic Treadmill*. It imagines U.S. economic growth at 1 percent a year—a difficult future for Duke. This condition could mean that Duke, with its aggressive buildup of power plants, might have too much capacity. Prices would fall, resulting in reduced profits or losses and employees being laid off.

The second scenario is called the *Market.com* scenario, wherein the Internet revolutionizes the buying and selling of electricity and natural gas. This condition would give buyers of energy a stronger market position relative to sellers such as Duke.

The third scenario is called *Flawed Competition,* which assumes continuing, uneven deregulation of the energy industry, much price volatility, and a U.S. economic growth rate of 3 percent or more. Duke executives believe that *Flawed Competition* is the most likely future, and it currently is the basis for their actions. As a result of the strong economy and high seasonal demand, summer price spikes are expected to continue for years to come. Imbalances in supply and demand are expected to persist among regions. "If we get the cycles right, we're successful. If we get the cycles wrong, we're less successful or unsuccessful," says Richard Priory, Duke's CEO.

The indicators don't yet point to the *Market.com* scenario. Only 4 of 23 signposts devised by the planning staff have materialized so far. If the *Market.com* scenario comes to pass, attracting customer acquisition of power through e-commerce would become especially important. To prepare for this contingency, Duke created an e-commerce unit in 1999.

What if the *Flawed Competition* scenario and its resulting price spikes

lead to a political backlash? Priory states: "All of this could roll back the momentum you have with deregulation, which is crucial to Duke's aggressive power-plant buildup. It would change our strategy rather dramatically. I don't see that on the horizon."

• • •

To learn more about Duke Energy, visit the company's home page at

http://www.duke-energy.com

FOSTERING CREATIVITY

3.

USE OSBORN'S CREATIVITY MODEL TO STIMULATE ADAPTIVE AND INNOVATIVE DECISIONS.

WEB INSIGHT

The BrainStore is a consulting firm that "brings imagination to work." Go to its *creative lab* at **http://www.brainstore.com**. Find the index list and click "creative lab." How is this lab described?

All planning and decision making needs to be supported strongly by creativity. *Creativity* is the ability to visualize, generate, and implement new ideas. Creative thinking increases the quality of solutions to many types of problems, helps stimulate innovation, revitalizes motivation and commitment by challenging individuals, and serves as a catalyst for effective team performance. For organizations, creativity is no longer optional—it is imperative. In particular, for total quality management initiatives to succeed, managers and employees alike need creative thinking skills.

THE CREATIVE PROCESS

The creative process, as suggested in Figure 9.1, usually involves five interconnected stages: preparation, concentration, incubation, illumination, and verification.[23]

Figure 9.1	*Stages of the Creative Process*

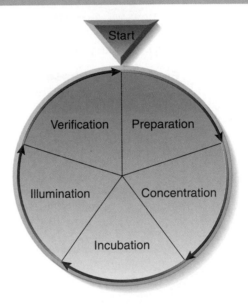

Preparation involves thoroughly investigating an issue or problem to ensure that all its aspects have been identified and understood. This stage involves searching for and collecting facts and ideas. Extensive formal education or many years of relevant experience is needed to develop the expertise required to identify substantive issues and problems. The preparation and concentration stages are consistent with Thomas Edison's statement that "creativity is 90 percent perspiration and 10 percent inspiration." Edison was responsible for more than a thousand patents, the most famous of which is the electric light bulb in 1879.[24]

Concentration involves focusing energies and resources on identifying and solving an issue or problem. A commitment must be made at this stage to implement a solution.

Incubation is an internal and unconscious ordering of gathered information. This stage may involve an unconscious personal conflict between what is currently accepted as reality and what may be possible. Relaxing, sometimes distancing oneself from the issue, and allowing the unconscious to search for possible issues or problems and solutions is important. A successful incubation stage yields fresh ideas and new ways of thinking about the nature of an issue or a problem and alternative solutions.

The *illumination stage* is the moment of discovery, the instant of recognition, as when a light bulb seems to be turned on mentally. The mind instantly connects an issue or a problem to a solution through a remembered observation or occurrence.

Verification is the testing of the created solution or idea. At this stage, confirmation and acceptance of the new approach is sought.

The knowledge and insights obtained from each stage of the creative process are often useful in addressing new issues and problems at the next *preparation* stage.

The Personal Creativity Inventory at the end of this chapter is a way for you to assess barriers to your own creative thought and innovative action. For now, we present A. F. Osborn's creativity model as an aid for fostering creative planning and decision making in organizations.

OSBORN'S CREATIVITY MODEL

Osborn's creativity model is a three-phase decision-making process that involves fact finding, idea finding, and solution finding. It is designed to help overcome blockages to creativity and innovation, which may occur for a variety of reasons. It is intended to stimulate freewheeling thinking, novel ideas, curiosity, and cooperation that in turn lead to innovative decisions.[25] It can be used with all types of groups (e.g., a manager and subordinates or a team). Sufficient time and freedom must be allowed for the model to work well, and some degree of external pressure and self-generated tension are helpful. However, too much pressure or threats from the wrong sources (e.g., an order from top management to determine within 10 days why quality has deteriorated) can easily undermine the process.

Fact-Finding Phase. Fact finding involves defining the issue or problem and gathering and analyzing relevant data. Although the Osborn creativity model provides some fact-finding procedures, they aren't nearly as well developed as the idea-finding procedures.[26] One way to improve fact finding is to begin with a broad view of the issue or problem and then proceed to define subissues or subproblems. This phase requires making a distinction between a symptom of an issue or a problem and an actual issue or problem. For example, a manager might claim that negative employee attitudes constitute a problem. A deeper investigation might reveal that negative employee attitudes are only symptoms of a festering issue. The issue may be a lack of feedback on how well employees are performing their jobs.

Idea-Finding Phase. Idea finding starts by generating tentative ideas and possible leads. Then the most likely of these ideas are modified, combined, and added to, if necessary. Osborn maintained that individuals can generate more good ideas by following two principles. First, defer judgment: Individuals can think up almost twice as many good ideas in the same length of time if they defer judgment on any idea until after they create a list of possible leads to a solution. Second, quantity breeds quality: The more ideas that individuals think up, the more likely they are to arrive at the potentially best leads to a solution.

To encourage uninhibited thinking and generate lots of ideas, Osborn developed 75 general questions to use when brainstorming a problem. ***Brainstorming*** is an unrestrained flow of ideas in a group with all critical judgments suspended. The group leader must decide which of the 75 questions are most appropriate to the issue or problem being addressed. Moreover, the group leader isn't expected to use all the questions in a single session. The following are examples of questions that could be used in a brainstorming session.

- How can this issue, idea, or thing be put to other uses?

- How can it be modified?

- How can it be substituted for something else, or can something else be substituted for part of it?

- How could it be reversed?

- How could it be combined with other things?[27]

A brainstorming session should follow four basic rules.

1. *Criticism is ruled out.* Participants must withhold critical judgment of ideas until later.

2. *Freewheeling is welcomed.* The wilder the idea, the better; taming down an idea is easier than thinking up new ones.

3. *Quantity is wanted.* The greater the number of ideas, the greater is the likelihood that some will be useful.

4. *Combination and improvement are sought.* In addition to contributing ideas of their own, participants should suggest how ideas of others can be turned into better ideas, or how two or more ideas can be merged into still another idea.[28]

These rules are intended to separate creative imagination from judgment. The two are incompatible and relate to different aspects of the decision-making process. The leader of one brainstorming group put it this way: "If you try to get hot and cold water out of the same faucet at the same time, you will get only lukewarm water. And if you try to criticize and create at the same time, you will not do either very well. So let us stick solely to *ideas*—let us cut out *all* criticism during this session.[29]

A brainstorming session should have from 5 to 12 or so participants in order to generate diverse ideas. This size range permits each member to maintain a sense of identification and involvement with the group. A session should normally run not less than 20 minutes or more than an hour. However, brainstorming could consist of several idea-generating sessions. For example, follow-up sessions could address individually each of the ideas previously generated. Table 9.3 presents the guidelines for leading a brainstorming session.[30]

T a b l e 9 . 3	**Guidelines for Leading a Brainstorming Session**
Basic leadership role	• Make a brief statement of the four basic rules.
	• State the time limit for the session.
	• Read the problem and/or related question to be discussed and ask, "What are your ideas?"
	• When an idea is given, summarize it by using the speaker's words insofar as possible. Have the idea recorded by a participant or on an audiotape machine. Follow your summary with the single word "Next."
	• Say little else. Whenever the leader participates as a brainstormer, group productivity usually falls.
Handling problems	• When someone talks too long, wait until he or she takes a breath (everyone must stop to inhale sometime), break into the monologue, summarize what was said for the recorder, point to another participant, and say "Next."
	• When someone becomes judgmental or starts to argue, stop him or her. Say, for example, "That will cost you one coffee or soda for each member of the group."
	• When the discussion stops, relax and let the silence continue. Say nothing. The pause should be broken by the group and *not* the leader. This period of silence is called the *mental pause* because it is a change in thinking. All the obvious ideas are exhausted; the participants are now forced to rely on their creativity to produce new ideas.
	• When someone states a problem rather than idea, repeat the problem, raise your hand with five fingers extended, and say, "Let's have five ideas on this problem." You may get only 1 or you may get 10, but you're back in the business of creative thinking.

Solution-Finding Phase. Solution finding involves generating and evaluating possible courses of action and deciding how to implement the chosen course of action. This phase relies on judgment, analysis, and criticism. A variety of planning and decision aids—such as those presented in this chapter and elsewhere in the book—can be used. To initiate the solution-finding phase, the leader could ask the team to identify from one to five of the most important ideas generated. The participants might be asked to jot down these ideas individually on a piece of paper and evaluate them on a five-point scale. A very important idea might get five points; a moderately important idea could get three points; and an unimportant idea could be assigned one point. The highest combined scores may indicate the actions or ideas to be investigated further.

Osborn's creativity model has been modified often and applied in a variety of ways.[31] The following Teamwork Competency feature highlights how IDEO Product Development, headquartered in Palo Alto, California, uses brainstorming.[32] The company is a renowned professional services firm that helps clients design and develop new products and, in the process, become more innovative. The creative process at IDEO is fostered through the extensive use of empowered design teams. These teams are staffed to take advantage of diverse perspectives, technical and creative skills, and ability to achieve goals jointly. Diverse views are encouraged and used to enhance the quality and creativity of decisions. At the same time, cooperation is fostered, and the teams are kept moving toward their goals.

TEAMWORK COMPETENCY

IDEO Brainstorms

IDEO projects last from a few weeks to several years, with the average being 10 to 12 months. Depending on the client's needs, results can range from sketches of products to crude working models to complete new products. Clients vary from venture-funded start-ups to multinational corporations in North America, Europe, and Japan. IDEO has developed part or all of more than 3,000 products in dozens of industries, including Apple's first computer mouse, AT&T's new consumer telephones, Oral B's "Squish Grip" toothbrushes for children, and Nike's sports sunglasses.

IDEO is unique in encouraging clients to participate in brainstorming sessions conducted by design teams. By going to a "brainstormer," clients gain insight and learn because they join IDEO designers in the creative process. Brainstorming sessions usually are initiated by a design team. The team members then invite other IDEO designers to help generate ideas for the project. These sessions are held in rooms with

five brainstorming rules written on the walls: defer judgment, build on the ideas of others, one conversation at a time, stay focused on the topic, and encourage wild ideas.

Designers who are also skilled facilitators lead the brainstorming sessions, enforce rules, write suggestions on the board, and encourage creativity and fun. Nearly all the designers are experienced at brainstorming. Typically, project members (or clients) introduce the project and describe the design issue or problem they face (e.g., How do you make fishing more fun and easier for neophytes?). Participants then generate ideas (e.g., Use the "slingshot" method to launch lures), often sketching them on paper or whiteboards. Many new projects start with a flurry of brainstorming sessions. Clients often attend them to describe their existing products and the new products that they want designed. Clients may also give detailed demonstrations before a brainstormer to explain the product or service, such as clients from a

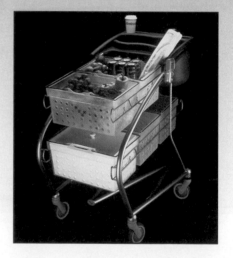

chain of hair salons who did haircuts at the Palo Alto office to demonstrate their work process. Twenty or so IDEO employees may be invited to brainstorming sessions in the early weeks of a project.

• • •

To learn more about IDEO Product Development, visit the company's home page at

http://www.ideo.com

Effectiveness. The Osborn creativity model is based on the assumption that most people have the potential for greater creativity and innovation in decision making than they use. Some research suggests that the same number of individuals working alone may generate more ideas and more creative ideas than do groups.[33] However, most of this research was conducted with students rather than employees and employee teams on the job. Unlike employees who have diverse knowledge and skills and who are brought together to brainstorm problems that have serious long-term consequences (as at IDEO), student groups are relatively homogeneous. Most students have a limited range of knowledge of the problems given to them and limited skills to apply to their solutions. Because students don't have to be concerned with real-world consequences, they may be less than fully committed to the process. Thus whether group brainstorming in a work setting is more or less effective than individuals working alone to generate ideas remains an open question.

Some evidence suggests that, under certain conditions, electronic brainstorming may be a better way to generate ideas than traditional face-to-face brainstorming.[34] One condition is when individuals from different organizational levels are in the same brainstorming group. **Electronic brainstorming** makes use of technology to input and automatically disseminate ideas in real time over a computer network to all team members, each of whom may be stimulated to generate additional ideas. For example, individuals may input ideas via the keyboard as they think of them. Every time an idea is entered, the team's ideas appear in random order on each person's screen. An individual can continue to see new sets of ideas in random order by pressing the appropriate key.[35] The random order format prevents the system from identifying who generates each idea.

FOSTERING QUALITY

4.

APPLY TWO QUALITY MANAGEMENT DECISION AIDS—BENCHMARKING AND THE DEMING CYCLE.

In Chapter 1, we defined *quality* as how well a good or service does what it is supposed to do—that is, how closely and reliably it satisfies the specifications to which it is built or provided. The most common meaning of *quality* is the extent to which a good or service meets and/or exceeds customers' expectations.[36] Consumers often apply the value dimension of quality when making purchasing decisions. *Consumer Reports* ranks goods and services on both quality and price to arrive at recommendations of "best-buys." The various perspectives of quality are, of course, appropriate in different circumstances. We review two of many planning and decision aids that focus on improving quality: benchmarking and the Deming cycle.

BENCHMARKING

Benchmarking is a systematic and continuous process of measuring and comparing an organization's goods, services, and practices against industry leaders anywhere in the world to gain information that will help the organization improve performance.[37] By identifying how such leading organizations achieved excellence in particular areas or processes, other organizations can determine how to develop their own strategic or tactical plans and processes to reach or exceed those levels. At the most fundamental level, benchmarking helps managers and employees learn from others.

Stages. As noted in Figure 9.2, benchmarking includes seven stages.[38] Stage 1 focuses on *defining the domain* to be benchmarked. This stage includes a careful assessment of the organization's own products and processes that are to be compared to benchmark products and processes. For example, common benchmarks used by airlines and rating services are percentage of on-time arrivals and amount of lost or misrouted baggage.

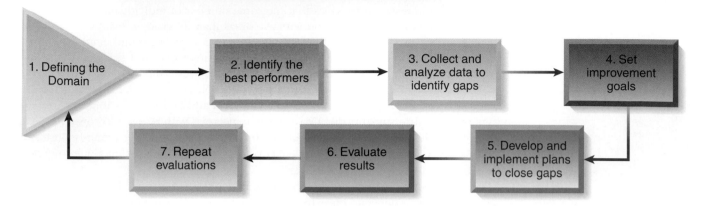

Figure 9.2   **The Benchmarking Process**

1. Defining the Domain

2. Identify the best performers

3. Collect and analyze data to identify gaps

4. Set improvement goals

5. Develop and implement plans to close gaps

6. Evaluate results

7. Repeat evaluations

Processes and outputs in functions such as manufacturing, finance, marketing, inventory management, transportation, accounting, legal services, human resources, and marketing may be benchmarked. Each function may be broken into more specific categories or processes for that purpose. For example, benchmarking in human resources may include the processes of recruiting, diversity enhancement, training, compensation, performance appraisal, recognition programs, and job design.

Benchmarking can be expensive and time consuming. Thus some people recommend that benchmarking be directed at the specific issues and processes that are likely to yield the greatest competitive advantage (e.g., core strategic competencies, managerial competencies, and the like). Others, such as the American Productivity and Quality Center (APQC), suggest that benchmarking be applied to all functions and processes to instill total quality throughout the organization.[39]

Stage 2 focuses on *identifying the best performers,* or best-in-class, for each function, process, and product to be benchmarked. They may include organizations in the firm's own industry or in other industries. For example, Xerox compared its warehousing and distribution process to that of L.L. Bean, the catalog and on-line sales company, because of Bean's excellent reputation in this area.

Stage 3 focuses on *collecting and analyzing data to identify gaps,* if any, between the function, product, or process being evaluated and that of the best-in-class organizations. The data collected need to focus on specific methods utilized, not simply on the results obtained. It is one thing to know that Wal-Mart has a superb warehouse distribution system, yet it is another thing to learn how Wal-Mart has achieved this level of excellence. Many sources of information are available for learning about best-in-class organizations. They include customers, suppliers, distributors, trade journals, company publications, newspapers, books on total quality, consultants, presentations at professional meetings, and even on-site interviews with people at the best-in-class organizations. This last source usually is easier to tap if the organizations aren't direct competitors.

The remaining steps are consistent with the typical planning phases: Stage 4 focuses on *setting improvement goals;* stage 5, *developing and implementing plans to close gaps;* stage 6, *evaluating results;* and stage 7, *repeating the evaluations* as necessary. Stage 7 suggests that benchmarking needs to be an ongoing process. Over time, the things benchmarked may remain the same or need to be revised. Revisions may include dropping and/or adding functions, products, or processes as issues, conditions, technology, and markets change.

Effectiveness. Benchmarking needs to be linked to other sources of information, such as changing customer expectations and preferences. Benchmarking always looks at the present in terms of how some process (logistics) or quality dimension is

WEB INSIGHT

The American Productivity and Quality Center (APQC) provides an *International Benchmarking Clearinghouse.* Go to the APQC Web site at *http://www.apqc.org* and click *International Benchmarking Clearinghouse.* What types of benchmarking information and services are provided?

being achieved by others. However, this approach may not be adequate for determining what should be done in the future or whether an organization should retain a function or process or contract it out. For example, an organization could contract out its computer operations to IBM or some other firm. When used simply to copy the best-in-class competitors, benchmarking may lead only to short-term competitive advantage. Finally, benchmarking needs to be used to complement and aid, not to substitute for, the creative and innovative efforts of the organization's own employees.[40] Benchmarking is often used to help an organization adapt but less commonly to innovate.

The following Communication Competency feature reports on how Samuel Johnson, general manager of Site Services at Cinergy Corporation, used benchmarking to improve effectiveness. The use of his communication competency in doing so is apparent.[41] Headquartered in Cincinnati, Ohio, Cinergy Corporation was created by the merger of the Cincinnati Gas & Electric Company and PSI Energy, Inc., the largest electric utility in Indiana.

COMMUNICATION COMPETENCY

Benchmarking in Site Services at Cinergy Corporation

Using standards of performance developed by the Building Owners and Managers Association (BOMA) and the International Facility Management Association (IFMA) Samuel Johnson and Site Services began a consistent, formal, and documented benchmarking process. Several years ago, it was put to the test. The following are Johnson's comments about the results of that test and the process that withstood it.

My boss went out and requested proposals from facilities management outsourcers and even gave them all my numbers. Amazingly, it solidified our organization's position within the company. All those firms came back and said "We can't do it as cheaply as you're doing it internally." From an overall facilities standpoint, we were providing services lower than anybody outside could do.

One thing I've really challenged my managers with is how they look at doing things. Just because we did it that way for the last 15 years it isn't necessarily the best way to do it. As the business changes and as the functions evolve internally, we have to be able to change. Change includes thinking of company associates as customers—internal customers—even to extending customer service training to administrative staff that field calls.

At Cinergy's Site Services, benchmarking is an ongoing process. At one point, we did it annually. Now, we're doing it every 6 months. The result is so refined that it even provides a comparative cost analysis for internal customers. We've created a document that when we do a job for one of our customers in a facilities area, we are able to say, "Be-

cause of benchmarking information, this is our cost; this is what it would have cost you if it were done by somebody else. This is how much we saved you in this particular function." Benchmarking is becoming more and more important; it's almost a core competency for my group. Everybody is being affected and made accountable cost-wise. The emphasis on costs can create some discrepancies in quality perceptions. As a result, we have developed service agreements with our business units. To me, it's an internal contract: "This is a level of housekeeping you'd like in your building."

• • •

To learn more about Cinergy Corporation, visit the company's home page at

http://www.cinergy.com

THE DEMING CYCLE

We provided some information on W. Edwards Deming, considered by some to be the "godfather" of the quality movement, in Chapter 2 (in the Quality Viewpoint section). One of the aids he advocated for improving quality is commonly known as the Deming cycle. Originally developed by Walter Shewhart, some call it the Shewhart cycle. Others refer to it as the PDCA cycle because it involves the four stages of plan (P), do (D), check (C), and act (A). As Figure 9.3 suggests, these stages unfold in sequence and continuously. Thus the **Deming cycle** comprises four stages—plan, do, check, and act—that should be repeated over time to ensure continuous learning and improvements in a function, product, or process.

Figure 9.3 **The Deming Cycle**

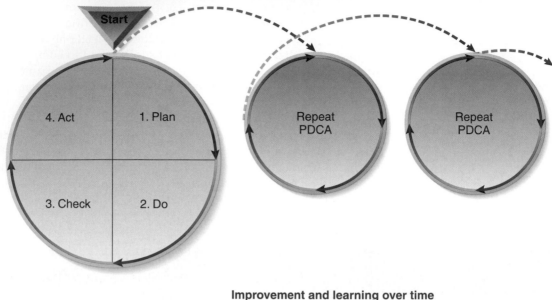

Improvement and learning over time

Three questions need to be answered during the *plan stage* of the Deming cycle: (1) What are we trying to accomplish? (2) What changes can we make that will result in improvement? (3) How will we know that a change is an improvement? The *plan stage* involves analyzing the current situation, gathering data, and developing ways to make improvements. The *do stage* involves testing alternatives experimentally in a laboratory, establishing a pilot production process, or trying it out with a small number of customers. The *check stage* requires determining whether the trial or process is working as intended, any revisions in it are needed, or it should be scrapped. The *act stage* focuses on implementing the process within the organization or with its customers and suppliers.[42] Benchmarking may be one of the aids used in the Deming cycle.

Application. The owner of Deluxe Diner, Billie Boyd, decided to do something about the long lines at lunchtime that occurred every day. During the *plan stage* she held several meetings with her employees. They identified four main aspects of this problem: (1) customers were waiting in line for as long as 15 minutes, (2) tables usually were available, (3) many of the customers were regulars, and (4) those taking orders and preparing food were getting in each others' way.

The employees offered various ideas. Boyd developed a plan that involved the following changes: (1) allow customers to fax their orders in ahead of time (rent a fax machine for one month), (2) install a preparation table for fax orders in the kitchen where there was ample room, and (3) devote one of the two cash registers to handling fax orders. To assess whether these changes had improved the situation, in the *do stage,* Boyd collected data on the number of customers in line, the number of empty tables, and the delay before customers were served. The length of the line and the number of empty tables were measured every 15 minutes during the lunch hour. When doing the 15-minute line check, she noted the last person in line and the elapsed time until that person was seated.

Next, the results of these measurements were observed for 3 weeks. Three improvements were detected during the *check stage.* Time in line dropped from 15 minutes to 5 minutes, on average. The line length was cut to a peak average of 12 people, and the number of empty tables declined slightly. Boyd held another meeting with her employees to discuss the results. In the *act stage,* they decided to purchase the fax machine, fill fax orders, and use both cash registers to handle walk-up and fax orders. Boyd thought that the Deming cycle was very helpful in resolving the problem and intends to use it again.[43]

CHAPTER SUMMARY

In this chapter, we focused on seven of the literally hundreds of planning and decision aids. They are aids that specifically foster knowledge management, forecasting, creativity, and quality management. These aids are useful in virtually all types of organizations, at all organizational levels, and in all functional areas.

1. **EXPLAIN KNOWLEDGE MANAGEMENT AS A MEANS OF CREATING AND UTILIZING AN INFORMATION BASE AND BUILDING ON AN ORGANIZATION'S INTELLECTUAL ASSETS.**

Knowledge management (KM) is the art and practice of obtaining and transforming information and utilizing intellectual assets to create value for an organization's employees and customers or clients. A supportive and enabling organizational culture is a prerequisite for the introduction and use of KM. Its three major components are an information base, enabling technologies, and the skills and abilities of people. Information and knowledge are increasingly more important assets and competitive weapons than an organization's physical assets. Knowledge management is most often applied to (1) collaboration among teams and departments; (2) improving service to customers or clients; and (3) tracking employees' capabilities, improving employee training, and performing other human resource functions.

2. **DESCRIBE THE BASIC FEATURES OF THE DELPHI TECHNIQUE, SIMULATION, AND SCENARIO FORECASTING AIDS.**

Forecasting is the process of estimating future events and conditions in an organization's environment. The Delphi technique is a process of consensus building among experts to arrive at such estimates. Simulation involves the use of models of real systems to test alternatives, often on a computer. Scenarios are written descriptions of possible futures. All three methods are especially relevant as aids in the strategic planning process.

3. **USE OSBORN'S CREATIVITY MODEL TO STIMULATE ADAPTIVE AND INNOVATIVE DECISIONS.**

Creativity is the ability to visualize, generate, and implement new ideas. The creative process usually involves five interconnected stages: preparation, concentration, incubation, illumination, and verification. Osborn's creativity model attempts to stimulate and reduce blocks of creativity and innovation. It helps decision makers address unstructured and ambiguous problems.

4. **APPLY TWO QUALITY MANAGEMENT DECISION AIDS—BENCHMARKING AND THE DEMING CYCLE.**

Quality management is concerned with improving how well a good, service, process does what it is supposed to do, as well as raising the standards and specifications for what it is supposed to do. In brief, benchmarking involves comparing an organization's functions, products, or processes with those of best-in-class organizations. This ongoing process is a sequence of seven stages: defining the domain, identifying the best performers, collecting and analyzing data to identify gaps, setting improvement goals, developing and implementing plans to close gaps, evaluating results, and repeating the evaluations. The Deming cycle includes four stages—plan, do, check, and act—that should be repeated over time to ensure continuous learning and improvement in functions, products, and processes.

KEY TERMS

Benchmarking, p. 257
Brainstorming, p. 254
Creativity, p. 253
Delphi technique, p. 248
Deming cycle, p. 259

Electronic brainstorming, p. 257
Extrapolation, p. 248
Forecasting, p. 248
Knowledge management (KM), p. 244
Osborn's creativity model, p. 254

Scenarios, p. 251
Simulation, p. 250
Virtual reality (VR), p. 250

QUESTIONS FOR DISCUSSION AND COMPETENCY DEVELOPMENT

1. Describe three similarities and/or differences in the components of knowledge management (KM) involved in the functioning of a team-based student project of which you were a member.

2. In what ways has an organization for which you have worked used or failed to use KM? Explain.

3. How might the Delphi technique be used to develop a forecast of the possible impacts of the Internet on the learning process in higher education?

4. Describe a personal experience that you've had with virtual reality. Which of its features might apply in a business setting?

5. Develop a negative scenario on the impact of the Internet on the work environment for college graduates in 2012.

6. Describe a personal situation that occurred within the past 6 months for which Osborn's creativity model would have been useful. Why would it have been useful?

7. Describe how benchmarking could be used to help plan improvements in one service or process (e.g., registration, advising, or financial aid) at your college or university. Who might you benchmark? Explain why.

8. **Competency Development: Global Awareness.** Visit the online knowledge management magazine *KM World Online* at ***http://www.kmworld.com/index.cfm***. In the *knowledge search* feature, enter the search term "global knowledge management" and click *FIND*. Select and read one of the articles identified. What did you learn?

9. **Competency Development: Strategic Action Competency.** The Royal Dutch/Shell Group is considered to be one of the leaders in the use of scenarios as a planning aid. Find its presentation of two energy scenarios at ***http://www. shell.com/royal-en/content/ 0,5028,25432-50913,00.html***. These scenarios are called *Sustained Growth* and *Demateri-alisation*. What are their key features? What conclusions are drawn by the Royal Dutch/Shell Group from these scenarios?

SELF-MANAGEMENT COMPETENCY INVENTORY

Personal Creativity

This inventory provides you the opportunity to assess, reflect on, and reduce possible personal barriers to creativity. For each of the statements in the questionnaire, use the following scale to express which number best corresponds to your agreement or disagreement with the statement.[44] Write that number in the blank to the left of each statement. Please do not skip any statements.

Strongly Agree 1	Agree Somewhat 2	Agree 3	Disagree 4	Strongly Disagree 5

_____ 1. I evaluate criticism to determine how it can be useful to me.

_____ 2. When solving problems, I attempt to apply new concepts or methods.

_____ 3. I can shift gears or change emphasis in what I am doing.

_____ 4. I get enthusiastic about problems outside of my specialized area of concentration.

_____ 5. I always give a problem my best effort, even if it seems trivial or fails to arouse enthusiasm.

_____ 6. I set aside periods of time without interruptions.

_____ 7. It is not difficult for me to have my ideas criticized.

_____ 8. In the past, I have taken calculated risks and I would do so again.

_____ 9. I dream, daydream, and fantasize easily.

_____ 10. I know how to simplify and organize my observations.

_____ 11. Occasionally, I try a so-called unworkable answer in hopes that it will prove to be workable.

_____ 12. I can and do consistently guard my personal periods of privacy.

_____ 13. I feel at ease with peers even when my ideas or plans meet with public criticisms or rejection.

_____ 14. I frequently read opinions contrary to my own to learn what the opposition is thinking.

_____ 15. I translate symbols into concrete ideas or action steps.

_____ 16. I see many ideas because I enjoy having alternative possibilities.

_____ 17. In the idea-formulation stage of a project, I withhold critical judgment.

_____ 18. I determine whether an imposed limitation is reasonable or unreasonable.

_____ 19. I would modify an idea, plan, or design, even if doing so would meet with opposition.

_____ 20. I feel comfortable in expressing my ideas even if they are in the minority.

_____ 21. I enjoy participating in nonverbal, symbolic, or visual activities.

_____ 22. I feel the excitement and challenge of finding solutions to problems.

_____ 23. I keep a file of discarded ideas.

_____ 24. I make reasonable demands for good physical facilities and surroundings.

_____ 25. I would feel no serious loss of status or prestige if management publicly rejected my plan.

_____ 26. I frequently question the policies, goals, values, or ideas of an organization.

_____ 27. I deliberately exercise my visual and symbolic skills in order to strengthen them.

_____ 28. I can accept my thinking when it seems illogical.

_____ 29. I seldom reject ambiguous ideas that are not directly related to the problem.

_____ 30. I distinguish between trivial and important physical distractions.

_____ 31. I feel uncomfortable making waves for a worthwhile idea even if it threatens team harmony.

_____ 32. I am willing to present a truly original approach even if there is a chance it could fail.

_____ 33. I can recognize the times when symbolism or visualization would work best for me.

_____ 34. I try to make an uninteresting problem stimulating.

_____ 35. I consciously attempt to use new approaches toward routine tasks.

_____ 36. In the past, I have determined when to leave an undesirable environment and when to stay and change the environment (including self-growth).

Scoring

Transfer your responses to the statements on page 262 and record them in the blanks provided below. Then add the numbers in each column, and record the column totals.

A	B	C	D	E	F
1. ___	2. ___	3. ___	4. ___	5. ___	6. ___
7. ___	8. ___	9. ___	10. ___	11. ___	12. ___
13. ___	14. ___	15. ___	16. ___	17. ___	18. ___
19. ___	20. ___	21. ___	22. ___	23. ___	24. ___
25. ___	26. ___	27. ___	28. ___	29. ___	30. ___
31. ___	32. ___	33. ___	34. ___	35. ___	36. ___

Totals:

___   ___   ___   ___   ___   ___

Interpretation

Take your scores from the scoring sheet and mark them with a dot in the score categories (cells) on the following graph. The vertical axis, which represents the possible column totals, ranges from 6 to 36. The horizontal axis represents the columns on your scoring sheet and ranges from A to F. The Key to Barriers at the end of this exercise identifies the category of barriers in each column. Connect the dots you have marked with a line. The high points represent your possible barriers to creativity as you see them. The higher the number in each column, the greater the barrier that factor represents in realizing your creative potential.

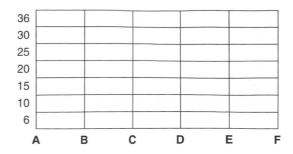

Key to Barriers

A = Barriers related to self-confidence and risk taking

B = Barriers related to need for conformity

C = Barriers related to use of the abstract

D = Barriers related to use of systematic analysis

E = Barriers related to task achievement

F = Barriers related to physical environment

Based on these results, are there any actions that you can and want to take to improve your creativity?

VIDEO CASE

SP Aviation and Firstbank

This video profiles two very different companies that both rely heavily upon commercial software to assist them with their planning and decision making.

SP Aviation is a small, 24-hour, on-call air charter company that specializes in transporting organs for transplant and time-critical computer components. Management wanted to develop a detailed business plan to guide the company's future direction and activities. To do so, it utilized software developed by JIAN, Inc., called Biz Plan Builder. JIAN's founder, Burke Franklin, describes this software as a device that simply allows users to edit a prepackaged business plan fit to their unique needs. Editing a standardized business plan, he argues, is much easier than writing a new plan from scratch. The Biz Plan Builder software provides all the basic components of a business plan. It begins by presenting a company overview whereby information is given on the management team's composition and any necessary staffing requirements. The product strategy part focuses on the various products (goods and services) that the company wants to sell. Next is an in-depth market analysis of the company's customers and competition. The marketing plan then details strategies for promoting and selling the firm's products. Finally, a financial plan is included that presents the company's financial statements and capital requirements.

Firstbank, the other company profiled in this video, is a multibank holding company located in Alma, Michigan. As a leading financial institution in the Midwest in terms of growth of assets and share price, Firstbank consistently faces the challenges of managing risk. Firstbank's executives recognize that, in their industry, changes that can have an immediate impact on the company's profitability may occur very rapidly. Two key variables that they must monitor involve changing interest rates and the status of the economy generally.

In monitoring the external environment and carrying out strategic planning, Firstbank's executives use integrated financial modeling software from the IPS-Sendero Corporation (formerly, Sendero, which recently merged with IPS), created specifically for the banking industry. The software allows management to define its future in terms of asset and liability management and get forecasts of economic conditions. It allows manageme to plore the ramifications of various potential decision the year by testing certain "what if" scenarios. It also helps management update information throughout the year and identify customer and industry trends. Firstbank's management views the software as an essential planning tool, enabling it to measure risk and return relationships and to gauge its service to customers, shareholders, and the communities it serves.

Both companies' planning and decision making abilities have been improved as a result of software designed to meet their specific needs.

Questions

1. How do the two software providers ensure that their products are current and adequately address the needs of their consumers?

2. Define *knowledge management* and then explain the role of decision-aid software (e.g., JIAN's and IPS-Sendero's) in fostering the three components of knowledge management.

To learn more about JIAN and IPS-Sendero, visit the companies' home pages at **http://www.jianusa.com** and **http://www.ips-sendero.com**.

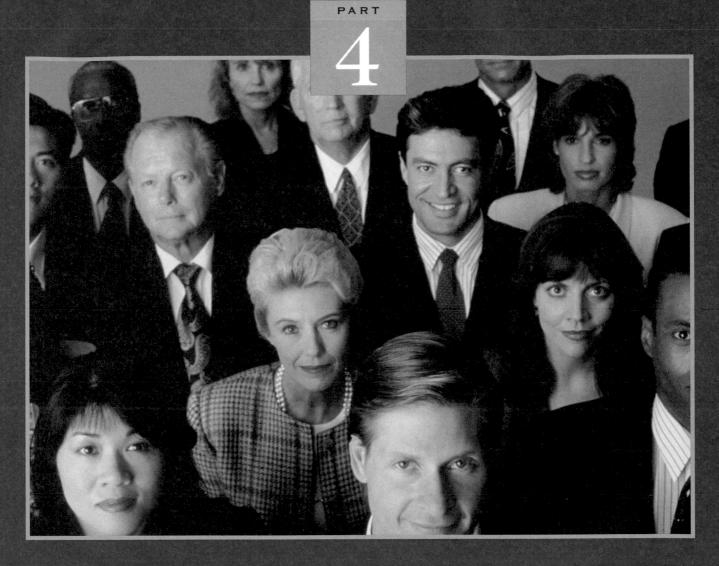

Organizing

CHAPTER 10
FUNDAMENTALS OF ORGANIZATION DESIGN

CHAPTER 11
CONTEMPORARY ORGANIZATION DESIGNS

CHAPTER 12
ORGANIZATIONAL CHANGE AND LEARNING

CHAPTER 13
MANAGING HUMAN RESOURCES

Fundamentals of Organization Design

LEARNING OBJECTIVES

AFTER STUDYING THIS CHAPTER YOU SHOULD BE ABLE TO:

1. EXPLAIN SEVERAL OF THE MAIN INGREDIENTS OF ORGANIZATION DESIGN.

2. OUTLINE THE FEATURES OF FOUR BASIC TYPES OF DEPARTMENTALIZATION.

3. DESCRIBE THREE OF THE PRINCIPLES FOR ACHIEVING COORDINATION WITHIN AND BETWEEN DEPARTMENTS.

4. DISCUSS THE FUNDAMENTAL CONCEPTS OF AUTHORITY IN ORGANIZATION DESIGN.

Chapter Outline

PREVIEW: REORGANIZATION OF THE IRS

INTRODUCTION TO ORGANIZATION DESIGN
ELEMENTS OF ORGANIZING
ORGANIZATIONAL STRUCTURE

BASIC TYPES OF DEPARTMENTALIZATION
FUNCTIONAL DEPARTMENTALIZATION
PLACE DEPARTMENTALIZATION
PLANNING AND ADMINISTRATION COMPETENCY: Starbucks' Organizational Structure
PRODUCT DEPARTMENTALIZATION
CUSTOMER DEPARTMENTALIZATION
STRATEGIC ACTION COMPETENCY: Novell Reorganizes
SELECTING AN ORGANIZATIONAL STRUCTURE

COORDINATION
UNITY OF COMMAND PRINCIPLE
SCALAR PRINCIPLE
SPAN OF CONTROL PRINCIPLE
COORDINATION AND DEPARTMENTALIZATION
TEAMWORK COMPETENCY: Cobra's Team Coordination

AUTHORITY
RESPONSIBILITY
ACCOUNTABILITY
DELEGATION
CENTRALIZATION AND DECENTRALIZATION
SELF-MANAGEMENT COMPETENCY: Tom Siebel
LINE AND STAFF AUTHORITY

CHAPTER SUMMARY

KEY TERMS

QUESTIONS FOR DISCUSSION AND COMPETENCY DEVELOPMENT

CASE FOR COMPETENCY DEVELOPMENT: PEACHTREE HOSPITAL

VIDEO CASE: JIAN

REORGANIZATION OF THE IRS

The National Commission on Restructuring of the Internal Revenue Service (IRS), created by the U.S. Congress, issued its report several years ago. It stated, in part, "As a guiding principle, the Commission believes that taxpayer satisfaction must become paramount at the new IRS and that the IRS should only initiate contact with a taxpayer if the agency is prepared to devote the resources necessary for a proper and timely resolution of the matter." The report addressed a number of organization design issues within the IRS and was followed by legislation. The legislation signed by the president stated, "The Act directs the Commissioner of Internal Revenue (the 'Commissioner') to develop and to implement a plan to reorganize the IRS." To implement this legislative mandate, top management of the IRS created a new or-

ganization design comprising four operating divisions and several other shared-service and functional units. Each operating division serves particular groups of taxpayers having similar needs and can be briefly described as follows.

- *Wage and Investment Income Division.* The vast majority of taxpayers (approximately 88 million filers, 116 million individual taxpayers) deal with this new division. It is based in Atlanta, Georgia, and has approximately 21,000 employees.

- *Small Business/Self-Employed Division.* This new division includes all corporations and partnerships with assets of less than $5 million. It is based in New Carrolton, Maryland, and has a staff of approximately 39,000. This division serves about 40 million filers.

- *Large and Mid-Size Business Division.* This new division serves approximately 170,000 filers from its Washington, D.C., headquarters. Its approximately 9,500 employees are divided into major industry groups.

- *Tax Exempt and Government Entities Division.* This division handles approximately 1.9 million tax-exempt filers. It is based in Washington, D.C., and has approximately 2,800 employees.

These changes in organization design, among many others, were made to support the revised IRS mission statement that provides for greater emphasis on serving the public and meeting the needs of taxpayers.[1]

To learn more about the Internal Revenue Service, visit the agency's home page at

http://www.irs.ustreas.gov/

INTRODUCTION TO ORGANIZATION DESIGN

1.

EXPLAIN SEVERAL OF THE MAIN INGREDIENTS OF ORGANIZATION DESIGN.

In Chapter 1, we defined *organizing* as the process of creating a structure of relationships that enable employees to carry out management's plans and meet organizational goals. Organizing was presented as one of four general managerial functions. The others are planning, leading, and controlling. **Organization design** includes the elements of the organizing function; their alignment and interrelationships with the planning, leading, and control functions; and the complex trade-offs that must be considered in achieving a "fit" among these functions and other aspects of the organization. The new organization design of the IRS features a new divisional structure (organizing function) and much more. For example, the new IRS Strategic Plan articulates the organization's goals, with which every organizational component is aligned. The organizational planning process developed new formal procedures for each operating division, dedicated to soliciting "customer" input on strategies to improve tax administration by, for example, simplifying return filing and payments.

Another aspect of the new IRS design relieves employees of having to try to stay current with much of the complex, ever-changing tax law. They no longer have to be concerned with provisions that are not relevant to the particular issues for which their particular division is responsible. This change allows managers and employees in a division to focus on the issues that are most important to their group of taxpayers. For example, management and employees of the Wage and Investment Income Division, although responsible for serving 75 percent of all taxpayers, will generally not have to be concerned with 83 percent of the tax code that ordinarily does not apply to the taxpayers handled by that division.[2]

There are few hard and fast rules for designing or redesigning an organization. Organization design is often the result of many decisions and historical circumstances. It may reflect various combinations of thoughtful analyses, managerial biases, political considerations, preferences of powerful external stakeholders, and historical circumstances. In a sense, an organization's design acts both as a "harness" to guide employees in performing their diverse tasks, and as a means of aligning and coordinating their efforts to help ensure that they all "pull" in the same direction. In this chapter, we cover the fundamental concepts, principles, and options for creating an organization design to help ensure alignment among the organization's parts, functions, and processes to implement its strategies and achieve its goals.[3]

ELEMENTS OF ORGANIZING

The four basic elements of the organizing function are specialization, standardization, coordination, and authority.[4] As suggested in Figure 10.1, these elements are interrelated, although we discuss them separately for purposes of clarity.

Figure 10.1 **Basic Elements of Organizing**

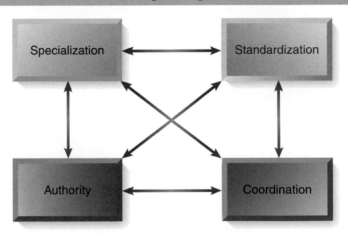

Specialization is the process of identifying particular tasks and assigning them to individuals, teams, departments, and divisions. For example, the Wage and Investment Income Division of the IRS specializes in serving the typical wage earner and having the relevant knowledge—tax laws, IRS regulations, court rulings, and the like—needed to do so. Within this division, there is further specialization in three major areas of taxpayer service. One of these areas involves the Customer Account Services (CAS) unit. It is responsible for taxpayer relationships having to do with filing; including processing submissions and payments; providing taxpayers with information on the status of their returns; and resolving errors; problems, and inconsistencies.[5]

Standardization is the process of developing uniform practices that employees are to follow in doing their jobs. These practices are intended to develop a certain amount of conformity and are expressed through written procedures, job descriptions, instructions, and rules relating to positions within the organization, performance of various tasks, and expected employee behaviors. Standardization permits managers to assess employee performance in relation to established responsibilities and performance indicators. Recruiting procedures, job descriptions, and application forms are used to standardize employee selection. On-the-job training programs develop standardized skills and reinforce values important to the organization's success. Although this process may seem mechanical, if jobs weren't standardized to some degree, many organizations couldn't achieve their goals.

Internal Revenue Service employees are expected to perform their jobs and demonstrate employee behaviors in certain standardized ways. The human resources (HR) and equal employment opportunity (EEO) units in the National Office Staff and the Office of Chief Counsel issue procedures and regulations that set standards for employees relative to their areas of specialization. For example, the Office of Chief Counsel issues regulations and legal interpretations for all IRS agents to follow uniformly. Even under its new organization design, standardization at the IRS is emphasized much more than in less mechanistic (bureaucratic) organizations. Recall the characteristics of bureaucratic organizations presented in Chapter 2: a formal system of rules (standardization), impersonality (standardization), and division of labor (specialization). In contrast, entrepreneurial firms are much less mechanistic than the IRS, UPS, and many other organizations. For example, Transmeta is a small entrepreneurial firm that makes microprocessors for mobile devices. It was founded in 1996, is headquartered in Santa Clara, California, and has 200 employees. Although it is entrepreneurial and therefore far from bureaucratic, even Transmeta has to rely on some specialization and standardization, especially in the manufacturing and quality control processes that production employees are expected to follow.[6]

Coordination involves the process and mechanisms used to integrate the tasks and activities of employees and organizational units. To some degree, virtually all organizations make use of rules, procedures, formal goals, and directions to help achieve the desired level of coordination. However, extra layers of management and the resulting additional personnel and amount of coordination required slow decision making and increase costs. Prior to reorganization of the IRS, eight intermediate levels of line and staff existed between a front-line employee and the deputy commissioner. Now there are typically only five levels.

The new organization design at the IRS substantially reduced the use of hierarchy to achieve coordination. The design significantly increases the use of direct two-way communication and decision making. Top management of the agency and each operating division consists of a set of teams, each of which is linked to the next level. For example, agency top management consists of the commissioner, deputy commissioners, key staff executives, and the heads of each operating division. The top management of each operating division consists of its head, deputy head, and its top four to six staff and line managers. In addition, many cross-unit councils and networks of individuals with special expertise have been created (e.g., human resources, finance, collections, examination, research, public affairs, etc.). This emphasis on teams facilitates the interchange of best practices and coordination.[7]

Authority is the right to make decisions of varying importance. For example, a first-level manager may have the authority to initiate an expenditure of up to $2,000 without prior review by the next level of management. In contrast, the president of the same organization may have the authority to initiate an expenditure of up to $100,000 without prior review and approval by the board of directors. Various organizations distribute authority differently. At 7-11 stores and other centralized organizations, a first-level manager may be required to obtain higher level approval before initiating an expenditure of even $2,000. At Johnson & Johnson and other highly decentralized organizations, a first-level manager may be given the authority to initiate expenditures of up to $10,000 and make job offers within certain guidelines without having to obtain prior higher level approvals.

Organizations may centralize certain functions and decentralize others. For example, on the one hand, the new organization design of the IRS centralized information system services. This realignment was made to provide more efficient, standardized, and compatible computer-based information services within and between units, as well as with taxpayers. Prior to the reorganization, the IRS used four separate and incompatible computer systems to collect taxes.[8] On the other hand, authority was largely decentralized to the four operating divisions, allowing them to make many types of decisions regarding implementation of laws and regulations for the classes of taxpayers they serve. Also, they were given more authority to make changes in procedures to serve those taxpayers better.

WEB INSIGHT

Review the organization chart for the U.S. Department of Justice. How many major subunits and levels are shown? Describe the specialized tasks and responsibilities for one of these subunits. Also click "text only version," go to *http://www.usdoj.gov/*, click "Organizations & Information" in the directory, and then click "Organization Chart."

ORGANIZATIONAL STRUCTURE

Organizational structure is the formal representation of working relationships that defines tasks by position and unit and indicates how they will be coordinated. An *organization chart* is a diagram that illustrates the relation of reporting relationships, functions, departments, divisions, and even individual positions within the organization. It is a "skeleton" representation of the organization's structure. Figure 10.2 shows the general organization chart for the IRS. Each of its operating divisions and other major units (e.g., Small Business and Self-Employed Division and Office of Chief Counsel) also has its own, more detailed organization chart.

Figure 10.2   **Portion of IRS Organizational Structure**

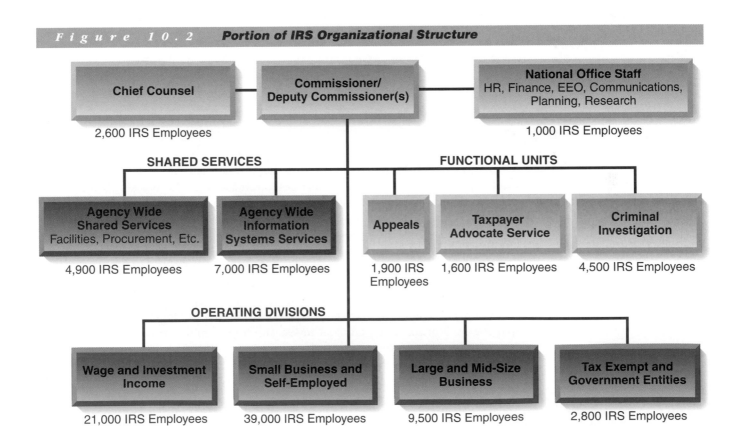

An organization chart provides four skeletal snapshots of an organization's structure.

- **Tasks.** The chart shows the range of tasks within the organization. As shown in Figure 10.2, tasks at the IRS range from information systems services to criminal investigation to serving large and mid-sized businesses.

Chapter 10 Fundamentals of Organization Design | **271**

- **Units.** Each box represents a unit, subunit, or position in the organization that is responsible for certain specialized tasks. The Taxpayer Advocate Service of the IRS shown in Figure 10.2 provides an independent system to ensure that tax problems that have not been resolved through normal channels are promptly and fairly handled.[9]

- **Levels of organization.** The chart may show the hierarchy from top management to entry-level employee, or it may show only the general outline of the hierarchy. Figure 10.2 shows only the major levels of the IRS hierarchy.

- **Lines of authority.** The solid lines connecting the boxes on the chart show which positions or units have authority over others. At the IRS, the Office of the Commissioner, which includes two deputy commissioners, has authority over all the operating divisions and other units. However, the operating divisions and other units have no authority over each other, as shown in Figure 10.2.

A potential benefit of an organization chart is that it provides some insight on how the pieces of the entire organization fit together. That is, it indicates how the various specialized functions performed relate to the whole. Thus everyone presumably knows who reports to whom and where to go with a particular problem. The chart also may help management detect gaps in authority or duplication of activities. A limitation of an organization chart is that it's just an idealized picture of the organization, sometimes without substantial validity. It simply can't show everything about an organization's structure or much about the way things often really get done. For example, it can't show who has the most political influence or how the vital informal channels of communication operate.

BASIC TYPES OF DEPARTMENTALIZATION

2.

OUTLINE THE FEATURES OF FOUR BASIC TYPES OF DEPARTMENTALIZATION.

Departmentalization subdivides work into jobs and tasks and assigns them to specialized units within an organization. It also includes devising standards for the performance of jobs and tasks. Departmentalization addresses two of the four basic elements of the organizing function: specialization and standardization. Management can use any of four basic types of departmentalization: by function, by place, by product, and by customer. Division of work is the first step in departmentalization. One key to effective departmentalization lies in organizing people, jobs, and tasks in such a way that decisions flow easily throughout the organization. Large, complex organizations, such as the IRS and GM actually use multiple forms of departmentalization to facilitate this flow and achieve their goals. As previously shown in Figure 10.2, the IRS is organized by function (e.g., criminal investigation and human resources), by product (e.g., agency wide information system services delivered to other IRS units), and by customer (i.e., the four operating divisions). Although not shown in Figure 10.2, the IRS is also organized by place (location) with its various field offices.

FUNCTIONAL DEPARTMENTALIZATION

Functional departmentalization groups employees into units according to their areas of expertise and the resources they draw on to perform a common set of tasks. Functional grouping is the most widely used and accepted form of departmentalization.[10] Recall that functions are the groups of activities that an organization performs (e.g., production, marketing, and finance). Functions vary widely, depending on the nature of the organization. For example, hospitals don't have production departments, but they do have functional units for admitting, emergency care, and surgery.

Grouping tasks and employees by function can be efficient and economical. It is particularly efficient for small organizations making a single product because it creates a clear hierarchy of authority and decision making. As suggested in Figure 10.3, functional departments may align naturally with key external stakeholders in the organization's environment. For example, finance specializes in dealing with creditors and debtors, purchasing with suppliers, marketing with current and prospective customers, and so on.

Figure 10.3   **Coping with Environmental Forces Through a Simple Functional Form of Organization**

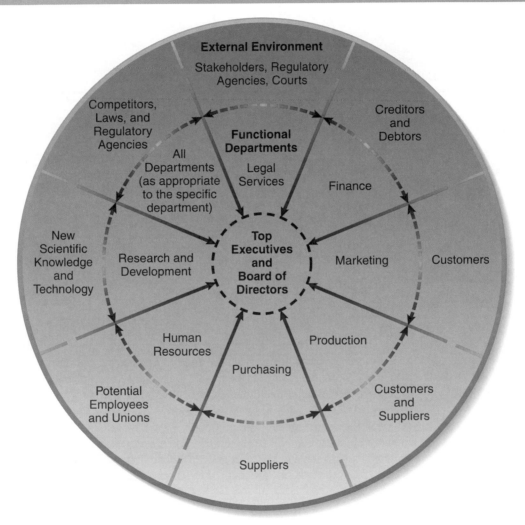

Large firms providing a single product and having customers with similar characteristics may also use functional departmentalization as their primary form of structure. Southwest Airlines is one organization that makes extensive use of this form of departmentalization, as shown in Figure 10.4.[11]

Potential Benefits. Departmentalization by function is economical because it results in a simple structure. It is often the best form for organizations that sell a narrow range

Figure 10.4   *Portion of Southwest Airlines' Organizational Structure*

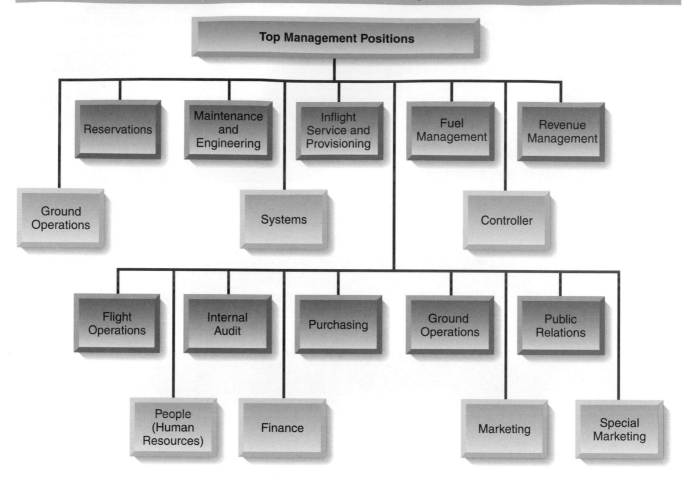

of goods and/or services mainly in one product and geographic market. Management creates one department for each primary function to be performed (e.g., production, marketing, and human resources). This structure keeps administrative expenses low because everyone in a department shares training, experience, and resources. Job satisfaction may increase if employees can improve their specialized skills by working with others in the same functional area. Employees can see clearly defined career paths within their own departments. As a result, the organization can more easily hire and promote employees who have or develop good problem-solving skills in each area of specialization. In brief, the potential benefits of functional departmentalization include

- supporting skill specialization,
- reducing duplication of resources and increasing coordination within the functional area,
- enhancing career development and training within the functional area,
- allowing superiors and subordinates to share common expertise, and
- promoting high-quality technical decision making.

Potential Pitfalls. The pitfalls of functional departmentalization become apparent when an organization provides highly diverse products (goods and/or services) or serves highly diverse customers. The problems with the previous use of functional departmentalization at the IRS finally became so great that they could no longer be ignored. Making decisions quickly becomes difficult when employees have to work their way through layers of structure for approvals. For example, a sales rep may lose a good account because she has to wait for the sales manager to get the production manager to make a scheduling decision. In addition, when there's friction between departments, managers have to spend time resolving the issues involved. Pinpointing the accountability and performance levels of employees who are performing separate functions may also be difficult. In other words, a top manager may not be able to determine easily which department—production, sales, or credit—is responsible for delays and declining profits.

Another pitfall is that top management may have a hard time coordinating the activities of employees in different departments. Moreover, functional departmentalization tends to de-emphasize the overall goals of the organization, with employees often focusing on departmental goals (e.g., meeting their own budgets and schedules). In brief, the potential pitfalls of functional departmentalization include

- inadequate communication between departments,
- conflicts over product priorities,
- difficulties with interdepartmental coordination,
- focus on departmental rather than organizational issues and goals, and
- development of managers who are experts only in narrow fields.

PLACE DEPARTMENTALIZATION

Place departmentalization groups most or all functions involving customers within a specific geographic area under one manager, rather than dividing functions among different managers or grouping all tasks in one central location. It is commonly used by organizations with large numbers of customers or key sources of raw materials in different locations. Many large companies, including Merrill Lynch, Caterpillar, and State Farm Insurance, use regional and district offices in addition to their functional units. Similarly, government agencies such as the IRS, Federal Reserve Board (12 regional banks), and the U.S. Postal Service use place departmentalization to provide direct services to their customers. For example, the Wage and Investment Division of the IRS, in addition to its headquarters office in Atlanta, Georgia, has regional offices in Buffalo, New York; Indianapolis, Indiana; St. Louis, Missouri; Greensboro, North Carolina; New Orleans, Louisiana; and the San Francisco Bay area, California, as well as smaller field offices throughout the country. Multinational firms often use this form of departmentalization to address cultural and legal differences, as well as other differences among geographic markets, in various countries.[12]

The following Planning and Administration Competency feature focuses on how Starbucks is organized to help implement its strategies.[13] As suggested in Figure 10.5, Starbucks makes extensive use of both place and functional departmentalization.

WEB INSIGHT

How is the Wage and Investment Income Division of the IRS organized? Read the description of the units in this division at *http://www.irs.ustreas.gov/news/wage-invest.html*.

PLANNING & ADMINISTRATION COMPETENCY

Starbucks' Organizational Structure

Starbucks CEO Howard Schultz and his top management team crafted a business strategy that enabled the company to become the largest specialty coffee retailer and roaster in the world. Headquartered in Seattle, Washington, Starbucks has annual sales of approximately $2 billion, 27,000 employees, and about 2,600 retail locations in North America, the United Kingdom, the Pacific Rim, and the Middle East. By far, the largest number is in continental North America—about 2,100 locations. However, the company is rapidly opening new retail locations throughout the world. In addition to coffee and espresso beverages, Starbucks sells a variety of pastries and confections, coffee-related accessories and equipment, and a line of premium teas in its stores. Top management stays abreast of the actions of competitors and has formed strategic partnerships (another dimension of organization design) with other firms. For example, Starbucks coffee is now served on all United Airlines flights. ITT Sheraton Hotels has its own catalogue of Starbucks products, offering shoppers espresso and cappuccino makers, cups, and related products.

Starbucks is vertically integrated and controls its coffee sources, roasting, and retail sales to ensure adherence to its strict standards. Figure 10.5 shows a portion of Starbucks' organizational structure, with examples of units organized by place and units organized by function. Three presidents and three executive vice presidents report directly to the CEO. In addition, but not shown, are senior vice presidents for various functions, including new business development, retail marketing and product development, law and corporate affairs, and communications and public areas.

For example, to ensure consistent customer service in all locations under the Retail North America unit, seven district managers (Southwest, East Coast, Canada, etc.) report to the president, Retail North America. The district managers implement operating guidelines, ranging from roasting practices to sales training. They are accountable for the specific operations and profitability of the stores in their areas. The district managers are involved in decisions regarding store locations, staffing and compensation, sales, store operations, and all other functions related to a store's profitability. They also are responsible for seeing that each new employee receives at least 25 hours of formal training. This training covers customer service, cash register operation, coffee brewing methods, and how to scoop coffee beans correctly.

Figure 10.5 also shows the use of place departmentalization for Starbucks Coffee International, Inc., which

is headed by a president. Reporting to the president are two corporate senior vice presidents (and presidents) of the UK and Asia Pacific units, respectively.

• • •

To learn more about Starbucks, visit the company's home page at

http://www.starbucks.com

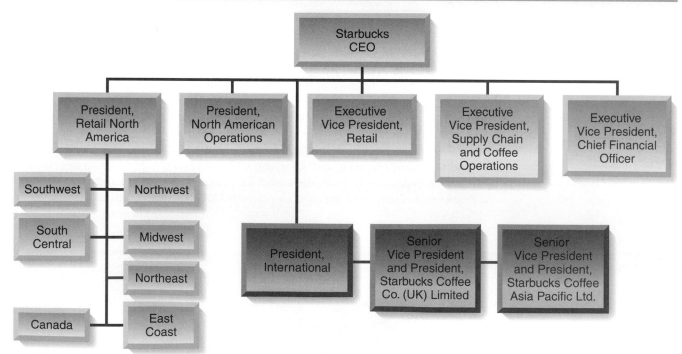

Figure 10.5   **Portion of Starbucks' Organizational Structure**

Starbucks CEO

- President, Retail North America
  - Southwest
  - South Central
  - Northwest
  - Midwest
  - Northeast
  - Canada
  - East Coast
- President, North American Operations
- Executive Vice President, Retail
  - President, International
  - Senior Vice President and President, Starbucks Coffee Co. (UK) Limited
  - Senior Vice President and President, Starbucks Coffee Asia Pacific Ltd.
- Executive Vice President, Supply Chain and Coffee Operations
- Executive Vice President, Chief Financial Officer

Potential Benefits. Place departmentalization allows an organization to focus on customer needs within a relatively small geographic area and to minimize the costs associated with transportation of goods or services. In brief, the potential benefits of place departmentalization include

- having facilities and the equipment used for production and/or distribution all in one place, saving time and costs;
- being able to develop expertise in solving problems unique to one location;
- gaining an understanding of customers' problems and desires; and
- getting production closer to raw materials and suppliers.

Potential Pitfalls. Organizing by location typically increases problems of control and coordination for top management. To ensure uniformity and coordination, organizations that use place departmentalization, such as Starbucks and the IRS, make extensive use of rules that apply to all locations. One reason for doing so is to guarantee a standard level of quality regardless of location, which would be difficult if units in various locations went their own separate ways. In brief, the potential pitfalls of place departmentalization include

- duplication of functions, to varying degrees, at each regional or individual unit location;
- conflict between each location's goals and organization goals; and
- added levels of management and extensive use of rules and regulations to coordinate and ensure uniformity of quality among locations.

PRODUCT DEPARTMENTALIZATION

Product departmentalization groups most or all functions into relatively self-contained units. Each unit may even have the full capability of designing, producing, and marketing its own goods and/or services. In their most developed form, these units are often called strategic business units (SBUs) or divisions. (See our discussion of SBUs in Chapter 7.) In a less developed form, product managers may be given full responsibility for the marketing and sale of their products. However, these product units rely on traditional functional units such as production (for manufacturing goods), finance (for approving credit and collecting debts), human resources (for recruiting personnel and setting personnel policies), and so on.

This form of organization is often adopted after the number and types of customers mushroom and the range of goods and services provided becomes too great for the efficient and effective handling of demands through only functional and/or place departmentalization.

WEB INSIGHT

Read the letter to investors in the most recent annual report for The Associates. Does its organizational structure appear to support the strategic issues discussed in the annual report? Find this annual report at *http://investor.theassociates.com*.

As indicated in Figure 10.6, the Associates First Capital Corporation (The Associates) makes extensive use of product and functional departmentalization.[14] The Associates is a large (some 33,000 employees), diversified financial services SBU of Citigroup. It provides finance, leasing, insurance, and related services to individual consumers and businesses in the United States and internationally. Examples of the unit's lines of business, including insurance, home equity, and U.S. consumer operations are shown in Figure 10.6. Each line of business provides a variety of financial services. For example, commercial operations include the financing and leasing of transportation, industrial, and communications equipment, auto fleet leasing, warehouse lending, municipal finance, and so on.

Potential Benefits. This form of organization enables managers and employees to become specialized and expert in a particular product (good or service) line. This benefit lessens only as the number and diversity of products provided by an organization increase. Management also can pinpoint costs, profits, problems, and successes accurately for each product line. In brief, the potential benefits of product departmentalization include

- permitting fast changes in a product line,
- allowing greater product line visibility,
- fostering a concern for customer demands,
- clearly defining responsibilities for each product line, and
- developing managers who can think across functional lines.

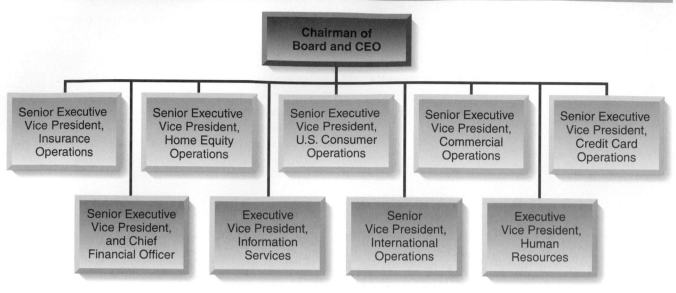

*Acquired by Citigroup in late 2000 and became a strategic business unit of that firm.

Potential Pitfalls. Because some or many functions are duplicated for each product line, resource utilization may be relatively inefficient. In addition, products with seasonal highs and lows in sales volumes may result in higher personnel costs. Coordination across product lines usually is difficult. Employees tend to focus on the goals for their particular products, rather than on broader company goals. This situation may create unhealthy competition within an organization for scarce resources. In brief, the potential pitfalls for product departmentalization include

- not allowing efficient utilization of skills and resources,
- not fostering coordination of activities across product lines,
- encouraging politics and conflicts in resource allocation across product lines, and
- limiting career mobility for personnel outside their own product lines.

CUSTOMER DEPARTMENTALIZATION

Customer departmentalization involves organizing around the types of customers being served. It is used when management wants to focus more on the customer's requirements than on the organization's skills (functional) or the brands it produces and sells (goods and services). It can also be used in combination with one or more of the other forms of departmentalization. That may often be the case in extremely large and complex organizations such as the IRS, which is organized to serve four main types of customers, and Ford Motor Company. In the increasingly service-oriented U.S. economy, the customer form of departmentalization is becoming increasingly common. Customer departmentalization is generally used to differentiate products and offer different terms to different customers (e.g., production of different models and volume discounts to large customers and nonprofit customers). This form of departmentalization indicates that management is sensitive to the needs of each customer group and that it has identified groups that have substantial sales potential.[15]

The following Strategic Action Competency feature describes Novell's recent reorganization based on customer departmentalization.[16] Headquartered in Provo, Utah, Novell is a major provider of software services to power and make secure all types of networks—the Internet, intranets, and extranets; wired to wireless; corporate and public—on all the leading computer operating systems. Novell's software provides the foundation for a single global network that supports numerous applications and forms of business. Novell has approximately 5,400 employees and $1.3 billion in annual revenues.

Novell had been experiencing problems with sales, profits, and customer service. In May 2000, Novell's management announced changes aimed at moving the company from a product to a market-driven (customer-driven) organization and sharpening the company's focus on new market opportunities. Novell now consists of four business groups (divisions), each of which has its own strategic focus and go-to-market strategy, including target markets and channels of distribution. These groups are depicted in Figure 10.7. In announcing this new organization design, Eric Schmidt, chairman and CEO, commented: "Our customers are at different stages in deploying their Internet strategies, and we recognize the need to focus our efforts around making the Net work for them regardless of where they are in that implementation. We're making these changes to align our business so that we can win in a dynamic and demanding marketplace. Ultimately, these actions will strengthen Novell's ability to deliver Net services software to customers including small to large enterprises, service providers, and dotcoms."

The four new business units are designed to provide market-driven technologies and services best suited to compete in their respective categories. In brief, these business groups are as follows.

- *Net Management*—this group focuses on providing solutions for existing and new enterprise customers and growing business around established product lines, including NetWare, GroupWise, BorderManager, and ZENworks.
- *Net Directory*—this group focuses on achieving directory service everywhere all the time with the goal being to provide directory "dialtone" for the Net. The group develops and delivers customer-driven software built on an NDS eDirectory such as DirXML, Single Sign On, and eGuide. Markets include both large enterprise customers and dotcoms.
- *Net Content*—this group focuses on content services including Novell's Internet Caching System (ICS) and other content distribution technologies currently under development. This group targets high-end Web hosters and other service providers, with the ultimate consumers being dotcom and eBusiness enterprises.
- *Novell Customer Services*—this group comprises consulting, education, and technical support services that maximize the business value of Novell's Net Management, Net Directory, and Net Content groups.

Whether this new organization design will be effective in supporting Novell's new strategies remains to be seen.

• • •

To learn more about Novell, visit the company's home page at

http://www.novell.com

Figure 10.7   **Portion of Novell's Organizational Structure**

Potential Benefits. This form allows the organization to focus more sharply on different types of customers' needs. In brief, the potential benefits of customer departmentalization include

- encouraging greater customer focus,
- clearly identifying key customers,
- enabling understanding of customer needs, and
- developing managers and employees who become customer advocates.

Potential Pitfalls. Customer departmentalization may lead to pressure on an organization to meet too many specialized customer demands. The result could be increased costs and substantially reduced profits. In brief, the potential pitfalls of customer departmentalization include

- not fostering coordination between divisions organized by customer group,
- encouraging politics and conflicts in resource allocation between divisions,
- making employees feel pressure from some customers to give them privileges not accorded others, and
- restricting problem solving to each group of customers.

SELECTING AN ORGANIZATIONAL STRUCTURE

No single type of departmentalization—functional, place, product, or customer—is best in all circumstances. Managers must select the structure that matches the organization's specific goals and needs.[17] Table 10.1 lists characteristics that can help managers decide which form of departmentalization to use in their particular situations. Clearly, the choice of structural pattern depends on a careful diagnosis of multiple strategic and environmental factors. Throughout our presentation, we have noted how two or more forms of departmentalization are often used in large and complex organizations.

Table 10.1	**Organizational Characteristics and Type of Departmentalization**
Organizational Characteristics	**Type of Departmentalization Favored**
Small size	Functional
Global or national scope	Place
Depends on customer needs	Customer
Essential to use scarce resources appropriately	Customer
Customer base is	
Diverse	Product
Stable	Functional or customer
Makes use of specialized equipment	Product
Requires skill specialization	Functional
High transportation costs for raw materials	Place or customer

COORDINATION

3.

DESCRIBE THREE OF THE PRINCIPLES FOR ACHIEVING COORDINATION WITHIN AND BETWEEN DEPARTMENTS.

As noted previously, *departmentalization* divides the organization's work and allows for specialization and standardization of jobs and tasks. However, to achieve organizational goals, employees, projects, and tasks have to be coordinated. Without it, employees' efforts are likely to result in delay, frustration, and waste. As shown previously in Figure 10.1, coordination is one of the basic elements of organizing.

Many managers believe that good people can make any organization design work. Although such managers may be overstating the case, employees who work well together are extremely valuable assets. A good analogy is basketball, where teamwork is essential. During practice sessions, coaches try to transform the individual players into one smoothly functioning team. Players learn their functions—guards, forwards, center—as part of a cooperative effort, see how each task relates to every other task, and relate these tasks to the whole. Coordination is required as the players execute their functions, particularly when they are called on to make adjustments in a game situation.

In this section, we present three traditional principles of coordination: the unity of command principle, the scalar principle, and the span of control principle. All are directly related to the planning and administration competency.

UNITY OF COMMAND PRINCIPLE

The **unity of command principle** states that an employee should have only one manager. Employees are supposed to know who is giving them directions and to whom they report. According to this principle, managers must minimize any confusion over who makes decisions and who implements them because uncertainty in this area can lead to ineffectiveness and morale problems.

SCALAR PRINCIPLE

The **scalar principle** states that a clear, unbroken chain of command should link every employee with someone at a higher level, all the way to the top of the organization. Tasks should be delegated clearly, with minimal overlapping or splitting of assignments.

If followed rigidly, the scalar principle would require that all job-related communications between employees in different product departments at the same level (e.g., Southwest regional manager and Northwest regional manager at Starbucks) be approved by their superior. Obviously, strict adherence to this principle would waste time and money—and be extremely frustrating. In practice, teams, committees, and informal communications across departmental lines facilitate problem solving and communication within the organization.

SPAN OF CONTROL PRINCIPLE

The **span of control principle** suggests that the number of people reporting directly to any one manager be limited because one manager can't effectively supervise a large number of subordinates. Span of control is a concept as old as organizations. In fact, it began with Roman military commanders' belief that narrow spans of control were effective in combat. The traditional viewpoint of management (Chapter 2) holds that the ideal number of subordinates reporting to any one manager should be no fewer than 4 and no more than 12.

Many organizations (including the IRS and Novell) are flattening their structures by reducing the number of management layers between the CEO and front-line employees. This approach broadens the span of control, with a greater number of employees reporting to each manager. Although there is no "correct" number of subordinates that a manager can supervise effectively, let's consider four of the key factors that may influence the span of control in any situation.

1. *The competence of both the manager and the employee.* If managers and/or employees are new to a task, they require more supervision than knowledgeable veteran managers and employees do.

2. *The similarity or dissimilarity of tasks being supervised.* At Starbucks, the span of control in the retail store area is broad because all managers can focus on one product: coffee and its accessories. The more numerous and dissimilar the products, the narrower the span of control should be.

3. *The incidence of new problems in the manager's department.* A manager should know enough about the operations of the department to understand precisely the problems that subordinates are likely to face. The more the manager knows about these factors, the broader the span of control can be.

4. *The extent of clear operating standards and rules.* Clear rules and standard operating procedures (SOPs) leave little to chance and lessen the need for adaptive decisions. At the local postal office, extensive rules govern the tasks and behaviors of employees. The greater the reliance on rules and SOPs, the broader the span of control may be because the rules do part of the controlling.[18]

COORDINATION AND DEPARTMENTALIZATION

In any organization, tension exists between coordination and departmentalization. When forces for organizationwide coordination are stronger than those for departmental autonomy, functional departmentalization may work best. Southwest Airlines (see Figure 10.4) has kept pace with the changing needs of the passengers it attempts to appeal to by using functional departmentalization. When a nonroutine problem arises, higher level managers and various teams quickly coordinate the actions of functional departments (e.g., reservations, flight operations, ground operations, and so on) to find a solution. Under such conditions, functional departmentalization may help ensure the degree of organizationwide coordination needed.

When forces for coordination and departmental autonomy are equal, a customer form of departmentalization may work best. The customer structure addresses the conflict between, say, the product manager's need to satisfy a customer and the functional department's need to provide technical help. Although not shown in Figure 10.7, Novell has both product and functional units within and under its new customer groups.

When forces for departmental autonomy are stronger than those for coordination, place or product departmentalization may work best. These units decide what is appropriate for only their market area or product, without having to focus on the impact of their decisions on other areas or product lines.

As noted previously, large and complex organizations (e.g., IRS, The Associates, Starbucks, and Novell) typically make use of two or more forms of departmentalization. In addition to the traditional forms of coordination, organizations are increasingly using various types of teams, committees, and task forces to facilitate coordination. The following Teamwork Competency feature reports on the use of teams as a means of coordination and decision making at the Cobra Metal Works, which is headquartered in Franklin Park, Illinois. Cobra develops and uses innovative approaches to machining airbag components.[19]

TEAMWORK COMPETENCY

Cobra's Team Coordination

Antoni Hirsch, who had spent 20 years in the contract machining business, established Cobra in 1997. He recognized that there were opportunities for someone who had an understanding of tooling, setups, and machining to carve out a niche by producing the highest quality airbag components. At Cobra, his management team consists of the quality, production, and purchasing department managers (functional departmentalization).

Cobra annually produces 1 to 1.5 million parts and operates 24 hours per day, 6 days per week. Teams on the factory floor run the jobs, following procedures that are clearly documented. The shop floor teams are encouraged to find better ways of processing parts. Whenever one of the teams believes that it has identified a process improvement, the team presents the idea to another team consisting of both management and shop floor employees

to determine whether the process should be modified. For example, changes to process sheets can't be made without approval by a team. "There may be eight machines running one part; the parts have to be produced identically," Hirsch says. He notes that if one person thought that he had a better way of doing something and simply made a change to the process, there would be no assured way of capturing this change. Consequently, inconsistencies

---

in parts would begin to appear—something that Cobra can't afford.

An interesting point about Cobra is that the company became QS9000 certified (total quality certification program) after its first year in business. "I wanted to get it right away," Hirsch says, explaining that he felt it important for the company to grow with quality procedures in place rather than adding them later. These procedures help ensure consistency (including high quality standards and tight coordination), which is certainly important in machining airbag components. To help ensure that the employees understand the importance of making good parts all the time, Hirsch makes the message quite simple: "We tell them if they don't make bad parts, the company makes more money; if the quality requirements are met [they chart and post internal reports and customer rejects so that everyone knows quality results in real time], then all of the employees receive quarterly bonuses. Good parts mean more money for one and all."

AUTHORITY

4.

DISCUSS THE
FUNDAMENTAL CONCEPTS
OF AUTHORITY IN
ORGANIZATION DESIGN.

Authority, the fourth basic element of organizing, is the right to make a decision and act. Authority is exercised, for instance, when a board of directors authorizes a bond issue to raise capital, when an executive approves a new advertising campaign, when a sales manager signs a contract with a client, when a production manager promotes an employee to first-line manager, when a manager fires someone, and when a self-managing team manages its work schedule. In short, authority is the glue of organization design.

In Chapter 2, we noted that Chester Bernard, president of New Jersey Bell Telephone Company from 1927 to 1948, held a somewhat different view of authority.[20] He maintained that authority flows from the bottom up, rather than from the top down. This view is known as the *acceptance theory of authority*. Bernard didn't think that an employee should analyze and judge every decision made by an immediate superior before either accepting or rejecting it. Rather, he thought that most decisions or orders fall within the subordinate's *zone of indifference,* which means that the subordinate will accept or obey them without serious question. If a decision or directive falls outside that zone, however, the subordinate may question whether to accept or reject it.

WEB INSIGHT

The Association for the Management of Organization Design is a professional organization formed to promote the knowledge and practice of organization design. Visit its home page at *http://www.amod2000.org* and click "Newsletter." What did you learn about organization design by reading one of its newsletters?

Authority implies both responsibility and accountability. That is, by exercising authority, employees accept the responsibility for acting and are willing to be held accountable for success or failure. When delegating tasks to others, managers should take care to match the responsibility they confer with authority and then insist on accountability for results.

RESPONSIBILITY

Responsibility is an employee's obligation to perform assigned tasks. The employee acquires this obligation upon accepting a job or a specific assignment. A manager is responsible not only for carrying out certain tasks but also for the actions of subordinates. At times, formal responsibilities may be assigned not just to a single individual but to a group, such as a board of directors, committee, or team. For example, in the new organization design for the IRS, federal legislation established a nine-member Oversight Board with specific responsibilities (and related accountability) to

- review and to approve annual and long-term strategic IRS plans;
- recommend candidates for commissioner and to review the commissioner's selection, evaluation, and compensation of senior IRS management;

- review and to approve the commissioner's plans for any major IRS reorganization; and

- review, approve, and submit to the secretary of the treasury the IRS budget prepared by the commissioner.[21]

ACCOUNTABILITY

Accountability is the expectation that employees will accept credit or blame for their performance. No manager can check everything an employee does. Therefore management normally establishes guidelines and performance standards within which responsibilities are to be carried out. This process may be undertaken in consultation with the employees who are being held accountable for those responsibilities.

Accountability flows from the bottom up. The news assistant of a newspaper is accountable to the senior reporter, the senior reporter is accountable to the editor, and the editor is accountable to the publisher. Accountability is the point at which authority and responsibility meet and is essential for effective performance. When either authority or responsibility are lacking, managers cannot judge a subordinate's accomplishments fairly. And when managers are reluctant to hold subordinates accountable for their tasks, subordinates can easily pass the buck for nonperformance. In the case of boards, committees, and teams, the judgments and assessments may fall on the group as a whole, rather than on just one of its members.

DELEGATION

Delegation is the process of giving authority to a person (or group) to make decisions and act in certain situations. Thus, in addition to holding an employee accountable for the performance of defined responsibilities, the manager gives the employee the authority to carry out the responsibilities effectively. Delegation starts when the structure of the organization is being established and work is divided. It continues as new jobs and tasks are added during day-to-day operations. Delegation should occur in conjunction with the assignment of responsibilities, as when a company president assigns to an executive assistant the task of preparing a formal statement for presentation to a congressional committee or when the head of a computer department instructs a programmer to debug a new management reporting system. In each case, the manager is giving authority to a subordinate.

Effective Delegation. The following practices are useful for achieving effective delegation.

1. *Establish goals and standards.* Individuals or teams should participate in developing the goals that they will be expected to meet. Ideally, they should also agree to the standards that will be used to measure their performance.

2. *Ensure clarity.* Individuals or teams should clearly understand the work delegated to them, recognize the scope of their authority, and accept their accountability for results.

3. *Involvement.* The challenge of the work itself won't always encourage individuals or groups to accept and perform delegated tasks well. Managers can motivate them by involving them in decision making, by keeping them informed, and by helping them improve their skills and abilities.

4. *Expect completed work.* Individuals or teams should be expected to carry a task through to completion. The manager's job is to provide guidance, help, and information—not to finish the task.

5. *Provide training.* Delegation can be only as effective as the ability of people to make the decisions necessary to perform the work and then actually to do the work. Managers should continually appraise delegated responsibilities and provide training aimed at building on strengths and overcoming deficiencies.

6. *Timely feedback.* Timely, accurate feedback should be provided to individuals or teams so that they may compare their performance to stated expectations and correct any deficiencies.[22]

Barriers to Delegation. Delegation can only be as effective as the ability of managers to delegate.[23] The greatest psychological barrier to delegation is fear. A manager may be afraid that, if subordinates don't do the job properly, the manager's own reputation will suffer. Such a manager may rationalize: "I can do it better myself." or "My subordinates aren't capable enough." or "It takes too much time to explain what I want done." In addition, some managers also may be reluctant to delegate because they fear that subordinates will do the work their own way, do it too well, and outshine the boss!

Among the organizational barriers that may block delegation is a failure to define authority and responsibility clearly. If managers themselves don't know what is expected or what to do, they can't properly delegate authority and responsibility to others.

The six practices for achieving effective delegation that we presented earlier provide a strong foundation for reducing barriers to delegation. In addition, managers need to accept that there are several ways to deal with problems and that their own ways of solving them aren't necessarily those that their subordinates will choose. Employees will make mistakes, but, whenever possible, they should be allowed to develop their own solutions to problems and learn from their mistakes.

CENTRALIZATION AND DECENTRALIZATION

Centralization and decentralization of authority are basic, overall management philosophies of delegation, that is, of where decisions are to be made. *Centralization* is the concentration of authority at the top of an organization or department. *Decentralization* is dispersal of a high degree of authority to lower levels of an organization or department. Decentralization is an approach that requires managers to decide what and when to delegate, to select and train personnel carefully, and to formulate adequate controls.

No Absolutes. Neither centralization nor decentralization is absolute in an organization. No one manager makes all the decisions, even in a highly centralized setting. Total delegation would end the need for middle and first-line managers. Thus there are only degrees of centralization and decentralization. In most organizations, some tasks are relatively centralized (e.g., payroll systems, purchasing, and human resource policies), and others are relatively decentralized (e.g., marketing and production).

Potential benefits to decentralization include the following.

1. It frees top managers to develop organizational plans and strategies. Lower level managers and employees handle routine, day-to-day decisions.

2. It develops lower level managers' self-management and planning and administration competencies.

3. Because subordinates often are closer to the action than higher level managers, they may have a better grasp of all the facts. This knowledge may enable them to make sound decisions quickly. Valuable time can be lost when a subordinate or team must check everything with a manager.

4. It fosters a healthy, achievement-oriented atmosphere among employees.

Key Factors. A variety of factors can affect management's decisions to centralize or decentralize authority in various areas of decision making. We briefly consider five of these factors.

- *Cost of Decisions.* Cost is perhaps the most important factor in determining the extent of centralization. As a general rule, the more costly the outcome, the more likely top management will make the final decision.

- *Uniformity of Policy.* Managers who value consistency favor centralization of authority. These managers may want to assure customers that everyone is treated equally in terms of quality, price, credit, delivery, and service. At Home Depot, for example, a nationwide home improvement sales promotion on paint requires that all stores charge the same price. Uniform policies have definite advantages for cost accounting, production, and financial departments. They also enable managers to compare the relative efficiencies of various departments. In organizations with unions, such as Ford and United Airlines, uniform policies also aid in the administration of labor agreements regarding wages, promotions, fringe benefits, and other personnel matters.

- *Competency Levels.* Many organizations work hard to ensure an adequate supply of competent managers and employees—an absolute necessity for decentralization. Lockheed Martin and Lucent Technologies, among others, believe that extensive training and practical experiences are essential to developing the competencies needed at lower levels. Also, they are willing to permit employees to make mistakes involving small costs so as to learn from them.

- *Control Mechanisms.* Even the most avid proponents of decentralization, such as DuPont, Cisco, and Marriott, insist on controls and procedures to avoid mistakes and to determine whether actual events are meeting expectations. For example, each hotel in the Marriott chain collects certain key data, including number of beds occupied, employee turnover, number of meals served, and the average amount that guests spend on food and beverages. Analysis of the data helps each manager control important aspects of the hotel's operation and compare it against the performance of others in the chain. If a hotel's operations don't fall within certain guidelines, top management may step in to diagnose the situation.[24]

- *Environmental Influences.* External factors (e.g., unions, federal and state regulatory agencies, and tax policies) affect the degree of centralization in an organization. For example, laws and government regulations regarding hours, wages, working conditions, and safety make it difficult to decentralize authority in those areas.

The following Self-Management Competency feature describes how Tom Siebel, founder and CEO of Siebel Systems, uses centralization.[25] His high levels of personal drive and self-awareness enable centralization in this stage of the development at Siebel Systems to work. Headquartered in San Mateo, California, Siebel Systems is a major provider of eBusiness application software. It has more than 5,200 employees, with operations in 28 countries and 100 offices around the world. The centralization of decision making at Siebel Systems appears to be primarily driven by Siebel's need for personal control and desire to provide maximum service to customers.

SELF-MANAGEMENT COMPETENCY

Tom Siebel

One afternoon Tom Siebel, CEO of Siebel Systems, was sitting in the offices of a big customer in New York City when he discovered a problem. The customer had bought millions of dollars' worth of Siebel's eBusiness software but was having trouble installing it. As soon as he got back to his San Mateo, California, headquarters, he dispatched a trusted senior executive to fly to New York and stay until the problem was solved to the customer's satisfaction. At least that's what Siebel thought would happen. But several days later when he walked into the conference room adjacent to his office for the company's regular Monday morning management meeting, Siebel was surprised to find the executive sitting there calmly drinking her coffee. She explained that instead of going to New York, she'd conducted a conference call with the customer and other Siebel employees and had sent one of her people to New York. Siebel grew red-faced and stated his disapproval: "I told you to go to New York and deal with it, not set up a conference call and delegate it." Siebel then excused the executive from the meeting so that she could book her flight.

Siebel asserts: "Running a business is a fundamentally rational process. We unemotionally put things on the table, look each other straight in the eye, and state the facts." If employees are offended by this management style, they're probably not right for Siebel Systems. Employees who perform are rewarded; those who don't are dismissed. Within each department, the performance of nearly everyone at Siebel is ranked (high to low). Every 6 months Siebel lops off the bottom 5 percent. He is intense, competitive, and driven.

Siebel set out to create a company of lock-step uniformity where the rules matter more than who is in charge. Nothing is too insignificant to merit a rule. So he decreed that every one of Siebel's 100 offices around the world have medium-blue carpeting and off-white walls. All desktops will be gray, the furniture honey maple, and the cubicle-to-office ratio 4 to1. When you

walk around Siebel Systems' headquarters in San Mateo, no matter what day of the week or which big customer is demanding a project that afternoon, the offices will be neat and orderly. No pizza boxes or Coke cans will be lying around because Siebel forbids employees to eat at their desks. It's not professional. Also not viewed as professional are employees playing foosball or assaulting each other with Nerf guns. There are no weekly beer busts or spontaneous parties involving tequila drinks. Office and cubicle décor is not subject to personal inspiration. Cartoons on your door or large Limp Bizkit posters are not allowed.

Siebel devised a system that both measures his employees' responsiveness to customers and encourages their ongoing solicitude. Every 6 months a Palo Alto firm, Prognostics, collects data from between 400 and 500 of Siebel's 2,500 customers and reports in detail how satisfied they are with specific departments and individuals. The

results are used to help decide how much Siebel employees will make in bonuses and commissions. Sales reps, for instance, don't get their full commissions until a year after sales—and then only if their scores are up to par.

• • •

To learn more about Siebel Systems, visit this company's home page at

http://www.siebel.com

LINE AND STAFF AUTHORITY

Line authority belongs to managers who have the right to direct and control the activities of employees who perform tasks essential to achieving organizational goals. Line authority thus flows down the organization through the primary chain of command, according to the scalar principle. In contrast, ***staff authority*** belongs to those who support line functions through advice, recommendations, research, technical expertise, and specialized services. For some issues, staff units may be given command or approval authority over line units. For example, a marketing department (line unit), might have to adhere to the mandates of human resources (staff unit) on how annual performance reviews are to be conducted. As previously shown in Figure 10.2, the IRS has national staff departments for human resources, finance, equal employment opportunity, communications, planning, and research, which together have some 1,000 employees. The directors of these departments report to the commissioner or a deputy commissioner. If staff services are used extensively throughout an organization, staff departments may need to be located relatively high in the hierarchy. In fact, most large and complex organizations—such as the IRS, The Associates, Southwest Airlines, and Novell—centralize general staff functions at the top. If a staff department provides necessary services to a specific line function, it should be located near that function, both physically and in terms of managerial authority. A staff specialist who performs some support functions that a line manager would otherwise have to perform usually reports directly to that line manager.

CHAPTER SUMMARY

In this chapter we focused primarily on fundamental concepts and ways of designing organizations. We build on these concepts and approaches in Chapter 11 to address the additional complexities in organization design due to (1) increasing levels of global activities, (2) the need to incorporate and use the explosion in information technologies, (3) the requirement for anticipating and responding to faster rates of environmental change, and (4) the need to be responsive to new employee expectations.

1. EXPLAIN SEVERAL OF THE MAIN INGREDIENTS OF ORGANIZATION DESIGN.

The four basic elements of organizing are (1) specialization—the process of identifying tasks and assigning them to individuals or teams trained specifically to perform them; (2) standardization—the process of developing procedures by which the organization promotes uniform and consistent performance; (3) coordination—the process of integrating tasks performed by separate individuals and groups; (4) and authority—the right to make decisions and take action. An organization chart provides a skeleton depiction of the interrelationships among these four elements.

2. OUTLINE THE FEATURES OF FOUR BASIC TYPES OF DEPARTMENTALIZATION.

The four primary types of departmentalization are (1) functional departmentalization—groups employees according to common tasks to be performed; (2) place departmentalization—groups functions and employees by geographic location; (3) product (goods or services) departmentalization—groups employees in self-contained units, each responsible for its own goods or services; and (4) customer departmentalization—groups employees to focus on specific customer needs.

3. DESCRIBE THREE OF THE PRINCIPLES FOR ACHIEVING COORDINATION WITHIN AND BETWEEN DEPARTMENTS.

Three basic principles may be used in coordinating employee activities: (1) the unity of command principle—holds that each employee should report to only one manager; (2) the scalar principle—holds that a clear unbroken chain of command should link every person in the organization with his or her superior; and (3) the span of control principle—holds that the number of subordinates who report directly to a particular manager should be limited.

4. DISCUSS THE FUNDAMENTAL CONCEPTS OF AUTHORITY IN ORGANIZATION DESIGN.

Authority is the fourth basic element of organizing. Three key concepts are central to this element: (1) responsibility—the obligation to perform assigned tasks; (2) accountability—the expectations that each employee (or team) will accept credit or blame for the results of his or her performance; and (3) delegation—the process of giving authority to a person (or group) to make decisions and act in certain situatins. Delegation is the assignment of authority to employees. Key management decisions must be made regarding the degree of centralization and decentralization of authority to various levels, units, and positions in the organization. Five of the factors that affect this decision are (1) cost, (2) uniformity of policy, (3) availability of talented employees and managers, (4) control mechanisms, and (5) environmental influences. The distribution of authority among units often varies by line and staff distinctions. Line authority normally flows down through the primary chain of command, according to the scalar principle, and is held by managers whose activities are central to achieving organizational goals. Staff authority is typically held by managers whose units support line activities by providing specialized information and services.

KEY TERMS

Accountability, p. 284
Authority, p. 270
Centralization, p. 285
Coordination, p. 270
Customer departmentalization, p. 278
Decentralization, p. 285
Delegation, p. 284
Departmentalization, p. 272

Functional departmentalization, p. 272
Line authority, p. 287
Organization chart, p. 271
Organization design, p. 268
Organizational structure, p. 271
Place departmentalization, p. 275
Product departmentalization, p. 277
Responsibility, p. 283

Scalar principle, p. 281
Span of control principle, p. 281
Specialization, p. 269
Staff authority, p. 287
Standardization, p. 269
Unity of command principle, p. 281

1. How do coordination and authority affect each other?

2. See Figure 10.2, which shows a portion of the IRS organizational structure. Identify all the fundamentals of organization design that are communicated by this organization chart.

3. What are two similarities and two differences between functional departmentalization and place departmentalization?

4. What are two similarities and two differences between product departmentalization and customer departmentalization?

5. How does the scalar principle support the unity of command principle?

6. Think of an organization for which you have worked (or currently work). Identify three specific examples of tensions between departmentalization and coordination that you have observed.

7. Think of an organization for which you have worked (or currently work). Describe the process and practices of delegation that you were able to observe. Were they effective? Explain.

8. **Competency Development: Global Awareness Competency.** Most organizations are members of professional and trade associations. These organizations must also use organization design concepts and approaches in serving their members. The French Federation of Insurance Companies is one such example. How is this professional organization structured? What bases of departmentalization are used for its 4 key departments and 17 standing committees? What are the key managerial roles? To answer these questions, visit this organization's Web site at *http://www.ffsa.com*.

9. **Competency Development: Communication Competency.** Buckman Laboratories Inc., headquartered in Memphis, Tennessee, provides advanced chemical treatment technologies and technical services to firms throughout the world. Robert Buckman, who retired from the firm in 2000, transformed the organization into a knowledge-sharing system. He decided to empower field staff to communicate with one another, rather than routing all information through managers in Memphis. At first, Buckman experienced nothing but trouble. Many managers hated yielding control over the flow of information.

   But Buckman persisted. He cajoled, telling managers they should think of themselves as mentors to their employees. If someone had a question, he or she should ask it; if someone had an answer, he or she should share it. He stroked the egos of frequent users. He let people know he was watching, ordering weekly statistics detailing each employee's use of the network.[26]

   What uses of authority, delegation, and coordination did Robert Buckman demonstrate through personal communication? For more information on Buckman Laboratories, visit this company's home page at *http://www.buckman.com*.

CASE FOR COMPETENCY DEVELOPMENT

Peachtree Hospital

The administrator and the human resource (HR) director of a large hospital were discussing problems of the hospital's organizational structure. It has been their practice to meet at least bimonthly to review the hospital's operations and staffing. The hospital had been open for less than a year, and the staff had spent the better part of its time recruiting and training employees. The administrator believed that sufficient "shake down" time had elapsed that hospital staff and organizational problems encountered would be "exceptions" to policies on the books. The administrator, however, was concerned with the high turnover (over 45 percent for nurses and licensed practitioners), absenteeism, uncleanliness of the wards, and loss of medical supplies.

The HR director felt that these problems still reflected "start-up" conditions and would be solved within another month or so. The administrator, who believed that the organization's charts, job descriptions, and policy manuals clearly covered all areas, couldn't understand the problems. Furthermore, all the personnel had been trained by the hospital, and many had several years' experience at other hospitals before coming to this hospital.

The HR director agreed with many of the points raised by the administrator but added that formal organization charts and job descriptions didn't ensure that employees would behave correctly. However, the HR director did agree to conduct a survey to determine the extent to which employees understood the organization and its policies.

Nearly all 1,200 of the hospital's administrators, doctors, nurses, technicians, maintenance workers, and others completed the questionnaire. It contained more than 150 items dealing with a variety of issues concerning the organization's structure and policies. The results were tabulated, and a summary was prepared for the administrator. The following were some of the important findings.

1. Twenty-five percent of the orderlies and maintenance employees felt that there was uncertainty concerning the nature of their jobs.

2. Thirty percent of the orderlies and maintenance employees felt that they often had difficulty obtaining job-related information from their supervisors.

3. Thirty percent of all employees could not name their immediate supervisor.

4. Thirty-five percent of the administrative staff felt that they were not given authority consistent with their responsibility.

5. Twenty percent of the nurses did not know their decision-making rights.

6. Forty percent of all employees did not know whether they were performing line or staff functions.

The hospital administrator was shocked when she read these statements.

Questions

1. What would be your response to the administrator if you were the HR director?

2. What are some of the authority and responsibility problems at Peachtree Hospital?

3. How might the administrator determine whether the current structure of the hospital was the most effective?

JIAN

Founded in Silicon Valley by CEO Burke Franklin in 1988, JIAN, Inc., has become a leader in providing time-saving business software templates. One of the company's key contributions in this area is the Biz Plan Builder software that provides a complete business plan. This software allows users to edit the standardized business plan and tailor it to their unique needs, rather than having to write a business plan from scratch. Editing the generic plan that his company provides, Franklin argues, is much easier than writing an entirely new business plan.

Making things easier for managers is also consistent with Franklin's decisions regarding the organization design of JIAN. Started as a small business in Franklin's home, JIAN soon experienced rapid growth and thus needed to change its organization design radically in order to continue that growth. At the time, most software companies tended to produce, develop, market, and distribute their products themselves and thus had organization designs reflecting that business strategy. Franklin chose not to follow suit, but instead to focus on what he considered to be the strengths of JIAN.

Rather than "doing it all" like other software companies, Franklin decided to outsource the production and distribution functions in order to concentrate on software development and marketing. Initially, the company selected a number of producers and distributors to provide specific process components. This approach led to a lot of "finger pointing" among producers and distributors when quality or distribution problems arose. Desiring to avoid such problems in the future but to continue outsourcing, Franklin changed JIAN's organizational structure to that of a virtual corporation.

He consolidated the various functions that were being outsourced. He also decided not only to outsource production and distribution, but the human resource function as well. To do so, he selected Bindco to handle all the production and distribution functions that had previously been divided among various firms, and Execustaff to handle all aspects of JIAN's human resource function. Bindco manufacturers the boxes, duplicates the disks, publishes the manuals, and performs a host of distribution tasks (e.g., processing orders over the Internet) to name just a few. Execustaff acts as a complete human resource department, doing all the recruiting, hiring, and firing of employees and implementing JIAN's employee policies and procedures.

These two companies, in essence, provide "one-stop shopping" to handle all of JIAN's outsourcing needs, allowing the company to focus on its core business—software development and marketing. JIAN's virtual organization design has enabled it to continue to grow, increased its flexibility, and allowed it to gain a competitive advantage in the marketplace.

Questions

1. What is the "secret" to the success of virtual corporations according to Burke Franklin, CEO of JIAN?

2. What types of relationships or what characteristics should exist to enable partners to succeed in a virtual corporation?

3. What type of departmentalization does JIAN use in its method of outsourcing?

To learn more about JIAN, visit the company's home page at *http://www.jianusa.com*.

Contemporary
Organization Designs

LEARNING OBJECTIVES

AFTER STUDYING THIS CHAPTER YOU SHOULD BE ABLE TO:

1. STATE THE ROLE OF STRATEGIC AND ENVIRONMENTAL FACTORS IN THE DEVELOPMENT AND ADOPTION OF CONTEMPORARY ORGANIZATION DESIGNS.

2. DESCRIBE THE ROLE OF TECHNOLOGY IN ORGANIZATION DESIGN.

3. DISCUSS THE IMPACT OF TWO BASIC INFORMATION PROCESSING FACTORS IN THE USE OF FOUR DESIGN STRATEGIES.

4. EXPLAIN THE FEATURES OF THREE CONTEMPORARY ORGANIZATION DESIGNS.

Chapter Outline

PREVIEW: DUKE POWER REORGANIZES

STRATEGIC AND ENVIRONMENTAL FACTORS

STRATEGIC CONSIDERATIONS
CHANGING ENVIRONMENT
ORGANIC ORGANIZATION

TECHNOLOGY FACTORS

TECHNOLOGICAL INTERDEPENDENCE
SERVICE TECHNOLOGIES

INFORMATION PROCESSING FACTORS

VERTICAL INFORMATION DESIGN STRATEGY
LATERAL INFORMATION DESIGN STRATEGY
PLANNING AND ADMINISTRATION COMPETENCY: FastCar Project
SLACK RESOURCES DESIGN STRATEGY
SELF-CONTAINED DESIGN STRATEGY
GLOBAL AWARENESS COMPETENCY: Yahoo!'s Design

THREE CONTEMPORARY ORGANIZATION DESIGNS

MATRIX ORGANIZATION
NETWORK ORGANIZATION
COMMUNICATION COMPETENCY: A Three-Firm Alliance Network
VIRTUAL ORGANIZATION
TEAMWORK COMPETENCY: AeroTech Builds Virtual Networks

CHAPTER SUMMARY

KEY TERMS

QUESTIONS FOR DISCUSSION AND COMPETENCY DEVELOPMENT

CASE FOR COMPETENCY DEVELOPMENT: FORD MOTOR'S TRANSFORMATION

VIDEO CASE: BINDCO, INC.

DUKE POWER REORGANIZES

Duke Power serves nearly 2 million customers in North and South Carolina. Several years ago, with deregulation coming, management realized that the company had to do a much better job of customer service if it was to survive the new competition. The organizational structure of Customer Operations, the business unit responsible for delivering electricity to customers, was not designed to enhance customer service. The unit was divided into four regional profit centers, with no provision for coordinating their efforts. The regional vice presidents were overwhelmed by an endless stream of administrative tasks and had little time for dealing with the details of customer service. Thus no one was responsible for how the company delivered value to customers.

To solve this organization design problem, Duke Power identified five core processes that together comprised the essential work that Customer Operations performed for customers: develop market strategies, acquire and maintain customers, provide reliability and integrity, deliver products and services, and calculate and collect revenues. A new unit was created for each process, and the unit managers report to Barbara Orr, vice president of process operations. In the new design, the regional vice presidents continue to manage their own workforces but are expected to work in partnership with the process units. The process units have only small staffs, but they have been given meaningful responsibility and authority over how the company operates. First, the process units define in detail how work will proceed, and the regional managers are expected to follow those designs. Second, the process units are respon-sible for setting performance targets, establishing budgets, and providing the budgets to the regions. The regional managers and their staffs continue to have authority over the people in their units, but they are evaluated on the basis of how well they meet the targets set by the process units. The regional budgets are, in large part, based on the amount of funds allocated by the process units to the regions. The new design has proven to be a great success, focusing the entire organization much more directly on the customer. Virtually every activity involved in serving customers has been redesigned from the bottom up.[1]

To learn more about Duke Power, visit the company's home page at

http://www.dukepower.com

STRATEGIC AND ENVIRONMENTAL FACTORS

1.

STATE THE ROLE OF STRATEGIC AND ENVIRONMENTAL FACTORS IN THE DEVELOPMENT AND ADOPTION OF CONTEMPORARY ORGANIZATION DESIGNS.

Duke Power is only one of many organizations that have adopted a new organization design to cope better with a variety of changes in their environments. Primary among those changes are anticipating and responding to customer expectations.

In Chapter 10 we provided insights for organization design by the more traditional methods of function, product, place, and customer; in this chapter we build on that foundation. Figure 11.1 outlines the focus of this chapter. First, we review several of the strategic and environmental factors that are influencing the adoption of contemporary organization designs. Because of the extensive coverage of these factors in previous chapters (especially Chapters 3, 4, and 7), our discussion of them here will be brief. Second, we review the increasing impact of technology and information processing factors on the strategic decision to adopt, in whole or in part, one or more of the contemporary organization designs reviewed—namely, the matrix organization, network organization, and virtual organization. However, we devote most of this chapter to design factors and issues related to the complexities of changing competitive environments, strategies, and technologies.

STRATEGIC CONSIDERATIONS

The practice of matching organization design to a firm's strategy isn't new. In his landmark study of 70 large organizations, Alfred Chandler found that the design of an organization follows its strategy.[2] The choice of organization design makes a difference because not all organizational forms support all strategies equally well. This structure-follows-strategy perspective is based on the idea that, like a plan, an organization's design should be a means to an end, not an end in itself. Thus there are few hard and fast

Figure 11.1   **Key Factors in Contemporary Organization Design**

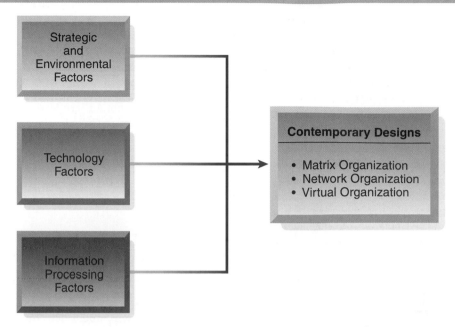

rules for designing or redesigning an organization. Every firm's organization design is the result of many decisions and historical circumstances. Moreover, there is no guarantee that any new organization design will improve an organization's performance. A new design, based on flawed assumptions or implemented through poor leadership, may actually make things worse by compounding errors rather than correcting them.[3]

At the same time, the relationship between strategy and organization design is reciprocal. How a firm is organized will influence its focus and time horizons, encouraging its managers and employees either to develop creative strategies or to maintain the status quo.[4] At Duke Power top management recognized that it had to do a much better job of customer service in the face of new competition—a strategic imperative. It recognized the inability of the current organization design to respond to this challenge. Through an extensive diagnosis, management identified five core processes that were crucial to improved customer service. A small unit for each process was created under a vice president of process operations. These units were given significant roles in the development of creative strategies and the authority to influence their consistent implementation across the four regional profit centers.

CHANGING ENVIRONMENT

The three organization designs that we present later in the chapter are intended to help management cope with a rapidly changing environment. A ***changing environment*** involves frequent and significant shifts in technology, customer expectations, products, competitors, and/or political forces. This type of environment is manifested in the following ways.

- In the information age new information technologies have radically sped up and changed the ways that people work, do business, communicate, and shop. These breakthroughs have altered the traditional limitations of time and space.

- Rising customer expectations are creating new pressures on organizations, which face the prospect of losing them to current and new competitors. Traditional customer loyalty no longer is a substitute for providing competitive prices for goods and services.

- Competitors—current and new—are continuously introducing improved and/or new goods and services that represent alternatives for the firm's customers.

- Government actions through political pressure, laws, and enforcement agencies come more quickly and with more force as a result of the political clout wielded by various interest groups for consumer protection, product safety, pollution control, and civil rights.[5]

Consider the following simple example of becoming more responsive to changing customer expectations. Rob Manning is the leader of the Delivery Products and Services unit, one of the five process units at Duke Power. He has worked with the regional units, with suppliers, and with his own 10-person staff to devise a new way to organize warehouse facilities. Parts that are required by installation crews, for example, are laid out the night before for easy pickup in the morning. Now, crews can load their trucks and be on the road in 10 minutes, a fraction of the 70 minutes previously required. The crews can do more installations in a day, so customers don't have to wait so long for service.[6]

ORGANIC ORGANIZATION

A strategic consideration in implementing contemporary organization designs is the need for top management to commit to operating as an organic organization. An *organic organization* encourages managers and subordinates to work together in teams and to communicate openly with each other. In fact, employees are encouraged to communicate with anyone who might help them solve a problem. Decision making tends to be decentralized. Authority, responsibility, and accountability flow to employees having the expertise required to solve problems as they arise. As a result, an organic organization is well suited to a changing environment. Additional features of an organic organization, in contrast to those of a mechanistic organization, are presented in Table 11.1.[7] In brief, a *mechanistic organization* is one in which management breaks activities into separate, highly specialized tasks, relies extensively on standardized rules, and centralizes decision making at the top. This type of organization may be most appropriate when an organization's environment is stable and predictable.

Table 11.1	Organic Versus Mechanistic Organizations

Organic	Mechanistic
• Tasks tend to be interdependent.	• Tasks are highly specialized.
• Tasks are continually adjusted and redefined through interaction and as situations change.	• Tasks tend to remain rigidly defined unless changed by top management.
• Generalized roles (responsibility for task accomplishment beyond specific role definition) are accepted.	• Specific roles (rights, obligations, and technical methods) are prescribed for each employee.
• Network structure of control, authority, and communication.	• Hierarchical structure of control, authority, and communication.
• Communication and decision making are both vertical and horizontal, depending on where needed information and expertise reside.	• Communication and decision making are primarily vertical, top-down.
• Communication emphasizes the form of mutual influence and advice among all levels.	• Communication emphasizes directions and decisions issued by superiors.

Duke Power had to become a more organic organization to implement its new design. Management recognized that the new design was more than a matter of establishing new management positions and reassigning responsibilities. As lines of authority were blurred, the way managers interacted with one another and with workers also had to change and leadership became as important as structure. Process leaders, for example, couldn't simply order workers to do their bidding. They had to work through the regional vice presidents. Rob Manning stated that his role requires "three critical skills: influence, influence, and influence." The regional vice presidents, for their part, have to negotiate with the process unit leaders to ensure that the process designs are sound, the process goals reasonable, and the resource allocations fair. The split in authority, in other words, makes cooperation unavoidable. If the various leaders don't work together, they will fail.[8]

TECHNOLOGY FACTORS

2.

DESCRIBE THE ROLE OF TECHNOLOGY IN ORGANIZATION DESIGN.

In previous chapters, we have frequently noted the importance of technology on a wide range of management issues, including organization design. Recall from Chapter 2 that *technology* is the method(s) used to transform organizational inputs into outputs. Technology greatly influences the size and shape of organizations and their products. Schools, banks, hospitals, governments, and retail stores all now rely heavily on technology. Therefore we can analyze its impact on organization design in a variety of settings—and its importance cannot be overstated.

TECHNOLOGICAL INTERDEPENDENCE

An organization's technology has a significant impact on its organization design because different types of technologies generate various types of internal interdependence. ***Technological interdependence*** is the degree of coordination required between individuals and departments to transform information and raw materials into goods and services.[9] There are three types of technological interdependence: pooled, sequential, and reciprocal. Figure 11.2 shows how they operate to coordinate the efforts of employees in order to achieve desired results.

Pooled interdependence. Illustrated in Figure 11.2(a), ***pooled interdependence*** involves little sharing of information or resources among individuals within a department or among departments in the performance of tasks. Although various departments contribute to overall organizational efforts, they work on their own specialized tasks. At

---

Figure 11.2   *Three Types of Technological Interdependence*

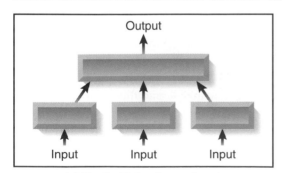

(a) Pooled interdependence

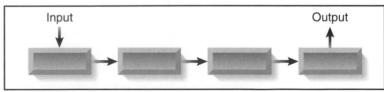

(b) Sequential interdependence

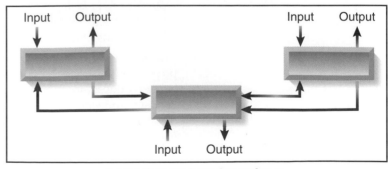

(c) Reciprocal interdependence

a Bank of America branch, for example, the savings, consumer loan, and commercial loan departments work independently of one another. Bank of America achieves coordination by requiring each department to meet certain standards and follow certain rules. These rules are consistent for all its banks in various states and apply to all routine transactions, such as check cashing and receiving deposits, with few exceptions.

Sequential interdependence. Illustrated in Figure 11.2(b), *sequential interdependence* involves the orderly step-by-step flow of information, tasks, and resources from one individual or team to another within the same department or from one department to another. That is, the output from department A becomes the input for department B, the output from department B becomes the input for department C, and so on. Mercedes-Benz uses standard methods and procedures at its Vance, Alabama, plant to manufacture its sport utility vehicles. These methods and procedures spell out the single exact and proper way to do every task. They were drawn up by engineers and posted at workstations for easy reference. Everything is spelled out, down to the proper way to tighten a lug nut. When an employee is finished with a hammer, guides (e.g., chalk body outlines) indicate exactly where it is to be laid. To ensure coordination of its workstations, managers must carefully schedule when parts arrive and leave each workstation.[10]

Reciprocal interdependence. Illustrated in Figure 11.2(c), *reciprocal interdependence* involves the need for every individual and department to work with every other individual and department; information and resources flow back and forth freely until the goal is achieved. For example, hospitals use resources from several departments (e.g., x-ray, nursing, surgery, and physical therapy) to restore a patient's health. Each specialist and department supplies some of the resources needed to help the patient. Doctors and professionals from each specialized area meet to discuss the patient's recovery. The method of coordination is mutual adjustment, achieved through team meetings.

Designing an organization to handle reciprocal interdependence and then managing it are extremely challenging. The design of the organization must allow for frequent communication among individuals and departments, and planning is essential. Because management can't easily anticipate all customer demands or solve all the problems that arise, managers must continually communicate to be sure that they understand the nature and scope of issues and problems—and to devise effective solutions.

SERVICE TECHNOLOGIES

The use of technology is fairly obvious in producing tangible goods. However, technology's role in the design of service organizations often is less obvious. The service sector of the U.S. economy now employs far more people than the manufacturing sector. In fact, services now account for 71 percent of the nation's total employment. Service organizations have grown rapidly both in number and size. The U.S. Bureau of Labor Statistics has forecasted that, through 2008, service-producing industries will account for virtually all the job growth in the United States.[11]

Two characteristics distinguish service organizations from manufacturing organizations.[12]

- *Intangibility.* The output of a service firm is intangible and thus cannot be stored. The output must be used immediately or lost forever. Holding seats in inventory on a plane or train is impossible. If these seats aren't sold prior to departure, the revenue is lost forever. Manufactured goods such as cars, TVs, and computers can be stored and sold later.

- *Closeness of the customer.* The customer or client is involved simultaneously in the production of services. Clients are consuming and evaluating services as they are being produced. In a very real sense, the employees of a travel agency are simultaneously producing and selling a service to their customers. Service employees deal directly with customers, but production employees in manufacturing are separated from their firm's customers.

These two features have an important implication for managers. The simultaneous production and consumption of services means that quality control cannot be achieved by the inspect-and-reject method traditionally used in manufacturing plants. Instead, quality control must occur at the point of service delivery. The service provider is responsible for ensuring quality of service during each interaction with the customer or client.

Types of Service Technologies. There are two basic types of service technologies: routine and nonroutine. Organizations operating in relatively stable environments and serving customers who are relatively sure of their needs use ***routine service technologies.*** Such organizations include retail stores, fast-food restaurants, banks, travel agencies, gas stations, and bookstores. They aren't so much involved with producing the service as with dispensing it. The information being exchanged is simple, and the tasks are standardized. The demand on the service provider is fairly precise, and thus employees interact with customers for only short periods of time. For example, the interaction between a teller at Bank of America and a customer who wants to make a deposit has all these characteristics.

Organizations operating in complex and changing environments and serving customers or clients who are unsure of their needs or imprecise about their problems use ***nonroutine service technologies.***[13] Customers or clients usually don't know how to solve their problems even when they can identify them. In this context, service providers—usually knowledge workers—continually encounter new problems, and variety is the norm, not the exception. Thus creativity and novelty are essential as the service provider develops techniques to fit the situation at hand. The types of service providers using nonroutine technologies include legal, accounting, brokerage, marketing and advertising, medical, and architectural firms. The focus is on communication between the knowledge worker and the client and the tasks and skills needed to serve the client's needs. A successful outcome depends on the client's willingness to give the service provider the information needed to find a satisfactory solution and to participate in its development.

Organization Design and Service Technology. Selected organization design features discussed in Chapter 10 (specialization, standardization, coordination, and authority) and their relationships with the two types of service technologies are shown in Table 11.2. Organizations using nonroutine service technologies tend to be organic. They are organized to foster process flexibility and decentralized decision making. Because the problems facing such an organization are often unique, reciprocal interdependence among employees is common. In contrast, organizations utilizing routine service technologies can be designed along more mechanistic lines. Well-defined standards are common because customers' or clients' needs are known. Decision making is often centralized in top management.

Table 11.2   *Organization Design and Links with Service Technologies*

Features	Service Technologies	
	Nonroutine	Routine
Needs of customers/clients	Unknown	Known
Design characteristics		
• Specialization	High	Low
• Standardization of activities	Low	High
• Span of management	Moderate	Wide
• Authority	Decentralized	Centralized
• Organization type	Organic	Mechanistic
• Environment	Changing	Stable
• Technological interdependence	Reciprocal	Pooled and/or sequential
Examples	Law firms, brokerage houses, marketing firms, and consulting firms	Retail stores, fast-food chains, and hotels/motels

We can further examine the way in which a service technology affects the design of an organization and the role of the customer in the service production process. Figure 11.3 illustrates the amount of customer participation in the process and the degree to which the organization tries to customize its offerings to satisfy unique customer needs.[14] Each combination presents the organization with different choices of technology. Let's explore the organization design implications for several different types of service.

In Quadrant A, customers simply need to tell the organization's employees what they want. The employees can routinely adjust their methods and behaviors to satisfy customers' needs. Organizations that provide services for a variety of customers who desire to have a home cleaned, lawn mowed, or routine car repairs (Midas Mufflers) are examples. Customers are price sensitive, and, in many instances, they could provide a service for themselves. They usually don't observe the actual performance of the work. Rather, they inspect the final product for quality. Sequential task interdependence permits standardization of tasks, and extensive rules and regulations govern employee behavior. The customer initially calls on the organization for service and then turns the process over to it.

Figure 11.3   Service Technology

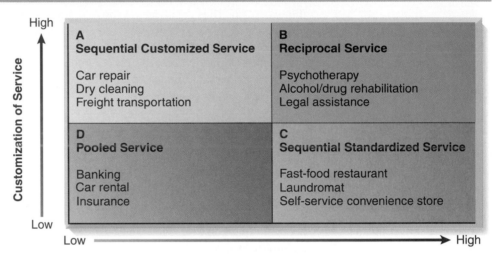

If customers have complex and unique problems, they are typically less price sensitive and not able to provide a service themselves; they will want the organization to provide customized solutions to their problems. Quadrant B of Figure 11.3 indicates that customers' problems require an organization's complex services, as in the provision of legal advice or medical treatment. The client (or patient) must actively participate by providing sensitive information before alternatives can be discussed. As the service provider learns more and more about the client's problem, various alternatives may become obvious, including the need for behavioral changes. As the client's behavior changes or other changes occur, the client communicates the effect of these changes back to the provider. This type of exchange leads to reciprocal interdependence between client and service provider. In such cases, the provider should have multiple skills for helping the client deal with the problem. Through conversations with the client, the service provider gains immediate feedback, which can help avoid costly and embarrassing misunderstandings.

Many services are purchased for mere convenience and are delivered with the use of sequential standardized service technology. Quadrant C in Figure 11.3 represents situations in which an employee greets a customer to find out what the customer wants. The employee notes the customer's desires on a document (e.g., a work order) and then passes it on to other employees to handle. Pizza Hut, Domino's, and Papa John's pizza parlors are examples of firms that use sequential standardized service technology to satisfy customer demand. The customer evaluates the organization's quality against known standards, such as time, cost, store hours, availability, accessibility, and taste preferences.

Banks, insurance companies, and movie theaters represent organizations in Quadrant D of Figure 11.3. The interdependence between customer and organization is pooled. Customers don't participate in the process after their initial request for service. The organization uses standard procedures to help achieve low costs. For example, at Alamo Car Rental the customer signs the rental agreement and looks over the car for damage (high customer participation). Then the customer gets the keys from the agent. Alamo doesn't communicate further with the customer until the car is returned (unless a breakdown or accident occurs).

INFORMATION PROCESSING FACTORS

3.

DISCUSS THE IMPACT OF
TWO BASIC INFORMATION
PROCESSING FACTORS
IN THE USE OF FOUR
DESIGN STRATEGIES.

Managers and professional employees spend considerable time sharing information in meetings, talking on the telephone, dictating letters and memos, receiving and sending e-mail, receiving reports, reading computer printouts, and so on. Information is the glue that holds the organization together. The design of an organization should be guided by the need to process information. Two factors must be considered in assessing this need.

1. Should management increase the organization's ability to process information and, if so, how?

2. Should management reduce the need to process information and, if so, how?

As suggested in Table 11.3, managers can increase an organization's ability to process information through a vertical information design strategy or a lateral information design strategy.[15] These strategies are especially useful when the people or departments involved are either sequentially or reciprocally interdependent. In contrast, managers can reduce the need to process information by either reducing the number of exceptions (problems) that occur or reducing the number of things to be considered when exceptions do occur. The two strategies shown in Table 11.3 to address this factor are the slack resources design strategy and self-contained design strategy.

Table 11.3	Information Processing Factors and Strategies
Factors	**Strategies**
Increase the ability to process information	• Vertical information design • Lateral information design
Decrease the need to process information	• Slack resources design • Self-contained design

VERTICAL INFORMATION DESIGN STRATEGY

The *vertical information design strategy* involves methods for sending information efficiently up and down the chain of command. These methods are typically computer based, which allows rapidly changing information to be constantly updated, giving managers the right information at the right time for planning, decision making, and coordinating activities. By bringing information to higher levels of management, vertical information fosters coordinated and centralized decision making.

The types of organizations that have effectively used the vertical information design strategy include Ticketmaster outlets, airline reservation departments, off-track betting parlors, and supermarkets. Most of these information systems are computerized. For example, Kroger, Safeway, and other supermarkets now use optical scanners at their checkout counters. As purchases pass over the eye of the scanner, the cost, item type, and related data are read directly from the Universal Product Code (UPC) into a computer. When the store manager wants to know how a special coupon affected a product's sales volume, the computer readily provides the information. The manager also can determine the percentage of sales from each department (e.g., produce, meat, and dairy) and track inventory. Finally, the vertical information design strategy allows the prices of items to be entered much faster than manual keying and virtually eliminates checkout errors.

Harrah's Entertainment, Inc., uses an extensive and successful vertical information design strategy. Through the use of Winners Information Network (WINet), top management formally communicates with customers to entice them to increase their loyalty to Harrah's. WINet keeps track of a customer's gaming activity, show and restaurant patronage, and room occupancy, among other things. In addition to supporting Harrah's target marketing efforts, this information is utilized with its point and reward program, which operates in much the same way as airline mileage incentive programs.[16]

LATERAL INFORMATION DESIGN STRATEGY

The *lateral information design strategy* involves methods that foster horizontal communication and decision making among individuals, teams, and departments. This strategy reduces the emphasis on communication and decision making through the vertical chain of command. Decision making is often placed in the hands of those who have the greatest and quickest access to information needed to make a decision. In contrast to the vertical information design strategy, which tends to centralize decision making by bringing information up to higher level managers and passing the decisions down to lower level managers and employees, the lateral information design strategy tends to decentralize decision making and fosters an organic organization.[17] The two primary methods of implementing this strategy are to (1) establish horizontal contact among employees, teams, or departments, or (2) create new positions to integrate information and decision making.

Rob Manning, the leader of the Delivery Products and Services unit at Duke Power, recognizes that part of his role is to integrate information and decision making. For example, Manning served in a lead role to change the way the company worked with its building-contractor customers. Duke Power was meeting only 30 to 50 percent of its commitments—laying cables by scheduled dates, for example—to those customers, which created serious problems for the customers. Homebuilders based much of their construction scheduling on Duke Power's promised dates. The employees making the commitments to the contractors didn't have an accurate picture of the availability of Duke's field workers. They could not ensure, therefore, that the needed employees would be in the right places on the scheduled dates. Manning and his team devised a new scheduling system that provides much more detailed information about the availability of field personnel, enabling more specific and accurate assignments to be made. They also designated specific people to negotiate commitment dates with contractors and keep both management and contractors apprised of changes. Finally, they underscored the importance of meeting commitments to customers by measuring the percentage of deadlines met and by publicizing each region's results daily. Duke Power now meets 98 percent of its construction commitments.[18]

The simplest form of lateral relations is to allow direct contact among employees, teams, or departments to solve a common problem to facilitate joint decision making. The following Planning and Administration Competency feature reports on a more sophisticated and complicated form of such lateral relations through the use of advanced information technologies at DaimlerChrysler.[19] The firm's FastCar project is intended to improve (1) information gathering, analysis, and problem solving; (2) planning and organizing the process of vehicle design; and (3) time management in the development of new vehicles.

DaimlerChrysler AG recently implemented a new Web-based initiative to augment existing systems and link all aspects of its vehicle design, production, and marketing operations. Officials at the Stuttgart, Germany-based automaker expect the infusion of new product development technology to speed vehicle development and trim costs.

The FastCar project includes the deployment of a Web infrastructure that provides closer communication among design, engineering, manufacturing, quality, finance, procurement, and sales and marketing units in the Chrysler division. Gary Dilts, senior vice president of e-connect platforms at DaimlerChrysler stated: "In the old system that worked sequentially, it took months before suppliers knew what was being done. Now, they won't be cutting tools based on

Assumption A, when we're working on Assumption C." For example, approved product design changes will be communicated instantly to other departments within DaimlerChrysler, as well as to external suppliers involved in equipping a new car.

The FastCar project will augment existing systems and let 4,100 internal employees and 5,000 external users communicate and access design changes over the Web. Navi Radjou, an analyst at Forrester Research, Inc., in Cambridge, Massachusetts, comments: "The real pain point is helping project managers in different operational units plan for ordering products and finding optimal parts. That part costs lots of money because there is traditionally little collaboration across units during the design phase." The FastCar project is intended to address

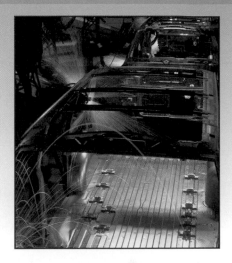

these issues through real-time lateral communication and decision making.

• • •

To learn more about DaimlerChrysler, visit the company's home page at

http://www.daimlerchrysler.com

SLACK RESOURCES DESIGN STRATEGY

The *slack resources design strategy* involves the stockpiling of extra resources—funds, personnel, and materials—to prepare an organization to respond to environmental changes. Slack resources can reduce the need to process information by minimizing the number and types of problems that are likely to arise. One form of slack resources is an organization's ability to lengthen production and delivery schedules or increase lead times. When an organization overestimates the length of time needed to complete a project, it creates slack—extra time—in the schedule that can be used for dealing with unexpected difficulties. The student who decides to enroll in 12 rather than 15 credit hours builds slack into his or her schedule—extra time that can be used for the enrolled courses or for something else entirely.

The slack resources design strategy tends to reduce departmental interdependence. For example, Eljer Industries, manufacturers of plumbing, heating, and ventilation products, maintains extra inventory of plumbing and ventilation products to meet unexpected demand. Less communication is needed among the purchasing, production, and sales departments because of this extra inventory. However, if only a minimal amount of finished goods inventory is kept on hand (no slack), the company's three departments must coordinate activities closely to avoid creating an unmanageable backorder situation. If backorders pile up, customer satisfaction drops because customers must wait longer than they anticipated for delivery of their orders.

However, creating slack resources has some negative cost and customer relations implications.[20] Increasing manufacturing lead time generates inventories that are expensive to store. At Eljer Industries, this extra cost is reflected in warehousing expenses, such as building construction or leasing costs and employee and energy costs to maintain the buildings. The money thus tied up isn't available for other purposes. Extending planning, budgeting, and scheduling time horizons may also lower performance expectations.

Moreover, some customers may not be able to live with extended schedules because of their own plans, commitments, or cost considerations.

SELF-CONTAINED DESIGN STRATEGY

The *self-contained design strategy* involves methods for assigning all activities, responsibilities, and resources for a specific product (good or service), project, or geographic region to one team, department, or strategic business unit (SBU). This strategy reduces the need to process information with other teams, departments, divisions, or SBUs. It effectively reduces the number of factors to be dealt with when exceptions or problems arise. The self-contained design strategy also involves choosing product or place rather than functional departmentalization. Recall from Chapter 10 that some organizations choose a product form of departmentalization because they are having problems with their functional organization designs. In a firm organized around products (e.g., Procter & Gamble, General Foods, and PepsiCo), each product group has its own resources for the functional areas of accounting, marketing, manufacturing, personnel, and finance. Each product line contains all or many of the resources needed to satisfy its customers' needs.

Organization by product line enables a company to achieve flexibility and adaptability. It also reduces the amount of information a manager needs to process, in two ways. First, product departmentalization limits the number of products and consumer demands that each unit must deal with. Within the organization, managers of one product line have little need to share information concerning manufacturing costs, delivery schedules, distribution channels, and the like with managers of other product lines. One manager's concerns aren't relevant to another's. Second, specialization across product lines is reduced. For example, in functional departmentalization, an accountant must know something about all the organization's products; in product departmentalization, an accountant needs to know something about only one product line. Thus uncertainty is reduced because all necessary information will pertain only to a limited set of product problems.

The following Global Awareness Competency feature reports on how Yahoo! has made effective use of a combination of the self-contained and lateral relations design strategies through the application of sophisticated information technologies to achieve a global presence.[21] Yahoo!, headquartered in Santa Clara, California, is a global Internet communications, commerce, and media company that offers a comprehensive branded network of services. The firm has more than 2,000 employees and annual sales revenue that exceed $600 million. Yahoo! offers its services to more than 156 million individuals each month and has more than 625 million page hits per day. Yahoo! makes money by selling advertising on its portal.[22] Its organization design is sensitive to language and cultural differences and the specific interests of its customers in various countries.

Yahoo!'s Design

Yahoo! has grown from its origins as a Web directory run from a trailer located on the Stanford University campus to a portal that operates 22 Web sites in 13 different languages directed from 16 offices located around the world.

Yahoo!'s success overseas springs from the fact that the company's international agenda is not that different from its overall plan. Yahoo!'s international divisions built a portal that was tailored to meet varying demand. "Yahoo! is the poster child for globalization," says Evan Neufeld, director of international research for Jupiter Communications. "They have conquered Europe one market at a time."

The Yahoo! portal is easy to use, but it is intricate and detailed below the surface. Yahoo! transported the original model from the United States to other regions of the world and diversified locally. Yahoo! projects the same look and feel for its site everywhere, but it serves up country-specific content and advertising. The firm's tactics include start early; construct barebones, country-specific foundation sites; and build up from there.

Running eight region-specific Web sites in Europe, the portal serves 20 million of the 38 million European Internet users. Yahoo!'s strongest markets are in the United Kingdom, France, and Germany. The company deals with more than 800 local advertisers across Europe (and more than 3,500 worldwide), and it has garnered advertising from major companies such as Renault, LVMH (Louis Vuitton Moët Hennessey), Lorél, and Heinz. It also serves as an outlet for U.S. companies advertising in Europe.

Yahoo! also identified partnerships and issues unique to targeted countries early on and now has 350 content partnerships in Europe. "Our principle was to build locally relevant services," says Fabiola Arrendondo, managing director of Yahoo! Europe. "We wanted local advertising, content, and e-commerce brand names that the users could recognize."

Yahoo! did not automatically transfer companies that were successful in the United States to Europe. Both CDnow and Amazon.com wanted exclusive European contracts with Yahoo!. Arrendondo refused because neither had fully developed a European distribution network. "I think it would have been a big mistake," she says in hindsight. "There was a clear need for good customer experience. We wanted local experience and most [U.S. e-commerce companies] didn't have local fulfillment." Instead, it established relations with bookseller Waterstone's and the music chain HMV.

• • •

To learn more about Yahoo!, visit the company's home page at

http://www.yahoo.com

THREE CONTEMPORARY ORGANIZATION DESIGNS

4.

EXPLAIN THE FEATURES OF THREE CONTEMPORARY ORGANIZATION DESIGNS.

The three contemporary designs discussed in this section work best in an organic organization and allow it to

- implement new and complex corporate and business-level strategies;
- quickly respond to important and changing environmental forces;
- facilitate technological interdependence, especially reciprocal interdependence; and
- increase the organization's ability to process information, especially through the use of the lateral information design strategy.

MATRIX ORGANIZATION

A **matrix organization** combines some features of the functional and product organization designs to increase the ability of managers and employees to process information. In a matrix organization, functional managers (e.g., engineering, manufacturing, and sales) and product managers (individual product lines) report to a matrix manager. The matrix manager's job is to coordinate the activities of the functional and product managers. Instead of reporting to separate higher level managers, they report to one general matrix manager who consolidates and integrates their activities.

Integration Process. A matrix design integrates activities and holds down costs by eliminating duplication of key functional activities—such as accounting, purchasing, and human resources—for each product line. The functional manager's responsibility is to identify the resources needed to perform a job, and the product manager's responsibility is to identify products that the organization can make to satisfy customers' needs. The matrix manager's job is to achieve an overall balance by coordinating the organization's functional and product activities to ensure delivery of the product on time and within budget. Figure 11.4 illustrates this balance. The functional and product managers need to work closely with each other (reciprocal interdependence) to make a matrix design work well.[23]

Matrix organizations require managers to demonstrate high levels of communication, teamwork, and self-management competencies. Often, human resources managers work with other managers and employees to help them learn how to make decisions organically rather than mechanistically. That is, they need to base decisions on expertise and persuasion rather than on rules, SOPs, formal roles, and hierarchical position. Disagreements must be dealt with through collaboration and problem solving rather than getting passed "upstairs." Coordination is achieved through extensive formal and informal meetings or in one-to-one conversations. Teams consisting of both product and functional managers and employees decide who will do what and when.[24]

Assessment. A matrix design permits the flexible sharing of employees across product lines. The job of the matrix manager is to assess new products, obtain resources for the entire division, and integrate the efforts of product and functional personnel. This

Figure 11.4   **Matrix Organization Design**

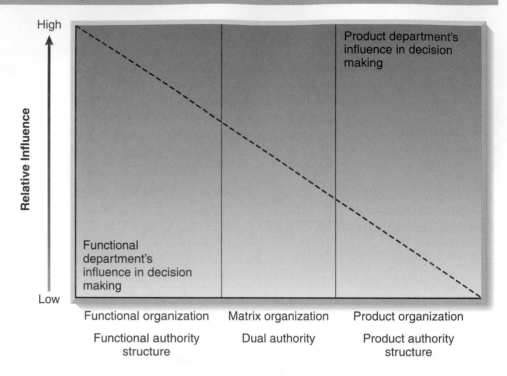

design helps achieve coordination to meet the dual demands of efficiency and changing customer expectations.

The potential problems associated with the matrix design include the reality that the maintenance of two management hierarchies (functional and product) is expensive. Further, the employees involved typically have two bosses: a functional and a product boss. Trying to decide who to listen to may create confusion and ambiguity for the employee. When the product is delivered and no new products are coming into the pipeline, layoffs usually follow. Therefore employees sometimes tend to prolong their tasks so that they can keep their jobs. Moreover, the expense of developing managers to behave as coaches and facilitators and not "bosses" can be high.

NETWORK ORGANIZATION

A *network organization* subcontracts some or many of its operations to other firms and coordinates them through various methods to accomplish specific goals.[25] For large and complex organizations, these "other firms" may also include strategic business units that are part of the same organization. The traditional functions of sales, accounting, and manufacturing may be provided by separate organizations or units in various locations connected by computer to the firm's headquarters. Contacts and working relationships in the network are facilitated by electronic means, as well as the more traditional personal meeting. Use of computer-based technologies permits managers to coordinate suppliers, designers, manufacturers, and others on a real-time basis.

Integration Process. People in network organizations can't operate effectively unless they can communicate quickly, accurately, and over great distances. When this capability exists, managers of network organizations can

- search globally for opportunities and resources;

- maximize the use of resources, whether owned by the organization or not;

- have the organization perform only those functions for which it has or can develop expertise; and

- outsource those activities that can be performed better and at less cost by others.

This design means that firms are added to or dropped from the network as needed to achieve defined goals. Organizations in the fashion, toy, publishing, motion picture, and software industries have used this design. Virtually all large retailers partially use this design by outsourcing the manufacturing function, and many outsource the distribution function. At Kmart, Wal-Mart, J.C. Penney, and other large retailers, corporate headquarters aggregates sales each night, as reported by each store over the electronic cash register point-of-sale information system. The system breaks product-line sales into item, cut, size, material, color, style, and number sold. Those data are then transmitted from corporate headquarters to contractors around the world. Within a few days or weeks, replacement merchandise is on the shelves.

WEB INSIGHT

Go to the Web site at *http://www.nike.com/ athletic/*. Search this site and list all the products sold under Nike's name but manufactured by others. Nike does no manufacturing.

Nike, one of the major firms in the athletic footwear and apparel sports industries, uses a network organization. The company employs only about 1,500 people at its Beaverton, Oregon, headquarters. Its success lies in its ability to design technologically advanced athletic shoes, athletic apparel, and accessories and to get them to the market quickly. Designers and market researchers at headquarters introduce new models. A small plant at headquarters makes prototype shoes and other items, which employees and athletes wear and test. Once the design has been finalized, it is faxed to suppliers in the Pan-Pacific region for mass production. Nike then distributes them to retailers throughout the world from its huge distribution warehouse in Memphis, Tennessee, home of FedEx.[26]

Alliances of companies increasingly function as a network of partners and reflect some of the features of network organizations. The network approach to alliance management is illustrated in the following Communication Competency feature.[27] It emphasizes the need for the effective transfer and exchange of information among alliance partners for a network to be effective.

COMMUNICATION COMPETENCY

A Three-Firm Alliance Network

Coca-Cola, McDonald's, and Disney have a three-way alliance network. Coca-Cola is the exclusive supplier to McDonald's and the Disney theme parks. The partners help each other set up new operations all over the world. McDonald's and Coca-Cola use the Disney cartoon characters in their marketing and advertising efforts. McDonald's, in turn, is a marketing and sales channel for Disney and Coca-Cola. New Disney film releases are often heavily promoted by McDonald's. This relationship benefits both companies: Higher sales at McDonald's increase the exposure of Coca Cola and Disney or vice versa.

The binding forces of this alliance are the companies' focus on families, their positions as market leaders in their respective industries, and the extremely large amount of business generated by the alliance. The agreements between the firms, however, are different. On the one hand, Disney and McDonald's have a formal alliance, as do Coca-Cola and Disney. On the other hand, Coca-Cola and McDonald's have no formal agreement. Figure 11.5 illustrates the integrating mechanisms in the alliance network.

The strength of these relationships also has its price, placing constraints on all three firms in making other choices. For example, a decision by Disney to switch from Coca-Cola to Pepsi would put in jeopardy its relationship with McDonald's, thereby possibly ruining a profitable alliance. Thus, next to its self-interest, Disney also has to consider the benefits of maintaining this network. Failing to recognize that strategic choices depend on the relationships among the partners can result in considerable ill will and costs because losing one alliance partner may well cause the loss of other partners.

• • •

To learn more about the three companies in this alliance, visit their home pages at

http://www.cocacolacompany.com/; *http://www.disney.go.com/investors/ index.html*; and *http://www. mcdonalds.com/corporate/ index.html*

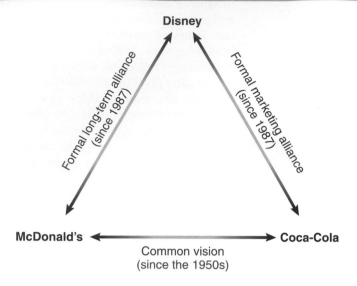

Assessment. A network design has several potential advantages.[28] First, fewer employees are needed because many production and service functions are outsourced and coordinated by means of computer-based and other information systems. Second, workforce flexibility and challenge are high because many employees are contractors who can respond quickly to changing tasks and new demands. Third, every company that joins the network is constantly subject to market pressures and demands. For example, if one of Nike's suppliers raises prices too much or the quality of its product declines, Nike can replace it with another firm fairly quickly. Fourth, the network organization tends to be highly flexible and adaptable to changing needs. For example, when Nike added a line of golf balls to its product portfolio in 2000, all it had to do was contract with an established golf ball manufacturer and specify how the Nike golf balls were to be marked and packaged.

As with each way of organizing, the network organization has several potential limitations.[29] First, there is little hands-on control. Operations aren't under one roof, and managers must adjust to relying on independent contractors and subcontractors to do the work. The network organization runs the risk that a contractor can't deliver as promised. Second, the ability of employees in the network, including a guiding network organization such as Nike, may find the network difficult to understand and manage if it changes too rapidly. As contractors change, new relationships need to be formed and these take time to develop. Finally, employee commitment to the network organization may be low. These employees may be loyal to the contractor that employs them, not to the key network firm. They realize that they may lose their jobs at any time if the key network firm decides to use a different contractor.

VIRTUAL ORGANIZATION

A *virtual organization* uses a number of advanced information technologies to integrate its employees, teams, and departments internally and with its network of subcontractors externally to achieve specific goals.[30] As suggested in this definition, the virtual organization builds on the features of the network organization. Both organization designs focus on forging alliances and partnerships with other organizations to pool and share skills, technology, and costs. However, the levels of reciprocal and sequential interdependencies in the virtual organization are much greater. They tend to be instantaneous—that is, anytime and anyplace—for the networked employees, functions, and organizations. The boundaries in a virtual organization, both internally and externally, are much more open than in a network organization because of the use of advanced information technologies that knit all partners together seamlessly. Because of this openness to information among the participants, the need for incredibly high levels of trust and collaboration are imperative.

Another imperative in a virtual organization is the availability and utilization of effective, reliable, and sophisticated information technologies (IT). Peter Keen, founder and chairman of Keen Innovations in Great Falls, Virginia, comments: "The technology architecture is the organizational structure. Your systems can't be down. After all, if you don't have a means of communication, a company can't function. And if your communication is all electronic, well, say no more."[31]

Integration Process. The integration process both vertically and laterally with employees and externally with the networked firms relies on an array of information technologies. In addition to the common methods of e-mail, fax, phone, hard copy documents, and the like now used by most organizations, the virtual organization often uses a number of other, more complex technologies in combination. Let's briefly consider just five of them.[32]

- *Interorganizational systems (IOS)* permit the coupling of transactions among organizations, making them more efficient and responsive. For example, Singapore's TradeNet system couples trade agents, government agencies, port authorities, freight forwarders, shipping companies, banks, and insurance companies with customers and immigration officials. The gains in efficiency and responsiveness are impressive. Clearing the port, which formerly required 2 to 4 days, may now take as little as 10 minutes.

- *Electronic commerce* provides the capability of buying and selling products and information via telephone lines, computer networks, and other electronic means. The Internet, the largest network of computer networks, is the medium usually favored for e-commerce because it allows an organization to cut service costs while increasing service delivery speed.

- *Extranets* provide specific external groups/organizations with limited access to an organization. For example, an organization's customers and suppliers can use extranets to acquire account information and coordinate shipments of their supplies. Package delivery firms make extensive use of extranets and promote responsiveness by giving customers access to the firm's internal tracking system. One of the best examples of this type of system is the FedEx package tracking system, which allows customers to trace the status of packages in transit.

- *Groupware* is a primary enabler of dispersed work teams because it facilitates efficient and accurate sharing of ideas, streamlines processes, and makes parallel task execution possible. These features enable teams to be more time and cost efficient. Groupware also helps team members to learn from each other's expertise. Groupware applications help coordinate tasks in three ways. First, the software makes available a common body of information. For example, a salesperson on the road can check the in-stock status of an item for a customer. Second, the software allows tracking of work flows so that group members can—from a remote location—collaborate on documents and projects. All members of a design team, for example, can use proprietary groupware to ensure that they're working with the most recent version of a drawing. Third, the software provides a means for communication and interactive discussions via e-mail bulletin boards and videoconferencing.

- *Intranets* are Web-based, firewall-protected networks that connect employees through common, hyperlinked interfaces to documents, messaging, and multimedia information sources. They promote communication and information sharing across internal boundaries. Also, intranets provide employees with access to newsletters, human resource information, calendars, product inventories, and recruiting data.

The in-depth use of these and other information technologies, in combination, create virtual organizations. In Chapter 20 we provide additional information on the increasing use of various information technologies, especially in virtual organizations.

The AeroTech Service Group, Inc., headquartered in St. Louis, Missouri, is a virtual organization. It creates software and provides services that ensure a secure gateway to internal networks for external customers, partners, and suppliers and that enable its customers to become virtual organizations. The following Teamwork Competency feature provides an example of how AeroTech's technologies enable teams in many companies to work together anyplace and anytime.[33]

The AeroTech Service Group has built a highly effective virtual factory. The open and flexible network accommodates users whose IT sophistication and relationships with one another vary greatly. Moreover, it permits teams to carry out a wide variety of collaborative tasks and is extremely secure.

To accommodate a broad range of tasks and users and to make its system as simple as possible to use, AeroTech employs protocols developed for the Internet. In addition, AeroTech permits network members to choose from a wide assortment of telecommunication methods and speeds. Members having minimal or sporadic needs access the system with modems, whereas more permanent participants (e.g., customers within large aerospace companies or the U.S. government) use dedicated high-bandwidth links.

Consider how McDonnell-Douglas and UCAR Composites, a $12 million manufacturer of tooling for high-performance composite components based in Irvine, California, use AeroTech's network to build prototypes of complex new parts rapidly. At McDonnell-Douglas computer-aided design (CAD) files are translated into the numerical-control machine code needed to operate UCAR's metal-cutting machines. Using standard Internet protocols over a dedicated high-speed link, McDonnell-Douglas then transfers the CAD file and the metal-cutting program to AeroTech's secure network node. AeroTech's system then forwards them to UCAR on normal phone lines.

Once information about the job has arrived in California, the UCAR engineering team can view the information on its own CAD/CAM systems and make last-minute program checks and any modifications needed. The team then transfers the cutting program to its machines and begins manufacturing the part. This method was particularly attractive to UCAR, which already had a paperless manufacturing operation.

Now it can feed the data directly into its manufacturing and quality-assurance systems. As a result, the cost of these transfers has fallen from $400 per file (for tapes and express mail) to $4—and can be carried out in seconds rather than days.

AeroTech also helps the electronic manufacturing community coordinate schedules better by allowing remote members to use scheduling software on one another's machines. A Department of Defense project manager in Washington, D.C., might use the system to access a McDonnell-Douglas mainframe and run the graphics-based program that maintains a project's schedule. The manager then could get early warnings of time and cost overruns by checking whether subcontractors were completing their subassemblies on time.

• • •

To learn more about the AeroTech Service Group, visit this company's home page at

http://www.aerotechsg.com

Assessment. The virtual organization offers many of the same advantages and has many of the same limitations as the network organization. In addition, the virtual organization has the potential for more cost savings and even faster and more automatic communication and decision-making processes. Because the Internet usually plays a key role in the virtual organization, security and privacy risks can be substantial. There is a constant need for monitoring the effectiveness of electronic "firewalls" and the continuous need to improve them. Also, the electronic openness to information among authorized users of the network requires even higher levels of trust than in the less automatically and instantly connected network organization. We discuss further the crucial role of trust in organizational collaboration and information sharing in Chapters 17 and 18. One of the major limitations of a virtual organization is the lack of much physical—face-to-face—interaction and the bonds of trust that are nurtured through such communication.[34]

In this chapter we built on the foundation of organization design established in Chapter 10. In doing so, we reviewed three important categories of factors that have prompted contemporary organization designs.

1. **STATE THE ROLE OF STRATEGIC AND ENVIRONMENTAL FACTORS IN THE DEVELOPMENT AND ADOPTION OF CONTEMPORARY ORGANIZATION DESIGNS.**

Ideally, an organization's design will help implement the key organizational strategies developed by management. At the same time, the organization's design may influence how managers and employees focus their time and energy. The main emphasis in this chapter was on concepts and designs that help an organization cope with a rapidly changing environment. Such an environment brings frequent and significant shifts in technology, customer expectations, products, competitors, and/or political forces. In such an environment, top management usually needs to make a commitment to operating as an organic organization. In contrast, a mechanistic organization may be effective in a highly stable environment.

2. **DESCRIBE THE ROLE OF TECHNOLOGY IN ORGANIZATION DESIGN.**

Three types of technological interdependence affect organizational design: pooled, sequential, and reciprocal. Pooled interdependence requires little sharing of information and other resources by individuals, teams, and departments, who work on specialized tasks. Sequential interdependence serializes the flow of information and other resources between individuals, teams, and departments to accomplish tasks. Reciprocal interdependence encourages the flow of information and other resources back and forth between individuals, teams, and departments to accomplish tasks. Two basic types of service technologies were reviewed—routine and nonroutine. Organizations using nonroutine service technologies tend to be organic.

3. **DISCUSS THE IMPACT OF TWO BASIC INFORMATION PROCESSING FACTORS IN THE USE OF FOUR DESIGN STRATEGIES.**

Two factors—presented as questions—guide the need to process information through an organization's design: (1) Should management increase the organization's ability to process information and, if so, how? and (2) Should management reduce the need to process information and, if so, how? Four design strategies address these factors. The vertical information design strategy involves methods that enable information to be sent efficiently up and down the chain of command. The lateral information design strategy involves methods that foster horizontal communication and decision making among individuals, teams, and departments. The slack resources design strategy involves stockpiling extra resources—funds, personnel, and materials—to prepare an organization to respond to environmental changes. The self-contained design strategy involves methods for assigning all activities, responsibilities, and resources for a specific product (good or service), project, or geographic region to one team, department, or strategic business unit.

4. **EXPLAIN THE FEATURES OF THREE CONTEMPORARY ORGANIZATION DESIGNS.**

Three contemporary organization designs help organizations (1) implement new strategies, (2) respond to changing environments, (3) facilitate technological interdependence, and (4) rapidly process information. The matrix organization combines some features of the functional and product organization designs to increase the ability of managers and employees to process information. A network organization subcontracts some or many of its operations to other firms and coordinates them to achieve specific goals. A virtual organization uses a number of advanced information technologies to integrate its employees, teams, and departments internally with each other and externally with its network of subcontractors to achieve specific goals. It represents an extension to the basic features of the network organization.

KEY TERMS

Changing environment, p. 295
Lateral information design strategy, p. 302
Matrix organization, p. 305
Mechanistic organization, p. 296
Network organization, p. 306
Nonroutine service technologies, p. 299

Organic organization, p. 296
Pooled interdependence, p. 297
Reciprocal interdependence, p. 298
Routine service technologies, p. 299
Self-contained design strategy, p. 304
Sequential interdependence, p. 298

Slack resources design strategy, p. 303
Technological interdependence, p. 297
Vertical information design strategy, p. 301
Virtual organization, p. 308

QUESTIONS FOR DISCUSSION AND COMPETENCY DEVELOPMENT

1. Think of an organization for which you have recently worked. In what ways are the organization's environment changing?

2. Did the organization you identified in Question 1 function organically or mechanistically? Use the dimensions shown in Table 11.1 to develop your response.

3. Did the departmental structure of the organization you identified in Question 1 match the nature of its technological interdependence? Explain.

4. How does the university or college in which you are enrolled make use of the vertical information design strategy?

5. How does Duke Power make use of the lateral information design strategy?

6. Assume that you are a matrix manager in a hi-tech organization. What competencies are likely to be especially important for your success in this position? Why?

7. What are the differences between a network organization and a virtual organization?

8. **Competency Development: Strategic Action Competency.** Shea Homes is one of four divisions of the J.F. Shea Co., Inc., headquartered in Los Angeles, California. This division builds residential units and develops master-planned communities throughout California, Arizona, Colorado, and North Carolina. Shea Homes operates as a network organization. Shea views its trade contractors as "TradePartners," a term that the company has trademarked. Paul Kalkbrenner, vice president/construction, comments: "These people are the lifeline of Shea Homes, not only because they supply the building materials, but also because their craftspeople actually construct the homes. They aren't subcontractors, they are an extension of Shea and treated as such."[35] To learn about Shea's strategy and the groups of people involved in the Shea Homes network, go to*http://www.sheahomes.com*. Click "Building a Shea Home" when that category comes on the screen, then click "People Involved," and finally click each category of people shown.

9. **Competency Development: Self-Management.** See the dimensions of the self-management competency in Table 1.7 on p. 25. In what ways are these dimensions likely to be important for your success in a virtual organization?

CASE FOR COMPETENCY DEVELOPMENT

Ford Motor Company's Transformation

Ford Motor Company was ranked fourth in revenues in the Fortune 500 list for 2000. Its revenues of more than $162 billion come from seven automotive brands (Aston-Martin, Jaguar, Volvo, Lincoln, Mercury, Ford, and Mazda) and four service divisions (Ford Credit, Hertz, Quality Care, and Quik-Fit). These businesses give Ford a presence in more than 200 countries and territories, with a workforce approaching 400,000 and 140 manufacturing plants.

Jacques A. (Jac) Nasser was named president and CEO of the company in 1999. Born in Lebanon and raised from age 4 in Australia, Nasser has been executive vice president of the company and president of Ford Automotive Operations. Before that, he was group vice president of product development. The following are excerpts from an extensive interview of Nasser.[36]

"When we look at e-commerce, we see a breakthrough in technology that comes along only once in a century. It will enable us to transform how we do business. In the past, we've been able to transform particular processes—such as an engineering process or a manufacturing process—but the speed and open architecture of this new technology allows us to integrate the diverse processes that make up a complex business in a way that was very difficult to do before. What used to happen was we would come up with new processes for manufacturing, engineering, logistics, sales, and marketing, but they weren't well-connected. Today, we need to be able to go from a creative idea to an assessment of demand, to design, engineering manufacturing, and logistics, all the way through to the relationship with our customers. That's the vision we have for this new technology.

How we apply it is interesting as well. We use it internally, in what I call Internet inside, in traditional business-to-business applications, in business-to-customer applications, and also to facilitate the ongoing relationship with customers. The technology is also applied inside our vehicles, through our Telematics initiative, which creates the Internet on wheels. As we've proceeded in these directions, we've tried to make sure that we had allied with the best technology partners: we feel that this technology is changing so rapidly that you don't want to be left out on an island of technology. You want to be linked to the people who can stay at the cutting edge, and you want to have as few filters as possible in their links with Ford.

The Auto Exchange—now called Covisint—the new supply-chain joint venture, is a great example of how we're using e-commerce business-to-business (B2B). We're boosting the effectiveness of the Internet inside program by giving 400,000 Ford employees around the world computers to use in their homes and get really familiar with using them.

Our initiatives will be successful if they allow us to run the business differently. For example, they should allow us to connect with our consumers so that we can tailor vehicle specifications—and new models—to them. They should allow our value chain to operate without frontiers. These initiatives shouldn't matter whether you're the dealer, the original equipment manufacturer, the tier-one supplier, the tier-two supplier, or whatever. Our new system should make the business more responsive, more efficient. It could be as big a transformation as Henry Ford's shift from craft manufacturing to mass production almost a hundred years ago."

Questions

1. What environmental factors are reflected in Jacques Nasser's remarks?

2. What strategic issues are reflected in his remarks?

3. What types of technological interdependence are illustrated in this case?

4. What contemporary organization design features are illustrated in Nasser's comments?

To learn more about the Ford Motor Company, visit this company's home page at ***http://www.ford.com.***

VIDEO CASE

Bindco, Inc.

Bindco, Inc., is a leading manufacturer and distributor of computer software and related products for firms such as Sun Microsystems and McCaffee. Bindco has evolved from a simple three-ring binding company (hence the name Bindco) to a firm engaged in providing virtually all the production and distribution services required of its software clients.

The company basically offers "turnkey manufacturing" to its clients by providing services such as printing instructional manuals; manufacturing floppy disks and compact disks; storing materials; designing, producing, and assembling kit boxes; handling all returned software; and operating an information system to facilitate all these activities. Bindco began providing production and distribution services after monitoring its external environment and anticipating the future needs of its clients. Management actively continues to monitor and anticipate trends in the software industry to gauge their impact on the company's capacity planning and decision-making process.

Bindco's emphasis on capacity planning is reflected in its continual forecasting of trends. The company utilizes a variety of forecasting methods, the basis for which is an aggressive information gathering process. It listens to the ideas, suggestions, and complaints of the ultimate consumers of its products. It surveys software resellers to get their opinions regarding the future of the market. And, it actively seeks the opinions of industry experts about the future of the computer software industry and monitors its competitors' activities. This approach has uncovered a number of trends regarding software demand (e.g., less use of diskettes and more use of CDs and emergence of the Internet). All have some impact on the company's capacity planning and decision making, and some even pose potential threats to the existence of Bindco and other software providers if they fail to adapt.

In response to the industry's risky and uncertain environment, Bindco's management faced three options. First, it could take the lead and anticipate demand for software development, marketing, and distribution and lead the competition. Second, it could closely follow demand for software products rather than lead, mimicking the actions of its competitors. Third, it could lag far behind demand by waiting for the next generation of software to be developed and new marketing and distribution methods to be put in place before acting.

The company's management chose to follow closely the demand for software development, marketing, and distribution rather than to lead it or lag far behind it. Management concedes that there is a "fine line" between keeping abreast of the latest technologies and innovations and having the ability to implement these changes quickly enough to capture a reasonable market share. The risks involve being either too late in responding to the changes in the industry or too early in committing to a technology that the industry and its customers won't embrace.

By adopting a strategy of closely monitoring its external environment, Bindco will constantly face many new problems and opportunities that will significantly affect its organization design, capacity planning, and operating decisions in the future.

Questions

1. Describe the main trends facing Bindco and the software industry. Then describe the impact they may have on the firm.

2. Would an organic or a mechanistic organizational structure favor Bindco in its current environment? Explain

3. Explain Bindco management's decision to follow demand closely in its industry.

To learn more about Bindco, Inc., visit the company's home page at ***http://www.bindco.com.***

Organizational Change and Learning

LEARNING OBJECTIVES

AFTER STUDYING THIS CHAPTER YOU SHOULD BE ABLE TO:

1. DESCRIBE FOUR TYPES OF ORGANIZATIONAL CHANGE.

2. EXPLAIN THE PLANNING PROCESS FOR ORGANIZATIONAL CHANGE.

3. IDENTIFY FOUR METHODS OF ORGANIZATIONAL CHANGE AND EXPLAIN HOW THEY CAN BE COMBINED.

4. DESCRIBE HOW INNOVATION RELATES TO ORGANIZATIONAL CHANGE.

5. DISCUSS HOW LEARNING ORGANIZATIONS DEAL WITH CHANGE.

Chapter Outline

PREVIEW: THE SPEED OF CHANGE AT HEWLETT-PACKARD

TYPES OF ORGANIZATIONAL CHANGE
DEGREE OF CHANGE
TIMING OF CHANGE
WHAT IS YOUR REACTION TO CHANGE?
SELF-MANAGEMENT COMPETENCY: Is Change Your Friend or Foe?

PLANNING FOR ORGANIZATIONAL CHANGE
ASSESS THE ENVIRONMENT
DETERMINE THE PERFORMANCE GAP
DIAGNOSE ORGANIZATIONAL PROBLEMS
ARTICULATE AND COMMUNICATE A VISION FOR THE FUTURE
DEVELOP AND IMPLEMENT A STRATEGIC PLAN FOR CHANGE
ANTICIPATE RESISTANCE AND TAKE ACTION TO REDUCE IT
TEAMWORK COMPETENCY: A Look Inside Outer Circle
MAKE PLANS TO FOLLOW UP

IMPLEMENTING CHANGE
TECHNOLOGY-BASED METHOD
ORGANIZATION REDESIGN METHOD
TASK-BASED METHOD
PEOPLE-ORIENTED METHOD
COMBINING METHODS OF CHANGE

ROLE OF INNOVATION IN ORGANIZATIONAL CHANGE
STRATEGIC IMPORTANCE OF INNOVATION
STRATEGIC ACTION COMPETENCY: E-Tailing Charges Up Retailing
TYPES OF INNOVATION
ARCHITECTURE FOR INNOVATION

LEARNING ORGANIZATIONS
SHARED LEADERSHIP
CULTURE OF INNOVATION
PLANNING AND ADMINISTRATION COMPETENCY: Learning Audits Improve Organizational Memory
CUSTOMER-FOCUSED STRATEGY
ORGANIC ORGANIZATION DESIGN
INTENSIVE USE OF INFORMATION

CHAPTER SUMMARY

KEY TERMS

QUESTIONS FOR DISCUSSION AND COMPETENCY DEVELOPMENT

CASE FOR COMPETENCY DEVELOPMENT: ROYAL DUTCH/SHELL

VIDEO CASE: CENTRAL MICHIGAN COMMUNITY HOSPITAL

THE SPEED OF CHANGE AT HEWLETT-PACKARD

In Silicon Valley, Hewlett-Packard (HP) has long been revered as the area's first "garage start-up." Founded in the 1930s, it grew steadily to become a complex, global company. In fact, by the end of the twentieth century, HP had become so complex that top management decided to split the company into more manageable parts. Reflecting just how much the company had changed, the split separated the core medical and instruments business on which the company was founded—which is now Agilent Technologies—from the computer side of the business. At about the same time, then-CEO Lew Platt announced he would leave HP, to be replaced by Carleton (Carly) Fiorina. Formerly an excutive at Lucent, Fiorina stepped into her new role as the first-ever outsider to serve as HP's CEO. Besides implementing the spin-off of Agilent Technologies, she was expected to lead HP through a radical transformation.

A successful company by many standards, HP nevertheless had been experiencing significant problems. While the rest of the industry was focused on customers, HP's product development process gave more weight to the preferences of the company's engineers than to the preferences of potential customers. And while other competitors were running on "Internet time" and experiencing rapid growth, both HP's decision-making processes and rate of growth lumbered along too slowly. According to Fiorina, the need for change at HP was urgent. "Time does not mean what it used to mean. In the Internet Age, things move very, very quickly. And we have to move quickly enough to catch up with that pace," she explains.

Fiorina's vision for change at HP was to preserve the best parts of the company and reinvent the rest. As part of HP's reinvention, it has entered into several new strategic alliances—a joint venture with Kodak, partnerships with Ford and Delta Air Lines, and a variety of strategic relationships with companies such as Yahoo!, Cisco, and Amazon.com. It has also reorganized its existing businesses into fewer, more clearly focused units. At the center of it all were the HP labs.

For Fiorina, the best parts of the company are its technological know-how and its culture, which values respect, integrity, teamwork, and contribution. HP's culture is strongly rooted in the company's early garage days. Today, a poster of the "Rules of the Garage" reminds employees that Bill Hewlett and Dave Packard believed that bureaucracy and company politics were stupid and destructive. Inventing something significant was the goal. In an effort to avoid the problems of bureaucracy, HP's past leaders encouraged decentralization. To avoid politics, they used a high-involvement approach to decision making and sought to reach consensus about major issues. But for a large company operating in the Internet Age, this approach is now considered too slow.

To speed things up at HP, Fiorina has adopted a take-charge, fast-paced style. When making decisions, she gets input but then makes it clear that she will decide what to do and move ahead with it. She explains her approach this way: "If you want people to speed up, *you* speed up. You don't talk about it, you do it. If you don't walk the talk, nothing will matter to the contrary. In fact, worse, the result will be cynicism, and that would be devastating."[1]

To learn more about organizational change at HP, visit the company's home page at

http://www.hp.com

TYPES OF ORGANIZATIONAL CHANGE

1.

DESCRIBE FOUR TYPES OF ORGANIZATIONAL CHANGE.

Organizational change refers to any transformation in the design or functioning of an organization. Effective managers understand when change is needed and are able to guide their organizations through the change process. Sometimes, the environment jolts the organization into making major changes. If a substantially new and better method of production becomes available, adopting that new method is likely to require major organizational change. In the steel industry, the new minimill production method cut the time required to make a ton of steel by about 60 percent. Steel producers such as Nucor Steel spent millions of dollars to build new plants. But adopting the minimill production method also meant that the jobs of steelworkers and their managers changed significantly, as did the competencies needed to perform those jobs. More recently, development of the Internet has required managers in almost every industry to rethink and radically change the way their organizations function.

DEGREE OF CHANGE

Massive changes in the way an organization operates occur occasionally, but more often change occurs in small steps. The desire to improve performance continuously in order to stay ahead of competitors is a common reason for smaller organizational changes.[2] When Procter & Gamble (P&G) created a new cleaning mop, only minor modifications in production and sales activities were required. Though small in magnitude, those changes were essential to customer acceptance of the new product. Successful organizations are equally adept at making both radical and incremental changes.

Radical. *Radical change* occurs when organizations make major adjustments in the ways they do business. Adopting a new organization structure, merging with another organization, or changing from a privately held to a publicly traded company are all examples of radical change. Radical change is relatively infrequent and generally takes a long time to complete. It can be stimulated by changes in the environment, by persistent performance declines, by significant personnel changes, or by a combination of all three factors. At Knight-Ridder, Inc., one of the largest newspaper chains in the United States, declining readership stimulated change. To rebuild its readership, the company launched a project called 25/43—so named because the goal was to increase readership among people between the ages of 25 and 43. Based on extensive input from readers, this project led to substantive changes in the way the company produced newspapers. Articles became shorter, topics were selected in part because of their potential interest to readers, and page layouts were redesigned. Equally significant was the change from a culture that gave priority to the preferences of editors and journalists to one that recognized that success required responding to the preferences of readers.[3]

At Hewlett-Packard, the Internet, declining share value, and a new CEO were the forces driving that company's radical change, including extensive restructuring of the business. Regardless of the cause, management undertakes radical change intentionally, often making huge investments in planning and implementing the change.[4]

Figure 12.1 illustrates a common framework for describing radical organizational change. Although it was introduced more than 50 years ago, most modern accounts of organizational change reflect the basic ideas shown. Developed by social scientist Kurt Lewin, the framework divides the change process into roughly three stages.[5] In Stage 1—unfreezing—management plans and prepares the members of the organization for a major transformation. A primary objective in this stage is to convince members of the organization of the need for change and to reduce their tendency to resist the change. In Stage 2—transitioning—most of the actual change occurs. Often this stage is described as the implementation process. Finally, in Stage 3—refreezing—the change is solidified. Ideally, changes remain in place once they have been made. But people tend to be creatures of habit, and habits are difficult to change. During refreezing, therefore, monitoring the intended outcomes and providing support for new behaviors are essential to minimize relapses to the old way of doing things.[6]

Figure 12.1   **Three Stages of Radical Change**

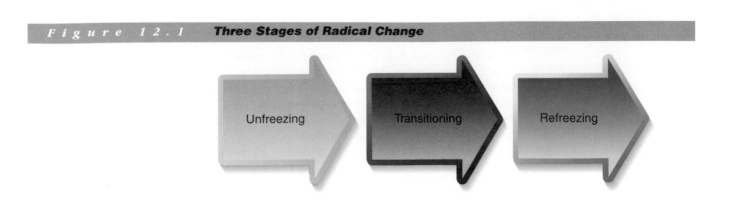

Unfreezing — Transitioning — Refreezing

Incremental. Radical change suggests that one "big bang" can transform an organization into something new. In contrast, ***incremental change*** is an ongoing process of evolution over time, during which many small changes occur routinely. After enough time has passed, the cumulative effect of these changes may be to transform the organization totally. Yet while they are occurring, the changes seem to be just a normal aspect of revising and improving the way that work gets done. As we discussed in Chapter 3, total quality management (TQM) is an approach that relies heavily on incremental organizational change. Employees routinely look for ways to improve products and services, and they make suggestions for changes day in and day out. Incremental change is also important in learning organizations, which we describe later in this chapter.

TIMING OF CHANGE

In addition to the differences in the magnitude of change are differences in the timing of change. Organizations may make radical changes in response to a crisis or because leaders have a bold new vision of what the future *could* be like. Similarly, organizations may make incremental changes as a reaction to past events or in anticipation of trends that have just begun to develop. Figure 12.2 illustrates how the degree and timing of change combine to form different types of change.

Figure 1 2 . 2	**Types of Organizational Change**

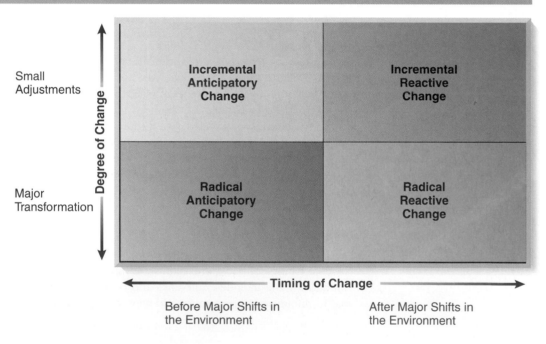

Reactive. *Reactive change* occurs when an organization is forced to change in response to some event in the external or internal environment. New strategic moves made by competitors and new scientific or technological discoveries are common reasons for reactive change. For many years, hospitals and other health-care organizations grew incrementally through evolutionary change. The external environment was relatively stable, allowing them to expand gradually by adding new services and increasing capacity. In the 1980s, the industry was jolted by new government regulations intended to reduce the mounting costs of health care. During the past 15 years, many hospitals have had to undergo large-scale, revolutionary changes in order to survive.[7]

Reactive change can be incremental or radical. If an organization adapts to a change in the environment without undergoing a substantial reorientation in its strategy or values, the change is reactive and incremental. When Citibank first introduced a new strategy for using ATM machines in New York City, it was an important event for competing banks. ATMs were already in use by other banks, but most banks had just one machine available on the outside of their buildings. Citibank installed several ATMs and enclosed the area in a vestibule that provided more security and privacy for customers. When it became clear that ATMs reduced costs and increased customer satisfaction, other banks had to react to this competitive move. To adapt, they added ATMs and placed them in less exposed locations, but they did not usually change their fundamental approach to doing business.[8]

Sometimes, reactive change takes the form of a new organization design. In response to a crisis, top-level executives may reassess their approach and decide to make fundamental changes. When Durk Jager became CEO of P&G, he tried to re-create that company to improve its sagging performance. His goal was to shake up the company's conservative and staid culture and turn it into a more entrepreneurial enterprise. Jager changed the company's processes for developing new products, conducting market tests, and making decisions about which products to promote. He closed several plants and cut thousands of jobs. Many of the managers who survived were moved into new jobs. New financial measures were adopted for assessing the company's progress. Unfortunately, Jager's reactive attempt to make radical change didn't succeed. A year after he began to make changes, the company's share price took a nosedive, falling 50 percent in six months, and Jager was replaced. Managers at P&G believed that Jager's biggest mistake was trying to change everything all at once. He didn't seem to realize how long organizations must plan and how carefully they must implement such radical transformations.[9]

Anticipatory. As the term suggests, *anticipatory change* occurs when managers make organizational changes in anticipation of upcoming events or early in the cycle of a new trend. The best-run organizations always look for better ways to do things in order to stay ahead of the competition. They constantly fine-tune their policies and practices, introduce technological improvements, and set new standards for customer satisfaction. Often, anticipatory change is incremental and results from constant tinkering and improvements. Occasionally, anticipatory change is discontinuous, however. Visionary leaders within the organization become convinced that major changes are needed even though there is no apparent crisis. Because there is no crisis, the change can be planned carefully and implemented gradually.

WHAT IS YOUR REACTION TO CHANGE?

Later in this chapter, we describe in more detail how change unfolds. Effective managers are comfortable with many types of changes. They know how to address the concerns of employees who embrace change and employees who find change difficult and stressful. Individual differences seem to play an important role in how people react to change. Some people thrive during change and even seek it out; others find change stressful and prefer to avoid it.[10] Before continuing, take a moment to answer the questions posed in the following Self-Management Competency feature. These questions are designed to provide insight into how you respond to change. After you have calculated your score, discuss it with other members of your class. Does everyone react to change the same way you do?

SELF-MANAGEMENT COMPETENCY

Is Change Your Friend or Foe?

INSTRUCTIONS

For each statement, circle "T" if the statement is true or circle "F" if the statement is false. There are no right or wrong answers. Rather, the intent is to help you explore your attitudes about change.

STATEMENT

T F 1. Among my friends, I'm usually the first person to try out a new idea or method.

T F 2. When I take vacations, I prefer to return to places I have been to already and know I will like.

T F 3. Compared to other people, I tend to change the way I look (hair, clothes) fairly often.

PLANNING FOR ORGANIZATIONAL CHANGE

2.

EXPLAIN THE PLANNING PROCESS FOR ORGANIZATIONAL CHANGE.

Organizational change can be unplanned and somewhat chaotic or planned and relatively smooth. By its very nature, chaotic change is difficult to manage. Nevertheless, large-scale organizational changes seldom occur without a bit of chaos. Organizations usually strive to minimize it by imposing some order on the change process. Change is most likely to be orderly when it has been planned. The planning process itself can help unfreeze the organization by convincing people of the need for change and involving them in decisions about how to change. The steps involved in planning for organizational change are shown in Figure 12.3. Although planned changes don't always proceed exactly as shown, planning generally precedes the implementation of major change initiatives.[11]

ASSESS THE ENVIRONMENT

As we described in Chapter 3, both the degree and rate of change in the environment have implications for organizations. The four environmental factors most responsible for stimulating organizational change are customers, technology, competitors, and the workforce. Other factors that may pressure organizations to change include globalization, technological advances, and the actions of important stakeholders, such as shareholders, government regulators, unions, and political action groups.[12] Environmental scanning activities ensure that organizations become aware of changes as they occur. Marriott Hotels, Hilton Hotels, and Bank of America use customer satisfaction surveys and other forms of market research to assess customers' preferences. Employee surveys

Figure 1 2 . 3 **Planning for Organizational Change**

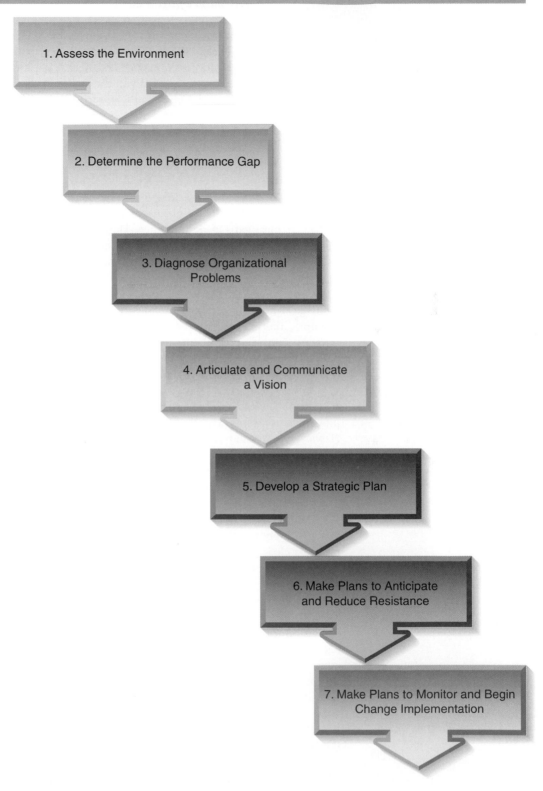

1. Assess the Environment

2. Determine the Performance Gap

3. Diagnose Organizational Problems

4. Articulate and Communicate a Vision

5. Develop a Strategic Plan

6. Make Plans to Anticipate and Reduce Resistance

7. Make Plans to Monitor and Begin Change Implementation

are a method of scanning the internal environment to assess the concerns of the work-force. Ed Zander, President of Sun Microsystems, Inc., uses "whack-o-meter" sessions to assess the environment. Each week, key decision makers meet to discuss competitors' moves and any implications that they may have for "whacking" the marketplace.[13]

DETERMINE THE PERFORMANCE GAP

A **performance gap** is the difference between what the organization wants to do and what it actually does. By determining the performance gap, managers provide clear answers to the question, What is wrong? Carly Fiorina's assessment of HP's environment led her to conclude that Hewlett-Packard needed to address a major performance gap: It was a hi-tech company that had failed to keep pace with the speed of change in the industry it helped create. In addition, it had failed to shift its mindset. Long after competitors such as Oracle, IBM, and EDS had shifted to a customer-focused approach to product design and development, HP's products were still designed to meet the standards of its own engineers.

WEB INSIGHT

By now, HP is well into its most recent change effort. What vision is CEO Carly Fiorina communicating at this stage, and how? Is the company still in transition, or is it refreezing? Visit the HP Web site at *http://www.hp.com* to make your assessment.

DIAGNOSE ORGANIZATIONAL PROBLEMS

The aim of **organizational diagnosis** is to identify the nature and extent of problems before taking action. Through diagnosis, managers develop an understanding of the reasons behind gaps in performance. They answer the question, *Why* do we have performance gaps? The idea that diagnosis should precede action may seem obvious, but its importance is often underestimated.[14] All too often results-oriented managers prematurely begin the change process and impatiently push for solutions before the nature of the problem itself is clear.

Organizations often hire outside consultants to assist with problem diagnosis. For example, interpersonal problems often require gathering sensitive information from employees. Outside consultants may be better able to conduct interviews and interpret data in an unbiased manner than insiders. In addition, consultants often have the expertise that the organization lacks to conduct and analyze attitude surveys properly.

Carly Fiorina relied heavily on employees to help her diagnose HP's organizational problems. As she toured the company during her first few months as CEO, she told employees to "send me 'The 10 Stupidest Things We Do!'" and promised to read them. Tom Hawley, the human resource director at Food Ingredient Specialties, also turned to employees to help diagnose organizational problems. To get people involved, he hired a blues band to perform during an off-site meeting. He then had employees spend some time actually writing and performing their *own* blues songs, describing problems in the company.[15]

ARTICULATE AND COMMUNICATE A VISION FOR THE FUTURE

Successful change efforts are guided by a clear vision for the future. Until leaders formulate a clear vision and persuade others to join them in being dedicated to that vision, they won't be able to generate the enthusiasm and resources needed for large-scale cultural change.[16]

To communicate the leader's vision, messages should be sent consistently and repeatedly through varying organizational channels by credible sources.[17] Communicating her vision for Hewlett-Packard was one of the most important items on Carly Fiorina's agenda during her first year as CEO. To begin, she went on a tour, visiting 20 sites in 10 countries. She also pushed mass distribution of voice-mail and e-mail messages, write-ups in the company magazine, and videotapes shown on the company's intranet. In describing the change processes that have been underway for several years at American Express, CEO Harvey Golub noted that, about the time he was completely sick of repeating the same message, people were just starting to hear it. Recognizing that different people prefer different modes of communication, Golub made sure that his vision for change was put in every form possible: memos, employee newspapers, videos, speeches, "white-papers" that provided supporting analysis, and so on.

DEVELOP AND IMPLEMENT A STRATEGIC PLAN FOR CHANGE

Although investments made in planning often produce significant improvements in productivity,[18] most companies begin substantial change efforts without a thoughtful, integrated plan.[19] A strategic plan for change should be the blueprint for action.

For major change efforts, the organization's strategic plan can be quite complex and not easily understood by the workforce because it includes proposals for all levels and all units involved in the change effort. However, in an organization structured by functional department, each department should develop a more focused plan based on the overall strategic plan; in an organization structured by region, more detailed plans for each region should be developed, and so on. Regardless of the approach used, the strategic plan should be adopted only after considering the full range of alternative methods for fostering change, which we describe in more detail later in this chapter. A strategic plan for change articulates the goals for change and describes the specific measures to be used to monitor and evaluate progress toward those goals. Finally, the strategic plan provides a timetable for implementation and evaluation.

Consider Alternatives. When developing a strategic plan for change, management should consider all feasible alternatives, along with their advantages and disadvantages. Complex issues and problems usually require multipronged solutions. All such solutions usually can't be implemented at the same time, so priorities must be established, taking into account both short- and long-term needs. For a plan to be effective, those who will be affected must buy into it. The best way to ensure that is through *early involvement*. That employees should be involved in planning change seems obvious, but even experienced managers often forget this principle.

Xerox has a long record of enlightened diversity management. One of its earliest successes involved a caucus group for African-American employees. In fact, it was so successful that the company decided to create a caucus group for female employees. However, the first attempt to establish a women's caucus—in the mid 1970s—failed. One explanation for the failure was that the women's caucus was designed to duplicate the existing African-American caucus instead of being designed specifically to address the concerns of female employees. A few years later, female employees at Xerox began to establish caucus groups on their own. Today, a dozen different women's caucuses in the company meet the many diverse needs of female employees.

Task forces, focus groups, surveys, hot lines, and informal conversations are but a few of the ways that managers can involve employees and other stakeholders in assessing the alternatives for change. There is little disagreement among change experts about the importance of involvement. How you get people involved is less important than doing it. However, it *is* important to be clear about what involvement means. If employees are led to believe that they'll have the final say when in fact their opinions are just one of many factors that'll affect decisions, involvement can backfire.

Set Goals. For change to be effective, goals should be set before the change effort is started. If possible, the goals should be (1) realistically attainable, (2) stated in clear and measurable terms, (3) consistent with the organization's overall goals and policies, and (4) attainable. For example, when a take-out pizza business in Virginia decided that it needed to improve driver safety, it began by collecting systematic information about behaviors (e.g., the extent to which drivers came to complete stops at intersections). Management shared the information with employees and asked them to set specific goals for improvement. During the months that followed, driving behavior was monitored and charts were used to inform employees of their progress toward meeting those goals. Employees participating in goal setting showed improvement in several areas of behavior, including some for which they hadn't even set specific goals.[20]

As part of the changes that Continental Airlines made to go "From Worst to First" airline according to the FAA, the company developed clear goals. Even the vice president of corporate communications admitted that the company had been in serious trouble: "This airline was probably, candidly, one of the least-respected airlines in corporate America. It could *not* get any worse than Continental in 1994." Two years later, Continental was celebrating its highest pretax profits ever. Its Go Forward plan set out the following strategic goals:

1. *Fly to win.* The goal was to achieve top-quartile industry profit margins.
2. *Fund the future.* To do so required reducing interest expense by owning more hub real estate.
3. *Make reliability a reality.* Specific goals included ranking among the top airlines on the four measurements used by the U.S. Department of Transportation (DOT).
4. *Working together.* Have a company where employees enjoy working and are valued for their contributions.

Specific goals linked to specific rewards were what made Continental's strategy meaningful. In 1995, one goal was to be ranked in the top five of the DOT on-time performance ratings. For each month the goal was achieved, employees would earn an extra $65. Two months later, Continental was in first place. The next year the goal and the reward were changed. Now employees could earn $100 for each month the company ranked first and $65 for each month it ranked second or third. Executives have goals and rewards, too. For example, employees regularly rate their managers on an employee survey. An outside consulting group analyzes the results, and executives' bonuses reflect their leadership performance as measured by the survey.[21]

ANTICIPATE RESISTANCE AND TAKE ACTION TO REDUCE IT

Few planned organizational change efforts go as smoothly as managers would like. Most run into some amount of resistance. To deal successfully with resistance, managers must learn to anticipate it and then head it off, if at all possible.

Experienced managers are all too aware of the various forms that resistance can take: immediate criticism, malicious compliance, sabotage, insincere agreement, silence, deflection, and in-your-face defiance are just a few examples.[22] Some managers don't even initiate needed changes because they feel incapable of overcoming expected resistance. Successful managers understand why people resist change and what can be done to overcome such resistance.

Some resistance to change may actually be useful. Employees can operate as a check-and-balance mechanism to ensure that management properly plans and implements change. Justifiable resistance that causes management to think through its proposed changes more carefully may result in better decisions. Effective change efforts rest on the ability of managers to overcome resistance. The commonly used methods for doing so are education, participation, and incentives.

In general, individuals—and sometimes even entire organizations—tend to resist change for four reasons: fear, vested interests, misunderstandings, and cynicism.[23]

Fear. To be able to reduce resistance to change, managers first of all must not be afraid of resistance—and then help employees not to be afraid of change or its consequences. Some people resist change because they fear that they'll be unable to develop the competencies required to be effective in the new situation. A common obstacle to organizational change is the reluctance of managers and employees to change their attitudes and learn the new behaviors that the organization requires. Even when employees understand and accept that they need to change, doing so often is difficult because they fear the consequences. When Mercedes-Benz Credit Corporation set out to restructure its operations in the United States, CEO Georg Bauer knew that fear could be a problem because restructuring often means downsizing. "It was absolutely essential to establish a no-fear element in this whole change process," he said. Rather than resist change, he wanted employees to help create a new, more efficient organization by expressing their ideas about where to cut and how to do work differently.[24]

Vested Interests. Fear often goes hand in hand with vested interests. People who have vested interests in maintaining things as they are often resist change.[25] This behavior seems to occur even when these people recognize the need for change. In one large study of 53 organizations, researchers found that merely convincing people of the need for change for the good of the organization did not necessarily reduce their resistance to it. They continued to resist the change if they believed that it conflicted with their own self-interests.[26]

Some managers initiate change believing that anyone with the same information would make the same decision. This assumption isn't always correct. Often top-level managers see change as a way to improve the organization. They may also believe that change will offer them new opportunities to develop their own competencies as they tackle new challenges. In contrast, employees may view proposed changes as upsetting the agreements between themselves and their employer. In particular, they may expect increased workloads and longer hours to be the only rewards for staying around to help implement a major organizational change.[27]

Georg Bauer of Mercedes-Benz attacked the combined problems of fear and vested interests in two ways. He empowered employees to make decisions about how to change their work, and he used financial incentives to convince employees that even cutting their own jobs wouldn't harm them. Empowering workers and giving them some control over the change process is an effective way to reduce the stress that employees experience during a change effort.[28] To align employees' self-interests with the company's interest, he offered the security of a new—and probably better—job to anyone bold enough to eliminate his or her current position. In this successful change effort, four entire layers of management vanished at the suggestion of the managers themselves.[29]

Misunderstandings. People resist change when they don't understand its implications. Unless quickly addressed, misunderstandings and lack of trust build resistance. Top managers must be visible during the change process to spell out clearly the new direction for the organization and what it will mean for everyone involved. Getting employees to discuss their problems openly is crucial to overcoming resistance to change.

GE's well-known Work-Out sessions help reduce misunderstandings between employees and managers by creating a two-way communication channel. After several years of trying to create change primarily through top-down directives, Jack Welch concluded that top management was too insulated from the reactions of the people on the assembly lines. At Work-Out sessions, employees throughout the company are brought together for a session of intense and frank discussion with a selected manager. Trained facilitators help run the sessions, which ensures that employees do most of the talking and that managers do most of the listening. Like trips to the gym, Work-Out sessions usually cause managers to work up a good sweat. Afterwards, managers can develop plans to help clear up any misunderstandings revealed by employees' comments during the session.

When wide-ranging changes are planned, managers should anticipate that misunderstandings will develop and take steps to minimize them. At Prudential Insurance, a specially designed game was used to help employees understand the implications of the company's impending change from a mutual association to a public company. Small groups of employees at all levels and in all types of jobs throughout the company were brought together to play the game, which was both informative and fun. Top management was convinced that this approach to informing the workforce about the implications of the change they were about to experience would enable the change process to go smoothly—and it did.

Cynicism. In some organizations, initiating change efforts is seen simply as something that new managers do to make their mark. Over time, employees see change efforts come and go much like the seasons of the year, as managers implement one fad after the other. Eventually, cynicism sets in and employees refuse to support yet another change "program." Without employee support the change efforts fail, which further contributes to cynicism.[30]

Organizations can reduce cynicism by involving employees throughout the change process. Research shows that participation, especially when it is voluntary, usually leads to commitment.[31] At IBM, which has undergone a major transformation during the past few years under CEO Lou Gerstner, full employee participation is credited with the company's revival. Managers such as John Patrick helped Gerstner by rallying people throughout the company around a common vision for the future. Patrick had been experimenting with Gopher, one of the early software programs used on the Internet. As he played with it, he realized that the Internet would change completely the future of computing. He shared this insight and a six-point plan for what IBM needed to do in a manifesto titled "Get Connected." His message generated immediate enthusiasm within the company, and before long a community of excited employees had formed to make it happen. Although Get Connected had no budget and no formal authority, within six months the team had created one of the first significant corporate Web sites. In another few months, IBM would create an Internet division and make John Patrick vice president and chief technology officer. Through his experiences, Patrick learned a great deal about making change happen.[32]

Nevertheless, participation can have its drawbacks. Sometimes employees are reluctant to participate, even when invited to do so. They may feel that they don't have the expertise needed to participate effectively. If cynicism has already set in, they may feel that it's a waste of their time to offer their ideas. Finally, if employees do get involved through participation, the process must be managed carefully to avoid wasting a lot of time and money.

When people are empowered to help guide an organization through major change, the participation that follows often requires a great deal of teamwork. The importance of teamwork in creating change is illustrated in the following Teamwork Competency feature.[33]

TEAMWORK COMPETENCY

A Look Inside Outer Circle

If you carry your lunch or snacks in a brightly colored nylon cooler hanging from a shoulder strap, you probably know about Outer Circle. Located in Chicago, this company employs 200 people. Together, they work as a team to gather ideas for new or better products. For example, thanks to one employee's observation that mothers were packing juice boxes with their children's lunches, the company redesigned the minicooler section of its lunch boxes. The idea for adding a shoulder strap was born after employees talked to workers at a local construction site. When the company needed a color scheme to fit the image of extreme sportsters, employees throughout the company pitched in to help. A stock boy brought in a

picture of silver sneakers. A marketing executive shared a photo of someone wearing a blue metallic shirt. A designer showed photos from a catalog of titanium bikes. From these ideas came the decision to use a metallic color scheme for the company's Z Series of products.

Since 1997, product design teams at Outer Circle have included employees from every department. According to CEO Larry Futterman, "Every functionary of the company needs to be involved in order for us to be profitable. It can't just be design people coming up with pretty pictures or marketing people coming up with good ideas." When the company was first founded, it got its ideas by knocking off those of its competitors. Now Outer

Circle is the one with the creative edge. "First they ignored us. Then they figured out we were here. Now they'll copy us," says Futterman.

MAKE PLANS TO FOLLOW UP

As the process of change unfolds, managers need to monitor employees' reactions as well as results. Measures of employee and customer satisfaction, new-product development, market share, profitability, and other results should be tracked to assess both short-term and longer-term consequences. The speed, degree, and duration of improvement should all be monitored. Ideally, the measures used for monitoring and follow-up should be closely tied to the goals and timetables established in the strategic plan for change.

Again, ideally, the results of a change process should be monitored continuously. However, because that usually is too costly and time-consuming, assessments typically are made at predetermined intervals. The first assessment should be made immediately after a change has been implemented.[34] To avoid jumping to premature conclusions, management should make another assessment later. Sometimes the second assessment reveals that the positive effects of change have worn off. Alternatively, a second assessment could reveal delayed positive effects. Misjudging the amount of time needed to see the positive results of a change process is perhaps the most common mistake that managers make.

IMPLEMENTING CHANGE

3.

IDENTIFY FOUR METHODS OF ORGANIZATIONAL CHANGE AND EXPLAIN HOW THEY CAN BE COMBINED.

Having decided that change is needed, managers have available to them many methods that they can use to make it happen. Here we discuss the four major methods depicted in Figure 12.4. Although we describe each method separately, some combination of these approaches is involved in most large organizational change efforts. Seldom can significant change be based on one of these approaches alone.[35]

Figure   12.4   **Methods for Creating Change**

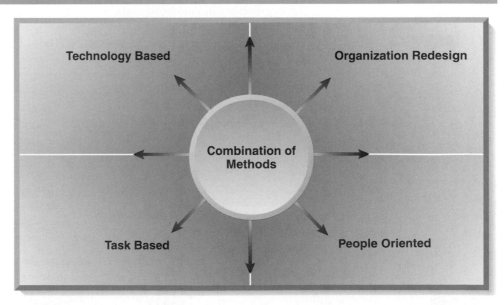

TECHNOLOGY-BASED METHOD

When an organization chooses the ***technology-based method*** for creating change, it focuses its attention on work flows, production methods, materials, and information systems. In 1908, Henry Ford changed the workplace by demonstrating how effective assembly-line technologies could be when he launched the mass production of cars. In that new age of mass consumption, the revolutionary assembly-line technology was ideal for making identical goods in volume.

Today, modern organizations are using information technology to achieve equally dramatic change. *Information technology* (IT) comprises complex networks of computers, telecommunications systems, and remote-controlled devices. As information technology continues to evolve, it is becoming increasingly easy for organizations to build links between suppliers, producers, distributors, and customers. At Wal-Mart, the electronic cash register monitors the goods sold, their prices, and the amounts remaining on hand (inventory). If the system recognizes that a store is low on Tide detergent, for example, an order is sent to the nearest distribution center to send more Tide to that store. When the distribution center's supply of Tide is low, the system automatically re-orders it from P&G. For organizations with Web sites, IT also provides an efficient method for communicating with customers. In addition to providing comments and feedback to companies, Web sites can be used to inform customers about changes in an organization's products and services. At the Yahoo! Web site, employees and customers hold a continuing electronic conversation about both the changes that customers request and the actions that Yahoo! takes in response.

Information technologies are also useful for breaking down barriers between departments, improving quality control, lowering costs, and increasing efficiencies. Alliant Foodservice, Inc., is a $6 billion distributor of food and supplies to restaurants, hotels, and hospitals. Formerly a division of Kraft, this old-economy company is built around a network of warehouses, trucks, and call centers. In an industry that hadn't changed much in more than 50 years, Alliant's top management realized that IT could be the basis for a total transformation of the business. In fact, the transformation envisioned was so radical that Alliant's top management decided to create a separate Web-based company that would partner with Alliant, while offering a new service to its small-business customers.

ORGANIZATION REDESIGN METHOD

The *organization redesign method* emphasizes internal structural changes: realigning departments, changing who makes decisions, and merging or reorganizing departments that sell the organization's products. Recall our discussion of the fundamentals of organization design in Chapters 10 and 11. The organization redesign method of change simply means moving from one form of organization to another. Sometimes the need for redesign follows directly from implementing new technologies. As Mellon Bank's customers became more comfortable using ATMs, the bank found that it needed 30 percent fewer branches. The remaining branches were redesigned to focus more on selling new products and offering new services than on cashing checks.[36]

Two basic approaches to organization redesign are changing the organization's structure and changing the organization's processes. Regardless of the redesign chosen, the intent usually is to clarify what gives the organization its leadership position with its customers. In other words, design changes should capitalize on the capabilities that differentiate the organization from its competitors. Businesses, goods, or services that don't contribute to this goal are candidates for elimination or sale.

Structural Redesign. *Restructuring* typically means reconfiguring the distribution of authority, responsibility, and control in an organization.[37] Authority, responsibility, and control change radically when entire businesses or divisions are combined or spun off. Thus, when Hewlett-Packard spun off its medical and instruments business, creating Agilent, it used radical organizational change.

Downsizing is another familiar approach to structural redesign. Downsizing is usually a reactive response to poor organizational performance, but this often-used method of change doesn't necessarily work. Although downsizing may improve financial performance in the short run, several studies have indicated that downsized firms end up in worse financial shape later.[38] However, no one knows whether such firms would have even survived without the changes undertaken. Regardless of how effective it may be in the long run, downsizing is a painful experience for both those who are let go and those who survive the cuts. The survivors often feel guilty because, somehow, they have been spared, but they also are anxious because they might be next. Survivors often have trouble maintaining a commitment to an organization when they might be "doing time" until the next round of layoffs is announced.[39]

Process Redesign. The ***process redesign method,*** also called ***reengineering,*** focuses on creating new ways to get work done. It often involves the redesign of processes related to logistics, manufacturing, and distribution. The goal is to design the most effective process for making and delivering a product.[40] Effective processes are those that cost the least while at the same time rapidly producing goods and providing services of excellent quality. Thus the starting point is to assess current processes from the customer's point of view.

Often, reengineering is interrelated with other key activities. Recall that many organizations are structured by function and that employees' reactions to change typically are based on its effect on their departments. However, reengineering requires employees to think across functions. Reengineering can reduce the amount of "hand-offs" between departments by increasing the amount of resources that are brought together simultaneously to meet customers' needs. Benefits may include faster delivery time, more accurate billing, and fewer defective products that must be returned.

At some companies, restructuring around processes involves improving the flow of work that cuts across multiple businesses, not just departments. Changes in the health-care industry led SmithKline Beecham to reevaluate the way its SBUs were structured. Before restructuring, it had four separate SBUs—pharmaceuticals, consumer health care, animal health, and clinical labs—each of which operated independently. When management evaluated customer demand, however, it concluded that the company should be restructured around three broad processes—care delivery, care management, and care coverage.[41]

TASK-BASED METHOD

The ***task-based method*** concentrates on changing specific employee job responsibilities and tasks. Whenever a job is changed—whether because of new technology or a redesign effort—tasks also change. Two dramatically different ways of changing a task are job simplification and job enrichment.

Job Simplification. The oldest task approach to change is job simplification. ***Job simplification*** involves the scientific analysis of tasks performed by employees in order to discover procedures that produce the maximum output for the minimum input. The job specification states the tasks to be performed, the work methods to be used, and the workflow to be obtained. Like reengineering, job simplification is founded on engineering concepts. Recall that the scientific management techniques developed by Frederick Taylor defined jobs and designed tasks on the basis of time-and-motion studies (see Chapter 2). But there is a big difference between these two approaches to change. Reengineering focuses on an entire process, which may involve many employees working in many parts of the organization. In contrast, the focus of job simplification is the work done by employees in a particular job.

The downside of job simplification is that it leads to low employee commitment and high turnover. Most current competitive challenges require a committed and involved workforce that is able to make decisions and experiment with new ways of doing things. Many people seek jobs that allow greater discretion and offer more of a challenge. Thus designing jobs with employee needs in mind requires a different approach.

Job Enrichment. Changing job specifications to broaden and add challenge to the tasks required and to increase productivity is called ***job enrichment.*** Job enrichment has four unique aspects. First, it changes the basic relationships between employees and their work. Job enrichment is based on the assumption that interesting and challenging work can be a source of employee satisfaction and involvement.

Second, job enrichment directly changes employee behaviors in ways that gradually lead to more positive attitudes about the organization and a better self-image. Because enriched jobs usually increase feelings of autonomy and personal freedom, employees are likely to develop attitudes that support the new job-related behaviors.

Third, job enrichment offers numerous opportunities for initiating other types of organizational change. Technical problems are likely to develop when jobs are changed, which offers management an opportunity to refine the technology used. Interpersonal problems almost inevitably arise between managers and subordinates and sometimes among coworkers who have to relate to one another in different ways. These situations offer opportunities for developing teamwork and communication competencies.

Finally, job enrichment can humanize an organization. Individuals can experience the psychological lift that comes from developing new competencies and doing a job well. Individuals are encouraged to grow and push themselves.

PEOPLE-ORIENTED METHOD

The ***people-oriented method*** includes a wide range of activities intended to improve individual competencies, attitudes, and performance levels. Technology, design, and task methods are used to improve organizational performance by changing the way work is done. The assumption is that employees will change as required by the changes made in their work settings.[42] In contrast, people-oriented approaches are used to create organizational change by focusing on changing employee perceptions, attitudes, competencies, and expectations. As these factors change, employees may then seek changes in the organization's technology, design, or tasks. According to this view, employees are the captains of change, not just the vessels for carrying it out.

WEB INSIGHT

What special competencies are needed by consultants who assist organizations in managing organizational change? To learn about the views of professionals in this field, visit the Web site of the Academy of Management's Division of Organizational Change and Development at *http://www.aom.pace.edu/odc*.

Many people-oriented methods for changing organizations are commonly grouped under the broad label of organization development. ***Organization development*** (OD) is a planned, long-range behavioral science strategy for understanding, changing, and developing an organization's workforce in order to improve its effectiveness.[43] Although OD methods frequently include design, technological, and task changes, their primary focus is on changing people. Three core sets of values define the OD approach to organizational change.

- *People values.* People have a natural desire to grow and develop. Organization development aims to overcome obstacles to individual growth and enable employees to give more to the organization. It stresses treating people with dignity and respect, behaving genuinely rather than playing games, and communicating openly.

- *Group values.* Acceptance, collaboration, and involvement in a group lead to expressions of feelings and perceptions. Hiding feelings or not being accepted by the group diminishes the individual's willingness to work constructively toward solutions to problems. Openness can be risky, but it can usually help people effectively plan solutions to problems and carry them out.

- *Organization values.* The way groups are linked strongly influences their effectiveness. Organization development recognizes the importance of starting the change process at the top and gradually introducing it throughout the rest of the organization. Top-level managers shouldn't attempt to introduce change at lower levels of the organization until they have begun to change themselves.

Of the many OD methods available, one of the most commonly used is survey feedback. ***Survey feedback*** allows managers and employees to provide feedback about the organization and receive feedback about their own behaviors.[44] Such information becomes the basis for group discussion and the stimulus for change. Accurate feedback from others about behaviors and job performance is one of the primary bases of OD.

Feedback is obtained by means of a questionnaire developed and distributed to all employees, who complete it and turn it in anonymously. The content of the questionnaire depends on the areas of most concern to the organization. Typically, however, employee surveys tap into employees' feelings of commitment and satisfaction, their assessments of the climate for innovation, the degree to which they feel that the organization is customer oriented, and their attitudes toward supervision and management practices.

Survey questionnaires used for obtaining feedback may be custom designed for the organization or standardized. The advantage of custom-designed questionnaires is that they focus on the topics of special interest to the organization. A disadvantage is that they can be difficult to interpret unless the same questions have been asked over a period of a few years. When information is available for a period of several years, a custom-designed questionnaire can be used to assess whether the organization is or isn't generally improving.

An alternative to a custom-designed questionnaire is a standardized questionnaire. A standardized questionnaire is one that has been developed for use in a wide variety of organizations. Often a standardized questionnaire has been developed according to scientific principles, so its users can be confident that the assessments it yields are valid reflections of the organization. Because standardized questionnaires often have been used by several organizations in the past, they allow an organization to compare its employees' responses to those of employees in other organizations. Benchmarking permits management to assess the degree to which employee attitudes match or diverge from the attitudes of employees in other organizations.

When employee surveys are designed to address issues of strategic importance, they can be used to enhance the organization's competitive advantage. For example, if the organization's strategy requires innovation and creativity, managers could use a survey to monitor whether employees feel that innovation and creativity are truly valued. If employees are cynical about management's latest attempts to stimulate innovation and creativity, the survey results should reveal this attitude. Thus survey feedback can be a useful tool that helps managers develop a better understanding of their organization. Table 12.1 describes one standardized questionnaire, called KEYS, that is often used for survey feedback. It's a survey that organizations can use to assess the extent to which employees perceive their workplace to be supportive of creativity and innovation. Based on the diagnosis that KEYS provides, management can determine whether changes are needed to improve the existing organizational climate. If improvements are needed, the results of the survey also provide information about which specific aspects of an organization's culture require change in order to be more supportive of creativity and innovation.[45]

T a b l e 1 2 . 1	**KEYS for Understanding the Organization**

KEYS includes 78 statements designed to assess perceptions of organizational creativity, autonomy and freedom, availability of resources, pressures, and impediments to creativity. Employees use a four-point scale to indicate the extent to which they agree with statements.

Examples of statements included in KEYS.

People are encouraged to solve problems creatively in this organization.

My supervisor serves as a good work model.

There is free and open communication within my work group.

Generally I can get the resources I need for my work.

I have too much work to do in too little time.

There are many political problems in the organization.

During the past 10 years, more than 15,000 employees from dozens of organizations have completed the KEYS survey. Research conducted on employees who work on creative projects has shown that scores on the KEYS questionnaire are higher in work units that produce creative results and lower in work units that produce less creative results. To learn more about KEYS, visit the Web site of the Center for Creative Leadership at *http://www.ccl.org/products/keys*.

COMBINING METHODS OF CHANGE

Organizational change is a complex undertaking. Usually, large-scale change efforts involve the use of a combination of methods. Because information is integral to the functioning of most organizations, any restructuring effort is likely to have implications for the design and use of information systems. In fact a new term, *e-engineering*, has recently been suggested as a description of reengineering initiatives that use Web-based technology as the primary method for managing business-to-business processes (e.g., purchasing and account management). After it merged with Allied Signal, Honeywell International used e-engineering to improve the functioning of engineers working on product development. Using the Web, engineers located throughout the United States can work as a virtual team to design everything from airline cockpits to electron microscopes.[46]

Likewise, in an era of employee empowerment and tight labor markets, imagining the implementation of large-scale, task-based change without using some form of employee survey is difficult. In one organization familiar to the authors, the CEO's effectiveness as a leader of change was evaluated primarily from the results of periodic employee surveys. When the CEO decided to reorganize the way work in the organization was to be done, he used the survey to solicit ideas, some of which he implemented. Several months after the change was initiated and again 2 years later, the survey showed that employees had lost confidence in the leader's ability to manage the change process. The CEO was dismissed by the company's board of directors.

ROLE OF INNOVATION IN ORGANIZATIONAL CHANGE

4.

DESCRIBE HOW
INNOVATION RELATES TO
ORGANIZATIONAL CHANGE.

I*nnovation* is the process of creating and implementing a new idea. When Jeff Bezos founded Amazon.com, he invented a new way for people to purchase books—over the Internet. Although they are not the same, change and innovation are closely related. Change often involves new ideas of some sort. The new idea may be the creation of a new product or process, or it can be an idea about how to change completely the way business is done. Successful organizations understand that both innovation and change are required to satisfy their most important stakeholders.

STRATEGIC IMPORTANCE OF INNOVATION

A dynamic, changing environment makes innovation and change as important—if not more important—for established organizations as they are for new organizations. Successful organizations can't rest on their prior successes. If they become complacent, competitors are sure to woo customers away. Organizational decline and even extinction may follow. Thus the ability to manage innovation and change is an essential part of a manager's competencies, as described in the following Strategic Action Competency feature.[47]

to design and build their own stuffed toy creations.

When the Mall of America in Bloomington, Minnesota, first opened in 1992, it was a one-of-a-kind experience that drew millions of shoppers from all over the world. At the time, a slow economy was more of a threat than e-tailing. To draw shoppers, the Mall of America offered entertainment such as an amusement park and an aquarium. Despite its success, other malls didn't bother to adopt this new approach to retailing until the Internet arrived. Today, the competition is pushing the innovation envelope. Simon Live Media is a joint venture by Simon Property and Time Warner that hopes to define the future of the industry. Their plan is to merge retail and e-tail in a multimedia collage of broadcasts, Web sites, live entertainment events, and the print medium. These innovations will create stiffer competition for dotcom companies. "The physical world is still the best medium ever invented," admits Jeff Bezos, CEO of Amazon.com.

• • •

To learn more about the latest developments in retailing, visit the International Council of Shopping Centers' home page at

http://www.icsc.org

When a company fails to innovate and change as needed, customers, employees, and even the larger community can all suffer. Eastman Kodak, headquartered in Rochester, New York, was the biggest employer in the region and the country's best-known name in photography. But when its main competitor, Tokyo-based Fuji, reduced the price of its color film by as much as 30 percent, Kodak's profits plummeted. To cut costs, Kodak announced that it would reduce its workforce by more than 10,000 people worldwide. Worried about job security, some of the 34,000 local employees cut back on their lunches at local restaurants, and when they did go to lunch they brought fewer smiles with them. George Fisher, who was CEO at the time, acknowledged the pain: "The anxiety that we create when we do things like we're doing is immense, and you can't help but generate some degree of ill will."[48] Eventually, Fisher himself became a victim of Kodak's lack of innovation and appropriate change efforts when he was asked to step down to make room for a new CEO.

TYPES OF INNOVATION

Because new ideas can take many forms, many types of innovation are possible. Three basic types of innovation are technical, process, and administrative.

Technical. The creation of new goods and services is one main type of innovation and is often referred to as *technical innovation.* Many technical innovations occur through basic R&D efforts intended to satisfy demanding customers who are always seeking new, better, faster, and/or cheaper products. For example, numerous technical innovations have spurred the shift to wireless communications systems. Even in the absence of a new product, innovation can still occur, however.

Process. *Process innovation* involves creating a new way of producing, selling, and/or distributing an existing good or service. The introduction of do-it-yourself online stock trading represents a process innovation. Honeywell's use of virtual teams for product design is another example of a process innovation. In the retail business, the introduction of personal shoppers was a significant, if low-tech, process innovation.

Administrative. *Administrative innovation* occurs when creation of a new organization design better supports the creation, production, and delivery of goods and services. In the 1970s, matrix organizations represented an administrative innovation intended to address the problems of earlier organizational designs. In the 1980s, many organizations began to experiment with flexible work schedules and telecommuting. Although these ideas had been around for some time, the widespread use of personal computers opened up new possibilities for implementing them on a large scale. Adopting a policy of flexible work schedules and/or telecommuting often means that an organization must find innovative ways to supervise and coordinate work effectively. Network and virtual organizations (see Chapter 11) are examples of more recent administrative innovations.

Convergence of Forms. The various types of innovation often go hand in hand. For example, the rapid development of business-to-business e-commerce represents process innovation. This new process required numerous technical innovations in computer hardware and software. As organizations began to use business-to-business e-commerce, administrative innovations soon followed. Furthermore, implementation of process innovations required organizational change. By necessity, doing something new means doing things differently. Thus innovation and organizational change go hand in hand.

Occasionally, the convergence of many types of innovation can fundamentally change the basis of competition within an industry.[49] That's the kind of challenge that appeals to Ted Waitt, founder and chairman of Gateway, Inc., the computer company. In his vision of the future, Waitt imagines that computers will be about as exciting, and profitable, as telephones. The opportunities for value and wealth creation will lie "beyond the box"—not in the hardware of the computer but in related gadgets and the services to which the computer provides access.[50]

ARCHITECTURE FOR INNOVATION

Because innovation is so important to success in a variety of industries, managers in all types of organizations are expected to help build infrastructures that encourage and support innovation and change. If an organization's basic infrastructure is in place before specific change initiatives are planned, the organization will be prepared to transform itself as needed. One of management's primary concerns should be to ensure that the organization maintains a state of readiness so that it can move quickly and effectively when innovation is needed. Building an infrastructure and maintaining a state of readiness require an architecture for innovation. Table 12.2 summarizes several key features of that architecture. Briefly, managers should

- develop a learning orientation among employees,

- foster workforce resilience, and

- provide a support system for innovation.[51]

Table 12.2	*Architecture for Innovation*

Learning Orientation

- Managers allow employees to identify and solve important problems.
- Managers openly discuss organizational successes and failures with employees.
- Formal and informal systems keep employees informed of customers' preferences and their evaluations of the services and products offered by the organization.
- Small-scale experiments are used to resolve emerging problems before they reach the crisis stage.

Resilient Workforce

- Hiring and promotion decisions are used to weed out people who resist change.
- Employees are trained in the fundamentals of organizational change and innovation.
- Because successful efforts are celebrated, employees have confidence in the organization's capacity for innovation and change.

Support for Innovation

- Formal and informal systems facilitate the free flow of knowledge throughout the organization.
- Reward and recognition systems encourage the development of competencies needed for innovation, including technical knowledge, teamwork, and communication.
- Key measures are monitored to assess the effectiveness of the process of innovation and the outcomes of innovation.

LEARNING ORGANIZATIONS

5.

DISCUSS HOW LEARNING ORGANIZATIONS DEAL WITH CHANGE.

A *learning organization* has both the drive and the capabilities to improve its performance continuously. It learns from past experiences, it learns from customers, it learns from various parts of the company, and it learns from other companies.[52] In learning organizations, successful innovation and change aren't events with clear-cut beginnings and endings. Rather, they are never-ending processes that have become part of the daily routine. Innovation and change are not infrequent and special—they are simply a way of organizational life. As one manager observed, this way of life helps a learning organization avoid organizational stupidity.

When an organization's environment is complex and dynamic, learning may require a lot of exploration and experimentation. Failures may be frequent, but so are unexpected achievements. When an organization's environment is more stable, learning is more likely to occur through a systematic process of testing alternative approaches.[53] In either situation, however, learning organizations change at a rate at least as fast as—or even faster than—the rate of change in their environments. Moreover, the learning process is managed systematically and professionally—it doesn't occur randomly.

Through continuous innovation and change, a learning organization creates a sustainable competitive advantage in its industry. Five distinctive features of learning organizations are illustrated in Figure 12.5:

- shared leadership,
- culture of innovation,
- customer-focused strategy,
- organic organization design, and
- intensive use of information.

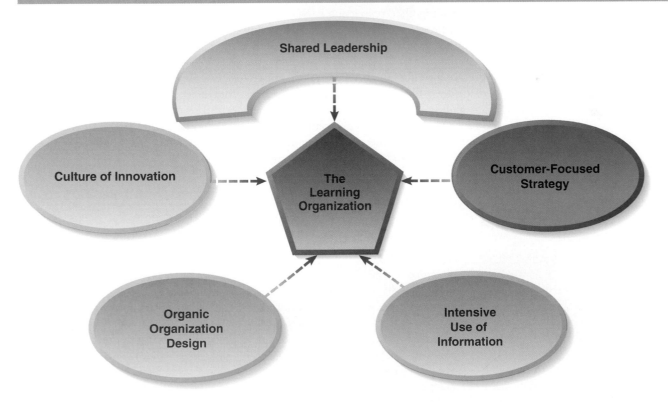

Figure 12.5   *Characteristics of a Learning Organization*

SHARED LEADERSHIP

In learning organizations, responsibility for making decisions, directing operations, and achieving organizational goals is shared among all employees. These leadership tasks aren't the responsibility of top-level managers alone. *Everyone* is encouraged to find ways to improve the organization and its products. At Yahoo!, all employees experiment constantly to satisfy customer demand. Yahoo! receives thousands of suggestions and comments from users who are eager for sites that suit their particular needs. Employees who read these submissions are fully empowered to make changes as they see fit.

Empowerment provides a way to integrate tasks and allow employees to buy into the organization's goals. At Nantucket Nectars, a participatory leadership style encourages employees to learn by allowing them to make their own mistakes. The founders of this company adopted this approach because they believed that it would yield better-quality beverages. When people discover better ways of doing their jobs, they see that their efforts *do* make a difference. That discovery in turn strengthens their involvement in making a better product and improving customer satisfaction.[54]

CULTURE OF INNOVATION

Shared leadership goes hand in hand with innovation. For learning organizations, successful innovation is a never-ending process that becomes part of the daily routine. Instead of being an infrequent and special event that takes people's attention away from the central work of the organization, it is the central work of the organization. At Southwest Airlines, empowered employees are always looking for better ways to meet customers' needs for low-cost, reliable air travel. When clerks suggested doing away with tickets, CEO Herb Kelleher encouraged them to experiment with this innovative idea on selected routes. Long before other airlines adopted the idea of electronic ticketing, Southwest airlines' passengers made reservations over the phone and received only a PIN number—no ticket was issued. At the gate, the PIN number is exchanged for a reusable boarding pass. Passengers who need a receipt get one promptly through the mail.[55]

Community. Learning organizations develop a sense of community and trust. Everyone works together, respecting each other and being able to communicate openly and honestly. Problems can't be avoided or handled by just passing them along to another department or up the hierarchy. Conflict and debate are accepted as responsible forms of communication. A sense of community also gives employees the feeling that they are important and are being treated fairly. Employees cooperate because they want to, not because they have to.[56] When people feel that they are part of a community, they are more willing to make the extra effort needed to find and fix problems. They are also are more likely to share their solutions with their coworkers. Preventing organizational memory loss is a problem that many learning organizations face, as described in the following Planning and Administration Competency feature.[57]

PLANNING & ADMINISTRATION COMPETENCY

Learning Audits Improve Organizational Memory

A professional who enters the job market today can expect to change jobs about every five years. In each job, the professional learns a great deal. Some of the learning is of a technical nature, which will probably be useful regardless of where the next job happens to be. But much of the professional's learning will be specific to the organization left behind: What was the real reason that the last client wasn't completely satisfied? Where are the inefficiencies in the system that should be eliminated? Unless this knowledge has been captured by the employer and passed on to others, it walks out the door when the

professional leaves. Soon, the organization finds itself left with mainly new employees, all of whom are struggling to learn their jobs and, at the same time, how the organization really operates.

When McKinsey & Co., a consulting firm, studied this problem at an automotive company, it discovered that 30 percent of the time spent solving problems was wasted. The problems had been solved before. The real problem, it seemed, was that no one who remembered was still around! Organizational memory loss is particularly severe when turnover is high.

Kraft General Foods has used learning audits for years to improve its organi-

zational memory. Over time, the company has accumulated huge amounts of valuable information. Learning audits typically center on a project. Throughout the project, key people periodically record what they are doing and thinking. The records capture their reasoning and can be studied by others in the company, enabling them to draw important lessons and inferences about the project.

• • •

To learn more about Kraft General Foods, visit the company's home page at

http://www.kraftfoods.com

Continuous Learning. Obviously, a learning organization can't succeed without employees who are willing to learn and change. Hence learning organizations encourage individual learning in numerous ways. One of the most successful ways is through empowerment, which places responsibility on employees for problem finding and problem solving.[58] Empowerment requires more involvement and learning than does simply having someone else make all the decisions. The flat, team-based structure found in learning organizations facilitates learning because employees are involved in a broad range of activities and work with others from whom they can learn. Formal training is another way to ensure continuous learning. For managers in particular, continuous learning is essential to develop the competencies needed by generalists who are knowledgeable in several areas, as opposed to specialists who understand only finance, production, marketing, or some other function.

CUSTOMER-FOCUSED STRATEGY

Learning organizations add value for customers by identifying needs—in some instances, even before customers have done so—and then developing ways to satisfy those needs. Customer-focused strategies reflect a clear understanding of how important customers are to the organization's long-term success and serve as the basis for aligning all its major activities.

At a time when many organizations and shareholders look no farther than the next quarterly financial report, acceptance of the need for a long-term perspective is crucial for a learning organization. The processes of learning and change simply take time. At Knight-Ridder, for example, declining newspaper circulation was anticipated long before it became a reality. As early as the 1970s, the company began experimenting with other forms of news delivery, including TV broadcasts, but eventually abandoned them as failures. During the 1980s, the company experimented with online business services and again had little success at first. Eventually, the learning paid off. With several years of experience behind it, the company bought Dialog Information Services, which was the world's largest online full-text information service. With this acquisition, Knight-Ridder was transformed from a traditional newspaper company to a leader in the provision of online business information.[59]

ORGANIC ORGANIZATION DESIGN

The design of learning organizations often reflects their emphasis on organic rather than mechanistic systems. In particular, they emphasize the use of teams, strategic alliances, and boundaryless networks.

Teams. In learning organizations, employees with dissimilar expertise form multidisciplinary teams. To encourage the free flow of ideas, these teams may be formed only as needed, on a project-by-project basis. "Bosses" are practically nonexistent. Team members have considerable autonomy to make key decisions and can take action without waiting for requests to crawl through a bureaucratic decision-making process. Compared to functional structures, team-based structures are more flexible and fluid. Knowledge flows more easily among members of the organization, which contributes to learning and creates opportunities for innovation.

Strategic Alliances. In addition to experimenting on their own, many learning organizations use strategic alliances with suppliers, customers, and even competitors as a method of learning. In Japan, Amgen, a biotech company, formed an alliance with Kirin Brewery. From Kirin, Amgen learned about fermentation processes, which are crucial for producing synthetic blood clotting protein. From Amgen, Kirin learned about amino acid–protein combinations that can act as catalysts to speed up the brewing process.[60]

Boundaryless Networks. Network structures, which we described in Chapter 11, maximize the linkages among organizations. Such linkages in turn provide learning opportunities and generate innovation in goods and services.[61] Network structures seem to work in part because they create a sense of community among a larger pool of people who share their diverse knowledge and expertise, using it to find creative solutions to difficult problems.[62]

INTENSIVE USE OF INFORMATION

Information is the lifeblood of learning organizations. To be effective they must undertake extensive scanning, be measurement oriented, and foster shared problems and solutions.

Scanning the Environment. In learning organizations, managers strive to be creators of change. Staying attuned to emerging trends is their passion. To ensure that they don't miss an important trend or change, learning organizations aggressively scan both the external and internal environments for information. As a result, large amounts of information are obtained from the external environment about how customers are reacting to current goods and services, how customers compare them to those of competitors, and whether new competitors may be on the horizon. Such information is essential to judgments concerning the need to create new products to meet customer demand. Information obtained from the internal environment indicates how employees feel about the organization, whether their attention is focused on customers, whether they feel energized to solve difficult problems, and whether key employees are likely to defect to competitors.

Measurement Oriented. Organizations learn in order to improve. To judge improvement, an organization needs to know where it was before and where it is now. Systematic measurement makes assessing improvement possible. In learning organizations, employees have access to data about customer satisfaction, profit and loss, market share, employee commitment, and competitors' strategies, among other things. Data are gathered, monitored, disseminated, and used throughout the organization. Employees believe that too much information is better than too little so that they can pick and choose what they need to perform their jobs most effectively.

Communication. Numerical data (measurements) aren't the only type of information considered important in learning organizations. "Soft" information—sometimes referred to as tacit knowledge or gossip—is valued too. Employees who serve customers day in and day out may not need to read the results of monthly customer satisfaction surveys to know where problems lie. The anecdotal evidence they gather through dozens of service encounters may be enough to begin seeing a pattern of pieces that all seem to fit together, make sense, and suggest needed improvements. When Xerox wanted to improve its service for customers, it hired an anthropologist to study how service reps went about their jobs. The anthropologist concluded that informal storytelling and conversations around the water cooler were important activities for sharing problems and solutions.[63]

By sharing information about the problems they face and the solutions they discover, employees minimize the number of times they reinvent the wheel and speed up the process of organizational learning. Coopers & Lybrand (which has since merged with PriceWaterhouse) identified the need to increase the amount and effectiveness of tacit knowledge sharing as one of its key strategic challenges. Its clients were scattered around the world, and they all demanded service that reflected cutting-edge practice. In this environment, Coopers & Lybrand's success depended on finding ways to transfer quickly the learning that occurs. With each consulting engagement, employees gain new insights and experiment with new solutions. The learning that occurs is useful for that specific engagement, and it may also be useful to another team sometime in the future. But most lessons can't be taught with numbers alone—detailed narrative explanations are also needed. Many organizations now use computer-aided systems for capturing and sharing "soft" information. Like e-mail, these systems allow for rapid and wide distribution of information. In addition, they enable organizations to store shared solutions in an electronic library. Later, users can access the library via index catalogs in which problems and solutions are grouped in meaningful categories. Although this technology is in its infancy, it promises to enhance organizational learning even when knowledge is widely dispersed in both space and time.[64]

CHAPTER SUMMARY

Whether they are newly established or mature, organizations of all types maintain their vitality by innovating, changing, and learning from their experiences. As their external environments become increasingly competitive and turbulent, the most effective organizations will be those that build innovation, change, and learning into their normal operations.

1. DESCRIBE FOUR TYPES OF ORGANIZATIONAL CHANGE.

Organizational changes vary in both degree and timing. In terms of degree, change can be radical or incremental. In terms of timing, change can be reactive or anticipatory. As shown in Figure 12.2, combinations of these possibilities create four basic types of change: radical reactive change, radical anticipatory change, incremental reactive change, and incremental anticipatory change.

2. EXPLAIN THE PLANNING PROCESS FOR ORGANIZATIONAL CHANGE.

Although change often involves a bit of chaos, organizations can usually reduce its amount and impact by carefully planning for major change. Through planning, the organization begins to unfreeze and prepares for the change. The key planning activities are (1) assessing the environment; (2) determining whether a performance gap exists and, if so, its nature and magnitude; (3) diagnosing organizational problems; (4) articulating and communicating a vision for the future; (5) developing a strategic plan for the change; (6) anticipating and making plans to reduce resistance; and (7) developing a way to monitor change and following up after the main initiatives have been implemented.

3. IDENTIFY FOUR METHODS OF ORGANIZATIONAL CHANGE AND EXPLAIN HOW THEY CAN BE COMBINED.

Many approaches to implementing change are possible. Four general methods are technology based, organization redesign, task based, and people oriented. The technology-based method often involves changing the way work is done by adopting new information technologies. The organization redesign method may involve changing the organizational structure and/or organizational processes. Organization redesign normally affects large portions of an organization. Downsizing and reengineering are examples of this method. The task-based method involves changing employees' jobs, either simplifying or enriching them. The people-oriented method can be used to change employee attitudes and behaviors. Survey feedback permits managers and employees to provide information about a range of topics, including job satisfaction, organizational commitment, and perceptions of supervisory and managerial behaviors. Change efforts often involve a combination of these methods.

4. DESCRIBE HOW INNOVATION RELATES TO ORGANIZATIONAL CHANGE.

Innovation is the process of creating and implementing a new idea. Three basic types of innovation are technical, process, and administrative. Organizational change refers to any transformation in the design or functioning of an organization. Generally, innovations require organizational change. Innovation and change are important to both new and established organizations, owing to the dynamic nature of the external environments of most organizations.

5. DISCUSS HOW LEARNING ORGANIZATIONS DEAL WITH CHANGE.

Organizations are redesigning themselves to become learning organizations capable of quickly adapting their practices to satisfy the needs of their customers. The basic features of such organizations are leadership that is shared, a culture that supports innovation, a strategy focused on customers, an organic organization design, and an intensive use of information. In a learning organization, change is not a special event; it's a natural part of the organization's continuous attempts to satisfy customers.

KEY TERMS

Administrative innovation, p. 333
Anticipatory change, p. 319
Incremental change, p. 318
Information technology (IT), p. 328
Innovation, p. 332
Job enrichment, p. 329
Job simplification, p. 329
Learning organization, p. 334

Organization development (OD), p. 330
Organization redesign method, p. 328
Organizational change, p. 316
Organizational diagnosis, p. 322
People-oriented method, p. 330
Performance gap, p. 322
Process innovation, p. 333
Process redesign method, p. 329

Radical change, p. 317
Reactive change, p. 318
Reengineering, p. 329
Restructuring, p. 328
Survey feedback, p. 330
Task-based method, p. 329
Technical innovation, p. 333
Technology-based method, p. 327

1. Which aspects of an organization's environment are more likely to lead to radical rather than incremental change? Explain.

2. Consider the four methods of change described in this chapter. Are some methods better suited to adaptive change or to reactive change? Can all these methods be used regardless of the timing of change? Why or why not?

3. Evaluate the statement: "We trained hard, but it seemed that every time we were beginning to form into teams, we would be reorganized. We tend to meet any new situation by reorganizing, and what a wonderful method it can be for creating the illusion of progress while producing confusion, inefficiency, and demoralization." (Petronius, 210 B.C.) Is the way you react to innovation and change a fixed aspect of your personality? Do you think you can develop the competencies needed to be effective in organizations experiencing change? Explain.

4. A manager once remarked, "No matter how much planning you do, the process of organizational change is always full of surprises." This is probably true, so why bother planning? Describe how planning can be useful even when anticipating everything that will happen during an organizational change is impossible.

5. The George Land World Class Innovation Award is given to companies in recognition of "best practices" in innovation management. What types of innovations have been central to the winners of this award—technical, administrative, or

process? To discover the answer, visit the Innovation Network at *http://www.thinksmart.com/articlesgeorgeland.html*.

6. Schools and colleges are supposed to be places of learning, but many fall short of being learning organizations. Choose a school or college with which you are familiar and explain how it could use one or more of the four basic change methods described in this chapter to become a more effective learning organization.

7. **Global Awareness Competency.** The process of organizational change requires extensive coordination among all parts of an organization. For global organizations, coordination can be particularly challenging. Describe how information technology can be used to address these issues. To learn about the current capabilities of information technology, visit the home page of *Computer Mediated Communications* magazine at *http://www.december.com/cmc/mag*.

8. **Communication Competency.** Time is a precious resource to managers, especially when they are in the process of major organizational change. Knowing that communication is important at that time, many rely heavily on formal outlets such as speeches and mass e-mailings. Describe the main advantages and disadvantages of using formal (versus informal) communication channels during times of change. Should informal communication be emphasized over formal communication at certain stages of the change process? Explain.

CASE FOR COMPETENCY DEVELOPMENT

Royal Dutch/Shell

No one should expect a company as big as Royal Dutch/Shell (known to many people simply as "Shell") to make major changes quickly. With 101,000 employees and $128 billion in annual revenues, it is one of the largest companies in the world. Worldwide, it has more than 47,000 filling stations, which serve more than 1 million customers daily. But Shell's size couldn't protect it from the intense competition being created by European hypermarkets, new competitors throughout the world, and business customers that needed a truly global supplier. In France, for example, sales declined by 50 percent in two years. If Shell couldn't find a way to boost its sales, it would have to exit this market.

Being able to predict how much time is enough time for such a company to enact change is no easy task. But Steve Miller, Shell's managing director, concluded that change was happening too slowly. Two years after Shell began a change initiative intended to transform the company, he felt that the company had little to show for the effort. It had reorganized and downsized. Beginning at the top, and working down, managers at each level had attended workshops that explained the changes needed. Performance had improved a bit, but morale

was low at corporate headquarters. The company's leaders agreed that Shell had to move into the Internet Age, but they couldn't agree on how to implement that idea and so the change effort stalled. Elsewhere in the company business seemed to be continuing just as it had been for years.

Miller believed that empowered employees would help the company find its way into the future. According to him, "once the folks at the grass roots find that they own the problem, they find that they also own the answer—and they improve things very quickly." Miller wanted every frontline employee to understand the new vision for Shell. To get that message across, Miller set aside half his time to work with the employees who needed to respond to the competitive threats the company faced. Week in and week out, he met with Shell employees at the grassroots level in 25 countries.

One of the challenges facing Shell was figuring out how better to use its 47,000 retail outlets to boost sales of all the company's products. To begin tackling that problem, Miller set up a five-day "retailing boot camp." Cross-functional teams (e.g., a trucker, a dealer, and a marketing employee) went to the "camp" and then went home to develop a new business plan. Later they returned to camp and received feedback on their plans from their peers.

After another cycle of revising their plans and getting more feedback, they went home to put their plans into action. After 2 more months, they returned to camp for a follow-up session that focused on what had worked, what had failed, and what they had learned. "The grassroots employees got to touch the new Shell, and participate in a give-and-take culture," Miller explained. "The energy of our employees spread to the managers above them. These frontline employees taught us to believe in ourselves again."

Miller admits that most of the people involved at the grassroots level found the process to be "scary as hell." Top management had convinced them that change was essential to their survival, but they didn't have confidence in their ability to solve the problems. That scared them. Miller was scared, too, because he had to let the process work without being in control of the results: "*They've* got to do it. You want to do it for them. You want to make it all come out right—but you can't. What you *can* do is feel for them." As scary as the process may be, Miller is convinced that creating change is a bottom–up task. "As people move up, they get further away from the work that goes on in the field—and as a result they tend to devalue it. People get caught up in broad strategic issues, legal issues, and stakeholder issues. But what really drives the business is the work that gets done down at the coalface [the frontline]."[65]

Questions

1. Refer to Figure 12.2 and the related discussion. What type of change was Shell undergoing? What seemed to trigger the company's realization that change was needed?

2. In a company the size of Shell, implementing substantial change without a solid plan to guide the process would be difficult. Describe how a plan for a top–down approach to change might differ from a plan for grassroots change.

3. Steve Miller understood that "the whole point of the exercise is to improve performance" because Shell couldn't ignore profitability. If you were Miller, how would you measure the success of your change effort? Explain your rationale.

4. To what extent does Shell seem to be a learning organization? What additional information do you need to make a full assessment of Shell as a learning organization?

To learn more about Royal Dutch/Shell, visit the company's homepage at *http://www.shell.com/royal-en*.

VIDEO CASE

Central Michigan Community Hospital

Central Michigan Community Hospital (CMCH) has provided the residents of Isabella County with high-quality health-care services since 1943. It is a 151-bed, nonsectarian, nonprofit, acute care hospital, which now grants practice privileges to more than 120 doctors and renders a wide variety of health-care services. The hospital is committed to quality and was rewarded for that commitment in 1994 by being named one of the top 100 hospitals in the United States. The following year, the hospital was one of 75 (of the previous 100) to exceed the median industry performance, gaining an honorable mention.

Despite past success CMCH's board, administration, and medical staff are confronting a great deal of uncertainty and must change to meet the challenges of today and the future. Patients, employees, insurance companies, and state and federal governments—all are demanding an ever higher quality of services while containing costs. The hospital and its leaders, like many others, are involved in a fundamental shift in emphasis in the health-care industry—from a complete focus on care toward a more balanced focus on care and business concerns. One concern at CMCH is that hospitals in nearby larger cities (within a 30-mile radius) can offer more attractive health-care packages and lure better paying customers away, leaving CMCH with poorer patients and those who are uninsured or underinsured. Another concern is that an increasingly older population will require more time for diagnosis and treatment, which might impede the hospital's ability to expand its emergency care.

The board, administration, and medical staff have responded to the changing needs of CMCH's constituencies and expressed its commitment to them in a variety of ways by (1) continuing to provide basic inpatient and outpatient health-care services; (2) beginning to collaborate with other health-care providers, employers, and consumers to provide access to a wide range of health-care products and services; (3) striving to improve the health of the community at large and its patients; and (4) seeking to develop better methods of meeting consumer needs for quality and value in an integrated health-care delivery system. Evidence of this commitment can be found throughout the hospital. For example, a major renovation to accommodate new equipment at CMCH recognizes the trend toward greater use of outpatient services, including diagnostic, therapeutic, behavioral, and surgical procedures.

Change is difficult for most individuals and organizations, but the problem is particularly salient in large health-care facilities. To be successful, CMCH will have to overcome resistance to change and implement decisions that will best position it to meet the demands of the rapidly changing health-care environment and remain a leader in its industry.

Questions

1. What types of changes should CMCH implement in order to respond to its environment and compete with other health-care providers in the region?

2. What are some of the recommendations for handling change that CMCH employees and administrators submitted?

3. How would you describe the types of organizational change being implemented at CMCH?

To learn more about Central Michigan Community Hospital, visit the organization's home page at *http://www.cmhs.org.*

Managing Human Resources

LEARNING OBJECTIVES

AFTER STUDYING THIS CHAPTER YOU SHOULD BE ABLE TO:

1. EXPLAIN HOW MANAGING HUMAN RESOURCES EFFECTIVELY CAN IMPROVE ORGANIZATIONAL PERFORMANCE.

2. IDENTIFY AND DISCUSS SEVERAL IMPORTANT LAWS AND GOVERNMENT REGULATIONS THAT AFFECT HOW ORGANIZATIONS MANAGE THEIR HUMAN RESOURCES.

3. STATE THE ELEMENTS OF HUMAN RESOURCE PLANNING.

4. EXPLAIN THE PROCESS THAT ORGANIZATIONS USE TO RECRUIT AND SELECT NEW HIRES.

5. DESCRIBE SEVERAL TYPES OF TRAINING AND DEVELOPMENT PROGRAMS.

6. EXPLAIN HOW MANAGERS USE PERFORMANCE INFORMATION TO IMPROVE EMPLOYEE JOB PERFORMANCE.

7. DISCUSS THE OBJECTIVES OF MONETARY COMPENSATION AND THE ELEMENTS OF A MONETARY COMPENSATION PACKAGE.

Chapter Outline

PREVIEW: SOUTHWEST AIRLINES

STRATEGIC IMPORTANCE
GAINING AND SUSTAINING COMPETITIVE ADVANTAGE
CONSEQUENCES FOR PROFITABILITY
SOCIAL VALUE

THE LEGAL AND REGULATORY ENVIRONMENT
EQUAL EMPLOYMENT OPPORTUNITY
GLOBAL AWARENESS COMPETENCY: Hiring Is No Laughing Matter for Cirque du Soleil
HEALTH AND SAFETY
COMPENSATION AND BENEFITS

HUMAN RESOURCE PLANNING
FORECASTS
COMPETENCY INVENTORIES

THE HIRING PROCESS
TEAMWORK COMPETENCY: At Dell, Everyone Is on the Recruiting Team
RECRUITMENT
SELECTION

TRAINING AND DEVELOPMENT
ORIENTATION TRAINING
BASIC SKILLS TRAINING
NEW-TECHNOLOGY TRAINING
TEAM TRAINING
CAREER DEVELOPMENT
PLANNING AND ADMINISTRATION COMPETENCY: Developing Leaders at Colgate-Palmolive
CROSS-CULTURAL TRAINING

PERFORMANCE APPRAISAL AND FEEDBACK
STRATEGIC ALIGNMENT
COMMUNICATION COMPETENCY: Making Improvements at Con-Way Transportation Services
EFFECTIVE PERFORMANCE APPRAISAL
PROVIDING FEEDBACK

COMPENSATION
ATTRACTING AND RETAINING EMPLOYEES
MAXIMIZING PRODUCTIVITY

CHAPTER SUMMARY

KEY TERMS

QUESTIONS FOR DISCUSSION AND COMPETENCY DEVELOPMENT

CASE FOR COMPETENCY DEVELOPMENT: THE MAGIC OF DISNEY BEGINS WITH HRM

VIDEO CASE: LaBELLE MANAGEMENT

SOUTHWEST AIRLINES

For nearly 30 years Southwest Airlines' successful low-cost, on-time, no-frills, no-allocated seats, no-meals approach to air travel has helped the company fly high above its competitors with hefty profit gains. In contrast to the industry as a whole, which has lost billions of dollars, Southwest's lean, mean flying machine has been continuously profitable for three decades. Since Southwest began selling shares of stock to the public in 1972, its value has increased by more than 21,000 percent.

Many observers believe that Southwest Airlines' special approach to managing human resources is one important reason for the company's continued success. Other airlines can copy its routes and use Boeing 737 aircraft, but they are hard-pressed to match the productivity of Southwest's employees. The number of passengers per Southwest employee is nearly double that of the industry average. And those passengers get excellent service. Nine times Southwest Airlines has won the industry's Triple Crown: (1) best on-time performance, (2) fewest lost bags, and (3) fewest passenger complaints in the same month. No competitor has achieved that level of performance even once.

Everyone in the organization, from Chairman Herb Kelleher to every new hire, understands the importance of outstanding productivity and service. Kelleher is famous for his strong belief that people make the difference and for his willingness to work alongside them at their jobs. To show their gratitude to Kelleher, one year the employees took out a full-page ad in *USA Today* to thank him. Among the things they thanked him for were

- remembering every one of their names,
- helping load baggage on Thanksgiving,
- giving *everyone* a kiss,
- singing at their holiday party,
- letting them wear shorts and sneakers to work, and
- being a friend, not just a boss.

Besides hiring only people who fit its unique culture, Southwest Airlines makes sure that employees understand the company's strategy and are motivated to do everything possible to continue the company's record of outstanding achievements. A profit-sharing program is one reason that Southwest's employees stay focused on the company's performance. An incident in Los Angeles illustrates the point: An agent from another airline asked to borrow a stapler. The Southwest agent went over with the stapler, waited for it to be used, and brought it back. The other agent asked, "Do you always follow staplers around?" The Southwest agent replied, "I want to make sure we get it back. It affects our profit sharing." Setting goals and targets for the performance of the company as a whole and never setting separate departmental goals is another way to ensure that employees all pull together. "At Southwest, we all work toward the same goal, and setting up different goals for different areas is likely to create a schism within the company," Kelleher asserts.

You might think that with all the pressure to perform, employees at Southwest Airlines might not have much fun. In fact, the opposite seems to be true. The company is famous for its wacky culture, which is part of the reason it was ranked No. 2 in *Fortune* magazine's list of the "100 Best Places to Work."[1]

To learn more about Southwest Airlines visit the company's home page at

http://www.southwest.com

STRATEGIC IMPORTANCE

1.

EXPLAIN HOW MANAGING HUMAN RESOURCES EFFECTIVELY CAN IMPROVE ORGANIZATIONAL PERFORMANCE.

Human resource management (HRM) encompasses the philosophies, policies, and practices that an organization uses to affect the behaviors of people who work for it. Included are activities related to staffing, training and development, performance review and evaluation, and compensation. Because the effective use of these activities can improve productivity and profitability, HRM is of strategic importance to an organization.[2]

Managing human resources is necessary in all organizations, from the smallest to the largest. At a minimum every company has jobs, which comprise sets of responsibilities. To get these jobs done, an organization hires people and compensates them for the work they do. To hire people an organization generally finds that it must recruit potential employees and then select among them. Few organizations continue to pay those who cannot or will not perform satisfactorily. At least some aspect of performance is generally measured—even if it is just keeping track of how many hours employees work. To help people know what they are supposed to do, some instruction and training are usually given, though these activities may be minimal.

Successful organizations see human resources as assets that need to be managed conscientiously and in tune with its needs. The most competitive organizations are working now to ensure that they have available tomorrow and a decade from now employees who are eager and able to address competitive challenges. Increasingly this effort involves attracting superior talent and stimulating such employees to perform at peak levels.

Even when the jobs they perform don't require them to be highly educated, people can make the difference between a company's success and failure. For example, companies selling online are learning that technology may not be able to replace salespeople completely. When iQVC.com, which received top scores on customer satisfaction, began allowing customers to chat online with an operator during the final stages of shopping, the percentage of shoppers who reached the checkout page of the Web site increased significantly. At Cameraworld.com, customers who use the company's Web site operator service make purchases far more often than customers who don't.[3]

GAINING AND SUSTAINING COMPETITIVE ADVANTAGE

As described in Chapter 7, a firm has a competitive advantage when all or part of the market prefers its goods and/or services. Companies seek ways to compete that can last a long time and cannot easily be imitated by competitors. As part of their strategies, some firms use their approaches to managing human resources to gain a sustainable competitive advantage. Several large research projects have generated substantial evidence linking HRM practices to profitability and productivity gains.[4] For example, one study involved asking thousands of employees to describe their jobs and their organizations. The responses were used to compile an index to reflect how much emphasis was placed on managing human resources. The results showed a strong association between emphasizing human resources and subsequent profitability.[5]

To gain sustainable competitive advantage through HRM, three conditions must be met:

- employees must be a source of value added,
- employees must be "rare" or unique in some way, and
- competitors must not be able to copy or imitate easily the company's approach to human resource management.

Employees Who Add Value. Like most intangibles, the value of an organization's employees doesn't appear on a balance sheet. Yet, intangibles such as the knowledge that employees have and the way that employees feel and behave, can be used to predict financial performance. Susan M. Smith knows this from experience. She was vice president of knowledge-based industries for the Royal Bank of Canada and subsequently became CEO of Royal Bank Growth Company. "It truly is a new economy," she says, "and the rules aren't written. We have to learn as we go and lend based on intellectual and intangible assets."[6] Investors seek companies with satisfied employees, recognizing that satisfied employees result in satisfied customers, especially in the services sector. Managers and employees who hate their jobs can't give the best possible service to customers. Conversely, when customers are happy, employees feel a sense of pride and satisfaction in their work and in being part of the organization.[7]

Employees Who Are Rare. To be a source of sustainable competitive advantage, the competencies of an organization's human resources must also be rare. If competitors can easily access the same pool of talent, that talent provides no advantage against competitors. When Lincoln Electric Company in Cleveland, Ohio, announced that it was planning to hire 200 production workers, it received more than 20,000 responses. When BMW announced that it had selected Spartanburg, South Carolina, as the site for its first U.S. production facility, it received more than 25,000 unsolicited requests for employment. Numbers this large allow Lincoln Electric and BMW to hire employees who are two to three times more productive than their counterparts in other manufacturing firms.

By being an employer of choice, organizations can gain access to the best available talent. In other words, "The Best Get the Best." Books and articles that purport to identify the "best" places to work are especially popular among students graduating from college, who view firms high in the rankings as desirable places to land their first postgraduation jobs. Dissatisfied workers who are looking for better employment situations read these lists too. Over time, a good reputation for attracting, developing, and keeping good talent acts like a magnet to draw the best talent to a firm.

An Approach That Can't Be Copied. Business practices that are easy for competitors to copy don't provide sources of sustained competitive advantage. Approaches to HRM that have evolved over a long period of time to meet the specific needs of an organization are the most difficult to copy. Some companies regularly scrutinize their approaches to managing human resources in order to improve continuously. FedEx is one such company. Years of relentless attention to how people are managed have helped it maintain a position of leadership in a highly competitive industry.

CONSEQUENCES FOR PROFITABILITY

Estimating the dollar value of investments in human resource activities (e.g., training programs and changes in organizational culture) is a topic of increasing interest to financial analysts and accountants. Until objective evaluation rules are developed, however, investors and shareholders must rely on their own judgments of how well a company manages its people. Organizations such as investment banks, consulting firms, and advertising agencies, have almost nothing of great value except their intangible human assets. Buying one of these companies often means acquiring only a customer (or client) list and some product brands (or contracts)—and the hope that the best people working there will stay and apply their talents for the new owner.[8] One study of companies floating initial public offerings (IPOs) showed that those attending to HRM issues are rewarded with more favorable initial investor reactions and tend to survive longer than companies that don't attend to such issues.[9]

Investors' judgments about the value of a company's human resources often are formed on the basis of reputation (e.g., rankings given by business publications) and by other forms of public recognition for excellence. For example, the Catalyst Award is given to organizations with outstanding initiatives to foster women's advancement into senior management. Another form of recognition of excellence in managing human resources is receipt of an Optima Award, sponsored by *Workforce* magazine. Trident Precision Manufacturing received the Optima Award for Financial Impact. It recognized the company's success in using better recruitment methods, increased training, employee involvement, and numerous other approaches to managing human resources to increase productivity by 73 percent and quadruple revenue over a ten-year period.[10]

SOCIAL VALUE

The financial consequences of how organizations manage human resources have received a great deal of attention in recent years, but these consequences are not the only ones that matter. During an era of seemingly constant restructuring and downsizing, many people have become aware of the social consequences of different approaches to managing human resources. When a large employer in a community is forced to downsize because of declining sales and profits, the entire community is affected. Similarly, if employers discriminate unfairly against some groups when making hiring decisions, the consequences of those discriminatory practices can ripple through the community for many years.

In the United States, society often judges organizations in terms of the fairness with which they treat their employees. People believe that fairness is a desirable social condition—everyone wants to be treated fairly and wants others to view them as being fair.[11] Companies that rank high as the best places to work generally emphasize fairness as part of their corporate cultures because fairness creates the feeling of trust that is needed to "hold a good workplace together."[12] When deciding which company to work for, potential employees evaluate whether a company pays a fair wage. If they feel unfairly treated after being hired, employees are likely to "vote with their feet" and seek employment elsewhere.[13]

Some companies make a point of addressing basic concerns such as fairness even when doing so is costly and perhaps even reduces profitability. In addition, many laws and government regulations act as restraints to protect workers from unfair and potentially harmful HRM practices. By complying with laws and government regulations, firms establish their legitimacy and gain acceptance and support from the community. Ultimately, they increase their chances for long-term survival.[14]

THE LEGAL AND REGULATORY ENVIRONMENT

2.

IDENTIFY AND DISCUSS SEVERAL IMPORTANT LAWS AND GOVERNMENT REGULATIONS THAT AFFECT HOW ORGANIZATIONS MANAGE THEIR HUMAN RESOURCES.

Through their elected government representatives, individual workers and organizations representing both management and labor influence the creation and enactment of federal, state, and local laws. Through their tax payments, organizations and their employees pay for the operations of a vast array of government agencies and courts that are responsible for interpreting and enforcing the laws. Thus employment laws should be considered not only as legal constraints but also as sources of information about the issues that potential employees are likely thinking about as they decide whether to join or leave an organization. The laws and regulations affecting how organizations manage human resources are numerous, and we can't begin to discuss all of them here. However, three significant categories of laws and regulations affecting HRM deserve comment:

- equal employment opportunity,
- health and safety protection, and
- compensation and benefits.

EQUAL EMPLOYMENT OPPORTUNITY

The laws regulating ***equal employment opportunity*** (EEO) are intended to eliminate discrimination in employment. The basic principle embodied in these laws is to ensure that job applicants and employees are judged on characteristics related to the work that they are being hired to do and on their job performance after being hired. In recent years, the number of EEO cases filed in federal courts has averaged about 23,000.[15]

One especially important EEO law is ***Title VII of the Civil Rights Act.*** As originally enacted in 1964, Title VII prohibited discrimination by employers, employment agencies, and unions on the basis of race, color, religion, sex, or national origin. A 1978 amendment prohibited discrimination against pregnant women. In 1991, a new version of the Civil Rights Act went into effect. It reinforces the intent of the Civil Rights Act of 1964 but states more specifically how cases brought under the act should proceed.[16] Other important employment discrimination laws cover age and disabilities.

Enforcement of U.S. EEO Laws. Power to enforce Title VII of the Civil Rights Act rests with the Equal Employment Opportunity Commission (EEOC). In carrying out its duties, the EEOC has the responsibility and authority to make rules, conduct investigations, make judgments about guilt, and impose sanctions. Thus the EEOC can prosecute companies that it believes are in violation of the law.

The EEOC's actions against Texaco illustrate this point. Based on employment data that companies are required to send routinely to the EEOC, Texaco appeared to engage in illegal discrimination. Many managers within the company ignored the company's nondiscrimination policies and allowed their personal prejudices to affect their managerial decisions and actions. The EEOC took Texaco to court and introduced such strong evidence that the company agreed to settle without continuing with a full trial. Texaco agreed to pay some $140 million to current and former aggrieved employees—the largest settlement ever for a case of racial discrimination. The company also agreed to begin a massive cultural change effort to eliminate discrimination.[17]

EEO in the Global Arena. Meeting legal requirements concerning employment practices requires a commitment to the principle of equal opportunity. The challenge is even greater for international firms because laws take many different forms in countries around the world. The following Global Awareness Competency feature provides insight into the international legal environment faced by Cirque du Soleil.[18] When making hiring decisions in various parts of the world, Cirque du Soleil must understand the legal constraints, as well as the cultural factors, that apply in each country.[19] The circus's management also must decide whether to accept local hiring practices in a country even if those practices would be considered discriminatory in another country. For example, in Singapore, including statements in job notices that describe the preferred sex, ethnicity, and age of potential applicants (e.g., Chinese female, 20 to 25 years old) is common and perfectly legal. Do you think that the circus should follow this practice when hiring in Singapore?

WEB INSIGHT

Describe the human resource management services available to firms sending employees overseas. You can learn about services that consulting firms offer by visiting the Hewitt Associates Web site at ***http://www. hewittassoc.com***, the Windham World Web site at ***http://www.windham.com***, and Arthur Andersen at ***http://www. arthurandersen.com***.

GLOBAL AWARENESS COMPETENCY

Hiring Is No Laughing Matter for Cirque du Soleil

Remember the last time you sat under the big top, watching clowns entertain and acrobats tumble across the floor? Perhaps you've even seen a performance of Cirque du Soleil—one of the most unique acts in the world. With corporate headquarters in Montreal and offices in Las Vegas, Nevada, and Amsterdam, Netherlands, Cirque du Soleil is an international entertainment company that employs more than 1,200 people representing 17 nationalities and speaking at least 13 different languages. Its main products include a permanent show that runs in Las Vegas and several touring shows that run in countries around the world.

In this business, people are clearly the company's most important asset, so managing human resources effectively is essential. Success is possible only with careful planning, recruitment, and selection. For its tours, Cirque relies heavily on temporary staff (temps) hired in each city—people who work as ushers, ticket sellers and takers, and security personnel. For a year of tours, that adds up to some 1,800 temps. Although Cirque employs them for only a few days, good temps are essential to the company's reputation because they have the most direct personal contact with customers. To be hired, applicants must conduct themselves well during an interview designed to assess attitude, experience, and skills.

For positions in the touring groups, the selection process is more intensive. Throughout these selection processes, the company must ensure that it adheres to all local labor laws. The following table illustrates differences in discrimination laws—just one aspect of employment conditions. Ideally, Cirque will also be sensitive enough to local conditions to be able to avoid practices that, although legal, are considered undesirable within local cultures.

• • •

To learn more about Cirque du Soleil, visit the company's home page at

http://www.cirquedusoleil.com

Who's Protected Where?

Country	Age	Sex	National Origin	Race	Religion	Marital Status
United States	Yes	Yes	Yes	Yes	Yes	No
France	Some	Yes	Yes	Yes	Yes	Yes
Venezuela	No	No	No	No	No	No
Canada	Yes	Yes	Yes	Yes	Yes	Yes
Hong Kong	No	No	No	No	No	No
Japan	No	Yes	Yes	Yes	Yes	No
Vietnam	No	Yes	No	Yes	Yes	No
Germany	No	Yes	Yes	Yes	Yes	No
Indonesia	No	No	No	No	No	No
United Kingdom	No	Yes	No	No	No	No
Singapore	No	No	No	No	No	No
Greece	No	Yes	No	Yes	Yes	Yes

HEALTH AND SAFETY

The *Occupational Safety and Health Act* (OSHA) of 1970 requires employers to provide a safe and healthful workplace with adequate protection against hazards that are likely to cause serious physical impairment or death. These hazards could be dangerous equipment, unsafe production processes, exposure to noxious chemicals, and the like. For jobs that are inherently dangerous (e.g., construction, foundry work, metal stamping, and coal mining) OSHA calls for the use of all appropriate safety precautions. In metal stamping, for instance, safety devices must be used so that the operator's limbs are in a safe zone before the machine can be operated. Spray painters commonly wear respirators to protect themselves from paint fumes. No matter how risky the job, the intent of OSHA is to ensure that employers do not expose employees to unsafe practices, thereby endangering their physical well-being.

The Occupational Safety and Health Act is also relevant to people who work in environments that may seem to be relatively safe. Each year, billions of dollars in productivity and medical costs are lost due to office worker injuries such as carpal tunnel syndrome and back strain. Carpal tunnel syndrome is caused by the types of repetitive motions required for typing. Poorly designed office furniture is a major cause of back strain. In 1999, the Clinton administration unveiled regulations that would require employers to protect office workers from such injuries. However, when the business community protested that the cost of compliance would be too high, the proposed regulations were quickly withdrawn.[20] A revised version of ergonomic regulations will likely be proposed in the future.[21]

Also of concern to office workers are the hazards of working in so-called "sick buildings." The U.S. standards that are now in place to protect workers from unhealthy air were developed primarily in industrial settings. They regulate substances such as benzene and formaldehyde, but they don't specifically protect workers from the chemicals, bacteria, and viruses that can create unhealthy office environments. According to some experts, modernization of OSHA regulations is sorely needed to protect U.S. workers. By comparison, the laws in countries such as France and Sweden are much more stringent. Even without such laws, however, businesses would benefit financially from improving the air quality of office buildings. According to one study, the financial benefits of improving office climate can be 8 to 17 times larger than the costs of the remedies. Such benefits accrue not only from improved health and reduced absenteeism, but also from better performance of computer circuit boards and telephone switches.[22]

COMPENSATION AND BENEFITS

Compensation and benefits practices are shaped by a plethora of laws and regulations. They cover taxation, nondiscrimination, fair wages, protection of children, hardship and overtime pay, and pension and welfare benefits.

Fair Labor Standards Act. Of the several laws that affect compensation and benefits practices, the primary one is the *Fair Labor Standards Act* (FLSA) of 1938, which specifies a national minimum wage and requires payment for overtime work by covered employees. In 1938, the minimum wage was set at $0.25/hour; in 2000, it was $5.75. Individual state and local governments can, and often do, set higher standards than those set at the federal level. The FLSA also includes provisions to protect children. For example, it prohibits minors under the age of 18 from working in hazardous occupations.

Equal Pay Act. Another important regulation affecting compensation practices is the *Equal Pay Act* of 1963, which requires that men and women be paid equally for doing equal work (in terms of skill, effort, responsibility, and working conditions) in the same organization. Suppose, for example, that a software company has mostly male programmers designing computer games and mostly female programmers designing Web sites for those games. If the levels of skill, effort, and responsibility are similar in these two jobs, the men and women should be paid equally—despite the fact that they aren't doing identical work.

Comparable Worth. Many states have extended the logic of the Equal Pay Act to require that men and women be paid equally for doing *comparable* work. ***Comparable worth*** legislation requires employers to assess the worth of all jobs and ensure that jobs of comparable worth are paid similarly. These state laws go beyond the narrow language of the federal law and hold that work that appears to be quite dissimilar (e.g., nurses and engineers) can be of comparable worth. If one occupation tends to be dominated by women and the other by men, chances are that the occupation dominated by women will be paid less. Such discrepancies may be due to historical factors, discrimination, or labor market conditions. For organizations covered by comparable worth laws, employers must demonstrate that pay discrepancies between men and women reflect differences in factors such as the skills and responsibilities associated with their work.

HUMAN RESOURCE PLANNING

3.

STATE THE ELEMENTS OF HUMAN RESOURCE PLANNING.

WEB INSIGHT

Read the IBM chairman's Letter to Shareholders in the company's most recent annual report, online at *http://www.ibm.com/AnnualReport*. Which strategic issues facing IBM have the greatest implications for human resource planning at the company?

Human resource planning involves forecasting an organization's human resource needs and developing steps to be taken to meet them. It consists of setting and implementing goals and actions needed to ensure that the right number and type of individuals are available at the appropriate time and place to fulfill organizational needs. Cirque du Soleil needs to do two types of human resource planning: for temporary staff and for permanent staff. The circus must continually plan for its staffing needs in the cities it tours. What are the days and hours during which temps will be needed? How many ticket sellers and takers, ushers, and security personnel will be needed? In addition, because the circus is growing rapidly, it must make plans to add permanent staff for both its traveling and permanent shows.

Human resource planning is tied directly to strategic planning (see Chapter 7). Typically, strategic goals are established first, followed by goals for managing human resources that will be consistent with the broader goals. Figure 13.1 illustrates this process.[23]

At the heart of human resource planning are two tasks: determining an organization's future human resource needs and determining the organization's current workforce capacity. With this information, managers can then use a variety of other HRM activities (e.g., recruiting, training, and compensation) to address any gaps between needed and available human resources. Typically, an organization's needs are determined by forecasts. The capacity of the organization's current workforce can be assessed using competency inventories.

FORECASTS

A variety of forecasting methods—some simple, some complex—can be used to determine an organization's human resource (HR) needs. More than 60 percent of all large firms utilize some type of forecasting to project their HR needs. However, such forecasts may not be very accurate. During times of growth, for example, foreseeing changing conditions that may cause a business downturn is difficult. Recognizing this forecasting problem, many companies try to avoid hiring too many people, who they may have to lay off later. Instead of hiring permanent workers to meet the demands of a growing business, many companies hire temporary workers or independent contractors.

Just as it is difficult to predict when business will slow, it also is difficult to predict when business will take off. When business is slow, many companies reduce their workforces by laying off employees. Then, often sooner than they expected, they find that they need to rehire these same people. According to one large study, approximately 25 percent of the companies that had trimmed their workforces were rehiring people the next year—either for their former jobs or for new permanent jobs. The true costs associated with forecast errors are difficult to quantify. But experienced managers understand

**HR Goals for
Expanding International
Operational Capacity**

- Select executives to include
  in a global talent pool for
  expatriate assignments.
- Develop models to predict
  better a person's likelihood
  of success or failure.
- Provide data to managers
  to guide their individual
  placement decisions.
- Develop an information
  system that includes
  information about talent
  available in the organization
  and the competencies
  needed for specific
  assignments.

**HR Goals to Foster
Continuous Learning**

- Help individuals take charge
  of their own growth and
  development.
- Provide feedback to individuals
  about their strengths and
  weaknesses.
- Provide resources to facilitate
  learning and inform employees
  of them.
- Conduct benchmarking studies
  to learn about cutting-edge
  practices in other organizations.

**HR Goals to Develop a
Team-Based Organization**

- Identify new skills and
  competencies needed for
  team work.
- Develop selection methods
  to evaluate potential new
  hires for teamwork skills.
- Provide training in teamwork
  skills.
- Introduce rewards and
  recognition to reinforce the
  development of teamwork
  skills.

Strategic Concerns

- Expand international
  operational capacity.
- Foster continuous learning.
- Develop a team-based
  organization.

that inaccurate forecasts can have many long-term consequences. For example, to rehire
a laid-off staff person, a company may have to offer higher pay. But though they may be
paid better, such employees now feel less loyalty to the firm. So, if better opportunities
come along, they may be more willing to change jobs than to stay put in anticipation of
a promotion or pay raise. By laying off workers, the company may have saved money in
the short term, but in the long term they may find that their labor costs go up.

COMPETENCY INVENTORIES

A *competency inventory* is a detailed file maintained for each employee that lists level
of education, training, experience, length of service, current job title and salary, and
performance history. For managers and potential managers, also included are measurements of their competency levels against the factors comprising the competency model
used throughout this textbook.[24] Our competency model is only one of many that could
be used. In fact, a recent survey of 217 companies revealed a total of 148 different competency models in use. There is a great deal of overlap among them, and their purpose
is the same: to keep track of the talent in the organization so that it can be nurtured and
used most effectively.

Many organizations use computerized HR information systems for storage and easy retrieval of vital job-related information. For example, Texas Instruments (TI) maintains such files on its thousands of employees. These files help the firm's top management spot gaps in human resources. When gaps exist between the needs of the organization and the current supply of talent in the organization managers can use a variety of other HR activities to fill them. Through staffing activities, they can hire more (or fewer) people, or they can begin hiring people with different competencies. If the organization has the right number of people, but some of those people need new skills, training activities may be used to address the gap. In the remainder of this chapter, we discuss these and other HR activities in more detail.

THE HIRING PROCESS

4.

EXPLAIN THE PROCESS THAT ORGANIZATIONS USE TO RECRUIT AND SELECT NEW HIRES.

The **hiring process** involves two primary activities: recruitment and selection. As illustrated in Figure 13.2, these activities are stimulated by vacancies in the organization. Vacancies may occur because employees leave the organization or because they have been moved to another position within the organization.

During recruitment, the organization develops a pool of job candidates from which to select qualified employees. Candidates are recruited, for example, by running ads, contacting employment agencies, and visiting college campuses. After recruiting candidates, the organization selects those who are most likely to perform well on the job.[25]

Figure 13.2 **The Hiring Process**

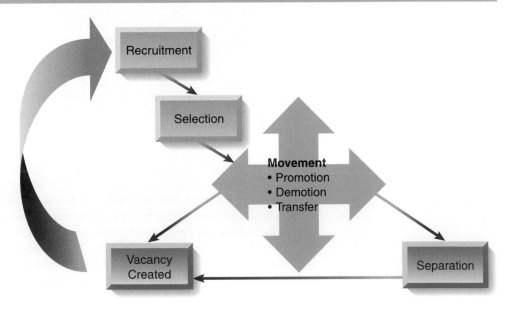

Those in an organization who have primary responsibility for the hiring process vary. In some organizations, hiring activities are centralized in a human resources department, and professional HR staff members do the recruiting and selection. In less centralized organizations, however, line managers often have most of the responsibility for hiring. In organizations that rely heavily on teamwork, team members often take most of the responsibility for hiring. At Dell Computer, everyone gets involved in hiring because it is so important to the company's success, as described in the following Teamwork Competency feature.[26]

As head of staffing for Dell Computer, Andy Esparza's job is to hire world-class people for a rapidly growing, world-class company. It's not a job he can do alone. He has more than 100 recruiters working with him, along with everyone else in the company. If they have a good recruit who's wavering because of competing offers, Esparza doesn't hesitate to call on CEO Michael Dell for help. "He'll pick up the phone right away, or use his car phone on his way home— whatever he needs to do to make that call. He's a great closer."

Esparza understands that just getting bodies in the door is not really the point. Dell wants to hire only the best. So, when a technician told him he had just discouraged his neighbor from applying for a job at Dell, Esparza was pleased. In the judgment of the technician, hiring the neighbor would have hurt the company.

Besides recommendations from employees—internal referrals—Dell attracts about one-third of new recruits through its Web site. In addition, Esparza created a "leads team." Like a SWAT team, its job is to act quickly and aggressively to tackle hiring problems— such as an unexpected vacancy in a key position. Acting almost like spies, the "leads team" studies newspapers, the Web, trade journals, and anything else they can think of to come up with the names of people who might consider a job change. Dips in stock prices, mergers, or plans for downsizing all provide clues. According to Esparza, "We look for people who might be a little uncomfortable in their jobs (and then) we jump on leads very, very quickly."

When good people are found, they often visit the company headquarters in Austin, Texas, before making a final decision. At this point, Esparza may involve other people from the community to help. When a recruit wanted to know about the ice-hockey opportunities for his son, a Junior Olympian, Esparza had the local youth league president meet with the candidate to provide the information. That was somewhat unusual. More typical would be involving realtors, medical experts, school administrators, and/or religious leaders, depending on candidates' particular concerns.

Esparza maintains that all his effort is worth it. "We feel we have an organization that's making history here. But our future depends on continuing to bring in great people—more and more of them. We want them, and we are willing to do a lot to get them."

• • •

To learn more about Dell Computer, visit the company's home page at

http://www.dell.com

RECRUITMENT

Recruitment is the process of searching, both inside and outside the organization, for people to fill vacant positions. Effective recruitment not only attracts individuals to the organization, but it also increases the chances of retaining them once they're hired. Larger organizations often develop systematic approaches to recruitment, whereas smaller organizations may do little more than rely on word of mouth.[27]

Labor Market Conditions. The external environment is particularly important for managers to consider when developing a recruiting program. If the local supply of qualified employees exceeds local demand, recruitment will be relatively easy. But when the local supply of qualified employees is limited, recruiting efforts must intensify. In recent years, U.S. unemployment has been low by historical standards, hovering just below 4 percent. Most employers face a shortage of skilled workers and managers. Forecasters expect this condition to continue into the foreseeable future.[28]

Failure to find effective ways to cope with a tight labor supply can doom an organization. When Charles Thomas, CEO of Pittsburgh-based Solid State Measurements, Inc., considered what it would take to achieve his objective of significant growth, he realized that he had a problem. "We had very good talent for running a $3 to $5 million company," he observed, "but we didn't have the talent for taking it to $25 million to $50 million in annual sales." At the time, Thomas was doing much of the top-level managerial work related to both day-to-day operations and marketing. To free up time for other things, he needed someone to help him create a top-level management team to take on some of this work. But even with the help of a search firm, it took nine months to find someone with the right strategic action competency. Thomas was surprised by how small the executive talent pool was. The number of searches being done by executive search firms is up by about 25 percent over past years, and finding the right candidate often takes twice as long as it did just a few years ago.

The shortage of talented managers puts pressure on all organizations. Even those that already have managerial talent in place can't relax because their employees are likely targets for poaching. The best ones won't hang around patiently, hoping for a promotion. If a competitor dangles an offer in front of them, chances are they'll take it unless they have strong incentives to stay where they are. Poaching talent from other companies may not be polite, but it's definitely popular.

Aggressive Recruitment Strategies. The shortage of technical talent looms large for many employers, but especially those in Silicon Valley, which needs two things to keep it going: bright ideas and bright people. Bright ideas are needed for continuous innovation and new products, and bright people are needed to fuel the growth of the booming hi-tech industry. These days, finding enough talented people seems to be more of a problem than coming up with new ideas, especially for companies that are desperately trying to grow.

During recent years, Cisco Systems has been hiring 4,000 to 5,000 new employees each quarter—accounting for nearly 10 percent of the total job growth in Silicon Valley. Usually, the best people already have good jobs, and often they're happy with their employers. Rather than rely on the pool of applicants that actively are looking for work, Cisco focuses on enticing passive job seekers with good potential. To figure out how to locate those people, Cisco first needs to learn how they spend their time. From group discussions with some of its current employees—the kind of people Cisco wants more of—Cisco's management knows that these folks don't spend their time looking through job ads. They're more likely to be surfing the Internet or attending art festivals and local home and garden fairs. At such events, Cisco recruiters work the crowds, pass out and collect business cards, and talk up the company. When an interested prospect is identified, that person is paired with a current Cisco employee who has similar interests and skills—a "friend." Friends serve both as screeners to help filter out unsuitable applicants and as advocates to convince the best candidates to accept job offers from Cisco. A thousand Cisco employees have volunteered to be part of the friends program. Do they do it to combat their own loneliness? Probably not. More likely, they're attracted to the generous referral fee and the free-trip lottery ticket that they receive if someone they've befriended is eventually hired.[29]

Other firms in the valley attack the recruiting problem by infiltrating local universities. Because of the shortage of engineers, competition for Stanford University graduates is fierce. To recruit them, some firms stake out particular classes and pursue an elaborate recruiting strategy. One such class is a computer science course that teaches people how to teach others to use computers. Students who complete this class then go on to work as teaching assistants in another computer course. If a company can hire one of these teaching assistants—or better yet, one of the two students who coordinate the work of the teaching assistants—it wins in two ways. First, it gains an employee who has excellent technical skills. Even better, it gets someone who has a direct connection to the students in the introductory class, who will be graduating in two years.[30]

SELECTION

Through recruitment, an organization finds people who are potential employees. The process of *employee selection* involves deciding which of these recruits should actually be hired and for which positions.[31] The decision about who to select often takes into account both a person's ability to do the job and how well that person is likely to fit into the organization. Jack Welch, CEO of General Electric, appreciated how important this activity is: "All we can do is bet on the people whom we pick," he says. "So my job is picking the right people."[32] Welch's most important selection decision was choosing his successor, Jeffrey R. Immelt, who will take over as GE's CEO in 2002.

The most common sources of information for making selection decisions are résumés, reference checks, interviews, and tests. Employers use the information they gain from these sources to select the best potential employees from a pool of applicants. Applicants, in turn, get a feel for the organization and job requirements from the content of the selection procedures and the way the organization treats applicants throughout the selection process. Well-qualified applicants who react negatively to either the content or process used during selection may decline the organization's job offer.[33]

Résumés. A well-written résumé is clear, concise, and easy to read and understand. It gives (1) personal data (name, address, and telephone number); (2) career objectives; (3) education (including grade point average, degree, and major and minor fields of study); (4) work experience (highlighting special skills and responsibilities); (5) descriptions of relevant competencies, activities, and personal information; and (6) the names, addresses, and telephone numbers of references. Many companies now accept electronic résumés submitted over the Internet. These companies may specify a format for a résumé, or even provide an electronic form to be completed. In such cases, complying with all the requirements for submitting a résumé is especially important because some of the companies also use software programs designed to scan for information and route the résumé to the appropriate person.

Reference Checks. Because résumés can be falsified easily, managers may request references and conduct reference checks. Many HR professionals routinely check educational qualifications, including schools attended, study major or majors, degrees awarded, and dates. An applicant's work experience is more difficult to check because employers often are reluctant to provide evaluations of former employees. Their concerns stem from successful lawsuits brought against employers by former employees who were given bad references. By law, organizations are required to provide only the job title and dates of employment of a former employee.

Interviews. In making a final selection, most organizations rely on a combination of interviews and tests. Although commonly used, interviews don't always predict on-the-job performance accurately. Research indicates that interviewers tend to decide about a person early in the interview and then spend the rest of the time seeking information to support that decision. But early impressions often are erroneous. Too often, managers form favorable impressions of candidates simply because they share superficial similarities with the manager (e.g., where they grew up or where they went to school). Managers may also let their stereotypes affect their judgments about individual candidates. Problems such as these made Home Depot decide to automate its staffing process. Because of its computerized approach to screening all job applicants, a qualified woman is now much more likely to end up in a job that uses all her skills instead of being put into a job that fits an interviewer's stereotype about the types of jobs that "women do best."[34]

Despite their potential drawbacks, interviews can be useful. The key to their success is developing a structured and systematic approach. The Taylor Group, a company that provides systems integration services, believes that its systematic approach to interviewing is the main reason that it is able to hire and retain the best talent in the industry. To get a job with the Taylor Group, submitting an electronic résumé is just the beginning of a long process. First, a telephone interview screens out people who aren't a good fit with the company's culture. About one in four applicants doesn't get past this first interview—often because their responses indicate that money is more important to them than having great coworkers and being at a place where they can keep learning. The next interview is usually held with the applicant's likely manager. The manager probes for attitudes toward teamwork and assesses past job experiences. Managers at the Taylor Group also use situational interviews. In a *situational interview,* the candidate is asked to describe or demonstrate how he or she would handle situations that are likely to arise on the job. Situational interviews are better predictors of performance than interviews that focus on past work.[35] A third interview is likely to involve a meeting with other people who would likely work with the new hire. For high-level positions, additional interviews with members of the top-management team would be the final hurdle.[36]

When you first enter the world of work, you probably will be interviewed many times before you're in a position to conduct interviews yourself. Typically, someone about to graduate from college goes through three types of employment interviews: on-campus, plant or office, and final selection.

Tests. Many organizations use tests to screen and select candidates. Capital One Financial Corporation tries to minimize its reliance on interviews, preferring written tests instead. Its own research shows that written tests predict job performance more accurately than interviews do. Based on test results from 1,600 of its employees, Capital One developed a four-hour battery of tests that it uses to screen applicants and select the most qualified.[37]

A common type of written test, the ***cognitive ability test,*** measures general intelligence; verbal, numerical, and reasoning ability, and the like. Such tests have proved to be relatively successful in predicting which applicants are qualified for certain jobs.

Written tests can also be used to measure personality. A ***personality test*** assesses the unique blend of characteristics that define an individual. In jobs that involve a great deal of contact with other people, such as sales agents and many types of service jobs, the personality characteristic *extraversion* is a good predictor of future job performance. Extraverts tend to be talkative, good-natured, and gregarious—traits that facilitate smooth interactions with customers and clients. Another personality characteristic of interest to many employers is conscientiousness. Conscientious people seem to have a strong sense of purpose, obligation, and persistence—all of which lead to high performance in almost any type of work situation.[38] Finally, honesty tests are becoming more common because employee theft costs U.S. businesses an estimated $40 billion annually.[39] An honesty test is a specialized paper-and-pencil measure of a person's tendency to behave dishonestly. Some honesty tests also predict the likelihood that people will break rules, abuse sick leave privileges, or use drugs at work.[40]

A ***performance test*** requires a candidate to simulate actual job tasks. One example is a code-writing test for computer programmers. Another example is an in-basket exercise. In this case, job candidates receive a stack of letters, e-mails, memos, telephone messages, faxes, and other items and are told to imagine that they have been promoted to a new position. They are given a specific amount of time to deal appropriately with these items. In most cases they will have the opportunity to explain or discuss their decisions in a follow-up interview.[41] At the BMW auto plant in South Carolina, job candidates work for 90 minutes on a simulated assembly line. They don't actually produce cars that will be sold, but they perform many of the tasks that are part of the job. To be hired, they must show more than their technical skills. They also must show the mental and physical stamina required to perform well in BMW's "aerobic workplace."[42]

TRAINING AND DEVELOPMENT

5.

DESCRIBE SEVERAL TYPES OF TRAINING AND DEVELOPMENT PROGRAMS.

When unemployment levels are high, employers can rather easily hire people who have the competencies needed to perform well in a job. But during labor shortages, hiring qualified new people becomes much more difficult. Instead, employers must help current employees develop the competencies needed by the company. By providing them with ***training,*** employers can help employees overcome their limitations and increase their productive capacities. By providing them with opportunities for ***development,*** employers can help employees attain the competencies needed to advance their careers.

Even if a company hired only the very best qualified people available, it would probably still need to invest in training and development. These activities can range from a 1-day orientation session to creation of a personalized, long-term career development plan. Different approaches generally are used to achieve different purposes.

ORIENTATION TRAINING

Almost all new hires need to "learn the ropes." Every organization has its own ways of doing things, which are important for new employees to understand. A few hours of training during the first day or two helps ease them into their jobs. When new employees are from different countries and cultures, this initial training is especially important in helping them adjust. At ACS International Resources, an IT consulting company, the CEO lectures new hires on everything from the company's strategic goals to the use of underarm deodorant. Cultural differences in approaches to personal hygiene often mean that new hires at ACS need to be trained to understand how the company's clients react to consultants who are not freshly showered and starched. "It's blunt, it's rude, but it works," says CEO Pantel. The training doesn't end with a lecture, however. During the first month or so, Pantel buys U.S.-style lunches for international hires and encourages them to watch some U.S. TV shows. He or someone else from the company might even show up at their homes on the weekend to take them grocery shopping or discuss the school system. The objective is simply to help international hires learn the ropes as quickly as possible.[43]

BASIC SKILLS TRAINING

Basic skills training may be needed by employees who are unable to read, write, do arithmetic, or solve problems well enough to perform even simple tasks. Such employees can't write letters to customers, read warning labels on chemical containers, or understand operating symbols on machines. Organizations spend large sums of money on remedial training for employees because they believe that if employees can master certain basic skills, they can perform a variety of jobs and deal with some of the new technologies in use.

NEW-TECHNOLOGY TRAINING

Another common reason that employees need to receive training is changing technology. Today, such changes occur almost continually in every industry, and most managers and employees need to keep up with them. In recent years, new technologies associated with the Internet have been the fundamental drivers of organizational change and the need for new competencies. At KPMG, a global consulting company, everyone—from senior partners to junior administrative assistants—goes through 50 hours of online training. Many people go through the curriculum just because they have to. But after they finish, some realize that it really helps them in their jobs. A marketing manager has found that the course helps her think in new ways about how to help clients build an intranet. Others have developed new research skills or gained new insights into copyright law issues. Perhaps most important, the company as a whole is beginning to understand better the changes that their clients are facing as they too adjust to the Internet. Such insights are bound to improve the quality of service provided to those clients.[44]

TEAM TRAINING

When an organization downsizes, merges with another firm, redesigns its production process, or develops a new approach to serving its customers, the jobs of many employees are likely to change in fundamental ways. Hence training and development often are needed to help employees adjust. Because teamwork often increases as a result of such changes, training programs often seek to enhance the teamwork competency.

When BP Norge decided to restructure around self-managing teams, its goals were to speed up decision making, reduce costs and cycle times, and increase innovation. Despite the strong business argument supporting a change to teamwork, the organization found that changing to it was difficult. Nine months of frustration led management to conclude that a training initiative was needed. A team of U.S. and Norwegian facilitators conducted two-day workshops, which were attended by a mix of people from all levels and functional specialties. Oil rig workers and senior managers sat side by side, as did Norwegians and Americans. Prior to the workshop, everyone watched a video that explained self-managed teams and showed how other organizations had used them successfully. Workshop participants also interviewed a few colleagues to find out what they thought about self-managed teams. At the workshop, discussion focused on understanding the process by which teamwork develops. The participants also began practicing the behaviors needed in their new team environment—taking risks, communicating their feelings, teaching others, and learning from others.[45]

CAREER DEVELOPMENT

Most people would not be satisfied to continue to do the same job year after year. They want to grow and move into new and better jobs. The intent of development programs is to improve an employee's competencies in preparation for future jobs. Before sending an employee to a development program, a needs analysis is made to identify that person's particular strengths and developmental needs. For beginning supervisors and managers, limitations often include an inability to set goals with others and to negotiate interpersonal conflicts. The following Planning and Administration Competency feature describes some of the other competencies that development programs can enhance.[46]

PLANNING & ADMINISTRATION COMPETENCY

Developing Leaders at Colgate-Palmolive

Nearly two centuries ago, Colgate-Palmolive (or just Colgate) sold mostly candles and soap. Today, it is one of the best-known consumer goods companies in the world. Its name-brand products, which generate nearly $10 billion annually in revenues, include Colgate soap, Ajax cleanser, Mennen deodorant, and dozens more.

Throughout most of its history, Colgate's approach to managing executive talent was simple: Just let the cream rise to the top, naturally. But a few years ago, top management began to question this approach. As they scanned the environment, Colgate's executives noted several trends that could create a shortage of managerial talent in the future—and they worried about how the company could

continue to grow if that happened. A plan was needed to ensure that there would be no talent shortage. A new unit, called People Development, was created to develop and implement a plan. Based on an extensive analysis of the external environment and forecasts of Colgate's needs, a profile of required leadership competencies was developed. Key competencies included business savvy, use of personal influence, global perspective, strong character, people management, and entrepreneurial action.

With a clear view of the types of leaders needed by the company, the People Development unit laid out a strategy for getting such people into place. The success of that strategy required (1) a commitment to identifying

"high potential" employees and giving them job assignments that allowed them to develop their leadership competencies, and (2) the active involvement of high-potential employees in managing their own careers. The table on the opposite page describes the components of a tool kit developed to assist high-potential employees at Colgate with career management. These employees give the new approach high marks. The next challenge is finding ways to extend elements of this developmental approach to the company's workforce worldwide.

• • •

To learn more about Colgate-Palmolive, visit the company's home page at

http://www.colgate.com

Components of a Tool Kit for Individual Development at Colgate-Palmolive

I. Overview of the Individual Development Process

Assess individual competencies and values

Define personal strengths, development needs, and options for career growth

Identify developmental actions

Craft individual development plan

Meet with manager to decide a course of action (based on preceding analysis)

Accept the challenge of implementing the plan

II. Worksheets for Individual Assessment

Competency assessment worksheets: assess strengths and weaknesses for a specified set of competencies

Personal values survey: assesses preferences for types of work environments, work relationships, work tasks, lifestyle needs, and personal needs

Development activities chart: describes on-the-job and off-the-job learning opportunities that can be used to develop key competencies

Global training grids: list all formal training programs offered by the company and explain how each relates to key competencies

Individual development plan: developed by the employee, this describes specific development goals and a course of action to be taken to achieve the goals

III. Defining and Understanding Global Competencies

This section of the tool kit is like a dictionary. It lists all the competencies considered to be important for various types of jobs throughout the company and describes the meaning of each competency. This section serves as a reference guide and encourages people across the company to use a common set of terms when discussing competencies and career development issues.

Many large companies, such as GE, McDonald's, Motorola, and Siemens, provide so many hours of developmental activities to so many employees that they have built company "universities," complete with classrooms, dorm rooms, and other amenities of a typical college campus. Organizations may encourage employees to attend these "universities" as part of a long-term strategy for developing a cadre of high-potential managers who, in several years, may become upper level managers. The developmental experiences are intended to broaden these managers' perspectives and prepare them for general (as opposed to functional) management positions. A key objective often is to develop a managers' strategic action competency.[47]

CROSS-CULTURAL TRAINING

One of the increasingly important challenges for organizations is preparing people to be expatriate employees working in a nation other than their home country. Without this preparation, such employees may not be able to take on and successfully complete a foreign assignment. Table 13.1 identifies some of the issues that organizations must address in preparing their employees for a foreign assignment.[48] Particularly important is cross-cultural training, including cultural awareness, language instruction, and practical assistance with matters of daily living. Such training improves employees' global awareness competency by creating sensitivity to the host country's culture and appreciation for it. Language training improves an expatriate employee's communication competency. Practical assistance with matters of daily living helps employees and their families adjust to life in the new environment, thereby enhancing their self-management competencies.

- What is the host country's business culture like? What is its management style? Do I have the skills I'll need to handle relationships with my employees?

- Will this assignment be good for my long-term career prospects? Can I expect to be promoted when I return? How will I be treated if I don't perform well in my new overseas job?

- What is the country like? What are its customs? Will I be able to adjust to the culture?

- Will my family be able to adjust to the new situation? Will my spouse be able to find suitable employment? Will my children be able to adjust to going to school in another country? How good is the educational system there?

- How will we learn enough of the new language to communicate effectively?

- Where will we live? How will the new housing arrangements compare to our current home? What will happen to our current home when we leave for the new assignment?

- What are the tax and other financial issues I will have to address as an expatriate? Who will be available to advise me on these topics? Will the company pay me in a way that protects my income from high foreign tax rates?

- How will our medical needs be taken care of? If someone in my family becomes seriously ill, will we be able to come back and receive treatment from our family physician?

PERFORMANCE APPRAISAL AND FEEDBACK

6.

EXPLAIN HOW MANAGERS USE PERFORMANCE INFORMATION TO IMPROVE EMPLOYEE JOB PERFORMANCE.

Performance appraisal is a formal, structured system for measuring, evaluating, and influencing an employee's job-related attributes, behaviors, and outcomes.[49] Its focus is on discovering how productive the employee is and whether he or she can perform as effectively or more effectively in the future. One of the primary responsibilities of managers is appraising the performance of their employees. Their assessments influence who is promoted, demoted, transferred, and dismissed—and the size of raises that employees receive. Increasingly, employees also are being asked to appraise the performance of their managers.

Performance appraisal, which necessarily reflects the past, isn't an end to be achieved. Rather, it's a means for moving into a more productive future. For performance appraisals to be effective, just doing them isn't sufficient; employees must *act* on them. Usually, supervisors are responsible for communicating the results of appraisals to their subordinates and helping them improve their performance. Conversely, subordinates usually are responsible for seeking honest feedback and using it to improve their performance.[50]

During a *performance feedback session,* manager and subordinate meet to exchange information and discuss how to improve performance. In many organizations, the discussion includes the manager's assessment of the employee, the employee's self-assessment, the assessment of team members, and even information from customers. Regular assessment of progress toward attaining goals helps employees remain motivated and solve problems as they arise. Regular feedback also encourages periodic reexamination of goals to determine whether they should be adjusted. This aspect of assessment is important regardless of whether the manager is giving the feedback or getting it! In a study that tracked the performance of managers for five years, researchers found that some managers who received appraisals by subordinates improved more than others. The managers who improved the most were the ones who met directly with their subordinates to discuss the appraisal results and what they could do to improve.[51]

STRATEGIC ALIGNMENT

Performance appraisal and feedback achieve their purposes when the process is integrated with achievement of strategic goals, aligning the goals of the individual with those of the organization. That is, the process of measuring performance and discus-

WEB INSIGHT

Read ProMES, an approach to measuring team performance, at *http://acs.tamu.edu/~promes*. Explain how this approach aligns team performance goals with an organization's strategic goals.

sions about how to improve performance focus clearly on the actions and behaviors that employees must exhibit and results that they must achieve to make a strategy come alive. In organizations having a low-cost strategy, such as Wal-Mart, ways to increase employee efficiency is stressed. In organizations pursuing a differentiated strategy based on outstanding customer service, such as Nordstrom or BMW, employees must be able to work in teams, solve customer problems collaboratively, and work without direct supervision. Therefore performance related to these strategies should be the focus.

When the performance appraisal and feedback process is aligned with strategic goals, discussions of performance are more likely to stay focused on organizational issues instead of personal issues. As the following Communication Competency feature illustrates, talking about people's performance requires sensitivity. Doing it well also requires making use of both informal and formal channels of communication.[52]

COMMUNICATION COMPETENCY

Making Improvements at Con-Way Transportation Services

Con-Way Transportation Services is a subsidiary of CNF, the giant shipping company. It's a company in which teams are prevalent, yet it had no centralized approach to evaluating team effectiveness. So the Information System Department decided to become trailblazers. To evaluate themselves, they developed the Team Improvement Review (TIR).

Daily life in the department is guided by their Team Agreement, a document that sets out how they do things. According to the department's manager, "It's pretty much the common law around here." The TIR separates feedback sessions, which focus on how to improve in the future, from salary reviews, which focus on the past. The team's reasoning was that people might not be candid in evaluating each other if they knew that doing so would affect salaries. Many experts agree with that reasoning.

Before a team improvement meeting, which occurs every three months,

members rate each other on 31 dimensions. To ensure that the feedback environment is "safe," these meetings usually take place with no managers present. In their place is a facilitator who helps the team manage the delicate process of providing feedback that improves rather than destroys team functioning. One trick that the team learned is to let an individual's self-assessment serve as the focus of the discussion. Each team member begins by listing a few of his or her strengths and weaknesses on a sheet of paper. The sheets are then passed around the group. By the time each sheet gets back to its owner, the sheet has comments from the other team members, indicating whether they agree or disagree with the items in the list and making suggestions for how and where to focus improvement efforts. The process encourages people to be honest with

themselves and, at the same time, creates a network of support for self-initiated change efforts.

• • •

To learn more about CNF Transportation, visit the company's home page at

http://www.cnf.com

Unfortunately, many organizations aren't successful in using performance appraisals strategically. One reason is that line managers do not fully understand the basics of this approach. They spend far more time acquiring technical skills than they do learning to manage human resources. Another roadblock to the effective use of performance appraisals is that managers fail to see the payoff for conducting them. In fact, many managers so dislike the associated paperwork and unpleasant confrontations with employees that they try to avoid the process entirely. Avoidance, of course, is shortsighted. Despite the challenges, organizations that make the effort to design and implement effective appraisal and feedback systems can expect their employees to trust the actions of management.[53]

EFFECTIVE PERFORMANCE APPRAISAL

During the past 50 years, hundreds of studies have revealed the shortcomings, failures, and abuses of performance appraisals and suggested ways to improve their accuracy and validity. Studies have examined the errors in judgment that managers make, the problems that can be created by poorly designed appraisal methods, the reluctance of managers to give employees negative appraisals, and even how employees use tactics such as ingratiation to influence their supervisors' evaluations of their performance.[54] The basic lesson learned from all this research is that accurately assessing the performance of subordinates is an extremely difficult managerial task. Fortunately, organizations can do several things to help managers be more accurate when conducting performance appraisals, as illustrated in Figure 13.3.

Figure 13.3	Improving Performance Appraisal Accuracy

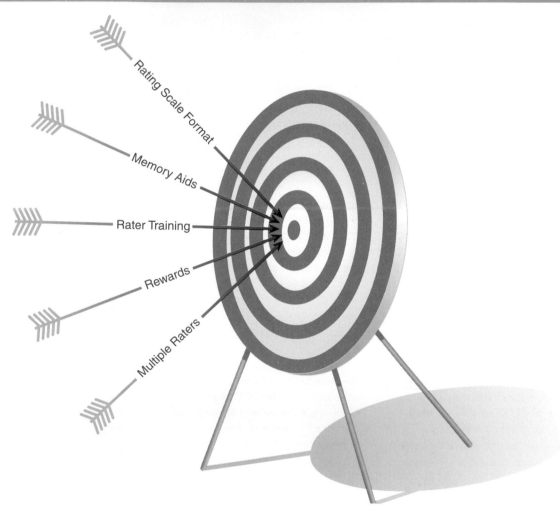

Rating Scale Format. Performance ratings tend to be more accurate when the rating scales used are precise. Each aspect of performance should be defined and rated separately and the scores then summed to determine the overall rating. In addition, managers shouldn't be asked to evaluate large groups of employees, especially all at the same time.

Memory Aids. Behavior diaries and critical incident files are useful memory aids.[55] Everyone involved in making appraisals should regularly record behaviors or outcomes—good or bad—that relate to an employee's or team's performance. Reviewing these records at the time of the performance appraisal helps ensure that the rater uses all available and relevant information.

Rater Training. Rating accuracy can also be improved through training that focuses on improving the observation skills of raters.[56] Training also builds confidence. A good training experience helps raters see that they *can* rate accurately and *can* handle the consequences associated with giving negative feedback.

Rewards. One cause of rating inaccuracy is a lack of rater motivation. Without rewards, raters may find it easier to give high ratings than to give accurate ratings. A straightforward way to increase rater motivation is to base salary increases, promotions, and assignments to key positions partly on performance as a rater. Ratings done in a timely and fair manner (as measured by employee attitude surveys) should be rewarded.

Multiple Raters. One innovative way to provide employees with feedback is the *360-degree appraisal system.*[57] This approach to performance appraisal has been available for several years, but only recently has it become easy to use, thanks to new Web-based software. It involves gathering assessments of an employee from a variety of sources—supervisors, subordinates, colleagues inside the organization, people outside the organization with whom the employee does business, and even an employee self-appraisal. The identities of specific individual assessors aren't disclosed to the employee. Multiple raters acting as a group—as they do at Con-Way—may be especially effective in producing accurate ratings, because discussion among team members helps overcome any individual's errors and biases.[58]

PROVIDING FEEDBACK

Many people feel uncomfortable providing performance feedback and are reluctant to do so, in part because the process often stimulates conflict. Such reluctance is as true for managers giving feedback to their subordinates as it is for subordinates giving feedback to their managers or peers. But providing feedback is important for improving performance. Feedback is most constructive when managers understand the potential for conflict and its possible sources. Being fully prepared and paying attention to issues of timing also make feedback constructive.

Understanding Sources of Conflict. Some conflict may be inevitable when a manager provides feedback to employees. By understanding the likely causes of conflict, however, managers can anticipate it and develop ways to handle the conflict.

One source of conflict during feedback sessions is competing goals. On the one hand, individuals want valid feedback that tells them where they stand and how they can improve. On the other hand, they want to verify their self-images and obtain valued rewards. Supervisors must strive to be both open and protective in helping employees meet both goals.[59]

Another source of conflict is the differing perspectives that supervisor and subordinate bring to the process. Low-performance situations accentuate a natural tendency to account for performance in a self-serving manner. For the subordinate, the focus is outward. Most salient are environmental forces (e.g., the supervisor, availability of supplies, and coworkers) that interfere with the subordinate's ability to perform. To protect their egos, employees explain their own poor performance by pointing to the difficulty of the task, unclear instructions, lack of necessary equipment, and other factors that often implicate the supervisor. For the supervisor, the focus is on the subordinate and her or his motivation and ability. Because supervisors also want to protect their egos, they may deny any responsibility for the subordinate's poor performance and instead blame poor performance solely on the employee's deficiencies.

Preparation. To signal the importance of performance discussions, the feedback session should be scheduled in advance. Also in advance, the manager and employee should agree on its purpose and content. Will the subordinate have an opportunity to evaluate the performance of the supervisor, or will the evaluation be one-way? Will the session be restricted to evaluating past performance or include suggestions for improving performance in the future, or will it involve both tasks? By discussing these issues ahead of time, both participants have time to prepare. Advance notice will also give an empowered subordinate sufficient time to update performance records and do a self-assessment.

Problem Solving. Carrying out an effective feedback session involves both coaching and counseling. Supervisors need to listen to and reflect back what subordinates say with regard to performance, its causes, and its outcomes. Too often, the interview process breaks down and supervisors end up telling employees how well or poorly they're doing and selling them on the merits of setting specific goals for improvement. This may seem efficient for supervisors, but subordinates feel frustrated trying to convince their superiors to listen to justifications for their performance levels.

A more effective approach is to conduct a problem-solving session. This approach centers on sharing perceptions of problems and identifying solutions to them. Active and open dialogue is established, and goals for improvement are set by mutual agreement. This type of discussion is difficult for most managers unless they have received prior training in it.

Follow-Up. Follow-up is essential to ensure that agreements made during the feedback session are met. Managers should verify that subordinates know what is expected of them, understand how they must perform to meet those expectations, and realize the consequences of good or poor behavior. Managers should also monitor behavior, provide feedback, and immediately reinforce new behaviors that match those desired. In the absence of continuing feedback and reinforcement, new behaviors will probably not become habit.

Team Feedback. Self-managing teams, such as those at Con-Way, frequently take full responsibility for developing and conducting their own performance appraisal and feedback processes. Team members are well acquainted with each other's strengths and weaknesses, so it makes sense that they become the primary performance evaluators. But team feedback is fraught with challenges. When team members evaluate each other, how should they use the information to provide feedback? Should someone outside the team conduct the feedback session? Should a team leader be designated for this task? Or should everyone on the team be involved in every feedback session?

The reality is that different teams handle feedback in different ways. At Con-Way, everyone on the team participates in providing feedback to everyone else, and feedback is provided during group discussions. The goal is to incorporate feedback sessions into the normal work routine. Many other organizations provide feedback in a more private setting. Often the manager to whom the team reports is responsible for collecting performance information from the team and discussing it with each team member privately.

More important than who delivers the feedback is how the person delivers it. Ideally, anyone who gives feedback has been trained in how to do so effectively. At Con-Way, teams are learning this invaluable skill by involving a professional facilitator in their feedback sessions. With sufficient practice and guidance, Con-Way teams should eventually develop enough skill and self-confidence to hold feedback sessions spontaneously and unassisted.

COMPENSATION

7.

DISCUSS THE OBJECTIVES OF MONETARY COMPENSATION AND THE ELEMENTS OF A MONETARY COMPENSATION PACKAGE.

At Southwest Airlines and most other companies, the *total* compensation that employees receive for the work they do includes a mix of both monetary and nonmonetary compensation. **Nonmonetary compensation** includes many forms of social and psychological rewards—recognition and respect from others and opportunities for self-development. For 9 years Steve O'Donnell was David Letterman's head writer. He's the one who came up with the idea of the show's now-famous top 10 lists. Did he ever get any special compensation for that particular contribution? "No. It never occurred to me," he says. "I'm probably the biggest simp about money of anybody over 12 years old. A pat on the back, making Dave happy, the thrill of hearing the audience laugh—that's what matters most."[60]

Clearly, there are many sources of nonmonetary rewards.[61] Jobs partly determine the social and psychological rewards associated with work. Opportunities for career growth and development, as well as the use of praise and recognition, also contribute to a corporate culture that makes employees feel good about coming to work. At Southwest Airlines, employment security is one of the many nonmonetary rewards employees receive. In an industry that experiences cyclical downturns about every five years, Southwest's no-furlough policy is unusual, giving the company a competitive advantage in the labor market.

Nonmonetary compensation is certainly important to employees. Indeed, it is one of the main factors that determines an organization's unique culture (discussed in Chapter 17). The focus of our discussion here, however, is monetary compensation. *Monetary compensation* includes direct payments such as salary, wages, and bonuses and indirect payments such as covering the costs of insurance plans. Indirect payments are generally referred to as *benefits* and they typically account for about one-third of an organization's total labor costs. In most organizations, base wages and salaries account for most of the direct compensation paid to employees, with bonuses and other forms of incentive pay making up the remainder. Within these two general categories of monetary compensation are many specific elements, as shown in Figure 13.4. The relative importance of these elements differs among organizations, as well as among employees.

Figure 13.4 **Elements of a Total Compensation System**

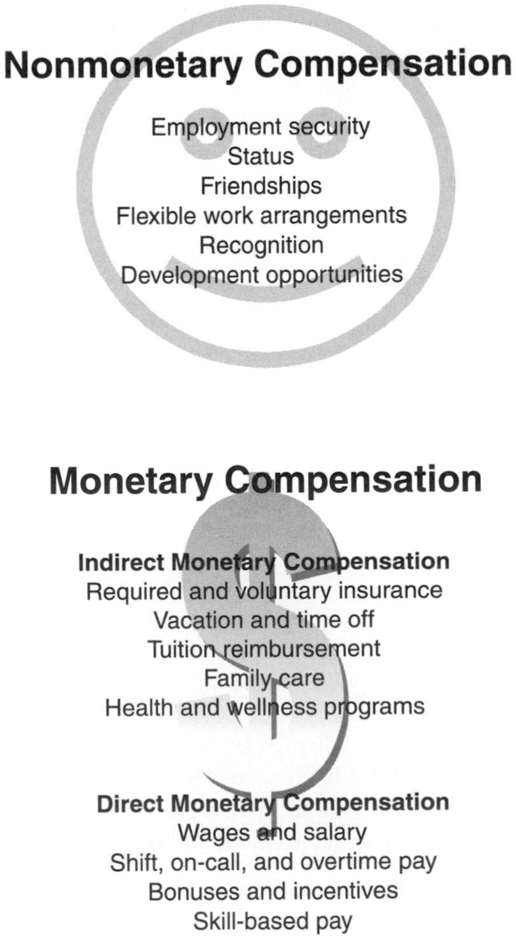

Nonmonetary Compensation

Employment security
Status
Friendships
Flexible work arrangements
Recognition
Development opportunities

Monetary Compensation

Indirect Monetary Compensation
Required and voluntary insurance
Vacation and time off
Tuition reimbursement
Family care
Health and wellness programs

Direct Monetary Compensation
Wages and salary
Shift, on-call, and overtime pay
Bonuses and incentives
Skill-based pay

Like many other aspects of an organization's approach to managing human resources, monetary compensation can facilitate (or interfere with) achieving various organizational goals. Two goals of particular relevance to compensation are (1) attracting and retaining the talent required for a sustainable competitive advantage and (2) maximizing productivity. The many elements of a monetary compensation system contribute in different ways to achieving these goals.

ATTRACTING AND RETAINING EMPLOYEES

In conjunction with an organization's recruitment and selection efforts, monetary compensation can help ensure that the rewards offered are sufficient to attract the right people at the right time for the right jobs.[62] Effective compensation systems appeal to employees' sense of fairness. *Pay fairness* refers to what people believe they deserve to be paid in relation to what others deserve to be paid. Unless compensation is perceived as externally competitive, the organization will have a difficult time attracting the best applicants. And unless it is internally fair, good employees (those that the organization wants to retain) are likely to leave.[63]

Three culprits that detract from perceptions of fairness are low pay, pay secrecy, and large pay differentials between the CEO and other executives at the top and employees at lower levels. Increasingly, employers must avoid these problems and also offer generous benefits to attract and retain the best talent.

Low Pay. Employees who are compensated above or on par with the market average are more likely to feel fairly paid than those who are paid below the going rate. Employers learn about the pay levels at other organizations through **wage and salary surveys.** These surveys provide systematic information from numerous companies about all aspects of compensation. Using this information, employers can judge how well they are paying relative to what competitors are paying.

Employees usually do not have good information about pay levels offered by other employers. They tend to rely on gossip and guesses to determine whether their pay is fair. Furthermore, when making their judgments about how their pay compares to the going rate in the market, some employees consider only their direct monetary compensation, whereas others pay more attention to benefits and nonmonetary compensation.

When comparing the pay they receive to the pay of others, most employees focus on base wages and salaries. Wages and salaries can be job based or competency based. With *job-based pay,* the hourly wage or annual salary is linked to the specific tasks that a person performs. So long as the task is performed at some minimally satisfactory level, the employee receives the agreed upon wage or salary. *Competency-based pay* links compensation to people's competencies—that is, their job-relevant skills, knowledge, and experience. Employees with higher competency levels receive higher pay than do those with lower competency levels. Thus competency-based pay encourages employees to develop their competencies, thereby becoming more valuable to the organization. As a result, the organization can be more flexible and adaptable to changing demands. With a more flexible workforce, the organization may need fewer employees and thus reduce human resource costs. Also, flexibility can enhance productivity and product quality.[64]

Pay Secrecy. Although it's illegal for employers to forbid employee discussions of pay, keeping pay secret is the norm in many U.S. organizations. According to organizational etiquette, asking others their salaries is generally considered rude. Managers usually favor pay secrecy, because it makes their lives easier. Without knowledge of what others are paid, employees are less likely to confront supervisors about inequitable pay, so managers don't have to justify their actions. Employers can increase the perceived fairness of a pay system by involving employees in its design, communicating the details of how pay is determined, and ensuring due process when problems arise.

Large Pay Differentials. During the past decade, employees at the middle and lower levels of organizations have watched the pay of those at the top rise rapidly at a time when increases in their own pay have been relatively modest. In the United States, the typical CEO is now paid $185 for every $1 paid to the lowest worker.[65] By comparison, the ratio in British, German, and French firms is less than $50 to $1, and the ratio in Japan is just $17 to $1.[66] Some employees sensitive to differences in the pay received by people at the top and bottom of organizations prefer to work for more egalitarian companies, such as Ben & Jerry's or Chaparral Steel, where the pay differential is not so great.

Benefits. Although the specific elements of benefits plans vary, these payments usually provide protection against health and accident-related problems and ensure income at retirement. Unlike direct compensation, which differs according to the job a person holds, full-time employees in an organization generally receive the same benefits. In some organizations, part-time employees receive the same benefits as full-time employees, but that is unusual.

WEB INSIGHT

Read the Family and Medical Leave Act at *http://www.dol.gov*. What are the costs and benefits of this law for employers? For employees?

Some benefits are required by law. These benefits include Social Security contributions, unemployment compensation, and workers' compensation. Other benefits are offered voluntarily by employers. Typically, larger organizations voluntarily offer health-care, life and disability insurance, and retirement pension or savings plans.

Benefits programs also include pay for time not at work—for instance, vacations, holidays, sick days, and absences for other reasons and short breaks during regular workdays. A growing category of benefits enables employees to enjoy a better lifestyle or to meet social or personal obligations while minimizing employment-related costs. Educational assistance and family care fall into this category. At Cisco, one of the benefits offered is having DSL lines installed in your home. Figure 13.5 illustrates the cost of benefits as a share of total labor costs for the "average" U.S. employee.[67]

Figure 13.5 **Compensation Paid as Employee Benefits and Earnings**

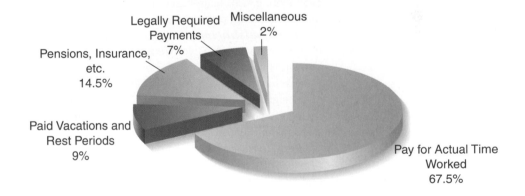

Legally Required Payments 7%
Miscellaneous 2%
Pensions, Insurance, etc. 14.5%
Paid Vacations and Rest Periods 9%
Pay for Actual Time Worked 67.5%

MAXIMIZING PRODUCTIVITY

Monetary compensation linked to the level of employee performance is referred to as **incentive pay,** which is intended to encourage superior performance. When pay is linked to strategically important behaviors and outcomes, it improves organizational productivity.[68] In the United States, many organizations are developing new compensation plans to fit new strategies. In these new systems, incentive pay plays a much bigger role than it did in the past.

In addition to increasing performance, incentive pay can reduce turnover among high performers. High performers are more motivated to stay with an organization when they are rewarded more generously than poor performers. In addition, incentive pay can be cost effective. Savings result from productivity improvements and from the organization's ability to match compensation costs and performance levels.

Individual Incentive Pay. Individual incentive pay is based on a person's performance—more pay for good performance, less pay for poor performance. Common forms of individual incentive pay include piece-rate incentives, commissions, bonuses, and merit pay. A *piece-rate incentive* is a fixed amount of pay for each unit of output produced. Sometimes used in manufacturing, piece-rate incentives tend to focus employees on those aspects of the job that increase output. Thus other useful activities such as machine maintenance or the training of new employees may be neglected.

Typically used with salespeople, a *commission* is compensation based on a percentage of total sales. Some salespeople work on a base salary plus commission. Others work on a straight commission basis, with all their direct compensation being incentive pay.

A *bonus* is a lump-sum payment given for achieving a particular performance goal. A bonus can represent a relatively small portion (e.g., 10 percent) or a large portion (e.g., 75 percent) of an employee's total direct pay. For instance, at CompUSA, a buyer paid a $45,000 salary earned a $120,000 bonus one year.[69]

Merit pay is the most widespread form of incentive pay. Whereas the other types of incentives have no permanent impact on an employee's base wages or salary, *merit pay* is a permanent increase in base pay linked to an individual's performance during the preceding year. Although employees generally prefer permanent pay raises, many companies have been reducing their reliance on merit pay because they believe other incentives are more effective for improving productivity.

Team and Organization Incentive Pay. Although individual incentive pay is an attractive compensation option for organizations, it isn't without problems. It works best when employees work more or less autonomously and the organization has an effective performance appraisal system. When people work in teams, individual performance is more difficult to assess. Furthermore, making pay distinctions among members of a team can result in friction. For these and other reasons, many companies are experimenting with team-based and organization-based incentive pay, including goalsharing, gainsharing, profit sharing, and stock ownership.[70]

With *goalsharing,* teams of employees receive bonuses for reaching strategically important goals. At Weyerhaeuser, the large forest and paper products company, goalsharing is used in its container board packaging and recycling plants. Bonuses are given for reaching goals related to safety, quality, waste, and costs. *Gainsharing* programs are designed to reward employees for making agreed upon *improvements* in productivity. At Owens Corning, gainsharing is used to reward manufacturing employees for reductions in the cost per pound of its products.[71]

Profit sharing is based on the actual profits that a business earns and rewards employees with a share of those profits. In this case, the entire organization is treated as one large team. At Lincoln Electric, in Cleveland, Ohio, employees often receive a profit sharing bonus that is worth as much as their base pay.

Stock-based incentive plans also treat the entire organization as a team. Stock-based incentives may take the form of stock options or an employee stock ownership plan. *Stock options* give employees the right to buy shares of the company's stock at a specified price. They are rewarded only if the share price goes up after they have exercised their options. Use of stock options as a form of incentive pay has exploded in recent years. For middle- to senior-level managers, it accounts for about 85 percent of their long-term incentive pay.[72]

Companies such as Microsoft, Wal-Mart, Kroger food stores, and AT&T use *employee stock ownership plans* (ESOPs) to provide employees throughout the organization with shares of their stock. A company contributes either shares of its stock or cash to purchase shares on the open market to the ESOP. The shares owned by the ESOP are then allocated to individual employee accounts. Employees become shareholders just like anyone else who invests in the company. Usually, the stock distributed to employees through an ESOP accounts for only a small portion of their total compensation. When employees see a clear link between their own performance and the value of their shares, stock ownership may increase motivation and commitment. If this link isn't clear, however, stock ownership is more likely to be perceived as a benefit that an employee gets just for being on the company's payroll.

CHAPTER SUMMARY

1. **EXPLAIN HOW MANAGING HUMAN RESOURCES EFFECTIVELY CAN IMPROVE ORGANIZATIONAL PERFORMANCE.**

Human resource management (HRM) is concerned with the philosophies, policies, and practices that affect the people who work for an organization. The various HRM activities should help the organization achieve its strategic goals and sustain a competitive advantage. Effective HRM has a positive impact on an organization's profitability and on the life of people in the community and the larger society.

2. **IDENTIFY AND DISCUSS SEVERAL IMPORTANT LAWS AND GOVERNMENT REGULATIONS THAT AFFECT HOW ORGANIZATIONS MANAGE THEIR HUMAN RESOURCES.**

Many laws and government regulations govern human resources management. Three important categories of laws and regulations are those that are intended to ensure equal employment opportunity, protect worker health and safety, and provide oversight of compensation and benefits. A few of the major U.S. laws that managers need to understand are Title VII of the Civil Rights Act, the Occupational Safety and Health Act, the Fair Labor Standards Act, and the Equal Pay Act.

3. **STATE THE ELEMENTS OF HUMAN RESOURCE PLANNING.**

Human resource planning is used to forecast the organization's HR needs and take steps to meet those needs. To determine future needs, forecasts often are used. To assess the capabilities of the current workforce, competency inventories may be used. If gaps are identified between the available competencies and those likely to be needed in the future, other HR activities can be designed to minimize or eliminate the gap.

4. **EXPLAIN THE PROCESS THAT ORGANIZATIONS USE TO RECRUIT AND SELECT NEW HIRES.**

The hiring process includes two main activities: recruitment of job applicants and selection of the best applicants. When labor is in short supply, recruitment activities become increasingly important. Selecting the right people to hire from the pool of applicants helps improve productivity and reduce turnover. In the selection process, the most common sources of information used to evaluate an applicant are résumés, reference checks, interviews, and various types of tests. Of these, tests generally do the best job of predicting performance.

5. **DESCRIBE SEVERAL TYPES OF TRAINING AND DEVELOPMENT PROGRAMS.**

Training programs help employees develop the competencies they need to perform their best in their current jobs. Orientation training, basic skills training, training in new technologies, team training, and cross-cultural training are types of programs used to improve workforce performance. Development programs help employees acquire and build on competencies that will enable them to continue to advance in their careers over the long term. They often provide employees with tools to assess their own strengths and weaknesses and develop personal plans for improvement.

6. **EXPLAIN HOW MANAGERS USE PERFORMANCE INFORMATION TO IMPROVE EMPLOYEE JOB PERFORMANCE.**

Performance appraisal is a formal, structured system for measuring job performance. During performance feedback sessions, managers and subordinates meet to exchange performance information and discuss how to improve performance. Performance appraisal and feedback are most effective when they are aligned with the organization's strategic goals, when managers make accurate judgments of performance, and when employees work with managers to use performance appraisal information as a basis for improving performance.

7. **DISCUSS THE OBJECTIVES OF MONETARY COMPENSATION AND THE ELEMENTS OF A MONETARY COMPENSATION PACKAGE.**

The compensation package is used to attract and retain qualified employees and then to motivate them to achieve high levels of performance. Monetary compensation includes both direct compensation and indirect compensation. Direct compensation consists of the base wage or salary and incentive pay. Job-based pay and competency-based pay are two methods of determining the base wage or salary. Incentive pay links at least part of an employee's pay to performance. It can also be linked to team and organizational performance. Indirect compensation includes benefits that are mandated by law and those that employers provide voluntarily. Social Security, unemployment compensation, and workers' compensation are benefits that employers must provide. Insurance and vacation pay are commonly offered benefits that are not required by law.

KEY TERMS

Bonus, p. 368
Cognitive ability test, p. 356
Commission, p. 368
Comparable worth, p. 350
Competency inventory, p. 351
Competency-based pay, p. 366
Development, p. 356
Employee selection, p. 354
Employee stock ownership plans, p. 368
Equal employment opportunity, p. 347
Equal Pay Act, p. 349
Fair Labor Standards Act, p. 349
Gainsharing, p. 368

Goalsharing, p. 368
Hiring process, p. 352
Human resource management, p. 344
Human resource planning, p. 350
Incentive pay, p. 367
Job-based pay, p. 366
Merit pay, p. 368
Monetary compensation, p. 365
Nonmonetary compensation, p. 364
Occupational Safety and Health Act, (OSHA), p. 349
Pay fairness, p. 366
Performance appraisal, p. 360

Performance feedback session, p. 360
Performance test, p. 356
Personality test, p. 356
Piece-rate incentive, p. 368
Profit sharing, p. 368
Recruitment, p. 353
Situational interview, p. 355
Stock options, p. 368
360-degree appraisal system, p. 363
Title VII of the Civil Rights Act, p. 347
Training, p. 356
Wage and salary surveys, p. 366

QUESTIONS FOR DISCUSSION AND COMPETENCY DEVELOPMENT

1. How does effective HRM address shareholders' concerns?

2. How does the international nature of Cirque du Soleil affect its training practices?

3. How can organizations use HRM practices to ensure that managers understand and abide by the primary laws and regulations that govern the hiring process?

4. Which types of training and development programs are likely to be most important for the following organizations: (a) a fast-food restaurant, (b) a software company located in New York City, and (c) a global consulting firm? Explain.

5. Some people believe that inaccurate performance appraisals are caused more by office politics and friendships than by inability of managers to be accurate. Do managers sometimes intentionally give inaccurate performance ratings? If so, why might that happen?

6. Describe the ideal compensation package that you would like to receive. Which elements of the package are most important to you? Why?

7. **Competency Development: Strategic Action.** Assume that you are a senior partner in Midland Ashby, a consulting firm. You are writing a proposal for an assignment in Indonesia. As part of the proposal you describe the members of the team who will work with the client, who you know has very "traditional" views about men and women. The person with the most expertise regarding the client's problem is a woman, so you list her as one of the team members. Your potential client states that a woman team member is unacceptable. Describe what you would do, and why. Consider the ethical, legal, and business conse-

quences of keeping her on the team versus removing her from consideration.

8. **Competency Development: Self-Management.** The following 10 questions might be asked during an employment interview. Some of them are illegal and should never be asked. Employers who ask illegal questions may be subject to prosecution for discrimination. Place a check mark in the appropriate column to indicate whether the question is legal or illegal. Before taking this quiz, visit the home page of the Equal Employment Opportunity Commission (EEOC) at *http://www.eeoc.gov*

	Legal	Illegal
1. How old are you?		
2. Have you ever been arrested?		
3. Do any of your relatives work for this organization?		
4. Do you have children, and if you do, what kind of child-care arrangements do you have?		
5. Do you have any handicaps?		
6. Are you married?		
7. Where were you born?		
8. What organizations do you belong to?		
9. Do you get along well with other men [or women]?		
10. What languages can you speak and/or write fluently?		

ANSWERS

The following evaluations provide clarification rather than strict legal interpretation because employment laws and regulations are constantly changing.

1. How old are you?
This question is legal but inadvisable. An applicant's date of birth or age can be asked, but telling the applicant that federal and state laws prohibit age discrimination is essential. Avoid focusing on age, unless an occupation requires extraordinary physical ability or training and a valid age-related rule is in effect.

2. Have you ever been arrested?
This question is illegal unless an inquiry about arrests is justified by the specific nature of the organization—for instance, law enforcement or handling controlled substances. Questions about arrests generally are considered to be suspect because they may tend to disqualify some groups. Convictions should be the basis for rejection of an applicant only if their number, nature, or recent occurrence renders the applicant unsuitable. In that case the question(s) should be specific. For example: Have you ever been convicted for theft? Have you been convicted within the past year on drug-related charges?

3. Do any of your relatives work for this organization?
This question is legal if the intent is to discover nepotism.

4. Do you have children, and if you do, what kind of child-care arrangements do you have?

Both parts of this question are currently illegal; they should not be asked in any form because the answers would not be job-related. In addition, they might imply gender discrimination.

5. Do you have any handicaps?
This question is illegal as phrased here. An applicant doesn't have to divulge handicaps or health conditions that don't relate reasonably to fitness to perform the job.

6. Are you married?
This question is legal, but may be discriminatory. Marriage has nothing directly to do with job performance.

7. Where were you born?
This question is legal, but it might indicate discrimination on the basis of national origin.

8. What organizations do you belong to?
As stated, this question is legal; it is permissible to ask about organizational membership in a general sense. It is illegal to ask about membership in a specific organization when the name of that organization would indicate the race, color, creed, gender, marital status, religion, or national origin or ancestry of its members.

9. Do you get along well with other men [or women]?
This question is illegal; it seems to perpetuate sexism.

10. What languages can you speak and/or write fluently?
Although this question is legal, it might be perceived as a roundabout way of determining an individual's national origin. Asking how a particular language was learned isn't permissible.

CASE FOR COMPETENCY DEVELOPMENT

THE MAGIC OF DISNEY BEGINS WITH HRM

The theme parks of the Walt Disney Company bring smiles to millions of customers from around the world. The company's sophisticated technical and creative staff makes experiences such as Sleeping Beauty's Castle possible, but for most customers these employees are out of sight and out of mind. Visitors are more immediately impressed by the costumed hosts and hostesses who take their tickets and help them on and off rides. Most of these hourly employees are students and older part-time workers. But they aren't just your typical students. They are an elite cadre who have been carefully selected, trained, and rewarded to deliver "Disney Courtesy."

Because most potential employees already know about the clean-cut and conservative image portrayed by Disneyland or Disney World employees, the company finds that most job applicants who wouldn't fit the image have already self-selected themselves from consideration. To be sure that everyone knows what to expect, however, one of the first steps in the hiring process involves showing applicants a video that details dress codes and rules of grooming and discipline. Next come 45-minute interviews. Interviewers ask standard questions and pay attention to how well applicants listen, smile, and respond. From the interviews, they judge how well applicants are likely to handle "guests" and how well they are likely to get along with other employees. Disney screens for communication and teamwork competencies, not technical skills.

Once hired, "cast-members" attend an eight-hour orientation program where they learn the company's history, philosophy, and standards for customer service. Here they also are introduced to their role in creating happiness—the most important, but least tangible aspect of a successful Disney experience. The message is delivered by trainers who exude the Disney spirit. You won't find corporate types in these classrooms. Instructors are more likely to be some of the best veteran cast members, dressed in full costume and showing through example what a job at Disney involves. Following orientation, new cast members receive 16 to 48 hours of "paired-training." This aspect of the training process is essentially one-on-one coaching by respected members of the troupe. Successful completion of training is required before new cast members are allowed to interact with customers on their own.

When a role is learned, it's performed repeatedly day after day. Supervisors and managers work hard to keep cast members fresh and focused on creating a feeling of magic. For example, one day a contest may be held to find the guest who has traveled the farthest, with a token prize for the winner. Disney also works hard to find ways to tell workers how much they are valued. For example, they offer service recognition awards, attendance awards, and banquets to mark the anniversaries of long-time employees. And one night a year the park is open only to employees and their families. Managers say thanks by dressing in costumes and operating the park themselves.

Questions

1. Why does Disney think that selecting people with communication and teamwork competencies is essential? Why don't they assess technical skills for their cast members?

2. Many of the jobs at Disney's amusement parks are routine and could easily lead to boredom. If you were a manager at Disney, how could you use performance appraisal and feedback to help keep cast members from letting the routine of their jobs interfere with the magical feeling that they're expected to create?

3. The Disney approach to managing human resources seems to give employees little freedom to be creative or develop new ways of doing things. Strict rules guide all aspects of behavior. Is this tight rein really necessary for the Disney parks to succeed? Why or why not? What problems might this approach to human resource management create for the company as it expands into other countries and cultures?

To learn more about the Walt Disney Company, visit the company's home page at *http://www.disney.com*.

VIDEO CASE

LaBelle Management

In 1948, the late Norman LaBelle opened the Pixie Hamburger Drive-In Restaurant complete with carhops and inexpensive food. The Pixie quickly became a popular place with both the local population and the fast-growing enrollment of Central Michigan University. Little did he know at the time that his two sons would later run the business and that it would eventually grow to more than 30 restaurants and hotels employing some 2,000 people.

LaBelle's growth has included both expansion and diversification into other types of restaurants. In 1972, the first Sweet Onion opened, followed 8 years later by a second. The Mt. Pleasant Big Boy Restaurants were started in 1982, and three more locations in Michigan were eventually added. Next came the Ponderosa Steakhouses, with three locations. By 1987, the company had assumed operation of the Michigan Division of Cafeteria at Dow Chemical and had added eight more Ponderosas in Indiana (since then, nine more Ponderosas have opened). By May 1995, LaBelle Management opened the Italian Oven Restaurant and a Bennigan's Irish Pub in Mt. Pleasant.

But restaurants comprised only part of the company's diversification efforts and its emergence as LaBelle Management. LaBelle started Comfort Inns in 1989. Then, in 1998, it acquired the Grand Beach Resort Hotel. In all, LaBelle Management now owns and operates 30 properties in Indiana and Michigan. They include hotels, resorts, conference centers, and freestanding restaurants located in resorts, major cities, small cities, suburbs, and small towns.

A common element in all its operations is the company's commitment to use of a comprehensive performance appraisal system. LaBelle's management views its system for employee appraisal as a two-way exchange between superior and subordinate whereby both benefit from the exchange of information and learn what each expects of the other. Formal performance appraisals are scheduled for each employee twice a year, but management believes in an open feedback system whereby feedback is given to employees on an ongoing basis (when they need it, not as long as 6 months later).

LaBelle uses different methods and criteria by which to evaluate its crew members and managers. Crew evaluations include such things as attitude, job performance, attendance, customer service, and teamwork. Manager appraisals focus on their human resource skills, leadership abilities, profitability of the operation, and degree of customer service.

LaBelle Management utilizes its performance appraisals for various administrative and developmental purposes. Its top management believes that managers should tell employees where they stand so that they know what they're doing right and what they're doing wrong. Top management views the performance appraisal system as a key to the company's continued success.

Questions

1. LaBelle Management uses different methods and criteria to evaluate personnel at different organizational levels, but all are evaluated in the same general way. How are they all evaluated?

2. For what specific purposes does LaBelle Management utilize performance appraisals?

3. Why does LaBelle Management believe that feedback must be directed to the superior from the subordinate, as well as to the subordinate from the superior?

To learn more about LaBelle Management, visit the company's home page at *http://www.labellemgt.com*.

Leading

CHAPTER 14
WORK MOTIVATION

CHAPTER 15
THE DYNAMICS OF LEADERSHIP

CHAPTER 16
ORGANIZATIONAL COMMUNICATION

CHAPTER 17
MANAGING WORK TEAMS

CHAPTER 18
ORGANIZATIONAL CULTURES AND CULTURAL DIVERSITY

Work Motivation

LEARNING OBJECTIVES

AFTER STUDYING THIS CHAPTER YOU SHOULD BE ABLE TO:

1. DESCRIBE THREE GENERAL FACTORS THAT INFLUENCE EMPLOYEES' MOTIVATION AT WORK.

2. EXPLAIN HOW MANAGERS AND THEIR SUBORDINATES CAN USE GOALS AND REWARDS TO IMPROVE PERFORMANCE.

3. STATE HOW JOB CONTENT AND ORGANIZATIONAL CONTEXT AFFECT MOTIVATION.

4. DESCRIBE HOW INDIVIDUAL DIFFERENCES IN NEEDS AND MOTIVES CAN AFFECT EMPLOYEES' WORK.

5. EXPLAIN HOW SEVERAL MOTIVATIONAL FORCES MAY COMBINE TO INFLUENCE AN EMPLOYEE'S WORK SATISFACTION AND PERFORMANCE.

6. DESCRIBE HOW UNDERSTANDING THE DYNAMICS OF MOTIVATION CAN HELP MANAGERS IMPROVE EMPLOYEE PERFORMANCE.

Chapter Outline

PREVIEW: MOTIVATION AT MEDI-HEALTH OUTSOURCING

THREE APPROACHES TO MOTIVATION
MANAGERIAL APPROACH
JOB AND ORGANIZATION APPROACH
INDIVIDUAL DIFFERENCES APPROACH
INTEGRATING THE APPROACHES

USING GOALS AND REWARDS TO IMPROVE PERFORMANCE
SETTING GOALS
TEAMWORK COMPETENCY: Goalsharing at Sears
OFFERING INCENTIVES AND REWARDS
SELF-MANAGEMENT
SELF-MANAGEMENT COMPETENCY: Here's Looking at You

EFFECTS OF JOB CONTENT AND ORGANIZATIONAL CONTEXT ON MOTIVATION
HERZBERG'S TWO-FACTOR THEORY
JOB CHARACTERISTICS
STRATEGIC ACTION COMPETENCY: Job Design at Whole Foods Markets
PERCEPTIONS OF EQUITY
GLOBAL AWARENESS COMPETENCY: The Challenge of International Compensation

INDIVIDUAL DIFFERENCES IN MOTIVATION
HIERARCHY OF NEEDS
MOVING THROUGH THE NEEDS HIERARCHY
LEARNED NEEDS

MOTIVATIONAL FORCES IN COMBINATION
BASIC EXPECTANCY THEORY
THE INTEGRATED EXPECTANCY MODEL

GUIDELINES FOR MANAGERS

CHAPTER SUMMARY

KEY TERMS

QUESTIONS FOR DISCUSSION AND COMPETENCY DEVELOPMENT

CASE FOR COMPETENCY DEVELOPMENT: MOTIVATING HI-TECH WORKERS

VIDEO CASE: VALASSIS COMMUNICATIONS

MOTIVATION AT MEDI-HEALTH OUTSOURCING

Medi-Health Outsourcing is a fast-growing, young company that helps hospitals and other health-care organizations manage patient records and documents for inclusion in national data bases. For founders Paula and Ron Lawlor, highly motivated employee are essential to a growing company, which may add as many as 60 or 70 new hospitals to its roster each year.

As president, Paula Lawlor has adopted a two-pronged motivation approach. On the one hand, she encourages employees to bring their personal lives into the workplace. "There are companies that don't want people to talk about their personal lives," she says. "But I say, 'bring it on.' If people can get

something off their chests for an hour, then I've got them for the next 10." The company's employee-friendly approach allows employees to bring their kids to work, work from home or from the beach, arrange their weekly schedules around family needs, and even take three months off without worrying about losing their jobs. When it comes to how people work, Lawlor's philosophy is pretty much that "anything goes."

When it comes to what work gets done, Lawlor has a clear philosophy: Employees are held accountable for performance results. She doesn't want rigid rules and management practices to stifle creativity and innovation, but she understands that setting and meeting challeng-

ing goals and deadlines are essential to business success. Most employees understand that this is the deal they've accepted. For example, if your job is to code documents for entry into a database, you might be given the goal of abstracting 100 records per week with 95 percent accuracy. If you meet the goal on Thursday, you can take the rest of the week off. Or, you can come to work and offer to take on other tasks—and some people do! Chuck Hammond admits that sometimes he feels that the company goes too far in accommodating employees, but he sees the performance payoff. "Sometimes I think we baby the heck out of them," he admits. "But when you ask them to do something, you just don't hear a lot of complaining."[1]

THREE APPROACHES TO MOTIVATION

1.

DESCRIBE THREE
GENERAL FACTORS THAT
INFLUENCE EMPLOYEES'
MOTIVATION AT WORK.

Motivation is a psychological state that is said to exist whenever internal and/or external forces trigger, direct, or maintain goal-directed behaviors. What motivates employees is a fundamental question that has long been of interest to managers and researchers alike. As a result, many different theories about work motivation have been suggested. Although each theory offers some insight into this complex topic, no single theory adequately addresses all aspects of motivation.

The many different theories of motivation can be easily grouped into three general approaches. We describe these general approaches and then discuss specific theories within each approach in more detail.

MANAGERIAL APPROACH

The managerial approach to motivating employees focuses on the behaviors of managers—in particular, their use of goals and rewards. According to this approach, Paula Lawlor's management practices for holding employees accountable for performance explain the high motivation levels of employees at Medi-Health Outsourcing.

The managers that employees work with on a day-to-day basis can directly motivate employees through personal, one-on-one communication. For example, they can work with employees to set realistic goals and then use recognition, praise, and monetary means to reward employees for achieving those goals. At Medi-Health Outsourcing, department managers set weekly goals for employees, and they reward employees who meet these goals by letting them work fewer hours.

JOB AND ORGANIZATION APPROACH

A second approach to motivating employees emphasizes the design of jobs and the general organizational environment. As described in Chapter 12, enriched jobs are more motivating than jobs that are narrow in scope. At Medi-Health, the job itself is part of the explanation for why people enjoy their work, but the organizational context also is important. In particular, employees appreciate the flexible work arrangements. Human resource management policies and practices are generally an important aspect of the organizational context. The appropriate benefits (e.g., paid vacations, sick leave, insurance, and child or elder care), reward structure (e.g., incentive pay), and development opportunities (e.g., education and mentoring) may attract new employees to the organization. Whether such policies serve to increase employee effort and desire to stay with the company depends partly on whether employees perceive them to be fair and equitable.

INDIVIDUAL DIFFERENCES APPROACH

The third approach to motivating employees treats motivation as a characteristic of the individual. According to this approach, an employee who is motivated at Medi-Health would be highly motivated in any organization.

Individual differences are the unique needs, values, competencies, and other personal characteristics that employees bring to their jobs. These characteristics vary from person to person. One person may be motivated to earn more money and prefer a job that offers such an opportunity. Another may be motivated by security, preferring a job that involves less risk of unemployment. Yet another may thrive on challenges and seek a position that stretches the person's competencies to the limit and helps the person develop new ones. Effective managers understand the individual differences that shape each employee's unique view of work and use this understanding to maximize each employee's effectiveness.

INTEGRATING THE APPROACHES

The three general approaches to motivation are most useful when they are combined and integrated. We show how this can be done at the end of this chapter. Most basic theories of motivation focus on only one factor (e.g., an individual's needs or the design of a job) affecting motivation at work. Only a few consider the ways in which various factors combine to affect the ebb and flow of a person's motivation over time. One that does so is expectancy theory, which we describe later in the chapter.

USING GOALS AND REWARDS TO IMPROVE PERFORMANCE

2.

EXPLAIN HOW MANAGERS AND THEIR SUBORDINATES CAN USE GOALS AND REWARDS TO IMPROVE PERFORMANCE.

Managers (e.g., first-line managers) who are in direct contact with employees may be the most important influences on the motivation levels of employees. When the Gallup Organization interviewed 80,000 people about their work, they found that employees tolerate a lot of negative aspects of their work if they work for a good manager. And if they have a bad manager, they are likely to look for another job.[2] Good managers, such as Paula Lawlor, understand the unique characteristics of each employee and are responsive to their differences. Applying the theories of individual differences can help managers work effectively with many different types of employees.

Good managers don't just make employees feel comfortable, however. They help them be productive. When Curt Coffman, coauthor of *First, Break All the Rules* and the Gallup Organization's study, was asked to describe the best managers, he replied, "A great manager is someone who says, You come and work with me and I'll help you be as successful as possible. I want you to be more successful than me."[3] Two proven ways to help employees be productive are to be sure that they have clear and challenging goals to strive for and to be sure that employees feel good about achieving those goals.

SETTING GOALS

Goals affect motivation in two ways: by increasing the amount of effort people choose to exert and by directing or channeling that effort. When employees accept a goal as something to strive for and then commit to achieving that goal, they essentially agree to exert the amount of effort required to do so. Put simply, **goal-setting theory** states that managers can direct the performance of their employees by assigning specific, difficult goals that employees accept and are willing to commit to. In addition, goal setting can be effective only if employees have the competencies needed to achieve the goals and receive feedback about their progress toward achieving them.

Numerous studies have documented that performance is improved when employees are guided by specific and difficult goals. In one of the most famous studies, goals were used to improve the efficiency of truck drivers hauling logs to lumber mills. Before goals were introduced, loggers were carrying loads that were well below their trucks' legal weight capacities. Goals were introduced to encourage the loggers to transport fuller loads. At first, drivers were given a vague, easy goal that was stated as "do your best." This goal had almost no effect on the size of loads the drivers hauled. Three months later, drivers were given the goal of carrying loads that were 94 percent of their trucks' capacities. Within a month, the average load had increased from less than 60 percent to more than 80 percent of capacity. Six months later, truckers were carrying loads that averaged over 90 percent of capacity. This improvement in efficiency was achieved without changing the compensation system or introducing organizational rewards for goal achievement. The goals themselves—and the competition they created among the logging crews—provided the motivation needed to improve performance.[4] Done correctly, goal setting has been shown to be equally effective for employees working in a wide range of jobs. Today, many of the basic principles from this theory are accepted as standard management practice for maximizing employee performance.[5]

Specific Goals. Specific goals are more effective motivators than are vague, ambiguous goals. For the loggers, the specific goal was to carry loads that averaged 94 percent of a truck's capacity. Such goals help focus attention on a well-defined task so that any effort expended by employees is more likely to translate into goal achievement. Specific goals also make it easier for employees to gauge how well they're doing. If a goal is specific, employees can quickly judge whether their efforts are paying off in terms of performance. Employees can then use this feedback to decide whether to continue using the same methods or try new approaches.[6]

Difficult Goals. To be effective, a goal should be challenging, but not so difficult that the employee believes that it can't be achieved. If goals are too easy, they don't give the employee any reason to exert extra effort. If they are too difficult, however, the employee will reject them as impossible and won't even bother trying to achieve them. General Electric's CEO, Jack Welch, is known for setting difficult but achievable goals. He calls them "stretch goals."

When judging whether a goal is too difficult, managers and employees have no easy rules to follow. One popular way is to use benchmarks as goals. Recall from our discussion of benchmarking in Chapter 9 that benchmarks are essentially role models that serve as examples of unusually good performance. For example, America West uses Southwest Airlines' rates of on-time departures and arrivals to set its own goals. Another popular standard for setting goals is past performance. At Southwest Airlines, setting goals to improve against its own excellent performance records may be more appropriate than to use other airlines as benchmarks. For example, one of Southwest's goals is to turn planes around (unload and load passengers) in 17 minutes. The norm for the industry is 42 minutes.[7]

Goal acceptance. Regardless of how the goal or performance standard is chosen, it will be effective only if the employee accepts it and feels a commitment to trying to attain it.[8] At one time, goals assigned by managers were considered to be just as effective as goals set jointly by a manager and subordinate. However, many managers believe that goals work best when the employee participates in goal setting. Doing so increases employee's willingness to accept goals, which is essential for the goals to be motivating.

Management by objectives (MBO) is a participative goal-setting technique used in many types of organizations in the United States. Generally, the MBO process begins with a conversation between manager and employee. During this conversation, past performance is reviewed and objectives (goals) for the future are identified. The manager and employee agree to a set of goals that both parties accept as appropriate, with the understanding that future performance evaluations and rewards will reflect the employee's progress toward the agreed-upon goals.

When employees are highly empowered, they may set their own goals. Because people generally feel committed to achieving goals they set themselves, this approach ensures goal acceptance. When employees feel that they are capable of high performance, their self-set goals may actually be higher than those that a manager would assign. However, employees who doubt their own capabilities are likely to set easy goals, which are less effective.

Feedback. Goal-setting works best when employees receive timely feedback about the progress they are making toward achieving their goals. As we explained in Chapter 13, performance feedback helps employees improve their performance. Even very simple forms of feedback (e.g., how well employees are doing compared to their goals) can be effective. When employees can see that they aren't performing well enough to reach their goals, they're likely to consider why and then change their methods or behaviors. One way is simply to try harder. If putting out more effort doesn't help, another way is to approach tasks differently.[9] Feedback is a signal that tells employees that they are doing well and should continue with their current approaches or that they aren't doing very well and should try new approaches.

Stephen Cooper, CEO and chairman of Etec Systems, a hi-tech manufacturer of expensive electronic equipment, used goal setting to turn the company around. When Cooper took over, it was losing $1 million a month. Believing in the power of goals both to motivate employees and to focus their attention, he set the goal of generating annual revenues of $500 million by 2000. To get there, he made sure that the company's 800 employees had written personal plans to guide their daily work. These one-page plans included five to seven goals, to which employees assigned priority rankings. For each goal, the employee had to state how progress would be measured.

As is typical in many organizations, goal setting starts at the top and then cascades down to lower levels. At Etec, a precision optics manager had a goal of increasing production volume by 30 percent and reducing cycle times by 10 percent. The six junior managers who reported to him, in turn, each had goals that were related to the manager's goals. The employees supervised by the junior managers all had daily checklists that reflected their managers' goals. At first there was no feedback system, and managers soon learned that small problems could turn into crises if employees weren't aware of them. Now, weekly feedback sessions let all the employees know what they should be doing, how much weight to give each assignment, and how their goals relate to the goals of other employees in the company. As a result, the company operates efficiently, yet can respond quickly to changes in its environment.[10]

WEB INSIGHT

Goal setting is so popular that goal-setting software packages are available to help people use this motivational tool. Learn about some of this software by visiting *http://www. goalsetting.com* and *http://www. motivator.com*. Do these programs seem to address all the elements needed for effective goal setting?

Team Goal Setting. Just as goals can improve the performance of individual employees, team goals can improve group performance.[11] Like individual goals, team goals work best if they are difficult, yet doable. To keep a team focused, it is best not to set too many team goals—usually no more than three to five. Also important in setting team goals is being sure that employees understand why it's important for them to achieve the goals. As described in the following Teamwork Competency feature, Sears is one example of a company that uses team goals to achieve a variety of business objectives.[12]

Goalsharing at Sears

As Sears, Roebuck and Company has learned, team goals work well and team rewards also work well. But goalsharing, which combines both, works even better. When Sears management compared stores that used goalsharing to those that didn't, it found that stores with goalsharing had 10 percent lower turnover among employees and similar improvements in customer service and sales performance.

With **goalsharing,** employees receive financial rewards for achieving team goals. At Sears, the "team" is usually defined as an individual store, and goalsharing is voluntary. If managers or employees are against the idea, top management doesn't impose goalsharing on them. According to Jane Floyd, Sears's director of strategic initiatives, goalsharing doesn't work if employees participate just because the boss tells them to. Employees need to believe in the process and feel committed to it.

Stores that choose to use goalsharing get to set their own goals. They do so by committee, with each store's committee representing a "diagonal slice" of employees from each level and functional area. As part of the process of communicating the team goals, employees attend sessions to discuss how achieving their goals will affect business results. Although goals differ somewhat from store to store, most stores have goals for improving customer service and satisfaction.

Consistent with good goal-setting practices, Sears also provides regular feedback, so the team knows how well it's doing. For example, if a store is focusing on improving customer service, the results of weekly customer satisfaction surveys are posted. If sales goals have been set, posted sales figures provide feedback. By measuring their performance against the goals, employees can see what they've achieved. Floyd also says that she can see results beyond those being measured. "You see ownership, people growing in ways they

never would," she says. "It's been difficult, but it's been worth it."

• • •

To learn more about Sears, Roebuck and Company, visit the company's home page at

http://www.sears.com

OFFERING INCENTIVES AND REWARDS

In some situations, managers can use goal setting to improve performance even if they don't offer any significant rewards to employees for achieving the goals. The idea of simply beating the goal may be all the motivation that some employees need. In most work situations, however, goals become more powerful when achieving them results in some type of tangible reward. Rewards for goal achievement increase motivation and performance because they strengthen the level of commitment that employees feel. Another explanation for the effectiveness of rewards is provided by reinforcement theory.

Reinforcement theory states that behavior is a function of its consequences. Positive consequences are referred to as rewards, and negative consequences are referred to as punishments. Psychologist B. F. Skinner developed and extended much of this approach to understanding what motivates behavior.[13] Skinner gained much public attention—and generated considerable controversy—when he revealed that he raised his children strictly by reinforcement principles.

The basic principles of reinforcement are simple. They state that behavior followed by pleasant consequences is more likely to be repeated and that behavior followed by unpleasant consequences is less likely to be repeated. For instance, suppose that your job involves helping modify the company's Web site. You come to a staff meeting with a proposal for letting customers search the Web site using everyday language instead of the hi-tech jargon used by the company's employees. If your manager praises your initiative and creativity, your behavior is rewarded. You probably will be motivated to come up with other innovations. However, if your manager gives you a disapproving look and says that the firm is perfectly happy with existing methods, you probably would feel put down or embarrassed in front of your colleagues. In effect, your behavior has been punished, indicating that you should modify that behavior in the future.

According to reinforcement theory, the behaviors currently seen in an organization are there because employees are being reinforced for them. On the one hand, if undesirable behaviors occur, it is because there are positive consequences for employees. On the other hand, if desirable behaviors are absent in the organization, it is because those behaviors lead to no positive consequences for employees. A manager who wants to change an employee's behavior must change the specific consequences of that behavior. Figure 14.1 shows the process by which pleasant and unpleasant consequences influence behavior.

Figure 14.1 **Process of Reinforcement and Behavior Change**

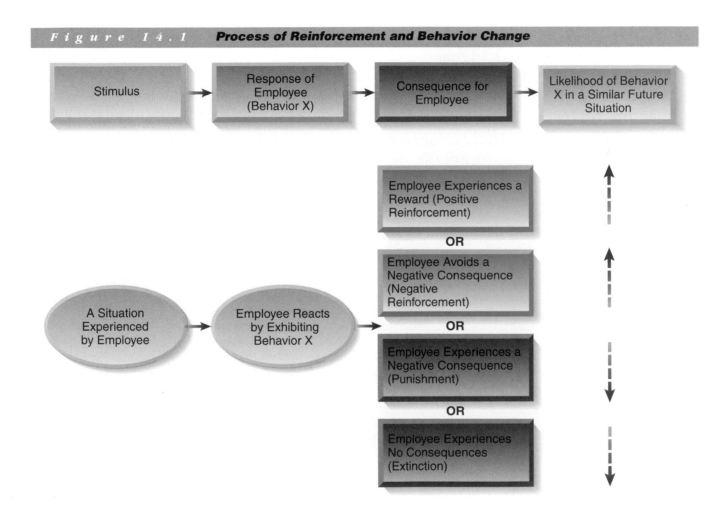

Behaviors, Not Outcomes. Whereas goal setting focuses directly on improving performance outcomes, reinforcement focuses on changing behaviors. For this reason, when reinforcement is used, it is sometimes referred to as **behavior modification.** A manager who follows the principles of reinforcement will almost certainly be able to modify employee behaviors to some extent. Whether those changes in behavior result in better performance, however, depends on whether the manager actually knows which behaviors result in better performance.

Behaviors that managers can most easily change by using reinforcement principles are those that can be easily measured.[14] Measurable behavior is action that can be observed and counted. Examples include smiling when a customer approaches, using a seat belt when driving a delivery truck, and wiping up spills when they occur on the shop floor. As Figure 14.1 suggests, a manager may increase the frequency of any of these behaviors by using positive reinforcement or negative reinforcement. To decrease any of these behaviors, a manager may use punishment or extinction. The concepts of reinforcement and punishment are easily understood because most individuals can readily recall at least one instance of a behavior being reinforced or punished. The concepts of negative reinforcement and extinction are sometimes more difficult to grasp, however. The reason is that both refer to the *absence* of behavioral consequences.

Reinforcement principles don't require that managers actually tell employees what they should strive to accomplish. The assumption is that employees can learn what is expected of them simply by experiencing the consequences of their behaviors. Of course, employees also learn by observing what happens to others in the organization. Fortunately, not everyone has to be punished before most learn that some behaviors are best avoided.

Positive reinforcement. *Positive reinforcement* increases the likelihood that a behavior will be repeated by using rewards to create a pleasant consequence. Any reward that encourages an individual to repeat a behavior can be classified as a positive reinforcer. Some common positive reinforcers used by organizations are praise, recognition of accomplishment, promotion, and salary increases. Most people regard these consequences as desirable. At Scitor, a systems engineering consulting firm, monetary bonuses are used as positive reinforcers for going above and beyond the call of duty. Staying *really* late, meeting a deadline that seemed impossible, and helping a colleague when it wasn't required are examples of the type of good citizenship that the company encourages. It rewards such behaviors by sending the employee a thank you card and enclosing a cash bonus of a few hundred dollars.[15]

Punishment. *Punishment* involves creating a negative consequence to discourage a behavior whenever it occurs. For example, disciplinary actions may be taken against an employee who comes to work late, fails to clean up the work area, or turns out too many defective parts. The disciplinary action might take the form of a verbal reprimand, a monetary fine, a demotion, or, if the employee persists, a suspension—all with the intention of discouraging the behavior.

Negative Reinforcement. When people engage in behavior to avoid unpleasant consequences, they experience **negative reinforcement.** Most students come to class on time to avoid a reprimand from the instructor. Similarly, most employees follow coffee break and lunch hour guidelines to avoid the disapproval of managers or coworkers. In both cases, these individuals are acting to avoid unpleasant results; when they are successful they are negatively reinforced. Note that, whereas punishment causes a behavior to occur less frequently, negative reinforcement causes the behavior to be repeated.

Extinction. *Extinction* is the absence of any reinforcement, either positive or negative, following the occurrence of a behavior. Usually, extinction occurs when the positive reinforcement that once normally resulted from the behavior is removed. Because the behavior no longer produces reinforcement, the employee stops engaging in it.

When extinction results in the decline of a disruptive behavior, the organization usually benefits. But extinction of beneficial behaviors occurs just as often, as illustrated in the following example. Jan Smith, a 7-11 store manager who seeks to reduce tardiness puts in place a plan to reward employees for coming to work and not taking days off. Smith begins to offer a small monetary bonus for perfect attendance. Absenteeism goes down, as planned. Then Smith feels pressured to reduce costs and decides to eliminate the bonus program. Soon absenteeism is higher than ever. What happened? Unfortunately, Smith has gotten everyone to overcome any barriers they encountered in getting to work on time in order to receive their bonuses. Removing the bonus they received for doing so caused extinction of the behavior.

Applying Reinforcement Principles. Positive reinforcement is the preferred approach for increasing desirable behavior in organizations, and extinction is the preferred approach for decreasing undesirable behaviors. Occasionally, punishment and negative reinforcement also may be needed, but managers often misuse these principles. The following is a typical example. Dan Caulfield, founder and CEO of a job-placement firm, spent countless hours trying to move from print to electronic communication. When he was confident that his employees had all the electronic tools they needed to work without paper, he became frustrated that employees didn't fully utilize the new systems. He tried using punishment to change their behavior. He walked through offices removing yellow paper stickers from computer monitors, crumpled up papers that he found on people's desks, and scrounged through desk drawers looking for whatever paper he could find. He threw it all into a barrel, dragged the barrel to the fire escape and set it ablaze as employees watched. Fines were introduced as a further deterrent: $1.00 per line for using the fax machine and 25 cents per page for printing a résumé. But as Caulfield eventually learned, this approach caused resentment among the employees.[16] With a better understanding of reinforcement, Caulfield would have known that offering rewards to the employees who used the least paper or found new ways to reduce the use of paper could have yielded the results he wanted. Table 14.1 provides some useful guidelines for managers to follow when applying the principles of reinforcement.

Table 14.1	**Six Guidelines for Using Reinforcement Theory**
Guideline	**Comment**
Don't reward all individuals equally.	To be effective, reinforcers should be based on performance. Rewarding everyone equally in effect reinforces poor or average performance and ignores high performance.
Failure to respond can also modify behavior.	Managers influence their subordinates by what they do not do as well as by what they do. For example, failing to praise deserving subordinates may cause them to perform poorly the next time.
Tell individuals what they can do to receive reinforcement.	Setting performance standards lets individuals know what they should do to be rewarded; they can then adjust their work habits to get these rewards.
Tell individuals what they are doing wrong.	If managers withhold rewards from subordinates without indicating why they're not being rewarded, the subordinates may be confused about what behaviors the manager finds undesirable. The subordinates may also feel that they're being manipulated.
Don't punish in front of others.	Reprimanding subordinates might sometimes be a useful way of eliminating an undesirable behavior. Public reprimand, however, humiliates subordinates and may cause all the members of the work group to resent the manager.

SELF-MANAGEMENT

Just as managers can use the principles of goal setting and reinforcement to change the behavior and performance of employees, so too can employees. With a bit of training, employees can learn to set their own goals, provide their own reinforcements, and even monitor their results over time. Taking an active self-management approach to job performance and career progress is one way to improve long-term outcomes, such as quicker promotions and higher salary levels.[17]

The effectiveness of self-management training was recently demonstrated for sales employees in an insurance company. During the period of a month, salespeople attended four training sessions that taught them about the principles of self-management.

The salespeople were then monitored for a year. Compared to a control group of salespeople who did not receive the training, those who completed self-management training reported that they felt better able to deal with difficult obstacles that might interfere with their jobs. They also greatly improved their sales performance. On average, they made 50 percent more sales calls, sold twice as many insurance policies, and generated three times as much revenue. To learn more about the steps involved in self-management, complete the table in the following Self-Management Competency feature.[18]

EFFECTS OF JOB CONTENT AND ORGANIZATIONAL CONTEXT ON MOTIVATION

3.

STATE HOW JOB CONTENT AND ORGANIZATIONAL CONTEXT AFFECT MOTIVATION.

Three theories that view the job and organization contexts as important determinants of behavior are Herzberg's two-factor theory, job characteristics theory, and equity theory. These theories consider organizational conditions that may not be under the control of an individual manager.

HERZBERG'S TWO-FACTOR THEORY

Do you believe that a happy worker is a productive worker? Many people assume that a good way to motivate employees is to increase their job satisfaction. According to Frederick Herzberg, however, the relationship between job satisfaction and motivation is more complicated than it seems.[19] To gain an understanding of that relationship, Herzberg studied 200 accountants and engineers. He asked participants to describe job experiences that produced good and bad feelings about their jobs. He discovered that the presence of a particular job characteristic, such as responsibility, might increase job satisfaction. However, the lack of that same characteristic didn't necessarily produce dissatisfaction. Conversely, if lack of a characteristic, such as job security, produced dissatisfaction, high job security didn't necessarily lead to satisfaction.

The study's results led to Herzberg's **two-factor theory,** which states that two separate and distinct aspects of the environment are responsible for motivating and satisfying employees. He used the terms *motivator factors* and *hygiene factors* to refer to these two aspects of the environment.

Motivator Factors. *Motivator factors* are aspects of job content and organizational context that create positive feelings among employees. Challenge of the work itself, responsibility, recognition, achievement, advancement, and growth are all motivator factors. These factors determine whether a job is exciting and rewarding. However, their presence alone doesn't guarantee that employees will be productive. Motivators lead to superior performance *only* if no dissatisfiers are present.

Hygiene Factors. *Hygiene factors* are the nontask characteristics of the work environment—the organizational context—that create dissatisfaction. They include compensation, level of responsibility, working conditions, company policies, supervision, coworkers, salary, formal status, and job security. Hygiene factors need to be present, at least to some extent, to avoid dissatisfaction. Lack of dissatisfaction alone will not motivate employees—that is, they won't generate feelings of excitement about the job and organization. Nevertheless, the absence of dissatisfying conditions is an essential condition for motivator factors to be effective. As described in Chapter 13, many of the fringe benefits offered by employers are attempts to remove potential sources of employee dissatisfaction. Figure 14.2 illustrates these basic components of Herzberg's two-factor theory.

WEB INSIGHT

How important does IBM's management think that motivator factors and hygiene factors are to employee motivation? To find out, read the information provided to job seekers at *http://www.ibm.com*.

The two-factor theory is based on the assumption that motivator and hygiene factors are similar for all employees. Individual differences among employees aren't recognized as being important. Therefore, in Herzberg's view, employers should be able to motivate all employees in the same way—by ensuring the presence of both hygiene and motivator factors. Studies that compare the importance of motivator and hygiene factors among different types of employees (e.g., those who work in the private sector versus the public sector or those who work in lower skill versus higher skill jobs) support this view.[20]

Figure 14.2   **Two-Factor Theory**

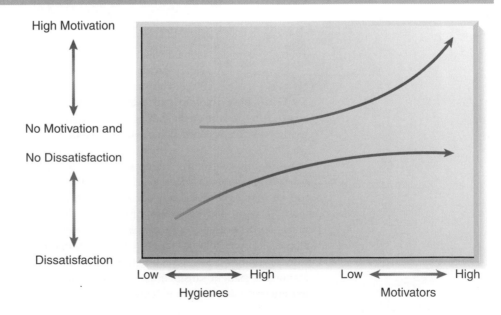

JOB CHARACTERISTICS

Developed by J. Richard Hackman and Greg Oldham, job characteristics theory is the most popular and extensively tested approach to designing jobs that employees enjoy and feel motivated to perform well. Figure 14.3 illustrates the components of this theory.[21] According to the *job characteristics theory,* one goal of designing work is to create jobs that employees will enjoy doing. People who enjoy the tasks they perform may not need the extra motivation of high pay and impressive job titles. In fact, according to a recent survey of 1,200 U.S. employees, the nature of the work they did was the most important factor (ahead of direct and indirect financial rewards and career concerns) in determining how people felt about staying with their current employer and how motivated they were to work hard.[22]

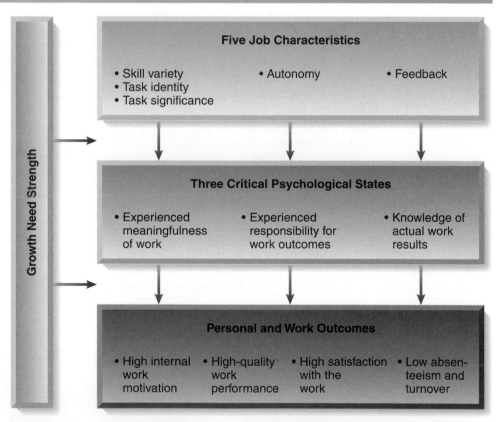

Figure 14.3   **Job Characteristics Theory**

Growth Need Strength

Five Job Characteristics

- Skill variety
- Task identity
- Task significance
- Autonomy
- Feedback

Three Critical Psychological States

- Experienced meaningfulness of work
- Experienced responsibility for work outcomes
- Knowledge of actual work results

Personal and Work Outcomes

- High internal work motivation
- High-quality work performance
- High satisfaction with the work
- Low absenteeism and turnover

Critical Psychological States. The job characteristics theory states that three *critical psychological states* are needed to create high levels of motivation in the workplace. *Experienced meaningfulness* refers to whether employees perceive their work as valuable and worthwhile. For example, people working in health care understand that their efforts can help save lives and improve the quality of people's lives. *Experienced responsibility* refers to whether employees feel personally responsible for the quantity and quality of their work. A surgeon who specializes in orthopedics is likely to experience a feeling of responsibility for the amount and quality of her or his work. *Knowledge of results* refers to the extent to which employees receive feedback about how well they are doing. Feedback can come from the task itself (e.g., successfully reviving a heart attack victim), or from other sources (e.g., the comments of colleagues or patient satisfaction surveys). When all three of these psychological states are experienced, motivation is high.[23]

Key Job Characteristics. The theory states that the three critical psychological states are affected by five key job characteristics. **Key job characteristics** are objective aspects of the job design that can be changed to improve the critical psychological states. **Skill variety** is the degree to which the job involves many different work activities or requires several skills and talents. **Task identity** is present when a job involves completing an identifiable piece of work, that is, doing a job with a clear beginning and outcome. **Task significance** is present when a job has a substantial impact on the goals or work of others in the company. **Autonomy** is present when the job provides substantial freedom, independence, and discretion to the individual in scheduling work and determining the procedures to be used in carrying out tasks. Finally, **feedback** is present when the outcome gives the employee direct and clear information about his or her performance. When all five key job characteristics are present at significant levels, employees feel involved in their work and exert more effort.[24]

Jobs that involve considerable amounts of cooperation and teamwork often have all these characteristics. As described in the following Strategic Action Competency feature, at Whole Foods Markets, jobs that are motivating fit the overall mission and values of the organization. They're a natural extension of a management philosophy based on employee empowerment.[25]

STRATEGIC ACTION COMPETENCY

Job Design at Whole Foods Markets

Founded by Texas hippies who were fond of health food, Whole Foods Markets has grown from one store to a company with more than 100 stores. What sets its stores apart from other grocery markets isn't just the food—it's also the company's democratic style of management. Seldom do employees receive mandates from above. Instead, coming up with their own mandates is part of the job. Each store is organized around self-managing teams. Teams are given goals that they're responsible for meeting, and then they're given a great deal of autonomy to find the best way to meet those goals. For example, if a holiday is coming up, a team decides how to arrange holiday schedules while also meeting the needs of customers. Teams also are accountable for results. For example, if a team comes in under budget, the team gets to keep the difference and split it among the team members. If it

comes in over budget, it builds up debt within the company, which can be erased by coming up with a plan to address the problem and showing some improvement. One indication of the level of autonomy in jobs is that team members decide whether a new hire will stay on a team, based on their evaluations during an initial probationary period. Because of the autonomy and responsibility given to Whole Foods Markets teams, task variety seems to follow naturally.

Feedback is present in many forms. Team leaders know that they can be voted out at any time. To ensure that that doesn't happen very often, team members let leaders know clearly how the team feels about them, and leaders make the effort to get feedback without actually having to take a vote. Feedback in the form of financial results is plentiful, too. In fact, employees get so much financial information that they are "insid-

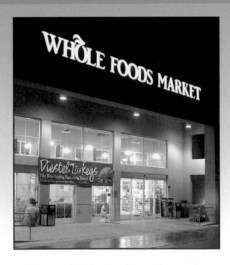

ers" according to the Securities and Exchange Commission's definition.

• • •

To learn more about Whole Foods Markets, visit the company's home page at

http://www.wholefoods.com

Growth Need Strength. Unlike the two-factor theory, job characteristics theory considers individual differences to be important in determining how an employee reacts to job content. In particular, employees' growth needs influence how they react to their jobs. **Growth need strength** is a desire for personal challenge, accomplishment, and learning. Employees with a strong growth need respond more favorably to enriched jobs, whereas employees with a weak growth need may experience enriched jobs as frustrating and dissatisfying. Research supports this aspect of the theory—enriched jobs aren't for everyone. Nevertheless, many people thrive in an environment characterized by jobs designed to give them a sense of responsibility and meaningfulness.

People with strong growth needs are just the type of people that Jamba Juice looks for when hiring general managers to run its stores. In selection interviews, the interviewers look for people who "think the glass is half full"—that is, they see opportunities and are eager to make the most of them. When it finds the right people, Jamba Juice puts them in a situation that guarantees they'll feel a sense of responsibility. Besides the challenging task of being in charge of Jamba Juice stores—retail outlets that sell made-to-order smoothies and a variety of healthy foods—general managers who succeed at expanding their businesses also experience significant personal financial gain.[26]

PERCEPTIONS OF EQUITY

Working at well-designed jobs is likely to make employees feel positive about their work, but it is no guarantee of satisfaction. Even when the job itself is enjoyable and motivating, people will probably be upset if they feel that they're not being treated fairly. **Equity theory** states that motivation levels can be enhanced or diminished by employees' judgments about whether the organization is treating them fairly. Employees determine whether they've been treated fairly by comparing the ratio of their inputs and outcomes to the ratios of others doing similar work. *Inputs* are what an employee gives to the job (e.g., time, effort, education, and commitment to the organization). *Outcomes* are what people get out of doing the job (e.g., the feelings of meaningfulness and responsibility associated with jobs, promotions, and increased pay).[27]

An example of equity comparison is presented in Table 14.2. It's a simple dollars-per-hour example to illustrate how the ratios work. In reality the ratios can be quite complex, involving factors that are quite difficult to quantify and compare. As a result of such a comparison, an employee or even a team will feel equitably rewarded, underrewarded, or overrewarded. Feelings of being overrewarded are probably rare, but when they occur they have beneficial consequences for employers. Overrewarded employees tend to perform better in their jobs and are better members of the organization than employees who haven't been so well rewarded.[28]

Table 14.2	The Equity Model of Motivation: Comparing Hourly Wages	
	Ratio Comparison	**Perception**
Equity	$\dfrac{\$50}{5 \text{ hrs. work}} = \dfrac{\$100}{10 \text{ hrs. work}} = \$10/\text{hr.}$ $\dfrac{\text{Outcomes (self)}}{\text{Inputs (self)}} = \dfrac{\text{Outcomes (other)}}{\text{Inputs (other)}}$	"I'm being treated equally."
Inequity	$\left[\dfrac{\$50}{5 \text{ hrs. work}} = \$10/\text{hr.}\right] < \left[\dfrac{\$100}{4 \text{ hrs. work}} = \$20/\text{hr.}\right]$ $\dfrac{\text{Outcomes (self)}}{\text{Inputs (self)}} < \dfrac{\text{Outcomes (other)}}{\text{Inputs (other)}}$	"I'm getting less than I deserve for my efforts."
Inequity	$\left[\dfrac{\$50}{5 \text{ hrs. work}} = \$10/\text{hr.}\right] > \left[\dfrac{\$25}{4 \text{ hrs. work}} = \$5/\text{hr.}\right]$ $\dfrac{\text{Outcomes (self)}}{\text{Inputs (self)}} > \dfrac{\text{Outcomes (other)}}{\text{Inputs (other)}}$	"I'm getting more than I deserve."

More typical are situations that result in employees feeling underrewarded. Trish Millines Dziko, executive director of Technology Access Foundation, recalls feeling underrewarded in her first job after college—long before she retired from Microsoft as a millionaire. After Dziko, an African American, had been in her new job a few months, a white woman (who eventually became her friend) was hired at a salary $10,000 higher than Dziko's. With a degree in computer science, Dziko was a quick study for the job. The new woman, who was the same age, had majored in psychology and had to attend a training course to learn about computers. Although Dziko may have been satisfied with her salary before this incident, from then on she felt underrewarded.[29]

Generally, six alternatives are available to employees who want to reduce their feelings of inequity:

- increase their inputs (e.g., time and effort) to justify higher rewards when they feel that they are overrewarded compared to others;

- decrease their inputs to compensate for lower rewards when they feel underrewarded;

- change the compensation they receive through legal or other actions (e.g., forming a union, filing a grievance, or leaving work early);

- modify their comparisons by choosing another person to compare themselves against;

- distort reality by rationalizing that the inequities are justified; or

- leave the situation (quit the job) if the inequities can't be resolved.

Some of these reactions can harm the organization. For example, high performers who feel that their pay is too low may leave the organization. As a result, the company loses their productive talents. If dissatisfied employees stay, they may react by withholding effort in order to restrict output or lower quality. Because feelings of inequity often cause frustration, they also lead people to behave in hostile and aggressive ways. A store clerk may be hostile to customers. A factory worker may deliberately sabotage equipment. Unfortunately, such hostility can even lead to such drastic reactions as killing former colleagues and managers.[30]

Perceived inequities often occur with respect to promotions, pay raises, and perquisites (perks). Pay inequities can be especially troublesome for organizations that compete in the international labor market, as explained in the following Global Awareness Competency feature.[31]

WEB INSIGHT

Visit Organization Resources Counselors at *http://www.orcinc.com* to learn about the type of information the firm makes available to employers of expatriates. How does information about living costs in other countries help employers address employees' equity perceptions?

GLOBAL AWARENESS COMPETENCY

The Challenge of International Compensation

The problem of perceived pay inequity is one that must be solved by the many companies that straddle the Canadian and U.S. border. Typically, employees who hold lower-level jobs are paid more in Canada than in the United States. In contrast, Canadian professionals and managers typically earn one third less than their U.S. counterparts, as shown in the following table. Demand for managers and professionals is strong in the United States, so many Canadians comparing inputs and outcomes to those of similar executives in the United States may conclude that they are underpaid and seek employment across the border. As more Canadian professionals and managers seek employment in the United States, Canadian companies face the possibility of a "brain drain."

To attract new talent and avoid losing their best employees, some Canadian companies try to minimize pay inequity by using a formula that blends the pay levels in the two countries. The following is an example of the formula used to determine the salary of a top information systems executive.

Weighted blending. A weight of 0.2 is given to pay rates in Canada, and a weight of 0.8 is given to pay rates in the United States. The exchange rate used to convert U.S. to Canadian dollars is 1.37. Thus

$$(0.2 \times \$98,000) + (0.8 \times \$110,000 \times 1.37) = \$140,160 \text{ Canadian.}$$

The formula takes into account managers' natural tendencies to compare their inputs and outputs to those of similar U.S. managers. Using the blended approach to setting the manager's pay helps reduce perceived inequities that might arise from such comparisons and knowing that subordinates are being paid as much as or more than the manager.

• • •

To learn more about international compensation practices, visit the home page of Windham International at

http://www.windhamint.com

Job	Canada	United States	Canadian Pay as a Percentage of U.S. Pay
CFO of $300-million packaging company	$161,000	$247,500	65%
Information systems executive	98,000	150,300	65
Treasurer	109,100	153,200	71
Machine operator	27,000	19,900	136
Salesclerk	24,500	16,800	146

Note: Amounts are in Canadian dollars.

To be effective in their roles, managers must strive to treat all members of the organization fairly. Doing so can pay huge dividends. Employees who are paid and treated fairly are more likely to believe in and be committed to what they do. In turn, they will become more trusting, honorable, and loyal employees and will work harder to exceed the expectations that managers have of them. In team situations, equitable treatment improves cooperation among team members.[32]

INDIVIDUAL DIFFERENCES IN MOTIVATION

4.

DESCRIBE HOW INDIVIDUAL DIFFERENCES IN NEEDS AND MOTIVES CAN AFFECT EMPLOYEES' WORK.

People differ from each other in many ways, having different abilities, personalities, values, and needs. During the past century, psychologists conducted thousands of studies designed to improve our understanding of such differences.[33] Here, we describe two views of how individual differences affect employee motivation in the workplace. Both approaches consider employees' needs to be the basis for differences in motivation. A **need** is a strong feeling of deficiency in some aspect of a person's life that creates an uncomfortable tension. That tension becomes a motivating force, causing the individual to take actions to satisfy the need, reduce the tension, and diminish the intensity of the motivating force.

HIERARCHY OF NEEDS

Psychologist Abraham Maslow believed that people have five types of needs, which he arranged in a **hierarchy of needs,** as shown in Figure 14.4: physiological (at the base), security, affiliation, esteem, and self-actualization (at the top). He suggested that, as a person satisfies each level of needs, motivation shifts to satisfying the next higher level of needs.[34]

Physiological needs are those for food, clothing, and shelter, which people try to satisfy before all others. For example, the primary motivation of a hungry person is to obtain food rather than, say, gain recognition for achievements. Thus people work for wages that will allow them to meet their physiological needs first.

Security needs include the desire for safety and stability, and the absence of pain, threat, and illness. People deprived of the means to satisfy security needs are motivated to fulfill them. Some workers express their security needs as a desire for a stable job with adequate medical, unemployment, and retirement benefits. Such people are likely

Figure 1 4 . 4   **Maslow's Hierarchy of Needs**

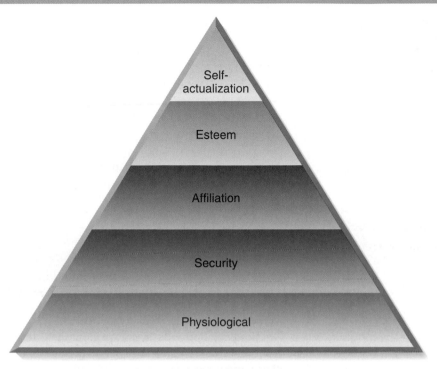

to be frustrated with current flexible staffing practices (e.g., emphasis on temporary workers to avoid providing benefits). Other workers express security needs as a desire for work that builds their competencies and ensures their long-term employability, and this concern is often more important than getting a bigger salary.

Affiliation needs are the desire for friendship, love, and belonging. Employees with high affiliation needs enjoy working closely with others. Employees with low affiliation needs may be content to work on tasks by themselves. When an organization doesn't meet affiliation needs, an employee's dissatisfaction may be expressed in terms of frequent absenteeism, low productivity, stress-related behaviors, and even emotional breakdown. A manager who recognizes that a subordinate is striving to satisfy affiliation needs might encourage others to work more closely with the employee and suggest that the employee participate in the organization's social activities.

Esteem needs are the desire for self-respect, a sense of personal achievement, and recognition from others. To satisfy these needs, people seek opportunities for achievement, promotion, prestige, and status—all of which symbolize their competence and worth. When the need for esteem is dominant, managers can promote job satisfaction and high-quality performance by providing opportunities for exciting, challenging work and recognition for accomplishments.

Self-actualization needs are the desire for personal growth, self-fulfillment, and the realization of the individual's full potential. Richard Branson, chairman of the Virgin Group, seems to be strongly motivated by the need for self-actualization. When explaining why he founded Virgin Atlantic Airlines and Virgin Records, he admits that part of the reason was to have fun but also important was to change things and make a difference. In the process of building new businesses, Branson himself developed and grew.[35] Managers who recognize this motivation in employees can help them discover the growth opportunities available in their jobs or create special growth opportunities for them. For example, at Merck, scientists can attend law school and become patent attorneys; at Hewlett-Packard, a parallel technical ladder was established so scientists could earn higher salaries without taking on management tasks. At both companies, managers also can offer employees special assignments, such as working on a task force that reports to top management. Such assignments often represent growth opportunities through which employees can develop their managerial competencies while continuing to utilize to the fullest their technical knowledge and skills.

MOVING THROUGH THE NEEDS HIERARCHY

People often equate individual differences with fixed traits that don't change much over time. In contrast to this view, Maslow believed that people move through the needs hierarchy by considering which needs have been satisfied and which needs remain to be satisfied. For any specific person, a need that was dominant three months ago may no longer be dominant, and a need that is dominant today may not be dominant next year. In Maslow's original formulation of the needs hierarchy, he viewed movement as occurring much as it does when people are moving up on an escalator—the only way to go is up. However, later research showed that movement through the hierarchy could actually go in both directions.

Always Moving Up.   To explain which need is dominant for someone at a particular time, Maslow proposed the satisfaction–progression hypothesis. The ***satisfaction–progression hypothesis*** states that a need is a motivator until it becomes satisfied. When a need is satisfied, it ceases to be a motivator and another need emerges to take its place. In general, lower level needs must be satisfied before higher level needs become strong enough to motivate behavior.

Research supports Maslow's view that, until their *basic* needs are satisfied, people won't be concerned with higher level needs. However, little evidence supports the view that people meet their needs precisely as suggested by Maslow's hierarchy (see Figure 14.4). Instead, it supports a reformulation of Maslow's hierarchy, called ERG theory.

Moving Up and Down.   Like Maslow, Clay Alderfer looked at motivation from a needs perspective. Instead of five categories of needs, however, his ***ERG theory*** specifies three needs categories: existence, relatedness, and growth.[36] Like Maslow's needs, these three needs are organized in a hierarchy.

Existence needs are the desires for material and physical well-being that are satisfied through food, water, air, shelter, working conditions, pay, fringe benefits, and the like. They are similar to Maslow's physiological and security needs combined. ***Relatedness needs*** are the desires to establish and maintain interpersonal relationships with other people, including family, friends, supervisors, subordinates, and coworkers. Relatedness is similar to Maslow's affiliation needs. ***Growth needs*** are the desires to be creative, to make useful and productive contributions, and to have opportunities for personal development. They are similar to Maslow's esteem and self-actualization needs combined.

ERG theory recognizes Maslow's satisfaction–progression hypothesis, but it also contains a frustration–regression hypothesis. The ***frustration–regression hypothesis*** holds that, when an individual is frustrated in meeting higher level needs, the next lower level needs reemerge and again direct behavior. For example, a finish carpenter who does highly creative trim work in houses may work for a contractor who builds from a limited number of floor plans with few trim options. Because the job doesn't provide a creative outlet, the frustrated carpenter may stop pursuing satisfaction of growth needs at work and instead regress to pursuing activities that satisfy his relatedness needs. An example would be socializing with other construction workers. Movement through the needs hierarchy resulting from satisfaction–progression and frustration–regression are illustrated in Figure 14.5.

The frustration–regression hypothesis suggests that managers should try to determine the cause of an employee's frustration and, if possible, work to remove blockages to needs satisfaction. If blockages can't be removed, managers should try to redirect the employee's behavior toward satisfying a lower level need. For example, a company's production technology may limit the growth opportunities for people in their jobs. If

Figure 14.5 **ERG Model of Motivation**

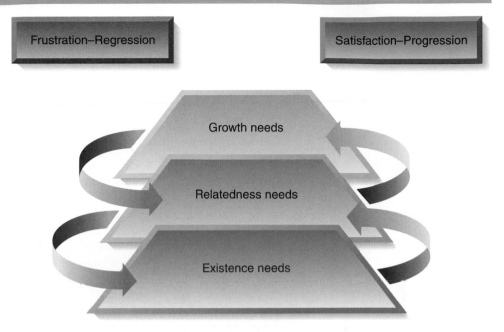

employees are frustrated because they can't be creative or develop new skills, they could be encouraged to focus on relating to their coworkers, which can also generate feelings of satisfaction.

LEARNED NEEDS

Maslow viewed the needs hierarchy as an inherent aspect of human beings. That is, anyone who satisfied all of the lower level needs in the hierarchy would be eventually be motivated by higher level needs. David McClelland proposed a different view of needs. His **learned needs theory** specifies that people acquire needs through interaction with the surrounding environment. In other words, the social contexts in which people live and work influence the learning of motivating needs and their strengths. When a need is acting as a determinant of a person's behavior, it is referred to as a *motive*. Three key motives are particularly useful for understanding the differences among individuals: affiliation, achievement, and power.[37]

Affiliation. The **affiliation motive** is a person's desire to develop and maintain close, mutually satisfying interpersonal relationships. Individuals with a strong affiliation motive tend to take into account the approval or disapproval that others may show toward their behavior, and they generally prefer to conform to group norms. People with weak affiliation motives care less about what others think and may be viewed as unsociable and not great team members, even if they perform their jobs well.

WEB INSIGHT

If a manager wanted to strengthen the achievement motivation of employees, how might he or she go about it? Read about achievement motivation training at *http://www.eiconsortium.org*. Would such training be a worthwhile investment?

Achievement. The **achievement motive** is the desire to succeed relative to some standard of excellence or in competitive situations. People with a high need for achievement often like to assume personal responsibility for setting their own goals and desire immediate and concrete feedback. Being achievement oriented has been found to predict performance in a variety of situations, including performance at work.[38] Lloyd Ward's strong need for achievement has been a driving force throughout much of his life. It helps explain how he became a basketball star at Michigan State University, despite his 5' 10" height and his insistence on taking tough engineering courses that would prepare him for a career after college. Getting a good education was a goal that Ward never lost sight of. According to one of his teammates, "He was probably the only guy on the team like that." A strong need for achievement also helps explain how Ward became only the second African American to lead a large U.S. company—Maytag.[39]

Power. The ***power motive*** is an individual's desire to influence and control others and the social environment. It is expressed in two ways: as *personal power* and as *socialized power*.[40] With personal power, people try to influence and control others merely to assert their dominance. With socialized power, individuals use their power to solve organizational problems and help the organization reach its goals. People who have a strong socialized power motive are likely to be viewed as effective managers and leaders.

Managing Multiple Motives. As people develop from childhood to adulthood, these three motives—for affiliation, achievement, and power—become relatively weak or relatively strong. For some people, one motive becomes clearly dominant, and the others become relatively unimportant. For other people, two or even all three of the motives may become fairly important. When more than one motive is strong, a person often faces situations that pose the challenge of trying to satisfy conflicting motives. For example, when subordinates don't perform as well as they should, managers often struggle with how to balance their affiliation motives against their achievement motives. Ed Zander has mastered this balancing act, to the benefit of himself, his family, and his colleagues at Sun Microsystems.

Most people know that Scott McNealy is cofounder and CEO of Sun Microsystems. But have you ever heard of the company's president, Ed Zander? Probably not, and that's okay with him. Zander is the person who coined the slogan, "We're the dot in dotcom." Before Sun used that slogan in its advertising, people had a hard time understanding what the company did. Today, most people recognize Sun Microsystems as a company that provides products that are vital to Internet operations. Some people refer to Zander as the executive behind the executive, referring to his immense importance to the success of Sun Microsystems. A strong achievement motive is reflected in his goals for Sun. Despite its success, he wants to remake the company so that it can become "the IBM of the Internet Age." Although Zander is not uninterested in power, his power motive appears to fit the pattern of socialized power rather than personal power. Becoming the person who controls everything doesn't seem to motivate him much. He's had offers to become CEO at competing firms—and has rejected them. "I've seen friends who wanted to run a company at all costs, but I don't stick pins in myself at night because I'm not CEO," he explains. There's little doubt that this view of power makes it easier for Zander to be supportive of other key players in the organization. Zander is also a good team player in the family home, perhaps because he also has a healthy desire for affiliation. Although he has always worked long hours, he also makes time to be a soccer coach and enjoy weekends with his family.[41]

MOTIVATIONAL FORCES IN COMBINATION

5.

EXPLAIN HOW SEVERAL MOTIVATIONAL FORCES MAY COMBINE TO INFLUENCE AN EMPLOYEE'S WORK SATISFACTION AND PERFORMANCE.

Each of the motivation theories described offers useful insights into motivation. To take maximum advantage of the theories, however, managers must be able to integrate them. In this section we describe an integrated view of motivation that incorporates many of the specific principles discussed so far in this chapter. But, before we do so, we need to present yet another theory of motivation—basic expectancy theory. This simple theory is the basis for the integrated view of motivation.

BASIC EXPECTANCY THEORY
Basic expectancy theory, as originally formulated by Victor Vroom, is a widely accepted model for explaining how people make decisions about how to behave. Expectancy

theory states that people choose among alternative behaviors by considering which behaviors will lead to the most desired outcomes (e.g., recognition or new challenges). Examples of behavioral choices that are related to work performance include whether to go to work or call in sick, whether to leave work at the official quitting time or stay late, and whether to exert a great deal of effort or to work at a more relaxed pace.

More specifically, **basic expectancy theory** states that people tend to choose behaviors that they believe will help them achieve their personal goals (e.g., a promotion or job security) and avoid behaviors that they believe will lead to undesirable personal consequences (e.g., a demotion or criticism). Thus it combines ideas from both reinforcement theory and goal-setting theory. By focusing on goals that are personally important rather than task related, it also takes into account individual differences in what people value.

When making behavioral choices, an employee normally considers three questions.

1. *The expectancy question:* If I make an effort, will I be able to perform the intended behavior?

2. *The instrumentality question:* If I perform the intended behavior, what will be the outcomes?

3. *The valence question:* How much do I value the outcomes associated with the intended behavior?

Expectancy. A person's estimate of how likely a certain level of effort will lead to improved performance is referred to as **expectancy.** Effort is the amount of physical and/or mental energy exerted to perform a task or to learn something new. In other words, how hard is the employee trying? At Nordstrom department stores, a salesperson's attempts to find a medium-sized blue-striped shirt is an example of effort. Effort refers solely to the energy expended—not to how successful it is. Performance could involve making more sales, creating a satisfied customer, and/or helping another salesperson do his or her job more effectively. Employees who believe that exerting more effort results in better performance generally show higher levels of performance than employees who don't believe that their efforts will pay off.[42]

Instrumentality. To be willing to expend the effort needed to achieve the desired performance, employees must believe that the performance will have some type of payoff. **Instrumentality** refers to a person's perception of how useful performance is for obtaining desired outcomes (or avoiding undesired outcomes). If an employee develops an innovative product design, will that person receive public recognition for this accomplishment? If an employee arrives at work on time, rather than being a few minutes late, will anyone else really care? If an employee's performance rating is outstanding, will the individual be paid more?

Goalsharing, gainsharing, and other forms of incentive pay (described in Chapter 13) are intended to create perceptions of high instrumentality. They don't always succeed, however. For managers whose pay is tied to movement in the company's share price, unpredictable market conditions or a single bad executive decision can have devastating consequences for the company's bonus pool, despite an overall excellent performance. Such events may result in a manager having a feeling of low instrumentality.

Valence. *Valence* is the value (weight) that an employee attaches to an outcome. Valences are personal; the same outcome may have a high valence for one person and a low valence for another. For example, a promotion from museum curator to the higher paying position of museum director would appeal more to an individual who values (places a high valence on) financial gain and increased responsibility than to an individual who values creativity and independence.

Like goal-setting theory, expectancy theory gives great weight to how people think about the future. The assumption is that people base rational choices about how to behave on the information available to them. Usually included in that information is some knowledge or prediction about how behavior affects performance levels and how performance levels affect outcomes such as pay and recognition. An important implication of this theory is that employers who offer incentives for performance must do more than simply design a good incentive plan. They must also communicate it effectively.

THE INTEGRATED EXPECTANCY MODEL

Figure 14.6 shows the integrated expectancy model.[43] In this model, satisfaction isn't viewed as a cause of high performance. Instead, it suggests that employees who perform well will feel more satisfied, assuming that their performance is rewarded appropriately.

Figure 14.6	The Integrative Expectancy Model

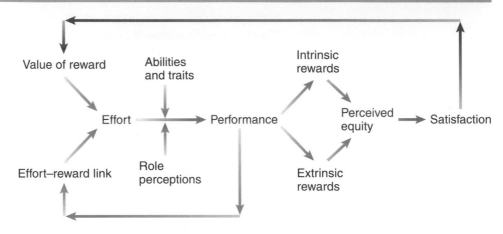

The foundation of this model is basic expectancy theory. Additions to the model suggest some conditions that may cause expectancies and instrumentalities to be lower than desired. Expectancies can be lower than optimal because of individual differences. Of particular importance are individual differences in employees' abilities, traits, and role perceptions. Instrumentalities can be lower than optimal because of perceived inequities and misalignment between the rewards available and those that employees value most.

Factors That Affect Expectancy. Individual abilities, traits, and role perceptions all influence how likely greater effort will translate into better performance. ***Ability*** is the individual's mastery of competencies required to do a job. If ability is low, high levels of effort may not result in high performance. ***Traits*** are stable personality characteristics that are difficult to change. If an employee doesn't have a trait that is important to job performance, more effort may not result in better performance. For example, an introvert who tries very hard to increase sales performance may simply not be as effective as an extrovert who tries equally hard. ***Role perceptions*** are the employee's beliefs about what is required to do the job successfully. Role perceptions are formed by many types of employee experiences, including interactions with customers, coworkers, and supervisors. Inaccurate role perceptions interfere with the link between effort and performance because the effort is misdirected. Managers can help clarify role perceptions by ensuring that employees have specific goals to strive for and by ensuring that an employee's various goals don't conflict.

Factors That Affect Instrumentality. Like equity theory, the integrated expectancy model suggests that perceived inequities are detrimental to motivation. Employees' perceptions of whether their rewards are equitable include their evaluations of both extrinsic and intrinsic rewards. ***Extrinsic rewards*** are supplied by the organization (e.g., a good salary, status, job security, and fringe benefits). These rewards are similar to the job context items that Herzberg called hygiene factors. ***Intrinsic rewards*** involve personal satisfaction (e.g., feelings of achievement and personal growth). These rewards are similar to Herzberg's motivator factors. Unlike Herzberg's, this model assumes that both types of rewards can be motivating for employees.

Finally, this model suggests that the level of satisfaction is determined by the difference between the rewards employees receive and the rewards they believe they *should* receive. Employees often compare the rewards they receive to the rewards others receive. If an employee believes that the comparison shows unfair treatment, dissatisfaction results. Satisfied employees focus on the positive aspects of their work, not the negative. They are therefore more likely to make a commitment to the organization than are dissatisfied employees. This commitment, in turn, translates into continued effort, better performance, and increasing rewards. Conversely, dissatisfied employees exert less effort, which results in declining performance and a general downward spiral to ineffectiveness.[44]

GUIDELINES FOR MANAGERS

6.

DESCRIBE HOW UNDERSTANDING THE DYNAMICS OF MOTIVATION CAN HELP MANAGERS IMPROVE EMPLOYEE PERFORMANCE.

Managers who understand what motivates employees and what detracts from employee motivation have a good basis for diagnosing and rectifying the causes of performance problems. Here we summarize some of practical lessons suggested by the motivation theories and research described in this chapter.

- **Design jobs with high motivating potential.** Jobs designed to meet the principles of job characteristics theory tend to be more satisfying than other jobs. To determine whether jobs need to be redesigned, managers should assess the degree to which employees experience their work as meaningful, feel personally responsible for their work outcomes, and receive adequate feedback.

- **State the behaviors and performance achievements that are desired and explain how they will be rewarded.** By working with employees to set specific and measurable goals, managers can clarify their expectations for employees. These goals may include job-specific performance goals as well as behaviors that extend beyond job tasks but are necessary for the organization to function effectively. When setting goals, managers should be careful not to fall into the trap of focusing only on goals that are easily quantified.[45]

- **Provide frequent and constructive feedback.** When employees are performing well, telling them so spurs them on. When employees are performing poorly, telling them so suggests that they consider a different approach to the task or intensify their efforts. Giving appropriate feedback can be difficult, however. As a general rule, feedback should focus on task performance and avoid criticizing personal characteristics that are difficult for employees to change.[46]

- **Provide rewards for desired behaviors and outcomes.** Employees tend to repeat behaviors that are rewarded, and they strive to achieve goals to which rewards are attached. When a gap exists between actual and desired behaviors and goal achievement, rewards and punishments are likely to be misaligned. Effective managers ensure that the formal and informal rewards and punishments experienced by employees are aligned with the organization's desired behaviors and goal achievement.

- **Provide rewards that employees value.** To be motivators, rewards must reflect the things that employees value. The rewards that employees want can be determined simply by asking them. Some employees value monetary rewards above everything else, whereas others value scheduling flexibility, the opportunity to work on special projects, training and development opportunities, and so on. Whenever possible, effective managers find ways to use various rewards to motivate a variety of employees.

- **Provide equitable rewards.** Employees make two types of comparisons when evaluating whether they have been rewarded fairly. One involves assessing their own accomplishments in terms of the rewards they receive. The second involves assessing their own accomplishments and rewards in terms of those of other employees. Effective managers recognize that employees' assessments of equity and fairness are basically subjective perceptions. Perceptions may partially reflect objective facts, but inaccurate assumptions and beliefs often play a role, too. Effective communication about rewards is essential. A well-designed reward system will have little motivational value if employees misunderstand the system and rely on inferences and rumor when assessing whether the system is fair.

- **Diagnose and remove barriers to performance.** Even when employees are highly motivated, other barriers to effective performance may exist. To remove these barriers, managers must first identify them. The theories described in this chapter suggest several questions that managers should explore when employees exhibit unsatisfactory performance.

  - Do employees understand what is expected of them?

  - Are the goals that have been set for employees specific, challenging, and clear?

  - Do employees feel committed to achieving the goals that have been set?

  - Do employees believe that they can improve their performance by putting in more effort?

  - Do employees have the competencies needed to perform the job well?

  - Is desirable behavior punished in any way? Is undesirable behavior rewarded in any way?

  - Do employees who perform at the highest levels receive the greatest rewards? If yes, do employees actually know that this result is true?

  - Do employees value the rewards offered by the organization? Are there other rewards they would value more?

  - Do employees feel that rewards are given out fairly and equitably?

CHAPTER SUMMARY

Ensuring that employees are motivated to work effectively is a primary managerial responsibility. Managers who are able to do so will be rewarded for their efforts with a workforce that expresses little dissatisfaction and exerts high levels of effort. To be effective, managers must understand the many factors that, in combination, can enhance or squelch motivation. The approaches to motivation described in this chapter provide useful insights about how to enhance the productivity of an organization's workforce.

1. DESCRIBE THREE GENERAL FACTORS THAT INFLUENCE EMPLOYEES' MOTIVATION AT WORK.

Work motivation is influenced by (1) an organization's goals and rewards, (2) the way jobs are designed and how equitably employees are treated, and (3) individual differences in needs and motives. None of these influences alone can fully explain employee motivation. Effective managers understand that the three factors work in combination.

2. EXPLAIN HOW MANAGERS AND THEIR SUBORDINATES CAN USE GOALS AND REWARDS TO IMPROVE PERFORMANCE.

Goal-setting theory states that performance improves when employees have specific, difficult goals that they accept and are committed to. Participative goal setting, one aspect of management by objectives, is an approach that managers can use to get employees to buy into goal setting. Providing feedback to employees about their progress toward those goals is important to their effectiveness. Reinforcement theory states that behavior is a function of its consequences. Positive reinforcement rewards an employee when a desired behavior occurs. Negative reinforcement occurs when an employee engages in a behavior to avoid unpleasant outcomes. Punishment provides negative outcomes that discourage repetition of a behavior. When a reinforcement that was offered in the past for a behavior is no longer available, extinction occurs. Positive and negative reinforcement should be used to encourage desired work behaviors, whereas punishment and extinction should be applied to discourage undesired work behaviors. The principles of goal setting and reinforcement can be used by managers to improve the performance of employees, and they also provide an effective approach to self-management.

3. **STATE HOW JOB CONTENT AND ORGANIZATIONAL CONTEXT AFFECT MOTIVATION.**

Herzberg's two-factor model states that factors in the work situation strongly influence satisfaction and performance. Motivator factors such as challenging work, responsibility, recognition, achievement, and growth create high levels of motivation. The presence of motivators should enhance performance. Hygiene factors, such as good working conditions and benefits, are important determinants of satisfaction and dissatisfaction. Hygiene factors can hurt employee performance if not present but don't necessarily increase performance when present.

Job characteristics theory states that three critical psychological states—experienced meaningfulness, experienced responsibility, and knowledge of results—lead to high motivation and job satisfaction. In turn, five job characteristics—skill variety, task identity, task significance, autonomy, and feedback—influence critical psychological states. Individuals with strong growth needs are likely to respond positively to jobs having these characteristics.

Equity theory is based on the assumption that employees want to be treated fairly. Employees judge fairness by comparing their own inputs and outcomes to those of others in the workplace. When inequities exist, employees feel dissatisfied and their performance drops.

4. **DESCRIBE HOW INDIVIDUAL DIFFERENCES IN NEEDS AND MOTIVES CAN AFFECT EMPLOYEES' WORK.**

Maslow's hierarchy of needs includes physiological, security, affiliation, esteem, and self-actualization needs. Alderfer's version of the needs hierarchy, the ERG theory, contains only three categories of needs: existence, relatedness, and growth. Need satisfaction causes people to move up the hierarchy and need frustration causes them to move down. The importance of a category of needs at any specific time in a person's life determines how strongly it influences a person's behavior. McClelland's learned needs model suggests that people acquire three motives—achievement, affiliation, and power—by interacting with their social environment. These motives have implications for what employees want from their work and how they interact with others, but they are not arranged in a hierarchy.

5. **EXPLAIN HOW SEVERAL MOTIVATIONAL FORCES MAY COMBINE TO INFLUENCE AN EMPLOYEE'S WORK SATISFACTION AND PERFORMANCE.**

Basic expectancy theory states that motivation is highest when employees feel that their efforts lead to improved performance (expectancy) and when performance is rewarded with outcomes that they value (instrumentality). The integrated expectancy model of motivation expands basic expectancy theory to incorporate concepts from other theories of motivation, including individual differences, goals, rewards, and equity perceptions.

6. **DESCRIBE HOW UNDERSTANDING THE DYNAMICS OF MOTIVATION CAN HELP MANAGERS IMPROVE EMPLOYEE PERFORMANCE.**

To improve the performance of employees, managers should design jobs with high motivating potential, clearly state what employees are expected to do, provide feedback as well as rewards, attend to employees' equity perceptions, and engage in continuous problem diagnosis and problem solving.

KEY TERMS

Ability, p. 396
Achievement motive, p. 393
Affiliation motive, p. 393
Affiliation needs, p. 391
Autonomy, p. 387
Basic expectancy theory, p. 395
Behavior modification, p. 381
Critical psychological states, p. 386
Equity theory, p. 388
ERG theory, p. 392
Esteem needs, p. 391
Existence needs, p. 392
Expectancy, p. 395
Experienced meaningfulness, p. 386
Experienced responsibility, p. 386
Extinction, p. 382
Feedback, p. 387

Frustration–regression hypothesis, p. 392
Goal-setting theory, p. 378
Goalsharing, p. 380
Growth need strength, p. 387
Growth needs, p. 392
Hierarchy of needs, p. 390
Hygiene factors, p. 385
Instrumentality, p. 395
Intrinsic rewards, p. 397
Job characteristics theory, p. 386
Key job characteristics, p. 387
Knowledge of results, p. 386
Learned needs theory, p. 393
Management by objectives, p. 379
Motivation, p. 376
Motivator factors, p. 385
Need, p. 390
Negative reinforcement, p. 382

Physiological needs, p. 390
Positive reinforcement, p. 382
Power motive, p. 394
Punishment, p. 382
Reinforcement theory, p. 380
Relatedness needs, p. 392
Role perceptions, p. 396
Satisfaction–progression hypothesis, p. 392
Security needs, p. 390
Self-actualization needs, p. 391
Skill variety, p. 387
Task identity, p. 387
Task significance, p. 387
Traits, p. 396
Two-factor theory, p. 385
Valence, p. 395

1. Pepper Oni manages a pizza shop. During the past few months, the pizza delivery drivers have received several traffic tickets and had three small accidents. No one has been seriously injured yet, but Oni is concerned. Using the principles of goal setting and reinforcement theory, develop a sixth-month plan to help Oni increase the frequency of safe driving behaviors and reduce the number of drivers' traffic tickets and accidents.

2. When Medi-Health managers hire new employees, they look for people who they think will feel satisfied in the company's unique culture. Which needs and motives are best satisfied by the Medi-Health environment? Which are likely to be most quickly frustrated? Explain.

3. When organizations downsize and lay off employees, the survivors of the downsizing often have increased workloads. According to equity theory, what are some of the possible reactions of the survivors that managers should expect? What can managers do to discourage negative reactions that employees may have if they feel that they're being treated unfairly?

4. When designing compensation packages for employees who are sent on international assignments, many employers offer "hardship" pay to employees moving from the United States to less developed countries. According to the two-factor theory, is this practice likely to improve the satisfaction of such employees? Is it likely to improve the motivation of such employees? Why or why not?

5. After visiting **http://www.wholefoods.com**, describe how the design of jobs at this company fits its overall mission and values. What are the implications of the company's approach to job design for its overall organizational structure?

6. Think about a specific job that you've had. Use the integrative model of expectancy theory to explain your motivation and performance. What aspects of the situation were motivating for you? What aspects of the situation interfered with your performance? How could a manager have used expectancy theory to improve your motivation and/or your performance?

7. **Planning and Administration Competency.** Use job characteristics theory to analyze the motivational aspects of this course. Focus on one critical psychological state and develop a plan that your instructor could follow to enhance your feelings of meaningfulness, responsibility, or knowledge of results.

8. **Communication Competency.** For many firms, hiring qualified employees is a key strategic action. Unless firms can attract the very best talent, they won't be able to compete successfully. Increasingly, a company's Web site is one of its most valuable communication tools for attracting talent. Visit the home pages of several hi-tech companies. Evaluate how effective these companies are likely to be in getting people to apply for jobs with them and eventually to accept job offers from them. Select one company and offer three suggestions for how they could improve their electronic job posting and recruiting efforts. The home pages of three companies that you might visit are those of Etec Systems at **http://www.etec.com**, IBM at **http://www.ibm.com**, and Microsoft at **http://www.microsoft.com**.

CASE FOR COMPETENCY DEVELOPMENT

Motivating Hi-Tech Workers

Steve Dorner isn't a household name, but Eudora, the e-mail software he invented, is. In fact, more than 18 million people use Eudora, a product owned by Qualcomm, Dorner's employer. A telecommunications company based in San Diego, Qualcomm purchased licensing and development rights, and eventually the Eudora trademark, from the University of Illinois at Champaign–Urbana. The university was Dorner's employer when he invented Eurdora, and it held all rights to his invention. When the university sold those rights for just under $1 million, he received no royalties. His invention became the world's leading Internet e-mail package, providing complete connectivity among virtually all types of personal computers. Contrast Dorner's situation with that of Mark Andreesen, who was an undergraduate student at Illinois. While Dorner was working on Eudora, Andreesen was working on a software program called Mosaic. Mosaic eventually became Netscape Navigator. As founder and CEO of Netscape, Andreesen was a millionaire by age 24.

After Eudora became a Qualcomm product, Dorner gave up his position at the university to go to work for Qualcomm so that he could continue working on Eurdora. His wife didn't want to move to San Diego, however, so he arranged to be a telecommuter. Giving employees wide latitude and respect is central to Qualcomm's culture. For his first two years as a Qualcomm employee, Dorner chose to work in a small windowless room that had been built as a bomb shelter under his house and was entered through a trap door. Then he moved into the family's woodworking shop, which has windows and heat, but still affords the isolation needed for him to stay focused on his work. These conditions suit Dorner fine. "After working four years at home," he said, "I never want to move back to an office."

Software programming is highly skilled work. According to one expert, "It's a young person's skill. It requires intense concentration. To do a good job, you have to have your mind wrapped around the whole program. . . . You have to be constantly focused on the goal." Dorner enjoys the creative aspects of the task, which he says include "figuring out the real problem people are trying to solve and the best way to solve the problem." Dorner also enjoys the contact he has with Eudora users, who send him about 100 e-mail messages a day. "It's very gratifying," he says, "but it can also make me feel a little hunted sometimes. I'm the one who has to, in the final analysis, deal with every single problem."[47]

Questions

1. How might Steve Dorner use self-management to maintain a high level of motivation and productivity?

2. Telecommuting can pose some special motivation and communication challenges for managers. Based on what you've learned about motivation in this chapter, what types of information should managers communicate to telecommuters such as Steve Dorner? Why?

3. Imagine that you were working on a team project with Steve Dorner and several other coworkers. Which of the guidelines for managers described in this chapter would be most useful for ensuring that the team makes satisfactory progress toward their goals? Give specific examples of how a manager could apply these principles to motivate the team.

To learn more about Qualcomm, visit the company's home page at ***http://www.qualcomm.com***. To learn more about Eudora, visit its home page at ***http://www.eudora.com***.

VIDEO CASE

Valassis Communications

As one of the nation's leading marketing services companies, Valassis Communications offers a variety of door-to-door marketing services for consumer package goods companies and franchise retailers. Accounting for more than 75 percent of the company's revenues is its flagship product, Free-Standing Inserts (FSIs). These are four-color booklets containing coupons and other promotional offers from leading consumer package goods companies. Through its FSIs, Valassis reaches almost 60 million households each week via Sunday newspapers and distributes nearly 90 percent of all coupons in the United States.

The Valassis Impact Promotions (VIP) division provides franchise retailers with a variety of specialty promotions that can be customized in unique shapes and sizes, highly targeted, and distributed by a variety of methods (e.g., zoned newspapers and direct mail). The VIP customer base is growing to include food services, telecommunications, and retail franchises.

Through its Targeted Marketing Services division, Valassis provides newspaper-delivered product samples and advertising, geo-demographic targeting capabilities, run-of-press advertising, and targeted solo print promotions. Valassis is now expanding its database and Internet services through its 50 percent ownership in an online coupon site (Save.com) and a stake in the Relationship Marketing Group.

According to *Fortune* magazine, Valassis is also one of the "Best 100 Companies" to work for in the United States. This achievement is due largely to the company's policies and actions to motivate its employees, both individually and in groups. Valassis management views its key to success as having a culture that is fun—and where goal-oriented individuals are rewarded for achieving their goals—and an environment that embraces flexibility and change.

Valassis has a performance-driven culture. Its executives want all employees to feel and behave like they are owners of the company and to believe that they will share in the rewards of the company. The company's pay-for-performance plan includes (1) base salary, (2) fringe benefits, (3) profit sharing, (4) stock purchases, and (5) "champion pay."

Pay is not the only motivation used at Valassis. Others include celebration of past achievements, comfortable employee facilities, various types of recognition awards, and many other programs that together help make employees enjoy coming to work and brag about their employer in their community.

Questions

1. Describe "champion pay" and explain why it is used as a motivator at Valassis Communications.

2. In addition to champion pay, what other actions has Valassis taken to motivate its employees?

3. Does Valassis engage more in goal-setting or reinforcement motivational strategies?

To learn more about Valassis Communications, visit the company's home page at ***http://www.valassis.com***.

Dynamics of Leadership

LEARNING OBJECTIVES

AFTER STUDYING THIS CHAPTER YOU SHOULD BE ABLE TO:

1. STATE THE TYPES OF POWER AND THEIR USE BY LEADERS.

2. DESCRIBE THE PERSONAL TRAITS ASSOCIATED WITH EFFECTIVE LEADERS.

3. EXPLAIN THE BEHAVIORS OF EFFECTIVE AND INEFFECTIVE LEADERS.

4. IDENTIFY CONTINGENCIES THAT MAY BE IMPORTANT TO THE EFFECTIVENESS OF LEADERS.

5. STATE THE KEY CHARACTERISTICS OF TRANSFORMATIONAL LEADERS.

6. DESCRIBE HOW ORGANIZATIONS DEVELOP LEADERS.

Chapter Outline

PREVIEW: DAVID POTTRUCK OF CHARLES SCHWAB

LEADERSHIP AND POWER
TYPES OF POWER
USE OF POWER

TRAITS AND LEADERS
EMOTIONAL INTELLIGENCE
SELF-MANAGEMENT COMPETENCY: Jack Morris's Emotional Intelligence
ETHICAL LEADERSHIP

BEHAVIORS AND LEADERS
THEORY X AND THEORY Y
MANAGERIAL GRID MODEL
COMMUNICATION COMPETENCY: From No to Yo!

CONTINGENCIES AND LEADERS
HERSEY AND BLANCHARD'S SITUATIONAL LEADERSHIP MODEL
VROOM–JAGO TIME-DRIVEN LEADERSHIP MODEL
TEAMWORK COMPETENCY: Conoco's Empowered Teams

TRANSFORMATIONAL LEADERS
VISIONARY
INSPIRATIONAL
THOUGHTFUL
CONSIDERATE
TRUSTWORTHY
CONFIDENT
STRATEGIC ACTION COMPETENCY: Ken Chenault of American Express

LEADERSHIP DEVELOPMENT
ON-THE-JOB LEARNING
ASSESSMENT AND TRAINING
COACHING AND MENTORING

CHAPTER SUMMARY

KEY TERMS

QUESTIONS FOR DISCUSSION AND COMPETENCY DEVELOPMENT

COMPETENCY DEVELOPMENT: YOUR LEADERSHIP STYLE PREFERENCE

VIDEO CASE: SUNSHINE CLEANING SYSTEMS

DAVID POTTRUCK OF CHARLES SCHWAB

David Pottruck is the president and co-CEO of the Charles Schwab Corporation. The mission of Schwab is "to provide customers with the most useful and ethical financial services in the world." Schwab has more than 18,000 employees located in some 360 offices and is a major provider of discount financial services via telephone and the Internet.

At one time, Pottruck's single-mindedness threatened his career. When he was head of marketing at Schwab back in the 1980s, then-president Larry Stupski told him he was "too forceful." Determined to win at all costs, Pottruck often bulldozed his way through colleagues' misgivings, rather than giving their opinions more consideration. Looking back, Pottruck says he was "too competitive; too driven, making everybody around me feel uncomfortable; a person whom a lot of my colleagues found oftentimes unappealing."

Pottruck began to change himself, an effort that he says is continuing. He states: "The role of leadership will either bring out the best in you or take you down." Dawn Lepore, the chief information officer (CIO) and vice chairperson at Schwab comments in reference to Pottruck: "If you're going to be leading a fast-paced company, you've got to be learning on the fly and reinventing the company. And to reinvent the company, you have to reinvent yourself."

Observers laud Pottruck's ability to anticipate change and act on it. "Schwab is a culture of change—of continual reinvention," says Harvard University Professor F. Warren McFarlan, who has studied the company's culture. Pottruck, he says, is "passionate about change, and those personal skills [around self-reinvention] are critical to that." Pottruck notes: "You cannot be successful in the technology world if you're not willing to change. You can't be a one-trick pony."

Beth Sawi, Schwab's chief administrative officer (CAO) and executive vice president, comments: "He's always had drive and energy, but he's matured as a leader." Back in the 1980s, when she worked for Pottruck in marketing, she found his hard-driving style difficult. "Every time I saw him, I'd come away with a long, long list of new things to do. It was just overwhelming. I felt like I couldn't win with this guy." Others felt the same, and in an effort to make him prioritize tasks, Pottruck's staff presented him with cutouts of a light bulb—for ideas that were just things to think about—and a gun—for things they had to "get done or else." Sawi recalls: "We said, 'You don't even have to say anything, just wave whichever one it is.' He has a very good sense of humor, and he's very good at accepting feedback. To this day he says, 'This is a gun; this is a light bulb.' "

Pottruck notes: "We have a very clear sense of what we need to do and we have been pursuing that path with relentlessness." Relentlessness but not ruthlessness. Pottruck says that modeling ethical behavior is a prime part of every business leader's job. "This is not an easy thing to do because we all have our weak moments. But we strive to be the best we can be. That's the responsibility that comes with the job. If you don't want the responsibility, don't take the job."[1]

To learn more about the Charles Schwab Corporation, visit the company's home page at

http://www.schwab.com

LEADERSHIP AND POWER

1.

STATE THE TYPES OF POWER AND THEIR USE BY LEADERS.

Leadership involves influencing others to strive to achieve one or more goals.[2] As David Pottruck learned, managers can't be leaders if they simply pressure or coerce others to comply with their wishes. Leadership focuses on interpersonal relationships, not simply the organization's strategies, systems, and structure. When Pottruck was a manager, he relied only on administrative controls. As a leader, Pottruck now inspires trust and constantly encourages others to innovate. He now listens and asks "what" and "why" questions. As a manager and leader, Pottruck has always strived to model ethical behaviors. As a leader, Pottruck has encouraged and supported leadership and risk taking throughout the organization. He comments that "I don't worry about failed projects. I worry about missed opportunities. . . . I worry about how we prevent our culture from being compromised or dissipated as we continue to grow so fast. We also don't want to lose our nimbleness, our ability to innovate, because we've started playing it safe or developed an arrogance about ourselves."[3]

David Pottruck's development as a leader is very instructive. First, he demonstrates that the multiple competencies needed to be an effective leader can be learned. Second, he reveals the importance of trust in leader–follower relationships. Third, he shows that leaders need to articulate and clarify the general direction and goals for followers. Fourth, he practices open, two-way communication. Fifth, he encourages and supports risk taking and innovation. Finally, he illustrates that leaders use various sources of power.

TYPES OF POWER

Power is the ability to influence the behavior of others. Leaders exercise power, and effective leaders know how to use it wisely. The types of power exercised by a leader reveal a great deal about why others follow that individual. One useful framework for understanding the power of leaders comprises five types of power: legitimate, reward, coercive, referent, and expert.[4] Effective leaders are likely to use all five types of power at various times.

Legitimate Power. *Legitimate power* is influence based on the leader's formal position in the organization's hierarchy. Access to resources, information, and key decision makers gives some leaders legitimate power in influencing events and passing information and rewards to subordinates. Such leaders are often said to have clout or political influence within an organization. Legitimate power can

- enable the hiring of a job candidate,
- obtain approval for expenditures beyond the budget,
- provide easy access to top people in the company, and
- ensure knowing early about important decisions and policy shifts.

Reward Power. *Reward power* is influence based on a leader's ability to satisfy followers' needs in return for performance of desired behaviors and results. In other words, employees act on a leader's requests or orders in the belief that their behaviors will be rewarded. The leader may be able to reward them with favorable job assignments, preferred vacation schedules, promotions, and/or pay raises.

Coercive Power. *Coercive power* is influence based on the ability of a leader to obtain compliance through fear or punishment. Punishment may take the form of official reprimands, less-desirable work assignments, pay cuts, demotions, suspensions, or even termination. Scott Rudin is the notoriously unpleasant producer of hit movies such as *The Truman Show* and *In & Out*. He is infamous for verbally abusing staffers, throwing phones, and demanding 16-hour workdays and 7-day workweeks. His former employees provide scathing reviews of him but insist that their names not be used. They say, "I would like to still work in this town." One of his former employees commented, "I think the people that work there—most of them hate him. Nobody likes him, everybody's miserable." Rudin is able to verbally abuse his employees because there are 100 applicants for every job. He pays enormous salaries for entry-level jobs—$70,000 to $100,000 (high reward power), and he doesn't mind seeing his staff turn over every two years.[5] Coercive power usually is less effective than reward power for the same reasons that punishment has a limited effect as a motivator (see Chapter 14). Some employees respond to coercion by falsifying performance reports, stealing company property, and exhibiting similar negative behavior, rather than improving their performance.

Referent Power. *Referent power* is influence based on followers' personal identification with the leader. The followers are apt to like, admire, and want to emulate the leader. Referent power usually is possessed by leaders who have admirable personal characteristics, charisma, and/or excellent reputations. To Dawn Lepore and numerous others at Schwab, David Pottruck has referent power. Lepore and Pottruck go back 16 years. She says that he taught her about the importance of building strong relationships and personal loyalty: "He leads with his heart as well as his head."[6]

Expert Power. *Expert power* is influence based on leader's knowledge and competencies. It is a key source of power for managers at the present time and will continue to be so in the future. Subordinates act on the leader's recommendations because of the leader's knowledge.

Since 1996, Schwab has been recasting itself as an Internet company on a brick-and-mortar base that includes more than 350 branches. "Schwab is writing the book" on Internet integration, says John Payne, a consultant at Cerulli Associates, Inc., a Boston-based research and consulting firm. Schwab currently manages about 42 percent of total online assets, or more than twice as much as its nearest rival. The leader of much of that success is Pottruck, who is in charge of executing Schwab's vision. Schwab's IT strategy is rooted in Pottruck's image of the company as "a technology firm that happens to be in the financial services business." Pottruck learned the ropes as an IT project manager at Citibank during the 1970s and has kept up with technology trends ever since. "He has such a keen knowledge and appreciation for technology that he's a wonderful thinking partner," Lepore says.[7] Also, recall Warren McFarlan's description of Pottruck in the Preview Case: Pottruck is "passionate about change, and those personal skills [around self-reinvention] are critical to that."

USE OF POWER

WEB INSIGHT

Leadership in Practice is an online magazine published quarterly. Read one of the main features in an issue of this magazine. What insights are provided on using power effectively? Go to *http://www.leadersandleadership.com/*.

A leader's use of different types of power, or clout, can lead to one of three types of behavior in employees: commitment, compliance, or resistance. *Committed* employees are enthusiastic about meeting their leader's expectations and strive to do so. Employees who merely *comply* with their leader's requests will do only what has to be done—usually without much enthusiasm. In most cases, *resistance* by employees will be expressed as appearing to respond to their leader's requests while not actually doing so or even intentionally delaying or sabotaging plans.[8]

Figure 15.1 suggests that expert and referent power tend to result in employee commitment, legitimate and reward power tend to result in compliance, and coercive power tends to result in resistance. Referent power usually leads to high levels of performance. Hence effective leaders are likely to rely on expert, referent, and reward power and use legitimate and coercive power only minimally. Legitimate power is effective when a manager simply requires an employee to perform a task that is within the employee's capabilities and job description. In some situations, coercive power may be effective in getting employees to comply with rules. In general, however, when leaders threaten or punish, the response is anger.

| *Figure 15.1* | **Consequences of Using Five Types of Power** |

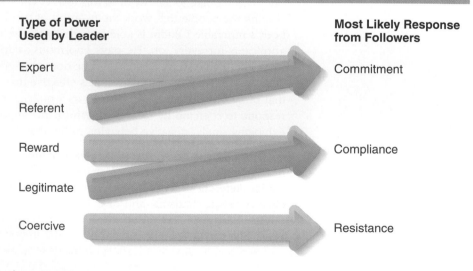

Various models and approaches explain and prescribe how effective leaders influence others. There is no single or simple answer to which style of leadership approach works best. We have grouped the models and approaches into four main categories: traits, behavioral, contingency, and transformational. Fifty years ago, traits models of leadership were the most popular. Gradually, the traits models were supplemented by behavioral models and then by contingency models. Currently, the transformational model has a large number of supporters, reflecting efforts of many leaders to transform outdated forms of organization into more competitive ones. In addition to the traits model, most models, especially the transformation model, identify various traits required for effective leadership.

TRAITS AND LEADERS

2.

DESCRIBE THE PERSONAL TRAITS ASSOCIATED WITH EFFECTIVE LEADERS.

Traits are the personal characteristics of individuals, including their physical, social, and personal attributes. Individuals' traits, when taken together, generally lead them to behave in fairly predictable ways over time and in various situations, and other people tend to describe them in those terms. The **traits model** suggests that the presence and absence of certain individual characteristics distinguish leaders from nonleaders. Of the many approaches to identifying—and perspectives of—traits for effective leadership, we briefly consider two: emotional intelligence and ethical leadership.

EMOTIONAL INTELLIGENCE

In recent years, the term *emotional intelligence* has received much attention for conveying traits of effective individuals, especially those in leadership roles. However, there is no agreed upon definition of the term.[9] For our purposes, **emotional intelligence** is a group of abilities and traits that enable individuals to recognize and understand their own and others' feelings and emotions and to use these insights to guide their own thinking and actions.[10] A number of traits have been included under the broad umbrella of emotional intelligence. When applied to leadership effectiveness, emotional intelligence includes traits such as the following.

- *Self-monitoring.* The ability to see the impact one has on people and to adapt.
- *Confidence.* The ability to recognize and appreciate one's own strengths and those of others.
- *Self-control.* The ability to rein in one's ego and desire for personal dominance.
- *Genuineness.* The ability to respect, and project, one's own authenticity.
- *Empathy.* The ability to understand, and work with, the needs and motivations of others.
- *Ownership.* The ability to accept responsibility for one's actions and their consequences.[11]

These traits and abilities should look familiar. They are aspects of several of our managerial competencies, including communication competency, teamwork competency, and self-management competency.

Please complete the brief questionnaire shown in Table 15.1, which illustrates traits of emotional intelligence.[12] Are your coworkers, manager, and close friends likely to rank you this way? When someone's emotional intelligence is being assessed in a work setting with a comprehensive questionnaire, a neutral third party should administer the instrument to coworkers and the individual. If the person being assessed is a manager, the questionnaire would also be administered to the person's subordinates.

As illustrated by David Pottruck's emotional growth, individuals can improve the level of emotional intelligence.[13] The Self-Management Competency feature on page 408 reports on the development and use of emotional intelligence by a marketing director for a division of a global food company. To preserve anonymity, he is referred to as "Jack Morris."[14]

Directions: *As honestly as you can,* estimate how you rate in the eyes of peers, superiors, and subordinates (if any) on each of the following traits. Place the number next to each statement that corresponds to your estimate. Use the following scale.

1 = Strongly disagree; 2 = Disagree; 3 = Undecided; 4 = Agree; 5 = Strongly agree

———— 1. I give credit for the work and ideas of others.

———— 2. I will apologize to another person—and mean it—if I make a personal attack in the heat of an argument.

———— 3. I do not take advantage of others, even if I think it will make me look good.

———— 4. I try to put myself in the "other person's shoes" when listening.

———— 5. I respect and relate well to people of diverse backgrounds.

———— 6. When I am angry with others, I can tell them about it in a nonthreatening way.

———— 7. I usually stay composed, positive, and unflappable even in trying moments.

———— 8. I can think clearly and stay focused on the task at hand under pressure.

———— 9. I am able to admit my own mistakes.

———— 10. I usually meet commitments and keep promises.

———— 11. I hold myself accountable for meeting my goals.

———— 12. I regularly seek fresh ideas from a wide variety of sources.

———— 13. I help other people feel better when they are down.

———— 14. I'm results oriented, with a strong drive to meet my objectives.

———— 15. Other people find it easy to confide in me.

———— 16. I readily make sacrifices to meet an important organizational goal.

———— 17. I actively seek opportunities to further the overall goals of the organization and enlist others to help me.

———— 18. I pursue goals beyond what's required or expected of me in my current job.

———— 19. I seek fresh perspectives, even if that means trying something totally new.

———— 20. I operate from an expectation of success rather than a fear of failure.

Scoring: Add the points next to each trait. A score of 75 or less may suggest the need for considerable personal development in emotional intelligence.

SELF-MANAGEMENT COMPETENCY

Jack Morris's Emotional Intelligence

Jack Morris was a classic pacesetter: high energy, always striving to find better ways to get things done, and too eager to step in and take over. Worse, Morris was prone to pounce on anyone who didn't seem to meet his standards, flying off the handle if a person merely deviated from completing a job in the way Morris thought best.

His leadership style had predictably disastrous impacts on the work climate, employees, and results. After two years of stagnant performance, Morris's manager suggested that he find a coach. Morris wasn't pleased but, realizing that his own job was on the line, he complied.

The coach he selected was an expert in teaching people how to increase their emotional intelligence and began with a 360-degree evaluation of Morris. The coach believed that a diagnosis from multiple viewpoints is essential in improving emotional intelligence be-

cause those who need the most help usually have blind spots. Morris rated himself more glowingly than did his subordinates, who gave him especially low grades on emotional self-control and empathy. Initially, Morris had some trouble accepting this feedback. But when his coach showed him how those weaknesses were tied to his inability to display effective leadership, Morris realized that he had to improve if he wanted to advance in the company.

Once Morris had zeroed in on areas for improvement and committed himself to making the effort, he and his coach worked up a plan to turn his job into a day-by-day learning laboratory. For instance, Jack discovered that he was empathetic when things were calm but that he turned on others in a crisis. This tendency hampered his ability to listen to what people were telling him at the very time he most needed to do so. Morris's plan required him to focus on his behavior during tough situations. As soon as he felt himself tensing up, he was to step back immediately, let the other person speak, and then ask clarifying questions. The point was to not act judgmental or hostile under pressure.

The change didn't come easily, but with practice Morris learned to defuse his flare-ups by entering into a dialogue instead of launching an attack. Although he didn't always agree with them, at least he gave people a chance to make their case. At the same time, he also practiced giving his subordinates more positive feedback and reminding them of how their work contributed to the unit's goals. And he restrained himself from micromanaging them.

Morris met with his coach every week or two to review his progress and get advice on specific problems. For instance, occasionally Jack found himself falling back on old habits and tactics—cutting people off, jumping in to take over, and blowing up in a rage. Almost immediately, he would regret it. So he and his coach dissected those relapses to figure out what triggered his regression and what to do the next time a similar situation arose. Over a six-month period, Morris made real improvement. His own records showed that he had reduced the number of flare-ups. The work climate in his unit had improved sharply, and its performance numbers were starting to creep upward.

ETHICAL LEADERSHIP

Recall our lengthy consideration of ethical concepts and actions in Chapter 6. We stated that being an ethical person means having certain moral traits and basing behaviors, including decision making, on ethical principles. The traits that executives most often associate with ethical leadership are honesty, trustworthiness, and integrity. As one executive commented, "If the person truly doesn't believe the ethical story and preaches it but doesn't feel it . . . that's going to show through. . . . But, a true ethical leader walks in and it doesn't take very long if you haven't met him before you think there's a person with integrity and candor and honesty."[15]

The comments that his colleagues and others made about David Pottruck suggest that employees at Schwab see him as an ethical leader. He expresses honestly his expectations of others. Because employees trust him, they are able to give him feedback about his leadership without fearing reprisals. He embraces the need for ethical behavior: "This is not an easy thing to do because we all have our weak moments. But we strive to be the best we can be. That's the responsibility that comes with the job. If you don't want the responsibility, don't take the job."

BEHAVIORS AND LEADERS

3.

EXPLAIN THE BEHAVIORS OF EFFECTIVE AND INEFFECTIVE LEADERS.

Behavioral models of leadership focus on differences in the actions of effective and ineffective leaders. In other words, they are based on what effective and ineffective leaders actually do: how they delegate tasks to subordinates, where and when they communicate with others, how they perform their roles, and so on. Thus traits are often associated with particular behaviors. Because leadership behaviors can be learned, individuals can become effective leaders with the proper encouragement and support.

THEORY X AND THEORY Y

Assumptions and beliefs about individuals and how to motivate them often influence a leader's behavior. One of the most widely cited and recognized models for recognizing differences in these assumptions and beliefs is Theory X and Theory Y, developed by Douglas McGregor in 1957. He coined these labels as a way of contrasting the conventional view of leadership in organizations with a view based on more adequate assumptions about human nature and human motivation.

Theory X Propositions. McGregor suggested that *Theory X* is a composite of propositions and underlying beliefs that take a command and control view of management based on a negative view of human nature. These propositions include the following.

- Management is responsible for organizing the elements of productive enterprise—money, materials, equipment, and people—in the interest of economic ends.

- With respect to people, management is a process of directing their efforts, motivating them, controlling their actions, and modifying their behaviors to fit the needs of the organization.

- Without active intervention by management, people would be passive—even resistant—to organizational needs. They must therefore be persuaded, rewarded, punished, and their activities controlled. Doing so is management's task—in managing both subordinate managers and employees.

Underlying these propositions, McGregor identified five beliefs that he contended many leaders hold, often implicitly, about people in general and their employees in particular. These underlying beliefs are as follows.

- People (employees) are by nature lazy—they work as little as possible.

- People (employees) lack ambition, dislike responsibility, and prefer to be led.

- People (employees) are inherently self-centered and indifferent to organizational needs.

- People (employees) are by nature resistant to change.

- People (employees) are gullible, not very bright, the ready dupe of the charlatan and the demagogue.[16]

When he published his propositions on Theory X and Theory Y in 1957, McGregor concluded:

> The human side of economic enterprise today is fashioned from propositions and beliefs such as these. Conventional organization structures, managerial policies, practices, and programs reflect these assumptions. . . . Management by direction and control . . . fails under today's conditions to provide effective motivation of human effort toward organizational objectives. It fails because direction and control are useless methods of motivating people whose physiological and safety needs are reasonably satisfied and whose social, egoistic, and self-fulfillment needs are predominant.[17]

Theory Y Propositions. McGregor contended that a different view of managing employees was needed—one based on more adequate assumptions about human nature and human motivation. *Theory Y* is a composite of propositions and beliefs that take a leadership and empowering view of management based on a positive view of human nature. These propositions and beliefs include the following.

1. Management is responsible for organizing the elements of productive enterprise—money, materials, equipment, and people—in the interest of economic ends.

2. Employees are *not* by nature passive or resistant to organizational needs. They have become so as a result of their experiences in organizations.

3. The motivation, the potential for development, the capacity for assuming responsibility, and the readiness to direct behavior toward organizational goals are all present in employees. Management does not put them there. It is management's responsibility to make it possible for people to recognize and develop these human characteristics for themselves.

4. The essential task of management is to arrange organizational conditions and methods of operation so that people can achieve their own goals *best* by directing *their own* efforts to achieve organizational objectives.[18]

According to McGregor:

*[Theory Y] involves a process primarily of creating opportunities, releasing potential, removing obstacles, encouraging growth, providing guidance. . . . And I hasten to add that it does **not** involve the abdication of management, the absence of leadership, the lowering of standards. . . . Theory X places exclusive reliance upon external control of human behavior, whereas Theory Y relies heavily on self-control and self-direction. It is worth noting that this difference is the difference between treating people as children and treating them as mature adults.*[19]

These seminal perspectives on Theory X and Theory Y spawned many new models, concepts, and approaches to management and leadership. Theory Y propositions are fundamental to major parts of our chapters on human resource management, change and innovation, motivation, leadership, communication, teams, organizational culture, and workplace diversity.

MANAGERIAL GRID MODEL

Developed by Robert Blake and Jane Mouton, the ***managerial grid model*** identifies five leadership styles that combine different degrees of concern for production and concern for people.[20] The model's optimal leadership style is based on Theory Y propositions and beliefs.

The five styles are plotted on the grid shown in Figure 15.2. At the lower left hand corner of the grid (point 1, 1) is the *impoverished style,* which is characterized by low concern for both people and production. The primary goal of managers who use this style is to stay out of trouble. They pass orders along to employees, go with the flow, and make sure that they can't be held accountable for mistakes. They exert the minimum effort required to get the work done and avoid being demoted or fired.

Figure 15.2   ***The Managerial Grid Model***

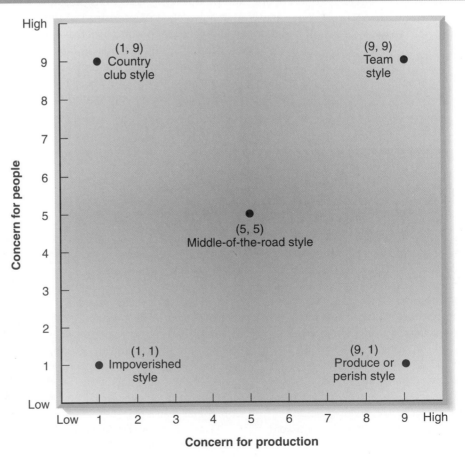

At the upper left-hand corner (point 1, 9) is the *country club style,* which is characterized by a high concern for people and a low concern for production. Managers who use this style try to create a secure, comfortable atmosphere and trust that their subordinates will respond with high performance. Attention to the need for satisfying relationships leads to a friendly, if not necessarily productive, atmosphere and work tempo.

A high concern for production and a low concern for people are reflected in the *produce or perish style* at the lower right-hand corner (point 9, 1). Managers who use this style don't consider employees' personal needs to be relevant to achieving the organization's objectives. In addition to tying pay to performance, they use their legitimate and coercive powers to pressure subordinates to meet production goals. They believe that operational efficiency results from arranging the work so that employees merely have to follow orders. When a company's profitability is falling, showing more concern for production may seem like the best thing a manager can do to turn the company around. This style is consistent with Theory X. Effective leaders realize that this approach is only a short-term solution, however.

At the middle of the grid (point 5, 5) is the *middle-of-the road style.* Managers who use this style seek a balance between workers' needs and the organization's productivity goals. Adequate performance is obtained by maintaining employee morale at a level sufficient to get the work done.

WEB INSIGHT

Team Leadership & Development is a firm committed to creating positive change within organizations by developing leadership skills. Describe its intervention program for developing team leaders. Go to *http://www.tlandd.com/*.

At the upper right-hand corner of the grid (point 9, 9) is the *team style.* It reflects high levels of concern for both people and production. Consistent with Theory Y, leaders who use this style attempt to establish teamwork and foster feelings of commitment among workers. By introducing a "common stake" in the organization's purposes, the leader builds relationships of trust and respect.

The following Communication Competency feature illustrates one of the many ways that Katherine Hudson communicates a high concern for both people and production.[21] Hudson is president and CEO of the Brady Corporation, headquartered in Milwaukee, Wisconsin. The firm provides solutions to problems of identification, including 30,000 products such as high-performance labels, signs and tapes, software, and printing systems. Hudson joined Brady in 1994 after 24 years in leadership roles at Eastman Kodak. She has received a number of awards for her leadership, including being named to the CIO Magazine Hall of Fame as one of the 12 most influential chief information officers during the 1990s.

COMMUNICATION COMPETENCY

From No to Yo!

From "No to Yo!" This is the welcoming phrase provided by Katherine Hudson in the President's Message on Brady Corporation's Web site. A strong sense of her communication competency and leadership style is reflected in this message, a portion of which follows.

Welcome to Brady Corporation's Website. I'm Katherine Hudson, president and CEO. As you surf this site, you'll learn about Brady's great products, great people, and our commitment to adding value in everything we do.

I was recently asked what one word would best describe the culture at

Brady Corporation. For us, the word is "Yo!" It's our corporate cheer. It means saying "yes" to change, information sharing, and cooperation. All of us at Brady are committed to working together in this spirit. It has moved us from an internal focus to a passion for our customers, from choosing between quality and speed to insisting on both, from competing internally to working together, and from focusing on short-term, line-item results to building for long-term, overall results.

In addition to operating under this concept of "Yo!," we also follow our five

Brady principles or *guiding values* to drive our decisions every day:

- Teamwork—We work together to achieve our vision.
- Customer Focus—We put our customers at the center of everything we do.
- Growth—We strive to grow our business and our capabilities as a company and as individuals.

- Value—By creating value for our customers, we create sustainable, long-term value for our shareholders.
- Honesty—Integrity is never compromised.

We believe that these are universally understood by all of our employees, customers and, of course, shareholders as the culture that will take us forward into the 21st century.

• • •

To learn more about the Brady Corporation, visit the company's home page at

http://www.bradycorp.com

Behavioral models have added to the understanding and practice of leadership. The focus has grown from who leaders *are* (traits) to what leaders *do* (behaviors). However, leadership behaviors that are effective in one situation aren't necessarily effective in another. Because the behavioral models failed to uncover leadership styles that were consistently effective in all situations, other models of leadership emerged. The next stage in the evolution of knowledge about leadership was the creation of contingency, or situational, models.

CONTINGENCIES AND LEADERS

4.

IDENTIFY CONTINGENCIES THAT MAY BE IMPORTANT TO THE EFFECTIVENESS OF LEADERS.

According to **contingency models** of leadership, the situation determines the best style to use.[22] Here we discuss two of the many contingency models of leadership: Hersey and Blanchard's situational model and the Vroom–Jago time-driven leadership model.

HERSEY AND BLANCHARD'S SITUATIONAL LEADERSHIP MODEL

Hersey and Blanchard's situational leadership model states that the levels of directive (similar to production centered) and supportive (similar to people centered) leader behaviors should be based on the level of readiness of the followers.[23]

Directive behavior occurs when a leader relies on one-way communication, spelling out duties and telling followers what to do and where, when, and how to do it. Directive leaders structure, control, and supervise employees.

Supportive behavior occurs when a leader relies on two-way communication, listening, encouraging, and involving followers in decision making. Being supportive doesn't mean just being nice. Katherine Hudson eliminates barriers to success by providing employees with the means to achieve their goals but, at the same time, demands excellence.

The contingency in this model is the degree of follower readiness. *Readiness* is a follower's ability to set high but attainable task-related goals and a willingness to accept responsibility for reaching them. Readiness is related to the task and not to the person's age. People have varying degrees of readiness, depending on their maturity, expertise, and experience in relation to the specific tasks that they undertake.

This model prescribes different combinations of directive and supportive leader behaviors for different levels of subordinates' readiness. Figure 15.3 portrays the relationship between Hersey and Blanchard's leadership styles and levels of follower readiness. The curve running through the four leadership quadrants (S4–S1) indicates the level of directive and/or supportive behavior that characterizes each style. The readiness level of the individual or team ranges from low to high.

WEB INSIGHT

The Center for Leadership Studies was founded by Paul Hersey. Go to its Web site at *http://www.situational.com/*, click "Leadership," and then click "Dr. Paul." Read the full interview of Dr. Hersey. Describe four additional insights you gained about this model.

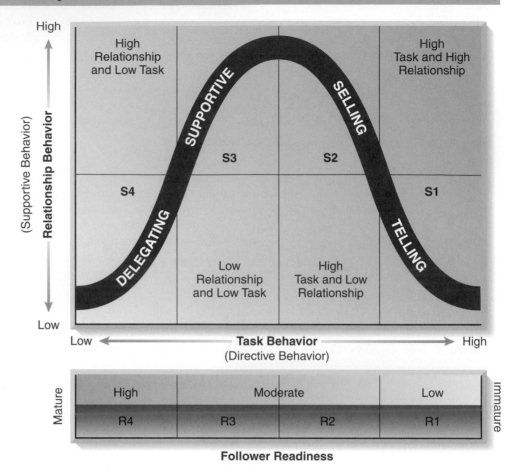

Follower Readiness

Leadership Styles. In using a ***telling style,*** the leader provides clear instructions and specific direction. When an employee first enters an organization, telling leadership may be most appropriate according to this model. Newcomers usually are committed, enthusiastic, and energetic. They are anxious to get started and learn. Because commitment is high, a lot of support from the leader isn't needed or appropriate.

As employees learn their jobs, a telling style is still considered important because the employees aren't yet ready to assume total responsibility for doing their jobs. However, a leader needs to begin using supportive behaviors in order to build employees' confidence and maintain their enthusiasm. In using a ***selling style,*** the leader provides direction, encourages two-way communication, and helps build confidence and motivation on the part of the follower. The leader still has responsibility for and controls decision making.

When followers feel confident performing their tasks and are ready to do so, the leader no longer needs to be directive. The leader maintains open communication by actively listening and assisting in followers' efforts to use what they have learned. In using a ***supportive style,*** the leader is encouraging and helpful to subordinates.

In using a ***delegating style,*** the leader sees followers as highly ready to accomplish particular tasks and both competent and motivated to take full responsibility for them. Even though the leader may still identify problems, the responsibility for carrying out plans is given to these mature followers. They are permitted to manage projects and decide how, when, and where tasks are to be done.

Assessment. Hersey and Blanchard's model has several limitations. First, can a manager actually change leadership style with each different situation? The answer to this question has important implications for managerial selection, placement, and promotion. Some people can read situations better and adapt their leadership style more effectively than others. For those who can't, what are the costs of training them to be able to do so? Do these costs exceed the potential benefits? Second, in a team, different employees are likely to be at different levels of readiness. Under this condition, what is the best leadership style? Finally, the model doesn't attempt to explain why employees at the same level of readiness perform differently. Does variation in performance reflect a lack of motivation, a lack of skills and abilities, or some combination of both?[24]

Hersey and Blanchard's situational leadership model has generated quite a bit of interest among practitioners and researchers, who are trying to find answers to at least some of the questions we posed.[25] The idea that leaders should be flexible with respect to the leadership style they use is appealing. An inexperienced employee may perform as well as an experienced employee if properly directed and closely supervised. An appropriate leadership style should also help followers gain more experience and become more competent. Thus, as a leader helps followers assume (acquire) more readiness, leadership style also needs to evolve. Therefore this model requires the leader to be constantly monitoring the maturity level of followers in order to determine the combination of directive and supportive behaviors that is most appropriate—not an easy task.

VROOM–JAGO TIME-DRIVEN LEADERSHIP MODEL

The ***Vroom–Jago time-driven leadership model*** prescribes a leader's choice(s) among five leadership styles based on seven contingency variables, recognizing the time requirements and other costs associated with each style.[26]

Contingency Variables. The Vroom–Jago time-driven leadership model focuses on seven contingency variables that should be assessed by the leader to determine which leadership style to use. Victor Vroom developed a Windows-based computer program called Expert System that enables a leader to record judgments about the extent to which a factor is present in a particular situation. A five-point scale is used: specifically, 5 = high presence, 3 = moderate presence, and 1 = low presence. We simplified the presentation here by using only a "high" or a "low" presence.

The seven contingency variables are as follows.

- *Decision significance*—the degree to which the problem is highly important and a quality decision is imperative. In brief, how important is the technical quality of this decision?

- *Importance of commitment*—the degree to which employees' personal willingness to support the decision has an impact on the effectiveness of implementation. Employees are more likely to implement enthusiastically a decision that is consistent with their goals, values, and understanding of the problem. In brief, how important is employee commitment to the decision?

- *Leader expertise*—the degree to which the leader has relevant information and competencies to understand the problem fully and select the best solution. In brief, does the leader believe that he or she has the ability and information to make a high-quality decision?

- *Likelihood of commitment*—the degree to which followers will support the leader's decision if it is made. Employees who trust the judgments of their leaders are more likely to be committed to the decision, even if they were not heavily involved in making it. In brief, if the leader were to make the decision, would employees likely be committed to it?

- *Team support*—the degree to which employees relate to the interests of the organization as a whole or a specific unit in solving the problem. In brief, do subordinates share the goals to be achieved by solving this problem?

- *Team expertise*—the degree to which the employees have the relevant information and competencies to understand fully the problem and select the best solution to it. In brief, does the leader believe that subordinates have the abilities and information to make a high-quality decision?

- *Team competence*—the degree to which team members have the abilities needed to resolve conflicts over preferred solutions and to work together in reaching a high-quality decision. In brief, are team members capable of handling their own decision-making process?

Leadership Styles. This model identifies five core leadership styles that vary in terms of the levels of decision-making freedom and participation available to a leader's subordinates. These styles are summarized in increasing levels of discretion and participation.

- *Decide style*—The leader makes the decision and either announces or sells it to the team. The leader may use his or her expertise and/or collect information from the team or others whom the leader believes can help solve the problem. The role of employees is clearly one of providing specific information that the leader requests, rather than generating or evaluating solutions.

- *Consult individually style*—The leader presents the problem to team members individually, getting their ideas and suggestions without bringing them together as a group. Then the leader makes the decision. This decision may or may not reflect the team members' influence.

- *Consult team style*—The leader presents the problem to team members in a meeting, gets their suggestions, and then makes the decision. This decision may or may not reflect the team members' suggestions.

- *Facilitate style*—The leader presents the problem to the team in a meeting and acts as a facilitator, defining the problem to be solved and the constraints within which the decision must be made. The objective is to get concurrence on a decision. Above all, the leader takes care to ensure that his or her ideas are not given any greater weight than those of others simply because of his or her position on the team. The leader's role is much like that of chairperson, coordinating the discussion, keeping it focused on the problem, and being sure that all the essential issues are discussed. The leader doesn't try to influence the team to adopt a particular solution and is willing to accept and implement any solution that the entire team supports.

- *Delegate style*—The leader permits the team to make the decision within prescribed limits. The team undertakes the identification and diagnosis of the problem, developing alternative procedures for solving it and deciding on one or more alternative solutions. The leader doesn't enter into the team's deliberations unless explicitly asked, but behind the scenes plays an important role, providing needed resources and encouragement. This style represents the highest level of subordinate discretion and participation.

Integrating Contingencies with Styles. The matrix shown in Table 15.2 integrates the model's seven contingencies with its five leadership styles.[27] This matrix begins on the left where the leader evaluates the significance of the problem—high (H) or low (L). The column headings denote the contingency variables that may or may not be present. The leader progresses across the matrix by selecting H or L for each relevant contingency variable. After determining the significance of the decision, the leader then evaluates the degree (H or L) to which employee commitment is important to implementation of the decision. Proceeding across the matrix, the leader records an H or L for only those contingency factors that call for a judgment, until the recommended leadership style is reached.

Decision Time. Leaders often must make decisions when time is of the essence. For example, air traffic control supervisors, emergency rescue squad leaders, and nuclear energy plant managers may have little time to get inputs from others before having to make a decision. The *decision-time penalty* is the negative result of decisions not being

Table 15.2 The Vroom–Jago Time-Driven Leadership Model

Problem	Decision Significance	Importance of Commitment	Leader Expertise	Likelihood of Commitment	Team Support	Team Expertise	Team Competence	Suggested Style
H	H	H	H	H	—	—	—	Decide
				L	H	H	H	Delegate
					H	H	L	Consult Team
					H	L	—	
					L	—	—	
			L	H	H	H	H	Facilitate
					H	H	L	Consult Individually
					H	L	—	
					L	—	—	
				L	H	H	H	Facilitate
					H	H	L	Consult Team
					H	L	—	
					L	—	—	
		L	H	—	—	—	—	Decide
			L	—	H	H	—	Facilitate
					H	L	—	Consult Individually
					L	—	—	
L	L	H	—	—	H	—	—	Decide
					L	—	H	Delegate
					L	—	L	Facilitate
		L	—	—	—	—	—	Decide

Note: An "H" indicates a high level of importance with that contingency variable, an "L" indicates a low level of importance, and a dashed line (—) indicates "not a factor."

made when needed. It is low when there are no severe pressures on the leader to make a quick decision.

Negative effects on what Vroom and Jago call "human capital" occur because the delegate and consult styles (especially the consult team version) use time and energy, which can be translated into costs even if there are no severe time constraints. Many managers spend almost 70 percent of their time in meetings and that time always has a value, although the precise costs of meetings vary with the reasons for them.

If participation has potential negative effects on human capital, it can also have positive effects, as discussed in Chapters 14 and 17. Participative leader behaviors help develop the technical and managerial competencies of employees, build teamwork, and foster loyalty and commitment to organizational goals. The Vroom–Jago model considers the trade-offs among four criteria by which a leader's decision-making style can be evaluated: decision quality, employee commitment to implementation, costs, and employee development. The consult and delegate styles are viewed as most supportive of employee development and commitment.

Assessment. If leaders can diagnose contingencies correctly, choosing the best leadership style for those situations becomes easier. These choices, in turn, will enable them to make high-quality, timely decisions. If the situation requires delegation, the leader must learn how to establish the desired goals and limitations and then let employees determine how best to achieve the goals within those limitations. If the situation calls for the leader alone to make the decision, the leader should be aware of potential positive and negative consequences of not asking others for their input.

This model does have limitations. First, most employees have a strong desire to participate in decisions affecting their jobs, regardless of the model's recommendation of a leadership style. If subordinates aren't involved in a decision, they are more likely to become frustrated and not be committed to the decision. Second, certain competencies of the leader play a key role in determining the relative effectiveness of the model. For example, in situations involving conflict, only leaders skilled in conflict resolution may be able to use the kind of participative decision-making strategy suggested by the model. A leader who hasn't developed this competency may obtain better results with a more directive style, even though this style is different from the style that the model proposes. Third, the model is based on the assumption that a decision is a one-time occurrence and addresses a single problem. Often, however, decision making goes through several cycles and involves solutions to larger problems.

The following Teamwork Competency feature reveals how Conoco makes extensive use of the facilitate and delegate leadership styles through the use of empowered teams at its LiquidPower flow improver plant in Bryan, Texas.[28] Conoco's vision is "to be recognized around the world as a truly great, integrated, international energy company that gets to the future first."

TEAMWORK COMPETENCY

Conoco's Empowered Teams

At Conoco's LiquidPower flow improver plant in Bryan, Texas, *associates* (not employees) produce material that increases the flow of crude oil through pipelines. The few managers in the plant are called "resources." They are expected to act more like advisers and coaches than supervisors to unleash fully the "power" in empowered teams. Paul Chomka, plant manager, explains: "Everybody in the plant reports to the plant manager. You can't get any flatter than that." David Nelson, manager of worldwide organizational development and director of Conoco University, the internal training and development arm of Conoco, adds: "Getting empowered teams is not easy. It takes a commitment from all levels of the organization to succeed. Every day I hear new stories about how our teams have provided innovative solutions and breakthrough results that would not have been possible without truly empowered employees."

At Conoco, team leaders receive training before they are "thrown in" to a coaching or facilitating role. As one

manager put it, "It's like getting 4 years of training in 18 months, but we believe in the benefits of intensive training." Conoco also advocates the concept of "felt leadership." Chomka comments that "everyone at Conoco has the ability to lead and is expected to lead at certain times." He notes that such a system invites positive "push back," or the expression and resolution of conflicting ideas that are important to releasing the innovative ability of empowered teams.

Visitors at the Texas Conoco plant were surprised to see team members take action to solve an automation problem during a recent plant tour. One observer commented: "People came out of nowhere, nobody gave any orders, there was no supervision, everyone did the work that needed to be done, and when they were finished they all went back to their normal routine. And the most impressive part was that no one at Conoco seemed to think it was that big of a deal! What would have taken most facilities 2 or 3 hours to fix took only about 20 minutes."

Associates do all the hiring. Prospective new hires are evaluated, not so much on skills as on behaviors. According to Chomka, "Empowered teams are not right for everyone. We can train people on the skills but we're looking for people who 'fit' with our empowered system. No one can assess that better than our associates."

Chomka concludes: "I don't believe you ever actually finish implementing empowered teams. As soon as we get to where we think we should be, we redefine the vision, it becomes more complex, and we keep changing and growing as our market demands." Adds David Nelson, "The success of our teams is really a testament to both the team leaders, who had the courage to let go and trust, and the team members that have embraced not only increased autonomy but increased accountability as well."

• • •

To learn more about Conoco, visit the company's home page at

http://www.conoco.com

TRANSFORMATIONAL LEADERS

5.

STATE THE KEY CHARACTERISTICS OF TRANSFORMATIONAL LEADERS.

The leaders of some organizations have increasingly realized that leadership is more than a matter of certain traits, specific behaviors, or particular contingencies. It is all of those things, but much more. The people needed to guide organizations in these changing times are often called transformational leaders. **Transformational leaders** inspire others with their vision, often promote this vision over opposition, and demonstrate confidence in themselves and their views.[29] They take an active and personal approach to influencing others. Transformational leaders alter feelings, desires, and expectations of others. They change perceptions of the possible and desirable. These leaders develop new approaches to long-standing problems and new options to open issues. Transformational leaders reflect excitement and enthusiasm and generate the same in others. They embrace risks to pursue new opportunities. They are empathetic and intuitive in their ability to relate with others and, in general, are high in emotional intelligence.

Figure 15.4 outlines the interrelated characteristics of transformational leaders. In the remainder of this section we discuss these characteristics separately. However, each transformational leader is a unique mosaic of these characteristics, which cannot be easily identified and assessed individually in practice. Each transformational leader is likely to be stronger in terms of some characteristics than others, but all are likely to be present.[30]

Figure 15.4	**Common Characteristics of Transformational Leaders**

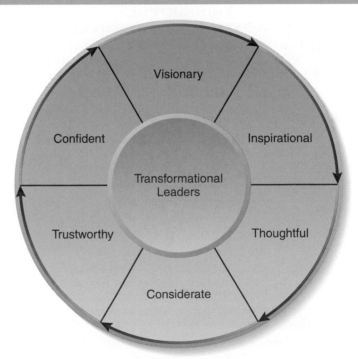

VISIONARY

Perhaps the dominant characteristic that transformational leaders possess is their ability to create a *vision* that binds people to each other and creates a new future. Dr. Martin Luther King, Jr.'s famous "I Have a Dream" speech galvanized a generation to support the civil rights movement in the United States. But transformational leaders must have more than just a vision. They also must have a road map for attaining it. What is important is that followers "buy into" that vision and that the leader has a plan to energize them to reach it.[31] Visionaries challenge old beliefs and ways of doing things. They strongly believe in their ideas, are able to communicate them clearly, and use them to excite others. Moreover, visionaries are typically intuitive, which has been described as "knowing something without knowing how we know it."[32]

INSPIRATIONAL

Transformational leaders are charismatic, but not all charismatic leaders are transformational leaders. A **charismatic leader** is a person who has the ability to influence others because of his or her inspirational qualities. The Greek word *kharisma* means "divine gift." Leaders with charisma have the power to obtain the devotion of followers. Followers of charismatic leaders attribute heroic and extraordinary abilities to them.[33] Charismatic leaders may benefit or harm an organization or society. Adolph Hitler was a charismatic leader to his followers but not to most people. He was an unethical, unbalanced, and immoral charismatic leader who focused on his own needs and was not open to criticism or suggestions.

Transformational leaders strive to be inspirational and ethical. They do not inspire others to follow them blindly. They listen carefully to followers, provide support and empowerment, and lead by example. They are flexible and open to criticism, but they will stand up for ideas even if they are unpopular.[34]

Over time, they inspire and develop their followers to become leaders. These leaders do not make fun of the opinions of others, regardless of their status and position. In essence, transformational leaders are role models for followers to emulate. Transformational leaders are the individuals whom people describe when asked to think about someone who had a major influence on their personal and professional development.

THOUGHTFUL

Transformational leaders are agents of thoughtful change and innovation. They challenge followers to build on their vision by offering innovative solutions and new ideas. They encourage positive thinking and problem solving. These leaders embrace taking risks, but base their actions on thoughtful analysis and discussion. Creativity is encouraged. Followers are expected and encouraged to question long-standing assumptions and practices. These leaders often focus on the "what" and "why" of problems, rather than the "who" on which to place blame. For these leaders, nothing is too good, too fixed, or too political that it can't be challenged or changed.

CONSIDERATE

Transformational leaders care about the needs of others and have a great capacity for empathy. They actively listen to concerns of employees, customers, suppliers, and the public. They are willing to accept responsibility when mistakes inevitably occur and do not look for scapegoats. They respect and value the contributions of all employees. Transformational leaders are often willing to sacrifice immediate personal gain for the benefit of others. They use their sources of power to move individuals and groups toward their visions but avoid the use of power for personal gain.[35]

TRUSTWORTHY

Transformational leaders strive to be ethical in their relations with others and are viewed as trustworthy. Employees who do not trust a leader will hesitate in following the leader's expressed vision and will interpret inspirational messages with skepticism. Transformational leaders are often known for their honesty under pressure, including straight talking and keeping commitments. They "walk the talk." In addition to being perceived as trustworthy, transformational leaders show trust in their followers. These leaders empower and delegate tasks to followers. They actively encourage a two-way flow of information and dialogue.[36]

CONFIDENT

Transformational leaders project optimism and self-confidence. Followers have to see that a leader is passionate about a vision and confident that it can be achieved—but not arrogant. Such leaders also exhibit confidence in their followers. They recognize that mistakes will be made and know that, if errors are not tolerated, followers will become too risk adverse.

Thus transformational leaders demonstrate a unique profile of traits, behaviors, and competencies. They aren't found only in top management positions in business organizations. They also are found in charitable organizations, civic and community groups, schools, student organizations, government agencies, small and large businesses, and every other type of organization. The individuals profiled in this chapter—David Pottruck of Charles Schwab Corporation, Katherine Hudson of Brady Corporation, and Paul Chomka of Conoco—can truly be called transformational leaders.

The following Strategic Action Competency feature reports on Ken Chenault who was appointed chairman and CEO of American Express in 2001 and who also possesses the attributes of a transformational leader.[37] Prior to assuming his current position, he served as its the company's president and COO. This account focuses on his leadership prior to assuming his new role. Chenault is one of the few African Americans who head a major global corporation. American Express provides an array of financial and travel-related services, including the recent development of online banking, mortgage, and brokerage services. The firm has more than 88,000 employees and annual sales of some $23 billion.[38]

STRATEGIC ACTION COMPETENCY

Ken Chenault of American Express

Since joining American Express in 1981, Ken Chenault has served American Express (AmEx) in a variety of positions, from director of strategic planning in the Merchandise Services division to president of the Consumer Card division. He displayed bold leadership during the early 1990s by persuading merchants—from airline companies to restaurants—not to leave the AmEx fold while internal feuds were being resolved at the company. As the executive handpicked to reduce costs, Chenault streamlined four divisions, creating a productive business unit and saving a substantial amount in operating costs.

Harvey Golub, then chairman and CEO, recommended to the board of directors that Chenault be his replacement. He commented: "There are qualities in leadership that can only be observed over time—how an individual deals with others, how he deals with adversity and complex issues, how he organizes his time and efforts, and deals with external constituencies. And Ken has demonstrated amply over the years his abilities. He's more than capable."

Golub and Chenault developed a three-prong growth strategy for the future. The plan calls for expanding the company's card network through banks

and financial institutions; expanding its financial and investment services; and increasing its market share in specialty segments, including small businesses and overseas markets. The glue that holds the growth strategy together is technology, through the Web and "smart cards." Chenault has crafted the new corporate agenda and intensified his focus on making AmEx bigger, stronger, and more ubiquitous. He comments: "Leaders must focus an organization on facing reality. Then they give them the confidence and support to inspire them to change that reality."

Louise Parent, executive vice president of American Express, observes that "Chenault has been relentless about performance and about measuring ourselves against the competition. He is the kind of person who inspires you to want to do your best. Part of the reason is his example."

David House, president of Establishment Service Worldwide for AmEx adds, "Ken has had tremendous courage in the face of adversity, and he's incredibly competitive. He really wants to win." According to House, he can persuade the proverbial Eskimo to purchase a cooler. In fact, House agreed to an interview with Chenault for a job in 1993 after previ-

ously turning the company down. "The only reason I accepted the interview was to meet Ken, whose name had come up several times when I was working at Reebok." At a dinner meeting, House intended to tell Chenault what he'd already told his wife—that he wouldn't accept a position as senior vice president for sales and field marketing for AmEx's U.S. Establishment Services unit.

He was surprised to hear the straightforward executive outline every reason why he shouldn't take the job. Chenault candidly pointed out that the card business was undergoing a major restructuring and that if his strategy didn't work, the company would go out of business. House states that "It was high risk, and that got me excited, along with the fact that [Chenault] had the integrity to tell me. Ken has the highest integrity of anyone I've ever met in business and personally, including my father."

One top-executive search firm consultant says that Chenault is a confident man who cares about bringing tangible results to his company's shareholders. "If a man at that level—black, white or green—doesn't have a certain amount of ego or fire, then he can't do the job. You have to be pleasant to be around,

but decisive and clinical about your decisions while remaining humane, and he has all those qualities."

• • •

To learn more about American Express, visit the company's home page at

http://www.americanexpress.com

LEADERSHIP DEVELOPMENT

6.

DESCRIBE HOW ORGANIZA-TIONS DEVELOP LEADERS.

A study conducted by the Conference Board asked executives to rate the leadership capacity of their organizations. The results were disturbing, showing that less than 10 percent of these executives rated their companies as excellent and that half rated their companies as fair or poor. This pessimism, combined with recognition of the importance of effective leadership, seems to explain why organizations invest millions of dollars and untold hours on efforts to improve leadership effectiveness.[39] These investments fall into three general categories: assigning people to positions to promote learning on the job, offering assistance through coaching and mentoring, and sending employees to formal leadership assessment and training programs.

ON-THE-JOB LEARNING

As we noted in Chapter 1, on-the-job learning is important for all aspects of managerial work. To develop leadership on the job requires that employees take jobs or project assignments that include leadership responsibilities. Early in a person's career, working as an individual contributor on team projects provides many opportunities for learning how to be an effective leader. Being a formal leader of a project allows an employee to use different types of power and observe how people react to the employee's attempts to influence them. Team leaders also can ask team members for candid feedback and suggestions for how to improve. Team members who aren't designated as the formal leader also can learn by observing the relationship between the leader and team and by practicing the use of referent and expert power.

When jobs with managerial responsibilities become available, opportunities for learning on the job expand considerably. Managerial jobs almost always require leadership—that is, they involve influencing others to make progress toward a goal. Although someone else may set the goal, managers are charged with inspiring others to become committed to the goal and to strive to achieve it.

ASSESSMENT AND TRAINING

Most large organizations don't rely solely on learning on the job to develop leaders. In addition, they ensure that their most talented employees receive formal leadership assessments and attend leadership training programs. Formal assessment and training may be conducted at the organization's own educational facilities, at a college or university, or by organizations such as the Center for Creative Leadership—a nonprofit organization dedicated to leadership research and education. Regardless of location, formal assessment and training programs generally include evaluating the individual's current approach to leadership and providing educational experiences designed to improve the individual's effectiveness as a leader. For employees in roles that involve leadership, providing feedback is a good way to improve their effectiveness. Not surprisingly, most leaders see themselves in a more positive light than their followers do. The best leaders have a realistic view of themselves and use feedback about their behavior to make improvements.[40]

At FedEx, selecting and developing a person to enter a leadership role takes 14 months. Each year, some 3,000 FedEx employees interested in leadership positions enter the company's Leadership Evaluation and Awareness Process (LEAP). Only 20 percent make it to the final stage. Why? According to a senior official at the company, three reasons account for people dropping out. First, they come to realize that leaders put in very long hours. Second, they realize that leadership carries an unrelenting sense of obligation—they are always representatives of FedEx, even when they aren't at work. Third, they realize that leadership involves intensive interactions with people. The self-evaluation included in FedEx's LEAP program opens the eyes of many potential leaders. According to the managing director of the FedEx Leadership Institute, "Too many people get into leadership for all the wrong reasons. They want power. They think it's the only way to advance. LEAP is a gate that everyone has to pass through. And those who pass through it are attuned to what it means to lead and to work effectively with other people."[41]

COACHING AND MENTORING

Whether held on a college campus or a corporate campus, most formal leadership development programs take place in designated settings. In contrast, leaders may hire a personal leadership coach or work with a mentor. Recall Jack Morris's experience, which illustrates how a coach can help a person improve leadership capabilities.

Personal coaches often provide an intensive leadership development experience. However, they can be quite expensive—costing several hundred dollars per hour—so few people can afford to hire them. For many managers, learning from a mentor is more feasible. *Mentors* most often are managers or senior colleagues in the organization who provide advice and guidance about a variety of career-related concerns. For managers, talking with mentors about how to develop more effective leadership behaviors is important to career advancement. In particular, mentors can help managers understand how others respond to their behaviors and point out weaknesses or blind spots. Mentors also serve as role models that individuals can emulate and provide valuable advice concerning the styles of leadership favored in the organization. Finally, mentors often assist managers in developing leadership capabilities by helping them obtain assignments that will foster on-the-job learning.[42]

In addition to what organizations do to develop leaders, individuals can develop their own leadership competencies by assessing their current approaches to leadership, developing action plans for improvement, and carrying out those plans. Throughout this book, we have given you an opportunity to learn about yourself by completing various questionnaires, address various discussion questions, analyze various cases, and reflect on various competency features. We hope that these activities are helping you develop your own leadership abilities.

CHAPTER SUMMARY

Leadership is central to the effectiveness of organizations. Employees at all levels of an organization can exercise leadership, which can take many forms. Because effective leadership is so important, numerous studies have been conducted in attempts to understand its nature. Each of numerous models explains some—but not all—aspects of effective leadership. Organizations interested in developing effective leaders often use these models as the basis for leadership development activities.

1. **STATE THE TYPES OF POWER AND THEIR USE BY LEADERS.**

Leadership involves influencing others to act to attain goals. Leaders rely on five types of power to exert influence: legitimate,

reward, coercive, referent, and expert. The most effective use of power results in followers who are committed to the leader's goals. The improper use of power may result in mere compliance or even resistance.

2. **DESCRIBE THE PERSONAL TRAITS ASSOCIATED WITH EFFECTIVE LEADERS.**

Traits are the personal characteristics of individuals, including their physical, social, and personal attributes. The traits model suggests that the presence and absence of certain individual characteristics distinguish leaders from nonleaders. The discussion of emotional intelligence presented one framework of leadership traits. Traits often associated with ethical leadership include honesty, trustworthiness, and integrity.

3. **EXPLAIN THE BEHAVIORS OF EFFECTIVE AND IN-EFFECTIVE LEADERS.**

Behavioral models of leadership provide a way of identifying effective leaders by their actions. We reviewed two of these models. The Theory X and Theory Y model states that leaders' behaviors reflect their basic assumptions about people. Theory X and Theory Y represent two quite different ways that leaders view their subordinates and thus manage them. The managerial grid model identifies various combinations of concern for people and production. They provide the basis for deriving five different styles of leadership—country club, impoverished, produce or perish, middle of the road, and team. In this model the team style is viewed as the ideal leadership style to strive for.

4. **IDENTIFY CONTINGENCIES THAT MAY BE IMPORTANT TO THE EFFECTIVENESS OF LEADERS.**

As with the behavioral models, there are a number of contingency leadership models. We discussed two of them. Hersey and Blanchard's situational leadership model indicates that leaders must adapt their leadership style to the readiness level of their followers. This model prescribes different combinations of directive and supportive leader behaviors for different levels of subordinates' readiness. It suggests four leadership styles—delegating, supportive, selling, and telling. The Vroom–Jago time-driven leadership model prescribes a leader's choices among five leadership styles based on seven contingency variables, recognizing the time requirements and other costs associated with each style. The five core leadership styles include: decide, consult individually, consult team, facilitate, and delegate. Both models are based on the assumption that leaders can be highly flexible in their use of leadership styles.

5. **STATE THE KEY CHARACTERISTICS OF TRANSFORMATIONAL LEADERS.**

Transformational leaders inspire others with their vision, often promote this vision over opposition, and demonstrate confidence in themselves and their views. They generally are visionary, inspirational, thoughtful, considerate, trustworthy, and confident.

6. **DESCRIBE HOW ORGANIZATIONS DEVELOP LEADERS.**

Organizations use three major approaches to develop leaders: placing employees in positions that promote learning on the job, providing employees with formal leadership assessments and training, and offering mentoring and coaching.

KEY TERMS

Behavioral models, p. 409
Charismatic leader, p. 420
Coercive power, p. 405
Contingency models, p. 413
Delegating style, p. 414
Directive behavior, p. 413
Emotional intelligence, p. 407
Expert power, p. 405
Hersey and Blanchard's situational leadership model, p. 413

Leadership, p. 404
Legitimate power, p. 405
Managerial grid model, p. 411
Mentors, p. 423
Power, p. 405
Readiness, p. 413
Referent power, p. 405
Reward power, p. 405
Selling style, p. 414
Supporting style, p. 414

Supportive behavior, p. 413
Telling style, p. 414
Theory X, p. 410
Theory Y, p. 410
Traits, p. 407
Traits model, p. 407
Transformational leaders, p. 419
Vroom–Jago time-driven leadership model, p. 415

QUESTIONS FOR DISCUSSION AND COMPETENCY DEVELOPMENT

1. Think of a leader that you know. Give examples of how this person uses sources of power to influence others.

2. Think of one of your good friends. Assess this person's emotional intelligence.

3. Describe a manager you have worked for in terms of Theory X or Theory Y. Give some examples of this manager's behaviors and attitudes that seem to be consistent with Theory X or Theory Y.

4. How are others likely to describe your leadership style in terms of the managerial grid? Why do you think they would characterize you this way?

5. In Hersey and Blanchard's situational leadership model, readiness of followers is a key contingency variable. Based on a recent job experience, did your manager appropriately recognize your "readiness" in work relations with you? Explain.

6. The Vroom–Jago time-driven leadership model emphasizes seven contingency variables in relation to a "decision-time" penalty. Think of a team or group decision-making situation in which you have been involved. Use Table 15.2 to assess that situation. Did the team or group leader use the correct leadership style based on this model? Explain.

7. **Self-Management Competency.** Numerous organizations offer leadership development programs. Investigate a leadership training program offered by one of the following organizations. Does the program utilize a leadership model based on traits, behaviors, contingencies, transformation, or a combination of these methods?

   • Education, Training and Development Resource Center for Business and Industry at ***http://www.tasl.com***.

   • Center for Creative Leadership at ***http://www.ccl.org***.

   • American Society for Training and Development at ***http://www.astd.org***.

8. **Planning and Administration Competency.** The workforce of many companies includes a diverse mix of people. However, diversity has not yet been achieved in high-level leadership positions of Fortune 500 companies. To assist companies interested in developing a pool of demographically diverse leaders, the U.S. Government's Glass Ceiling Commission developed 12 recommendations for business and government organizations. What are these recommendations? What are their implications for the design of a company's leadership development programs? The commission's recommendations are described at ***http://www.dol. gov/dol/_sec/public/media/reports/ceiling.htm***.

CASE FOR COMPETENCY DEVELOPMENT

Your Leadership Style Preference[43]

This questionnaire measures your preferences for certain styles of leadership behavior. It is intended to help you better understand and develop your leadership competency. For the questionnaire to be useful, you must answer the questions honestly. There are no "right" or "wrong" answers. Trying to figure out the best answer only makes the results useless for improving your self-awareness and understanding. Some of these questions ask you to make difficult choices. Please base these choices only on your personal preferences.

The questions ask you to describe how you treat those reporting to you. If you have never managed others, try to imagine what you would do if you were in fact managing others. Pick the statement that best describes how you think you would behave.

Instructions

Read each pair of statements. For each pair, pick the statement—(a) or (b) and so on—that *best* describes your own management behaviors and preferences and place an X next to it. In some cases, you will probably feel that both statements describe you fairly well, but you still must pick only the one that describes you best. In other cases, you might feel that neither statement describes you at all. Even so, you must pick one—the one that is the least inaccurate. You will not be able to score this questionnaire when you finish unless you have picked only one statement from each pair.

1. —— a. I take the time to explain to employees exactly what I expect of them.
   —— b. Employees should be responsible for determining what is expected of them on the job.
2. —— c. I am pleasant toward employees but I avoid getting too friendly.
   —— d. I respond to employees in a warm and friendly manner.
3. —— e. I help employees set specific high goals for themselves.
   —— f. I allow employees to find their own ways to do their jobs better.
4. —— g. I try to get employees to work together as a team.
   —— h. I try to keep a proper distance from individual employees.
5. —— b. As long as the job gets done I don't care how employees go about doing it.
   —— a. I make clear to employees exactly how I want the job done.
6. —— c. Employees know when they have done a good job and don't need me to tell them.
   —— d. I tell employees how much I appreciate their efforts.
7. —— f. I take employees' limits into account and don't expect too much of them.
   —— e. I provide employees with the information they need to plan their work effectively.
8. —— g. I provide opportunities for employees to get together to share ideas and information.
   —— h. I make productive use of the time when others are speaking to prepare my own arguments.
9. —— a. I encourage employees to try out new work-related ideas.
   —— b. I expect employees to adhere to and maintain standard work procedures.
10. —— d. I treat employees with respect and as equals.
    —— c. I respect effective employees, but I don't pretend to be at their level.

11. —— f. I expect employees to solve their own work problems.

—— e. I make sure that employees have the resources they need to do a good job.

12. —— h. I emphasize to employees their own responsibility for their work.

—— g. I am understanding when employees come to me with their problems.

13. —— b. I expect employees to figure out for themselves how things should be done.

—— a. I express clearly to employees my views about the ways things should be done.

14. —— c. There's little point in encouraging employees' ideas because almost all that they come up with were tried long ago.

—— d. I ask employees for their ideas and let them know that their suggestions are desired and appreciated.

15. —— e. I expect a great deal from employees in terms of performance.

—— f. I avoid giving employees specific numerical goals or targets.

16. —— g. I show employees that I am personally concerned about them.

—— h. I prefer to deal with employees privately and one-to-one rather than involving a group.

17. —— b. I decide myself what will be done as well as how to do it.

—— a. If employees want to know how to do a specific task or activity, they know there are established procedures they can follow.

18. —— c. With so much always changing, there's no point in worrying employees with details too far in advance.

—— d. I let employees know of changes well in advance so that they can prepare.

19. —— f. I let employees know that I expect them to do their best.

—— e. I help employees get the training they need to perform their jobs effectively.

20. —— h. I rarely spend time in group meetings with employees.

—— g. I show employees that I really listen to them.

21. —— a. I make clear assignments of particular employees to specific tasks.

—— b. I find it best to let employees sort out informally who is best for which assignment.

22. —— c. I screen out all unimportant interactions with employees and attend only to those that are really important, to minimize disruptions to my own work.

—— d. I make sure that employees find me accessible to them and interested in their concerns.

23. —— e. I make sure that employees clearly understand my role and responsibilities.

—— f. When employees know and carry out their job responsibilities, there is little need for me to get involved.

24. —— g. I show a great deal of concern for employees' personal welfare.

—— h. I respect employees' privacy and right to have personal concerns left alone.

25. —— b. As long as the work gets done, employees can keep to their own schedules.

—— a. I prepare specific work schedules for employees to define their responsibilities and coordinate their work.

26. —— c. I permit employees to try out new ideas that seem unlikely to have an adverse effect on productivity.

—— d. I listen to employees' ideas for doing things better and make changes based on their suggestions.

27. —— f. I ask employees to do their best without setting overly specific standards.

—— e. I make sure that all employees understand the specific standards of performance that apply to their work.

28. —— h. Employees accept the fact that I'm the boss, so there is no need for constant explanations of my actions.

—— g. I make sure that when I take actions or make decisions affecting them, employees understand the reasons.

29. —— a. I let employees know the standards and regulations that I expect them to follow.

—— b. Employees can develop their own informal standards and work rules, so long as the job gets done.

30. —— c. I try to get all the relevant information before making an important decision.

—— d. I consult with employees before making important decisions about the work.

Directions for Scoring

1. Count the number of times you picked "a." Put the number here: ——

2. Count the number of times you picked "e." Put the number here: ——

3. To get your Task Behavior Score, add the two numbers and put the total here: ——

   Task Behavior Score

4. Count the number of times you picked "d." Put the number here: ——

5. Count the number of times you picked "g." Put the number here: ——

6. To get your Relationship Behavior Score, add the two numbers and put the total here: ——

   Relationship Behavior Score

7. Plot your scores on the following chart. Find your Task Behavior Score on the vertical axis first, and draw a horizontal line across the chart at this level. Then find your Relationship Behavior Score on the horizontal axis and from this point draw a vertical line up the chart. Note: all responses are not scored in this questionnaire.

Interpretation: Most research on leadership suggests that the best style of leadership depends somewhat on the situation. The scores on this questionnaire cannot tell you how well you are able to adapt your leadership style to different situations. What it can tell you is something about the leadership style that is most natural to you. By plotting your scores on the chart, you can see clearly just what your overall tendency is.

Uninvolved (Delegating style): Low on both Task and Relationship Behaviors

Participating (Selling style): High on both Task and Relationship Behaviors

Friendly (Supportive style): Low on Task and High on Relationship Behaviors

Controlling (Telling style): High on Task and Low on Relationship Behaviors

Understanding your own typical pattern of behavior will probably help you find ways to improve on it or change it to meet varying situations.

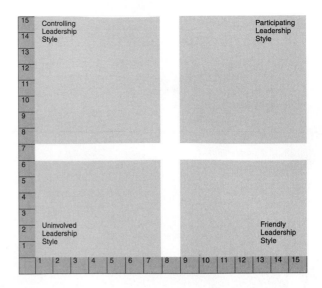

VIDEO CASE

Sunshine Cleaning Systems

As one of the largest contract cleaning companies in the state of Florida, Sunshine Cleaning Systems, Inc., has more than 1,000 employees and annual revenues exceeding $10 million. The company specializes in pressure cleaning, janitorial service, and window cleaning. The company's success is evident by the long list of clients it serves, including the Miami Dolphins training center, the Orlando Arena (home of the Orlando Magic), the Florida Turnpike Authority, the Florida Citrus Bowl, the Fort Lauderdale Airport, and numerous banks, restaurants, and convention centers. The company is expanding beyond the state of Florida and has landed a window cleaning contract for all 11 museums of the Smithsonian Institution in Washington, D.C.

The success of Sunshine Cleaning can, in large measure, be traced to the leadership of the company's CEO, Larry Calufetti. A former major league baseball player, Calufetti applies many of the principles he learned during his days as a player to his "coaching" style of leadership. Under his direction, all the managers of this privately held corporation have to use the coaching leadership style. Calufetti is convinced that this approach is the key to motivating and leading employees to accomplish the company's goals.

Seven major principles comprise Sunshine's coaching leadership style. First, leading by example, Sunshine management supports and respects all its employees and believes, further, that all of them should treat others as they want to be treated. Second, management believes that, just like their counterparts in baseball, managers need to train and teach employees how to do their tasks correctly. Third, management supplies employees with all the necessary tools and supplies they need to do their jobs well. Fourth, employees need to feel responsible for their jobs and take pride in doing good work—and, in the process, develop a special *esprit de corps* that translates into better performance.

Fifth, management encourages innovation from its employees by openly soliciting new ideas from them. Sixth, it utilizes various rewards, both financial and informal, to build loyalty to the organization and sustain its family atmosphere. Finally, the company develops its employees (as a baseball coach would), helping them find their niches and maximizing their effectiveness. As part of this development program, the company promotes from within so that employees view their work as a career opportunity, not just another job.

With the company's growth and significantly lower than average turnover rate (in an industry with a history of high turnover), the coaching leadership style at Sunshine Cleaning Systems is an apparent big league hit.

Questions

1. How does coaching differ from managing?

2. Why does Sunshine's management stress the cross-training of employees?

3. For what practical reasons does Sunshine's management emphasize responsibility and innovation and reward employees for exhibiting these traits?

To learn more about Sunshine Cleaning Systems, visit the company's home page at ***http://www.sunshinecleaning.com***.

Organizational Communication

Chapter Outline

PREVIEW: GORDON BETHUNE AT CONTINENTAL AIRLINES

THE COMMUNICATION PROCESS
SENDER (ENCODER)
RECEIVER (DECODER)
MESSAGE
STRATEGIC ACTION COMPETENCY: Feng Shui at Nortel Communications
CHANNELS
FEEDBACK
SELF-MANAGEMENT COMPETENCY: Are You Open to Feedback?
PERCEPTION

IMPACT OF INFORMATION TECHNOLOGY
ELECTRONIC MAIL
THE INTERNET
TELECONFERENCING
THE DOWNSIDE OF INFORMATION TECHNOLOGY
PLANNING AND ADMINISTRATION COMPETENCY: A Hip Workplace

HURDLES TO EFFECTIVE COMMUNICATION
ORGANIZATIONAL HURDLES
INDIVIDUAL HURDLES
COMMUNICATION COMPETENCY: Translation Blunders
ELIMINATING HURDLES

FOSTERING EFFECTIVE COMMUNICATION

CHAPTER SUMMARY

KEY TERMS

QUESTIONS FOR DISCUSSION AND COMPETENCY DEVELOPMENT

CASE FOR COMPETENCY DEVELOPMENT: COMMUNICATION INVENTORY

VIDEO CASE: BURKE, INC.

GORDON BETHUNE AT CONTINENTAL AIRLINES

When Michelle Meissner, Continental Airlines director of human resources, joined the airline in 1995, the working environment was terrible. "It was a horrible place to work," she says. Continental wasn't meeting its financial goals and was about to enter its third bankruptcy; employees didn't trust management and had lost confidence in top management.

Since then, however, things have changed. Continental has enjoyed 21 consecutive quarters of profitability, has among the highest revenue per seat per mile in the industry, and ranks high in consumer satisfaction. Perhaps best of all, recently the company was named as one of *Fortune*'s 100 best places to work.

The key to Continental's dramatic turnaround has been the leadership and communication of CEO Gordon Bethune and COO Greg Brenneman. Their visibility, involvement, and commitment to Continental's goals have made them credible communicators. Frequent communication occurs with all employees at Continental. Employees often see Bethune and other managers in an airport break room talking about what's going on. Both Bethune and Brenneman eat lunch in the office café, not at their desks, and ask employees to join them. During these informal chats they learn the "bad news" from gate attendants, mechanics,

reservation agents, and others who might lack the courage to make an appointment to see them in their offices.

To improve communication throughout the 50,000-employee organization, Bethune and his team established what they call the Go Forward Plan. It has four components.

- Achieve top-quartile industry financial margins.

- Reduce interest expense and develop our franchise hubs for future growth.

- Have an industry-leading product that our employees are proud to sell.

- Have a company where employees enjoy coming to work every day and are valued for their contributions.

To communicate these four points clearly and to implement the plan, the company's managers are expected to walk the talk. Every year, employees receive a survey that asks questions such as "Has your leader informed you about the Go Forward Plan?" and "Has your leader set measurable, specific goals based on the Go Forward Plan?" Leaders who score well on these assessments are rewarded with bonuses. Those who don't, according to Meissner, "aren't around much longer."

Bethune communicates directly through e-mail with all employees every Friday evening. His commitment to full disclosure means sharing both bad and good news—no sugar coating. What's he communicating? He reports on how the company's stock performed during the week, on-time performance, baggage handling performance, number of e-mail tickets purchased, revenue per available seat, passenger load factor, number of passenger boardings, average price for a gallon of fuel, amount of fuel consumed, and so on.

These communications are from his perspective. Every month in Houston, Texas, Continental has an open house where employees, their families, and their friends can learn more about Continental's operations. Some employees are even flown in from other hubs to attend these open houses. Such face-to-face communication builds trust and credibility. A monthly newsletter is sent to the homes of all employees. Every 6 months, Bethune goes to several of Continental's hubs (e.g., Cleveland and Newark), gives a formal presentation on company issues, and listens to employees.[1]

To learn more about Continental Airlines, visit the company's home page at

http://www.continental.com

THE COMMUNICATION PROCESS

1.

EXPLAIN THE MAIN ELEMENTS OF THE COMMUNICATION PROCESS.

Whether the organization is an airline, school district, bank, transportation system, or manufacturing plant, effective communication is essential. Communication is to an organization as the bloodstream is to a person. Just as a person can develop hardening of the arteries, which impairs physical efficiency, an organization can develop blockages of communication channels, which impair its effectiveness. Just as heart bypass surgery may be necessary to save a person's life, an organization may have to revamp its communications system to survive. And, just as heart patients can do more harm than good if they overreact to their health problems by exercising too strenuously, an organization may go overboard trying to repair a history of poor communication with employees.

Without *effective* communication, managers can accomplish little, which is why we included communication as one of the six key managerial competencies. Recall that communication can be formal or informal, verbal or nonverbal, and may take many forms, including face-to-face interactions, phone calls, faxes, e-mail, notes posted on bulletin boards, letters, memos, reports, videos, and oral presentations. In this chapter, we examine how organizational communication takes place, identify key hurdles to communication, and explore ways of improving communication in organizations.

Communication is the transfer and exchange of information and understanding from one person to another through meaningful symbols.[2] It is a process of sending, receiving, and sharing ideas, attitudes, values, opinions, and facts. Communication requires both a sender, who begins the process, and a receiver, who completes the communication link. When the receiver provides feedback that the message was received as intended, the communication cycle is complete.

In organizations, managers use the communication process to carry out their four functions (planning, organizing, leading, and controlling). Because they must have access to relevant information in order to make sound decisions, effective managers build networks of contacts who facilitate information gathering, interpretation, and dissemination. These contacts help managers become the nerve centers of their organizations. Much like radar screens, managers scan the environment for changes that could affect the organization and share this information with others. Once made, decisions are quickly disseminated to those who will help carry them out.

In contrast, ineffective managers often leave employees in the dark about what is happening. Poor communication seems to be a particular problem during downsizing, when managers' and employees' stress levels soar. Poor communication allows rumors to replace facts, fosters animosities between departments and teams, and impedes successful organizational change. Under such circumstances, poor communication seems to be the single most important reason for poor strategy implementation.

Most managers spend a large part of their working day communicating with superiors, peers, customers, and others; writing memos, letters, and reports; and talking with others on the phone. In doing so, they are engaged in the communication process, which involves six basic elements: sender (encoder), receiver (decoder), message, channels, feedback, and perception. Figure 16.1 shows how these elements interact during the communication process.[3] Managers and employees who are concerned with improving communication competency need to be aware of these elements and how they contribute

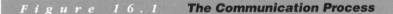

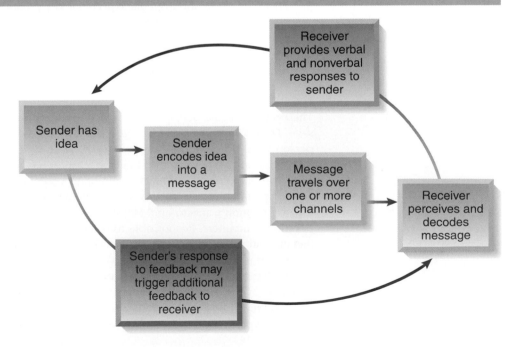

Figure 16.1   The Communication Process

to successful communication. We discuss the roles of the sender and the receiver first because they are the actors in the process.

SENDER (ENCODER)

The **sender** is the source of information and the initiator of the communication process. The sender tries to choose the type of message and the channel that will be most effective. The sender then encodes the message.

Encoding translates thoughts or feelings into a medium—written, visual, or spoken—that conveys the meaning intended. Imagine that you are planning to apply for a job. You will get the best response by first learning about the channels of communication used by the organization. Many employers now prefer to accept applications via the Internet, so you should begin by visiting the organization's Web site. From there, you often can determine which job openings exist and the procedures that the company uses to process applications for employment. If the organization accepts electronic applications, you're likely to get a faster response to your inquiry by using this method.[4] If the organization has no Web site, you can begin the process by calling to find out whether an opening exists, then writing a letter, and then phoning again to confirm that your letter had been received.

Regardless of whether you apply electronically or use a traditional letter, your application should convey certain ideas and impressions. For example, you should explain why you're interested in that particular company. You also need to provide background information about your qualifications for the job and explain how you think the job will further your career. When you transfer these ideas into speech or to an electronic memo or to paper, you are encoding your message. To increase encoding accuracy, apply the five principles of communication to the form of communication you're using.

1. *Relevancy.* Make the message meaningful and significant, carefully selecting the words, symbols, or gestures to be used.

2. *Simplicity.* Put the message in the simplest possible terms, reducing the number of words, symbols, or gestures used to communicate your intended thoughts and feelings.

3. *Organization.* Arrange the message as a series of points to facilitate understanding. Complete each point in a message before proceeding to the next.

4. *Repetition.* Restate key points of the message at least twice. Repetition is particularly important in spoken communication because words may not be clearly heard or fully understood the first time.

5. *Focus.* Focus on the essential aspects, or key points, of the message. Make the message clear and avoid unnecessary detail. In spoken communication, emphasize significant points by changing your tone of voice, pausing, gesturing, or using appropriate facial expressions. In written communication, underline or italicize key sentences, phrases, or words.

RECEIVER (DECODER)

The **receiver** is the person who receives and decodes (or interprets) the sender's message. **Decoding** translates messages into a form that has meaning to the receiver. The person who receives your electronic application or letter about a summer job reacts to it first on the basis of whether the organization has any openings. If it doesn't, the receiver probably won't pay much attention to your inquiry. If there are openings, the receiver probably will compare what you wrote about yourself to the type of person that the organization wants to hire. Monica Powell is one of The Associates First Capital Corporation's recruiters. Responsible for recruiting at more than 60 colleges and universities around the country, she's learned to decode messages efficiently. She takes no more than a half a minute to judge a résumé. She prefers a standard résumé—if she receives one printed on pink paper with a color photo she'll "try to look beyond it." She searches for key information, including job experience, campus leadership, grades, and hometown. Why hometown? She says that it helps her judge the likelihood of a student's accepting a job in one of the cities where The Associates has facilities.[5]

Both encoding and decoding are influenced by personal factors, such as education, personality, socioeconomic, family, work history, culture, and gender, among others.[6] Some research suggests that women are more concerned with the feelings and reactions of the person with whom they're speaking than men are. They focus on seeking and giving more support and try to gain consensus. When men use qualifiers such as "perhaps," "maybe," "sort of," or "I guess," they are often perceived as warm and polite; when women use such qualifiers, they are often perceived as weak and unassertive. Men are more concerned with status and trying to maintain the upper hand in a conversation. Men are more likely to interrupt others who are talking, and women are interrupted more often than men. Whereas women try to create intimacy in conversations, men focus on establishing their independence. For example, women are more likely to frame orders as questions (Can you meet me at my office? rather than Come to my office).

One of the main requirements of the receiver is the ability to listen. *Listening* involves *paying attention to* the message, not merely hearing it. Of the 75 percent or more of their time that managers spend in communicating, about half is spent listening to others. Becoming a better listener is an important way for people to improve their communication skills. Studies have shown that most people can recall immediately only about 50 percent of what someone tells them. Two months later, they can recall only about 25 percent. That's why effective communication often involves the use of several media, such as written reports, memos, newsletters, and e-mail, in addition to the telephone, face-to-face conversations, and speeches.

Ten guidelines for effective listening are presented in Table 16.1. Try using them the next time you're having a conversation with someone. You'll be surprised at how much effective listening improves the communication process.

T a b l e 1 6 . 1	*Guidelines for Effective Listening*

1. Remember that listening is not just about receiving information—how you listen also sends a message back to the message sender.
2. Stop talking! You can't listen if you're talking.
3. Show a talker that you want to listen. Paraphrase what's been said to show that you understand.
4. Remove distractions.
5. Avoid prejudging what the person thinks or feels. Listen first, then make judgments later.
6. Try to see the other person's point of view.
7. Listen for total meaning. This includes both the content of the words and the feeling or attitude underlying the words.
8. Attend to both verbal and nonverbal cues.
9. Go easy on argument and criticism, which put people on the defensive and may make them "clam up" or become angry.
10. Before each person leaves, confirm what has been said.

MESSAGE

The *message* contains the verbal (spoken and written) symbols and nonverbal cues representing the information that the sender wants to convey to the receiver. Like a coin, a message has two sides, and the message sent and the message received aren't necessarily the same. Why? First, encoding and decoding of the message may vary because of differences in the sender's and the receiver's backgrounds and viewpoints. Second, the sender may be sending more than one message.

Recruiters such as Monica Powell, as well as managers and employees generally, use three types of messages: nonverbal, verbal, and written. The use of nonverbal messages is extremely important, although many individuals don't recognize this fact. Accordingly, we discuss nonverbal messages at greater length than the other two types.

Nonverbal Messages. All messages not spoken or written constitute nonverbal messages. *Nonverbal messages* involve the use of facial expressions, eye contact, body movement, gestures, and physical contact (collectively often called *body language*) to convey meaning. When people communicate in person, as much as 60 percent of the content of the message is transmitted through facial expressions and other methods of nonverbal communication.[7]

Recruiter Monica Powell sees each student for only 30 minutes, so every bit of information she can get is important. A smile and strong handshake create an excellent first impression. Powell admits that first impressions based on nonverbal cues can be misleading but that they are hard to ignore. She uses her understanding of nonverbal communication to gather information about the candidate during the interview.[8] The ability to interpret facial expressions is an important part of communication. Eye contact is a direct and powerful way of communicating nonverbally. In the United States, social rules suggest that in many social situations brief eye contact is appropriate. However, if eye contact is too brief, people may interpret it as a sign of aloofness or untrustworthiness. Conversely, people often interpret prolonged eye contact as either a threat or a sign of romantic interest, depending on the context. A good poker player watches the eyes of the other players as new cards are dealt. Pupil dilation often betrays whether the card(s) just dealt improved the player's hand.

With regard to *body language*, the body and its movement—particularly movements of the face and eyes, which are very expressive—tell a lot about a person. As much as 50 percent of the content of a message may be communicated by facial expression and body posture and another 30 percent by inflection and the tone of speech. The words themselves may account for only 20 percent of the content of a message.[9]

The meaning of nonverbal communication varies by cultures. For example, the smile that Powell saw on the face of a candidate may indicate happiness or pleasure in the United States, but for Asians, it can also be a sign of embarrassment or discomfort. In the United States, maintaining eye contact is the sign of a good communicator; in the Middle East, it is an integral part of successful communication; but for the Chinese and Japanese, it can indicate distrust. Many Americans shake hands to greet people, whereas Middle Easterners of the same sex kiss on the cheek.

With regard to *space*, how close you are to another person, where you sit or stand, and how you arrange your office can have a significant impact on communication. *Proxemics* is the study of ways that people use physical space to convey messages. Think how you would feel if you walked into class midway through the term and someone was sitting in "your" seat. You'd probably feel angry because your space, or territory, had been invaded. To test how important your territory is to you, complete the questionnaire shown in Figure 16.2.[10]

The distances that people feel comfortable with when communicating vary greatly by culture. South Americans and Southern and Eastern Europeans prefer closeness. Asians, Northern Europeans, and North Americans prefer not to be as close. These behaviors reflect a culture's overall tendency to be high contact or low contact. People in high-contact cultures like to stand close and touch each other. High-contact cultures usually are in warmer climates; their peoples tend to have greater interpersonal orientation and are perceived as interpersonally "friendly." Those from low-contact cultures prefer to stand farther apart and touch infrequently. These cultures are often in cooler climates; their peoples tend to be task oriented and interpersonally "cool." Figure 16.3 shows the approximate placement of various countries along the high-to-low contact culture continuum. For example, in Japan, strict rules of etiquette guide seating behavior. If businesspeople are traveling together on a train, the most senior executive sits next to the window, facing the direction in which the train is moving. In a taxi, the "top" seat is behind the driver and the most junior seat is next to the driver. In elevators, the senior person stands in the rear in the center facing the door and the most junior person stands near the buttons.[11]

Spatial arrangements in corporate offices in North America send many signals to members of an organization.[12] In some organizations, such as Texaco, American Airlines, and

Figure 16.2 **How Territorial Are You?**

Instructions: Circle one number to answer each question as follows:

1. Strongly agree
2. Agree
3. Not sure
4. Disagree
5. Strongly disagree

	1	2	3	4	5
1. If I arrive at my apartment (room) and find my roommate sitting in my chair, I am annoyed if he/she doesn't at least offer to get up immediately.	1	2	3	4	5
2. I do not like anyone to remove anything from my desk without first asking me.	1	2	3	4	5
3. If a stranger puts a hand on my shoulder when talking to me I feel uncomfortable.	1	2	3	4	5
4. If my suit jacket is lying on the back of a chair and another student comes in and chooses to sit in the chair, I feel that he or she should ask me to move my jacket or choose another seat.	1	2	3	4	5
5. If I enter a classroom and "reserve" a chair with a notebook, I am annoyed and offended upon my return to find my book moved and someone sitting in "my" seat.	1	2	3	4	5
6. If a person who is not a close friend of mine gets within a foot from my face to talk to me, I will either back off or uncomfortably hold my ground.	1	2	3	4	5
7. I do not like strangers walking into my room (apartment).	1	2	3	4	5
8. If I lived in an apartment, I would not want the landlord to enter for any reason without my permission.	1	2	3	4	5
9. I do not like my friends or family borrowing my clothes without asking me first.	1	2	3	4	5
10. If I notice someone staring at me in a restaurant, I become annoyed and uncomfortable.	1	2	3	4	5

To score and interpret your responses, add the numbers you circled for all 10 statements. Then compare your total with the following definitions:

10–25 points: *Highly territorial.* Your instincts for staking out and protecting what you consider yours are high. You strongly believe in your territorial rights.

26–39 points: *Ambiguous but territorial.* You may act territorial in some circumstances but not in others. You feel differently about different types of space.

40–50: *Not territorial.* You disagree with the entire concept of territoriality. You dislike possessiveness, protectiveness, and jealousy. The concept of private ownership is not central to your philosophy of life.

Texas Instruments (TI), top managers have larger offices, windows with better views, plusher carpets, and higher quality furnishings than middle managers have. Meriting a personal secretary, a seat at the head of the table at meetings, a chauffeured limousine, use of a private dining room, and the ability to summon employees for discussion—

Figure 16.3 **Examples of Cultures on the Cultural Contact Continuum**

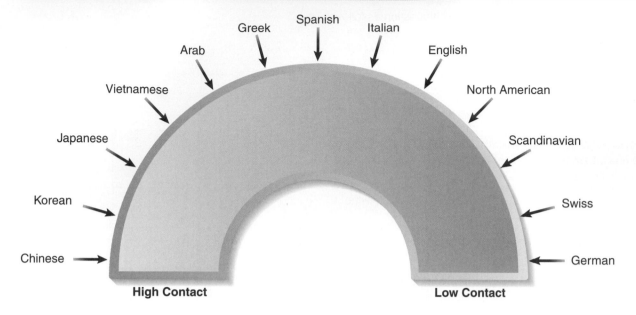

all send messages via the use of space. Organizations that seek to have a more egalitarian culture, such as Lucent Technologies and Southwest Airlines, intentionally avoid these status symbols. Most managers don't have the opportunity to plan and design the buildings in which their people will work. However, many do have the opportunity to plan floor layouts and the style and arrangement of office furniture, the tables and chairs used to furnish meeting rooms, and similar elements of work space.

As the following Strategic Action Competency feature illustrates, making decisions about the environment in which people work can be an important administrative responsibility. When Nortel Networks, a Canadian telecommunications firm, moved its global headquarters from downtown Toronto to suburban Brampton, it based its building design on the layout of ancient Rome and the concepts of feng shui.[13] The building has two main arteries (entrances) that form the central focus of the building. Extending from them are pathways providing access to Nortel's neighborhoods (departments). Nortel's CEO Roy Dohner doesn't occupy a formal office. He sits at a desk attached to his secretary's cubicle. If he has paperwork to do, he works at that spot. If he has a meeting, he connects his laptop in a convenient place somewhere in the building. Otherwise, he may be working at home or in one of Nortel's branch offices.

WEB INSIGHT

Nortel Networks interacts with customers in more than 150 countries worldwide, in many different languages. To learn more about Nortel's global customer communications, visit the company's Web site at *http://www.nortelnetworks.com*.

STRATEGIC ACTION COMPETENCY

Feng Shui at Nortel Networks

What is feng shui? **Feng shui** literally means wind (feng) and water (shui). In design, it refers to the Chinese science and art of creating harmony between people and their environment. When Nortel designed its new building, a feng shui consultant was hired. Employees from headquarters were asked to fill out a survey focusing on their areas of concern and to review the organization's communication needs. The consultant talked with people about the location of entrances, evaluated indoor air pollution levels, reviewed where people and teams gathered to make decisions, and studied places to maximize sales of new products and minimize theft. After gathering these data, the consultant prepared a geomantic (landscape design) chart for management.

This chart provides a personnel energy blueprint of the building that reveals problem areas and areas that might be underutilized. Enhancements to ensure greater utilization could include better use of light, space, color, natural landscape, position of furniture, office ergonomics, and aesthetics. Nortel included seven indoor "parks," a Zen garden, a full-service branch of the Canadian Imperial Bank of Commerce, fitness centers, basketball and volleyball courts, a physiotherapy area, a dry cleaning service, and an Ooops Café. The Docklands—the shipping and receiving area—features

an imposing 20-foot-tall graffiti mural created by 12 local street artists. There is even a "spirituality room" so that employees of various religious beliefs can pray and meditate—and even wash their feet if they're Muslim.

• • •

To learn more about Nortel's headquarters, visit the company's home page at

http://www.nortel.com

In terms of *personal appearance,* you've undoubtedly heard the expression, "Clothes make the person." Style consultants for major corporations believe that the way a person dresses definitely communicates something to others. You should ask yourself: Is the way I'm dressed going to hurt or help my business relationships? Like it or not, people judge you partly on the basis of how you look. If you're dressed appropriately, customers and others may see you as a more competent person than someone who dresses inappropriately. Of course, what is *appropriate* depends on the organization. A conservative suit fits in well on Wall Street but looks out of place in Silicon Valley.

Posture also communicates meaning by signaling a person's degree of self-confidence or interest in what is being discussed. The more interested you are, the more likely you are to lean toward the person who is talking. Conversely, leaning away may communicate a lack of interest. Similarly, tension and anxiety typically show in a person's legs and feet. People often are able to hide tension from the waist up but may give themselves away by crossing their legs tightly and tapping their feet.[14]

Verbal Messages. Employees communicate verbally more often than in any other way. Spoken communication takes place face to face, over the telephone, and via other electronic media. Most people prefer face-to-face communication because nonverbal messages are an important part of it. But some people prefer written communications because it allows them to choose and weigh their words more carefully before sending the message. When emotions run high, or someone is writing in a second language, weighing words carefully can be advantageous.

Effective verbal communication requires the sender to (1) encode the message in words (and nonverbal cues) that will convey it accurately to the receiver, (2) convey the message in a well-organized manner, and (3) try to eliminate distractions. At Ace Cash Express, loan officers must be especially good at sending verbal messages. Many customer transactions involve the use of long written documents, filled with legal and financial jargon. Loan officers assume that most customers won't read these documents, even though they are required to sign them. Therefore loan officers take responsibility for conveying verbally the messages contained in the written documents. They translate the jargon into everyday language and then summarize what the documents say for the customer, checking to be sure that the customer understands the key points.

Written Messages. Although spoken communication is quicker than written communication and allows the sender and receiver to interact, organizations use many forms of written messages (e.g., reports, memoranda, letters, e-mail, and newsletters). Such messages are most appropriate when information has to be collected from or distributed to many people at scattered locations and when keeping a record of what was sent is necessary. The following are some guidelines for preparing effective written messages.

1. The message should be drafted with the receiver clearly in mind.

2. The contents of the message should be well thought out ahead of time.

3. The message should be as brief as possible, without extraneous words and ideas. Important messages should be prepared in draft form first and then polished. If the message has to be long, a brief summary should be presented on the first page. This summary should clarify the main points and contain page references to details on each item.

4. The message should be carefully organized. The most important point should be stated first, then the next most important point, and so on. Thus, even if the receiver reads only the first few points, the essentials of the message will get across. Giving the message a title makes the subject clear. Using simple words and short, clear sentences make the message more readable and easily understood.

CHANNELS

The **channel** is the path a message follows from the sender to the receiver. **Information richness** is the information-carrying capacity of the channel. Not all channels can carry the same richness of information.[15] Written communications are low in richness. Customer and employee surveys are a form of written communication that many organizations rely on heavily despite their lack of information richness. Surveys usually ask people to express their opinions about various topics by choosing from multiple-choice options. Customers might be asked to indicate whether they were delighted, just satisfied, or disappointed with the customer service they received. Employees might be asked to indicate whether they strongly agree, agree, disagree, or strongly disagree with a statement such as My manager treats me with respect. This form of communication facilitates quantitative analyses, but it limits the type and amount of information received from customers and employees. Only the information written down is received. Channels low in richness are considered to be *lean* because they are effective mainly for sending specific data and facts.

As Figure 16.4 indicates, face-to-face interaction is the richest communication channel. It conveys several cues simultaneously, including spoken and nonverbal information. Face-to-face interaction also provides immediate feedback so that comprehension can be checked and misinterpretations corrected. Managers can gather additional information about how customers and employees feel about the organization and its products by speaking with them personally. Focus groups are a structured form of face-to-face communication that often are used to gauge customers' reactions to products. The telephone is somewhat less rich than face-to-face communication, but not as lean as written surveys. The First National Bank of Chicago changed its approach to customer satisfaction surveys in order to obtain richer information. The bank discontinued its mail survey and began to conduct telephone surveys. Managers were trained to interview customers and were responsible for acting on their responses. Directly hearing the voices of customers added richness and perspective to the information provided.

| **Figure 16.4** | **Information Richness of Channels** |

Information Channel		**Information Richness**
Face-to-face discussion		Highest
Telephone conversations		High
Written letters/memos (individually addressed)		Moderate
Formal written documents (unaddressed bulletins or e-mail)		Low
Formal numeric documents (printouts, budget reports)		Lowest

In addition to selecting a level of information richness, individuals must choose among several *types* of channels for communicating with others. They include downward, upward, and horizontal formal channels and informal channels, such as the grapevine and networking (or caucus) groups.

Downward Channels. ***Downward channels*** involve all the means of sending messages from management to employees. For instance, the L.L. Bean mail-order headquarters in Freeport, Maine, receives more than 250,000 communications (e.g., phones calls, faxes, and e-mail messages) a day during the holiday season for 20,000 outdoor items ranging from socks to flannel shirts to hunting bows to tents.[16] To communicate effectively with L.L. Bean's 4,000 employees, managers use downward channels to convey

- how to handle special promotional items;
- job descriptions, detailing duties and responsibilities;
- policies and procedures, explaining what is expected of employees and the organization's rules and employee benefits;
- feedback about an individual's job performance; and
- news of activities and events that management believes employees should participate in (charitable organizations, blood drives, and the like).

Managers frequently use downward communication effectively as a channel, but it may be the most misused channel because it provides little opportunity for employees to respond. In fact, the fundamental problem with downward communication is that it is too often one way. It's a lean channel that doesn't encourage feedback from those on the receiving end. To correct this problem, managers should urge employees to use upward channels.

Upward Channels. Some managers don't see the value of encouraging employees to participate in setting goals and planning and formulating policies. The result is a failure to provide upward channels of communication. ***Upward channels*** are all the means used by employees to send messages to management. Such channels may be the only formal means that employees have for communicating with higher level managers in the organization. Upward communication includes providing feedback on how well employees understand the messages they have received via downward channels. Moreover, it enables employees to voice their opinions and ideas. If it is effective, upward communication can provide an emotional release and, at the same time, give employees a chance to participate, the feeling that they are being listened to, and a sense of personal worth. Most important, employees often have excellent suggestions for improving efficiency and effectiveness, as Gordon Bethune found out when he became CEO of Continental Airlines.

At Cirque du Soleil, upward channels are as strong as downward channels.[17] Specific methods for communicating upward include direct personal contacts and three publications circulated regularly within the company. One publication is *The Ball*, which features a column called BYOB—Be Your Own Bitch. Employees use it to complain, gripe, and rib without censorship. "This is part of the way we do things," explained Marc Gagnon, vice president of human resources. One message indicated that the writer felt that the Dutch employees were being treated better than the Canadians. This information was quite useful because it allowed the company to head off certain issues before they could become crises. *The Ball* also informs employees of events and activities taking place at company locations around the world.

WEB INSIGHT

Cirque du Soleil takes its communication skills outside the company to help youth at risk around the world. Find out more about its programs for troubled young people by visiting Cirque du Soleil's Web site at *http://www.cirquedusoleil.com*.

Besides its publications, Cirque du Soleil uses employee focus groups to help design new initiatives and develop new policies. "We look for three things," explained Gagnon. "Make sure the proposed policy is clear and they understand it; see if they agree with it, or if they disagree with it and why; and see if we have any chance to get people to use it. People are allowed to say 'no' to a policy."

Upward channels provide many benefits, but managers need to be aware of the problems that can plague upward communication. First, most employees don't want their superiors to learn anything negative about them, so they may screen out bad news. Most employees try to impress their superiors by emphasizing their contributions to the organization. Some may even try to make themselves look better by putting others down. Second, an employee's personal anxieties, aspirations, and attitudes almost always color what is communicated. Would you tell a potential employer of the bad things you've heard about the organization? If you really wanted the job, you probably wouldn't be so bold. Finally, the employee may be competing for the manager's job and thus remains silent in the hope of being recommended for it when the manager is promoted and moves to another position.

Realizing that employees aren't always comfortable giving direct upward feedback has led many companies to provide another alternative—anonymously contacting a third party. At Pillsbury, employees can call a recording machine and sound off. Verbatim transcripts are prepared of each call and forwarded to the CEO and other top-level managers, with no identification about the gender or any other detectable caller characteristics. The objective was to let the company's senior managers hear the views of employees, without causing employees to be fearful of what might happen to them for voicing their concerns and criticisms. Employees began using the service to share all sorts of information. They noted that a clock in one bakery always ran five minutes fast, identified locations that didn't carry particular products on the shelves, suggested new pizza toppings, and complained so much about slow expense reimbursements that the company overhauled some of its accounting procedures. By calling to express their appreciation, employees also made a hero of a manager who closed down operations during a snowstorm.[18] Other companies that actively encourage upward communication include Rite Aid, Eastman Kodak, and Brown-Ferris Industries. In each case, the CEO encourages open griping and pays particular attention when the same comment is made repeatedly.

Horizontal Channels. *Horizontal channels* are all the means used to send and receive messages across departmental lines, with suppliers, or with customers. This type of channel is especially important in network organizations (see Chapter 11). Essential to the success of a network organization is maintaining effective communication among customers, suppliers, and employees in various divisions or functional areas. Nike outsources the manufacturing of its athletic shoes and apparel to manufacturers throughout the world. It needs effective horizontal communication channels to link suppliers with information about market demand in order to schedule production and shipping efficiently.

Horizontal channels are formal if they follow prescribed organizational paths. Messages communicated horizontally usually are related to coordinating activities, sharing information, and solving problems. Horizontal channels are extremely important in today's team-based organizations, where employees must often communicate among themselves to solve their clients' production or process problems.

Informal Channels. So far we have concentrated on formal channels of communication. Equally important, however, are informal channels of communication. *Informal channels* are all the nonformal means for sender and receiver to communicate downward, upward, and horizontally. The *grapevine* is an organization's informal communication system, along which information can travel in any direction. The term comes from a Civil War practice of hanging telegraph lines loosely from tree to tree, like a grapevine. In organizations, the path that messages follow along the grapevine is based on social interaction, not organization charts.

At Xerox's Palo Alto Research Center (PARC), informal channels are essential to its success. The company learned just how important informal channels were when it began looking for ways to boost productivity. Management hired a social anthropologist to observe closely the behavior of technicians who repaired copiers (tech reps) in an effort to improve efficiency. The consultant saw that tech reps often made a point of spending time with each other but not with customers. They would hang around the parts warehouse or the coffeepot and swap stories from the field. The consultant recognized the importance of these informal conversations to tech rep performance. Through their stories, the reps shared knowledge and generated new insights about how to repair machines better. Xerox concluded that tech rep performance could be improved by increasing this type of communication, so the company issued two-way radio headsets to the reps.[19]

Informal channels of communication have been recognized by many organizations as so important that they encourage and provide support for employees' efforts to strengthen them. *Employee network groups* are informal groups that organize regularly scheduled social activities to promote informal communication among employees who share a common interest or concern. In many organizations, network groups form to bring together minority employees. For example, at Sara Lee, Motorola, IBM, and many other large organizations, numerous caucus groups exist for members of particular ethnic groups. Caucus groups for women also are quite common. According to a survey of Fortune 500 companies, such groups have grown rapidly during the past decade. Participants benefit from the business information shared during meetings, as well as from the friendships they form and the contacts they make. At Sara Lee, women's leadership councils operate within specific divisions of the company to support career development and offer networking opportunities for women. To ensure their effectiveness, John Bryan, CEO, regularly reviews developmental activities of female and minority employees.[20]

External Networking. Managers and employees also spend considerable time meeting with peers and others outside the organization. They attend meetings of professional associations, trade shows, and other gatherings. As a result, they may develop various close, informal relationships with talented and interesting people outside the organization. People use these networks to help each other, trading favors and calling on each other's resources for career advancement or other types of information and support.

Bill Case, founder of Integrated Change Ware Systems, recognized how important networking is to growing businesses. He organized Star Light, which meets once a month in Richardson, Texas, for managers of small companies to network and discuss business issues. The club's activities are supported by organizations such as *Dallas Business* magazine, American Express, and TI and draws some 100 attendees per meeting. The goal is to provide small-business owners with some insights into problems and issues surrounding mergers and acquisitions. Venture capitalists, bankers, and consultants often attend these breakfast meetings to learn about the newest small business in the Dallas area. Jeff Barton, marketing manager at TI, also attends because TI doesn't want to miss out on opportunities to acquire a business started by "three-guys in a garage" that turns out to be another Apple Computer Corporation. Case is frequently sought after as a speaker for other groups of small-business entrepreneurs because of his intimate knowledge of their organizational challenges and financial problems.[21]

FEEDBACK

Feedback is the receiver's response to the sender's message. It's the best way to show that a message has been received and to indicate whether it has been understood. As Gordon Bethune and his staff found out at Continental Airlines, lots of information gets filtered and lost between top management and those who work daily with Continental's customers. You shouldn't assume that everything you say or write will be understood exactly as you intend it to be. If you don't encourage feedback, you're likely to misjudge how much others understand you. Thus you'll be less effective than those who encourage feedback.

When managers are asked to rank the communication skills they find crucial to their success on the job, they consistently place feedback at the top of the list. Managers spend more than half their time listening to others. Because most people speak at a rate of 100 to 150 words per minute and the brain is capable of thinking at a rate of 400 to 500 words per minute, people often daydream. Therefore feedback is needed to ensure that messages sent are accurately received. The following Self-Management Competency feature allows you to assess your openness to receiving feedback.[22]

When answering these 11 questions, use the following rating scale.

1. Strongly disagree
2. Disagree
3. Slightly disagree
4. Slightly agree
5. Agree
6. Strongly agree

_____ 1. I seek information about my strengths and weaknesses from others as a basis for self-improvement.

_____ 2. When I receive negative feedback about myself from others, I do not get angry or defensive.

_____ 3. In order to improve, I am willing to be self-disclosing to others (i.e., share my feelings and beliefs).

_____ 4. I am very much aware of my personal style of gathering information and making decisions.

_____ 5. I am very much aware of my own interpersonal needs when it comes to forming relationships with other people.

_____ 6. I have a good sense of how I cope with situations that are ambiguous and uncertain.

_____ 7. I have a well-developed set of personal standards and principles that guide my behavior.

_____ 8. I feel very much in charge of what happens to me, good and bad.

_____ 9. I seldom, if ever, feel angry, depressed, or anxious without knowing why.

_____ 10. I am conscious of the areas in which conflict and friction most frequently arise in my interactions with others.

_____ 11. I have a close personal relationship with at least one other person with whom I can share personal information and personal feelings.

SCORING KEY

Skill Area   **Total**

Self-disclosure and openness to feedback from others (items 1, 2, 3, 9, 11)   _____

Awareness of own values, cognitive style, change orientation, and interpersonal orientation (items 4, 5, 6, 7, 8, 10)   _____

Grand Total _____

COMPARISON DATA

Compare your scores to three standards: (1) the maximum possible (66); (2) the scores of other students in your class; and (3) the scores of a norm group consisting of more than 500 business students. In comparison to the norm group, if you scored

55 or above,	you are in the top quartile.
52–54,	you are in the second quartile.
48–51,	you are in the third quartile.
47 or below,	you are in the bottom quartile.

Whenever a message is sent, the actions of the sender affect the reactions of the receiver. The reactions of the receiver, in turn, affect later actions of the sender. If the sender receives no response, the message was never received or the receiver chose not to respond. In either case, the sender is alerted to the need to find out why the receiver didn't respond. Upon receiving rewarding feedback, the sender continues to produce the same kind of message. When feedback is *not* rewarding, the sender eventually changes the type of message.

Receiver reactions also tell the sender how well goals are being achieved or tasks are being accomplished. However, in this case the receiver exerts control over the sender by the type of feedback provided. The sender must rely on the receiver for an indication of whether the message was received and understood. Such feedback assures the sender that things are going as planned or brings to light problems that have to be solved. Lands' End, OxyChem, Holiday Inn, and other companies have guidelines for providing effective feedback. According to these guidelines, feedback should have the following characteristics.[23]

1. *It should be helpful*. If the receiver of the message provides feedback that adds to the sender's information, the feedback is likely to be seen as constructive.

2. *It should be descriptive rather than evaluative*. If the receiver responds to the message in a descriptive manner, the feedback is likely to be effective. If the receiver is

highly critical (or judgmental), the feedback is likely to be ineffective or even cause a breakdown in communication.

3. *It should be specific rather than general.* The receiver should respond specifically to points raised and questions asked in the message. If the receiver responds in generalities, the feedback may indicate evasion or lack of understanding.

4. *It should be well timed.* The reception—and thus the effectiveness—of feedback is affected by the context in which it occurs. Giving performance feedback to a person during a round of golf or at a luncheon is different from giving the same person this feedback in the office. Informal settings usually are reserved for social as opposed to performance-based feedback.

5. *It should not overwhelm.* Spoken communication depends heavily on memory. Accordingly, when large amounts of information are involved, spoken feedback is less effective than written feedback. People tend to "tune in and out" of conversations. They may fail to grasp what the speaker is saying if the message is too long and complex.[24]

PERCEPTION

Perception is the meaning given to a message by either sender or receiver. Perceptions are influenced by what people see, by the ways they organize these elements in memory, and by the meanings they attach to them. The ability to perceive varies from person to person. Some people having entered a room only once can later describe it in detail, whereas others can barely remember anything about it. Thus the mental ability to notice and remember is important. How people interpret what they perceive is affected by their pasts. A clenched fist raised in the air by an employee on strike and walking the picket line could be interpreted as either an angry threat to the organization *or* as an expression of union solidarity and accomplishment. The attitudes that people bring to a situation color their perceptions of it.

Some problems in communication can be traced to two problems of perception: selective perception and stereotyping. **Selective perception** is the process of screening out information that a person wants or needs to avoid. Many people "tune out" TV commercials. Most everyone has been accused at one time or another of listening only to what they want to hear. Both are examples of selective perception. In organizations, employees sometimes do the same thing. Manufacturing employees pay close attention to manufacturing problems, and accounting employees pay close attention to debits and credits. Such employees tend to filter out information about other areas of the organization and focus on information that is directly related to their own jobs.

Stereotyping is the process of making assumptions about individuals solely on the basis of their belonging to a certain gender, race, age, or other category. Stereotyping distorts reality by suggesting that all people in a category have similar characteristics, which simply isn't true.

During the 1990s, organizations became increasingly sensitive to the potential negative consequences of stereotyping based on a person's gender, race, ethnicity, age, or sexual orientation. As they have sought to manage workforce diversity more effectively, many organizations—including General Mills and Allstate—have developed training programs and other taken other initiatives to reduce the negative personal and organizational consequences of stereotyping. We discuss workforce diversity further in Chapter 18.

In summary, then, the message sent, the channel of communication used, and the ability to respond all depend on a person's perceptions. Encoding and decoding skills are based on a person's ability to perceive a message and situation accurately. Developing the ability to send and receive messages accurately is central to being an effective manager.

IMPACT OF INFORMATION TECHNOLOGY

2.

DESCRIBE THE ROLE
OF INFORMATION
TECHNOLOGY IN THE
COMMUNICATION
PROCESS.

New information technologies are rapidly changing the methods of communication available to managers and employees alike—and thus the channels of communication they use. These technologies are changing not only the manner in which managers and employees communicate with each other, but they also are changing the ways they make decisions. Telephone answering machines (voice mail), fax machines, teleconferencing, closed-circuit television systems, computerized report preparation, videotaping, and computer-to-computer transmission are examples of communication methods developed during the past 25 years. Here, we review three of these technologies: electronic mail, the Internet, and teleconferencing.

ELECTRONIC MAIL

Electronic mail (e-mail) uses computer text composition and editing to send and receive written information quickly, inexpensively, and efficiently. In seconds, messages are transmitted from the sender's computer to the receiver's. They are read at the receiver's convenience. Senders and receivers usually process their own e-mail. They don't have to give messages to, or receive messages from, secretaries or telephone operators. Messages appear on (and disappear from) video screens with no hard copies produced, unless one is specifically desired. Electronic mail has become popular with managers for several reasons. First, a manager doesn't have to wait long for a response because information usually can be sent, returned, and recalled in moments. Second, e-mail is relatively inexpensive because it can "piggyback" on computer, telephone, and other equipment that companies already have in place. Third, it increases productivity by eliminating the need for the paper-handling steps required in traditional interoffice or intercompany communication systems. One significant disadvantage has been observed in companies that use e-mail extensively: Employees who might never confront coworkers face-to-face are less hesitant to explode at others via e-mail, a phenomenon called *flaming*.

Texas Instruments began using e-mail more than a decade ago. Today thousands of PCs connect TI's more than 36,000 employees at locations throughout the world, along with its more than 3,500 customers. The system covers the United States and plants in more than a dozen foreign countries. If TI's CEO Tom Engibous needs to send a message to a plant manager in Tokyo, Japan, he can call Tokyo. However, 3:00 P.M. in Texas is equivalent to 2:00 A.M. in Japan, so timing (as well as cost) make the telephone a less than optimal method. E-mail enables Engibous to send a message before leaving work in the evening and to have an answer waiting on his computer when he arrives for work the next morning. In terms of cost, e-mail is 90 percent less expensive than overseas calls and letters and 75 percent less costly than telex. Engibous believes that e-mail and other automated office techniques have had positive effects on research and development at TI. Producing state-of-the-art products and services at affordable prices requires that everyone in the organization have access to global information that can improve their performance.[25]

E-mail has dramatically changed the way people can work. No longer is it necessary for an employee to live within commuting distance of the organization's office. Telecommuting allows organizations to recruit and hire people who may never come to the office and can live anywhere in the world. Allowing employees to telecommute expands the pool from which an employer can select new hires and can also help in promoting existing employees who prefer not to relocate.

THE INTERNET

The *Internet* is a loosely configured, rapidly growing web of thousands of corporate, educational, and research computer networks around the world. The U.S. Department of Defense created it in 1969, and it was designed to survive a nuclear war. Rather than route messages through central computers, the Internet makes use of thousands of computers linked by thousands of different paths. Each message sent bears an address code that speeds it toward its destination. Messages usually arrive in seconds; only on rare occasions do they vanish into cyberspace. The Internet is like any other communications device in that a user can get a busy signal. With thousands of Internet groups and e-mail lists, sometimes the traffic is heavy and a user might have to wait a short time to connect to the system.

The privacy of information sent over the Internet is limited, and finding methods to make information secure is a high priority of both researchers and users. But because information on the Internet is potentially available to almost anyone in the world, it also offers almost unlimited communication opportunities. If you have been completing the Web Insights in each chapter and Questions for Discussion and Competency Development at the end of each chapter in this textbook, you are already quite familiar with the Internet.

TELECONFERENCING

Communicating via e-mail offers many conveniences, but a major drawback is that the information sent is primarily in written form. The Internet is more information rich, easily transmitting increasingly high-quality video and sound. New technological developments are quickly transforming the Internet into a high-fidelity communications tool. Teleconferencing technology, which combines television and telephone technologies, is another high-fidelity communications tool that organizations use to facilitate discussions among people dispersed throughout the world. Unlike traditional conference calls over the telephone, teleconferencing allows participants to see each other's body language and to jointly view materials such as blueprints, charts, graphs, and even product prototypes. Also, it can be used in combination with other information technology, such as *groupware*, which is an aid to group problem solving and decision making.

THE DOWNSIDE OF INFORMATION TECHNOLOGY

Information technologies can expand the communication capabilities of individuals and organizations exponentially. In recent years, organizations have spent billions of dollars on these technologies in the hope of improving communication among employees and among employees and external stakeholders, such as suppliers and customers. L.L. Bean uses information technology to scan résumés of prospective employees, reducing the time needed to fill a position from an average of 60 to 90 days to 45 days.[26] E-recruiting software that works like an advanced search engine scans for key words that point to an applicant's credentials. The program flags only those résumés that satisfy specific requirements for a particular position. Employment decisions take into account the organization's overall strategy and the location of the store. Unfortunately, if a candidate's résumé doesn't contain any of the key words, the candidate won't be interviewed.

Information technology should play an important role in helping an organization achieve its goals. As illustrated in the following Planning and Administration Competency feature, attracting and retaining hi-tech workers are high priorities for many organizations.[27]

PLANNING & ADMINISTRATION COMPETENCY

A Hip Workplace

Farm, Inc., a Toronto-based communication design organization, hunts for ways to attract and retain hi-tech workers. The firm recently redesigned the interior of the Bulldog Group's building to provide the Toronto firm's customers and employees with a sense of fun and excitement. Kitchens, cappuccino bars, schmoozing zones, and napping couches were all incorporated into the design.

The main reception and brainstorming area, a few steps down from street level, is dominated by long bar tables where employees eat their lunch, kick around ideas, and meet clients.

There is music, a microwave, and a fridge stocked with beer and champagne, for special occasions. Employees bring their lunch or just hang out—and park their bicycles behind the bar. By seeking and sharing the latest information, employees have a good feel for what's going on and how that affects their own interests. The bar tables provide an opportunity for employees to voice their opinions without fear of reprisal. The attitude is that facts are friendly, and it is therefore a good thing for people to know what's going on.

Throughout the building are small private offices, a compact boardroom, and small enclaves where employees can have private conversations with other employees or customers. Some enclaves even have couches where employees can stretch out and nap if they so desire. Like many hi-tech firms, the Bulldog Group often employs contract (freelance) workers and provides areas where they can work while at the firm.

HURDLES TO EFFECTIVE COMMUNICATION

3.

IDENTIFY HURDLES TO COMMUNICATION AND DESCRIBE WAYS TO ELIMINATE THEM.

One of the first steps in communicating more effectively is to identify hurdles to the process. These hurdles hinder the sending and receiving of messages by distorting, or sometimes even completely blocking, intended meanings. We divided these impediments into organizational and individual hurdles—although there is obviously some overlap—and listed them in Table 16.2.

Table 16.2	*Barriers to Communication*

Organizational

Authority and status levels

Specialization of task functions by members

Different goals

Status relationships among members

Individual

Conflicting assumptions

Semantics

Emotions

ORGANIZATIONAL HURDLES

Channels of communication, both formal and informal, are largely determined by organization design. Hierarchical organizations have more levels of authority and greater differences in status among their members. Flat organizations have relatively few authority levels and tend to be more egalitarian in terms of status. The degree of specialization present in the organization also may affect clear communication, as can the presence of conflicting goals.

Authority and Status Levels. A person holding a higher formal position than another person has a higher level of authority. A person who is held in higher esteem than another person, regardless of their positions, has a higher status. Authority level and status often go hand in hand, but not always. *Status* is a person's social rank in a group, which often is determined by a person's characteristics, in addition to the person's formal position. When status and authority level differ, communication problems are likely to occur.

The more levels in the organization—and the farther the receiver is from the sender—the more difficult effective communication becomes. Figure 16.5 illustrates the loss of understanding as messages are sent downward through a formal communication channel. To minimize this problem, top managers increasingly are using live video presentations or videotapes to deliver the same message to employees at all of an organization's locations. In doing so, these managers use both verbal and nonverbal messages and cut out intervening receivers and senders to increase the probability that the original messages will be received intact. Many organizations use videotapes when moving managers to new locations. Such presentations can introduce the managers, reinforce the reason(s) for the relocation, and emphasize the need for employee cooperation during the changeover.

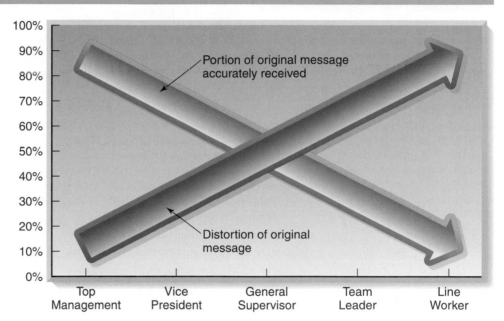

Figure 16.5 *Levels of Understanding for a Message from the CEO*

Even when communicating with others at the same level of authority, status can interfere with the process. In group discussions, members having higher status speak more and have more influence than members having lower status. This phenomenon is difficult to overcome, and it has been observed in both computer-mediated (exchange of e-mail messages) and face-to-face discussion groups. When computer-mediated group discussions were first introduced, many people expected them to mute the effects of status on communication. Instead such information technologies often reinforce existing status relationships and magnify their effects on communication.

In organizations with flat hierarchies, such as Southwest Airlines, Sun Hydraulics, and Chapparal Steel, authority levels may not interfere with communication, but status is likely to come into play. Temporary employees, for example, often report feeling as if they are being treated as second-class workers. Often they are excluded from meetings, not invited to social functions, and denied team-based reward systems. In other words, they seldom hear news as it travels through the grapevine and miss the many advantages of being part of informal communication networks. Not surprisingly, then, nearly one of four managers reports that friction between permanent and temporary workers is a significant disadvantage of relying on temporary employees to create flexible staffing levels and reduce costs.[28]

Specialization. As knowledge becomes more specialized, professionals in many fields develop their own jargon, or shorthand, to simplify communication among themselves. That often makes communication with people outside a particular field difficult. For example, a tax accountant and a marketing research manager might have trouble communicating successfully. Moreover, in an attempt to make themselves indispensable, some people intentionally use the language of specialization to obscure what's going on. Employees often use specialized language when trying to "snow" others. When a plumber wrote to the U.S. Department of Housing and Urban Development (HUD) to find out whether using hydrochloric acid to unclog drains was safe, a HUD bureaucrat wrote back: "The efficacy of hydrochloric acid is indisputable, but corrosive acid is incompatible with metallic permanence." The plumber wrote back saying he agreed and was using it. A fax message from the bureaucrat arrived immediately at the plumber's shop. It read: "Don't use hydrochloric acid. It eats the hell out of pipes." Then the plumber understood.

Different Goals. If each department has its own goals, these goals can interfere with the organization's overall performance. Herb Kelleher, CEO of Southwest Airlines, doesn't set departmental goals because he believes that they would create conflicts between departments. Such conflicts can be direct consequences of competing interests, or they may simply arise from misunderstandings created by the different perspectives of the people involved. However, open communication between people with differing goals speeds problem solving and improves the quality of solutions. At ARAMARK, a large managed-services organization, each of its seven divisions—campus dining, business dining, sports and recreation, facilities management, maintenance, hospital, and correctional—has its own goals for revenue, account retention, and gaining new accounts. The goal of the campus-dining director is to serve student dining needs. Some colleges also outsource their maintenance and facilities needs, so it would be logical for the campus-dining director to look into a campus's needs in these other two areas. Unfortunately, most campus-dining directors narrowly focus on their own goals and neglect reaching out to help the organization reach its overall goals in the other areas. Why? Because their rewards are based on achieving their own unit's goals, not those of the entire organization.

INDIVIDUAL HURDLES

The Center for Creative Leadership at Greensboro, North Carolina, estimates that half of all managers and 30 percent of top managers have some difficulty communicating with others.[29] Through an intense training session at the center, managers can learn how to improve their communication competencies. The center's staff works with participants who believe that their messages are clear and effective when, in fact, they aren't. Their words, phrases, and references may be clear to some individuals, puzzling to others, and obscure to still others. These problems can be caused by semantics and emotions.

Semantics. The study of the way words are used and the meanings they convey is called *semantics.* Misinterpretation of word meanings can play a large role in communication failure. When two people attribute different meanings to the same words but don't realize it, a communication hurdle exists. Consider what happened when a sales rep phoned in a special order to her company's shipping department. She asked that it be shipped "as soon as possible," expecting these words to ensure that the order was given top priority. Five days later, the sales rep got a call from the irate customer wanting to know when the order would be delivered. Upon checking with the shipping department, the sales rep found that the order was being shipped that day. After some shouting, she realized that, in the shipping department, "as soon as possible" meant that the request did *not* need to be given top priority.

Problems caused by semantics are compounded when people who speak different languages attempt to communicate. As described in the following Communication Competency feature, imprecise translations cause many blunders in international business dealings.[30]

The largest number of blunders in advertising promotions in foreign countries are caused by faulty translation. Slang terms, idioms, and local dialects have all contributed to the many marketing mishaps that have occurred as organizations expanded into global markets. Here are some examples that illustrate how small language differences create big advertising blunders.

- Exxon's original Japanese brand was Esso, which means "stalled car" when pronounced phonetically in Japanese. Discovering this problem, Exxon chose Enco as a replacement, not realizing that it referred to a sewage disposal truck.

- When Budweiser tried to translate its slogan, King of Beer, into Spanish it discovered that Beer (*cerveza*) is a noun of the feminine gender, leaving them with Queen of Beer as a slogan.

- The soft drink Fresca was marketed in Mexico without a change in brand name. The company later discovered that fresca is slang for lesbian in Mexico.

- The Marlboro cigarette brand is well known for its American cowboy sitting on a horse symbolizing the frontier spirit of America. In Hong Kong, people see him as a low-status laborer.

- Tiffany sells glassware in sets of five in Japan because the word four translates to *shi,* which means "death" in Japanese.

- During the 1994 soccer World Cup, both McDonald's and Coca-Cola imprinted the Saudi Arabian flag, which includes sacred words from the Koran, on disposable packaging. Doing so offended the Saudis.

To avoid such blunders, companies should routinely have messages translated back to the original language to ensure the accuracy of the original translation—a process called *backtranslation*. If the original message and the backtranslated version agree, the translated version probably will not have unexpected meanings. Even backtranslation is not foolproof, however, because the meanings of words often depend on the context in which they are used—especially in high-context cultures (e.g., Arab, Japanese, and Chinese). In these cultures, communication involves sending and receiving many subtle cues. Nonverbal cues, intonation subtleties, and inferences are all essential aspects of communication. The Japanese often talk around a point without ever stating it directly. From their perspective, it is the responsibility of the listener to discern the message from the context. German, Scandinavian, and Anglo cultures are low-context cultures that place more emphasis on the precise meanings of words and terms.[31]

Emotions. An *emotion* is a subjective reaction or feeling. Remembering experiences, an individual recalls not only events but also the feelings that accompanied them. Thus when people communicate, they convey emotions as well as facts and opinions. The sender's feelings influence encoding of the message and may or may not be apparent to the receiver. The receiver's feelings affect decoding of the message and the nature of the response.

Misunderstandings owing to differences in what arouses people's emotions often accompany cross-cultural communication. In Japan, for example, feelings of embarrassment and shame are more easily aroused during social interactions than they are in Western cultures. Furthermore, these emotions aren't easily detected by people not socialized in the Japanese culture. Consequently, Westerners are likely to create situations that cause their Japanese counterparts to feel embarrassment and shame without realizing it—and thus seem insensitive.

Although there are many other cultural differences in how people experience and express emotions, there are also many similarities. Rather than being hurdles to communication, these similarities aid communication. In particular, the antecedents of some emotions—anger, happiness, disgust, fear, sadness, and surprise—seem to be similar in most cultures, as are the facial expressions that accompany the emotions.[32] These similarities mean that nonverbal cues are less likely to be misinterpreted when emotions are involved.

ELIMINATING HURDLES

Regardless of how much information is needed to create feelings of overload in individuals, every organization is capable of producing that volume of information and more. Therefore you should set up a system that identifies priority messages for immediate attention. One way of doing so is to ask others to bring you information only when significant deviations from goals and plans occur (known as *exception reporting*). When everything is going as planned, you don't need a report. And if you want to empower your subordinates, let them know that they don't need to send you a copy of all those e-mail messages.

Regulate the Flow of Information. If you receive too much information you will suffer from information overload. How much information is too much varies from one person to the next and may even be different for today's Generation Y. It has grown up in an environment where 10–30-second TV commercials are normal and students do homework with their Walkmans turned on. MTV and video games that may lead to information overload by older people are normal for today's students.

Regardless of how much information is needed to create the sensation of information overload, every organization is capable of producing volumes of information. Therefore you should set up a system that identifies priority messages for immediate attention. Some e-mail software packages allow senders to put "red flags" next to their messages, indicating urgency to recipients.

Encourage Feedback. You should follow up to determine whether important messages have been understood. Feedback lets you know whether the other person understands the message accurately. Feedback doesn't have to be verbal; in fact, actions often speak louder than words. The sales manager who describes desired changes in the monthly sales planning report receives feedback from the report itself when it is turned in. If it contains the proper changes, the manager knows that the message was received and understood. Similarly, when you talk to a group of people, look for nonverbal feedback that will tell you whether you are getting through to them.

Simplify the Language. Because language can be a hurdle, you should choose words that others will understand. Your sentences should be concise, and you should avoid jargon that others won't understand or that may be misleading. In general, understanding is improved by simplifying the language used—consistent, of course, with the nature of your intended audience.

Listen Actively. You need to become a good listener as well as a good message sender. Recently, several organizations have developed training programs to improve employee listening. Such programs often emphasize that listening is an active process in which listeners and speakers share equal responsibility for successful communication. The following are some characteristics of active listeners.[33]

- *Appreciative:* listens in a relaxed manner, seeking enjoyment, knowledge, or inspiration.

- *Empathic:* listens without judging, is supportive of the speaker, and learns from the experiences of others.

- *Comprehensive:* listens to organize and make sense of information by understanding relationships among ideas.

- *Discerning:* listens to get complete information, understand the main message, and determine important details.

- *Evaluative:* listens in order to make a decision based on the information provided.

Restrain Negative Emotions. Like everyone else, you convey emotions when communicating, but negative emotions can distort the content of the message. When emotionally upset, you are more likely than at other times to phrase a message poorly. The simplest answer in such a situation is to call a halt until you and the other people involved can restrain your emotions—that is, until all of you can be more descriptive than evaluative.

Use Nonverbal Cues. You should use nonverbal cues to emphasize points and express feelings. Recall the methods of nonverbal communication that we've presented. You need to be sure that your actions reinforce your words so that they don't send mixed messages.

Use the Grapevine. As a manager, you couldn't get rid of the grapevine in an organization even if you tried, so you should use it to send information rapidly, test reactions before announcing a final decision, and obtain valuable feedback. Also, the grapevine frequently carries destructive rumors, reducing employee morale and organizational effectiveness. By being "plugged into" the grapevine, you can partially counteract this negative effect by being sure that relevant, accurate, meaningful, and timely information gets to others.

FOSTERING EFFECTIVE COMMUNICATION

4.

STATE THE GUIDELINES FOR FOSTERING EFFECTIVE COMMUNICATION.

To be an effective communicator, you must understand not only the communication process depicted earlier in Figure 16.1, but also the guidelines for fostering effective communication. These guidelines, presented throughout the chapter, are summarized in the following list. We have expressed them in terms of the American Management Association's seven guidelines that you can use to improve your communication skills.[34]

- *Clarify your ideas before communicating.* Analyze the topic or problem to clarify it in your mind before sending a message. Communication often is ineffective because the message is inadequately planned. Part of good message planning is considering the goals and attitudes of those who will receive the message.

- *Examine the true purpose of the communication.* Before you send a message, ask yourself what you really want to accomplish with it. Decide whether you want to obtain information, convey a decision, or persuade someone to take action.

- *Consider the setting in which the communication will take place.* You convey meanings and intent by more than words alone. Trying to communicate with a person in another location is more difficult than doing so face to face.

- *Consult with others, when appropriate, in planning communications.* Encourage the participation of those who will be affected by the message. They can often provide a viewpoint that you might not have considered.

- *Be mindful of the nonverbal messages you send.* Tone of voice, facial expression, eye contact, personal appearance, and physical surroundings all influence the communication process. The receiver considers both the words and the nonverbal cues that comprise your message.

- *Take the opportunity to convey something helpful to the receiver.* Considering the other person's interests and needs often presents opportunities to the sender. You can make your message clearer by imagining yourself in the other's position. Effective communicators really try to understand the message from the listener's point of view.

- *Follow up the communication.* Your best efforts at communication can be wasted unless you succeed in getting your message across. You should follow up and ask for feedback to find out whether you succeeded. You can't assume that the receiver understands your message; feedback in some form is necessary.

If you follow these recommendations, you will improve your ability to communicate effectively. Unfortunately, when communication does break down, people often waste time and energy trying to figure out who is at fault, provoking a defensive reaction that further inhibits effective communication.

WEB INSIGHT

The American Management Association offers a full range of managerial development programs throughout the world. How may its members profit from AMA's expertise in communication? View its Web site at *http://www.amanet.org*.

CHAPTER SUMMARY

Effective communication is essential to many aspects of human endeavor, including organizational life. For managers, the communication competency is the foundation upon which managerial effectiveness is built. Through communication, managers gather and interpret information that they then use to plan, set goals, and make strategic decisions. Strategic decisions, in turn, must be communicated throughout the organization, where they are used to guide planning and team activities. In cross-cultural situations, the global awareness competency supports effective communication.

1. EXPLAIN THE MAIN ELEMENTS OF THE COMMUNICATION PROCESS.

The communication process comprises six elements: the sender (encoder), the receiver (decoder), the message, channels, feedback, and perception. Of the many possible forms of nonverbal communication, managers should be particularly aware of—and able to use effectively—space, physical appearance, and body language. Channels of communication are both formal and informal. Formal channels are downward, upward, and horizontal. Managers most frequently use downward channels to send messages to the various levels of the organization. Upward channels allow employee participation in decision making and provide feedback to management. Horizontal channels are used among peers in different departments and are especially important in network organizations. Informal channels—the grapevine and network groups—often are as important as formal channels of communication. Managers can never eliminate the grapevine and thus should learn to use it to send messages and receive feedback.

2. DESCRIBE THE ROLE OF INFORMATION TECHNOLOGY IN THE COMMUNICATION PROCESS.

Information technology increases the speed and convenience of communication and information transfer. E-mail, the Internet, and teleconferencing are three types of information technology that affect the communication process in organizations. Although information technology often makes communication easier, it can lead to information overload, lower quality communication, and deteriorating social relationships.

3. IDENTIFY HURDLES TO COMMUNICATION AND DESCRIBE WAYS TO ELIMINATE THEM.

Hurdles to communication hinder the sending and receiving of messages by distorting or even blocking intended meanings. Hurdles can be either organizational or individual. Organizational hurdles may result from the design of the organization itself, from differences in status, from the jargon that often grows up around highly specialized tasks, and from differing goals. Individual hurdles may result from conflicting assumptions on the part of the sender and receiver, from misinterpretation of meaning, and from misunderstanding of emotional reactions.

4. STATE THE GUIDELINES FOR FOSTERING EFFECTIVE COMMUNICATION.

Guidelines for effective communication include clarifying ideas, examining the purpose of communicating, considering the setting, consulting with others, being mindful of nonverbal messages, taking the opportunity to convey something helpful to the receiver, following up, and being sure that actions taken support the communication.

KEY TERMS

Channel, p. 438

Communication, p. 431

Decoding, p. 432

Downward channels, p. 439

Electronic mail, p. 444

Emotion, p. 449

Employee network groups, p. 441

Encoding, p. 432

Feedback, p. 441

Feng shui, p. 436

Grapevine, p. 440

Horizontal channels, p. 440

Informal channels, p. 440

Information richness, p. 438

Internet, p. 444

Listening, p. 433

Message, p. 433

Nonverbal messages, p. 434

Perception, p. 443

Proxemics, p. 434

Receiver, p. 432

Selective perception, p. 443

Semantics, p. 448

Sender, p. 432

Status, p. 446

Stereotyping, p. 443

Upward channels, p. 439

QUESTIONS FOR DISCUSSION AND COMPETENCY DEVELOPMENT

1. What communication channels does Gordon Bethune use most often at Continental Airlines? When is each channel most effective?

2. What is feng shui? To learn more about it and how architects use it to design buildings, go to *http://www.geomancy.net*.

3. How does information technology affect how you communicate?

4. What are some of the downsides to sending messages via e-mail? Using the Internet to communicate?

5. Why do communication difficulties arise in organizations?

6. The world is a busy and confusing place, and people are constantly bombarded by multiple messages. How do you simplify these messages in order to reduce the confusion?

7. Open office (cubicles) designs are becoming increasingly popular in organizations. Describe the pros and cons of open office designs for communication processes. You might consult **http://www.cubeoffice.com/steel3.htm** for some interesting ideas.

8. **Competency Development: Teamwork Competency.** AT&T, Lucent Technologies, British Petroleum, and many other organizations are using virtual teams for numerous projects. How does a team that comes together electronically communicate effectively? For information, go to **http://www.att.com/learningnetwork** and **http://www.seanet.com/~daveg** for clues on how these two organizations use virtual teams effectively.

9. **Competency Development: Global Awareness Competency.** Besides taking foreign language lessons, what other activities could you participate in to avoid communication blunders overseas? What benefits would be associated with improving this competency? For further information go to **http://www.intl-businesslink.com**.

CASE FOR COMPETENCY DEVELOPMENT

Communication Inventory[35]

The following statements relate to how your manager and you communicate on the job. There are no right or wrong answers. Respond honestly to the statement, using the following scale.

1. **Strongly Agree**
2. **Agree**
3. **Uncertain**
4. **Disagree**
5. **Strongly Disagree**

_____ 1. My manager criticizes my work without allowing me to explain.

_____ 2. My manager allows me as much creativity as possible in my job.

_____ 3. My manager always judges the actions of his or her subordinates.

_____ 4. My manager allows flexibility on the job.

_____ 5. My manager criticizes my work in the presence of others.

_____ 6. My manager is willing to try new ideas and to accept other points of view.

_____ 7. My manager believes that he or she must control how I do my work.

_____ 8. My manager understands the problems that I encounter in my job.

_____ 9. My manager is always trying to change other people's attitudes and behaviors to suit his or her own.

_____ 10. My manager respects my feelings and values.

_____ 11. My manager always needs to be in charge of the situation.

_____ 12. My manager listens to my problems with interest.

_____ 13. My manager tries to manipulate subordinates to get what he or she wants or to make himself or herself look good.

_____ 14. My manager does not try to make me feel inferior.

_____ 15. I have to be careful when talking to my manager so that I will not be misinterpreted.

_____ 16. My manager participates in meetings with employees without projecting his or her higher status or power.

_____ 17. I seldom say what really is on my mind because it might be twisted and distorted by my manager.

_____ 18. My manager treats me with respect.

_____ 19. My manager seldom becomes involved in employee conflicts.

_____ 20. My manager does not have hidden motives in dealing with me.

_____ 21. My manager is not interested in employee problems.

_____ 22. I feel that I can be honest and straightforward with my manager.

_____ 23. My manager rarely offers moral support during a personal crisis.

_____ 24. I feel that I can express my opinions and ideas honestly to my manager.

_____ 25. My manager tries to make me feel inadequate.

_____ 26. My manager defines problems so that they can be understood but does not insist that his or her subordinates agree.

_____ 27. My manager makes it clear that he or she is in charge.

_____ 28. I feel free to talk to my manager.

_____ 29. My manager believes that if a job is to be done right, he or she must oversee it or do it.

_____ 30. My manager defines problems and makes his or her subordinates aware of them.

_____ 31. My manager cannot admit that he or she makes mistakes.

_____ 32. My manager tries to describe situations fairly without labeling them as good or bad.

_____ 33. My manager is dogmatic; it is useless for me to voice an opposing point of view.

_____ 34. My manager presents his or her feelings and perceptions without implying that a similar response is expected from me.

_____ 35. My manager thinks that he or she is always right.

_____ 36. My manager attempts to explain situations clearly and without personal bias.

Communication Inventory Scoring and Interpretation Sheet

Place the numbers that you assigned to each statement in the appropriate blanks. Then add them together to determine a subtotal for each communication category. Place the subtotals in the proper blanks and add your scores. Place an X on the graph to indicate what your perception is of your organization or department's communication. You may wish to discuss with others their own perceptions and interpretations.

Part I: Defensive Scores

Evaluation

Question 1 _____

Question 3 _____

Question 5 _____

Subtotal _____

Neutrality

Question 19 _____

Question 21 _____

Question 23 _____

Subtotal _____

Control

Question 7 _____

Question 9 _____

Question 11 _____

Subtotal _____

Superiority

Question 25 _____

Question 27 _____

Question 29 _____

Subtotal _____

Strategy

Question 13 _____

Question 15 _____

Question 17 _____

Subtotal _____

Certainty

Question 31 _____

Question 33 _____

Question 35 _____

Subtotal _____

Subtotals for Defensive Scores

Evaluation _____

Control _____

Strategy _____

Neutrality _____

Superiority _____

Certainty _____

Total _____

| 18 | 25 | 30 | 35 | 40 | 45 | 50 | 55 | 60 | 65 | 70 | 75 | 80 | 85 | 90 |

Defensive   Defensive to Neutral   Neutral to Supportive   Supportive

Part II: Supportive Scores

Provisionalism

Question 2 _____

Question 4 _____

Question 6 _____

Subtotal _____

Spontaneity

Question 20 _____

Question 22 _____

Question 24 _____

Subtotal _____

Empathy

Question 8 _____

Question 10 _____

Question 12 _____

Subtotal _____

Problem Orientation

Question 26 _____

Question 28 _____

Question 30 _____

Subtotal _____

Equality

Question 14 _____

Question 16 _____

Question 18 _____

Subtotal _____

Description

Question 32 _____

Question 34 _____

Question 36 _____

Subtotal _____

Subtotals for Supportive Scores

Provisionalism _____

Empathy _____

Equality _____

Spontaneity _____

Problem Orientation _____

Description _____

Total _____

| 18 | 25 | 30 | 35 | 40 | 45 | 50 | 55 | 60 | 65 | 70 | 75 | 80 | 85 | 90 |

Supportive   Supportive to Neutral   Neutral to Defensive   Defensive

Questions

1. What communication skills would you like to improve?

2. What did you learn about your communication competency from this exercise?

3. What steps will you take to become a more effective communicator?

Burke, Inc.

Based in Cincinnati, Ohio, Burke, Inc., is a leading international firm in marketing research that has been providing its services to blue chip companies since 1931. Because of its long and successful history, the company believes that it has researched virtually every category of products, services, and business and marketing topics on behalf of its clients.

The company provides full-service custom marketing research, analysis, and consulting for consumer and business-to-business goods and services companies to help them understand marketplace dynamics worldwide. The services that Burke offers include product testing, brand equity research, pricing research, market segmentation, image and positioning studies, and a wide range of marketing research protocols targeted at both tactical and strategic business issues.

Burke describes itself as being in the knowledge business, and being uniquely qualified to uncover insights into marketplace dynamics anywhere in the world. The success that this company has enjoyed during the past 70 years is, in large measure, a result of effectively communicating the knowledge gleaned from its research to its clients.

To do so successfully, the company has embraced several technologies that have changed the face of business communication. For instance, Burke researchers and analysts make extensive use of electronic mail (e-mail) to improve written internal (within the organization) and external (with clients) communication. In fact, with some clients (e.g., Sun Microsystems), the company relies entirely on electronically communicated data with no paper being physically sent to them.

Another technology that Burke utilizes to increase the efficiency of its oral communications is teleconferencing. Teleconferences are held with both the company's clients and members of its own organization (many of whom are often dispersed geographically). Burke's management believes that videoconferencing has not yet achieved the potential that many thought it would quickly attain. This technology is currently limited by each group of participants having to meet physically in central teleconferencing rooms. This restriction can be inconvenient or untenable for many organizations and their clients. Teleconferencing, however, does not have this limitation and allows for diverse groups of individuals to meet literally from their own desks.

Finally, Burke is a strong advocate for the increased use of Internet technology as means of both collecting data and transferring results of its data analysis. The Internet allows Burke and many other organizations to collect and disseminate information quickly, both within an office and throughout the world.

Burke's extensive utilization of these three technologies illustrates their increasing use by organizations in improving business communication.

Questions

1. What should managers consider when deciding whether to use each of the three communication technologies (e-mail, teleconferencing or videoconferencing, and the Internet) presented in this video?

2. In what ways can the use of e-mail and the Internet improve written communication?

3. With regard to the communication process and the decoder/receiver in particular, what potential problems do the Internet and e-mail present to the sender, as opposed to other technologies such as teleconferencing?

To learn more about Burke, Inc., visit the company's home page at *http://www.burke.com*.

Managing Work Teams

LEARNING OBJECTIVES

AFTER STUDYING THIS CHAPTER YOU SHOULD BE ABLE TO:

1. EXPLAIN THE IMPORTANCE OF WORK TEAMS.

2. IDENTIFY FOUR TYPES OF WORK TEAMS.

3. STATE THE MEANING AND DETERMINANTS OF TEAM EFFECTIVENESS.

4. DESCRIBE THE INTERNAL TEAM PROCESSES THAT CAN AFFECT TEAM PERFORMANCE.

5. EXPLAIN HOW TO DIAGNOSE AND REMOVE BARRIERS TO POOR TEAM PERFORMANCE.

Chapter Outline

PREVIEW: **SELF-MANAGED TEAMS TAKE OFF AT GENERAL ELECTRIC**

IMPORTANCE OF WORK TEAMS
WORK TEAMS COMPARED TO OTHER GROUPS
WHY ORGANIZATIONS USE WORK TEAMS

TYPES OF WORK TEAMS
PROBLEM-SOLVING WORK TEAMS
FUNCTIONAL WORK TEAMS
MULTIDISCIPLINARY WORK TEAMS
SELF-MANAGING WORK TEAMS
COMMUNICATION COMPETENCY: Quiet, She's Listening

A FRAMEWORK FOR TEAM EFFECTIVENESS
EFFECTIVENESS CRITERIA
EFFECTIVENESS DETERMINANTS

INTERNAL TEAM PROCESSES
TEAMWORK COMPETENCY: Team Assessment Survey
DEVELOPMENTAL STAGES
FEELINGS
BEHAVIORAL NORMS
PLANNING AND ADMINISTRATION COMPETENCY: These Norms Aren't Normal

DIAGNOSING THE CAUSES OF POOR TEAM PERFORMANCE
TEAM DESIGN
GLOBAL AWARENESS COMPETENCY: NCR's Virtual Teams
CULTURE
TEAM MEMBER SELECTION
TEAM TRAINING
REWARD SYSTEMS

CHAPTER SUMMARY

KEY TERMS

QUESTIONS FOR DISCUSSION AND COMPETENCY DEVELOPMENT

CASE FOR COMPETENCY DEVELOPMENT: THE UTILITY OF EMPOWERED TEAMS

VIDEO CASE: VALASSIS COMMUNICATIONS

SELF-MANAGED TEAMS TAKE OFF AT GENERAL ELECTRIC

In Durham, North Carolina, 170 GE employees work in nine teams to produce the GE90 jet engines that Boeing will install in its new, long-range 777 aircraft. Each team "owns" the engines it builds—from the beginning of the assembly process to getting the engine loaded on a truck for delivery. As a team begins each engine, about the only instruction it receives is the date on which the engine is to be shipped from the plant.

Producing engines is the goal of each team, but that goal can be reached only if a team effectively manages itself. Besides producing an 8.5-ton engine from 10,000 individual parts, team members order tools and parts; schedule their vacations, training, and overtime; make adjustments to the production process to improve their efficiency; monitor product quality; and take responsibility for diagnosing and resolving problems that arise among team members.

Decisions about these and all other issues that the teams face are made by consensus. Each employee understands that living with ideas that they don't necessarily agree with is part of the job. They don't blame others when things go wrong because they are the ones who make the decisions. The process of reaching agreement is so much a way of life at the plant that people routinely talk about "consensusing" on this or that.

The one boss at the plant—plant manager Paula Sims—keeps everyone's attention focused on the common goal: making perfect jet engines quickly, cheaply, and safely. At the strategic level, her job is first to be sure that the efforts of all the teams are coordinated so that together their decisions optimize the plant's performance, and then to free up resources for growth and improvement.

As one employee explained, aviation mechanics at this plant enjoy a job that's unlike any other in the industry: "I came from Northrop Grumman where I was working on a B-2 bomber. That plane, which used stealth technology, was as hi-tech as you can get. But someone else wrote the assembly process. Here, I write the process—at the mechanic level. There, I was on a 'team,' but I also had a supervisor. He had a boss. And there were other bosses above him. In two years of working there, I never saw the plant manager. Every day, my boss would just hand me my job. I had no input at all—none. I'm much happier here."[1]

To learn more about GE's Aircraft Engine business, visit the company's home page at

http://www.geae.com

IMPORTANCE OF WORK TEAMS

1.

EXPLAIN THE IMPORTANCE OF WORK TEAMS.

In everyday conversation, the terms *group* and *team* often are used interchangeably, but in this chapter we distinguish between the two. Here, *group* is the more general term, and *team* is a special type of group. Teams and groups are both important to organizational life, but for different reasons.

WORK TEAMS COMPARED TO OTHER GROUPS

A *group* is two or more individuals who come into personal and meaningful contact on a continuing basis.[2] Employees often form groups that have little to do with completing tasks required by their employer, such as bowling leagues and parent-support groups. Only some groups in an organization are formed for the purpose of doing the organization's work, and it is these groups that generally are referred to as *work teams*.

Informal Groups. An *informal group* consists of a small number of individuals—usually 3 to 12—who frequently participate together in activities and share feelings for the purpose of meeting their mutual needs. Five employees who by chance happen to sit at the same lunch table in their company's cafeteria are not a group. Although they have personal contact, it isn't likely to be highly meaningful and most likely is just a brief, one-time event. Suppose, however, that the five employees regularly seek each other out and almost always eat lunch together. As their interactions become more meaningful and they develop expectations for each other's behavior, the five employees become an informal group. Informal groups may support, oppose, or have no interest in organizational goals, rules, or higher authority.

An organization's management practices often influence the development of informal groups. For example, during the summer of 2000, pilots at United Airlines decided not to work overtime because top management had not negotiated a new contract with them. The pilots banded together in informal groups at United's major hubs in Denver, Chicago, and Los Angeles, and agreed to refuse to fly overtime. Angry customers who were left stranded at airports vowed never to fly United Airlines again. In contrast, an organization may encourage employees to participate in more positive informal groups, such as those based on shared hobbies or other interests. The friendships formed in such informal groups are greatly valued by many employees and may result in their feeling a greater sense of loyalty toward their employer. In Chapter 18, we consider the importance of other types of groups in more detail.

Work Teams. A *work team* consists of a small number of employees with complementary skills who work together on a project, are committed to a common purpose, and are accountable for performing tasks that contribute to achieving an organization's goals.[3] Work teams—the focus of this chapter—go by many different names. A few of the terms used to describe work teams are shown in Figure 17.1.

| *Figure 17.1* | **Terms for Work Teams** |

Empowered teams
Autonomous work groups
Crews
Self-managing teams
Cross-functional teams
Quality circles
Project teams
Task forces
High-performance teams
Emergency response teams
Committees
Councils

Generally, work teams range in size from 2 to about 20 members. About 15 members belong to each of the nine teams at GE's aircraft engine plant in Durham. The GE/Durham teams are similar to work teams in many other ways, too. Most important is that the members of each work team have a shared goal that they can achieve only if they communicate with each other. The requirement that team members communicate with each other differentiates work teams from organizations. Members of an organization often share a goal but not all of them need to communicate with each other in order to achieve that goal.

A recent study by the Center for the Study of Work Teams at the University of North Texas revealed just how pervasive teams have become in organizations. Based on recent trends, the researchers estimated that 50 percent or more of the employees work in teams at 80 percent of the Fortune 500 companies. Furthermore, whereas work teams were found mostly in manufacturing operations a few years ago, they have now spread throughout the service sector.[4]

The importance of teams is reflected in the amount of time that managers and others spend in team meetings. Many top managers report spending 50 percent or more of their time in team meetings; first-line managers and professionals may spend between 20 and 50 percent of their time in such meetings.[5] These team meetings range from quick huddles in someone's office to voice-mail exchanges to planning retreats lasting several days.

WHY ORGANIZATIONS USE WORK TEAMS

WEB INSIGHT

The image of engineers that many people have is that they work mostly alone in labs or cubicles. How important are work teams in engineering and why? To find out, visit *http://www.ieee.org* and conduct a search using the key word "work team."

Automakers estimate that developing a new model requires as many as 7 million engineering hours. At Toyota and Honda, developing a new car requires as many as 1,000 engineers working in teams for 3 years. At Microsoft, creating a new version of Windows requires writing more than 10 million lines of code. Producing that amount of code takes 400–500 people working together for approximately three years. Management's first challenge is figuring out how to divide the mountains of work involved in such complex projects. Its second challenge is integrating the efforts of the individuals and teams working on the projects to ensure that they achieve the organization's goals.

The specific goals to be achieved by work teams differ from team to team and organization to organization. They depend partly on the needs of the particular customers being served. In a large study of U.S. and Canadian companies, half the managers who responded believed that improving team processes to focus on customers was the strategic initiative having the greatest potential for ensuring their organizations' success.[6] Moreover, the main reasons that managers give for organizing work around teams are generally similar for a variety of organizations. They include serving customers better through innovation, speed, cost reduction, and quality improvement.[7]

Innovation. Creative thinking, which is the bedrock of new product ideas, is increased by bringing together people having a variety of experience and expertise to address a common problem or task.[8] At Microsoft, teams are essential to developing innovative products. Whether the product is another version of Windows or a new Internet service, managers at Microsoft address innovation and product development challenges by organizing employees into numerous work teams and then synchronizing their activities. Each team has a clear and limited product vision and a time limit for completing its work. Teams working on the same project are in constant communication with each other. Almost all major development efforts take place at Microsoft headquarters, which makes face-to-face communication and problem solving easy.

Speed. In addition to introducing more ideas, teams can also reduce the time required for product development. They do so by replacing serial development with parallel development. In the past, the development process involved completion by one function (e.g., basic research) of its task and then forwarding the item to the next function (e.g., prototyping), and so on until all the functions had completed their tasks in sequence. With parallel development, many tasks are done at the same time and are closely coordinated among the functions. Parallel development cuts the amount of time spent in the development cycle, or what is often called *time to market*.

Teams also can speed up customer service activities. When Trade Insurance Services reorganized into teams, it emphasized its expectations for speedier services, calling the new initiative *FAST*—for flexible account services teams. These work teams include policy underwriters, salespeople, and claims specialists who work together to serve each customer.[9]

Cost. Like many other companies, reducing costs and responding more quickly to customers were key reasons for Jostens' decision to organize around teams. Jostens manufactures a variety of products, the best known being class rings. Before Jostens re-organized work around teams, employees were producing 16 rings per employee per day. After the entire manufacturing facility was switched to self-managing teams, the employees produced 25 rings per person per day. The entire process—from receipt of a work order to shipping of the finished product—was shortened from 30 calendar days to just 10 calendar days.[10]

Quality. Excellent quality is a primary goal of work teams. In fact, at GE/Durham, the goal is to build perfect jet engines. Specifications routinely require fittings with error margins of less that one 1,000th of an inch. The engines they build will be used in air-planes that fly 10,000 miles without stopping. The drive for perfection really matters at this plant. As one employee put it, "I've got a three-year-old daughter, and I figure that every plane we build engines for has someone with a three-year-old daughter riding on it." A bad engine could destroy hundreds of lives and even alter the course of history.

TYPES OF WORK TEAMS

2.

IDENTIFY FOUR TYPES
OF WORK TEAMS.

Although the strategic goals to be achieved by work teams—innovation, speed, cost reduction, and quality—may be much the same, the specific goals of work teams often differ greatly. Work teams also differ in other important ways, including their longevity and membership. The *longevity* of a work team may be quite short, or it may be permanent. On the one hand, a short-lived team comprising lawyers, invest-ment bankers, and other specialists might be formed to help a company go public and then disband after the initial public offering (IPO). On the other hand, NASA's mission control team has been in existence for several decades.

The *membership* of work teams can also differ greatly from one situation to another. Sometimes all members of a team work in the same department. Other times, work teams include employees from several different departments or even people from dif-ferent organizations, such as employees working with suppliers and customers. Thus different types of work teams suit different purposes.[11] Problem-solving, functional, multidisciplinary, and self-managing work teams are four common types of work teams, and each has a different purpose.

PROBLEM-SOLVING WORK TEAMS

A *problem-solving work team* usually consists of employees from different areas of an organization whose purpose is to consider how something can be done better. Such a team may meet one or two hours a week on a continuing basis to discuss ways to improve quality, safety, productivity, or morale. Quality circles are the most familiar example of a relatively permanent and enduring problem-solving work team. Not all problem-solving teams have indefinite life spans, however. Temporary task forces are a familiar example of problem-solving teams that exist just long enough to deal with a specific problem. When Xerox needed to find a solution to a design problem for a product using photoreceptors that had to "rest" for 24 hours in the dark, it turned to a problem-solving team. The team discovered the causes of the problem, developed an improved design, and saved the company $266,000 the first year.[12]

Quality Circles. A *quality circle* (also called a TQM team) is a group of employees who meet regularly to identify, analyze, and propose solutions to various types of work-place problems. Meetings usually lasting an hour or so are held once every week or two during or after regular working hours. Quality circles at Navistar International, Johnson & Johnson, and Exxon/Mobil, among others, don't address just one problem and then disband. They are expected to look for and propose solutions to quality-related prob-lems *continually*. Members often are given overtime pay if a quality circle meets after work. They normally receive eight or more hours of formal training in decision-making and team processes, which they apply in their meetings. Quality circles normally don't have the authority to implement their proposed solutions, which are presented to management for further consideration and action.

Task Forces. As its name suggests, a *task force* is a team that is formed to accomplish a specific, highly important task for an organization. Task forces often meet intensively during the course of a few weeks or months and then disband. Task force members usually are expected to continue working at their normal jobs during the duration of the task force. Also typical of task forces is diversity in the backgrounds and expertise of the members. Managers often create task forces to help accomplish strategic reorientation, to help gather data about the external environment, and to help design approaches for implementing a new strategy.

Signicast Corporation used a problem-solving task force when management decided to build new facilities. Headquartered in Milwaukee, Wisconsin, Signicast manufactures precision castings of metal parts using blueprints supplied by customers such as Harley Davidson and John Deere. When top management decided to build a new facility, it wanted to design the best facility of its type in the world. To do so required taking advantage of everyone's expertise—from the top to the bottom of the organization. A team of five executives would develop an idea and then ask employees to evaluate it and suggest revisions. "Sometimes those meetings would go on for hours," recalled Robert Schuemann, a member of the executive team. "Sometimes there were even multiple meetings to discuss one item." Many policies and procedures were adopted only after the employees had an opportunity to vote on them.[13]

FUNCTIONAL WORK TEAMS

A *functional work team* includes members from a single department who jointly consider issues and solve problems common to their area of responsibility and expertise. For example, at ConAgra, a diversified international food company, a functional team could be the purchasing manager and the purchasing agents in the department. Their goals might include minimizing costs and ensuring that beef supplies are available to stores when needed. To achieve their goals, these work team members need to coordinate their activities constantly, sharing information on price changes and demand for various products. At Next Door Food Stores, the audit department formed functional teams in order to improve the company's relationships with customers—in this case, the store managers.

Functional work teams formed for the purpose of completing their daily tasks are quite stable, enduring for as long as the organization maintains its same basic structure. In contrast, a functional work team brought together as a task force to look at a specific issue or problem would disband as soon as it had completed its specific assignment.

MULTIDISCIPLINARY WORK TEAMS

Multidisciplinary work teams provide several important competitive advantages if they are properly formed and managed. In particular, they often are used to speed up design, production, and services processes or to enhance creativity and innovation.[14]

A *multidisciplinary work team* may consist of employees from various functional areas and sometimes several organizational levels who collectively have specific goal-oriented tasks. In this respect, multidisciplinary teams are like task forces. However, they differ from task forces in one important way: They are the primary vehicles for accomplishing the core work of the organization. The work assigned to multidisciplinary teams at Lockheed Martin includes designing technology, meeting with customers and suppliers, and developing new products for the U.S. Navy. The use of such teams is spreading rapidly and crosses all types of organizational boundaries.[15]

A product development team is a common type of multidisciplinary work team. It exists for the period of time required to bring a product to market, which could vary from a couple of months to several years. As already noted, Microsoft is one of many companies using product development teams extensively. In the telecommunications and electronics industries, multidisciplinary R&D teams bring together experts having a variety of knowledge and backgrounds to generate ideas for new products and services. To ensure that the products appeal to customers, the work teams may include representatives from marketing and the products' eventual end users.

SELF-MANAGING WORK TEAMS

In the United States, manufacturers have been steadily moving to self-managing work teams during the past two decades. A *self-managing work team* normally consists of employees who work together daily to make an entire product or deliver an entire service. The members all may be from a single functional area, but more often such teams are multidisciplinary, as illustrated in Figure 17.2. The teams at GE/Durham are self-managing work teams.

WEB INSIGHT

Read about the Orpheus Chamber Orchestra at *http://www.orpheusnyc.com*. How does this self-managing team handle the tasks that usually are done by an orchestra's music director?

Figure 17.2   **Members of a Self-Managing Work Team**

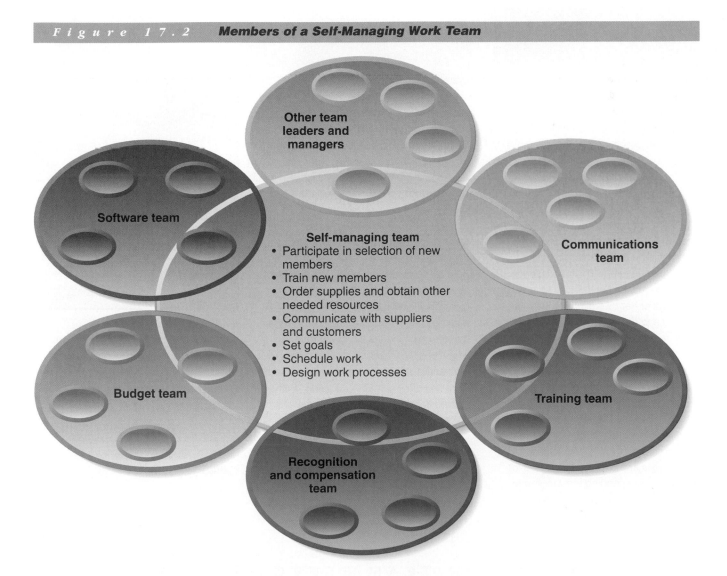

- **Other team leaders and managers**
- **Software team**
- **Communications team**
- **Budget team**
- **Training team**
- **Recognition and compensation team**

Self-managing team
- Participate in selection of new members
- Train new members
- Order supplies and obtain other needed resources
- Communicate with suppliers and customers
- Set goals
- Schedule work
- Design work processes

The distinctive feature of a self-managing work team is the level of responsibility that the team itself has for various managerial tasks, including scheduling members' work and vacations, rotating job tasks and assignments among members, ordering materials, deciding on team leadership (which may rotate among members), providing feedback to team members, setting performance goals, and monitoring progress toward team goals. To a large extent, the team as a whole—not just its leader—decides both what the team needs to do and how to do it. When it is truly empowered, a self-managing team does more than simply take over administrative duties. It also has a strong commitment to the organization's mission, the autonomy needed to control its own activities, belief in itself, and a chance to see directly the impact of its efforts.[16]

Organizations designed around self-managing teams are very flat—but not so flat that there are *no* managers. At GE/Durham, for example, one plant manager is responsible for more than 140 employees. For that manager, communication competency is especially important. As explained in the following Communication Competency feature, the plant manager's effectiveness depends heavily on her skillful use of informal communication.[17]

Quiet, She's Listening

In her 4 years as the plant manager responsible for GE's jet engine production teams, Paula Sims learned that communicating what you intend to isn't always easy. Sims described her plant manager's job as "the most challenging four years of my life—and also the most rewarding. To do it well requires a different level of listening skills—significantly different. More and more of what I do involves listening to people, to teams, to councils, to ideas, trying to find common themes."

In this culture of continuous feedback, one reason Sims listens so carefully is to monitor her own effectiveness. She learned early on that her actions could be easily misinterpreted. Recalling an incident from her early days, she explained, "An employee came to me and said, 'Paula, you realize that you don't need to follow up with us to make sure we're doing what we agreed to do. If we say we'll do something, we'll do it. You don't need to micro-manage us.'" At most plants, following up is just part of a manager's job. But here it was sending the wrong message. Because she always followed up,

people concluded that she didn't trust them. The real problem was that she had not yet learned the plant's behavioral norms about decision making.

Sims also listens when the plant is trying to solve a problem. At other companies, the title of manager is almost synonymous with "decision maker." At GE/Durham, however, the manager actually makes only about a dozen major decisions each year. For all other decisions she either relies heavily on input from plant employees or the employees actually make the decisions. The plant manager is responsible for being sure that the employees know about problems and for informing the GE managers to whom she reports about the solutions they come up with. But to get those solutions, the plant manager generally is expected to listen, not decide. For a major issue, such as reducing costs or improving safety, a task force is formed to decide how to address it. The plant manager informs the task force and everyone else about the issue and explains why resolving it is important. Then the task force

takes responsibility for coming up with a plan for doing so. When a plan is agreed upon, the plant manager informs the managers above her of how the plant intends to proceed and enlists their support.

• • •

To learn more about GE's Aircraft Engine business, visit the company's home page at *http://www.geae.com*.

A FRAMEWORK FOR TEAM EFFECTIVENESS

3.

STATE THE MEANING AND DETERMINANTS OF TEAM EFFECTIVENESS.

The increasing popularity of team-based organizational structures reflects the belief that teams can achieve outcomes that could not be achieved by the same number of individuals working alone. But as many organizations are discovering, the payoff from teams isn't automatic. Although teams offer great potential, that potential isn't always realized. Even when teams do fulfill their potential, team members and their organizations may experience unanticipated negative side effects, such as lingering political fights and turnover.

EFFECTIVENESS CRITERIA

The first step in fostering team effectiveness involves knowing how to assess it. Figure 17.3[18] shows several effectiveness criteria for evaluating work teams. **_Effectiveness criteria_** measure the outcomes achieved by individual members and the team as a whole. A particular work team may be effective in some respects and ineffective in others. For example, a team may take longer than expected to make a decision. Thus, on speed and cost criteria, the team may seem ineffective. But the team's decision may be highly creative and make the team's primary customer feel very satisfied with the output. Thus, on creativity and customer satisfaction, the team would be viewed as effective. Similarly, individual members of the team may feel that their own work is slowed by having to get agreement from other team members before they proceed. But through discussion, individuals develop a better understanding of other perspectives and gain new technical knowledge and skills. Whether the work team is viewed as effective overall depends on the relative importance of the various effectiveness criteria applied.

Figure 17.3	**Effectiveness Criteria for Work Teams**

Team Effectiveness		
Task completion	**Team development**	**Stakeholder satisfaction**
Accuracy	Team cohesiveness	Customer satisfaction with team's procedures and outputs
Speed	Team flexibility	Team satisfaction with team's procedures and outputs
Creativity	Team preparedness for new tasks	Satisfaction of other teams with the team's procedures and outputs
Cost		

Individual Effectiveness		
Task performance	**Relationships with others**	**Personal development**
Speed	Increased understanding of other perspectives	Develop competencies (teamwork, communication, strategic action, global awareness, planning and administration, and self-awareness)
Accuracy	Build others' trust in you	Develop network of colleagues within and outside the organization
Creativity	New friendships	Gain technical knowledge and skills
Efficiency		

EFFECTIVENESS DETERMINANTS

The second step in achieving team effectiveness involves knowing about the various factors that determine how well the team is doing with respect to the effectiveness critieria. Figure 17.4 illustrates several factors that work in combination to determine team effectiveness. Effectiveness is determined by three main sets of influences: the external context in which the team operates, team design, and internal team processes. When teams are ineffective, managers must be able to diagnose and correct the causes of the teams' problems and poor team performance.[19]

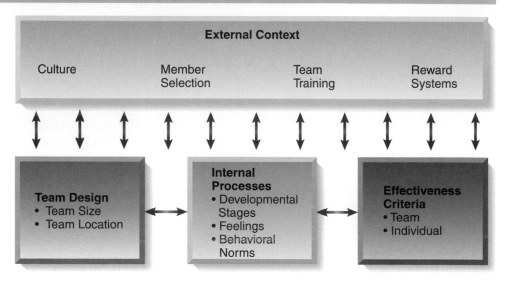

Figure 17.4 **A Model of Work Team Functioning**

Teamwork always presents challenges. Managers who understand its nature and challenges are in the best position to take advantage of teamwork and anticipate some of the problems that often crop up when teams are used.

Internal team processes may be the most immediate cause of performance problems. When a team experiences internal problems, however, the root cause of those problems may lie elsewhere. The team members may be doing the best they can but under adverse circumstances. Their internal problems may be due to the design of the team or to aspects of the external context.

INTERNAL TEAM PROCESSES

4.

DESCRIBE THE INTERNAL TEAM PROCESSES THAT CAN AFFECT TEAM PERFORMANCE.

Internal team processes include the development of the work team over time, personal feelings, and behavioral norms. In effective work teams, these processes support cooperation among team members and coordination of their work.[20] When a team leader and individual team members learn how to manage the team's internal processes, they improve the likelihood of the team's being effective.

A tool for assessing a work team's internal processes is presented in the following Teamwork Competency feature. Before continuing, take a few minutes to complete the Team Assessment Survey for a team to which you belong. If you were using this survey in an organization, you would want to ask *all* members of the team you described to complete the survey.[21]

Team Assessment Survey

INSTRUCTIONS

This survey can be used to help a team assess its internal processes. It should be completed individually by each team member, who should indicate the extent to which he or she thinks the team exhibits the following characteristics and behaviors.

Questions	To a Very Small Extent		To Some Extent		To a Very Large Extent
1. Team members understand the range of backgrounds, skills, preferences, and perspectives in the team.	1	2	3	4	5
2. Team member differences and similarities have been effectively focused on achieving team goals.	1	2	3	4	5
3. The team cannot integrate diverse viewpoints.	5	4	3	2	1
4. Members view themselves as a team, not as a collection of individuals with their own particular jobs to do (e.g., they work interdependently, have joint accountability, and are committed to joint goals).	1	2	3	4	5
5. Team members have articulated a clear set of goals.	1	2	3	4	5
6. The team's goals are not motivating to members.	5	4	3	2	1
7. Team members agree on what goals and objectives are important.	1	2	3	4	5
8. The team has an effective work structure. It understands what work needs to be done, when work needs to be completed, and who is responsible for what.	1	2	3	4	5
9. It is not clear what each person in the team is supposed to do.	5	4	3	2	1
10. Team members have devised effective timetables and deadlines.	1	2	3	4	5
11. Team members have a clear set of norms that cover most aspects of how to function.	1	2	3	4	5
12. Team members take arguments personally and get angry easily.	5	4	3	2	1
13. Every team member does his or her fair share of the work.	1	2	3	4	5
14. A few members do most of the work.	5	4	3	2	1
15. A few people shirk responsibility or hold the team back.	5	4	3	2	1
16. Team members are imaginative in thinking about new or better ways to perform team tasks.	1	2	3	4	5
17. All team members participate in decision making.	1	2	3	4	5
18. Team members have the resources, information, and support they need from people outside team boundaries.	1	2	3	4	5
19. Team meetings are well organized.	1	2	3	4	5
20. Team meetings are not productive.	5	4	3	2	1
21. Coordination among members is a problem. People seem not to know what to do and when to do it for smooth team functioning.	5	4	3	2	1
22. Team members express their feelings freely in the team.	1	2	3	4	5
23. Team members support each other.	1	2	3	4	5
24. Team members are not effective at decision making.	5	4	3	2	1

To assess the overall quality of the team's internal processes, simply add all the numbers you circled and divide by 24 (the total number of items in the survey). A score of 4 or higher indicates that you judge the team's internal processes as generally quite positive. A score less than 4 but greater than 2.5 indicates that you feel the team is doing satisfactorily overall but that several areas need improvement. A score of 2.5 or lower indicates that you believe the team's internal functioning is quite poor.

The team leader should compute the team's average score for each question. For example, suppose that a team had four members and that they gave these responses to question 1: The first person circled 3, the second person circled 4, the third person circled 5, and the fourth person circled 4. Then the team's average for question 1 is $(3 + 4 + 5 + 4)/4 = 4$.

After computing the average score for each question, the team leader should provide feedback to the team. Effective feedback involves acknowledging the things that the team seems to be doing well (e.g., questions with an average of 4 or higher), and identifying the things that need to be improved immediately (e.g., questions with an average of 2.5 or lower).

After setting priorities for the areas needing improvement, the team leader and team members should agree on a schedule for making those improvements. At the end of that time, the leader should again ask team members to respond to the Team Assessment Survey. When the reassessment results have been calculated, team members should determine whether satisfactory progress has been made in addressing the issues previously identified. If they find that it hasn't, they should continue to make adjustments and reassessments, as needed.

People with little experience working in teams often expect a team to be fully functioning immediately, but that rarely happens. Observations of newly formed work teams reveal that coordination and integration tend to develop over a period of time. Team members usually need to spend some time together before the team can jell—knowing this fact of team life reduces needless frustration. The establishment of trust and clear behavioral norms usually precedes effective task completion.[22]

DEVELOPMENTAL STAGES

A team's internal processes usually change over time. Like individuals, teams develop their skills the more they use them. Team functioning generally improves after the team has been together awhile. The developmental stages that teams commonly go through are shown in Figure 17.5. The vertical axis indicates that work teams develop along a *continuum of maturity,* which ranges from low, or immature (e.g., inefficient and ineffective), to high, or mature (e.g., efficient and effective). The horizontal axis represents a *continuum of time together,* which ranges from start (e.g., the first team encounter) to end (e.g., the point at which the team adjourns).[23] In general, the speed of team development seems to reflect the team's deadlines. Work teams tend to develop slowly at first. Then, as deadlines approach, team members feel more pressure to perform and often respond by resolving or setting aside personal differences in order to complete the task.

No particular period of time is needed for a team to progress from one stage to the next. For example, a work team whose members have effective interpersonal skills and high initial commitment to the team's goals could move rapidly to the performing stage. In contrast, a committee that is skeptical about whether its work is really valued by the organization and which also experiences early conflict among its members may never make much progress and even disband without producing a recommendation or report.

A work team may adjourn in a variety of ways. It may simply stop meeting and continue to exist only on paper. It may meet rarely and engage only in routine tasks. Its membership may change (e.g., adding, losing, or changing members), weakening its purpose or commitment. It may be terminated officially by the authority that created it.

Figure 17.5 also shows the possibility of a team ending at each stage or recycling to a previous stage. For example, a mature work team could lose the majority of its members in a short period of time to promotion, retirement, and/or rotation of membership. With so many new members, the team may recycle to an earlier stage of development. The stages identified represent general tendencies, and teams may develop by going through repeated cycles rather than linearly, as shown. Also, each stage simply reveals the *primary* issues facing team members. Behaviors from other stages may occur at times within each stage.

Figure 17.5 **The Development of Work Teams**

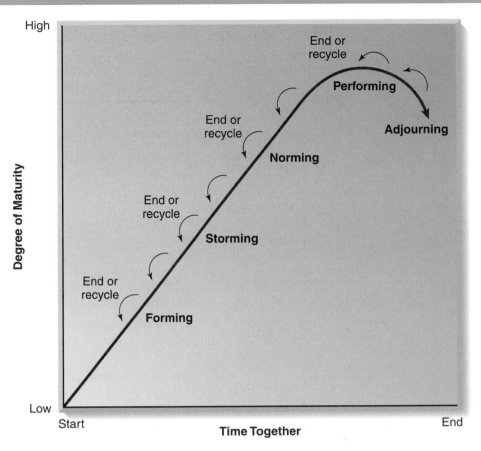

Forming. During the *forming stage,* a work team focuses on orientation to its goals and procedures. The amount of information available and the manner in which it is presented are crucial to work team development. Most members may be anxious about what the team and they, as individual members, are supposed to do. In newly formed teams, relationships often are guarded, cautious, and noncommittal. Understanding leadership roles and getting acquainted with other team members facilitate development.

Storming. The *storming stage* begins when competitive or strained behaviors emerge. Initially, the storming process may involve resistance and impatience with the lack of progress. A few dominant members may begin to force an agenda without regard for the needs of other team members. Team members may challenge the leader, or they may isolate themselves from team discussion. If conflict spreads, frustration, anger, and defensive behavior (especially the self-serving "look out for yourself" kind) may appear. Team members might think: Our problem is that we don't want to resolve our conflicts; we thrive on them, and though it may be counterproductive, conflict seems to be a way of life for now.

If conflict is suppressed and not permitted to occur, resentment and bitterness may result, which in turn can lead to apathy or abandonment. Although conflict resolution often is the goal of work teams during the storming stage, conflict management generally is what is achieved. In fact, conflict management is a more appropriate goal because maintaining conflict at a manageable level is a desirable way to encourage a work team's growth and development.[24]

Norming. In the *norming stage,* team members become increasingly positive about the team as a whole, the other members as individuals, and what the team is doing. At the beginning of the norming stage, the dominant view might be: We are in this together, like it or not, so let's make the most of it. Thus the team members may begin to develop a sense of belonging and commitment. Task-related and role behaviors of members increasingly are resolved through cooperation, open communication, and the acceptance of mutual influence. The rules of behavior that are widely shared and enforced by team members develop. If the work team gets to the end of this stage, most members may like their involvement a great deal.

Sometimes, however, the work team focuses too much on "we-ness," harmony, and conformity. When that happens, team members may avoid task-related conflicts that need to be resolved to achieve optimal performance. That in turn may cause the quality and/or quantity of performance to slip.

Performing. By the *performing stage,* members usually have come to trust and accept each other. To accomplish tasks, diversity of viewpoints (rather than we-ness) is supported and encouraged. Members are willing to risk presenting "wild" ideas without fear of being put down by the team. Careful listening and giving accurate feedback to others focus team members on the team's tasks and reinforce a sense of clear and shared goals. Leadership within the team is flexible and may shift among members in terms of who is most capable of solving a particular problem. The team accepts the reality of differences and disagreements and works on them cooperatively and enthusiastically. The team tries to reach consensus on important issues and to avoid internal politics. The following characteristics lead to high levels of team performance.

- Members direct their energies toward the twin goals of getting things done (task behaviors) and building constructive interpersonal ties and processes (relationship behaviors).

- Members have adopted procedures for making decisions, including how to share leadership.

- Members have achieved trust and openness among themselves.

- Members have learned to receive help from and give help to one another.

- Members experience a sense of freedom to be themselves while feeling a sense of belonging with others.

- Members have learned to accept and deal with conflicts.

- Members know how to diagnose and improve their own functioning.[25]

The degree to which one or more of these characteristics is absent determines the extent to which teams are likely to be ineffective.

Adjourning. The *adjourning stage* involves terminating task behaviors and disengaging from relationships. This stage isn't always planned and may be rather abrupt. However, a planned team conclusion often involves recognition for participation and achievement and an opportunity for members to say personal good-byes. Adjournment of a work team charged with a particular task should be set for a specific time and have a recognizable ending point. However, many work teams (e.g., the executive committee of an organization's board of directors) are ongoing. As members turn over, some recycling through earlier stages rather than adjournment may occur. Staggered terms of appointment can minimize the amount of recycling required.

FEELINGS

Throughout the stages of a work team's development, team members experience a variety of *feelings,* which reflect the emotional climate of a group. The four feelings most likely to influence work team effectiveness and productivity are trust, openness, freedom, and interdependence. The more these feelings are present, the more likely the work team will be effective and the members will be satisfied.[26] These feelings probably are present in a formal or informal group to which you belong if you *agree* with the following statements.

- *Trust:* Members have confidence in each other.

- *Openness:* Members are really interested in what others have to say.
- *Freedom:* Members do what they do out of a sense of responsibility to the group, not because of pressure from others.
- *Interdependence:* Members coordinate and work together to achieve common goals.

The greater the degree to which the four feelings are present, the greater is the level of group cohesiveness.

Cohesiveness is the strength of members' desires to remain on the team and their commitment to it. It is a reflection of the members' feelings toward one another and the team as a whole. Team members may feel strongly committed to the team, even if they don't feel strongly committed to the organization.[27] Cohesiveness can't be dictated by managers, team leaders, or other work team members. A cohesive team can work effectively for or against organizational goals.[28] For example, a cohesive team with negative feelings toward the organization may promote performance standards that limit productivity and pressure individual members to conform to them. In contrast, a cohesive team with positive feelings toward the organization may support and reinforce high quality and increased productivity.

BEHAVIORAL NORMS

Although how people feel is an important aspect of teamwork, how people actually behave may be even more important. **Behavioral norms** are the rules of behavior that are widely shared and enforced by members of a work team. Their main function is to regulate and standardize the behaviors viewed as important by team members.[29] Norms may specify how much members should do, how customers should be treated, the importance that should be assigned to quality, what members should wear, what kinds of jokes are acceptable, how members should feel about the organization, how they should deal with their managers, and so on.

A team norm exists when three criteria have been met.[30] First, there is a standard of appropriate behavior for team members. For example, at Foxboro Company, there are standards for the lower and upper limits of production for the team as a whole and for individual members. Second, members must generally agree on the standard. If most members have widely varying opinions about how much work is enough, for example, the team doesn't have a productivity norm. Third, the members must be aware that the team supports the particular standard through a system of rewards and punishments. For example, a member who produces fewer electronic process control systems per day than the work team norm may get the silent treatment until he or she complies with that norm. When a team member isn't contributing fully to team performance but still shares in team rewards, that person is referred to as a **free rider.**

Effective managers understand that they can shape the norms that develop within work teams. As described in the following Planning and Administration Competency feature, Chef Michael Schlow at Radius, a Boston restaurant, uses frequent staff meetings to develop and sustain the behavioral norms that account for some of his restaurant's popularity with diners.[31]

PLANNING & ADMINISTRATION COMPETENCY

These Norms Aren't Normal

In Boston's financial district, Radius is a popular spot for lunch and dinner. The food is a major reason for its appeal, but good food isn't enough to satisfy the demanding clients of this restaurant. According to co-owner and chef Michael Schlow, teamwork among the staff members is another key. "This restaurant is about creating something bigger than any of us could accomplish alone," he says. In the true spirit of a team-based organization, Schlow believes that *To-gether Everyone Accomplishes More.*

The work at Radius is organized around functional teams: a meat team, a fish team, a pastry team, and so on. Each team is responsible for everything related to its specialty. The fish team, for example, buys, cleans, and prepares the fish. At most restaurants, a different individual is responsible for each of these tasks. To make the work more exciting for employees and to provide them with opportunities for career growth, employees rotate from one team station to the next. Although these rotations mean that Schlow must spend more time planning for how his staff will be deployed, they pay off by helping employees develop an appreciation for the contributions of all the teams involved in preparing a meal.

The work teams at Radius also support a norm that favors continual learning. One way that Schlow supports the norm of learning is by assigning one person each day the task of researching a bit of information about food and presenting what she or he learned to the others of the restaurant's staff. And Schlow gives them occa-

sional tests to see how much they've learned!

Each week, employees attend a series of meetings that further enforce many of the norms required for the team to perform effectively. These meetings usually involve people from several different functional teams. A weekly meeting of chefs, waiters, and food runners focuses on how to describe and present each course of the meal. Schlow uses daily meetings of all kitchen staff to remind his employees that they should always be thinking about ways to use as much of each ingredient as possible, in order to cut down on waste. A nightly meeting of service staff is used to reinforce the importance of recognizing repeat customers.

Do Schlow's efforts make a difference? According to a recent graduate of the Culinary Institute of America, the norms at Radius are immediately noticeable. "The first time I walked into Radius, the whole atmosphere was beautiful," he

said. "You could tell people really believed in what they were doing. I knew this place was for me."

• • •

To learn more about Michael Schlow and Radius, visit the restaurant's home page at

http://www.bostonchefs.com

Norms concerning how to handle conflicts within the team are especially important for teams that engage in a lot of problem solving and decision making. Social pressures to maintain friendships and avoid disagreements can lead to work team members agreeing to a decision based more on personal feelings than on facts and analysis. When team norms stifle conflict, groupthink can develop. **Groupthink** is an agreement-at-any-cost mentality that results in ineffective work team decision making and may lead to poor solutions. The fundamental problem underlying groupthink is pressure on members to concede and accept what other members think. The likelihood of groupthink increases when

- peer pressure to conform is great,
- a highly directive leader presses for a particular interpretation of the problem and course of action,
- the need to process a complex and unstructured issue under crisis conditions exists, and
- the group is isolated.[32]

Instead of stifling conflict, a better approach to handling disagreements is to engage in productive controversy. **Productive controversy** occurs when team members value different points of view and seek to draw them out to facilitate creative problem solving. To ensure constructive controversy, work team members must establish ground rules to keep them focused on issues rather than people and defer decisions until various issues and ideas are explored. By framing decisions as collaborations aimed at achieving the best possible results and following procedures that equalize sharing of power and responsibility, team members can focus on their common goal and avoid becoming embroiled in battles of egos.[33]

DIAGNOSING THE CAUSES OF
POOR TEAM PERFORMANCE

5.

**EXPLAIN HOW TO
DIAGNOSE AND REMOVE
BARRIERS TO POOR TEAM
PERFORMANCE.**

When teams fail to perform as well as they are supposed to, there may be many reasons for their failure. Typically, the first thing that people think about are the internal processes, which we have already discussed. Effective teams and their leaders consider whether negative internal team processes are responsible for poor performance, but they don't stop there.[34] Teams don't exist in a vacuum, and their internal processes don't unfold in isolation. The external forces acting on a team may also be the cause of team performance problems. The ***external system*** comprises outside conditions and influences that exist before and after the team is formed. Important features of the external system to consider include team design, culture, team member selection, team training, and the reward system.[35]

TEAM DESIGN

The design choices involved in creating a work team are numerous. We have already discussed the importance of choices concerning team goals, team duration, and team membership. Here we focus on two additional design choices: team size and team location.

Team Size. As the number of team members increases, changes occur in the team's internal decision-making processes. The optimal team size seems to be from four to eight members, depending on the team's tasks. A good rule of thumb to remember is that understaffed teams tend to outperform overstaffed teams.[36] Members of teams with more than a dozen members generally have difficulty communicating with each other. Increasing team size also causes the following effects.

- Demands on leader time and attention are greater. The leader becomes more psychologically distant from the other team members. This problem is most serious in self-managing work teams, where more than one person can take on leader roles.

- The team's tolerance of direction from the leader is greater, and the team's decision making becomes more centralized.

- The team atmosphere is less friendly, the actions are less personal, more cliques form within the team, and, in general, team members are less satisfied.

- The team's rules and procedures become more formalized.[37]

For innovative decision making, the ideal work team size is probably between five and nine members.[38] If a work team has more than nine members, separate cliques might form. If larger teams are required for some reason, the use of subteams may be a solution to the problem of size. The purpose of subteams is to encourage all team members to share ideas when analyzing problems, information, and alternative solutions. The full team can then meet to discuss subteam assessments and recommendations. In some instances, different subteams work on the same set of problems and then share and discuss their conclusions with the entire team. The leader of a large work team needs to be aware of the possibility that subteams, or cliques, may form on their own, each with its own leader and agenda. Although more resources are available to large teams, these resources can create a backlash that hurts overall team effectiveness if each unofficial subteam or clique lobbies strongly for its own position.

Team Location. The term ***team proximity*** refers to the location of a team's members. Two aspects of team location are (1) proximity to other work teams and members of the organization and (2) team members' proximity to each other.

The ideal proximity among teams depends on the work being done. When many teams are working together on a single project, close coordination among the teams is needed. At Microsoft, teams benefit from being near others in the organization. Members of different teams can meet at the snack shop or water cooler to fill each other in on developments within their respective teams. Problem solving readily occurs as the need arises. For some work teams, however, performance is improved when the team is removed from the daily activities of the organization. Recall the discussion of corporate intrapreneurship in Chapter 5. Innovation and creativity are essential to successful intrapreneurship, but the bureaucracy and political intrigue often found in large corporations can stifle them. Consequently, intrapreneurial teams at 3M, Lincoln Electric, and Black & Decker frequently set up skunk works operations in a remote location—such as an old warehouse or someone's garage. Isolated from outside distractions, the intrapreneurs are able to focus on the future without having to battle the status quo.

WEB INSIGHT

Visit the Project Management Forum at *http://www.pmforum.org*. If you were to become a professional project manager, how could you use the resources available to improve your ability to manage a global, virtual project management team?

The location of team members often depends on where the talent needed for a task happens to be. In virtual teams, team members usually work in widely scattered geographic locations. A ***virtual work team*** meets and does its tasks without everyone being physically present in the same place or even at the same time. Virtual work teams can be functional, problem solving, multidisciplinary, or self-managing. As described in the following Global Awareness Competency feature,[39] communications technologies such as the Internet, voice mail, and video, allow virtual work teams to extend the reach of organizations far beyond their traditional physical and cultural boundaries.

GLOBAL AWARENESS COMPETENCY

NCR's Virtual Teams

When NCR was founded more than a century ago, it produced and sold cash registers. Back then, employees of the National Cash Register (NCR) Company knew nothing about working in virtual teams—the term hadn't even been coined and the technology necessary for such teams to function hadn't even been thought of, much less invented. Today, such teams are vital to the firm's survival. Although you may still be able to buy an antique cash register from NCR, most of the company's customers are more interested in products such as its WorldMark enterprise computer server. A virtual team of more than 1,000 people working in 17 locations created this product. The U.S. team members were scattered across five states, and they in turn worked with others who lived in Ireland, India, and China. With such a complex project (imagine designing a computer that weighs about 10 tons!), the most amazing feat of this team may have been completing its work on time and within budget.

One factor contributing to its success was that everyone on the team understood his or her mission and its importance. In addition, all the team members knew the basics of good project management—setting goals, identifying tasks and the ultimate results to be achieved, scheduling work, and so on. And, perhaps most important, this team had the benefit of using the latest and best communications technologies. As they worked together each day, they relied heavily on a continuously available high-speed, full-bandwidth communications link through which they could send audio, video, and data signals. The team nicknamed this link "Worm Hole." In science fiction stories, wormholes make it possible for people to be transported instantly from galaxy to galaxy. NCR's "Worm Hole" didn't actually transport people from one location to another—but it came close. Team members could see everyone at all the locations, visually present material to each other, exchange documents, use flip charts, and discuss or argue about any topic. In just 11 months, this team created a new generation of computer systems.

• • •

To learn more about NCR, visit the company's home page at

http://www.ncr.com

Many of the principles of effective teamwork that apply to face-to-face team activities also apply to virtual work teams. At NCR, for example, the project management skills used by the virtual team that designed WorldMark would have been needed even if all the team members had worked in the same location. However, other principles for designing and managing virtual work teams address their special nature.[40] As organizations expand into global consumer and labor markets, managing virtual work teams will be an increasingly important managerial responsibility. It is an aspect of global awareness competency that managers can develop by staying informed of developments in communications technology and in practices being adopted by the companies with the most experience in this aspect of organization design. The following are some of the current best practices for managing virtual work teams.[41]

- *Use a variety of communication technologies.* Software designed especially for electronic meetings can be a good way to supplement video or telephone conference calls. Software that facilitates language translations can make written communication easier for global team members.

- *Pay attention to the quality of the communication transmissions.* Low-quality voice transmissions are frustrating and demotivating for team members, especially when they are listening to a person with a strong accent. Video images should be clear and large enough to reveal subtle expressions and body language.

- *Encourage the team members to discuss cultural differences.* These differences usually become apparent quickly when people meet face to face. They may be less noticeable during electronic meetings, but they are no less important.

- *Be sure that someone is responsible for facilitating the communication process.* A good facilitator doesn't allow anyone to be a passive observer. A good facilitator may also occasionally contact participants individually to be sure they feel that their opinions are being heard.

- *Encourage team members to interact one on one, without feeling obligated to copy every e-mail message to the entire team.* This approach can help prevent misunderstandings from needlessly escalating into crises.

- *Train team members to match their choice of technology to the task.* Fax, e-mail, and a company's intranet work well for disseminating information. Conference calls and video conferencing are more appropriate for holding important discussions and making major decisions.

For virtual teams that will be working together for several months or years, a few additional principles should be followed, within time and budget constraints.

- To help the team members develop trust more quickly, hold an initial face-to-face meeting. Discuss the team's purpose and clarify the roles and responsibilities of each team member.

- Whenever possible, individual team members should visit others, even if the entire team can't be assembled.

- Schedule periodic face-to-face meetings to refresh connections and minimize "out-of-site, out-of-mind" attitudes.

CULTURE

Both the societal and organizational cultures within which work teams operate are important aspects of their external contexts. Differences in norms for team behavior often reflect differences in national culture. In some cultures, such as China, Malaysia, and Thailand, societal values support striving for harmony and cohesiveness and avoiding open conflict. In the more individualistic cultures of the United States and Canada, people feel more comfortable when they are able to express their opinions and have their views taken seriously by other team members. At the same time, however, U.S. and Canadian cultures value friendly relationships among coworkers, so too much conflict feels uncomfortable.[42] In an international work team, the natural tendency of team members is to behave according to the norms of their countries. When different cultures are present, misunderstandings are the likely result if team members are not familiar with the cultures represented on the team.

Even within the United States, norms vary greatly between teams. A study of executive teams revealed that norms concerning conflict differed greatly from one team to the next. About half the teams studied reported that the team members argued most of the time. In these teams, everyone felt free to voice opinions and share ideas. One executive described his team's pattern for handling conflict this way: "We scream a lot, then laugh, and then resolve the issues." In several other teams, however, there was little open conflict—in fact, some teams actually had too little conflict.[43]

Regardless of national cultures, work teams can function well if they are supported by the organization's culture. Organizations that support participation by lower level employees increase the likelihood that work teams will embrace organizational goals and authority relations, rather than attempt to undermine them.[44] When individualistic employees are empowered through self-managing work teams, they gain more control and influence over their work. Because having control is important in individualistic cultures, employees working in self-managing teams often report being very satisfied with their work.[45]

TEAM MEMBER SELECTION

The characteristics needed in an employee who works in relative isolation are different from those needed in an employee who must work in a team environment. In work teams, the personality trait of *agreeableness* seems to be especially important, for example.[46] Such people seek to find areas of common understanding with the members of the team. When areas of agreement are known, team members may also be able to accept their differences more easily.

Of the six managerial competencies, communication and teamwork are essential for working in *all* types of teams. If the team is self-managed and everyone shares all aspects of a task, more technical skills often are needed by each team member. Planning and administration competency also is extremely important for members of self-managing teams. When teams are used to coordinate the activities of organizational units spread throughout the world, global awareness competency is especially important.[47]

Personality traits are difficult to change, and both technical skills and managerial competencies develop slowly over time. For these reasons, team-based organizations often use intensive and sophisticated selection procedures when hiring new employees. The GE/Durham plant is a good example. When the plant was started, management decided that all job candidates would have to be FAA-certified mechanics. FAA certification requires two years of training and is something that no other GE plant requires of all job candidates. First-rate mechanical skills are just one of the 11 areas that job applicants must possess to get a job. Others include helping skills, teamwork, communication, coaching, and flexibility. As one current employee remembers, the interview process—lasting eight hours—was especially grueling: "That was one heck of an experience. I talked to five different people. I participated in three group activities with job candidates. I even had to do a presentation: I had 15 minutes to prepare a 5-minute presentation." Through these activities, GE assessed the teamwork and communication competencies that these mechanics would have to rely on day in and day out in doing their new jobs.

TEAM TRAINING

Even in organizations that are effective in selecting employees capable of working well in teams, team training can be beneficial. Perhaps more than any other organization, NASA understands that training comes before effective teamwork. Before astronauts are sent into space to live in a community that relies heavily on teamwork for survival, NASA has them working together every day for a year or two in order to become a team. They share office space, spend countless hours together in flight simulators, and rehearse everything from stowing their flight suits to troubleshooting malfunctions. Formal training in procedures is part of the experience, but it isn't everything. NASA realizes that teamwork training also involves helping teammates get to know each other and develop confidence in each other.

WEB INSIGHT

Which aspects of the external system are most important to the success of space station teams? To learn more about the space station, visit *http://spaceflight.nasa.gov/shuttle/*.

Most organizations can't afford to give team members a year or two of training before teams begin working on their tasks. They look for quicker ways to achieve the same objectives that NASA has for its training program. For example, at Mabe, an appliance manufacturer with plants located throughout Latin America, employees receive two to three weeks of training each year. To support teamwork, the training teaches employees about setting goals, learning how to measure results, and deciding what needs to be measured.[48] Regardless of how many hours of team training organizations require, their goals usually are the same—to train team members to perform a variety of managerial and leadership activities and to enhance team cohesiveness. For some teams, such as airline flight crews, team members may also need specialized training to ensure that they respond appropriately to rare and unexpected events, such as equipment failure, when lives are at risk.[49] Organizations that invest resources to train teams can increase both team and organizational effectiveness.[50]

Management and Leadership Training. Work teams of all types are being empowered to perform tasks that previously weren't employees' responsibility. Figure 17.6 shows a wide range of tasks that could be assigned to a work team. The vertical axis indicates the degree to which the team is self-managing. The greater the degree of self-management, the more the team has authority, responsibility, and general decision-making discretion for tasks. The horizontal axis indicates the amount and range of competencies required of team members for handling an increasing number and complexity of tasks. The more self-managing a team is, the more important it is for team members to receive training that will enhance all their management competencies.

F i g u r e 1 7 . 6	**Examples of Tasks Performed in Self-Managing Work Teams**

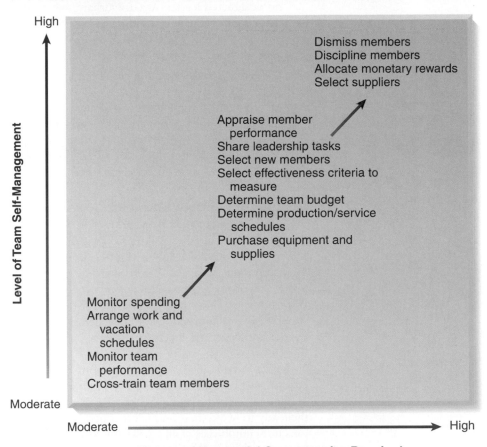

Degree of Managerial Competencies Required

We've already described leadership development in some detail in Chapter 15. That discussion applies particularly to situations where there is one designated leader. Often, however, the task of leadership is shared among all members of the team. In such circumstances, all can benefit from a discussion of the key leadership responsibilities that they'll be sharing, which include the following.

- *Managing meetings.* People who resist teamwork often point to time wasted in meetings as a big source of dissatisfaction. True, teams do need to meet, one way or another, but team meetings should never be a waste of time. Training team members to run meetings properly can make meetings more efficient. Team members can then share the key leadership role (e.g., scheduling a meeting, developing an agenda, recording ideas and decisions, and communicating with others outside the team), rotating through these responsibilities during the life of the team.

- *Supporting disagreement.* A skillful team leader supports disagreement that stimulates innovative solutions while minimizing the risk of bad feelings. Disagreement can be productive if members are open to differences within the team and if they separate idea generation from idea evaluation. Team members also need to understand that the absence of disagreement on a work team may be as destructive as too much disagreement to the team's proper functioning. The use of decision-making aids, such as brainstorming, the nominal group technique, devil's advocacy, and dialectical inquiry, creates productive controversy and can result in better quality decisions that team members can fully accept.[51]

- *Committing to a team decision.* Making a final decision when team members disagree can be relatively easy if final decisions ultimately rest with a team leader. Reaching a final decision that everyone will endorse is more difficult when there is no designated leader. At GE/Durham, where decisions are made by consensus, all team members receive training in how to come to a consensus. Their training also ensures that they understand that they won't be allowed to moan or drag their feet after the team's decision has been made.

- *Using group-based technologies.* For virtual teams (whose members may be widely scattered), as well as some co-located teams (all of whose members are at the same location), training may be needed to develop the teams' abilities to use technologies that support their work. Group decision support systems (GDSS) can be particularly useful. A GDSS is an interactive, computer-based system that combines communication, computer, and decision-making technologies to support group meetings. Using such a system can help a team effectively process information when making a group decision.[52]

Building Team Cohesiveness. To develop team cohesiveness, many organizations use experientially based adventure training. Such training often is held in a camplike environment and includes navigating river rapids, scaling cliffs, or completing a ropes course. Evart Glass Plant, a division of Chrysler Corporation, involved its entire 250-person staff in such training as a way to prepare its employees for working in self-managed work teams. Union members and managers trained side by side during employees' normal work hours. A hi-lo driver (similar to a forklift operator), a maintenance person, a shift supervisor, and a receptionist found themselves working together as a team throughout their training. After each activity, trainers led a discussion about the experience to identify the lesson to be learned from it. Table 17.1 describes a few of the activities and associated lessons from the company's specially designed one-day program. Was the training effective? Surveys and personal interviews were conducted to assess employees' reactions, and the results were positive. Employees commented that people now were going out of their way to help others and felt that people were doing a better job of seeking out opinions from employees at all levels. Employees also got to know each other. Explained one engineer, "Personally, I hadn't been on third shift very long and found there were three people on that shift that I had the wrong opinion of. I saw they were real go-getters and they stayed positive throughout the experience; I was surprised." Overall, the training helped break down personal walls that people had built around themselves and helped them see the benefits of being a contributing member of a team.[53]

Experiential training is an effective way to develop cohesiveness, but used alone it isn't likely to result in optimal teamwork. Teams can also benefit from more formal training. In addition to covering organization-specific procedures for obtaining resources, cost accounting, progress reports, and the like, team members may benefit from learning about the stages of team development. If they understand how teams normally develop, they are less likely to become easily frustrated during the early forming and storming

Table   17.1   **Examples of Team Training Activities and Objectives**

The Challenging Activity	The Teamwork Lesson
Juggle several objects simultaneously (e.g., tennis balls, hackey sacs, and koosh balls) as a team.	Although everyone has a different role, each person touches and affects the outcome.
Find the path hidden in a carpet maze and move each member through it in a limited amount of time.	Teams must find and use each individual's hidden strengths (e.g., a good memory and the abilitiy to move quickly). Doing so allows the team as a whole to succeed.
Balance 14 nails on the head of a nail that has been pounded into a supporting block of wood, creating a free-standing structure without supports.	Things that may seem impossible can be achieved when people work together.
Draw a vehicle that represents the training team and signify which part of the vehicle each member represents.	Each member has different strengths and bringing these strengths together leads to task success.

stages of their own team's development. Formal team training can also help members realize the importance of norms to their performance and stimulate the team to develop norms that aid rather than hinder it.

REWARD SYSTEMS

As described in Chapters 13 and 14, reward systems inform employees about how to direct their energies and reinforce them for making valuable contributions to the organization. When employees work in a single team most of the time and it is essentially the employee's entire job, establishing team performance measures and using them to determine rates of pay is relatively easy. In most organizations, however, people aren't assigned full time to a single team. Their primary responsibilities may derive from a job that they perform essentially as an individual, with work team participation added to their regular duties. Or most of a person's regular duties may require working on teams, but over the course of a year the person may serve on five or six different teams.

Most experts agree that different team structures call for different reward systems. Thus, rather than prescribing a specific approach to rewarding work teams, understanding the basic choices involved in tailoring a reward system to an organization's situation is more useful. Regardless of the details of a team-based reward system, employees need to understand it and managers need to endorse and support it.[54] Table 17.2 lists several questions that managers should consider when designing and evaluating team reward systems. With so many choices, perhaps the best way to develop an appropriate reward system is to assign the task to an empowered, multidisciplinary, well-trained work team.

Table   17.2   **Choices in Designing Reward Systems for Work Teams**

- How can nonmonetary rewards be used to recognize excellent team performance?
- What portion of a person's total monetary rewards should be linked to performance of the team (versus the performance of the individual or the business unit)?
- If rewards are to be linked to results, which effectiveness criteria should be used to evaluate team results? Individual results?
- How should rewards be distributed among the members of a team? Should they all receive equal reawrds? If not, on what basis should people receive differential rewards?
- Who should be responsible for the allocation of rewards among team members: team members, a team leader, someone outside the team?
- For global teams, how should cultural differences among members of the team and the pay systems used in different countries be addressed?

One of the most striking things about today's organizations is their reliance on work teams. The trend toward greater reliance on team-based structures is the reason that teamwork competency is one of the six key managerial competencies that are the focus of this textbook. The model of work team functioning presented in this chapter is intended to help you improve your teamwork competency.

1. **EXPLAIN THE IMPORTANCE OF WORK TEAMS.**
The popularity of team-based organizational structures reflects the belief that teamwork offers the potential to achieve outcomes that couldn't be achieved by individuals working in isolation. Several strategic objectives lead organizations to design their structures around work teams, including customers' demands for innovation, faster response times, better quality, and lower prices.

2. **IDENTIFY FOUR TYPES OF WORK TEAMS.**
A work team is a special type of group. Most work teams consist of a small number of identifiable, interdependent employees who are held accountable for performing tasks that contribute to achieving an organization's goals. Members of a work team have a shared goal and must interact with each other to achieve it. The four most common types of work teams are problem-solving, functional, multidisciplinary, and self-managing. Three key differences among work teams are the nature of their goals, their duration, and their membership. Different types of work teams suit different organizational purposes.

3. **STATE THE MEANING AND DETERMINANTS OF TEAM EFFECTIVENESS.**
The primary components of a model of work team functioning are the external system, team design, internal team processes, and criteria for assessing the team's effectiveness. Effectiveness criteria measure the outcomes achieved by individual members and the team as a whole. A particular work team may be effective in some respects and not in others. Internal processes include the development of the work team over time, personal feelings, and behavioral norms. Through these processes, team members develop and integrate their behaviors. The choices involved in creating a team, including goals, membership, size, location and duration, are numerous. Virtual work teams are an increasingly common choice in global and hi-tech organizations. A team's external system comprises outside conditions and influences that exist before and after the team is formed. Its components include the societal and organizational culture, member selection, team training, and reward system.

4. **DESCRIBE THE INTERNAL TEAM PROCESSES THAT CAN AFFECT TEAM PERFORMANCE.**
Teams tend to develop over time, moving through several developmental stages. These stages include forming, storming, norming, performing, and adjourning. Teams may move through these stages in a variety of ways. In effective teams, members develop feelings of trust, openness, freedom, and interdependence. These feelings allow team members to cooperate and coordinate their actions. Behavioral norms also develop within a work team. They function to regulate and standardize behaviors within the team. Norms concerning how to handle conflict and controversy are especially important for effective team decision making.

5. **EXPLAIN HOW TO DIAGNOSE AND REMOVE BARRIERS TO POOR TEAM PERFORMANCE.**
When teams are ineffective, the source of the problem may be internal team processes. However, poor internal processes may be caused by factors in the team's external system. Managers who accurately diagnose the causes of work team problems will be able to take appropriate corrective actions.

KEY TERMS

Adjourning stage, p. 470
Behavioral norms, p. 471
Cohesiveness, p. 471
Effectiveness criteria, p. 465
External system, p. 473
Feelings, p. 470
Forming stage, p. 469
Free rider, p. 471
Functional work team, p. 462

Group, p. 458
Groupthink, p. 472
Informal group, p. 458
Internal team processes, p. 466
Multidisciplinary work team, p. 462
Norming stage, p. 469
Performing stage, p. 470
Problem-solving work team, p. 461
Productive controversy, p. 472

Quality circle, p. 461
Self-managing work team, p. 463
Storming stage, p. 469
Task force, p. 462
Team proximity, p. 473
Virtual work team, p. 474
Work team, p. 459

1. Why are work teams so prevalent in organizations?

2. Describe how work teams develop. What dangers are present at each stage of development?

3. Martha Stalwart manages a Pizza Hut in Tuscaloosa, Alabama. Business is good, but from the grapevine she's learned that there is a lot of conflict among her team of 20 employees. She's not sure whether the conflict is something to be concerned about, or whether it's normal. She's asked you how to evaluate the situation. What are your recommendations?

4. Outdoor adventure training is a popular approach to team-building. Is this type of training best suited for speeding up the development of the team, creating positive feelings, or building appropriate group norms? Learn about team training based on outdoor activities by visiting the Web site *http://www.team-builder.co.uk*.

5. Choose two organizations that you are familiar with (e.g., your school, your employer, a local community group, or a department store in your town). For each organization, list the work teams that appear to be present, identify the types of teams (functional, multidisciplinary, problem-solving, or self-managing), and explain why the organization needs those particular types of teams.

6. You have an opportunity to take a new job as work team leader in an organization. Before you accept the offer, you want to assess whether the organization is likely to provide a supportive environment for the team. What questions would you ask about the organization to determine whether the environment is supportive?

7. In many schools, one of the most interesting student work teams is the one assigned to create a class yearbook. Suppose that you were a member of this team. Refer to Figure 17.3 and then list the criteria that could be used to assess the effectiveness of the yearbook team.

8. **Competency Development: Strategic Planning.** As the owner of a small business that offers marketing services, you believe that your staff needs to understand how to work effectively in teams, including teams whose members are mostly the employees of your clients. You plan to send several of your employees to a teamwork training program. Investigate three training programs offered at universities or by consultants. List the strengths and weaknesses of each. Then rank order the three programs, assigning 1 to the program that you think is most comprehensive and 3 to the program that you think is least comprehensive. To get started, visit the home pages of the International Institute for Learning at *http://www.iil.com*, Team Leadership Results at *http://www.team-leadership.com*, and Outward Bound at *http://www.outwardbound.org*.

9. **Competency Development: Self-Management.** Jobweb is one of many electronic services that provide information about job openings for recent college graduates. This particular Web site often also lists the results of recent surveys concerning the competencies and experience that employers are looking for. Visit Jobweb and similar Web sites to learn more about how your teamwork competency is likely to affect employers' evaluations of your candidacy for a job. Compared to other competencies, how important is the teamwork competency? What types of experience should you try to get now in order to convince potential employers that you have developed your teamwork competency? The Jobweb home page is at *http://www.jobweb.org*.

CASE FOR COMPETENCY DEVELOPMENT

The Utility of Empowered Teams

AES Corporation supplies electricity to public utilities and steam to industrial companies. Headquartered in Arlington, Virginia, it operates 90 plants in 35 countries. The company expects continued rapid growth in the years ahead as more and more governments deregulate their utilities.

To create a work environment that is both fun and supportive of its strategy of operational excellence, AES adopted a de-

centralized structure. Every employee is encouraged to participate in strategic planning and new plant design. To minimize layers of management, the company chose to organize around multiskilled teams and to have no functionally organized corporate staff. Scott Gardner graduated from Dartmouth and joined an AES team that was developing a $200 million cogeneration plant in San Francisco. "It involved a lot of work and few people to do it," he recalled. Among the tasks he took on were negotiating with the community over the plant's water system and buying and selling pollution credits. Most of the company's plants operate without shift supervisors. Cofounder and chairman Roger Sant explains the logic: "If Dennis [referring to Dennis Bakke, the CEO] and I had to lead everything, we couldn't have grown as much as we have. People would bring deals for us to approve, and we would have a huge bottleneck." As a result, in 5 years the company grew from 600 to 6,000 employees. These employees have enriched jobs and plenty of authority to make decisions. At AES, managers and their teams make the decisions. Team leaders are expected to seek the advice of whomever they think appropriate and then take responsibility for the decisions made. AES believes that its team-based structure fits the company's four basic values.

- *Integrity and wholeness.* The goal is that the things AES people say and do in all parts of the company should fit together with truth and consistency.

- *Fairness.* AES wants to treat its people, customers, suppliers, shareholders, governments, and communities fairly. This value requires that employees routinely question the relative fairness of alternative courses of action.

- *Fun.* AES wants employees to flourish in the use of their gifts and skills and thereby enjoy the time they spend at AES.

- *Social responsibility.* The company believes that it should be involved in projects that provide social benefits, such as lower costs to customers, safety, reliability, and environmental cleanliness.

AES's approach has worked well in the United States, but it doesn't always transfer well to other cultures. This issue is a challenge for the company because over two-thirds of its operations are now overseas. When AES joined with a Belgian company and purchased a plant in Ireland, the Irish managers found that relinquishing their authority was difficult. A U.S. employee had to go to Ireland to instill the company's values at the new location. Slowly, some managers began to see that their employees could make good decisions, but CEO Bakke says the changes have taken too long. "The managers just didn't trust the employees to turn over power," he observed.

In many countries, the biggest problem that AES faces is the overstaffing of existing facilities. When AES buys these facilities or enters into a joint venture relating to them, AES must cut staff. Central to the AES philosophy is the idea of giving people big jobs with big responsibilities and getting rid of as many bosses as possible. According to employee Michael Cranna, "There are two reasons why teams are successful at AES: the type of people we have here and the environment in which they work. People tend to be independent and thrive in a loose environment where roles and responsibilities are not always clearly defined. The environment at AES is one where responsibility is pushed down to the lowest level possible, encouraging everyone to take ownership for not only their piece of the project, but for the project in its entirety." To succeed, employees must be willing to accept these responsibilities and then draw on a team of people who can help them make the right decisions.

In 1998, AES began to initiate changes in its pay systems to support its team environment. Bakke is critical of U.S. laws that require nonmanagement employees to be paid strictly on an hourly basis. He believes that such laws are a major hindrance to creating a fun, meaningful, and empowered workplace. Although he can't do much to change those laws, in other countries AES has begun to introduce changes. Plants in Argentina, Pakistan, England, and South America are moving to an all-salaried format. Oscar Prieto described his experience with changing the pay system in Argentina: "We broke all the rules. No bosses. No time records. No shift schedule. No assigned responsibilities. No administration. And guess what? It worked!"[55]

Questions for Discussion

1. What work team effectiveness criteria seem to be most important to AES cofounders Dennis Bakke and Roger Sant?

2. Suppose that you were in charge of campus recruiting for AES. What qualities would you look for in job candidates and how would you determine whether a candidate possessed those qualities?

3. In which countries or cultures is AES likely to have the most difficulty applying its management principles? In which countries or cultures is it likely to have the least difficulty? Explain.

4. Do you agree with Dennis Bakke's opinion concerning the negative consequences of paying people on an hourly basis? Is an all-salaried system more appropriate for a team-based organization? Why or why not?

5. Besides pay, what other aspects of the external system at AES are likely to be important to the success of its work teams?

To learn more about AES, visit the company's home page at *http://www.aesc.com*.

Valassis Communications

A leading marketing services company, Valassis Communications offers consumer package goods and franchise retailers a variety of products (goods and services), including free-standing inserts (FSIs), Valassis impact promotions (VIPs), and targeted marketing services. The flagship product for the company is its FSIs, or four-color booklets containing coupons and other promotional offers from leading consumer goods companies. Reaching 58 million households each week through more than 400 Sunday newspapers, Valassis effectively distributes nearly 90 percent of all the coupons in the United States. FSIs account for approximately 95 percent of the company's revenue. The VIP division provides franchise retailers with a variety of specialty promotions that are customized to clients' needs and distributed by a variety of methods (e.g., zoned newspapers and direct mail). The Targeted Services division provides various services, including product sampling and advertising delivered via newspapers, geodemographic targeting, run-of-press advertising, and targeted solo print promotions.

As a leader in the sales promotion industry for more than 29 years, Valassis Communications is a publicly held NYSE corporation with annual sales exceeding $795 million. Employing more than 1,600 employees in the United States and Canada, it has been designated one of the "100 Best Companies to Work for in America." One reason for its continued success is its commitment to teamwork.

Valassis utilizes the team approach to accomplish its goals because management believes that even its best employees require the knowledge and expertise of others to do their jobs well. Exchanging thoughts and working together, management believes, results in a synergistic effect (i.e., the quantity and quality of work produced by teams will be greater than that produced by individuals working alone). Management also believes that a "fun" approach allows the company to remain flexible and to meet the unique needs of its customers.

To encourage and support the use of teamwork at Valassis, the company has taken several steps. First, jobs are deliberately designed so that employees are required to work with others and share their unique perspectives and experiences. Management often makeups teams by first defining the problem or outcome desired, and then assembling the various in-house "experts" to address it. The physical layout of open cubicles contributes to the corporate culture of promoting teamwork by encouraging employees to communicate with one another.

Valassis also recruits individuals who display behaviors that contribute to effective teamwork, and the company continually encourages them to further develop their teamwork competencies. Communication competency is another important quality that Valissis looks for when hiring. By employing individuals with these competencies and promoting their use and mastery through its policies and decisions, Valassis has created an environment that rewards both the individual and the company for teamwork.

Questions

1. With regard to teamwork, why does Valassis promote the MOVE and "Make it Happen Day" programs?

2. Why does Valassis promote cross-training of its employees?

To learn more about Valassis Communications, visit the company's home page at *http://www.valassis.com*.

Organizational Cultures and Cultural Diversity

LEARNING OBJECTIVES

AFTER STUDYING THIS CHAPTER YOU SHOULD BE ABLE TO:

1. DESCRIBE THE CORE ELEMENTS OF A CULTURE.

2. COMPARE AND CONTRAST FOUR TYPES OF ORGANIZATIONAL CULTURES.

3. DISCUSS SEVERAL TYPES OF SUBCULTURES THAT MAY EXIST IN ORGANIZATIONS.

4. EXPLAIN WHY MANAGING CULTURAL DIVERSITY IS IMPORTANT AND DESCRIBE SEVERAL ACTIVITIES REQUIRED TO MANAGE IT SUCCESSFULLY.

Chapter Outline

PREVIEW: ARCHITECTS BUILD A NEW CULTURE

THE ELEMENTS OF A CULTURE
ASSUMPTIONS
VALUES AND NORMS
SOCIALIZATION
SYMBOLS
LANGUAGE
NARRATIVES
PRACTICES

BASIC TYPES OF ORGANIZATIONAL CULTURE
BUREAUCRATIC
CLAN
TEAMWORK COMPETENCY: Mayo Clinic's Patient-Centered Culture
ENTREPRENEURIAL
MARKET
ORGANIZATIONAL IMPLICATIONS

ORGANIZATIONAL SUBCULTURES
SUBCULTURES REFLECTING NATIONAL DIFFERENCES
SUBCULTURES REFLECTING WITHIN-COUNTRY DIFFERENCES
SUBCULTURES REFLECTING INDUSTRY DIFFERENCES
SUBCULTURES REFLECTING OCCUPATIONAL DIFFERENCES
IMPLICATIONS OF ORGANIZATIONAL SUBCULTURES

MANAGING CULTURAL DIVERSITY
ORGANIZATIONAL GOALS FOR MANAGING CULTURAL DIVERSITY
PLANNING AND ADMINISTRATION COMPETENCY: More Women Become Partners at Deloitte and Touche
ASSESSING THE ORGANIZATION
DEVELOPING A PLAN
COMMUNICATION COMPETENCY: GM Executives Listen Up
IMPLEMENTATION
SELF-MANAGEMENT COMPETENCY: Diversity Knowledge Quiz
MONITORING AND ADJUSTING

CHAPTER SUMMARY

KEY TERMS

QUESTIONS FOR DISCUSSION AND COMPETENCY DEVELOPMENT

CASE FOR COMPETENCY DEVELOPMENT: CRACKING AVON'S GLASS CEILING

VIDEO CASE: W. B. DONER, INC.

ARCHITECTS BUILD A NEW CULTURE

When the Cuningham Group, an architectural firm in Minneapolis, Minnesota, decided to merge with Solberg + Lowe Architects with offices in Los Angeles, California, and Phoenix, Arizona, the top management teams in both organizations thought that their cultures would meld easily. For the Cuningham Group, the goal of the merger was to expand geographically and to broaden its range of projects. Already well-known for its educational and hotel buildings, the group's management wanted to begin doing design work for the entertainment industry. Partners Rick Solberg and Doug Lowe of Solberg + Lowe were well-known for their work in hotels and the entertainment industry, but economic conditions in the Los Angeles area meant that they needed to look for opportunities elsewhere. As is often the case, the managers at both firms discovered that, although analyzing whether a merger makes financial and strategic sense is easy, successfully merging two corporate cultures is much more difficult.

When Cuningham and his team visited the offices of Solberg + Lowe, they liked the look and feel of the work environment. The physical spaces reminded them of their own offices, and they could see that the principal partners still liked to be actively involved in project design. "I felt it would be easy for me to work there," recalled Cuningham. Solberg recalls feeling the same way when he visited Minneapolis. "I wanted to see live, vibrant contributors on the ownership side. I didn't want a bunch of dead initials on the door." What he and his partner saw led them to conclude, "This is where we'd want to be." Subsequent visits to each others' homes reinforced their beliefs that the two teams would work well together.

The honeymoon lasted less than a year. By then, the fundamental value differences between the two firms became more apparent. Although neither had a formal dress code, the Minnesotans often wore ties to work, whereas the staff in Los Angeles and Phoenix preferred knit shirts. The Minnesota group worked a full 5-day week, but on Friday afternoons, they couldn't reach anyone in Phoenix or Los Angeles because those offices routinely closed at midday on Friday. "At first we wondered if they were just lazier than we were. But we just had to adjust" admits Cuningham.

Communication patterns within the firms also differed. The Cuningham Group didn't hold nearly as many meetings as Solberg + Lowe. And when they did meet, there was always a clear agenda. Solberg and Lowe admit that some of their partners' meetings were more like family fights than discussions between professionals. Solberg and Lowe's frankness with each other was beneficial, but the screaming shocked Cuningham's team, which Solberg described as using a "Minnesota nice" style. There were even differences in how the two firms handled bill collections. The easygoing approach of Solberg + Lowe meant that they didn't press people whom they considered trustworty for overdue payments. Cuningham disapproved: "If you don't pay your gas bill, they cut off your gas. It isn't mean or kind; it's just policy. And it has to be the same for everyone," he explained.

Five years after the merger, the two groups are working together well enough to consider expanding again through another merger. This time, Solberg says that he will make an even greater effort to ensure that there is totally open communication with the other management team, as well as with the staff. "You can't hold anything back. Chances are, what you're concealing will be the problem. Better to find out today than after you've committed to the transaction."[1]

To learn more about the Cuningham Group, visit the firm's home page at

http://www.cuninghamgroup.com

THE ELEMENTS OF A CULTURE

1.

DESCRIBE THE CORE ELEMENTS OF A CULTURE.

A *culture* is the unique pattern of shared assumptions, values, and norms that shape the socialization, symbols, language, narratives, and practices of a group of people.[2] As illustrated in Figure 18.1, these elements form the base of a culture but they can't be observed directly. They can only be inferred from a culture's more visible elements—its socialization activities, symbols, language, narratives, and practices. At Solberg + Lowe, the shared assumptions, values, and norms created a familylike atmosphere that contrasted with the more professional atmosphere created by the shared assumptions, values, and norms of the Cuningham Group.

Figure 18.1 **The Culture Iceberg**

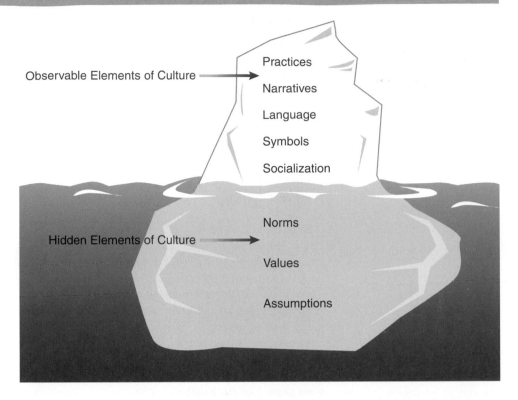

Herb Kelleher, CEO of Southwest Airlines, believes that his company's culture is the key to its success. When asked whether the real secret to his success wasn't simply keeping costs low, Kelleher slammed his fist on the table and shouted back that culture has *everything* to do with Southwest's success because competitors can't copy its culture.[3] Southwest's powerful organizational culture is a key aspect of the company's overall strategy and the primary reason for its success.[4] Its effective management begins with an understanding of the elements of culture.

Cultures develop in both large and small groups of people. In this chapter, we focus on organizational cultures and subcultures. In doing so, however, we recognize that an organization's culture is influenced by larger societal and industry cultures.

ASSUMPTIONS

Shared assumptions are the underlying thoughts and feelings that members of a culture take for granted and believe to be true. Solberg and Lowe's frankness with each other was beneficial, but the screaming shocked Cuningham's team, which Solberg described as using a "Minnesota nice" style. There were even differences in how the two companies handled bill collections. The easygoing approach at Solberg + Lowe—reflected in the practice of not pressing people to pay their bills—was associated with assumptions about who was trustworthy. Cuningham assumed that pressing people to pay their bills was just a normal part of business relationships, which had little to do with feelings of personal trust. Another example is the loosely knit "open source" community of Linux software programmers who share the assumption that software code should be openly available so that anyone anywhere can modify it or create new code to enhance a software's capability. This assumption contrasts sharply with the assumption held by most software producers who believe that code should be proprietary and that secrecy is required in order to make a profit.

VALUES AND NORMS

A *value* is a basic belief about something that has considerable importance and meaning to individuals and is stable over time. In organizations with cultures that support TQM, employees value continuous improvement and information sharing.[5] At Southwest Airlines, "having fun" is a shared value. And, as described in Chapter 6, many contemporary organizations are striving to ensure that all employees value ethical and socially responsible conduct.

As we explained in Chapter 17, norms are rules for the behaviors of group members. There we discussed norms as elements of the internal processes of work teams. When a norm is shared throughout an organization, it becomes an element of the organization's culture. As for teams, the main function of norms in organizations is to regulate and standardize behavior. When members of an organization engage in behaviors that violate the norms, they can expect expressions of disapproval. When behavior conforms to the norms, members receive the approval of their peers and others in the organization.

SOCIALIZATION

Socialization is a process by which new members are brought into a culture.[6] The most powerful way to do so is through consistent role modeling, teaching, coaching, and enforcement by others in the culture. At the societal level, socialization takes place within the family, in schools and religious organizations, and through the media. At the industry level, socialization often occurs through organized activities conducted by industry associations. In organizations, socialization typically begins subtly during the hiring process. It then becomes more apparent during orientation and training events soon after the new hire begins work. In the Linux open source community, socialization occurs over the Internet, where norms such as "don't dump on others" and "make nice" are posted electronically.

SYMBOLS

A *symbol* is anything visible that can be used to represent an abstract shared value or something having special meaning. Symbols are the simplest and most basic observable form of cultural expression. They may take the form of logos, architecture, uniforms, awards, and many other tangible expressions. At the first big get-together of all the staff from Solberg + Lowe and the Cuningham Group, the Minnesotans were given a surfboard signed by all the Solberg + Lowe staff members, symbolizing their sun-drenched lifestyles. The Minnesotans, who hosted the event, greeted their new colleagues with an assortment of scarves, hats, and gloves.

LANGUAGE

Language is a shared system of vocal sounds, written signs, and/or gestures used to convey special meanings among members of a culture.[7] Herb Kelleher is a master at using language to maintain and differentiate his company's culture. Consider these cultural statements: "Work should be fun . . . it can be play . . . enjoy it." "Work is important . . . don't spoil it with seriousness." "We give more for less, not less for less." "Fly the luv airline." "We dignify the CUSTOMER." The word *customer* is always capitalized. Letters of commendation and appreciation to employees are known as "Love Reports." "We are family" is a metaphor used to refer to all employees.

NARRATIVES

Narratives are the unique stories, sagas, legends, and myths in a culture. They often describe the unique accomplishments and beliefs of leaders over time, usually in heroic and romantic terms.[8] Originally, a story may be based on historical fact, but as the story gets told and retold, the facts may be embellished with fictional details. The party that Cuningham threw for his newly merged staff became the topic of a lasting narrative in that company. In what seemed like an extravagant move, Cuningham flew the entire staff of Solberg + Lowe plus their spouses, children, and significant others to Minnesota for a holiday party in January. That event is still talked about and recognized as an expression of how much the company values its people and its assumption that people who know and like each other will work together better than people who don't know or like each other.

PRACTICES

The most complex but observable cultural element is shared practices, which include taboos and ceremonies. **Taboos** are culturally forbidden behaviors. A taboo at Johnson & Johnson is to put profits ahead of ethical responsibilities to doctors, nurses, and patients. When people join the company, they receive a copy of the Johnson & Johnson credo, which states this taboo.

Ceremonies are elaborate and formal activities designed to generate strong feelings. Usually they are carried out as special events.[9] In most societies, ceremonies celebrate the birth, marriage, and death of the society's members. In many organizations, ceremonies are used to recognize special achievements and honor retiring employees. At Apple Computer, Steve Jobs hosts an elaborate annual ceremony at which the company introduces its new products. Jobs assumes that his company's unique product designs will be stolen if competitors learn about them during the development phase, so he invests great effort in keeping new designs as secret as possible. This secrecy heightens the excitement during the ceremony, where even Apple's own employees are surprised and delighted as Jobs reveals the firm's new products.[10]

BASIC TYPES OF ORGANIZATIONAL CULTURE

2.

COMPARE AND CONTRAST FOUR TYPES OF ORGANIZATIONAL CULTURES.

Cultural elements and their relationships create a pattern that is distinct to an organization, just as a personality is unique to an individual. As with a classification of individuals that share some common characteristics, several general types of organizational culture can be described. One useful type is presented in Figure 18.2. The vertical

| Figure 18.2 | **Types of Organizational Cultures** |

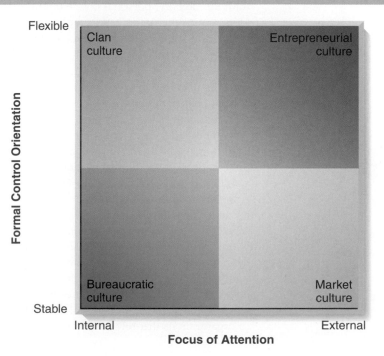

axis reflects the relative formal control orientation, ranging from stable to flexible. The horizontal axis reflects the relative focus of attention, ranging from internal functioning to external functioning. The four quadrants represent four pure types of organizational culture: bureaucratic, clan, entrepreneurial, and market.[11] In a culturally homogeneous organization, one of these basic types of culture will predominate.

Different organizational cultures may be appropriate under different conditions, with no one type of culture being ideal for every situation. However, some employees may prefer one over another. As you read about each type of culture, consider which best fits your preferences. An employee who works in an organization that fits the person's view of an ideal culture tends to be committed to the organization and optimistic about its future.[12]

BUREAUCRATIC

In a *bureaucratic culture,* the behavior of employees is governed by formal rules and standard operating procedures, and coordination is achieved through hierarchical reporting relationships. Recall that the long-term concerns of a bureaucracy are predictability, efficiency, and stability. The focus of attention is on the internal operations of the organization. To ensure stability, the tasks, responsibilities, and authority for all employees are clearly spelled out. Rules and processes that apply to most situations are developed, and employees are socialized to believe that their duty is to "go by the book" and follow legalistic procedures. Behavioral norms support formality over informality.[13]

Bureaucratic cultures often are found in organizations that produce standardized goods and/or services. They are particularly common in local, state, and federal governments. Governments create rules in their efforts to ensure that all citizens are treated the same, regardless of their backgrounds, wealth, or status. These same values often are reflected in the organizational cultures of such organizations.

CLAN

An internal focus also characterizes a clan culture. However, compared to bureaucratic cultures, in a clan culture control over behavior is more subtle. Few formal rules and procedures exist. Instead, the behaviors of employees in a *clan culture* are shaped by tradition, loyalty, personal commitment, extensive socialization, and self-management. Members of the organization recognize an obligation beyond the simple exchange of labor for a salary. They understand that contributions to the organization (e.g., hours worked per week) may exceed any contractual agreements. The clan culture achieves unity with a long and thorough socialization process. Long-time employees serve as mentors and role models for newer members. These relationships perpetuate the organization's values and norms over successive generations of employees. Members of a clan culture are aware of their unique history, which is likely to be documented in some way. They also celebrate their culture's traditions in various rites. Members have a shared image of the organization's style and manner of conduct. Public statements reinforce its values. At Southwest Airlines, Friday afternoon parties in Dallas and the widely publicized antics of cofounder Herb Kelleher are a strong tradition that support the company's fun-loving culture.

In a clan culture, members share feelings of pride in membership. They have a strong sense of identification and recognize their need to work together. The promotion-from-within career pattern results in an extensive network of colleagues whose paths have crossed and who have shared similar experiences. Shared goals, perceptions, and behavioral tendencies foster communication, coordination, and integration. Peer pressure to adhere to important norms is strong. As described in the following Teamwork Competency feature, the combination of cultural elements found in a clan culture is well-suited to organizations that rely heavily on teamwork, such as the Mayo Clinic.[14]

Each year, nearly half a million patients are treated by the 2,000 physicians and 35,000 allied staff who work in the Mayo Clinic. The philosophy behind the Mayo Clinic was developed a century ago by two Minnesota physicians—Doctors Charlie and Will Mayo. Their philosophy for practicing medicine was that two heads are better than one and that five heads are even better! That philosophy is reflected in the Mayo Clinic's mission statement:

> Mayo will provide the best care to every patient every day through integrated clinical practice, education, and research.

Symbolizing the integration of practice, education, and research in the interest of protecting patients' health is the clinic's logo of three interlocked shields.

At Mayo, the value of teamwork is evident everywhere. Doctors are encouraged to include social workers, spiritual advisors, and psychiatrists as members of the team working with a patient. Dr. Lynn Hartmann explained the team concept: "We work in teams, and

each team is driven by the medical problems involved in a case and the patient's preferences. Sometimes that means that a team must be expanded—or taken apart and reassembled."

The importance of doctors consulting with each other when treating patients is reflected in the language used at the clinic. All doctors use the term "consultants" to refer to each other. To ensure that economic forces don't interfere with teamwork, all doctors are paid a salary. The high value placed on teamwork also shows up in the way patients are treated. They can be as actively involved in their own diagnosis and treatment as they wish. Governance of the clinic is by teamwork, too. Committees of doctors make decisions ranging from how to decorate the lobby to how patient billings should be handled to when and where to expand the clinic and its services.

The Mayo approach is unique, so how does the clinic find physicians who fit its culture? Most of them have been "Mayo-ized" through a process of careful selection and extensive socialization. For physicians who trained at Mayo, the

culture is taught from the beginning of their careers. Their days in training also give Mayo consultants time to observe whether they fit the culture. "You can tell early on. You watch people, day in an day out, and you quickly tell who has the attitude as well as the aptitude," explained neurologist Robert Brown.

• • •

To earn more about the Mayo Clinic, visit the organization's home page at

http://www.mayo.edu

WEB INSIGHT

Access the Web site of Federal-Mogul at *http://www.federal-mogul.com* and read about the company's values and vision. What type of culture does the company have? Does the Fel-Pro culture seem to have survived?

Fel-Pro, an auto-parts maker in Skokie, Illinois, had a clan culture. When Chairman Richard Snell of Federal-Mogul approached Fel-Pro about buying the company, he was told that a deal could be worked out only if Fel-Pro's culture was protected. The Fel-Pro culture valued maintaining a family atmosphere. It operated a summer camp for children of its employees, always sent parents a U.S. Treasury Bond upon the arrival of a new child, and funded scholarships for employees and their children. Teamwork among employees was promoted, and turnover was unusually low. The family programs cost the company 57 cents per worker hour, and company data indicated that employees who took advantage of the programs were more likely than others to participate in team problem solving and offer suggestions for operational improvements. Although he worried about how Federal-Mogul's employees might react, Snell agreed to continue operating Fel-Pro's summer camp for at least two years and to continue the scholarship fund for at least five years.[15]

ENTREPRENEURIAL

In an ***entrepreneurial culture,*** the external focus and flexibility create an environment that encourages risk taking, dynamism, and creativity. There is a commitment to experimentation, innovation, and being on the leading edge. This culture doesn't just quickly react to changes in the environment; it creates change. Effectiveness means providing new and unique products and rapid growth. Individual initiative, flexibility, and freedom foster growth and are encouraged and well rewarded. As described in Chapter 5, entrepreneurs must be keenly focused on aspects of the external environment, including customers, competitors, and potential sources of funding. Regardless of whether an organization is a start-up company or a more established firm, this focus on the external environment will be evident in an entrepreneurial culture. As is true in organizations with clan cultures, flexibility is another important aspect of entrepreneurial cultures.

An entrepreneurial culture suits a new company's start-up phase. During the 1990s, Internet-based start-ups such as Yahoo! and Amazon.com were well known for their entrepreneurial cultures. An entrepreneurial culture also fits well with the demands faced by employees who are seeking to create and develop new products within the environment of a larger company—such as those who work in skunk-works units. However, for managing products and services that have already been brought to market and may be entering later stages of the product life cycle, a market culture may be more appropriate. By 2000, for example, many who had happily invested in dotcom start-ups when they were unprofitable now began to pressure those same companies to produce financial results for shareholders.

MARKET

In a ***market culture,*** the values and norms reflect the importance of achieving measurable and demanding goals, especially those that are financial and market-based (e.g., sales growth, profitability, and market share). Hard-driving competitiveness and a profits orientation prevail throughout the organization. CEO Christos Cotsakos describes the market culture of E*Trade this way: "At E*Trade, we're an attacker. We're predatory. We believe we have a God-given right to market share."[16] Other companies with strong market cultures include PepsiCo, ARAMARK, Frito-Lay, and Citigroup, among others.

As the term implies, the focus of a market culture is outward. Although the market being served may be quite dynamic, the organization usually strives for some internal stability. When a person is hired at Frito-Lay, the obligations of each party are agreed upon in advance and the relationship between individual and organization is contractual. The employee is responsible for delivering results, and Frito-Lay promises a specified level of rewards in return. The contract, renewed annually if each party adequately performs its obligations, is utilitarian because each party uses the other to further its own goals. Thus, rather than promoting a feeling of membership in a social system, a market culture values independence and individuality. For example, the salesperson who increases sales will make more money, and the firm will earn more profits through the salesperson's greater sales volume.

A market culture doesn't exert much informal social pressure on an organization's members. Superiors' interactions with subordinates largely consist of negotiating performance–reward agreements and/or evaluating requests for resource allocations. Social relations among coworkers aren't emphasized, and few economic incentives are tied directly to cooperating with peers. Managers in one department are expected to cooperate with managers in other departments only to the extent necessary to achieve their performance goals.

Colgate-Palmolive adopted a market culture in order to survive in the highly competitive consumer products business. The career of one manager, Lois Juliber, illustrates the challenges that managers face when working in a market culture. As head of North American operations, she sharply reduced costs and reorganized business processes, cutting the time needed to deliver orders by 25 percent. In an earlier assignment as head of Asian operations, she had doubled sales and tripled profits in just 3 years. With these successes behind her, Juliber was given the assignment of achieving similar goals globally by integrating the company's scattered manufacturing and operating procedures.[17]

ORGANIZATIONAL IMPLICATIONS

Organizational culture has the potential to enhance organizational performance, individual satisfaction, the sense of certainty about how problems are to be handled, and other aspects of worklife. However, if an organizational culture gets out of step with the changing expectations of external stakeholders, it can hinder effectiveness.[18]

The need to determine which attributes of an organization's culture should be preserved and which should be modified is constant. In the United States during the 1980s, many companies began changing their cultures to be more responsive to customers' expectations for high-quality products and excellent customer service. During the 1990s, when unemployment levels reached historic lows and labor shortages made it difficult for organizations to take advantage of market opportunities, many top managers began to reassess how well their organizational cultures fit the expectations of their workforces. Rapid rates of globalization and the need for business models that are effective in a variety of countries continue to press organizations to scrutinize their cultures.[19] As described in Chapter 12, the need for continual innovation and change is causing many an organization to become more of a learning organization. Finally, the continuation of merger and acquisition activities has focused attention on the importance of understanding, assessing, and melding differing organizational cultures. As Figure 18.3 shows, many executives recognize that they have often failed to merge cultures successfully.[20]

Figure 18.3 **Meeting the Merger Challenge**

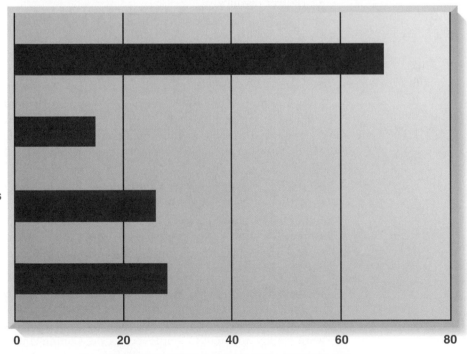

Percentage of Experienced Executives Agreeing

Regardless of the reason, when an organization focuses on understanding its culture, it is likely to discover that it doesn't have *one* organizational culture. Instead, it probably has several subcultures. Before an organization can improve its overall culture, it must first understand these organizational subcultures.

ORGANIZATIONAL SUBCULTURES

3.

DISCUSS SEVERAL TYPES
OF SUBCULTURES THAT
MAY EXIST IN
ORGANIZATIONS.

For an organizational culture to be of any consequence, it must have a base of shared assumptions, values, and norms. At the same time, however, various individuals and groups in the organization may hold different assumptions, values, and norms. An **organizational subculture** exists when assumptions, values, and norms are shared by some—but not all—organizational members.

It's not unusual to find several subcultures within a single organization. Before they merged, the cultures of the Cuningham Group and Solberg + Lowe were similar in many ways. No doubt, both were shaped by the assumptions, values, and norms that pervade their profession. Yet, even after five years of existence as a unified organization, distinct subcultures rooted in past histories persisted at the firm's three offices.

Organizational subcultures occur for a variety of reasons. As with the Cuningham Group and Solberg + Lowe merger, subcultures are likely to exist after established organizations come together to form a new organization. Organizational subcultures also are common in international firms, where societal cultures combine with organizational cultures to create distinct subcultures. In domestic companies, subcultures may emerge among employees from different demographic groups or among employees working in different divisions or occupations. Because subcultures are so common in organizations, managing cultural diversity has emerged as a key business issue in recent years.

SUBCULTURES REFLECTING NATIONAL DIFFERENCES

We described some of the cultural differences that exist among countries in Chapter 3. Recall that such differences can be described in terms of the following dimensions.

- Power distance
- Uncertainty avoidance
- Individualism
- Masculinity
- Confucian dynamics

In organizations that operate in several countries, subcultures that reflect these national differences are likely to exist even when there is a common organizational culture. At each location where a multinational company has operations, organizational and societal cultures in combination create a unique organizational subculture.

SUBCULTURES REFLECTING WITHIN-COUNTRY DIFFERENCES

Experienced travelers know that societal cultures are not uniform within a country. Subcultures in a country can be based on many factors. In the United States, the most salient subcultures are those based on geographic region and ethnicity. Demographic characteristics other than ethnicity may also be sources of subcultures, including gender, age, family status, religion, and sexual orientation.

Geographic Region. National culture may change dramatically from one side of a mountain range to the other, from north to south, and from seashore to landlocked interior. The U.S. subcultures found in midwestern Minnesota and western Los Angeles were readily apparent to employees of the Cuningham Group and Solberg + Lowe. A study of more than 700 managers in large cities in each of China's six major regions suggests that there are at least three distinct subcultures in China: one in the southeast, another in the northeast, and a third covering much of the central and western parts of the country. The subculture of the southeast region is the most individualistic, whereas the subculture of the central and western areas is the most collectivistic. The culture of the northeast region falls between these two extremes. Thus a manager whose company operates at several locations in China needs to understand the organizational subcultures that are based on these regional differences.[21]

Ethnicity. In China, the regions in which people live are closely associated with their ethnicity. In Europe, where immigration across country borders has been minimal until quite recently, ethnicity is closely associated with a person's nationality.[22] In the United States, where the population is much more mobile, people from a variety of ethnic backgrounds are found in every region. Nearly 1 in 10 workers in the United States today is foreign born—the highest rate in 70 years. In a surging economy, immigrants have been an essential source of workers for many industries.[23]

Among workers born in the United States, many still identify with the ethnic groups of their ancestors, who may have come to this country one, two, or several generations ago. The dominant ethnic groups in the United States, as defined by the Census Bureau, are described in Table 18.1.[24] Note that each of the six main categories of ethnicity used for census purposes includes more specific geographic or ethnic groups that people may identify with more readily.

Table 18.1	Ethnic Categories Used in the U.S. 2000 Census
Ethnic Category	**Description**
Hispanic or Latino	A person of Cuban, Puerto Rican, South American, Central American, or other Spanish culture or origin, regardless of race.
American Indian or Alaska Native	A person with origins in the original peoples of North, South, or Central America who maintains tribal affiliation and community attachment.
Asian	A person with origins in any of the original peoples of the Far East, Southeast Asia, or the Indian subcontinent, including Cambodia, China, India, Japan, Korea, Malaysia, Pakistan, the Philippine Islands, Thailand, and Vietnam.
Black or African American	A person with origins in any of the black racial groups in Africa.
Native Islander or other Pacific Islander	A person with origins in any of the original peoples of Hawaii, Guam, Samoa, or other Pacific Islands.
White	A person with origins in any of the original peoples of Europe, the Middle East, or North Africa.

Census counts of people in the categories shown in Table 18.1 are, at best, rough estimates of the proportion of workers who identify with each ethnic group's culture. The identity of many people is influenced by more than one ethnic group. For others, the cultures of their ancestors have little effect on their daily lives. Although their consequences are difficult to quantify, ethnic subcultures can have a significant impact on an organization.

Other Subcultures. Characteristics such as ethnicity, age, gender, and religion are typically referred to as *demographics*. We have already described some ethnic subcultures and noted that they may or may not be associated with geographic regions. Other demographic subcultures are seldom associated with geographic regions. Men and women live in every region, as do members of different generations and people with and without children. The fact that people with different demographic backgrounds live side by side doesn't mean that they share the same culture, however. Employees within each generation (or even each age cohort) tend to share a subculture distinct from the subcultures of other generations. Similarly, although many cultural groupings include both men and women, the experiences of men and women within a culture may be quite distinct. In addition, subcultures based in religion, marital and family status, sexual orientation, and other unifying life experiences typically are found within larger societal cultures.

SUBCULTURES REFLECTING INDUSTRY DIFFERENCES

Dutch researcher Geert Hofstede, who is best known for his studies of societal cultures (see Chapter 3), has also studied industry cultures. His research indicates that industry cultures can be compared by using the dimensions shown in Figure 18.4.[25]

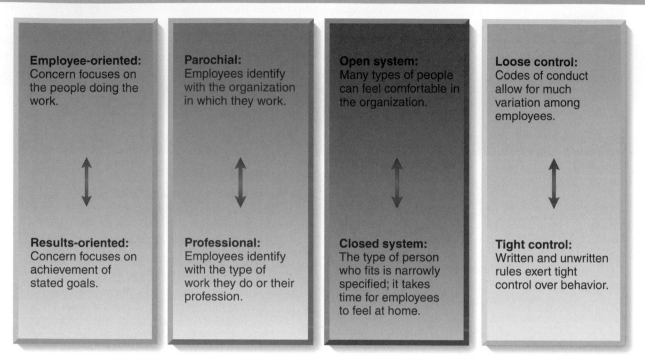

Figure 18.4 Dimensions for Describing Industry Cultures

Employee-oriented: Concern focuses on the people doing the work.

Results-oriented: Concern focuses on achievement of stated goals.

Parochial: Employees identify with the organization in which they work.

Professional: Employees identify with the type of work they do or their profession.

Open system: Many types of people can feel comfortable in the organization.

Closed system: The type of person who fits is narrowly specified; it takes time for employees to feel at home.

Loose control: Codes of conduct allow for much variation among employees.

Tight control: Written and unwritten rules exert tight control over behavior.

As an industry, higher education has long been more people oriented than results oriented. It is also a relatively closed system that requires several years of training to enter and whose members exert strong control over who is allowed to remain (e.g., through granting or denying tenure). The entertainment industry is also relatively people oriented, with the concerns of artists being at least as important as the concerns of entertainment consumers. Relative to higher education, it is more open, however. A wide variety of people, some with relatively little specific experience, can easily move into the industry and expect to achieve success.

When SBUs in a company compete in different industries, industry-based subcultures often clash. Andersen Worldwide has experienced debilitating internal conflicts for several years, owing in part to the two different subcultures that have evolved in its accounting and consulting units. Founded in 1913, the accounting firm of Arthur Andersen was so internally cohesive that employees were sometimes referred to as "Androids." In 1954, the firm began its consulting activities, which focused on information technology. For years, people who specialized in accounting and consulting coexisted. All new hires attended a four-week school located in Illinois, where they were exposed to rigorous training and mentorship programs. Consultants didn't need in-depth knowledge of accounting, but they were expected to pass the CPA exam nevertheless. Most of the people who became partners had been with the firm their entire careers. By the 1980s, however, industry-based differences had emerged within the firm. Some partners in the consulting business came to the firm later in their careers and weren't CPAs. The consultants began

WEB INSIGHT

Andersen Worldwide is an organization that has two distinct subcultures: those of the accounting and the consulting units. How would you categorize the organizational cultures of Arthur Andersen (go to *http://www.arthurandersen.com*) and Accenture (go to *http://www.accenture.com*)—bureaucratic, clan, entrepreneurial, or market?

to question the assumption that the two businesses were better off combined than they would be as separate firms. The consultants eventually persuaded the accountants to establish Andersen Consulting as a separate business unit. The consulting division was located in Los Angeles, and the accounting division was located in Chicago. Face-to-face meetings between the two groups were rare, and the adversarial relationship between the presidents of the two divisions was public knowledge. The two business units continued to grow apart, each with its own culture and vision of the future. Battles between the units peaked in 2000, when they entered arbitration in order to settle disagreements about the nature of their respective legal obligations. The arbitrator's ruling cleared the way for the two businesses essentially to sever their relationship completely.[26] In 2001, Andersen Consulting formalized the separation when it announced that it changed its name to Accenture.

SUBCULTURES REFLECTING OCCUPATIONAL DIFFERENCES

Subcultures within organizations often reflect business or functional specialties (e.g., manufacturing, R&D, accounting, engineering, marketing, and human resources). Occupational socialization practices can be strong sources of cultural indoctrination, especially for professionals. For them, the socialization period begins in college and continues as long as they identify with their chosen professions. Professional associations often formulate their own mission statements, codes of ethics, and standards for professional practice. Together, these values and norms can create a shared world view that is understood and generally accepted within the profession—but is largely unknown to outsiders. Organizational structures that group members of a profession in functionally defined departments reinforce and sustain occupation-based subcultures.

As described elsewhere, one of the goals of TQM and reengineering efforts is to integrate the subcultures that divide functional specialties and thereby reduce the conflicts that often go hand-in-hand with them. Fragmented subcultures can also be stitched together by changing the physical layout of work space, rotating employees among departments, linking monetary rewards to the achievement of goals that require collaborative effort, and organizing around work teams.[27]

IMPLICATIONS OF ORGANIZATIONAL SUBCULTURES

Sometimes organizational subcultures coexist peacefully within an overall organizational culture; at other times subcultures are a major source of continuing conflict.[28] Managers have many different views about whether subcultures are "good" or "bad" for business. Some managers believe that organizations function best when they have a single strong organizational culture. Other managers believe that the presence of many subcultures can be a source of creativity and change.

Strong Organizational Culture. An organization is said to have a ***strong culture*** when the more observable cultural elements project a single, consistent message. In such organizations, managers and employees share a common behavioral style. They use the same basic approach to solve problems, meet goals, and deal with important customers, suppliers, and other stakeholders. They share common norms that guide how they relate to one another. Results are measured the same way throughout the organization. And a common set of rules governs the use of rewards and punishments.[29] In other words, a strong organizational culture results in predictable, well-specified behavior patterns.

A strong organizational culture doesn't just happen. It's cultivated by management, learned and reinforced by employees, and passed on to new employees. In a ***monolithic organization*** the organizational culture is determined by a single majority culture or subculture, and members of other cultures or subcultures are expected to adopt the norms and values of the majority. In many large U.S. organizations, the norms and values of white, American, heterosexual men are dominant. That is, the norms of this group determine the norms of the entire organization. Employees who are different in any respect often feel that, in order to succeed, they must adjust their behaviors at work to fit those norms. However, in many medium-sized and small businesses, the norms are those of other cultures. For example, Wall Street Strategies, a business that provides advice on stock selection, is a monolithic organization in which the norms reflect the values of the African-American men who work there.[30]

Multiple Subcultures. A strong organizational culture can be beneficial for a business, but depending on the particular nature of the culture, it may also have some negative consequences. A pluralistic organizational culture is one alternative model for managing subcultures. Compared to monolithic organizations, ***pluralistic organizations*** are more mixed in their cultural composition. The norms are still those of a dominant culture or subculture, which members of the organization are expected to follow, but members from other cultural backgrounds fill a variety of jobs at all levels in the organization. Cultural differences are accepted as part of the work environment, and each subculture attempts to maintain its own set of norms and values. Many pluralistic companies are located in large urban centers, such as New York City, where small and medium-sized hi-tech companies hire immigrants to fill approximately one-third of their technical jobs. Muffin Head Productions is typical. Owner Haim Ariav describes his small company as the United Nations of multimedia because 5 of his 16 employees are immigrants.[31]

Many managers believe that the presence of distinct subcultures in an organization can be beneficial and should be valued. Michael Critelli, chairman and CEO of Pitney Bowes, puts it this way: "There is no limit to what we can accomplish if we can crack the code of valuing diversity on a global basis as we move forward into the 21st century."[32] Disney CEO and chairman Michael Eisner expresses a similar view: "We believe in diversity because the more diverse you are as an organization, the more diverse are the opinions that get expressed. That will make us more creative."[33] At Ford, the rationale for valuing the perspectives present in different subcultures focuses on customers. According to Mary Ellen Heyde, director of Ford's Lifestyle Vehicles unit, "If you have a diverse workforce, then you know that the customer's point of view will always be represented." The design and marketing teams for Ford's Windstar minivan, which is bought mostly by women, included many women. Their involvement in the project accounts for features such as the "sleeping baby mode" for overhead lights.[34] At UPS, bilingual support centers have been set up in southern California to serve the area's many foreign-born entrepreneurs.

Many U.S. organizations are in the process of transforming themselves from monolithic organizations to pluralistic organizations. Others are attempting to transform themselves from pluralistic to multicultural organizations. Recall that in Chapter 1 we defined a *multicultural organization* as having a workforce representing the full mix of cultures found in the population at large, along with a commitment to utilize fully these human resources. A multicultural organization's culture reflects a blending of many cultures and subcultures, with no one culture or subculture dominating the others. From this blending, a new type of culture emerges.

The notion of a multicultural organization remains more of an ideal than a reality, although some progress toward this ideal is evident. Nevertheless, interviews with employees in organizations that are recognized as being "America's best companies for minorities" indicate that members of minority subcultures often feel dominated and undervalued by members of the majority. Figure 18.5 summarizes some of the results from a poll conducted in 2000 by the Council on Economic Priorities. Respondents worked in the 50 "best" companies identified by *Fortune* magazine, where minorities are well represented on the board and in the managerial ranks.[35] Because members of subcultures in many organizations report having these and other negative experiences,[36] managing diversity effectively is an increasingly important goal at many U.S. companies.

Figure 18.5 **Experiences of Minority Employees in the "Best" Companies**

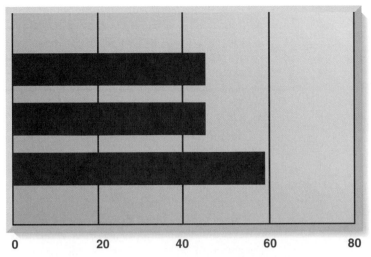

Observed a double standard in delegation of assignments

Personally been a target of racial or cultural jokes

Held back anger for fear of being seen as having a chip on shoulder

0   20   40   60   80

Percentage of Minorities Who Reported Each Experience

MANAGING CULTURAL DIVERSITY

4.

EXPLAIN WHY MANAGING CULTURAL DIVERSITY IS IMPORTANT AND DESCRIBE SEVERAL ACTIVITIES REQUIRED TO MANAGE IT SUCCESSFULLY.

C*ultural diversity* encompasses the full mix of the cultures and subcultures to which members of the workforce belong. Subcultures with which employees may identify include all those described earlier in this chapter.

When efforts to manage diversity first began in the 1980s, the term *diversity* was applied to the mix of people from various racial and ethnic backgrounds. Today, however, efforts to manage diversity effectively usually involve finding ways to manage people representing the wide variety of subcultures found in an organization, regardless of the basis for those subcultures—nationality, occupation, ethnicity, age, gender, and many other factors. Some experts believe that addressing such a broad array of diversity issues may be detrimental to improving the treatment and career outcomes of ethnic minorities. Others believe that eventually the new, more inclusive approach to managing diversity is likely to pay off for members of all subcultures.[37] The particular approach an organization takes to managing diversity depends partly on the goals it hopes to achieve.[38]

ORGANIZATIONAL GOALS FOR MANAGING CULTURAL DIVERSITY

We have already suggested that there are many reasons for managers to be concerned about managing diversity effectively. The three main goals that most organizations strive to achieve are complying with laws and regulations, creating a positive culture for employees, and creating economic value.

Legal Compliance. Complying with laws and regulations that prohibit discrimination, such as Title VII of the Civil Rights Act, is a necessary first step for any organization that seeks to manage diversity effectively. The basic premise of such laws and regulations is that employment decisions should be based on job-related qualifications, not membership in a demographic group. Affirmative action regulations, which have recently become quite controversial, go a bit further.[39] The basic premise of these regulations is that organizations should actively recruit job applicants to build a workforce that reflects the demographics of the qualified labor force locally. To monitor their progress, employers generally assess various employment numbers and ratios. These measures include female and minority hiring numbers, offer/acceptance ratios, turnover and retention rates, promotion patterns, downsizing decisions, and compensation levels.[40]

Of course, simply monitoring numbers isn't sufficient to ensure legal compliance. As Coca-Cola learned, a company must take action to change the numbers if they suggest a pattern of discrimination. Coca-Cola managers used to take pride in the company's diversity. But that pride quickly vanished when a group of four employees filed a lawsuit. Subsequently, 2000 other employees joined in the case. The employees pointed out that the company's overall numbers looked acceptable only because minorities were hired into low-level jobs. After being hired, they claimed, minorities were denied promotions, pay raises, and other benefits because of their race. Management eventually agreed to a settlement valued at more than $192 million. They also agreed to allow a panel of outsiders to spend four years monitoring Coke's treatment of women and minorities. Top management acknowledged that the company's culture needed to change and instituted new practices that tied managers' compensation to achieving diversity goals.[41]

Some organizations that initially monitored their numbers primarily because of concerns about legal compliance discovered that the numbers could also be used to gain insights into other problems. At the accounting firm of Deloitte and Touche, employment numbers alerted the partners to a disturbing trend. A decade ago, the CEO publicly admitted the existence of a problem when figures revealed that only 5 percent of the company's partners were women and that the turnover for women was 30 percent. The turnover rates and promotion patterns for men and women signaled the need to change the company's approach to managing gender diversity. As described in the following Planning and Administration Management Competency feature, the numbers have been transformed since the company introduced changes aimed at making it more "women friendly."[42]

PLANNING & ADMINISTRATION COMPETENCY

More Women Become Partners at Deloitte and Touche

When Diana O'Brien left Deloitte and Touche in 1990 to work elsewhere, she was just one of many women who had concluded that she needed a change. Subsequently, partners at Deloitte and Touche realized that what really needed changing was the company's culture. A decade later, the new culture is so good that Diana O'Brien decided to return. "Before I left, I couldn't have a life and still do consulting. Now, enough has changed that I have been able to do that," she explains. One of the most significant changes has been the company's new flexible work arrangements.

To help the company create a new culture, Deloitte and Touche formed an outside group comprising a former U.S. Secretary of Labor, the first female member of the New York Stock Exchange, and other notables. The group met quarterly and set achievement goals for the company. Within three years, the company had developed a new set of worklife policies designed to make worklife more family-friendly for men and women alike. These policies now include compressed work weeks, flexible work arrangements, telecommuting, job sharing, and two weeks of paid child-care leave. Compensation is prorated for employees who work a reduced work week, but in every other way, the company signals that there is no penalty for taking advantage of the new policies. For Jeff McLane, the new policies have made it possible to have a more balanced personal life, which includes training to compete as an Olympic cyclist. For Diana O'Brien, who was promoted to partner while working an alternative schedule, the policies make it possible to raise a family that includes triplets diagnosed with autism.

Some of the alternative arrangements are offered only to high-performing employees, so managers have a great deal of say about how particular employees are treated. To ensure that managers are fair, the company keeps track of who is permitted to work flexibly. To ensure that the arrangements don't hurt employee performance, managers are trained to manage flexibly. And for good measure, the company also tracks employees' attitudes about the policies. In a recent survey of those taking advantage of the new policies, 95 percent said they would have left had it not been for the company's flexible approach.

• • •

To learn more about Deloitte and Touche, visit the firm's home page at

http://www.us.deloitte.com/

Creating a Positive Culture. As the Deloitte and Touche example demonstrates, an organization can begin to assess whether people from different backgrounds and with different needs are being given job opportunities that match their capabilities by analyzing various employment statistics. Nevertheless, managers shouldn't fall into the trap of using records kept to monitor legal compliance as a basis for drawing conclusions about how employees are matched to jobs or feel about their work situations.

A positive organizational culture is one in which everyone feels equally integrated into the larger system. Members of majority and minority subcultures feel respected; everyone has an equal chance to express views and influence decisions; and everyone has similar access to both formal and informal networks within the organization. The most common methods used to assess organizational culture are employee surveys and focus groups. Questionnaires may be used to ask employees individually or in focus-group discussions whether they feel valued and whether they feel that everyone is equally valued; the degree of respect, sensitivity, and fairness managers show toward employees from different subcultures; and how employees feel about their future career opportunities.

In addition to asking employees directly about the organizational culture, some organizations conduct cultural audits to evaluate the language used in organizational documents and advertising, the visible symbols that decorate public spaces, the types of awards given to employees, the types and quality of food available in the company cafeteria, policies regarding holidays and absences, and the types of social activity sponsored by the organization, among other items. Cultural audits often reveal that the organizational culture reflects the values and preferences of some subcultures while ignoring those of others. When such discrepancies are found, simple changes often can be made to create a more positive organizational culture.

Creating Economic Value. A third reason that organizations are striving to manage diversity effectively is because they believe that they can use diversity to create greater economic value.[43] With a diverse workforce and positive organizational culture in place, many managers believe that their companies will be able to

- develop products and services for new markets,
- attract a broader range of customers,
- improve customer satisfaction and increase business from repeat customers, and
- reduce costs, including those associated with litigation.

Denny's is an organization whose negative corporate culture resulted in blatantly poor customer service for African-American customers and several consecutive years of financial losses. In 1993, on the same day that it settled one federal suit for discriminating against customers in California, six black Secret Service agents waited nearly an hour before being served in a Denny's restaurant in Maryland. This wasn't an isolated incident. Such poor customer treatment was condoned by Denny's managers all over the country. As one news reporter put it, "Diversity was a concept as foreign to its all-white management team as foie gras was to a Denny's menu." The suit that the six agents filed against Denny's was the third such suit filed that year. Meanwhile, competitors such as McDonald's had established strong links to minority communities and developed many loyal customers. The costs to Denny's of settling these and similar suits were enormous. As part of one settlement, Denny's paid $54 million to 295,000 aggrieved customers.

In the Denny's case, there is little doubt that corporate culture contributed to the company's financial decline during the 1980s and early 1990s. Even before the problems at Denny's were being reported in the media, a consulting firm hired to help the company improve its financial performance told management that its organizational culture was a problem. "The lack of diversity was the first issue we identified," according to Bill Boggs, a managing partner of the consulting firm. "I told the senior managers that Flagstar [the parent company] was in a strategically dangerous position, since their customers are certainly not all white males." Then-CEO Jerry Richardson replied that he had "just never thought about it." Five years later, Richardson was finally replaced by Ron Petty, the former head of Burger King. Since then, Denny's has effected a stunning cultural and financial turnaround. In fact, the transformation has been so complete that Denny's parent company, Advantica, was rated by *Fortune* as the best company for minority employees in 2000.[44]

To date, little research is available publicly to document the economic benefits of a diverse workforce and positive organizational culture. Some companies use proprietary information to establish the economic benefits of diversity. Others simply believe that there is a link and don't offer research evidence to support their view. One manager was convinced of the value of his company's diversity efforts when he and a team of his managers attended a meeting with one of their company's largest customers. Somewhat to his surprise, there wasn't a single white male on the customer's side of the table. When they expressed an interest in his company's diversity efforts, he was fortunate to be able to point to an excellent record, despite appearances on his own side of the table. The CEO of another company with a less than stellar record was forced to recognize that the success of his business could depend on learning to manage diversity better. One of his most important distributors—a woman—recently criticized him about it at a meeting. And the manager of a mutual fund that owns millions of his company's shares—an African American—also chided him on the topic. Christine Lagarde, chairperson of Baker & McKenzie, one of the largest law firms in the world, agrees that customers expect to see diversity in the companies that they do business with. As more and more corporations hire women as high-level corporate counselors, law firms are getting the message that they need to have similarly integrated legal teams.[45]

Undoubtedly, personal experiences with customers and clients have convinced some CEOs that managing diversity poorly is risky business. But what may have grabbed the most attention of CEOs was the stock plunge that Texaco experienced after it settled a widely publicized discrimination lawsuit. At $175 million, the cost of the settlement itself was substantial. However, that paled in comparison to the nearly $1 billion decline in market value that occurred in the days immediately following the discovery of a tape recording in which a high-level executive was heard making racist remarks that were apparently accepted without comment by the other executives who were present. Texaco's share price later recovered, and management has since earned praise for its efforts to improve the company's organizational culture. But the cost of this episode to the company and its employees was enormous.[46]

Organizations that succeed in managing diversity do so because top management is committed to achieving legal compliance, instituting a positive organizational culture, and using diversity to create economic value. Such managers recognize that significant organizational changes may be needed to achieve these goals, and they are willing to commit resources to making such changes. As described in Chapter 12, considerable investments of time, money, and people are necessary to carry out successfully any type of large-scale organizational change. As shown in Figure 18.6, understanding the goals to be achieved is the first step in moving from a monolithic to a pluralistic or multicultural organization. Once the commitment to specific goals has been made, other required steps include

- assessing the current organization and understanding its history,
- designing a strategic plan for creating change,
- implementing a large number and variety of targeted change efforts, and
- monitoring change efforts against goals, and making adjustments as needed.

ASSESSING THE ORGANIZATION

Traditional organizational practices tend to minimize cultural diversity in various ways. Recruiting practices emphasize finding candidates from "reliable" sources. Interviews screen out candidates who "don't fit." Socialization and training practices produce uniform ways of thinking and behaving. Attendance policies and pay practices standardize work schedules. Centralization often limits the amount of discretion that managers can exercise in addressing the special needs of employees.

Figure 18.6 **Phases of Diversity Management Change Efforts**

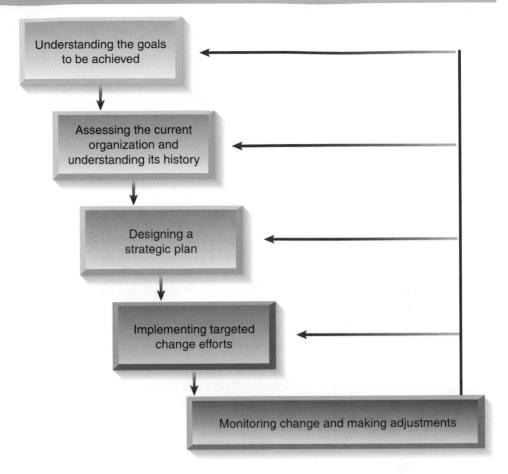

Many such practices were adopted by organizations for valid reasons. Standardization and centralization often evolve to increase efficiency and ensure the fair (equal) treatment of employees. Before managers begin designing new approaches to managing diversity, they first need to be sure that they understand how current practices affect the amount and nature of diversity—both in the organization as a whole and within its smaller units. Some types of homogeneity may be appropriate, or even essential, to effective operations and thus should be retained if justified after careful evaluation.

DEVELOPING A PLAN

As described in Chapters 7 and 12, the process of planned organizational change involves assessing the environment and determining performance gaps. This aspect of the planning process calls for setting specific goals that are linked to a clear vision for the future, making plans for how to involve all relevant stakeholders, and setting a clear and realistic timetable.

Vision. Articulating and communicating a clear vision of how the future can be better is essential in developing a plan for change. Until leaders formulate a clear vision and persuade others to join them in being dedicated to that vision, they won't be able to generate the enthusiasm and resources needed for large-scale cultural change. Most experts agree that the CEO is the key to articulating a vision of a new organizational culture that supports and builds on diversity. Unless the CEO is a tireless advocate and exemplar of the new culture, others in the organization are not likely to believe that change is important. In addition, the CEO may need to make a persuasive business case for changing the culture. The question to be answered is this: If the organization has been successful up to now, why does it need to change?

Involvement. For the plan to be effective, those who are affected must buy into it. The best way to ensure that they do so is through early involvement. That employees should be involved seems obvious, but often this principle is forgotten, even by experienced managers. Xerox has a long record of enlightened diversity management. One of its earliest successes involved a caucus group for African-American employees. In fact, it was so successful that the company decided to create a caucus group for female employees. However, the first attempt to establish a women's caucus—in the mid 1970s—failed. One explanation for the failure was that the women's caucus was designed to duplicate the existing African-American caucus instead of being designed specifically to address the concerns of female employees. A few years later, female employees at Xerox began to establish caucus groups on their own. Eventually a dozen different women's caucuses emerged: Some are national, some are regional, and some are specific to one location; some are for minority women and others aren't; and some are for exempt employees and others are for nonexempt employees.

When General Motors initiated cultural change, one of the goals was to create a work environment in which all voices were heard. To explore what that might involve, GM created eight employee groups representing

- Asians,
- blacks,
- gays and lesbians,
- Hispanics,
- non-U.S. citizens working in the United States,
- people with disabilities,
- white males, and
- women.

Some 500 employees participated in these groups. They polled workers in their constituencies, investigated what other companies were doing, and drafted suggestions for senior management concerning how to remove barriers to productivity and improve the company's standing in the marketplace. This work took about a year and set the stage for discussions with senior management, as described in the following Communication Competency feature.[47]

GM Executives Listen Up

Years ago, the workforce at Detroit-based General Motors wasn't very diverse. Even today, 78 percent of GM workers aged 55 and over are white males. The new GM workforce looks completely different. Of those aged 25 and under, only 49 percent are white males. To tap into the ideas and talents of today's more diverse workforce, GM created Employee Resource Groups (ERGs) and asked for their input in the development of business policies and practices. According to Lorna Utley, director of diversity initiatives, "the whole purpose of the resource groups was to recommend specific steps that could enhance GM's implementation of management imperatives, things that are important to the success of our company from a cultural and organizational standpoint."

The ERGs developed their suggestions over a period of several months. Then they were invited to present their ideas to the senior leadership team. A two-step process was used. The first feedback session consisted of a small number of representatives from an ERG sitting down to discuss their recommendations face-to-face with two members

of the top-executive team. Recalls one ERG representative, "That was pretty open and candid and probably in the long run more beneficial to do it that way because there are certain issues that always arise when you get before a large group." In effect, this was a rehearsal for the second session, when the leadership of each ERG met with the strategy board to present its recommendations formally.

How were the ERGs' recommendations received? A month after the strategy board heard the recommendations, it announced which ones were to be adopted. Some were adopted verbatim, others were revised for adoption, and many were scrapped. A suggestion made by both the women's ERG and the gay and lesbian ERG was to revise the company's "escort" policy. The old policy provided travel expenses for a spouse to accompany an employee on certain types of business trips. The new, revised policy allows for expenses to be paid for

anyone the employee wants to bring as his or her guest. Other suggestions that were eventually adopted included establishing a mobility center to focus on the needs of disabled and aging workers and extending medical and dental benefits to same-sex partners.

By acting quickly to make some of the recommendations a reality, top management communicated that it was listening and taking the suggestions seriously. The challenge now is to keep the dialogue open because the ERGs were temporary task forces that disbanded after making their recommendations. One way that GM management hopes to keep communication open is by supporting "affinity groups" that might reconvene along lines similar to those of the ERGs. With management's

approval, they could use the company's meeting rooms, faxes, e-mail accounts, and so on. And GM's senior leaders would continue to listen to their concerns and suggestions. The company is also undertaking the largest employee survey in its history. All 391,000 employees in this global firm will be asked for their opinions concerning several cultural issues. Through the survey, the company seeks to ensure that all voices get heard—not just the loudest.

• • •

To learn more about General Motors, visit the company's home page at

http://www.gm.com

Timing. Planned organizational change usually follows an evolutionary—not revolutionary—path. Realistic expectations about how quickly change will occur are important to the long-term success of change efforts. Usually, change occurs more slowly than expected. Xerox began changing its culture more than 30 years ago and continues to do so. Although meaningful changes in corporate cultures occur slowly, not all useful initiatives require decades to implement. At Texaco, for example, the promotion rates for African Americans doubled in two years after the CEO began to hold managers accountable for managing diversity. At GM, changes in the company's "escort policy" were made in a matter of several weeks.

Sometimes the slowness of change is merely frustrating. At other times unrealistic expectations cause change efforts to be abandoned prematurely. For this reason, some change experts endorse a "small-wins" approach to change. The idea behind this strategy is to work on identifying the little everyday things that create difficulties for members of subcultures and then work to correct the problems as quickly as possible. For example, using this approach, one company discovered that its norms regarding time created more difficulties for women than men. Time was treated as an "unbounded" resource. Meetings frequently were rescheduled at the last minute, ran past normal working hours, and started late. Lack of discipline in the use of meetings left people feeling overloaded and sapped creativity. Once the problem was identified and labeled (as "unbounded time"), the norm began to shift and managers made sure that new people learned the new norm. Within less than a year, the culture supported an "informal *and* disciplined" approach to meetings.[48] Clearly, different problems require different solutions and time frames. Learning from the experiences of change experts and other organizations may be the best way for a manager to develop a timetable for cultural change.

IMPLEMENTATION

The list of methods that organizations can use to manage cultural diversity is quite long and varied. Thus managers need to target specific efforts and set priorities for implementing them. One targeted change effort that can be used quickly is simply to terminate employees who create a negative atmosphere by engaging in harassment or other clearly

WEB INSIGHT

A person's mobility can be affected by age, size, general health, vision, and physical impairments. After visiting the Web site of the National Organization on Disability at *http://www.nod.org*, describe ways in which a facility that you know about is "friendly" or "unfriendly" to a diverse population of users.

inappropriate or disruptive behavior.[49] Assessing compensation levels and making needed adjustments is another type of targeted change effort. Women around the world generally earn less than men in the same types of job, according to data collected by the United Nations. Frustrated with this situation, many are leaving the corporate world, often to set up their own businesses.[50] In the United States, numerous studies have shown that women tend be paid less than men even when their education, experience, skills, performance, and job assignments are equivalent. Such pay differentials generally have negative consequences for organizational culture. Female employees often feel unfairly treated and become resentful. These feelings may result in higher turnover rates for women, which can in turn be demoralizing for other women. By changing their procedures for setting pay rates to reduce the role of subjective judgments, organizations can quickly signal their intention to move from being a monolithic organization toward becoming a pluralistic or multicultural organization.[51]

Perhaps the most common targeted action that organizations take is to send employees to diversity training sessions. Training programs vary greatly, but most attempt to provide basic information about cultural differences and similarities and sensitize participants to the powerful role that culture plays in determining their work behavior. How informed are you about issues of cultural diversity? To get a sense of how well you are able to separate myth from fact, take the Diversity Knowledge Quiz presented in the following Self-Management Competency feature.

SELF-MANAGEMENT COMPETENCY

Diversity Knowledge Quiz

Indicate whether each statement is True or False. Correct answers are given later in the chapter.

1. T F Joy and fear are feelings that can be accurately recognized from facial expressions, regardless of which cultures people are from.

2. T F A person who is older than 65 and living in one of the world's developing regions is three times more likely to be working than a person of that age living in a developed region.

3. T F Worldwide, about 50 percent of women between the ages of 15 and 64 are in the labor force.

4. T F Most Americans with Japanese heritage come from families who have lived in the United States for two or three generations.

5. T F During the past decade, college graduation rates have been declining for men and increasing for women.

6. T F Most people could count on their fingers the number of female and minority CEOs who head one of the 500 largest firms in the United States.

7. T F In America's 10 largest cities, an average of one in four persons is of Latino origin.

8. T F Compared to other demographic groups, gay men tend to be better educated and hold higher paying jobs.

9. T F Compared to other employees, those with disabilities have better safety records on the job.

10. T F Mental speed slows down slightly but steadily beginning at about age 30, but performance of many complex mental tasks continues to improve steadily as people age.

11. T F As recently as 1970, interracial marriages were illegal in some parts of the United States.

12. T F Almost all Fortune 500 firms indicate that they are implementing initiatives to manage diversity.

13. T F The proportion of companies with at least one woman board director is greater among Fortune 500 companies than among companies ranked 501 through 1,000.

For the correct answers, refer to page 510.

An organization's choice of specific efforts may reflect the nature of diversity that is important for the organization, the goals set, the actions of other organizations in the industry, and so on. At Dayton Hudson much of the focus is on customers, and specific targeted change efforts include providing seating that older customers can use to rest their feet for a few minutes, putting baby-changing stations in the men's lounges, and providing diversity training to demonstrate how mistaken employees can be when they base inferences about customers on appearance alone.

Texaco's comprehensive plan for creating cultural change, agreed to as part of its lawsuit settlement, focuses more on the treatment of employees than the treatment of customers. It includes the activities listed in Table 18.2, many of which are typically found in plans developed by other organizations.[52]

Table 18.2	Texaco's Cultural Change Initiatives

Recruitment and Hiring

- Ask search firms to identify wider arrays of candidates
- Enhance the interviewing, selection, and hiring skills of managers
- Expand college recruitment at historically minority colleges

Identifying and Developing Talent

- Form a partnership with INROADS, a nationwide internship program that targets minority students for management careers
- Establish a mentoring process
- Refine the company's global succession planning system to improve identification of talent
- Improve the selection and development of managers and leaders to help ensure that they are capable of maximizing team performance

Ensuring Fair Treatment

- Conduct extensive diversity training
- Implement an alternative dispute resolution process
- Include women and minorities on all human resources committees throughout the company

Holding Managers Accountable

- Link managers' compensation to their success in creating "openness and inclusion in the workplace"
- Implement 360-degree feedback for all managers and supervisors
- Redesign the company's employee attitude survey and begin using it annually to monitor employee attitudes

Improve Relationships with External Stakeholders

- Broaden the company's base of vendors and suppliers to incorporate more minority- and women-owned businesses
- Increase banking, investment, and insurance business with minority- and women-owned firms
- Add more independent, minority retailers and increase the number of minority managers in company-owned gas stations and Xpress Lube outlets

Implementing such changes will take many years, and many challenges will arise along the way. Among the most difficult challenges that Texaco and other companies face as they attempt to implement change are

- managing the reactions of members of the dominant culture, who may feel that they have lost some of the power they had previously held and exercised;
- synthesizing the diversity of opinions from individuals and using them as the basis for reaching meaningful agreement on issues; and
- avoiding real and perceived tokenism and quota systems that can help the organization achieve its quantitative goals but can be destructive to developing a positive culture.[53]

Perhaps the biggest challenge to managers, however, is understanding that cultural diversity can have many organizational consequences. For example, on the one hand, diversity can enhance a team's ability to solve problems creatively. On the other hand, the price of such creativity may be heightened conflict within the team. Similarly, changing the mix of men and women in a team or department toward a 50–50 split may improve the attitudes of the women involved while irritating the men. Managers shouldn't expect that diversity-related initiatives affect members of the organization in uniformly positive ways. They should be prepared to weigh carefully which costs they are willing to incur in order to achieve which gains.[54]

MONITORING AND ADJUSTING

When an organization offers a new product (good or service) in the marketplace, it almost always uses one or more numerical indicators to measure its success. When the development and sale of a product is successful, the people who contributed to that success often are recognized and rewarded. Many organizations apply these same principles to the introduction of diversity-related changes, and doing so seems to pay off. Research shows that the success of diversity training initiatives is greater in organizations that evaluate the effectiveness of the training and in those that offer rewards to managers who make diversity-related improvements in their business units. At Dow Chemical, managers are encouraged to promote women at a rate at least equal to that of men. Hoechst Celanese bases numerical targets for its workforce on analysis of the available labor pool and ties managers' bonuses to their performance on diversity initiatives (e.g., training programs, mentoring, and developing employees for promotion).[55]

Not all organizations accept this approach, however. For example, Colgate-Palmolive doesn't buy the idea of numerical goals. Others worry that attempts to quantify results may backfire because things often get worse before they get better. After R. R. Donnelley & Sons started its cultural change efforts, black employment fell from 8 percent to 6 percent of the total. The small number of black employees, in turn, led the company to ask those who remained to attend multiple diversity training sessions to ensure that their views were represented. Employees found the training sessions to be stressful, and some resented having to attend multiple sessions, especially in light of the declining minority employment.[56] Some indicators commonly show negative effects, whereas others show the opposite. Managers unfamiliar with such patterns may react to early negative results by withdrawing their support for continued change efforts. Concerns about what the data indicate shouldn't be addressed by halting change efforts. Better ways to avoid such problems include setting realistic timetables and being careful to collect data that are consistent with the goals for change.

Any organizational change effort can run into unanticipated problems, and diversity interventions are no exception. Cultural awareness training programs may backfire if they seem to reinforce stereotypes or highlight cultural differences that employees have tried to erase in order to fit into the company's culture. Special skill-building programs offered only to some subgroups also can feed negative stereotyping, or they may be viewed as giving the target group an unfair advantage. Employees assigned to work in markets that match their cultural backgrounds may view that as limiting rather than maximizing the contributions that they can make. Affirmative action programs may create a stigma for all members of groups targeted to benefit. As a result, even the best-qualified people are presumed to have acquired their positions because of their demographic attributes rather than on the basis of merit. Networking or caucus groups may lead to increased segregation and fragmentation.[57] Problems such as these seem to arise in organizations when employees become focused on their cultural differences rather than on their common goals. Ultimately, managing diversity successfully involves developing a strong organizational culture that values cultural differences and ensures that the talents of all employees are used to their fullest extent.

CHAPTER SUMMARY

The thoughts, feelings, motivations, and behaviors of employees reflect an organization's culture and subcultures. Subcultures in an organization may reflect the influence of cultures within societies, industries, occupations, and various other social groupings. The greater the variety of subcultures in an organization, the more difficult it is to create a strong overarching organizational culture and the greater is the need to actively manage cultural diversity.

1. DESCRIBE THE CORE ELEMENTS OF A CULTURE.

A culture is the unique pattern of shared assumptions, values and norms that shape the socialization activities, language, symbols, and practices that unite members of a group and maintain their distinction relative to nonmembers. Assumptions are the underlying thoughts and feelings that are taken for granted and believed to be true. Values are basic beliefs about a condition that has considerable importance and meaning to individuals and is stable over time. Socialization is a systematic process by which new members are brought into a culture and taught the norms for behavior. A symbol is anything visible that can be used to represent an abstract shared value or something having special meaning. Language is a shared system of vocal sounds, written signs, and/or gestures used to convey special meanings among members. Narratives are the unique stories, sagas, legends, and myths in a culture. Shared practices include taboos (forbidden behaviors) and rites and ceremonies (formal activities that generate strong feelings).

2. COMPARE AND CONTRAST FOUR TYPES OF ORGANIZATIONAL CULTURES.

Each organization's culture is unique. Nevertheless, four general types of organizational cultures that are useful for comparing organizations are bureaucratic, clan, entrepreneurial, and market cultures. They are characterized by differences in formal control (ranging from stable to flexible) and focus of attention (ranging from internal to external).

3. DISCUSS SEVERAL TYPES OF SUBCULTURES THAT MAY EXIST IN ORGANIZATIONS.

The cultural diversity of a workforce reflects the range of subcultures to which employees belong. In multicultural organizations, the organizational culture reflects a blending of all the subcultures found within the organization. Monolithic organizations are dominated by a single majority subculture, and members of other subcultures are expected to follow the norms and accept the values of the majority. Pluralistic organizations are more mixed in their cultural composition, but members of the organization are still expected to adopt the norms of a dominant subculture.

4. EXPLAIN WHY MANAGING CULTURAL DIVERSITY IS IMPORTANT AND DESCRIBE SEVERAL ACTIVITIES REQUIRED TO MANAGE IT SUCCESSFULLY.

Concern about effectively managing workforce diversity reflects three types of organizational goals: complying with EEO laws and regulations, creating a positive organizational culture that makes work enjoyable for employees, and improving organizational performance. Managing cultural diversity in order to achieve these objectives is a long-term process requiring substantial investments of time, money, and people. All are necessary to implement any type of large-scale organizational change. The activities required to change an organization from one that values cultural homogeneity to one that values and builds on cultural diversity include understanding the goals to be achieved, assessing the current organization and understanding its history, designing a strategic plan for creating change, implementing a large number and variety of targeted change efforts, measuring the effects of change efforts, and making adjustments as needed.

KEY TERMS

Bureaucratic culture, p. 490
Ceremonies, p. 489
Clan culture, p. 490
Cultural diversity, p. 499
Culture, p. 486
Entrepreneurial culture, p. 491

Language, p. 488
Market culture, p. 492
Monolithic organization, p. 497
Narratives, p. 488
Organizational subculture, p. 494
Pluralistic organizations, p. 498

Shared assumptions, p. 487
Socialization, p. 488
Strong culture, p. 497
Symbol, p. 488
Taboos, p. 489
Value, p. 488

QUESTIONS FOR DISCUSSION AND COMPETENCY DEVELOPMENT

1. Choose an organization that you know well. List examples of socialization activities, symbols, language, narratives, and practices that capture the essence of the organization's culture. What assumptions and values are reflected in the cultural elements you identified?

2. Suppose that you are interested in determining whether an organization's culture is strong or weak. State three things you could do to assess the strength of the organization's culture.

3. Review Figure 18.2. Which type of organizational culture would you prefer to work in? Why would you choose it?

4. The European Business Network for Social Cohesion seeks to provide a network of expertise in implementing diversity practices. Visit this organization's Web site at *http://www.csreurope.org* to learn about what it considers to be the best practice in the area of diversity management. In what ways are the practices they recommend for organizations conducting business in Europe similar to or different from those that might be recommended in the United States?

5. Consider the diversity initiatives at Texaco presented in Table 18.2. For each item on that list, state which of the three types of organizational diversity goals it addresses. Has Texaco failed to address any important goals? Explain.

6. **Competency Development: Global Awareness.** The CIA World Fact Book provides detailed information about factors such as the geography, economics, and cultures of many countries. To access it, go to *http://www.odci.gov/cia/publications/factbook/index.html.* Choose a country with which you are unfamiliar and learn as much as you can about its national culture. Suppose that your employer sends you to this culture for 2 weeks. Your assignment is to evaluate whether the company's new fast-food sandwich made with chicken and cheese is likely to sell well. How can you use what you learned about the culture to help your company judge how well the sandwich will sell? What suggestions would you make about marketing this product in this country (what to emphasize and what to avoid)?

7. **Competency Development: Strategic Action.** Suppose that you've been appointed to a task force to make suggestions for diversity initiatives at the Coca-Cola Company. Visit its home page at *http://www.coca-cola.com* to learn what the company is doing now. What would you add to its current efforts? Be sure to state the goals to be met by the initiatives you recommend adding.

ANSWERS FOR THE DIVERSITY KNOWLEDGE QUIZ
All the statements are true.

CASE FOR COMPETENCY DEVELOPMENT

Cracking Avon's Glass Ceiling

Avon Products, Inc., employs women from various backgrounds. Founded in 1886, the firm's products were familiar to almost everyone in the generations that preceded Generation X. More than 2 million "Avon Ladies" sell its cosmetics door to door around the world, and there are more women in powerful executive positions at Avon than at any other Fortune 500 company. Approximately 40 percent of its global managers are women, and more than 20 percent of its professionals and managers are people of color. Those figures indicate what can be achieved after two decades of paying attention to diversity.

In the 1970s and well into the 1980s, Avon's approach to diversity was to strive to "do the right thing." Influenced by the Civil Rights era, the firm has had aggressive affirmative action programs in place for many years. But, ironically, managers at the company were slow to realize that the influx of women into corporate America had important consequences for home-based cosmetics sales. Fewer customers were at home to sell to, and fewer women were available to be recruited as Avon representatives. As a result, by the mid 1980s, Avon's profitability had slumped.

Financial problems have a way of getting the attention of managers. At Avon, poor financial performance signaled a need to become more responsive to a changing consumer market. Multiculturalism was recognized as an important element in meeting customer demand and gaining the competitive advantage. A variety of cultural diversity initiatives were launched. Middle managers were sent to Morehouse College in Atlanta for leadership development training, which included a session on why and how diversity can provide a competitive advantage. The entire management team participated in awareness training provided by leading diversity consultants affiliated with the American Institute for Managing Diversity. Management launched a multicultural planning research project to evaluate the company's policies and practices regarding promotion. Its purpose was to identify potential barriers to the advancement of women and minorities. More than 100 people from corporate headquarters and several profit centers participated in the project, including most of the company's senior managers. Based on findings from the project, management developed a five-year plan with specific goals.

Throughout the 1990s, Avon's approaches to managing cultural diversity were widely reported. Executives' annual hunting trips to the rod and gun club were discontinued. Women got showers and lockers in their bathrooms, just like the men had. The company's season tickets for the Knicks and Yankees were swapped for the New York City Ballet and the New York Philharmonic. The company had earned a reputation for being progressive. Its culture had changed. When other companies sought to benchmark their own diversity efforts, they often compared themselves to Avon. All these events occurred under the leadership of chairman and CEO James E. Preston.

In 1997, Preston indicated that he would probably retire within a year. At the same time, he announced several promotions within the company. The promotions put six executives, three of whom were women, in place for possible succession. When speculation arose about whether the next CEO would likely be a woman, Preston said, "I would be very surprised if it wasn't the case. We have more women in senior-, middle-, and lower-level management than any other company I know of." After that comment, *Fortune* reported that "now the Avon execs who are concerned about whether they will get a fair shot at the top job are *the men.*" *The men* included Avon's president and chief operating officer Ed Robinson. *The men* realized that they had stiff competition. Susan Kropf, president of Avon U.S., had presided over manufacturing and was credited with dominating global markets when she was head of the Emerging Markets unit. Edwina Woodbury, chief financial and administrative officer, was in the spotlight for her efforts to overhaul Avon's inefficient ways and free cash for growth. Andrea Jung, president of global marketing and new business—and widely considered a hotshot talent—had held previous executive positions at Bloomingdale's, I. Magnin, and Neiman Marcus before Preston lured her to Avon. Christina Gold, a Canadian who had taken over U.S. operations in 1993, was credited with saving the company from a revolt by Avon ladies who were disgruntled with her predecessor's cost-cutting tactics.

On December 12, 1997, the headlines that shocked many observers read: "Avon calls on a man to lead it." The man was Charles Perrin, former CEO of Duracell International, the battery company. Preston explained the decision: "We wanted someone who had been there and done it. We wanted someone who had experience as a chief executive of a global company. A lot has been made of the gender issue. But the first responsibility of the Avon board is to place Avon in the hands of someone who can lead it." And what about the promising men and women with experience inside Avon as well as many executives in the cosmetics and retailing industry? "They are just a few years away," explained Preston.

Just two years after Preston made this prediction, Charles Perrin stepped down as CEO, more than a year before his contract expired. By then, two of the women who were passed over when he stepped down had left the company, which was now in a slump. His successor was Andrea Jung. On the day her appointment was announced, the company's share price rose by nearly 7 percent. Now, as one of only four women heading a Fortune 500 company, her job is to turn the company around.[58]

Questions for Discussion

1. What can you tell about Avon's culture after visiting the company's home page? Which of the four types of organizational cultures shown in Figure 18.2 seems to describe this company best?

2. Jung appears to have cracked the glass ceiling at Avon. Now she has to deliver by improving the company's performance. What if she doesn't succeed? Will the board be more or less reluctant to fire her compared to a male CEO? Explain your logic.

3. If you were a high-level manager at Avon, would Jung's appointment to CEO have any consequences for your longer term career expectations? For example, when Perrin was appointed CEO, high-ranking women left the firm. Are high-ranking men likely to leave now?

4. Because Jung is a Chinese-American female, most people would expect her to value diversity at Avon. As a leader, does she need to make issues involving Avon's culture and diversity a high priority? Why or why not?

To learn more about Avon Products, visit the company's home page at ***http://avon.com***.

W. B. Doner, Inc.

In the world of advertising agencies, there is a trend toward acquisition and merger that has resulted in very large companies who bundle specialties and services for their clients. W. B. Doner, Inc., a medium-sized international advertising agency, has decided to buck that trend and remain independent.

The Southfield, Michigan–based advertising agency, with nine offices in various parts of the United States, is one of the largest independent agencies in the world. It is no slouch when it comes to landing and keeping major accounts such as Mazda, Coca-Cola, and American Greetings. Its 1999 billings totaled approximately $1.5 billion. Also, despite its independent status, over the past three years the company has become one of the fastest-growing agencies in terms of increased billings and revenues. *Adweek* magazine named W. B. Doner one of its 1999 Agencies of the Year, and in a separate evaluation ranked the company among the top four agencies in the country, based on management, growth, and creativity.

In an interview with Office.com, Chairman and CEO Alan Kaltar was quoted as saying, "Being bigger does not equal being better, and our business model has been working very well." Part of that business model has been the development of a flexible and innovative corporate culture, which is pervasive in the organzation. Although many of the larger firms in the industry have very formal and structured cultures, W. B. Doner's executives believe that its distinctive culture rewards entrepreneurship behavior and creativity and at the same time requires teamwork among its employees.

The core values of W. B. Doner's corporate culture can be summarized in the words of the company's founder: "[Be] cre-ative first, all other things second." In other words, the organization supports its employees in pursuing the best ideas for its clients and will not allow anything to get in the way of the attainment of that goal. For example, the company intentionally hires entrepreneurial individuals who enjoy the freedom and responsibility of work that doesn't involve much direction or supervision. Instead, individuals are encouraged to think "outside of the box" or work on their own if needed. Although employees are encouraged to think on their own, all ideas are subject to open and honest critique from coworkers. Management believes that constructive criticism is essential in developing the best ideas for clients. The company also offers an annual "heart, head and funny bone" award to the employee who best typifies the organization's corporate culture and perpetuates its core values.

Finally, at W. B. Doner, regardless of where an idea originates (the top, the middle, or the bottom), all ideas are critiqued. Debates and discussions of ideas often become intense, but the company does not permit them to become personal; criticism of individuals isn't permitted. W. B. Doner makes this clear distinction to encourage all employees to express their opinions openly to allow the best ideas to emerge and eventually be presented to clients.

Questions

1. What forms of inappropriate behavior are identified for employees of W. B. Doner?

2. What type of organizational culture exists at W. B. Doner?

To learn more about W. B. Doner, Inc., visit the company's home page at ***http://www.doner.com***.

Controlling and Evaluating

CHAPTER 19
CONTROLLING IN ORGANIZATIONS

CHAPTER 20
INFORMATION MANAGEMENT TECHNOLOGY

Controlling in Organizations

LEARNING OBJECTIVES

AFTER STUDYING THIS CHAPTER YOU SHOULD BE ABLE TO:

1. EXPLAIN THE FOUNDATIONS OF CONTROL.

2. DISCUSS WAYS THAT ORGANIZATIONS CAN CREATE EFFECTIVE CONTROLS.

3. IDENTIFY THE SIX PHASES OF THE CORRECTIVE CONTROL MODEL.

4. DESCRIBE THE PRIMARY METHODS OF ORGANIZATIONAL CONTROL.

Chapter Outline

PREVIEW: FEDEX IS ON TIME

FOUNDATIONS OF CONTROL

PREVENTIVE AND CORRECTIVE CONTROLS
SOURCES OF CONTROL
PATTERNS OF CONTROL
STRATEGIC ACTION COMPETENCY: Kodak's SUN Plant

CREATING EFFECTIVE CONTROLS

COST–BENEFIT MODEL
CRITERIA FOR EFFECTIVE CONTROLS
SELF-MANAGEMENT COMPETENCY: Tim Koogle, CEO of Yahoo.com

CORRECTIVE CONTROL MODEL

DEFINE THE SUBSYSTEM
IDENTIFY KEY CHARACTERISTICS
SET STANDARDS
COLLECT INFORMATION
MAKE COMPARISONS
DIAGNOSE AND CORRECT PROBLEMS
PLANNING AND ADMINISTRATION COMPETENCY: Computer Monitoring

PRIMARY METHODS OF CONTROL

MECHANISTIC AND ORGANIC CONTROL
MARKET CONTROL
FINANCIAL CONTROL
COMMUNICATION COMPETENCY: Hospice of Central Kentucky
AUTOMATION-BASED CONTROL

CHAPTER SUMMARY

KEY TERMS

QUESTIONS FOR DISCUSSION AND COMPETENCY DEVELOPMENT

CASE FOR COMPETENCY DEVELOPMENT: ETHICAL BEHAVIORS IN THE OFFICE

VIDEO CASE: BINDCO CORPORATION

FedEx Is On Time

Annually, U.S. organizations spend more than $87 billion on loading, unloading, sorting, reloading, and delivering packages to customers. Frederick Smith, founder and CEO of FedEx, has been winning the battles against most of his competitors in this intensively competitive industry because of FedEx's well-developed control system. FedEx operates an $18 billion delivery system from its eight U.S. and seven international hubs. It operates more than 630 airplanes, 42,500 vehicles, and 44,400 drop-off locations. It delivers more than three million express packages to customers in more than 200 countries. When Smith first started FedEx about 20 years ago, he knew that it was in the information business. He stressed that knowledge about the cargo's origin, present whereabouts, destination, estimated time of arrival, price, and shipping cost were as important to customers as safe delivery. Today, FedEx wants to be known as the "Clipper ships of the computer age."

The control system that makes FedEx unique is its centralized sorting facilities—in Memphis and Indianapolis, and its newest hub in Dallas, which mirrors the efficiency of its other hubs. All packages arrive at a hub for sorting by midnight. A DC-10 with more than 50,000 pounds of packages (or some

131,000 packages) is unloaded within 30 minutes. The packages are unloaded directly into a giant warehouse containing an elaborate conveyor belt system. The packages are sorted frantically because all must be loaded onto outgoing planes that take off for their intended destinations by 3:00 A.M. Within six minutes from the time a package is placed on one of the intake ramps, the conveyor system scans, sorts, and redirects the item to a container ready to be loaded onto an outgoing plane. Planes arrive at their local sorting destinations before 6:00 A.M. Ground couriers then transport packages to local offices and on to receivers. Its bar-coding process enables FedEx to monitor a customer's package movement at every step of its journey. FedEx has installed computer terminals in the offices of its largest 100,000 customers, and it has given 650,000 customers its proprietary software so that they can label their own packages. FedEx receives electronic notification from them to pick up and then ships and delivers those packages.

During the day, contact is maintained with ground couriers by means of the digitally assisted dispatch system. This system enables the company to leave messages at the couriers' vans even when they are unoccupied. The use of hand-held transceivers by couriers has

enabled FedEx to reduce customer-billing errors and maintain constant contact with couriers. FedEx also uses this system to find out how satisfied its 200,000 employees are with its policies.

FedEx forecasts that, over the next ten years, the global express–transportation market is likely to grow rapidly. Because most manufacturers have shifted to just-in-time inventory, expensive parts must be shipped quickly all over the world. To do so constantly, FedEx has established partnerships with global firms. Temic Semiconductor, a division of Mercedes-Benz with annual sales of $1 billion, and FedEx formed a partnership that enabled Temic to close eight warehouses and set up one global warehouse at Subic Bay in the Philippines. A customer placing an order with Temic receives confirmation within 30 seconds. Notice is sent electronically to the manufacturing plant, which makes and sends products to Subic Bay where FedEx receives them and ships them to customers. In Asia, orders can be received and shipped within 8 hours; within 48 hours they reach their final U.S. and European destinations. This arrangement saves Temic more than $5.5 million annually.[1]

To learn more about FedEx, visit the company's home page at

http://www.fedex.com

FOUNDATIONS OF CONTROL

1.

EXPLAIN THE FOUNDATIONS OF CONTROL.

Control involves the processes for ensuring that behaviors and performance conform to an organization's standards, including rules, procedures, and goals.[2] To most people the word *control* has a negative connotation—of restraining, forcing, delimiting, watching, or manipulating. Many shopping malls employ security guards during the peak season to keep tight surveillance on shoppers' cars and on shoppers themselves when they are returning to their cars with goods. Most convenience stores (e.g., 7-11 and self-service gasoline stations, among others) have surveillance cameras that videotape customer movements throughout the store but especially when they approach the cashier. Most employees and many shoppers resent such practices because of their deeply held values of freedom and individualism. For this reason, controls often are the focus of controversy and policy struggles within organizations.

However, controls are both useful and necessary. Effective control was one of the keys to FedEx's increased profits during the past decade. An important part of that control system was the ability to track customers' parcels at each stage of collection, shipment, and delivery. We can illustrate the need for controls by describing how control interacts with planning, with specific reference to FedEx's operations.

- Planning is the formal process of developing goals, strategies, tactics, and standards and allocating resources. Controls help ensure that decisions, actions, and results are consistent with those plans. At FedEx, its controls help identify which customers generate the greatest profits and which actually end up costing the company. FedEx closes accounts that aren't profitable to serve, such as those in small, widely scattered locations.

- Planning prescribes desired behaviors and results. Controls help maintain or redirect *actual* behaviors and results. At FedEx, customer service employees are supposed to answer a customer's question within 140 seconds. Managers are evaluated annually by their superiors and workers. If assessments fall below an established level, managers may be replaced.

- Managers and employees can't effectively plan without accurate and timely information. Controls provide much of this essential information. The Internet has enabled FedEx to attract and hold new customers by providing them with crucial information as needed. Customers can log onto the Internet and follow the progress of their packages. By partnering with Temic and other organizations—and providing timely information about services and costs, along with parcel tracking, to them and their customers—FedEx has been able to expand rapidly its customer base. More than 2.5 million customers are connected electronically with FedEx.

- Plans indicate the purposes to be served by controls. Controls help ensure that plans are implemented as intended. Thus planning and control complement and support each other.

PREVENTIVE AND CORRECTIVE CONTROLS

There are two general types of organizational controls: preventive and corrective.[3] **Preventive controls** are mechanisms intended to reduce errors and thereby minimize the need for corrective action. For example, most major banks and credit unions have developed methods to increase the security of their ATMs and the customers who use them. Jerome Sviglas, a credit card and electronic security consultant, says that financial institutions need to screen and rotate employees who maintain ATMs, place ATMs in well-lighted areas or inside 24-hour convenience stores, change the encryption key on ATMs every six months, and establish and advertise a rapid response to ATM abuse. Similarly, air traffic controllers help prevent crashes by ensuring that airline pilots follow well-defined standards, rules, and procedures during take-offs and landings.

Rules and regulations, standards, recruitment and selection procedures, and training and development programs function primarily as preventive controls. They direct and limit the behaviors of managers and employees alike. The assumption is that, if managers and employees comply with these requirements, the organization is likely to achieve its goals. Thus preventive controls are needed to ensure that rules, regulations, and standards are being followed and are working. FedEx's ability to pick up and deliver more than three million packages a day in some 200 countries depends on its employees' ability to conform to FedEx's standards.

Corrective controls are mechanisms intended to reduce or eliminate unwanted behaviors or results and thereby achieve conformity with the organization's regulations and standards. Thus an air traffic controller exercises corrective control by instructing pilots to change altitude and direction to avoid other planes. At FedEx, dispatchers send messages to drivers to express dissatisfaction with the amount of time they're taking to complete their routes.

SOURCES OF CONTROL

The four primary sources of control in most organizations are stakeholders, the organization itself, groups, and individuals. These sources are shown in Table 19.1, along with examples of preventive and corrective controls for each.

	Types of Control	
Source of Control	**Preventive**	**Corrective**
Stakeholders	Maintaining quotas for hiring personnel in protected classes	Changing recruitment policies to attract qualified personnel
Organization	Using budgets to guide expenditures	Disciplining an employee for violating a "No Smoking" safety regulation in a hazardous area
Group	Advising a new employee about the group's norm in relation to expected level of output	Harassing and socially isolating a worker who doesn't conform to group norms
Individual	Deciding to skip lunch in order to complete a project on time	Revising a report you have written because you are dissatisfied with it

Stakeholder control is expressed as pressures from outside sources on organizations to change their behaviors. Recall that stakeholders may be unions, government agencies, customers, shareholders, and others who have direct interests in the well-being of an organization. During the past decade, organizations were increasingly pressured to reduce pollution, save energy, and produce more environmentally safe goods. The Environmental Protection Agency (EPA) estimates that building-related illnesses, such as those caused by contaminated air, cost U.S. organizations more than $260 billion a year in lost productivity. Boeing reports that employees in its "healthier" buildings are about 10 percent more productive than employees located in other plants. General Motors has pledged to cut its energy use by 20 percent from 1995 levels by 2002.[4] In addition, many consumers are demanding that companies provide environmentally safe products and often are willing to pay extra for "green marketed" products. ***Green marketing*** involves marketing of goods and services considered environmentally friendly that make their organizations "environmentally responsible." Organizations use green marketing not only to increase consumer approval, but also to cut costs. By using recyclable packaging materials for its hair-care products, Cosmair has saved several hundred thousand dollars annually. McDonald's uses one million pounds of recycled materials per year and has challenged its suppliers to provide and use recycled products and materials. Environmental friendliness impresses a broad range of stakeholders.[5]

Organizational control comprises the formal rules and procedures for preventing or correcting deviations from plans and for achieving desired goals. Examples include rules, standards, budgets, and audits. ***Group control*** comprises the norms and values that group members share and maintain through rewards and punishments. Examples include acceptance by the group and punishments, such as giving group members the silent treatment, which we described in Chapters 17 and 18.

Individual self-control comprises the guiding mechanisms that operate consciously and unconsciously within each person. Standards of professionalism are becoming an increasingly important aspect of individual self-control. Becoming a professional involves acquiring detailed knowledge, specialized skills, and specific attitudes and ways of behaving. The entire process may take years of study and socialization. In

WEB INSIGHT

General Motors is committed to protecting the environment. To learn more about the company's environmental principles and the controls necessary to enforce them, visit GM's Web site at *http://www.gm.com.*

doing their work, certified public accountants, lawyers, engineers, business school graduates, and physicians, among others, are expected to exercise individual self-control based on the guiding standards of their professions.

PATTERNS OF CONTROL

Stakeholder, organizational, group, and individual controls form patterns that differ widely from one organization to another. Strong organizational cultures, the characteristics of which we described in Chapter 18, usually produce mutually supportive and reinforcing organizational, group, and individual controls. One of the cultural values of the Ritz-Carlton Hotel is that "we are ladies and gentlemen serving ladies and gentlemen." It is an extremely powerful cultural statement because of the dignity it gives to the act of serving. At Ritz-Carlton Hotels, bellhops, drivers, room attendants, telephone operators, maintenance workers, and front-desk people experience what many employees in other organizations do not—a feeling of being respected.

In our discussions of motivation, leadership, and teams, we focused on managerial practices used to achieve employee loyalty, which often is influenced by an organization's control systems. In 1986, when Kodak developed its first "disposable" camera, industry analysts predicted that the camera would never be a success. By 2000, single-use cameras have become a $2.5 billion market, with an annual growth rate of nearly 30 percent. To supply the market, Kodak built a $50 million factory in Guadalajara, Mexico. It is one of the most advanced, high-volume, high-speed factories in the world, producing 120,000 single-use cameras a day for export to the United States, Canada, Japan, and Latin America. The following Strategic Action Competency feature highlights the types of controls that Kodak uses in that factory.[6]

STRATEGIC ACTION COMPETENCY

Kodak's SUN Plant

Kodak employs more than 1,200 people at its SUN plant in Guadalajara, Mexico. These employees assemble and package more than 5,000 cameras per hour. Each camera consists of 26 separate parts, most of which are manufactured on-site. In the course of a year, these employees will handle more than 1 billion parts and export more than 40 million cameras. According to the plant manager, the plant was built to maximize speed but also to maintain a defect rate of less than 1 percent.

To achieve these results, Kodak designed the SUN plant so that managers could see the entire operation. "In most factories, the people at the front end have no idea of what's happening at the back end," says Joe Brennen, materials manager for SUN. "So, if there's a quality problem somewhere along the line, a product can pile up before anyone knows about it and before the problem gets fixed. That can't happen here."

When the corrective control system reported that a shipment of circuit boards from China contained an unusual number of defects, Brennen and his team went into action immediately. Because these boards are an essential component of flash cameras, waiting for another shipment would have meant shutting down the plant. The alternative was to weed out faulty boards through extra quality tests during assembly. But the assembly line was designed to allow for only one flash test. The team's solution was to give the employees a short work break and use that time to reconfigure the assembly line to include extra workstations. Within fifteen minutes, not only was the plant up and running at 100 percent, but employees were able to perform the additional quality tests that were needed.

Kodak is also sensitive to environmental issues. After the customer has used a Fun Saver camera, he or she sends it to a film developer. The film developer separates the film and sends the camera to SUN for recycling. SUN recycles more than 8 million cameras

annually, or about 70 percent of all Fun Saver cameras that it produces, reusing 86 percent of the material from those cameras. Kodak hopes that, in the future, fewer "throwaway" cameras will actually be thrown away.

• • •

To learn more about Kodak, visit the company's home page at

http://www.kodak.com

One way to develop and measure the effectiveness of formal organizational controls is to compare their costs and benefits. Such a cost–benefit analysis addresses three basic questions.

1. For what desired behaviors and results should organizational controls be developed?

2. What are the costs and benefits of the organizational controls required to achieve the desired behaviors and results?

3. What are the costs and benefits of utilizing alternative organizational controls to obtain the desired behaviors and results?

Monfort, Inc., a meatpacking subsidiary of ConAgra Foods, discovered that annual medical costs for employees had increased to more than $5 million, largely because of premature and low birth–weight babies. The director of human resources showed top management that medical claim costs and lost earnings owing to parental leave surrounding pregnancy and childbirth could be reduced if the company established a neonatal program for employees reluctant to seek prenatal care. Management provided incentives, including $50 up front and a car seat when the baby was born to jumpstart the program. As a result, Monfort, Inc.'s, medical costs dropped from $5.5 million to $2.3 million in one year, and the average hospital stay for premature and low birth–weight babies following birth dropped from 17 to 11 days in just three years. Monfort's efforts to control costs resulted in preventive care that also had great value to employees and their families[7]

COST–BENEFIT MODEL

Figure 19.1 shows a cost–benefit model for gauging the effectiveness of an organization's control system. The horizontal axis indicates the amount of organizational control, ranging from low to high. The vertical axis indicates the relationship between the costs and benefits of control, ranging from zero to high. For simplicity, the cost-of-control curve is shown as a direct function of the amount of organizational control. The two break-even points indicate where the amount of organizational control moves from a net loss to a net benefit and then returns to a net loss. Although the optimal amount of control is difficult to calculate, effective managers probably come closer to achieving it than do ineffective managers.

Managers have to consider trade-offs when choosing the amount of organizational control to use. With too little control, costs exceed benefits and the controls are ineffective. As the amount of control increases, effectiveness also increases—up to a point. Beyond a certain point, effectiveness declines with further increases in the amount of control exercised. For example, an organization might benefit from reducing the average managerial span of control from 21 to 16 employees. However, to reduce it further to 8 employees would require doubling the number of managers. The costs of the increased control (managers' salaries) might far outweigh the expected benefits. Such a move might also make workers feel *micromanaged*. That, in turn, could lead to increased dissatisfaction, absenteeism, and turnover. Obviously, some of these costs and benefits can be difficult to quantify.

Eighty-one percent of large U.S. organizations engage in some kind of drug screening of their employees. According to the American Management Association, about 2 percent of these organizations use hair analysis. A major selling point is that hair analysis has a so-called wide detection window. Although urine tests generally detect drug use during the previous week, hair tests can reveal the use of any illegal substance as far back as a month or more. Employees at Bic Corporation, the retail chain Sports Authority, and GM have complained that this analysis can expose genetic information contained in DNA, such as hereditary defects or a predisposition to certain diseases. Opponents of hair testing argue that insurance companies could use genetic information to deny coverage, or a company could deny a person promotions because he or she is likely to suffer a major illness later in life.[8]

Figure 19.1 **Cost–Benefit Model of Organizational Control**

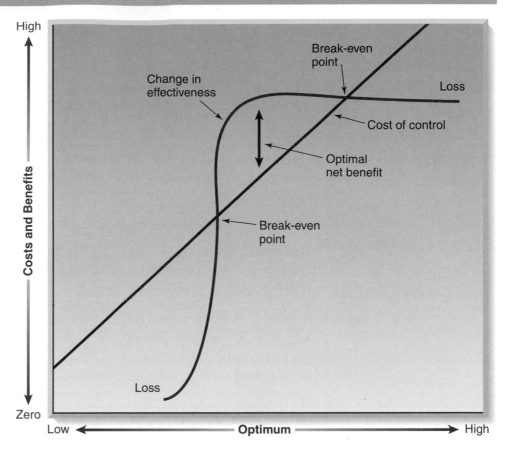

CRITERIA FOR EFFECTIVE CONTROLS

Designing effective organizational controls and control systems isn't simple because many issues must be considered. However, control systems are more likely to be effective if they are linked to desired goals and are objective, complete, timely, and acceptable. These criteria refine and make more specific the ideas presented in the cost–benefit model.

As suggested by the assessment method shown in Table 19.2, a control may more or less satisfy each of these criteria. A particular control or control system should be designed and evaluated in terms of all five criteria. The total score from such an assessment can range from a low of 5 to a high of 25. The higher the total score, the greater is the likelihood that the control or control system is effective. Organizational controls that fail reasonably to satisfy the five criteria actually may do more harm than good.

Table 19.2 **Assessment of Organizational Controls**

Criteria	Scale				
	Strongly Disagree	Disagree	Undecided	Agree	Strongly Agree
1. It is linked to desired goals.	1	2	3	4	5
2. It is objective.	1	2	3	4	5
3. It is complete.	1	2	3	4	5
4. It is timely.	1	2	3	4	5
5. It is acceptable.	1	2	3	4	5

WEB INSIGHT

The "ladies and gentlemen" of the Ritz-Carlton staff are constantly reminded of The Gold Standards of the hotel by a card they carry in their pockets. What are these standards? They can be accessed at *http://www.ritzcarlton.com*.

Linkage to Desired Goals. Control or control systems should be linked to the strategic goals of the organization. These goals often include improving customer service, protecting the organization's assets, and improving the quality of the goods and/or services it produces. FedEx has information systems—including bar codes and hand-held tracking devices—that provide fast and profitable service to its customers. Similarly, Ritz-Carlton Hotels treat employees as ladies and gentleman, yet exercise formal controls. The hotel chain believes that, as a result, its employees will help guests in ways that will benefit both them and the hotel.

Objective. An objective control or control system is impartial and can't be manipulated by employees for personal gain. In the United States, the Financial Accounting Standards Board (FASB) and several government agencies devote a great deal of effort to developing and monitoring principles and practices to ensure that financial statements objectively and as accurately as possible reflect reality. Thus a control system for assessing an organization's effectiveness must be based on multiple criteria.

Complete. A complete control or control system encompasses all the behaviors and goals desired by the organization. A purchasing manager evaluated solely on the basis of cost per order may allow quality to slip. A computer salesperson at Gateway evaluated only on the basis of sales volume may ignore after-sales service. Thus balancing quantitative (measurable) and qualitative (subjective) controls is necessary.

Timely. A timely control or control system provides information when it is needed most. Timeliness may be measured in seconds for evaluating the safe movement of trains and planes or in terms of months for evaluating employee performance. Computer-based information systems have played a major role in increasing the timely flow of information. The computerized cash registers at Wal-Mart give store managers daily data on each department's sales, as well as profitability measures for the entire store.

Acceptable. To be effective a control or control system must be recognized as necessary and appropriate. If a control system is widely ignored, managers need to find out why. Perhaps the controls should be dropped or modified, should be backed up with rewards for compliance and punishments for noncompliance, or should be linked more closely to desired results.

Meg Whitman, CEO of eBay; Rick Braddock, CEO of Priceline.com; James Barksdale, CEO of Netscape; and other dotcom managers face severe control problems as competition intensifies. Often, dotcoms have highly advanced technologies but no definite control systems to turn these technologies into profitable goods and services. Unsuccessful dotcoms, such as Webvan and HomeGrocer, have leaders who refuse to give up their notions about command and control, which can stifle growth and cause their companies to miss opportunities in fast-changing markets. The following Self-Management Competency feature highlights how Tim Koogle, CEO of Yahoo!, established an effective control system at his company.[9]

SELF-MANAGEMENT COMPETENCY

Tim Koogle, CEO of Yahoo.com

Yahoo! became the second dotcom company to join Standard and Poor's 500-stock index in 2000. Yahoo! achieved this feat in three years, or less than half the time it took AOL. To make it the largest Internet portal in 21 coun-

tries, Koogle had to craft Yahoo!'s expansion from a simple search engine to a strong consumer service brand. More than 105 million people visit Yahoo! monthly, and annual revenues exceeded $575 million recently. Today,

Yahoo!'s network, which includes everything from e-mail to news to auctions, is targeting new buyers through an upbeat video. Koogle's goal is to make Yahoo! the largest media company in the world.

To reach this goal, Koogle has created a control system that lets him share power and responsibility with his staff without losing control. At Yahoo!, there is no such thing as weekly face-to-face management meetings. Every week, 30 top managers receive an e-mail from the finance department summarizing all key measures of Yahoo!'s operations and the major executive decisions made during the week. Managers communicate with Koogle via e-mail in response to the weekly numbers. This free-flowing communication keeps Yahoo!'s managers up to date on all the organization's key indicators. Senior managers rarely find themselves in a position of waiting to hear from Koogle. Koogle says that he "zooms in and out" of many meetings to understand what's going on in Yahoo!'s divisions but that he never second-guesses a manager's operational decision. Yahoo!'s managers are accountable for their results because they have been empowered to make decisions. In Koogle's words, they "own the results."

• • •

To learn more about Yahoo!, visit the company's home page at

http://www.yahoo.com

CORRECTIVE CONTROL MODEL

3.

IDENTIFY THE SIX PHASES OF THE CORRECTIVE CONTROL MODEL.

The ***corrective control model*** is a process for detecting and eliminating or reducing deviations from an organization's established standards.[10] This process relies heavily on information feedback and responses to it. As shown in Figure 19.2, the corrective control model has six interconnected phases: (1) define the subsystem (an individual, a department, or a process), (2) identify the key characteristics to be measured, (3) set standards, (4) collect information, (5) make comparisons, and (6) diagnose problems and make corrections.

Figure 19.2 **Corrective Control Model**

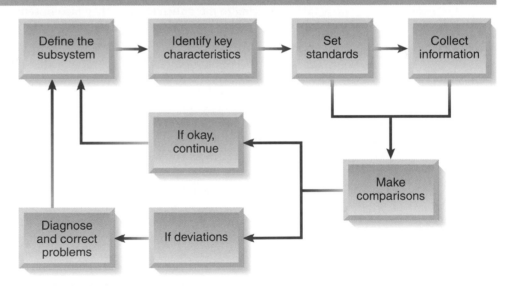

DEFINE THE SUBSYSTEM

A formal control subsystem might be created and maintained for an employee, a work team, a department, or an entire organization. The control mechanisms could focus on specific inputs, transformation processes, or outputs. Input controls often limit the amount by which raw materials used in the transformation process can vary from the organization's standards. For example, breweries use elaborate controls (including inspections and laboratory testing) to guarantee that the water and grains they use to make beer meet predetermined standards. Such controls ensure that the correct quantity and quality of inputs enter the production process.

Many formal controls are applied during production (the transformation process). For Budweiser, Coors, Miller, and other brewers, they include timing the cooking of the brew, monitoring the temperature in the vats, sampling and laboratory testing of the brew at each stage of the process, and visual inspection of the beer prior to final packing. Finally, output controls are used. For brewers, they range from specifying the levels of distributor inventories to monitoring consumer attitudes toward the beer and its marketing.

IDENTIFY KEY CHARACTERISTICS

The key types of information to be obtained about a person, team, department, or organization must be identified. Establishing a formal corrective control system requires early determination of the characteristics that can be measured, the costs and benefits of obtaining information about each characteristic, and whether variations in each characteristic are likely to affect performance.

After identifying them, managers must choose the characteristics to be measured. The **_principle of selectivity_** (also known as Pareto's law) holds that a small number of characteristics always account for a large number of effects. In brewing beer, three characteristics that greatly influence the final product's quality are water quality, temperature, and length of brewing time. Failing to control these few vital characteristics can account for large variations in results.

SET STANDARDS

Standards are criteria for evaluating qualitative and quantitative characteristics and should be set for each characteristic measured. One of the most difficult, but important, aspects of doing business in a foreign country is to adjust to differences in standards. Owing to the difficulties that they face in setting standards that apply in widely differing cultures and markets, many global organizations have adopted the strategy of _thinking globally, but acting locally_. Cisco, a computer networking organization, discovered that customer standards varied from country to country. In Japan, Cisco found that office buildings often lack the space required for installing the company's complex electrical equipment, so it had to design network routers that would fit under a person's desk. In France, buyers insisted that at least some product components be French made and demanded that Cisco use French-based organizations to test its products.[11]

Cultural and cross-cultural differences also are apparent in various human interactions, including language, nonverbal communication, religion, time, space, color, numbers, degree of materialism, customs, status symbols, and food preferences. For example, different time standards are reflected in differing approaches to work. U.S. and Canadian executives expect meetings to begin and end at certain times, but Latins typically arrive late and aren't concerned about ending meetings on time. Why? Their standard for time isn't based on deadlines, but rather on a series of events: First, they do a task; when that is finished, they move on to the next task; and so on. Similarly, Indonesians have "rubber time"; to them, time is elastic. If something comes up that is more important than business, such as a wedding, business gets postponed. In Nigeria, a starting time for a meeting is only an approximation, and tardiness is readily accepted. Thus global organizations must observe standards set by cultures, rather than apply standards that the organizations are accustomed to and would prefer to set.[12]

Increasingly, control systems are being based on performance standards (performance goals). Of the many possible types of performance standards, the following are but a few examples from five different functional areas.

- _Inventory:_ Monthly finished goods inventory should be maintained at the sales level forecast for the following two-month period.

- _Accounts receivable:_ Monthly accounts receivable should be no more than the dollar value of the previous month's sales.

- *Sales productivity:* The dollar value of sales per salesperson should be $1,000 greater than the comparable month for the previous year and $12,000 greater annually.

- *Employee turnover:* The turnover of field sales personnel should be no more than 2 per 100 salespeople per month and no more than 20 per 100 salespeople annually.

- *Production waste:* Waste should amount to no more than $50 per month per full-time production worker, or no more than $600 per year per full-time production worker.

COLLECT INFORMATION

Information on each of the standards can be collected manually or automatically. Examples of the latter are the electronic counting devices used at Disney World to count the number of people who use each ride or the turnstiles at libraries that count the number of people who enter.

If the individual or group whose performance is to be controlled collects information, its validity must be checked. Employees and managers have an incentive to distort or conceal information if they will be criticized or punished for negative results. Moreover, when formal controls emphasize punishment, strong group controls (see Chapter 17 for a list) often emerge to distort the information reported to management. Such reporting often obscures responsibility for failure to meet standards or achieve goals.

Top managers may create special departments or rely on existing functional departments to collect information by monitoring or auditing certain activities. Mick McGill, executive vice president of human resources at The Associates First Capital Corporation, collects data from the U.S. Department of Labor and the company's competitors to determine, for example, whether starting salaries for various jobs are sufficient and whether affirmative action guidelines are being followed. Similarly, John Stillo, executive vice president in the controller's department of The Associates, collects and analyzes information to verify that income and expenditures are being recorded in accordance with established accounting standards.

MAKE COMPARISONS

Comparisons are needed to determine whether what *is* happening is what *should be* happening. In other words, information about actual results must be compared with performance standards. Such comparisons allow managers and team members to concentrate on deviations or exceptions. At Tom's of Maine, an operator is supposed to package 81 tubes of toothpaste a minute. If all operators reach or surpass this goal, the production process is operating efficiently. If there is no apparent difference between what is and what should be happening, operations normally continue without any change.

DIAGNOSE AND CORRECT PROBLEMS

Diagnosis involves assessing the types, amounts, and causes of deviations from standards. Action can then be taken to eliminate those deviations and correct problems. However, the fact that a characteristic can be controlled doesn't necessarily mean that it should be controlled. Computer-based management information systems often help in overcoming inadequacies in corrective controls.

Suppose that you have just gotten your midterm examination back and have received a D. You immediately start typing an e-mail message to a friend, ranting about your terrible instructor and how you're thinking about getting other students to give him poor faculty evaluations at the end of the semester. You begin to have second thoughts, decide that complaining might be a dumb idea, and don't send the e-mail message. However, unbeknownst to you every character you typed on your school's computer has been stored for the faculty to see. You get a call from the faculty member saying that he would like to see you after your next class.

Can something like that actually happen? The answer is a definite *yes!* Many organizations are installing software that monitors their employees' computer activity, both online and off-line—every message sent, every Web site visited, every file formatted, and even every key stroke entered—to control abuses. Collecting such data is easy and cheap. For example, a company on the Internet at http://www.winwhatwhere.com sells a surveillance program for under $100 that allows a company to analyze how any employee is using its computers.

About 20 percent of Fortune 1,000 companies, along with some federal agencies, now have so-called monitoring software, according to International Data Corporation, and that figure is expected to jump to 80 percent shortly. About 12 percent of companies don't notify their employees of their monitoring activities. The following Planning and Administration feature highlights some of the issues surrounding this type of control system.[13]

Computer Monitoring

Managers at a New York City import–export company suspected that two employees were robbing it. Corporate Defense Strategies (CDS) of Maywood, New Jersey, advised the firm to install a software program that could secretly log every single stroke of the suspects' computer keys and send an encrypted e-mail report to CDS. Investigators revealed that the two employees were deleting orders from the corporate books after processing them, pocketing the revenues, and building their own company from within. The program picked up on their plan to return to the office late one night to steal a large shipment of electronics. Police hid in the rafters of the firm's warehouse, and when the suspects entered they were arrested. The pair were charged with embezzling $3 million over 2½ years, a sizable amount of revenue for a $25 million-a-year firm.

Programs such as those developed by CDS and Websense are legal. According the American Bar Association (ABA), employers are free to monitor an employee's use of their networks so long as they don't violate labor and antidiscrimination laws. Some union con-

tracts limit an employer's ability to monitor during downtime, such as lunch hours and coffee breaks, but they typically don't bar monitoring altogether. Although federal law prohibits wiretapping and monitoring of private phone conversations without a court order, it doesn't preclude an employer from monitoring its own systems.

A survey by the Computer Security Institute and the FBI found that 71 percent of the respondents had detected unauthorized access to their computer by others and that 79 percent of employees abuse their Internet privileges. Chevron Corporation paid $2.2 million to four female employees who claimed that they had been sexually harassed because of jokes sent via the company's network. To end such abuses, Chevron stated that it needed to monitor all employees' e-mail transmissions. Xerox fired 40 employees for what it deemed inappropriate use of the Internet, and the New York Times fired 23 workers for sending what were considered to be obscene e-mail messages via company computers. The American Civil Liberties Union (A.C.L.U.) indicates

that the vast majority of employees are unaware of the extent to which monitoring goes on. The Privacy Rights Clearinghouse (*http:// www.privacyrights.org*) distributes documents that spell out the rights of individuals and employers.

● ● ●

To learn about computer monitoring at work, visit the home pages of

http://www.corporatedefense.com
and
http://www.websense.com

PRIMARY METHODS OF CONTROL

4.

**DESCRIBE THE PRIMARY
METHODS OF
ORGANIZATIONAL
CONTROL.**

Throughout this textbook, we have discussed various aspects of control and have indicated how a firm's strategy helps focus (control) employee behavior.[14] For example, compared to the Ritz-Carlton, Marriott's Hampton Inns provide low-cost accommodations. Therefore Marriott's control systems focus on maintaining a low-cost strategy. In terms of human resource management, performance appraisal systems help managers assess the behaviors of employees and compare them to performance standards. Deviations are noted and corrective controls are used to reduce or eliminate problems.

In this section we explore six primary methods of organizational control. Two are basic to the type of organization: mechanistic and organic controls. One reflects external considerations: market controls. Two are functional: financial and accounting controls. And one is technological: automation controls. We also provide examples of specific control methods utilized by organizations.

As Figure 19.3 illustrates, all organizations utilize some combination of mechanistic and organic control methods in conjunction with their market, financial, accounting, and automation-based controls. The methods available have the potential for complementing one another or working against one another. Thus management should select and assess control methods in relation to one another when deciding which to apply.

Figure 19.3   Relationships among Primary Organizational Control Methods

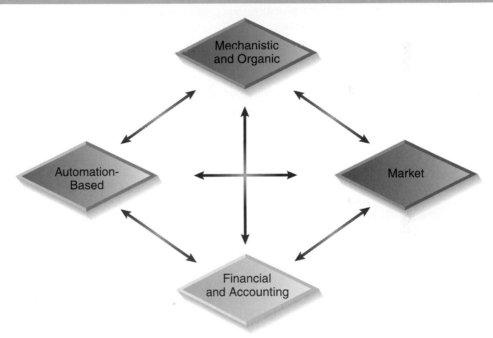

MECHANISTIC AND ORGANIC CONTROL

Mechanistic control involves the extensive use of rules and procedures, top–down authority, tightly written job descriptions, and other formal methods for preventing and correcting deviations from desired behaviors and results. Mechanistic controls are an important part of bureaucratic management (see Chapters 2, 11, and 18). In contrast, *organic control* involves the use of flexible authority, relatively loose job descriptions, individual self-controls, and other informal methods for preventing and correcting deviations from desired behaviors and results. Organic control reflects organic management (see Chapter 11).

Organic control is consistent with a clan culture. In clan-type organizational cultures, such as The Associates, Johnson & Johnson, and Home Depot, members share pride in membership and a strong sense of identification with management. In addition, peer pressure to adhere to certain norms is considerable. Teams of self-managed employees control themselves with little direction from a supervisor. These self-managed teams use many organic controls, which create a supportive environment for members to learn new tasks.

Table 19.3 contrasts the use of mechanistic and organic control methods. For example, detailed rules and procedures are used whenever possible in mechanistic control. In contrast, detailed rules and procedures are used only when necessary in organic control. However, an organization or its units doesn't have to use totally bureaucratic or totally organic control methods. The la Madeleine French Bakery & Cafe headquartered in Dallas has grown to 62 restaurants since 1991. Mechanistic controls are used to enforce uniform and highly detailed safety rules throughout the organization. In contrast, the manager of each restaurant uses organic controls to build team spirit in day-to-day operations.

Table 19.3	*Mechanistic and Organic Control Methods*
Mechanistic Control Methods	**Organic Control Methods**
Use of detailed rules and procedures whenever possible	Use of detailed rules and procedures only when necessary
Top–down authority, with emphasis on positional power	Flexible authority, with emphasis on expert power and networks of influence
Activity-based job descriptions that prescribe day-to-day behaviors	Results-based job descriptions that emphasize goals to be achieved
Emphasis on extrinsic rewards (wages, pensions, status symbols)	Emphasis on both extrinsic and intrinsic rewards (meaningful work)
Distrust of teams, based on an assumption that team goals conflict with organizational goals	Use of teams, based on an assumption that team goals and norms assist in achieving organizational goals

WEB INSIGHT

Have you ever wondered how Coca-Cola controls the number of vending machines there are in Japan? To answer this and other questions about its worldwide control systems, visit Coca-Cola's Web site at *http://www.coke.com.*

Coca-Cola, American Airlines, Gillette, and other major organizations have large numbers of departments, which can differ widely in their emphasis on mechanistic or organic control and create departmental subcultures. The use of mechanistic control in certain departments and organic control in others don't necessarily reduce a firm's overall effectiveness.[15] For example, at Coca-Cola the syrup production department operates in a relatively stable environment, whereas the bottling department operates in a changing environment. Managers of these two departments are likely to choose different ways to divide and manage the work. The syrup production manager probably will choose a more bureaucratic control system, and the bottling manager probably will choose a more organic control system. One consequence of use of the organic system was that bottling managers recognized that consumers in different countries didn't perceive Coca-Cola the same way and had differerent product requirements. For example, in Spain, refrigerators are smaller than in other countries. As a result, two-liter bottles didn't fit in the refrigerators, and sales were lost until the bottling department redesigned the container.

MARKET CONTROL

Market control involves the collection and evaluation of data related to sales, prices, costs, and profits for guiding decisions and evaluating results. The idea of market control emerged from economics, and dollar amounts provide effective standards of comparison. To be effective, market control mechanisms generally require that

- the costs of the resources used in producing outputs be measured monetarily,
- the value of the goods and services produced be defined clearly and priced monetarily, and
- the prices of the goods and services produced be set competitively.

Two of the control mechanisms that can satisfy these requirements are profit-sharing plans and customer monitoring.

Profit-Sharing Plans. Recall from Chapter 13 that profit-sharing plans provide employees with supplemental income based on the profitability of an entire organization or a selected subunit.[16] The subunit may be a strategic business unit, a division, a store in a chain, or other organizational entity. Profit-sharing plans generally are used to

- increase employee identification with the organization's profit goals, allowing greater reliance on individual self-control and group controls;

- achieve a more flexible wage structure, reflecting the company's actual economic position and controlling labor costs;

- attract and retain workers more easily, improving control of selection and lowering turnover costs; and

- establish a more equitable reward system, helping to develop an organizational culture that recognizes achievement and performance.

At least three important factors influence whether the goals of a profit-sharing plan can be achieved. First, employees must believe that the plan is based on a reasonable, accurate, and equitable formula. The formula, in turn, must be based on valid, consistently, and honestly reported financial and operating information. Second, employees must believe that their efforts and achievements contribute to profitability. Third, employees must believe that the size of profit-based incentives will increase proportionally as profitability increases. These factors also are crucial in determining the effectiveness of gainsharing plans. Recall that gainsharing plans pass on the benefits of increased productivity, cost reductions, and improved quality through regular cash bonuses to employees.

Customer Monitoring. *Customer monitoring* consists of ongoing efforts to obtain feedback from customers concerning the quality of goods and services. Such monitoring is done to prevent problems or learn of their existence and solve them. Customer monitoring is being used increasingly in corrective control, in an attempt to assess or measure customers' perceptions of service and quality.[17] Based on such assessments, management may take action to prevent the loss of further business because of customer dissatisfaction.

Service providers use customer monitoring often. Staples, the office supply chain founded in 1986, tracks consumer purchases by offering a membership card good for discounts and special promotions. This system allows Staples to know its customers' purchasing habits well. Because of its cash-register data, which tracks buying preferences, quantities, and frequency, Staples doesn't need to use mass mailings and generic coupons. Instead, it targets specific customer segments for selected coupons, mailings, and promotions. Hotels and restaurants may ask customers to judge the quality of their service by completing a "customer satisfaction card." After purchases of their products, many firms follow up with telephone interviews or mail questionnaires to obtain information from customers. Lexus reimburses dealers for performing 1,000- and 7,500-mile checkups at no cost to Lexus owners. After the car has been serviced, the customer is asked to fill out a survey regarding the adequacy of the service. An independent marketing research firm enters the data into a computer and then sends it on to Lexus headquarters in California by satellite transmission. As a result, Lexus can track all service work done anywhere in its system and compare the quality of service provided by its dealers.[18]

FINANCIAL CONTROL

Financial control includes the mechanisms for preventing or correcting the misallocation of resources.[19] External auditors, usually certified public accounting firms (e.g., Arthur Andersen, Ernst & Young, and KPMG) and/or internal auditing departments (e.g., accounting, controller, and treasurer), monitor the effectiveness of financial control. The primary responsibility of external auditors is to the shareholders. The auditors' role is to assure shareholders that the firm's financial statements present its true financial position and are in conformity with generally accepted accounting principles.

Because there are so many financial control mechanisms, we focus on only three of the essential ones: comparative financial analysis, budgeting, and activity-based costing.

Comparative Financial Analysis. Evaluation of a firm's financial condition for two or more time periods is called *comparative financial analysis.* When data are available from similar firms, they are used in making comparisons.[20] Industry trade associations often collect information from their members and publish it in summary form. Publicly owned firms publish income statements, balance sheets, and other financial statements. These sources often are used by managers and outsiders to assess changes in the firm's financial indicators and to compare its financial health with that of other firms in the same industry. Companies that have multiple production facilities (e.g., GM, Toyota, Bridgestone/Firestone, and IBM), retail outlets (e.g., Pier 1, J.C. Penney, and Kohl's), restaurants (e.g., Taco Bell, Olive Garden, and Red Lobster), hotels (e.g., Marriott, Holiday Inn, and Sheraton) compare the financial records of all units for control purposes.

The technique most commonly used is ratio analysis. *Ratio analysis* involves selecting two significant figures, expressing their relationship as a fraction, and comparing its value for two periods of time or with the same ratio of similar organizations. Of the many types of possible ratios, those most commonly used by organizations are profitability, liquidity, activity, and leverage. They are summarized in Table 19.4.[21]

Table 19.4	Examples of Commonly Used Financial Ratios		
Type	**Example**	**Calculation**	**Interpretation**
Profitability	Return on investment (ROI)	$\dfrac{\text{Net income}}{\text{Total investment}}$	Profitability of investment
Liquidity	Current ratio	$\dfrac{\text{Current assets}}{\text{Current liabilities}}$	Short-term solvency
Activity	Inventory turnover	$\dfrac{\text{Sales}}{\text{Inventory}}$	Efficiency of inventory management
Leverage	Debt ratio	$\dfrac{\text{Total debt}}{\text{Total assets}}$	How an organization finances itself

Return on investment (ROI) generally is considered to be the most important profitability ratio because it indicates how efficiently the organization is using its resources. A ratio value greater than 1.0 indicates that the organization is using its resources effectively. The *current ratio* indicates an organization's ability to pay bills on time. A current ratio should be well above 1:1, and a ratio of 2:1 indicates that a firm is financially sound. A low current ratio might mean that the organization has unnecessary inventory, a lot of cash sitting idle, or heavy accounts receivable that are difficult to collect. *Inventory turnover* indicates the average number of times that inventory is sold and restocked during the year. A high ratio means efficient operations—a relatively small amount of money is tied up in inventory—enabling the organization to use its resources elsewhere. *Debt ratio* is computed to assess an organization's ability to meet its long-term financial commitments. A value of 0.35 indicates that the organization has $0.35 in liabilities for every $1.00 of assets. The higher this ratio, the poorer credit risk the organization is perceived to be by financial institutions. Generally, organizations with debt ratios above 1.0 are considered to be relying too much on debt to finance their operations.

Financial ratios have little value unless managers know how to interpret them. For example, an ROI of 10 percent doesn't mean much unless it is compared to the ROIs of other organizations in the same industry. A firm with an ROI of 5 percent in an industry where the average ROI is 11 percent might be performing poorly. An inventory turnover rate of 5 at Pep Boys, Chief Auto Parts, and other auto-supply stores might be excellent but would be disastrous for Kroger, Grand Union, Safeway, and other large supermarkets for which an inventory turnover rate of 15 is common. Organizations can improve their inventory turnover rates by offering "specials" to stimulate customer demand, lowering prices, or not carrying items that move slowly.

Budgeting. *Budgeting* is the process of categorizing proposed expenditures and linking them to goals. Budgets usually express the dollar costs of various tasks or resources. For example, at Lockheed Martin Aerospace production budgets may be based on hours of labor per unit produced, machine downtime per thousand hours of running time, wage rates, and similar information. The main budget categories usually include labor, supplies and materials, and facilities (property, buildings, and equipment).

Budgeting has three primary purposes: (1) to help in planning work effectively; (2) to assist in allocating resources; and (3) to aid in controlling and monitoring resource utilization during the budget period. When managers assign dollar costs to the resources needed, they sometimes realize that proposed tasks aren't worth the cost; they can then modify or abandon the proposals.

Budgeting for completely new tasks usually requires forecasting conditions and estimating costs. Budgeting for established tasks is easier because historical cost data are available. In either case, those who prepare budgets must exercise judgment about what is likely to happen and how it will affect the organization. Budgets often are developed for a year and then broken down by month. Managers thus are able to track progress in meeting a budget as the year unfolds—and to take corrective action as necessary.

The control aspect of budgeting may be either corrective or preventive. When budgeting is used as a corrective control, the emphasis is on identifying deviations from the budget. Deviations indicate the need to identify and correct their causes or to change the budget itself.

The power of a budget, especially when used as a preventive control, depends on whether it is viewed as an informal contract that has been agreed to or a club to bludgeon those who don't stay within their budgets. One study asked first-line managers about their companies' budgets. The question was: "Do you feel that budgets or standards are frequently a club held over the head of the manager to force better performance?" Twenty percent of the 204 respondents replied "yes" and 68 percent answered "no." Most managers and employees who must live by budgets accept their use by top management as a control mechanism. However, some managers and employees view budgets with fear and hostility. This reaction usually occurs when an organization enforces budget controls with threats and punishment.[22]

There is no single classification system for budgets. Specific individuals, sections, projects, teams, committees, departments, divisions, or SBUs may be given budgets within which they are expected to operate. The following are the most common types of budgets used in business.

- *Sales budget*—a forecast of expected revenues, generally stated by product line on a monthly basis and revised at least annually.

- *Materials budget*—expected purchases, generally stated by specific categories, which may vary from month to month because of seasonal variations and inventory levels.

- *Labor budget*—expected staffing and benefits levels, generally stated by number of individuals and dollars for each job category.

- *Capital budget*—targeted spending for major tangible assets (e.g., new or renovated headquarters building, new factory, or major equipment), often requiring a time horizon beyond a year.

- *Research and development budget*—targeted spending for the development or refinement of products, materials, and processes.

- *Cash budget*—expected flow of monetary receipts and expenditures (cash flow), generally developed at least once a year for each month of the year.

The types of budgets and budget categories used are strongly influenced by organization design and organizational culture. An organization having a functional structure usually has a budget for each function (e.g., marketing, production, finance, and human resources). However, an organization having a product structure usually has a budget for each product line. For example, United Technologies has five distinct product lines—Pratt & Whitney, Carrier, Otis, UT Automotive, and Flight Systems. Management has found that this type of budgeting enables its control system to measure effectively the contributions of each product line.

Activity-Based Costing. *Activity-based costing* (ABC) is a system that focuses on activities as the fundamental cost centers.[23] An *activity* is any event that drives costs, including energy consumed, miles driven, computer hours logged, quality inspections made, shipments made, and scrap/rework orders filled.

In contrast to most financial control mechanisms, ABC focuses on the work activities associated with operating a business. The number of these activities usually depends on the complexity of operations. The more complex the organization's operations, the more cost-driving activities it is likely to have. Equally important, managers have discovered that not all products have the same mix of these activities. If a product doesn't require the use of an activity, its cost would be zero for that activity.

At Carrier's air conditioning plant in Tyler, Texas, one low-volume product requires frequent machine setups, has many intricate parts that generate numerous purchase orders, and requires constant inspections to maintain quality. A second, high-volume product requires few machine setups, few purchase orders, and few quality inspections. If Carrier were to ignore the differences in these two products in terms of their cost-driving activities and simply assign a general overhead cost to the products on the basis of volume, the high-volume product would bear most of the overhead cost. This approach would seriously distort actual unit costs for each product. As a result, Carrier could make production mistakes, and overall profitability would hide the impact of these mistakes. The company could carry unprofitable products and customers because winners would more than offset losers. It could survive with misleading cost allocations and without knowing the real costs of its individual business processes—but profits would not be as high as they could be.

Figure 19.4 depicts a model of the flow of information in activity-based costing, which is viewed from two perspectives: cost and process. The *cost view* reflects the flow of costs from resources to activities and from activities to products and services. At Lucent Technologies plant in Dallas, Texas, one of the activities is materials handling. The resources consumed in moving materials from one location to another at the plant is traced to each product, based on the number of times an item has been moved. This cost view is the key concept underlying activity-based costing: *Resources are consumed by activities, and activities are consumed by products and services.*

Figure 19.4 **Activity-Based Costing Model**

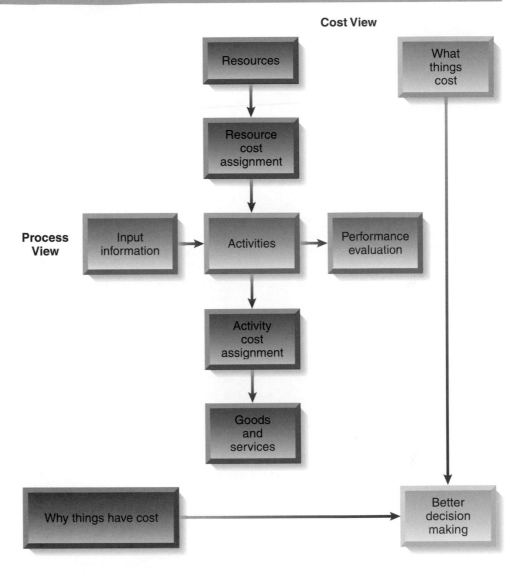

The *process view* reflects the lateral flow from costs of input information to activities and from activities to performance evaluation, or the observed transactions associated with an activity. In the case of materials handling at Lucent, information is gathered on the number of times that an item is moved to determine the extent of activity during a period. This information provides the activity data needed to complete the costing of products. It also provides the data needed for performance evaluation.[24]

Today some service organizations are also using ABC to communicate to their employees which activities are driving up costs. The Hospice of Central Kentucky (HCK) also used ABC to negotiate rates with insurance companies. The hospice operates under a managed-care model, with insurance companies providing per visit and per diem reimbursement. Shorter lengths of stay, higher costs for many terminal patients, and indigent care strain the resources of this managed-care facility. The following Communication Competency feature highlights how HCK used the ABC approach to communicate the need to cut costs, manage its hospice more effectively, and negotiate more favorable rates with insurance carriers.[25]

The Hospice of Central Kentucky (HCK) established a cross-functional team to determine the costs of things based on a patient day. The team realized that patients with lower acuity require less care and are subject to care over a longer period of time, whereas patients with higher acuity require more intense care over a shorter period of time. Because the per diem reimbursement doesn't vary in relation to acuity, the lower acuity cases subsidize the higher acuity cases.

To understand better the extent to which patients in various stages of acuity demanded hospice resources, the cross-functional team identified activities at the hospice. The team traced costs for 6 months to get a good picture of them. To be useful, the resources required by a cost driver must be measurable or there must be some way to estimate them. The differences between the traditional way of accounting for costs and the activity-based costing system are shown in the following table. The data on the left are the *accounting police,* or the traditional cost categories. These data tell managers whether they have overspent their budgets. The data on the right define the same costs in *everyday language,* pro-viding cost information for managers and employees, not for accountants. Employees can relate much better to this language because it is easy to understand and logical.

The hospice was able to improve its efficiency by pinpointing activities that drove costs—accounting/finance, management, and information systems. Employees involved in these activities are much more intensely involved with the patients in imminent death situations than with other patients. For example, ABC analysis revealed that the cost per patient day dramatically increased as the patient approached death, rising from $35.53 for a patient not near death to $381.57 per day for a patient near death.

Communicating these results to all employees in the hospice let everyone know that total length of stay needed to be increased by admitting more patients at the less acute stage of illness because patients entering the acute phase strained the system financially. The hospice was also able to negotiate better contracts with private insurance carriers. Armed with more accurate information, HCK's management determined

that the insurance carrier could select a payment type at admission, but couldn't change the payment type later. When faced with this choice, most insurance carriers selected the per diem type of payment that was financially advantageous to the hospice.

• • •

To learn more about Hospice of Central Kentucky, visit this organization's home page at

http://www.ubalt.edu/bereavement/ hospky.htm

Traditional		Activity-Based Costing	
Salaries	$70,000	Prereferral	$24,700
Benefits	16,000	Referral	10,900
Supplies	10,000	Admission	2,000
Depreciation	27,500	Postadmission	3,700
Pharmacy	5,000	Postdeath	1,500
Total	**$128,500**	Bereavement	12,700
		Postbereavement	15,100
		Patient Care	
		Medical services	5,600
		Reception	8,500
		Acctg/finance	13,600
		Info-systems	6,200
		Billing	2,900
		Volunteer services	3,400
		Total	**$128,000**

Using activity-based costing yields at least four benefits.[26] First, all costs are pinpointed by activity instead of many of them being charged to overhead. Employees understand that their activities are translated into costs that define the performance level of their units and the organization as a whole. The system also gives them an incentive to think about how to reduce costs. Second, cost allocations are based on the portion of activities that can be directly traced to a finished product itself, as opposed to production volume. Third, costs associated with an activity for a particular product can now be traced. For example, at HCK, each activity was divided by the number of patient days associated with the cost. Prereferral interviews, testing, and similar activities cost HCK $322.58 per patient, whereas the receptionist who answered calls was charged $1.11 per patient. This result showed HCK managers that the best way to control costs is to control the activities that generate them in the first place. Managers can identify activities that are being performed that have little impact on profits but are costing a lot of money. Finally, the use of ABC shifts managers' thinking from traditional cost analysis to managerial decision making. Information technology is essential in gathering ABC information and combining not just cost information but also nonfinancial information and performance measures. As managers and employees become more aware of activity-based costing and the information available from it, they will become more proficient in differentiating profitable and unprofitable activities.

The benefits of activity-based costing are offset somewhat by two limitations. First, managers must still make some arbitrary cost allocations based on volume. In many organizations, obtaining accurate product costs is difficult because so many costs relate to buildings, land, and equipment. Second, high measurement costs are associated with multiple activity centers and cost drivers. For example, at a hospital, automatically recording the results each time a nurse takes someone's blood pressure would be unreasonably expensive. Similarly, at Chase Bank or Bank of America, recording the length of time that a teller and customer talk would be extremely difficult. Even if it were feasible, it might not be a good idea because most banks don't want tellers rushing customers and minimizing customer contact.

AUTOMATION-BASED CONTROL

Automation involves the use of self-regulating devices and processes that operate independently of people. Automation usually involves linking machines with other machines to perform tasks. *Machine control* utilizes self-regulating instruments or devices to prevent and correct deviations from preset standards. The use of machines in business has gone through several significant stages of development. Machines initially increased productivity by giving employees better physical control over certain tasks. Eventually the interaction of employee and machine created a mutual control system. Then a new threshold was reached with automation.

Machine control of other machines takes over part of the managerial control function. That is, machines can now participate in the control process with managers. For example, computers in oil refineries collect data, monitor, and make automatic adjustments during refining processes. The impact of such automatic machine control on management has been reported in a number of studies. One researcher found that the introduction of an advanced automated system in one large factory reduced the number of middle management jobs by 34 percent.[27]

There has been a steady shift toward machine control in production operations. It began with machines being given control of some production tasks, as when automatic sensors replaced visual inspection in steel production. With the advent of assembly lines and mass-production technology, machines supplemented rules and regulations as a way of directly controlling production workers. In continuous process or robotic operations, machines actually control other machines.

Advanced machine control is a distinctive feature at Swatch Watch.[28] In 1978, when Ernest Thomke founded that watch company in Bienne, Switzerland, he realized that Swiss manufacturers long ago had lost much of their market share to the Japanese. Although they still dominated the luxury segment of the market, the Swiss were suffering from the Far East's onslaught. He decided to revolutionize the industry by making a watch that would sell for no more than $30, could be manufactured cheaply, was of high quality, required no repair, and would sell 10 million pieces in the first 3 years. These goals were so high that to reach them by using or improving on existing technologies was impossible. He designed a manufacturing process that enabled Swatch Watch to use the latest machine controls to reach those goals. Traditionally, as many as 30 independent organizations were involved in the production of a single watch. Skilled craftsman made parts of the watch in hundreds of tiny shops, each of them specializing in only a few parts. The parts were then sold to firms that put entire watches together.

The Swatch differed with regard both to its construction and the process used to manufacture it. First, the case included both an outer shell and a container to which individual parts could be directly attached. This technology required advanced computer-aided design and computer-aided manufacturing (CAD/CAM) technology and the extensive use of robotics. Second, the number of components was reduced from 91 in a traditional watch to 51. New materials were developed for the case, the glass, and micromotor. Also, a new assembly technology was designed and a pressure diecasting process perfected. Third, screws no longer were used to attach parts. Components were riveted and welded together ultrasonically. Because the crystal was also welded to the case, the watch was guaranteed to be water-resistant to a depth of 100 feet. Fourth, the strap was integrated into the case and assembled at the same time the case was made. Finally, the only part with a limited life expectancy (of about three years), the battery, was inserted into the bottom of the case and the opening closed with a cover. The Swatch was officially introduced in Switzerland on March 1, 1983. During the first four months, 25,000 were sold. Sales in the United States of this $30 colorful watch grew from 100,000 pieces in 1983 to more than 4 million (revenue of $2.3 billion) pieces by 2000.

CHAPTER SUMMARY

In this chapter we examined how organizations use various controls to achieve their goals. After considering the basic foundations of control, we highlighted the criteria for effective control systems. Next, we looked at a corrective control model and detailed the steps involved in its use. We then discussed primary types of financial and nonfinancial controls, including activity-based costing.

1. EXPLAIN THE FOUNDATIONS OF CONTROL.
The foundations of organizational control are (1) the type of control, (2) the source of control, (3) the pattern of control, and (4) the purpose of control. Preventive controls, such as rules, standards, and training programs, are designed to reduce the number and severity of deviations that require corrective action. In contrast, corrective controls are designed to bring unwanted results and behaviors in line with established standards or goals. There are four sources of organizational control: stakeholders, the organization itself, groups, and individuals. Patterns of the different kinds of control vary from mutually reinforcing to independently operating to conflicting.

2. DISCUSS WAYS THAT ORGANIZATIONS CAN CREATE EFFECTIVE CONTROLS.
The effectiveness of formal organizational controls is measured in terms of costs and benefits. The cost–benefit model highlights the trade-offs that occur with increases or decreases in control. At some point, increasing controls ceases to be effective. The effectiveness of specific controls is evaluated according to whether they achieve desired results and are objective, complete, timely, and acceptable.

3. **IDENTIFY THE SIX PHASES OF THE CORRECTIVE CONTROL MODEL.**

The corrective control model comprises six interconnected phases: (1) define the subsystem, (2) identify the characteristics to be measured, (3) set standards, (4) collect information, (5) make comparisons, and (6) diagnose and correct any problems.

4. **DESCRIBE THE PRIMARY METHODS OF ORGANIZATIONAL CONTROL.**

The primary methods of organizational control are (1) mechanistic (2) organic, (3) market, (4) financial, and (5) automation-based. Effective managerial control usually requires using multiple methods of control in combination.

KEY TERMS

Activity-based costing, p. 532
Automation, p. 535
Budgeting, p. 531
Comparative financial analysis, p. 530
Control, p. 516
Corrective control model, p. 523
Corrective controls, p. 517
Customer monitoring, p. 529

Financial control, p. 529
Green marketing, p. 518
Group control, p. 518
Individual self-control, p. 518
Machine control, p. 535
Market control, p. 528
Mechanistic control, p. 527
Organic control, p. 527

Organizational control, p. 518
Preventive controls, p. 517
Principle of selectivity, p. 524
Ratio analysis, p. 530
Stakeholder control, p. 518
Standards, p. 524

QUESTIONS FOR DISCUSSION AND COMPETENCY DEVELOPMENT

1. What types of control does FedEx use?

2. How do you or how would you feel about your organization monitoring your PC at work?

3. What are the characteristics of the control system at Yahoo!?

4. International discussions about intellectual property rights are ongoing. What controls may governments use to enforce intellectual property rights?

5. Describe the key characteristics of the corrective control model as they apply to your bank.

6. Think of an organization in which you have worked or are currently working. What are some examples of control used in this organization?

7. What is activity-based costing? Visit a local fast-food restaurant and apply this model of control to its operation.

8. **Competency Development: Teamwork.** Steve Robinson and Truett Cathy, founders of Chick-Fil-A, have developed a unique control system to breed loyalty in an industry noted for fierce competition and high manager turnover (between 40 and 50 percent). What kind of conrtrol system did they install at Chick-Fil-A? To learn more about Chick-Fil-A's control system, go to its home page at ***http://www.chickfila.com***.

9. **Competency Development: Global Awareness.** Many U.S. companies have located some or all of their manufacturing facilities in other countries. Nike, for example, has received a great deal of criticism for the employment conditions in its manufacturing plants abroad. How has Nike tried to control the working conditions in foreign plants that it does not own? To understand Nike's global control systems, go to Nike's home page at ***http://www.nike.com***.

Ethical Behaviors in the Office

The following questionnaire lists behaviors that you and others might engage in on the job. For each item, circle the number that best indicates the frequency with which you would engage in that behavior. Then put an X over the number that you think best describes how others you know behave. Finally, put a check mark beside that behavior if you believe that management should design a system to control that behavior.[29]

Behavior	Most of the time	Often	About half the time	Seldom	Never
1. Blaming an innocent person or a computer for errors that you made.	5	4	3	2	1
2. Passing on information that was told in confidence.	5	4	3	2	1
3. Falsifying quality reports.	5	4	3	2	1
4. Claiming credit for someone else's work.	5	4	3	2	1
5. Padding an expense account by more than 5 percent.	5	4	3	2	1
6. Using company supplies for personal use.	5	4	3	2	1
7. Accepting favors in exchange for preferred treatment.	5	4	3	2	1
8. Giving favors in exchange for preferred treatment.	5	4	3	2	1
9. Asking a person to violate company rules.	5	4	3	2	1
10. Calling in sick to take a day off when you weren't sick.	5	4	3	2	1

Behavior	Most of the time	Often	About half the time	Seldom	Never
11. Hiding errors.	5	4	3	2	1
12. Taking longer than necessary to do the job.	5	4	3	2	1
13. Doing personal business on company time.	5	4	3	2	1
14. Taking a longer lunch hour without approval.	5	4	3	2	1
15. Seeing a violation and not reporting it.	5	4	3	2	1
16. Overlooking boss's error to prove loyalty.	5	4	3	2	1
17. Asking an aide to lie about your whereabouts.	5	4	3	2	1
18. Telling coworkers that you are going somewhere when actually you are going somewhere else.	5	4	3	2	1

Questions

1. What are the differences between the most and least frequently occurring behaviors?

2. What are the most important behaviors that should be controlled? Why? What do they reveal about your own preferences for control?

3. How would management go about establishing programs for controlling them?

Bindco Corporation

The Bindco Corporation was one of the largest, independently owned software manufacturing turnkey service providers in the country. The company provided a variety of services to its clients, including (1) operations management (e.g., electronic services, manufacturing, warehousing, inventory management, order fulfillment and distribution, and package design and manufacturing); (2) component services (e.g., printing, binding, demand publishing, media mastering and replication, and loose-leaf products and multimedia packaging); and (3) fulfillment operations for software and related products. Founded in the Silicon Valley in 1981, the company had locations in Los Angeles, San Diego, and Redwood City, California. In 1994, the company opened its first European subsidiary in Amsterdam, Holland.

However, Bindco recently merged with ZBR Publications, Inc., to form a new company, GlobalWare Solutions. With the combined resources of both companies, GlobalWare Solutions today has annual revenues in excess of $100 million. The merger marked a major step toward creation of a worldwide, sole-source provider for the computer hardware/software and information-based industry. The company provides its customers with an "end-to-end" business solution for the global management and delivery of digital content, information, and physical products. Customers include Sun Microsystems, The Learning Company, Cannon Information Systems, and Hewlett-Packard.

GlobalWare Solutions is headquartered in Haverhill, Massachusetts, in a state-of-the-art, 300,000-square-foot facility. Its European division is based in Amsterdam (a 50,000-square-foot facility). The West Coast division (the 250,000-square-foot Bindco facility highlighted in the video) is still at Bindco's original Redwood City, California, location.

To satisfy the needs of its clients and numerous customers, Bindco implemented a large number of control systems to ensure quality and efficiency. The company is ISO 9000 compliant and utilizes a pervasive team of quality assurance inspectors who conduct production-line investigations and generate weekly reports. Furthermore, all personnel are trained extensively in the general quality assurance methods utilized by the company.

Other more specific control measures are in place at the Bindco facility. Personnel examine each software disk for any flaws or physical defects. To combat mislabeling, employees utilize scanners to conduct bar code labeling inspections. All electronic artwork, which is generated by clients, is proofed and shown to them before it goes to press. Assembly kits are sampled, and prototype testing is based on diagrams illustrating the method by which products are to be packaged. Extremely sensitive scales are used to ensure that each product package includes the proper mix of CDs, manuals, and floppy disks.

Bindco prides itself on the ability of its control measures to keep defects to a minimum, maintain high product quality, and ensure customer satisfaction.

Questions

1. Is Bindco's use of "personal accountability" an effective control technique?

2. Do the organizational control measures at Bindco represent preventive controls, corrective controls, or both?

To learn more about GlobalWare Solutions, visit the company's home page at *http://www.globalwaresolutions.com*.

Information Management Technology

LEARNING OBJECTIVES

AFTER STUDYING THIS CHAPTER YOU SHOULD BE ABLE TO:

1. EXPLAIN THE ROLE OF INFORMATION AS A MANAGEMENT RESOURCE.

2. DESCRIBE SIX COMMON INFORMATION MANAGEMENT TECHNOLOGIES.

3. IDENTIFY THE PRIMARY FACTORS IN THE DESIGN OF INFORMATION SYSTEMS.

4. STATE THE ETHICAL ISSUES INVOLVED IN INFORMATION TECHNOLOGIES.

Chapter Outline

PREVIEW: AVIS GOES WIRELESS

ROLE OF INFORMATION IN ORGANIZATIONS
DATA AND INFORMATION
VALUE-ADDED RESOURCE
PLANNING AND ADMINISTRATION COMPETENCY: Pillsbury's Data Mining

COMMON INFORMATION TECHNOLOGIES
INTERNET
EXTRANET
INTRANET
STRATEGIC ACTION COMPETENCY: Countrywide's Internet Challenge
DECISION SUPPORT SYSTEM
EXPERT SYSTEM
GROUP DECISION SUPPORT SYSTEM
TEAMWORK COMPETENCY: MS2 Accelerate

DESIGNING INFORMATION SYSTEMS
INFORMATION NEEDS
SYSTEM CONSTRAINTS
GOALS
DEVELOPMENT STAGES
EFFECTIVE IMPLEMENTATION

ETHICS AND INFORMATION TECHNOLOGIES
COMPUTER ETHICS
SELF-MANAGEMENT COMPETENCY: Computer Ethics Survey
PRIVACY ISSUES

CHAPTER SUMMARY

KEY TERMS

QUESTIONS FOR DISCUSSION AND COMPETENCY DEVELOPMENT

CASE FOR COMPETENCY DEVELOPMENT: A B2B RELATIONSHIP

VIDEO CASE: ARCHWAY COOKIES

AVIS GOES WIRELESS

Avis began to implement broadband wireless local area networks (LANs) at 4 of its 700 car locations in 2000. Among other features, this high-speed wireless technology allows Avis to capture digital signatures from customers in real time and transmit the signed documents directly to the company's centralized information system. Since 1984, Avis lot attendants have used handheld wireless packet data terminals. But owing to their relatively low bandwidth, packet radios can't handle signatures and other applications.

Vicki DeMarco, executive vice president for information technology at Avis Rental Car, says that "the system provides a complete wireless infrastructure that will extend beyond check-in and checkout. It will also support maintenance, repairs, and training. . . . It will help make our overall operation more

efficient." With the new technology, billing information is transmitted to wireless LAN access points at an airport. It's then transmitted to a local PC or server, which in turn feeds into the company's central information system.

Avis has incorporated the wireless LAN technology into its airport shuttle bus fleet, letting customers check in while proceeding to the lot. The terminal on the shuttle transmits the data to the Avis corporate system when it's within range of the LAN, usually within a couple hundred feet.

The four airports at which this technology was tested were Chicago's O'Hare, New York's LaGuardia, San Francisco, and Pittsburgh—with each representing various levels of difficulty of installation. For example, LaGuardia posed less of a challenge than the new central rental-car building at the San Francisco airport, where Avis operates

on multiple levels. In a location such as San Francisco, Avis may need to install as many as 20 LAN access points, whereas at smaller airports, it probably will need only 2: one for the counter, and one for the lot.

Bob Egan is an analyst at Gartner Group, Inc., in Stamford, Connecticut, which makes technology forecasts. He comments: "To my knowledge, Avis is the first rental car company to adopt wireless LANs to support its operations. The Avis rollout is indicative of how this is the year [2000] of the wireless LAN. There are a wide range of businesses expected to adopt the technology to support an increasingly mobile workforce with mobile applications that tie into enterprise systems."[1]

To learn more about Avis, visit the company's home page at

http://www.avis.com/company/home

ROLE OF INFORMATION IN ORGANIZATIONS

1.

EXPLAIN THE ROLE OF INFORMATION AS A MANAGEMENT RESOURCE.

Throughout this book, we have noted that organizations process and store vast amounts of data that employees and managers turn into useful information to make decisions. We have also discussed the substantial role of information technologies in this undertaking. *Information technologies* (ITs) are the computer-based electronic systems that help individuals and organizations assemble, store, transmit, process, and retrieve data and information.[2] The broadband wireless LANs introduced by Avis are an example of one such new technology. Avis management installed the LAN to improve the effectiveness (doing the right things better) and efficiency (doing the right things at less cost) of its data and information flows. The system achieves better customer service by allowing Avis to capture digital signatures from customers, allowing customers to check in while proceeding to the lot on the shuttle bus, and allowing customers to pick up and drop off vehicles more quickly. The impacts are even greater in terms of improved administrative processes and reduced costs. For example, billing information is automatically transmitted from a LAN to a local PC or server, which in turn, automatically feeds into the firm's central information system. This process helps reduce errors by lot attendants and automatically transmits data and information on the need for vehicle maintenance or repair. These and other automatic mechanisms have improved the efficiency of the company's field employees by cutting the labor time required per vehicle rental transaction. They also have enabled employees and managers to make better decisions.

DATA AND INFORMATION

The terms *data* and *information* often are used interchangeably, but incorrectly. **Data** are facts and figures. Every organization, such as Avis, processes data about its operations to create current, accurate, and reliable information. Many decisions require data such as market statistics, operating costs, inventory levels, sales figures, customer profiles, and the like. However, raw data are much like raw materials—not very useful until they are processed. Processing data involves comparison, classification, analysis, and summarization to transform them into usable and valuable information.[3] Thus the relationship of data to information is the same as that of raw materials to components of finished goods or various aspects of services. For example, through Avis's LANs, numerous types of data are collected—departure and arrival times/dates, miles driven, methods of payment, mechanical problems (if any) with the vehicle, vehicle damage (if any), and so on. These and other data are summarized and compared against standards of service and vehicle performance. Using such analyses of the data, employees create information to help meet Avis's efficiency and effectiveness goals.

Information is the knowledge derived from data that have been transformed to make them meaningful and useful. In effect, data are subjected to a *value-added process* that yields meaningful information for decision making. Individuals use their *knowledge*—concepts, tools, and categories—to create, store, apply, and share information. Recall our discussion of knowledge management in Chapter 9. Knowledge can be stored in a book, in a person's mind, or in a computer program as a set of instructions that gives meaning to streams of data.[4] At Avis, use of the broadband wireless LAN technology improves the knowledge base needed to support customer service, maintenance, repairs, and employee training.

VALUE-ADDED RESOURCE

Compared to physical resources, the value of information isn't easily documented. The value added to data, especially through the use of information technologies, is determined by those who use the resulting information to achieve desired goals. Such organizational goals may include (1) maintaining or increasing market share, (2) avoiding catastrophic losses, (3) creating greater flexibility and adaptability, (4) improving the quality of goods and services, (5) maximizing revenue, and (6) minimizing costs.[5] Managers and employees at different organizational levels and in diverse units and teams have different information needs. Information in various forms and amounts is essential to the specific types of decisions they must make to serve their customers, whether internal or external to the organization.

Higher level managers typically are interested in information on overall organizational performance and new product ideas. Detailed information on daily production and quality at each manufacturing plant isn't likely to be as useful to them as it is to self-managing teams in the plants. These teams need specific and timely information about the availability of raw materials, changes in productivity, rates of defects, and other operating characteristics. To salespeople, detailed information on the suppliers of raw materials probably has little value. Sales personnel want to know the amounts and types of goods and services that can be promised for delivery at certain times and at what prices.

Information must have benefits over and above that of the raw data to be considered a value-added resource.[6] Figure 20.1 shows four common interrelated criteria used to assess the value of information: quality, relevance, quantity, and timeliness.

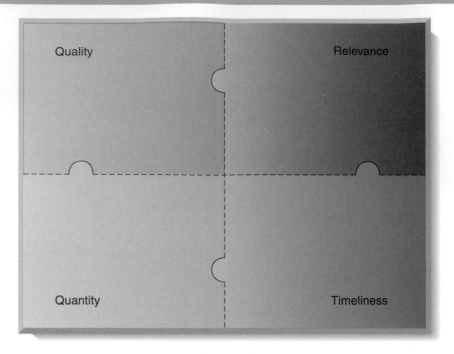

Quality. The quality of information is its accuracy in portraying reality. The more accurate the information, the higher is its quality. Quality required varies according to the needs of those who will use the information. Employees responsible for production inventory control need high-quality (precise) information about the amounts of raw materials available and resupply schedules required to meet production schedules and customers' delivery expectations. Marketing managers concerned with five-year sales forecasts might be able to use lower quality (less precise) information, such as general market trends and sales projections. Such long-term forecasting can't be developed quickly or easily from detailed daily or weekly sales data.

Relevance. The relevance of information is the extent to which it directly assists decision making. Managers and employees often receive information that is of little use. For example, a self-managing production team needs detailed information about production schedules, inventory levels, and promised delivery dates in order to make decisions about scheduling employees for overtime, vacations, training, and the like. This information is relevant to the provision of quality goods at the times desired by customers. These team members don't need detailed information about how the organization developed its global strategy or even what it is. However, the relevance of information can differ for the same person or function at different times. For example, summer sales estimates prepared in January may not be relevant to Mattel managers trying to project demand for toys during next December's holiday season. But summer sales figures may be very useful the following October when those same managers are trying to project next summer's demand before setting production goals.

WEB INSIGHT

Go the Web site for PerkinElmer at ***http:// www.perkinelmer.com/***. What do you think of the quality, relevance, quantity, and timeliness of information on this Web site?

Quantity. Quantity is the amount of information available when people need it. More information isn't always better. In fact, too much can lead to information overload, particularly if the extra information isn't relevant to the decisions being made.[7] Information—relevant or not—costs time and money, and information overload can reduce effectiveness. Gregory Summe is CEO of PerkinElmer, Inc., a hi-tech company that makes instruments and related products, headquartered in the Boston area. Summe often felt overloaded with the quantity of e-mail that he was getting. To make screening messages easier, he set up his Microsoft Outlook e-mail package to show just the first paragraph of any e-mail message. He stated: "The e-mail disease is that everybody tends to copy everyone. I view that as complexity and slowdown." He urged subordinates to reduce such copying by saying to them that "this distribution list looks way too long. Why copy 50 people? If that many people need to see items, I view it as an organizational problem." When he's on the road, Summe says, "I have my secretary screen my e-mail and fax me the ones I need to respond to."[8]

Timeliness. Timeliness means the receipt of needed information before it ceases to be useful for decision-making purposes. Top managers at IBM who must make strategic plans for new plants and products are interested in aggregated production and sales information on a monthly and annual basis. In contrast, production employees and managers at its Boulder, Colorado, facility need daily—and sometimes even hourly or minute-by-minute—information concerning operations to ensure that they meet their production schedules. If they received such information only quarterly or even monthly, it wouldn't be timely, would probably severely harm the quality and amount of outputs, and would likely disrupt promised deliveries to customers.

These four criteria—quality, relevance, quantity, and timeliness—are interrelated and are essential to the provision of information that serves as a value-added management resource. The following Planning and Administration Competency feature describes some of the ways that Pillsbury's new software and information system is enabling it to develop value-added information.[9] Minneapolis, Minnesota–based Pillsbury is a strategic business unit of Diageo, a multinational corporation headquartered in London that has about 17,000 employees, and annual sales of more than $6 billion. It is a major food company that sells brands such as Pillsbury, Häagen-Dazs, Green Giant, Old El Paso, Totinós, JENOs, and Progresso.[10]

PLANNING & ADMINISTRATION COMPETENCY

Pillsbury's Data Mining

As part of a group of 150 employees, Fred Hulting led the development of new software called *NetStat* for Pillsbury to handle the analysis of masses of data. With the ability to share information instantly, the company is accelerating the design of manufacturing lines from Illinois to Switzerland. Market analysts throughout this 70-country global firm are also able to dissect consumer data more efficiently and effectively—even by regional tastes. Within a couple of years, Hulting expects the software to be as common on Pillsbury desktops as photos and statues of the plump, blue-eyed doughboy, Poppin' Fresh. Hulting claims that "we'll reach everyone who sits at a desk. We will change the way people are doing their jobs."

Long considered a marketing leader, Pillsbury ships 437 million cases of food a year. It excels by having an intimate knowledge of its products and how consumers feel about them. To gain this knowledge, Pillsbury compiles masses of data. For example, it gathers customer data by encouraging consumers to call an 800 number printed on every product package. Consumer relations staff answer some 3,500 calls a day, logging the comments into a database that's organized into categories, such as "manufacturing code" and consumer likes and dislikes.

Toaster Strudel is a frozen breakfast pastry. Thousands of people called or wrote, saying, "Your fruit flavors are good, but how come you don't offer chocolate?" Analysis of those calls led to a chocolate-flavored version introduced in 2000. But from start to finish, the process took months, as marketing and R&D per-

sonnel developed reports on consumers' strudel preferences. To produce the reports, Pillsbury's staff of analysts had to interpret the data. "We had to go in and dig around," says Sally S. Shlosberg, vice president for consumer relationships. It took Shlosberg's group several days just to analyze the data to come up with the right chocolate flavor to be used. With NetStat, Pillsbury personnel are able to undertake such analyses instantly.

NetStat software resides on Pillsbury's Web server, allowing data from any worker's disk drive or machinery on the plant floor to be input. NetStat then shares the data with another software program, S-Plus, which crunches the numbers instantly and returns them to NetStat to be downloaded to the originating site. Moreover, because NetStat functions on the Web, employees lo-cated anywhere in the world—in a plant or on a sales call or in an administrative office—can log onto the program and access the data stored there.

• • •

To learn more about Pillsbury, visit the company's home page at

http://www.pillsbury.com

COMMON INFORMATION TECHNOLOGIES

2.

DESCRIBE SIX COMMON INFORMATION MANAGEMENT TECHNOLOGIES.

Computer-based information technologies continue to develop and improve at a breathtaking pace, becoming less expensive, more effective, and ever more powerful. The most conservative forecasts claim that the cost–performance relationship for these technologies as a whole will continue to improve by 15 percent or more annually into the foreseeable future.[11]

In this section, we review six interrelated information technologies being used to support a wide range of managerial functions. These technologies are the Internet, extranet, intranet, decision support systems, expert systems, and group decision support systems.

INTERNET

In previous chapters (especially Chapters 11 and 16), we discussed the dramatic impacts of the Internet on many organizational strategies, processes, and functions. Recall that the *Internet* is a loosely configured, rapidly growing web of thousands of corporate, educational, and research computer networks around the world. In essence, it is a network of networks and is often referred to as the information superhighway. The Internet is available to anyone with a computer and a modem, and by now you should be very familiar with it. Internet access usually provides four primary capabilities.[12]

- *Electronic mail* (e-mail) enables users to send, receive, and forward messages from people all over the world. Users can then reply to, save, file, and categorize received messages. E-mail makes participation in electronic conferences and discussions possible.

- *Telnet* enables users to log in to remote computers and to interact with them. Users' computers are remotely connected to computers at other locations but act as if they were directly connected.

- *File Transfer Protocol* (FTP) enables users to move files and data from one computer to another. Users can download magazines, books, documents, software, music, graphics, and much more.

- *World Wide Web* (the Web) is a set of standards and protocols that enables users to access and input text, documents, images, video, and sound on the Internet. The Web is nonlinear by design, permitting users to jump from topic to topic, document to document, and site to site. The Web requires the use of a ***browser***—an application that allows users to download documents, view them on their own computer monitors, and even make copies of them. Major browsers include Netscape Navigator, Microsoft Internet Explorer, AOL, Hotjava, iCab, Lynx, and Mosaic. The World Wide Web is quite young—the first Web browser was introduced in 1993. A browser is supported by a ***search engine***—a program that allows users to sift through millions of documents on the Internet to locate user-specified data and information. Widely used search engines include Yahoo!, Netscape, MSN, Lycos/Hotbox, GO/Infoseek, Excite, and AltaVista.

Tim Berner-Lee invented the Web and currently serves as director of the World Wide Web Consortium at the Massachusetts Institute of Technology. He comments:

> *I developed the Web with three purposes in mind. The first was to give people up-to-date information at their fingertips by giving them the personal power to hypertext. [Note: The term **hypertext** generally refers to any text that contains links to other documents—words or phrases (often in a different color)—that can be selected (clicked on) and then result in another document being retrieved and displayed.] The second goal was the realization of an information space that everyone could share and contribute their ideas and solutions to. Part three was the creation of agents to integrate the information that is out there with real life. Enormous amounts of information would no longer be lost.*[13]

The capabilities of the Internet are building blocks for the explosion in information technology applications; they can be applied anytime and anywhere. Throughout this book, we have presented examples of how organizations and individuals are developing new strategic applications through the Internet.[14]

Use of the Internet by business and the public has been explosive. Consider a few facts and near-term forecasts. Global use of the Internet increased from 40 million individuals in 1996 to about 400 million by 2001. Adults with home Internet access increased from 10 million in 1994 to about 50 million in 1999 and is forecasted at 105 million adults by 2003. Online U.S. retail commerce (e-commerce) was about $50 billion in 2000 and is projected to reach more than $180 billion by 2004. Business to business (B2B) commerce via the Internet was about $275 billion in 2000 and is projected to exceed $1 trillion ($1,000 million) by 2004.[15]

EXTRANET

An *extranet* is a wide area network (WAN) that links an organization's employees, suppliers, customers, and other key stakeholders electronically. Unlike the Internet, the general public doesn't have access to an extranet. A firm's extranet is intended to provide fast, reliable, secure, and low-cost computer-to-computer communication for a wide range of applications—everything from sales, marketing, online publishing, and customer service, to product development, directory and database services, employee communications, work-group projects, and electronic commerce.

Four technologies are essential to an extranet: the Web, the Internet, groupware applications (e.g., Lotus Notes), and firewalls. A *firewall* is a combination of computer hardware and software that controls access to and transmission of particular sets of data and information, often referred to as a *private network*. Network identification numbers and passwords are elementary components of a firewall. By setting up an extranet with a firewall, a company can allow suppliers or customers to access via the Web certain information stored on the company's internal computer-based system while maintaining the security of that information.[16]

Few companies are more sensitive to security concerns than Lockheed Martin Corporation's Tactical Aircraft Systems, which decided to bid on the contract to build a new fighter aircraft—called the Joint Strike Fighter—for the U.S. Defense Department. The company built an extranet to develop, manage, and coordinate the proposal with suppliers and partners around the world. But it had two unusual security concerns: It was dealing with classified information, and some companies that were partners for certain aspects of the proposal were competitors on other projects.

Lockheed Martin implemented a dual password system for the extranet. One log-on ID and a password were needed to get past the firewall, and a second log-on ID and a password were needed to get to the proposal information. In addition, Lockheed wanted data to be encrypted during transmission to provide additional security. So it set up a virtual private network connection to accommodate transmissions from British Aerospace and Northrop Grumman Corporation. As part of an analysis to assure itself that its internal systems wouldn't be compromised, Lockheed hired a company to try to break into them. The attempt failed. The extranet produced significant cost savings by eliminating the need to copy and distribute information involving the proposal. It also cut turnaround time by at least 90 days.[17]

INTRANET

An *intranet* is a private or semiprivate, internal network that uses the infrastructure and standards of the Internet and the Web. Access is normally limited to an organization's employees through the use of firewalls. Sensitive data and information—such as salaries, performance appraisals, and choice of fringe benefits—can be restricted to particular authorized employees. An intranet enables employees to communicate with each other and to access internal information and databases for which they have been cleared, through their desktop or laptop computers.[18] An intranet can be used to link employees at a single site and at diverse geographic locations, even throughout the world. The use of intranets is growing rapidly. The following are four common applications.

- Organizations have volumes of policies and procedures that they want their employees to be aware of and use when appropriate. Unfortunately, most of the time, a set of policies and procedures sits on a shelf somewhere and collects dust. Employees may not even know that the policies and procedures exist or how to find a current version. With an intranet, the organization merely sets up a Web server (identical to the Web servers used for the Internet), places the linked policies and procedures on it, and provides an address for the online policies and procedures to the employees.

- There are a variety of human resource management uses for intranets. An increasing number of organizations want to help employees understand their fringe benefits packages, including their 401(k) retirement plan options. The intranet often includes a program that allows employees to consider "what-if" scenarios regarding their retirement investments and other benefits.

- Employees sometimes feel that they're the last to know about a company's accomplishments or activities (perhaps learning from the local newspaper that the company won an award or hired a new vice president). With an intranet, such announcements can be made available internally first (allowing employees to know about an event before it becomes public knowledge). Information can also be linked to related documents so that employees can relate a specific news item to the larger context of an event if they so desire (by pursuing the links).

- Intranets may be used to present issues, problems, and solutions to all employees. These postings can be linked to an internal problem management system that tracks employee requests and their resolutions. By combining the intranet with the organization's e-mail system, employees can send and receive e-mail to support staff and/or use the intranet for online problem solving.[19]

Increasingly, the Internet, extranets, and intranets are becoming interrelated information technologies frequently used by employees in doing their work. Countrywide Credit Industries, the nation's largest independent residential mortgage lender and servicer, provides one such example. The following Strategic Action Competency feature focuses on the challenges faced by the company's top management in developing and implementing a coherent Internet strategy for the firm.[20] Countrywide is headquartered in Calabasas, California, and has offices throughout the United States.

Countrywide Credit Industries learned how politics can affect the introduction of an e-commerce strategy. CEO Angelo Mozilo and Stanford Kurland, who runs the Countrywide Home Loans subsidiary, saw early on that Countrywide's business was a natural for the Web (Internet): The firm was in a highly competitive industry, consumers were knowledgeable about rates and cost, and information was intensive. Countrywide had always considered itself a technological innovator. In 1996, the company set up a separate unit to offer mortgages online. Back-end support remained where it had always been in the company, but those employees were unenthusiastic about helping the new operation. Kurland states that "our first stumble was trying to set up an independent unit. There was tremendous resistance to incorporating it with the fulfillment services inside our company."

Meanwhile, a number of units in the company launched their own Web initiatives. Besides making loans, Countrywide sells insurance and loans to third parties and operates other financial businesses. Thirty different Web projects were under way in late 1998, when Countrywide folded the Internet mortgage loan–origination efforts into one company unit. Its manager quickly left. Countrywide's online business started growing faster, but it divisions remained highly protective of their own information resources and Web projects. Kurland hired David Espenschied to improve the overall usability and coordination of Countrywide's online efforts. Espenschied quickly recognized the obstacles created by multiple Web operations. He commented: "Each business division had its own Web development and quality assurance operation, and even created tools like their own calculators and credit evaluators. It was a waste of resources. And the Web site was disjointed from the standpoint of navigation."

Espenschied, who was in the corporate marketing department, didn't have the authority to eliminate the inefficiency, duplication, and confusion, so Mozilo hired a Web consulting firm, Agency.com. It developed the case for a separate electronic division to integrate Web resources. Countrywide set up the division in early 2000, despite opposition from some units. Espenschied is CEO of the new operation, which includes both Web site developers and corporate marketers. Departments come to the unit for technical work, but individual divisions still control which activities are put online. Kurland comments: "Now, every division has to comply with the same set of standards, infrastructure is centralized, and we haven't affected the entrepreneurial spirit of the various divisions.

Mozilo asserts that "the changes the Web is bringing to the financial services industry are just beginning. We haven't seen anything yet. The mortgage will become truly a commodity, almost an auction process. Those companies that resist will die."

• • •

To learn more about Countrywide Credit Industries, visit the company's home page at

http://www.countrywide.com/

DECISION SUPPORT SYSTEM

A *decision support system* (DSS) is a complex set of computer hardware and software that allows end users—usually managers and professionals—to analyze, manipulate, format, display, and output data in different ways. Such a system aids decision making because the user can pull together data from different sources, view them in formats that may differ from the original formats, and create information from them. The system allows data and information to be printed out or presented in the form of charts or graphs. The goal of a DSS is to help individuals or teams improve the quality of decision making in connection with recurring, but unstructured, tasks that require human judgment.

A DSS enables decision makers to represent aspects of the environment (e.g., customer purchasing practices) and economic developments (e.g., changes in prices and inflation) in a model and quickly to evaluate many alternatives and assumptions. Actually, you may be familiar with DSS and not even know it. If you've used an electronic spreadsheet, such as Lotus 1-2-3, Multiplan, Javelin, EXCEL, or QUATRO, you've used one form of DSS software. These electronic spreadsheets will automatically recalculate a quantity when you change the value of any of the variables in a formula.

The following DSS capabilities give the decision maker flexibility and the ability to explore various alternatives easily and quickly.[21]

- *Data collection and organization capabilities.* Current DSSs often have links to external databases and intranets, enabling rapid creation of a specialized internal database. A ***database*** is an organized collection of facts, figures, documents, and the like that have been stored for easy access and efficient use. The computerized card catalog at a library is a database. Another type of database consists of the files describing customers' buying behavior, which are kept by many retailers and credit card companies. The term *data warehouse* rather than *database* is increasingly being used.

- *"What-is?" capabilities.* The current status of projects and developments can be obtained from the DSS, external databases, or other internal databases.

- *"What-if?" capabilities.* The decision maker can propose alternative actions and test their likely consequences.

- *Goal-seeking capabilities.* Actions to be taken to achieve a goal specified by the decision maker can be provided.

- *Presentation and report generation capabilities.* The user can create various types of tables, graphs, text, pictures, art, audio, and video displays.

DSSs are being made more user-friendly through a variety of new software tools, such as ***data visualization,*** the graphical representation of a data collection, often in an interactive form. The most useful data visualization applications are interactive models and graphs that let users examine the underlying data to reorganize and compare them to create useful information. Interactive maps, 3-D models, and scatter charts enable users to observe data changes in real time.[22]

Consider how data visualization enhanced the DSS at Oshkosh B'Gosh, the maker of children's clothing, headquartered in Oshkosh, Wisconsin. Jon Dell Antonia, the company's CIO, comments: "Visualizing data really helps us pinpoint data anomalies and intuitively see what's happening in the data. Say, for example, we're getting lots of items returned from retailers. We can drill into the visual model for the data about what plants made the items that are being returned. If they primarily came from one plant, then we may have a manufacturing problem. But if the returns are coming primarily from one retailer, then we know we don't have a product quality issue, but instead might need to talk to that customer (retailer). This type of analysis used to take us days and days to do. Now it can take minutes."[23]

EXPERT SYSTEM

An ***expert system*** is a computer program based on the decision-making processes of human experts that stores, retrieves, and manipulates data, diagnoses problems, and makes limited decisions based on detailed information about a specific problem. It helps users find solutions by posing a series of questions about a specific situation and then offering solutions based on the information it receives in response. The primary characteristics of an expert system include the following.

- It is programmed to use factual knowledge, if-then rules, and specific procedures to solve certain complex problems. If-then rules are logical steps of progression toward a solution.

- It is based on the decision-making process used by effective managers or specialists when they search among possible alternatives for a "good enough" solution.

- It provides programmed explanations, so the user can follow the assumptions, line of reasoning, and process leading to the recommended alternative.[24]

An expert system has problem-solving capabilities within a specific area of knowledge, and if requested, can explain its path of reasoning to the user. An expert system is an application of ***artificial intelligence*** (AI), or the ability of a properly programmed computer system to perform functions normally associated with human intelligence, such as comprehending spoken language, making judgments, and even learning.[25]

Consider the application of an expert system by the Meiji Life Insurance Company. As one of the major life insurance companies in Japan, Meiji offers more than 30 insurance products. The company was finding it difficult to ensure that all the insurance sales staff had the expertise and the latest knowledge required to provide the best advice and service to customers. As a result, Meiji developed an expert system to help staff select the most suitable products and present the reasons for them to customers. The knowledge base in the expert system contains 47 decision tasks, and decision rules for selecting each type of insurance plan were developed. The system was designed so that, when the details of a customer are entered, the system assesses the suitability of all the plans and presents the best five in priority order. The system takes only 3 to 4 seconds to analyze the information and make the selections.[26]

GROUP DECISION SUPPORT SYSTEM

A *group decision support system* (GDSS) is a set of software, hardware, and language components that support a team of people engaged in decision making. A GDSS aims to improve the process of team decision making by removing common communication barriers, providing techniques for guiding the decision process, and systematically directing the pattern, timing, or content of the discussion. Facilitators play a crucial role, allowing the participants to concentrate on issues rather than struggling to learn how to use the technology themselves.[27]

Some executives and managers aren't highly proficient on a computer, which must be taken into account in designing and implementing GDSS systems. A requirement that all parties be highly computer proficient to use support systems, such as GDSS, is likely to minimize their use. Slowness in manipulating data and the resulting frustration may even lead to disinterest and lack of support. Even computer-literate users need time to become familiar with the GDSS. A typical GDSS room might contain a series of terminals or workstations linked by some form of computer-based network, a large main screen visible to everyone and controlled by the facilitator, a photocopying whiteboard on which to record the options as they emerge, and a three-color video projector or large monitor. Increasingly, GDSSs are being made to operate through the use of intranet technology.

The following Teamwork Competency feature reports on the development of a GDSS and related tools by MS2, Inc., that can operate "any place, anytime."[28] The firm was founded in 1998, is headquartered in Mountain View, California, and has approximately 60 employees. The firm developed MS2 Accelerate, a Web-based groupware portal for coordinating collaborative functions.

computer-related equipment and software that enables organizations to communicate effectively with their customers. It uses MS2 Accelerate to coordinate the work of product teams scattered around the world. Approximately 30 people in Aspect's marketing department and more than 100 people in its engineering department use MS2 Accelerate to collaborate on documents via a central Web site. David Puglia, Aspect's vice president of product planning comments: "Product release cycles have been shortened, quality has improved, and the work is being done by fewer people."

• • •

To learn more about MS2, Inc., visit the company's home page at

http://www.ms2.com

DESIGNING INFORMATION SYSTEMS

3.

IDENTIFY THE PRIMARY FACTORS IN THE DESIGN OF INFORMATION SYSTEMS.

Five primary interrelated factors affect the design of information systems: (1) information needs, (2) system constraints, (3) goals, (4) development stages, and (5) implementation issues.[29]

INFORMATION NEEDS

Organizations sometimes develop information systems without an adequate understanding of their true needs or the costs involved. An organization wouldn't construct a new manufacturing plant unless it was essential. Information system development should be approached in the same way. Any proposed information system needs to fit the organization's overall mission and strategy. In other words, the information system should make sense in terms of organizational strategies, financial and technical resources, customers, competitors, and desired return on investment. Questions that need to be asked include: Is the organization planning to change or add to its customer base or its goods and services? What are the current financial constraints? Do competitors use such technology? What type, quality, relevance, quantity, and timeliness of data and information do employees currently use?

The transformation of raw data into information and then into decisions is illustrated in Figure 20.2. Note that knowledge of the environment (box 1) progresses from disorganized data to refined and sharply focused information (box 6).

Figure 20.2   ***Evolution in Information Needs***

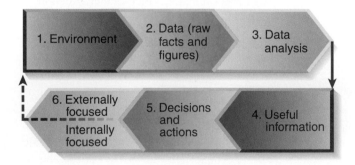

Information needs vary by organizational level, function, and individual employee—and according to the type of decision to be made. Decision-making activities occur at three levels: strategic, tactical, and operational. The characteristics of information most used by managers and employees at these levels are summarized in Table 20.1: scope, aggregation level, time horizon, currency, frequency of use, and type. Strategic decisions require information from external sources, such as customers, suppliers, and competitors. For example, should Motorola expand its manufacturing capacity in China or other countries? The information is broad in scope, highly aggregated, future oriented, and both qualitative and quantitative. In contrast, information needs for operational decisions are substantially different. Operational decisions basically require internal information (e.g., inventory levels) that is well defined, detailed, reported daily or weekly, precise, and quantitative. Tactical decisions, which are of most concern to middle managers and professionals, represent the middle ground between strategic and operational decisions. For example, if J.C. Penney were to centralize its merchandise buying decisions at its headquarters in Plano, Texas, what impact would this decision have on the jobs of the store managers who traditionally have performed this function?

T a b l e 2 0 . 1	*Information Requirements by Decision Level*		
	Requirement		
Information Characteristic	**At Operational Level**	**At Tactical Level**	**At Strategic Level**
Scope	Narrow, well defined		Broadly defined
Aggregation level	Detailed		Composite
Time horizon	Historical		Future-oriented
Currency	Recent		Long-term
Frequency of use	Continuous		Periodic
Type	Quantitative		Qualitative and quantitative

SYSTEM CONSTRAINTS

System constraints are the limitations on the discretion available to decision makers and may be internally or externally imposed. External constraints vary from organization to organization and may include government regulations, supplier requirements, global competitors, and customer demands. For example, government regulations require automobile manufacturers to produce cars with safety features such as seatbelts that protect passengers, exhaust systems that emit limited amounts of certain chemicals, and engines that meet fuel efficiency standards.

Internal constraints are created by the organization itself. Probably the most common internal constraint on the development of an information system is cost. The best available information technology may be very costly. That's true even though the price–performance relationships for information technologies continue to improve dramatically year by year. Another internal constraint is lack of support from employees and top management. Without their support, or with only their limited support, an information system isn't likely to be successful.

GOALS

Goals should focus on the purposes that the information will serve, who will use it, and how it will be used. One goal for most expert systems is for them to serve as investigative tools, that is, for answering "what-if" questions such as: What would happen if Pizza Hut relied on more overtime to meet an increase in demand rather than adding more employees? Goals also should be established for the number and type of operating personnel and the system's cost. Setting goals provides the direction for developing and implementing the information system.

DEVELOPMENT STAGES

An information system may be created in various ways. However, the basic underlying development process generally is the same.[30] Figure 20.3 shows the four stages of information systems development. The dashed arrows indicate feedback loops, illustrating that the process is never cut and dried.

Figure 20.3 **Stages in Information Systems Development**

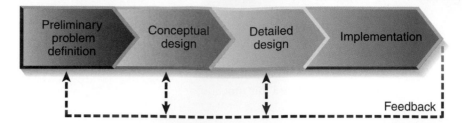

Preliminary Problem Definition. A team of information users, with technical support personnel, may be given the tasks of determining information needs, rough cost estimates, constraints, and goals.

Conceptual Design. The conceptual design stage should be primarily user-led, although system development experts should act as resource people for the team. During this stage, information generated in the preliminary problem definition stage is used to develop alternative designs. They are evaluated in terms of how well they satisfy organizational needs and goals. More accurate cost estimates are obtained at this stage. This evaluation usually leads to preliminary selection of specific system characteristics for further review. However, it also my lead back to the problem definition stage.

Detailed Design. During the detailed design stage, performance specifications are established. The team selects or develops hardware and software components. Information system experts are heavily involved, mapping information flows, preparing specialized programs, and defining databases. They also create a prototype of the information system and evaluate, test, refine, and reevaluate it until the stated requirements are satisfied. Users are still involved, but their role is primarily advisory at this stage. If problems arise, returning to the conceptual design stage or even to a reanalysis of the problem definition may be necessary.

Testing. During the final stage, models of information systems are connected and users begin testing the system. As operational problems are identified and corrected, one module after another is added. Eventually, the entire system is assembled and tested for all conceivable types of errors. Corrections continue to be made by the team until the information system's performance satisfies all the performance criteria. At that point, the information system is ready to be phased into the organization for full-time use.

EFFECTIVE IMPLEMENTATION

Although each information system has unique characteristics, seven main factors commonly influence the effective implementation of information systems. Figure 20.4 shows these system building blocks, which emerge during the initial stages of system design and development, continue through testing, and then become important to everyday operations.[31] Information system users should be involved in the design process. Their input gives system designers an accurate picture of current work flows, costs, and time requirements for various functions. This input helps in the identification of current operational inefficiencies that the new system should correct. The effective implementation of new information systems usually requires strong, visible support from management. Like any major organizational change effort, information technology applications must involve managers in order to succeed. A thorough evaluation of time and cost requirements is necessary. The development of new information systems usually requires more time and costs than originally anticipated.

Any significant new technology normally should be introduced in phases. A new information system, such as PeopleSoft, can't just be turned on and the old system abandoned at the same time. Too many things can and will go wrong: The new system doesn't work as expected, it generates bad information, few employees know how to use it, and so on. When the system is implemented in phases, problems owing to

7. System backup

4. Phased implementation

5. Thorough testing

6. Training and documentation

1. User information

2. Top-management support

3. Time and cost evaluation

design glitches and unforeseen events can be managed. Testing of both hardware and software is needed. Testing should be performed on individual modules, on sets of modules as the system is assembled, and then on the entire system before it becomes fully operational. The testing process should anticipate probable errors as well as those that aren't likely to occur. The introduction of new technologies requires training of users and adequate documentation of operational procedures. An information system is of little value if no one knows how to use it properly.

Computer systems are notorious for developing problems, especially software problems, at the wrong time. If users are too dependent on a single information system, they may believe that the quicker the fix, the better. Quick system fixes may overlook real problems that lead to other problems. A backup procedure—or even access to a backup computer system—will give analysts time to track down such problems, carefully evaluate them, and properly correct them. This approach can't ensure a problem-free future, but it does encourage solutions that are less likely to create additional problems.

In global firms, system implementation needs to account for cultural and political considerations in various countries. Consider the sensitivity of DHL Worldwide Express's management in the development and implementation of its Web site. A leading international document and package delivery company, DHL operates in 233 countries and territories. It found that cultural differences can turn seemingly routine technology-building chores into difficult decisions. For instance, in choosing icons for Web pages, the "A OK" sign in the United States is a sign of approval but tantamount to an obscene gesture in Australia. And color schemes can prove offensive if not tailored to a country because in various cultures blue, white, red, and yellow are regarded as colors of death and mourning. DHL's Web site reflects this knowledge.

On DHL's corporate Web site, shippers can check pages that present an array of relevant information on all countries being shipped to. As a gesture of DHL's efforts to be sensitive to various countries, the company includes the following statement on its "Visit a Country" page, which includes links to the DHL services in each country served:

> *DHL encourages the countries within the Network to establish their own Web sites. These sites offer you more detailed information, and localized services that are not available on the corporate site often in the local language [as well as English]. Use the list below to visit a DHL country Web site.*[32]

The corporate Web site includes various categories of information for each country served, including drop-off locations, country DHL office locations, import guidelines, and country demographics.

4.

A s computer-based information technologies become pervasive, concern with their ethical—and unethical or criminal—use has become more important in the United States, Canada, and other countries characterized as information societies.

COMPUTER ETHICS

Computer ethics is concerned with the nature and social impact of information technologies and the formulation of policies for their appropriate use.[33] An increasing number of individuals and organizations are concerned with computer ethics. The ethical issues surrounding computers arise from their unique technological characteristics, including the following.

- Computers make mistakes that no human being would make.

- Computers communicate over great distances at high speed and low cost.

- Computers have huge capacities to store, copy, erase, retrieve, transmit, and manipulate information quickly and economically.

- Computers have the effect of radically distancing (depersonalizing) originators, users, and subjects of programs and data from each other.

- Computers may collect and store data for one purpose that can easily be used for another purpose and be kept for long periods of time.[34]

The Computer Ethics Institute, a professional association headquartered in Washington, D.C., was formed because of the growing concerns with the ethical use of computer technology. It has issued a "ten commandments" of computer ethics, which are listed in Table 20.2.[35] The commandments provide an ethical code of conduct for guidance in situations that may not be covered by law.

Table 20.2	**Ten Commandments of Computer Ethics**

1. Thou shalt not use a computer to harm other people.
2. Thou shalt not interfere with other people's computer work.
3. Thou shalt not snoop around in other people's files.
4. Thou shalt not use a computer to steal.
5. Thou shalt not use a computer to bear false witness.
6. Thou shalt not copy or use proprietary software for which you have not paid.
7. Thou shalt not use other people's computer resources without authorization or proper compensation.
8. Thou shalt not appropriate other people's intellectual output.
9. Thou shalt think about the social consequences of the program you are writing or the system you design.
10. Thou shalt use a computer in ways that show consideration and respect for your fellow humans.

The following Self-Management Competency feature gives you an opportunity to assess and develop further your understanding of computer ethics.[36] Recall that the self-management competency includes (1) acceptance of responsibility for continuous self-development and learning, (2) willingness to learn and relearn continually, as changed situations call for new skills and perspectives, and (3) application of clear personal standards of integrity and ethical conduct.

INSTRUCTIONS

Twenty statements appear in this survey. You should evaluate each statement by using the following 5-point scale.

1	2	3	4	5
True	Somewhat True	Neither True nor False	Somewhat False	False

If you think that a statement is *true,* record a 1 next to it. If you think that a statement is *neither true nor false,* place a 3 next to it, and so on. Don't skip any statement.

_____ 1. The courts have provided clear guidance on who should have access to electronic mail at work.

_____ 2. Employees are usually informed by employers if their voice mail is going to be monitored.

_____ 3. Medical records are not available to employers.

_____ 4. Most organizations have clear written policies and procedures regarding the use of electronic mail.

_____ 5. The confidentiality of faxes is generally well maintained.

_____ 6. Nothing inherent in computer technology raises unique ethical questions.

_____ 7. Public perceptions of computers and computer professionals generally have been good.

_____ 8. Computer professionals have a level of influence that is matched by equivalent levels of organizational controls and professional association guidance.

_____ 9. The best way to deter unethical behavior in the use of computers is through legal deterrents and remedies.

_____ 10. The best way to deter unethical behavior in the use of computers is through professional codes of conduct.

_____ 11. The majority of computer science graduates have had at least one course in computer ethics by the time they graduate.

_____ 12. There are many controls over what information is kept on private citizens, who keeps it, and who can access it.

_____ 13. The majority of businesses in the United States have well-documented policies regarding what employee information is kept in personnel databases and who has access to it.

_____ 14. Computerized medical records pose no greater danger to privacy and potential for misuse than do paper records.

_____ 15. Electronic bulletin boards are fairly well "policed" and do not contain potentially harmful information.

_____ 16. The majority of computer crimes are reported, and the perpetrators are successfully prosecuted.

_____ 17. Computer abuse, such as gaining unauthorized access to a system or placing a virus or other potentially damaging program in a computer, is a minor problem.

_____ 18. Software theft, including unauthorized copying of software, is clearly a problem, but monetary losses are not yet significant.

_____ 19. Although failures of computer systems have been reported in the media, none have resulted in serious injury or significant property loss.

_____ 20. Because computer ethics is a relatively new application of older ethical concepts to new technology, there is little understanding about what can and should be done.

SCORING

Sum the point values for statements 1–20. The total points may range from 20 to 100. Most experts on computer ethics would consider a perfect score to be 100; that is, all statements are considered to be *false.*

• • •

To learn more about computer ethics, visit the home page of the Computer Ethics Institute at

http://www.brook.edu/ITS/CEI/CEI_HP.HTM

PRIVACY ISSUES

The amount and types of information available about most individuals in the United States and Canada to just about any business (or individual in that business) or government agency is astounding. Some of this information originates with individuals when they borrow money, participate in a government program, or purchase goods with a credit card. Consumers and borrowers routinely give information voluntarily to retailers and creditors so that they can purchase goods on credit.[37] At least once a month, banks, retailers, credit card companies, and mail-order houses send computer tapes or other electronic files detailing their customers' purchases and payment activities to credit bureaus.

The three large credit rating companies—TRW, Trans Union, and Equifax—maintain credit information on more than 170 million people in the United States. This information is accessible in a matter of seconds to merchants, clerks, and, in essence, just about anyone. A group of newspaper journalists, who acquired and published the credit rating of Dan Quayle, a former U.S. vice president, illustrates this situation. In addition to credit ratings, a large amount of information on nearly everyone in the United States—ranging from medical histories and insurance information to buying habits—is stored in computer-readable form and widely disseminated among credit bureaus, resellers of data purchased from bureaus, and many businesses.[38] The information that used to be inaccessible or very difficult to obtain is now instantly available for use by almost anyone. Protection of privacy through the legal system, organizational and managerial policies and practices, self-regulation through professional and trade associations, and consumer groups hasn't caught up with technological developments.

WEB INSIGHT

Go to the Web site for BBB OnLine at *http://www.bbbonline.org/*. This site is a subsidiary of the Council of Better Business Bureaus. Click "The Code." Describe the six principles in the code of online business practices.

One step in the direction of trying to reestablish online "rights of privacy" was taken in 2000 by the Council of Better Business Bureaus, headquartered in Arlington, Virginia. One component of their initiative is the "Privacy Seal Program," which participating and approved companies can use and display on their Web sites. For consumers, the program is designed to help Internet users identify companies that stand behind their privacy policies and have met the program requirements of notice, choice, access, and security in the use of personally identifiable information. Among other things, the program requires a site to disclose how it intends to use the information being collected, mandates that consumers be allowed to opt out of data collection, and requires site operators to obtain parental permission to collect data on children.[39]

Some critics of the online invasion of privacy crisis assert that such voluntary industry efforts are inadequate. They contend that more governmental regulation and enforcement of privacy protections are needed for both consumers and employees.[40]

CHAPTER SUMMARY

In this chapter, we surveyed several important issues and capabilities related to the use and management of information technologies (ITs). Through the Internet and extranets, ITs have a profound impact on providing "anytime/anyplace" links among employees, suppliers, customers, government agencies, and the public. Some experts suggest that new information technologies are having as dramatic an impact on employees and organizations as the Industrial Revolution more than a hundred years ago had on transforming agriculturally based economies and cultures to industrial and urban economies and cultures.

1. EXPLAIN THE ROLE OF INFORMATION AS A MANAGEMENT RESOURCE.

Organizations are using information technologies and systems as strategic assets. Information is a value-added resource derived by transforming data to make them useful. Knowledge is used by individuals to create, store, share, and apply information. Four interrelated criteria may be used to assess the value of information: quality, relevance, quantity, and timeliness.

2. DESCRIBE SIX COMMON INFORMATION MANAGEMENT TECHNOLOGIES.

Information management technologies continue to become more efficient, effective, and powerful. Through real-time communications networks, the basic managerial functions of planning, organizing, leading, and controlling are dramatically changing, rapidly improving, and quickly becoming more closely linked. Six important, interrelated information technologies are the Internet, extranet, intranet, decision support systems, expert systems, and group decision support systems.

3. IDENTIFY THE PRIMARY FACTORS IN THE DESIGN OF INFORMATION SYSTEMS.

The design of systems should begin with a determination of information needs. This assessment should be linked to the organization's market-related goals and strategies. System constraints, which are the internal and external limitations on decision-making discretion, should be identified and evaluated. Within these constraints, goals for the information system need to be formulated. The development stages for the system should be clearly specified. These stages include preliminary problem definition (which normally reflects the information needs, system constraints, and system goals), conceptual design, detailed design, testing, and implementation.

4. **STATE THE ETHICAL ISSUES INVOLVED IN INFORMATION TECHNOLOGIES.**

The unethical and criminal uses of information technologies are of increasing concern in the United States, Canada, and other information-dependent societies. Ethical issues arise from the unique characteristics of computers and related information technologies. The "ten commandments" of computer ethics reflect the need for radically different attitudes and actions on the part of many individuals and the media toward computer crime and the unethical use of computer-based technologies. Privacy issues also are central to computer ethics. The private and government sectors haven't yet come up with sufficient controls to stem the current wide-open access to and use of all types of data and information about individuals.

KEY TERMS

Artificial intelligence, p. 550
Browser, p. 546
Computer ethics, p. 556
Data, p. 543
Data visualization, p. 550
Database, p. 550

Decision support system, p. 549
Expert system, p. 550
Firewall, p. 547
Group decision support system, p. 551
Hypertext, p. 547
Information, p. 543

Information technologies, p. 542
Intranet, p. 548
Search engine, p. 546
System constraints, p. 553

QUESTIONS FOR DISCUSSION AND COMPETENCY DEVELOPMENT

1. Recall the Preview feature on the use of new wireless technology by the Avis Rental Car Company. What applications of wireless technology have you observed and experienced? How would you evaluate the effectiveness of those uses?

2. Computer-based information technologies are reducing the number of management levels in many organizations. Why?

3. How effective is your college's student registration system in terms of quality, relevance, quantity, and timeliness?

4. Identify three ways that your life is affected by the Internet.

5. Identify a decision that you have recently made (or are making). What information technologies did you use or might you use to make this decision?

6. What are three differences between intranets and expert systems?

7. Has your sense of "right to privacy" been reduced or violated by computer-based information technologies? Explain.

8. **Competency Development: Strategic Action.** Covisint is a business to business (B2B) online purchasing alliance owned by Ford, GM, DaimlerChrysler, Nissan, and Renault. These automakers expect to achieve cost reductions through greater pricing leverage over an estimated 50,000 suppliers. Go to Covisint's home page at ***http://www.covisint.com/***. Click "FAQ" (frequently asked questions). Identify three of those questions of interest to you and click each of them. What did you learn?

9. **Competency Development: Communication.** GroupVine is a Web site that fosters "public discussions" or "invitational discussions." "Public discussions" are open and available to anyone and may be created by anyone. "Invitational discussions" are for members only. In both categories, users may view and respond on the board via PCs and wireless technologies. GroupVine is free to users. Go to GroupVine at ***http://www.groupvine.com***. Click "discussions" and then click "public discussions." Click the "computers and Internet" discussion category, which includes a number of public discussions. Click one of them. What types of information, including questions, did it contain?

A B2B Relationship

Business-to-business (B2B) e-commerce isn't new to Buffalo Hospital Supply Company. For more than a decade, the Buffalo, N.Y.–based distributor has been using electronic data interchange (EDI) to buy and then sell its line of health-care products and equipment, primarily to hospitals and long-term-care nursing homes in New York and Pennsylvania. The company has taken a major step onto the Internet by making its product catalog available online via Medibuy.com, Inc., a San Diego–based B2B health-care exchange.

Gary Skura, CEO of Buffalo Hospital Supply, comments: "What Medibuy allows us to do is put our catalog on their site for anybody to use. It tears down the geographic barriers and makes us much more of a global company. It also lets us branch out to sell beyond hospitals and nursing homes."

Buffalo Hospital Supply didn't spend any money on technology or professional services to begin selling its products on the Internet. Medibuy.com has done all the systems integration work, including customizing contract pricing data for Buffalo's various customers. Before it signed on with Medibuy.com, Buffalo Hospital Supply had been developing its own Web site. But it dropped the project in favor of moving to the Internet through the services of Medibuy.com.

The company's customers can access real-time availability and shipping information because the Medibuy.com site connects customers to the supplier's in-house ordering system. Robert Witt, chief technology officer at Medibuy.com, comments: "We have seamless integration, so the buyer doesn't feel they have left the Medibuy site, but they're actually using the [supplier's] price files. The advantage of that is the likelihood of much higher accuracy."

Medibuy.com does most of the systems integration work necessary to hook up buyers and suppliers to the Web site. Witt states: "We have a very robust implementation methodology, under which we send in an integration manager with a series of tools that identifies which suppliers a hospital needs to deal with to conduct business." Because it has this information, Medibuy.com also knows what kind of traffic volumes to anticipate, and that helps with its own planning of network and Web site capacity.

Medibuy.com furnishes buyers with detailed monthly reports of all their purchasing activities. This information helps pinpoint high-volume suppliers, which hospitals can then target as candidates for contract renegotiation. Witt also notes that hospitals will now be able to reduce the number of times their employees go off prenegotiated contracts to purchase the same items. Thus, through Medibuy.com, hospitals can aggregate better their purchases and negotiate better contracts.

Medibuy.com's pricing model allows free use by buyers, whereas suppliers such as Buffalo Hospital Supply pay a transaction fee of less than 1 percent of the total for each order that comes in over the exchange. One of the biggest ways a supplier can recoup these costs is in the significant savings achieved by processing orders electronically, rather than by phone or fax.

But pricing is also where things can get sticky. Skura, for example, says that he's willing to pay a fee for new business that comes in via the Web site but that he doesn't want to pay for Web-based orders from existing customers who now use EDI (about 60 percent of Buffalo's incoming orders) or do business with the company manually. "I'm not keen on giving [Medibuy.com] money for that," Skura says. "We're still negotiating."[41]

Questions

1. What are three benefits to Buffalo Hospital Supply Company, Medibuy.com, and hospitals in this B2B relationship?

2. What are three potential long-term risks to Buffalo Hospital Supply Company in this B2B relationship?

3. What are three potential long-term risks to Medibuy.com in this B2B relationship?

To learn more about Medibuy.com, visit the company's home page at *http://medibuy.com/.*

Archway Cookies

When the founders of Archway Cookies, Harold and Ruth Swanson, baked their first batch of soft oatmeal cookies in 1936, they had no idea that their efforts would one day lead to their becoming the third largest cookie producer in the United States. Headquartered in Battle Creek, Michigan, Archway produces more than 1 billion cookies annually at its two company-owned and four licensed bakeries in the United States and Canada.

As the homestyle cookie maker has grown, so too has its need for a sophisticated management information system. Initially, the firm relied on manual paper and pencil record keeping and later on three distinct software packages for its general ledger, inventory, and payables/receivables. These efforts were not integrated and information sharing was nonexistent. As a result, management lacked precise cost information for use in budgeting and control decisions. Moreover, the marketing function was left entirely on its own.

Archway's management realized that it needed one database that would provide timely and accurate information, on which it could base business and management decisions. Management also realized that individuals at different levels within the organization needed access to different types of information. For example, top management needed general information for making strategic decisions, whereas lower-level managers required specific information about production in real time for measurement and control purposes. These and similar concerns led management to develop and install a new, comprehensive MIS.

As soon as the new management information system was implemented, the company began to realize a number of benefits. For example, the MIS provided managers with access to all kinds of needed information in a timely manner. It also reduced operating costs through increased efficiency, including tighter inventory and production controls, which resulted in the system soon paying for itself. Finally, the system produced various financial reports, enabling management to measure results against goals and forecasts.

As with implementation of any significant organizational change, the new system at Archway initially met with some resistance and unanticipated problems had to be addressed. But an integrated MIS is there to stay. "To provide the best Home Style baked products from our family to yours," as promised in its mission statement, Archway will continue to embrace and utilize the most relevant MIS technologies available.

Questions

1. What challenges face organizations such as Archway Cookies when they first implement a management information system?

2. What two concerns about management information systems are highlighted in the Archway video that managers should consider?

To learn more about Archway Cookies, visit the company's home page at *http://www.archwaycookies.com*.

Endnotes

CHAPTER 1

[1] Adapted from R. D. Hof, H. Green, and D. Brady. Suddenly, Amazon's books look better. *Business Week,* February 21, 2000, pp. 78–84; J. Quittner. An eye on the future: Jeff Bezos merely wants Amazon.com to be earth's biggest seller of everything. *Time,* December 27, 1999, pp. 56–68; P. Sellers. Bezos on Buffett: Skeptical of Internet mania, the founder and CEO of Amazon.com is spreading the gospel according to Buffett. *Fortune,* November 22, 1999, pp. 220–222; T. Corrigan. The quintessential figure of electronic commerce. *Financial Times,* December 7, 1999, pp. 8–9.

[2] Our definition of competencies is adapted from the definition by M. W. McCall, Jr. *High Flyers: Developing the Next Generation of Leaders.* Boston: Harvard Business School Press, 1998; the Career Planning Competency Model developed by Bowling Green State University, as described in its Web site http://www.bgsu.edu (February 8, 2000).

[3] The lists incorporate the competencies identified by others, including R. L. Davis. *Successful Manager's Handbook.* Minneapolis: Personnel Decisions, 1992; B. Howland. *The Prospector.* Greensboro, N.C.: Center for Creative Leadership, 1999; personal conversations with J. Weekley, Senior Vice President, Paragon, Inc., Dallas, Texas, January 2000.

[4] M. Halkias. Penney moves to centralize function of 1,150 stores. *Dallas Morning News,* January 15, 2000, pp. 15D, 16D.

[5] Personal conversation with L. A. Dimpfel, Vice President, Worldwide Olympic Technology Systems, IBM, Dallas, Texas, January 16, 2000.

[6] The top apparel brands in the U.S. *Women's Wear Daily,* January 24, 2000, pp. 15–25.

[7] G. Colvin. How to be a great CEO. *Fortune,* May 24, 1999, pp. 104–126.

[8] P. Moser. The McDonald's mystique. *Fortune,* July 4, 1988, pp. 112–116.

[9] S. Greco. There's no place like in-house. *Inc.,* February 1999, p. 38.

[10] L. Buchanan. The taming of the crew. *Inc.,* August 1999, pp. 28–40.

[11] G. Kinkead. In the future people like me will go to jail. *Fortune,* May 24, 1999, pp. 190–200.

[12] A. M. Francesco and B. A. Gold. *International Organizational Behavior.* Upper Saddle River, N.J.: Prentice Hall, 1998, p. 48.

[13] Adapted from J. R. Johnson. Rising through the ranks. *Industrial Distribution,* January 1999, pp. 46–49; Company Secrets. *Inc. Tech.,* 1, 1999, p. 40; D. Fenn. Personnel best. *Inc.,* February 2000, pp. 75–85.

[14] J. P. Briscoe and D. T. Hall. Grooming and picking: Leaders using competency frameworks: Do they work? *Organizational Dynamics,* autumn 1999, pp. 37–52; B. L. Kedia and A. Mukherji. Global managers: Developing a mindset for global competitiveness. *Journal of World Business,* 34, 1999, pp. 230–251.

[15] S. K. Hoon-Halbauer. Managing relationships within Sino-foreign joint ventures. *Journal of World Business,* 34, 1999, pp. 344–370.

[16] J. P. Walsh, E. Wang, and K. R. Xin. Same bed, different dreams: Working relationships in Sino American joint ventures. *Journal of World Business,* 34, 1999, pp. 69–93.

[17] Personal conversation with C. Koski, Global Marketing Manager, Celanese Ltd., Dallas, Texas, February 2000.

[18] Adapted from T. Petzinger. In search of the new world of work. *Fast Company,* April 1999, pp. 214–224; http://www.cemex.com.

[19] M. Buckingham and C. Coffman. *First, Break All the Rules.* New York: Simon and Schuster, 1999.

[20] J. R. Katzenbach and J. Santamaria. Firing up the front line. *Harvard Business Review,* May–June 1999, pp. 107–115; D. I. Jung and B. J. Avolio. Effects of leadership style and followers cultural orientation on performance in group and individual task conditions. *Academy of Management Journal,* 42, 1999, pp. 208–218; C. E. Nicholls, H. W. Lane, and M. B. Brechu. Taking self-managed teams to Mexico. *Academy of Management Executive,* 13(3), 1999, pp. 15–25.

[21] Adapted from L. L. Thompson. *Making The Team: A Guide for Managers.* Upper Saddle River, N.J.: Prentice Hall, 2000, p. 56. Also see M. K. DeVries. High-performance teams: Lessons from the Pygmies. *Organizational Dynamics,* winter 1999, pp. 66–77.

[22] P. Labarre. What's new, what's hot. *Fast Company,* January 1999, p. 78.

[23] J. A. Petrick, R. F. Scherer, J. D. Brodzinski, J. F. Quinn, and M. F. Ainina. Global leadership skills and reputational capital: Intangible resources for sustainable competitive advantage. *Academy of Management Executive,* 13(1), 1999, pp. 58–70.

[24] E. Weldon and W. Vanhonacker. Operating a foreign-invested enterprise in China: Challenges for managers and management researchers. *Journal of World Business,* 34, 1999, pp. 94–107.

[25] Adapted from http://www.thecoca-colacompany.com/news and H. Unger. Coke cutbacks show company went down wrong path. *Dallas Morning News,* January 30, 2000, p. 6H. Also see H. Thomas, T. Pollock and P. Gorman. Global strategic analyses: Frameworks and approaches. *Academy of Management Executive,* 13(1), 1999, pp. 70–83; R. D. Ireland and M. A. Hitt. Achieving and maintaining strategic competitiveness in the 21st century: The role of strategic leadership. *Academy of Management Executive,* 13(1), 1999, pp. 43–57.

[26] M. Waldrop. The trillion-dollar vision of Dee Hock. *Fast Company,* October/November 1996, pp. 75–86.

[27] S. W. Wellington. *Women of Color in Corporate Management: Opportunities and Barriers.* New York: Catalyst, 1999;

S. Branch. MBAs are hot again—and they know it. *Fortune,* April 14, 1997, pp. 155–157.

28 E. Van Velsor and J. B. Leslie. Why executives derail: Perspectives across time and cultures. *Academy of Management Executive,* 9(1), 1995, pp. 62–72; M. McCall. *High Flyers: Developing the Next Generation of Leaders.* Boston: Harvard Business School Press, 1998; R. Charan and G. Colvin. Why CEOs fail. *Fortune,* June 21, 1999, pp. 69–78.

29 M. V. Uzumeri. ISO 9000 and other metastandards: Principles of management practice? *Academy of Management Executive,* 11(1), 1997, pp. 21–36.

30 A. Grove. *Only the Paranoid Will Survive.* New York: Bantum, 1999.

31 A. Vining and S. Globerman. A conceptual framework for understanding the outsourcing decision. *European Management Journal,* 17(6), 1999, pp. 645–649; B. S. Klass, J. McClendon, and T. Gainey. HR outsourcing and its impact. *Personnel Psychology,* 52(1), 1999, pp. 113–129.

32 R. A. Pitts and D. Lei. *Strategic Management: Building and Sustaining Competitive Advantage.* Cincinnati: South-Western, 2000, pp. 342–346.

33 D. Lei, J. W. Slocum, Jr., and R. A. Pitts. Designing organizations for competitive advantage. *Organizational Dynamics,* winter 1999, pp. 24–38; T. K. Das and B. Teng. Managing risks of strategic alliances. *Academy of Management Executive,* 13(4), 1999, pp. 50–62.

34 http://www.ameristat.org (February 10, 2000).

35 T. Simons, L. H. Pelled, and K. A. Smith. Making use of difference: Diversity, debate, and decision comprehensiveness in top management teams. *Academy of Management Journal,* 42, 1999, pp. 662–674.

36 P. R. Gamble and D. A. Gibson. Executive value and decision-making: The relationship of culture and information flows. *Journal of Management Studies,* 36, 1999, pp. 217–219; C. M. Pearson and J. Chong. Contributions of job content and social information on organizational commitment and job satisfaction. *Journal of Occupational and Organizational Psychology,* 70, 1997, pp. 357–375.

37 S. W. Wellington. *Women of Color in Corporate Management.* New York: Catalyst, 1999, pp. 69–71.

38 P. F. Drucker. Knowledge-worker productivity: The biggest challenge. *California Management Review,* winter, 41(2), 1999, pp. 79–80; P. Simonsen. Do your managers have the right stuff? *Workforce,* August 1999, 78(8), 47–51.

39 N. B. Kurland and D. E. Bailey. Telework: The advantages and challenges of working here, there, anywhere, and anytime. *Organizational Dynamics,* autumn 1999, pp. 53–68.

40 A. Lipparini and L. Fratocchi. The capabilities of the transnational firm: Accessing knowledge and leveraging interfirm relationships. *European Management Journal,* 17(6), 1999, pp. 655–667.

41 J. Selmer. Effects of coping strategies on sociocultural and psychological adjustment of Western expatriate managers. *Journal of World Business,* 34, 1999, pp. 41–51; A. Haasen.

M-Class: The making of the new Daimler-Benz. *Organizational Dynamics,* spring 1999, pp. 74–78.

CHAPTER 2

1 Adapted from T. Fujimoto. *The Evolution of a Manufacturing System at Toyota.* New York: Oxford University Press, 2000; P. S. Adler, B. Goldoftas, and D. I. Levine. Flexibility versus efficiency: A case study of model changeovers in the Toyota production system. *Organization Science,* 10(1), 1999, pp. 43–68; R. DeMeis, J. Gonzalez, J. Lewis, and C. J. Murray, A parade of new technology. *Design News,* October 4, 1999, pp. 80–85.

2 M. Weber. *The Theory of Social and Economic Organization,* trans. by M. A. Henderson and T. Parsons. New York: Free Press, 1947.

3 B. O'Reilly. The power merchant. *Fortune,* April 17, 2000, pp. 148ff.

4 B. O'Reilly. They've got mail. *Fortune,* February 7, 2000, pp. 101–112; B. Leonard. A neatly wrapped welfare-to-work package. *HR Magazine,* 44, 1999, pp. 35–37; Greenwald, J. Hauling UPS's freight. *Time,* January 29, 1999, p. 59.

5 W. McKinley, M. A. Mone, and G. Moon. Determinants and development of schools in organization theory. *Academy of Management Review,* 24, 1999, pp. 634–648.

6 Interview with C. Fitzgerald, Director, Wireless Internet, Ericsson Inc., April 2000, Dallas, Texas. Also see L. M. Andersson and C. M. Pearson. Tit for tat? The spiraling effect of incivility in the workplace. *Academy of Management Review,* 24, 1999, pp. 452–471.

7 P. S. Adler. Building better bureaucracies. *Academy of Management Executive,* 13(4), 1999, 36–49; A. H. Van de Ven, D. E. Polley, R. Garud, and S. Venkataraman. *The Innovation Journey.* New York: Oxford University Press, 1999.

8 F. W. Taylor. *Scientific Management.* New York: Harper & Row, 1947, pp. 66–71.

9 P. Evans and T. S. Wurster. *Blown to Bits: How the Economics of Information Systems Transforms Strategy.* Boston: Harvard Business School Press, 2000.

10 L. J. Krajewski and L. P. Ritzman. *Operations Management: Strategy and Analysis,* 5th ed. Reading, Mass.: Addison-Wesley, 1997.

11 H. Fayol. *General and Industrial Management.* London: Pitman & Sons, 1949.

12 M. P. Follett. *Prophet of Management.* Boston: Harvard Business School Press, 1995.

13 Whole Foods Market. *Corporate Meetings and Incentives,* 18(6), 1999, pp. 14–18; J. Reed and R. Cunningham. *Team Member General Information Guidebook.* Austin, Tex.: Whole Foods Market, 1998; J. B. Raskin. Does Whole Foods Market lack moral fiber? *Business and Society Review,* 82, summer 1992, pp. 26–30.

14 C. Barnard. *The Functions of the Executive.* Cambridge, MA: Harvard University Press, 1938.

15 E. Mayo. *The Social Problems of an Industrial Civilization.* Boston: Harvard Business School, 1945; E. S. O'Connor. The

politics of management thought: A case study of the Harvard Business School and the human relations school. *Academy of Management Review,* 24, 1999, pp. 117–131.

[16] L. Thompson. *Making the Team,* Upper Saddle River, N.J.: Prentice Hall, 2000; B. L. Kirkman and B. Rosen. Powering up teams. *Organizational Dynamics,* winter 2000, pp. 67–79.

[17] Adapted from R. Ferner. Share it all with employees, *Inc. Tech,* 1, 1999, p. 48; B. P. Sunoo. Campbell's global growth. *Workforce,* 77(4), 1998, pp. 27–29.

[18] S. Brickson. The impact of identity orientation on individual and organizational outcomes in demographically diverse settings. *Academy of Management Review,* 25(1), 2000, pp. 82–101.

[19] R. D. Klassen and D. C. Whybark. The impact of environmental technologies on manufacturing performance. *Academy of Management Journal,* 42, 1999, pp. 599–615.

[20] Adapted from S. F. Brown. Wrestling new wealth from the supply chain. *Fortune,* November 9, 1998, pp. 204L–204P; S. Avery. Use of online tools helps to leverage buying power. *Purchasing,* April 22, 1999, pp. 18–19; Online purchasing frees buyers for strategic work. *Purchasing,* December 16, 1999, pp. 194–195.

[21] C. Nielson. *Quantitative Analysis for Marketing Decision Making: Bringing Essential Concepts into the Classroom.* Cincinnati: South-Western, 1997.

[22] P. C. Nutt. Surprising but true: Half the decisions in organizations fail. *Academy of Management Executive,* 13(4), 1999, pp. 75–90; M. T. Frohlich and J. R. Dixon. Information systems adaptation and the successful implementation of advanced manufacturing technologies. *Decision Sciences,* 30, 1999, pp. 921–959; B. B. Flynn and E. J. Flynn. Information-processing alternatives for coping with manufacturing environment complexity. *Decision Sciences,* 30, 1999, pp. 1021–1052.

[23] J. Lee and D. Miller. Strategy, environment and performance in two technological contexts: Contingency theory in Korea. *Organization Studies,* 17(5), 1996, pp. 729–751.

[24] L. L. Berry. *The Soul of Service.* New York: Free Press, 1999.

[25] M. Walton. *The Deming Method.* New York: Dodd Mead, 1986.

[26] T. E. Vollmann, W. L. Berry, and D. C. Wybark. *Manufacturing Planning and Control.* Burr Ridge, IL: Irwin, 1997.

[27] K. Seiders and L. L. Berry. Service fairness: What it is and why it matters. *Academy of Management Executive,* 12(2), 1998, pp. 8–21; M. H. Meyer and A. DeTore. Product development for services. *Academy of Management Executive,* 13(3), 1999, pp. 64–65.

[28] A. Haasen. M-Class: The making of the new Daimler-Benz. *Organizational Dynamics,* spring 1998, pp. 74–78.

[29] J. Y. Murray and M. Kotabe. Sourcing strategies of U.S. service companies: A modified transaction-analysis. *Strategic Management Journal,* 20(9), 1999, pp. 791–797.

[30] R. A. Pitts and D. Lei. *Strategic Management: Building and Sustaining Competitive Advantage.* Cincinnati: South-Western, 2000, pp. 61–64; N. Blodgett. Service organizations increas-

ingly adopt Baldrige model. *Quality Process,* 32(12), 1999, pp. 74–77.

[31] Adapted from http://www.marlow.com; D. Kunde. Quality rewarded. *Dallas Morning News,* October 19, 1994, p. 1D; T. Steinert-Threkeld. Dallas company wins Baldrige award. *Dallas Morning News,* October 10, 1991, p. 1Aff.

[32] Adapted from M. Hornblower. Wake up and smell the protest. *Time,* April 17, 2000, p. 58; V. Vishwanath and D. Harding. The Starbucks effect. *Harvard Business Review,* 78(2), 2000, pp. 17–18; K. Strauss. Howard Schultz. *Nation's Restaurant News,* January 2000, pp. 162–164; N. Weiss. How Starbucks impassions workers to drive growth. *Workforce,* 77(8), 1998, pp. 60–65; Masters in business. *Inc.,* 20(10), 1998, pp. 126–127.

CHAPTER 3

[1] Adapted from E. M. Bossong-Martincs. *Standard & Poor's Industry Survey. Healthcare Pharmaceuticals.* New York: Standard & Poors, 1999; J. P. Lathrop, G. D. Ahlquist, and D. G. Knott. Health care's new e-marketplace. *Strategy + Business,* Second Quarter 2000, pp. 34–43; http://www.activemedia-guide.com/pharmaceutical_industry.htm. May 10, 2000.

[2] J. J. Hoffman. Institutional evolution and change: Environmentalism and the U.S. chemical industry. *Academy of Management Journal,* 42, 1999, pp. 351–371.

[3] W. A. McEachern. *Economics: A Contemporary Introduction,* 4th ed. Cincinnati: South-Western, 1997, p. 2.

[4] Adapted from C. Meyer. What's the matter? *Business 2.0,* March 2000, pp. 193–196; M. Sawney. Making new markets. *Business 2.0,* March 2000, pp. 202–211; D. F. Spulber. Clock wise. *Business 2.0,* March 2000, pp. 212–215; D. Tapscott. Minds over matter. *Business 2.0,* March 2000, pp. 220–229.

[5] Meyer. pp. 193–196.

[6] Sawney, pp. 197–201.

[7] Spulber, pp. 201–204; L. L. Barry. *Discovering the Soul of Service.* New York: Free Press, 1999.

[8] Tapscott, pp. 220–229.

[9] M. R. Solomon and E. W. Stuart. *Marketing: Real people, real choices.* 2nd ed. Upper Saddle River, N.J.: Prentice Hall, 2000, pp. 63–65.

[10] S. Kilman. Monsanto avoids gene controversy by quitting bid. *Wall Street Journal,* December 22, 1999, p. C24ff; J. Gillis and A. Swardson. Plans shattered, Monsanto seeks to right itself. *International Herald Tribune,* October 28, 1999, pp. 11–13. Also visit the company's home page at: http://www.monsanto.com.

[11] S. L. Berman. A. C. Wicks, S. Kotha, and T. M. Jones. Does stakeholder orientation matter? The relationship between stakeholder management models and firm financial performance. *Academy of Management Journal,* 42, 1999, pp. 488–506.

[12] J. W. Kelinson and P. Tate. The 1998–2008 job outlook in brief. *Occupational Outlook,* 44, 2000, pp. 2–12.

[13] Kelinson and Tate, pp. 2–12.

[14] T. Bland. Diversity is about companies reaching potential. *Kansas City Business Journal,* February 25, 2000, pp. 18–24;

T. Simons, L. H. Pelled, and K. A. Smith. Making use of difference: Diversity, debate and decision comprehensiveness in top management teams. *Academy of Management Journal,* 42, 1999, pp. 662–673.

[15] Adapted from P. Dass and B. Parker. Strategies for managing human resource diversity: From resistance to learning. *Academy of Management Executive,* 13(2), 1999, pp. 68–69; S. K. Schneider and G. B. Northcraft. Three social dilemmas of workforce diversity in organizations: A social identity perspective. *Human Relations,* 52(11), 1999, pp. 1445–1460; J. A. Dolan and L. Giles-Brown. Realizing the benefits of diversity: A wake-up call. *The Public Manager: The New Bureaucrat,* 28, 1999, pp. 51–55.

[16] A. D. Bhappu. The Japanese family: An institutional logic for Japanese corporate networks and Japanese management. *Academy of Management Review,* 25(2), 2000, pp. 409–415; N. J. Adler. *International Dimensions of Organizational Behavior,* 3rd ed. Cincinnati: South-Western, 1997; F. Trompenaars and C. Hampden-Turner. *Riding the Waves of Culture.* New York: McGraw-Hill, 1998.

[17] G. Hofstede. *Culture's Consequences: International Differences in Work-Related Values.* London: Sage, 1980; G. Hofstede and M. H. Bond. The Confucian connection: From cultural roots to economic growth. *Organizational Dynamics,* spring 1988, pp. 4–21.

[18] Adapted from Hofstede and Bond, pp. 12–13.

[19] K. Melymuka. There's something about Ketty Brown; is your IT staff just going through the motions? Eli Lilly project manager Ketty Brown had that problem until she came up with her own way to motivate her people. *Computerworld,* December 6, 1999, pp. 56–57.

[20] M. E. Porter. *Competitive Strategy: Techniques for Analyzing Industries and Competitiveness.* New York: Free Press, 1980; R. M. Hodgetts. A Conversation with Michael E. Porter: A Significant extension toward operational improvement and positioning. *Organizational Dynamics,* summer 1999, pp. 24–33.

[21] B. D. Henderson. The anatomy of competition. *Journal of Marketing,* 47(2), 1983, pp. 7–11. Also see P. Moran and S. Ghoshal. Markets, firms and the process of economic development. *Academy of Management Review,* 24(3), 1999, pp. 390–412.

[22] Bossong-Martines, p. 20.

[23] V. Cohen. Merck's strategy in the pharmaceutical industry. Dallas, TX: Unpublished paper, Cox School of Business, Southern Methodist University, Dallas, TX, May 2000; Personal conversations with V. Cohen, professional representative, Merck, Dallas, TX, May 2000; R. F. White and S. Fraley, Imperfect competition, price-fairness, and the pharmaceutical. *Online Journal of Ethics,* http://www.depaul.edu/ethics/icpfpi.html., May 7, 2000.

[24] Adapted from http://www.merck.com/overview/philosophy.html, April 30, 2000; http://www.merck.com/overview/speech/042500.htm., April 30, 2000; http://www.hoovers.com., April 30, 2000.

[25] J. F. Brett, G. B. Northcraft, and R. L. Pinkley. Stairways to heaven: An interlocking self-regulation model of negotiation. *Academy of Management Review,* 24(3), 1999, pp. 435–451.

[26] H. von Bertrab. *Negotiating NAFTA.* Westport, Conn.: Praeger, 1997.

[27] M. L. Marks and P. H. Mirvis. Managing mergers, acquisitions, and alliances. *Organizational Dynamics,* winter 2000, pp. 35–47; B. L. Simonin. Ambiguity and the process of knowledge transfer in strategic alliances. *Strategic Management Journal,* 20, 1999, pp. 595–624.

[28] D. Lei and J.W. Slocum, Jr. Responding to inflection points: Leveraging technology to renew competitive advantage. Dallas, Texas: Unpublished working paper, Cox School of Business, Southern Methodist University, Dallas, Texas, May 2000.

[29] R. R. Callister, M. K. Kramer, and D. B. Turban. Feedback seeking following career transitions. *Academy of Management Journal,* 42, 1999, pp. 429–438.

[30] Adapted from http://www.aarp.org., and http://www.aarp.org/ontheissues/issueAARPVote.html. May 1, 2000.

[31] R. D. Klassen and D. C. Whybark. The impact of environmental technologies on manufacturing performance. *Academy of Management Journal,* 42, 1999, pp. 599–615; R. J. Arend. Emergence of entrepreneurs following exogenous technological change. *Strategic Management Journal,* 20, 1999, pp. 31–48; K. Werbach. Syndication: The emerging model for business in the Internet era. *Harvard Business Review,* May–June 2000, pp. 84–96.

[32] M. Knight. Levi's launches a new blueprint for denim: Engineered jeans collection reinvents brand's basic look. *Daily News Record,* January 14, 2000, pp. 1Aff. Also see R. Gulati and J. Garino. Getting the right mix of bricks and clicks. *Harvard Business Review,* May–June 2000, pp. 107–117.

[33] It's digital, it's encrypted—it's postage. *Wall Street Journal,* September 21, 1998, pp. B1ff. Also see D. Tapscott, D. Ticoll, and A. Lowy. *Digital Capital: Harnessing the Power of the Business Web.* Boston: Harvard Business School Press, 2000.

[34] Motorola brings chip coordinators to China. *Xinhua News,* April 28, 2000, p. 100811; http://www.motorola.com.

[35] Adapted from R. A. Pitts and D. Lei. *Strategic Management: Building and Sustaining Competitive Advantage.* Cincinnati: South-Western, 2000, pp. 26–28.

CHAPTER 4

[1] Adapted from M. Frazier. P&G no longer playing the predictable Goliath. *Business Courier Serving Cincinnati-Northern Kentucky,* January 28, 2000, p. 3; D. Starkman. Strike by Finnish paper workers is seen boosting industry, increasing prices. *Wall Street Journal,* April 12, 2000, p. A2; K. Brooker. Plugging the leaks at P&G. *Fortune,* February 21, 2000, pp. 44–45; E. Neuborne and R. Berner. Warm and fuzzy won't save Procter & Gamble. *Business Week,* June 26, 2000, p. 48; E. Nelson and N. Deogun. Lafley takes on Gamble: New P&G chief faces challenge in balancing firm's old, new brands. *Wall Street Journal,* June 12, 2000, p. C1.

2 W. R. Feist, J. A. Heely, M. H. Lu, and R. L. Nersesian. *Managing a Global Enterprise*. Westport, Conn.: Quorum Books, 1999.

3 Feist, Heely, Lu, and Nersesian, p. 5.

4 R. Ramamurti. Risks and rewards in globalization of telecommunications in emerging economies. *Journal of World Business,* 35(2), 2000, pp. 149–170.

5 A. Schuh. Global standardization as a success formula for marketing in Central Eastern Europe. *Journal of World Business,* 35(2), 2000, pp. 133–148; S. L. McGaughey, P. W. Liesch, and D. Poluson. An unconventional approach to intellectual property protection. *Journal of World Business,* 35(1), 2000, pp. 1–20.

6 S. A. Zahr. The changing rules of global competitiveness in the 21st century. *Academy of Management Executive,* 13 (1), 1999, pp. 36–42.

7 Interview with John O'Dwyer, Global Manager, Celanese Chemical Corporation, Dallas, TX, July 11, 2000.

8 http://www.calsunshine.com, July 2000.

9 J. W. Slocum, Jr. and D. Lei. Designing global strategic alliances: Integrating cultural and economic factors. In G. P. Huber and W. H. Glick, *Organizational Change and Redesign.* New York: Oxford University Press, 1993, pp. 285–322.

10 http://www.image-entertainment.com, July 2000.

11 H. Thomas, T. Pollock, and P. Gorman. Global strategic analyses: Frameworks and approaches. *Academy of Management Executive,* 13(1), 1999, pp. 70–82.

12 R. D. Ireland and M. A. Hitt. Achieving and maintaining strategic competitiveness in the 21st century: The role of strategic leadership. *Academy of Management Executive,* 13(1), 1999, pp. 43–57.

13 T. Kostova and S. Zaheer. Organizational legitimacy under conditions of complexity: The case of the multinational enterprise. *Academy of Management Review,* 24(1), 1999, pp. 64–81.

14 L. E. Palich and L. R. Gomez-Mejia. A theory of global strategy and firm efficiencies: Considering the effects of cultural diversity. *Journal of Management,* 25, 1999, pp. 587–607.

15 Adapted from http://www.boeing.com, July 2000, and R. A. Pitts and D. Lei. *Strategic Management: Building and Sustaining Competitive Advantage.* Cincinnati: South-Western, 2000, pp. 216–217.

16 R. M. Kanter and T. D. Dretler. Global strategy and its impact on local operations: Lessons from Gillette Singapore. *Academy of Management Executive,* 12(4), 1998, pp. 60–69; R. Saner, L. Yiu, and M. Sondergaard. Business diplomacy management: A core competency for global companies. *Academy of Management Executive,* 14(1), 2000, pp. 80–92.

17 A. L. Appell and R. Jenner. Revitalizing Asia by shifting from patronage to meritocracy. Paper presented at Pan Pacific Conference, Gold Coast, Australia, May 31, 2000.

18 T. Crampton. Officials warn Asia to fight corruption. *International Herald Tribune,* February 12, 2000, pp. 13–14; J. Glasser. The software sopranos. *U.S. News & World Report,* February 7, 2000, pp. 14–16. Also see http://users.aol.com/ptroost/piracy.htm, July 2000, and J. M. Oetzel, R. A. Bettis, and M. Zenner. Country risk measures: How risky are they? *Journal of World Business,* in press.

19 http://www.usinfo.gov/topical/econ/bribes/trp922.htm, July 2000; A guide to graft: Transparency International surveys corruption. *Economist* (U.K.), October 30, 1999, pp. 114–115.

20 Adapted from D. Fairlamb. Robert Wilson: Managing political risk. *Institutional Investor,* November 1992, pp. 23–25; and http://www.riotinto.com, July 2000.

21 Sugar solution. *Economist* (U.S.), April 22, 2000, p. 58.

22 W. A. McEachern. *Economics: A Contemporary Introduction.* Cincinnati: South-Western, 1997, pp. 537–538.

23 M. A. Geo-JaJa, and G. L. Mangum. The Foreign Corrupt Practices Act's consequences for U.S. trade. *Journal of Business Ethics,* 24(3), 2000, pp. 245–256.

24 http://www.wto.org, July 2000.

25 http://users.aol.com/ptroost/piracy.htm, July 2000.

26 L. Zgabjar. When NAFTA's free trade gets costly, program can help. *Kansas City Business Journal,* February 11, 2000, p. 17.

27 T. Stundza. Trade approaches $600 billion. *Purchasing,* March 9, 2000, p. 70. Also see http://www.mac.doc.gov/nafta/nafta2.htm, July 2000.

28 Adapted from H. W. Lane, M. B. Brechu, and D. T. A. Wesley. Mabe's president Luis Berrondo Avalos on teams and industry competitiveness. *Academy of Management Executive,* 13(3), 1999, pp. 8–10, and http:www.mabe.com.mx, July 2000.

29 Competition policy. *European Policy Analyst,* July–August 2000, pp. 31–32. This entire issue is dedicated to issues facing countries in the European Union.

30 F. Williams. The Americas: U.S. subsidy plan irks EU. *Financial Times,* July 1, 2000, p. 7ff.

31 http://www.europa.eu.int, July 2000.

32 M. Harvey and M. M. Novicevic. Staffing global marketing positions: What we don't know can make a difference. *Journal of World Business,* 35(1), 2000, pp. 80–94.

33 J. P. Walsh, E. P. Wang, and K. R. Xin. Same bed, different dreams: Working relationship in Sino–American joint ventures. *Journal of World Business,* 34(1), 1999, pp. 69–93.

34 Adapted from M. Torrcelli. Culture at work. In A. M. Francesco and B A. Gold, *International Organizational Behavior.* Upper Saddle River, N.J.: Prentice-Hall, 1998, pp. 3–4.

35 M. R. Evans. Japanese economy stumbles toward recovery. *Industry Week,* April 3, 2000, p. 96; G. N. Soutar, R. Grainger, and H. Pamela. Australian and Japanese values stereotypes: A two-country study. *Journal of Internal Business Studies,* 30(1), 1999, pp. 203–216.

36 R. Neff. A new Japan. *Business Week,* October 25, 1999, pp. 69–78.

37 A. D. Bhappu. The Japanese family: An institutional logic, Japanese corporate networks, and Japanese management. *Academy of Management Review,* 25, 2000, pp. 409–415.

[38] N. Hirakubo. The end of lifetime employment in Japan. *Business Horizons,* November–December 1999, pp. 41–46.

[39] Adapted from D. Cyr. Sierra Systems' CEO Grant Gisel on high technology alliances. *Academy of Management Executive,* 13(2), 1999, pp. 13–17; D. Cyr. High-tech–high-impact: Creating Canada's competitive advantage through technology alliances. *Academy of Management Executive,* 13(2), 1999, pp. 17–28.

CHAPTER 5

[1] B. Einhorn. Portal combat. *Business Week,* January 17, 2000, pp. 96–97; B. Schlender, How a virtuoso plays the Web. *Fortune,* March 6, 2000, pp. F-79–F-85; L. Himelstein, H. Green, and R. Siklos, Yahoo! The company, the strategy, the stock. *Business Week,* September 7, 1998; Yahoo! history. Company home page at http://www.yahoo.com/info/investor, March 9, 2000.

[2] G. Gendron. The origin of the species. *Inc.,* February 2000, pp. 105–114; D. L. Sexton and F. I. Seale. *Leading Practices of Fast Growth Entrepreneurs: Pathways for High Performance.* Kansas City, MO: National Center for Entrepreneurship Research, 1996.

[3] J. Theroux. *Ben & Jerry's Homemade Ice Cream Inc.: Keeping the Mission(s) Alive.* Boston: Harvard Business School Press, 1991.

[4] U1: Jake Burton. *Fast Company,* April 2000, p. 122.

[5] A. Alvarez. Millenium voices: Women business experts offer their business and financial projections. CNNFN Online, January 1, 2000, at http://cnn.com/2000/01/personalfinance/century women; S. Shane. Explaining variation in rates of entrepreneurship in the United States: 1899–1988. *Journal of Management,* 22, 1996, pp. 747–781.

[6] G. S. Becker. Global Silicon Valleys? First, kill all the subsidies. *Business Week,* March 27, 2000, p. 26. For a detailed discussion of the concept of entrepreneurship, see M. H. Morris. *Entrepreneurial Intensity: Sustainable Advantages for Individuals, Organizations, and Societies.* Westport, Conn.: Quorum Books, 1998.

[7] S. N. Mehta. As ideas beget entrepreneurs, so does a plan. *Wall Street Journal,* February 19, 1997, pp. B1, B2.

[8] B. Einhorn, P. Engardio, and M. Kripalani. In search of new growth engines. *Business Week,* November 29, 1999, pp. 68–74.

[9] C. Yang, A. Borrus, and S. B. Garland. Between Silicon Valley and Silicon Alley: How the areas around Washington, D.C., became a high-tech haven. *Business Week,* August 30, 1999, pp. 168–178.

[10] J. Kotkin. The best 4 small-business cities. *The State of small business,* 1997, pp. 58–69; Outside the U.S., privatization of government activities is spurring entrepreneurial behavior. To learn about this trend, see S. A. Zahara, R. D. Ireland, I. Gutierrez, and M. A. Hitt. Privatization and entrepreneurial transformation: Emerging issues and a future research agenda. *Academy of Management Review,* 25, 2000, pp. 509–524; A. Spicer, G. McDermott, and B. Kogut. Entrepreneurship and privatization in Central Europe: The tenuous balance between destruction and creation. *Academy of Management Review,* 25, 2000, pp. 630–649.

[11] J. Holusha, Providing a helping hand to Internet startups. *New York Times,* March 5, 2000, p. 9.

[12] M. Hopkins and J. L. Seglin. Americans@work: The state of small business, *Inc.,* 1997, pp. 77–85; J. P. Kotter. *The New Rules: How to Succeed in Today's Post-Corporate World.* New York: Free Press, 1995.

[13] Kotter; A. Tannenbaum. Worker satisfaction found to be higher at small companies. *Wall Street Journal,* May 5, 1997, p. B2; S. N. Mehta. It's easier for MBAs to find jobs at small firms. *Wall Street Journal,* July 8, 1997, p. B2; D. Whitford. Is Fidelity losing it? *Fortune,* January 13, 1997; L. A. Winokur. Big doubts: Small business isn't necessarily a steppingstone to a corporate career. *Wall Street Journal,* May 22, 1997, p. R24; E. Felsenthal. High court makes it easier for workers to sue small firms because of job bias. *Wall Street Journal,* January 15, 1997, p. B2; J. A. Tannenbaum. The pocketbook issue: Striking it rich. *Wall Street Journal,* May 22, 1997, p. R4; S. N. Mehta. Top down: Two entrepreneurs talk about how they try—sometimes with limited success—to provide workers with the benefits many of them seek. *Wall Street Journal,* May 22, 1997, p. R25.

[14] S. D. Solomon. Fit to be tired. *1999 Inc. 500,* pp. 89–98.

[15] *1999 Inc. 500 Almanac.*

[16] D. P. Moore and E. H. Buttner. *Women Entrepreneurs: Moving Beyond the Glass Ceiling.* Thousand Oaks, Calif.: Sage, 1997.

[17] S. K. Kassicieh, R. Radosevich, and J. Umbarger. A comparative study of entrepreneurship incidence among inventors in national laboratories. *Entrepreneurship Theory and Practice,* spring 1996, pp. 33–49.

[18] For example, see R. G. McGrath and I. MacMillan. *The Entrepreneurial Mindset.* Boston: Harvard Business School Press, 2000. R. A. Baron. Psychological perspectives on entrepreneurship: Cognitive and social factors in entrepreneurs' success. *Current Directions in Psychological Science,* 9(1), 2000, pp. 15–18; B. A. Baron and G. D. Markham, Beyond social capital: How social skills can enhance entrepreneurs' success. *Academy of Management Executive,* 14(1), 2000, pp. 106–116; P. D. Reynolds, W. D. Bygrave, N. M. Carter, S. Manigart, C. M. Mason, G. D. Meyer, and K. G. Shaver (eds.), *Frontiers in Entrepreneurship Research.* Babson Park, MA: Babson College Press, 1998.

[19] D. C. McClelland. Characteristics of successful entrepreneurs. *Journal of Creative Behavior,* 21, 1987, pp. 219–233; P. B. Robinson and E. A. Sexton. The effect of education and experience on self-employment success. *Journal of Business Venturing,* 9, 1994, pp. 141–156.

[20] C. Ghosh. The comeback queen. *Forbes,* September 20, 1999, pp. 86–87.

[21] H. Page. Like father, like son? Entrepreneurial history repeats itself. *Entrepreneur,* 20, 1997, pp. 45–53; M. Virarelli. The birth of new enterprises. *Small Business Economics,* 3(3),

1991, pp. 215–233; M. P. Bhave. A process model of entrepreneurial venture creation. *Journal of Business Venturing, 9,* 1994, pp. 223–243.

22 S. Birley and P. A. Westhead. A taxonomy of business start-up reasons and their impact on firm growth and size. *Journal of Business Venturing, 9,* 1994, pp. 7–32.

23 I. M. Kunii. The web spinners. *Business Week,* March 13, 2000, pp. 81–88; http://www.sbholdings.com, March 8, 2000.

24 D. L. Sexton and F. I. Seale. *Leading Practices of Fast Growth Entrepreneurs: Pathways for High Performance.* Kansas City, MO: National Center for Entrepreneurship Research, 1996.

25 The 25 top managers: Jobs's juggling act. *Business Week,* January 10, 2000, p. 69; P. Burrows and R. Grover. Steve Jobs, movie mogul: Can he build Pixar into a major studio? *Business Week,* November 23, 1998.

26 J. G. Longenecker, C. W. Moore, and J. W. Petty. *Small Business Management: An Entrepreneurial Emphasis.* Cincinnati: South-Western, 1994, pp. 161–296.

27 R. D. Hisrich. Entrepreneurship/Intrapreneurship. *American Psychologist, 45,* 1990, pp. 209–222.

28 G. J. Castrogiovanni. Pre-startup planning and the survival of new small businesses: Theoretical linkages. *Journal of Management, 22,* 1996, pp. 801–822.

29 W. E. Watson, L. D. Ponthieu, and J. W. Critelli. Team interpersonal process effectiveness in venture partnerships and its connection to perceived success. *Journal of Business Venturing, 10,* 1995, pp. 393–411.

30 R. A. Baron and G. D. Markham, Beyond social capital: how social skills can enhance entrepreneurs' success. *Academy of Management Executive, 14,* 2000, pp. 106–115; R. C. Hill and M. Levenhagen. Metaphors and mental models: Sensemaking and sensegiving in innovative and entrepreneurial activities. *Journal of Management, 21,* 1995, pp. 1057–1074.

31 N. Munk, Why women find Estée Lauder mesmerizing. *Fortune,* May 25, 1998, pp. 97–104; G. Mirabell, Beauty queen: Estée Lauder. *Time 100,* http://www.time.com/time/time100/profile/lauder, March 4, 2000; the company's home page at http://www.elcompanies.com/investor/.

32 K. Fitzsimmons. No comparison. *Wall Street Journal,* May 22, 1997, pp. R10, R18.

33 Adapted from J. Finegan. Pipe dreams. *Inc.,* August 1994, pp. 64–72.

34 Castrogiovanni, pp. 801–822.

35 W. A. Sahlma. How to write a great business plan. *Harvard Business Review,* July–August 1997, pp. 98–108; A. Bhide. The questions every entrepreneur must answer. *Harvard Business Review,* November–December 1996, pp. 120–130.

36 Source: Adapted from Longenecker, Moore, and Petty.

37 D. Whitford. Never too small to manage. *Inc.,* February 1997, pp. 56–61.

38 A. C. Cooper and K. W. Artz. Determinants of satisfaction for entrepreneurs. *Journal of Business Venturing, 10,* 1995, 439–457.

39 I. J. Dugan. The baron of books. *Business Week,* June 29, 1998, pp. 109–115.

40 E. Schonfeld. Tech report: Cool companies. *Fortune,* July 7, 1997, pp. 84–110.

41 Adapted from Sexton and Seale.

42 J. Rae-Dupee. Bankrollers: L. John Doerr. *Business Week e.biz* (special supplement), September 27, 1999, p. EB 40; M. S. Malone. John Doerr's start-up manual. *Fast Company,* February–March 1997, pp. 82–87.

43 N. M. Carter, W. B. Gartner, and P. D. Reynolds. Exploring start-up event sequences. *Journal of Business Venturing, 11,* 1996, pp. 151–166.

44 N. M. Carter, M. Williams, and P. D. Reynolds. Discontinuance among new firms in retail: The influence of initial resources, strategy, and gender. *Journal of Business Venturing, 12,* 1997, pp. 125–145.

45 B. Zider. How venture capital works. *Harvard Business Review,* November–December 1998, pp. 131–139; also see S. Reed, New world financiers, old world startups. *Business Week,* February 14, 2000.

46 S. Greco. gct$$$now.com. *Inc.,* September 1999, pp. 35–38.

47 N. Brodsky and B. Burlingham. My life as an angel. *Inc.,* July 1997, pp. 43–48.

48 H. J. Sapienza and M. A. Korsgaard. Procedural justice in entrepreneur–investor relations. *Academy of Management Journal, 39,* 1996, pp. 544–574; D. M. Cable and S. Shane. A prisoner's dilemma approach to entrepreneur-venture capitalist relationships. *Academy of Management Review, 22,* 1997, pp. 142–176.

49 Datamine: The 2000 *Inc.* 500 Almanac. *Inc.,* October, 2000, pp. 57–65; see also J. M. Bloodgood, H. J. Sapienza, and J. G. Almeida. The internationalization of new high-potential U.S. ventures: Antecedents and outcomes. *Entrepreneurship Theory and Practice,* summer 1996, pp. 61–76.

50 U1: Didier Benchimol. *Fast Company,* January–February, 2000, p. 111.

51 B. M. Oviatt and P. Phillips McDougall. Global start-ups: Entrepreneurs on a worldwide stage. *Academy of Management Executive, 9,* 1995, pp. 30–79.

52 M. Selz. Caught in the crossfire. *Wall Street Journal,* May 22, 1997, p. R15.

53 C. Hayes. Business dynamos: Women business achievers. *Black Enterprise,* August 1998, pp. 58–79.

54 Based on information provided on the company's Web site at http://www.babyjogger.com, February 29, 2000; M. Baechler. The death of a marriage. *Inc.,* April 1994, pp. 74–78.

55 G. Hamel *Leading the Revolution.* Boston: Harvard Business School Press, 2000. G. T. Lumpkin and G. G. Dess. Clarifying the entrepreneurial orientation construct and linking it

to performance. *Academy of Management Review,* 21, 1996, pp. 135–172; S. A. Zahra. Governance, ownership, and corporate entrepreneurship: The moderating impact of industry technological opportunities. *Academy of Management Journal,* 39, 1996, pp. 1713–1735; J. S. Hornsby, D. W. Naffziger, D. F. Kuratko, and R. V. Montagno. An interactive model of corporate entrepreneurship. *Entrepreneurship: Theory and Practice,* winter 1993, pp. 29–38.

56 G. Pinchott III. *Intrapreneurship.* New York: Harper & Row, 1985.

57 U1: Art Fry. *Fast company,* April 2000, p. 100.

58 Perspectives: How can big companies keep the entrepreneurial spirit alive? *Harvard Business Review,* 1995, pp. 183–192; T. L. Peters and R. H. Waterman, Jr. *In Search of Excellence.* New York: Harper & Row, 1982.

59 Lumpkin and Dess; M. E. McGill and J. W. Slocum, Jr. *The Smarter Organization: How to Adapt to Meet Marketplace Needs.* New York: John Wiley & Sons, 1994.

60 E. Schine. The mountain man of office gear. *Business Week,* May 5, 1997, pp. 114–117; company home pages for Gaiam (http://www.gaiam.com) and Corporate Express (http://www.corporate-express.com), March 19, 2000.

CHAPTER 6

1 B. Morris. Idealist on board: This Ford is different. *Fortune,* April 3, 2000, pp. 123–146: K. Bradsher. Ford said to plan improved mileage in sport utilities. *New York Times,* July 27, 2000, pp. 1, 22; D. Welch and L. Woellert. The eco-car. *Business Week,* August 14, 2000, pp. 62–68; L. Greenhalgh. Ford motor company's CEO Jac Nasser on transformational change, e-business, and environmental responsibility. Academy of Management Executive, 14(3), 2000, pp. 46–51.

2 A. A. Atkinson, J. H. Waterhouse, and R. B. Wells. A stakeholder approach to strategic performance measurement. *Sloan Management Review,* spring 1997, pp. 25–37.

3 G. F. Franke, D. F. Crown, and D. F. Spake. Gender differences in ethical perceptions of business practices: A social role theory perspective. *Journal of Applied Psychology,* 82, 1997, pp. 920–934.

4 R. H. Franke. Fraud: Bringing light to the dark side of business. *Academy of Management Executive,* 10, 1996, pp. 93–95.

5 J. W. Weiss. *Business Ethics: A Managerial, Stakeholder Approach.* Belmont, Calif.: Wadsworth, 1994.

6 J. Steinberg. New rallying cry on campus: Stockholder power! *New York Times,* November 1999, p. 8.

7 C. Haddad. Why big tobacco can't be killed. *Business Week,* April 24, 2000, pp. 68–71; B. Meier. Cigarette makers in a $368 billion accord to curb lawsuits and curtail marketing. *New York Times,* June 21, 1997, pp. A1, A10; B. Meier. White House's bottom line is reported in tobacco deal. *New York Times,* September 8, 1997, p. A3.

8 Source: S. E. Jackson and R. S. Schuler. *Managing Human Resources: A Partnership Perspective.* Cincinnati: South-Western, 2000. Used with permission.

9 M. S. Bauccus and D. A. Bauccus. Paying the piper. An empirical examination of longer-term financial consequences of illegal corporate behavior. *Academy of Management Journal,* 40, 1997, pp. 129–151.

10 For a discussion of how cultural differences can affect the ethical choices of business leaders, see R. N. Kanungo and M. Mendonca. *Ethical Dimensions of Leadership.* Thousand Oaks, CA: Sage, 1996.

11 R. E. Thaler-Carter. Social Accountability 8000: A social guide for companies or another layer of bureaucracy? *HR Magazine,* June 1999, pp. 105–112; Social responsibility code starting to attract attention. *Worldlink,* July 1999, p. 2.

12 D. L. Swanson. Toward an integrative theory of business and society: A research strategy for corporate social performance. *Academy of Management Review,* 24, 1999, pp. 506–521.

13 F. Navran. Are your employees cheating to keep up? *Workforce,* August 1997, pp. 58–61; other related studies are summarized in J. Krohe, Jr. Ethics are nice, but business is business. *Across the Board,* April 1997, pp. 16–22.

14 P. L. Moore. This scandal changes everything. *Business Week,* February 28, 2000, pp. 140–143.

15 L. Kohlberg. The cognitive-developmental approach to moral education. In P. Scharf (ed.), *Readings in Moral Education.* Minneapolis: Winston Prisa, 1978, pp. 36–51; G. D. Boxterand and C. A. Rarick. Education and moral development of managers: Kohlberg's stages of moral development and integrative education. *Journal of Business Ethics,* 6, 1987, pp. 243–248.

16 Source: Marshall Sashkin. Used with permission.

17 M. Schminke, M. L. Ambrose, and T. W. Noel. The effect of ethical frameworks on perceptions of organizational justice. *Academy of Management Journal,* 40, 1997, 1198–1207; J. S. Mill. *Utilitarianism.* Indianapolis: Bobbs-Merrill, 1957 (originally published 1863).

18 M. A. Friedman. Friedman doctrine: The social responsibility of business is to increase its profits. *New York Times Magazine,* September 13, 1970, pp. 32ff.

19 J. Q. Wilson. Adam Smith on business ethics. *California Management Review,* fall 1989, pp. 59–72.

20 L. Holyoke. How HR measures impact on corporate donations. *Workforce,* June 1997, p. 23.

21 C. Vogel. Armani gift to the Guggenheim revives issue of art and commerce. *New York Times,* December 15, 1999, pp. E1, E3: D. Barstow. After 'Sensation' furor, museum group adopts guidelines on sponsors. *New York Times,* August 3, 2000, pp. E1, 3; G. B. Voss, D. M. Cable, and Z. G. Voss. Linking organizational values to relationships with external constituents: A study of nonprofit professional theaters. *Organizational Science,* 11, 2000, pp. 33–347.

22 S. M. Puffer and D. J. McCarthy. Finding the common ground in Russian and American business ethics. *California Management Review,* winter 1995, pp. 29–46.

23 J. D. Aram. *Presumed Superior: Individualism and American Business.* Englewood Cliffs, N.J.: Prentice-Hall, 1993.

24 M. Velasquez, D. V. Moberg, and G. F. Cavanagh. Organizational statesmanship and dirty politics: Ethical guidelines for the organizational politician. *Organizational Dynamics,* autumn 1983, pp. 65–80.

25 M. Gowen, S. Ibarreche, and C. Lackey. Doing the right things in Mexico. *Academy of Management Executive,* 10, 1996, pp. 74–81.

26 A. Bernstein. Down and out in Silicon Valley. *Business Week,* March 27, 2000, pp. 78–92.

27 R. E. Kidwell, Jr., and N. Bennett. Employee reactions to electronic control systems. *Group & Organization Management,* 19, 1994, pp. 203–218; F. Jossi. Eavesdroppers in cyberspace. *Business Ethics,* May/June 1994, pp. 22–25; D. R. Comer. Crossroads: A case against workplace drug testing. *Organization Science,* 5, 1994, pp. 259–267.

28 T. E. Weber. Mainstream sites accept ads selling x-rated. *Wall Street Journal,* January 16, 1997, p. B10.

29 J. A. Rawls. *A Theory of Justice.* Cambridge, Mass.: Harvard University Press, 1971; J. A. Greenberg. A taxonomy of organizational justice theories. *Academy of Management Review,* 12, 1987, pp. 9–22; J. Greenberg and K. S. Scott. Why do workers bite the hand that feeds them? Employee theft as a social exchange process. *Research in Organizational Behavior,* 18, 1996, pp. 111–156.

30 C. Goldin. *Understanding the Gender Gap: An Economic History of American Women.* New York: Oxford University Press, 1990; B. Reskin and I. Padavic. *Women and Men at Work.* Thousand Oaks, CA: Pine Forge Press, 1994.

31 D. Leonhardt. Order of compensation universe reflects pull of new economy. *New York Times,* April 2, 2000, Section 3, pp. 1, 12–17; J. Reingold, Executive pay. *Business Week,* April 17, 2000, pp. 100–112; D. M. Gold. Pressing the issue of pay inequity. *New York Times,* February 7, 1999, p. 11.

32 R. Folger and M. A. Konovsky. Effects of procedural and distributive justice on reactions to pay raise decisions. *Academy of Management Journal,* 32, 1989, pp. 115–130; and B. P. Niehoff and R. H. Moorman. Justice as a mediator of the relationship between methods of monitoring and organizational citizenship behavior. *Academy of Management Journal,* 36, 1993, pp. 527–556.

33 B. Bemmels and J. R. Foley. Grievance procedure research: A review and theoretical recommendations. *Journal of Management,* 22, 1996, pp. 359–384; and P. Feuille and D. R. Chachere. Looking fair or being fair: Remedial voice procedures in nonunion workplaces. *Journal of Management,* 21, 1995, pp. 27–42.

34 W. C. Kim and R. A. Mauborgne. Procedural justice and managers' in-role and extra-role behavior: The case of the multinational. *Management Science,* April 1996, pp. 499–513.

35 A. Carroll and A. K. Buchholtz. *Business and Society: Ethics and Stakeholder Management.* Cincinnati: South-Western, 2000.

36 K. Bradsher. Ford to sell gasoline-electric vehicle in 2003. *New York Times,* April 7, 2000, p. C17; E. Thornton. Envirocars: The race is on. *Business Week,* February 8, 1999, pp. 74–76.

37 For a review of this perspective, see T. Donaldson and L. E. Preston. The stakeholder theory of the corporation: Concepts, evidence, and implications. *Academy of Management Review,* 20, 1995, pp. 65–91.

38 M. B. E. Clarkson. A stakeholder framework for analyzing and evaluating corporate social performance. *Academy of Management Review,* 20, 1995, pp. 92–117; Donaldson and Preston; R. E. Freeman. *Strategic Management: A Stakeholder Approach.* Boston: Pittman/Ballinger, 1994; T. M. Jones. Instrumental stakeholder theory: A synthesis of ethics and economics. *Academy of Management Review,* 20, 1995, pp. 404–437.

39 R. O. Crockett, A new company called Motorola. *Business Week,* April 17, 2000, pp. 88–92; Q. Hardy. Motorola, broadsided by the digital era, struggles for a footing. *Wall Street Journal,* April 22, 1998, pp. A1, A14; D. Roth. Motorola lives! *Fortune,* September 27, 1999, pp. 305–306; R. Tetzeli. And now for Motorola's next trick. *Fortune,* April 28, 1997, p. 130.

40 Many companies have found that their incentive systems cause unwanted behaviors. This is an important topic, which we discuss in more depth in Chapters 13 and 14.

41 Verena Dobnik. Study: Chinese workers abused while making Nike, Reebok shoes. Associated Press. *Corpus Christi Caller-Times,* September 21, 1997, p. A8; A. Chan. Boot camp at the shoe factory. *Washington Post,* November 3, 1996, pp. C1, C4.

42 L. Lee. Can Nike still do it? *Business Week,* February 21, 2000, pp. 120–128; A. Bernstein. Sweatshops: No more excuses. *Business Week,* November 6, 1999, pp. 104–106; S. Greenhouse. Nike identifies plants abroad making goods for universities. *New York Times,* October 8, 1999, pp. C1, C6.

43 T. Lewin. Equal pay for equal work is no. 1 goal for women. *New York Times,* September 5, 1997, p. A20.

44 To learn more about cash balance plans, see J. O'Rouke. Retirement benefits innovation. *ACA News,* February 2000, pp. 14–18.

45 A. Borrus. Commerce reweaves the social fabric. *Business Week,* August 28, 2000, pp. 187–189. To learn how researchers attempt to measure corporate social performances, see B. M. Ruf, K. Muralidhar, and K. Paul. The development of a systematic, aggregate measure of corporate social performance. *Journal of Management,* 24, 1998, pp. 119–133.

46 As quoted in *Fast Company,* September 1999, p. 142.

47 P. C. Judge. Is it rainforest crunch time? *Business Week,* July 1996, pp. 70–71; B. Cohen and J. Greenfield. *Ben & Jerry's Double-Dip Capitalism: Lead with Your Values and Make Money Too.* New York: Simon & Schuster, 1997.

48 C. L. Hays. Shops rally to Ben & Jerry's cause(s). *New York Times,* January 25, 2000.

49 Adapted from B. Leonard. Supporting volunteerism, *HRM Magazine,* June 1998, pp. 84–93.

50 Based on information provided at http://www.ron-brown-award.org.

51 How refreshing. *HR World,* May/June 1999, pp. 14–18.

52 Recent research and theory are described in a special issue of *The Academy of Management Journal* (Special Research Forum: The management of organizations in the natural environment.) 43(4), 2000.

53 World Commission on Environment and Development. *Our Common Future*. New York: Oxford University Press, 1987. For more recent discussions see R. E. Freeman, J. Pierce, and R. Dodd. *Environmentalism and the New Logic of Business*. New York: Oxford University Press, 2000.

54 C. Fishman. Agenda: I want to pioneer the company of the next industrial revolution. *Fast Company,* April–May 1999, pp. 236–142.

55 C. A. Raiborn, B. E. Joyner, and J. W. Logan. ISO 14000 and the bottom line. *Quality Progress,* November 1999, pp. 89–93. To learn more about the ISO 14000 standards, see R. Hillary. *The Eco-Management Audit Scheme: A Practical Guide*. Hillsdale, N.J.: Lawrence Erlbaum, 1993.

56 Adapted from M. A. Berry and D. A. Rondinelli. Proactive corporate environmental management: A new industrial revolution. *Academy of Management Executive,* 12 (2), 1998, pp. 38–50.

57 S. Sharma and H. Vredenburg. Proactive corporate environmental strategy and the development of competitively valuable organizational capabilities. *Strategic Management Journal,* 19, 1998, pp. 729–753.

58 B. J. Feder. Chemistry cleans up a factory. *New York Times,* July 18, 1999, Section 3, pp. B1, B11.

59 K. H. Hammonds, W. Zellner, and R. Melcher. Writing a new social contract. *Business Week,* March 11, 1997, pp. 60–61; Clarkson.

60 For a detailed discussion of how managers can attempt to make decisions that respect the concerns of competing stakeholders, see T. Donaldson and T. W. Dunfee. *Ties That Bind: A Social Contracts Approach to Business Ethics*. Boston: Harvard Business School Press, 1999.

61 Examples of other alliances that have been developed to promote socially responsible business are described in S. Sagawa and E. Segal. *Common Interest, Common Good: Creating Value Through Business and Social Sector Partnerships*. Boston: Harvard Business School Press, 2000.

62 D. Edgington. From steak holders to stakeholders. *Inc.,* March 1997, p. 24.

63 M. Treacy and F. Wiersema. *The Discipline of Market Leaders: Choose Your Customers, Narrow Your Focus, Dominate Your Market*. Reading, Mass.: Addison-Wesley, 1997.

64 M. J. Schmit and S. P. Allscheid. Employee attitudes and customer satisfaction: Making the theoretical and empirical connections. *Personnel Psychology,* 48, 1995, pp. 521–536; C. A. Lengnick-Hall. Customer contributions to quality: A different view of the customer-oriented firm. *Academy of Management Review,* 21, 1996, pp. 791–824; and P. S. Goodman, M. Fichman, F. J. Lerch, and P. R. Snyder. Customer–firm relationships, involvement, and customer satisfaction. *Academy of Management Journal,* 38, 1995, pp. 1310–1324.

65 S. Scherreik, A conscience doesn't have to make you poor. *Business Week,* May 1, 2000, pp. 204–208; T. Gutner. Do the right thing—it pays. *Business Week,* August 28, 2000, p. 286. A. A. Atkinson, J. H. Waterhouse, and R. B. Wells. A stakeholder approach to strategic performance measurement. *Sloan Management Review,* spring 1997, pp. 25–37; T. M. Jones. Instrumental stakeholder theory: A synthesis of ethics and economics. *Academy of Management Review,* 20, 1995, pp. 404–437; R. D. Klassen and C. P. McLaughlin. The impact of environmental management on firm performance. *Management Science,* August, 1996, pp. 1199–1216; D. B. Turban and D. W. Greening. Corporate social performance and organizational attractiveness to prospective employees. *Academy of Management Journal,* 40, 1997, pp. 658–672.

66 J. T. Mahoney, A. S. Huff, and J. O. Huff. Toward a new social contract theory in organization science. *Journal of Management Inquiry,* 3, 1994, pp. 153–168.

67 Data from Vasin, Heyn & Company at http://www.vhcoaudit.com/SRArticles, April 5, 2000; MHC International at http://www.win.com.pl/critics, April 5, 2000.

68 J. P. Near and M. P. Miceli. Effective whistle-blowing. *Academy of Management Review,* 20, 1995, pp. 679–708.

69 P. Elkind. A merger made in hell. *Fortune,* November 9, 1998, pp. 135–149.

70 Adapted from J. P. Near and M. P. Miceli. Whistle-blowing: Myth and reality. *Journal of Management,* 22, 1996, pp. 507–526; Near and Miceli. Effective whistle-blowing; M. P. Miceli and J. P. Near. *Blowing the Whistle: The Organizational Implications for Companies and Their Employees*. New York: Lexington Books, 1992.

71 Near and Miceli. Effective whistle-blowing.

72 J. P. Near, T. M. Dwarkin, and M. P. Miceli. Explaining the whistle-blowing process: Suggestions from power theory and justice theory. *Organization Science,* 4, 1993, pp. 393–411.

73 Adapted from J. Makower. *Beyond the Bottom Line: Putting Social Responsibility to Work for Your Business and the World*. New York: Simon & Schuster, 1994.

74 S. J. Wells, Turn employees into saints? *HR Magazine,* December 1999, pp. 48–58.

75 Adapted from the company's home page; R. Lieber and A. Wyant. Working, naturally. *Fast Company,* August, 2000, pp. 139–148. J. Laabs. Mixing business with passion. *Workforce,* March 2000, pp. 80–92; A. Adelson, Casual, Worker-friendly, and a Money-maker, Too. *New York Times,* June 30, 1996, p. F8; C. Callicott. How Green Is Your Gear? *Hudson Valley Sports,* September/October 1996; E. O. Wells. Lost in Patagonia. *Inc.,* August 1992, pp. 91–95.

CHAPTER 7

1 Adapted from R. A. McGinn. The race to build next-generation networks. *California Management Review,* 42(2), 2000, pp. 123–132; S. Rosenbush. Can Rich McGinn revive Lucent? *Business Week,* June 24, 2000, pp. 182–184.

[2] G. Colvin. America's most admired companies. *Fortune,* February 21, 2000, pp. 108–118.

[3] J. M. Liedtka. Linking strategic thinking with strategic planning. *Strategy & Leadership,* 26(4), 1998, pp. 30–35.

[4] R. A. McGinn, p. 127.

[5] For a discussion of different approaches to strategy formation, see H. Mintzberg and J. Lampel. Reflecting on the strategy process. *Sloan Management Review,* 40(4), 1999, pp. 21–30.

[6] M. A. Hitt, R. D. Ireland, and R. E. Hoskisson. *Strategic Management: Competitiveness and Globalization,* 4th ed. Cincinnati: South-Western, 2001.

[7] M. Borden. When big growth happens to small companies. *Fortune,* March 6, 2000, pp. 385–386. Also see Alteon WebSystems Web site at http://www.alteonwebsystems.com (June 19, 2000).

[8] C. O'Gorman and R. Doran. Mission statements for small and medium-sized businesses. *Journal of Small Business Management,* 37(4), 1999, pp. 59–66; M. G. Brown. Improving your organization's vision. *Journal for Quality and Participation,* 21(5), 1998, pp. 18–21.

[9] Vision and mission statements are from the Web sites for Lucent Technologies. http://www.lucent.com (June 16, 2000); Cisco Systems. http://www.cisco.com (June 16, 2000); and Dell Computer. http://www.dell.com (June 16, 2000).

[10] R.A. McGinn, p. 125.

[11] J. M. Liedtka. Strategic planning as contributor to strategic change: A generative model. *European Management Journal,* 18(2), 2000, pp. 195–206.

[12] J. Surowiecki. The return of Michael Porter. *Fortune,* February 1, 1999, pp. 135–138; M. E. Porter. *On Competition.* Boston: Harvard Business School Publishing, 1998.

[13] M. Dell. *Direct from Dell: Strategies That Revolutionized Industry.* New York: HarperBusiness, 1999; M. Dell. The dell advantage. Keynote Address Available at Michael Dell Speech Archive. http://www.del.com (March 3, 1999).

[14] Adapted from Cisco Systems, Inc. *Hoover's Online.* http://www.hoovers.com (June 13, 2000); Management's discussion and analysis. Cisco's *Annual Report 1999.* http://www.cisco.com (June 13, 2000); K. T. Greenfeld. Do you know CISCO? *Time,* January 17, 2000, pp. 72–74.

[15] P. Sellers. Why Pepsi needs to become more like Coke. *Fortune,* March 3, 1997, pp. 26–27; J. A. Byrne. PepsiCo's new formula. *Business Week,* April 10, 2000, pp. 172–184.

[16] M. Ligos. Clicks and misses. *Sales & Marketing,* June 2000, pp. 68–76; J. Negley. Wal-Mart & Toys "R" Us: The best of the century. *Discount Store News,* 2000, pp. 42–46; I. Mount. Toys "R" Us: Beware the giraffe. *Ecompany,* September 2000, pp. 159–164.

[17] D. Shand. Proflowers.com. *Computerworld,* April 10, 2000, p. 86; C. Zimmerman. Site blooms with caching. *Internetweek,* January 31, 2000, p. 21; http://www.proflowers.com (June 25, 2000).

[18] Growth strategy. http://www.cemex.com (June 18, 2000).

[19] T. M. Grubb and R. B. Lamb. *Capitalize on Merger Chaos.* New York: Free Press, 2000.

[20] G. Colvin, p. 108.

[21] Business portfolio. http://www.ge.com/investor/annuals.htm (June 20, 2000).

[22] *GE 1999 Annual Report.* http://www.ge.com/annual99/letter/ (June 20, 2000). Also see R. Slater. *Jack Welch & the G.E. Way: Management Insights and Leadership of the Legendary CEO.* Blacklick, OH: McGraw-Hill, 1998.

[23] C. W. L. Hill and G. R. Jones. *Strategic Management: An Integrated Approach,* 5th ed. Boston: Houghton Mifflin, 2001.

[24] P. A. Gaughan. *Mergers, Acquisitions and Corporate Restructuring.* Somerset, N.J.: John Wiley & Sons, 1999; R. Wise and P. Baungartner. Go downstream: The new profit imperative in manufacturing. *Harvard Business Review,* 77(5), 1999, pp. 133–141.

[25] Lucent Technologies, *1999 Annual Report.* http://www.lucent.com/investor (June 20, 2000).

[26] Junglee: Enabling comparison shopping on the web. *Red Herring Magazine,* September 1, 1998, p. 3.

[27] United Airlines press release May 24, 2000. http://www.united.com (June 18, 2000); W. Zellner, D. Carney, and M. Arndt. How many airlines will stay aloft? *Business Week,* June 19, 2000, pp. 50–51.

[28] GE Cisco Industrial Networks. http://www.gecisco.com/about_ge_cisco/ (June 21, 2000).

[29] C. J. Loomis. AOL + TWX = ???. *Fortune,* February 7, 2000, pp. 81–84; R. Siklos and C. Yang. Welcome to the 21st century. *Business Week,* January 24, 2000, pp. 36–44.

[30] *GE 1999 Annual Report.* http://www.ge.com/investor/annuals.htm (June 20, 2000). Also see: G. Hamel. *Leading the Revolution.* Boston: Harvard Business School Publishing, 2000.

[31] R. A. Burgelman. *Strategy in Destiny: How Strategy-Making Shapes a Company's Future.* New York: Free Press, 2000; C. C. Markides. *All the Right Moves: A Guide to Crafting Breakthrough Strategies.* Boston: Harvard Business School Publishing, 1999.

[32] S. Briggs and W. Keogh. Integrating human resource strategy and strategic planning to achieve success. *Total Quality Management,* 10(4/5), 1999, pp. 447–453; R. J. Grossman. Measuring up. *HR Magazine,* 45(1), 2000, pp. 28–35.

[33] Adapted from C. Daniels. To hire a lumber expert, click here. *Fortune,* April 3, 2000, pp. 267–268. Also go to the home page of Home Depot at http://www.homedepot.com (June 24, 2000). Click on *Company Information* and then find *Careers* in the *Company Information Categories.*

[34] Letter to shareholders. *Home Depot 1999 Annual Report.* http://www.homedepot.com (June 23, 2000).

[35] B. Mascarenhas, A. Baveja, and M. Jamil. Dynamics of core competencies in leading multinational companies. *California*

Management Review, 40(4), 1998, pp. 117–132; T. R. V. Davis. Different service firms, different core competencies. *Business Horizons,* 42(5), 1999, pp. 23–33.

[36] B. Mascarenhas, A. Baveja, and M. Jamil, 120, 123; A.S. Huff (Ed.). Citigroup's John Reed and Stanford's James March on management research and practice. *Academy of Management Executive,* 14(1), 2000, pp. 52–64; P. Sellers. Behind the shootout at Citigroup. *Fortune,* March 20, 2000, pp. 27–32.

[37] A. Shepherd. Outsourcing IT in a changing world. *European Management Journal,* 17(1), 1999, pp. 64–84; P. Burrows. Technology on tap. *Business Week,* June 19, 2000, pp. 74–84.

[38] A. S. Horowitz. Extreme outsourcing: Does it work? *Computerworld,* May 10, 1999, pp. 50–51.

[39] Adapted from D. Lyons. Michael Dell's second act. *Forbes,* April 17, 2000, pp. 208–214; K. L. Kramer, J. Dedrick, and S. Yamashiro. Refining and extending the business model with information technology. *Information Society,* 16(1), 2000, pp. 5–21.

[40] B. Fryer. When something clicks. *Inc. Tech 2000,* No. 1, 2000, pp. 63–72.

[41] A survey of business and the Internet: The net imperative. *The Economist,* June 26, 1999, pp. 1–40.

[42] M. E. Porter. *Michael Porter on Competition.* Boston: Harvard Business School Publishing, 1998.

[43] N. Venkatraman. Five steps to a dotcom strategy: How to find your footing on the Web. *Sloan Management Review,* 41(3), 2000, pp. 15–28.

[44] About E*Trade. http://www.etrade.com (June 26, 2000).

[45] N. Dawar and T. Frost. Competing with the giants: Survival strategies for local companies in emerging markets. *Harvard Business Review,* 77(2), 1999, pp. 119–129.

[46] P. H. Fuchs et al. Strategic integration: Competing in the age of capabilities. *California Management Review,* 42(3), 2000, pp. 118–147; C. A. O'Reilly III and J. Pfeffer. *Hidden Value: How Great Companies Achieve Extraordinary Results with Ordinary People.* Boston: Harvard Business School Publishing, 2000.

[47] J. Collins. Turning goals into results: The power of catalytic mechanisms. *Harvard Business Review,* 77(4), 1999, pp. 71–82.

[48] B. I. Kirkman and B. Rosen. Powering up teams. *Organizational Dynamics,* 28(3), 2000, pp. 48–65.

[49] Excerpts from Letter to shareholders. *1999 IBM Annual Report.* Available at http://www.ibm.com/annualreport/1999/letter/letter_01.html (June 28, 2000). Also see: G. Hamel. Waking up IBM: How a gang of unlikely rebels transformed big blue. *Harvard Business Review,* 78(4), 2000, pp. 137–146.

CHAPTER 8

[1] Adapted from S. Alexander. Like performing a brain transplant. *Computerworld,* May 8, 2000, p. 9.

[2] P. Evans and T. S. Wurster. *Blown to Bits: How the New Economics of Information Transforms Strategy.* Boston: Harvard Business School Publishing, 1999.

[3] E. F. Harrison. *The Managerial Decision-Making Process,* 5th ed. Boston: Houghton Mifflin, 1999.

[4] D. Lupton. *Risk.* New York: Routledge, 1999.

[5] C. Dahle. Risky business. *Fast Company,* July–August 1999, pp. 70–72.

[6] The story of E*Trade: http://www.etrade.com (July 7, 2000).

[7] Adapted from Form 10-K for E*Trade Group, Inc. Filed with U.S. Securities and Exchange Commission. May 15, 2000. Go to http://www.hoovers.com, keystroke "E*Trade," and click "GO." Find and click "Real-time SEC filings" in the index for E*Trade.

[8] G. Gotz. Strategic timing of adoption of new technologies under uncertainty. *International Journal of Industrial Organization,* 18(2), 2000, pp. 369–379.

[9] Adapted from N. G. Carr. On the edge: An interview with Akamai's George Conrades. *Harvard Business Review,* 78(3), 2000, pp. 118–125. Also see M. W. Kramer. Motivation to reduce uncertainty: A reconceptualization of uncertainty reduction theory. *Management Communication Journal,* 13, 1999, pp. 305–316.

[10] R. Bohn. Stop fighting fires. *Harvard Business Review,* 78(4), 2000, pp. 83–91.

[11] S. Crainer. *The 75 Greatest Management Decisions Ever Made: . . . and 21 of the Worst.* New York: AMACOM, 1999.

[12] W. J. Altier. *The Thinking Manager's Toolbox: Effective Processes for Problem Solving and Decision Making.* New York: Oxford University Press, 1999.

[13] Adapted from D. N. Sull. Why good companies go bad. *Harvard Business Review,* 77(4), 1999, pp. 42–52.

[14] Adapted from C. Fishman. This is a marketing revolution. *Fast Company,* May 1999, pp. 204–218.

[15] For more information on Lands' End, visit the company's home page at http://www.landsend.com.

[16] Adapted from F. Hayes. Convergence. *Computerworld,* May 15, 2000, p. 58.

[17] T. J. Clark. *Success through Quality: Support Guide for the Journey to Continuous Improvement.* Milwaukee: American Society for Quality, 1999.

[18] B. Dale and H. Bunney. *Total Quality Management Blueprint.* Malden, MA: Blackwell, 1999.

[19] Adapted from T. A. Stewart. Making decisions in real time. *Fortune,* June 26, 2000, pp. 332–333.

[20] K. M. Eisenhardt. Strategy as strategic decision making. *Sloan Management Review,* 40(3), 1999, pp. 65–81.

[21] Adapted from R. Crockett. Chow (on) line. *Business Week E. Biz,* June 5, 2000, pp. 84–90.

[22] J. Freeman. Efficiency and rationality in organizations. *Administrative Science Quarterly,* 44, 1999, pp. 163–175.

[23] J. C. Picken and G. G. Dess. Right strategy, wrong problem. *Organizational Dynamics,* 27(1), 1999, pp. 35–49. For more information on Greyhound Lines, visit the company's home page at http://www.greyhound.com.

24 M. Ray and R. Myers. *Creativity in Business.* Garden City, NY: Doubleday, 1986, pp. 94–96.

25 C. Lentzsch. Taking care of customers one at a time. *Greyhound Today Newsletter,* April 23, 1999, p. 1.

26 J. Frooman. Stakeholder influence strategies. *Academy of Management Review,* 24, 1999, pp. 191–205.

27 Adapted from J. H. Gittell. Paradox of coordination and control. *California Management Review,* 42(3), 2000, pp. 101–117. Also see A. E. Tenbrunsel and D. M. Messick. Sanctioning systems, decision frames and cooperation. *Administrative Science Quarterly,* 44, 1999, 684–707.

28 L. R. Beach. *The Psychology of Decision Making: People in Organizations.* Thousand Oaks, CA: Sage, 1997.

29 H. A. Simon. *Administrative Behavior: A Study of Decision-Making Processes in Administrative Organizations,* 4th ed. New York: Free Press, 1997; A. Rubinstein. *Modeling Bounded Rationality.* Cambridge, MA: MIT Press, 1998.

30 J. M. Roach. Simon says: Decision making is a "satisficing" experience. *Management Review,* January 1979, pp. 8–9.

31 E. H. Foreman. How additional information can lead to inferior decisions—A paradox. *Decision Line,* July 1993, p. 3.

32 L. W. Busenitz. Entrepreneurial risk and strategic decision making: It's a matter of perspective. *Journal of Applied Behavioral Science,* 35, 1999, pp. 325–340.

33 M. Harvey and M. Novicevic. The trials and tribulations of addressing global organizational ignorance. *European Management Journal,* 17, 1999, pp. 431–443.

34 J. M. Beyer et al. The selective perceptions of managers revisited. *Academy of Management Journal,* 40, 1997, pp. 717–737.

35 G. Klein and K. E. Weick. Decisions: Making the right ones, learning from the wrong ones. *Across the Board,* June 2000, pp. 16–22.

36 J. Frooman. Stakeholder influence strategies. *Academy of Management Review,* 24, 1999, pp. 191–205; J. Pfeffer. *Managing With Power: Politics and Influence in Organizations.* Boston: Harvard Business School Press, 1992.

37 E. B. Smith. Flour settles whistle-blower suit for $8.4 million. *Knight-Ridder/Tribune News,* June 23, 1997, p. 623B.

38 Adapted from G. Baum. Stop the politics. *Forbes ASAP,* April 3, 2000, pp. 122–126.

39 A. Bernstein and P. Dwyer. This package is a heavy one for the Teamsters. *Business Week,* August 18, 1997, pp. 40–42.

40 D. A. Buchanan, R. Badham, and D. Buchanan. *Power, Politics, and Organizational Change: Winning the Turf War.* Thousand Oaks, CA: Corvin Press, 1999.

41 J. Pfeffer. *New Directions for Organization Theory.* New York: Oxford University Press, 1997.

42 T. A. Stewart. Get with the new power game. *Fortune,* January 13, 1997, p. 58.

43 Adapted from L. McCauley. Measure what matters. *Fast Company,* May 1999, pp. 97–106.

44 Adapted from D. Wallace. The company simply refused to pay. *Business Ethics,* March/April 2000, p. 18.

CHAPTER 9

1 Adapted from W. C. Rappleye, Jr. Knowledge management: A force whose time has come. *Across the Board,* June 2000, special section—unpaginated; KPMG Web site at http://www.kpmg.com/about/ (July 20, 2000).

2 R. Abbott. Knowledge synthesis for innovation and competitive advantage. Invited paper by AIOPI. Available online at http://www.aiopi.org.uk/. Click "articles"; find this article and click it (April 26, 2000); C. Lucier and J. D. Toprsilieri. Steal this idea: Knowledge remains the strongest force for business-building. *Strategy & Business.* Third Quarter, 2000, pp. 21–24.

3 Adapted from KPMG Consulting's knowledge management online fact sheet. http://www.kpmgconsulting.com/kpmgsite/service/km/factsheet.html (July 20, 2000); M. T. Hansen, N. Nohria, and T. Tierny. What's your strategy for managing knowledge? *Harvard Business Review,* 77(2), 1999, pp. 106–116.

4 Adapted from Practicing Knowledge Management: Turning experience and information into results. (White paper by Microsoft Corporation; no author given.) Available online at http://www.microsoft.com (August 16, 2000); R. Cross and L. Baird. Technology is not enough: Improving performance by building organizational memory. *Sloan Management Review,* 41(3), 2000, pp. 69–78.

5 Adapted from W. C. Rappleye, Jr.

6 Adapted from W. C. Rappleye, Jr.

7 M. H. Zack. Managing codified knowledge. *Sloan Management Review,* 40(4), 1999, pp. 45–58; N. M. Dixon. *Common Knowledge: How Companies Thrive by Sharing What They Know.* Boston: Harvard Business School Press, 2000.

8 G. Von Krogh, K., Ichijo, and I. Nonaka. *Enabling Knowledge Creation: How to Unlock the Mystery of Tacit Knowledge and Release the Power of Innovation.* New York: Oxford University Press, 2000; S. L. Pan and H. Scarbrough. Knowledge management in practice: An exploratory case study. *Technology Analysis & Strategic Management,* 11(3), 1999, pp. 359–374.

9 About Mitre. Available online at http://www.mitre.org/about (July 21, 2000).

10 Adapted from T. Field. The Mitre Corp.: Common knowledge. *CIO Magazine,* February 1, 1999. Available online at http://www.cio.com/archive/020199_mitre.html (July 23, 2000); D. Young. An audit tale. *CIO Magazine,* May 1, 2000. Available online at http://www.cio.com/archive/050100_mitre.html (July 23, 2000).

11 IT Projections. Available at http://www.e-forecasting.com/index.html/. Click "IT Projections" in the index listing (August 16, 2000). Web site provided by Informetrica, Inc.

12 J. V. Crosby. *Cycles, Trends, and Turning Points: Practical Marketing and Sales Forecasting Techniques.* Chicago: NTC, 2000.

[13] Adapted from J. Huber. Trend track: Experts tell you how to spot tomorrow's hottest trends. *Business Startups,* January 1995, pp. 49–51; C. Russell. *The Baby Boom Americans Aged 35 to 54* 2nd ed. Ithaca, NY: New Strategist, 1999.

[14] C. E. Sahakian. *The Delphi Method.* Skokie, IL: Corporate Partnering Institute, 1997.

[15] G. Rowe and G. Wright. The Delphi technique as a forecasting tool: Issues and analysis. *International Journal of Forecasting,* 15(4), 1999, pp. 353–375.

[16] Adapted from T. A. Stewart. The dance gets trickier all the time. *Fortune,* May 27, 1997, pp. 127–129.

[17] P. Waurzyniak. Virtual models gain favor. *Manufacturing Engineering,* 124(4), 2000, pp. 34–46.

[18] S. Sullivan. Virtual fire. *Risk Management,* January 2000, p. 8.

[19] P. Schwartz. *The Art of the Long View: Planning for the Future in an Uncertain World.* New York: Doubleday, 1996.

[20] K. Tucker. Scenario planning. *Association Management,* April 1999, pp. 70–75.

[21] G. Ringland, K. Todd, and P. Schwartz. *Scenario Planning: Managing for the Future.* Somerset, NJ: John Wiley & Sons, 1998.

[22] Adapted from B. Wyscocki, Jr. Soft landing or hard? Firm test strategy on 3 views of future. *Wall Street Journal,* July 7, 2000, pp. A1, A6.

[23] This section draws on A. G. Robinson and S. Stern. *Corporate Creativity: How Innovation and Improvement Actually Happen.* San Francisco: Berrett-Koehler, 1997; T. Richards. *Creativity and the Management of Change.* Malden, MA: Blackwell, 1999.

[24] P. Israel. *Edison: A Life of Invention.* New York: John Wiley & Sons, 1999.

[25] A. F. Osborn. *Applied Imagination,* 3rd rev. ed. New York: Scribner's, 1963.

[26] P. B. Paulus and Huei-Chang Yang. Idea generation in groups. A basis for creativity in organizations. *Organizational Behavior and Human Decision Processes,* 82(1), 2000, pp. 76–87.

[27] A. F. Osborn, pp. 229–290.

[28] A. F. Osborn, pp. 155–158.

[29] A. F. Osborn, p. 156.

[30] Adapted from A. F. Osborn, pp. 166–196.

[31] G. Bachman. Brainstorming deluxe. *Training & Development,* January 2000, pp. 15–17; F. Hurt. Beyond brainstorming. *Successful Meetings,* June 2000, pp. 81–82.

[32] Adapted from R. I. Sutton and T. A. Kelly. Creativity doesn't require isolation. Why product designers bring visitors "backstage." *California Management Review,* Fall 1997, pp. 75–91; E. Brown. A day at innovation U. *Fortune,* April 12, 1999, p. 28.

[33] R. A. Malaga. The effect of stimulus modes and associative distance in individual creativity support systems. *Decision Support Systems,* 29(2), 2000, pp. 125–141.

[34] D. J. DeTombe. Moments of support by a groupware brainstorming tool in handling complex technical policy problems. *European Journal of Operational Research,* 119(2), pp. 267–281. Also see A. Pinsonneault et al. Electronic brainstorming: The illusion of productivity. *Information Systems Research,* 10(2), 1999, pp. 110–133.

[35] A. R. Dennis et al. Structuring time and task in electronic brainstorming. *MIS Quarterly,* 23(1), 1999, pp. 95–108.

[36] B. Dale and H. Bunney. *Total Quality Blueprint.* Malden, MA: Blackwell, 1999, pp. 1–36.

[37] M. Simpson, D. Kondouli, and P. H. Wai. From benchmarking to business process re-engineering: A case study. *Total Quality Management,* 10(4/5), 1999, pp. 5717–5724.

[38] M. T. Czarnecki. *Managing by Measuring: How to Improve Your Organization's Performance Through Effective Benchmarking.* New York: AMACOM, 1999.

[39] To learn more about these issues, visit the home page for the American Productivity and Quality Center International Benchmarking Clearinghouse at http://www.apqc.org (July 22, 2000).

[40] K. N. Dervitsiotis. Benchmarking and business paradigm shifts. *Total Quality Management,* 11(4/6), 2000, pp. S641–S647.

[41] Adapted from L. K. Monroe. Benchmarking for success. *Buildings,* May 2000, pp. 44–48.

[42] W. E. Deming. *The New Economics for Industry, Government, and Education.* Cambridge, MA: Center for Advanced Engineering Study, Massachusetts Institute of Technology, 1993; G. R. Russell. The Deming cycle extended to software development. *Production and Inventory Management Journal,* 39(3), 1998, pp. 32–37.

[43] Adapted and modified from G. Langley, K. Nolan, and T. Nolan. The foundation of improvement. Presented at the Sixth Annual International Deming's User's Group Conference. Cincinnati, August 1992; J.W. Dean, Jr., and J. R. Evans. *Total Quality: Management, Organization, and Strategy.* St. Paul: West, 1994, pp. 81–82.

[44] L. P. Martin. Inventory of barriers to creative thought and innovation action. Reprinted from J. William Pfeiffer (ed.), *The 1990 Annual: Developing Human Resources.* San Diego: University Associates, 1990, pp. 138–141. Used with permission.

CHAPTER 10

[1] Adapted from *Report of National Commission on Restructuring the Internal Revenue Service,* June 1997. Available at http://www.house.gov/natcommirs/intro.htm; Pillsbury Madison & Sutro LLP. Internal Revenue Service restructuring and reform act of 1998. Tax bulletin, August 1998. Available at http://www.pmstax.com/gen/bull9808.shtml (August 20, 2000); P. M. Bakery, Jr. Shape of restructured IRS becoming clearer. *Accounting Today,* May 10–May 23, 1999, pp. 10–11; *IRS Modernization Update.* IR-199940 Bulletin. Washington, DC: Internal Revenue Service, April 19, 1999.

[2] Adapted from *Modernizing America's Tax Agency.* Washington, DC: Internal Revenue Service, 1999, pp. 33–34.

[3] D. A. Nadler and M. I. Tushman. *Competing by Design: The Power of Organizational Architecture.* New York: Oxford University Press, 1998.

[4] R. L. Daft. *Organization Theory and Design,* 7th. ed. Cincinnati: South-Western, 2001.

[5] Adapted from *Meet the New IRS Wage and Investment Operating Division.* Available at http://www.irs.ustreas.gov/news/wage-invest.html (August 22, 2000).

[6] M. Gimein. Transmeta. *Fortune,* June 26, 2000, pp. 104–105.

[7] *Modernizing America's Tax Agency,* p. 38.

[8] *Modernizing America's Tax Agency,* pp. 33, 37.

[9] *Taxpayer Advocate Service.* Available at http://www.irs.ustreas.gov/ind_info/advocate.html (August 25, 2000).

[10] M. E. McGill and J. W. Slocum, Jr. *The Smarter Organization: How to Build a Business That Learns to Adapt to Marketplace Needs.* New York: John Wiley & Sons, 1994, pp. 93–96.

[11] Adapted from *Southwest Airlines Company Annual Report 1999.* Dallas: Southwest Airlines Company, 2000.

[12] A. Rugman and J. D'Cruz. *Multinationals as Flagship Firms.* New York: Oxford University Press, 2000.

[13] Adapted from *Starbucks Annual Report 1999.* Seattle, Washington: Starbucks Corporation, 2000; H. Schultz and D. J. Yang. *Pour Your Heart into It: How Starbucks Built a Company One Cup at a Time.* Westport, CT: Hyperion Press, 1999; L. Lee. Now, Starbucks uses its bean. *Business Week,* February 14, 2000, pp. 92, 97.

[14] Adapted from *Associates First Capital Corporation Annual Report 1999.* Irving, TX: Associates First Capital Corporation, 2000.

[15] G. S. Day. *The Market Driven Organization: Understanding, Attracting, and Keeping Valuable Customers.* New York: Free Press, 2000.

[16] Adapted from Novell aligns organization to capture new market opportunities. Novell press release, May 23, 2000. Available at http://www.novell.com/press/archive/2000/05/pr00074.html; C. Haney and T. Weiss. Novell reorganizes after bad showing. *Computerworld,* May 29, 2000, p. 28; A. Wittmann. Novell: Greatness beyond the gap. *Network Computing,* August 21, 2000, pp. 44–48.

[17] D. J. Ketchen, Jr., and Associates. Organizational configurations and performance: A meta-analysis. *Academy of Management Journal,* 40, 1997, pp. 222–240.

[18] D. Nadler and M. I. Tushman. *Competing by Design: The Power of Organizational Architecture.* New York: Oxford University Press, 1997.

[19] Adapted from G. S. Vasilash. More than machining millions of parts per year: How Cobra is competitive. *Automotive Manufacturing & Production,* January 2000, pp. 56–58.

[20] C. Bernard. *The Functions of an Executive.* Cambridge, MA: President and Fellows of Harvard University, 1938.

[21] Internal Revenue Service restructuring and reform act of 1998.

[22] R. B. Nelson. *Empowering Employees through Delegation.* Burr Ridge, IL: Irwin, 1994, pp. 17–38.

[23] M. A. Johnston. Delegation and organizational structure in small businesses: Influences of manager's attachment patterns. *Group & Organization Management,* 25, 2000, pp. 4–21.

[24] Interview with R. Hinton, president of Burgundy Group, July 1997.

[25] Adapted from M. Warner. Confessions of a control freak. *Fortune,* September 4, 2000, pp. 130–140; About Siebel Systems. Available at http://www.siebel.com (August 29, 2000).

[26] Adapted from S. Thurm. What do you know? *Wall Street Journal,* June 21, 1999, pp. R10, R19; C. M. Means. Bob Buckman steps aside. Press release, Buckman Laboratories, May 8, 2000. Available at http://www.buckman.com/eng/StevePro.htm.

CHAPTER 11

[1] Adapted from M. Hammer and S. Stanton. How process enterprises really work. *Harvard Business Review,* November–December 1999, pp. 108–120.

[2] A. D. Chandler. *Strategy and Structure.* Cambridge, MA: MIT Press, 1962.

[3] E. H. Bowman et al. When does restructuring improve economic performance? *California Management Review,* winter 1999, pp. 33–54.

[4] D. A. Nadler and M. L. Tushman. The organization of the future: Strategic imperatives and core competencies for the 21st century. *Organizational Dynamics,* summer 2000, pp. 45–60.

[5] G. Hamel. *Leading the Revolution.* Boston: Harvard Business School Press, 2000.

[6] M. Hammer and S. Stanton, p. 112.

[7] Adapted from T. Burns and G. M. Stalker. *The Management of Innovation.* London: Tavistock, 1961, 119–122.

[8] M. Hammer and S. Stanton, p. 113.

[9] J. D. Thompson. *Organizations in Action.* New York: McGraw-Hill, 1967, pp. 51–67; K. E. Weick. *Making Sense of the Organization.* Malden, MA: Blackwell, 2001.

[10] C. Gresov and R. Drazin. Equifinality: Functional equivalence in organization design. *Academy of Management Review,* 22, 1997, pp. 403–428.

[11] BLS releases new 1998–2008 employment projections. November 30, 1999. Available at http://stats.bls.gov/news.release/ecopro.nro.htm (September 25, 2000).

[12] L. L. Berry, K. Seiders, and L. G. Gresham. The common traits of successful retailers. *Organizational Dynamics,* Autumn 1997, pp. 7–23.

[13] R. Metters and V. Vargas. Organizing work in service firms. *Business Horizons,* July–August 2000, pp. 23–32.

[14] J. L. Heskett, W. E. Sasser, Jr., and L. A. Schlesinger. *The Service Profit Chain.* New York: Free Press, 1997.

[15] J. R. Galbraith. *Competing with Flexible Lateral Designs.* Reading, MA: Addison-Wesley, 1994.

[16] J. Cope. Harrah's entertainment bets big on its new IT structure. *Computerworld,* July 3, 2000, p. 32; C. Brinkley. Harrah's builds database about patrons. *Wall Street Journal,* September 3, 1997, pp. B1, B8.

[17] A. Pettigrew, S. Massini, and T. Numagami. Innovative forms of organising in Europe and Asia. *European Management Journal,* 18, 2000, pp. 259–273.

[18] M. Hammer and S. Stanton, p. 114.

[19] Adapted from L. Copeland. DaimlerChrysler drives FastCar Web initiative. *Computerworld,* August 14, 2000, p. 12.

[20] N. Nohria and R. Gulati. Is slack good or bad for innovation? *Academy of Management Journal,* 39, 1996, pp. 1245–1264; J. L. C. Cheng and I.L. Kesner. Organizational slack and response to environmental shifts: The impact of resource allocation patterns. *Journal of Management,* 23, 1997, pp. 1–18.

[21] Adapted from C. Pickering. The world's local yokel. *Business 2.0.* May 2000, pp. 188–191.

[22] Adapted from Yahoo!, Inc. Capsule, *Hoover's Online,* September 27, 2000. Available at http://www.hoovers.com; S. Lucey. Should you Yahoo!? *Red Herring,* September 8, 2000, pp. 12–14.

[23] R. L. Daft. *Organizational Theory and Design.* Cincinnati: South-Western, 2000; D. Cackowski. Object analysis in organizational design: A solution for matrix organizations. *Project Management Journal,* 31, 2000, pp. 44–52.

[24] S. A. Mohrman, J. R. Galbraith, and E. E. Lawler (eds.). *Tomorrow's Organization: Crafting Winning Capabilities in a Dynamic World.* San Francisco: Jossey-Bass, 1998.

[25] E. E. Lawler III. *From the Ground Up: Six Principles for Building the New Logic Corporation.* San Francisco: Jossey-Bass, 1996; M. Castells. *The Rise of the Network Society.* Malden, MA: Blackwell, 2000.

[26] E. Randall. The Nike story? Just tell it. *Fast Company,* January–February 2000, pp. 44–45; T. Vanderbilt. *The Sneaker Book: Anatomy of an Industry and Icon.* Nevada City, CA: New Press, 1998.

[27] Adapted from G. Duysters, A. DeMan, and L. Wildeman. A network approach to alliance management. *European Management Journal,* 17, 1999, pp. 182–187; The cool rationalist. *Economist,* June 15, 1998, pp. 4–5, 11–12.

[28] C. Shapiro and H. R. Varian. *Information Rules: A Strategic Guide to the Network Economy.* Boston: Harvard Business Review, 1999; M. Ebers (ed.). *The Formation of Inter-Organizational Networks.* New York: Oxford University Press, 1999; I. F. Wilkinson, L-G. Mattson, and G. Easton. International competitiveness and trade promotion policy from a network perspective. *Journal of World Business,* 35, 2000, pp. 275–299.

[29] N. Nohria and S. Ghoshal. *The Differentiated Network: Organizing Multinationals for Value Creation.* San Francisco: Jossey-Bass, 1997.

[30] Adapted from C. B. Kavan, C. S. Saunders, and R. E. Nelson. Virtual@virtual.org. *Business Horizons,* September–October 1999, pp. 73–82; W. M. Fitzpatrick and D. R. Burke. Form, functions, and financial performance realities for the virtual organization. *S.A.M Advanced Management Journal,* Summer 2000, pp. 13–20.

[31] J. Chutchian-Ferranti. Virtual corporation. *Computerworld,* September 13, 1999, p. 64.

[32] Adapted from M. Claude Boudreau et al. Going global: Using information technology to advance the competitiveness of the virtual transnational organization. *Academy of Management Executive,* November 1998, pp. 120–128; W. B. Werther, Jr. Structure-driven strategy and virtual organization design. *Business Horizons,* March–April 1999, pp. 13–18; Y. Malhotra (ed.). *Knowledge Management and Virtual Organizations.* New York: Idea Group, 2000.

[33] Adapted from D. M. Upton and A. McAfee. The real virtual factory. In D. Tapcott (ed.), *Creating Value in the Network Economy.* Boston: Harvard Business School Publishing, 1999, pp. 69–106; AreoTech Service Group. Available at http://www.aerotechsg.com (October 2, 2000).

[34] W. F. Cascio. Managing in a virtual workplace. *Academy of Management Executive,* August 2000, pp. 81–90; W. J. Orlikowski. Using technology and constituting structures: A practice lens for studying technology in organizations. *Organization Science,* 11, 2000, pp. 404–428; M. K. Ahuja and K. M. Carley. Network structure in virtual organizations. *Organization Science,* 10, 1999, pp. 741–757; T. Kayworth and D. Leidner. The global virtual manager: A prescription for success. *European Management Journal,* 18, 2000, pp. 183–194.

[35] H. McCune. Creating quality. *Professional Builder,* October 1999, pp. 61–67.

[36] Adapted from L. Greenhalgh (interviewer). Ford Motor Company's CEO Jac Nasser on transformational change, e-business, and environmental responsibility. *Academy of Management Executive,* August 2000, pp. 46–51.

CHAPTER 12

[1] Q. Hardy. All Carly all the time. *Forbes,* December 13, 1999, pp. 138–144; C. Fiorina. Speech at Hewlett-Packard Shareholders Meeting, February 29, 2000 (accessed at http://www.hp.com on September 24, 2000); P. Sellers. Powerful women: These women rule. *Fortune,* October 25, 1999.

[2] M. Beer and N. Nohria. *Breaking the Code of Change.* Boston: Harvard Business School Press, 2000; R. A. Johnson. Antecedents and outcomes of corporate refocusing. *Journal of Management,* 22, 1996, pp. 439–483.

[3] N. A. Wishart, J. J. Elam, and D. Robey. Redrawing the portrait of a learning organization: Inside Knight-Ridder, Inc. *Academy of Management Executive,* 10, 1996, pp. 7–20. For an in-depth discussion of the importance of matching cultures and strategies, see A. C. Bluedorn and E. F. Lundgren. A culture-match perspective for strategic change. In R. W. Woodman and W. A. Pasmore (eds.), *Research in Organizational Change and Development,* 7, 1993, pp. 137–179.

[4] K. E. Weick and R. E. Quinn. Organizational change and development. *Annual Review of Psychology,* 1999, 50, pp. 361–386.

[5] K. Lewin. *Field Theory in Social Science.* New York: Harper & Row, 1951; C. Hendry. Understanding and creating organizational change through learning theory. *Human Relations,* 49, 1996, pp. 621–641.

[6] This and other stage models are reviewed in A. A. Armenakis and A. G. Bedeian. Organizational change: A review of

theory and research in the 1990s. *Journal of Management,* 25, 1999, 293–315.

[7] A. Meyer, G. Brooks, and J. Goes. Environmental jolts and industry revolutions: Organizational responses to discontinuous change. *Strategic Management Journal,* 11, 1990, 93–110.

[8] D. A. Nadler, R. B. Shaw, and A. E. Walton. *Discontinuous Change: Leading Organizational Transformations.* San Francisco: Jossey-Bass, 1995.

[9] D. Leonhardt. Weak outlook leads to shake-up at Procter & Gamble. *New York Times,* June 9, 2000, pp. C1, C5.

[10] T. A. Judge et al. Managerial coping with organizational change: A dispositional perspective. *Journal of Applied Psychology,* 84, 1999, 107–122.

[11] M. S. Poole et al. *Organizational Change Processes.* Oxford, UK: Oxford University Press, 2000; M. I. Tushman and C. A. O'Reilly III. *A Practical Guide to Leading Organizational Change and Renewal.* Boston: Harvard Business School Press, 1997.

[12] S. B. Bacharach, P. Bamberger, and W. J. Sonnenstuhl. The organizational transformation process: The micropolitics of dissonance reduction and the alignment of logics of action. *Administrative Science Quarterly,* 41, 1996, pp. 477–506.

[13] M. Stepanek. How fast is net fast? *Business Week E-Biz,* November 1, 1999, pp. EB 52–54.

[14] G. P. Huber and W. H. Glick. *Organizational Change and Redesign.* New York: Oxford University Press, 1993. Also see A. Howard and Associates. *Diagnosis for Organizational Change: Methods and Models.* New York: Guilford, 1994.

[15] A. Muoio. The change-agent blues. *Fast Company,* May 2000, pp. 44–45.

[16] For more details about the role of top management in communicating during organizational change, see Delta Consulting Group. *Strategic Communication: A Key to Implementing Change.* New York: Delta Consulting Group, 1999.

[17] D. M. Rousseau and S. A. Tijoriwala. What's a good reason to change? Motivated reasoning and social accounts in promoting organizational change. *Journal of Applied Psychology,* 84, 1999, pp. 514–528.

[18] M. J. Koch and R. G. McGrath. Improving labor productivity: Human resource management policies do matter. *Strategic Management Journal,* 17, 1996, pp. 335–354.

[19] J. E. McCann III and M. Buckner. Redesigning work: Motivations, challenges and practices in 181 companies. *Human Resource Planning,* 17(4), 1994, pp. 23–41.

[20] T. D. Ludwig and E. S. Geller. Assigned versus participative goal setting and response generalization: Managing injury control among professional pizza deliverers. *Journal of Applied Psychology,* 82, 1997, 253–261.

[21] G. Flynn. A flight plan for success. *Workforce,* July 1997, pp. 72–78.

[22] R. Maurer. *Beyond the Wall of Resistance.* Austin, TX: Bard Books, 1996.

[23] K. Skoldberg. Tales of change. *Organization Science,* 5, 1994, pp. 219–238.

[24] T. Petzinger. George Bauer put burden of downsizing into employees' hands. *Wall Street Journal,* May 10, 1996, p. B1.

[25] J. M. Pennings, H. Barkema, and S. Douma. Organizational learning and diversification. *Academy of Management Journal,* 37, 1994, pp. 608–641

[26] J. Clarke, C. Ellett, J. Bateman, and J. Rugutt. Faculty receptivity/resistance to change, personal and organizational efficacy, decision deprivation and effectiveness in research I universities. Paper presented at the Twenty-first Annual Meeting of the Association for the Study of Higher Education, Memphis, Tennessee, 1996.

[27] P. Strebel. Why do employees resist change? *Harvard Business Review,* May–June 1996, pp. 86–106.

[28] M. McHugh. The stress factor: Another item for the change management agenda? *Journal of Organizational Change Management,* 10, 1997, pp. 345–362.

[29] T. Petzinger, Jr., p. B1.

[30] J. Dean, P. Brandes, and R. Dharwadkar. Organizational cynicism. *Academy of Management Review,* 23, 1998, pp. 341–352; A. E. Reichers, J. P. Wanous, and J. T. Austin. Understanding and managing cynicism about organizational change. *Academy of Management Executive,* 11, 1997, p. 48.

[31] J. E. Mathieu and D. M. Zajkac. A review and meta-analysis of the antecedents, correlates, and consequences of organizational commitment. *Psychological Bulletin,* 108, 1990, pp. 171–194; J. F. Brett, W. L. Cron, and J. W. Slocum, Jr. Economic dependency on work: A moderator of the relationship between organizational commitment and performance. *Academy of Management Journal,* 38, 1995, pp. 261–271; R. E. Allen, M. A. Lucero, and K. L. Van Norman. An examination of the individual's decision to participate in an employee involvement program. *Group & Organization Management,* 22, 1997, pp. 117–143; W. C. Kim and R. Mauborgne. Fair process: Managing the knowledge economy. *Harvard Business Review,* July–August 1997, pp. 65–75.

[32] G. Hamel. Waking up IBM: How a gang of unlikely rebels transformed Big Blue. *Harvard Business Review,* July–August 2000, pp. 137–146; E. Randall. IBM's grassroots revival. The real story of how Big Blue found the future, got the net, and learned to love the People in Black. *Fast Company,* October–November 1997, pp. 102–200.

[33] R. Wherry. Out of the box. *Forbes,* September 20, 1999, p. 94.

[34] I. L. Goldstein. Training in work organizations. In M. D. Dunnette and L.M. Hough (eds.), *Handbook of Industrial and Organizational Psychology,* 2nd ed., vol. 2. Palo Alto, CA: Consulting Psychologists Press, 1991, pp. 507–620.

[35] For a detailed review of the effectiveness of various change programs, see B. A. Macy and H. Izumi. Organizational change, design, and work innovation: A meta-analysis of 131 North American field studies—1961–1991. In R. W. Woodman and W. A. Pasmore (eds.), *Research in Organizational Change and Development,* 7, 1993, pp. 235–313.

[36] C. Hymowitz. Task of managing changes in workplace takes a careful hand. *Wall Street Journal,* July 1, 1997, p. B1.

37 R. L. DeWitt. The structural consequences of downsizing. *Organization Science,* 4, 1993, pp. 30–40.

38 V. B. Wayman and S. Werner. The impact of workforce reductions on financial performance: A longitudinal perspective. *Journal of Management,* 26, 2000, pp. 341–363.

39 W. F. Cascio. Financial consequences of employment-change decisions in major U.S. corporations. *Academy of Management Journal,* 40, 1997, pp. 1175–1189.

40 E. Brynjolfsson, A. A. Renshaw, and M. V. Alstyne. The matrix of change. *Sloan Management Review,* Winter 1997, pp. 37–54; M. Hammer and J. Champy. *Reengineering the Corporation.* New York: HarperCollins, 1993; M. Hammer. *Beyond Reengineering: How the Processs-Centered Organization Is Changing Our Lives.* New York: HarperBusinesss, 1996; J. Champy. *Reengineering Management: The Mandate for New Leadership.* New York: HarperBusiness, 1996.

41 D. A. Garvin. Leveraging processes for strategic advantage. *Harvard Business Review,* September–October 1995, pp. 77–90.

42 P. J. Robertson, D. R. Roberts, and J. I. Porras. An evaluation of a model of planned organizational change: Evidence from a meta-analysis. In R. W. Woodman and W. A. Pasmore (eds.), *Research in Organizational Change and Development,* 7, 1993, pp. 1–39.

43 P. Bate, R. Khan, and A. Pye. Toward a culturally sensitive approach to organization structuring: Where organization design meets organization development. *Organization Science,* 11, 2000, pp. 197–211; J. I. Porras and P. J. Robertson. Organizational development: Theory, practice, and research. In M. D. Dunnette and L. M. Hough (eds.); T. T. Baldwin, C. Danielson, and W. Wiggenhorn. The evolution of learning strategies in organizations: From employee development to business redefinition. *Academy of Management Executive,* 11(4), 1997, 47–58.

44 A. I. Kraut. *Organizational Surveys: Tools for Assessment and Change.* San Francisco: Jossey-Bass, 1996.

45 Adapted from T. M. Amabile. How to kill creativity. *Harvard Business Review,* September–October 1998, pp. 77–87; T. M. Amabile et al. Assessing the work environment for creativity. *Academy of Management Journal,* 39, 1996, pp. 1154–1184; T. M. Amabile. *KEYS: Assessing the Climate for Creativity.* Greensboro, NC: Center for Creative Leadership, 1995.

46 J. Reingold and M. Stepanek. Why the productivity revolution will spread. *Business Week,* February 14, 2000, pp. 112–118.

47 J. Ginsburg and K. Morris. Xtreme retailing. *Business Week,* December 20, 1999, pp. 120–128.

48 Associated Press. Kodak's hometown feels little security. *Dallas Morning News,* November 13, 1997, p. 4D.

49 G. Hamel. Strategy as revolution. *Harvard Business Review,* July–August 1996, pp. 69–82.

50 S. V. Brull. Gateway's big gamble. *Business Week E-Biz,* June 5, 2000, pp. EB26–36.

51 A. Hargadon and R. I. Sutton. Building an innovation factory. *Harvard Business Review,* May–June 2000, pp. 157–166;

J. L. McCarthy. *A Blueprint for Change: A Conference Report.* (No. 1149-96-CH). New York: Conference Board, 1996; T. J. Galpin. *The Human Side of Change.* San Francisco: Jossey-Bass, 1996; Price Waterhouse. *Better Change: Best Practices for Transforming Your Organization.* Burr Ridge, IL: Irwin, 1995; B. Schneider, A. P. Brief, and R. A. Guzzo. Creating a climate and culture for sustainable organizational change. *Organizational Dynamics,* 24(4), 1996, pp. 6–19.

52 E. C. Nevis, A. J. DiBella, and J. M. Gould. Understanding organizations as learning systems. *Sloan Management Review,* Winter 1995, 73–85; P. Senge, *The Fifth Discipline: The Art and Practice of the Learning Organization.* New York: Doubleday, 1990; D. A. Garvin. Building a Learning Organization. *Harvard Business Review,* July–August 1993 78–91; P. Senge et al. *The Dance of Change.* New York: Doubleday, 1999.

53 Y.-T. Cheng and A. H. Van de Ven. Learning the innovation journey: Order out of chaos. *Organization Science,* 7, 1996, pp. 593–614.

54 B. P. Sunoo. Nantucket Nectars' recipe for participation. *Workforce,* May 1998, pp. 25–26.

55 T. Maxon. Southwest to go "ticketless" on all routes January 31. *Dallas Morning News,* January 11, 1995, p. 1D; M. E. McGill and J. W. Slocum, Jr. *The Smarter Organization: How to Build an Organization That Learns to Adapt to Marketplace Needs.* New York: John Wiley & Sons, 1994; M. DePree. *Leadership Is an Art.* New York: Doubleday, 1992.

56 C. Kim and R. Mauborgne. Fair process: Managing in the knowledge economy. *Harvard Business Review,* July–August 1997, pp. 65–75; R. Pascale, M. Millimann, and L. Gioja. Changing the way we change. *Harvard Business Review,* November–December 1997, pp. 127–139.

57 A. Kransdorrf. Fight organizational memory lapse. *Workforce,* September 1997, pp. 34–39.

58 J. P. MacDuffie. The road to "Root Cause": Shop-floor problem-solving at three auto assembly plants. *Management Science,* 43, 1997, pp. 479–502.

59 N. A. Wishart, J. J. Elam, and D. Robey.

60 D. Lei, J. W. Slocum, Jr., and R. A. Pitts. Building cooperative advantage: Managing strategic alliances to promote organizational learning. *Journal of World Business,* 32(3), 1997, pp. 203–223; R. C. Hill and D. Hellriegel. Critical contingencies in joint venture management: Some lessons from managers. *Organization Science,* 5, 1994, pp. 594–607.

61 J. B. Goes and S. H. Park. Interorganizational links and innovation: The case of hospital services. *Academy of Management Journal,* 40, 1997, pp. 673–696.

62 R. M. Grant. Prospering in dynamically-competitive environments: Organizational capability as knowledge integration. *Organization Science,* 7, 1996, pp. 357–411; J. P. Liebeskind et al. Social networks, learning, and flexibility: Sourcing scientific knowledge in new biotechnology firms. *Organization Science,* 7, 1996, pp. 428–443.

63 J. S. Brown and P. Duguid. Capturing knowledge without killing it. *Harvard Business Review,* May–June 2000, pp. 73–80.

64 P. S. Goodman and E. D. Darr. Exchanging best practices through computer-aided systems. *Academy of Management Executive,* 10(2), 1996, pp. 7–19.

65 R. Pascale. Change how you define leadership and you change how you run a company. *Fast Company,* April–May 1998, pp. 110–120; G. Hamel. Reinvent your company. *Fortune,* June 12, 2000, pp. 99–118.

CHAPTER 13

1 For more details about the HR practices at Southwest Airlines, see R. Levering and M. Moskowitz. The 100 best. *Fortune,* January 10, 2000, pp. 80–103; S. E. Jackson and R. S. Schuler, *Managing Human Resources: A Partnership Perspective.* Cincinnati: South-Western, 2000; N. Wong. Let spirit guide leadership. *Workforce,* February 2000, pp. 33–35; K. Freiberg and J. Freiberg, *Nuts! Southwest Airlines' Crazy Recipe for Business and Personal Success.* Austin, TX: Bard Press, 1996; F. E. Whittlesey, CEO Herb Kelleher discusses Southwest Airlines' people culture: How the company achieves competitive advantage from the ground up. *ACA Journal,* Winter 1995, pp. 8–25.

2 Strategic HRM is described in detail in R. S. Schuler and S. E. Jackson (eds.), *Strategic Human Resource Management.* Oxford, UK: Blackwell, 1999, and in *Human Resource Strategy: Formulation, Implementation, and Impact.* Thousand Oaks, CA: Sage, 2000.

3 T. J. Mullaney. Needed: The human touch. *Business Week E-Biz,* December 13, 1999, pp. EB58–EB59.

4 *High Performance Work Practices and Firm Performance.* U.S. Department of Labor: Washington, DC, 1993.

5 G. S. Hansen and B. Wernerfelt. Determinants of firm performance: Relative importance of economic and organizational factors. *Strategic Journal of Management,* 10, 1989, pp. 399–411.

6 T. A. Stewart. Real assets, unreal reporting. *Fortune,* July 6, 1997, pp. 207–208.

7 M. Buckingham and C. Coffman. *First Break All the Rules.* New York: Simon and Schuster, 1999; L. Grant. Happy workers, happy returns. *Fortune,* January 12, 1998, p. 81; G. E. Fryzell and J. Wang. The Fortune Corporation "Reputation" Index: Reputation for what? *Journal of Management,* 20, 1994, pp. 1–14; M. J. Schmit and S. P. Allscheid. Employee attitudes and customer satisfaction: Making the theoretical and empirical connections. *Personnel Psychology,* 48, 1995, pp. 521–536; C. A. Lengnick-Hall. Customer contributions to quality: A different view of the customer-oriented firm. *Academy of Management Review,* 21, 1996, pp. 791–824; P. S. Goodman et al. Customer-firm relationships, involvement, and customer satisfaction. *Academy of Management Journal,* 38, 1995, pp. 1310–1324.

8 C. Handy. A better capitalism. *Across the Board,* April 1998, pp. 16–22.

9 T. M. Welbourne and A. O. Andrews. Predicting the performance of initial public offerings: Should human resource management be in the equation? *Academy of Management Journal,* 39, 1996, pp. 891–919.

10 J. J. Laabs. Quality drives Trident's success. *Workforce,* February 1998, pp. 44–49.

11 M. A. Konovsky. Understanding procedural justice and its impact on business organizations. *Journal of Management,* 26, 2000, pp. 489–511; J. Greenberg. Looking fair vs. being fair: Managing impressions of organizational justice. In B. M. Staw and L. L. Cummings (eds.), *Research in Organizational Behavior,* vol. 12. Greenwich, CT: JAI Press, 1990, pp. 111–157.

12 W. C. Kim and R. Mauborgne. Fair process: Managing in the knowledge economy. *Harvard Business Review,* July–August 1997, pp. 65–75; R. Levering. *A Great Place to Work.* New York: Random House, 1988. Also see F. Fukuyama. *Trust: The Social Virtues and the Creation of Prosperity.* New York: Free Press, 1995.

13 J. C. Morrow, P. C. Morrow, and E. J. Mullen. Intraorganizational mobility and work-related attitudes. *Journal of Organizational Behavior,* 17, 1996, pp. 363–374.

14 J. W. Meyer and B. Rowan. Institutionalized organizations: Formal structure as myth and ceremony. *American Journal of Sociology,* 1977, pp. 340–363; W. R. Scott. The adolescence of institutional theory. *Administrative Scientific Quarterly,* 1987, pp. 493–511; L. G. Zucker. Institutional theories of organization. *Annual Review of Sociology,* 13, 1987, pp. 443–464.

15 Number of EEO lawsuits appears to be "leveling off." *HR Magazine,* June 2000, p. 27; S. Siwolop. Recourse or retribution? Employers are taking on disgruntled workers in court. *New York Times,* June 7, 2000, pp. C1, C6.

16 P. E. Varca and P. Pattison. Evidentiary standards in employment discrimination: A view toward the future. *Personnel Psychology,* 46, 1993, p. 239.

17 K. Eichenwald. The two faces of Texaco: The right policies are on the books, but not always on the job. *New York Times,* November 10, 1996, pp. A1–A3; A. Bryant. How much has Texaco changed? A mixed report card on anti-bias efforts. *New York Times,* November 2, 1997, Section 3, pp. 1, 16, 17.

18 C. Hall. Ringmasters turn a circus into an empire. *Dallas Morning News,* February 8, 1998, pp. H1–H2; G. Flynn. Acrobats, aerialists, and HR: The big top needs big HR. *Workforce,* August 1997, pp. 38–45. Table adapted from L. B. Pincus and J. A. Belohlav. Legal issues in multinational business strategy: To play the game you have to know the rules. *Academy of Management Executive,* 10(3), 1996, pp. 52–62; J. P. Begin. *Dynamic Human Resource Systems: Cross-National Comparisons.* New York: de Gruyter, 1997; R. Orzechowski and B. Berret. Setting up shop in Vietnam. *Global Workforce,* May 1998, pp. 24–27.

19 For a discussion of how culture impacts hiring practices, see A. M. Ryan et al. An international look at selection practices: Nation and culture as explanations for variability in practice. *Personnel Psychology,* 52, 1999, pp. 359–391.

20 J. Carey. OSHA's ergo-rules: Business, hold your fire. *Business Week,* December 4, 1999, p. 54.

21 R. W. Thompson. Setting OSHA's agenda. *HR Magazine,* December 1999, pp. 94–102; M. Conlin. Is your office killing you? *Business Week,* June 6, 2000, pp. 114–122.

22 M. Conlin.

23 S. E. Jackson and R. S. Schuler. *Managing Human Resources: A Partnership Perspective.* Cincinnati: South-Western, 2000. Used with permission.

24 E. E. Lawler III and G. E. Ledford, Jr. New approaches to organizing: Competencies and the decline of the bureaucratic model. In C. L. Cooper and S. E. Jackson (eds.), *Creating Tomorrow's Organizations: Handbook for Future Research in Organizations.* Chichester, UK: John Wiley & Sons, 1997, pp. 231–249.

25 For a comprehensive review, see J. A. Breaugh and M. Starke. Research on employee recruitment: So many studies, so many remaining questions. *Journal of Management,* 26, 2000, pp. 405–434.

26 C. Salter. Andy Esparza knows what success sounds like. *Fast Company,* December, 1999, pp. 218–222.

27 A. E. Barber et al. A tale of two job markets: Organizational size and its effects on hiring practices and job search behavior. *Personnel Psychology,* 52, 1999, pp. 841–867. Also see A. Barber. *Recruiting Employees: Individual and Organizational Perspectives.* Thousand Oaks, CA: Sage, 1998.

28 R. W. Judy. Labor forecast: Gray skies, worker drought continues. *HR Magazine: HR in the 21st century* (special issue), January 2000, pp. 18–26.

29 R. Levering and M. Moskowitz. The 100 best. *Fortune,* January 10, 2000, pp. 80–103; P. Nakache. Cisco's recruiting edge. *Fortune,* September 29, 1997, pp. 275–276; K. Ferguson. Cisco high. *Business Week E-Biz,* June 3, 2000, pp. 102–103.

30 J. Aley. The heart of Silicon Valley. *Fortune,* July 7, 1997, pp. 66–74.

31 For more details, see J. F. Kehoe (ed.), *Managing Selection in Changing Organizations.* San Francisco: Jossey-Bass, 2000.

32 A. Fisher. The world's most admired companies. *Fortune,* October 27, 1997, pp. 220–240.

33 A. M. Ryan and R. E. Ployhart. Applicants' perceptions of selection procedures and decisions: A critical review and agenda for the future. *Journal of Management,* 26, 2000, pp. 565–606.

34 C. Daniels. To hire a lumber expert, click here. *Fortune,* April 3, 2000, pp. 267–270.

35 M. A. McDaniel et al. The validity of employment interviews: A comprehensive review and meta-analysis. *Journal of Applied Psychology,* 79, 1994, pp. 599–616.

36 D. Mochari. The screen machine. *Inc. 500,* 1999, pp. 198–199.

37 M. McNamee. We try to minimize face-to-face interviews. *Business Week,* November 22, 1999, p. 178.

38 J. Y. Murray and M. Kotabe. Sourcing strategies of U.S. service companies: A modified transaction-analysis. *Strategic Management Journal,* 20, 1999, pp. 791–797.

39 B. P. Neihoff and R. J. Paul. Causes of employee theft and strategies that HR managers can use for prevention. *Human Resource Management,* Spring 2000, pp. 51–65; J. C. Wimbush and D. R. Dalton. Base for employee theft: Convergence

of multiple methods. *Journal of Applied Psychology,* 82, 1997, pp. 756–764; S. Greengard. Theft control starts with HR strategies. *Personnel Journal,* April 1993, pp. 80–91; H. J. Bernardin and D. K. Cooke. Validity of an honesty test in predicting theft among convenience store employees. *Academy of Management Journal,* 36, 1993, pp. 1097–1108.

40 D. Ones, S. C. Viswesvaran, and F. L. Schmidt. Comprehensive meta-analysis of integrity test validities: Findings and implications for personnel selection and theories of job performance. *Journal of Applied Psychology* (monograph), 78, 1993, pp. 679–703.

41 A. Tziner, S. Ronen, and D. A. Hacohen. A four-year study of an assessment center in a financial corporation. *Journal of Organizational Behavior,* 14, 1993, pp. 225–237.

42 P. Carbonara. Hire for attitude: Train for skill. *Fast Company,* April–May 1996, pp. 64–71.

43 Orientation: Welcome to America. *Inc. 500,* 1999, pp. 208–211.

44 R. Balu. KPMG faces the Internet test. *Fast Company,* March 2000, pp. 50–52.

45 M. Moravec, O. J. Johannessen, and T. A. Hjelmas. Thumbs up for self-managed teams. *Management Review,* July/August 1997, pp. 234–241; S. E. Prokesch. Unleashing the power of learning: An interview with British Petroleum's John Browne. *Harvard Business Review,* September–October 1997; Moravec, O. J. Johannessen, and T. A. Hjelmas. We have seen the future and it is self-managed. *PM Network,* September 1997, pp. 20–22.

46 J. Conner and C. A. Smith. Developing the next generation of leaders: A new strategy for leadership development at Colgate-Palmolive. In E. M. Mone and M. London (eds.), *HR to the Rescue: Case Studies of HR Solutions to Business Challenges.* Houston: Gulf, 1998.

47 R. V. Gerbman. Corporate universities 101. *HR Magazine,* February 2000, pp. 101–106.

48 Adapted from S. Taylor and N. Napier. Working in Japan: Lessons from women expatriates. *Sloan Management Review,* Spring 1996, pp. 76–84; C. Gould. What's the latest in global compensation? *Global Workforce,* July 1997, pp. 17–20; Executives overseas. *HR Focus,* March 1997, pp. 6–7; L. Grant. That overseas job could derail your career. *Fortune,* April 14, 1997, p. 166.

49 For a review, see R. D. Arvey and K. R. Murphy. Performance evaluation in work settings. *Annual Review Psychology,* 49, 1998, pp. 141–168.

50 For a discussion of how performance standards can affect employee satisfaction and motivation, see P. Bobko and A. Colella. Employee reactions to performance standards: A review and research propositions. *Personnel Psychology,* 47, 1994, pp. 1–29.

51 A. G. Walker and J. W. Smither. A five-year study of upward feedback: What managers do with their results matters. *Personnel Psychology,* 52, 1999, pp. 393–423.

52 G. Imperato. How to give good feedback. *Fast Company,* September 1998, pp. 144–156.

53 R. C. Mayer and J. H. Davis. The effect of the performance appraisal system on trust for management: A field quasi-experiment. *Journal of Applied Psychology,* 84, 1999, pp. 123–136.

54 For a recent discussion, see J. W. Smither (ed.), *Performance Appraisal: State of the Art in Practice.* San Francisco: Jossey-Bass, 1998.

55 T. J. Maurer, J. K. Palmer, and D. K. Ashe. Diaries, checklists, evaluations, and contrast effects in measurement of behavior. *Journal of Applied Psychology,* 78, 1993, pp. 226–231.

56 N. M. A. Hauensstein. Training raters to increase accuracy of appraisals and the usefulness of feedback, in J. W. Smither (ed.), 1998, pp. 404–442.

57 W. W. Tornow and M. London (eds.). *Maximizing the Value of 360-Degree Feedback.* Greensboro, NC: Center for Creative Leadership, 1999.

58 R. F. Martell and M. R. Borg. A comparison of the behavioral rating accuracy of groups and individuals. *Journal of Applied Psychology,* 78, 1993, pp. 43–50.

59 J. Lefkowitz. The role of interpersonal affective regard in supervisory performance ratings: A literature review and proposed causal model. *Journal of Occupational and Organizational Psychology,* 73, 2000, pp. 67–80; M. Beer. Performance appraisal: Dilemmas and possibilities. *Organizational Dynamics,* Winter 1981, p. 26; A. Zander. Research on self-esteem, feedback and threats to self-esteem. In A. Zander (ed.), *Performance Appraisals: Effects on Employees and Their Performance.* New York: Foundation for Research in Human Behavior, 1963.

60 A. Farnham. How to nurture creative sparks. *Fortune,* January 10, 1994, p. 98.

61 T. B. Weiss. Show me more than the money. *HR Focus.* November 1997, pp. 3–4.

62 A. E. Barber and R. D. Bretz, Jr. Compensation, attraction and retention. In S. L. Rynes and B. Gerhart (eds.), *Compensation in Organizations: Current Research and Practice.* San Francisco: Jossey-Bass, 2000; D. M. Cable and T. A. Judge. Pay preferences and job search decisions: A person-organization fit perspective. *Personnel Psychology,* 47, 1994, pp. 339–348.

63 J. Davis and C. Harris. Retaining your hot skills employees—Use dollars and sense. *ACA Journal,* First Quarter 2000, pp. 47–56; C. O. Trevor, B. Gerhart, and J. W. Boudreau. Voluntary turnover and job performance: Curvilinearity and the moderating influences of salary growth on promotions. *Journal of Applied Psychology,* 82, 1997, pp. 44–61.

64 For a comparison of different forms of base pay, see F. M. Brennen and M. Coil. Comparing alternative base pay methods. *ACA News,* June 1999, pp. 21–25.

65 Readers on CEO pay: Many are angry, a few really think the big guy is worth it. *Fortune,* June 8, 1998, p. 296.

66 For additional data, see *CEO Pay: A Comprehensive Look.* Scottsdale, AZ: American Compensation Association, 1997.

67 S. E. Jackson and R. S. Schuler. *Managing Human Resources: A Partnership Perspective.* Cincinnati: South-Western, 2000. Used with permission.

68 R. L. Heneman, G. E. Ledford, Jr., and M. T. Gresham. The changing nature of work and its effects on compensation design and delivery. In S. L. Rynes and B. Gerhart (eds.), *Compensation in Organizations: Current Research and Practice.* San Francisco: Jossey-Bass, 2000.

69 S. M. Puffer. CompUSA's CEO James Halpin on technology, rewards, and commitment. *Academy of Management Executive,* May 1999, pp. 29–36.

70 J. S. DeMatteo, L. T. Eby, and E. Sundstrom. Team-based rewards: Current empirical evidence and directions or future research. *Research in Organizational Behavior,* 20, 1998, pp. 141–184.

71 P. K. Zingheim and J. R. Schuster. Value is the goal. *Workforce,* February 2000, pp. 56–61.

72 M. M. Engel. Update on trends in stock option and long-term incentive plans. *ACA Journal,* Third quarter 1999, pp. 42–48; J. Dolmat-Connell. Magic potion or passing fad? *ACA News,* April 2000, pp. 38–49.

CHAPTER 14

1 D. Fenn. Personnel best. *Inc.,* February 2000, pp. 75–83.

2 B. Buckingham and C. Coffman. *First, Break All the Rules.* New York: Simon & Schuster, 1999.

3 It's the manager, stupid. *Fortune* (interview by magazine's editors), October 25, 1999, pp. 366–367.

4 G. P. Latham and J. J. Baldes. The practical sigificance of Locke's theory of goal setting. *Journal of Applied Psychology,* 60, 1975, pp. 122–124.

5 E. A. Locke. Motivation, cognition, and action: An analysis of studies of task goals and knowledge. *Applied Psychology: An International Review,* 49, 2000, pp. 408–429; E. A. Locke. Toward a theory of task motivation and incentives. *Organizational Behavior and Human Performance,* 3, 1968, pp. 157–189; E. A. Locke and G. P. Latham. *A Theory of Goal Setting and Task Performance.* Englewood Cliffs, NJ: Prentice-Hall, 1990.

6 G. P. Latham and G. H. Seijts. The effects of proximal and distal goals on performance on a moderately complex task. *Journal of Organizational Behavior,* 20, 1999, pp. 421–429. Also see P. M. Gollwitzer. Implementation intentions: Strong effects of simple plans. *American Psychologist,* 54, 1999, pp. 493–503; D. VandeWalle, W. L. Cron, and J. W. Slocum, Jr. The role of goal orientation following performance feedback. *Journal of Applied Psychology,* in press.

7 To learn more about how goal setting is similar to benchmarking, see L. Mann, D. Samson, and D. Dow. A field experiment on the effects of benchmarking and goal setting on company sales performance. *Journal of Management,* 24, 1998, pp. 73–96.

8 A. D. Stajkovic and F. Luthans. Self-efficacy and work-related performance: A meta-analysis. *Psychological Bulletin,* 124, 1998, pp. 240–261.

9 J. E. Sawyer et al. Analysis of work group productivity in an applied setting: Application of a time series panel design.

Personnel Psychology, 52, 1999, pp. 927–967; D. VandeWalle. A goal orientation model of feedback seeking behavior. *Human Resource Management Review,* in press.

[10] E. Matson. The discipline of high-tech leaders. *Fast Company,* April/May 1997, pp. 34–36.

[11] J. Wegge. Procrastination in group goal setting: Some novel findings and a comprehensive model as a new ending to an old story. *Applied Psychology: An International Review,* 49, 2000, pp. 498–516; A. M. O'Leary-Kelly, J. J. Martocchio, and D. D. Fink. A review of the influence of group goals on group performance. *Academy of Management Journal,* 37, 1994, pp. 1285–1301.

[12] C. Garvey. Goalsharing scores. *HR Magazine,* April 2000, pp. 99–106.

[13] B. F. Skinner. *Contingencies of Reinforcement.* New York: Appleton-Century-Crofts, 1969; B. F. Skinner. *Beyond Freedom and Dignity.* New York: Bantam, 1971; B. F. Skinner. *About Behaviorism.* New York: Knopf, 1974.

[14] F. Luthans and A. D. Stajkovic. Reinforce for performance: The need to go beyond pay and even rewards. *Academy of Management Executive,* 12 (2), 1999, pp. 49–57; A. D. Stajkovic and F. Luthans. A meta-analysis of the effects of organizational behavior modification on task performance, 1975–1995. *Academy of Management Journal,* 40, 1997, pp. 1122–1149.

[15] C. Daniels. "Thank-you" is nice, but this is better. *Fortune,* November 22, 1999, p. 370.

[16] J. Macht. Pulp addiction. *Inc. Technology,* 1, 1997, pp. 43–46.

[17] S. E. Seibert, J. M. Crant, and M. L. Kraimer. Proactive personality and career success. *Journal of Applied Psychology,* 84, 1999, pp. 416–427.

[18] Adapted from C. A. Frayne and M. J. Geringer. Self-management training for improving job performance: A field experiment involving sales people. *Journal of Applied Psychology,* 85, 2000, pp. 361–372; C. A. Frayne and M. J. Geringer. A social cognitive approach to examining joint venture general managers. *Group and Organizational Management,* 19, 1994, pp. 240–262.

[19] F. Herzberg, B. Mausner, and B. Snyderman. *The Motivation to Work.* New York: John Wiley & Sons, 1959.

[20] C. L. Jurkiewicz and T. K. Massey, Jr. What motivates municipal employees: A comparison study of supervisor and non-supervisory employees. *Public Personnel Management,* 26, 1997, pp. 367–376.

[21] *Source:* J. R. Hackman and G. R. Oldham. *Work Redesign.* Reading, MA: Addison-Wesley, 1980, p. 83. Reprinted with permission. Also see N. G. Dodd and D. C. Ganster. The interactive effects of variety, autonomy, and feedback on attitudes and performance. *Journal of Organizational Behavior,* 17, 1996, pp. 329–347.

[22] P. W. Mulvey, G. E. Ledford, and P. V. LeBlanc. Rewards of work: How they drive performance, retention, and satisfaction. *WorldatWork Journal,* Third quarter, 2000, pp. 6–28.

[23] R. W. Renn and R. J. Vandenberg. The critical psychological states: An underrepresented component in job characteristics model research. *Journal of Management,* 21, 1995, pp. 279–303.

[24] S. P. Brown and T. W. Leigh. A new look at psychological climate and its relationship to job involvement, effort, and performance. *Journal of Applied Psychology,* 81, 1996, pp. 358–368.

[25] E. Simon. Corporate democracy. *Star Ledger,* Newark, New Jersey, November 8, 1999, pp. 23, 27. Also see R. Forrester. Empowerment: Rejuvenating a potent idea. *Academy of Management Executive,* 14(3), 2000, pp. 67–77.

[26] B. P. Sunoo. Blending a successful workforce. *Workforce,* March 2000, pp. 44–48.

[27] J. S. Adams. Toward an understanding of equity. *Journal of Abnormal and Social Psychology,* 67, 1963, pp. 422–436.

[28] A. S. Tsui et al. Alternative approaches to the employee–organization relationship: Does investment in employees pay off? *Academy of Management Journal,* 40, 1997, pp. 1089–1121.

[29] Trish Millines Dziko. *Fast Company,* August, 2000, p. 85.

[30] K. Aquino et al. Integrating justice constructs into the turnover process: A test of a referent cognitions model. *Academy of Management Journal,* 40, 1997, pp. 1208–1227; R. E. Kidwell, Jr., and N. Bennett. Employee propensity to withhold effort: A conceptual model to intersect three avenues of research. *Academy of Management Review,* 18, 1993, pp. 429–456; J. Schaubroek, D. R. May, and F. W. Brown. Procedural justice explanations and employee reactions to economic hardship: A field experiment. *Journal of Applied Psychology,* 79, 1994, pp. 455–161; M. A. Konovsky and S. D. Pugh. Citizenship behavior and social exchange. *Academy of Management Journal,* 37, 1994, pp. 656–669; J. Greenberg. Employee theft as a reaction to underpayment inequity: The hidden costs of pay cuts. *Journal of Applied Psychology,* 75, 1990, pp. 561–568; J. Greenberg. Stealing in the name of justice: Informational and interpersonal moderators of theft reactions to underpayment inequity. *Organizational Behavior and Human Decision Processes,* 54, 1993, pp. 81–103.

[31] This example is based on actual practice in one particular company.

[32] M. Bloom. The performance effects of pay dispersion on individuals and organizations. *Academy of Management Journal,* 42, 1999, pp. 25–50.

[33] See R. Kanfer and P. L. Ackerman. Individual differences in work motivation: Further explorations of a trait framework. *Applied Psychology: An International Review,* 49, 2000, pp. 470–482; K. R. Murphy (ed.), *Individual Differences and Behavior in Organizations.* San Francisco: Jossey-Bass, 1996.

[34] A. H. Maslow. *Motivation and Personality,* 2nd ed. New York: Harper & Row, 1970. Also see D. H. Shapiro, Jr., C. E. Schwartz, and J. A. Astin. Controlling ourselves, controlling our world. Psychology's role in understanding positive and negative consequences of seeking and gaining control. *American Psychologist,* 51, 1996, pp. 1213–1230.

[35] Richard Branson. *Fast Company.* August 2000, p. 78.

[36] C. P. Alderfer. *Existence, Relatedness and Growth: Human Needs in Organizational Settings.* New York: Free Press, 1972.

[37] K. Sokolowski et al. Assessing achievement, affiliation, and power motives, all at once—The Multi-Motive-Grid (MMG). *Journal of Personality Assessment,* 74, 2000, pp. 126–145; D. C. McClelland. *Motivational Trends in Society.* Morristown, NJ: General Learning Press, 1971.

[38] M. L. Ambrose and C. T. Kulick. Old friends, new faces: Motivation research in the 1990s. *Journal of Management,* 25, 1999, pp. 231–292.

[39] D. Leonhardt. The saga of Lloyd Ward. *Business Week,* August 9, 1999, pp. 59–70.

[40] D. C. McClelland. The two faces of power. *Journal of International Affairs,* 24, 1970, pp. 29–47.

[41] P. Burrows. The man who "dot.commed" Sun. *Business Week E-Biz,* December 13, 1999, pp. EB62–EB70.

[42] W. Van Erde and H. Thierry. Vroom's expectancy models and work-related criteria: A meta-analysis. *Journal of Applied Psychology,* 81, 1996, pp. 575–586.

[43] Source: From L. W. Porter and E. E. Lawler III. *Managerial Attitudes and Performance.* Homewood, IL: Irwin, 1968, p. 165. Used with permission.

[44] D. H. Lindsley, D J. Brass, and J. B. Thomas. Efficacy-performance spirals: A multilevel perspective. *Academy of Management Review,* 20, 1995, pp. 645–678; R. W. Griffeth and P. W. Hom. The employee turnover process. *Research in Personnel and Human Resources Management,* 13, 1995, pp. 245–293. Note, however, that the link between satisfaction and turnover may be weaker for employees with high financial requirements. See J. F. Brett, W. L. Cron, and J. W. Slocum, Jr. Economic dependency on work: A moderator of the relationship between organizational commitment and performance. *Academy of Management Journal,* 38, 1995, pp. 261–271.

[45] For a discussion of this and other common pitfalls, see S. Kerr. An academy classic: On the folly of rewarding A, while hoping for B. *Academy of Management Executive,* 9, 1995, pp. 7–16.

[46] A. N. Kluger and A. DeNisi. The effects of feedback interventions on performance: A historical review, a meta-analysis, and a preliminary feedback intervention theory. *Psychological Bulletin,* 119, 1996, pp. 254–284.

[47] J. Thomas. Satisfaction in job well done is only reward for e-mail software inventor. *New York Times,* January 21, 1997, p. A10.

CHAPTER 15

[1] Adapted from K. Melymuka. Taking stock. *Computerworld,* June 26, 2000, pp. 66–67; J. Nocera. A mug only 20,000 employees could love. *Ecompany.com,* June 2000, pp. 159–166; M. Leuchter. Schwab—A potent competitor. *USBanker,* May 2000, pp. 44–45; L. Lee and David S. Pottruck. *Business Week,* September 27, 1999, pp. EB51–EB52.

[2] P. G. Northouse. *Leadership Theory and Practice,* 2nd ed. Thousand Oaks, CA: Sage, 2000.

[3] M. Leuchter, p. 45.

[4] C. C. Cogliser and C. A. Schriesheim. Exploring work unit context and leader–member exchange: A multilevel perspective. *Journal of Organizational Behavior,* 21, 2000, pp. 487–511.

[5] T. Carvell. Your staff hates you. *Fortune,* September 28, 1998, pp. 200–206.

[6] K. Melymuka, p. 67.

[7] K. Melymuka, p. 67.

[8] J. O. Whitney, T. Parker, and S. Noble. *Power Plays: Shakespeare's Lessons in Leadership and Management.* Old Tappan, NJ: Simon & Schuster, 2000; B. Lee and S. R. Covey. *The Power Principle: Influence with Honor.* New York: Fireside, 1998.

[9] R. Bar-On and J. D. Parker (eds.). *The Handbook of Emotional Intelligence: Theory, Development, Assessment, and Application at Home, School and in the Workplace.* New York: John Wiley & Sons, 2000.

[10] Q. Nguyen Huy. Emotional capability, emotional intelligence and radical change. *Academy of Management Review,* 24, 1999, pp. 325–345.

[11] A. G. Robertson and C. L. Walt. The leader within. *Outlook,* June 1999, pp. 19–23.

[12] Adapted from T. Schwartz. How do you feel? *Fast Company,* June 2000, pp. 297–314; A. Fisher. Success secret: A high emotional IQ. *Fortune,* October 26, 1998, pp. 293–298; N. S. Schutte et al. Development and validation of a measure of emotional intelligence. *Personality and Individual Differences,* 25, 1998, pp. 167–177.

[13] D. P. Goleman. *Working with Emotional Intelligence.* New York: Doubleday Dell, 1998.

[14] Adapted from D. Goleman. Leadership that gets results. *Harvard Business Review,* March–April 2000, pp. 78–90.

[15] L. Klebe Treviño, L. Pincus Hartman, and M. Brown. Moral person and moral manager: How executives develop a reputation for ethical leadership. *California Management Review,* Summer 2000, pp. 128–142.

[16] D. McGregor. The human side of enterprise. *Management Review,* 46(11), 1957, pp. 22–28, reprinted in *Reflections: The SOL Journal,* Fall 2000, pp. 6–14; G. Heil et al. *Douglas McGregor, Revisited: Managing the Human Side of the Enterprise.* New York: John Wiley & Sons, 2000.

[17] D. McGregor, p. 11 (reprint).

[18] D. McGregor, p. 12 (reprint).

[19] D. McGregor, p. 12 (reprint). Also see D. McGregor. *The Human Side of the Enterprise.* New York: McGraw-Hill, 1960.

[20] R. R. Blake and J. S. Mouton. *The Managerial Grid.* Houston: Gulf, 1985; C. T. Lewis and S. M. Jobs. Conflict management: The essence of leadership. *Journal of Leadership Studies,* November 1993, pp. 47–60.

21 From No to Yo!. Available at http://www.bradycorp.com. Click "President's Message."

22 G. A. Yukl. *Leadership in Organizations,* 4th ed. Englewood Cliffs, NJ: Prentice-Hall, 1997.

23 P. Hersey, K. H. Blanchard, and D. E. Johnson. *Management of Organizational Behavior: Leading Human Resources,* 8th ed. Englewood Cliffs, NJ: Prentice-Hall, 2001.

24 K. H. Blanchard, D. Zigarmi, and R. B. Nelson. Situational leadership after 25 years: A retrospective. *Journal of Leadership Studies,* November 1993, pp. 21–36.

25 W. E. Norris and R. P. Vecchio. Situational leadership theory: A replication. *Group & Organization Management,* 17, 1992, pp. 331–343.

26 Adapted from V. H. Vroom. Leadership and the decision-making process. *Organizational Dynamics,* Spring 2000, pp. 82–94.

27 V. H. Vroom. New developments in leadership and decision making. *OB News.* Briarcliff Manor, NY: Organizational Behavior Division of the Academy of Management, headquartered at Pace University, Spring 1999, 5. Copyright © Victor Vroom, 1998. Used with permission.

28 Adapted from B. L. Kirkman and B. Rosen. Powering up teams. *Organizational Dynamics,* Winter 2000, pp. 48–66.

29 C. P. Egri and S. Herman. Leadership in the North American environmental sector: Values, leadership styles, and contexts of environmental leaders and their organizations. *Academy of Management Journal,* 43, 2000, pp. 571–604; F. J. Yammarino, W. D. Spangler, and A. J. Dubinsky. Transformational and contingent reward leadership: Individual dyad and group levels of analysis. *Leadership Quarterly,* 9, 1998, pp. 27–54.

30 Adapted from H. H. Friedman, M. Lingbert, and K. Giladi. Transformational leadership: Instituting revolutionary change in accounting. *National Public Accountant,* May 2000, pp. 8–11; B. J. Avolio. *Full Leadership Development: Building the Vital Forces in Organizations.* Thousand Oaks, CA: Sage, 1999.

31 L. Larwood et al. Structure and meaning of organizational vision. *Academy of Management Journal,* 39, 1995, pp. 740–769.

32 H. Rubin. Can we develop the ability to have visions, *Fast Company,* August 2000, pp. 238–242.

33 A. J. Alessandra and T. Allissandra. *Charisma: Seven Keys to Developing the Magnetism That Leads to Success.* New York: Warner Books, 2000.

34 J. A. Conger. Charismatic and transformational leadership in organizations: An insider's perspective on the developing streams of research. *Leadership Quarterly,* 10, 1999, pp. 145–179.

35 J. J. Sosik and L. E. Megerian. Understanding leader emotional intelligence and performance: The role of self–other agreement on transformational leadership perceptions. *Group & Organization Management,* 24, 1999, pp. 367–390.

36 B. M. Bass. Ethics, character, and authentic transformational leadership behavior. *Leadership Quarterly,* 10, 1999, pp. 187–217.

37 Adapted from M. Whigham-Desir. Leadership has its rewards. *Black Enterprise,* September 1999, pp. 73–85.

38 American Express Company. *Hoover's Online.* Available at http://hoovers.com (October 12, 2000).

39 M. A. Berman. Sweating the soft stuff. *Across the Board,* January 1998, pp. 39–43. Also see P. Taffinder. *The Leadership Crash Course: A 6-Step Self-Development Program.* Dover, NH: Kogan Page.

40 M. W. McCall, Jr. *High Flyers: Developing the Next Generation of Leaders.* Boston: Harvard Business School Press, 1997; J. Conner. Developing the global leaders of tomorrow. *Human Resource Management,* Summer/Fall, 2000, pp. 147–157.

41 H. Row. Is management for me? That is the question. *Fast Company.* February–March 1998, pp. 50–52. Also see J. P. Briscoe and D. T. Hall. Grooming and picking leaders using competency frameworks: Do they work? *Organizational Dynamics,* Autumn 1999, pp. 37–52.

42 J. A. Conger and B. Benjamin. *Building Leaders: How Successful Companies Develop the Next Generation.* San Francisco: Jossey-Bass, 1999.

43 Copyright © 1998 Marshall Sashkin. Used with permission. No further reproduction without written permission.

CHAPTER 16

1 Adapted from L. Grensing-Pophal. Follow me. *HR Magazine,* February 2000, pp. 36–45. http://www.continental.com (July 18, 2000).

2 J. T. Wood. *Communication in Our Lives.* New York: Wadsworth, 1997.

3 J. Penrose, R. W. Rasberry, and R. Myers. *Advanced Business Communications.* Cincinnati: South-Western, 2001.

4 T. J. Hess, L. P. Rees, and T. R. Rakes. Using autonomous software agents to create the next generation of decision support systems. *Decision Sciences,* 31(1), 2000, pp. 1–32; D. Straub and E. Karahanna. Knowledge worker communications and recipient availability: Towards a task closure explanation of media choice. *Organization Science,* 9(2), 1998, pp. 160–174.

5 Personal communication with M. Powell, Director, College Recruiting. The Associates First Capital Corporation, Irving, Texas, August 1, 2000. Also see J. A. Breaugh and M. Starke. Research on employee recruitment: So many studies, so many remaining questions. *Journal of Management,* 26, 2000, pp. 405–434.

6 D. Tannen. *Talking from 9 to 5.* New York: William Morrow, 1994.

7 M. Munter. *Guide to Managerial Communication: Effective Business Writing and Speaking,* 5th ed. Englewood Cliffs, NJ: Prentice-Hall, 1999.

8 K. M. Hiemstra. Shake my hand: Making the right first impression in business with nonverbal communications. *Business and Communication Quarterly,* 62(4), 1999, pp. 71–74; A. M. Ryan and R. E. Ployhart. Applicants' perceptions of se-

lection procedures and decisions: A critical review and agenda for the future. *Journal of Management,* 26, 2000, pp. 565–606.

[9] S. Martin. The role of nonverbal communications in quality improvement. *National Productivity Review,* 15(1), 1995, pp. 27–40.

[10] Adapted from J. W. Gibson and R. M. Hodgetts. *Organizational Communication: A Managerial Perspective.* Orlando: Academic Press, 1986, p. 99.

[11] Based on E. Hall. *Understanding Cultural Differences.* Yarmouth, ME: Intercultural Press, 1989; M. Munter; Workplace potpourri: Strict etiquette in Japanese firms lives on. *Manpower Argus,* August 1996, p. 11.

[12] F. Becker and F. Steele. *Workplace by Design: Mapping the High-Performance Workscape.* San Francisco: Jossey-Bass, 1995.

[13] Adapted from B. P. Sunoo. Redesign for a better work environment. *Workforce,* February 2000, pp. 39–46.

[14] C. M. Solomon. Communications in a global environment. *Workforce,* November 1999, pp. 50–56.

[15] J. R. Carlson and R. W. Zmud. Channel exposition theory and the experiential nature of media richness perceptions. *Academy of Management Journal,* 42, 1999, pp. 153–170.

[16] S. Collett. New L.L. Bean store may hike IT costs 40%. *Computerworld,* May 31, 1999, pp. 8–9.

[17] G. Flynn. Acrobats, aerialists, and HR: The big top needs big HR. *Workforce,* August 1997, pp. 38–45.

[18] J. S. Lubin. Dear boss: I'd rather not tell you my name, but. . . . *Wall Street Journal,* June 18, 1997, p. B1.

[19] D. Krackhardt and J. B. Hanson. Informal networks: The company behind the chart. *Harvard Business Review,* July–August 1993, pp. 104–113.

[20] S. W. Wellington. *Women of Color in Corporate Management: Opportunities and Barriers.* New York: Catalyst, 1999, pp. 78–80.

[21] Personal communication with W. N. Case, President, Integrated Change Ware Systems, Dallas, Texas, July 26, 2000.

[22] Adapted from D. A. Whetten and K. S. Cameron. *Developing Management Skills.* Reading, MA: Addison-Wesley, 1998, pp. 36–37. Used with permission.

[23] D. VandeWalle. A goal orientation model of feedback-seeking behavior. *Human Resource Management,* in press.

[24] C. D. Mortensen. *Miscommunication.* Thousand Oaks, CA: Sage, 1997.

[25] http://www.ti.com (August 30, 2000).

[26] B. Barth. L.L. Bean streamlines hiring process. *Women's Ware Daily,* July 5, 2000, pp. 14–15.

[27] Adapted from V. Galt. Hip workplaces seen as hot recruiting tool. *The Globe and Mail,* Toronto, Ontario, Canada, August 9, 2000, p. B9.

[28] A. Cameron. The hidden organisational costs of using nonstandard employment. *Personnel Review,* 29(2), 2000, pp.

188–203; C. L. Cooper. The changing psychological contract at work. *European Business Journal,* 11(3), 1999, pp. 115–125.

[29] R. Moxley. *Leadership and Spirit.* San Francisco: Jossey-Bass, 1999.

[30] Adapted from M. R. Solomon and E. W. Stuart. *Marketing,* 2nd ed. Upper Saddle River, NJ: Prentice-Hall, 2000, pp. 95–102.

[31] C. Tinsley. Models of conflict resolution in Japanese, German, and American cultures. *Journal of Applied Psychology,* 83, 1999, pp. 316–323; G. Golzen. Language barriers. *HR World,* July/August 1999, pp. 13–20.

[32] L. K. Stroh and P. M. Caliguri. Increasing global competitiveness through effective people management. *Journal of World Business,* 33(1), 1998, pp. 1–17.

[33] C. M. Solomon. Communicating in a global environment. *Workforce,* November 1999, p. 54.

[34] These guidelines are abridged from *Ten Commandments for Good Communications.* New York: American Management Association, 1955.

[35] Adapted from J. S. Osland, D. A. Kolb, and I. M. Rubin. *Organizational Behavior: An Experiential Approach,* 7th ed. Upper Saddle River, NJ: Prentice-Hall, 2001, pp. 150–151; J. I. Castican and M. A. Schneidler. Communication climate inventory. In J. W. Pfeffer and L. D. Goodstein (eds.). *The 1984 Annual: Developing Human Resources.* Copyright ©1984 by Pfeiffer and Company, San Diego, CA. Used with permission.

CHAPTER 17

[1] C. Fishman. Engines of democracy. *Fast Company,* October 1999, pp. 175–202.

[2] E. J. Lawler and B. Markovsky (eds.). *Social Psychology of Groups: A Reader.* Greenwich, CT: JAI Press, 1995.

[3] R. A. Guzzo. Fundamental considerations about work groups. In M. A. West (ed.), *Handbook of Work Group Psychology.* New York: John Wiley & Sons, 1996; J. R. Katzenbach and D. K. Smith. The discipline of teams. *Harvard Business Review,* March–April 1993, pp. 111–120; M. A. West, C. S. Borrill, and K. L. Unsworth. Team effectiveness in organizations. In C. L. Cooper and I. T. Robertson (eds.), *International Review of Industrial-Organizational Psychology.* Chichester, UK: John Wiley & Sons, 1998.

[4] C. Joinson. Teams at work. *HR Magazine,* May 1999, pp. 30–36.

[5] N. Steckler and N. Fondas. Building team leader effectiveness: A diagnostic tool. *Organizational Dynamics,* Winter 1995, pp. 20–35.

[6] *The Hay Report: Compensation and Benefits Strategies for 1997 and Beyond.* New York: Hay Group, 1997.

[7] H. Axel. Teaming in the global arena. *Across the Board,* February 1997, p. 56; G. M. Parker, K. B. Clark, and S. C. Wheelwright. *The Product Development Challenge: Competing Through Speed, Quality, and Creativity.* Boston: Harvard Business School Press, 1995; S. A. Mohrman and A. M.

Mohrman, Jr. *Designing and Leading Team-Based Organizations: A Workbook for Organizational Self-Design*. San Francisco: Jossey-Bass, 1997.

[8] P. B. Paulus. Groups, teams and creativity: The creative potential of idea-generating groups. *Applied Psychology: An International Review*, 49, 2000, pp. 237–262.

[9] Business Wire. Intercargo subsidiary announces Flexible Account Service Teams—"FAST." *Today's News on the Net* at http://www.businesswire.com (January 21, 1998).

[10] Described at http://www.jostens.com/ (January 1998).

[11] J. R. Galbraith. *Competing with Flexible Lateral Organizations*. Reading, MA: Addison-Wesley, 1994.

[12] C. Joinson.

[13] B. Nagler. Recasting employees into teams. *Workforce*, January 1998, pp. 101–106.

[14] G. M. Parker, K. B. Clark, and S. C. Wheelwright.

[15] R. L. Cross, A. Yan, and M. R. Louis. Boundary activities in "boundaryless" organizations: A case study of a transformation to a team-based structure. *Human Relations*, 56, 2000, pp. 841–859.

[16] B. L. Kirkman and B. Rosen. Powering up teams. *Organizational Dynamics*, Winter 2000, pp. 48–66.

[17] C. Fishman.

[18] Adapted from S. E. Jackson, K. E. May, and K. Whitney. Understanding the dynamics of diversity in decision making teams. In R. A. Guzzo, E. Salas, and Associates (eds.), *Team Effectiveness and Decision Making in Organizations*. San Francisco: Jossey-Bass, 1995, pp. 204–261; D. C. Borwhat, Jr. How do you know if your work teams work? *Workforce*, May 1997 (suppl.), p. 7; D. R. Denison, S. L. Hart, and J. A. Kahn. From chimneys to cross-functional teams: Developing and validating a diagnostic model. *Academy of Management Journal*, 39, 1996, 1005–1023; M. Cianni and D. Wnuck. Individual growth and team enhancement: Moving toward a new model of career development. *Academy of Management Executive*, 11, 1997, pp. 105–113.

[19] B. D. Janz, J. A. Colquitt, and R. A. Noe. Knowledge worker team effectiveness: The role of autonomy, interdependence, team development, and contextual support variables. *Personnel Psychology*, 50, 1997, pp. 877–904; G. L. Stewart and M. R. Barrick. Team structure and performance: Assessing the mediating role of intrateam process and the moderating role of task type. *Academy of Management Journal*, 43, 2000, pp. 146–163. For extensive descriptions of research relevant to each of the four components, see M. A. West (ed.), *Handbook of Work Group Psychology*. Chichester, UK: John Wiley & Sons, 1996.

[20] M. D. Zalezny, E. Salas, and C. Prince. Conceptual and measurement issues in coordination: Implications for team behavior and performance. In K. Rowland and G. Ferris (eds.), *Research in Personnel and Human Resource Management*, 13, 1995, pp. 81–115; D. E. Hyatt and T. M. Ruddy. An examination of the relationship between work group characteristics and performance: Once more into the breech. *Personnel Psychology*, 59, 1997, pp. 553–573.

[21] Copyright © South-Western College Publishing. All rights reserved. The items listed here are based on a version of this survey that appears in South-Western's *Team Handbook*, 1996.

[22] K. T. Dirks. The effects of interpersonal trust on work group performance. *Journal of Applied Psychology*, 84, 1999, pp. 445–555; A. Edmondson. Psychological safety and learning behavior in work teams. *Administrative Science Quarterly*, 44, 1999, pp. 350–383; T. L. Simons and R. S. Peterson. Task conflict and relationship conflict in top management teams: The pivotal role of intragroup trust. *Journal of Applied Psychology*, 85, 2000, pp. 102–111.

[23] *Source:* Adapted and modified from B. W. Tuckman and M. A. C. Jensen. Stages of small-group development revisited. *Group and Organization Studies*, 2, 1977, pp. 419–442; B. W. Tuckman. Developmental sequence in small groups. *Psychological Bulletin*, 63, 1965, pp. 384–389; S. Worchel. You can go home again: Returning group research to the group context with an eye on developmental issues. *Small Group Research*, 25, 1994, pp. 205–223; C. J. G. Gersick. Marking time: Predictable transitions in task groups. *Academy of Management Journal*, 32, 1989, pp. 274–309.

[24] R. S. Dooley and G. E. Fryxell. Attaining decision quality and commitment from dissent: The moderating effects of loyalty and competence in strategic decision-making teams. *Academy of Management Journal*, 42, 1999, pp. 389–402.

[25] M. J. Stevens and M. A. Campion. The knowledge, skill, and ability requirements for teamwork: Implications for human resource management. *Journal of Management*, 20, 1994, pp. 503–530; A. M. O'Leary, J. J. Martocchio, and D. D. Frink. A review of the influence of group goals on group performance. *Academy of Management Journal*, 37, 1994, pp. 1285–1301.

[26] C. W. Mueller et al. Employee attachment and noncoercive conditions of work. *Work and Occupations*, 21, 1994, pp. 179–212.

[27] J. W. Bishop and E. D. Scott. *Journal of Applied Psychology*, 85, 2000, pp. 439–450.

[28] R. A. Cooke and J. L. Szumal. The impact of group interaction styles on problem-solving effectiveness. *Journal of Applied Behavioral Science*, 30, 1994, pp. 415–437; J. M. Rabbie. Determinants of ingroup cohesion and outgroup hostility. *International Journal of Group Tensions*, 23, 1993, pp. 309–328.

[29] J. R. Hackman. Group influences on individuals in organization. In M. D. Dunnette and L. M. Hough (eds.), *Handbook of Industrial and Organizational Psychology*, 2nd ed., vol. 3. Palo Alto, CA: Consulting Psychologists Press, 1992, pp. 199–267.

[30] A. Zander. *Making Groups Effective*, 2nd ed. San Francisco: Jossey-Bass, 1994.

[31] G. Imperator. Their specialty? Teamwork. *Fast Company*, January–February, 2000, 54–56.

[32] B. Mullen et al. Group cohesiveness and quality of decision making: An integration of tests of the groupthink hypothesis. *Small Group Research*, 25, 1994, pp. 189–204; S. M. Miranda. Avoidance of groupthink: Meeting management using

group support systems. *Small Group Research,* 25, 1994, pp. 105–136.

[33] A. Nahavandi and E. Aranda. Restructuring teams for the re-engineered organization. *Academy of Management Executive,* 8, 1994, pp. 58–68; K. M. Eisenhardt, J. L. Kahwajy, and L. J. Bourgeois III. How management teams can have a good fight. *Harvard Business Review,* July–August 1997, pp. 77–85.

[34] For a discussion of how managers and team members handle disciplinary problems, see R. C. Liden et al. Management of poor performance: A comparison of manager, group member and group disciplinary decisions. *Journal of Applied Psychology,* 84, 2000, pp. 835–851.

[35] S. Adams and L. Kydoniefs. Making teams work: Bureau of Labor Statistics learns what works and what doesn't. *Quality Progress,* January 2000, pp. 43–48; R. Ginnett. The essentials of leading a high-performance team. *Leadership in Action,* 18(6), 1999, pp. 1–5; P. E. Tesluk and J. E. Mathieu. Overcoming roadblocks to effectiveness: Incorporating management of performance barriers into models of work group effectiveness. *Journal of Applied Psychology,* 84, 1999, pp. 200–217; V. U. Druskat and D. C. Kayes. The antecedents of team competence: Toward a fine-grained model of self-managing team effectiveness. *Research on Managing Groups and Teams,* 2, 1999, pp. 221–231.

[36] D. C. Ganster and D. J. Dwyer. The effects of understaffing on individual and group performance in professional and trade occupations. *Journal of Management,* 21, 1995, pp. 175–190.

[37] A. P. Hare. Group size. *American Behavioral Scientist,* 24, 1981, pp. 695–708; R. Albanese and D. D. Van Fleet. Rational behavior in groups: The free-riding tendency. *Academy of Management Review,* 10, 1985, pp. 244–255.

[38] E. Sundstrom, K. P. DeMeuse, and D. Futrell. Work teams: Applications and effectiveness. *American Psychologist,* 45, 1990, pp. 120–133; K. G. Smith et al. Top management team demography and process: The role of social integration and communication. *Administrative Science Quarterly,* 39, 1994, pp. 412–438.

[39] J. Lipnack and J. Stamps. Virtual teams: The new way to work. *Strategy & Leadership,* January–February 1999, pp. 14–19. Also see E. Carmel. *Global Software Teams: Collaborating Across Borders and Time Zones.* Upper Saddle River, NJ: Prentice-Hall, 1999.

[40] W. R. Pape. Group insurance: Virtual teams can quickly gather knowledge even from far-flung staff. *Inc. Tech,* no. 2, 1997, pp. 29–31. An interesting study showing how computer-mediated group decision making differs from face-to-face influence is P. L. McLeod et al. The eyes have it: Minority influence in face-to-face and computer-mediated group discussion. *Journal of Applied Psychology,* 82, 1997, pp. 706–718. Also see D. Armstrong and P. Cole. Managing distances and differences in geographically distributed work groups. In S. E. Jackson and M. N. Ruderman (eds.), *Diversity in Work Teams: Research Paradigms for a Changing Workplace.* Washington, DC: American Psychological Association, 1996, pp. 187–215.

[41] Adapted from A. M. Townsend, S. M. DeMarie, and A. R. Hendrickson. Virtual teams: Technology and the workplace of the future. *Academy of Management Executive,* 12(3), 1998, pp. 17–29; C. Grove and W. Hallowell. Spinning your wheels? Successful global teams know how to gain traction. *HRM Magazine,* April 1998, pp. 25–28; Communication processes for virtual organizations. *Organization Science* (special issue), 10(6), 1999.

[42] For a comparison of the United States and several European countries, see J. B. Leslie and E. VanVelsor. *A Cross-National Comparison of Effective Leadership and Teamwork: Toward a Global Workforce.* Greensboro, NC: Center for Creative Leadership, 1998.

[43] K. M. Eisenhardt, J. L. Kahwajy, and L. J. Bourgeois III. Conflict and strategic choice: How top management teams disagree. *California Management Review,* 39, 1997, pp. 42–62.

[44] A. Sagie. Participative decision making and performance: A moderator analysis. *Journal of Applied Behavioral Science,* 30, 1994, pp. 227–246; W. A. Kahn and K. E. Kram. Authority at work: Internal models and their organizational consequences. *Academy of Management Review,* 19, 1994, pp. 17–50.

[45] For a discussion of the consequences of mixing employees from different cultures within a single team, see E. Elron. Top management teams within multinational corporations: Effects of cultural heterogeneity. *Leadership Quarterly,* 8(4), 1997, pp. 393–412; J. A. Wagner III. Studies of individualism–collectivism: Effects on cooperation in groups. *Academy of Management Journal,* 38, 1995, pp. 152–172; P. C. Earley and E. M. Mosakowski. Creating hybrid team cultures: An empirical test of international team functioning. *Academy of Management Journal,* 43, 2000, pp. 26–49.

[46] G. A. Neuman and J. Wright. Team effectiveness: Beyond skills and cognitive ability. *Journal of Applied Psychology,* 84, pp. 376–389.

[47] J. Martin. Mercedes: Made in Alabama. *Fortune,* July 7, 1997, pp. 150–158.

[48] H. W. Lane, M. B. Brechu, and D. T. A. Wesley. Mabe's President Luis Berrondo Avalos on teams and industry competitiveness. *Academy of Management Executive,* 13(3), 1999, pp. 9–11.

[49] See M. J. Waller. The timing of adaptive group responses to nonroutine events. *Academy of Management Journal,* 42, 1999, pp. 127–137.

[50] E. Salas, C. A. Bowers, and E. Eden. *Improving Teamwork in Organizations: Applications of Resource Management and Training.* Englewood Cliffs, NJ: Lawrence Erlbaum, 2001; R. A. Guzzo and M. W. Dickson. Teams in organizations: Recent research on performance and effectiveness. *Annual Review of Psychology,* 47, 1996, pp. 307–308;

[51] J. W. Dean, Jr., and M. P. Sharfman. Does decision process matter? A study of strategic decision making effectiveness. *Academy of Management Journal,* 39, 1996, pp. 368–396; P. W. Mulvey, J. F. Viega, and P. M. Elsass. When teammates raise a white flag. *Academy of Management Executive,* 10, 1996, pp. 40–49; R. L. Priem, D. A. Harrison, and N. K. Muir. Structured conflict and consensus outcomes in group decision making. *Journal of Management,* 21, 1995, pp. 691–710.

[52] S. S. K. Lam and J. Schaubroeck. Improving group decisions by better pooling information: A comparative advantage of group decision support systems. *Journal of Applied Psychology,* 85, 2000, pp. 565–573.

[53] H. Campbell. Adventures in teamland: Experiential training makes the lesson fun. *Personnel Journal,* May 1996, pp. 56–62.

[54] J. McAdams and E. J. Hawk. Making group incentives work. *WorldatWork,* Third quarter, 2000, pp. 28–39; G. Parker, J. McAdams, and D. Zielinski. *Rewarding Teams: Lessons from the Trenches.* San Francisco: Jossey-Bass, 2000.

[55] A. Markels. Power to the people. *Fast Company,* February–March 1998, pp. 155–165; L. Woelert. Not acting at all like a utility. *Business Week,* December 13, 1999, pp. 94–98; S. Wetlaufer. Organizing for empowerment: An interview with AES's Roger Sant and Dennis Bakke. *Harvard Business Review,* January–February 1999, pp. 110–123.

CHAPTER 18

[1] C. Caggiano. Merge now, pay later. *Inc.,* April 2000, pp. 86–96.

[2] H. M. Trice and J. M. Beyer. *The Culture of Work Organizations.* Englewood Cliffs, NJ: Prentice-Hall, 1993, pp. 1–32; D. R. Denison. What is the difference between organizational culture and organizational climate? A native's point of view on a decade of paradigm wars. *Academy of Management Review,* 21, 1996, pp. 619–654.

[3] G. Colvin. The changing art of becoming unbeatable. *Fortune,* November 24, 1997, pp. 299–300.

[4] The culture wars (An interview with Allan Kennedy). *Inc.,* 20th Anniversary Issue, 1999, pp. 107–108.

[5] T. G. Powell. Total Quality Management as competitive advantage: A review and empirical study. *Strategic Management Journal,* 16, 1995, pp. 15–37.

[6] N. J. Allen and J. P. Meyer. Organizational socialization tactics: A longitudinal analysis of links to newcomers' commitment and role orientation. *Academy of Management Journal,* 33, 1990, pp. 847–858.

[7] H. M. Trice and J. M. Beyer. *The Culture of Work Organizations.*

[8] H. M. Trice and J. M. Beyer. *The Culture of Work Organizations.*

[9] H. M. Trice and J. M. Beyer. Cultural leadership in organizations. *Organization Science,* 2, 1991, pp. 149–169.

[10] J. Hyatt. Founder king. *Inc.,* 20th Anniversary Issue, 1999, pp. 97–98.

[11] Adapted from R. Hooijberg and F. Petrock. On cultural change: Using the competing values framework to help leaders execute a transformational strategy. *Human Resource Management,* 32, 1993, pp. 29–50; R. E. Quinn. *Beyond Rational Management: Mastering the Paradoxes and Competing Demands of High Performance.* San Francisco: Jossey-Bass, 1988.

[12] S. G. Harris and K. W. Mossholder. The affective implications of perceived congruence with culture dimensions during organizational transformation. *Journal of Management,* 22, 1996, pp. 527–547.

[13] D. A. Morand. The role of behavioral formality and informality in the enactment of bureaucratic versus organic organizations. *Academy of Management Review,* 20, 1995, pp. 831–872.

[14] P. Roberts. The best interest of the patient is the only interest to be considered. *Fast Company,* April, 1999, pp. 149–162.

[15] R. A. Melcher. Warm and fuzzy, meet rough and tumble. *Business Week,* January 26, 1998, p. 38

[16] L. Lee. Tricks of E*Trade. *Business Week E-Biz,* February 7, 2000, pp. EB18–EB31.

[17] G. Grant. Outmarketing P&G. *Fortune,* January 12, 1998, pp. 150–152; T. Parker-Pope. Colgate's Total grabs big share in early sales. *Wall Street Journal,* March 6, 1998, p. B6; Harvard Business School Bulletin Online at http://www.hbs.edu (September 2, 2000).

[18] D. R. Denison and A. K. Mishra. Toward a theory of organizational culture and effectiveness. *Organization Science,* 6, 1995, pp. 204–222.

[19] M. J. Mandel. The new economy: It works in America. Will it go global? *Business Week,* January 31, 2000, pp. 73–77

[20] P. Giles. The importance of HR in making your merger work. *Workspan,* August, 2000, pp. 16–20. Also see A.T. J. Tetenbaum. Beating the odds of merger & acquisition failure: Seven key practices that improve the chance for expected integration and synergies. *Organizational Dynamics,* Autumn 1999, 22–36; S. DeVoge and S. Spreier. The soft realities of mergers. *Across the Board,* December 1999, pp. 27–32.

[21] D. A. Ralston et al. The cosmopolitan Chinese manager: Findings of a study on managerial values across the six regions of China. *Journal of International Management,* 2, 1996, pp. 79–109.

[22] For projections about the future of immigration in Europe, see B. Crossette. Europe stares at a future built by immigrants. *New York Times,* January 2, 2000, section 4, pp. 1, 4.

[23] W. Zellner and M. Arndt. Keeping the hive humming: Immigrants may prevent the economy from overheating. *Business Week,* April 24, 2000, pp. 50–52; S. Greenhouse. Foreign workers at highest level in seven decades. *New York Times,* September 4, 2000, pp. A1, A12.

[24] M. Minehan. A new twist on the census. *HR Magazine,* December 1999, pp. 60–64.

[25] Adapted from G. Hofstede. *Cultures and Organizations: Software of the Mind.* New York: McGraw-Hill, 1995; G. Hofstede et al. Measuring organizational cultures: A qualitative and quantitative study of twenty cases. *Administrative Science Quarterly,* 35, 1990, pp. 286–316.

[26] *Wall Street Journal,* February 26, 1998, p. A9; A. Bryant. The Andersen family feud: Two units split on new leadership. *New York Times,* June 28, 1997, pp. B35, B37; D. Whitford. Arthur, Arthur. . . . *Fortune,* November 10, 1997, pp. 169–178; D. Leonhardt. Andersen Consulting's chief makes e-commerce a new goal. *New York Times,* November 2, 1999, p. C3; R. O. Crockett. Next stop, splitsville. *Business Week,* January 18,

1999, pp. 100–102; Andersen Consulting wins arbitration case: Will formally separate from Arthur Andersen. Arbitrator's News Release at http://newsroom.ac.com/news/arbitration/release.html/ (September 6, 2000).

27 A. Majchrzak and Q. Wang. Breaking the functional mindset in process organizations. *Harvard Business Review,* September–October 1996, pp. 93–99.

28 H. M. Trice and J. M. Beyer. *The Culture of Work Organizations,* pp. 175–253; R. Goffee and G. Jones. What holds the modern company together? *Harvard Business Review,* November–December 1996, pp. 133–148.

29 E. H. Schein. What is culture? In P. J. Frost et al. (eds.), *Reframing Organizational Culture.* Newbury Park, CA: Sage, 1991, pp. 243–253.

30 L. E. Wynter. Rare black firm on Wall Street learns how to make its way. *Wall Street Journal,* March 4, 1998, p. B1; G. N. Powell. Reinforcing and extending today's organizations: The simultaneous pursuit of person–organization fit and diversity. *Organizational Dynamics,* Winter 1998, pp. 50–61. For a description of what it is like for gay men to work in the monolithic culture of an American automobile company, see A. Gilmore. Revelations: My life as a gay executive. *Fortune,* September 8, 1997, pp. 106–110. For the results of a study of how culture affects gay and lesbian workers, see N. E. Day and P. Schoenrade. Staying in the closet versus coming out: Relationships between communication about sexual orientation and work attitudes. *Personnel Psychology,* 50, 1997, pp. 147–163. For insights into the experiences of employees with disabilities, see A. Colella. Organizational socialization of newcomers with disabilities: A framework for future research. *Research in Personnel and Human Resource Management,* 14, 1996, pp. 351–417.

31 For a detailed case study that contrasts pluralistic and multicultural organizations, see J. A. Gilbert and J. M. Ivancevich. Valuing diversity: A tale of two organizations. *Academy of Management Executive,* 14, 2000, pp. 93–105.

32 Pitney Bowes web page, http://www.pitneybowes.com (June 5, 2000).

33 S. Wetlaufer. Common sense and conflict: An interview with Disney's Michael Eisner. *Harvard Business Review,* January–February, 2000, pp. 113–124.

34 Mary Ellen Heyde. *Fast Company,* April, 2000, p. 112.

35 S. H. Mehta. What minorities really want. *Fortune,* July 10, 2000, pp. 181–186; E. LaBlanc, L. Vanderkam, and K. Vella-Zarb. America's best 50 companies for minorities. *Fortune,* July 10, 2000, pp. 190–200.

36 See R. J. Grossman. Race in the workplace. *HR Magazine,* March, 2000, pp. 41–45.

37 R. J. Grossman. Is diversity working? *HR Magazine,* March 2000, pp. 47–50.

38 E. Y. Cross. *Managing diversity—The Courage to Lead.* Westport, CT: Quorum Books, 2000.

39 A study of how the design of affirmative action policies affect reactions to them is reported in D. A. Kravita and S. L. Klineberg. Reactions to two versions of affirmative action among whites, blacks, and hispanics. *Journal of Applied Psychology,* 85, 2000, pp. 597–611.

40 M. L. Wheeler. *Corporate Practices in Diversity Measurement: A Research Report.* New York: Conference Board, 1996.

41 G. Winter. No instant results expected from Coke bias case. *New York Times,* November 18, 2000, pp. C1, C3; C. L. Constance. Coke's black employees step up pressure to resolve a racial discrimination lawsuit. *New York Times,* March 23, 2000, pp. C1, C9; A. Harrington. Prevention is the best medicine. *Fortune,* July 10, 2000, p. 188,

42 K. Townsend. Female partners double thanks to gender initiative. *Financial Times,* May 8, 2000, p. 35.

43 G. Robinson and K. Dechant. Building a business case for diversity. *Academy of Management Executive,* 11(3), 1997, pp. 21–31.

44 F. Rice. Denny's changes its spots. *Fortune,* May 13, 1996, pp. 133–142; E. LaBlanc, L. Vanderkam, and K. Vella-Zarb, pp. 190–200.

45 M. Petersen. Her partners call her Ms. Chairman. *New York Times,* October 9, 1999, pp. C1, C4.

46 K. Labich. No more crude at Texaco. *Fortune,* September 6, 1999, pp. 205–212; Rooting out racism. *Business Week,* January 10, 2000, pp. 66–67.

47 J. Cook. Taking the diversity tour. *Human Resources Executive,* May 16, 2000, pp. 80–83; K. Bradsher. Big carmakers extend benefits to gay couples. *New York Times,* June 9, 2000, pp. B1, C12.

48 D. E. Meyerson and J. K. Fletcher. A modest manifesto for shattering the glass ceiling. *Harvard Business Review,* January–February, 2000, pp. 127–136.

49 For a discussion of how harassment affects workers, see K. T. Schneider, R. T. Hitlan, and P. Radhakrishnan. An examination of the nature and correlates of ethnic harassment experiences in multiple contexts. *Journal of Applied Psychology,* 85, 2000, pp. 3–12.

50 *Manpower Argus,* March 1996, p. 5; P. Dwyer, M. Johnson, and K. L. Miller. Out of the typing pool, into career limbo. *Business Week,* April 15, 1996, pp. 92–94.

51 C. J. Whalen. Closing the pay gap. *Business Week,* August 28, 2000, p. 38; F. D. Blau and L. M. Kahn. *Journal of Economic Perspectives* (in press).

52 Source: Adapted from V. C. Smith. Texaco outlines comprehensive initiatives. *Human Resource Executive,* February 1997, p. 13; A. Bryant. How much has Texaco changed? A mixed report card on anti-bias efforts. *New York Times,* November 2, 1997, section 3, p. 1ff; Texaco's workforce diversity plan, as reprinted in *Workforce,* March 1997 (suppl.).

53 J. R. W. Joplin and C. S. Daus. Challenges of leading a diverse workforce. *Academy of Management Executive,* 11(3), 1997, pp. 32–47.

54 C. M. Riordan and L. M. Shore. Demographic diversity and employee attitudes: An empirical examination of relational demography within work units. *Journal of Applied Psychology,* 82, 1997, pp. 342–358; B. Lawrence. The black box of

organizational demography. *Organization Science,* 8, 1997, pp. 1–22; S. E. Jackson and A. Joshi. Research on domestic and international diversity in organizations: A merger that works. In N. Anderson et al. (eds.), *Handbook of Work and Organizational Psychology.* Thousand Oaks, CA: Sage, 2001.

[55] L. Himelstein and S. A. Forest. Breaking through. *Business Week,* February 17, 1997, pp. 64–70.

[56] A. Markels. A diversity program can prove divisive. *Wall Street Journal,* January 30, 1997, pp. B1, B5.

[57] D. A. Thomas and R. J. Ely. Making differences matter: A new paradigm for managing diversity. *Harvard Business Review,* September–October 1996, pp. 79–90; M. E. Heilman, C. J. Block, and P. Stathatos. The affirmative action stigma of incompetence: Effects of performance information ambiguity. *Academy of Management Journal,* 40, 1997, pp. 603–625; R. A. Friedman. Defining the scope and logic of minority and female network groups: Can separation enhance integration? *Research in Personnel and Human Resource Management,* 14, 1996, pp. 307–349.

[58] S. Rose. Remaking the Avon lady. *Money,* February 2000, pp. 46–49; N. Byrnes. Avon: The new calling. *Business Week,* September 18, 2000, pp. 136–148; D. Canedy. Opportunity knocks at Avon: Passed over before, a woman is named chief executive; I. J. Dugan. Why Avon called a "nonwoman." *Business Week,* March 16, 1998, pp. 57–60; L. Wayne and K. N. Gilpin. Avon calls on a man to lead it: Female cosmetics executives passed over for the top post. *New York Times,* December 12, 1997, pp. C1, C7; T. Parker-Pope. Ding Dong! Avon calls up six executives, putting them in line for top positions. *Wall Street Journal,* March 26, 1997, p. B7; B. Morris. If women ran the world, it would look a lot like Avon. *Fortune,* July 21, 1997, pp. 74–79; R. R. Thomas, Jr. *Beyond Race and Gender.* New York: Amacon, 1991.

CHAPTER 19

[1] Adapted from http://www.fedex.com (September 21, 2000); FedEx Logistic, Inc. *American Shipper,* 42(7), 2000, pp. 93ff; R. O. Mason et al. Absolutely, positively operations research: The FedEx story. *Interfaces,* 27(2), 1997, pp. 17–36.

[2] G. R. Weaver, L. K. Trevino, and P. L. Cochran. Corporate ethics programs as control systems: Influences on executive commitment and environmental factors. *Academy of Management Journal,* 42, 1999, pp. 41–57.

[3] R. Simmons. *Levers of Control: How Managers Use Innovative Control Systems to Drive Strategic Renewal.* Boston: Harvard University Press, 1995.

[4] L. Andersson and T. S. Bateman. Individual environmental initiative: Championing natural environmental issues in U.S. business organizations. *Academy of Management Journal,* 43, 2000, pp. 548–570; L. Otto. Growing green. *Journal of Property Management,* January 2000, pp. 43ff.

[5] H. Meyer. The greening of corporate America. *Journal of Business Strategy,* 21(1), 2000, pp. 38–45; P. Bansal and K. Roth. Why companies go green: A model of ecological responsiveness. *Academy of Management Journal,* 43, 2000, pp. 717–736.

[6] Adapted from L. Chadderdon. Fast focus. *Fast Company,* May 1999, pp. 147–155.

[7] S. Duff. Work-life benefits shedding fuzzy image in favor of hard numbers. *Employee Benefits,* November 15, 1999.

[8] D. May. Testing by necessity. *Occupational Health and Safety,* 68(4), 1999, pp. 48–51; http://www.amanet.org/research/specials/monit/ (November 15, 1999).

[9] Adapted from M. Gimein. CEOs who manage too much. *Fortune,* Septmber 4, 2000, pp. 235–242; Timothy Koogle. *Business Week,* September 27, 1999, p. EB26; A class act at Yahoo! *Business Week,* January 10, 2000, p. 67.

[10] T. Lowe and J. L. Machin. *New Perspectives on Managerial Control.* New York: Macmillan, 1987.

[11] G. T. Hult, B. D. Keillor, and R. Hightower. Value product attributes in an emerging market: A comparison between French and Malaysian consumers. *Journal of World Business,* 35, 2000, pp. 206–220.

[12] S. H. Ang. The power of money: A cross-cultural analysis of business-related beliefs. *Journal of World Business,* 35, 2000, pp. 43–60; S. S. Standifird and R. S. Marshall. The transaction cost advantage of guanxi-based business practices. *Journal of World Business,* 35, 2000, pp. 21–42.

[13] Adapted from C. Faltermayer. Cyberveillance: Managers are increasingly monitoring employees' computer activity—Every message sent, website visited, and key stroked. *Time,* August 14, 2000, pp. B22ff; http://www.privacyrights.org (September 4, 2000).

[14] F. R. Reichfeld and P. Schefter. E-loyalty: Your secret weapon on the web. *Harvard Business Review,* July–August 2000, pp. 105–114; L. L. Berry. *Discovering the Soul of Service: The Nine Drivers of Sustainable Business Success.* New York: Free Press, 1999.

[15] F. H. Fabian. Keeping the tension: Pressures to keep the controversy in the management discipline. *Academy of Management Review,* 25, 2000, pp. 350–371.

[16] O. Azfar. Innovation in labor contracts: On the adoption of profit sharing in Canadian labor contracts. *Industrial Relations,* 39(2), 2000, pp. 291–311.

[17] S. Sharma, R. W. Niedrich, and G. Dobbins. A framework for monitoring customer satisfaction. *Industrial Marketing Management,* 28(3), 1999, pp. 232–233.

[18] Personal communication with Carl Sewell, President, Sewell Lexus, Dallas, Texas.

[19] S. K. McEvily, S. Das, and K. McCabe. Avoiding competence substitution through knowledge sharing. *Academy of Management Review,* 25, 2000, pp. 294–311.

[20] K. G. Palepu, P. M. Healy, and V. L. Bernard. *Business Analysis & Valuation,* 2nd ed. Cincinnati: South-Western, 2000.

[21] C. P. Stickney and R. L. Weil. *Financial Accounting,* 9th ed. Fort Worth, TX: Dryden, 2000.

[22] S. S. Rao. ABCs of cost control. *Inc.Tech,* 2, 1997, pp. 79–81.

[23] G. Cokins. Learning to love ABC. *Journal of Accountancy,* 188(2), 1999, pp. 37–40.

24 D. T. Hicks. Yes, ABC is for small business, too. *Journal of Accountancy*, 188(2), 1999, pp. 41–43.

25 Adapted from S. J. Baxendale and V. Dornbusch. Activity-based costing for a hospice. *Strategic Finance*, Spring 2000, pp. 65–70.

26 G. Cokins.

27 D. R. Anderson, D. J. Sweeney, and T. A. Williams. *Quantitative Methods for Business*, 7th ed. Cincinnati: South-Western, 1997.

28 M. Kletter. A tale of time: Fortunes of watch companies. *Women's Wear Daily*, January 24, 2000, pp. 2–5; B. Pappas. Transparent eyeball. *Forbes*, May 17, 1999, pp. 45–46; B. Murray. A very smart watch. *U.S. News & World Report*, September 27, 1997, pp. 54–55.

29 Adapted from L. R. Jaunch et al. *The Management Experience: Cases, Exercises and Readings*, 4th ed. Chicago: Dryden, 1986, pp. 254–255.

CHAPTER 20

1 Adapted from B. Brewin. Avis goes wireless to fuel efficiency. *Computerworld*, July 24, 2000, pp. 1, 85.

2 R.C. Nickerson. *Business and Information Systems*. Old Tappan, NJ: Prentice-Hall, 2000; T. H. Davenport. *Mission Critical: Realizing the Promise of Enterprise Systems*. Boston: Harvard Business School Press, 2000.

3 J. Han and M. Kamber. *Data Mining: Concepts and Techniques*. San Francisco: Morgan Kaufmann, 2000.

4 P. Westerman. *Data Warehousing: Using the Wal-Mart Model*. San Francisco: Morgan Kaufmann, 2000.

5 P. Evans and T. S. Wurster. *Blown to Bits: How the New Economics of Information Transforms Strategy*. Boston: Harvard Business School Press, 1999.

6 M. Kolbasuk McGee and C. Wilder. It's official: IT adds up. *Informationweek*, April 17, 2000, pp. 46–63.

7 J. S. Brown and P. Duguid. *The Social Life of Information*. Boston: Harvard Business School Press, 2000.

8 W. M. Buckeley. The view from the top. *Wall Street Journal*, June 21, 1999, p. R6.

9 Adapted from R.O. Crockett. A digital doughboy. *Business Week E-Biz*, April 3, 2000, pp. EB79–EB86.

10 About Pillsbury. Available at http://www.pillsbury.com (October 25, 2000).

11 G. Gilder. Hot piping. *Forbes ASAP*, February 23, 1998, pp. 110–120.

12 G. W. Keen, W. Mougayar, and T. Torregrossa. *The Business Internet and Intranets: A Manager's Guide to Key Terms and Concepts*. Boston: Harvard Business School Press, 1998.

13 The founder's message. *Forbes ASAP*, December 1, 1997, p. 65.

14 J. Keyes. *Internet Management*. Boca Raton, FL: CRC Press, 2000.

15 Stats: Web growth. *Browser News*. Online weekly magazine available at http://www.upsdell.com/browsernews/ (October 18, 2000).

16 D. L. Clark. *IT Manager's Guide to Virtual Private Networks*. Blacklick, OH: McGraw-Hill-College, 2000.

17 Adapted from K. Blough. In search of more secure extranets. *Informationweek*, November 1, 1999, pp. 94–100.

18 K. Terplan and S. Zamir. *Intranet Performance Management*. Boca Raton, FL: CRC Press, 2000.

19 E. Callahan. *The Power of Intranets*. LaVergne, LA: Microsoft Press, 1999.

20 Adapted from D. Kirkpatrick. ePocalypse! now. *Ecompany.com*, September 2000, pp. 87–94.

21 D. M. Steiger. Enhancing user understanding in a decision support system: A theoretical basis and framework. *Journal of Management Information Systems*, 15, 1998, pp. 199–220.

22 S. Deck. Data visualization. *Computerworld*, October 11, 1999, p. 77.

23 S. Deck, p. 77.

24 P. Jackson. *Introduction to Expert Systems*, 3rd ed. Harlow, England: Addison Wesley Longman, 1999.

25 R. Kurzweil. *The Age of Spiritual Machines*. New York: Viking Press, 1999.

26 The life insurance plan selection system at the Meiji Life Insurance Company. Available online at http://www.attar.com. Click "User Case Stories" and then click "Meiji Mutual Life Insurance" (October 19, 2000).

27 A. M. Townsend et al. Technology at the top: Developing strategic planning support systems. *S.A.M. Advanced Management Journal*, Winter 2000, pp. 31–37.

28 D. Essex. Teamware offering that's tailor made. *Computerworld*, April 10, 2000, p. 90; J. Maynard. MS2: Better product lifecycle processes through automated best practices consistency. Aberdeen Group, September 1, 2000. Available at http://www.aberdeen.com (October 26, 2000).

29 R. McLeod, Jr. and G. Schell. *Management Information Systems*, 8th ed. Old Tappan, NJ: Prentice-Hall, 2001.

30 G. M. Doss and S. McDermott (eds.). *IS Project Management Handbook*. Old Tappan, NJ: Prentice-Hall, 2000.

31 G. B. Davis (ed.). *The Blackwell Encyclopedic Dictionary of Management Information Systems*. Cambridge, MA: Blackwell, 1997.

32 Adapted from M. Halper. Everyone in the knowledge pool. *Computerworld: Global Innovation Series*, December 8, 1997, pp. 8–13; and DHL Worldwide Express Web site at http://www.dhl.com (October 20, 2000).

33 J. Weckert and D. Adeney. *Computer and Information Ethics*. Westport, CT: Greenwood, 1997.

34 R. M. Baird, R. Mays Ramsower, and S. E. Rosenbaum (eds.). *Cyberethics: Social and Moral Issues in the Computer Age*. Amherst, NY: Prometheus, 2000.

35 Source: Computer Ethics Institute, Washington, DC, October 20, 2000.

[36] Adapted from D. Kelsey. Computer ethics: An overview of the issues. *Ethics: Easier Said Than Done,* 15, 1991, pp. 30–33; T. E. Weber. Does anything go? *Wall Street Journal,* December 8, 1997, pp. R29, R31.

[37] S. Garfinkel. *Database Nation: The Death of Privacy in the 21st Century.* San Francisco: O'Reilly & Associates, 2000.

[38] C. J. Sykes. *The End of Privacy.* New York: St. Martin's Press, 2000.

[39] About the privacy program. *BBB OnLine.* Available at http://www.bbbonline.org/ (October 21, 2000).

[40] H. Green, M. France, and M. Stepanek. Online privacy: It's time for rules in wonderland. *Business Week,* March 20, 2000, pp. 83–96; J. Rosen. *The Unwanted Gaze: The Destruction of Privacy in America.* New York: Random House, 2000.

[41] Adapted from J. King. How to do B2B. *Computerworld,* February 28, 2000, pp. 48–49; S. Hensley. Just call it gpo.com: Internet deals change the supply biz. *Modern Healthcare,* April 10, 2000, pp. 30–32.

Organization and Internet Index

A T & T, 125, 174
http://www.att.com

AARP, 95, 96
http://www.aarp.org

Academy of Management, 330
http://www.aom.pace.edu

Accenture, 208, 496, 497
http://www.accenture.com

ACS International Resources, 357

ACT*1 Personnel Services, 150
http://www.act1personnel.com

AeroTech Service Group, 310
http://www.aerotechsg.com

AES Corporation, 215, 481
http://www.aesc.com

Akami Technologies, 223
http://www.akami.com

Algorithmics, Inc., 222
http://www.algorithmics.com

Alliant Foodservice, Inc., 228, 328
http://www.alliantfs.com

Allied Signal, 332
http://aerospace.alliedsignal.com

Alteon WebSystems, 193
http://www.alteonsystems.com

Amazon.com, 4, 10, 15, 16, 97, 202
http://www.amazon.com

America Online, 202
http://www.aol.com

America West, 378
http://www.americawest.com

American Airlines, 232
http://www.americanairlines.com

American Express, 322, 421
http://www.americanexpress.com

American Federation of Labor (AFL), 43
http://www.aflcio.org

American Management Association, 451
http://www.amanet.org

American Productivity and Quality
Center, 258
http://www.apqc.org

American Society for Training and
Development, 357
http://www.astd.org

Amgen, 337
http://www.amgen.com

Andersen Consulting (now Accenture),
208, 496, 497
http://www.accenture.com

Apple Computer, 489
http://www.apple.com

ARAMARK, 448
http://www.aramark.com

Archway Cookies, 561
http://www.archwaycookies.com

Arthur Andersen, 348, 496
http://www.arthurandersen.com

Arvin Industries, 63
http://www.Arvin.com

Associates First Capital Corp., 277, 432,
525
http://www.theassociates.com

Autumn Harp, 143

Avis, 542
http://www.avis.com

Avon Products, 510–511
http://www.avon.com

Baby Jogger Company, 152
http://www.babyjogger.com

Baker & McKenzie, 502

Barnes and Noble, 147
http://www.barnesandnoble.com

Ben & Jerry's Ice Cream, 135, 174, 187
http://www.benjerry.com

Bindco Corporation, 313, 539
http://www.bindco.com

BMW of North America, 356
http://www.bmwusa.com

Body Shop, 143
http://www.bodyshop.com

Boeing, 112, 113
http://www.boeing.com

BP Norge, 358
http://www.bp.com

Brady Corporation, 412
http://www.bradycorp.com

Buckman Laboratories Inc., 289
http://www.buckman.com

Budweiser, 524
http://www.budweiser.com

Bureau of the Census, 148, 495
http://www.census.gov

Burger King, 69
http://www.burgerking.com

Burke, Inc., 455
http://www.burke.com

Burton Snowboards, 75, 135
http://www.burton.com

Business Resource Software, 550
http://www.a-businessplan.com

Caesar's Palace, 60
http://www.caesars.com/palace

California Public Employees Retirement
System (CALPERS), 178–179
http://www.calpers.ca.gov

California Sunshine, 109
http://www.hiddenvilla.com

Cameraworld.com, 211, 345
http://www.camerworld.com

Campbell Soup, 56
http://www.campbellsoup.com

Capital One Financial Corp., 226, 356
http://www.capitalone.com

Career Transition, 146

Celanese Chemical Corporation, 15, 108
http://www.celanese.com

Celemi, 250
http://www.celemi.com

Cemex, 1, 25, 199
http://www.cemex.com

Cendant, 161, 181
http://www.cendant.com

Center for Creative Leadership, 331
http://www.ccl.org

Center for Leadership Studies, 413
http://www.situational.com

Center for the Study of Work Teams, 459

Central Michigan Community Hospital,
341
http://www.cmhs.org

Chapparal Steel, 52

Charles Schwab, 404, 406
http://www.schwab.com

Chick-Fil-A, 537
http://www.chickfila.com

Chrysler, 178, 478
http://www.chrysler.com

Cinergy Corp., 259
http://www.cinergy.com

Cirque du Soleil, 348, 350, 439
http://www.cirquedusoleil.com

Cisco Systems, 27, 194, 196, 227, 354,
367, 524
http://www.cisco.com

Citigroup, 208, 319
http://www.citigroup.com

CNF Transportation, 361
http://www.cnf.com

CNN, 153
http://www.cnn.com

Cobra Metal Works, 282

Coca-Cola, 22, 111, 118, 307, 528, 500
http://www.coca-cola.com

Colgate-Palmolive, 358–359, 492, 508
http://www.colgate.com

Community Grocers, 178

Computer Ethics Institute, 556
http://www.brook.edu/ITS/CEI

Conoco, 418
http://www.conoco.com

Continental Airlines, 323, 430, 439, 441
http://www.continental.com

Con-Way Transportation Services, 361, 364
http:/www.con-way.com

Cornell University, 162
http://www.cornell.edu

Corporate Defense Strategies, 526
http://www.corporatedefense.com

Council of Better Business Bureaus, 558
http://www.bbbonline.org

Countrywide Credit Industries, 549
http://www.countrywide.com

Covisint, 559
http://www.covisint.com

Cuningham Group, 486, 487, 488, 494
http://www.cuninghamgroup.com

DaimlerChrysler, 303
http://www.daimlerchrysler.com

Dayton Hudson, 506
http://www.dhc.com

Dell Computer, 6, 12, 194, 195, 210, 352–353
http://www.dell.com

Deloitte and Touche, 500, 501
http://www.us.deloitte.com

Deloitte Consulting, 300
http://www.dc.com

Denny's, 501
http://www.denny's.com

DHL Worldwide Express, 555
http://www.dhl.com

Disney, 307, 371–372, 498, 501
http://www.disney.com

Dixon Ticonderoga, 81
http://www.dixonticonderoga.com

Dow Chemical, 177–178, 508
http://www.dow.com

Duke Energy, 252
http://www.duke-energy.com

Duke Power, 294, 296, 302
http://www.dukepower.com

Dunkin Donuts, 169
http://www.dunkindonuts.com

E*TRADE, 213, 223, 492
http://www.etrade.com

eBay, 12
http://www.ebay.com

Edward Lowe Foundation, 193
http://www.edge.lowe.org/search.htm

Eli Lilly and Company, 89
http://www.lilly.com

Enforcement Technology (ETEC), 131
http://www.autocite.com

Ericsson, 49
http://www.ericsson.com

Ernst & Young, 141
http://www.ey.com

Estee Lauder, 143
http://www.elcompanies.com

Etec Systems, 379
http://www.etec.com

Ethics Resource Roundtable, 183
http://www.ethics.org

Eudora, 400
http://www.eudora.com

FAA, 476
http://www.faa.gov

Fannie Mae, 175
http://www.fanniemae.com

Farm, Inc., 445

Federal-Mogul, 491
http://www.federal-mogul.com

FedEx, 6, 516
http://www.fedex.com

First National Bank of Chicago, 438

Flagstar, 501
http://www.flagstar.com

Fluor Corporation, 236
http://www.fluor.com

Ford Motor Company, 65, 160, 167, 172, 185, 312, 498
http://www.ford.com

Freddie Mac, 175
http://ww1.freddiemac.com

French Federation of Insurance Companies, 289
http://www.ffsa.com

Gateway, 334
http://www.gateway.com

General Electric Aircraft Engines, 458, 459, 461, 463, 464, 476, 478
http://www.geae.com

General Electric, 7, 95, 199, 200, 203, 325, 354, 378
http://www.ge.com

General Foods, 174

General Mills, 28
http://www.generalmills.com

General Motors, 169, 418, 504–505
http://www.gm.com

GlobalWare Solutions, 539
http://www.globalwaresolutions.com

Goldman, Sachs and Company, 126
http://www.gs.com

Green Mountain Coffee, Inc., 220, 221, 231
http://www.greenmountaincoffee.com

Greyhound Lines, 229
http://www.greyhound.com

GroupVine, 559
http://www.groupvine.com

H.B. Fuller, 12
http://www.gluelink.com

Harrah's Entertainment, Inc., 302
http://www.harrahs.com

Heartland-By-Products, 117

Hewitt Associates, 348
http://www.hewittassoc.com

Hewlett-Packard, 8, 316–317, 322, 391
http://www.hp.com

Home Depot, 206, 355
http://www.homedepot.com

Honda, 172
http://www.honda.com

Honeywell, 19, 25, 332
http://www.honeywell.com

Hospice of Central Kentucky, 533, 534, 535
http://www.ubalt.edu/bereavement/hospky.htm

Hudson's Sommerset Store, 217
http://www.targetcorp.com

IAMS 143
http://www.IAMS.com

IBM, 9, 215, 153, 174, 325
http://www.ibm.com

IDEO Product Development, 256
http://www.ideo.com

IEEE, 460
http://www.ieee.org

Image Entertainment, Inc., 110
http://www.image-entertainment.com

Integrated Change Wear Systems, 441

Intel, 26
http://www.intel.com

Interface, 12, 176

Internal Revenue Service, 60, 61, 268, 270, 271
http://www.irs.ustreas.gov

International Business Ethics, 183
http://www.business-ethics.org

International Council of Shopping
   Centers, 333
http://www.icsc.org

International Organization for
   Standardization, 176

IPS-Sendero, 264
http://www.ips-sendero.com

iQVC.com, 345
http://iqvc.com

Jamba Juice, 388
http://www.jambajuice.com

JCPenney, 7
http://www.jcpenneyinc.com

JIAN, 71, 291
http://www.jianusa.com

Johnson & Johnson, 489
http://www.jnj.com

Jolliebee Foods, 213
http://www.jollibee.com

Jostens, 460–461
http://www.jostens.com

KFC, 51
http://www.kentuckyfriedchicken.com

Kirin Brewery, 337
http://www1.kirin.co.jp

Knight-Ridder, 317, 337
http://www.knight-ridder.com

Knowledge Inc.,.com, 245
http://www.knowledgeinc.com

Kodak, 333, 519
http://www.kodak.com

KPMG, 244, 357
http://www.kpmg.com

Kraft General Foods, 336
http://www.kraftfoods.com

LaBelle Management, 372
http://www.labellemgt.com

Lands' End, 100, 227
http://www.landsend.com

Levi Strauss, 97, 183
http://www.us.levi.com

Lexus, 63, 529
http://www.lexus.com

Lincoln Electric, 345, 368
http://www.lincolnelectric.com

Lockheed Martin Corp., 93, 184, 462, 547
http://www.lockheedmartin.com

Lucent Technologies, 192, 193,
   194, 197, 199, 202, 436, 532
http://www.lucent.com

Lucky Hot Dogs, 11

Mabe, 121, 122
http://www.mabe.com.mx

Marlow Industries, 66
http://www.marlow.com

Martha by Mail, 140
http://www.marthastewart.com

Marthastore, 140

Mayo Clinic, 491
http://www.mayo.edu

Maytag, 394
http://www.maytag.com

McDonald's, 226, 307
http://www.mcdonald's.com

MCI Communications, 135–136
http://www.worldcom.com

McKinsey & Company, 336
http://www.mckinsey.com

Medibuy.com, 560
http://www.medibuy.com

Medi-Health Outsourcing, 376

Meji Life Insurance Co., 551
http://www.attar.com

Mercedes-Benz, 64, 298, 324, 325
http://www.usa.mercedes-benz.com

Merck, 69, 90, 91, 92, 391
http://www.merck.com

Meredith Corporation, 210
http://www.meredith.com

Microsoft, 389, 460, 462
http://www.microsoft.com

Midvale Steel Company, 49

Mitre Corp., 247
http://www.mitre.org

Monsanto, 80
http://www.monsanto.com

Montfort, Inc., 520

Motorola, 98, 99, 173
http://www.Motorola.com

MS2, Inc., 551
http://www.ms2.com

Muffin Head Productions, 498
http://www.muffinhead.com

Nantucket Nectars, 336
http://www.juiceguys.com/home.php

NASA, 461, 476
http://spaceflight.nasa.gov

Nashua Corporation, 62
http://www.Nashua.com

National Association of Manufacturers,
   93
http://www.nam.org

National Gypsum, 28
http://national-gypsum.com

National Whistleblower Association,
   181
http://www.whistleblower.org

NCR, 474
http://www.ncr.com

Net Impact, 165
http://www.netimpact.org

Next Door Food Stores, 241, 462
http://www.nextdoor1.com

Nike, 10, 26, 140, 174, 307, 537
http://www.nike.com

Nortel Networks, 432
http://www.nortelnetworks.com

Nortel Telecommunications, 436
http://www.nortelnetworks.com

North American Free Trade Agreement
   (NAFTA), 120, 121
http://www.mac.doc.gov/nafta

Northwestern Mutual Life Insurance,
   143
http://www.northwesternmutual.com

Novell, 279
http://www.novell.com

Nucor Steel, 316
http://www.nucor.com

Orpheus Chamber Orchestra, 463
http://www.orpheusnyc.com

OshKosh B'Gosh, 550
http://www.oshkoshbgosh.com

Outer Circle, 326

Owens Corning, 239, 368
http://www.owenscorning.com

Patagonia, 186
http://www.patagonia.com

Penguin Group, 20, 21
http://www.penguin.com

PepsiCo, 197
http://www.pepsico.com

PerkinElmer, 544
http://www.perkinelmer.com

Phar-Mor, 161

Phone.com, 236
http://www.phone.com

Pillsbury, 545
http://www.pillsbury.com

Pitney-Bowes, 97, 498
http://www.pitneybowes.com

Pixar Animation Studios, 141–142
http://www.pixar.com

PriceWaterhouseCoopers, 168, 338
http://www.pwcglobal.com

Procter & Gamble, 78, 106, 246, 317, 319, 328
http://www.pg.com

Proflowers.com, 199
http://www.proflowers.com

Project Management Forum, 474
http://www.pmforum.org

Prudential Insurance, 325
http://www.prudential.com

Purple Moon, 147–148
http://purple-moon.com

Qualcomm, 400
http://www.qualcom.com

Radius, 471–472
http://www.bostonchefs.com

Rio Tinto Corporation, 116
http://www.riotinto.com/ok.html

Ritz-Carlton Hotel, 519, 522
http://www.ritzcarlton.com

Royal Dutch/Shell Group, 262, 340–341
http://www.shell.com

Rubbermaid, 100
http://www.Rubbermaid.com

S.C. Johnson Wax, 234
http://www.scjohnson.com

Scitor, 382
http://www.scitor-corp.com

Sears, Roebuck and Company, 43, 173, 380
http://www.sears.com

Second Chance Body Armor, 39
http://www.secondchance.com

Shea Homes, 312
http://www.sheahomes.com

Shell Oil Company, 80
http://www.shell.com

Siebel Systems, 286
http://www.siebel.com

Siecor Corporation, 49

Sierra Systems Consultants, 129, 130
http://www.sierrasys.com

Signicast, 462
http://www.signicast.com

Small Business Administration, 136
http://www.sba.gov and http://www.sbaonline.sba.gov

SmithKline Beecham, 329
http://www.sb.com

Softbank, 140
http://www.sbholdings.com

Solid State Measurements, 353
http://www.ssm-inc.com

Solomon R. Guggenheim Museum, 168
http://www.guggenheim.org

Sonnet Supply Company, 13, 15
http://www.sonnetsuply.com

Sonoco Products, 81
http://www.sonoco.com

Sony Corporation, 6, 47
http://www.sony.com

Southwest Airlines, 18, 436, 232, 274, 336, 344, 365, 378, 448, 487, 488, 490
http://www.southwest.com

Staples, 65, 529
http://www.staples.com

Starbucks, 69, 70, 275
http://www.starbucks.com

StrideRite, 69
http://www.striderite.com

Students for Responsible Business (renamed Net Impact), 165
http://www.netimpact.org

Sun Microsystems, 107, 211, 239, 321, 394
http://www.sun.com

Sunshine Cleaning Systems, 70, 427
http://www.sunshinecleaning.com

Swatch Watch, 536
http://www.swatch.com

Taylor Group, 355

Teachers Insurance and Annuity Association, 178
http://www.tiaa-cref.org

Team Leadership & Development, 412
http://www.tlandd.com

Texaco, 347, 502, 507
http://www.texaco.com

Texas Instruments, 352, 435, 444
http://www.ti.com

Thomas Consumer Electronics, 58, 59, 62
http://www.thomson-multimedia.com

Time Warner, 202
http://www.timewarner.com

Toshiba Corporation, 126
http://www.toshiba.com

Toyota, 42, 58, 62, 63, 81, 172
http://www.Toyota.com

Toys "R" Us, 197
http://www.toysrus.com

Trade Insurance Services, 460

Transmeta, 270
http://www.transmeta.com

Travelocity.com, 207
http://www.travelocity.com

U.S. Food and Drug Administration, 76
http://www.fda.com

U.S. Bureau of Labor Statistics, 298
http://www.bls.gov

United Airlines, 202, 459
http://www.ual.com/site/primary/

United Parcel Service, 9, 498
http://www.ups.com

US Airways, 202
http://www.USAirways.com

Valassis Communications, 401, 483
http://www.valassis.com

Virgin Atlantic, 391
http://www.fly.virgin.com

Visa, 23
http://www.visa.com

Wall Street Strategies, 498

Wal-Mart, 78, 94
http://www.walmart.com

W. B. Doner, 512
http://www.doner.com

Websense, 526
http://www.websense.com

Whole Foods Markets, 54, 387
http://www.wholefoodsmarket.com/company

Windham International, 390
http://windhamint.com

Windham World, 348
http://www.windham.com

World Trade Organization, 119
http://www.wto.or

World Wide Web Consortium, 547
http://www.w3.org

Xerox, 106, 246, 323, 337, 440, 461, 504
http://www.xerox.com

Yahoo!, 10, 134, 141, 157, 304, 335, 522, 523
http://www.yahoo.com

Yale University, 162
http://www.yale.edu

Name Index

Note: The (*n*) in selected entries designates an end-note. The page number(s) with the *n* indicates the page on which the note reference appears, while the page number with the E-prefix indicates the page where the note can be found in its entirety.

Abbott, R., 245*n*, E-13
Ackerman, P. L., 390*n*, E-22
Adams, J. S., 388*n*, E-22
Adams, S., 473*n*, E-27
Adelson, A., 186*n*, E-10
Adeney, D., 556*n*, E-31
Adler, N. J., 84*n*, E-4
Adler, P. S., 42*n*, 49*n*, E-2
Ahlquist, G. D., 76*n*, E-3
Ahuja, M. K., 310*n*, E-16
Ainina, M. F., 21*n*, E-1
Albanese, R., 473*n*, E-27
Alderfer, C. P., 392, 392*n*, E-23
Alessandra, A. J., 420*n*, E-24
Alexander, S., 220*n*, E-12
Aley, J., 354*n*, E-20
Allen, Bob, 174
Allen, N. J., 488*n*, E-28
Allen, R. E., 325*n*, E-17
Allissandra, T., 420*n*, E-24
Allscheid, S. P., 179*n*, 345*n*, E-10, E-19
Almeida, J. G., 149*n*, E-7
Alstyne, M. V., 329*n*, E-18
Altier, W. J., 226*n*, E-12
Amabile, T. M., 331*n*, E-18
Ambrose, M. L., 167*n*, 393*n*, E-8, E-23
Anderson, D. R., 535*n*, E-31
Anderson, N., 508*n*, E-30
Anderson, Ray, 12, 176
Andersson, L. M., 49*n*, 518*n*, E-2, E-30
Andreessen, Marc, 157, 400
Andrews, A. O., 346*n*, E-19
Ang, S. H., 524*n*, E-30
Antonia, Jon Dell, 550
Appell, A. L., 114*n*, E-5
Aquino, K., 389*n*, E-22
Aram, J. D., 168*n*, E-8
Aranda, E., 472*n*, E-27
Arend, R. J., 96*n*, E-4
Ariav, Haim, 498
Armani, Giorgio, 168
Armenakis, A. A., 317*n*, E-16
Armstrong, D., 474*n*, E-27
Arndt, M., 202*n*, 495*n*, E-11, E-28
Artz, K. W., 146*n*, E-7
Arvey, R. D., 360*n*, E-20
Ashe, D. K., 362–363*n*, E-21
Astin, J. A., 390*n*, E-22
Atkinson, A. A., 161*n*, 179*n*, E-8, E-10
Austin, J. T., 325*n*, E-17
Avolio, B. J., 19*n*, 419*n*, E-1, E-24
Axel, H., 460*n*, E-25
Azfar, O., 529*n*, E-30

Bacharch, S. B., 320*n*, E-17
Bachman, G., 256*n*, E-14
Badham, R., 237*n*, E-13
Baechler, Mary, 152, 152*n*, E-7
Baechler, Phil, 152
Bailey, D. E., 28*n*, E-2
Baird, L., 245*n*, E-13
Baird, R. M., 556*n*, E-31
Bakery, P. M., Jr., 268*n*, E-14
Bakke, Dennis, 482, 482*n*, E-28
Baldes, J. J., 378*n*, E-21
Baldwin, T. T., 330*n*, E-18
Balu, R., 357*n*, E-20
Bamberger, P., 320*n*, E-17
Bansal, P., 518*n*, E-30
Barber, A. E., 353*n*, 366*n*, E-20, E-21
Barkema, H., 324*n*, E-17
Barksdale, James, 522

Barnard, Chester, 54–55, 55*n*, 283, E-2
Barnard, Seph, 137
Baron, B. A., 138*n*, E-6
Bar-On, R., 407*n*, E-23
Baron, R. A., 138*n*, 142*n*, E-6, E-7
Barrick, M. R., 466*n*, E-26
Barry, L. L., 79*n*, E-3
Barstow, D., 168*n*, E-8
Barth, B., 445*n*, E-25
Barton, Jeff, 441
Bass, B. M., 420*n*, E-24
Bate, P., 330*n*, E-18
Bateman, J., 325*n*, E-17
Bateman, T. S., 518*n*, E-30
Bauccus, D. A., 162*n*, E-8
Bauccus, M. S., 162*n*, E-8
Bauer, Georg, 324, 324*n*, 325, E-17
Baum, G., 236*n*, E-13
Baungartner, P., 202*n*, E-11
Baveja, A., 208*n*, E-11, E-12
Baxendale, S. J., 533*n*, E-31
Beach, L. R., 232*n*, E-13
Becker, F., 434*n*, E-25
Becker, G. S., 135*n*, E-6
Bedeian, A. G., 317*n*, E-16
Beer, M., 317*n*, 363*n*, E-16, E-21
Begin, J. P., 348*n*, E-19
Belohlav, J. A., 348*n*, E-19
Bemmels, B., 171*n*, E-9
Benchimol, Didier, 149, 149*n*, E-7
Benjamin, B., 423*n*, E-24
Bennett, N., 169*n*, 389*n*, E-9, E-22
Berkheimer, Colette, 152
Berman, M. A., 422*n*, E-24
Berman, S. L., 80*n*, E-3
Bernard, C., 283*n*, E-15
Bernard, V. L., 530*n*, E-30
Bernardin, H. J., 356*n*, E-20
Berner, R., 106*n*, E-4
Bernstein, A., 169*n*, 174*n*, 237*n*, E-9, E-13
Berret, B., 348*n*, E-19
Berry, L. L., 62*n*, 64*n*, 298*n*, 526*n*, E-3, E-15, E-30
Berry, M. A., 177*n*, E-10
Berry, W. L., 63*n*, E-3
Bethune, Gordon, 430, 439, 441
Bettis, R. A., 114*n*, E-5
Beyer, J. M., 234*n*, 486*n*, 488*n*, 497*n*, E-13, E-28, E-29
Bezos, Jeff, 4, 4*n*, 7, 9, 15, 16-17, 24, 333, E-1
Bhappu, A. D., 84*n*, 126*n*, E-4*n*, E-5*n*
Bhave, M. P., 139*n*, E-7
Bhide, A., 145*n*, E-7*n*
Birley, S., 140*n*, E-7
Bishop, J. W., 471*n*, E-26
Blake, R. R., 411*n*, E-23
Blake, Robert, 411
Blanchard, K. H., 413–415, E-24
Bland, T., 82*n*, E-3
Blau, F. D., 506*n*, E-29
Blodgett, N., 66*n*, E-3
Bloodgood, J. M., 149*n*, E-7
Bloom, M., 390*n*, E-22
Blough, K., 548*n*, E-31
Bluedorn, A. C., 317*n*, E-16
Bobko, P., 360*n*, E-20
Boggs, Bill, 501
Bohn, R., 224*n*, E-12
Bond, M. H., 85*n*, E-4
Booker, Joe, 193
Borden, M., 193*n*, E-11
Borg, M. R., 363*n*, E-21
Borrill, C. S., 459*n*, E-25
Borrus, A., 136*n*, 174*n*, E-6, E-9
Borwhat, D. C., Jr., 465*n*, E-26
Bossong-Martines, E. M., 76*n*, 90*n*, E-3, E-4
Boudreau, J. W., 366*n*, E-21
Boudreau, M. Claude, 309*n*, E-16
Bourgeois, L. J., III, 471*n*, 475*n*, E-27

Bowerman, Bill, 140
Bowers, C. A., 477*n*, E-27
Bowman, E. H., 295*n*, E-15
Boxterand, G. D., 165*n*, E-8
Boyd, Billie, 260
Braddock, Rick, 522
Bradsher, K., 161*n*, 172*n*, 504*n*, E-8, E-9, E-29
Brady, D., 4*n*, E-1
Branch, S., 24–25*n*, E-2
Brandes, P., 325*n*, E-17
Branson, Richard, 391, 391*n*, E-23
Brass, D. J., 397*n*, E-23
Breaugh, J. A., 352*n*, 432*n*, E-20, E-24
Breaux, John, 117
Brechu, M. B., 19*n*, 121*n*, 476*n*, E-1, E-5, E-27
Brenneman, Greg, 430
Brennen, F. M., 366*n*, E-21
Brennen, Joe, 519
Brett, J. F., 92*n*, 325*n*, 397*n*, E-4, E-17, E-23
Bretz, R. D., Jr., 366*n*, E-21
Brewin, B., 542*n*, E-31
Brickson, S., 57*n*, E-3
Brief, A. P., 334*n*, E-18
Briggs, S., 204*n*, E-11
Brinkley, C., 302*n*, E-15
Briscoe, J. P., 14*n*, 423*n*, E-1, E-24
Brodsky, Norm, 149, 149*n*, E-7
Brodzinski, J. D., 21*n*, E-1
Brooker, K., 106*n*, E-4
Brooks, G., 318*n*, E-17
Brown, E., 256*n*, E-14
Brown, F. W., 389*n*, E-22
Brown, J. S., 338*n*, 544*n*, E-18, E-31
Brown, Ketty, 88*n*, E-4
Brown, M. G., 194*n*, 409*n*, E-11, E-23
Brown, Michael, 17
Brown, S. F., 58*n*, E-3
Brown, S. P., 387*n*, E-22
Brull, S. V., 334*n*, E-18
Bryant, A., 347*n*, 497*n*, 507*n*, E-19, E-28, E-29
Bryant, Michael, 146
Brynjolfsson, E., 329*n*, E-18
Buchanan, D. A., 237*n*, E-13
Buchanan, L., 11*n*, E-1
Buchholtz, A. K., 171*n*, E-9
Buckeley, W. M., 545*n*, E-31
Buckingham, B., 377*n*, E-21
Buckingham, M., 18*n*, 345*n*, E-1, E-19
Buckner, M., 322*n*, E-17
Bunney, H., 227*n*, 257*n*, E-12, E-14
Burgelman, R. A., 204*n*, E-11
Burke, D. R., 308*n*, E-16
Burlington, B., 149*n*, E-7
Burns, T., 296*n*, E-15
Burrows, P., 141*n*, 208*n*, 394*n*, E-7, E-12, E-23
Burton, Jake, 135, 135*n*, E-6
Busenitz, L. W., 234*n*, E-13
Buttner, E. H., 138*n*, E-6
Bygrave, W. D., 138*n*, E-6
Byrne, J. A., 197*n*, E-11
Byrnes, N., 511*n*, E-30

Cable, D. M., 149*n*, 168*n*, 366*n*, E-7, E-8, E-21
Cackowski, D., 305*n*, E-16
Caggiano, C., 486*n*, E-28
Caliguri, P. M., 449*n*, E-25
Callahan, E., 548*n*, E-31
Callicott, C., 186*n*, E-10
Callister, R. R., 95*n*, E-4
Cameron, A., 447*n*, E-25
Cameron, K. S., 441*n*, E-25
Campbell, H., 478*n*, E-28
Campion, M. A., 470*n*, E-26
Canedy, D., 511*n*, E-30
Carbonara, P., 356*n*, E-20
Carey, J., 349*n*, E-19
Carley, K. M., 310*n*, E-16
Carlson, J. R., 438*n*, E-25

Carmel, E., 474n, E-27
Carney, D., 202n, E-11
Carr, N. G., 223n, E-12
Carroll, A., 171n, E-9
Carter, Larry, 227
Carter, N. M., 138n, 148n, E-6, E-7
Carvell, T, 405n, E-23
Cascio, W. F., 310n, 329n, E-16, E-18
Case, Bill, 441
Case, W. N., 441n, E-25
Castagna, Vanessa, 7, 8
Castells, M., 306n, E-16
Castican, J. I., 453n, E-25
Castrogiovanni, G. J., 142n, 145n, E-7
Caulfield, Dan, 383
Cavanagh, G. F., 168n, E-9
Chachere, D. R., 171n, E-9
Chadderdon, L., 518n, E-30
Chamberlin, Monte, 58-59, 62
Chambers, John, 27
Champy, J., 329n, E-18
Chan, A., 174n, E-9
Chandler, A. D., 294n, E-15
Chandler, Alfred, 294
Charan, R., 24–25n, E-2
Chenault, Ken, 421
Cheng, J. L. C., 303n, E-16
Cheng, Y.-T., 335n, E-18
Chomka, Paul, 421
Chong, J., 28n, E-2
Chouinard, Yvon, 186
Chutchian-Ferranti, J., 309n, E-16
Cianni, M., 465n, E-26
Clark, D. L., 547n, E-31
Clark, K. B., 460n, 462n, E-25, E-26
Clark, T. J., 227n, E-12
Clarkson, M. B. E., 172n, E-9
Clinton, William, 12
Cochran, P. L., 516n, E-30
Coffman, Curt, 18n, 345n, 377, 377n, E-1, E-19, E-21
Cogliser, C. C., 405n, E-23
Cohen, Ben, 135, 174–175, 174n, 187, E-9
Cohen, V., 90n, E-4
Coil, M., 366n, E-21
Cokins, G., 532n, 535n, E-30, E-31
Cole, P., 474n, E-27
Colella, A., 360n, 498n, E-20, E-29
Collett, S., 439n, E-25
Collins, J., 215n, E-12
Colquitt, J. A., 466n, E-26
Colvin, G., 10n, 24–25n, 192n, 199n, 487n, E-1, E-2, E-11, E-28
Comer, D. R., 169n, E-9
Conger, J. A., 420n, 423n, E-24
Conlin, M., 349n, E-19, E-20
Conner, J., 358n, 422n, E-20, E-24
Conrades, George, 223–224
Constance, C. L., 500n, E-29
Conway, William, 62
Cook, J., 504n, E-29
Cooke, D. K., 356n, E-20
Cooke, R. A., 471n, E-26
Cooper, A. C., 146n, E-7
Cooper, C. L., 351n, 447n, 459n, E-20, E-25
Cooper, Stephen, 379
Cope, J., 302n, E-15
Copeland, L., 302n, E-16
Corrigan, T., 4n, E-1
Cotsakos, Christos, 492
Covey, S. R., 406n, E-23
Coyle, Shirley, 225
Crainer, S., 225n, E-12
Crampton, T., 114n, E-5
Crant, J. M., 383n, E-22
Crawford, Lee, 169
Critelli, J. W., 142n, E-7
Critelli, Michael, 498
Crockett, R. O., 173n, 228n, 497n, 545n, E-9, E-12, E-28, E-31
Cron, W. L., 325n, 378n, 397n, E-17, E-21, E-23
Crosby, J. V., 248n, E-13
Cross, E. Y., 499n, E-29

Cross, R. L., 245n, 462n, E-13, E-26
Crossette, B., 495n, E-28
Crown, D. F., 162n, E-8
Cummings, L. L., 346n, E-19
Cunningham, R., 54n, E-2
Cyr, D., 129–130n, E-6
Czarnecki, M. T., 257n, E-14

Daft, R. L., 269n, 305n, E-15, E-16
Dahle, C., 222n, E-12
Dale, B., 227n, 257n, E-12, E-14
Dalton, D. R., 356n, E-20
Danaher, Cynthia, 46
Daniels, C., 205n, 355n, 382n, E-11, E-20, E-22
Danielson, C., 330n, E-18
DaPrile, Mike, 42
Darr, E. D., 338n, E-19
Das, S., 529–530n, E-30
Das, T. K., 27n, E-2
Dass, P., 82–83n, E-4
Daus, C. S., 507n, E-29
Davenport, T. H., 542n, E-31
Davis, B. L., 5n, E-1
Davis, G. B., 554n, E-31
Davis, J. H., 361n, 366n, E-21
Davis, T. R. V., 208n, E-12
Dawar, N., 213n, E-12
Day, G. S., 278n, E-15
Day, N. E., 498n, E-29
D'Cruz, J., 275n, E-15
Dean, J. W., Jr., 260n, 325n, 478n, E-14, E-17, E-27
Dechant, K., 501n, E-29
Deck, S., 549n, 550n, E-31
Dedrick, J., 210n, E-12
Dell, Michael, 12, 195–196, 195n, 210-211, 210n, E-11, E-12
DeMan, A., 307n, E-16
DeMarco, Vicki, 542
DeMarie, S. M., 474n, E-27
DeMarines, Victor A., 247-248
DeMatteo, J. S., 368n, E-21
Dembo, Ron, 222
DeMeis, R., 42n, E-2
DeMeuse, K. P., 473n, E-27
Deming, W. Edwards, 62, 67, 225, 233, 259, 260n, E-14
DeNisi, A., 397n, E-23
Denison, D. R., 465n, 486n, 493n, E-26, E-28
Dennis, A. R., 257n, E-14
Deogun, N., 106n, E-4
DePree, M., 336n, E-18
Dervitsiotis, K. N., 259n, E-14
Dess, G. G., 152n, 154n, 230n, E-7, E-8, E-12
DeTombe, D. J., 257n, E-14
DeTore, A., 64n, E-3
DeVoge, S., 493n, E-28
DeVries, M. K., 19n, E-1
DeWitt, R. L., 328n, E-18
Deyo, Nancy, 147
Dharwadkar, R., 325n, E-17
Diana (Princess), 46
DiBella, A. J., 334–335n, E-18
Dickson, M. W., 477n, E-27
Dickson, William, 55, 56
Dilts, Gary, 303
Dimpfel, Lois A., 9, 9n, E-1
Dirks, K. T., 468n, E-26
Dixon, J. R., 60n, E-3
Dixon, N. M., 246n, E-13
Dobbins, G., 529n, E-30
Dobbs, Lou, 153
Dobnik, Verena, 174n, E-9
Dodd, N. G., 386n, E-22
Dodd, R., 175n, E-10
Doerr, John, 148, 148n, E-7
Dohner, Roy, 436
Dolan, J. A., 82–83n, E-4
Dolmat-Connell, J., 368n, E-21
Donaldson, T., 172n, 178n, E-9, E-10
Dooley, R. S., 469n, E-26
Doran, R., 194n, E-11
Dornbusch, V., 533n, E-31
Dorner, Steve, 400–401

Doss, G. M., 553n, E-31
Douma, S., 324n, E-17
Dow, D., 378n, E-21
Drazin, R., 298n, E-15
Dretler, T. D., 113n, E-5
Drucker, P. F., 28n, E-2
Druskat, V. U., 473n, E-27
Dubinsky, A. J., 419n, E-24
Duff, S., 520n, E-30
Dugan, I. J., 147n, 511n, E-7, E-30
Duguid, P., 338n, 544n, E-18, E-31
Dunfee, T. W., 178n, E-10
Dunnette, D., 327n, 330n, 471n, E-17, E-18, E-26
Duysters, G., 307n, E-16
Dwarkin, T. M., 183n, E-10
Dwyer, D. J., 473n, E-27
Dwyer, P., 237n, 506n, E-13, E-29
Dyer, Jeffery, 63
Dziko, Trish Millines, 389, 389n, E-22

Earley, P. C., 476n, E-27
Easton, G., 308n, E-16
Eaton, Robert, 178
Ebers, M., 308n, E-16
Eby, L. T., 368n, E-21
Eden, E., 477n, E-27
Edgington, D., 178–179n, E-10
Edmondson, A., 468n, E-26
Egan, Bob, 542
Egri, C. P., 419n, E-24
Eichenwald, K., 347n, E-19
Einhorn, B., 134n, 135n, E-6
Eisenhardt, K. M., 227n, 472n, 475n, E-12, E-27
Eisner, Michael, 20, 498
Elam, J. J., 317n, 337n, E-16, E-18
Ellett, C., 325n, E-17
Ellett, J. Clarke, 325n, E-17
Elron, E., 476n, E-27
Elsass, P. M., 478n, E-27
Ely, R., 43, 508n, E-30
Engardio, P., 135n, E-6
Engel, M. M., 368n, E-21
Engibous, Tom, 444
Esparza, Andy, 352n, 353, E-20
Essex, D., 551n, E-31
Estridge, Philip, 153
Evans, J. R., 260n, E-14
Evans, M. R., 125n, E-5
Evans, P., 50n, 221n, 543n, E-2, E-12, E-31

Fabian, F. H., 528n, E-30
Fairlamb, D., 116n, E-5
Faltermayer, C., 526n, E-30
Farnham, A., 365n, E-21
Fayol, Henri, 51–52, 51n, 53, 54, E-2
Feder, B. J., 177n, E-10
Feist, W. R., 107n, E-5
Felsenthal, E., 136n, E-6
Fenn, D., 13n, 376n, E-1, E-21
Ferner, Ron, 56, 56n, E-3
Ferris, G., 466n, E-26
Feuille, P., 171n, E-9
Field, T., 247n, E-13
Fields, Debbie, 46
Filo, David, 134, 141, 157
Finegan, J., 143n, E-7
Fink, D. D., 379n, E-22
Fiorina, Carleton (Carly), 17, 316, 322
Fisher, A., 354n, 407n, E-20, E-23
Fishman, C., 458n, 464n, E-12, E-25, E-26
Fitzgerald, C., 49n, E-2
Fitzpatrick, W. M., 308n, E-16
Fitzsimmons, K., 143n, E-7
Fletcher, J. K., 505n, E-29
Floyd, Jane, 380
Flynn, B. B., 60n, E-3
Flynn, E. J., 60n, E-3
Flynn, G., 324n, 348n, 439n, E-17, E-19, E-25
Foley, J. R., 171n, E-9
Folger, R., 171n, E-9
Follett, M. P., 54, 54n, E-2
Fondas, N., 460n, E-25
Forbest, Walter, 181

Ford, Bill, Jr., 161, 172
Ford, Henry, 161, 327
Foreman, E. H., 234n, E-13
Forest, S. A., 508n, E-30
Forrester, R., 387n, E-22
Fox, Vicente, 108
Fraley, S., 90n, E-4
France, M., 558n, E-32
Francesco, A. M., 13n, 124n, E-1, E-5
Franke, G. F., 162n, E-8
Franke, R. H., 162n, E-8
Fratocchi, L., 29n, E-2
Frayne, C. A., 384n, E-22
Frazier, M., 106n, E-4
Freeman, J., 229n, E-12
Freeman, R. E., 172n, 175n, E-9, E-10
Freiberg, J., 344n, E-19
Freiberg, K., 344n, E-19
Friedman, H. H., 419n, E-24
Friedman, Milton, 167, 167n, E-8
Friedman, R. A., 508n, E-30
Frink, D. D., 470n, E-26
Frohlich, M. T., 60n, E-3
Frooman, J., 230n, 235n, E-13
Frost, P. J., 497n, E-29
Frost, T., 213n, E-12
Fry, Art, 153, 153n, E-8
Fryer, B., 211n, E-12
Fryzell, G. E., 345n, 469n, E-19, E-26
Fuchs, P. H., 213n, E-12
Fujimoto, T., 42n, E-2
Fukuyama, F., 346n, E-19
Futrell, D., 473n, E-27
Futterman, Larry, 326

Gagnon, Marc, 439
Gainey, T., 26n, E-2
Galbraith, J. R., 301n, 305n, 461n, E-15, E-16, E-26
Galpin, T. J., 334n, E-18
Galt, V., 445n, E-25
Galvin, Christopher, 173
Gamble, P. R., 28n, E-2
Gandhi, M., 46
Ganster, D. C., 386n, 473n, E-22, E-27
Gantt, Henry, 51, 53
Gardner, Scott, 481–482
Garfinkel, S., 557n, E-32
Garino, J., 97n, E-4
Garland, S. B., 136n, E-6
Gartner, W. B., 148n, E-7
Garud, R., 49n, E-2
Garvey, C., 379n, E-22
Garvin, D. A., 329n, 334–335n, E-18
Gaughan, P. A., 202n, E-11
Geller, E. S., 323n, E-17
Gendron, G., 135n, E-6
Geo-JaJa, M. A., 118n, E-5
Gerbman, R. V., 359n, E-20
Gerhart, B., 366n, 367–368n, E-21
Geringer, M. J., 384n, E-22
Gersick, C. J. G., 468n, E-26
Gerstner, Louis, Jr., 215, 325–326, 326
Ghosh, C., 139n, E-6
Ghoshal, S., 89n, 308n, E-4, E-16
Gibson, D. A., 28n, E-2
Gibson, J. W., 434n, E-25
Giladi, K., 419n, E-24
Gilbert, J. A., 498n, E-29
Gilbreth, Frank, 50, 51, 53
Gilbreth, Lillian, 50, 53
Gilder, G., 546n, E-31
Giles, P., 493n, E-28
Giles-Brown, L., 82–83n, E-4
Gillis, J., 80n, E-3
Gilmartin, Raymond, 92
Gilpin, K. N., 511n, E-30
Gimein, M., 270n, 522n, E-15, E-30
Ginsburg, J., 332n, E-18
Gioja, L., 336n, E-18
Gisel, Grant, 129–130
Gittell, J. H., 231n, E-13
Glasser, J., 114n, E-5
Glick, W. H., 110n, 322n, E-5, E-17

Globerman, S., 26n, E-2
Goes, J., 318n, 337n, E-17, E-18
Goffee, R., 497n, E-29
Gold, B. A., 13n, 124n, E-1, E-5
Gold, Christina, 511
Gold, D. M., 170n, E-9
Goldin, C., 170n, E-9
Goldoftas, B., 42n, E-2
Goldstein, I. L., 327n, E-17
Goleman, D. P., 407n, E-23
Gollwitzer, P. M., 378n, E-21
Golub, Harvey, 322, 421
Golzen, G., 449n, E-25
Gomez-Mejia, L. R., 112n, E-5
Gompers, Samuel, 43
Gonzalez, J., 42n, E-2
Goodman, P. S., 179n, 338n, 345n, E-10, E-19
Goodstein, L. D., 453n, E-25
Gorman, P., 22n, 110n, E-1, E-5
Gotz, G., 223n, E-12
Gould, C., 359n, E-20
Gould, J. M., 334–335n, E-18
Gowen, M., 169n, E-9
Grainger, R., 125n, E-5
Grant, G., 493n, E-28
Grant, L., 359n, E-20
Grant, R. M., 338n, E-18
Greco, S., 11n, 149n, E-1, E-7
Green, H., 4n, 134n, 558n, E-1, E-6, E-32
Greenberg, J. A., 170n, 346n, 389n, E-9, E-19, E-22
Greenfeld, K. T., 196n, E-11
Greenfield, J., 135, 174n, 187, E-9
Greengard, S., 356n, E-20
Greenhalgh, L., 161n, 312n, E-8, E-16
Greenhouse, S., 174n, 495n, E-9, E-28
Greening, D. W., 179n, E-10
Grensing-Pophal, L., 430n, E-24
Gresham, L. G., 298n, E-15
Gresham, M. T., 367–368n, E-21
Gresov, C., 298n, E-15
Griffeth, R. W., 397n, E-23
Grossman, R. J., 204n, 499n, E-11, E-29
Grove, Andy, 26n, 79, E-2
Grove, C., 474n, E-27
Grover, R., 141n, E-7
Grubb, T. M., 199n, E-11
Gulati, R., 97n, 303n, E-4, E-16
Gutierrez, I., 136n, E-6
Gutner, T., 179n, E-10
Guzzo, R. A., 334n, 459n, 465n, 477n, E-18, E-25, E-26, E-27

Haasen, A., 29n, 64n, E-2, E-3
Hackman, J. Richard, 386, 386n, 471n, E-22, E-26
Hacohen, D. A., 356n, E-20
Haddad, C., 162n, E-8
Halkias, M., 7n, E-1
Hall, C., 348n, E-19
Hall, D. T., 14n, 423n, E-1, E-24
Hall, E., 434n, E-25
Hallowell, W., 474n, E-27
Halper, M., 555n, E-31
Hamel, G., 152n, 203n, 216n, 295n, 326n, 334n, 341n, E-7, E-11, E-12, E-15, E-17, E-18, E-19
Hammer, M., 294n, 296n, 302n, 329n, E-15, E-16, E-18
Hammonds, K. H., 178n, E-10
Hampden-Turner, C., 84n, E-4
Han, J., 543n, E-31
Handy, C., 346n, E-19
Haney, C., 278n, E-15
Hansen, G. S., 345n, E-19
Hansen, M. T., 245n, E-13
Hanson, J. B., 441n, E-25
Harding, D., 70n, E-3
Hardy, Q., 173n, 316n, E-9, E-16
Hare, A. P., 473n, E-27
Hargadon, A., 334n, E-18
Harkin, Ruth, 116
Harrington, A., 500n, E-29
Harris, C., 366n, E-21
Harris, S. G., 490n, E-28
Harrison, D. A., 478n, E-27

Harrison, E. F., 221n, E-12
Hart, S. L., 465n, E-26
Hartman, L. Pincus, 409n, E-23
Hartmann, Lynn, 491
Harvey, M., 123n, 234n, E-5, E-13
Hauenstein, N. M. A., 363n, E-21
Hawk, E. J., 479n, E-28
Hayes, C., 150n, E-7
Hayes, F., 227n, E-12
Hays, C. L., 175n, E-9
Healy, P. M., 530n, E-30
Heely, J. A., 107n, E-5
Heil, G., 410n, E-23
Heilman, M. E., 508n, E-30
Hellriegel, D., 337n, E-18
Henderson, B. D., 89, 89n, E-4
Hendrickson, A. R., 474n, E-27
Hendry, C., 317n, E-16
Heneman, R. L., 367–368n, E-21
Hensley, S., 560n, E-32
Herman, S., 419n, E-24
Hersey, Paul, 413–415, 413n, E-24
Herzberg, Frederick, 384–385, 384n, E-22
Heskett, J. L., 300n, E-15
Hess, T. J., 432n, E-24
Hewlett, Bill, 316
Heyde, Mary Ellen, 498, 498n, E-29
Hickey, Fred, 210
Hicks, D. T., 533n, E-31
Hiemstra, K. M., 434n, E-24
Hightower, R., 524n, E-30
Hill, C. W. L., 200n, E-11
Hill, R. C., 142n, 337n, E-7, E-18
Hillary, R., 177n, E-10
Himelstein, L., 134n, 508n, E-6, E-30
Hinton, R., 286n, E-15
Hirakubo, N., 127n, E-6
Hirsch, Antoni, 282–283
Hisrich, R. D., 142n, E-7
Hitlan, R. T., 506n, E-29
Hitt, M. A., 22n, 111nE-5, 136n, 193n, E-1, E-6, E-11
Hjelmas, T. A., 358n, E-20
Hock, Dee, 23–24
Hodgetts, R. M., 89n, 434n, E-4, E-25
Hof, R. D., 4n, E-1
Hoffman, J. J., 77n, E-3
Hofstede, Geert, 85, 85n, 86n, 496n, E-4, E-28
Holthouse, Don, 246
Holusha, J., 136n, E-6
Holyoke, L., 167n, E-8
Hom, P. W., 397n, E-23
Hooijberg, R., 490n, E-28
Hoon-Halbauer, S. K., 15n, E-1
Hopkins, M., 136n, E-6
Hornblower, M., 70n, E-3
Hornsby, J. S., 152n, E-8
Horowitz, A. S., 208n, E-12
Hoskisson, R. E., 193n, E-11
Hough, L. M., 327n, 330n, 471n, E-17, E-18, E-26
House, David, 421
Howard, A., 322n, E-17
Howland, B., 5n, E-1
Howroyd, Janice Bryant, 150
Huber, G. P., 110n, 322n, E-5, E-17
Huber, J., 248n, E-14
Hudson, Katherine, 412–413, 421
Huff, A. S., 179n, E-10
Huff, J. O., 179n, E-10
Hughes, Catherine, 139
Hult, G. T., 524n, E-30
Hyatt, D. E., 466n, E-26
Hyatt, J., 489n, E-28
Hymowitz, C., 328n, E-17

Ibarreche, S., 169n, E-9
Ichijo, K., 247n, E-13
Imperato, G., 361n, 471n, E-20, E-26
Ireland, R. D., 22n, 111n, 136n, 193n, E-1, E-5, E-6, E-11
Israel, P., 253n, E-14
Ivancevich, J. M., 498n, E-29
Izumi, H., 327n, E-17

Jackson, Jesse, 46
Jackson, P., 550n, E-31
Jackson, S. E., 162n, 344n, 350n, 351n, 367n, 465n, 474n, 508n, E-8, E-19, E-20, E-21, E-26, E-27, E-30
Jager, Durk, 106, 319
Jago, 417
Jamil, M., 208n, E-11, E-12
Janz, B. D., 466n, E-26
Jaunch, L. R., 538n, E-31
Jenner, R., 114n, E-5
Jensen, M. A. C., 468n, E-26
Jobs, S. M., 141–142, 411n, 489, E-23
Johannessen, O. J., 358n, E-20
Johnson, D. E., 413n, E-24
Johnson, J. R., 13n, E-1
Johnson, M., 506n, E-29
Johnson, R. A., 317n, E-16
Johnson, Samuel, 259
Johnston, M. A., 285n, E-15
Joinson, C., 460n, 461n, E-25, E-26
Jones, G. R., 200n, 497n, E-11, E-29
Jones, T. M., 80n, 172n, 179n, E-3, E-9, E-10
Joplin, J. R. W., 507n, E-29
Joshi, A., 508n, E-30
Jossi, F., 169n, E-9
Joyner, B. E., 177n, E-10
Judge, P. C., 174n, E-9
Judge, T. A., 319n, 366n, E-17, E-21
Judy, R. W., 353n, E-20
Juliber, Lois, 492
Jung, Andrea, 511
Jung, D. I., 19n, E-1
Jurkiewicz, C. L., 385n, E-22

Kahn, J. A., 465n, E-26
Kahn, L. M., 506n, E-29
Kahn, W. A., 476n, E-27
Kahwajy, J. L., 472n, 475n, E-27
Kamber, M., 543n, E-31
Kanfer, R., 390n, E-22
Kanter, R., 113n, E-5
Kanungo, R. N., 163n, E-8
Karahanna, E., 432n, E-24
Kassicieh, S. K., 138n, E-6
Katzenbach, J. R., 19n, 459n, E-1, E-25
Kavan, C. B., 308n, E-16
Kayes, D. C., 473n, E-27
Kayworth, T., 310n, E-16
Kedia, B. L., 14n, E-1
Keen, G. W., 546n, E-31
Keen, Peter, 309
Kehoe, J. F., 354n, E-20
Keillor, B. D., 524n, E-30
Kelinson, J. W., 82n, E-3
Kelleher, Herb, 46, 336, 344, 448, 487, 488, 490, E-19
Kelly, T. A., 256n, E-14
Kelsey, D., 556n, E-32
Kennedy, Allan, 487n, E-28
Keogh, W., 204n, E-11
Kerr, S., 397n, E-23
Kesner, I. L., 303n, E-16
Ketchen, D. J., Jr., 280n, E-15
Keyes, J., 547n, E-31
Khan, R., 330n, E-18
Kidwell, R. E., Jr., 169n, 389n, E-9, E-22
Kilman, S., 80n, E-3
Kim, C., 336n, E-18
Kim, W. C., 171n, 325n, 346n, E-9, E-17, E-19
King, J., 560n, E-32
King, Martin Luther, Jr., 46, 419
Kinkead, G., 12n, E-1
Kirkman, B. I., 56n, 215n, 418n, 464n, E-3, E-12, E-24, E-26
Kirkpatrick, D., 548n, E-31
Klass, B. S., 26n, E-2
Klassen, R. D., 57n, 96n, 179n, E-3, E-4, E-10
Klein, G., 235n, E-13
Kletter, M., 536n, E-31
Klineberg, S. L., 499n, E-29
Kluger, A. N., 397n, E-23
Knight, M., 97n, E-4
Knight, Phil, 10, 174

Knott, D. G., 76n, E-3
Koch, M. J., 322n, E-17
Kogut, B., 136n, E-6
Kohlberg, L., 165n, E-8
Kolb, D. A., 453n, E-25
Konarski, John, 332
Kondouli, D., 257n, E-14
Konovsky, M. A., 171n, 346n, 389n, E-9, E-19, E-22
Koogle, Tim, 10, 134, 522–523, 522n, E-30
Korsgaard, M. A., 149n, E-7
Koski, Christine, 15, 16n, E-1
Kostova, T., 111n, E-5
Kotabe, M., 65n, 356n, E-3, E-20
Kotha, S., 80n, E-3
Kotkin, J., 136n, E-6
Kotter, J. P., 136n, E-6
Krackhardt, D., 441n, E-25
Kraimer, M. L., 383n, E-22
Krajewski, L. J., 51n, E-2
Kram, K. E., 476n, E-27
Kramer, K. L., 210n, E-12
Kramer, M. K., 95n, E-4
Kramer, M. W., 223n, E-12
Kransdorrf, A., 336n, E-18
Kraut, A. I., 330n, E-18
Kravita, D. A., 499n, E-29
Kripalani, M., 135n, E-6
Krohe, J., Jr., 164n, E-8
Kropf, Susan, 511
Kulick, C. T., 393n, E-23
Kunde, D., 66n, E-3
Kunii, I. M., 140n, E-7
Kuratko, D. F., 152n, E-8
Kurland, N. B., 28n, E-2
Kurzweil, R., 550n, E-31
Kydoniefs, L., 473n, E-27

Laabs, J. J., 346n, E-19
Labarre, P., 20–21n, E-1
Labich, K., 502n, E-29
LaBlanc, E., 498n, E-29
Lackey, C., 169n, E-9
Lafley, A. G., 106
Lagarde, Christine, 502
Lam, S. S. K., 478n, E-28
Lamb, R. B., 199n, E-11
Lampel, J., 193n, E-11
Lane, H. W., 19n, 121n, 476n, E-1, E-5, E-27
Langley, G., 260n, E-14
Larwood, L., 419n, E-24
Latham, G. P., 378n, E-21
Lathrop, J. P., 76n, E-3
Lauder, Estée, 143
Lawler, E. E., III, 305n, 306n, 351n, 396n, E-16, E-20, E-23
Lawler, E. J., 458n, E-25
Lawlor, Paula, 376, 377
Lawlor, Ron, 376
Lawrence, B., 508n, E-29
LeBlanc, P. V., 386n, E-22
Ledford, G. E., Jr., 351n, 367–368n, 386n, E-20, E-21, E-22
Lee, B., 406n, E-23
Lee, J., 60n, E-3
Lee, L., 174n, 275n, 404n, 492n, E-9, E-15, E-23, E-28
Lefkowitz, J., 363n, E-21
Lei, D., 26n, 27n, 66n, 94n, 101n, 110n, 112n, 337n, E-2, E-3, E-4, E-5, E-18
Leidner, D., 310n, E-16
Leigh, T. W., 387n, E-22
Lengnick-Hall, C. A., 179n, 345n, E-10, E-19
Lentzsch, Craig, 230, 230n, E-13
Leonard, B., 47n, 175n, E-2, E-9
Leonhardt, D., 170n, 319n, 394n, 497n, E-9, E-17, E-23, E-28
Lepore, Dawn, 404
Lerch, F. J., 179n, E-10
Leslie, J. B., 24–25n, 475n, E-2, E-27
Letterman, David, 364
Leuchter, M., 404n, E-23
Levenhagen, M., 142n, E-7
Levering, R., 344n, 346n, 354n, E-19, E-20

Levine, D. I., 42n, E-2
Lewin, K., 317n, E-16
Lewin, T., 174n, E-9
Lewis, C. T., 411n, E-23
Lewis, J., 42n, E-2
Liden, R. C., 473n, E-27
Lieber, R., 186n, E-10
Lieberskind, J. P., 338n, E-18
Liedtka, J. M., 192n, 195n, E-11
Liesch, P. W., 108n, E-5
Ligos, M., 198n, E-11
Linder, Bob, 236–237
Lindsley, D. H., 397n, E-23
Lingbert, M., 419n, E-24
Lipnack, J., 474n, E-27
Lipparini, A., 29n, E-2
Livermore, Ann, 8
Locke, E. A., 378n, E-21
Logan, J. W., 177n, E-10
London, M., 358n, 363n, E-20, E-21
Longenecker, J. G., 142n, 145n, E-7
Loomis, C. J., 203n, E-11
Louis, M. R., 462n, E-26
Lowe, Doug, 486, 487
Lowe, T., 523n, E-30
Lowy, A., 97–98n, E-4
Lu, M. H., 107n, E-5
Luberski, Tim, 109
Lubin, J. S., 440n, E-25
Lucero, M. A., 325n, E-17
Lucey, S., 304n, E-16
Lucier, C., 245n, E-13
Ludwig, T. D., 323n, E-17
Lumpkin, G. T., 152n, 154n, E-7, E-8
Lundgren, E. F., 317n, E-16
Lupton, D., 222n, E-12
Luthans, F., 378n, 381n, E-21, E-22
Lynton, Michael, 20–21
Lyons, D., 210n, E-12

MacDuffie, J. P., 337n, E-18
Machin, J. L., 523n, E-30
Macht, J., 383n, E-22
Mackery, John, 54
MacMillan, I., 138n, E-6
Macy, B. A., 327n, E-17
Mahoney, J. T., 179n, E-10
Majchrzak, A., 497n, E-29
Makower, J., 184n, E-10
Malaga, R. A., 257n, E-14
Malhotra, Y., 309n, E-16
Mallett, Jeffrey, 134
Malone, M. S., 148n, E-7
Mandel, M. J., 493n, E-28
Mangum, G. L., 118n, E-5
Manigart, S., 138n, E-6
Mann, L., 378n, E-21
Manning, Rob, 296–297
Markels, A., 482n, 508n, E-28, E-30
Markham, G. D., 138n, 142n, E-6, E-7
Markides, C. C., 204n, E-11
Markopoulos, Andrew, 217
Markovsky, B., 458n, E-25
Marks, M. L., 93n, E-4
Marlow, Raymond, 66
Marshall, R. S., 524n, E-30
Martell, R. F., 363n, E-21
Martin, J., 476n, E-27
Martin, L. P., 262n, E-14
Martin, S., 434n, E-25
Martocchio, J. J., 379n, 470n, E-22, E-26
Mascarenhas, B., 208n, E-11, E-12
Maslow, Abraham, 390–392, 390n, 392, E-22
Mason, C. M., 138n, E-6
Mason, Earl, 228
Mason, R. O., 516n, E-30
Massey, T. K., Jr., 385n, E-22
Massini, S., 302n, E-16
Mathieu, J. E., 325n, 473n, E-17, E-27
Matson, E., 379n, E-22
Mattson, L-G., 308n, E-16
Mauborgne, R., 171n, 325n, 336n, 346n, E-9, E-17, E-18, E-19

Maurer, R., 324n, E-17
Maurer, T. J., 362–363n, E-21
Mausner, B., 384n, E-22
Maxon, T., 336n, E-18
May, D. R., 389n, 520n, E-22, E-30
May, K. E., 465n, E-26
Mayer, R. C., 361n, E-21
Maynard, J., 551n, E-31
Mayo, Charlie, 491
Mayo, Elton, 55, 55n, 56, E-2
Mayo, John S., 107
Mayo, Will, 491
McAdams, J., 479n, E-28
McAfee, A., 310n, E-16
McCabe, K., 529–530n, E-30
McCall, M. W., Jr., 4n, 422n, E-1, E-24
McCann, J. E., III, 322n, E-17
McCarthy, D. J., 168n, E-8
McCarthy, J. L., 334n, E-18
McCauley, L., 239n, E-13
McClelland, David, 138, 138n, 393, 393n, 394n,
    E-6, E-23
McClendon, J., 26n, E-2
McCune, H., 312n, E-16
McDaniel, M. A., 355n, E-20
McDermott, G., 136n, E-6
McDermott, S., 553n, E-31
McDougall, P. Phillips, 149n, E-7
McEachern, W. A., 78n, 118n, E-3, E-5
McEvily, S. K., 529–530n, E-30
McFarlan, F. Warren, 404
McGaughey, S. L., 108n, E-5
McGee, M. Kolbasuk, 543n, E-31
McGill, M. E., 154n, 272n, 336n, E-8, E-15, E-18
McGinn, Richard, 192, 192n, 194, 195n, E-10,
    E-11
McGrath, R. G., 138n, 322n, E-6, E-17
McGregor, Douglas, 409, 410–411, 410n, E-23
McHugh, M., 325n, E-17
McKinley, W., 47n, E-2
McLaughlin, C. P., 179n, E-10
McLeod, P. L., 474n, E-27
McLeod, R., Jr., 552n, E-31
McNamee, M., 356n, E-20
McNealy, Scott, 394
Means, C. M., 289n, E-15
Megerian, L. E., 420n, E-24
Mehta, S. N., 135n, 136n, 498n, E-6, E-29
Meier, B., 162n, E-8
Meir, Golda, 46
Meissner, Michelle, 430
Melcher, R. A., 178n, 491n, E-10, E-28
Melymuka, K., 88n, 404n, 405n, E-4, E-23
Mendonca, M., 163n, E-8
Messick, D. M., 231n, E-13
Metters, R., 299n, E-15
Meyer, A., 318n, E-17
Meyer, C., 78n, E-3
Meyer, G. D., 138n, E-6
Meyer, H., 518n, E-30
Meyer, J. P., 488n, E-28
Meyer, J. W., 347n, E-19
Meyer, M. H., 64n, E-3
Meyerson, D. E., 505n, E-29
Miceli, M. P., 181n, 182n, 183n, E-10
Mill, J. S., 167n, E-8
Millenium, A. Alvarez, 135n, E-6
Miller, D., 60n, E-3
Miller, K. L., 506n, E-29
Miller, Steve, 340–341
Millimann, M., 336n, E-18
Minehan, M., 495n, E-28
Mintzberg, H., 193n, E-11
Mirabell, G., 143n, E-7
Miranda, S. M., 472n, E-26
Mirvis, P. H., 93n, E-4
Mishra, A. K., 493n, E-28
Moberg, D. V., 168n, E-9
Mochari, D., 356n, E-20
Moffat, Joan, 69–70
Mohrman, A. M., Jr., 460n, E-25–26
Mohrman, S. A., 305n, 460n, E-16, E-25
Mone, E. M., 358n, E-20

Mone, M. A., 47n, E-2
Monroe, L. K., 259n, E-14
Montagno, R. V., 152n, E-8
Moon, G., 47n, E-2
Moore, 145n, E-7
Moore, C. W., 142n, E-7
Moore, D. P., 138n, E-6
Moore, P. L., 164n, E-8
Moorman, R. H., 171n, E-9
Moran, P., 89n, E-4
Morand, D. A., 490n, E-28
Moravec, M., 358n, E-20
Morris, B., 161n, 511n, E-8, E-30
Morris, Jack, 408–409, 423
Morris, K., 332n, E-18
Morris, M. H., 135n, E-6
Morrow, J. C., 347n, E-19
Morrow, P. C., 347n, E-19
Mortensen, C. D., 443n, E-25
Mosakowski, E. M., 476n, E-27
Moser, P., 10n, E-1
Moskowitz, M., 344n, 354n, E-19, E-20
Mossholder, K. W., 490n, E-28
Mougayar, W., 546n, E-31
Mount, I., 198n, E-11
Mouton, Jane, 411, 411n, E-23
Moxley, R., 448n, E-25
Mueller, C. W., 470n, E-26
Muir, N. K., 478n, E-27
Mukhcrji, A., 14n, E-1
Mullaney, T. J., 345n, E-19
Mullen, B., 472n, E-26
Mullen, E. J., 347n, E-19
Mulvey, P. W., 386n, 478n, E-22, E-27
Munk, N., 143n, E-7
Munter, M., 434n, E-24
Muoio, A., 322n, E-17
Murphy, K. R., 360n, 390n, E-20, E-22
Murphy, Robert "Joe," 178–179
Murray, B., 536n, E-31
Murray, C. J., 42n, E-2
Murray, J. Y., 65n, 356n, E-3, E-20
Myers, R., 230n, 431n, E-13, E-24

Nadler, D., 269n, 282n, 295n, 319n, E-15, E-17
Naffziger, D. W., 152n, E-8
Nagler, B., 462n, E-26
Nahavandi, A., 472n, E-27
Napier, N., 359n, E-20
Nasser, Jacques A. (Jac), 312, 312n, E-16
Navarro, Linda, 13, 15, 25
Navran, F., 164n, E-8
Near, J. P., 181n, 182n, 183n, E-10
Neff, R., 126n, E-5
Negley, J., 198n, E-11
Neihoff, B. P., 356n, E-20
Nelson, David, 418
Nelson, E., 106n, E-4
Nelson, R. B., 285n, 415n, E-15, E-24
Nelson, R. E., 308n, E-16
Nersesian, R. L., 107n, E-5
Neuborne, E., 106n, E-4
Neufeld, Evan, 304–305
Neuman, G. A., 476n, E-27
Nevis, E. C., 334–335n, E-18
Nguyen Huy, Q., 407n, E-23
Nguyen Tuy, 49
Nicholls, C. E., 19n, E-1
Nickerson, R. C., 542n, E-31
Niedrich, R. W., 529n, E-30
Niehoff, B. P., 171n, E-9
Nielson, C., 59n, E-3
Noble, S., 406n, E-23
Nocera, J., 404n, E-23
Noe, R. A., 466n, E-26
Noel, T. W., 167n, E-8
Nohria, N., 245n, 303n, 308n, 317n, E-13, E-16
Nolan, K., 260n, E-14
Nolan, T., 260n, E-14
Nonaka, I., 247n, E-13
Norris, W. E., 415n, E-24
Northcraft, G. B., 82–83n, 92n, E-4

Northouse, P. G., 404n, E-23
Novicevic, M. M., 123n, 234n, E-5, E-13
Numagami, T., 302n, E-16
Nutt, P. C., 60n, E-3

O'Connor, E. S., 55n, E-2
O'Donnell, Steve, 364
O'Dwyer, John, 109n, E-5
Oetzel, J. M., 114n, E-5
O'Gorman, C., 194n, E-11
Oldham, G. R., 386, 386n, E-22
O'Leary-Kelly, A. M., 379n, 470n, E-22, E-26
Ones, D., 356n, E-20
O'Reilly, B., 47n, E-2
O'Reilly, C. A., III, 213n, 320n, E-12, E-17
Orlikowski, W. J., 310n, E-16
O'Rourke, J., 174n, E-9
Orr, Barbara, 294
Orzechowski, R., 348n, E-19
Osborn, A. F., 254, 254n, 255n, E-14
Osland, J. S., 453n, E-25
Otto, L., 518n, E-30
Oviatt, B. M., 149n, E-7

Packard, Dave, 316
Padavic, I., 170n, E-9
Page, H., 139n, E-6
Palepu, K. G., 530n, E-30
Palich, L. E., 112n, E-5
Palmer, J. K., 362–363n, E-21
Pamela, H., 125n, E-5
Pan, S. L., 247n, E-13
Pantel, 357
Pape, W. R., 474n, E-27
Pappas, B., 536n, E-31
Parent, Louise, 421
Park, S. H., 337n, E-18
Parker, B., 82–83n, E-4
Parker, G. M., 460n, 462n, 479n, E-25, E-26, E-28
Parker, J. D., 407n, E-23
Parker, T., 406n, E-23
Parker-Pope, T., 493n, 511n, E-28, E-30
Pascale, R., 336n, 341n, E-18, E-19
Pasmore, W. A., 317n, 327n, 330n, E-16, E-17,
    E-18
Patrick, John, 326
Pattison, P., 347n, E-19
Paul, K., 174n, E-9
Paul, R. J., 356n, E-20
Paulus, P. B., 254n, 460n, E-14, E-26
Payne, John, 406
Pearson, C. M., 28n, 49n, E-2
Pelled, L. H., 28n, 82n, E-2, E-4
Pennings, J. M., 324n, E-17
Penrose, J., 431n, E-24
Percy, Ethel, 95
Perrin, Charles, 511
Peters, T. L., 153n, E-8
Petersen, M., 502n, E-29
Peterson, R. S., 468n, E-26
Petrick, J. A., 21n, E-1
Petrock, F., 490n, E-28
Pettigrew, A., 302n, E-16
Petty, J. W., 142n, 145n, E-7
Petzinger, T., 17n, 324n, 325n, E-1, E-17
Pfeffer, J. W., 213n, 235n, 237n, 262n, 453n, E-12,
    E-13, E-14, E-25
Picken, J. C., 230n, E-12
Pickering, C., 304n, E-16
Pierce, J., 175n, E-10
Pinchott, G., III, 153n, E-8
Pincus, L. B., 348n, E-19
Pinkley, R. L., 92n, E-4
Pinsonneault, A., 257n, E-14
Pitts, R. A., 27n, 66n, 101n, 112n, 337n, E-2, E-3,
    E-4, E-5, E-18
Platt, Lew, 316
Ployhart, R. E., 355n, 434n, E-20, E-24
Polley, D. E., 49n, E-2
Pollock, T., 22n, 110n, E-1, E-5
Poluson, D., 108n, E-5
Ponthieu, L. D., 142n, E-7
Poole, M. S., 320n, E-17

Porras, J. I., 330n, E-18
Porter, L. W., 396n, E-23
Porter, M. E., 89n, 195, 195n, 206, 212n, E-4, E-11, E-12
Pottruck, David S., 404-405, 404n, 405, 407, 421, E-23
Powell, G. N., 498n, E-29
Powell, Monica, 432, 432n, 433, 434, E-24
Powell, T G., 488n, E-28
Preston, James E., 511
Preston, L. E., 172n, E-9
Prevo, Jim, 220, 230-231
Priem, R. L., 478n, E-27
Prince, C., 466n, E-26
Priory, Richard, 252
Prokesch, S. E., 358n, E-20
Puffer, S. M., 168n, 368n, E-8, E-21
Pugh, S. D., 389n, E-22
Pye, A., 330n, E-18

Quayle, Dan, 558
Quinn, J. F., 21n, E-1
Quinn, R. E., 317n, 490n, E-16, E-28
Quittner, J., 4n, E-1

Rabbie, J. M., 471n, E-26
Radhakrishnan, P., 506n, E-29
Radosevich, R., 138n, E-6
Rae-Dupee, J., 148n, E-7
Raiborn, C. A., 177n, E-10
Rakes, T. R., 432n, E-24
Ralston, D. A., 494n, E-28
Ralston, Paul, 143
Ramamurti, R, 107n, E-5
Ramsower, R. Mays, 556n, E-31
Randall, E., 307n, 326n, E-16, E-17
Rao, S. S., 531n, E-30
Rappleye, W. C., Jr., 244n, 246n, E-13
Rarick, C A., 165n, E-8
Rasberry, R. W., 431n, E-24
Raskin, J. B., 54n, E-2
Rawls, J. A., 170n, E-9
Ray, M., 230n, E-13
Reed, J., 54n, E-2
Rees, L. P., 432n, E-24
Reichers, A. E., 325n, E-17
Reichfeld, F. R., 526n, E-30
Reingold, J., 170n, 332n, E-9, E-18
Renn, R. W., 386n, E-22
Renshaw, A. A., 329n, E-18
Reséndez, Homero, 17, 25
Reskin, B., 170n, E-9
Reynolds, P. D., 138n, 148n, E-6, E-7
Rice, F., 502n, E-29
Richardson, Jerry, 501–502
Ringland, G., 252n, E-14
Riordan, C. M., 508n, E-29
Ritzman, L. P., 51n, E-2
Roach, J. M., 233n, E-13
Roberts, D. R., 330n, E-18
Roberts, P., 490n, E-28
Robertson, A. G., 407n, E-23
Robertson, I. T., 459n, E-25
Robertson, P. J., 330n, E-18
Robey, D., 317n, 337n, E-16, E-18
Robinson, A. G., 253n, E-14
Robinson, Ed, 511
Robinson, G., 501n, E-29
Robinson, P. B., 138n, E-6
Roethlisberger, Fritz, 55, 56
Roger, James, 228
Rondinelli, D. A., 177n, E-10
Ronen, S., 356n, E-20
Roosevelt, Franklin Delano, 53
Rose, S., 511n, E-30
Rosen, B., 56n, 215n, 418n, 464n, E-3, E-12, E-24, E-26
Rosen, J., 558n, E-32
Rosenbaum, S. E., 556n, E-31
Rosenbush, S., 192n, E-10
Rossman, Alain, 236, 237
Roth, D., 173n, E-9
Roth, K., 518n, E-30

Rousseau, D. M., 322n, E-17
Row, H., 423n, E-24
Rowan, B., 347n, E-19
Rowe, G., 248n, E-14
Rowland, K., 466n, E-26
Rubin, H., 420n, E-24
Rubin, I. M., 453n, E-25
Rubinstein, A., 232n, E-13
Ruddy, T. M., 466n, E-26
Ruderman, M. N., 474n, E-27
Rudin, Scott, 405
Ruf, B. M., 174n, E-9
Rugman, A., 275n, E-15
Rugutt, J., 325n, E-17
Russell, Cheryl, 248, 248n, E-14
Russell, G. R., 260n, E-14
Ryan, A. M., 348n, 355n, 434n, E-19, E-20, E-24
Rynes, S. L., 366n, 367-368n, E-21
Rysavy, Jirka, 156

Sagawa, S., 178n, E-10
Sagie, A., 476n, E-27
Sahakian, C. E., 248n, E-14
Sahlma, W. A., 145n, E-7
Salas, E., 465n, 466n, 477n, E-26, E-27
Salter, C., 352n, E-20
Samson, D., 378n, E-21
Saner, R., 113n, E-5
Sanger, Steve, 28
Sant, Roger, 482, 482n, E-28
Santamaria, J., 19n, E-1
Sapienza, H. J., 149n, E-7
Sargent, Susan, 11
Sashkin, Marshall, 165n, E-8
Sasser, W. E., Jr., 300n, E-15
Saunders, C. S., 308n, E-16
Sawney, M., 78n, 79n, E-3
Sawyer, J. E., 379n, E-21
Scarbrough, H., 247n, E-13
Schaubroeck, J., 389n, 478n, E-22, E-28
Schefter, P., 526n, E-30
Schein, E. H., 497n, E-29
Schell, G., 552n, E-31
Scherer, R. F., 21n, E-1
Scherreik, S., 179n, E-10
Schine, E., 156n, E-8
Schlender, B., 134n, E-6
Schlesinger, L. A., 300n, E-15
Schlow, Michael, 471–472
Schmeidler, M. A., 453n, E-25
Schmidt, Eric, 279
Schmidt, F. I., 356n, E-20
Schminke, M., 167n, E-8
Schmit, M. J., 179n, 345n, E-10, E-19
Schneider, B., 334n, E-18
Schneider, K. T., 506n, E-29
Schneider, S. K., 82–83n, E-4
Schoenrade, P., 498n, E-29
Schonfeld, E., 148n, E-7
Schriesheim, C. A., 405n, E-23
Schuh, A., 108n, E-5
Schuler, R. S., 162n, 344n, 350n, 367n, E-8, E-19, E-20, E-21
Schuster, J. R., 368n, E-21
Schutte, N. S., 407n, E-23
Schwartz, C. E., 390n, E-22
Schwartz, P., 251n, 252n, E-14
Schwartz, T., 407n, E-23
Scott, E. D., 471n, E-26
Scott, K. S., 170n, E-9
Scott, W. R., 347n, E-19
Seale, F. I., 135n, 141n, E-6, E-7
Sears, Richard W., 43
Segal, E., 178n, E-10
Seglin, J. L., 136n, E-6
Seibert, S. E., 383n, E-22
Seiders, K., 64n, 298n, E-3, E-15
Seijts, G. H., 378n, E-21
Sellers, P., 4n, 197n, 208n, E-1, E-11, E-12
Selmer, J., 29n, E-2
Selz, M., 150n, E-7
Senge, P., 334-335n, E-18

Sewell, Carl, 529n, E-30
Sexton, D. L., 135n, 141n, E-6, E-7
Sexton, E. A., 138n, E-6
Shand, D., 199n, E-11
Shane, S., 135n, 149n, E-6, E-7
Shapiro, C., 308n, E-16
Shapiro, D. H., Jr., 390n, E-22
Sharfman, M. P., 478n, E-27
Sharma, S., 177n, 529n, E-10, E-30
Shaver, K. G., 138n, E-6
Shaw, R. B., 319n, E-17
Shepherd, A., 208n, E-12
Shewhart, Walter, 259
Shlosberg, Sally S., 545–546
Shore, L. M., 508n, E-29
Siebel, Tom, 286–287
Siklos, R., 134n, 203n, E-6, E-11
Simmons, R., 517n, E-30
Simon, E., 387n, E-22
Simon, H. A., 232, 232n, 233, E-13
Simonin, B. L., 93n, E-4
Simons, T. L., 28n, 82n, 468n, E-2, E-4, E-26
Simonsen, P., 28n, E-2
Simpson, Jean, 239–240
Simpson, M., 257n, E-14
Sims, Paula, 464
Siwolop, S., 347n, E-19
Skinner, B. F., 380n, E-22
Skoldberg, K., 324n, E-17
Skura, Gary, 560
Slater, R., 200n, E-11
Slocum, J. W., Jr., 27n, 94n, 110n, 154n, 272n, 325n, 336n, 337n, 378n, 397n, E-2, E-4, E-5, E-8, E-15, E-17, E-18, E-21, E-23
Smith, Adam, 167n, E-8
Smith, C. A., 358n, E-20
Smith, D. K., 459n, E-25
Smith, E. B., 236n, E-13
Smith, Frederick, 516
Smith, Jan, 382
Smith, K. A., 28n, 82n, E-2, E-4
Smith, K. G., 473n, E-27
Smith, Susan M., 345
Smith, V. C., 507n, E-29
Smither, J. W., 360n, 362n, 363n, E-20, E-21
Snell, Richard, 491
Snyder, P. R., 179n, E-10
Snyderman, B., 384n, E-22
Sokolowski, K., 393n, E-23
Solberg, Rick, 486, 487
Solomon, C. M., 437n, 450n, E-25
Solomon, M. R., 80n, 448n, E-3, E-25
Solomon, S. D., 137n, E-6
Sondergaard, M., 113n, E-5
Sonnenstuhl, W. J, 320n, E-17
Sosik, J. J., 420n, E-24
Soutar, G. N., 125n, E-5
Spake, D. F., 162n, E-8
Spangler, W. D., 419n, E-24
Spicer, A., 136n, E-6
Spreier, S., 493n, E-28
Spulber, D. F., 78n, 79n, E-3
Stajkovic, A. D., 378n, 381n, E-21, E-22
Stalker, G. M., 296n, E-15
Stamps, J., 474n, E-27
Standifird, S. S., 524n, E-30
Stanton, S., 294n, 296n, 302n, E-15, E-16
Starke, M., 352n, 432n, E-20, E-24
Starkman, D., 106n, E-4
Stathatos, P., 508n, E-30
Staw, B. M., 346n, E-19
Steckler, N., 460n, E-25
Steele, F., 434n, E-25
Steiger, D. M., 549n, E-31
Steinberg, J., 162n, E-8
Steinert-Threkeld, T., 66n, E-3
Stepanek, M., 321n, 332n, 558n, E-17, E-18, E-32
Stern, S., 253n, E-14
Sternberg, Tom, 65
Stevens, M. J., 470n, E-26
Stewart, G. L., 466n, E-26
Stewart, T. A., 227n, 239n, 250n, 345n, E-12, E-13, E-14, E-19

Stickney, C. P., 530n, E-30
Stiller, Robert, 220
Stillo, John, 525
Strahan, Jerry, 11
Strasser, Adolph, 43
Straub, D., 432n, E-24
Strauss, K., 70n, E-3
Strebel, P., 325n, E-17
Stroh, L. K., 449n, E-25
Stroucken, Albert, 12
Stuart, E. W., 80n, 448n, E-3, E-25
Stundza, T., 120n, E-5
Stupski, Larry, 404
Sull, D. N., 210n, 226n, E-12
Sullivan, S., 251n, E-14
Summe, Gregory, 544
Sundstrom, E., 368n, 473n, E-21, E-27
Sunoo, B. P., 56n, 336n, 388n, 436n, E-3, E-18, E-22, E-25
Surowiecki, J., 195nnE-11
Sutton, R. I., 256n, 334n, E-14, E-18
Swanson, D. L., 164n, E-8
Swardson, A., 80n, E-3
Sweeney, D. J., 535n, E-31
Sykes, C. J., 558n, E-32
Szumal, J. L., 471n, E-26

Taffinder, P., 422n, E-24
Talbot, Doug, 11
Tannen, D., 433n, E 24
Tannenbaum, A., 136n, E-6
Tapscott, D., 78n, 97–98n, E-3, E-4
Tate, P., 82n, E-3
Taylor, F. W., 49–50n, 49n, 51, 53, 54, 57, 329, E-2
Taylor, S., 359n, E-20
Tenbrunsel, A. E., 231n, E-13
Teng, B., 27n, E-2
Terplan, K., 548n, E-31
Tesluk, P. E., 473n, E-27
Tetenbaum, A. T. J., 493n, E-28
Tetzeli, R., 173n, E-9
Thaler-Carter, R. E., 163n, E-8
Theroux, J., 135n, E-6
Thierry, H., 395n, E-23
Thomas, Charles, 353
Thomas, D. A., 508n, E-30
Thomas, H., 22n, 110n, E-1, E-5
Thomas, J. B., 397n, 401n, E-23
Thomas, R. R., Jr., 511n, E-30
Thomke, Ernest, 536
Thompson, J. D., 297n, E-15
Thompson, L. L., 19n, 56n, E-1, E-3
Thompson, R. W., 349n, E-19
Thornton, E., 172n, E-9
Thurm, S., 289n, E-15
Ticoll, D., 97–98n, E-4
Tierny, T., 245n, E-13
Tijoriwala, S. A., 322n, E-17
Tinsley, C., 449n, E-25
Todd, K., 252n, E-14
Toprsilieri, J. D., 245n, E-13
Tornow, W. W., 363n, E-21
Torrcelli, M., 124, 124n, 125, E-5
Torregrossa, T., 546n, E-31
Towne, Henry R., 42–43
Townsend, A. M., 474n, 551n, E-27, E-31
Townsend, K., 500n, E-29
Treacy, Michael, 179, 179n, E-10
Treviño, L. Klebe, 409n, 516n, E-23, E-30
Trevor, C. O., 366n, E-21
Trice, H. M., 486n, 488n, 497n, E-28, E-29
Trompenaars, F., 84n, E-4
Tsui, A. S., 388n, E-22
Tucker, K., 252n, E-14
Tuckman, B. W., 468n, E-26
Turban, D. B., 95n, 179n, E-4, E-10
Turillo, Mike, 244, 246
Turner, Ted, 225
Tushman, M. I., 269n, 282n, 295n, 320n, E-15, E-17
Tziner, A., 356n, E-20

Umbarger, J., 138n, E-6
Unsworth, K. L., 459n, E-25

Upton, D. M., 310n, E-16
Uzumeri, M. V., 26n, E-2

Vandenberg, R. J., 386n, E-22
Vanderkam, L., 498n, E-29
Van de Ven, A. H., 49n, 335n, E-2, E-18
VandeWalle, D., 378n, 379n, 442n, E-21, E-22, E-25
Van Erde, W., 395n, E-23
Van Fleet, D. D., 473n, E-27
Vanhonacker, W., 22n, E-1
Van Norman, K. L., 325n, E-17
Van Velsor, E., 24–25n, 475n, E-2, E-27
Varca, P. E., 347n, E-19
Vargas, V., 299n, E-15
Varian, H. R., 308n, E-16
Vasilash, G. S., 282n, E-15
Vecchio, R. P., 415n, E-24
Velasquez, M., 168n, E-9
VellaZarb, K., 498n, E-29
Venkataraman, S., 49n, E-2
Venkatraman, N., 213n, E-12
Viega, J. F., 478n, E-27
Vining, A., 26n, E-2
Virarelli, M., 139n, E-6
Vishwanath, V., 70n, E-3
Visweswaran, S. C., 356n, E-20
Vogel, C., 168n, E-8
Vollmann, T. F., 63n, E-3
Von Bertrab, H., 93n, E-4
Von Krogh, G., E-13
Voss, G. B., 168n, E-8
Voss, Z. G., 168n, E-8
Vredenburg, H., 177n, E-10
Vroom, V. H., 394, 415–418, 416n, E-24

Wagner, J. A., III, 476n, E-27
Wai, P. H., 257n, E-14
Waitt, Ted, 334
Waldrop, M., 24n, E-1
Walker, A. G., 360n, E-20
Wallace, D., 239n, E-13
Waller, M. J., 477n, E-27
Walsh, J. P., 15n, 124n, E-1, E-5
Walt, C. L., 407n, E-23
Walton, A. E., 319n, E-17
Walton, M., 62n, E-3
Wang, E. P., 15n, 124n, E-1, E-5
Wang, J., 345n, E-19
Wang, Q., 497n, E-29
Wanous, J. P., 325n, E-17
Ward, Lloyd, 393
Warner, M., 286n, E-15
Waterhouse, J. H., 161n, 179n, E-8, E-10
Waterman, R. H., Jr., 153n, E-8
Watson, W. E., 142n, E-7
Waurzyniak, P., 250n, E-14
Wayman, V. B., 328n, E-18
Wayne, L., 511n, E-30
Weaver, G. R., 516n, E-30
Weber, Max, 45, 45n, 53, 54, E-2
Weber, T. E., 170n, 556n, E-9, E-32
Weckert, J., 556n, E-31
Weekley, J., 5n, E-1
Wegge, J., 379n, E-22
Weick, K. E., 235n, 297n, 317n, E-13, E-15, E-16
Weil, R. L., 530n, E-30
Weiss, J. W., 162n, E-8
Weiss, T. B., 278n, 365n, E-15, E-21
Welbourne, T. M., 346n, E-19
Welch, D., 161n, E-8
Welch, Jack, 7, 200, 203, 325, 354, 378
Weldon, E., 22n, E-1
Wellington, S. W., 24n, 28n, 441n, E-1, E-2, E-25
Wells, E. O., 186n, E-10
Wells, R. B., 161n, 179n, E-8, E-10
Wells, S. J., 184n, E-10
Werbach, K., 96n, E-4
Werner, S., 328n, E-18
Werner, B., 345n, E-19
Werther, W. B., 309n, E-16
Wesley, D. T. A., 121n, 476n, E-5, E-27
West, M. A., 459n, 466n, E-25, E-26

Westerman, P., 543n, E-31
Westhead, P. A., 140n, E-7
Wetlaufer, S., 482n, 498n, E-28, E-29
Whalen, C. J., 506n, E-29
Wheeler, M. L., 500n, E-29
Wheelwright, S. C., 460n, 462n, E-25, E-26
Wherry, R., 326n, E-17
Whetten, D. A., 441n, E-25
Whigham-Desir, M., 421n, E-24
White, R. F., 90n, E-4
Whitford, D., 146n, 497n, E-7, E-28
Whitman, Meg, 12, 522
Whitney, J. O., 406n, E-23
Whitney, K., 465n, E-26
Whittlesey, F. E., 344n, E-19
Whybark, D. C., 57n, 96n, E-3, E-4
Wicks, A. C., 80n, E-3
Wiersema, F., 179n, E-10
Wiersema, Fred, 179
Wiggenhorn, W., 330n, E-18
Wildeman, L., 307n, E-16
Wilder, C., 543n, E-31
Wilkinson, I. F., 308n, E-16
Williams, F., 122n, E-5
Williams, M., 148n, E-7
Williams, T. A., 535n, E-31
Wilson, J. Q., 167n, E-8
Wilson, Kemmons, 225
Wilson, Robert, 116, 116n, E-5
Wimberly, Jim, 232
Wimbush, J. C., 356n, E-20
Winokur, L. A., 136n, E-6
Winter, G., 500n, E-29
Wise, R., 202n, E-11
Wishart, N. A., 317n, 337n, E 16, E-18
Witt, Robert, 560
Wittmann, A., 278n, E-15
Wnuck, D., 465n, E-26
Woellert, L., 161n, 482n, E-8, E-28
Wood, J. T., 431n, E-24
Woodman, R. W., 317n, 327n, 330n, E-16, E-17, E-18
Worchel, S., 468n, E-26
Wright, G., 248n, E-14
Wright, J., 476n, E-27
Wurster, T. S., 50n, 221n, 543n, E-2, E-12, E-31
Wyant, A., 186n, E-10
Wybark, D. C., 63n, E-3
Wynter, L. E., 498n, E-29
Wyscocki, B., Jr., 252n, E-14

Xin, K. R., 15n, 124n, E-1, E-5

Yammarino, F. J., 419n, E-24
Yan, A., 462n, E-26
Yanashiro, S., 210n, E-12
Yang, C., 136n, 203n, E-6, E-11
Yang, D. J., 275n, E-15
Yang, H.-C., 254n, E-14
Yang, Jerry, 134, 141, 157
Yiu, L., 113n, E-5
Young, D., 247n, E-13
Yukl, G. A., 413n, E-24

Zack, M. H., 246n, E-13
Zahara, S. A., 136n, 152n, E-6, E-8
Zaheer, S., 111n, E-5
Zahr, S. A., 108n, 110n, E-5
Zajkac, D. M., 325n, E-17
Zalezny, M. D., 466n, E-26
Zamir, S., 548n, E-31
Zander, A., 363n, 471n, E-21, E-26
Zander, Ed, 321, 394
Zellner, W., 178n, 202n, 495n, E-10, E-11, E-28
Zenner, M., 114n, E-5
Zgabjar, L., 120n, E-5
Zider, B., 149n, E-7
Zielinski, D., 479n, E-28
Zigarmi, D., 415n, E-24
Zimmerman, C., 199n, E-11
Zingheim, P. K., 368n, E-21
Zmud, R. W., 438n, E-25
Zucker, L. G., 347n, E-19

Subject Index

AAMCO Transmissions, 147
Abbott Labs, 89
Ability, expectancy and, 396
Acceptance theory of authority, 55, 283
Accountability, 284
Accutron, 96
Ace Cash Express, 437
Acer (Taiwan), 101
Achievement motive, 393–94
  in entrepreneurs, 138–39
ACS International Resources, 357
ACT*1 Personnel Services, 150
Active inertia, 226
Activity-based costing, 532–33, 535
Adaptive decisions, 226–27
Adidas, 173
Adjourning stage, 470
Administrative innovation, 333
Administrative management, 51–52
AeroTech Service Group, 310
AES Corporation, 481–82
Affiliation motive, 393
Affiliation needs, 391
Affirmative action, 499
Affirmative social responsibility, 179–80
Aggressive recruitment strategies, 354
Agilent Technologies, 316
Airborne, 48
Air Product, 15
Akamai Technologies, 223–24
Alamo Car Rental, 301
Alcon Laboratories, 107
Algorithmics, Inc., 222
Alliance
  defined, 93–94
  strategy for, 110–11, 202
Alliant Foodservice, Inc., 227–28, 328
Allied Signal, 332
Allstate Insurance Company, 222, 443
Alta Vista, 547
Alteon WebSystems, 193
Alternative solutions
  comparing and evaluating, 230–31
  implementing, 231
Amazon.com, 4, 15, 16–17, 24, 43, 47, 79, 148,
    202, 305, 316, 333, 492
AMD, 101
American Airlines, 27, 43, 210, 231–32, 434, 528
American Association of Retired Persons (AARP),
    77, 93, 95–96
American Brands, 66
American Express Company, 112, 113, 322, 421–22
American Home Products, 90
American Productivity and Quality Center (APQC),
    258
American Society of Mechanical Engineers
    (ASME), 42–43
American Telephone & Telegraph Co. (AT&T), 54,
    65, 93, 124, 125, 174, 180, 192, 194, 207,
    256, 368
America Online (AOL), 94, 203, 210, 546
America Online (AOL) Time Warner, 204, 209
America West, 378
Ameritrade, 79, 97
Amgen, 337
Andersen, Arthur, Consulting, 208, 496, 497, 530
Angel, 149
Anheuser Busch, 175
Anticipatory change, 319–20
Apple Computer Corporation, 90, 100, 111, 256,
    441, 489
Applied Magnetics, 101
ARAMARK, 448–49, 492
Arbor Day Foundation, 156
Architecture for innovation, 334
Artificial intelligence (AI), 550
Arvin Industries, 63, 83

Asahi Chemical, 94
The Associates First Capital Corporation, 49, 90,
    277, 282, 432, 525, 527
Association of Southeast Asian Nations (ASEAN),
    119–20
Assumptions, shared, 487
AST Computers, 207
AST Research, 100
Atlantic Richfield, 93
Attributes, measuring, 65
Audubon Society, 80
Aurora Biosciences, 92
Authority
  in administrative management, 51
  in decision making, 270–71
  as organizational hurdle, 446
  in organization design, 283–87
  protection of, 48
  structure of, 45–46
Automation-based control, 535–36
Autonomy, 387
Autumn Harp, 143
Availability bias, 234
Aventis, 91
Avis Rental Car, 542, 543
Avon Products, Inc., 43, 510–11

Baby Jogger Company, 152
Backtranslation, 449
Backward integration strategy, 202
Baker & McKenzie, 502
Baldrige, Malcolm, National Quality Award, 175
Bally's, 60
BankBoston, 175
Bank of America, 298, 320, 535
Barnes and Noble, 4, 97, 147
Barriers to entry, 207
Basic expectancy theory, 394–96
Basic skills training, 357
Bass Pro Shops, 332–33
Bayer AG (Germany), 107
L. L. Bean, 97, 186, 258, 439
Behavioral norms in work teams, 471–72
Behavioral viewpoint of management, 53–57, 67
Behavior modification, 381–82
Behaviors of leaders, 409–13
Bell Labs, 199
Benchmarking, 244, 257–59, 378
Benefits, 349
Ben & Jerry's Ice Cream, 135, 174–75, 187
Bennigan's Irish Pub, 372
Best Buy, 58, 100
Bethlehem Steel, 49–50
Bic Corporation, 520
Bindco Corporation, 539
Black & Decker, 474
Blockbuster Video, 47
Bloomingdale's, 511
BMW, 213, 345, 356, 361
Body language, 434
Body Shop International PLC, 143
Boeing, 93, 112–13, 518
Bonus, 368
Borden's, 135
Borders, 4, 97
Boston Consulting Group, 89
Boundaryless networks, 337–38
Bounded rationality model of decision making,
    232–35
BP Norge, 358
Brady Corporation, 412–13, 421
Brainstorming, 254–55
  electronic, 257
  guidelines for leading session in, 255
Bribe, 118
Bridgestone/Firestone, 530
British Aerospace, 548

British Airways, 27, 113
Brown, Ron, Award for Corporate Leadership, 175,
    176, 179
Browning-Ferris, 80
Browser, 546
Brundtland Commission of the United Nations,
    175–76
Budgeting, 531–32
Budweiser Beer, 449, 524
Buffalo Hospital Supply, 560
Buhrman, 156
Bureaucracy
  benefits of, 47
  costs of, 47
Bureaucratic culture, 490
Bureaucratic management, 45–49
Bureaucratic orientation, ranking organizations by,
    47
Burger King, 45, 110, 226, 502
Burton Snowboards, 135
Business(es)
  deciding whether to start or buy, 146–47
  family, 137
  small, 136
  types of, 198–200
Business-level strategy, 204
Business plan, 145–46
  components of, 145
Business-to-business (B2B) e-commerce, 560

Cable News Network (CNN), 203, 225
Caesar's Palace, 60
California Public Employees Retirement System
    (CALPERS), 178
California Sunshine, 109
Calyx & Corolla, 139
Cameraworld.com, 211, 345
Campbell Soup, 56
Canada-United States Free Trade Agreement, 120
Canadian Airlines, 27
Canon, 51, 101
Capital budget, 532
Capital One Financial Corporation, 226, 356
Capital requirements, 90
Career development, 358–59
CarPoint, 79
Carrier, 532
Cartel, 118
Cash balance plan, 174
Cash budget, 532
Caterpillar, 47, 112, 275
Cathay Pacific, 27
Celanese Chemical Corporation, 15, 108–9
CEMEX, 17, 199, 200
Cendant, 181
Center for Creative Leadership, 422
Centralization, 52, 285–86
Ceremonies, 489
Cerulli Associates, Inc., 406
Change. See also Organizational change
  anticipatory, 319–20
  developing and implementing strategic plan for,
    322–24
  incremental, 318
  radical, 317
  reactive, 318–19
Change Ware Systems, 441
Changing environment, 295–96
Channels, 438–41
Chaparral Steel, 52, 447
Charismatic authority, 46
Charismatic leader, 420
Chase Bank, 535
Chief Auto Parts, 531
Chrysler Corporation, 178, 478
Cincinnati Gas & Electric Company, 259
Cinergy Corporation, 259

Circuit City, 58, 100
Cirque du Soleil, 348, 350, 439
Cisco Systems, 24, 27, 47, 60–61, 192, 194, 196, 227, 286, 316, 354, 524
Citibank, 406
CitiGroup, 208, 492
Citizen, 96
Civil Rights Act (1964), 162
   Title VII of, 347, 499
Clan culture, 490
Clean Air Act (1990), 80
Closed system, 58
CNNFN, 153
Coaching, 423
Cobra, 282–83
Coca-Cola, 22–23, 43, 93, 110, 111, 118, 307, 449, 500, 528
Code of ethics, 164
Coercive power, 405
Cognitive ability test, 356
Cohesiveness, 471
Colgate-Palmolive, 358, 492–93, 508
Collectivism, 87, 125
Columbia Hospital Corporation of America, 164
Commission, 368
Communication. *See also* Organizational
   communication
   defined, 431
   formal, 15–16
   grapevine, 440, 451
   informal, 15
Communication competency,14
   for entrepreneurs, 142–43
Communication Competency
   AARP, 95
   Benchmarking in Site Services at Cinergy Corporation, 259
   Estée Lauder Built an Image and a Brand, 143
   From No to Yo!, 412
   GM Executives Listen Up, 504
   GE's Social Architecture, 200
   Hospice of Central Kentucky, 534
   Linda Navarro of Sonnet Supply, 13
   Making Improvements at Con-Way Transportation Services, 361
   Quiet She's Listening, 464
   Supply-Chain Management at Thomson, 58
   A Three-Firm Alliance Network, 307
   Translation Blunders, 449
Communicator, 203
Community, 336
Community Grocers, Inc., 178–79
Compaq Computer, 100, 207
Comparable worth, 350
Comparative financial analysis, 530–31
Compensation, 349, 364–69
   international, 389–90
Competencies. *See also* Managerial competencies
   core, 208
   defined, 4
Competency-based pay, 366
Competency inventories, 351–52
Competitive advantage, gaining and sustaining, 345–46
Competitive forces in industry, 89–92
Competitors, 89
   in diagnosing opportunities and threats, 207
Complexity, 108
CompuServe, 203
Computer ethics, 556
Computer Ethics Institute, 556
Computer Ethics Survey, 557
Computer Sciences Corporation (CSC), 208
ConAgra Foods, 462, 520
Concentric diversification strategy, 202–3
Concrete information bias, 234
Confidence, 420–21
Conflicts of interest, 167–68
Confucian dynamism, 88
Conglomerate diversification strategy, 203
Congress of Industrial Organizations (CIO), 53
Conoco, 95, 418, 421

Consideration, 420
Consorcio Aga, 111
Consumer Reports, 257
Continental Airlines, 323–24, 430, 439, 441
Contingencies, 60–62
   assessing, 61–62
   leaders and, 413–18
   planning for, 193
   variables, 60–61, 415–16
Contingency viewpoint of management, 60–62, 67
Continuous improvement, 227
Continuous learning, 337
Control. *See* Organizational control
Controlling, 9–10
Convenience, 92
Convergence, 227
Con-Way Transportation Services, 361
Coopers & Lybrand, 338
Co-optation, 237
Coordination, 270, 280–83
   departmentalization and, 282
Coors Beer, 524
Copyrights, 91
Core competencies, 208
Corporate Express, 156
Corporate level strategy, 200–203
Corporate social responsibility. *See also* Ethics
   evaluating performance in, 179–80
   importance of, 160–65
   managing, 172–80
Corrective controls, 517, 523–26
Corridor principle, 140
Corruption, 114–15
Cosmair, 518
Cost-benefit model, 520
Cost leadership strategy, 213
Countertrade, 109–10
Countrywide Credit Industries, 548, 549
Craig, Jenny, Diet Centers, 147
Creativity, fostering, 253–57
Critical psychological states, 386
Cross-cultural training, 359–60
Cultural audits, 501
Cultural diversity, managing, 499–508
Cultural forces, 84–88
   in global management, 123–27
Cultural values, identifying, 85–86
Culture, 84. *See also* Organizational culture
   defined, 486
   enabling, 247
   of innovation, 336–37
   for work teams, 475–76
Cuningham Group, 486, 488, 494
Current ratio, 530
Customer convenience, 79
Customer departmentalization, 278–80
Customer-focused strategy, 337
Customers, 91
   concerns of, 172–74
   in diagnosing opportunities and threats, 207
   in knowledge management, 246
   monitoring, 529

DaimlerChrysler, 160, 302, 303
Data, 543
Database, 550
Data visualization, 550
Dayton Hudson, Inc., 217, 506
Debt ratio, 531
Decentralization, 285–86
Decision making, 48–49, 220–37
   models of, 228–37
   risk in, 222–23
   role of, 220–24
   uncertainty in, 223
Decisions. *See also* Planning and decision aids
   adaptive, 226–27
   basic types, 224–28
   innovative, 227–28
   rational, 228
   routine, 226

Decision support system (DSS), 549–50
Decision-time penalty, 416–17
Decoding, 432
Deere, John, 462
Delegating style of leader, 414
Delegation, 284–85, 414
   barriers to, 285
Dell Computer, 6, 12, 43, 90, 100, 194, 195–96, 207, 210–11, 230, 352, 353
Deloitte and Touche, 500, 501
Delphi questionnaires, 248–49
Delphi technique, 94, 244, 248–50
Delta Air Lines, 316
Deluxe Diner, 260
Deming cycle, 244, 259–60
Deming Prize, 122
Demographics, 82, 495
Denny's, 501, 502
Departmentalization, 280
   coordination and, 282
   customer, 278–80
   functional, 272–75
   place, 275–77
   product, 277–78
Developmental stages of work teams, 468–70
DHL Worldwide Express, 48, 555
Dialog Information Services, 337
Differentiation, product, 90
Differentiation strategy, 213
Directive behavior, 413
Discipline, 51
Disney, Walt, Company, 20, 307, 371–72, 498
Disposal Soft Goods, 106
Distribution, role of technology in, 97–99
Distributive justice principle, 170
Divergence
   in goals, 237
   in solutions, 237
Diversification, 197–98
Diversity
   increasing, 82
   managing cultural, 499–508
   in workforce, 28
Diversity Knowledge Quiz, 506
Division of labor, 45, 51
Dixon Ticonderoga, 81
Domestic instability, 114
Dominant-business firm, 199
Domino's Pizza, 147
Donnelley, R. R., & Sons, 508
Dot.com companies, 140
Dow Chemical, 177–78, 508
Downsizing, 26, 328–29
Downward channels, 439
Duke Energy, 252
Duke Power, 294, 295, 296–97, 302
Dunkin' Donuts, 169
DuPont, 15, 208, 286

Early Winters, 97
Eastman Kodak, 333, 412–13
eBay, 12, 79, 522
Economic climate, 114
Economics, 78–79
Economic value, creating, 501–2
Economies of scale, 90
Economy, global, 106–8
Edmund's, 79
EDS, 17, 208, 322
Edward Jones, 24
Effectiveness criteria, 465, 466
Efficiency, 167
e-Forecasting.com, 248
Electrolux, 81
Electronic brainstorming, 257
Electronic commerce, 309
Electronic mail, 444, 546
Emotional intelligence, 407–8
Emotions, 449
Employees
   attracting and retaining, 366–67
   concerns of, 174

Employees (continued)
network groups for, 441
selection of, 354–56
Employee stock ownership plans (ESOPs), 368–69
Employment-at-will, 162
Enabling culture, 247
Enabling technologies, 245, 246–47
Encoding, 432
Enterprise resource planning (ERP), 220, 230
Entrepreneurs, 132–57
assessing market of, 147–48
assessing potential of, 143–45
characteristics of, 137–45
culture for, 491–92
deciding whether to start or buy a business, 146–47
defined, 134–35
development of activities for, 134–37
environment encouragement of, 135–36
finding funding, 148–50
global, 149–50
in large organizations, 152–54
managerial competencies of, 141–43
in managing family start-up, 150–52
motivations of, 146
personal attributes of, 138–40
planning for, 145–52
serial, 140
technical proficiency of, 140–41
Environment, 76–89
assessing, in planning for organizational change, 320–22
changing, 295–96
encouragement of entrepreneurial activity by, 135–36
general, 77–78
natural, 175–78
in organization design, 294–97
Environmental forces, 74–103
competitive forces as, 89–92
cultural forces as, 84–88
demographics as, 82–84
new economics as, 78–79
political-legal forces as, 92–96
stewardship as, 80–82
technological changes as, 96–99
Environmental Protection Agency (EPA), 518
Environmental stewardship, 80–82
Environment management
competitive forces in industry in, 89–92
political-legal forces in, 92–96
technological change in, 96–99
Equal Credit Opportunity Act, 92
Equal Employment Opportunity Commission (EEOC), 347
Equal employment opportunity (EEO), 347
Equal Pay Act, 349
Equifax, 558
Equity, 52
perceptions of, 388–90
Equity theory, 388
ERG theory, 392
Ericsson, 47, 98
Ernst & Young, 530
Esprit de corps, 52
E-Stamp, 97
Esteem needs, 391
ETEC Systems, 379
Ethics, 161. See also Corporate social responsibility
combining approaches to, 171–72
encouraging, 181–84
forces that shape conduct, 161–65
importance of, 160–65
information technologies and, 556–58
justice approach to, 170–71
leadership in, 409
moral rights approach to, 168–70
norms in, 179
utilitarian approach to, 167–68
Ethnicity, 495
E*Trade, 79, 97, 213, 223, 492
European Union (EU), 119–20, 122–23
Eco-Management and Audit Scheme (EMAS), 176

EXCEL, 549
Exception reporting, 450
Excite, 148, 547
Existence needs, 392
Expectancy, 395
factors that affect, 396
Experienced meaningfulness, 386
Experienced responsibility, 386
Expert power, 405
Expert system, 550–51
Explicit knowledge, 245
Export Administration Act (1979), 114
Exporting strategy, 109–10
External networking, 441
External system, 473
Extinction, 382
Extortion, 118
Extranets, 309, 547–48
Extrapolation, 248
Extrinsic rewards, 396
Exxon/Mobil, 15, 93, 156, 449, 461

Fact-finding phase in creativity, 254
Fair Labor Standards Act (FLSA) (1938), 349
Fairness principle, 171
False Claims Act, 182
Family business, 137
managing start-up, 150–52
Fannie Mae, 175
Farm, Inc., 445–46
Farmer's Insurance, 14, 222
Fear of resistance, 324
Federal Communications Commission (FCC) (1934), 93
Federal Drug Administration (FDA), 12–13
Federal Express (FedEx), 6, 28, 43, 48, 49, 65, 179, 199, 222, 307, 422–23, 516, 517, 522
Feedback
in organization communication, 441–43
in performance appraisal, 360–64
in survey, 330–31
in systems viewpoint of management, 58
team, 364
in work motivation, 379, 387
Feelings in work teams, 470–71
Fel-Pro, 491
Femininity, 88
Feng shui, 436
Fields, Debbie, Cookies, 46
File Transport Protocol (FTP), 546
Finance strategies, 204
Financial Accounting Standards Board (FASB), 522
Financial control, 529–35
Firewall, 547
First-line managers, 10–11
First National Bank of Chicago, 438
Flaming, 444
Flight Systems Management, 532
Flour Corporation, 236
Focus strategy, 213
Food and Drug Administration (FDA) (1927), 93
Ford Motor Company, 10, 65, 111, 160, 167, 172, 213, 252, 278, 312–13, 316, 498
Forecasting, 248
Delphi technique in, 248–50
in human resource planning, 350–51
scenarios in, 251–52
simulation in, 250–51
Foreign conflict, 114
Foreign Corrupt Practices Act (1977), 118
Formal communication, 15–16
Forming stage, 469
Forward integration strategy, 202
Franchising, 110, 147
Freddie Mac Foundation, 175
Freedom of conscience and speech, 170
Free rider, 471
Freewheeling, 255
Fresca, 449
Frito-Lay, 112, 492
Frustration-regression hypothesis, 392–93
Fuji, 113, 333

Fuller, H. B., Brush Company, 12–13
Functional departmentalization, 272–75
Functional foremanship, 50
Functional-level strategy, 204–5
Functional managers, 8
Functional work teams, 462
Funds, finding, by entrepreneurs, 148–49

Gainsharing, 368, 395
Gambler's fallacy bias, 235
Gantt chart, 51
Gardeners Eden, 139
Gartner Group, Inc., 542
Gateway, Inc., 100, 207, 334
GE Capital Services, 8
GE Cisco Industrial Networks, 202
GEICO, 79
Genentech, 148
General Agreement on Tariffs and Trade (GATT) (1947), 119–20
General Electric (GE), 7–8, 58, 63, 95, 108, 121, 199–200, 201–2, 203, 204, 209, 230, 325, 354, 359, 378, 458, 459, 476
General Electric (GE) Medical Systems, 204
General environment, 77–78
Generale Occidentale (France), 107
General Foods, 174, 304
General goals, 230
General managers, 8
General Mills, 28, 110, 111, 443
General Motors (GM), 10, 12, 83, 94, 110, 160, 169, 213, 226, 272, 504–5, 518, 520, 530
Generic competitive strategies model, 212–13
Geographic region, 494
Gillette, 528
Glaxo Wellcome, 90
Global awareness competency, 21
Global Awareness Competency
The Challenge of International Compensation, 389–90
Coca-Cola, 22–23
Hiring Is No Laughing Matter for Cirque Du Soleil, 348
Mabe, 121–22
Masayoshi Son Builds a Conglomerate from Start-ups, 140
Motorola in China, 98–99
NCR's Virtual Teams, 474
Social Accountability 8000 Guidelines Provide Direction, 163–64
Yahoo!'s Design, 304–5
Global competition, 88
Globalization, 29
Global management, 104–30
cultural forces in, 123–27
economy in, 106–8
in international business, 108–13
political-legal forces in, 113–19
Global strategic alliances, 110
Global strategy, 112–13
Global trade agreements, 119–23
GlobalWare Solutions, 539
Goals
developing, 205–6
divergence in, 237
in improving performance, 377–84
organizational, 194–95
for managing cultural diversity, 499–502
setting, 230, 323–24
Goal-setting theory, 378
Goalsharing, 368, 380, 395
GO/Infoseek, 547
Goods, substitute, 90, 208
Government Employees Insurance Company (GEICO), 14
Government regulation, 90
Grace, W. R., 80
Grand Union, 107, 531
Grapevine communication, 440, 451
Grease payments, 118–19
Great Basin Bird Conservancy, 186
Green Giant, 545
Green marketing, 518

Green Mountain Coffee, Inc., 220, 230–31
Greyhound Lines, 229, 230
Group decision support system (GDSS), 551
Groups, 458
  control, 518
  informal, 458–59
Groupthink, 472
Groupware, 309
Growth needs, 392
Growth need strength, 387–88
Growth strategies, 202–3
Gruman Aircraft, 93
Guggenheim, Solomon R., Museum, 168
Gypsum, 28

Häagen-Dazs, 545
Hardee's, 45
Harley Davidson, 462
Harrah's Entertainment, 60, 302
Hasbro, 108
Hawthorne effect, 55
Hawthorne Illumination Tests, 55
Haymarket Affair, 43
HBO, 203, 204
Health and safety, 349
Healtheon, 148
Heartland-By-Products, 117
Heineken, 175
Herzberg's two-factor theory, 384–85
Hewlett-Packard, 8, 17, 46, 100, 101, 156, 207, 316, 317, 322, 391
Hierarchical structure, 45
Hierarchy of needs, 390–92
Hilton Hotels, 320
Hiring process in human resource management, 352–56
Hitachi, 112, 127
Hoeschst AG, 76, 84
Holiday Inn, 110, 225, 442, 530
Home Depot, 204, 206, 355
HomeGrocer, 522
Honda, 51, 172, 213, 460
Honeywell International, 19, 332
Horizontal channels, 440
Horizontal integration strategy, 202
Hospice of Central Kentucky (HCK), 533, 534, 535
Hotjava, 546
Hudson's Department Stores, 217
Human resource management, 344–69
  benefits in, 349–50, 367
  compensation in, 349–50, 364–69
  equal employment opportunity in, 347–48
  health and safety in, 349
  hiring process in, 352–56
  legal and regulatory environment in, 347–50
  performance appraisal and feedback in, 360–64
  planning in, 350–52
  as primary means of control, 526–27
  recruitment in, 353–54
  selection in, 354–56
  strategic importance of, 344–47
  training and development in, 356–60
Hygiene factors, 385
Hypertext, 547

I. Magnin, 511
i2 Technologies, 216
IBM, 9, 85, 90, 98, 100, 101, 129, 153, 174, 175, 207, 208, 215–16, 322, 325–26, 441, 530, 545
iCab, 546
Idea-finding phase in creativity, 254–55
IDEO Product Development, 256
Ignorance, 234
Illumination stage in creativity, 253
iMediation, 149
Impersonality, 45
Incentive pay, 367–69, 395
Incentives, offering, 380–83
Incremental change, 318
Incubation in creativity, 253
Incubator organizations, 136
Independence, desire for, in entrepreneurs, 139

Individual differences approach to motivation, 377, 390–94
Individualism, 87
Individual self-control, 518–19
Industry, competitive forces in, 89–92
Informal channels, 440–41
Informal communication, 15
Informal groups, 458–59
Information
  collecting, 525
  defined, 543
  intensive use of, 338
  limited, 234
  needs, 552–53
  quality of, 544
  quantity of, 544–45
  relevance of, 544
  role of, in organizations, 542–46
  as value-added resource, 543–46
Information processing biases, 234–35
Information processing factors, 301–5
Information revolution, 107
Information richness, 438
Information technologies, 328, 540–61
  common, 546–52
  designing systems in, 552–55
  downside of, 445
  ethics and, 556–58
  impact of, 444–46
  role of information in organizations, 542–46
Infrastructure, 114
Initial public offerings (IPOs), 193, 346, 461
Initiative, 52
Innovation, 332
  administrative, 333
  architecture for, 334
  culture of, 336–37
  in organizational change, 332–34
  process, 333
  technical, 333
  types of, 333–34
Innovation Net, 245–46
Innovative decisions, 227–28
Inputs, 58
  in quality control process, 62–63
Inspirational, 420
Institute for Research on Intercultural Cooperation, 85
Instrumentality, 395
  factors that affect, 396–97
Integrated expectancy model, 396–97
Intel, 51, 79, 98, 101, 112, 179
Intelligence, emotional, 407–8
Interdependence
  pooled, 297–98
  reciprocal, 298
  sequential, 298
  technological, 297–98
Interenterprise human capital, 79–80
Interface, 12
InterFIRE VR, 251
Internal team processes, 466–72
International Association of Machinists and Aerospace Workers, 93
International business
  alliance strategy for, 110–11
  exporting strategy for, 109–10
  franchising strategy for, 110
  global strategy for, 112–13
  licensing strategy for, 110
  multidomestic strategy for, 111–12
International compensation, 389–90
International Council of Shopping Centers, 332–33
International Ladies Garment Workers Union, 115
International Longshoremen's Association, 115
International Network Services, 202
International Standards Organization (ISO), 122
  14000 standards, 176
Internet, 444–45, 546–47
Internet brokerage, 97
Interorganizational systems (IOS), 309
Interviews, 355
Intranets, 309, 548

Intrapreneurship, 153
  fostering, 153–54
Intrinsic rewards, 397
Inventory turnover, 530
Involvement, 504
iQVC.com, 345
Italian Oven Restaurant, 372
ITT Sheraton Hotels, 275

Jamba Juice, 388
Japan, value systems in, 125–27
Japan Airlines, 113
Javelin, 549
Jefferson Smurfit, 81
JENOs, 545
Jiffy Lube, 147
Job and organization approach to motivation, 376–77
Job-based pay, 366
Job characteristics, 386–88
  key, 387
Job content, effects of, on motivation, 384–90
Job enrichment, 329–30
Job simplification, 329
Johnson, S. C., Wax, 234
Johnson & Johnson, 43, 180, 270, 461, 489, 527
Joint ventures, 94
Jolliebee Foods, 213
Jostens, 460–61
Junglee Corporation, 202
Justice approach to ethical judgments, 170–71

Keen Innovations, 309
Kellogg's, 110
Kentucky Fried Chicken (KFC), 51, 110, 197
Kirin Brewery, 337
Kmart, 140, 307
KMPG, 357
Knight-Ridder, Inc., 317, 337
Knowledge management, 79, 244
  drivers in, 245
  fostering, 245–48
  targets in, 245–46
Knowledge of results, 386
Knowledge workers, 28
Kodak, 49, 96, 113, 316, 519
Kohler Company, 137
Kohl's, 530
Komatsu, 112
KPMG, 244, 246, 247, 530
Kraft General Foods, 135, 336
Kroger food stores, 368, 531
Kyorin Pharmaceutical Co., Ltd., 91
Kyoto Protocol, 12

LaBelle Management, 372
Labor, division of, 45
Labor budget, 532
Labor market conditions, 353–54
LA Gear, 173
Lands' End, 97, 186, 227, 442
Language, 124–25, 488
Large organizations, entrepreneurship in, 152–54
Lateral information design strategy, 302
Lauder, Estée, Companies, 143
Law of small numbers bias, 234
Laws and regulations, 162–63
Leaders
  behaviors of, 409–13
  confident, 420–21
  considerate, 420
  contingencies and, 413–18
  inspirational, 420
  thoughtful, 420
  traits of, 407–9
  transformation, 419–22
  trustworthy, 420
  visionary, 419–20
Leadership, 9, 402–27
  defined, 404
  development, 422–23
  ethical, 409
  power and, 404–7

Subject Index | SI-4

Leadership (continued)
  shared, 335–36
  styles of, 416
  time-driven model of, 415–18
Lear Corporation, 176–77
Learned needs theory, 393–94
Learning, continuous, 337
Learning audits, 336
Learning organizations, 334–38
  customer-focused strategy for, 337
  intensive use of information in, 338
  organic organization design for, 337–38
Legal and regulatory environment for human resource management, 347–50
Legal compliance, 499–500
Legislative and political activities, 180
Legitimate power, 405
Leshan Radio Factory, 98
Levels of organization, 272
Lexmark, 101
Lexus, 65, 83, 213, 529
Licensing strategy, 110
Life and safety, 168–69
Lifelong career commitment, 46
Liggett, 66
Lilly, Eli, and Company, 76, 89
Lincoln Electric Company, 345, 368
Lines of authority, 272
Linux, 487
Listening, 433, 450
  guidelines for effective, 433
Lobbying, 93
Lockheed-Martin, 90, 93, 112, 184, 286, 462, 531, 547–48
Logitech, 149
Lotus 1-2-3, 549
Louisiana-Pacific, 80
Lucent Technologies, 43, 107, 192, 194, 197, 200, 202, 286, 436
Lucky Gold Star, 46
Lucky Hot Dogs, 11
Lufthansa, 113
Lycos/Hotbox, 547
Lynx, 546

Mabe, 121–22, 476
Machine control, 535
Macroenvironment, 77–78
Madeleine French Bakery & Cafe, 528
Management. See also Managerial competencies
  administrative, 51–52
  behavioral viewpoint of, 53–57, 67
  bureaucratic, 45–49
  contingency viewpoint of, 60–62, 67
  defined, 7–8
  in dynamic environment, 4–29
  evolution of, 42–67
  fostering knowledge, 245–48
  global, 104–30
  integration of viewpoints, 66–67
  levels of, 10–13
  quality viewpoint of, 62–66, 67
  scientific, 49–51
  scope of, 8
  systems viewpoint of, 57–60, 67
  traditional viewpoint of, 42–53, 67
  of work teams, 456–82
Management action plans, 81–82
Management by objectives (MBO), 379
Management Review magazine, 225
Managerial competencies, 4, 5, 14
  communication, 14–16, 58–59, 141, 142–43, 143, 200, 259, 307, 361, 412–13, 449, 464, 514–15, 534
  defined, 4
  developing, 25
  global awareness, 21–23, 98–99, 121–22, 140, 163–64, 304–5, 348, 389–90, 474
  integration of, 66–67
  planning and administration, 16–18, 48, 116, 142, 181, 203, 247–48, 275–76, 336, 358, 445–46, 526, 545–46
  self-assessment inventory of, 32–38

self-management, 23–25, 85–86, 144–45, 165–66, 223–24, 286–87, 319–20, 384, 408–9, 442, 506, 522–23, 557
  strategic action, 20–21, 66, 91–92, 112–13, 141–42, 177–78, 195–96, 228, 252, 279, 387, 421–22, 436–37, 519, 549
  teamwork, 18–20, 56, 125, 142, 236–37, 256, 282–83, 310, 326, 353, 380, 418, 491, 551
Managerial grid model, 411–13
Managerial implications, 88
Managerial Values Profile, 165–66
Managers. See also Managerial competencies
  defined, 7
  effectiveness in, 4
  first-line, 10–11
  functional, 8
  general, 8
  general functions, 8–10
  guidelines for, in work motivation, 397–98
  middle, 11–12, 29
  motivation and, 376
  skills of great, 14
  small-business, 13–14
  top, 12
Manufacturing, role of technology in, 97
Maquiladora plants, 120
Market control, 528–29
Market culture, 492–93
Market development strategy, 210
Marketing strategies, 204
Market penetration strategy, 210
Markets, 79
  assessing, for entrepreneurs, 147–48
Marlboro, 449
Marlow Industries, 66
Marriott Hotels, 42, 60, 110, 286, 320, 526, 530
Marshall Field's, 217
Martha by Mail catalog, 140
Masayoshi Son, 140
Masculinity, 87–88
Materialism, 127
Materials budget, 532
Matrix organization, 305–6
Matsushita, 101, 127
Mattel, 49, 108
Mayo Clinic, 491
Maytag, 65
Mazda, 110, 213
McDonald's, 45, 47, 106, 110, 147, 180, 226, 307, 359, 449, 518
McDonnell-Douglas, 112, 310
MCI Communications, 49, 135–36, 207
Measuring by variable, 64
Mechanistic control, 527
Mechanistic organization, 296
Medibuy.com, 560
Medi-Health Outsourcing, 376
Meiji Life Insurance Company, 551
Mellon Bank, 328
Memory aids, 362–63
Mentoring, 423
Mercedes-Benz, 29, 64, 213, 298, 324, 325
Merck, 76, 89, 90, 91–92, 391
Meredith Corporation, 210
Merit pay, 368
Merrill Lynch, 113, 275
Mervyn's, 217
Message, 433–38
Microelectronics and communications technologies, 199
Micron, 207
Microsoft, 49, 93, 129, 207, 368, 460, 462–63, 546
Microsystems, Inc., 321
Middle management, 7
Middle managers, 11–12, 29
Midvale Steel Company, 49
Miles Laboratories, 107
Miller Beer, 524
Mission in strategic decision making, 194, 205–6
Mitre Corporation, 247–48
Mitsubishi, 127
Mitsui, 127
Monetary compensation, 365

Monfort, Inc., 520
Monitoring, in offering new product to marketplace, 508
Monolithic organization, 497
Monsanto, 80
Moral rights approach to ethical judgments, 168–70
Mosaic, 546
Most favored nation principle, 119
Motivation. See also Work motivation
  understanding your, 146
Motivator factors, 385
Motorola, 93, 98–99, 101, 111, 173, 359, 441
MS2, 551–52
MSN, 547
Muffin Head Productions, 498
Multicultural organization, 28, 498
Multidisciplinary work teams, 462–63
Multidomestic strategy, 111–12
Multinational corporation, 108
Multiplan, 549
Multiple raters, 363
Multiple subcultures, 498
Munsingwear, 43
Mutual Life Insurance Company, 143
Myers, 66

Nanjing Panda Electronics, 98
Narratives, 488–89
Nashua Corporation, 62
National Association of Manufacturers (NAM), 93
National Cash Register (NCR) Company, 474
National Chamber of Commerce, 93
National Commission on Restructuring of the Internal Revenue Service, 268
National Resources Defense Council, 80
National Semiconductor, 101
Natural duty principle, 171
Natural environment, concerns about, 175–78
Navistar International, 461
NBC, 93
NEC, 46
Needs, 390
  hierarchy of, moving through, 392–93
  hierarchy of, 390–92
Negative reinforcement, 382
Negotiation, 15, 92–93
Neiman Marcus, 511
Nestlé, S. A., 107, 110, 111
NetCare professional services, 199
Netscape Communications, 129, 148, 157, 522, 547
Netscape Navigator, 203
Network organization, 306–8
New Balance, 173
New entrants in diagnosing opportunities and threats, 207
New Jersey Bell Telephone Company, 55, 283
New-technology training, 357
Next Door Food Stores, 462
N-Geners, 79–80
Niche, 213
Nike, 10, 42, 115, 173, 174, 307–8
Nissan, 110, 127
Nokia, 26, 29
Nonmonetary compensation, 364–65
Nonroutine service technologies, 299
Nonverbal messages, 434–37, 451
Nordstrom, 361, 395
Norming stage, 469–70
Norms, 488
  behavioral, in work teams, 471–72
  societal, and culture, 162
Nortel Telecommunications, 192, 436–37
North American Free Trade Agreement (NAFTA), 80, 119–21
Northern Telecom, 98
Northrop Grumman Corporation, 548
Novell, 278–79, 281, 282
Nucor Steel, 81, 316

Objective probability, 222
Occupational Safety and Health Act (OSHA) (1970), 168, 349
Office Depot, 106

Old El Paso, 545
Olive Garden, 530
Olivetti, 111
Oneworld, 27
On-the-job learning, 422
Open system, 58
Operating strategy, 179
Operational goals, 230
Operations research group, 57
Operations strategies, 204
Oracle, 129, 322
Oral B, 256
Order, 52
Organic control, 527
Organic organization, 296–97
  design, 337
Organizational change
  combining methods of, 331–32
  defined, 316
  degree of, 317–18
  implementing, 327–32
  innovation in, 332–34
  organizational redesign method for, 328–29
  people-oriented method for, 330–31
  planning for, 320–27
  reaction to, 319
  task-based method for, 329–30
  technological-based method for, 327–28
  timing of, 318–19
  types of, 316–20
Organizational communication, 428–54. *See also*
    Communication
  channels in, 438–41
  electronic mail in, 444
  feedback in, 441–43
  fostering effective, 451
  hurdles to effective, 446–51
  impact of informational technology, 444–46
  Internet in, 444–45
  message in, 433–38
  perception in, 443
  process of, 430–43
  receiver in, 432–33
  sender in, 432
  teleconferencing in, 445
Organizational context, effects of, on motivation, 384–90
Organizational control, 513–39
  automation-based, 535–36
  corrective, 517
  corrective model for, 523–26
  creating effective, 520–23
  criteria for effective, 521–22
  defined, 516
  financial, 529–35
  foundations of, 516–19
  human resource management in, 526–27
  market, 528–29
  mechanistic, 527
  organic, 527
  patterns of, 519
  performance appraisal systems, 526–27
  preventive, 517
  primary methods of, 526–36
  sources of, 518–19
Organizational culture, 164, 183–84
  elements of, 486–89
  types of, 489–93
Organizational diagnosis, 322
Organizational goals, 194–95
  achieving, 167
  for managing cultural diversity, 499–502
Organizational hurdles to organizational communication, 446–48
Organizational structure, 271–72
  selecting, 280
Organizational subcultures, 494–99
Organization chart, 271
Organization design, 268–72
  authority and, 283–87
  coordination and, 280–83
  defined, 268
  departmentalization and, 272–80

information processing factors, 301–5
  lateral information, 302
  matrix, 305–6
  network, 306–8
  organic, 337–38
  self-contained, 304
  service technology and, 299–301
  slack resources, 303–4
  strategic and environmental factors in, 294–97
  technology factors, 297–301
  vertical information, 301–2
  virtual, 308–10
Organization of Petroleum Exporting Countries
    (OPEC), 118
Organization redesign method, 328–29
Organizations
  assessing, 502–3
  defined, 5–7
  development of, 330
  entrepreneurship in large, 152–54
  learning, 334–38
  matrix, 305–6
  mechanistic, 296
  multicultural, 28
  organic, 296–97, 337
  ranking, by bureaucratic orientation, 47
  reasons for using work teams, 460–61
  restructuring of, 26–27
  role of information in, 542–46
Organizing, 9
  defined, 268
  elements of, 269–71
Orientation training, 357
Osborn's creativity model, 254–57
Oshkosh B'Gosh, 550
Otis, 532
Outer Circle, 326
Outputs, 58
  in quality control process, 64
Outsourcing, 26–27, 208
Overseas Private Investment Corporation (OPIC),
    116
Owens Corning, 368
Owners
  shareholders and, 178
  small-business, 136
OxyChem, 442

Packard Bell, 100
Papa John's, 301
Pareto's law, 524
Patagonia, 186
Patents, 91
Pay fairness, 366
Peachtree Hospital, 289–90
Penguin Group, 20
Penney, J. C., Company, 7, 94, 226, 307, 530, 553
People-oriented method, 330–31
Pep Boys, 531
PepsiCo, 110, 111, 197, 304, 492
Perception, 443
Performance
  diagnosing causes of poor team, 473–79
  improving through goals and rewards, 377–84
Performance appraisal, 360–64
  defined, 360
  effective, 362–63
  feedback session in, 360
  providing, 363–64
  systems for, 526–27
Performance gap, 322
Performance test, 356
Performing stage, 470
PerkinElmer, timeliness of, 545
Personal attributes of entrepreneurs, 138–40
Personal Creativity Inventory, 254
Personality test, 356
Pfizer Corporation, 76
Pfizer Warner-Lambert, 89
Pharmaceutical industry, 76, 77
Philip Morris, 66, 111
Philips, 98, 101
Phone.com, 236–37

Physiological needs, 390
Piece-rate incentive, 368
Pier I, 530
Pillsbury, 135, 545–46
Pitney Bowes, 97, 98, 498
Pixar Animation Studios, 141–42
Pizza Hut, 197, 301
Place departmentalization, 275–77
Planning, 8–9. *See also* Strategic planning
  adverse outcomes and, 231–32
  contingency, 193
  continuing, 212
  for entrepreneurs, 145–52
  function, 192–93
  in human resource management, 350–52
  for organizational change, 320–27
  phases of, 205–12
  tactical, 196
Planning and administration competency, 16
  of entrepreneurs, 142
Planning & Administration Competency
  Computer Monitoring, 526
  Contrasting Controls at American and Southwest
    Airlines, 231
  Developing Leaders at Colgate-Palmolive, 358
  FastCar Project, 303
  GE's Operating System, 203
  A Hip Workplace, 445–46
  Homero Resendez of CEMEX, 17
  How Could They Not Know, 181
  Learning Audits Improve Organizational Memory, 336
  Mitre's Introduction of Knowledge Management,
    247–48
  More Women Become Partners at Deloitte and
    Touche, 500
  Pillsbury's Data Mining, 545–46
  Rio Tinto Corporation, 116
  Starbucks' Organizational Structure, 275–76
  These Norms Aren't Normal, 471
  United Parcel Service, 48
Planning and adverse outcomes, 303, 471–72,
    500
Planning and decision aids, 244–60
  in fostering creativity, 253–57
  in fostering forecasts, 248–52
  in fostering knowledge management,
    245–48
  in fostering quality, 257–60
Pluralistic organizations, 498
Political climate, 114
Political-legal forces, 92–96
  in global management, 113–19
Political mechanisms, 117–19
Political model of decision making, 235–37
Political risks, 113–14
  assessing, 114–16
Polyfoam Packers, 81
Pooled interdependence, 297–98
Portland Electric, 45
Positive culture, creating, 501
Positive reinforcement, 382
Post-It Notes, 153
Power, 235
  defined, 405
  types of, 405–6
  use of, 406–7
Power distance, 86
Power motive, 394
Pratt & Whitney, 532
Preparation in creativity, 253
Preventive controls, 517
Priceline.com, 522
PriceWaterhouseCoopers (PWC), 164
Privacy, 169–70
Privacy Act (1974), 169
Privacy issues, 557–58
Private network, 547
Privatization, 108
Probability, 222
  objective, 222
  subjective, 222–23
Problem definition, divergence in, 235–36

Problems
  defining and diagnosing, 229–30
  diagnosing and correcting, 525–26
  types of, 224
Problem solving, 364
Problem-solving work team, 461–62
Procedural justice, 171
Process innovation, 333
Process redesign method, 329
Process view, 533
Procter & Gamble (P&G), 42, 65, 78, 106, 111,
    245–46, 304, 317, 319, 328
Product departmentalization, 277–78
Product development strategy, 210
Product differentiation, 90
Productive controversy, 472
Productivity, maximizing, 367–69
Profitability, consequences for, 346
Profit center, 111
Profit sharing, 368, 529
Proflowers.com, 199, 204
Progresso, 545
ProScanbrands, 58
Protectionism, 117–18
Proxemics, 434
PSI Energy, Inc., 259
Pulsar, 96
Puma, 173
Punishment, 382
Purple Moon, 147–48

Qantas, 27
Qualcomm, 400–401
Quality, 62
  fostering, 257–60
  importance of, 65–66
Quality circles, 461–62
Quality control process, 62–65
Quality of information, 544
Quality viewpoint of management, 62–66,
    67
Quantitative techniques, 59–60
Quantity of information, 544–45
Quantum, 101
QUATRO, 549
Questionnaires, Delphi, 248–49
Questions
  strategic, 197–98
  what if, 251–52
Quota, 117

Radical change, 317
Radio One, 139
Radio Shack, 29, 100
Radius, 471–72
Rain Forest Rescue, 156
Rater training, 363
Rating scale format, 362
Ratio analysis, 530
Rational decision, 228
Rationality, 47
Rational-legal authority, 46
Rational model of decision making, 228–32
RCA, 58
Reactive change, 318–19
Readiness of followers, 413
Read-Rite, 101
Receiver (decoder), 432–33
Reciprocal interdependence, 298
Recruitment, 353–54
Red Lobster, 530
Red tape, 48
Reebok, 173
Reengineering, 329
Reference checks, 355
Referent power, 405
REI, 186
Reinforcement theory, 380
Related-business firm, 199
Related diversification, 202–3
Relatedness needs, 392
Relevance of information, 544
Reliable process, 208

Remuneration, 52
Representation, 94
Research and development budget, 532
Resistance, anticipating, and taking action to re-
    duce, 324–26
Resource allocations, 196
Resource commitment, 108
Responsibility, 283–84
  affirmative social, 179–80
  corporate social, 160–65, 172–80
  experienced, 386
Results, controlling and diagnosing, 211
Résumés, 355
Return on investment (ROI), 530
Reward power, 405
Rewards, 363
  in improving performance, 377–84
  offering, 380–83
  for work teams, 479
Rhome-Polulenc, SA, 76
Rhore-Poulence Ericcson, 111
Rio Tinto Corporation, 116
Risk in decision making, 222–23
Ritz-Carlton Hotel, 519, 522, 526
Robbins, A. H., Pharmaceutical, 77–78
Role perceptions, expectancy theory, 396
Routine decisions, 226
Routine service technologies, 299
Royal Bank Growth Company, 345
Royal Crown Cola Company, 111
Royal Dutch/Shell, 12, 340–41
Rules, 45

Safety-Kleen, 81
Safeway, 531
Sales budget, 531
Salient, Inc., 239–40
Samsung, 46, 94
SAP, 129, 216
Sara Lee, 441
SAS Institute, 24
Satisfaction-progression hypothesis, 392
Satisficing, 232–33
Scalar chain, 52
Scalar principle, 281
Scapegoating, 236
Scenarios, 244, 251–52
Schering-Plough Corporation, 76
Schwab, Charles, Corporation, 79, 404, 405, 406,
    421
Scientific management, 49–51
Scitor, 382
Seagate, 101
Sealtest, 135
Search engine, 546–47
Sears, Roebuck and Company, 43, 94, 140, 173,
    380
Securities and Exchange Commission (SEC), 93,
    223
Security needs, 390–91
Seiko-Epson, 96, 101
Selective perception, 234, 443
Selectivity, principle of, 524
Self-actualization needs, 391–92
Self-confidence in entrepreneurs, 139
Self-contained design strategy, 304
Self-management, 383–84
Self-management competency, 23
Self-Management Competency
  Are You Open to Feedback?, 442
  Computer Ethics Survey, 557
  Diversity Knowledge Quiz, 506
  George Conrades, Akamai Technologies, 223–24
  Is Change Your Friend or Foe?, 319–20
  Jack Morris's Emotional Intelligence, 408–9
  Managerial Values Profile, 165–66
  Tim Koogle, CEO of Yahoo.com, 522–23
  Tom Siebel, 286–87
  What Are Your Cultural Values?, 85–86
  Your Entrepreneurial Quotient, 144–45
Self-managing work teams, 463–64
Self-sacrifice in entrepreneurs, 139
Selling style of leaders, 414

Semantics, 448–49
Sender (encoder), 432
Sequential interdependence, 298
Serial entrepreneur, 140
Service provider networks, 199
Services, substitute, 90, 208
Service technologies, 298–301
  organization design and, 299–301
  types of, 299
7-11 stores, 270, 382
SGS-Thompson, 111
Shared assumptions, 487
Shared leadership, 335–36
Shareholders, owners and, 178
Shell Oil Company, 15, 80, 116, 180
Sheraton, 530
Siebel Systems, 216, 286–87
Siecor Corporation, 47, 49
Siemens, 94, 111, 359
Sierra Club, 80
Sierra Systems Consultants, 129–30
Sigma, 63
Signicast Corporation, 462
Simon and Schuster, 20
Simulation, 244, 250–51
Single-business firm, 199
Situational approach, 60
Situational interview, 355
Situational leadership model, 413–15
Six Sigma Quality, 203
Six sigma rule, 63, 99
Skill variety, 387
Skunkworks, 154
Slack resources design strategy, 303–4
Small Business Administration (SBA), 136
Small Business Advancement National Center, 146
Small Business Development Centers, 146
Small-business managers, 13–14
Small Business Network Development Forum, 15
Small-business owners, 136
SmithKline Beecham, 329
Social Accountability 8000 certification guidelines,
    163–64
Social architecture, 200
Social audits, 180
Social change, views of, 123–24
Socialization, 94–95, 488
Social pressures, response to, 180
Social Security Administration, 53
Social value, 346–47
Societal norms and culture, 162
Society, concerns of, 174–75
Softbank, 140
Solberg & Lowe Architects, 486, 488–89, 494
Solid State Measurements, Inc., 353
Solution-finding phase in creativity, 256
Solutions
  divergence in, 237
  types, 225
Sonnet Supply Company, 13, 15
Sonoco Products Company, 81
Sony, 6, 101
Southwest Airlines, 18, 24, 46, 65, 113, 231–32,
    273, 336, 344, 364, 365, 378, 436, 447, 448,
    487, 488, 490
Span of control principle, 281–82
Specialization, 269, 448
Sports Authority, 520
Sprint, 207
Staff, stability and tenure of, 52
Staff authority, 287
Stakeholders, 172
  concerns of, 172–79
  control of, 518
Stamp Master, 97
Standardization
  in organizational control, 524–25
  in organizational design, 269–70
Staples, 65, 529
Starbucks, 69–70, 275–76, 282
State Farm Insurance, 66, 275
Statistical process control, 63
Status as organizational hurdle, 446

Stereotyping, 443
Stewardship, environmental, 80–82
Stock options, 368
Storming stage, 469
Strategic action competency, 20–21
Strategic Action Competency
  Alliant Foodservice Innovates, 228
  Boeing, 112–13
  Countrywide's Internet Challenge, 549
  Dell's New Growth Strategies, 210
  Dow Cleans Up Its Act, 177–78
  Duke Energy's Scenarios, 252
  E-Tailing Charges Up Retailing, 332
  Feng Shui at Nortel Telecommunications,
    436–37
  Job Design at Whole Foods Markets, 387
  Ken Chenault of American Express, 421–22
  Kodak's Sun Plant, 519
  Marlow Industries Delivers Quality, 66
  Merck, 91–92
  Novell Reorganizes, 279
  Picture This, 141–42
Strategic alignment, 360–61
Strategic alliances, 27, 337
Strategic business unit, 201–2, 277
Strategic factors in organization design, 294–97
Strategic importance
  of human resource management, 344–47
  of innovation, 332–33
Strategic planning, 193–96, 206. See also Planning
  business-level, 204
  corporate-level, 200–203
  developing and implementing, for change,
    322–24
  focus of, 197
  functional-level, 204–5
  generic competitive model for, 212–13
  human resource planning and, 350
  levels of diversification in, 197–200
  planning function in, 192–93
  preparing plan in, 211
  resource allocation in, 196
Strategic questions, 197–98
Strategies, 195
  business-level, 204
  corporate-level, 200–203
  developing, 209–11
  functional-level, 204
  role of technology in, 96–97
Strauss, Levi, & Company, 97, 180, 183
Strengths, diagnosing, 208–9
Strong organizational culture, 497–98
Structural redesign, restructuring, 328–29
Subcultures. See Organizational subcultures
Subjective probability, 222–23
Subsidy, 117–18
Substitute goods and services, 90, 208
Sun Hydraulics, 447
Sun Microsystems, 111, 129, 148, 156, 394
Suppliers, 91
  in diagnosing opportunities and threats, 207–8
Supply-chain management, 58–59
Supporting style of leaders, 414
Supportive behavior, 413
Survey feedback, 330–31
Sustainable development, 175–76
Swatch Watch, 96, 536
Symbols, 488
System concepts, 57–58
Systems analysis, 57
Systems viewpoint of management, 57–60, 67
  assessing, 60

Taboos, 489
Tacit knowledge, 245
Taco Bell, 197, 226, 530
Tactical planning, 196
  focus of, 197
  preparing plan in, 211
Tandy Corporation, 29
Tango! simulation, 250
Tape Resources, 137
Target Corporation, 217

Tariff, 117
Task-based method, 329–30
Task forces, 462
Task identity, 387
Tasks, 271
  significance, 387
Taylor Group, 355
Teachers Insurance and Annuity Association
    (TIAA), 178
Team and organization incentive pay, 368
Team Assessment Survey, 467–68
Team proximity, 473–75
Teams, 337. See also Work teams
  feedback, 364
  goal setting, 379
  in knowledge management, 245–46
  training, 357–58
Teamsters, 115
Teamwork competency, 17
Teamwork Competency
  Aerotech Builds Virtual Networks, 310
  At Dell, Everyone Is on the Recruiting Team,
    353
  Cobra's Team Coordination, 282–83
  Conoco's Empowered Teams, 418
  Goalsharing at Sears, 380
  Honeywell, 19
  IDEO Brainstorms, 256
  A Look Inside Outer Circle, 326
  Marianne Torrcelli of AT&T, 125
  Mayo Clinic's Patient-centered Culture, 491
  MS2 Accelerate, 551
  Phone.com's Aversion to Politics, 236–37
  Share It with Employees, Soup to Nuts, 56
  Team Assessment Survey, 467
Technologics, 61
  changes in, 96–99
  changing, 28, 327–28
  in distribution, 97–99
  enabling, 246–47
  incompatibility with changing, 49
  innovation in, 333
  interdependence in, 297–98
  in manufacturing, 97
  in organization design, 297–301
  proficiency of entrepreneurs in, 140–41
  service, 298–301
  in strategy, 96–97
Technology Access Foundation, 389
Telcordia Technologies, 216
Teleconferencing, 445
Telling style of leaders, 414–15
Telnet, 546
Temic, 517
Temple-Inland, 81
Tengelmann Group (Germany), 107
Tests, 356
Texaco, 160, 347, 434
Texas Instruments (TI), 112, 192, 352, 435, 444
Theory X, 409, 410
Theory Y, 409, 410–11
Thomson, 58–59, 62
Threats, diagnosing, 206–8
3M, 153, 474
360-degree appraisal system, 363
Tiffany, 449
Time-and-motion study, 50
Time-driven leadership model, 415–18
Timeliness of information, 545
Time orientation, 124
Time to market, 460
Time Warner, 203
Timex, 96
Timing, 505
TNT, 203
Tom's of Maine, 525
Top managers, 12
Toshiba Corporation, 101, 111, 126, 127
Total quality management (TQM), 62, 318, 488,
    497
  philosophy of, 67
  programs in, 172
Totinós, 545

Touch of Class, 97
Toyota, 42, 43, 46, 57, 63, 81, 127, 172, 213, 225,
    460, 530
Toys "R" Us, 197–98
Trade Insurance Services, 460
Traders of the Lost Arts, 156
Traditional authority, 45
Traditional viewpoint of management, 42–53,
    67
  assessing, 52–53
Training
  in human resources management, 356–60
  of leaders, 422–23, 477–78
  of work teams, 476–79
Traits
  defined, 408
  expectancy and, 396
  of leaders, 407–9
Traits model, 407
Transformation leaders, 419–22
Transformation operations, 63
Transformation processes, 58
Transmeta, 270
Transparency International, 115
Transparency principle, 119
Trans Union, 558
Travelocity, 79
Trustworthy, 420
Truthfulness, 169
Truth in Lending Act, 92
TRW, 558

Uncertainty
  avoiding, 86–87
  in decision making, 223
Union of Concerned Scientists, 80
United Airlines, 202, 275, 459
United Parcel Service (UPS), 9, 47, 48, 237, 270
U.S. Postal Servie (USPS), 9
United States, value systems in, 125–27
U.S. Airways, 202
United Technologies, 111, 532
Units, 272
Unity of command principle, 51, 281
Unity of direction, 51
Unrelated-business firm, 199–200
Upward channels, 439–40
UT Automotive, 532
Utilitarian approach to ethical judgments, 167–68

Valassis Communications, 401
Valence, 395–96
Value-added resource, information as, 543–46
Values, 78–79, 488
Value systems, 84, 125–27
Venture capitalists, 148–49
Verbal messages, 437
Verification in creativity, 254
Vertical information design strategy, 301–2
Vested interests, 324–25
Video Privacy Protection Act (1988), 169
Virgin Atlantic Airlines, 391
Virgin Group, 391
Virgin Records, 391
Virtual organization, 308–10
Virtual reality, 250–51
Virtual work team, 474
Visa, 23
Vision
  in developing cultural diversity, 503–4
  in strategic decision making, 194
Visionary leaders, 419
Vision statement, 194
Vitro, 94
Volkswagen, 111
Volvo, 177

Wage and salary surveys, 366
Wainwright Industries, 39
Wal-Mart, 78, 94, 179, 258, 307, 328, 368
Warner Brothers Studios, 203, 204
Warner-Lambert, 76
Waste Management, 80

Weaknesses, diagnosing, 208–9
Webvan, 522
Wellman, 81
Wells Fargo, 79
Wendy's, 45
Western Digital, 101
Western Electric Company, 55
Westinghouse, 43
"What if" questions, 251–52
Whistle-blowing, 181–83
Whole Foods, 54, 387
Wiley, John & Sons, 20
Williams-Sonoma, 139
Winners Information Network (WINet), 302
Win-win solutions, finding, 178–79
WOL-AM, 139
Workers
   incompatibility with values of, 49
   knowledge of, 28
Workforce
   changing, 27–28
   diversity in, 28
   in knowledge management, 246
Work-in-progress inspections, 63

Work motivation, 374–401
   approaches to, 376–77
   basic expectancy theory in, 394–96
   effects of job content and organizational context
      on, 384–90
   forces in combination, 394–97
   goals and rewards in improving performance,
      377–84
   guidelines for managers, 397–98
   individual differences in, 390–94
   integrated expectancy model in, 396–97
Work teams, 456–82. *See also* Teams
   behavioral norms for, 471–72
   building cohesiveness, 478–79
   culture of, 475–76
   defined, 459–60
   developmental stages for, 468–70
   diagnosing causes of poor performance, 473–79
   feelings in, 470–71
   framework for effectiveness, 464–66
   functional, 462
   importance of, 458–61
   internal team processes for, 466–72
   location of, 473–75

multidisciplinary, 462–63
reasons for organizational use of, 460–61
reward systems for, 479
selection of members, 476
self-managing, 463–64
size of, 473
training for, 476–79
types of, 461–64
virtual, 474
World Cup, 449
World Trade Organization (WTO), 119–20
World Wide Web (WWW), 546
Written messages, 437–38
Wrongdoing, organizational practices for minimizing, 183

Xerox, 106, 246, 323, 440–41, 504

Yahoo!, 10, 134, 141, 157, 304–5, 316, 328, 492,
   522–23, 547
Your Entrepreneurial Quotient, 144–45

Zone of indifference, 283